COMPUTER
SIMULATION
OF
HUMAN
BEHAVIOR

The Wiley Series in

MANAGEMENT AND ADMINISTRATION

ELWOOD S. BUFFA, *Advisory Editor*
University of California, Los Angeles

MANAGEMENT SYSTEMS, SECOND EDITION
Peter P. Schoderbek
OPERATIONS MANAGEMENT: PROBLEMS AND MODELS, THIRD EDITION
Elwood S. Buffa
PROBABILITY FOR MANAGEMENT DECISIONS
William R. King
PRINCIPLES OF MANAGEMENT: A MODERN APPROACH, THIRD EDITION
Henry H. Albers
MODERN PRODUCTION MANAGEMENT, THIRD EDITION
Elwood S. Buffa
CASES IN OPERATIONS MANAGEMENT: A SYSTEMS APPROACH
James L. McKenney and Richard S. Rosenbloom
ORGANIZATIONS: STRUCTURE AND BEHAVIOR, VOLUME I, SECOND EDITION
Joseph A. Litterer
ORGANIZATIONS: SYSTEMS, CONTROL AND ADAPTATION, VOLUME II
Joseph A. Litterer
MANAGEMENT AND ORGANIZATIONAL BEHAVIOR:
A MULTIDIMENSIONAL APPROACH
Billy J. Hodge and Herbert J. Johnson
MATHEMATICAL PROGRAMMING: AN INTRODUCTION TO THE
DESIGN AND APPLICATION OF OPTIMAL DECISION MACHINES
Claude McMillan
DECISION MAKING THROUGH OPERATIONS RESEARCH
Robert J. Thierauf and Richard A. Grosse
QUALITY CONTROL FOR MANAGERS & ENGINEERS
Elwood G. Kirkpatrick
PRODUCTION SYSTEMS: PLANNING, ANALYSIS AND CONTROL
James L. Riggs
SIMULATION MODELING: A GUIDE TO USING SIMSCRIPT
Forrest P. Wyman
BASIC STATISTICS FOR BUSINESS AND ECONOMICS
Paul G. Hoel and Raymond J. Jessen
BUSINESS AND ADMINISTRATIVE POLICY
Richard H. Buskirk
INTRODUCTION TO ELECTRONIC COMPUTING: A MANAGEMENT
APPROACH
Rodney L. Boyes, Robert W. Shields and Larry G. Greenwell
COMPUTER SIMULATION OF HUMAN BEHAVIOR
John M. Dutton and William H. Starbuck
INTRODUCTION TO GAMING: MANAGEMENT DECISION SIMULATIONS
John G. H. Carlson and Michael J. Misshauk

COMPUTER SIMULATION OF HUMAN BEHAVIOR

EDITED BY

JOHN M. DUTTON

New York University

WILLIAM H. STARBUCK

International Institute of Management

JOHN WILEY & SONS, INC. 1971

New York | London | Sydney | Toronto

Library of Congress Catalogue Card Number: 70-159284

ISBN 0-471-22850-8

Printed in the United States of America.

10 9 8 7 6 5 4 3 2 1

CONTENTS

COMPUTER
SIMULATION
OF
HUMAN
BEHAVIOR

INTRODUCTION

THE PLAN OF THE BOOK

JOHN M. DUTTON

WILLIAM H. STARBUCK

This book is concerned with the description of human behavior and the implementation of one technology for making descriptive statements about human behavior. The research studies included here follow traditional scientific strategy in marshalling observed facts to make credible their theoretical assumptions or conclusions, but they use a nontraditional strategy for logical inference. Assumptions are stated as computer programs that simulate the structures of the real world, and inferences are drawn by operating a computing machine.

Machine analogies date at least to the beginning of the twentieth century. In the first issue of the *American Journal of Psychology* in 1887, C. S. Peirce discussed the inability of logical machines to replicate human thought, and I. Fisher's doctoral dissertation of 1892 drew analogies between the operation of competitive economic systems and the operation of hydraulic systems. Several machine analogs were built and operated during the first half of the twentieth century, but each was a special-purpose machine having narrow capabilities. The development and widespread distribution of the general-purpose computer stimulated the creation of socially accepted languages for discussing physical analogies and eliminated the need for hardware construction. By 1960, simulation programs had been written, or were in the process of being written, in all of the social sciences, and by 1965, simulation had become a widely used methodology.

This adoption process has not had universal acceptance. It was Peirce's point in 1887 that, although logical machines might duplicate the systematic and rational aspects of human thought, they could never capture the complex essence of the human being. The same argument has been repeated and repeated ever since, and articles stating this viewpoint or debating it comprise the largest single subpopulation of publications on descriptive simulation—even outnumbering the articles which state that simulation can solve all problems.

Of course, similar skepticism has attended the development of behavioral theory in other forms, but only mathematical theories have encountered skepticism of the type and degree simulation has encountered. The implied parallel between mathematics and simulation is not spurious because simulation models are essentially empirical cousins of mathematical theories, sharing a similar dedication to logical rigor and inexorable consequences. However, where the mathematical theorist depends on his intellect to establish connections between premises and their implications, the simulator depends on a machine; and where the mathematical theorist obtains results that simultaneously characterize general classes of events, the simulator invariably obtains particular realizations of events.

3

SOME ADVANTAGES AND DISADVANTAGES OF SIMULATION

Simulation's most prominent attractions are intelligible results and freedom from the constraints of mathematical ignorance. People who cannot distinguish a Lagrange multiplier from an eigenvalue can solve difference equations or find constrained optima. People having advanced mathematical training are no longer restricted to analytically convenient assumptions, and they can explore the implications of irregular, nonlinear relations. The outputs of a program may include a "yes" or "no"; a sentence in natural language; a graph, or diagram, or table; or a deck of punched cards ready for statistical analyses. If the program does not reason like Walter Felch, it surely talks like him.

Simulation also imposes a modest degree of logical rigor on the theorist, and encourages him to analyze the temporal structure of the modeled processes. Unless the program contains enough assumptions to produce an output, no output occurs, and it follows that an operating program includes sufficient assumptions for the outputs produced. Machine errors aside, the logic relating assumptions to outputs is impeccable. Verbal and mathematical theories are not always complete, and because their creators are more fallible than machines, such theories often contain logical errors. Because computing machines operate sequentially, a well-defined temporal sequence is inherent in every operating program, and the model-builder is forced to specify this sequence. He must at least consider which operations precede which operations, and in so doing, he takes a first step toward causal identification.

For each of these advantages, however, there is a corresponding disadvantage. Temporal specification and sufficient assumptions are required even when the model-builder has too little information to specify them realistically, and the desire to make his program operate is likely to induce him to substitute conjecture for investigation. Computer languages and hardware configurations differ in the operations they facilitate or make difficult, so that two programs intended to implement the same conceptual model on different machines are likely

to produce distinctly different outputs and may bear little resemblance in computational method. The fact that a program is sufficient to produce its outputs is no guarantee that the outputs derive from the model-builder's assumptions in the way he intended; simulations have been published in which the outputs were almost entirely independent of the model-builders' conceptual models, and almost entirely dependent on what the model-builders perceived as programming techniques. The flexibility of output formats has induced some model-builders to devote more effort to achieving realistic outputs than to achieving realistic associations between outputs and inputs.

Moreover, the fact that a problem can be solved in ignorance of the underlying mathematical theory does not repeal the implications of that theory. Simulation outputs are necessarily particular solutions obtained from particular parameter values and particular values of exogenous variables (such as random numbers), and the character of the solution may shift in nonintuitive ways as a function of the experimental numbers used. As a result, experimentation with the simulation program may not reveal the potential range of output behaviors and may leave the model-builder with no clear understanding of the general relations between inputs and outputs.

In the extreme case, simulation leads to "Bonini's paradox." A model is built in order to achieve understanding of an observed causal process, and the model is stated as a simulation program in order that the assumptions and functional relations may be as complex and realistic as possible. The resulting program produces outputs resembling those observed in the real world, and inspires confidence that the real causal process has been accurately represented. However, because the assumptions incorporated in the model are complex and their mutual interdependencies are obscure, the simulation program is no easier to understand than the real process was. As Bonini concluded, "We cannot explain completely the reasons why the firm behaves in a specific fashion. Our model of the firm is highly complex, and it is not possible to trace out the behavior pattern throughout the firm. . . . Therefore, we cannot pinpoint the explicit causal mechanism in the model" [1].

Of course, the existence of a credible simulation model offers the opportunity for experimentation that would be impossible in the real situation. The program becomes a captive subject who will attempt whatever the experimenter asks, who will forget on command his previous experimental experiences, and who will exactly repeat his previous behaviors an indefinite number of times. But in the case of a really complicated program, the cost of machine time is so high that only a few experiments are possible, and the experimental results are likely to be unintelligible under statistical examinations that assume linearity and normality.

HOW THE BOOK IS ORGANIZED

One purpose of this book is to examine issues like the above ones, or more precisely, to provide a framework within which the reader can examine such issues himself. The opening four chapters raise methodological issues in a broadly suggestive way, and the final ten chapters attack specific methodological problems and suggest routes to solution. However, the core of the book is a collection of research studies that use simulation but do not often discuss methodology per se. These case studies provide contexts within which the reader can ask:

How intricate is the modeled behavior?

How complex must a model be to portray the behavior?

Why did the model-builder use simulation? How would a mathematical or verbal model have constrained him?

How could the simulation model have been stated more effectively? How does the model contribute to understanding?

How valid or realistic is the model? On what basis is its validity established, or if validity is not established, what information would be necessary to establish it?

Has simulation facilitated scientific progress in this case? How could the research effort have been allocated more effectively?

The case study approach has been adopted instead of abstract discussion of methodological issues because simulation is an inelegant and pragmatic solution to real research problems.

To develop a methodological viewpoint in a substantive vacuum, evokes an artificial homogeneity in the concept of simulation, leaves one with little basis for asking whether simulation is the most effective methodological choice, and focuses attention on the internal structure of the model—its elegance and sophistication—rather than on the relation of the model to the modeled phenomena. The case studies make clear that simulation is different things to different users: a problem one man can solve only by simulation, another man would solve with a mathematical model, and a third man would leave as an imprecise set of verbal statements. Most of the studies use techniques far below the feasible level of sophistication, and could have been made more productive had the model-builder been aware of and adopted the best available technology. Yet simulation technique is an irrelevant consideration if simulation should not have been used, or if the model bears little resemblance to the modeled behavior.

One consequence of this viewpoint is that the book gives slight attention to the properties of simulation languages, to the considerations which suggest the choice of one language over another, or to specific programming techniques like the construction of pseudorandom number generators. These can be significant issues: programming and testing may be much easier in one language than another, and nonrandom "random" numbers may badly distort a model's behavior. However, other books and articles cover these subjects, and more importantly, software problems have much lower priority than substantive problems.

One should first assemble evidence about the processes to be modeled, and ask whether a complete and detailed (to the point of being operational) model is warranted and desirable. If it is, the likely second step is to gather more data to support the assumptions of the model or to serve as the model's inputs. Third comes the specification and design of validation procedures: the kinds of real world data that will be needed and obtainable, the outputs the model should generate, and the system for selecting outputs to generate—ordinary random sampling is almost always inefficient. Fourth, the model can be designed conceptually, beginning with general verbal and mathematical descriptions and ending with a logical flow diagram. Finally, a simulation language can be selected and the model programmed.

It should be obvious that, given the massive investment made before programming begins, a small investment in exploring alternative languages and selecting an appropriate one is likely to be worthwhile. However, it should also be obvious that the characteristics of the language should not dictate the structure of the model, since the model is the basic scientific product and different models amount to different statements about the nature of human behavior. Two models having different internal structures but producing the same outputs from the same inputs are not equivalent: they imply different beliefs on the part of the model-builder about the causal processes he is modeling, and they imply different directions for future theoretical and empirical research. Therefore, the most important criterion for selecting a simulation language is that it admits the full versatility of a general-purpose computer and allows the model-builder to express his beliefs accurately. In addition, the language should be available on a large number of existing machines and should be expected to be available on most future machines. The model-builder must avoid being caught with a model that has been made obsolete by technological change or a change in his own organizational affiliation, and he should be able to communicate the model to other research workers in a form they can utilize.

Selection and Organization of the Case Studies

We debated organizing the case studies according to academic disciplines such as psychology, sociology, or traffic engineering; according to problem areas such as voting behavior, business decision making, or national economic systems; or according to simulation classes such as queuing models, simultaneous difference equations, or massive data problems. The first two schemes would have placed similar models in several different categories, and would have involved too many categories to cover without extensive redundancy. The third scheme would have clumped together studies having distinctly different modeling objectives and would have implicitly suggested that the formulations used

were the kinds of formulations that should have been used.

Therefore, we invented a classification scheme having some properties of a disciplinary or problem area scheme, but involving only four broad classes which should be associated with the type of simulation model used. The four classes are:

A. Models of individual human beings.
B. Models of individuals who interact with one another.
C. Models of individuals who aggregate without interacting.
D. Models of individuals who both aggregate and interact.

These characterize the way the model-builder chose to define his problem, that is, his intent rather than his model, but intent should be associated with the kind of model adopted. The aggregative classes C and D should make more extensive use of probability distributions and stochastic formulations than the nonaggregative classes A and B. The interactive classes B and D should make more extensive use of forecasting and feedback functions than the noninteractive classes A and C. Both distinctions are related to the kinds of validation procedures that should be adopted.

At the same time, there should be correspondence between the model classes and the substantive problems studied. For example, studies by psychologists could fall into any of the four categories, but nearly all fall into category C because of the disciplinary tradition that the proper object of study is a group average. Similarly, nearly all studies of national economic systems fall into category D because individual variables represent the aggregates of many individual decisions and these decisions are treated as simultaneous functions of one another.

By arranging the case studies in four sections, one for each model class, and by including the same number of studies in each section, we hope we have achieved a more uniform coverage of modeling techniques and subject matters than one would obtain by a random sample of the studies that have been done. Each section includes six studies, and within this numeric constraint, they have been selected to display

(a) unusually conscientious efforts to validate the models with empirical data and (b) a wide range of applications to social science and social engineering problems. For example, the section on aggregation and interaction would be composed almost entirely of macroeconomic models of the United States if the studies had been chosen solely on the basis of validation effort, and this section would include only one such model had variance in subject matter been the only criterion. The introduction to each section lists studies which we consider to be strong alternatives to those included, so the reader can make substitutions that fit his interests.

Within each section, the studies are sequenced according to the type of validation attempted (type 3, type 2, and then type 1 as these types are defined in the next chapter); and within validation types, the studies are sequenced chronologically. We have not attempted to lead the reader into comparisons among studies, partly because we think comparisons across sections are as informative as comparisons within sections, and partly because we think the book's rationale implies that the reader should make these comparisons himself. The process of discovery is more valuable to learn than the content of the discoveries we think we have made.

The reader may be surprised that applied studies outnumber "pure" science studies among those included here. We were—because application or the lack of it was not among our selection criteria. After the fact, however, the emphasis on application seems wholly reasonable. For one thing, our criteria stressed systematic empiricism, and people who do applied studies frequently take care that their models are empirically valid. Nonapplied studies are often purely hypothetical or depend on unsystematic, qualitative measures of validity because, we suspect, the costs of error are low. For another thing, simulation is fundamentally an inelegant solution method for intractable problems. Nonapplied scientists have greater opportunity to redefine their problems to make elegant solutions feasible, and they place higher value on elegant and general solutions. The applied scientist is more likely to accept problems in the form in which he finds them.

The Introductory Section

This chapter is the first of four intended to introduce the reader to simulation as a tool for descriptive social science. The next chapter traces the history of computer simulation of human behavior, and in the process, presents more detail on our classifications of studies. The chapter by Dutton and Briggs explains the mechanics of model construction and further discusses the role of simulation in scientific research. Finally, Gregg and Simon explore the interrelation between simulation models and mathematical models, and the comparative advantages of each.

FINANCE AND RESOURCE ACKNOWLEDGMENTS

The studies included in this book were facilitated by resource contributions from the following institutions:

Chapter 2, Cornell University and Southern Methodist University; 3, Purdue University and Harbridge House; 4, U.S. Public Health Service; 5, Ford Foundation and Rand Corporation; 6, Ford Foundation; 7, Carnegie Corporation; 8, Ford Foundation; 9, Pennsylvania State University; 10, Krannert Charitable Trust and Purdue Research Foundation; 11, Ford Foundation and Carnegie-Mellon University; 12, Purdue University; 13, Illinois Institute of Technology; 14, Ford Foundation and Rensselaer Polytechnic Institute; 15, Ford Foundation and University of Pittsburgh; 16, Ford Foundation, Richard D. Irwin Foundation, and University of Michigan; 17, System Development Corporation and Michigan State University; 18, Simulmatics Corporation; 19, U.S. Public Health Service; 20, U.S. Bureau of Public Roads; 21, U.S. Bureau of Public Roads; 22, Harvard University; 23, Ford Foundation, Leob Foundation, Social Science Research Council, and Columbia University; 24, George Philbrick Associates; 25, University of Pennsylvania; 26, U.S. Office of Education; 27, U.S. Office of Business Economics; 28, Board of Governors of the Federal Reserve System; 29, Rand Corporation; 30, Netherlands Organization for Pure Research; 31, U.S. Office of Naval Research, Western Management Science Institute,

Carnegie-Mellon University, and Stanford University; 32, U.S. Air Force; 33, System Development Corporation; 34, Johns Hopkins University; 35, Rand Corporation; 36, University of California; 37, Ford Foundation; 38, National Science Foundation.

REFERENCES

1. C. P. Bonini, 1963. *Simulation of information and decision systems in the firm.* Englewood Cliffs, N.J.: Prentice-Hall; p. 136. Second edition in 1967 by Markham Publishing of Chicago. 5B.

2

THE HISTORY OF SIMULATION MODELS

WILLIAM H. STARBUCK

JOHN M. DUTTON

This is a report on a project that failed to reach its initial goal. The goal was a complete and exhaustive bibliography of the English-language literature on computer simulation of human behavior. An exhaustive bibliography would be valuable to users of simulation, of course, but it would also be a data source within which one could investigate the adoption and diffusion of an intellectual technology. Computer simulation is a technological invention in much the same sense that the electric toothbrush, the Bessemer furnace, and the deep-water well are technological inventions; but simulation is a more ambiguous concept existing in a more abstract and intellectual world. Although there have been quantitative and systematic studies of the adoption and diffusion of the electric toothbrush, the Bessemer furnace, and the deep-water well, we know of no comparable studies of the adoption and diffusion of intellectual technologies like simulation.

Probably there are no systematic studies of intellectual technologies because the first requirement is a nearly exhaustive bibliography. The bibliographic search process is inherently nonrandom and biased, and the bias can only be

removed by expanded coverage of the document population. Of course, random sampling is impossible when the document population is unknown. However, an exhaustive bibliography is no mean feat. During a year of intensive effort, in which roughly 12,000 articles and documents were examined, we discovered 1921 relevant items that were published before 1969. These are estimated to represent only three-fourths of what has been written, but the search had to be abandoned because our heuristics for high-yield search were depleted.[1] Each additional item would have required significantly more time to locate than the average for items already found, and the time it would take to achieve 100 percent coverage appeared very long indeed.

An attempt was made to test and measure the completeness of our bibliography's coverage. The test was based on a bibliography compiled by Werner and Werner [21], which we discovered after our bibliography was essentially finished. Werner and Werner did not define a

---

[1] We still have about forty references to documents which we have not been able to locate in the United States or which we found too late to borrow through interlibrary loans.

relevant document as we did,[2] but 326 of the publications they cited are relevant or probably relevant by our standards. Of these 326 publications, 266 had been discovered during our previous search and 60 were added to our search as a result of seeing their bibliography.[3] If their bibliography is a representative sample from the document population, our bibliography included 82 percent of the population before we saw their bibliography, and includes 84 percent of the population now.[4] However, Werner and Werner's bibliography is even less likely to be representative than our own because theirs is only one-sixth as large. Moreover, we used some of the same search procedures they used. The duplication rate between the two bibliographies is undoubtedly higher than the duplication rate between two representative samples, and 84 percent is an optimistic estimate of our bibliography's coverage. If half of the 266 items originally included in both bibliographies were automatic inclusions that would be in any broad-scope bibliography on simulation, our bibliography now covers 71 percent of the document population. The conjectured 50 percent automaticity seems high enough—considering the substantial differences in the two bibliographies' criteria for relevance—to make 71 percent a pessimistic estimate of our bibliography's coverage.

Thus we present a bibliography containing 71 to 84 percent of the literature. Since we examined the documents cited in all other bibliographies we found, we are sure this bibliography is much more complete than any other published so far. But then Icarus flew much higher than any man had so far. Although the bibliography suggests some interesting characteristics of technological evolution, some questions cannot be explored, and the probable biases in the data must constantly be anticipated. In particular, we cannot say: how many journals have published simulation studies; how many journals have published one or two studies as compared to how many have published numerous studies; how many authors have published simulation studies; how many authors have published one or two studies as compared to how many have published several studies; how many different subject matters have been explored by means of simulation.

The bibliography almost certainly understates the number of authors, journals, and subjects associated with small numbers of publications. An author, journal, or subject with many publications has a high probability of being cited elsewhere and a high probability of being discovered through bibliographic search. Of course, authors tend to cite themselves, to cite studies on the same subject, and to cite publications in the same journal. We systematically investigated the citations in the studies we found, so we tended to find additional studies by the same authors, in the same journals, and on the same subjects. Moreover, when we found a journal containing several simulation studies, we exhaustively searched every issue of the journal, thereby turning up additional publications in the same journal, on the same subject, and by the same authors.

The bibliography is undoubtedly also biased with respect to publication dates, incorporating relatively fewer very early and very recent publications and relatively more publications from the late 1950s and early 1960s. Publications from before 1950 are difficult to find partly because they are rare and partly because the terms computer and simulation were not used;

---

[2] Werner and Werner include progress reports on research grants, short abstracts of speeches, news reports, a financial report, documents written in languages other than English, doctoral dissertations that are neither included in *Dissertation Abstracts* nor immediately available in other forms, and documents that are secret or confidential and are unavailable to the public. They also include one item for which we searched very extensively without being able to establish that it ever existed in written form. We have excluded all of these as not falling within the document domain that interests us. Moreover, Werner and Werner do not restrict their bibliography to computer simulations of human behavior. They include games, man-machine simulations, hand simulations, mathematical models, uses of computers for data processing, studies of artificial intelligence, and simulations of physical systems.

[3] Of the Werner and Werner citations, 265 were in our bibliography before we saw theirs, 50 were added to our bibliography on Werner and Werner's lead, and 17 may be relevant but we have not been able to acquire and inspect them at the time of this writing. On the basis of authors and titles, 6 of the 17 are probably not relevant; 10 are probably relevant and were brought to our attention by Werner and Werner; and 1 is probably relevant but we had been trying to obtain it for some time.

[4] These percentages apply only to pre-1969 items. Our coverage of 1969 and 1970 items is erratic and low.

rarity and the absence of standardized terms meant that the studies were indexed and classified by other criteria. Publications during the last few years are difficult to find because they have not yet been cited and because library acquisition introduces a time-lag between publication and visibility. Presumably there is a general interaction between these temporal biases and the author–journal–subject biases mentioned above, since who wrote about what subjects changed through the years.

The nature of these temporal biases can be demonstrated graphically. It is argued that the present bibliography is underrepresentative of very old and very new publications because its coverage is less than exhaustive. If so, much smaller bibliographies should be even more distorted. Two smaller bibliographies are available for comparison: the one by Werner and Werner, which was compiled about one year before our bibliography was, and an ancestor of our bibliography that was compiled by John Dutton and Harold E. Bailey about 18 months before ours was. Both bibliographies contain 326 references, and both show 1965 as the peak

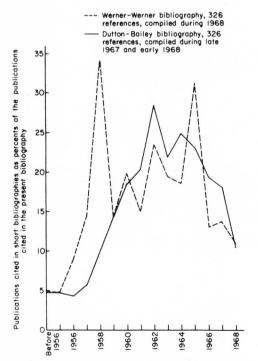

Figure 1 Temporal distributions of citations in two short bibliographies.

publication year, with the rate of publication dropping off during 1966 to 1968. Our bibliography was compiled later and it shows the peak publication year as 1966. Figure 1 graphs the citations in the short bibliographies as percentages of the citations in the long one, and both graphs display the expected low yields early and late. It can be assumed that our bibliography distorts the temporal distribution of the document population in somewhat this same fashion, and that analogous distortions occur with respect to authors, journals, and subject matters.

However, despite these biases and limitations in our data, we can show that simulation studies have become more systematic and empirical over time, and that this evolution has been produced by changes in who simulates rather than by changes in the work patterns of individual researchers. On the average, studies by a given author or group of authors have become less systematic and empirical over time.

Before these patterns can be demonstrated, and in order that the reader can interpret our bibliographic categories, we must explain how the publications have been sorted into substantive and methodological categories. The next two sections of this chapter explain how we defined a computer simulation of human behavior and how classification codes were assigned to the studies found. Then the last section presents observations about the historical evolution of simulation technology.

COMPUTER SIMULATION OF HUMAN BEHAVIOR

Many very well known studies are not included in our bibliography. The probability is negligible that such studies have been omitted out of ignorance. Instead, about five-sixths of the articles and documents we examined have been omitted intentionally.

One reason for omitting studies was their unavailability. Approximately one-fourth of the citations in other articles and bibliographies turned out to be erroneous in one detail or another, and approximately one-half percent of the citations either could be proven never to have existed or could not be proved to exist in 1969. Consequently, our bibliography includes only articles and documents we physically sighted, and errors in our citations are restricted to errors of transcription and typography or to errors in our choices among citation formats. The reader can assume that a document physically existed in 1969 corresponding to each entry in the bibliography. The only exception is that some doctoral dissertations have been cited and classified on the basis of abstracts printed in *Dissertation Abstracts*.[5]

But unavailability accounts for a very small proportion of the omitted studies. The main reason for omitting studies was that they did not directly discuss computer simulation of human behavior, by our definition of that topic. A publication might be cited by several of the studies in our bibliography, and yet be omitted because it did not mention computers or simulation. Even if the publication mentioned computer simulation, it could be omitted because it discussed simulation in a context not directly relevant to the description of human behavior. Conversely, some studies included in the bibliography did not contain the words computer or simulation, and did not say that the description of human behavior was a primary objective.

We defined computer simulation as a model or representation entirely realized through a mechanical system. The mechanical system did not have to be called a computer—and of course the systems conceived before 1940 were not called computers—but the system did have to be mechanically complete, and the author of the system did have to characterize it as an analog of some real-world process. Thus, simulation games and man-machine simulations[6] were

omitted because portions of the models were not mechanical; hand simulations and mathematical models were omitted unless the publication explicitly anticipated machine realization;[7] some computer programs were omitted because their authors characterized them as data-processing procedures that did not represent reality. Insofar as possible, we took the author of a study to be the ultimate authority as to whether the study was a model or analog and as to whether machine realization was intended; but we also tried to discover and interpret such subtle clues as footnotes acknowledging the assistance of computation centers and descriptions of computation methods.

Two of our bibliographic categories, MS and MG, include methodological studies that extend to contexts beyond human-behavior simulation. The rule was that a methodological publication should be included in the bibliography unless it explicitly identified a context other than human behavior. All the other bibliographic categories are restricted to descriptive models of human behavior. Studies of artificial intelligence were included when intelligence was defined by comparison to human behaviors or when the systems' components were modeled on human processes, but they were omitted when intelligence was defined abstractly without reference to human characteristics.[8] Simulations of physical systems such as nuclear reactions or electric fields were omitted, as were simulations of partially human systems, such as factories, in which the human components were left implicit.[9] In mixed cases, the bibliographic classifications characterize only the portions of

---

[5] Dissertations were virtually the only documents included and classified on the basis of abstracts, because in the case of dissertations one can be sure that a reference document actually exists. Abstracts themselves were excluded from the bibliography unless they were so long as to comprise short articles.

Also excluded as unavailable were a few documents that came into our hands fortuitously even though they bore the designations "secret" or "confidential." Our rule was that documents should be examined if they were available to the general public in 1969, whereas documents that had restricted circulations in 1969 should be ignored.

[6] A few man-machine simulations are included on the ground that a subset of the system was a self-complete computer simulation. In these cases, the bibliographic classification describes only the subset. An example is I. D. Pool and A. R. Kessler, 1965: The Kaiser, the Tsar, and the computer: information processing in a crisis [14].

[7] Omitted, for example, was W. M. Morgenroth, 1964: A method for understanding price determinants [12].

[8] For example, the bibliography includes O. G. Selfridge, 1956: Pattern recognition and learning [15]; and it does not include O. G. Selfridge, 1959: Pandemonium: a paradigm for learning [16]. Three other publications excluded as being concerned with artificial intelligence are: L. A. Hiller, Jr. and L. M. Isaacson, 1959: *Experimental music* [9]; N. J. Nilsson, 1965: *Learning machines* [13]; and M. D. Seversky, 1966: Retail forecasting [17].

[9] Typical publications excluded as not being concerned with human behavior are: M. S. Bartlett, 1957: Measles periodicity and community size [2]; D. A. D'Esopo, H. L. Dixon, and B. Lefkowitz, 1960: A model for simulating an air-transportation system [6]; F. K. Tan and J. M. Burling, 1967: Manufacturing planning using simulation [18]; and W. O. Turner, 1963: Traffic simulation [20].

the models that purported to describe human behavior. For example, several models of factories and their markets have explicitly treated the markets as aggregations of human consumers, but have treated the factories as aggregations of machines whose human operators were implicit at best. These studies were classified on the basis of their market components, the factory components being interpreted as irrelevant physical systems.

Obviously the human being is himself a physical system, and a model of, for example, the human circulatory system could be considered a model of human behavior. However, we chose to exclude physiologically oriented studies as not representing the kinds of behavior that interest us—a decision which immediately posed the necessity of defining a boundary between relevant and irrelevant behaviors. We finally defined relevant human behaviors to be those displaying at least one of four properties: (1) learning, (2) perceptual gestalt, (3) choice, or (4) social effects. Thus, most studies of aural perception and the majority of human-operator studies have been omitted because they examined the human as a time-invariant mechanical system; some neural models are included and some excluded, depending on whether they represented learning; most studies of visual perception are included because the model-builders in this area have emphasized learning and pattern recognition.[10]

We also excluded publications on the subjects of simulation hardware or software. One use of the term simulation makes it synonymous with computation on an analog or analog-digital machine, and many publications have discussed the effectiveness of alternative, analog

hardware configurations. Of course, many publications have also discussed the effectiveness of alternative programming languages for digital machines, some languages being intended specifically for simulation uses and some being general-purpose languages adaptable to simulation uses. Rather than establish a fairly subtle relevance criterion for discussions of hardware and software, we excluded all publications that were devoted exclusively to implementation techniques.[11] The only discussions of hardware and software in the bibliography are ones which presented conceptions of substantive modeling tasks, and their bibliographic classifications are based on their treatments of substantive problems.

Figure 2 (see p. 14) shows the time distribution of publications in our bibliography. The apparent leveling off in 1967 and 1968 is probably attributable to our ignorance, instead of to a leveling of the actual publication rate, and the publication rate is probably underestimated for the early years in comparison to the recent years.

Nevertheless, the graph demonstrates that machine simulation existed both as a concept and as an operational technology long, long before general-purpose computers were developed. Obviously, the existence of the invention did not induce its widespread adoption. Even if the early publication rates were three or four times those shown, the curve's appearance would suggest the presence of inhibiting forces. The inhibiting forces were probably less mechanical than cultural. The very earliest publications described practical, if unbuilt, mechanical devices. By 1915 there was an electrical "dog" that strongly resembled the mechanical "turtles" of the 1950s, and the learning machines of the 1930s were not unlike the simple neural models of the 1950s. Although model-builders may not have recognized its applicability, the hardware created for telephone exchanges and electrical accounting machines would have enabled the

---

[10] Studies of "animal" or "mammalian" behaviors are included when the authors appeared to have used these terms generically as categories that included humans as a subset, and they were excluded when it appeared that the authors meant animal-as-opposed-to-human behaviors. One article excluded on this basis, for instance, was E. C. Tolman, 1939: Prediction of vicarious trial and error by means of the schematic sowbug [19].

Examples of publications excluded on the ground that they were physiologically oriented are: E. R. Caianiello, A. deLuca, and L. M. Ricciardi, 1967: Reverberations and control of neural nets [3]; R. L. Cosgriff and G. E. Briggs, 1960: *Accomplishments in human operator simulation* [5]; D. B. Fry and P. Denes, 1958: The solution of some fundamental problems in mechanical speech recognition [7]; and R. Wyman, 1962: A nerve net simulation [22].

[11] Typical hardware–software exclusions are: T. H. Barker, 1966: *A computer program for simulation of perceptrons and similar neural networks: users manual* [1]; D. Gross and J. Ray, 1965: A general purpose forecast simulator [8]; and D. Longley, 1964: An analogue computer application in operations research [11]. On the other hand, the bibliography includes H. S. Krasnow, 1969: Simulation languages: facilities for experimentation, because of its substantive relevance [10].

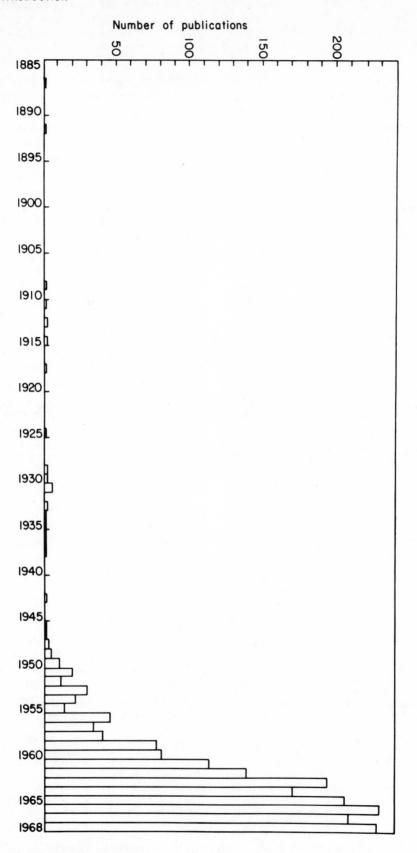

Figure 2 All categories combined.

construction of quite elaborate models. On the other hand, simulation was viewed with the kind of antideterministic skepticism that attended mathematical modeling, and the model-builders tended to perceive their models as demonstration devices rather than as tools which could disclose theoretical implications. The failure to exploit simulation's analytic potentials meant that there were few benefits from actually constructing working models, and the professional skepticism meant that what benefits there were had to be primarily intrinsic to the model-builder himself. Thus, there was little incentive to utilize the hardware which existed, or even to discover what hardware did exist.

The general-purpose computer facilitated the satisfaction of latent modeling demands. It reduced the amount of esoteric expertise a model-builder had to have, and reduced the time and dollar costs of model building. More complex models, warranting greater professional recognition, could be constructed with the time and money originally allocated to a single research study. Computer languages and concepts conveyed more information per unit of publication space than had mechanical and electrical diagrams, and were understood by more people. Indeed, the creation of a socially accepted language for describing machine analogies was probably a more influential contribution than was the actual fabrication and distribution of hardware, although the former might not have happened without the latter, and doubtless would have been ignored if it had.

The advent of the computer was also associated with increased benefits from simulation. First, the computer facilitated statistical computations and thereby increased the frequency of systematic comparisons between theory and data. Systematic analyses made formal theoretical statements more productive and accelerated the professional acceptance of mathematical and semimathematical models—the adoption curve for mathematical models probably bears a strong resemblance to the adoption curve for simulation models. Second, the computer was publicized as a mechanical marvel, and the fact that the machines operated rapidly and produced intelligible outputs was no small part of their romance. Those who built simulation

models were oriented toward exploring the models' behaviors under various input conditions, and such explorations readily assumed the aspect of logical analyses. Simulation became a tool as well as an illustration. Finally, the Manhattan project and postwar atomic-energy projects made the computer into a pseudorandom number generator and Monte Carlo machine. Computer simulations did not have to be viewed as deterministic, highly rational, and mechanical representations of man—though they were of course—and the opponents of mechanistic models were better able to accept pseudorandom models.[12]

BIBLIOGRAPHIC CLASSIFICATIONS

Based on our interpretation of its relevance to computer simulation of human behavior, each entry in the bibliography has been assigned a two-character classification code. The first character in the code—1, 2, 3, 4, 5, 6, 7, 8, or M —describes the type of empiricism used. The second character—A, B, C, D, S, or G—describes the general subject category.

Study types describe the relation between a model and real-world data. They represent an attempt to discover whether simulation studies have become increasingly systematic and empirical through the years.

Such an evolution could appear at the level of the individual author. If a model-builder wrote articles at each stage of his involvement

---

[12] It would be interesting to compare the time-series of publication rates with time-series of available computer capacities. We conjecture that the existence of computers evoked methodological and speculative publications, and that the availability of computers produced operating models. Thus, total publications (Figure 2) probably accelerated before model-builders had access to machines, and probably rose more rapidly than machine capacities throughout the early and middle 1950s. Unfortunately, the expected temporal bias in the bibliography would distort the publication-rate changes during the late 1940s and early 1950s, and we have been unable to discover appropriate time-series of computer capacities. Census statistics merge computer sales with cash register sales, and they provide no directly relevant price indices for converting sales to real output. Of course, it is the total stock (assets) of computers rather than the output (sales) which is needed; and for the present purposes, the stock available for simulation modeling should be separated from the stock reserved for routine accounting and data processing.

with a particular study, and if his study progressed gradually toward an average degree of systematic validation, there might be a sequence something like this:

1. Simulation is a good idea.
2. A simulation project has begun; this is what the model probably will look like.
3. A model exists; the structural characteristics of the model resemble, at least qualitatively, the structure of the real world.
4. Outputs from the model have been compared with real-world data, and there is at least a qualitative similarity between the two.

If the problem were sufficiently important and the model-builder sufficiently persistent, later versions of the model might be based on more systematic observations of the structure of the real world, and the model's outputs might be generated through a systematic experimental design and then compared quantitatively to real-world data.

The evolution could also appear at the social level. During the early years, the initial visibility of simulation as a technological alternative might evoke publications discussing simulation's advantages and disadvantages and postulating how simulation should be done; but there might be comparatively few models built, both because it would not be obvious how to build them, and because people needing working models might avoid an untried technology. Since heavy investments in model construction might displace investments in data collection and model testing, and since journals might be willing to substitute novelty for sophistication, the first models built and published might be only weakly and qualitatively analogous to the real world. The foregoing effects would be reinforced if the people attracted to simulation in its earliest days had atypically strong interests in the qualitative, philosophical properties of new research technologies, while people in the disciplinary mainstreams were either content with traditional methods or too immersed in empirical problems to notice new theoretical alternatives. As time passed, simulation's general characteristics might become too well known to be worth writing about; people originally attracted by simulation's newness might shift their interests to newer

alternatives; the publication of working models might call forth increasingly rigorous empirical standards and might draw the attention of people who want to build more working models; an accumulation of substantively strong studies might filter into the disciplinary mainstreams.

The codes assigned to uncover such evolutionary patterns characterize each publication as being: a methodological discussion, a description of a model that will be (but has not been) built, or a description of a working model. Descriptions of working models were further classified according to how precise and systematic were the comparisons between the model and the real world, and according to whether real-world data were used to document the model's inputs and structure, the model's outputs, or both. The code symbols are presented in Table 1, together with the percentages of publications assigned each symbol. Percentages are given both for all documents published before 1969 and for documents published from 1958 to 1966, the period for which the bibliography should be most complete. The 1958 to 1966 period includes 1256 publications, about 65 percent of the bibliography.

Whether the real-world data were used in a prior or posterior fashion was often ambiguous, and in these cases, we tried to interpret the model-builder's intent rather than substitute our own criteria. However the prior-posterior issue is the only dimension of Table 1 in which the model-builder's criteria were allowed to dominate ours, and many authors may disagree with our classifications of their work. For example, nearly half of the entries in the bibliography are labelled M. This is a high percentage; but had authors' preferences dominated, the percentage would have been much higher. We minimized the number of type M publications by classifying on the basis of a model whenever a model was described, even if the author treated the model as an illustrative example and if the example was not the main thrust of the publication's content. This rule was adopted because we believe that working models are the most influential stimuli motivating the acceptance and adoption of new research methods and because we believe that models, rather than philosophies, have determined simulation's contributions to science.

TABLE 1   Codes Identifying Study Types

| The content of the publication | The use made of real-world data and the kind of measurement employed | | Code symbol | Percentage of publications assigned this code | |
	Data used to demonstrate the realism of a model's formulation or its inputs—prior use of data	Data used to demonstrate the realism of a model's outputs—posterior use of data		Published between 1958 and 1966	Published before 1969
Description of a working model; that is, the hardware or program was operative	Quantitative measurement	Quantitative measurement	1	3.8	4.0
	Quantitative measurement	Quantitative or negligible measurement	2	5.0	5.4
	Qualitative or negligible measurement	Quantitative measurement	3	7.6	6.8
	Qualitative measurement	Qualitative measurement	4	2.9	2.9
	Qualitative measurement	Negligible measurement	5	10.6	9.9
	Negligible measurement	Qualitative measurement	6	3.4	3.9
	Negligible measurement	Negligible measurement	7	12.6	12.5
Description of a proposed or inoperative model	Not relevant	Not relevant	8	7.8	6.8
Methodological discussion which does not present a working model	None	None	M	46.2	47.8

The numeric codes do not indicate a publication's goodness or badness. They are independent of the properties of a model itself—its innovativeness, imaginativeness, sophistication, realism, completeness, or complexity. We could think of no criteria for such properties that would be duplicatable and relatively free of personal prejudices. Moreover, we suspect that Newton's laws are important less because they possess admirable properties than because they work, and we conjecture that social acceptance of descriptive simulation models has been heavily influenced by those studies that have tried to demonstrate their validity by rigorous and impersonal standards. Therefore studies were classified according to the ways in which correspondence between the model and reality was measured, a classification readers should be able to replicate but which captures only some of a study's virtues.

Each study was evaluated on two dimensions: (1) its use of data to ensure that inputs to the model were realistic, or to ensure that the structure of the model was realistic, or both; and (2) its use of data to demonstrate that the model behaved realistically. Each dimension could take three values: quantitative measurement, qualitative measurement, or negligible measurement. The norm for quantitative measurement was a numerical table of any sort; the numbers did not have to be analyzed by formal statistical methods. In fact, a better term might be systematic measurement, because analyses of qualitative data were classified as quantitative measurements when the analyses were detailed and systematic ones, for example, a line-by-line analysis of a problem-solving protocol. The norm for qualitative measurement was a list of qualitative properties such as "learning," "oscillation," or "stability"; the study did not necessarily have to explain why the author believed the model or the real-world system possessed the stated properties, although most studies did. The norms for negligible measurement were either an unsubstantiated claim that the model was realistic or a characterization of the model's properties in highly ambiguous terms such as "intelligence." Obviously, the adoption of a mathematical function on grounds of its computational convenience, or the description of a model's behaviors unaccompanied by statements that the real-world system showed similar behaviors were classified as instances of negligible measurement. In all cases, we avoided introducing our own beliefs as readers—whether we believe that intelligent systems learn or whether we believe that economic systems oscillate—and tried to adhere to the explicit statements of the original authors.

Altogether, 311 studies were classified as instances of quantitative measurement—types 1, 2, and 3—and 320 studies were classified as instances of qualitative measurement—types 4 5, and 6. Another 240 studies involved only negligible measurements—type 7. The implication is that in the population of published simulation models, 28 percent reflected the belief that empirical measurements are essentially unnecessary; and the remaining 72 percent were almost equally split between those fitting the judgment that the rewards from making more rigorous measurements exceeded the costs of making them, and those fitting the judgment that the costs exceeded the rewards. The quantitative and qualitative studies also differed in their emphases on prior versus posterior uses of data. The distributions given in Table 2 indicate that the quantitative studies were a little more likely to use data in a balanced way for both prior and posterior verifications than the qualitative studies were. When there was imbalance between prior and posterior, the quantitative studies much more frequently emphasized posterior tests of model's outputs, and the qualitative studies much more frequently emphasized prior uses of data to verify models' structures or inputs. One interpretation would be that when only qualitative measurements were made, more model-builders valued data that were useful for model formulation, whereas when quantitative measurements were made, qualitative input and structure data were already available, and so more model-builders valued data that would verify their models' outputs.

Inoperative models (type 8) were distinguished from operative models because there is no guarantee that a simulation model is logically sufficient or accurate until it has actually been

TABLE 2   Emphases on Prior and Posterior Uses of Data

	Studies published between 1958 and 1966		Studies published before 1969	
	Percentages of quantitative studies—types 1, 2, and 3	Percentages of qualitative studies—types 4, 5, and 6	Percentages of quantitative studies—types 1, 2, and 3	Percentages of qualitative studies—types 4, 5, and 6
Balanced emphases on prior and posterior—types 1 or 4	23	17	24	18
Emphasis on prior—types 2 or 5	30	63	33	59
Emphasis on posterior— types 3 or 6	46	20	42	23
Totals	100	100	100	100

implemented. An example is provided by G. P. E. Clarkson's prizewinning dissertation: *Portfolio selection: a simulation of trust invest-ment* (1962) [4]. Page 3 of Clarkson's report stated that "a heuristic model, written as a computer program, simulates the procedures used in choosing investment policies for accounts, in evaluating the alternatives pre-sented by the market, and in selecting the required portfolios"; and p. 27 explained that "the trust investment model is stated in terms of a heuristic, computer model. . . . The pro-gram is written in an information processing language I.P.L.V. and is presented in Appendix C." However, footnotes on page 60 said that the computer program in Appendix C was not the simulation model, but a data-processing program to compute statistics about each stock —such as the average percentage change in price over recent years—and then to select the most promising stocks for investment con-sideration.[13] "As mentioned earlier the IBM 7090 was not large enough to permit the entire model to be processed at one time. Hence the final two stages (the formulation of the invest-ment policy and the selection of a portfolio) of the investment model were hand simulated."[14]

The decision to hand simulate led to a number of errors and deficiencies in the report of the study. First, the model was incomplete. The selection of stocks involved search through a sequence of industries, and since search stopped as soon as all funds had been expended whether all relevant industries had been examined, the sequence of industries was a critical parameter. Yet the report did not discuss the search sequence. The modeled investment officer reported to us that he searched alphabetically, and portions of Clarkson's report implied an alphabetic search,[15] but the published trace of the model's processing (pages 83–89) followed the sequence: MI, A, C, MA, OI, A, UG, UE, R, OD, I. There were several more minor omissions as well.[16]

Second, one can infer that there were errors in the descriptions of the model.[17]

Third, Clarkson presented a trace of the model's processing, which appears to have deviated from the described model. Page 49 said:

The selector takes the first company from the in-dustry that is at the head of this list and applies a set of tests to it. . . . The set of tests are qualitative in nature and are applied, in turn, to the companies within each industry. Unless the value of some attribute is very much out of line with what it should be, the selector will accept the first company that is processed. If, for some reason, the first company does not pass the tests, the selector moves on to the second company and repeats the process. If no company from that industry is able to pass through the set of tests, the selector moves on the next industry. If, after processing all industries, funds remain to be invested, the selector returns to the first industry from which no selection was made and recommences

[13] That is, the program computed stock "attri-butes" from raw data and then identified stocks appropriate for inclusion in the "A" list. As was explained, "the mechanisms [in the program] are not intended to be a reproduction of the analytic procedures used by the trust officer each time he selects a new portfolio." They were "an approxi-mation of the processes he has used over the years in order to build up a set of measures by which performance of a company can be judged." Clarkson presented neither prior nor posterior data about this portion of the model, and the most reasonable interpretation is that it is more an input generator than a functional part of the model.

[14] Strictly speaking, Clarkson's study should not have been classified as an inoperative model because we found no indication that future machine simu-lation was intended. However, a great many people had the impression that the study was a machine simulation, and they might not have understood why we had said its contribution was solely meth-odological, or why we said it was based on negligible measurement.

[15] The lists on pp. 106–108 are alphabetic.

[16] Tests T_7 and T_{10} on p. 110 involve "stability of earnings" and "stability of dividends," but we found no definitions of these variables either in the text (pp. 33–38) or in the program (pp. 113–137). It is not clear how test T_5 (pp. 110–111) was performed. Test T_{15} on p. 110 was not defined. "Dividend payout" was included in the attribute list, but did not appear on the flow diagrams for stock selection. In addition, the descriptions on pp. 39–43 of attribute computation and "A" list selection appear to have been erroneous and/or incomplete, but readers familiar with IPL-V have recourse to the program.

[17] *Probably:* The consequence of a "No" answer to test T_1 on p. 50 should have been entry into another test rather than rejection. On p. 110, the consequences of T_7 should have been (Not B, B); the consequences of the right-hand T_{11} should have been (No, Yes); and the consequences of T_{13} should have been (Not B, B) on the left and (B, Not B) on the right. On p. 111, the consequences of T_9 should have been (A, Not A). On p. 110, T_{10} was incorrectly described; it should have been labeled "stability of dividends."

processing. This time processing begins at that test that immediately follows the spot where the selector stopped on the first run through. As soon as a company is selected, the scanner and selector move on to the next industry.

The trace did not follow these rules: companies from the automobile industry were examined at two different points in the search, even though all other eligible industries had not been searched before the automobile industry was considered a second time; and an electric utility company was evaluated immediately after another electric utility company had been evaluated and selected for investment. What is more, the trace computed the numbers of shares to buy in a fashion somewhat different from that diagrammed in the text.[18]

Fourth, Clarkson compared four stock portfolios generated by the model with four portfolios chosen by the investment officer; the generated portfolios were impressively similar to the actual ones. However, the model-generated portfolios were not consistent with the model as it was described in the text. Three of the portfolios contained two stocks from the electric utility industry and the fourth portfolio contained two stocks from the "miscellaneous" industry, yet according to the text quoted in the preceding paragraph, at most one stock could be chosen from each industry. The industries searched were chosen from lists of eligible industries consistent with a client's goals; three of the four portfolios contained stocks from industries that were not eligible for evaluation.[19] For four stocks, included in two of the four portfolios, the numbers of shares to be

purchased were not consistent with the diagrammed computation rules.[20]

An inquiry to Clarkson confirmed that the model had been incompletely described. The utility industries and the "miscellaneous" industry were not subject to the one-stock-per-industry constraint; the lists of eligible industries were erroneous; the rules for computing how many shares to buy differed from those diagrammed. Unfortunately, however, the entire model cannot now be reconstructed because "all the cards and tapes, protocols and other such material has long since vanished." This is a serious substantive loss: Clarkson's model had higher predictive accuracy against field-collected data than any model of sophisticated thought published before or since, and further study of the model might both add to understanding of thought and show the way to more accurate models. The model's value would have been much greater and the various difficulties would have been avoided if the model had been an operating computer program, if the program had been written in a language most readers could understand, and if the program had been reproduced in Clarkson's report.

[18] The computation of shares for the last-selected stock (p. 89) considered the total funds remaining unspent. Although the rule was logical, it was not included in the flow diagram (p. 112). Moreover, the diagram implied that there was no intermediate storage, the diagram being entered at the top each time a stock was selected for investment; whereas the trace behaved as if the average amount spent on each stock was computed in advance of the search for stocks to buy, and then the number of shares of a selected stock was computed from this dollar target.

Also, the traces for Socony Mobil, Libbey Owens Ford, and Phillips Petroleum differed from the diagram on p. 110. But this is probably because the diagram mislabeled the consequences of T_{13} (see footnote 17 above). As diagrammed, T_{13} said high-priced stocks were preferred to low-priced stocks, price being measured as a multiple of annual earnings.

[19] Not eligible, that is, according to the lists printed on p. 108. The portfolios on pp. 63 and 65 contained stocks from the insurance, electric utility, and gas utility industries although these industries were omitted from the "income and growth" list. (The headings on Table 3, p. 63, were obviously erroneous.) The portfolio on p. 67 included International Harvester from the agricultural machinery industry, which did not appear on the "income" list. These difficulties are not easily explained by simple typographic omissions in the printing of p. 108, because of statements made elsewhere about the numbers of stocks on each list and about the number of lists on which utility stocks appeared (pp. 48 and 70–72).
Furthermore, American Home Products appeared in the "growth" portfolio on p. 73, although the proprietary drug industry was not included in p. 108's "growth" list.

[20] According to the diagram on p. 112, the shares in the portfolio on p. 62 should have been (75, 50, 10, 65, 55) instead of (60, 50 10, 60, 45). If the diagram was incomplete in that shares of the last stock bought should have been computed from the funds remaining, one of the five stocks on p. 62 would have had a smaller number of shares than shown above. Also according to the diagram, p. 65 should have designated 95 shares of Continental Insurance instead of 100. In a letter, Clarkson explained that the number of shares was rounded to 100 whenever the diagram indicated a purchase of more than 90.

Then ambiguities in the text could be resolved by referring to the program, and there would be guarantees of consistency and completeness for the model and for the model's outputs. Because simulation programs are difficult to describe accurately with words and figures, and because error-free hand simulation is practically impossible even with models much simpler than Clarkson's, to gain the rigor simulation offers one must actually use a computer.

Subject categories, specified with the second classification character, correspond directly to the major sections of this book. The letter A denotes studies of individual human beings, the criterion being whether the model represented an entity having a name such as John Smith or Mary Brown. B denotes studies of individual people who interact with other individual people. C denotes studies of aggregated individuals, where the behavioral measures were summed or averaged across many people, but the aggregated people did not interact with one another (at least in the model). D denotes studies of aggregates that interact, or studies of aggregated interactions, or both. Thus 2A denotes a type 2 study of individuals, and 8C denotes a type 8 study of aggregated individuals.

Most methodological studies are coded MA, MB, MC, or MD because they were assigned to subject categories whenever a subject emphasis could be identified. However, some methodological discussions were too diffuse to assign to a subject category; these are coded MG. And other methodological publications emphasized the development of a highly systematic and formal simulation technology; since these form a distinctive subset, they are coded MS irrespective of their subject emphases. Consequently there are 38 code classifications—MS, MG, and the 36 combinations of (1, 2, 3, 4, 5, 6, 7, 8, M) with (A, B, C, D).

At least, the foregoing was the original design. In practice we found almost no studies properly classifiable in category B—studies of two or more identifiable individuals who based their behaviors on expectations about the others' behaviors or who exchanged information and chose actions jointly. Therefore category B was enlarged to include portions of categories A, C, and D. Now category B encompasses studies of single individuals (category A) or studies of

hypothetical "average" individuals obtained by aggregation (categories C and D) in which the model incorporated (a) forecasts of another's behaviors, (b) messages received from another, or (c) explicit responses to another's behaviors. We also established some arbitrary ground rules for placing methodological (type M) studies in subject categories. Unless there was a strong reason to deviate: all discussions of "intelligent machines" and of simulation of thought were classified MA; all discussions of Monte Carlo were classified MC; and all discussions of systems simulation and macroeconomic simulation were classified MD.

Table 3 summarizes the subject categories and gives the percentages of publications assigned to each. Table 4 shows how the publication frequencies of study types varied from one subject category to another and identifies the categories containing high and low percentages of each type. Because the methodological publications tend to dominate the frequency distributions, the type M studies were deleted from the distributions before the high–low judgments for types 1 to 8 were made.

The four categories form a similarity ordering —A, D, B, C—in which closer elements have larger correlations between their distributions. Category A includes a strikingly high proportion of methodological discussions, reflecting the popularity of debating whether machines can simulate thought and the popularity of projecting thought simulation into a robot-populated future. A also contains a surplus of proposed models and a deficiency of models based on systematically collected data, and the low frequency of type 3A combined with the high frequency of type 6A suggest the substitution of qualitative posterior tests for quantitative ones.[21] Anticipating the findings about technological development over time, category A looks like a technology in a comparatively rudimentary state of development.

Category D contains a high percentage of models that were unverified or verified with negligible measurements; and the surplus of 2D combined with the deficiencies of both 3D and

---

[21] The introduction to this book's section on studies of individuals outlines some ways in which category A studies are based on unusual substantive premises as well.

TABLE 3   Codes Identifying Subject Categories

The object of study	Criteria	Code symbol	Percentage of publications assigned this code	
			Published between 1958–1966	Published before 1969
Individuals	Modeled people who could probably be identified by name	A	30.5	30.8
Individuals who interact	Identifiable people or hypothetical "average" people who forecast, react to, or communicate with others	B	4.8	4.7
Individuals who aggregate	People who are added together and do not interact	C	25.0	23.2
Individuals who aggregate and interact	People who are added together and who interact with one another either before or after being added	D	23.7	23.5
Simulation methodology— type M	Emphasis on systematic, formal methods such as statistical techniques	S	6.1	7.7
Simulation methodology— type M	Too general to assign to categories A, B, C, D, or S	G	9.9	10.1

6D suggest that prior verifications have taken precedence over posterior ones.[22]

The low frequency of methodological publications in category B could well be an artifact of our classification rules. Types MA, MC, and MD were each associated with broad topics of discussion, and MB was not. Otherwise, B is the category most like the average of the four—which is an unsurprising result considering that B is mostly composed of studies that belong in the other three categories under strict application of the category definitions.

Category C contains very low percentages of proposed models, models based on negligible measurements, and models based on balanced-prior-to-posterior qualitative measurements. The implication is that C should contain a high proportion of operating models that were verified with quantitatively measured data. It does, but the frequency of posterior verifications is more unusual than the frequency of prior or balanced-prior-and-posterior verifications. Again anticipating the findings about technological development over time, category C looks like a technology in a comparatively advanced state of development.[23]

Reliability

During the literature search, we recorded cases where a publication was classified twice. Forty-four such cases occurred. These are too few to warrant reporting in detail—for example, the single case involving category B implies that all category B studies were misclassified,

[22] If this pattern suggests schizophrenia, the inference is tenable. See the introduction to studies of individuals who aggregate and interact.

[23] The introduction to studies of individuals who aggregate proposes that this advanced development may result from comparatively simple models.

TABLE 4 Distributions of Study Types Within Each Subject Category

Study types	Category A 1958–1966	Category A To 1969	Category B 1958–1966	Category B To 1969	Category C 1958–1966	Category C To 1969	Category D 1958–1966	Category D To 1969	Categories S and G 1958–1966	Categories S and G To 1969	Comparisons Very low	Comparisons Low	Comparisons High	Comparisons Very high
Type 1	2.9	2.9	5.0	5.5	6.4	5.4	4.7	6.6				A,B,D	C	
Type 2	.8	1.2	10.0	9.9	8.9	9.4	8.7	10.2			A		B,C	D
Type 3	3.9	3.0	16.7	15.4	18.8	18.7	4.0	3.5			A,D			B,C
Subtotal for quantitative measurement	7.6	7.1	31.7	30.8	34.1	33.5	17.4	20.4			A	D	B	C
Type 4	3.9	3.7	3.3	4.4	2.9	3.4	3.7	3.3			C	B,D		A
Type 5	8.1	6.9	16.7	14.3	15.9	16.2	14.1	14.2				A,B	C,D	A
Type 6	4.2	6.1	5.0	3.3	6.1	5.6	1.7	2.2			D	B	C	A
Type 7	11.2	10.3	20.0	25.3	11.5	14.2	22.5	20.6			C	B	A	D
Subtotal for qualitative or negligible measurement	27.4	27.1	45.0	47.3	36.3	39.3	41.9	40.3				B,C	A,D	
Type 8	9.1	7.6	10.0	12.1	6.1	4.9	12.8	11.7			C	B	D	A
Type MX where X is A, B, C, or D	55.9	58.2	13.3	9.9	23.6	22.2	27.9	27.7			B	C,D		A
Type MS									38.3	43.4				
Type MG									61.7	56.6				
Subtotal for methodological discussions	65.0	65.8	23.3	22.0	29.6	27.2	40.6	39.4			B	C,D		A

[a] Comparisons are based on the 1958–1966 data with MX publications excluded, except of course, from comparisons involving type M. The judgments denote: Very low $< .7P <$ Low $< P <$ High $< 1.3P <$ Very high, where P is the mean percentage across the four categories.

and the two cases involving type MS imply that all MS studies were correctly classified. But they can be used for computing pessimistic estimates of the classifications' overall reliabilities. The estimates are pessimistic because the main reason for examining publications twice was that we found reasons to suspect that the earlier classifications were wrong.[24]

The reliability estimates are given in Table 5. The heading "different from the first but similar to it" means (a) the two classifications do not differ both in subject category and in model type, and (b) the differences occur in only one dimension of the category or type space, for example, aggregation or interaction, prior or posterior. Thus 3A would be "similar" to 1A, 6A, 3B, or 3C and would be "significantly different" from all other classes; 5C would be "similar" to 2C, 4C, 7C, 5A, or 5D.

CHANGES WITH TIME

Figure 3 shows the annual publication rates for each subject category, and for each year from 1946 to 1968. The absolute rates are indicated by solid lines and the percentage rates by dashed lines. The erratic shifts in percentages during the early years result from the small numbers, of course.

---

[24] The usual procedure of replicating a randomly chosen subset of the classifications has not been used because it would produce optimistic estimates of the reliabilities—probably very near 100 percent. The classifier's memory produces a fundamentally ineradicable bias in second readings.

Category A was almost the only subject discussed before 1948, at which time category C appeared. Thereafter, category A's share has fallen—despite drastic increases in the numbers of A studies—until A's share from 1966 to 1968 was approximately one-fifth. The largest shares during recent years were held by categories C and D, each of which comprised about one-fourth of all publications, and the publication rates for categories B, C, D, S, and G seem to be continuing to rise. The publication rate for category A appears to have stabilized near its 1961 value, but this perception could be produced by less complete enumeration of the 1966, 1967, and 1968 publications. Publications in classes MA and MG tend to be widely dispersed across journals and books; they are more difficult to find than the other classes and therefore more liable to be incompletely enumerated.

Figure 4 indicates how the distributions among model types changed with time. As before, small numbers produce erratic percentage shifts during the early years, so the percentages for all categories combined have been computed from three-year moving sums as well as from annual data. In the moving-sum graph, the year graphed is the last of the three years included in each sum; for example, the percentages for the 1954 to 1956 period are graphed above 1956.

It is evident there has been change over time and the changes occurring within the separate subject categories were generally similar. Each graph begins with 100 percent of the publi-

TABLE 5   Classification Reliabilities

Estimated frequencies of a second classification that is:	Percentages considering only the subject category	Percentages considering only the model type	Percentages considering both the subject category and the model type
Exactly the same as the first	71	65	45
Different from the first but similar to it	22	21	39
Significantly different from the first	8	14	16
Totals	100	100	100

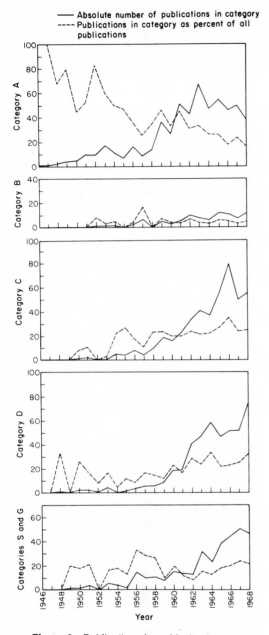

Figure 3 Publications by subject category.

cations in the methodological classes, and ends with the methodological percentage decreasing. Each graph also begins with no publications in the quantitative classes, and ends with the quantitative percentage increasing. The percentages of studies using qualitative or negligible measurements vary considerably during the early years and then stabilize around nearly

constant values. In the three-year sums for example, the qualitative percentage jumped from 0 to 20 in 1948, fell to 11 in 1949, and then oscillated between 21 and 33—with negligible trend—from 1950 to 1968.

These patterns are wholly consistent with the prior expectations about technological development that induced us to classify publications by study types in the first place. That is, they are consistent with the expected evolution at the social level. The data do not support our expectations about technological evolution in the works of individual authors.

Analyses of authors' publication histories are inevitably founded on fallacious assumptions. In order to perceive changes over time, one must observe authors who published in more than one year; and to perceive subtle and complex changes over time, one must observe authors who published in several years. But the people who published in N years differed from

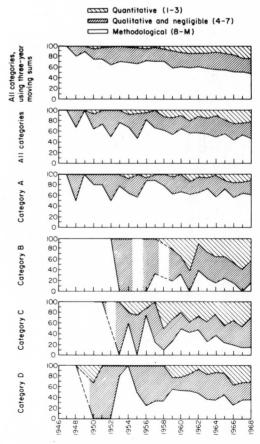

Figure 4 Percentage distribution by model types.

TABLE 6   Changes in Document Sample Associated with Successively Longer Publication Sequences by One Author

	Authors in the bibliography who are represented by at least N publications				Authors in the bibliography who are represented by publications during at least N different years			
	Numbers of	Percentages of publications in types:			Numbers of	Percentages of publications in types:		
N	authors	1, 2, and 3	4, 5, 6, and 7	8 and M	authors	1, 2, and 3	4, 5, 6, and 7	8 and M
1[a]	1433	17.2	28.6	54.3	1433	17.2	28.6	54.3
2	297	16.8	25.9	57.3	254	16.5	25.1	58.4
3	126	14.4	25.8	59.8	96	16.3	26.7	57.0
4	75	15.7	27.4	57.0	41	13.5	27.1	59.4
5	40	12.6	29.8	57.6	15	3.9	23.6	72.4
6	21	14.4	26.3	59.3	7	3.9	27.3	68.8
7	12	9.7	23.9	66.4	5	4.8	24.2	71.0
8	7	3.8	24.4	71.8	5	4.8	24.2	71.0

[a] The first row characterizes all publications in the bibliography, and the percentages differ from those in Table 1 because 1969 and 1970 publications are included here. The total number of publications is 2034.

those who published in $N-1$ years or in $N+1$ years, and the differences were much more fundamental than differences in names. As a result, the evolutionary patterns characterizing authors who published in N years do not accurately characterize the authors who published over shorter or longer spans.

Table 6 shows the consequences of increasing the numbers of successive publications or successive years of publication. Since there have been very few authors who published more than two or three contributions to the simulation literature,[25] statistics on long publication histories have to be computed from small, volatile numbers. More significantly, the percentage of quantitative studies decreases, and the percentage of methodological studies increases when one looks at longer histories. One reason is that, on the average, methodological publications require less original work than do operating models based on systematic empiricism; long publication histories can be achieved by emphasizing projects that demand small amounts of

work. In addition, the authors who published in five or more years began publishing when simulation was still seen as a new and innovative technology,[26] and five-eighths of their publications were concentrated in category A.[27] Both characteristics are consistent with an emphasis on methodological philosophy.

The rising percentages of types 8 and M with increasing years of publication actually result from a blend of effects. Table 7 shows how people who terminated after N years differed from people who continued to publish for $N+1$ years or more. Predictably, continuers published type 8 studies more frequently than did terminaters—a proposed model being an improbable finale[28]—and the frequency of type 8 publications decreased as the number of preceding publications increased. However, the type M frequencies varied more subtly. For terminaters,

[25] In instances of multiple authorship, the term author denotes a unique combination of people. For example, Newell is a different author from Newell-Simon or from Newell-Shaw-Simon, but Newell-Simon is equivalent to Simon-Newell.

[26] Within the set of 15 authors, the first date of publication ranges from 1947 to 1961, and the correlation is $-.68$ between first date and number of years published.

[27] Of 127 publications, 79 were in A, 37 in D, 6 in C, 3 in G, 2 in S, and none in B.

[28] Some of the studies classified as terminal in Table 7 are probably misclassified due to the artificial truncation of the bibliography in 1968–1970. Thus the actual frequencies of termination after a type 8 publication are lower than those shown.

the frequency of methodological publications was fairly constant and independent of N. For continuers, the methodological frequency fell to 39 percent when $N = 2$ and then increased with N. Apparently methodological discussions are moderately popular beginnings for series, but less popular as series components during the second and third years; and it is only among authors of long series that methodology reaches its maximum popularity.

There is no way to choose a homogeneous subset of the authors that is both representative of all authors and also large enough to provide reliable statistics. However, among the available alternatives, the most reasonable subset to analyze seems to be the 41 authors who published in at least four years. Two or three years are not enough to allow for nonlinear trends, and the authors who published in five or more years are too few and too eccentric.

Figure 5 (see p. 28) graphs the distributions of study types across the four years and graphs the percentages of authors whose publications became more or less empirical.[29] The labels "much more empirical" and "much less empirical" describe changes across the sets 1–3, 4–7, and 8–M; for example, the transition from type 2 to type 7 would be classified as much

[29] In Figure 5 and in Tables 6 to 9, each datum is the average value of one author's publications during one year, M being computed as nine. Thus in principle, a type 2 plus a type 8 are treated as equivalent to a type 5. In practice, there were few such extreme cases. For authors who published more than once, 93 percent of the author-years were homogeneous within the sets 1–3, 4–7, and 8–M, and 2 percent more were homogeneous within the set 7–M.

less empirical, whereas the transition from type 4 to type 7 would not.

The second highest likelihood was that the second year's publications would be more empirical than the first year's were, and the minimum likelihood was that the second year's publications would be less empirical than those of the first year. Of the second year's publications, 51 percent described operating models and 17 percent involved quantitative measurements—both figures are maxima across the four years. Thus, the second year's publications were distinctly more empirical and more systematic than the first year's, a change which is consistent with the previously observed advancement of simulation at the social level, and which is consistent with our hypotheses.

Unfortunately, the pattern of change reversed after the second year. There was a high likelihood that the third year's publication would be less empirical than the second year's had been, and the percentage of methodological publications began to rise. The trend continued into the fourth year—more methodological discussions and fewer operating models—except there was a maximum likelihood of no change between the third and fourth years, and the changes that did occur were more frequently extreme ones. One gets the clear impression that, having established their credentials for expertise during the second year, many authors were retiring from active model-building and assuming the roles of elder statesmen who generalize from their experiences.

Because 41 authors are so few and potentially unrepresentative, Figure 5 also graphs the

TABLE 7   Percentages of Type 8 and Type M Publications During Year N

	Percentages for authors who published in only N years		Percentages for authors who published in more than N years	
N	Type 8	Type M	Type 8	Type M
1	5	46	13	46
2	8	53	12	39
3	2	58	5	44
4	4	50	0	67
Average for 5–10	5	50	7	84

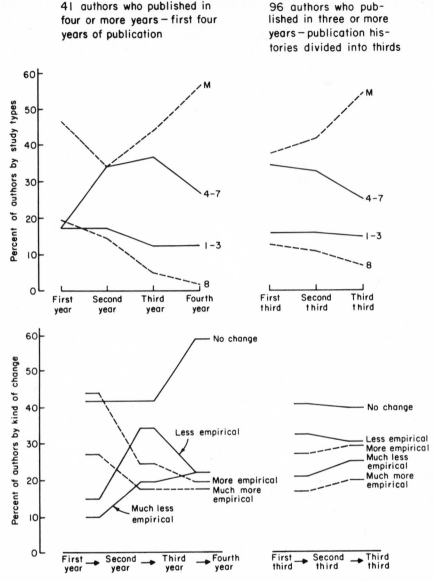

Figure 5   Distributions of model types in successive publication periods and distributions of changes between periods.

publication patterns among the 96 authors who published in three or more years. In these graphs, however, the unit of analysis is not one year but one-third of an author's publication history; for example, an author who published in six years is represented in each third by his average publication type during two years.[30] The resulting patterns for the first, second, and third thirds strongly resemble the patterns for the second, third, and fourth years. This is approximately what one would expect given that the mean year numbers for the successive thirds are 1.4, 2.7, and 3.8.

[30] When the number of years was not evenly divisible by three, the history was partitioned to distribute the numbers of publications most evenly among the thirds. The mean numbers of years aggregated in the successive thirds are 1.36, 1.33, and 1.11.

Table 8 shows year-to-year transition matrices. Since one row of the observed matrices had to be computed from only six cases, and three rows had to be computed from only seven cases each, the observed matrices have low reliabilities. Somewhat more reliable matrices can be computed if one is willing to assume that the changes across the three matrices were linear ones; this reduces the number of estimated parameters from 18 to 12. Such least-squares matrices assuming linear trends are also presented in Table 8.[31] The fit is rather good, the mean absolute error being only 4 percent. The largest errors are those in the second row of the second matrix.

The largest frequencies in the transition matrices fall on the major diagonals, and with two exceptions the frequencies decrease with increasing distance from the major diagonals.

Thus, an author's next publications were more likely to resemble his last ones than to be different. The two exceptions to this proposition occur in the first rows of the second and third matrices, where quantitative studies were more frequently followed by methodological discussions than by qualitative studies. These exceptions are explained by the time-gradients presented in Table 9. From year-to-year, the

[31] Each entry in the transition matrix was assumed to have the form $A + BN$, N being the year; and the parameters were constrained by the fact that, across each row, the sum of the A's had to be 100 and the sum of the B's had to be zero. Each row's parameters were estimated separately—four free parameters estimated from nine observations. The B's are given in Table 9.

Obviously the assumed linear change is not a serious hypothesis about long-run changes. The estimated matrix for transitions from year five to year six would contain two negative elements.

TABLE 8   Transition Matrices Based on 41 Authors Who published in Four or More years

Observed Transition Matrices: Frequencies of Types Given the Type During the Preceding Year

Type during first year	Type during second year			Type during second year	Type during third year			Type during third year	Type during fourth year		
	1–3	4–7	8–M		1–3	4–7	8–M		1–3	4–7	8–M
1–3	57	29	14	1–3	57	14	29	1–3	50	17	33
4–7	29	57	14	4–7	0	64	36	4–7	20	40	40
8–M	4	30	67	8–M	10	25	65	8–M	0	20	80

Estimated Transition Matrices: Least-Squares Estimates Assuming Linear Trends

Type during first year	Type during second year			Type during second year	Type during third year			Type during third year	Type during fourth year		
	1–3	4–7	8–M		1–3	4–7	8–M		1–3	4–7	8–M
1–3	57	27	16	1–3	54	20	26	1–3	51	13	36
4–7	21	62	17	4–7	16	54	30	4–7	12	45	43
8–M	6	30	64	8–M	5	25	71	8–M	3	20	77

transition matrices changed so as to increase the likelihood of a methodological publication and to decrease the likelihood of a quantitative or qualitative publication; qualitative publications lost ground more rapidly than did quantitative ones. The trend patterns are the same in all three rows, but the largest trends are associated with authors who last published qualitative studies, and the smallest trends are associated with authors who last published methodological studies. The consistency of the patterns across rows and columns is striking.[32]

It is evident that the pattern of change that characterized technological advancement on the social level was not produced by evolution in the works of individual authors. After the second year, the publication histories of most authors ran counter to the social trend. The aggregate pattern of increasingly systematic empiricism was produced by changes in the population of authors as methodological innovators retired and the technology was absorbed into the mainstream of social science research.

[32] In fact, the time-gradients in the second column are all about 2.3 times the gradients in the first column, and the magnitudes of the gradients in each row are correlated with the time-zero value of the major diagonal element in the row. The free parameters could be reduced from 12 to 9 with negligible loss in the fit.

THE BIBLIOGRAPHY

The bibliography appears following this chapter as an alphabetic list containing complete information about each citation. The citation format varies slightly depending on the kind of publication.

The format for articles in serials:
> Author, Date. Title of article in roman type. *Title of Serial in Italics and with Initial Capitals*, *Volume* (Issue): Pages. Classification code.

The format for chapters or sections in books:
> Author, Date. Title of section in roman type. *Title of book in italics* (Editor, if any); City of publication: Publisher, Volume number if any, Pages. Classification code.

The format for complete books or documents that are intended for public circulation:
> Author, Date. *Title in italics*. City of publication: Publisher, Document number if relevant. Classification code.

The format for dissertations, manuscripts, or documents that are not intended for public circulation:
> Author, Date. *Title in italics*. "Working paper" or "Doctoral dissertation," Source institution, Document number if relevant. Classification code.

Similar formats are used for publications cited in the anthology's text.

TABLE 9   Estimated Time-Gradients for Frequencies in the Transition Matrices

Type during year N	Type during year $N+1$		
	1–3	4–7	8–M
1–3	−3	−7	+10
4–7	−4	−9	+13
8–M	−2	−5	+7

REFERENCES

1. T. H. Barker, 1966. *A computer program for simulation of perceptions and similar neural networks: users manual.* Ithaca, N.Y.: Cornell University Cognitive Systems Research Program.
2. M. S. Bartlett, 1957. Measles periodicity and community size. *Journal of the Royal Statistical Society, Series A, 120*(1): 48–60.
3. E. R. Caianiello, A. deLuca, and L. M. Ricciardi, 1967. Reverberations and control of neural nets. *Kybernetik, 4*(1): 10–18.
4. G. P. E. Clarkson, 1962. *Portfolio selection: a simulation of trust investment.* Englewood Cliffs, N.J.: Prentice-Hall. 8A.
5. R. L. Cosgriff, and G. E. Briggs, 1960. *Accomplishments in human operator simulation.* New York: American Society of Mechanical Engineers, Paper No. 60-AV-40.
6. D. A. D'Esopo, H. L. Dixon, and B. Lefkowitz, 1960. A model for simulating an air-transportation system. *Naval Research Logistics Quarterly, 7*(3): 213–220.
7. D. B. Fry, and P. Denes, 1958. The solution of some fundamental problems in mechanical speech recognition. *Language and Speech, 1*(1): 35–58.
8. D. Gross, and J. Ray, 1965. A general purpose forecast simulator. *Management Science, 11*(6): B-119-135.
9. L. A. Hiller, Jr., and L. M. Isaacson, 1959. *Experimental Music.* New York: McGraw-Hill.
10. H. S. Krasnow, 1969. Simulation languages: facilities for experimentation. *The design of computer simulation experiments,* (T. H. Naylor, ed.); Durham: Duke University Press, Chapter 16. MG.
11. D. Longley, 1964. An analogue computer application in operations research. *Electronic Engineering, 36*: 378–381.
12. W. M. Morgenroth, 1964. A method for understanding price determinants. *Journal of Marketing Research, 1*(3): 17–26.
13. N. J. Nilsson, 1965. *Learning machines.* New York: McGraw-Hill.
14. I. D. Pool, and A. R. Kessler, 1965. The Kaiser, the Tsar, and the computer: information processing in a crisis. *American Behavioral Scientist, 8*(9): 31–38. 7B.
15. O. G. Selfridge, 1956. Pattern recognition and learning. *Information theory* (C. Cherry, ed.); London: Butterworths, 345–353. MA.
16. O. G. Selfridge, 1959. Pandemonium: a paradigm for learning. *Mechanisation of thought processes* (D. V. Blake and A. M. Uttley, eds.); London: H. M. Stationery Office, Volume 1, 513–531.
17. M. D. Seversky, 1966. Retail forecasting. *Datamation, 12*(8): 28–34.
18. F. K. Tan, and J. M. Burling, 1967. Manufacturing planning using simulation. *Conference of the AIIE, Proceedings of the Eighteenth Annual:* 261–266.
19. E. C. Tolman, 1939. Prediction of vicarious trial and error by means of the schematic sowbug. *Psychological Review, 46*(4): 318–336.
20. W. O. Turner, 1963. Traffic simulation. *Bell Laboratories Record, 41*(9): 346–350.
21. R. Werner, and J. T. Werner, 1969. *Bibliography of simulations: social systems and education.* La Jolla, California: Western Behavioral Sciences Institute, Contract OEC-1-7-071027-4273. MG.
22. R. Wyman, 1962. A nerve net simulation. *Behavioral Science, 7*(2): 250–252.

BIBLIOGRAPHY OF SIMULATION STUDIES

R. P. Abelson: see J. D. Carroll and see I. D. Pool.

R. P. Abelson, 1963. Computer simulation of "hot" cognition. *Computer simulation of personality* (S. S. Tomkins and S. Messick, eds.); New York: Wiley, 277–298, 8A.

R. P. Abelson, 1964. Mathematical models of the distribution of attitudes under controversy. *Contributions to mathematical psychology* (N. Frederiksen and H. Gulliksen, eds.); New York: Holt, Rinehart, and Winston, 141–160, 5C.

R. P. Abelson, 1965. Lectures on computer simulation. *Mathematics and social sciences* (S. Sternberg, V. Capecchi, T. Kloek, and C. T. Leenders, eds.); The Hague: Mouton, 443–482, 5C.

R. P. Abelson, 1965. Storage of beliefs. *Computers for the humanities?* (G. W. Pierson, ed.); New Haven: Yale University, 134–136, 8A.

R. P. Abelson, 1968. Simulation of social behavior. *The handbook of social psychology* (G. Lindzey and E. Aronson, eds.); Reading, Mass.: Addison-Wesley, Volume 2, 274–356, MG.

R. P. Abelson and A. Bernstein, 1963. A computer simulation model of community referendum controversies. *Public Opinion Quarterly, 27* (1): 93–122, 2C.

R. P. Abelson and J. D. Carroll, 1965. Computer simulation of individual belief systems. *American Behavioral Scientist, 8* (9): 24–30, 7A.

D. I. Abrams: see E. B. Roberts.

J. W. Abrams: see G. S. Shaw.

C. C. Abt, 1964. War gaming. *International Science and Technology, 32*: 29–37 and 96–98, MD.

C. C. Abt, 1968. *Computer applications to social and economic problem-solving.* Working paper, Abt Associates Incorporated, MD.

C. C. Abt, J. Blaxall, M. Gorden, J. C. Hodder, J. J. McDonnell, M. O. Rosen, and M. Zonis, 1966. Survey of the state of the art: social, political, and economic models and simulations. *Technology and the American economy, Appendix volume V: applying technology to unmet needs* (U. S. National Commission on Technology, Automation, and Economic Progress); Washington: U. S. Government Printing Office, 203–250, MG.

S. S. Ackerman, 1966. Simulation of social action programs. *Information processing 1965* (International Federation for Information Processing, W. A. Kalenich, ed.); Washington: Spartan, Volume 2, 416–417, 7C.

H. E. Adams, R. E. Forrester, J. F. Kraft, and B. B. Oosterhout, 1961. *CARMONETTE: a computer-played combat simulation.* Bethesda: Johns Hopkins University Operations Research Office, Technical Memorandum ORO–T–389, AD–257012, 5D.

J. A. Adams and C. E. Webber, 1963. A Monte Carlo model of tracking behavior. *Human Factors, 5*(1): 81–102, 3C.

R. H. Adams and J. L. Jenkins, 1960. Simulation of air operations with the air-battle model. *Operations Research, 8*(5): 601–615, 7C.

F. L. Adelman: see I. Adelman.

I. Adelman, 1963. Long cycles — a simulation experiment. *Symposium on simulation models* (A. C. Hoggatt and F. E. Balderston eds.); Cincinnati: South-Western, 152–181, 1D.

I. Adelman, 1965. Discussion (of G. Fromm's "Forecasting, policy simulation, and structural analysis"). *American Statistical Association, 1964 Proceedings of the Business and Economic Statistics Section*: 22–23. MD.

I. Adelman. 1968. Simulation: economic processes. *International encyclopedia of the social sciences* (D. L. Sills, ed.); New York: Macmillan, Volume 14, 268–273, MD.

I. Adelman and F. L. Adelman, 1959. The dynamic properties of the Klein-Goldberger model. *Econometrica, 27*(4): 596–625, 1D.

C. Adler, 1931. Remarks of Dr. Cyrus Adler at the opening of the round table conference. *Proceedings of the American Philosophical Society, 70*(3): 309–311, MA.

I. Adler, 1961. Thinking machines and the brain. *Thinking machines*; New York: Day, 180–184, MA.

I. Adolfsson: see H. Hyrenius.

J. M. Agostini: see N. Steinberg.

J. M. Aitken, 1963. Simulation of traffic conditions at an uncontrolled T–junction. *Traffic Engineering & Control, 5*(6): 354–358, 5D.

M. S. Alba, 1967. *Microanalysis of the socio-dynamics of diffusion of innovation: a simulation study.* Doctoral dissertation, Northwestern University, 3D.

W. E. Alberts, 1956. System simulation. *American Institute of Industrial Engineers, Proceedings of the Annual National Conference, 7*(3): 1–6, MD.

W. E. Alberts, 1957. Report to the eighth AIIE national conference on the system simulation symposium. *Journal of Industrial Engineering, 8*(6): 366–369. Also published in 1958 under the title "Report to the eighth AIIE national convention on the system simulation symposium" in *Report of system simulation symposium* (D. G. Malcolm, ed.); New York: American Institute of Industrial Engineers, 1–5, MG.

H. R. Alker, Jr., 1968. *Computational equations for MARXSIM.* Working paper, Yale University, 8D.

H. R. Alker, Jr., 1968. *Computer simulations: bad mathematics but good social science?* Working paper, Center for Advanced Study in the Behavioral Sciences, MD.

H. R. Alker, Jr., 1968. *Computer simulations, conceptual frameworks and coalition behavior.* Working paper, Yale University. To be published in *The study of coalition behavior* (Groennings, Kelley, and Leiserson, eds.), 8D.

H. R. Alker, Jr., 1969. *Computer simulations of integration processes.* Working paper, Massachusetts Institute of Technology, 8D.

M. Allais: see P. C. Mahalanobis.

G. Allen: see J. W. Gyr.

M. Allen, 1962. A concept attainment program that simulates a simultaneous-scanning strategy. *Behavioral Science, 7*(2): 247–250, 7A.

M. Allen, 1962. *A detailed simulation of a non-stock production leveling problem.* Masters thesis, Massachusetts Institute of Technology, 7D.

J. Almond, 1965. Traffic assignment to a road network. *Traffic Engineering & Control, 6*(10): 616–617 and 622, 6C.

N. M. Amosov, 1967. *Modeling of thinking and the mind.* New York: Spartan, MA.

A. E. Amstutz: see H. J. Claycamp.

A. E. Amstutz, 1966. Development, validation, and implementation of computerized microanalytic simulations of market behavior. *Proceedings of the fourth international conference on operational research* (D. B. Hertz and J. Melese, eds.); New York: Wiley-Interscience, 241–262, 1D.

A. E. Amstutz, 1966. *Management use of computerized micro–analytic behavioral simulations.* Working paper, Massachusetts Institute of Technology Sloan School of Management, Paper No. 169–66, 1D.

A. E. Amstutz, 1967. *Computer simulation of Competitive market response.* Cambridge, Mass.: MIT Press, 1D.

A. E. Amstutz, 1968. Discussant (of papers by Kotler, Starr, and Weber). *Systems* (D. M. Slate and R. Ferber, eds.); Urbana: University of Illinois Bureau of Economic and Business Research, 99–103, MD.

C. J. Ancker, Jr.: see A. V. Gafarian.

A. R. Anderson, 1964. Selected bibliography. *Minds and machines*; Englewood Cliffs, N. J.: Prentice-Hall, 109–114, MA.

N. S. Anderson, 1961. Comments on the use of computers in psychological research. *Behavioral Science*, 6(3): 266–270, MG.

T. E. Anderson, E. A. Kidd, and K. R. Laughery, 1968. *Urban intersection study — Volume II: a computer simulation model of driver behavior at intersections.* Buffalo: Cornell Aeronautical Laboratory, Report VJ–2120–V–2, 1D.

W. H. L. Anderson and J. Cornwall, 1961. Problems of growth policy. *Review of Economics and Statistics* 43(2): 163–174, 2D.

S. E. Andersson, 1966. A Monte Carlo model for simulation of tank battles. *BIT, Nordisk Tidskrift for Informations-behandling*, 6(2): 89–100, 7B.

A. Ando and F. Modigliani, 1969. Econometric analysis of stabilization policies. *American Economic Review*, 59(2): 296–314, 3D.

J. H. Andreae, 1964. STELLA: a scheme for a learning machine. *Automatic and remote control, theory* (International Federation of Automatic Control, V. Broida, ed.); London: Butterworths, 497–502, 7A.

A. M. Andrew, 1959. The Conditional Probability Computer. *Mechanisation of thought processes* (D. V. Blake and A. M. Uttley, eds.); London: H. M. Stationery Office, Volume 2, 945–946, 7A.

A. M. Andrew, 1959. Learning machines. *Mechanisation of thought processes* (D. V. Blake and A. M. Uttley, eds.); London: H. M. Stationery Office, Volume 2, 475–505, MA.

A. M. Andrew, 1963. *Brains and computers.* London: Harrap, MA.

E. S. Angel and G. A. Bekey, 1968. Adaptive finite-state models of manual control systems. *IEEE Transactions on Man-Machine Systems*, MMS-9(1): 15–20, 4A.

A. J. Angyan: see H. Zemanek.

A. J. Angyan, 1959. Machina reproducatrix. *Mechanisation of thought processes* (D. V. Blake and A. M. Uttley, eds.); London: H. M. Stationery Office, Volume 2, 933–943, 4A.

H. I. Ansoff and D. P. Slevin, 1968. An appreciation of industrial dynamics. *Management Science*, 14(7): 383–397, MD.

G. Antunes: see K. Janda.

L. Apostel, 1965. On cybernetic foundations for deductive and inductive logic. *Third international congress on cybernetics*; Namur, Belgium: Association Internationale de Cybernétique, 419–458, MA.

M. A. Arbib, 1964. *Brains, machines, and mathematics.* New York: McGraw-Hill, MA.

M. A. Arbib, 1969. Memory limitations of stimulus-response models. *Psychological Review*, 76(5): 507–510, MA.

A. G. Arkadev and E. M. Braverman, 1967. *Computers and pattern recognition.* Washington: Thompson Book, MA.

P. Armer, 1961. Attitudes toward intelligent machines. *First Bionics Symposium* (*Living prototypes — the key to new technology*, J. C. Robinette, ed.); Wright-Patterson AFB: Wright Air Development Division, TR 60-600, 13–39, MA.

P. Armer, 1966. "Intelligent" machines. *The evolving society* (A. M. Hilton, ed.); New York: Institute of Cybercultural Research, 113–117, MA.

W. R. Arnheim, 1968. Artificial intelligence: a case study. *The MBA*, 3(1): 43–47, 4A.

H. J. Arnold, B. D. Bucher, H. F. Trotter, and J. W. Tukey, 1956. Monte Carlo techniques in a complex problem about normal samples. *Symposium on Monte Carlo methods* (H. A. Meyer, ed.); New York: Wiley, 80–88, MS.

K. Arnold: see D. D. Lamb.

R. Arnold: see D. D. Lamb.

E. R. Arzac, 1967. The dynamic characteristics of Chow's model: a simulation study. *Journal of Financial and Quantitative Analysis*, 2(4): 383–397, 3D.

W. R. Ashby, 1947. The nervous system as physical machine: with special reference to the origin of adaptive behaviour. *Mind*, 56(221): 44–59, MA.

W. R. Ashby, 1948. Design for a brain. *Electronic Engineering*, 20(250): 379–383, 6A.

W. R. Ashby, 1952. *Design for a brain.* New York: Wiley; second edition in 1960, 6A.

W. R. Ashby with R. W. Gerard, J. B. Wiesner, W. Pitts, J. H. Bigelow, J. Z. Young, W. S. McCulloch, G. Bateson, G. E. Hutchinson, H. Klüver, G. von Bonin, H. Quastler, F. Fremont-Smith, and J. R. Bowman, 1953. Homeostasis. *Ninth conference on cybernetics, Transactions* (*Cybernetics*, H. Von Foerster, ed.); New York: Josiah Macy, Jr. Foundation, 73–108, 6A.

W. R. Ashby, 1959. The mechanisation of habituation. *Mechanisation of thought processes* (D. V. Blake and A. M. Uttley, eds.); London: H. M. Stationery Office, Volume 1, 95–113, 4A.

W. R. Ashby, 1959. A simple computer for demonstrating behaviour. *Mechanisation of thought processes* (D. V. Blake and A. M. Uttley, eds.); London: H. M. Stationery Office, Volume 2, 947–949, 6A.

W. R. Ashby, 1961. What is an intelligent machine? *Joint Computer Conference, Western Proceedings, 19*: 275–280, MA.

W. R. Ashby, 1962. Simulation of a brain. *Computer applications in the behavioral sciences* (H. Borko, ed.); Englewood Cliffs, N. J.: Prentice-Hall, 452–467, MA.

W. R. Ashby, 1963. Cybernetics today and its future contribution to the engineering-sciences. *General Systems*, 8: 207–212, MA.

W. R. Ashby, 1965. Brain and computer. *Third international congress on cybernetics*; Namur, Belgium: Association Internationale de Cybernétique, 778–793, MA.

W. R. Ashby, 1966. Modeling the brain. *IBM scientific computing symposium on simulation models and gaming, Proceedings*; White Plains, N. Y.: IBM Data Processing Division, 195–206, MA.

R. L. Ashenhurst, 1959. Computer capabilities and management models. *Contributions to scientific research in management*; Los Angeles: University of California, 47–58, MD.

A. E. Ashford: see A. W. McEachern.

R. Ashworth, 1968. A note on the selection of gap acceptance criteria for traffic simulation studies. *Transportation Research*, 2(2): 171–175, MD.

M. Asimow: see R. C. Sprowls.

Association for Computing Machinery, 1962. Computer simulation of city traffic. *Communications of the ACM*, 5(4): 224–226, 4D.

M. L. Athavale, 1968. Manufacturing lead time determination by GPSS simulation. *Digest of the second conference on applications of simulation* (A. Ockene, ed.); New York: Institute of Electrical and Electronic Engineers, Publication No. 68C60SIM, 99–100, 7C.

R. J. Atkins: see M. Hamburg.

R. C. Atkinson, 1961. The observing response in discrimination learning. *Journal of Experimental Psychology*, 62(3): 253–262, 3C.

F. Attneave, 1967. Criteria for a tenable theory of form perception. *Models for the perception of speech and visual form* (W. Wathen-Dunn, ed.); Cambridge: MIT Press, 56–67, MA.

A. F. Ax: see A. B. Clymer.

R. E. Bach, Jr., L. Dolanský, and H. L. Stubbs, 1962. Some recent contributions to the Lanchester theory of combat. *Operations Research*, 10(3): 314–326, 7B.

M. A. Baer and H. Zeigler, 1967. Computers and political science: a review article. *Computers and the Humanities*, 1(4): 135–143, MG.

H. D. Baernstein: see C. L. Hull.

H. D. Baernstein and C. L. Hull, 1931. A mechanical model of the conditioned reflex. *Journal of General Psychology*, 5(1): 99–106, 6A.

D. E. Bailey: see R. S. Lehman.

C. T. Baker: see B. P. Dzielinski.

F. B. Baker, 1965. CASE: a program for simulation of concept learning. *Joint Computer Conference, Fall Proceedings*, 27(1): 979–984, 5A.

F. B. Baker, 1967. The internal organization of computer models of cognitive behavior. *Behavioral Science*, 12(2): 156–161, MA.

N. R. Baker: see R. E. Nance.

N. R. Baker and R. E. Nance, 1968. The use of simulation in studying information storage and retrieval systems. *American Documentation*, 19(4): 363–370, 5D.

F. E. Balderston and A. C. Hoggatt, 1962. *Simulation of market processes*. Berkeley: University of California, 7D.

F. E. Balderston and A. C. Hoggatt, 1963. Simulation models: analytic variety and the problem of model reduction. *Symposium on simulation models* (A. C. Hoggatt and F. E. Balderston, eds.); Cincinnati: South-Western, 182–191, MD.

R. F. Bales, A. S. Couch, and P. J. Stone, 1962. The interaction simulator. *Harvard symposium on digital computers and their applications*; Cambridge: Harvard University Press, 305–314, 8B.

R. F. Bales, M. M. Flood, and A. S. Householder, 1952. *Some group interaction models*. Working paper, Rand Corporation, RM-953, 8B.

J. L. Balintfy: see T. H. Naylor.

R. J. Ball: see J. A. C. Brown.

R. J. Ball, 1963. The Cambridge model of economic growth. *Economica*, 30(118): 180–190, MD.

R. J. Ball, 1967. Economic model building for control. *Advancement of Science*, 23(188): 625–642, 1D.

R. J. Ball, 1968. Econometric model building. *Mathematical model building in economics and industry* (C.E.I.R.); New York: Hafner, 15–30, MD.

R. J. Ball and T. Burns, 1968. An econometric approach to short-run analysis of the U. K. economy, 1955–66. *OR, Operational Research Quarterly*, 19(3): 225–256, 3D.

R. B. Banerji, 1960. An information processing program for object recognition. *General Systems*, 5: 117–127, 8A.

H. B. Barbe: see A. N. Crowther.

B. Barber: see D. Brand.

L. D. Barbosa, 1961. *Studies on traffic flow models*. Working paper, Ohio State University Engineering Experiment Station, Report EES 202A-1, 1A.

M. Barenfeld: see H. A. Simon.

P. L. Bargellini, 1965. Considerations on man versus machines for space probing. *Advances in computers, Volume 6* (F. L. Alt and M. Rubinoff, eds.); New York: Academic Press, 195–227, MA.

N. N. Barish: see N. Hauser.

T. Barna: see J. A. C. Brown and see R. M. Solow.

S. Barnoon and H. Wolfe, 1968. Scheduling a multiple operating room system: a simulation approach. *Health Services Research*, *3*(4): 272–285, 5C.

I. Barr: see E. W. Paxson.

I. Barr, 1964. *A net to simulate Morse-code learning*. Working paper, Rand Corporation, RM-3850-PR, 5A.

R. L. Barringer: see I. M. Robinson.

D. J. Bartholomew, 1967. *Stochastic models for social processes*. New York: Wiley, 5D.

R. F. Barton, 1967. A generalized responsiveness (elasticity) function for simulations. *Behavioral Science 12*(4): 337–343, MS.

A. Battersby, 1967. Simulating a despatcher. *Digital simulation in operational research* (S. H. Hollingdale, ed.); London: English Universities Press, 148–152, 7A.

R. A. Bauer and R. D. Buzzell, 1964. Mating behavioral science and simulation. *Harvard Business Review*, *42*(5): 116–124, MG.

W. F. Bauer, 1958. The Monte Carlo method. *SIAM Journal on Applied Mathematics*, *6*(4): 438–451, MS.

D. C. Baxter: see R. E Gagné.

R. C. Baxter: see J. P. Carstens.

Bay Area Simulation Study, 1968. *Jobs, people and land*. Berkeley: University of California Center for Real Estate and Urban Economics, 2D.

R. M. Bayevskiy: see V. V. Parin.

G. W. Baylor and H. A. Simon, 1966. A chess mating combinations program. *Joint Computer Conference, Spring Proceedings, 28*: 431–447, 5A.

N. W. Bazley and P. J. Davis, 1960. Accuracy of Monte Carlo methods in computing finite Markoff chains. *Journal of Research of the National Bureau of Standards, Section B: Mathematical Sciences, 64B*(4): 211–215, MS.

E. M. L. Beale and P. A. B. Hughes, 1966. A computer assessment of media schedules. *OR, Operational Research Quarterly, 17*(4): 381–411, 2C.

R. W. Becker and E. B. Parker, 1963. A model for simulation of attitude change within an individual. *Paul J. Deutschmann memorial papers in mass communications research* (W. A. Danielson, ed.); Cincinnati: Scripps-Howard Research, 45–49, 8A.

M. Beckmann, C. B. McGuire, and C. B. Winsten, 1955. A Monte Carlo experiment. *Studies in the economics of transportation*; New Haven: Yale University Press, 44–45, 5C.

J. G. Beebe-Center: see G. A. Miller.

S. Beer, 1966. *Decision and control*. New York: Wiley, MG.

S. Beer, 1969. *Futures for simulation*. Working paper, Science in General Management Limited (Sigma), MG.

A. G. Beged Dov, C. D. Carmichael, S. T. Ferguson, I. E. Mitchell, and W. H. Struble, 1968. Production programming by revenue curve analysis. *Digest of the second conference on applications of simulation* (A. Ockene, ed.); New York: Institute of Electrical and Electronic Engineers, Publication No. 68C60SIM, 53–54, 5C.

R. I. Beggs: see C. H. Springer.

M. H. Beiby, 1968. Traffic simulation by digital computer. *Traffic Engineering & Control 10*(1): 21–23 and 27, MD.

G. A. Bekey: see E. S. Angel.

A. C. Bell: see T. B. Sheridan.

D. A. Bell, 1964. *Intelligent machines*. London: Pitman, MA.

R. E. Bellman: see N. L. Gilbreath.

R. E. Bellman, 1960. Simulation and stimulation. *Report of the second system simulation symposium* (W. E. Alberts and D. G. Malcolm, eds.) ; American Institute of Industrial Engineers, 1–9, MG.

R. E. Bellman, 1967. Mathematical models of the mind. *Mathematical Biosciences, 1*(2): 287–304, MA.

R. E. Bellman, M. B. Friend, and L. Kurland, 1963. *Psychiatric interviewing and multistage decision processes of adaptive type*. Working paper, Rand Corporation, RM-3732-NIH, MB.

R. E. Bellman, M. B. Friend, and L. Kurland, 1964. *On the construction of a simulation of the initial psychiatric interview*. Working paper, Rand Corporation, RM-4044-NIH, 8A.

R. E. Bellman, M. B. Friend, and L. Kurland, 1966. *A simulation of the initial psychiatric interview*. Working paper, Rand Corporation, R-449-RC, 5B.

C. Ben, R. J. Bouchard, and C. E. Sweet, Jr., 1965. An evaluation of simplified procedures for determining travel patterns in a small urban area. *Highway Research Record, 88*: 137–170, 1C.

F. E. Bender, 1966. *An analysis of a firm and industry facing a seasonal demand: a computer simulation of the broiler industry*. Doctoral dissertation, University of North Carolina at Raleigh, 7D.

F. G. Benhard, 1959. *Simulation of a traffic intersection on a digital computer*. Masters thesis, University of California at Los Angeles, 7C.

B. Benjamin, W. P. Jolly, and J. Maitland, 1960. Operational research and advertising: theories of response. *OR, Operational Research Quarterly, 11*(4): 205–218, 3C.

A. M. Bennett, 1967. The use of simulation techniques in the analysis of a command control and communications system. *Digital simulation in operational research* (S. H. Hollingdale, ed.); London: English Universities Press, 218–226, 7B.

E. M. Bennett and J. W. Degan, 1961. The diagnostic process in men and automata. *IEEE Transactions on Man-Machine Systems, MMS-2*(2): 68-72, MA.

G. K. Bennett and L. B. Ward, 1933. A model of the synthesis of conditioned reflexes. *American Journal of Psychology, 45*(2): 339–342, 6A.

J. C. Benson, 1962. *A programme to simulate on a Pegasus II computer the behaviour of traffic at a single intersection controlled by vehicle-actuated traffic signals.* Working paper, Road Research Laboratory, Laboratory Note No. LN/182/JCB, 7C.

O. Benson, 1961. A simple diplomatic game. *International politics and foreign policy* (J. N. Rosenau, ed.); Glencoe, Ill.: Free Press, 504–511, 7D.

O. Benson, 1962. Simulation of international relations and diplomacy. *Computer applications in the behavioral sciences* (H. Borko, ed.); Englewood Cliffs, N. J.: Prentice-Hall, 574–595, 7D.

S. Ben-Tuvia: see S. Ehrenfield.

H. M. Berger: see B. O. Koopman.

E. C. Berkeley: see L. E. S. Green, see G. G. Hawley, and see E. F. Murphy.

E. C. Berkeley, 1949. *Giant brains.* New York: Wiley, MA.

E. C. Berkeley, 1951. Light sensitive electronic beast. *Radio Electronics, 23*(3): 46–48, 7A.

E. C. Berkeley, 1952. Avenues for future developments in computing machinery. *Computers and Automation, 1*(4): 19–20, MA.

R. R. Berman, 1967. Simulation as a problem-solving technique. *American Society of Civil Engineers, Proceedings, 93*(PL1): 21–45, MG.

R. Bernhard, 1963. Towards a chemical kinetic brain model. *Cybernetica, 6*(3): 158–173. Also published in 1964 in *Journal of Theoretical Biology, 6*(2): 244–257, MA.

A. Bernstein: see R. P. Abelson and see I. D. Pool.

J. M. Beshers, 1965. Birth projections with cohort models. *Demography, 2*: 593–599, 8C.

J. M. Beshers, 1965. Substantive issues in models of large-scale social systems. *Computer methods in the analysis of large-scale social systems* (J. M. Beshers, ed.); Cambridge: MIT-Harvard Joint Center for Urban Studies, 85–91, MD.

J. M. Beshers, 1967. Computer models of social processes: the case of migration. *Demography, 4*(2): 838–842, MC.

J. M. Beshers, 1967. *Population processes in social systems.* New York: Free Press, 5C.

J. M. Beshers, 1968. The demographic model: empirical and policy aspects. *The Regional Science Association, Papers and Proceedings, 21*: 165–169, 5D.

R. L. Beurle, 1956. Properties of a mass of cells capable of regenerating pulses. *Royal Society of London, Philosophical Transactions, Series B: Biological Sciences, 240*(B669): 55–94, MA.

H. W. Bevis, 1959. A model for predicting urban travel patterns. *Journal of the American Institute of Planners, 25*(2): 87–89, 3C.

W. E. Biddle, 1965. The reality of the image as illustrated by hypnosis and the computer. *American Journal of Clinical Hypnosis, 8*(1): 8–9, MA.

J. L. Biermann, 1963. Traffic analysis, forecast and assignment by means of electronic computers. *International Road Safety and Traffic Review, 11*(1): 21–23 and 35, 5C.

K. Blake and G. Gordon, 1964. Systems simulation with digital computers. *IBM Systems Journal, 3*(1): 14–20, MG.

R. W. Blanning: see J. R. Emshoff.

J. Blaxall: see C. C. Abt.

R. L. Bleyl, 1964. Simulation of traffic flow to compare regular and flashing traffic signal operation. *Institute of Traffic Engineers, Proceedings, 34*: 152–161, 5D.

H. D. Block, 1962. The Perceptron: a model for brain functioning. I. *Reviews of Modern Physics, 34*(1): 123–135, 5A.

S. H. Block, 1963. *A neural net for adaptive behavior.* Working paper, Rand Corporation, RM-3868-PR, 4A.

A. M. Blum, 1964. Digital simulation of urban traffic. *IBM Systems Journal, 3*(1): 41–50, 7C.

J. Blum, 1967. Modelling, simulation and information system design. *Information system science and technology* (D. E. Walker, ed.); Washington: Thompson, 301–306, MG.

G. P. Blunden and H. S. Krasnow, 1967. The process concept as a basis for simulation modeling. *SCi Simulation, 9*(2): 89–93, MG.

W. R. Blunden: see W. R. McDonald and see R. L. Pretty.

D. G. Bobrow, 1964. *Natural language input for a computer problem solving system.* Doctoral dissertation, Massachusetts Institute of Technology, 7A.

D. G. Bobrow, 1964. A question-answering system for high school algebra word problems. *Joint Computer Conference, Fall Proceedings, 26*: 591–614, 7A.

D. G. Bobrow, J. B. Fraser, and M. R. Quillian, 1967. Automated language processing. *Annual review of information science and technology, Volume 2* (C. A. Cuadra, ed.); New York: Interscience, 161–186, MA.

R. Boguslaw, 1965. *The new utopians.* Englewood Cliffs, N. J.: Prentice-Hall, MA.

R. Boguslaw and R. H. Davis, 1969. Social process modeling: a comparison of a live and computerized simulation. *Behavioral Science, 14*(3): 197–203, 3B.

M. M. Bongard, 1961. Modelling of the process of recognition in a digital computer. *Biophysics, 6*(2): 143–156, 7A.

C. P. Bonini, 1962. A simulation of a business firm. *Joint Computer Conference, Spring Proceedings, 21*: 33–37, 5B.

C. P. Bonini, 1963. *Simulation of information and decision systems in the firm.* Englewood Cliffs, N. J.: Prentice-Hall; second edition in 1967 by Markham Publishing of Chicago, 5B.

C. P. Bonini, 1964. Simulating organizational behavior. *New perspectives in organization research* (W. W. Cooper, H. J. Leavitt, and M. W. Shelly); New York: Wiley, 276–288, 5B.

C. P. Bonini, 1964. Simulation of organizational behavior. *Management controls* (C. P. Bonini, R. K. Jaedicke, and H. M. Wagner, eds.); New York: McGraw-Hill 91–101, 7D.

E G Boring, 1946. Mind and mechanism. *American Journal of Psychology*, *59*(2): 173–192, MA.

H. Borko, 1965. Integrating computers into behavioral science research. *Joint Computer Conference, Fall Proceedings*, *27*(1): 527–532, MG.

Boston College Seminar Research Bureau, 1961. *Travel in the Boston region 1959-1980, Volume II — trip distribution procedures*. Boston: Boston College, 2C.

R. J. Bouchard: see C. Ben.

R. J. Bouchard and C. E. Pyers, 1965. Use of gravity model for describing urban travel. *Highway Research Record*, *88*: 1–43, 1C.

J. M. Boughton and T. H. Naylor, 1968. *Simulation experiments with a monetary policy model*. Working paper, Duke University, 2D.

J. M. Boughton, E. H. Brau, T. H. Naylor, and W. P. Yohe, 1969. An econometric model for monetary policy. *American Statistical Association, 1968 Proceedings of the Business and Economic Statistics Section*: 365– 370, 8D.

J. M. Boughton, E. H. Brau, T. H. Naylor, and W. P. Yohe, 1969. A policy model of the United States monetary sector. *Southern Economic Journal*, *35*(4): 333–346, 8D.

H. D. Bouland, 1967. Truck queues at country grain elevators. *Operations Research*, *14*(4): 649–659, 5C.

M. D. F. Boulton, N. J. Hopkins, J. B. Fain, and W. W. Fain, 1966. Comparing results from a war game and a computer simulation. *Proceedings of the fourth international conference on operational research* (D. B. Hertz and J. Melese, eds.); New York: Wiley-Interscience, 739–753, 3D.

P. Le Bourgeoist 1968. Simulation study of a series of synchronized intersections. *Digest of the second conference on applications of simulation* (A. Ockene, ed.); New York: Institute of Electrical and Electronic Engineers, Publication No. 68C60SIM, 212–217, 7C.

W. G. Bouricius and J. M. Keller, 1959. Simulation of human problem-solving. *Joint Computer Conference, Western Proceedings*, *15*: 116–119, 7A.

L. W. Bowden, 1965. *Diffusion of the decision to irrigate: simulation of the spread of a new resource management practice in the Colorado northern high plains*. Chicago: University of Chicago Department of Geography, Research Paper No. 97, 3D.

G. H. Bower: see T. R. Trabasso and see G. Wolford.

E. H. Bowman and R. B. Fetter, 1957. Monte Carlo analysis. *Analysis for production management*; Homewood, Ill.: Irwin, 297–312, MG.

E. H. Bowman and R. B. Fetter, 1967. Simulation and heuristics. *Analysis for production and operations management*; Homewood, Ill.: Irwin, 413–476, MG.

D. E. Boyce: see H. R. Hamilton.

D. E. Boyce and R. W. Cote, 1966. Verification of land use forecasting models: procedures and data requirements. *Highway Research Record*, *126*: 60–65, MC.

D. E. Boyce and S. E. Goldstone, 1966. A regional economic simulation model for urban transportation planning. *Highway Research Record*, *149*: 29–41, 2D.

D. F. Boyd, 1964. *The emerging role of enterprise simulation models*. Working paper, IBM Advanced Systems Development Division, 5D.

D. F. Boyd, 1966. Enterprise models: a new management technique. *Industrial Management Review*, *8*(1): 55–70, 7D.

D. F. Boyd and H. S. Krasnow, 1963. Economic evaluation of management information systems. *IBM Systems Journal*, *2*(March): 2–23, 7D.

D. F. Boyd, H. S. Krasnow, and A. C. R. Petit, 1964. Simulation of an integrated steel mill. *IBM Systems Journal*, *3*(1): 51–56, 7D.

J. M. Braasch, 1966. Business games, programmed players, and individual decision-making profiles—basic technique. *Proceedings of the fourth international conference on operational research* (D. B. Hertz and J. Melese, eds.); New York: Wiley-Interscience, 959–973, 7A.

H. Bradner, 1937. A new mechanical "learner". *Journal of General Psychology*, *17*(2): 414–419, 5A.

R. Brain, 1962. Traffic simulation for urban areas. *Traffic Engineering & Control*, *3*(9): 534–537, MC.

S. N. Braines, 1962. Matrix structure in simulation of learning. *IEEE Transactions on Information Theory*, *IT-8*(5): S-186–190, 8A.

M. C. Branch, 1966. *Planning*. New York: Wiley, MG.

D. Brand: see D. M. Hill.

D. Brand, B. Barber, and M. Jacobs, 1967. Technique for relating transportation improvements and urban development patterns. *Highway Research Record*, *207*: 53–67, 3C.

N. M. Branston, 1968. Activity regulation in perceptrons. *Collected technical papers, Volume 3* (F. Rosenblatt, ed.); Ithaca, N. Y.: Cornell University Cognitive Systems Research Program, Report No. 12, 79–138, MA.

P. Bratley: see J. P. Thorne.

P. Bratley and D. J. Dakin, 1968. A limited dictionary for syntactic analysis. *Machine intelligence 2* (E. Dale and D. Michie, eds.); New York: American Elsevier, 173–181, 7A.

P. Bratley, H. Dewar, and J. P. Thorne, 1967. Recognition of syntactic structure by computer. *Nature*, *216*(5119): 969–973, 7A.

E. H. Brau: see J. M. Boughton.

M. L. Braunstein and O. F. Coleman, 1967. An information-processing model of the aircraft accident investigator. *Human Factors*, *9*(1): 61–70, 1A.

M. L. Braunstein, K. R. Laughery, and J. B. Siegfried, 1963. *Computer simulation of driver behavior during car following: a methodological study*. Working paper: Cornell Aeronautical Laboratory, YM-1797-H-1, 8A.

M. L. Braunstein, K. R. Laughery, and J. B. Siegfried, 1964. Computer simulation of the automobile driver: a model of the car follower. *Highway Research Record*, *55*: 21–28, 8A.

E. M. Braverman: see A. G. Arkadev.

A. S. Bregman, 1966. Is recognition memory all-or-none? *Journal of Verbal Learning and Verbal Behavior*, *5*(1): 1–6, 3C.

A. S. Bregman and D. W. Chambers, 1966. All-or-none learning of attributes. *Journal of Experimental Psychology*, *71*(6): 785–793, 3C.

M. E. Brenner, 1963. *Correlated and selective sampling applied to the simulation of some inventory systems.* Doctoral dissertation, Johns Hopkins University, MS.

M. E. Brenner, 1963. Selective sampling—a technique for reducing sample size in simulation of decision-making problems. *Journal of Industrial Engineering*, *14*(6): 291–296, MS.

M. E. Brenner, 1965. A relation between decision making penalty and simulation sample size for inventory systems. *Operations Research*, *13*(3): 433–443, MS.

M. E. Brenner, 1966. A cost model for determining the sample size in the simulation of inventory systems. *Journal of Industrial Engineering*, *17*(3): 141–144, MS.

R. Breton, 1965. *Output norms and productive behavior of industrial work groups.* Working paper, Johns Hopkins University, 5B.

W. G. Briggs: see J. M. Dutton.

W. G. Briggs, 1960. *Baseball-o-mation, a simulation study.* Boston: Harbridge House, 2B.

W. G. Briggs, 1965. *Some notes on digital computer simulation.* Boston: Harbridge House, 2B.

H. J. Brightman, E. E. Kaczka, and B. H. Shane, 1969. *A simulation model of individual behavior in a work group.* Working paper, University of Massachusetts, Paper 69-821-1, 2B.

H. J. Brightman, E. E. Kaczka, and B. H. Shane, 1969. *A simulation model of individual behavior in a work group.* Working paper, University of Massachusetts, Paper 69-822-2-(55), 3B.

E. R. Broad, Jr., 1968. Simulation of a rapid-exit industrial parking structure. *Digest of the second conference on applications of simulation* (A. Ockene, ed.); New York: Institute of Electrical and Electronic Engineers, Publication No. 68C60SIM, 205–211, 5C.

D. E. Broadbent, 1957. A mechanical model for human attention and immediate memory. *Psychological Review*, *64*(3): 205–215, 8A.

S. R. Broadbent, 1963. Advertising and computers. *Journal of the Market Research Society*, (11): 22–23, MC.

S. R. Broadbent, 1965. *Computer Assessment of Media, the LPE media model.* London: The London Press Exchange, 2C.

S. R. Broadbent, 1965. *Media planning and computers by 1970.* London: The Thomson Organisation, MC.

S. R. Broadbent, 1965. A year's experience of the LPE media model. *Eleventh annual conference, Proceedings*; New York: Advertising Research Foundation, 51–56, 5C.

S. R. Broadbent, 1966. Media planning and computers by 1970. *Applied Statistics*, *15*(3): 234–256, MC.

A. Broberg, 1963. A computer method for traffic assignment developed and used in Stockholm. *International Road Safety and Traffic Review*, *11*(3): 27–31, MC.

W. H. Brockman, 1966. *A stimulus conditioning learning model and its application to pattern recognition.* Doctoral dissertation, Purdue University, 3C.

K. Brodman, 1960. Diagnostic decisions by machine. *IEEE Transactions on Bio-Medical Engineering*, *BME-7*(3): 216–219, 5A.

G. E. Brokke, 1959. Program for assigning traffic to a highway network. *Highway Research Board Bulletin*, *244*: 89–97, 7C.

G. E. Brokke and W. L. Mertz, 1958. Evaluating trip forecasting methods with an electronic computer. *Highway Research Board Bulletin*, *203*: 52–75, 3C.

F. C. Brooks, 1965. The stochastic properties of large battle models. *Operations Research*, *13*(1): 1–17, MS.

L. Brotman and J. Minker, 1957. Digital simulation of complex traffic problems in communications systems. *Operations Research*, *5*(5): 670–679, 5C.

L. Brotman and B. Seid, 1960. Digital simulation of a massed-bomber, manned-interceptor encounter. *Operations Research*, *8*(3): 421–423, 7B.

A. Brown: see J. R. N. Stone.

A. Brown, 1963. Industrial outputs in 1970. *British Association for Commercial and Industrial Education, Papers presented at the BACIE spring conference* (*Economic growth and manpower*): 15–26, 5D.

A. Brown, 1965. *A programme for growth, Volume 6: exploring 1970.* London: Chapman and Hall, 5D.

G. W. Brown, 1956. Monte Carlo methods. *Modern mathematics for the engineer* (E. F. Beckenbach, ed.); New York: McGraw-Hill, 279–303, MG.

J. A. C. Brown: see J. R. N. Stone.

J. A. C. Brown, J. P. Lewis, R. J. Ball, C. E. V. Leser, T. Barna, R. M. Goodwin, L. Johansen, F. R. Oliver, C. van de Panne, M. McManus, A. Smith, J. Johnston, and L. R. Klein, 1964. Discussion on the paper by L. R. Klein. *Econometric analysis for national economic planning* (P. E. Hart, G. Mills, and J. K. Whitaker, eds.); London: Butterworths, 169–178, MD.

J. S. Brown: see J. W. Gyr.

L. A. Brown, 1965. *Models for spatial diffusion research—a review*. Working paper, Northwestern University Department of Geography, Research Report No. 10, MD.

L. A. Brown, 1968. Diffusion dynamics. *Lund Studies in Geography, Series B, 29*: 1–94, MD.

L. A. Brown, 1968. *Diffusion processes and location*. Philadelphia: Regional Science Research Institute, MD.

M. Brown and P. Taubman, 1962. A forecasting model of Federal purchases of goods and services. *American Statistical Association, 1961 Proceedings of the Business and Economic Statistics Section*: 146–154, 1D.

R. G. Brown, 1958. A general-purpose inventory-control simulation. *Report of system simulation symposium* (D. G. Malcolm, ed); New York: American Institute of Industrial Engineers, 6–16, 7C.

W. B. Brown, 1967. Model-building and organizations. *Academy of Management Journal, 10*(2): 169 178, MG.

J. J. Browne, 1967. Simulation of public transportation operations. *American Institute of Industrial Engineers, Proceedings of the Annual National Conference, 18*: 301–306, 7C.

J. J. Browne and J. J. Kelly, 1968. Simulation of elevator system for world's tallest buildings. *Transportation Science, 2*(1): 35–56, 2D.

R. P. Browning, 1962. Computer programs as theories of political processes. *Journal of Politics, 24*(3): 562–582, MG.

R. P. Browning, 1968. Hypotheses about political recruitment: a partially data-based computer simulation. *Simulation in the study of politics* (W. D. Coplin, ed.); Chicago: Markham, 303–325, 2C.

R. P. Browning, 1969. *Quality of collective decisions*. Working paper, Michigan State University, 5B.

R. P. Browning, 1969. *Computer simulation of political bargaining*. Working paper, Michigan State University, 8B.

H. W. Bruck, S. H. Putman, and W. A. Steger, 1966. Evaluation of alternative transportation proposals: the Northeast Corridor. *Journal of the American Institute of Planners, 32*(6): 322–333, MD.

J. M. Bruggeman: see K. W. Heathington.

J. M. Bruggeman and K. W. Heathington, 1969. *Sensitivity to various parameters of a demand-scheduled-bus system computer simulation model*. Working paper, Northwestern University; to be published by the Highway Research Board, 7C.

R. D. Brunner, 1968. Some comments on simulating theories of political development. *Simulation in the study of politics* (W. D. Coplin, ed.); Chicago: Markham, 329–342, 8D.

J. A. Bubenko, Jr., 1968. Simulating a "management game" with programmed decisions. *Digest of the second conference on applications of simulation* (A. Ockene, ed.); New York: Institute of Electrical and Electronic Engineers, Publication No. 68C60SIM, 222–229, 5B.

B. D. Bucher: see H. J. Arnold.

D. J. Buckley, 1962. Road traffic headway distributions. *Australian Road Research Board, Proceedings 1*(1): 153–183, MD.

C. R. Budrose: see T. B. Roby.

R. J. Bueno, 1966. *Some practical solutions to two statistical problems in simulation*. Masters thesis, University of California at Los Angeles, MS.

E. S. Buffa: see A. Reisman.

E. S. Buffa, 1963. Simulation models. *Models for production and operations management*; New York: Wiley, 505–568, MG.

R. Buhler: see P. Kunstadter.

J. H. Buhr, T. C. Meserole, and D. R. Drew, 1968. A digital simulation program of a section of freeway with entrance and exit ramps. *Highway Research Record, 230*: 15–31, 7D.

M. Bunge, 1956. Do computers think? *British Journal for the Philosophy of Science, 7*(26): 139–148, MA.

D. S. Burdick: see T. H. Naylor.

D. S. Burdick and T. H. Naylor, 1966. Design of computer simulation experiments for industrial systems. *Communications of the ACM, 9*(5): 329–339, MS.

D. S. Burdick and T. H. Naylor, 1969. Response surface designs. *The design of computer simulation experiments* (T. H. Naylor, ed); Durham: Duke University Press, Chapter 4, MS.

D. S. Burdick and T. H. Naylor, 1969. Response surface methods in economics. *Review of the International Statistical Institute, 37*(1): 18–35, MS.

Bureau of Public Roads, 1963. *Calibrating and testing a gravity model for any size urban area*. Washington: Bureau of Public Roads, MC.

Bureau of Public Roads, 1963. *Calibrating and testing a gravity model with a small computer*. Washington: Bureau of Public Roads, MC.

A. R. Burgess, 1962. Comments on "Simulation in the application of wage incentives to multiple machines." *Journal of Industrial Engineering, 13*(4): 264–267, MB.

T. Burns: see R. J. Ball.

D. B. Burrell, 1967. Obeying rules and following instructions. *Philosophy and cybernetics* (F. J. Crosson and K. M. Sayre, eds); Notre Dame, Indiana: University of Notre Dame Press, 203–232, MA.

A. J. Burton and R. G. Mills, 1960. New applications of business computers. *Electronic computers and their business applications*; London: Ernest Benn, 294–296. MG.

R. R. Bush, 1963. Estimation and evaluation. *Handbook of mathematical psychology* (R. D. Luce, R. R. Bush, and E. Galanter, eds.); New York: Wiley, Volume 1, 429–469, MS.

R. R. Bush and F. Mosteller, 1955. *Stochastic models for learning*. New York: Wiley, 3C.

R. R. Bush and F. Mosteller, 1959. A comparison of eight models. *Studies in mathematical learning theory* (R. R. Bush and W. K. Estes, eds.); Stanford: Stanford University Press, 293–307, 3C.

R. R. Bush, E. H. Galanter, and R. D. Luce, 1959. Tests of the "beta model". *Studies in mathematical learning theory* (R. R. Bush and W. K. Estes, eds.); Stanford: Stanford University Press, 382–399, 3C.

D. D. Bushnell, 1967. Applications of computer technology to the improvement of learning. *The computer in American education* (D. D. Bushnell and D. W. Allen, eds.); New York: Wiley, 59–76. MG.

N. P. Buslenko, 1964. Application of the Monte Carlo method to the investigation of mass service or congestion processes, including queueing. *Method of statistical testing* (Y. A. Shreider, ed.); Amsterdam: Elsevier, 127–155. Also published in 1966 under the title *The Monte Carlo method*; London: Pergamon; 184–215, MC.

D. L. Bussard, 1968. Communication network design using message flow simulation. *Digest of the second conference on applications of simulation* (A. Ockene, ed.); New York: Institute of Electrical and Electronic Engineers, Publication No. 68C60SIM, 198–201, 5C.

G. R. Bussey, 1965. Computer experiments in motor learning. *Joint Computer Conference, Fall Proceedings*, *27*(1): 753–774, 5A.

J. N. Buxton, 1961. Monte Carlo simulations on computers. *New Scientist*, *9*(226): 678–679, MC.

R. D. Buzzell: see R. A. Bauer.

R. D. Buzzell, 1964. Benton & Bowles, Inc.—Service Bureau Corporation. *Mathematical models and marketing management*; Boston: Harvard University, 180–199, 7D.

R. D. Buzzell, 1964. Everclear Plastics Company. *Mathematical models and marketing management*; Boston: Harvard University, 112–135, 5C.

R. A. Byerly, 1960. *The use of mathematical models in the analysis and improvement of bank operations.* Chicago: NABAC Research Institute, Confidential Research Bulletin *1*(5): 12–19, MC.

R. Byrne: see D. D. Lamb.

C-E-I-R, 1963. *The Signal Corps ground combat simulator: theory, organization and structure of the model.* Fort Huachuca, Ariz.: C-E-I-R, AD-410799, 7D.

A. J. Cacioppo, 1960. *Possibilities for simulation of human dynamics and perception.* New York: American Society of Mechanical Engineers, Paper No. 60-AV-39, MA.

M. L. Cadwallader, 1959. The cybernetic analysis of change in complex social organizations. *American Journal of Sociology*, *65*(2): 154–157, MD.

E. R. Caianiello, 1961. Outline of a theory of thought-processes and thinking machines. *Journal of Theoretical Biology*, *1*(2): 204–235, 8A.

E. R. Caianiello, 1964. Mathematical and physical problems in the study of brain models. *Neural theory and modeling* (R. F. Reiss, ed.); Stanford: Stanford University Press, 98–104, MA.

E. T. D. Calhoun, 1962. Why machines will never think. *Automation* (M. H. Philipson, ed.); New York: Vintage, 180–212, MA.

W. B. Calland, 1959. Traffic forecasting for freeway planning. *Journal of the American Institute of Planners*, *25*(2): 82–86, 3C.

H. C. Calpine: see B. van der Pol.

J. F. Calvert: see R. H. Strotz.

T. W. Calvert and F. Meno, 1969. An approach to modelling the nervous system with applications to the cerebellum. *Simulation and modeling conference* (R. U. Benson, ed.); Pittsburgh: Pittsburgh chapters of ACM, IEEE-EC, and IEEE-SSC, and Midwest SCi, 207–212, 8A.

E. W. Campbell, 1956. A mechanical method for assigning traffic to expressways. *Highway Research Board Bulletin*, *130*: 27–46. Also published in 1958 in *Traffic Engineering*, *28*(5): 9–14 and 35, MC.

V. E. Cangelosi and J. G. March, 1966. An experiment in model building. *Behavioral Science*, *11*(1): 71–75, MA.

B. L. Capehart, 1967. *Digital simulation of the homeostat modified to show memory and learning.* Doctoral dissertation, University of Oklahoma, 5A.

B. L. Capehart and R. A. Terry, 1968. Digital simulation of the homeostat modified to show memory and learning. *IEEE Transactions on Systems Science and Cybernetics*, SSC-4(2): 188–190, 5A.

G. J. Caras, 1968. Computer simulation of a small information system. *American Documentation*, *19*(2): 120–122, 7D.

J. R. Carbonell, 1966. A queueing model of many-instrument visual sampling. *IEEE Transactions on Man-Machine Systems*, MMS-7(4): 157–164, 6A.

J. R. Carbonell, J. L. Ward, and J. W. Senders, 1968. A queueing model of visual sampling: experimental validation. *IEEE Transactions on Man-Machine Systems*, MMS-9(3): 82–87, 3A.

B. R. Carlson, 1964. Industrial dynamics. *Management Services*, *1*(2): 32–39, 7D.

B. R. Carlson, 1964. An industrialist views industrial dynamics. *Industrial Management Review*, *6*(1): 15–20, MD.

R. H. Carlson, 1968. Better schedules—automatically. *IEEE Transactions on Engineering Management*, EM-15(4): 188-192, 7D.

M. Carlsson: see H. Hyrenius.

C. D. Carmichael: see A. G. Beged Dov.

B. Carnahan: see D. L. Katz.

J. B. Carroll, 1962. Computer applications in the investigation of models in educational research. *Harvard symposium on digital computers and their applications*; Cambridge: Harvard University Press, 48–58, 5C.

J. D. Carroll: see R. P. Abelson.

J. D. Carroll, R. P. Abelson, and W. Reinfeld, 1963. *A computer program which assesses the credibility of assertions*. Working paper, Yale University, 7A.

J. D. Carroll, Jr.: see R. L. Creighton.

J. D. Carroll, Jr., 1959. A method of traffic assignment to an urban network. *Highway Research Board Bulletin, 224*: 64–71, 7C.

T. W. Carroll: see G. J. Hanneman.

T. W. Carroll, 1969. *SINDI 2: simulation of innovation diffusion in a rural community of Brazil*. East Lansing: Michigan State University Computer Institute for Social Science Research, Technical Report 8, 1B.

T. W. Carroll and R. V. Farace, 1968. *Systems analysis, computer simulation, and survey research: applications to social research in developing countries*. Working paper, Michigan State University Department of Communication, MG.

T. W. Carroll and G. J. Hanneman, 1968. Two models of innovation diffusion. *Digest of the second conference on applications of simulation* (A. Ockene, ed.); New York: Institute of Electrical and Electronic Engineers, Publication No. 68C60SIM, 158–162, 2B.

A. G. Carruthers: see R. M. Solow.

J. P. Carstens, R. C. Baxter, and J. Reitman, 1966. Economic models for rail systems. *IEEE Transactions on Systems Science and Cybernetics, SSC-2*(2): 128–134, 7C.

D. A. Carter, A. Colker, and J. Leib, 1968. Simulation model for vocational educational facility planning. *Journal of Industrial Engineering, 19*(2): 68–75, 7C.

E. E. Carter and K. J. Cohen, 1967. The use of simulation in selecting branch banks. *Industrial Management Review, 8*(2): 55–69, 7C.

M. Carter: see S. L. Levy.

C. L. Case, 1968. Traffic prognosis by comprehensive simulation. *Traffic Engineering & Control, 10*(4): 178–180, MC.

S. Ceccato, 1965. Suggestions for anthropology: the machine which observes and describes. *The use of computers in anthropology* (D. H. Hymes, ed.); The Hague: Mouton, 465–500, 5A.

S. Ceccato, 1965. Towards the automation of mental activities. *Third international congress on cybernetics*; Namur, Belgium: Association Internationale de Cybernétique, 473–476, MA.

F. J. Cesario: see H. R. Hamilton.

D. W. Chambers: see A. S. Bregman.

J. C. Chambers and S. K. Mullick, 1968. Strategic new product planning models for dynamic situations. *IEEE Transactions on Engineering Management, EM-15*(3): 100–108, MD.

A. M. Chammah: see An. Rapoport.

A. Chapanis, 1961. Men, machines, and models. *American Psychologist, 16*(3): 113–131, MA.

F. S. Chapin, Jr.: see T. G. Donnelly.

F. S. Chapin, Jr., 1965. A model for simulating residential development. *Journal of the American Institute of Planners, 31*(2): 120–125, 5C.

F. S. Chapin, Jr., and S. F. Weiss, 1962. *Factors influencing land development*. Chapel Hill: University of North Carolina Institute for Research in Social Science, 8C.

F. S. Chapin, Jr. and S. F. Weiss, 1968. A probabilistic model for residential growth. *Transportation Research, 2*(4): 375–390, 1C.

A. Chapuis and E. Droz, 1958. *Automata*. Neuchatel: Editions du Griffon, MA.

G. Charlesworth, 1961. Science and the road traffic problem. *Impact of Science on Society, 11*(3): 183–196, MC.

Y. I. Cherniak, 1963. The electronic simulation of information systems for central planning. *Economics of Planning, 3*(1): 23–40, 8D.

Y. I. Cherniak, 1964. Electronic simulation of planning systems in the U.S.S.R. *Data Processing, 6*(1): 18–23, MD.

H. Chernoff, 1969. Sequential designs. *The design of computer simulation experiments* (T. H. Naylor, ed.); Durham: Duke University Press, Chapter 5, MS.

A. L. Chernyavskii, 1967. Computer simulation of the process of solving complex logical problems. *Automation and Remote Control, 28*(1): 145–167, MA.

C. H. Cherryholmes, 1966. *The House of Representatives and foreign aid: a computer simulation of roll call voting*. Doctoral dissertation, Northwestern University, 3D.

C. H. Cherryholmes and M. J. Shapiro, 1969. *Representatives and roll calls*. New York: Bobbs-Merrill, 1D.

H. Chestnut, 1962. Modeling and simulation. *Electrical Engineering, 81*(8): 609–613, MG.

Chicago Area Transportation Study, 1960. *Final report, Volume II: data projections*. Chicago: Chicago Area Transportation Study, 2C.

D. N. Chorafas, 1965. *Systems and simulation*. New York: Academic Press, MG.

N. K. Choudry, Y. Kotowitz, J. A. Sawyer, and J. W. L. Winder, 1968. *An annual econometric model of the Canadian economy, 1928–1966*. Working paper, University of Toronto, 2D.

K. Chu: see T. H. Naylor.

K. Chu and T. H. Naylor, 1965. A dynamic model of the firm. *Management Science, 11*(7): 736–750, 7C.

S.-H. Chung, 1968. Neurophysiology of the visual system. *Recognizing patterns* (P. A. Kolers and M. Eden, eds.); Cambridge: MIT Press, 82–101, MA.

C. W. Churchman, 1963. An analysis of the concept of simulation. *Symposium on simulation models* (A. C. Hoggatt and F. E. Balderston, eds.); Cincinnati: South-Western, 1–12, MG.

J. C. R. Clapham, 1958. A Monte Carlo problem in underground communications. *OR, Operational Research Quarterly, 9*(1): 36–54, 2C.

J. C. R. Clapham and H. D. Dunn, 1957. Communications in collieries. *First international conference on operational research, Proceedings* (M. Davies, R. T. Eddison, and T. Page, eds.); Baltimore: Operations Research Society of America, 291–305, 5C.

C. E. Clark, 1960. *Importance sampling in Monte Carlo analyses.* Working paper, System Development Corporation, TM-505, MS.

C. E. Clark, 1960. The utility of statistics of random numbers. *Operations Research, 8*(2): 185–195, MS.

C. E. Clark, 1961. Importance sampling in Monte Carlo analysis. *Operations Research, 9*(5): 603–620, MS.

D. Clark, T. Rands, and R. I. Tricker, 1969. Hybrid simulation of business systems. *Journal of Management Studies, 6*(3): 281–292, 7D.

G. E. Clark, Jr., P. F. Michelsen, and B. Urban, 1957. Analogue computer solutions of Lanchester's equations with constant coefficients. *War gaming, Cosmagon, and Zigspiel* (No editor); Bethesda: Johns Hopkins University Operations Research Office, ORO-SP-12, AD-235892, 65–78, 5D.

J. A. Clark: see E. M. Rogers.

W. A. Clark: see B. G. Farley.

W. A. Clark and B. G. Farley, 1955. Generalization of pattern recognition in a self-organizing system. *Joint Computer Conference, Western Proceedings, 7:* 86–91, 4A.

G. P. E. Clarkson, 1962. *Portfolio selection: a simulation of trust investment.* Englewood Cliffs, N. J.: Prentice-Hall, 8A.

G. P. E. Clarkson, 1963. Interactions of economic theory and operations research. *Models of markets* (A. R. Oxenfeldt, ed.); New York: Columbia University Press, 339–361, MG.

G. P. E. Clarkson, 1963. A model of the trust investment process. *Computers and thought* (E. A. Feigenbaum and J. Feldman, eds.); New York: McGraw-Hill, 347–371, 8A.

G. P. E. Clarkson, 1963. A model of trust investment behavior. *A behavioral theory of the firm* (R. M. Cyert and J. G. March); Englewood Cliffs, N. J.: Prentice–Hall, 253–267, 8A.

G. P. E. Clarkson and A. H. Meltzer, 1960. Portfolio selection: a heuristic approach. *Journal of Finance, 15*(4): 465-480, 8A.

G. P. E. Clarkson and W. F. Pounds. 1963. Theory and method in the exploration of human decision behavior. *Industrial Management Review, 5*(1): 17–27, MA.

G. P. E. Clarkson and H. A. Simon, 1960. Simulation of individual and group behavior. *American Economic Review, 50*(5): 920–932, MA.

C. J. Clawson, 1959. Quantifying motivation research to predict consumer behavior. *Advancing marketing efficiency* (L. H. Stockman, ed.); Chicago: American Marketing Association, 54–70, MC.

H. J. Claycamp and A. E. Amstutz, 1968. Simulation techniques in the analysis of marketing strategy. *Applications of the sciences in marketing management* (F. M. Bass, C. W. King, and E. A. Pessemier, eds.); New York: Wiley, 113–150, 4D.

W. C. Clemens, Jr., 1968. A propositional anlysis of the international relations theory in TEMPER—a computer simulation of cold war conflict. *Simulation in the study of politics* (W. D. Coplin, ed.); Chicago: Markham, 59–101, 5D.

D. J. Clough, J. B. Levine, G. Mowbray, and J. R. Walter, 1965. A simulation model for subsidy policy determination in the Canadian uranium mining industry. *CORS Journal, 3*(3): 115–128, 7D.

A. B. Clymer, 1960. *Accomplishments in human simulation.* New York: American Society of Mechanical Engineers, Paper No. 60-AV-26, MA.

A. B. Clymer, 1969. The modeling and simulation of big systems. *Simulation and modeling conference* (R. U. Benson, ed.); Pittsburgh: Pittsburgh chapters of ACM, IEEE-EC, and IEEE-SSC, and Midwest SCi, 107–118, MD.

A. B. Clymer, 1969. *The modeling of hierarchical systems.* Working paper, Author, MD.

A. B. Clymer and A. F. Ax, 1960. *Possibilities for human simulation.* New York: American Society of Mechanical Engineers, Paper No. 60-A-V37, MA.

A. B. Clymer and G. F. Graber, 1964. Trends in the development and applications of analog simulations in biomedical systems. *SCi Simulation, 2*(4): 41–59, MA.

R. M. Coe, 1964. Conflict, interference, and aggression: computer simulation of a social process. *Behavioral Science, 9*(2): 186–196, 1B.

J. F. Cogswell: see R. L. Egbert.

J. F. Cogswell, 1962. *Clinical diagnostic models via computer simulation.* Working paper, System Development Corporation, SP-976, 8C.

J. F. Cogswell, 1965. Systems analysis and computer simulation in the implementation of media. *Audiovisual Instruction, 10*(5): 384–386, 8D.

J. F. Cogswell, R. L. Egbert, D. G. Marsh, and F. A. Yett, 1963. *Construction of school simulation vehicle.* Working paper, System Development Corporation, TM-1409, 8D.

J. F. Cogswell, R. L. Egbert, D. G. Marsh, and F. A. Yett, 1963. *Purpose and strategy of the school simulation project.* Working paper, System Development Corporation, TM-1493/101/00, 8D.

J. F. Cogswell, R. L. Egbert, D. G. Marsh, and F. A. Yett, 1964. *New solutions to implementing instructional media through analysis and simulation of school organization.* Working paper, System Development Corporation, TM-1809, 8D.

J. F. Cogswell, R. L. Egbert, D. G. Marsh, and F. A. Yett, 1965. Construction and use of the school simulation vehicle. *Journal of Educational Measurement, 2*(1): 5–14, 3C.

B. P. Cohen, 1958. A probability model of conformity. *Sociometry, 21*(1): 69–81, 3C.

B. P. Cohen, 1963. *Conflict and conformity.* Cambridge: M. I. T. Press, 3C.

J. Cohen, 1955. Can there be artificial minds? *Analysis, 16*(2): 36–41, MA.

J. Cohen, 1966. *Human robots in myth and science.* London: George Allen & Unwin, MA.

J. E. Cohen, 1966. *A model of simple competition.* Cambridge: Harvard University Press, 3D.

K. J. Cohen: see E. E. Carter.

K. J. Cohen, 1960. *Computer models of the shoe, leather, hide sequence.* Englewood Cliffs, N. J.: Prentice-Hall, 1D.

K. J. Cohen, 1960. Simulation of the firm. *American Economic Review, Papers and Proceedings, 50*(2): 534–540, MD.

K. J. Cohen, 1967. Computer simulation. *Handbook of business administration* (H. B. Maynard, ed.); New York: McGraw-Hill, MG.

K. J. Cohen and R. M. Cyert, 1961. Computer models in dynamic economics. *Quarterly Journal of Economics, 75*(1): 112–127, MD.

K. J. Cohen and R. M. Cyert, 1965. Simulation of organizational behavior. *Handbook of organizations* (J. G. March, ed.); Chicago: Rand McNally, 305–334, MB.

K. J. Cohen and R. M. Cyert, 1965. *Theory of the firm.* Englewood Cliffs, N. J.: Prentice-Hall, MB.

K. J. Cohen, R. M. Cyert, J. G. March, and P. O. Soelberg, 1963. A general model of price and output determination. *Symposium on simulation models* (A. C. Hoggatt and F. E. Balderston, eds.); Cincinnati: South-Western, 250–289, 5D.

R. H. Cohen: see J. G. Taylor.

S. I. Cohen, 1966. The rise of management science in advertising. *Management Science, 13*(2): B-10-28, MG.

K. M. Colby: see L. Tesler.

K. M. Colby, 1963. Computer simulation of a neurotic process. *Computer simulation of personality* (S. S. Tomkins and S. Messick, eds.); New York: Wiley, 165–179, 8A.

K. M. Colby, 1964. Experimental treatment of neurotic computer programs. *Archives of General Psychiatry, 10*(3): 220–227, 4A.

K. M. Colby, 1965. Applications of stochastic and computer models to the process of free association. *Mathematical explorations in behavioral science* (F. Massarik and P. Ratoosh, eds.); Homewood, Ill.: Irwin, 112–117, MA.

K. M. Colby, 1965. Computer simulation of neurotic processes. *Computers in biomedical research* (R. W. Stacy and B. D. Waxman, eds.); New York: Academic Press, Volume 1, 491–503, 4A.

K. M. Colby, 1967. Computer simulation of change in personal belief systems. *Behavioral Science, 12*(3): 248–253, 7A.

K. M. Colby and H. Enea, 1967. Heuristic methods for computer understanding of natural language in context-restricted on-line dialogues. *Mathematical Biosciences, 1*(1): 1–25, 7A.

K. M. Colby and H. Enea, 1968. Machine utilization of the natural language word "good". *Mathematical Biosciences, 2*(1/2): 159–163, MA.

K. M. Colby and J. P. Gilbert, 1964. Programming a computer model of neuroses *Journal of Mathematical Psychology, 1*(2): 405–417, 5A.

K. M. Colby, J. B. Watt, and J. P. Gilbert, 1966. A computer method of psychotherapy. *Journal of Nervous and Mental Disease, 142*(2): 148–152, 7A.

M. Cole, 1965. Search behavior: a correction procedure for three-choice probability learning. *Journal of Mathematical Psychology, 2*(1): 145–170, 2C.

J. S. Coleman: see J. Kirk and see F. Waldorf.

J. S. Coleman, 1960. *Analysis of social structures and simulation of social processes with electronic computers.* Working paper, Johns Hopkins University Department of Social Relations, 2D.

J. S. Coleman, 1961. Analysis of social structures and simulation of social processes with electronic computers. *Educational and Psychological Measurement, 21*(1): 203–218, MD.

J. S. Coleman, 1964. Mathematical models and computer simulation. *Handbook of modern sociology* (R. E. L. Faris, ed.); Chicago: Rand McNally, 1027–1062, MD.

J. S. Coleman, 1965. The use of electronic computers in the study of social organization. *European Journal of Sociology, 6*(1): 89–107, MD.

J. S. Coleman and F. Waldorf, 1962. *Study of a voting system with computer techniques.* Working paper, Johns Hopkins University, 4D.

J. S. Coleman, E. Heau, R. Peabody, and L. Rigsby, 1964. Computers and election analysis: the "New York Times" project. *Public Opinion Quarterly, 28*(3): 418–446, 3C.

O. F. Coleman: see M. L. Braunstein.

A. Colker: see D. A. Carter, see G. H. Kruschwitz and see D. D. Lamb.

R. H. Collcutt: see J. A. Farmer.

G. H. Collins, Jr., 1968. Data processing in occupational health. *Archives of Environmental Health, 17*(6): 957–959, MG.

N. R. Collins: see L. E. Preston.

Connecticut Development Commission and Connecticut Highway Department, 1962. *The Connecticut interregional land use/transportation program, a program of integrated planning for long-range land use and transportation development of the State of Connecticut, prospectus.* Working paper, Connecticut Interregional Planning Program, 8C.

Connecticut Highway Department: see Connecticut Development Commission.

Connecticut Highway Department, 1961. *Hartford area traffic study report, Volume* 1. Hartford: Connecticut Highway Department, fourth printing, 1C.

T. Constantine, 1964. Simulation by electronic digital computer. *Traffic Engineering & Control, 5*(12): 706–709, MD.

R. W. Conway, 1961. Some comments on the simulation of management control systems. *Management Technology, 1*(3): 1–5, MG.

R. W. Conway, 1963. Some tactical problems in digital simulation. *Management Science, 10*(1): 47–61, MS.

R. W. Conway, 1966. Simulation in operations. *Selected papers on operational gaming* (A. G. Feldt, ed.); Ithaca: Cornell University 27–36, MG.

R. W. Conway, B. M. Johnson, and W. L. Maxwell, 1959. Some problems of digital systems simulation. *Management Science, 6*(1): 92–110, MG.

V. J. Cook: see J. D. Herniter.

V. J. Cook and J. D. Herniter, 1968. Preference measurement in a new product demand simulation. *Marketing and the new science of planning* (R. L. King, ed.); Chicago: American Marketing Association, 316–322, 5A.

S. L. Coombs, M. Fried, and S. H. Robinovitz, 1968. An approach to election simulation through modular systems. *Simulation in the study of politics* (W. D. Coplin, ed.); Chicago: Markham, 286–299, 5D.

R. N. Cooper, 1969. Macroeconomic policy adjustment in interdependent economies. *Quarterly Journal of Economics, 83*(1): 1–24, 5D.

W. D. Coplin, 1968. Introduction—simulation as an approach to the study of politics. *Simulation in the study of politics* (W. D. Coplin, ed.); Chicago: Markham, 1–5, MG.

W. D. Coplin, 1968. Summary. *Simulation in the study of politics* (W. D. Coplin, ed.); Chicago: Markham, 343-349, MG.

T. Corlett and D. Richardson, 1969. An examination of some of the tolerances in press media schedule evaluations. *Journal of the Market Research Society, 11*(2): 107–124, MC.

C. R. Corner, 1965. *Simulation of human thought.* MBA thesis, Washington State University, 3A.

J. Cornwall: see W. H. L. Anderson.

J. Cornwall, 1959. Economic implications of the Klein-Goldberger model. *Review of Economics and Statistics, 41*(2): 154–161, 2D.

R. L. Cosgriff, 1964. Transportation simulation. *Highway conference on the future of research and development in traffic surveillance, simulation, and control, Proceedings*; Washington: U. S. Department of Commerce, 123–126, MG.

A. J. Cote, Jr., 1967. *The search for the robots.* New York: Basic Books, MA.

R. W. Cote: see D. E. Boyce.

A. S. Couch: see R. F. Bales.

J. G. Cox: see J. H. Mize.

J. J. Coyle: see T. H. Eighmy.

S. W. Cragin, Jr., P. J. Fernald, G. F. Mader, D. T. Nowacki, C. Porten, P. M. Pruzan, D. J. Rylander, B. O. B. Williams, and L. M. Wilson, 1959. *Simulation.* Groton, Connecticut: Simulation Associates, MG.

K. J. W. Craik, 1943. *The nature of explanation.* Cambridge: Cambridge University Press, MA.

G. Cramer: see R. E. Zimmerman.

D. Crane, 1962. Computer simulation: new laboratory for the social sciences. *Automation* (M. H. Philipson, ed.); New York: Vintage, 339–354, MG.

D. B. Crane, 1966. A simulation model of corporation demand deposits. *Analytical methods in banking* (K. J. Cohen and F. S. Hammer, eds.); Homewood, Ill.: Irwin, 483–519, 4C.

J. R. Crawford, 1963. *Simulation methods and model design.* Working paper, System Development Corporation, TM-765/000/00, MG.

J. P. Crecine, 1964. *TOMM (time oriented metropolitan model).* Working paper. Pittsburgh Department of City Planning, CRP Technical Bulletin 6, 5D.

J. P. Crecine, 1967. A computer simulation model of municipal budgeting. *Management Science, 13*(11): 786–815, 1B.

J. P. Crecine, 1968. Computer simulation in urban research. *Public Administration Review, 28*(1): 66–77, MG.

J. P. Crecine, 1968. *A dynamic model of urban structure.* Working paper, Rand Corporation, P-3803, 7D.

J. P. Crecine, 1968. A simulation of municipal budgeting: the impact of problem environment. *Simulation in the study of politics* (W. D. Coplin, ed); Chicago: Markham, 115–146, 1B.

J. P. Crecine, 1969. *Governmental problem solving: a computer simulation of municipal budgeting.* Chicago: Rand McNally, 1B.

J. P. Crecine, 1969. *Spatial location decisions and urban structure: a time-oriented model.* Working paper, University of Michigan, 5D.

R. L. Creighton: see J. R. Hamburg.

R. L. Creighton, J. D. Carroll, Jr., and G. S. Finney, 1959. Data processing for city planning. *Journal of the American Institute of Planners, 25*(2): 96–103, MC.

J. E. Cremeans, 1968. The trend in simulation. *Computers and Automation, 17*(1): 44–48, MG.

J. W. Crichton and J. H. Holland, 1959. *A new method of simulating the central nervous system using an automatic digital computer.* Ypsilanti: University of Michigan Willow Run Laboratories, Report 2144-1195-M, 8A.

R. J. Crom and W. R. Maki, 1965. A dynamic model of a simulated livestock-meat economy. *Agricultural Economics Research, 17*(3): 73–83, 2D.

F. J. Crosson, 1967. Memory, models, and meaning. *Philosophy and cybernetics* (F. J. Crosson and K. M. Sayre, eds.); Notre Dame, Indiana: University of Notre Dame Press, 183–202, MA.

F. J. Crosson and K. M. Sayre, 1963. Modeling: simulation and replication. *The modeling of mind* (K. M. Sayre and F. J. Crosson, eds.); Notre Dame: University of Notre Dame Press, 3–24, MA.

A. N. Crowther and H. B. Barbe, 1967. Forecasting by land use/traffic model technique. *Traffic Engineering & Control, 9*(4): 182–184 and 189, MC.

C. B. Crumb: see G. G. Hawley.

J. T. Culbertson, 1953. *Sense data in robots and organisms.* Working paper, Rand Corporation, P-378, MA.

J. T. Culbertson, 1965. Some uneconomical robots. *Automata studies* (C. E. Shannon and J. McCarthy, eds.); Princeton: Princeton University Press, 99–116, 8A.

J. T. Culbertson, 1963. *The minds of robots.* Urbana: University of Illinois Press, MA.

T. A. Culshaw, R. W. J. Morris, and P. G. Pak-Poy, 1966. Comparison of traffic signal controllers using computer simulation—some preliminary results. *Australian Road Research Board Proceedings, 3*(1): 471–482, 7C.

W. E. Cushen, 1954. *Generalized battle games on a digital computer.* Working paper, Johns Hopkins University Operations Research Office, Technical Memorandum ORO-T-263, PB-165215, 4B.

W. E. Cushen, 1957. The philosophy of war gaming. *War gaming, Cosmagon, and Zigspiel* (No editor); Bethesda: Johns Hopkins University Operations Research Office, ORO-SP-12, AD-235892, 1–14, MC.

W. E. Cushen, 1957. TOBOGGAN—tank battle games. *War gaming, Cosmagon, and Zigspiel* (No editor); Bethesda: Johns Hopkins University Operations Research Office, ORO-SP-12, AD-235892, 95–121, 8B.

G. Cutuly, 1969. Simulation for the planning of new manufacturing systems. *Simulation and modeling conference* (R. U. Benson, ed.); Pittsburgh: Pittsburgh chapters of ACM, IEEE-EC, and IEEE-SSC, and Midwest SCi, 20–23, MD.

R. M. Cyert: see K. J. Cohen.

R. M. Cyert, 1966. A description and evaluation of some firm simulations. *IBM scientific computing symposium on simulation models and gaming, Proceedings*; White Plains, N. Y.: IBM Data Processing Division, 3–19, MB.

R. M. Cyert and J. G. March, 1959. Research on a behavioral theory of the firm. *Contributions to scientific research in management*; Los Angeles: University of California, 59–67, MB.

R. M. Cyert and J. G. March, 1963. *A behavioral theory of the firm.* Englewood Cliffs, N. J.: Prentice-Hall, 2B.

R. M. Cyert, E. A. Feigenbaum, and J. G. March, 1959. Models in a behavioral theory of the firm. *Behavioral Science, 4*(2): 81–95, 3B.

R. M. Cyert, J. G. March, and C. G. Moore, Jr., 1962. A model of retail ordering and pricing by a department store. *Quantitative techniques in marketing analysis* (R. E. Frank, A. A. Kuehn, and W. F. Massy, eds.); Homewood, Ill.: Irwin, 502–522, 1A.

D. J. Dankin: see P. Bratley.

P. Dale: see An. Rapoport.

D. J. Daley, 1968. Monte Carlo estimation of the mean queue size in a stationary GI/M/1 queue. *Operations Research, 16*(5): 1002–1005, MS.

W. C. Dalleck, 1958. Operational model of a waiting line problem. *Report of system simulation symposium* (D. G. Malcolm, ed.); New York: American Institute of Industrial Engineers, 20–23, 5C.

J. A. Daly, R. D. Joseph, and D. M. Ramsey, 1965. Perceptrons as models of neural processes. *Computers in biomedical research* (R. W. Stacy and B. D. Waxman, eds.); New York: Academic Press, Volume 1, 525–545, MA.

W. Darnton: see T. Ploughman.

F. K. Dashiell and W. W. Fain, 1966. Solution of the extended Lanchester equations used in a tactical warfare simulation programme. *CORS Journal, 4*(2): 89–96, MS.

I. M. Datz, 1966. Simulated shipping. *Datamation, 12*(2): 61–63, 7D.

M. H. David, 1965. *Design of simulation models of the household sector.* Working paper, University of Wisconsin Social Systems Research Institute, Workshop on the Economic Behavior of Households, Paper 6503, MS.

C. H. Davidson and E. C. Koenig, 1967. Simulating the real thing. *Computers*; New York: Wiley, 402–423, MG.

M. Davidson and E. Scott, 1963. *Simulation techniques and their application.* Working paper, System Development Corporation, SP-1133, MG.

H. Davis: see D. L. Trautman.

H. Davis, 1954. Simulation with general-purpose computers. *Analysis and simulation of vehicular traffic flow* (D. L. Trautman, H. Davis, J. Heilfron, E. C. Ho, J. H. Mathewson, and A. Rosenbloom); Los Angeles: University of California Institute of Transportation and Traffic Engineering, Research Report No. 20, 27–33, MC.

P. J. Davis: see N. W. Bazley.

R. H. Davis: see R. Boguslaw.

R. F. Dawson and H. L. Michael, 1966. Analysis of on-ramp capacities by Monte Carlo simulation. *Highway Research Record*, 118: 1–20, 2D.

R. H. Day and E. H. Tinney, 1968. How to cooperate in business without really trying: a learning model of decentralized decision making. *Journal of Political Economy, 76*(4): 583–600, 5B.

R. L. Day: see A. A. Kuehn.

R. L. Day, 1965. Simulation of consumer preference. *Journal of Advertising Research, 5*(3): 6–10, 3C.

G. W. Dean: see A. N. Halter.

R. E. Dear, 1961. *Multivariate analyses of variance and covariance for simulation studies involving normal time series.* Working paper, System Development Corporation, FN-5644, MS.

J. W. Degan: see E. M. Bennett.

A. D. DeGroot, 1964. Chess playing programs. *Indagationes Mathematicae, 26*(4): 385–398, MA.

W. B. Delano: see H. J. Leonard.

P. de Latil, 1957. *Thinking by machine.* Boston: Houghton Mifflin, MA.

F. DeLeeuw, 1964. Financial markets in business cycles: a simulation study. *American Economic Review, Papers and Proceedings, 54*(3): 309–323, 6D.

F. DeLeeuw, 1965. A model of financial behavior. *The Brookings quarterly econometric model of the United States* (J. S. Duesenberry, G. Fromm, L. R. Klein, and E. Kuh, eds.); Chicago: Rand McNally, 464–530, 8D.

F. DeLeeuw and E. Gramlich, 1968. The Federal Reserve-MIT econometric model. *University of Michigan, Fifteenth Annual Conference on the Economic Outlook*: 51–109. Also published in *American Statistical Association, 1967 Proceedings of the Business and Economic Statistics Section*: 36–50; and reprinted in *Federal Reserve Bulletin, 54*(1): 11–40, 1D.

DeLeuw, Cather & Company, 1964. Simulation. *Effect of control devices on traffic operations—interim report*; Washington: National Cooperative Highway Research Program, Report 11, 65–69, MD.

DeLeuw, Cather & Associates, 1966. *Peninsula area transportation study, Commonwealth of Virginia, Volume I: Survey findings and data projections.* Chicago: DeLeuw, Cather & Associates, 2C.

P. Denes: see D. B. Fry.

E. F. Denison, F. Modigliani, and L. R. Klein, 1964. Comments (on L. R. Klein's "A postwar quarterly model"). *Models of income determination* (National Bureau of Economic Research); Princeton: Princeton University Press, 36–57. MD.

D. C. Dennett, 1968. Machine traces and protocol statements. *Behavioral Science, 13*(2): 155–161, MA.

W. B. Denton, 1965. *An information processing model of human concept learning.* Doctoral dissertation, University of Texas, 3C.

M. Desai, 1966. An econometric model of the world tin economy, 1948–1961. *Econometrica, 34*(1): 105–134, 2D.

W. H. Desmonde, 1964. *Computers and their uses.* Englewood Cliffs, N. J.: Prentice-Hall, MG.

Detroit Metropolitan Area Traffic Study, 1956. *Report on the Detroit Metropolitan Area Traffic Study, Part II—future traffic and a long range expressway plan, March, 1956.* Detroit: Detroit Metropolitan Area Traffic Study, 2C.

J. A. Deutsch, 1953. A new type of behaviour theory. *British Journal of Psychology, 44*(4): 304–317, MA.

J. A. Deutsch, 1954. A machine with insight. *Quarterly Journal of Experimental Psychology, 6*(1): 6–11, 6A.

K. W. Deutsch, 1951. Mechanism, teleology, and mind. *Philosophy and Phenomenological Research, 12*(2): 185–223, MA.

S. Deutsch, 1967. *Models of the nervous system.* New York: Wiley, MA.

P. J. Deutschmann, 1962. *A machine simulation of attitude change in a polarized community.* Working paper, Inter-American Program for Information to the People, 8C.

P. J. Deutschmann, 1962. *A machine simulation of information diffusion in a small community.* Working paper, Inter-American Program for Information to the People, 8D.

P. J. Deutschmann, 1962. *A model for machine simulation of information and attitude flow.* Working paper, Inter-American Program for Information to the People, 8D.

H. Dewar: see P. Bratley and see J. P. Thorne.

J. H. Dickins: see N. H. Jennings.

E. Dickman: see D. D. Lamb.

G. W. Dickson, 1965. *Decision making in purchasing.* Doctoral dissertation, University of Washington, 3A.

G. W. Dickson, 1969. A generalized simulation model of vendor selection. *Management action* (C. E. Weber and G. Peters, eds.); Scranton: International Textbook, 115–136, 8C.

W. R. Dill, 1963. Using computers to design and to test organizational structures. *Marketing and the computer* (W. Alderson and S. J. Shapiro, eds.); Englewood Cliffs, N. J.: Prentice-Hall, 220–232, MG.

W. R. Dill, D. P. Gaver, jr. and W. L. Weber, 1966. Models and modelling for manpower planning. *Management Science, 13*(4): B-142-167. MG.

R. M. Dinkel, 1965. Population growth and economic development: recent U. S. history and computer models of analysis. *Social Forces, 43*(4): 461–470, MC.

J. R. Dirksen: see R. P. Shumate.

G. G. Dobson, 1969. Tyneside conurbation traffic assignment study. *Traffic Engineering & Control, 10*(10): 513–516, 4C.

N. Dodd: see D. M. Hill and see N. A. Irwin.

L. Dolanský: see R. E. Bach.

T. G. Donnelly, F. S. Chapin, Jr., and S. F. Weiss, 1964. *A probabilistic model for residential growth.* Chapel Hill: University of North Carolina, 6C.

J. J. Donovan, 1967. *Investigations in simulation and simulation languages*. Doctoral dissertation, Yale University, MS.

R. Dorfman: see P. C. Mahalanobis.

R. Dorfman, 1965. Formal models in the design of water resource systems. *Water Resources Research*, *1*(3): 329–336, MG.

J. R. Dorfwirth, 1963. Traffic analysis, forecast and assignment by means of electronic computers. *International Road Safety and Traffic Review*, *11*(1): 24–28, 4C.

W. S. Dorn and H. J. Greenberg, 1967. Monte Carlo methods. *Mathematics and Computing*; New York: Wiley, 470–473. MC.

A. S. Douglas, 1967. A review of operational research applications of digital simulation. *Digital simulation in operational research* (S. H. Hollingdale, ed.); London: English Universities Press, 143–147, MG.

N. J. Douglas, Jr.: see W. A. Steger.

N. J. Douglas, Jr., and W. A. Steger, 1964. Choices (s. d. s. e.) in a large scale modeling effort: the Pittsburgh simulation model. *Second Annual Conference on Urban Planning Information Systems and Programs, Proceedings* (*Urban information and policy decisions*, C. D. Rogers, ed.), 167–187, 5D.

R. A. Douglas: see J. R. Walton.

R. A. Douglas and J. R. Walton, 1962. *The simulation on a digital computer of rural highway configurations and the movement of traffic, Final report*. Working paper, North Carolina State University Engineering Research Department, Project ERD-110-F, 3D.

R. T. Douty: see D. L. Katz.

J. S. Drake and L. A. Hoel, 1969. Some modeling considerations in statewide transportation planning. *Simulation and modeling conference* (R. U. Benson, ed.); Pittsburgh: Pittsburgh chapters of ACM, IEEE-EC, and IEEE-SSC, and Midwest SCi, 24–36, MD.

D. R. Drew: see J. H. Buhr.

P. G. Drew, S. Swerling, and A. B. Fonda, 1968. Cyberail simulation. *Digest of the second conference on applications of simulation* (A. Ockene, ed.); New York: Institute of Electrical and Electronic Engineers, Publication No. 68C60SIM, 262–265, 7C.

H. L. Dreyfus, 1967. Why computers must have bodies in order to be intelligent. *Review of Metaphysics*, *21*(1): 13–32, MA.

E. Droz: see A. Chapuis.

E. Duckstad, K. E. Duke, R. G. Spiegelman, B. Lefkowitz, and A. Painter, 1962. Economic, population and trip projections. *City-county highway plan for San Mateo County*; San Jose: G. S. Nolte and Associates, 92–114, 2C.

W. L. Duda: see N. Rochester.

B. C. Duer, 1966. The use of multidimensional search techniques in large scale simulation. *Simulation in Business and Public Health, Proceedings*, *1*: 11–20, MS.

J. S. Duesenberry and L. R. Klein, 1965. Introduction: the research strategy and its application. *The Brookings quarterly econometric model of the United States* (J. S. Duesenberry, G. Fromm, L. R. Klein, and E. Kuh, eds); Chicago: Rand McNally, 2–32, 8D.

J. S. Duesenberry, O. Eckstein, and G. Fromm, 1960. A simulation of the United States economy in recession. *Econometrica*, *28*(4): 749–809, 1D.

D. J. Duffy: see N. Hauser.

D. J. Duffy, N. Hauser, and R. Roda, 1967. A computer simulation model of a police communication system. *Law enforcement science and technology* (S. A. Yefsky, ed.); Washington: Thompson, Volume 1, 101–105, 2C.

K. E. Duke: see E. Duckstad and see R. G. Spiegelman.

J. W. Duncan: see H. R. Hamilton.

H. D. Dunn: see J. C. R. Clapham.

J. M. Dutton: see W. H. Starbuck.

J. M. Dutton, 1962. Simulation of an actual production scheduling and work flow control system. *International Journal of Production Research*, *1*(4): 21–41, 8B.

J. M. Dutton, 1964. Production Scheduling—a behavioral model. *International Journal of Production Research*, *3*(1): 3–27, 8A.

J. M. Dutton and W. G. Briggs, 1971. Simulation model construction. *Computer simulation of human behavior* (J. M. Dutton and W. H. Starbuck, eds.); New York: Wiley, MG.

J. M. Dutton and W. H. Starbuck, 1967. How Charlie estimates run-time. *Research toward the development of management thought* (M. P. Hottenstein and R. W. Millman, eds); Academy of Management, 48–63, 1A.

J. M. Dutton and W. H. Starbuck, 1971. Finding Charlie's run-time estimator. *Computer simulation of human behavior* (J. M. Dutton and W. H. Starbuck, eds.); New York: Wiley, 1A.

C. H. Dym, 1968. *The national model: final report*. Washington: IBM Advanced Systems Development Division, Contract OEO 2293, 5D.

B. P. Dzielinski, C. T. Baker, and A. S. Manne, 1963. Simulation tests of lot size programming. *Management Science*, *9*(2): 229–258, 7C.

T. E. Easterfield, 1961. A short cut in a class of simulation problems. *OR, Operational Research Quarterly*, *12*(4): 221–225, MS.

D. D. Eberhardt: see L. R. Howard.

J. P. Eckert, 1962. How the electronic computer works. *The computer in advertising* (Central Media Bureau, eds.); New York: Association of National Advertisers, C1-C10, MA.

O. Eckstein: see J. S. Duesenberry.

Economic Commission for Europe, 1967. *Macro-economic models for planning and policy-making.* Geneva: United Nations, Publication No. E.67.II.E.3, MD.

A. M. Economos, 1968. A financial simulation of a proposed computer leasing company. *Digest of the second conference on applications of simulation* (A. Ockene, ed.); New York: Institute of Electrical and Electronic Engineers, Publication No. 68C60SIM, 48–49. 7C.

A. M. Economos, 1969. A financial simulation for risk analysis of a proposed subsidiary. *Management Science*, 15(12): B-675-682, 5C.

M. Eden, 1963. Human information processing. *IEEE Transactions on Information Theory*, IT-9(4): 253–256, MA.

M. Eden, 1968. Other pattern recognition problems and some generalizations. *Recognizing patterns* (P. A. Kolers and M. Eden, eds.); Cambridge: MIT Press, 196–225, MA.

J. A. Edwards, 1962. Simulating traffic flow patterns on a computer. *Data Processing*, 4(3): 192–196, 7D.

R. L. Egbert: see J. F. Cogswell.

R. L. Egbert, 1963. The computer in education: malefactor or benefactor. *Joint Computer Conference, Fall Proceedings*, 24: 619–630, MG.

R. L. Egbert and J. F. Cogswell, 1963. *System analysis and design in schools.* Working paper, System Development Corporation, SP-1141, MD.

R. L. Egbert and J. F. Cogswell, 1963. *System design in the Bassett High School.* Working paper, System Development Corporation, TM-1147, 8D.

S. Ehrenfeld: see N. Hauser and see E. Richman.

S. Ehrenfeld and S. Ben-Tuvia, 1962. The efficiency of statistical simulation procedures. *Technometrics*, 4(2): 257–275, MS.

W. F. Eicker, 1968. Systems technology applied to the social symbiosis of mental health. *IEEE systems science and cybernetics conference, San Francisco, October 14–16, 1968*; New York: Institute of Electrical and Electronic Engineers, Publication No. 68C23SSC, 8D.

T. H. Eighmy and J. J. Coyle, 1967. *Toward a simulation of land use for highway interchange communities.* Working paper, Pennsylvania State University Institute for Research on Land and Water Resources, Research Publication Number 51, 8D.

J. W. Elliott, 1967. *A computerized macroeconomic forecasting system.* Doctoral dissertation, University of Southern California, 1D.

D. G. Ellson, 1935. A mechanical synthesis of trial-and-error learning. *Journal of General Psychology*, 13(1): 212–218, 5A.

S. E. Elmaghraby, 1966. Computers in engineering design. *The design of production systems*; New York: Reinhold, 406–457, MG.

S. E. Elmaghraby, 1968. The role of modeling in IE design. *Journal of Industrial Engineering*, 19(6): 292–305, MG.

W. M. Elsasser, 1958. *The physical foundation of biology.* London: Pergamon, MA.

J. R. Emshoff, R. W. Blanning, and A. G. Rao, 1966. *A behavioral model of the Prisoner's Dilemma.* Working paper, University of Pennsylvania, 3B.

J. Endicott: see R. L. Spitzer.

H. Enea: see K. M. Colby and see L. Tesler.

A. Engel and J. J. Kennedy, 1965. Modelling dynamic economic problems on the analog computer. *International Journal of Computer Mathematics*, 1(4): 289–311, MD.

S. Enke, 1951. Equilibrium among spatially separated markets: solution by electric analogue. *Econometrica*, 19(1): 40–47, 7D.

R. A. Enlow and A. A. B. Pritsker, 1969. *Planning R & D projects using GERT.* Working paper, Arizona State University Engineering Research Center, 7D.

H. F. Erdley: see O. J. M. Smith.

R. L. Ernest: see T. H. Rockwell.

G. Ernst: see A. Newell.

J. Esherick, 1962. *The systems approach in the design professions: possibilities and problems.* Working paper, University of California at Berkeley, MD.

D. H. Evans, 1963. Applied multiplex sampling. *Technometrics*, 5(3): 341–359, MS.

G. W. Evans, II, G. F. Wallace, and G. L. Sutherland, 1967. *Simulation using digital computers.* Englewood Cliffs, N. J.: Prentice-Hall, MG.

M. K. Evans, 1969. Computer simulation of nonlinear econometric models. *The design of computer simulation experiments* (T. H. Naylor, ed.); Durham: Duke University Press, Chapter 19, MD.

M. K. Evans, 1969. *An econometric model of the French economy.* Paris: Organisation for Economic Co-Operation and Development, 1D.

M. K. Evans, 1969. *Macroeconomic activity.* New York: Harper & Row, MD.

M. K. Evans and L. R. Klein, 1967. *The Wharton econometric forecasting model.* Philadelphia: University of Pennsylvania, 1D.

T. G. Evans, 1964. A heuristic program to solve geometric-analogy problems. *Joint Computer Conference, Spring Proceedings*, 25: 327–338, 6A.

H. Fagin, 1962. Penn Jersey study. *Traffic Engineering & Control*, *3*(11): 660–662 and 667, 8D.

J. B. Fain: see M. D. F. Boulton and see W. W. Fain.

W. W. Fain: see M. D. F. Boulton and see F. K. Dashiell.

W. W. Fain, J. B. Fain, and H. W. Karr, 1966. A tactical warfare simulation program. *Naval Research Logistics Quarterly*, *13*(4): 413–436, 7D.

W. R. Fair, 1953. Analogue computations of business decisions. *Operations Research*, *1*(4): 208–219, 8D.

A. A. Fairthorne: see B. van der Pol.

R. V. Farace: see T. W. Carroll.

B. G. Farley: see W. A. Clark.

B. G. Farley, 1964. The use of computer technics in neural research. *Neural theory and modeling* (R. F. Reiss, ed.); Stanford: Stanford University Press, 43–72, MA.

B. G. Farley and W. A. Clark, 1954. Simulation of self-organizing systems by a digital computer. *IEEE Transactions on Information Theory*, *PGIT-4*: 76–84, 5A.

J. A. Farmer and R. H. Collcutt, 1967. Experience of digital simulations in a large O. R. group. *Digital simulation in operational research* (S. H. Hollingdale, ed.); London: English Universities Press, 166–180, MG.

N. A. Fattu, 1951. Computational technics. *Review of Educational Research*, *21*(5): 415–431, MC.

N. A. Fattu, 1965. An introduction to simulation. *Fourth annual Phi Delta Kappa symposium on educational, research* (*Simulation models for education*, N. A. Fattu and S. Elam, eds.); Bloomington, Ind.: Phi Delta Kappa, 1–27, MG.

E. A. Feigenbaum: see R. M. Cyert and see H. A. Simon.

E. A. Feigenbaum, 1959. *An information processing theory of verbal learning*. Working paper, Rand Corporation, P-1817; also doctoral dissertation, Carnegie-Mellon University, 3A.

E. A. Feigenbaum, 1961. The simulation of verbal learning behavior. *Joint Computer Conference, Western Proceedings*, *19*: 121–132, 3A.

E. A. Feigenbaum, 1963. Artificial intelligence research. *IEEE Transactions on Information Theory*, *IT-9* (4): 248–253, MA.

E. A. Feigenbaum, 1964. *Computer simulation of human behavior*. Working paper, Rand Corporation, P-2905, MA.

E. A. Feigenbaum and J. Feldman, 1963. Simulation of cognitive processes. *Computers and thought* (E. A. Feigenbaum and J. Feldman, eds.); New York: McGraw-Hill, 269–276, MA.

E. A. Feigenbaum and H. A. Simon, 1961. Comment: the distinctiveness of stimuli. *Psychological Review*, *68*(4): 285–288, 3C.

E. A. Feigenbaum and H. A. Simon, 1961. Forgetting in an association memory. *Association for Computing Machinery, Proceedings*, *16*: 2C–2, 6A.

E. A. Feigenbaum and H. A. Simon, 1963. Elementary Perceiver and Memorizer: review of experiments. *Symposium on simulation models* (A. C. Hoggatt and F. E. Balderston, eds.); Cincinnati: South-Western, 101–138, 3A.

E. A. Feigenbaum and H. A. Simon, 1963. Generalization of an elementary perceiving and memorizing machine. *Information processing 1962* (International Federation for Information Processing, C. M. Popplewell, ed.); Amsterdam: North-Holland, 401-405, 6A.

E. A. Feigenbaum and H. A. Simon, 1963. Performance of a reading task by an elementary perceiving and memorizing program. *Behavioral Science*, *8*(1): 72–76, 3A.

L. Fein, 1965. The structure and character of useful information-processing simulations. *Joint Computer Conference, Fall Proceedings*, *27*(1): 277–282. Also published in *SCi Simulation*, *5*(6): v-vii, MA.

J. Feldman: see E. A. Feigenbaum.

J. Feldman, 1959. *An analysis of predictive behavior in a two-choice situation*. Doctoral dissertation, Carnegie-Mellon University, 1A.

J. Feldman, 1961. Simulation of behavior in the binary choice experiment. *Joint Computer Conference, Western Proceedings*, *19*: 133–144, 1A.

J. Feldman, 1962. Computer simulation of cognitive processes. *Computer applications in the behavioral sciences* (H. Borko, ed.); Englewood Cliffs, N. J.: Prentice-Hall, 336–359, MA.

J. Feldman and J. F. Hanna, 1966. The structure of responses to a sequence of binary events. *Journal of Mathematical Psychology*, *3*(2): 371–387, 3C.

J. Feldman F. M. Tonge, and H. Kanter, 1963. Empirical explorations of a hypothesis-testing model of binary choice behavior. *Symposium on simulation models* (A. C. Hoggatt and F. E. Balderston, eds.); Cincinnati: South-Western, 55–100, 1C.

R. J. Feldmann: see G. A. Pask.

E. N. Ferentzy, 1965. Computer simulation of human behavior and concept formation in music composition. *Computational Linguistics* (*Magyar Tudomanyos Akademia, Budapest*), *4*: 93–106, 8A.

J. Ferguson: see W. N. McPhee.

S. T. Ferguson: see A. G. Beged Dov.

P. J. Fernald: see S. W. Cragin, Jr.

R. B. Fetter: see E. H. Bowman and see J. D. Thompson.

R. B. Fetter, 1965. Simulation of the activity in a maternity suite. *Computers for the humanities?* (G. W. Pierson, ed); New Haven: Yale University, 125–129, 5C.

R. B. Fetter and J. D. Thompson, 1965. The simulation of hospital systems. *Operations Research*, *13*(5): 689–711, 1C.

R. B. Fetter and J. D. Thompson, 1966. Patients' waiting time and doctors' idle time in the outpatient setting. *Health Services Research, 1*(1): 66–90, 7C.

W. R. Fey, 1962. An industrial dynamics case study. *Industrial Management Review, 4*(1): 79–99. A 1966 revision was published in *Some theories of organization* (A. H. Rubenstein and C. J. Haberstroh, eds.); Homewood, Ill.: Irwin, 519–539, 4D.

W. R. Fey, 1962. An industrial dynamics study of an electronic components manufactureer. *American Production and Inventory Control Society Annual Conference Proceedings*: 248–263, 4D.

J. E. Fidler, 1963. A computer program to forecast population growth. *Upstate New York Transportation Studies Notes, 2*: 1–4, 5C.

J. E. Fidler, 1967. Commercial activity location model. *Highway Research Record, 207*: 68–84, 3C.

S. Fifer, 1961. The analogue computer in economics. *Analogue computation*; New York: McGraw-Hill, Volume IV, 1274–1277, MD.

N. V. Findler, 1963. Some further thoughts on the controversy of thinking machines. *Cybernetica, 6*(1): 47–52, MA.

N. V. Findler, 1965. Human decision making under uncertainty and risk: computer-based experiments and a heuristic simulation program. *Joint Computer Conference, Fall Proceedings, 27*(1): 737–752, 8A.

N. V. Findler, 1966. An information processing theory of human decision making under uncertainty and risk. *Kybernetik, 3*(2): 82–93, 3A.

N. V. Findler, 1967. Computer studies on human decision making under uncertainty and risk. *Australian computer conference, Proceedings of the third, Canberra, 16th May to 20th May, 1966* (G. N. Lance and T. Pearcey, eds.); Chippendale: Australian Trade Publications, 215–225, 8A.

J M. Finger: see T. H. Naylor.

D. G. Fink, 1966. *Computers and the human mind.* Garden City, N. J.: Anchor, MA.

G. S. Finney: see R. L. Creighton.

O. Firschein: see M. Fischler.

M. Fischler, R. L. Mattson, O. Firschein, and L. D. Healy, 1962. An approach to general pattern recognition. *IEEE Transactions on Information Theory, IT-8*(5): S-64-73, 7A.

I. Fisher, 1892. Mathematical investigations in the theory of value and prices. *Transactions of the Connecticut Academy of Arts and Sciences, 9*(1): 1–124, 8B.

I. N. Fisher, 1968. *Credit expansion in a multibank system.* Working paper, Rand Corporation, P-3860, 7B.

R. B. Fisher, 1964. Simulation of traffic flows at one-way restrictions. *Australian Road Research Board Proceedings. 2*(1): 212–219, 5D.

G. S. Fishman, 1967. Problems in the statistical analysis of simulation experiments: the comparison of means and the length of sample records. *Communications of the ACM, 10*(2): 94–99, MS.

G. S. Fishman, 1967. *Statistical considerations in computer simulation experiments.* Working paper, Rand Corporation, P-3608, MG.

G. S. Fishman, 1968. The allocation of computer time in comparing simulation experiments. *Operations Research, 16*(2): 280–295. See the erratum in *Operations Research, 16*(5): 1087, MS.

G. S. Fishman, 1968. *Digital computer simulation: input-output analysis.* Working paper, Rand Corporation, RM-5540-PR, MS.

G. S. Fishman, 1968. Estimating reliability in simulation experiments. *Digest of the second conference on applications of simulation* (A. Ockene, ed.); New York: Institute of Electrical and Electronic Engineers, Publication No. 68C60SIM, 6–10, MS.

G. S. Fishman and P. J. Kiviat, 1965. *Spectral analysis of time series generated by simulation models.* Working paper, Rand Corporation, RM-4393-PR, MS.

G. S. Fishman and P. J. Kiviat, 1967. The analysis of simulation-generated time series. *Management Science, 13*(7): 525–557, MS.

G. S. Fishman and P. J. Kiviat, 1967. *Digital computer simulation: statistical considerations.* Working paper, Rand Corporation, RM-5387-PR, MS.

G. S. Fishman and P. J. Kiviat, 1968. The statistics of discrete-event simulation. *SCi Simulation, 10*(4): 185–195, MS.

C. D. Flagle, 1960. Simulation techniques. *Operations research and systems engineering* (C. D. Flagle, W. H. Huggins, and R. H. Roy, eds.); Baltimore: Johns Hopkins Press, 425–447, MG.

C. D. Flagle, 1966. Simulation techniques applicable to public health administration. *Simulation in Business and Public Health, Proceedings, 1*: 140–143, MC.

A. Fleisher, 1965. The uses of simulation. *Computer methods in the analysis of large-scale social systems* (J. M. Beshers, ed.); Cambridge: MIT-Harvard Joint Center for Urban Studies, 144–146, MG.

R. Flesch, 1953. How to talk about computers. *Computers and Automation, 2*(5): 17–18, MA.

M. M. Flood: see R. F. Bales.

M. M. Flood, 1954. On game-learning theory and some decision-making experiments. *Decision processes* (R. M. Thrall, C. H. Coombs, and R. L. Davis, eds.); New York: Wiley, 139–158, 6A.

M. M. Flood, 1954. A stochastic model for social interaction. *Transactions of the New York Academy of Sciences, 16*(4): 202–205, 6C.

L. J. Fogel, 1957. The human computer in flight control. *IEEE Transactions on Computers, C-6*(3): 195–202, MA.

L. J. Fogel, A. J. Owens, and M. J. Walsh, 1964. On the evolution of artificial intelligence. *Fifth national symposium on human factors in electronics, Proceedings*; New York: Institute of Electrical and Electronic Engineers, 63–76, 3A.

L. J. Fogel, A. J. Owens, and M. J. Walsh, 1966. Avenues toward artificial intelligence. *Artificial intelligence through simulated evolution*; New York: Wiley, 3–10, MA.

A. B. Fonda: see P. G. Drew.

S. E. Forbush, 1957. The use of sequential sampling procedures for acceptance tests of computers and applications to Monte Carlo battle games. *War gaming, Cosmagon, and Zigspiel* (No editor); Bethesda: John Hopkins University Operations Research Office, ORO-SP-12, AD-235892, 35–47, MS.

J. W. Forrester, 1957. Systems technology and industrial dynamics. *Technology Review, 59*(8): 417–422 and 428–432, MD.

J. W. Forrester, 1958. Industrial dynamics: a major breakthrough for decision makers. *Harvard Business Review, 36*(4): 37–66, 7D.

J. W. Forrester, 1958. New frontiers. *Joint Computer Conference, Eastern Proceedings, 14*: 5–10, MD.

J. W. Forrester, 1959. Advertising: a problem in industrial dynamics. *Harvard Business Review, 37*(2): 100–110, 7D.

J. W. Forrester, 1961. *Industrial dynamics*. Cambridge, Mass.: MIT Press, MD.

J. W. Forrester, 1963. Industrial dynamics. *The encyclopedia of management* (C. Heyel, ed.); New York: Reinhold, 313–319, MD.

J. W. Forrester, 1963. Simulative approaches for improving knowledge of business processes and environments. *International management congress, Thirteenth CIOS: human progress through better management*; New York: Council for International Progress in Management (USA), 234–238, MD.

J. W. Forrester, 1965. Modeling of market and company interactions. *Marketing and economic development* (P. D. Bennett, ed.); Chicago: American Marketing Association, 353–364, 7D.

J. W. Forrester, 1966. Modeling the dynamic processes of corporate growth. *IBM scientific computing symposium on simulation models and gaming, Proceedings*; White Plains, N. Y.: IBM Data Processing Division, 23–42, MD.

J. W. Forrester, 1968. Industrial dynamics—after the first decade. *Management Science, 14*(7): 398–415. MD.

J. W. Forrester, 1968. Industrial dynamics—a response to Ansoff and Slevin. *Management Science, 14*(9): 601–618, MD.

J. W. Forrester, 1968. Market growth as influenced by capital investment. *Industrial Management Review, 9*(2): 83–105, 7D.

J. W. Forrester, 1968. Structure and dynamics of feedback systems in marketing. *Systems* (D. M. Slate and R. Ferber, eds.); Urbana: University of Illinois Bureau of Economic and Business Research, 9–35, 7D.

J. W. Forrester, 1969. A deeper knowledge of social systems. *Technology Review, 71*(6): 21–31, 7D.

J. W. Forrester, 1969. *Urban dynamics*. Cambridge: MIT Press, 4D.

R. E. Forrester: see H. E. Adams.

D. F. Foster: see I. E. Robinson.

P. Fox and F. G. Lehman, 1967. Digital computer simulation of automobile traffic. *Traffic Quarterly, 21*(1): 53–66, MG.

P. Fox and F. G. Lehman, 1967. A digital simulation of car following and overtaking. *Highway Research Record, 199*: 33–41, 7B.

P. D. Fox and C. H. Kriebel, 1967. An empirical study of scheduling decision behavior. *Journal of Industrial Engineering, 18*(6): 345–360, 2A.

J. G. F. Francis and R. S. Lott, 1965. A simulation programme for linked traffic signals. *Second international symposium on the theory of road traffic flow, London 1963, Proceedings* (J. Almond, ed); Paris; Organisation for Economic Co-operation and Development, 257–259, 5C.

M. Francki, 1968. The problem of confidence and three methods of variance reduction in the simulation of queueing. *Australian Road Research Board Proceedings, 4*(1): 567–580, MS.

A. L. Frank, 1968. The use of experimental design techniques in simulation. *Digest of the second conference on applications of simulation* (A. Ockene, ed.); New York: Institute of Electrical and Electronic Engineers, Publication No. 68C60SIM, 11–12, MS.

R. E. Frank: see W. F. Massy.

S. Frankel, 1955. On the design of automata and the interpretation of cerebral behavior. *Psychometrika, 20*(2): 149–162, 4A.

J. M. Frankovich: see A. S. Manne.

L. R. Franks, 1966. A case study of service level behavior in a telephone answering system. *Journal of Industrial Engineering, 17*(8): 423–429, 5C.

J. B. Fraser: see D. G. Bobrow.

D. E. Freeman, 1966. Discrete systems simulation . . . a survey and introduction. *SCi Simulation, 7*(3): 142–148, MG.

M. Fried: see S. L. Coombs.

L. Friedman, 1963. A model of goal-directed behavior. *Artificial intelligence* (B. W. Pollard, ed.); New York: Institute of Electrical and Electronics Engineers, S-142, 65–82. 8A.

L. S. Friedman: see D. D. Lamb.

M. P. Friedman, T. R. Trabasso, and L. Mosberg, 1967. Tests of a mixed model for paired-associates learning with overlapping stimuli. *Journal of Mathematical Psychology, 4*(2): 316–334, 3C.

M. B. Friend: see R. E. Bellman and see N. L. Gilbreath.

D. D. Friesen: see J. W. Loughary.

D. D. Friesen, 1965. *The validation of an automated counseling system*. Doctoral dissertation, University of Oregon, 3A.

N. H. Frijda, 1966. *Towards a model of human memory*. Working paper, University of Amsterdam Psychology Laboratory, 8A.

N. H. Frijda, 1967. Problems of computer simulation. *Behavioral Science, 12*(1): 59–67, MA.

N. H. Frijda and L. Meertens, 1967. *The simulation of human information retrieval*. Working paper, University of Amsterdam Psychology Laboratory, 5A.

R. Frisch: see P. C. Mahalanobis.

R. Frisch, 1948. Repercussion studies at Oslo. *American Economic Review, 38*(3): 367–372, MD.

D. Fromm: see W. L. L'Esperance.

G. Fromm: see J. S. Duesenberry.

G. Fromm, 1965. Forecasting, policy simulation, and structural analysis: some comparative results of alternative models. *American Statistical Association, 1964 Proceedings of the Business and Economic Statistics Section*: 6–17, MD.

G. Fromm, 1966. Recent monetary policy: an econometric view. *National Banking Review, 3*(3): 299–306, 2D.

G. Fromm, 1969. Utility theory and the analysis of simulation output data. *The design of computer simulation experiments* (T. H. Naylor, ed.); Durham: Duke University Press, Chapter 18, 2D.

G. Fromm and L. R. Klein, 1965. The Brookings-S.S.R.C. quarterly econometric model of the United States: model properties. *American Economic Review, 55*(2): 348–361, MD.

G. Fromm and P. Taubman, 1968. *Policy simulations with an econometric model*. Washington: Brookings Institution, 2D.

D. B. Fry and P. Denes, 1959. An analogue of the speech recognition process. *Mechanisation of thought processes* (D. V. Blake and A. M. Uttley, eds.); London: H. M. Stationery Office, Volume 1, 377–384, 4A.

K. S. Fu: see E. E. Gould, see D. E. Knoop and see J. T. Tou.

G. R. Funkhouser, 1968. *A general mathematical model of information diffusion*. Working paper, Stanford University Institute for Communication Research, 1C.

K. P. Furness, 1962. Estimation of traffic by gravity model. *Traffic Engineering & Control, 3*(11): 663–667, MC.

K. P. Furness, 1965. Time function iteration. *Traffic Engineering & Control, 7*(7): 458–460, MC.

J. H. Gaddum, 1966. The neurological basis of learning. *Aspects of learning and memory* (D. Richter, ed.); New York: Basic Books, 38–72, MA.

A. V. Gafarian and C. J. Ancker, Jr., 1966. Mean value estimation from digital computer simulation. *Operations Research, 14*(1): 25–44, MS.

A. V. Gafarian and J. E. Walsh, 1966. Statistical approach for validating simulation models by comparison with operational systems. *Proceedings of the fourth international conference on operational research* (D. B. Hertz and J. Melese, eds.); New York: Wiley-Interscience, 702–705, MG.

A. V. Gafarian and J. E. Walsh, 1966. *Statistical approach for validating simulation models by comparison with operational systems—illustrated for traffic flow*. Working paper, System Development Corporation, SP-2367, MD.

A. V. Gafarian, E. Hayes, and W. W Mosher, Jr., 1967. The development and validation of a digital simulation model for design of freeway diamond interchanges. *Highway Research Record, 208*: 37–78, 5C.

G. A. Gagné: see W. W. Wierwille.

R. E. Gagné and D. C. Baxter, 1968. Techniques for the design of linear digital simulations. *SCi Simulation, 11*(2): 87–96, MS.

L. Gainen, 1968. Computer simulation. *Complete system analysis* (A. F. Goodman, L. Gainen, and C. O. Beum, Jr.); Los Angeles: McDonnell Douglas Astronautics Company, 23–37, MG.

P. Galambos, 1960. Two scientific-management techniques. *Data Processing, 2*(1): 48–53, MG.

E. H. Galanter: see R. R. Bush, see M. Kochen and see G. A. Miller.

E. H. Galanter, 1966. Organization. *Textbook of elementary psychology*; San Francisco: Holden-Day, 305–396, MA.

E. H. Galanter and G. A. Miller, 1960. Some comments on stochastic models and psychological theories. *Mathematical methods in the social sciences, 1959* (K. J. Arrow, S. Karlin, and P. Suppes, eds.); Stanford: Stanford University Press, 277–297, MA.

H. P. Galliher, 1958. Monte Carlo simulation studies. *Report of system simulation symposium* (D. G. Malcolm, ed.); New York: American Institute of Industrial Engineers, 24–27, 8C.

H. Galper, 1968. The timing of Federal expenditure impacts. *Budget concepts for economic analysis* (W. Lewis, Jr., ed.); Washington: Brookings, 95–109, 2D.

H. Galper, 1969. The impacts of the Vietnam War on defense spending: a simulation approach. *Journal of Business, 42*(4): 401–415, 2D.

H. Galper and E. Gramlich, 1968. A technique for forecasting defense expenditures. *Review of Economics and Statistics, 50*(2): 143–155, 1D.

H. B. Gamble and D. L. Raphael, 1965. *A microregional analysis of Clinton County, Pennsylvania, Volume I*. Working paper, Pennsylvania State University, Pennsylvania Regional Analysis Group, 2C.

H. B. Gamble and D. L. Raphael 1966. *A microregional analysis of Clinton County, Pennsylvania, Volume II*. Working paper, Pennsylvania State University, Pennsylvania Regional Analysis Group, 2C.

B. J. Garner: see E. J. Taaffe.

W. L. Garrison, 1960. Notes on the simulation of urban growth and development. *Occasional Papers in Geography*, *1*: 1–6, MC.

W. L. Garrison, 1962. Toward simulation models of urban growth and development. *Lund Studies in Geography, Series B*, *24*: 91–108 (Proceedings of the IGU symposium in urban geography, Lund 1960), MD.

R. A. Gaskill, 1965. Fact and fallacy in digital simulation. *SCi Simulation*, *5*(5): 309–313, MS.

A. Gauld, 1966. Could a machine perceive? *British Journal for the Philosophy of Science*, *17*(1): 44–58, MA.

D. P. Gaver, Jr.: see W. R. Dill.

D. P. Gaver, Jr., 1969. *Statistical methods for improving simulation efficiency*. Working paper, Carnegie-Mellon University, MS.

J. W. Gavett, 1968. *Production and operations management*. New York: Harcourt, Brace & World, MG.

D. C. Gazis, G. F. Newell, P. Warren, and G. H. Weiss, 1967. The delay problem for crossing an *n* lane highway. *Vehicular traffic science, Proceedings of the third international symposium on the theory of traffic flow* (L. C. Edie, R. Herman, and R. Rothery, eds.); New York: American Elsevier, 267–279, 7D.

R. F. Gebhard, 1963. A limiting distribution of an estimate of mean queue length. *Operations Research*, *11*(6): 1000-1003, MS.

M. A. Geisler, 1959. *Simulation techniques*. Working paper, Rand Corporation, P–1808, MG.

M. A. Geisler, 1962. *A statistical approach to simulation*. Working paper, Rand Corporation, P–2543, MS.

M. A. Geisler, 1964. The sizes of simulation samples required to compute certain inventory characteristics with stated precision and confidence. *Management Science*, *10*(2): 261–286, MS.

M. A. Geisler, 1964. A test of a statistical method for computing selected inventory model characteristics by simulation. *Management Science*, *10*(4): 709–715, MS.

H. L. Gelernter and N. Rochester, 1958. Intelligent behavior in problem-solving machines. *IBM Journal of Research and Development*, *2*(4): 336–345, 7A.

T. Generes, 1968. Job shop heuristics and statistical inference in a taxicab simulation. *Digest of the second conference on applications of simulation* (A. Ockene, ed.); New York: Institute of Electrical and Electronic Engineers, Publication No. 68C60SIM, 235–236, 7C.

D. H. Gensch, 1967. *A computer simulation model for selecting advertising schedules*. Doctoral dissertation, Northwestern University, 2C.

D. H. Gensch, 1968. Computer models in advertising media selection. *Journal of Marketing Research*, *5*(4): 414–424, MC.

D. H. Gensch, 1969. A computer simulation model for selecting advertising schedules. *Journal of Marketing Research*, *6*(2): 203–214, 2C.

F. George, 1963. Cybernetics and systems analysis. *Scientific Business*, *1*(1): 78–85. Reprinted in *Journal of the Market Research Society*, (11): 24–29, MA.

F. H. George, 1956. Logical networks and behavior. *Bulletin of Mathematical Biophysics*, *18*(4): 337–348, MA.

F. H. George, 1957. Logic and behaviour. *Science News*, *45*: 46–60, MA.

F. H. George, 1958. Probabilistic machines. *Automation Progress*, *3*(1): 19–21, 5A.

F. H. George, 1959. *Automation cybernetics and society*. New York: Philosophical Library, MA.

F. H. George, 1962. *The brain as a computer*. Oxford: Pergamon, MA.

F. H. George, 1962. Thinking and language in computers. *Cybernetica*, *5*(4): 265–275, MA.

F. H. George. 1963. Finite automata and the nervous system. *Progress in brain research, Volume 2: nerve, brain and memory models* (N. Wiener and J. P. Schadé, eds.); Amsterdam: Elsevier, 37–52, MA.

F. H. George, 1965. Analogues of thinking. *Third international congress on cybernetics*; Namur, Belgium: Association Internationale de Cybernétique, 459–472, MA.

F. H. George, 1965. *Cybernetics and biology*. San Francisco: Freeman, MA.

F. H. George, 1968. Formation and analysis of concepts and hypotheses on a digital computer. *Mathematical Biosciences*, *3*(1/2): 91–113, 6A.

F. H. George and D. J. Stewart, 1967. Computer programming and learning theory. *Automation theory and learning systems* (D. J. Stewart, ed.); Washington: Thompson, 73–88, MA.

L. Gérardin, 1968. *Bionics*. New York: McGraw-Hill, MA.

D. L. Gerlough: see J. H. Mathewson.

D. L. Gerlough, 1954. Analogs and simulators for the study of traffic problems. *Sixth California Street and Highway Conference, Proceedings*; Los Angeles: University of California Institute of Transportation and Traffic Engineering, 82–83, 8C.

D. L. Gerlough, 1955. *Simulation of freeway traffic on a general-purpose discrete variable computer*. Doctoral dissertation, University of California at Los Angeles. 7D.

D. L. Gerlough, 1956. Simulation of freeway traffic by an electronic computer. *Highway Research Board, Proceedings*, *35*: 543–547. 7D.

D. L. Gerlough, 1959. Traffic inputs for simulation on a digital computer. *Highway Research Board, Proceedings*, *38*: 480–492, MC.

D. L. Gerlough, 1964. Simulation of traffic flow. *An introduction to traffic flow theory* (D. L. Gerlough and D. G. Capelle, eds.); Washington: Highway Research Board Special Report 79, 97–118, MG.

D. L. Gerlough and J. H. Mathewson, 1956. Approaches to operational problems in street and highway traffic—a review. *Operations Research*, *4*(1): 32–41, MC.

D. L. Gerlough and F. A. Wagner, Jr., 1965. Simulation of traffic in a large network of signalized intersections. *Second international symposium on the theory of road traffic flow, London 1963, Proceedings* (J. Almond, ed.); Paris: Organisation for Economic Co-operation and Development, 249–252, 3C.

M. L. Gerson and R. B. Maffei, 1963. Technical characteristics of distribution simulators. *Management Science, 10*(1): 62–69, MC.

D. Gerwin, 1969. *Budgeting public funds.* Madison: University of Wisconsin Press, 1B.

D. Gerwin, 1969. A process model of budgeting in a public school system. *Management Science, 15*(7): 338–361, 1B.

R. Gettig: see H. Ozkaptan.

D. T. Gianturco: see T. H. Naylor.

B. Giffler, 1966. Simulation models in production scheduling and inventory control. *Simulation in Business and Public Health, Proceedings, 1*: 27–35, MG.

J. P. Gilbert: see K. M. Colby.

J. P. Gilbert and E. A. Hammel, 1966. Computer simulation and analysis of problems in kinship and social structure. *American Anthropologist, 68*(1): 71–93, 7C.

N. L. Gilbreath, R. E. Bellman, M. B. Friend, and L. Kurland, 1964. *Construction of a simulation process for initial psychiatric interviewing.* Working paper, Rand Corporation, P-2933, 8B.

R. W. Gillespie: see E. P. Holland.

M. J. Gilman, 1968. A brief survey of stopping rules in Monte Carlo simulations. *Digest of the second conference on applications of simulation* (A. Ockene, ed.); New York: Institute of Electrical and Electronic Engineers, Publication No. 68C60SIM, 16–20, MS.

L. D. Gilstrap and R. J. Lee, 1961. Learning machines. *First Bionics Symposium (Living prototypes—the key to new technology,* J. C. Robinette, ed.); Wright-Patterson AFB: Wright Air Development Division, TR 60-600, 437–450, MA.

A. S. Ginsberg, 1965. *Simulation programming and analysis of results.* Working paper, Rand Corporation, P-3141, MG.

W. H. Glanville, 1955. Road safety and traffic research in Great Britain. *Operations Research, 3*(3): 283–299, 5C.

A. Glickstein: see S. L. Levy.

A. Glickstein, 1963. Analytical methods in transportation: digital simulation of traffic. *American Society of Civil Engineers, Proceedings, 89*(EM6): 1–13, 7D.

A. Glickstein and S. L. Levy, 1961. Application of digital simulation techniques to highway design problems. *Joint Computer Conference, Western Proceedings, 19*: 39–50, 7D.

V. M. Glushkov, 1965. Teaching theory of one class of perceptrons. *International Journal of Computer Mathematics, 1*(3): 199–220, MA.

B. E. Goetz. 1960. Monte Carlo solution of waiting line problems. *Management Technology, 1*(1): 2–11, MC.

R. J. Goldacre, 1960. Can a machine create a work of art? *Second international congress on cybernetics*; Namur, Belgium: Association Internationale de Cybernétique, 683–697, MA.

S. E. Goldstone: see D. E. Boyce, see H. R. Hamilton and see W. L. Swager.

R. F. Gonzalez: see C. McMillan.

I. J. Good, 1959. Could a machine make probability judgments? Part I. *Computers and Automation, 8*(1): 14–16, MA.

I. J. Good, 1959. Could a machine make probability judgments? Part II. *Computers and Automation, 8*(2): 24–26, MA.

H. H. Goode, 1951. Simulation—its place in systems design. *Proceedings of the IEEE, 39*(12): 1501–1506, MG.

H. H. Goode and R. E. Machol, 1957. Simulation. *System engineering*; New York: McGraw-Hill, 403–407, MG.

H. H. Goode and W. C. True, 1958. *Simulation and display of four inter-related vehicular traffic intersections.* Working paper, University of Michigan, 7D.

H. H. Goode, C. H. Pollmar, and J. B. Wright, 1956. The use of a digital computer to model a signalized intersection. *Highway Research Board, Proceedings, 35*: 548–557, 7D.

R. M. Goodwin: see J. A. C. Brown.

M. Gorden: see C. C. Abt.

M. Gorden, 1968. Comments on Clemens' paper. *Simulation in the study of politics* (W. D. Coplin, ed.); Chicago: Markham, 101–104, MG.

C. K. Gordon, Jr., 1963. In defense of the search for the pretercomputer. *Cybernetica, 6*(2): 57–75, MA.

G. Gordon: see K. Blake.

G. Gordon and K. Zelin, 1968. *A simulation study of emergency ambulance service in New York City.* Working paper, IBM New York Scientific Center, Report No. 320-2935, 2C.

G. R. Gordon: see J. Surkis.

I. D. Gordon and A. J. Miller, 1966. Right turn movements at signalized intersections. *Australian Road Research Board Proceedings, 3*(1): 446–459, 6D.

S. Gorn, 1959 On the mechanical simulation of habit-forming and learning. *Information and Control, 2*(3): 226–259, MA.

C. C. Gotlieb: see L. E. S. Green.

M. H. Gotterer, 1963. A study of the effects of delays in changes in a work force. *Symposium on simulation models* (A. C. Hoggatt and F. E. Balderston, eds.); Cincinnati: South-Western, 192–202, 7D.

D. L. Gottheil and R. E. Pendley, 1966. Appendix: a partial bibliography of books, articles, and unpublished materials on simulation in international relations. *IBM scientific computing symposium on simulation models and gaming, Proceedings*; White Plains, N. Y.: IBM Data Processing Division, 273–278, MD.

E. E. Gould and K. S. Fu, 1966. Adaptive model of the human operator in a time-varying control task. *Second annual NASA-university conference on manual control*; Washington: National Aeronautics and Space Administration, 85–97, 8A.

P. Gould, 1964. A note on research into the diffusion of development. *Journal of Modern African Studies*, 2(1): 123–125, MD.

G. F. Graber: see A. B. Clymer.

M. G. Grace, R. W. J. Morris, and P. G. Pak-Poy, 1964. Some aspects of intersection capacity and traffic signal control by computer simulation. *Australian Road Research Board Proceedings*, 2(1): 274–302, 5C.

E. Gramlich: see F. DeLeeuw and see H. Galper.

E. M. Gramlich, 1968. Measures of the aggregate demand impact of the Federal budget. *Budget concepts for economic analysis* (W. Lewis, Jr., ed.); Washington: Brookings, 110–127, MD.

F. Graves, 1966. Computer models and public policy. *Research and education for regional and area development* (W. R. Maki and B. J. L. Berry, eds.); Ames: Iowa State University Press, 263–274, 8D.

G. W. Gray, 1936. Thinking machines. *Harper's Magazine*, 172(March): 416–425, MA.

R. S. Graybeal, 1967. A simulation model of residential development. *Regional Science Association, Third Far East Conference, Proceedings*: 199–208, 5C.

J. Grayson, 1961. The electronic invasion. *Nerves, brain and man*; New York: Taplinger, 206–218, MA.

B. F. Green, Jr., 1959. Non-computational uses of digital computers. *Behavioral Science*, 4(2): 164–167, MG.

B. F. Green, Jr., 1961. Computer models of cognitive processes. *Psychometrika*, 26(1): 85–91, MA.

B. F. Green, Jr., 1963. *Digital computers in research.* New York: McGraw-Hill, MG.

B. F. Green, Jr., 1964. Intelligence and computer simulation. *Transactions of the New York Academy of Sciences*, 27(1): 55–63, MA.

D. H. Green: see M. G. Hartley.

D. H. Green, 1966. *Direct digital control of simulated traffic intersections.* Doctoral dissertation, University of Manchester, 7D.

D. H. Green, 1967. Control of oversaturated intersections. *OR, Operational Research Quarterly*, 18(2): 161–173, 7D.

D. H. Green and M. G. Hartley, 1966. The simulation of some simple control policies for a signalized intersection. *OR, Operational Research Quarterly*, 17(3): 263–278, 7D.

G. R. Green, 1968. *Multiplier paths and business cycles: a simulation approach.* Working paper, U. S. Department of Commerce, 2D.

L. E. S. Green, E. C. Berkeley, and C. C. Gotlieb, 1959. Conversation with a computer. *Computers and Automation*, 8(10): 9–11, 7B.

P. E. Green, 1963. Bayesian decision theory in pricing strategy. *Journal of Marketing*, 27(1): 5–14, 5C.

P. E. Green and D. S. Tull, 1966. Information from simulation. *Research for marketing decisions*; Englewood Cliffs, N. J.: Prentice-Hall, 404–438, MC.

H. J. Greenberg: see W. S. Dorn.

M. Greenberger: see G. H. Orcutt.

M. Greenberger, 1961. Simulation and the problem of air traffic control. *Industrial Management Review*, 2(2): 27–42, MC.

M. Greenberger, 1961. Simulation of a complex economic system. *Second international conference on operational research, Proceedings* (J. Banbury and J. Maitland, eds.); New York: Wiley, 511–517, 5C.

M. Greenberger, 1965. A new methodology for computer simulation. *Computer methods in the analysis of large-scale social systems* (J. M. Beshers, ed); Cambridge: MIT-Harvard Joint Center for Urban Studies, 147–162, MG.

M. Greenberger, 1966. Simulation and a house-heating problem. *Behavioral Science*, 11(2): 143–147, MA.

P. H. Greene, 1959. An approach to computers that perceive, learn, and reason. *Joint Computer Conference, Western Proceedings*, 15: 181–186, MA.

P. H. Greene, 1960. A suggested model for information representation in a computer that perceives, learns, and reasons. *Joint Computer Conference, Western Proceedings*, 17: 151–164, MA.

P. H. Greene, 1964. New problems in adaptive control. *Computer and information sciences* (J. T. Tou and R. H. Wilcox, eds.); Washington: Spartan, 410–456, MA.

R. M. Greene, Jr., 1960. *Representation of human functions in business system simulations.* Working paper, System Development Corporation, FN-3745, 8B.

P. S. Greenlaw: see R. D. Smith.

L. T. Gregg, 1964. A digital computer technique for operator performance studies. *Fifth national symposium on human factors in electronics, Proceedings*; New York: Institute of Electrical and Electronic Engineers, 44–51, MA.

L. T. Gregg, 1965. On computer simulation of human operator performance. *SCi Simulation*, 5(1): 61–68, MA.

L. W. Gregg: see K. R. Laughery.

L. W. Gregg, 1967. Internal representations of sequential concepts. *Concepts and the structure of memory* (B. Kleinmuntz, ed.); New York: Wiley, 107–142, 1A.

L. W. Gregg and H. A. Simon, 1967. An information-processing explanation of one-trial and incremental learning. *Journal of Verbal Learning and Verbal Behavior*, 6(5): 780–787, 3C.

L. W. Gregg and H. A. Simon, 1967. Process models of simple concept formation. *Journal of Mathematical Psychology*, 4(2): 246–276, MS.

R. L. Gregory, 1967. Will seeing machines have illusions? *Machine intelligence 1* (N. L. Collins and D. Michie, eds.); New York: American Elsevier, 169–177, MA.

J. S. Griffith, 1965. On the stability of brain-like structures. *General Systems*, 10: 91–96, MA.

R. L. Grimsdale, R. W. Mathers, and F. H. Sumner, 1963. An investigation of computer-controlled traffic signals by simulation. *Institution of Civil Engineers, Proceedings*, 25(6645): 183–192, 5C.

R. B. Grove: see W. R. Reitman.

E. L. Gruenberg: see H. E. Tompkins.

E. L. Gruenberg, 1954. The concept of thinking. *Computers and Automation*, 3(4): 18–21, MA.

E. L. Gruenberg, 1954. Reflective thinking in machines. *Computers and Automation*, 3(1): 12–19, 26, and 28, MA.

E. L. Gruenberg, 1955. Thinking machines and human personality. *Computers and Automation*, 4(4): 6–9, MA.

R. L. Gue, 1966. Signal flow graphs and analog computation in the analysis of finite queues. *Operations Research*, 14(2): 342–350, MC.

G. T. Guilbaud, 1959. *What is cybernetics?* New York: Criterion Books, MA.

J. P. Guilford, 1967. Computer simulation of thinking. *The nature of human intelligence*; New York: McGraw-Hill, 342–344, MA.

C. R. Guinn: see J. R. Hamburg.

J. E. Gullahorn: see J. T. Gullahorn.

J. E. Gullahorn, 1966. Initial efforts in validating a computer model of social behavior. *Psychological Reports*, 19(3): 786, 6C.

J. T. Gullahorn and J. E. Gullahorn, 1963. A computer model of elementary social behavior. *Computers and thought* (E. A. Feigenbaum and J. Feldman, eds.); New York: McGraw-Hill, 375–386. Reprinted in *Behavioral Science*, 8(4): 354–362, 5B.

J. T. Gullahorn and J. E. Gullahorn, 1964. *Approaches to testing theories of organization design*. Working paper, System Development Corporation, SP-1238/000/01, MD.

J. T. Gullahorn and J. E. Gullahorn, 1964. Computer simulation of human interaction in small groups. *Joint Computer Conference, Spring Proceedings*, 25: 103-113. Reprinted in *SCi Simulation*, 4(1): 50–61, 2B.

J. T. Gullahorn and J. E. Gullahorn, 1965. A computer experiment in elementary social behavior. *IEEE Transactions on Systems Science and Cybernetics*, SSC-1(1): 45–51, 3C.

J. T. Gullahorn and J. E. Gullahorn, 1965. The computer as a tool for theory development. *The use of computers in anthropology* (D. H. Hymes, ed.); The Hague: Mouton, 427–448, 5B.

J. T. Gullahorn and J. E. Gullahorn, 1965 *Computer simulation of role conflict resolution*. Working paper, System Development Corporation, SP-2261/000/00, 3C.

J. T. Gullahorn and J. E. Gullahorn, 1965. Some computer applications in social science. *American Sociological Review*, 30(3): 353–365, 3C.

K. Gunderson, 1964. The imitation game. *Mind*, 73(290): 234–245, MA.

W. A. Gunn, 1964. Airline system simulation. *Operations Research*, 12(2): 206–229, 2C.

J. W. Gyr, J. S. Brown, R. Willey, and A. Zivian, 1966. Computer simulation and psychological theories of perception. *Psychological Bulletin*, 65(3): 174–192, 8A.

J. W. Gyr, J. Thatcher, and G. Allen, 1962. Computer simulation of a model of cognitive organization. *Behavioral Science*, 7(1): 111–116, 5A.

W. J. Haas, 1964. A description of a project to study the research library as an economic system. *Association of Research Libraries, Minutes*, 63: 40–46, 7D.

T. Haavelmo: see P. C. Mahalanobis.

T. Hägerstrand, 1957. Migration and area. *Lund Studies in Geography, Series B*, 13: 27–158, 6D.

T. Hägerstrand, 1965. Aspects of the spatial structure of social communication and the diffusion of information. *The Regional Science Association, Papers and Proceedings*, 16: 27–42. 6D.

T. Hägerstrand, 1965. A Monte Carlo approach to diffusion. *European Journal of Sociology*, 6(1): 43–67, 3D.

T. Hägerstrand, 1965. Quantitative techniques for analysis of the spread of information and technology. *Education and economic development* (C. A. Anderson and M. J. Bowman, eds.); Chicago: Aldine, 244–280, 6D.

T. Hägerstrand, 1967. On Monte Carlo simulation of diffusion. *Quantitative Geography* (W. L. Garrison and D. F. Marble, eds.); Evanston: Northwestern University, Volume 1, 1–32, 6D.

L. H. Haibt: see N. Rochester.

F. A. Haight, 1964. Annotated bibliography of scientific research in road traffic and safety. *Operations Research*, 12(6): 976–1039, MC.

G. H. Haines, Jr., 1961. The Rote Marketer. *Behavioral Science*, 6(4): 375–365, 3B.

G. H. Haines, Jr., 1968. The use of alternative models on a set of consumer data. *Marketing and the new science of planning* (R. L. King, ed.); Chicago: American Marketing Association, 386–392, 3C

P. C. Haines, 1964. *Air traffic control—models and myths.* London: C-E-I-R, MD.

M. Halle: see S. J. Keyser.

A. N. Halter and G. W. Dean, 1965. *Simulation of a California range-feedlot operation.* Working paper, University of California Division of Agricultural Sciences (Davis), Giannini Foundation Research Report No. 282, 5A.

J. H. Halton, 1960. On the efficiency of certain quasi–random sequences of points in evaluating multi-dimensional integrals. *Numerische Mathematik, 2*(2): 84–90, MS.

J. H. Halton and D. C. Handscomb, 1957. A method for increasing the efficiency of Monte Carlo integration. *Journal of the Association for Computing Machinery, 4*(3): 329–340, MS.

J. R. Hamburg: see G. T. Lathrop.

J. R. Hamburg and R. L. Creighton, 1959. Predicting Chicago's land use pattern. *Journal of the American Institute of Planners, 25*(2): 67–72, 5C.

J. R. Hamburg and C. R. Guinn, 1966. *A modal-choice model—description of basic concepts.* Working paper, New York State Department of Public Works Subdivision of Transportation Planning and Programming, Publication TPOO-130-01, MC.

M. Hamburg and R. J. Atkins, 1967. Computer model for new product demand. *Harvard Business Review, 45*(2): 107–115, 4C.

M. J. Hamburger: see A. A. Kuehn.

H. R. Hamilton: see W. L. Swager.

H. R. Hamilton, S. E. Goldstone, F. J. Cesario, D. C. Sweet, D. E. Boyce, and A. L. Pugh, III, 1966. *Final report on a dynamic model of the economy of the Susquehanna River basin to Susquehanna River Basin Utility Group.* Columbus, O.: Battelle Memorial Institute, 2D.

H. R. Hamilton, S. E. Goldstone, J. W. Milliman, A. L. Pugh, III, E. B. Roberts, and A. Zellner, 1969. *Systems simulation for regional analysis.* Cambridge: MIT Press, 2D.

H. R. Hamilton, S. E. Goldstone, D. C. Sweet, N. M. Kamrany, R. D. Schultz, J. W. Duncan, D. E. Boyce, A. L. Pugh, III, and E. M. Roberts, 1964. *Progress report on a dynamic model of the economy of the Susquehanna River basin to Susquehanna River Basin Utility Group.* Columbus, O.: Battelle Memorial Institute, 2D.

E. A. Hammel: see J. P. Gilbert.

C. Hammer, 1961. Computers and simulation. *Cybernetica, 4*(4): 204–294, MG.

J. M. Hammersley, 1956. Conditional Monte Carlo. *Journal of the ACM, 3*(2): 73–76, MS.

J. M. Hammersley, 1960. Monte Carlo methods for solving multivariable problems. *Annals of the New York Academy of Sciences, 86*(3): 844–874, MS.

J. M. Hammersley and D. C. Handscomb, 1964. *Monte Carlo methods.* New York: Wiley, MS.

J. M. Hammersley and J. G. Mauldon, 1956. General principles of antithetic variates. *Cambridge Philosophical Society, Proceedings, 52*(3): 476–481, MS.

J. M. Hammersley and K. W. Morton, 1954. Poor man's Monte Carlo. *Journal of the Royal Statistical Society, Series B, 16*(1): 23–38, MS.

J. M. Hammersley and K. W. Morton, 1956. A new Monte Carlo technique: antithetic variates. *Cambridge Philosophical Society, Proceedings, 52*(3): 449–475, MS.

R. W. Hamming, 1963. Intellectual implications of the computer revolution. *The American Mathematical Monthly, 70*(1): 4–11, MA.

D. C. Handscomb: see J. H. Halton and see J. M. Hammersley.

D. C. Handscomb, 1958. Proof of the antithetic variates theorem for $n > 2$. *Cambridge Philosophical Society, Proceedings, 54*(2): 300–301, MS.

D. C. Handscomb, 1969. Variance reduction techniques: theoretical. *The design of computer simulation experiments* (T. H. Naylor, ed.); Durham: Duke University Press, Chapter 12, MS.

A. Hanken: see T. H. Rockwell.

J. F. Hanna: see J. Feldman.

J. F. Hanna, 1965. *The methodology of the testing of learning models, with applications to a new stimulus discrimination model of two-choice behavior.* Eugene: University of Oregon, MS.

J. F. Hanna, 1966. A new approach to the formulation and testing of learning models. *Synthese, 16*(3): 344–380, MS.

J. F. Hanna, 1971. Information-theoretic techniques for evaluating simulation models. *Computer simulation of human behavior* (J. M. Dutton and W. H. Starbuck, eds.); New York: Wiley, MS.

G. J. Hanneman: see T. W. Carroll.

G. J. Hanneman, 1968. *A computer simulation model of the innovation decision process in the diffusion of innovations.* Working paper, Michigan State University Department of Communication, 5D.

G. J. Hanneman, 1969. *A computer simulation of information diffusion in a peasant community.* Master's thesis, Michigan State University, 1D.

G. J. Hanneman and T. W. Carroll, 1969. *SINDI 1: simulation of information diffusion in a peasant community.* East Lansing: Michigan State University Project on Diffusion of Innovations in Rural Societies, Technical Report No. 7, 1D.

G. J. Hanneman, T. W. Carroll, E. M. Rogers, J. D. Stanfield, and N. Lin, 1969. Computer simulation of innovation diffusion in a peasant village. *American Behavioral Scientist, 12*(6): 36–45, 1D.

B. Hanon, 1965. The use of simulation in the analysis of business systems. *American Behavioral Scientist, 8*(9): 4–7, MS.

W. B. Hansen: see D. M. Hill.

W. G. Hansen: see T. R. Lakshmanan.

W. G. Hansen, 1960. Land use forecasting for transportation planning. *Highway Research Board Bulletin,* *253*: 145–151, MC.

W. G. Hansen, 1962. Evaluation of gravity model trip distribution procedures. *Highway Research Board Bulletin, 347*: 67–76, 1C.

A. P. Hare, 1961. Computer simulation of interaction in small groups. *Behavioral Science, 6*(3): 261–265, 3B.

A. P. Hare and R. Richardson, 1966. *Computer simulation of small group decisions.* Working paper, Haverford College, 3B.

A. P. Hare, R. Richardson, and H. Scheilblechner, 1968. *Computer simulation of small group decisions.* Working paper, Haverford College, 3B.

V. C. Hare, Jr., 1964. Systems analysis. *Progress in operations research, Volume II* (D. B. Hertz and R. T. Eddison, eds.); New York: Wiley, 123–158, MG.

V. C. Hare, Jr., 1967. System simulation. *Systems analysis*; New York: Harcourt, Brace & World, 358–410, MG.

J. Harling, 1958. Simulation techniques in operational research. *OR, Operational Research Quarterly, 9*(1): 9–21. Reprinted under the title "Simulation techniques in operations research—a review" in *Operations Research, 6*(3): 307–319, MG.

H. H. Harman, 1961. Simulation: a survey. *Joint Computer Conference, Western Proceedings, 19*: 1–9, MG.

F. K. Harmston, 1966. *Some simulation experiments with regard to a state-region of the United States.* Doctoral dissertation, University of Missouri, 5D.

R. W. Harrington, 1966. Simulation and public health. *Simulation in Business and Public Health, Proceedings, 1*: 148–151, MG.

B. Harris: see I. S. Lowry.

B. Harris, 1961. *Regional growth model—activity distribution sub-model.* Working paper, Penn Jersey Transportation Study, Paper 7, 8C.

B. Harris, 1961. Some problems in the theory of intra-urban location. *Operations Research, 9*(5): 695–721, MD.

B. Harris, 1962. *Linear programming and the projection of land uses.* Working paper, Penn Jersey Transportation Study, Paper 20, 8D.

B. Harris, 1965. New tools for planning. *Journal of the American Institute of Planners, 31*(2): 90–94, MC.

B. Harris, 1966. *Basic assumptions for a simulation of the urban residential housing and land market.* Working paper, University of Pennsylvania Institute for Environmental Studies, 8D.

B. Harris, 1966. The uses of theory in the simulation of urban phenomena. *Highway Research Record, 126*: 1–16. Reprinted in the *Journal of the American Institute of Planners, 32*(5): 258–273, MG.

B. Harris, 1968. Computers and urban planning. *Socio-Economic Planning Sciences, 1*(3): 223–230, MD.

B. Harris, 1968. Quantitative models of urban development: their role in metropolitan policy-making. *Issues in urban economics* (H. S. Perloff and L. Wingo, Jr., eds.); Baltimore: Johns Hopkins Press, 363–412, MD.

B. Harris, J. Nathanson, and L. Rosenburg, 1966. *Research on an equilibrium model of metropolitan housing and model locational cloice, interim report.* Working paper, University of Pennsylvania Institute for Environmental Studies, 2C.

C. C. Harris, Jr., 1966. *Suburban development as a stochastic process.* Working paper, University of California Center for Real Estate and Urban Economics, 5C.

J. O. Harrison, Jr., 1957. TATOO—a tank battle on the digital computer. *War gaming, Cosmagon, and Zigspiel* (No editor); Bethesda: Johns Hopkins University Operations Research Office, ORO-SP-12, AD-235892, 79–94, 8B.

S. Harrison: see J. E. Jacoby.

E. M. Harth, 1966. Brain models and thought processes. *Automata theory* (E. R. Caianiello, ed.); New York: Academic Press, 201–217, 4A.

M. G. Hartley: see D. H. Green and see S. I. Saleeb.

M. G. Hartley, 1968. *Modelling techniques for traffic studies.* Doctoral dissertation, University of Manchester, 7C.

M. G. Hartley, 1969. The Manchester traffic simulator. *University of Manchester, Advance, 6*, MD.

M. G. Hartley, 1969. Performance of a switching policy applied to a set of intersections. *Transportation Research, 3*(1): 91–100, 7C.

M. G. Hartley, 1969. A switching policy for a pair of intersections. *Transportation Research, 3*(1): 79–90, 7C.

M. G. Hartley and D. H. Green, 1965. Study of intersection problems by simulation on a special purpose computer. *Traffic Engineering & Control, 7*(3): 219–223 and 229, MD.

J. J. Hartman, 1966. *Annotated bibliography on simulation in the social sciences.* Ames: Iowa State University, MG.

Harvard Computational Laboratory, 1952. Simple learning by a digital computer. *Association for Computing Machinery, Proceedings, Toronto* (September): 55–61, 6A.

C. B. Haselgrove, 1961. A method for numerical integration. *Mathematics of Computation, 15*(76): 323–337, MS.

D. P. Hattaway, E. D. Hietanen, and R. W. Rothfusz, 1966. Training a machine to read with nonlinear threshold logic. *Electronics, 39*(17): 86–93, 7A.

N. Hauser: see D. J. Duffy, see D. L. Katz and see J. Surkis.

N. Hauser and D. J. Duffy, 1967. Analysis of complex systems by computer simulation. *Law enforcement science and technology* (S. A. Yefsky, ed.); Washington: Thompson, Volume 1, 635–643, MD.

N. Hauser, N. N. Barish, and S. Ehrenfeld, 1966. Design problems in a process control simulation. *Journal of Industrial Engineering, 17*(2): 79–86, MS.

M. Havass, 1964. A simulation of musical composition, synthetically composed folkmusic. *Computational Linguistics (Magyar Tudomanyos Akademia, Budapest), 3:* 107–128, 4C.

J. K. Hawkins, 1961. Self-organizing systems—a review and commentary. *Proceedings of the IEEE, 49*(1): 31–48, MA.

G. G. Hawley, S. A. Scharff, C. B. Crumb, and E. C. Berkeley, 1953. "How to talk about computers"—discussion. *Computers and Automation, 2*(6): 9–12, MA.

G. B. Hawthorne, Jr., 1964. Digital simulation and modelling. *Datamation, 10*(10): 25–29, MG.

J. C. Hay, F. C. Martin, and C. W. Wightman, 1960. The Mark I perceptron—design and performance *IEEE International Convention Record, 8*(2): 78–87, 7A.

R. F. C. Hayden, 1963. Computers and the administration of justice. *Joint Computer Conference, Fall Proceedings, 24:* 609–617, MG.

E. Hayes: see A. V. Gafarian.

E. Hayes, 1966. Programming a digital simulation model of a freeway diamond interchange. *Twenty-first national conference of the ACM, Proceedings;* Washington: Thompson, 117–129, 7C.

R. H. Hayes, 1969. The expected value of sample information. *The design of computer simulation experiments* (T. H. Naylor, ed.); Durham: Duke University Press, Chapter 15, MS.

R. M. Hayes, 1964. Simulation and modeling in the information sciences. *Second Annual Conference on Urban Planning Information Systems and Programs, Proceedings (Urban Information and policy decisions,* C. D. Rogers, ed.), 77–95, MG.

W. W. Haythorn, 1962. Group composition in an isolation environment. *Fourth IBM Medical Symposium, Proceedings:* 151–161, 8B.

G. F. Healea, 1966. *Evolutionary methods as applied to simulation models.* Master's thesis, University of Washington, MS.

L. D. Healy: see M. Fischler.

T. L. Healy, 1964. *On the solution of queuing problems by computer simulation.* Dayton: National Cash Register Company, OP-8-15, MS.

K. E. Heanue and C. E. Pyers, 1966. A comparative evaluation of trip distribution procedures. *Highway Research Record, 114:* 20–37, 3C.

K. W. Heathington: see J. M. Bruggeman.

K. W. Heathington and J. M. Bruggeman, 1969. The use of computer simulation to analyze a demand-scheduled-bus system. *Simulation and modeling conference* (R. U. Benson, ed.); Pittsburgh: Pittsburgh chapters of ACM, IEEE-EC, and IEEE-SSC, and Midwest SCi, 64–69, 7C.

K. W. Heathington and G. J. Rath, 1968. Computer simulation for transportation problems. *Traffic Quarterly, 22*(2): 271–281, MG.

K. W. Heathington, J. Miller, R. R. Knox, G. C. Hoff, and J. M. Bruggeman, 1968. Computer simulation of a demand-scheduled bus system offering door-to-door service. *Highway Research Record, 251:* 26–40, 7C.

E. Heau: see J. S. Coleman.

G. B. Hegeman, 1965. Dynamic simulation for market planning. *Chemical & Engineering News, 43*(1): 64–71, MC.

D. M. Heien, 1968. *An econometric model of U. S. government revenues and expenditures.* Working paper, U. S. Department of Labor, 8D.

D. M. Heien, 1968. *An econometric model of United States government revenues and expenditures.* Doctoral dissertation, George Washington University, AD-669464, 8D.

J. Heilfron: see D. L. Trautman.

J. F. Helliwell, L. H. Officer, H. T. Shapiro, and I. A. Stewart, 1968. *RDX1—a quarterly model of the Canadian economy.* Working paper, Bank of Canada, 1D.

W. Helly, 1961. Simulation of bottlenecks in single-lane traffic flow. *Theory of traffic flow* (R. Herman, ed.); Amsterdam: Elsevier, 207–238, 2C.

C. Helm, 1967. Computer simulation techniques for research on guidance problems. *Personnel and Guidance Journal, 46*(1): 47–52, 6A.

C. E. Helm, 1965. Simulation models for psychometric theories. *Joint Computer Conference, Fall Proceedings, 27*(1): 727–736, 3C.

O. Helmer and N. Rescher, 1959. On the epistemology of the inexact sciences. *Management Science, 6*(1): 25–52, MG.

G. C. Hemmens, 1968. *Analysis and simulation of urban activity patterns.* Working paper, University of North Carolina, MC.

J. D. Herbert and B. H. Stevens, 1960. A model for the distribution of residential activity in urban areas. *Journal of Regional Science, 2*(2): 21–36, 8D.

J. D. Herbert and B. H. Stevens, 1960. *A model for the distribution of residential activity in urban areas.* Working paper, Penn Jersey Transportation Study, Paper 2, 8D.

R. E. Herlihy: see C. H. Springer.

C. F. Hermann, 1968. Simulation: political processes. *International encyclopedia of the social sciences* (D. L. Sills, ed.); New York: Macmillan, Volume 14, 274–281, MD.

J. D. Herniter: see V. J. Cook and see B. Norek.

J. D. Herniter and V. J. Cook, 1967. $NOMMAD_1$: normative models of market acceptance determination. Working paper, Marketing Science Institute, P-43-5, 5C.

J. D. Herniter and R. A. Howard, 1964. Stochastic marketing models. *Progress in operations research, Volume II* (D. B. Hertz and R. T. Eddison, eds.); New York: Wiley, 33–96, 7A.

J. D. Herniter and J. Wolpert, 1967. Coalition structures in the three-person non-zero-sum game. *Peace Research Society, Papers, 8*: 7–108, 6D.

J. D. Herniter, V. J. Cook, and B. Norek, 1969. *Microsimulation of purchase behavior for new and established products.* Working paper, Michigan State University Computer Institute for Social Science Research, 1C.

J. D. Herniter, A. Williams, and J. Wolpert, 1967. Learning to cooperate. *Peace Research Society, Papers, 7*: 67–82, 6D.

R. F. Hespos, 1963. Simulation as an aid to staffing a customer service function. *Management Technology, 3*(2): 160–166, 7C.

W. Heuser: see T. Ploughman.

P. Hewett, R. Keigher, S. Meaker, and H. Montague, 1959. *A final report of the AG-1 sensitivity studies.* Working paper, Technical Operations, Incorporated, Operations Model Evaluation Group Staff Memorandum 59-4, 5C.

M. P. Heyes, 1968. Synthetic trip prediction models. *Traffic Engineering & Control, 10*(3): 131–133, MC.

E. D. Hietanen: see D. P. Hattaway.

D. M. Hill, 1965. A growth allocation model for the Boston region. *Journal of the American Institute of Planners, 31*(2): 111–120, 3C.

D. M. Hill and N. Dodd, 1962. Travel mode split in assignment programs. *Highway Research Board Bulletin, 347*: 290–301, MC.

D. M. Hill, D. Brand, and W. B. Hansen, 1966. Prototype development of statistical land-use prediction model for Greater Boston region. *Highway Research Record, 114*: 51–70, 3C.

F. S. Hillier and G. J. Lieberman, 1967. Simulation. *Introduction to operations research*; San Francisco: Holden-Day, 439–476, MS.

J. A. Hillier, 1962. A review of developments in area traffic control. *Australian Road Research Board, Proceedings, 1*(1): 416–426, MD.

J. A. Hillier, 1963. Use of computers for traffic analysis, forecast and assignment. *International Road Safety and Traffic Review, 11*(1): 34–35, 5C.

J. A. Hillier, P. D. Whiting, and J. G. Wardrop, 1954. *The automatic delay computer.* Working paper, Road Research Laboratory (Harmondsworth), Research Note RN/2291/JAH.PDW.JGW, 3C.

A. M. Hilton: see M. A. Rothman.

H. Hinomoto: see J. D. Singer.

D. R. Hinson: see J. W. Horn.

D. L. Hintzman, 1967. *Explorations with a discrimination net model for paired associate learning.* Doctoral dissertation, Stanford University, 3C.

D. L. Hintzman, 1967. Some tests of a discrimination net theory: paired-associate learning as a function of stimulus similarity and number of responses. *Journal of Verbal Learning and Verbal Behavior, 6*(5): 809–816, 3C.

D. L. Hintzman, 1968. Explorations with a discrimination net model for paired-associate learning. *Journal of Mathematical Psychology, 5*(1): 123–162, 3C.

D. L. Hintzman, 1968. Learning and memory in a discrimination net. *Computer Studies in the Humanities and Verbal Behavior, 1*(4): 191–199, 6C.

A. A. Hirsch: see M. Liebenberg.

E. C. Ho: see D. L. Trautman.

J. C. Hodder: see C. C. Abt.

R. Hodgen, 1964. Traffic assignment studies. *Traffic Engineering & Control, 5*(12): 710–713, MC.

J. D. Hodges, Jr., 1964. The decision-making function in system simulation—an approach. *Fifth national symposium on human factors in electronics, Proceedings*; New York: Institute of Electrical and Electronic Engineers, 294–303, MA.

L. A. Hoel: see J. S. Drake.

G. C. Hoff: see K. W. Heathington.

P. J. Hoffman: see N. Wiggins.

W. Hoffman and R. Pavley, 1959. Applications of digital computers to problems in the study of vehicular traffic. *Joint Computer Conference, Western Proceedings, 13*: 159–161, 6C.

J. D. Hogan, 1966. Long-range planning. *Society of Actuaries, Transactions, 18*(4): D305-D327, 5C.

J. D. Hogan, 1966. The use of operations research in field planning. *IBM symposium in operations research in the insurance industry, Proceedings*; Los Angeles: International Business Machines Corporation, 29–73, 7C.

J. D. Hogan, 1968. Statistical analysis for corporate simulation. *American Statistical Association, 1967 Proceedings of the Business and Economic Statistics Section*: 229–239, 5D.

A. C. Hoggatt: see F. E. Balderston.

A. C. Hoggatt, 1957. *Simulation of the firm.* Doctoral dissertation, University of Minnesota, 7B.

A. C. Hoggatt, 1959. A simulation study of an economic model. *Contributions to scientific research in management*; Los Angeles: University of California, 127–142, 7D.

A. C. Hoggatt, 1965. On stabilizing a large micro-economic simulation model. *Logistics Review and Military Logistics Journal*, *1*(3): 21–28, MS.

A. C. Hoggatt, 1966. Statistical techniques for the computer analysis of simulation models. *Studies in a simulated market* (L. E. Preston and N. R. Collins); Berkeley: University of California, 91–122, MS.

A. D. C. Holden: see D. L. Johnson.

A. D. C. Holden and D. L. Johnson, 1963. Simulation of human problem-solving methods. *National Electronics Conference, Proceedings*, *19*: 489–496, 7A.

E. P. Holland, 1958. *An analog model for studying economic development problems*. Cambridge: MIT Center for International Studies, Report C/58-6. Also a doctoral dissertation at Massachusetts Institute of Technology, 8D.

E. P. Holland, 1958. *Analog simulation of an economy beginning to develop*. Cambridge: MIT Center for International Studies, Report C/58-17, 7D.

E. P. Holland, 1962. Principles of simulation. *Science, technology and development, Volume 8: organization, planning and programming for economic development* (J. H. Durston and N. J. Meiklejohn, eds.); Washington: U. S. Government Printing Office, 106–118, 7D.

E. P. Holland, 1962. Simulation of an economy with development and trade problems. *American Economic Review*, *52*(3): 408–430, 5D.

E. P. Holland, 1965. Principles of simulation. *American Behavioral Scientist*, *9*(1): 6–10, MD.

E. P. Holland and R. W. Gillespie, 1963. *Experiments on a simulated underdeveloped economy: development plans and balance-of-payments policies*. Cambridge: MIT Press, 5D.

E. P. Holland, B. Tencer, and R. W. Gillespie, 1960. *A model for simulating dynamic problems of economic development*. Cambridge: MIT Center for International Studies, C/60-10, 8C.

J. H. Holland: see J. W. Crichton and see N. Rochester.

S. H. Hollingdale and G. C. Tootill, 1965. Simulation or equation-solving. *Electronic computers*; Baltimore: Penguin, 81–88, MG.

I. Holmberg: see H. Hyrenius.

W. K. Holstein and W. R. Soukup, 1962. *Simulation*. Lafayette, Ind.: Purdue University, Institute Paper No. 23, 7C.

C. C. Holt: see W. E. Schrank.

C. C. Holt, 1965. Validation and application of macroeconomic models using computer simulation. *The Brookings quarterly econometric model of the United States* (J. S. Duesenberry, G. Fromm, L. R. Klein, and E. Kuh, eds.); Chicago: Rand McNally, 636–650, MS.

C. C. Holt, F. Modigliani, and H. A. Simon, 1955. A linear decision rule for production and employment scheduling. *Management Science*, *2*(1): 1–30, 5C.

E. M. Hoover, 1966. *Computerized location models for assessing of indirect impacts of water resources projects*. Working paper, Washington University Institute for Urban and Regional Studies, 7D.

N. J. Hopkins: see M. D. F. Boulton.

J. W. Horn, D. B. Stafford, D. R. Hinson and G. L. Reed, 1964. *An investigation to correlate synthetic land use origin and destination techniques to field conducted origin and destination surveys, final report*. Raleigh: University of North Carolina at Raleigh Highway Research Program, MS.

S. J. Horwitz: see N. F. Morehouse.

A. S. Householder: see R. F. Bales and see J. L. Rogers.

A. S. Householder, 1951. *Neural nets for "Toad Ti"*. Working paper, Rand Corporation, RM-671, 8A.

A. S. Householder, 1953. The Monte Carlo method. *Principles of numerical analysis*; New York: McGraw-Hill, 242–246, MG.

C. I. Hovland: see E. B. Hunt.

C. I. Hovland, 1960. Computer simulation of thinking. *American Psychologist*, *15*(11): 687–693, MA.

C. I. Hovland, 1963. Computer simulation in the behavioral sciences. *The behavioral sciences today* (B. R. Berelson, ed.); New York: Basic Books, 77–88, MA.

C. I. Hovland and E. B. Hunt, 1960. Computer simulation of concept attainment. *Behavioral Science*, *5*(3): 265–267, 5C.

B. E. Howard, 1966. Nonlinear system simulation. *SCi Simulation*, *7*(4): 205–211, MS.

J. A. Howard and W. M. Morgenroth, 1968. Information processing model of executive decisions. *Management Science*, *14*(7): 416–428, 8A.

L. R. Howard and D. O. Eberhardt, 1967. Airline simulation for analysis of commercial airplane markets. *Transportation Science*, *1*(3): 131–157, 2D.

R. A. Howard: see J. D. Herniter.

W. D. Howard, 1961. The computer simulation of a colonial socio-economic system. *Joint Computer Conference, Western Proceedings*, *19*: 613–622. 5D.

M. G. Howat, 1965. *A digital computer simulation of driver overtaking, following and passing*. Working paper, Cornell Aeronautical Laboratory, VK-1938-V-1, 2C.

E. P. Howrey, 1969. *Dynamic properties of a condensed version of the Wharton model*. Working paper, University of Pennsylvania, MS.

E. P. Howrey and H. H. Kelejian, 1969. Computer simulation versus analytical solutions. *The design of computer simulation experiments* (T. H. Naylor, ed.); Durham: Duke University Press, Chapter 10, MS.

D. S. Huang and M. D. McCarthy, 1967. Simulation of the home mortgage market in the late sixties. *Review of Economics and Statistics*, *49*(4): 441–450, 2D.

P. Huggins, 1960. Two experimental learning machines. *Electronics & Power*, *6*(72): 702–705, 6A.

P. A. B. Hughes: see E. M. L. Beale.

C. L. Hull: see H. D. Baernstein and see R. G. Kreuger.

C. L. Hull, 1930. Simple trial-and-error learning: a study in psychological theory. *Psychological Review*, *37*(3): 241–256, MA.

C. L. Hull and H. D. Baernstein, 1929. A mechanical parallel to the conditioned reflex. *Science*, *70*(1801): 14–15, 6A.

T. E. Hull, 1966. Simulation. *Introduction to computing*; Englewood Cliffs, N. J.: Prentice–Hall, 158–169, MG.

E. B. Hunt: see C. I. Hovland.

E. B. Hunt, 1962. *Concept learning: an information processing problem*. New York: Wiley, 8A.

E. B. Hunt, 1963. Simulation and analytic models of memory. *Journal of Verbal Learning and Verbal Behavior*, *2*(1): 49–59, 3A.

E. B. Hunt, 1965. The evaluation of somewhat parallel models. *Mathematical explorations in behavioral science* (F. Massarik and P. Ratoosh, eds.); Homewood, Ill.: Irwin, 37–55, MS.

E. B. Hunt and C. I. Hovland, 1961. Programming a model of human concept formulation. *Joint Computer Conference, Western Proceedings*, *19*: 145–155, 1A.

E. B. Hunt, J. Marin, and P. J. Stone, 1966. *Experiments in induction*. New York: Academic Press, 3C.

J. McV. Hunt, 1961. *Intelligence and experience*. New York: Ronald, MA.

J. S. Hunter and T. H. Naylor, 1969. Experimental designs for computer simulation experiments. *The design of computer simulation experiments* (T. H. Naylor, ed.); Durham; Duke University Press, Chapter 2, MS.

C. C. Hurd, 1954. Simulation by computation as an operations research tool. *Operations Research*, *2*(2): 205–207, MG.

C. C. Hurd, 1955. Computing in management science. *Management Science*, *1*(2): 103–114, MG.

E. G. Hurst, Jr., and A. B. McNamara, 1967. Heuristic scheduling in a woolen mill. *Management Science*, *14*(4): B-182-203, 1A.

R. Hurst: see J. W. Loughary.

R. H. Hurtubise, 1969. Sample sizes and confidence intervals associated with a Monte Carlo simulation model possessing a multinomial output. *SCi Simulation*, *12*(2): 71–77, MS.

B. G. Hutchinson: see J. F. Morrall.

B. G. Hutchinson, W. A. McLaughlin, and J. H. Shortreed, 1966. Planning urban transportation systems. *Australian Road Research Board Proceedings*, 3(1): 87–128, MC.

G. K. Hutchinson, 1964. *The design and simulation of a management information and control system*. Doctoral dissertation, Stanford University, 7D.

S. H. Hymans, 1970. The trade-off between unemployment and inflation: theory and measurement. *Readings in money, national income, and stabilization policy* (W. L. Smith and R. L. Teigen, eds.); Homewood, Ill.: Irwin, second edition, 2D.

H. Hyrenius and I. Adolfsson, 1964. *A fertility simulation model*. Göteborg: University of Göteborg, 5C.

H. Hyrenius, I. Adolfsson, and I. Holmberg, 1966. *Demographic models: DM2*. Göteborg: University of Göteborg, 4C.

H. Hyrenius, I. Holmberg, and M. Carlsson, 1967. *Demographic models: DM3*. Göteborg: University of Göteborg, 3C.

S. Ichimura, L. R. Klein, S. Koizumi, K. Sato, and Y. Shinkai, 1964. A quarterly econometric model of Japan, 1952–1959. *Osaka Economic Papers*, *12*(2): 19–44, 5D.

S. Ichimura, L. R. Klein, S. Koizumi, K. Sato, and Y. Shinkai, 1964. A quarterly econometric model of Japan, 1952–1959: data appendix. *Osaka Economic Papers*, *13*(1): 21–62, 5D.

Y. Ijiri, 1962. *Computer simulation of Yule distribution models*. Working paper, Carnegie-Mellon University, MC.

Y. Ijiri and H. A. Simon, 1964. Business firm growth and size. *American Economic Review*, 54(2): 77–89, 5C.

R. M. Ilfeld, 1967. Dispatcher model and repair man simulation. *Some new models of human decision making*; Masters thesis, Massachusetts Institute of Technology, 73–114, 4C.

D. Ingerman, 1968. Simulation of a railed automated highway. *Digest of the second conference on applications of simulation* (A. Ockene, ed.); New York: Institute of Electrical and Electronic Engineers, Publications No. 68C60SIM, 58–61, 7C.

G. Ingram: see L. Uhr.

International Business Machines, 1966. *Bibliography on simulation*. White Plains, N. Y.: IBM Technical Publications Department, Form 320-0924, MG.

N. A. Irwin, 1965. Review of existing land-use forecasting techniques. *Highway Research Record*, *88*: 182–216, MG.

N. A. Irwin and H. G. von Cube, 1962. Capacity restraint in multi-travel mode assignment programs. *Highway Research Board Bulletin*, *347*: 258–289, 3C.

N. A. Irwin, N. Dodd, and H. G. von Cube, 1961. Capacity restraint in assignment programs. *Highway Research Board Bulletin*, *297*: 109–127, 3C.

A. G. Ivakhnenko, 1963. Inductive and deductive methods of cognition as a basis for building two principal types of learning systems. *Principles of the design of self-learning systems—USSR* (State Publishing House of Technical Literature, Kiev, 1962); Washington: Joint Publications Research Service, JPRS No. 18181, 133–155, MA.

T. E. Ivall, 1956. Computers of the future. *Electronic computers*; London: Iliffe, 245–259, MA.

D. N. Jackson, 1963. Strategic problems in research on computer models of personality. *Computer simulation of personality* (S. S. Tomkins and S. Messick, eds.); New York: Wiley, 101–111, MA.

J. R. Jackson: see A. J. Rowe.

R. R. P. Jackson, 1964. Design of an appointments system. *OR, Operational Research Quarterly, 15*(3): 219–224, 5A.

R. R. P. Jackson and D. G. Nickols, 1959. The economics of the hiring of private wires in Great Britain—a simulation study. *OR, Operational Research Quarterly, 10*(1): 22–40, 5C.

W. C. Jacob, 1964. A review of computer applications in statistics. *ICC Bulletin, 3*(1): 1–21, MC.

M. Jacobs: see D. Brand.

L. Jacobson and P. J. McGovern, Jr., 1962. Computer simulation of a national economy. *Computers and Automation, 11*(8): 14–16, MD.

J. E. Jacoby and S. Harrison, 1960. *Efficient experimentation with simulation models*. Washington, D. C.: Technical Operations Incorporated, Report 60-2, MS.

J. E. Jacoby and S. Harrison, 1962. Multi-variable experimentation and simulation models. *Naval Research Logistics Quarterly, 9*(2): 121–136, MS.

K. Janda, G. Antunes, and W. Skogan, 1967. *Intersocietal computer simulation: the governmental structure routine*. Working paper, Northwestern University Department of Political Science, 5B.

W. E. Jarmain, ed., 1963. *Problems in industrial dynamics*. Cambridge: MIT Press, MG.

E. T. Jaynes: see M. A. Rothman.

J. P. Jeanniot and P. J. Sandiford, 1963. Some airline applications of Monte-Carlo system simulations. *Information processing 1962* (International Federation for Information Processing, C. M. Popplewell, ed); Amsterdam: North-Holland, MG.

G. Jefferson, 1949. The mind of mechanical man. *British Medical Journal, 1949*(1-4616): 1105–1110, MA.

J. L. Jenkins: see R. H. Adams.

H. S. Jennings, 1909. The work of J. von Uexküll on the physiology of movements and behavior. *Journal of Comparative Neurology, 19*(3): 313–336, MA.

N. H. Jennings, 1958. Computer simulation of peak hour bus operation. *Report of system simulation symposium* (D. G. Malcolm, ed.); New York: American Institute of Industrial Engineers, 28–31, 5C.

N. H. Jennings and J. H. Dickins, 1958. Computer simulation of peak hour operations in a bus terminal. *Management Science, 5*(1): 106–120, 2C.

W. N. Jessop, 1956. Monte Carlo methods and industrial problems. *Applied Statistics, 5*(3): 158–165, MC.

L. Johansen: see J. A. C. Brown and see R. M. Solow.

B. M. Johnson: see R. W. Conway.

D. L. Johnson: see A. D. C. Holden.

D. L. Johnson and A. D. C. Holden, 1964. A problem-solving machine with the capacity to learn from its experience. *SCi Simulation, 3*(2): 71–76, 7A.

D. L. Johnson and A. D. C. Holden, 1966. Computer learning in theorem proving. *IEEE International Convention Record, 14*(6): 51–60. Reprinted in *IEEE Transactions on Systems Science and Cybernetics, SSC-2*(2): 115–123, 6A.

E. S. Johnson, 1961. *The simulation of human problem solving from an empirically derived model*. Doctoral dissertation, University of North Carolina, 8A.

E. S. Johnson, 1964. An information-processing model of one kind of problem solving. *Psychological Monographs, 78*(4): 1–31, 8A.

G. O. Johnson, 1964. Utilization of an automated planning file. *The cybernetic approach to urban analysis* (L. M. Swanson and G. O. Johnson, eds.); Los Angeles: University of Southern California, 55–67, MD.

H. J. Johnson and S. S. Smith, 1961. Simulation in the application of wage incentives to multiple machines. *Journal of Industrial Engineering, 12*(6): 428–430, 7B.

M. C. Johnson, 1964. Adaptive computer model. *Journal of Educational Psychology, 55*(1): 66–70, 6C.

W. M. Johnson: see T. B. Sheridan.

J. Johnston: see J. A. C. Brown.

W. P. Jolly: see B. Benjamin.

C. H. Jones, 1967. Parametric production planning. *Management Science, 13*(11): 843–866, 7C.

L. V. Jones, 1963. Beyond Babbage. *Psychometrika, 28*(4): 315–331, MA.

N. Jordan, 1961. *Why we cannot build "thinking machines" (at least at present)*. Working paper, Rand Corporation, P-2258, MA.

N. O. Jørgensen, 1961. Determination of the capacity of road intersections by model testing. *Ingeniøren, 5*(3): 99–104, 3D.

E. Joseph: see R. E. Zimmerman.

R. D. Joseph: see J. A. Daly.

R. C. Joyner, 1968. Computer simulation of concept learning by individuals in a minimum social situation. *Digest of the second conference on applications of simulation* (A. Ockene, ed.); New York: Institute of Electrical and Electronic Engineers, Publication No. 68C60SIM, 163–165, 3C.

R. W. Judy and J. B. Levine, 1965. *A new tool for educational administrators.* Toronto: University of Toronto Press, 7D.

I. W. Kabak, 1968. Stopping rules for queuing simulations. *Operations Research, 16*(2): 431–437, MS.

I. W. Kabak, 1968. Stopping rules for queuing simulations: non independent tours. *Digest of the second conference on applications of simulation* (A. Ockene, ed.); New York: Institute of Electrical and Electronic Engineers, Publication No. 68C68SIM, 13–15, MS.

M. Kabrisky, 1966. *A proposed model for visual information processing in the human brain.* Urbana: University of Illinois Press, 2A.

E. E. Kaczka: see H. J. Brightman.

E. E. Kaczka, 1966. *The impact of some dimensions of managerial climate on the performance of industrial organizations.* Doctoral dissertation, Rensselaer Polytechnic Institute, 2B.

E. E. Kaczka and R. V. Kirk, 1967. Managerial climate, work groups, and organizational performance. *Administrative Science Quarterly, 12*(2): 253–272, 2B.

E. E. Kaczka and W. A. Wallace, 1965. Management simulation for optimizing decision-making. *Industrial Management, 7*(4): 6 and 13, MG.

J. Kagdis and M. R. Lackner, 1962. *Introduction to management control systems research.* Working paper, System Development Corporation, TM-708/100/00, 7D.

J. Kagdis and M. R. Lackner, 1963. A management control systems simulation model. *Management Technology, 3*(2): 145–159, 7D.

J. Kagdis and M. R. Lackner, 1963. *The modeling of management control.* Working paper, System Development Corporation, SP–1213, MG.

H. Kahn, 1950. Random sampling (Monte Carlo) techniques in Neutron attenuation problems—I. *Nucleonics, 6*(5): 27–33 and 37, MS.

H. Kahn, 1950. Random sampling (Monte Carlo) techniques in Neutron attenuation problems—II. *Nucleonics, 6*(6): 60–65, MS.

H. Kahn, 1951. Modification of the Monte Carlo method. *Seminar on scientific computation, November, 1949, Proceedings* (IBM Applied Science Department and C. C. Hurd, eds.); New York: International Business Machines, 20–27, MS.

H. Kahn, 1954. *Applications of Monte Carlo.* Working paper, Rand Corporation, RM-1237-AEC, revised 1956, MS.

H. Kahn, 1956. Use of different Monte Carlo sampling techniques. *Symposium on Monte Carlo methods* (H. A. Meyer, ed.); New York: Wiley, 146–190, MS.

H. Kahn and I. Mann, 1956. *Techniques of systems analysis.* Working paper, Rand Corporation, RM-1829, MG.

H. Kahn and I. Mann, 1957. *Monte Carlo.* Working paper, Rand Corporation, P-1165, MS.

H. Kahn and A. W. Marshall, 1953. Methods of reducing sample size in Monte Carlo computations. *Operations Research, 1*(5): 263–278, MS.

J. F. Kain: see J. H. Niedercorn.

J. F. Kain, 1964. The development of urban transportation models. *The Regional Science Association, Papers and Proceedings, 14*: 147–173, 4D.

N. M. Kamrany: see H. R. Hamilton and see W. L. Swager.

L. P. Kane: see T. G. Miller, Jr.

B. Kanner, 1963. Simulation. *American Association of Advertising Agencies, Papers from the 1962 region conventions, A.A.A.A. Eastern Annual Conference,* MC.

H. Kanter: see J. Feldman.

R Karg: see D. D. Lamb.

H. W. Karr: see W. W. Fain.

S. Kashin, A. J. Syvertsen, and M. L. Landsman, 1968. *The Queens-Long Island traffic demand model.* New York: Peat, Marwick, Livingston & Co., 1C.

J. Kates, 1963. Traffic analysis, forecast and assignment by means of elctronic computers. *International Road Safety and Traffic Review, 11*(1): 28–34, 3C.

L. D. Kattsoff, 1954. Brains, thinking and machines. *Methodos, 6*(24): 279–286, MA.

A. Katz, 1959. An industrial dynamic approach to the management of research and development. *IEEE Transactions on Engineering Management,* EM-6(3): 75–80, 8D.

D. L. Katz, B. Carnahan, R. T. Douty, N. Hauser, E. L. McMahon, J. R. Zimmerman, and W. D. Seider, 1966. Simulation. *Computers in engineering design education, Volume I: summary report;* Ann Arbor: University of Michigan College of Engineering, 13–28, MG.

J. H. Katz, 1963. Simulation of a traffic network. *Communications of the ACM, 6*(8): 480–486, 6C.

G. M. Kaufman, R. Penchansky, and B. Marshall, 1968. Simulation study of union health and welfare funds. *Industrial Management Review, 10*(1): 41–59, 4C.

H. Kaufman, 1967. An experimental investigation of process identification by competitive evolution. *IEEE Transactions on Systems Science and Cybernetics,* SSC-3(1): 11–16, MS.

I. M. Kay, 1966. An executive's primer on simulation. *Data Processing Magazine, 8*(10): 52–57, MG.

R. Keigher: see P. Hewett.

H. H. Kelejian: see E. P. Howrey.

J. H. Kell, 1960. A theory of traffic flow on urban streets. *Institute of Traffic Engineers, Western Section Proceedings, 13*: 66–70, 3C.

J. H. Kell, 1962. Analyzing vehicular delay at intersections through simulation. *Highway Research Board Bulletin, 356*: 28–39, 7D.

J. H. Kell, 1963. Intersection delay obtained by simulating traffic on a computer. *Highway Research Record, 15*: 73–97, 7D.

J. H. Kell, 1963. Results of computer simulation studies as related to traffic signal operation. *Institute of Traffic Engineers, Proceedings, 33*: 70–107, 3D.

J. H. Kell, 1964. Simulation of the intersection. *Highway conference on the future of research and development in traffic surveillance, simulation, and control, Proceedings*; Washington: U. S. Department of Commerce, 127–143, 2D.

J. M. Keller: see W. G. Bouricius.

C. R. Kelley, 1967. A psychological approach to operator modeling in manual control. *Third annual NASA-university conference on manual control*; Washington: National Aeronautics and Space Administration, 165–180, MA.

C. R. Kelley, 1968. *Manual and automatic control.* New York: Wiley, MA.

G. A. Kelly, 1963. Aldous, the personable computer. *Computer simulation of personality* (S. S. Tomkins and S. Messick, eds.); New York: Wiley, 221–229, MA.

J. J. Kelly: see J. J. Browne.

P. M. Kelly, 1961. Problems in bio-computer design. *First Bionics Symposium (Living prototypes—the key to new technology*, J. C. Robinette, ed.); Wright-Patterson AFB: Wright Air Development Division, TR 60-600, 215–237, MA.

R. F. Kelly, 1968. The search component of the consumer decision process—a theoretic examination. *Marketing and the new science of planning* (R. L. King, ed.); Chicago: American Marketing Association 273–279, MA.

R. Kemball-Cook, 1961. Solving production problems by the Monte Carlo method. *Mass Production, 37*(7): 49–53, MC.

J. G. Kemeny, J. L. Snell, and G. L. Thompson, 1966. Computer simulation. *Introduction to finite mathematics*; Englewood Cliffs, N. J.: Prentice-Hall, second edition, 447–458, MG.

H. H. Kendler, 1961. Problems in problem-solving research. *Current trends in psychological theory*; Pittsburgh: University of Pittsburgh Press, 180–207, MA.

H. H. Kendler, 1964. The concept of the concept. *Categories of human learning* (A. W. Melton, ed.); New York: Academic Press, 211-236, MA.

Z. Kenessey, 1967. The beginnings of simulation research in Hungary. *Computer uses in the social sciences, Proceedings of the working conference*; Vienna: Institut für Höhere Studien und Wissenschaftliche Forschung Wien, MG.

J. J. Kennedy: see A. Engel.

T. W. Kerlin, 1967. Sensitivities by the state variable approach. *SCi Simulation, 8*(6): 337–345, MS.

F. J. Kern, 1966. *An application of pattern recognition techniques to social systems modeling.* Doctoral dissertation, University of Oklahoma, MG.

J. P. Kerr, 1964. City planning and planning for future governmental services and revenue means. *The cybernetic approach to urban analysis* (L. M. Swanson and G. O. Johnson, eds); Los Angeles: University of Southern California, 142–149, MC.

R. B. Kershner, 1960. A survey of systems engineering tools and techniques. *Operations research and systems engineering* (C. D. Flagle, W. H. Huggins, and R. H. Roy, eds.); Baltimore: Johns Hopkins Press, 140–172, MG.

W. Kessen, 1963. Strong and weak simulation—mimic or model. *Computer simulation of personality* (S. S. Tomkins and S. Messick, eds.); New York: Wiley, 273–276, MA.

A. R. Kessler: see I. D. Pool.

A. R. Kessler and I. D. Pool, 1965. Crisiscom: a computer simulation of human information processing during a crisis. *IEEE Transactions on Systems Science and Cybernetics, SSC-1*(1): 52–58, 5B.

N. Keyfitz and A. Tyree, 1967. Computerization of the branching process. *Behavioral Science, 12*(4): 329–336, 5C.

S. J. Keyser and M. Halle, 1968. What we do when we speak. *Recognizing patterns* (P. A. Kolers and M. Eden, eds.); Cambridge: MIT Press, 64–80, MA.

S. M. Khanna and C. R. Noback, 1963. Neural nets and artificial intelligence. *Artificial intelligence* (B. W. Pollard, ed.); New York: Institute of Electrical and Electronics Engineers, S-142, 83–88D, 5A.

J. M. Kibbee, 1960. Management control simulation. *Management control systems* (D. G. Malcolm and A. J. Rowe, eds.); New York: Wiley, 300–320, 8D.

E. A. Kidd: see T. E. Anderson and see K. R. Laughery.

E. A. Kidd and K. R. Laughery, 1966. Computer model of driving behavior: the highway intersection situation. *Highway Research Record, 118*: 96–97, 7A.

M. D. Kilbridge and L. Wester, 1966. An economic model for the division of labor. *Management Science, 12*(6): B-255-269, 2B.

M. D. Kilbridge, R. P. O'Block, and P. V. Teplitz, 1969. A conceptual framework for urban planning models. *Management Science, 15*(6): B-246-266, MD.

D. W. W. King: see D. R. Rexworthy.

E. P. King and R. N. Smith, 1966. Simulation in an industrial environment. *IBM scientific computing symposium on simulation models and gaming, Proceedings*; White Plains, N. Y.: IBM Data Processing Division, 43–55, MD.

G. W. King, 1953. The Monte Carlo method as a natural mode of expression in operations research, *Operations Research, 1*(2): 46–51, MG.

G. W. King, 1956. Applied mathematics in operations research. *Modern mathematics for the engineer* (E. F. Beckenbach, ed.); New York: McGraw-Hill, 211–242, MG.

S. J. King, 1968. A heuristic model of the human visual perception system. *Collected technical papers, Volume 3* (F. Rosenblatt, ed.); Ithaca, N. Y.: Cornell University Cognitive Systems Research Program, Report No. 12, 9–31, 8A.

S. Kinoshita: see H. Ueno.

J. Kirk and J. S. Coleman, 1963. *The use of computers in the study of social structure: interaction in a 3-person group.* Working paper, Johns Hopkins University, 4B.

R. V. Kirk: see E. E. Kaczka.

G. R. Kiss, 1967. Networks as models of word storage. *Machine intelligence 1* (N. L. Collins and D. Michie, eds.); New York: American Elsevier, 155–167, 8A.

P. J. Kiviat: see G. S. Fishman and see A. A. B. Pritsker.

P. J. Kiviat, 1967. *Digital computer simulation: modeling concepts.* Working paper, Rand Corporation, RM-5378-PR, MG.

D. Klahr, 1966. A computer simulation of the paradox of voting. *American Political Science Review, 60*(2); 384–390, 7B.

D. Klahr and H. J. Leavitt, 1967. Tasks, organization structures, and computer programs. *The impact of computers on management* (C. A. Myers, ed.); Cambridge: MIT Press, 107–139, MD.

J. P. Kleijnen, 1968. *Increasing the reliability of estimates in the simulation of systems: negative and positive correlation between runs.* Working paper, Katholieke Hogeschool, Tilburg, MS.

J. P. Kleijnen, 1968. *The use of multiple ranking and multiple comparison procedures in the simulation of business and economic systems.* Working paper, Katholieke Hogeschool, Tilburg. MS.

J. P. Kleijnen, 1969. A comment on the paper by Handscomb and Moy. *The design of computer simulation experiments* (T. H. Naylor, ed.); Durham: Duke University Press, Chapter 14, MS.

J. P. Kleijnen, T. H. Naylor, and T. H. Wonnacott, 1968. *The use of multiple ranking procedures to analyze simulations of business and economic systems.* Working paper, Duke University Econometric System Simulation Program, Paper No. 24, MS.

L. R. Klein: see J. A. C. Brown, see E. F. Denison, see J. S. Duesenberry, see M. K. Evans, see G. Fromm, and see S. Ichimura.

L. R. Klein, 1964. A postwar quarterly model: description and applications. *Models of income determination* (National Bureau of Economic Research); Princeton: Princeton University Press, 11–36, 1D.

L. R. Klein, 1964. The Social Science Research Council econometric model of the United States. *Econometric analysis for national economic planning* (P. E. Hart, G. Mills, and J. K. Whitaker, eds.); London: Butterworths, 129–168, 2D.

L. R. Klein, 1967. On the possibility of another '29. *University of Michigan, Fourteenth Annual Conference on the Economic Outlook*: 45–87, 2D.

L. R. Klein, 1969. Estimation of interdependent systems in macroeconomics. *Econometrica, 37*(2): 171–192, MS.

L. R. Klein and J. Popkin, 1961. An econometric analysis of the postwar relationship between inventory fluctuations and changes in aggregate economic activity. *Inventory fluctuations and economic stabilization* (U. S. Congress, Joint Economic Committee); Washington: U. S. Government Printing Office, Part III. 69–89, 1D.

S. Klein: see R. F. Simmons.

S. Klein, 1966. Historical change in language using Monte Carlo techniques. *MT, Mechanical Translation and Computational Linguistics, 9*(3): 67–82, 7D.

T. A. Klein, 1964. *The performance implications of brand advertising: simulation of a typical market for packaged whole milk.* Doctoral dissertation, Ohio State University, 7D.

B. Kleinmuntz, 1963. A portrait of the computer as a young clinician. *Behavioral Science, 8*(2): 154–156, 8A.

B. Kleinmuntz, 1963. Profile analysis revisited: a heuristic approach. *Journal of Counseling Psychology, 10*(4): 315–321, 5A.

B. Kleinmuntz, 1964. MMPI decision rules for the identification of college maladjustment: a digital computer approach. *Psychological Monographs, 77*(14): 1–22, 5A.

B. Kleinmuntz, 1966. Some studies in medical diagnostic problem solving by machine. *Information processing 1965* (International Federation for Information Processing, W. A. Kalenich, ed.); Washington: Spartan, Volume 2, 624–625, 8C.

B. Kleinmuntz, 1968. The processing of clinical information by man and machine. *Formal representation of human judgement* (B. Kleinmuntz, ed.); New York: Wiley, 149–186, 4C.

L. Klem: see D. B. Yntema.

J. Klír, 1965. The general system as a methodological tool. *General Systems, 10* 29–42, MS.

J. Klír, 1967. Processing of general system activity. *General Systems, 12*: 193–198, MS.

J. Klír and M. Valach, 1967. *Cybernetic modelling.* London: Iliffe, MG.

D. E. Knoop and K. S. Fu, 1964. An adaptive model of the human operator in a control system. *Fifth national symposium on human factors in electronics, Proceedings*; New York: Institute of Electrical and Electronic Engineers, 252–265, 6A.

R. R. Knox: see K. W. Heathington.

M. Kochen, 1957. Group behavior of robots. *Computers and Automation*, 6(3): 16–21 and 48, 7B.

M. Kochen, 1961. An experimental program for the selection of "disjunctive hypotheses". *Joint Computer Conference, Western Proceedings, 19*: 571–578, 7A.

M. Kochen, 1961. Experimental study of 'hypothesis-formation' by computer. *Information theory* (C. Cherry, ed.); London: Butterworths, 377–402, MA.

M. Kochen, 1963. Some mechanisms in hypothesis selection. *Symposium on mathematical theory of automata, New York, 1962, Proceedings*; Brooklyn: Polytechnic Press, 539–613, 7A.

M. Kochen and E. H. Galanter, 1958. The acquisition and utilization of information in problem solving and thinking. *Information and Control, 1*(3): 267–288, 8A.

M. Kochen, D. M. MacKay, M. E. Maron, M. J. Scriven, and L. Uhr, 1967. Computers and comprehension. *The growth of knowledge* (M. Kochen, ed.); New York: Wiley, 230–243, MA.

E. C. Koenig: see C. H. Davidson.

H. E. Koenig, 1965. Mathematical models of socio-economic systems: an example. *IEEE Transactions on Systems Science and Cybernetics, SSC-1* (1): 41–45, MG.

R. H. Kohr, 1967. On the identification of linear and nonlinear systems. *SCi Simulation, 8*(3): 165–174, MS.

S. Koizumi: see S. Ichimura.

R. G. Kokat, 1966. The economic component of a regional socio-economic model. *Fourth Annual Conference on Urban Planning Information Systems and Programs, Proceedings*, 73–88, 5D.

P. A. Kolers, 1968. Some psychological aspects of pattern recognition. *Recognizing patterns* (P. A. Kolers and M. Eden, eds.); Cambridge: MIT Press, 4–61, MA.

F. A. Koomanoff, 1966. Introduction (to simulation of railroad operations). *Simulation of railroad operations*; Chicago: Railway Systems and Management Association, MG.

B. O. Koopman and H. M. Berger, 1967. Use and misuse of simulations. *Digital simulation in operational research* (S. H. Hollingdale, ed.); London: English Universities Press, 19–25, MG.

T. C. Koopmans: see P. C. Mahalanobis.

J. Korbel: see G. H. Orcutt.

G. A. Korn, 1965. Hybrid computer Monte Carlo techniques. *SCi Simulation, 5*(4): 234–245, MS.

P. Kotler, 1965. The competitive marketing simulator—a new management tool. *CMR, California Management Review, 7*(3): 49–60, 8D.

P. Kotler, 1965. Competitive strategies for new product marketing over the life cycle. *Management Science, 12*(4): B-104-119, 7D.

P. Kotler, 1965. Evaluating competitive marketing stratergies through computer simulation. *Marketing and economic development* (P. D. Bennett, ed.); Chicago: American Marketing Association, 338–353, 7D.

P. Kotler, 1968. Computer simulation in the analysis of new-product decisions. *Applications of the sciences in marketing management* (F. M. Bass, C. W. King, and E. A. Pessemier, eds.); New York: Wiley, 283–331, 7C.

P. Kotler, 1968. Decision processes in the marketing organization. *Systems* (D. M. Slate and R. Ferber, eds.); Urbana: University of Illinois Bureau of Economic and Business Research, 57–70, 8B.

K. Kotovsky: see H. A. Simon.

Y. Kotowitz: see N. K. Choudry.

J. F. Kraft: see H. E. Adams and see R. E. Zimmerman.

R. Kraft and C. J. Wensrich, 1961. *Monte Carlo methods: a bibliography covering the period 1949 to June 1961*. Livermore: University of California Lawrence Radiation Laboratory, UCRL-6581, MC.

R. Kraft and C. J. Wensrich, 1964. *Monte Carlo methods, a bibliography covering the period 1949–1963*. Livermore: University of California Lawrence Radiation Laboratory, UCRL-7823, MC.

J. F. Kramer: see I. D. Pool.

H. S. Krasnow: see G. P. Blunden and see D. F. Boyd.

H. S. Krasnow, 1964. *Characteristics of simulation models*. Working paper, IBM Advanced Systems Development Division, Memorandum S-21, MG.

H. S. Krasnow, 1968. The process view and management systems. *Simulation programming languages* (J. N. Buxton, ed.); Amsterdam: North-Holland, 1–10, MD.

H. S. Krasnow, 1969 Simulation languages: facilities for experimentation. *The design of computer simulation experiments* (T. H. Naylor, ed.); Durham: Duke University Press, Chapter 16, MG.

J. G. Kreifeldt: see T. B. Sheridan.

V. I. Kremyanskiy, 1960. Certain peculiarities of organisms as a "system" from the point of view of physics, cybernetics, and biology. *General Systems, 5*: 221–230, MA.

H. Kretz: see H. Zemanek.

R. G. Kreuger and C. L. Hull, 1931. An electro-chemical parallel to the conditioned reflex. *Journal of General Psychology, 5*(2): 262–269, 6A.

P. Kribs, 1964. *SHARE digital simulation glossary*. Working paper, System Development Corporation, SP-1562, MG.

C. H. Kriebel: see P. D. Fox.

C. H. Kriebel, 1967. Operations research in the design of management information systems. *Operations research and the design of management information systems* (J. F. Pierce, Jr., ed.); New York: Technical Association of the Pulp and Paper Industry, STAP No. 4, 375–390, MD.

N. B. Krim, 1934. *Electrical circuits illustrating mammalian behavior and their possible engineering value*. Bachelor of Science thesis, Massachusetts Institute of Technology, 4A.

C. Kruger, 1963. *An overview of current and potential uses of simulation in sociological research.* Working paper, System Development Corporation, SP–363, 8D.

G. H. Kruschwitz and D. D. Lamb, 1968. *CAP impact model.* Pittsburgh: Consad Research Corporation, 5D.

G. H. Kruschwitz, A. Colker, and D. D. Lamb, 1969. A community-action-program impact model. *Socio-Economic Planning Sciences, 3*(1): 37–63, 5D.

K. A. Krusemark: see W. W. Murphy.

J. Kubanoff, 1953. "Timothy"—a robot electronic turtle. *Electronics World, 49*(4): 35–38 and 150–153, 7A.

A. A. Kuehn, 1962. Complex interactive models. *Quantitative techniques in marketing analysis* (R. E. Frank, A. A. Kuehn, and W. F. Massy, eds.); Homewood, Ill.: Irwin, 106–123, MD.

A. A. Kuehn, 1966. Simulation of consumer behavior. *American Statistical Association, 1965 Proceedings of the Business and Economic Statistics Section*: 39–42, MC.

A. A. Kuehn and R. L. Day, 1963. Simulation and operational gaming. *Marketing and the computer* (W. Alderson and S. J. Shapiro, eds.); Englewood Cliffs, N. J.: Prentice-Hall, 234–247, MG.

A. A. Kuehn and M. J. Hamburger, 1963. A heuristic program for locating warehouses. *Management Science, 9*(4): 643–666, MD.

A. A. Kuehn and A. C. Rohloff, 1967. Simulation of promotional effects. *Promotional decisions using mathematical models* (P. J. Robinson, ed.); Boston: Allyn and Bacon, 142 and 145, MC.

P. Kugel, 1963. Contemplative computers. *Artificial intelligence* (B. W. Pollard, ed.); New York: Institute of Electrical and Electronics Engineers, S-142, 31–43, MA.

E. Kuh, 1965. Econometric models: is a new age dawning? *American Economic Review, Papers and Proceedings, 55*(2): 362–369, MD.

P. Kunstadter, R. Buhler, F. F. Stephan, and C. F. Westoff, 1963. Demographic variability and preferential marriage patterns. *American Journal of Physical Anthropology, 21*(4): 511–519, 7D.

L. Kurland: see R. E. Bellman and see N. L. Gilbreath.

A. R. Lacey, 1960. Men and robots. *Philosophical Quarterly, 10*(38): 61–72, MA.

D. C. Lach: see P. B. Wilson.

M. R. Lacker: see J. Kagdis.

M. R. Lackner, 1964. *Digital simulation and system theory.* Working paper, System Development Corporation, SP–1612, MD.

M. R. Lackner, 1966. A process oriented scheme for digital simulation modeling. *Information processing 1965* (International Federation for Information Processing, W. A. Kalenich, ed.); Washington: Spartan, Volume 2, 413–414, MG.

T. R. Lakshmanan and W. G. Hansen, 1965. Market potential model and its application to a regional planning problem. *Highway Research Record, 102*: 19–41, 2C.

T. R. Lakshmanan and W. G. Hansen, 1965. A retail market potential model. *Journal of the American Institute of Planners, 31*(2): 134–143, 3C.

D. D. Lamb: see G. H. Kruschwitz.

D. D. Lamb, 1967. *Research of existing land use models.* Pittsburgh: Southwestern Pennsylvania Regional Planning Commission, MD.

D. D. Lamb, E. Dickman, L. S. Friedman, T. Soltman, R. Byrne, J. Snatchko, R. Karg, R. Arnold, A. Schwartz, A. Colker, and K. Arnold, 1969. *An urban-regional model of small area change for southeastern Michigan.* Pittsburgh: Consad Research Corporation, 2C.

J. J. Lamb, 1962. Evaluation of tactical communications effectiveness by computer simulation. *IEEE National Convention on Military Electronics, Conference Proceedings, 6*: 162–167, 7D.

S. M. Lamb, 1965. Linguistic data processing. *The use of computers in anthropology* (D. H. Hymes, ed.); The Hague: Mouton, 159–188, MD.

M. L. Landsman: see S. Kashin.

G. T. Lathrop and J. R. Hamburg, 1965. An opportunity-accessibility model for allocating regional growth. *Journal of the American Institute of Planners, 31*(2): 95–103, 7D.

G. T. Lathrop, J. R. Hamburg, and G. F. Young, 1965. Opportunity-accessibility model for allocating regional growth. *Highway Research Record, 102*: 54–66, 5C.

J. B. Lathrop and J. E. Walsh, 1958. Some practical simulations of operations. *Journal of Industrial Engineering, 9*(5): 392–396, 7D.

G. E. Laudon (G. E. L. Ostenso), 1963. *Development of a generalized cafeteria simulator.* Doctoral dissertation, University of Winconsin, 6C.

K. R. Laughery: see T. E. Anderson, see M. L. Braunstein, and see E. A. Kidd.

K. R. Laughery, 1961. *An information processing analysis of problem solving behavior.* Doctoral dissertation Carnegie-Mellon University, 1A.

K. R. Laughery, 1969. Computer simulation of short-term memory: a component-decay model. *The psychology of learning and motivation: Advances in research and theory, Volume III* (J. T. Spence and G. H. Bower, eds.); New York: Academic Press, 6C.

K. R. Laughery and L. W. Gregg, 1962. Simulation of human problem-solving behavior. *Psychometrika, 27*(3): 265–282, 1A.

K. R. Laughery and E. A. Kidd, 1968. *Urban intersection study—Volume I: summary report.* Buffalo: Cornell Aeronautical Laboratory, Report VJ-2120-V-1, 1D.

R. C. Lawlor, 1962. Information technology and the law. *Advances in computers, Volume 3* (F. L. Alt and M. Rubinoff, eds.); New York: Academic Press, 299–352, MG.

H. J. Leavitt: see D. Klahr.

A. M. Lee and P. A. Longton, 1959. Queueing processes associated with airline passenger check-in. *OR, Operational Research Quarterly, 10*(1): 56–71, 2C.

D. B. Lee, Jr., 1968. *Models and techniques for urban planning.* Buffalo: Cornell Aeronautical Laboratory, Report VY-2474-G-1. Reprinted in *Urban models and household disaggregation: an empirical problem in urban research;* doctoral dissertation, Cornell University, 1–266 and 359–372, MC.

E. M. Lee, 1957. A model of combat with both space and time variables. *War gaming, Cosmagon, and Zigspiel* (No editor); Bethesda: Johns Hopkins University Operations Research Office, ORO-SP-12, AD-235892, 157–180, 8D.

R. J. Lee: see L. O. Gilstrap.

B. Lefkowitz: see E. Duckstad.

B. Lefkowitz, 1962. *The San Mateo County trafficways's project.* Working paper, Stanford Research Institute, MC.

E. LeGrande, 1963. The development of a factory simulation using actual operating data. *Management Technology, 3*(1): 1–19, 7C.

F. G. Lehman: see P. Fox.

R. S. Lehman and D. E. Bailey, 1968. Basic simulation techniques. *Digital computing;* New York: Wiley, 217–231, MG.

J. Leib: see D. A. Carter.

K. N. Leibovic, 1962. Learning theory in biological systems and machines. *Cybernetica, 5*(2): 116–134, MA.

C. Leicester, 1963. The composition of manpower requirements. *British Association for Commercial and Industrial Education, Papers presented at the BACIE spring conference (Economic growth and manpower):* 38–53, 5D.

H. J. Leonard and W. B. Delano, 1965. Distribution model for short and long distance travel. *Traffic Engineering & Control, 7*(6): 390–395, 3C.

W. W. Leontief: see P. C. Mahalanobis.

C. E. V. Leser: see J. A. C. Brown and see R. M. Solow.

W. L. L'Esperance, G. Nestel, and D. Fromm, 1969. Predictions and policy analysis with an econometric model of a state. *American Statistical Association, 1968 Proceedings of the Business and Economics Statistics Section:* 317–328, 1D.

C. Levert and J. van Galen, 1968. Mathematical and statistical details on the simulation of MARKOFF-type stochastic processes on an electronic computer. *Computing, 3*(1): 65–75, MS.

B. M. Levin: see R. E. Schofer.

M. L. Levin, 1968. *An analytical approach to the study of interpersonal influence networks.* Working paper, Emory University Department of Sociology and Anthropology, 3B.

M. L. Levin, 1970. *A simulation model of the flow of influence in social systems.* Working paper, Emory University Department of Sociology, 3B.

E. Levine, 1966. Generic features of military simulations. *Information processing 1965* (International Federation for Information Processing, W. A. Kalenich, ed.); Washington: Spartan, Volume 2, 412–413, MB.

J. B. Levine: see D. J. Clough and see R. W. Judy.

S. L. Levy: see A. Glickstein and see P. A. Perchonok.

S. L. Levy, 1965. Simulation of the freeway. *Highway conference on the future of research and development in traffic surveillance, simulation, and control, Proceedings;* Washington: U.S. Department of Commerce, 166–174, 7D.

S. L. Levy, M. Carter, and A. Glickstein, 1965. Traffic and simulation. *Second international symposium on the theory of road traffic flow, London 1963, Proceedings* (J. Almond, ed.); Paris: Organisation for Economic Co-operation and Development, 253-256, 7D.

J. P. Lewis: see J. A. C. Brown.

R. M. Lewis and H. L. Michael, 1963. Simulation of Traffic flow to obtain volume warrants for intersection control. *Highway Research Record, 15*: 1–43, 2D.

T. S. Lewis: see C. J. Moore.

J. C. R. Licklider, 1967. Dynamic modeling. *Models for the perception of speech and visual form* (W. Wathen-Dunn, ed.); Cambridge: MIT Press, 11–25, MG.

M. Liebenberg, A. A. Hirsch, and J. Popkin, 1966. A quarterly econometric model of the United States: a progress report. *Survey of Current Business, 46*(5): 13–39, 1D.

G. J. Lieberman: see F. S. Hillier.

N. Lin: see G. J. Hanneman, see E. M. Rogers and see J. D. Stanfield.

N. Lindgren, 1962. Bionics—Part III: brain models and neural nets. *Electronics, 35*(9): 41–45, MA.

R. K. Lindsay, 1960. *The reading machine problem.* Doctoral dissertation, Carnegie-Mellon University, 7A.

R. K. Lindsay, 1961. *Toward the development of a machine which comprehends.* Working paper, University of Texas, 7A.

R. K. Lindsay, 1963. Inferential memory as the basis of machines which understand natural language. *Computers and thought* (E. A. Feigenbaum and J. Feldman, eds.); New York: McGraw-Hill, 217–233, 7A.

R. K. Lindsay, 1964. *A heuristic parsing procedure for a language learning program.* Working paper, University of Texas, 7A.

T. Y. Ling, 1966. *The structural characteristics of economic simulation models: a survey and outlook*. Working paper, IBM Advanced Systems Development Division, TR-17-7176, MD.

T. Y. Ling, 1968. *Mathematical expressions of the IBM preliminary simulation model of a hypothetical economy*. Working paper, IBM Advanced Systems Development Division, 5D.

T. Y. Ling, 1968. *Statistical design and analysis of deterministic simulation experiments with a static, socioeconomic model of the United States*. Working paper, IBM Advanced Systems Development Division, MS.

T. Y. Ling, 1969. A statistical concept of statics and dynamics in simulation experiments. *The design of computer simulation experiments* (T. H. Naylor, ed.); Durham: Duke University Press, Chapter 9, MS.

J. W. Lingner: see M. C. Sheps.

A. J. Lipinski, 1964. Planning for the company growth. *National Association of Accountants Bulletin*, *46*(3): 37–41, 7C.

A. J. Lipinski, D. W. Ross, and D. M. Salmon, 1968. Development and application of a simple product development and marketing strategy model. *Digest of the second conference on applications of simulation* (A. Ockene, ed.); New York: Institute of Electrical and Electronic Engineers, Publication No. 68C60SIM, 57a–57b, 5C.

B. Lipstein, 1966. Toward a theory of simulation. *American Statistical Association, 1965 Proceedings of the Business and Economic Statistics Section:* 32–38, MC.

A. D. Little, Inc., 1950. Monte Carlo at work. *Industrial Bulletin of Arthur D. Little, Inc., 270*: 3–4, MC.

A. D. Little, Inc., 1966. *Model of San Francisco housing market*. Working paper, A. D. Little, Inc., C-65400, 4D.

J. D. C. Little, 1966. A model of adaptive control promotional spending. *Operations Research, 14*(6): 1075–1097, 7C.

T. C. Liu, 1963. An exploratory quarterly econometric model of effective demand in the postwar U.S. economy. *Econometrica, 31*(3): 301–348, 2D.

J. Loeb, 1918. An artificial heliotropic machine. *Forced movements, tropisms, and animal conduct;* Philadelphia: Lippincott, 68–69, MA.

J. C. Loehlin, 1962. The personality of Aldous. *Discovery, 23*(7), 23–26, 5A.

J. C. Loehlin, 1963. A computer program that simulates personality. *Computer simulation of personality* (S. S. Tomkins and S. Messick, eds.); New York: Wiley, 189–211, 5A.

J. C. Loehlin, 1965. "Interpersonal" experiments with a computer model of personality. *Journal of Personality and Social Psychology, 2*(4): 580–584, 6B.

J. C. Loehlin, 1968. *Computer models of personality*. New York: Random House, MA.

K. R. London, 1968. *Introduction to computers*. London: Faber and Faber, MG.

P. A. Longton: see A. M. Lee.

Los Angeles Regional Transportation Study, 1963. *Volume I: base year report 1960*. Los Angeles: Los Angeles Regional Transportation Study, 1C.

Los Angeles Regional Transportation Study, 1968. *1980 progress report*. Los Angeles: Transportation Association of Southern California, 2C.

A. J. Lotka, 1925. Correlating apparatus not peculiar to living organisms. *Elements of physical biology;* Baltimore: Williams and Wilkins, 340–342 and 381–383, 7A.

R. S. Lott: see J. G. F. Francis.

J. W. Loughary, D. D. Friesen, and R. Hurst, 1966. Autocoun: a computer-based automated counseling system. *Personnel and Guidance Journal, 45*(1): 6–15, 1A.

Louisiana Department of Highways, 1962. *New Orleans metropolitan area transportation study, 1960-1980, Volume II—outlook for the future*. Baton Rouge: Louisiana Department of Highways Traffic and Planning Section, 1C.

I. S. Lowry, 1963. Location parameters in the Pittsburgh model. *The Regional Science Association, Papers and Proceedings, 11:* 145–165, 8D.

I. S. Lowry, 1964. *A model of metropolis*. Working paper, Rand Corporation, RM-4035-RC, 1D.

I. S. Lowry, 1968. Seven models of urban development: a structural comparison. *Urban development models* (G. C. Hemmens, ed.); Washington: Highway Research Board, Special Report 97, 121–146 MD.

I. S. Lowry, B. Harris, and K. J. Schlager, 1966. Discussion of land use forecasting concepts. *Highway Research Record, 126:* 32–37, MG.

J. R. Lucas, 1961. Minds, machines and Gödel. *Philosophy, 36*(137): 112–127, MA.

R. D. Luce: see R. R. Bush.

R. D. Luce and P. Suppes, 1965. Preference, utility, and subjective probability. *Handbook of mathematical psychology* (R. D. Luce, R. R. Bush, and E. Galanter, eds.); New York: Wiley, Volume 3, 249–310, 5C.

L. B. Lusted, 1965. Computer techniques in medical diagnosis. *Computers in biomedical research* (R. W. Stacy and B. D. Waxman, eds.); New York: Academic Press, Volume 1, 319–338, 7A.

L. B. Lusted, 1968. *Introduction to medical decision making*. Springfield, Ill.: C. C. Thomas, MA.

A. A. Lyapunov, 1963. Some questions on the teaching of automata. *Principles of the design of self-learning systems—USSR* (State Publishing House of Technical Literature, Kiev, 1962); Washington: Joint Publications Research Service, JPRS No. 18-181, 180–185, MG.

J. C. McAnulty: see R. H. Strotz.

J. McCarthy, 1959. Programs with common sense. *Mechanisation of thought processes* (D. V. Blake and A. M. Uttley, eds.); London: H. M. Stationery Office, Volume 1, 77–84, 8A.

M. D. McCarthy: see D. S. Huang.

K. McConlogue: see R. F. Simmons.

D. D. McCracken, 1955. The Monte Carlo method. *Scientific American, 192*(5): 90–96, MG.

M. C. McCracken, 1967. Simulation in economics. *SCi Simulation, 9*(1): 49–50, MD.

W. S. McCulloch: see H. E. Tompkins.

W. S. McCulloch, 1949. The brain as a computing machine. *Electrical Engineering, 68*(6): 492–497, MA.

W. S. McCulloch, 1950. Machines that know and want. *Brain and behavior, a symposium* (W. C. Halstead, ed.); Berkeley: University of California Press (*Comparative Psychology Monographs, 20*(1): 39–50, MA.

W. S. McCulloch, 1951. Why the mind is in the head. *Cerebral mechanisms in behavior* (L. A. Jeffress, ed.): New York: Wiley, 42–57. Reprinted in *Dialectica, 4*(3): 192–205, MA.

W. S. McCulloch, 1957. Biological computers. *IEEE Transactions on Computers, C-6*(3): 190–192, MA.

W. S. McCulloch and J. Pfeiffer, 1949. Of digital computers called brains. *The Scientific Monthly, 69*(6): 368–376, MA.

W. R. McDonald and W. R. Blunden, 1968. The application of linear programming to the determination of road traffic desire line patterns. *Australian Road Research Board Proceedings, 4*(1): 153–164, 7C.

J. J. McDonnell: see C. C. Abt.

A. W. McEachern, E. M. Taylor, J. R. Newman, and A. E. Ashford, 1968. The juvenile probation system. *American Behavioral Scientist, 11*(3): 1–45, 8C.

R. McGinnis, 1966. A simulation approach to stochastic mobility processes. *Simulation in Business and Public Health, Proceedings, 1*: 168–174, 5C.

R. McGinnis, 1968. A stochastic model of social mobility. *American Sociological Review, 33*(5): 712–722, 5C.

R. McGinnis and J. White, 1967. *Simulation experiments on a stochastic attraction model.* Working paper, Cornell University, 7C.

P. J. McGovern, 1960. Computer conversation compared with human conversation. *Computers and Automation, 9*(9): 6–11, 6C.

P. J. McGovern, Jr.: see L. Jacobson.

C. B. McGuire: see M. Beckmann.

R. E. Machol: see H. H. Goode.

C. S. McIntosh: see J. D. Thompson.

J. O. McIntosh, 1961. *On the decision of a simple conditioned-response machine.* Bedford, Massachusetts: Air Force Cambridge Research Laboratories. AD-264230, MA.

D. M. MacKay: see M. Kochen, see B. van der Pol and see J. O. Wisdom.

D. M. MacKay, 1951. Mindlike behaviour in artefacts. *British Journal for the Philosophy of Science, 2*(6): 105–121, MA.

D. M. MacKay, 1954. On comparing the brain with machines. *Advancement of Science, 10*(40): 402–406. Reprinted in *American Scientist, 42*(2): 261–268, MA.

D. M. MacKay, 1956. The epistemological problem for automata. *Automata studies* (C. E. Shannon and J. McCarthy, eds.); Princeton: Princeton University Press, 235–251, MA.

D. M. MacKay, 1956. Towards an information-flow model of human behaviour. *British Journal of Psychology, 47*(1): 30–43, MA.

D. M. MacKay, 1957. Information theory and human information systems. *Impact of Science on Society, 8*(2): 86–101. An abridged and revised version with the title "Information theory in the study of man" was published in 1964 in *Readings in psychology* (J. Cohen, ed.); London: Allen and Unwin, 214– 235, MA.

D. M. MacKay, 1959. Operational aspects of intellect. *Mechanisation of thought processes* (D. V. Blake and A. M. Uttley, eds.); London: H.M. Stationery Office, Volume 1, 39–65, MA.

D. M. MacKay, 1960. Modelling of large-scale nervous activity. *Models and analogues in biology* (Fourteenth symposium of the Society for Experimental Biology, J. W. L. Beament, ed.); New York: Academic Press, 192–198, MA.

D. M. MacKay, 1962. The use of behavioural language to refer to mechanical processes. *British Journal for the Philosophy of Science, 13*(50): 89–103, MA.

D. M. MacKay, 1965. A mind's eye view of the brain. *Progress in brain research, Volume 17: cybernetics of the nervous systems* (N. Wiener and J. P. Schadé, eds.); Amsterdam: Elsevier, 321–332, MA.

D. M. MacKay, 1966. Information in brains and machines. *Information processing 1965* (International Federation for Information Processing, W. A. Kalenich, ed.); Washington: Spartan, Volume 2, 637–643, MA.

D. M. MacKay, 1967. Ways of looking at perception. *Models for the perception of speech and visual form* (W. Wathen-Dunn, ed.); Cambridge: MIT Press, 25–43, MA.

W. McKay: see H. Mechanic.

J. L. McKenney, 1967. A clinical study of the use of a simulation model. *Journal of Industrial Engineering, 18*(1): 30–35, MD.

J. L. McKenney, 1967. Critique of: "Verification of computer simulation models." *Management Science, 14*(2): B-102–103, MS.

J. L. McKenney, 1967. Guidelines for simulation model development. *Information system science and technology* (D. E. Walker, ed.); Washington: Thompson, 169–173, 4D.

S. C. McLaughlin: see M. A. Rothman.

W. A. McLaughlin: see B. G. Hutchinson.

J. McLeod, 1968. Advances in simulation. *Advances in computers, Volume 9* (F. L. Alt and M. Rubinoff, eds.); New York: Academic Press, 23–49, MG.

J. McLeod, 1968. *Simulation.* New York: McGraw-Hill; reprints of articles from *SCi Simulation*, MG.

E. L. McMahon: see D. L. Katz.

M. McManus: see J. A. C. Brown and see R. M. Solow.

C. McMillan and R. F. Gonzalez, 1965. *Systems analysis.* Homewood, Ill.: Irwin, MG.

A. B. McNamara: see E. G. Hurst, Jr.

R. McNaughton, 1961. The theory of automata, a survey. *Advances in computers, Volume 2* (F. L. Alt, ed.); New York: Academic Press, 379–421, MG.

W. N. McPhee, 1961. Note on a campaign simulator. *Public Opinion Quarterly*, 25(2): 184–193, 5D.

W. N. McPhee, 1963. Natural exposure and the theory of popularity. *Formal theories of mass behavior;* New York: Free Press, 104–168, 3C.

W. N. McPhee and J. Ferguson, 1962. Political immunization. *Public opinion and congressional elections* (W. N. McPhee and W. A. Glaser, eds.); New York: Free Press, 155–179, 3D.

W. N. McPhee and R. B. Smith, 1962. A model for analyzing voting systems. *Public opinion and congressional elections* (W. N. McPhee and W. A. Glaser, eds.); New York: Free Press, 123–154, 5D.

W. N. McPhee, J. Ferguson, and R. B. Smith, 1963. A theory of informal social influence. *Formal theories of mass behavior* (W. N. McPhee); New York: Free Press, 74–103, 7D.

L. F. McPherson, III, 1965. Organizational change: an industrial dynamics approach. *Industrial Management Review*, 6(2): 51–63, 7D.

L. F. McPherson, III, A. L. Pugh, III, E. B. Roberts, and J. W. Wilcox, 1966. *Advanced systems analysis of textile industry problems.* Working paper, Pugh-Roberts Associates, PB 170390, 5D.

W. H. McWhinney, 1964. Simulating the communication network experiments. *Behavioral Science*, 9(1): 80–84, 4B.

G. F. Mader: see S. W. Cragin, Jr.

R. B. Maffei: see M. L. Gerson and see H. N. Shycon.

P. C. Mahalanobis, R. Frisch, H. O. A. Wold, W. W. Leontief, T. Haavelmo, T. C. Koopmans, L. Pasinetti, M. Allais, E. Schneider, R. Dorfman, and J. R. N. Stone, 1965. Discussion (of J. R. N. Stone's "The analysis of economic systems"). *Study week on the economic approach to development planning;* Chicago: Rand McNally, 89–113 (Pontificiae acadamiae scientiarum scripta varia 28), MD.

J. Maitland: see B. Benjamin.

W. R. Maki: see R. J. Crom.

D. G. Malcolm, 1958. New method pre-tests ideas. *Nation's Business*, 46(2): 64–68, MG.

D. G. Malcolm, 1958. System simulation—a fundamental tool for industrial engineers. *Journal of Industrial Engineering*, 9(3): 177–187, MG.

D. G. Malcolm, 1960. Bibliography on the use of simulation in management analysis. *Operations Research*, 8(2): 169–177, MD.

D. G. Malcolm, 1960. The use of simulation in management analysis. *Report of the second system simulation symposium* (W. E. Alberts and D. G. Malcolm, eds.); American Institute of Industrial Engineers, 11–26, MG.

D. G. Malcolm and A. J. Rowe, 1961. Computer-based control systems. *CMR, California Management Review*, 3(3): 4–15, MG.

R. Malm, G. Olsson, and D. Wärneryd, 1966. Approaches to simulations of urban growth. *Geografiska Annaler, Series B*, 48B(1): 9–22, 6C.

J. C. Maloney, 1962. The use of computers in advertising today. *The computer in advertising* (Central Media Bureau, eds.); New York: Association of National Advertisers, D1-D22, MC.

T. J. Manetsch, 1965. *Simulation and systems analysis of the United States softwood plywood industry.* Doctoral dissertation, Oregon State University, 4D.

T. J. Manetsch, 1966. Transfer function representation of the aggregate behavior of a class of economic processes. *IEEE Transactions on Automatic Control*, AC-11(4): 693–698, MS.

T. J. Manetsch, 1967. The United States plywood industry—systems study. *IEEE Transactions on Systems Science and Cybernetics*, SSC-3(2): 92–101, 4D.

I. Mann: see H. Kahn.

I. Mann and L. S. Shapley, 1960. *Values of large games, IV: evaluating the electoral college by Monte Carlo techniques.* Working paper, Rand Corporation, RM-2651, 7D.

A. S. Manne: see B. P. Dzielinski.

A. S. Manne and J. M. Frankovich, 1953. Electronic calculating methods for handling the excess capacity problem. *Review of Economics and Statistics*, 35(1): 51–58, 4B.

J. G. March: see V. E. Cangelosi, see K. J. Cohen and see R. M. Cyert.

J. G. March, 1962. The business firm as a political coalition. *Journal of Politics*, 24(4): 662–678, MD.

J. I. Marcum, 1962. *Inference of Monte Carlo properties from the solution of a known problem.* Working paper, Rand Corporation, RM-3184–PR, MS.

J. Marin: see E. B. Hunt.

M. E. Maron: see M. Kochen and see H. E. Tompkins.

M. E. Maron, 1962. Design principles for an intelligent machine. *IEEE Transactions on Information Theory*, IT-8(5): 3-179-185, 5A.

M. E. Maron, 1962. *Mechanisms underlying predictive behavior for an intelligent machine.* Working paper, Rand Corporation, RM-3011-PR, MA.

M. E. Maron, 1963. *Artificial intelligence and brain mechanisms.* Working paper, Rand Corporation, RM-3522-PR, MA.

M. E. Maron, 1964. *The logic of interrogating a digital computer.* Working paper, Rand Corporation, P-3006, MA.

M. E. Maron, 1965. On cybernetics, information processing, and thinking. *Progress in brain research, Volume 17: cybernetics of the nervous system* (N. Wiener and J. P. Schadé, eds.); Amsterdam: Elsevier, 118–138, MA.

D. G. Marsh: see J. F. Cogswell.

A. W. Marshall: see H. Kahn.

A. W. Marshall, 1956. The use of multi-stage sampling schemes in Monte Carlo computations. *Symposium on Monte Carlo methods* (H. A. Meyer, ed.); New York: Wiley, 123–140, MS.

A. W. Marshall, 1958. *Experimentation by simulation and Monte Carlo.* Working paper, Rand Corporation, P-1174, MG.

B. Marshall: see G. M. Kaufman.

W. S. Marshall, 1967. Simulating communication network experiments. *Management Science, 13*(10): B-656–665, 3B.

B. V. Martin: see H. J. Wootton.

E. W. Martin, Jr., 1959. Simulation in organizational research. *Business Horizons, 2*(3): 68–77, MG.

F. C. Martin: see J. C. Hay.

F. F. Martin, 1968. *Computer modeling and simulation.* New York: Wiley, MG.

F. N. Marzocco, 1964. Simulation of learning processes. *Fifth national symposium on human factors in electronics, Proceedings;* New York: Institute of Electrical and Electronic Engineers, 77–80, 5C.

R. A. Mash: see A. E. Shaw.

J. L. Massey, 1967. Information, machines, and men. *Philosophy and cybernetics* (F. J. Crosson and K. M. Sayre, eds.); Notre Dame, Indiana: University of Notre Dame Press, 37–69, MA.

F. Massnick, 1959. Computers simulating men. *Computers and Automation, 8*(10): 17–18, 7A.

W. F. Massy and R. E. Frank, 1965. The study of consumer purchase sequences using factor analysis and simulation. *American Statistical Association, 1964 Proceedings of the Business and Economic Statistics Section:* 412–421, 3C.

W. F. Massy and J. D. Savvas, 1964. Logical flow models for marketing analysis. *Journal of Marketing, 28*(1): 30–37, MA.

R. W. Mathers: see R. L. Grimsdale.

J. H. Mathewson: see D. L. Gerlough and see D. L. Trautman.

J. H. Mathewson, D. L. Trautman, and D. L. Gerlough, 1955. Study of traffic flow by simulation. *Highway Research Board, Proceedings, 34:* 522–530, 8D.

R. Mattessich, 1961. Budgeting models and system simulation. *Accounting Review, 36*(3): 384–397, 7C.

R. L. Mattson: see M. Fischler.

J. Mauchly: see H. E. Tompkins.

J. G. Mauldon: see J. M. Hammersley.

W. L. Maxwell: see R. W. Conway.

C. S. Mayer, 1964. *Interviewing costs in survey research.* Ann Arbor: University of Michigan Bureau of Business Research, 2D.

C. S. Mayer, 1964. Pretesting field interviewing costs through simulation. *Journal of Marketing, 28*(2): 47–50, 5D.

W. Mays, 1951. The hypothesis of cybernetics. *British Journal for the Philosophy of Science, 2*(7): 249–250, MA.

W. Mays, 1952. Can machines think? *Philosophy, 27*(101): 148–162, MA.

M. Mead: see H. Von Foerster.

S. Meaker: see P. Hewett.

H. Mechanic and W. McKay, 1966. *Confidence intervals for averages of dependent data in simulations II.* Working paper, IBM Advanced Systems Development Division, TR-17-202, MS.

L. Meertens: see N. H. Frijda.

L. Mehl, 1959. Automation in the legal world. *Mechanisation of thought processes* (D. V. Blake and A. M. Uttley, eds.); London: H.M. Stationery Office, Volume 2, 757–779, MA.

R. C. Meier, 1967. The application of optimum-seeking techniques to simulation studies: a preliminary evaluation. *Journal of Financial and Quantitative Analysis, 2*(1): 31–51, MS.

R. C. Meier, W. T. Newell, and H. L. Pazer, 1969. *Simulation in business and economics.* Englewood Cliffs, N.J.: Prentice-Hall, MS.

R. L. Meier, 1961. The simulation of social organization. *Behavioral Science, 6*(3): 232–248, MD.

W. A. Meinhart, 1966. Artificial intelligence, computer simulation of human cognitive and social processes, and management thought. *Academy of Management Journal, 9*(4): 294–307, MG.

J. L. Meiry: see A. E. Preyss.

R. M. Meisel, 1966. Monte Carlo techniques for simulation and design. *Electro-Technology, 78*(4): 48–51, MC.

H. F. Meissinger, 1960. The use of parameter influence coefficients in computer analysis of dynamic systems. *Joint Computer Conference, Western Proceedings, 17:* 181–192, MS.

D. Meister, 1964. Methods of predicting human reliability in man-machine systems. *Human Factors, 6*(6): 621–646, MC.

A. H. Meltzer: see G. P. E. Clarkson.

F. Meno: see T. W. Calvert.

G. P. Meredith, 1960. The communication of scientific concepts and models of semantic mechanisms. *Advancement of Science, 17*(66): 110–117, 5A.

J. H. H. Merriman and D. W. G. Wass, 1959. To what extent can administration be mechanized? *Mechanisation of thought processes* (D. V. Blake and A. M. Uttley, eds.); London: H.M. Stationery Office, Volume 2, 811–818, MA.

R. L. Merritt, 1967. Political science and computer research. *Computers in humanistic research* (E. A. Bowles, ed.); Englewood Cliffs, N.J.: Prentice-Hall, 90–107, MC.

W. L. Mertz: see G. E. Brokke.

W. L. Mertz, 1961. Review and evaluation of electronic computer traffic assignment programs. *Highway Research Board Bulletin, 297:* 94–105, MC.

T. C. Meserole: see J. H. Buhr.

S. Messick, 1963. Computer models and personality theory. *Computer simulation of personality* (S. S. Tomkins and S. Messick, eds.); New York: Wiley, 305–317, MA.

J. Meszar, 1953. Switching systems as mechanized brains. *Bell Laboratories Record, 31*(2): 63–69, MA.

N. Metropolis and S. Ulam, 1949. The Monte Carlo method. *Journal of the American Statistical Association, 44*(247): 335–341, MG.

Metropolitan Toronto Planning Board, 1964. *Report on the metropolitan Toronto transportation plan.* Toronto: Metropolitan Toronto Planning Board, 4C.

H. A. Meyer, 1956. Bibliography. *Symposium on Monte Carlo methods* (H. A. Meyer, ed.); New York: Wiley, 283–370, MC.

J. R. Meyer, 1962. Computers in economics. *Harvard symposium on digital computers and their applications*: Cambridge: Harvard University Press, 252–261, MD.

M. Meyer, 1911. *The fundamental laws of human behavior.* Boston: R. G. Badger, MA.

M. Meyer, 1913. The comparative value of various conceptions of nervous function based on mechanical analogies. *American Journal of Psychology, 24*(4): 555–563, M A.

R. F. Meyer and H. B. Wolfe, 1961. The organization and operation of a taxi fleet. *Naval Research Logistics Quarterly, 8*(2): 137–150, 7C.

H. L. Michael: see R. F. Dawson and see R. M. Lewis.

P. F. Michelsen: see G. E. Clark, Jr.

B. F. Miessner, 1915. A new solution for the problem of selectivity in torpedo control. *Purdue Engineer, 15*(8): 34–41, 7A.

M. W. Mikulak, 1966. Cybernetics and Marxism-Leninism. *The social impact of cybernetics* (C. R. Dechert, ed.); Notre Dame, Ind.: University of Notre Dame Press, 129–159, MA.

D. Milledge and M. J. Mills, 1960. Forecasting election results. *Computer Journal, 2*(4): 195–198, 6C.

A. J. Miller: see I. D. Gordon.

E. T. Miller, 1967. *Investigation of traffic simulation models for a signalized street network.* Doctoral dissertation, Texas A. & M. University, 6C.

G. A. Miller: see E. H. Galanter.

G. A. Miller, 1957. A note on the remarkable memory of man. *IEEE Transactions on Computers, C-6*(3): 194–195, MA.

G. A. Miller, 1962. The study of intelligent behavior. *Harvard symposium on digital computers and their applications*; Cambridge: Harvard University Press, 7–22, MA.

G. A. Miller, 1965. Computers, communication, and cognition. *Advancement of Science, 21*(93): 417–430, MA.

G. A. Miller and J. G. Beebe-Center, 1956. Some psychological methods for evaluating the quality of translations. *MT, Mechanical Translation and Computational Linguistics, 3*(3): 73–80, MS.

G. A. Miller, E. H. Galanter, and K. H. Pribram, 1960. *Plans and the structure of behavior.* New York: Holt, Rinehart and Winston, MA.

J. Miller: see K. W. Heathington.

K. S. Miller and F. J. Murray, 1953. A mathematical basis for an error analysis of differential analyzers. *Studies in Applied Mathematics, 32*(2/3): 136–163, MS.

T. G. Miller, Jr., and L. P. Kane, 1965. Strategies for survival in the aerospace industry. *Industrial Management Review, 7*(1): 19–35, 7D.

V. E. Miller, 1963. Area control by digital computer. *Traffic Engineering & Control, 5*(6): 359–363, MD.

V. E. Miller, 1963. Traffic survey analysis by electronic computer. *Traffic Engineering and Control, 4*(12): 657–662, MC.

V. E. Miller, 1965. The analysis of traffic surveys by electronic computers. *Second international symposium on the theory of road traffic flow, London 1963, Proceedings* (J. Almond, ed.); Paris: Organisation for Economic Co-operation and Development, 277–278, MC.

J. W. Milliman: see H. R. Hamilton.

M. J. Mills: see D. Milledge.

R. G. Mills: see A. J. Burton.

J. Minami, 1966. *Air defense war game model of the Japanese Air Defense Force.* Working paper, Air Staff Office, Japan Air Self Defense Force, 7C.

J. Minker: see L. Brotman.

M. L. Minsky: see H. E. Tompkins.

M. L. Minsky, 1961. A selected descriptor-indexed bibliography to the literature on artificial intelligence. *IEEE Transactions on Man-Machine Systems, MMS-2*(1): 39–55, MA.

M. L. Minsky, 1961. Steps toward artificial intelligence. *Proceedings of the IEEE, 49*(1): 8–30, MA.

M. L. Minsky, 1965. Matter, mind and models. *Information processing 1965* (International Federation for Information Processing, W. A. Kalenich, ed.); Washington: Spartan, Volume 1, 45–49, MA.

M. L. Minsky and D. G. Selfridge, 1961. Learning in random nets. *Information theory* (C. Cherry, ed.); London: Butterworths, 335–347, MA.

P. Mintz: see C. J. Stokes.

I. E. Mitchell: see A. G. Beged Dov.

M. Mitchner and R. P. Peterson, 1957. An operations-research study of the collection of defaulted loans. *Operations Research, 5*(4): 522–545, 7C.

I. I. Mitroff, 1967. *A study of simulation-aided engineering design.* Doctoral dissertation, University of California at Berkeley, 5A.

I. I. Mitroff, 1968. Simulating engineering design—a case study on the interface between technology and social psychology of design. *IEEE Transactions on Engineering Management, EM-15*(4): 178–187, 7A.

I. I. Mitroff, 1969. Fundamental issues in the simulation of human behavior: a case in the strategy of behavioral science. *Management Science, 15*(12): B-635-649, MS.

J. H. Mize and J. G. Cox, 1968. *Essentials of simulation.* Englewood Cliffs, N.J.: Prentice-Hall, MG.

F. Modigliani: see A. Ando, see E. F. Denison, and see C. C. Holt.

A. Modin, 1963. Developing interbranch balances for economic simulation. *Economics of Planning, 3*(2): 104–116, 8D.

M. Mogel, 1962. Voting simulation: the manufacture of consent. *Automation* (M. H. Philipson, ed.); New York: Vintage, 355–370, MC.

A. T. Mollegen, Jr., 1968. On the optimum structure for war-game simulations. *Digest of the second conference on applications of simulation* (A. Ockene, ed.); New York: Institute of Electrical and Electronic Engineers, Publication No. 68C60SIM, 230–232, MB.

W. F. Monroe, 1966. Objectivity and automated management decisions. *Journal of Industrial Engineering, 17*(3): 133–140, MD.

H. Montague: see P. Hewett.

D. B. Montgomery and G. L. Urban, 1969. *Management science in marketing.* Englewood Cliffs, N.J.: Prentice-Hall, MG.

C. G. Moore, Jr.: see R. M. Cyert.

C. G. Moore, Jr., 1968. The heuristic programming of marketing decisions. *Marketing and the new science of planning* (R. L. King, ed.); Chicago: American Marketing Association, 41–49, MA.

C. G. Moore, Jr., 1968. Simulation of organizational decision making: a survey. *Simulation in the study of politics* (W. D. Coplin, ed.); Chicago: Markham, 183–226, MA.

C. G. Moore, Jr., 1969. A descriptive model of the industrial purchasing process: the supplier selection routine. *Management action* (C. E. Weber and G. Peters, eds.); Scranton: International Textbook, 76–114, 8C.

C. G. Moore, Jr., 1969. Simulating actual decision-making processes in organizations: a progress report. *Management action* (C. E. Weber and G. Peters, eds.); Scranton: International Textbook, 285–315, MG.

C. G. Moore, Jr., and C. E. Weber, 1969. Buyer decisions and simulated buyer decisions. *Management action* (C. E. Weber and G. Peters, eds.); Scranton: International Textbook, 41–46, 1A.

C. G. Moore, Jr. and C. E. Weber, 1969. A comparison of the planning of sales by two department store buyers. *Management action* (C. E. Weber and G. Peters, eds.); Scranton: International Textbook, 19–40, 2A.

C. J. Moore and T. S. Lewis, 1960. Digital simulation of discrete flow systems. *Communications of the ACM, 3*(12): 659–660 and 662, 7D.

E. F. Moore, 1956. Gedanken-experiments on sequential machines. *Automata studies* (C. E. Shannon and J. McCarthy, eds.); Princeton: Princeton University Press, 129–153, MS.

E. G. Moore, 1966. Models of migration and the intra-urban case. *Australian and New Zealand Journal of Sociology, 2*(1); 16–37, MC.

C. R. Moores: see J. W. Morrison, Jr.

N. Moray, 1963. *Cybernetics.* New York: Hawthorn Books, MA.

N. Moray, 1967. Where is capacity limited? a survey and a model. *Acta Psychologica, 27*: 84–92, MA.

N. F. Morehouse: see R. H. Strotz.

N. F. Morehouse, R. H. Strotz, and S. J. Horwitz, 1950. An electro-analog method for investigating problems in economic dynamics: inventory oscillations. *Econometrica, 18*(4): 313–328, 7D.

T. B. Morgan, 1961. The people-machine. *Harper's, 222*(1328): 53–57, MC.

W. M. Morgenroth: see J. A. Howard.

G. W. Morgenthaler, 1961. The theory and application of simulation in operations research. *Progress in operations research, Volume I* (R. L. Ackoff, ed.); New York: Wiley, 363–419, MG.

K. Mori, 1966. Simulation analysis of fluctuations and growth of the Japanese economy: 1955–1960. *Postwar economic growth in Japan* (R. Komiya, ed.); Berkeley: University of California Press, 189–207, 3D.

J. F. Morrall, M. P. Ness, and B. G. Hutchinson, 1968. Traffic prediction models for central business district planning. *Australian Road Research Board Proceedings, 4*(1): 112–133, 2C.

R. L. Morrill, 1962. Simulation of central place patterns over time. *Lund Studies in Geography, Series B, 24:* 109–120 (Proceedings of the IGU symposium in urban geography, Lund 1960), 7D.

R. L. Morrill, 1963. The development of spatial distributions of towns in Sweden: an historical-predictive approach. *Annals of the Association of American Geographers, 53*(1): 1–14, 3D.

R. L. Morrill, 1965. Migration and the spread and growth of urban settlement. *Lund Studies in Geography, Series B, 26:* 1–208, 1D.

R. L. Morrill, 1965. The Negro ghetto: problems and alternatives. *Geographical Review, 55*(3): 339–361, 3C.

R. W. J. Morris: see T. A. Culshaw and see M. G. Grace.

·J. W. Morrison, Jr., and C. R. Moores, 1962. *The application of analog computers to traffic intersection problems.* Working paper, Arizona State University, 1C.

P. M. Morse, 1960. Operations research. *Frontiers of numerical mathematics* (R. E. Langer, ed.); Madison: University of Wisconsin Press, 69–77, MG.

K. W. Morton: see J. M. Hammersley.

K. W. Morton, 1956. On the treatment of Monte Carlo methods in text books. *Mathematics of Computation, 10*(56): 223–224, MS.

K. W. Morton, 1957. A generalisation of the antithetic variate technique for evaluating integrals. *Studies in Applied Mathematics, 36*(3): 289–293, MS.

L. Mosberg: see M. P. Friedman.

W. W. Mosher, Jr.: see A. V. Gafarian.

J. Moshman, 1958. The application of sequential estimation to computer simulation and Monte Carlo procedures. *Journal of the ACM, 5*(4): 343–352, MS.

J. Moshman, 1964. The role of computers in election night broadcasting. *Advances in computers, Volume 5* (F. L. Alt and M. Rubinoff, eds.); New York: Academic Press, 1–21, 6C.

F. Mosteller: see R. R. Bush.

A. Moustacchi, 1964. The interpretation of shadow prices in a parametric linear economic programme. *Econometric analysis for national economic planning* (P. E. Hart, G. Mills, and J. K. Whitaker, eds.); London: Butterworths, 205–224, 7D.

G. Mowbray: see D. J. Clough.

A. Mowshowitz: see Am. Rapoport.

W. A. Moy, 1965. *Sampling techniques for increasing the efficiency of simulations of queuing systems.* Doctoral dissertation, Northwestern University, MS.

W. A. Moy, 1969. Variance reduction techniques: practical. *The design of computer simulation experiments* (T. H. Naylor, ed.); Durham: Duke University Press, Chapter 13, MS.

R. W. Moyer: see W. W. Murphy.

P. Mueller, 1963. Principles of temporal pattern recognition in artificial neuron nets with application to speech recognition. *Artificial intelligence* (B. W. Pollard, ed.); New York: Institute of Electrical and Electronics Engineers, S-142, 137–144, 4A.

M. G. Mugglin: see W. R. Sutherland.

S. K. Mullick: see J. C. Chambers.

E. F. Murphy and E. C. Berkeley, 1953. Automatic computers on election night. *Computers and Automation, 2*(1): 27–28, 6C.

W. W. Murphy, K. A. Krusemark, and R. W. Moyer, 1968. Increased crew activities scheduling effectiveness through the use of computer techniques. *Human Factors, 10*(1): 57–62, 7B.

F. J. Murray: see K. S. Miller.

C. A. Muses, 1962. The logic of biosimulation. *Aspects of the theory of artificial intelligence* (C. A. Muses, ed.); New York: Plenum, 115–163, MA.

B. L. Myers and C. E. Weber, 1969. Purchase planning for department store buyers. *Management action* (C. E. Weber and G. Peters, eds.); Scranton: International Textbook, 61–75, 1A.

J. C. Myers, 1968. *Project Seal: simulation experiments in adaptive learning.* Working paper, University of California at Berkeley Management Science Laboratory, Report 7, 3A.

E. Naddor, 1963. Markov chains and simulations in an inventory system. *Journal of Industrial Engineering, 14*(2): 91–98, 7C.

A. L. Nagar, 1966. *Stochastic simulation of the Brookings economic model.* Working paper, Brookings Institution, 2D.

J. B. Naines: see R. H. Strotz.

R. E. Nance: see N. R. Baker.

R. E. Nance, 1967. Systems analysis and the study of information systems. *American Documentation Institute, Proceedings, 4*: 70–74, 8D.

R. E. Nance, 1968. *Strategic simulation of a library/user/funder system.* Doctoral dissertation, Purdue University, 7D.

R. E. Nance and N. R. Baker, 1969. *An industrial dynamics model of a university library.* Working paper, Southern Methodist University, 5D.

B. Nanus, 1965. The management uses of simulation. *Data Processing, 7*(2): 65–69, MG.

A. V. Napalkov, 1963. Information processes of the brain. *Progress in brain research, Volume 2: nerve, brain and memory models* (N. Wiener and J. P. Schadé, eds.); Amsterdam: Elsevier, 59–69, MA.

J. Nathanson: see B. Harris.

National Bureau of Standards, 1962. City traffic simulated by computer. *Computers and Automation*, *11*(5): 23–26, 5D.

J. A. Navarro: see J. G. Taylor.

T. H. Naylor: see J. M. Broughton, see D. S. Burdick, see K. Chu, see J. S. Hunter, see J. P. Kleijnen, see W. E. Sasser, see J. M. Vernon, and see W. H. Wallace.

T. H. Naylor, 1965. The economic theory of the firm: three tools of analysis. *Quarterly Review of Economics and Business*, *5*(4): 33–49, MD.

T. H. Naylor, 1968. *Bibliography on simulation and gaming*. Working paper, Duke University, MG.

T. H. Naylor, 1969. *Corporate simulation models*. Working paper, Duke University, MG.

T. H. Naylor and J. M. Finger, 1967. Verification of computer simulation models. *Management Science*, *14*(2): B-92–101, MS.

T. H. Naylor and D. T. Gianturco, 1966. Computer simulation in psychiatry. *Archives of General Psychiatry*, *15*(3): 293–300, MG.

T. H. Naylor and J. M. Vernon, 1969. *Microeconomics and decision models of the firm*. New York: Harcourt, Brace & World, MD.

T. H. Naylor, J. L. Balintfy, D. S. Burdick, and K. Chu, 1966. *Computer simulation techniques*. New York: Wiley, MG.

T. H. Naylor, D. S. Burdick, and W. E. Sasser, 1967. Computer simulation experiments with economic systems: the problem of experimental design. *Journal of the American Statistical Association*, *62*(320): 1315–1337, MS.

T. H. Naylor, D. S. Burdick, and W. E. Sasser, 1967. Design of computer simulation experiments for economic systems. *American Statistical Association, 1966 Proceedings of the Business and Economic Statistics Section:* 388–401, MS.

T. H. Naylor, W. H. Wallace, and W. E. Sasser, 1967. A computer simulation model of the textile industry. *Journal of the American Statistical Association*, *62*(320): 1338–1364, 1D.

T. H. Naylor, K. Wertz, and T. H. Wonnacott, 1967. Methods for analyzing data from computer simulation experiments. *Communications of the ACM*, *10*(11): 703–710, MS.

T. H. Naylor, K. Wertz, and T. H. Wonnacott, 1968. Some methods for evaluating the effects of economic policies using simulation experiments. *Review of the International Statistical Institute*, *36*(2): 184–200, MS.

T. H. Naylor, K. Wertz, and T. H. Wonnacott, 1969. Spectral analysis of data generated by simulation experiments with econometric models. *Econometrica*, *37*(2): 333–352, MS.

U. Neisser: see M. A. Rothman.

U. Neisser, 1961. Time-analysis of logical processes in man. *Joint Computer Conference, Western Proceedings*, *19:* 579–585, MA.

U. Neisser, 1963. The imitation of man by machine. *Science*, *139*(3551): 193–197, MA.

U. Neisser, 1963. The multiplicity of thought. *British Journal of Psychology*, *54*(1): 1–14, MA.

U. Neisser, 1966. Computers as tools and as metaphors. *The social impact of cybernetics* (C. R. Dechert, ed.), ed.); Notre Dame, Ind.: University of Notre Dame Press, 71–93, MA.

U. Neisser, 1967. *Cognitive psychology*. New York: Appleton-Century-Crofts, MA.

D. J. Nelson, 1963. A fundamental error theory for analog computers. *IEEE Transactions on Computers*, *C-12*(5): 541–550, MS.

R. T. Nelson, 1967. Labor and machine limited production systems. *Management Science*, *13*(9): 648–671, 7D.

M. Nerlove, 1966. A tabular survey of macro-economic models. *International Economic Review*, *7*(2): 127–175, MD.

M. P. Ness: see J. F. Morrall.

G. Nestel: see W. L. L'Esperance.

P. R. Newcomb, 1957. The analysis of war gaming. *War gaming, Cosmagon, and Zigspiel* (No editor): Bethesda: Johns Hopkins University Operations Research Office, ORO-SP-12, AD-235892, 285–298, MS.

A. Newell: see H. A. Simon.

A. Newell, 1962. Some problems of basic organization in problem-solving programs. *Self-organizing systems—1962* (M. C. Yovits, G. T. Jacobi, and G. D. Goldstein, eds.); Washington: Spartan, 393–423. Also published in 1963 in *ICC Bulletin*, *2*(2): 99–119, MA.

A. Newell, 1963. *A guide to the General Problem-Solver program GPS-2-2*. Working paper, Rand Corporation, RM-3337-PR, 7A.

A. Newell, 1963. Learning, generality and problem-solving. *Information processing 1962* (International Federation for Information Processing, C. M. Popplewell, ed.); Amsterdam: North-Holland, 407–412, MA.

A. Newell and G. Ernst, 1965. The search for generality. *Information processing 1965* (International Federation for Information Processing, W. A. Kalenich, ed.); Washington: Spartan, Volume 1, 17–24, MA.

A. Newell and H. A. Simon, 1956. The logic theory machine, a complex information processing system. *IEEE Transactions on Information Theory*, *IT-2*(3): S-61–79, 8A.

A. Newell and H. A. Simon, 1961. Computer simulation of human thinking. *Science*, *134*(3495): 2011–2017, 3A.

A. Newell and H. A. Simon, 1961. GPS, a program that simulates human thought. *Lernende Automaten* (H. Billing, ed.); Munich: R. Oldenbourg KG, 109–124, 1A.

A. Newell and H. A. Simon, 1961. The simulation of human thought. *Current trends in psychological theory;* Pittsburgh: University of Pittsburgh Press, 152–179, 1A.

A. Newell and H. A. Simon, 1962. *Heuristic programs and algorithms.* Pittsburgh: Carnegie-Mellon University, CIP-39, MS.

A. Newell and H. A. Simon, 1963. Computers in psychology. *Handbook of mathematical psychology* (R. D. Luce, R. R. Bush, and E. Galanter, eds.); New York: Wiley, Volume 1, 361–428, MA.

A. Newell and H. A. Simon, 1964. Problem-solving machines. *International Science and Technology, 36:* 48–62 and 96, MA.

A. Newell and H. A. Simon, 1965. Programs as theories of higher mental processes. *Computers in biomedical research* (R. W. Stacy and B. D. Waxman, eds.); New York: Academic Press, Volume 2, 142–172, MA.

A. Newell and H. A. Simon, 1965. Simulation of human processing of information. *Computers and computing* (F. A. Ficken, J. Heller, P. D. Lax, D. H. Lehmer, and R. D. Richtmyer, eds.); Buffalo: Mathematical Association of America, *The American Mathematical Monthly, 72*(2, Part II): 111–118 MA.

A. Newell and H. A. Simon, 1968. Simulation: individual behavior. *International encyclopedia of the social sciences* (D. L. Sills, ed.); New York: Macmillan, Volume 14, 262–268, MA.

A. Newell, J. C. Shaw, and H. A. Simon, 1956. *Problem solving in humans and computers.* Working paper, Rand Corporation, P-387, MA.

A. Newell, J. C. Shaw, and H. A. Simon, 1957. Empirical explorations of the Logic Theory Machine, a case study in heuristic. *Joint Computer Conference, Western Proceedings, 11:* 218–230, 7A.

A. Newell, J. C. Shaw, and H. A. Simon, 1958. Chess-playing programs and the problem of complexity. *IBM Journal of Research and Development, 2*(4): 320–335, 8A.

A. Newell, J. C. Shaw, and H. A. Simon, 1958. Elements of a theory of human problem solving. *Psychological Review, 65*(3): 151–166, MA.

A. Newell, J. C. Shaw, and H. A. Simon, 1959. A report on a general problem-solving program for a computer. *Computers and Automation, 8*(7): 10–17. Reprinted in 1960 under the title "Report on a general problem-solving program" in *Information processing* (International Federation for Information Processing, S.de Picciotto, ed.); Paris: UNESCO, 256–264, 5A.

A. Newell, J. C. Shaw, and H. A. Simon, 1959. *Report on the play of chess player I-5 of a book game of Morphy vs. Duke Karl of Brunswick and Count Isouard.* Pittsburgh: Carnegie-Mellon University, CIP-21, MA.

A. Newell, J. C. Shaw, and H. A. Simon, 1960. A variety of intelligent learning in a General Problem Solver. *Self-organizing systems* (M. C. Yovits and S. Cameron, eds.); New York: Pergamon, 153–189, 7A.

A. Newell, J. C. Shaw, and H. A. Simon, 1962. The processes of creative thinking. *Contemporary approaches to creative thinking* (H. E. Gruber, G. Terrell, and M. Wertheimer, eds.); New York: Atherton, 63–119, 6A.

G. F. Newell: see D. C. Gazis.

W. T. Newell: see R. C. Meier.

W. T. Newlyn, 1950. The Phillips/Newlyn hydraulic model. *Yorkshire Bulletin of Economic and Social Research, 2*(2): 111–127, 2D.

J. R. Newman: see A. W. McEachern.

Niagara Frontier Transportation Study, 1966. *Final report, Volume two: travel.* Albany: New York State Department of Public Works Subdivision of Transportation Planning and Programming, 2C.

R. S. Nickerson: see T. J. Roby.

D. G. Nickols: see R. R. P. Jackson.

J. H. Niedercorn and J. F. Kain, 1963. An econometric model of metropolitan development. *The Regional Science Association, Papers and Proceedings, 11:* 123–143, 2D.

C. R. Noback: see S. M. Khanna.

A. S. Noble, 1968. Problems of building a model of a company. *Mathematical model building in economics and industry* (C.E.I.R.); New York: Hafner, 71–80, MG.

O. C. Nord, 1963. *Growth of a new product.* Cambridge: MIT Press, 5D.

B. Norek: see J. D. Herniter.

B. Norek and J. D. Herniter, 1968. *NOMMAD$_2$, a 360/65 FORTRAN IV program for simulating demand for new products in frequently purchased consumer good categories.* Working paper, Marketing Science Institute, P-43-11, 7C.

A. Norman: see M. F. Snell.

D. A. Norman, 1968. Toward a theory of memory and attention. *Psychological Review, 75*(6): 522–536, MA.

M. R. Norman, 1967. *Solving a non-linear econometric model.* Working paper, University of California at Santa Barbara, MS.

D. T. Nowacki: see S. W. Cragin, Jr.

J. D. Nystuen, 1959. *Geographical analysis of customer movements and retail business locations.* Doctoral dissertation, University of Washington, 6C.

J. D. Nystuen, 1967. A theory and simulation of intraurban travel. *Quantitative Geography* (W. L. Garrison and D. F. Marble, eds.); Evanston: Northwestern University, Volume 1, 54–83 6C.

R. W. Obermayer, 1964. Simulation, models, and games; sources of measurement. *Human Factors,* 6(6): 607–619, MG.

R. P. O'Block: see M. D. Kilbridge.

A. C. Oettinger, 1952. Programming a digital computer to learn. *Philosophical Magazine, 43*(347): 1243–1263, MA.

A. G. Oettinger: see H. E. Tompkins.

L. H. Officer: see J. F. Helliwell.

C. Ohlin and P. Warren, 1963. *An approach to street traffic simulation.* Lidingo, Sweden: IBM Nordiska Laboratorier, 7C.

F. R. Oliver: see J. A. C. Brown.

E. Olsen, 1967. Regional income differences: a simulation approach. *The Regional Science Association, Papers and Proceedings, 20:* 7–17, 5D.

G. Olsson: see R. Malm.

B. B. Oosterhout: see H. E. Adams.

G. H. Orcutt, 1960. Simulation of economic systems. *American Economic Review, 50*(5): 893–907, MD.

G. H. Orcutt, 1961. Microanalytic models of socioeconomic systems: a new approach to forecasting. *University of Michigan, Ninth Annual Conference on the Economic Outlook:* 64–74, 5C.

G. H. Orcutt, 1963. Views on simulation and models of social systems. *Symposium on simulation models* (A. C. Hoggatt and F. E. Balderston, eds.); Cincinnati: South-Western, *22*–221–236, MD.

G. H. Orcutt, 1965. Data needs for computer simulation of large-scale social systems. *Computer methods in the analysis of large-scale social systems* (J. M. Beshers, ed.); Cambridge: MIT-Harvard Joint Center for Urban Studies, 189–198, MD.

G. H. Orcutt, 1965. Simulation of economic systems: model description and solution. *American Statistical Association, 1964 Proceedings of the Business and Economic Statistics Section:* 186-193. Also published in 1966 in *IBM scientific computing symposium on simulation models and gaming, Proceedings;* White Plains, N.Y.: IBM Data Processing Division, 59–76, MD.

G. H. Orcutt, 1967. Comments by Guy H. Orcutt. *The transfer of technology to developing countries* (Airlie House Conference, D. L. Spencer and A. Woroniak, eds.); New York: Praeger, 145–146, MD.

G. H. Orcutt, M. Greenberger, J. Korbel, and A. M. Rivlin, 1961. *Microanalysis of socioeconomic systems.* New York: Harper, 1C.

G. E. L. Ostenso: see G. E. Laudon.

J. L. Overholt, 1969. Factorial designs. *The design of computer simulation experiments* (T. H. Naylor, ed.); Durham: Duke University Press, Chapter 3, MS.

R. E. Overstreet, 1971. Simulation models of the Prisoner's Dilemma game. *Computer simulation of human behavior* (J. M. Dutton and W. H. Starbuck, eds.); New York: Wiley, 3B.

R. E. Overstreet and M. Pilisuk, 1967. *Simulation models of sequential choices in the Prisoner's Dilemma.* Working paper, Purdue University, 3B.

A. J. Owens: see L. J. Fogel.

H. Ozkaptan and R. Gettig, 1963. Computer simulation of man-integrated systems. *Behavioral Science.* 8(3): 259–266, 8D.

H. Pack, 1968. Formula flexibility: a quantitative appraisal. *Studies in economic stabilization* (A. Ando, E. C. Brown, and A. F. Friedlaender, eds.); Washington: Brookings Institution, 5–40, 2D.

D. W. Packer, 1964. *Resource acquisition in corporate growth.* Cambridge: MIT Press, 7D.

E. S. Page, 1965. On Monte Carlo methods in congestion problems. *Operations Research, 13*(2): 291–305, MS.

J. M. Paige and H. A. Simon, 1966. Cognitive processes in solving algebra word problems. *Problem solving* (B. Kleinmuntz, ed.); New York: Wiley, 51–119, 3A.

A. Painter: see E. Duckstad.

P. G. Pak-Poy: see T. A. Culshaw and see M. G. Grace.

P. G. Pak-Poy, 1962. Some current trends in traffic theory and practice. *Journal of the Institution of Engineers, Australia, 34*(4-5): 89–96, MC.

W. D. Panyan, 1969. Urban traffic simulation model. *Simulation and modeling conference* (R. U. Benson, ed.); Pittsburgh: Pittsburgh chapters of ACM, IEEE-EC, and IEEE-SSC, and Midwest SCi, 37–43, 5C.

V. V. Parin and R. M. Bayevskiy, 1967. Simulation. *Introduction to medical cybernetics;* Washington: National Aeronautics and Space Administration, TT F-459, 45–54, MA.

E. B. Parker: see R. W. Becker.

D. F. Parkhill, 1962. Distributed state response pattern recognition systems. *1961 Rochester conference on data acquisition and processing in biology and medicine* (K. Enslein, ed.); New York: Pergamon, 63–75, 4A.

H. Parlow, 1966. Lift operation and computers: a simulation of performance. *The Architects' Journal, 143*(12): 747–753, 5C.

L. Pasinetti: see P. C. Mahalanobis.

G. A. Pask, 1958. Organic control and the cybernetic method. *Cybernetica, 1*(3): 155–173, MA.

G. A. Pask, 1959. Artificial organisms. *General Systems, 4:* 151–170, 6A.

G. A. Pask, 1959. Physical analogues to the growth of a concept. *Mechanisation of thought processes* (D. V. Blake and A. M. Uttley, eds.); London: H.M. Stationery Office, Volume 2, 879–922, 4A.

G. A. Pask, 1961. *An approach to cybernetics.* London: Hutchinson, MA.

G. A. Pask, 1962. The simulation of learning and decision-making behaviour. *Aspects of the theory of artificial intelligence* (C. A. Muses, ed.); New York: Plenum, 165–210, MS.

G. A. Pask, 1963. A discussion of the cybernetics of learning behaviour. *Progress in brain research, Volume 2: nerve, brain and memory models* (N. Wiener and J. P. Schadé, eds.); Amsterdam: Elsevier, 177–214, MA.

G. A. Pask, 1964. A discussion of artificial intelligence and self-organization. *Advances in computers, Volume 5* (F. L. Alt and M. Rubinoff, eds.); New York: Academic Press, 109–226, MA.

G. A. Pask and R. J. Feldmann, 1966. Tests for a simple learning and perceiving artifact. *Cybernetica*, 8(2): 75–90, 5A.

R. Pavley: see W. Hoffman.

E. W. Paxson, 1963. *A neutral net for the recall of sequences*. Working paper, Rand Corporation, RM-3872-PR, 5A.

E. W. Paxson and I. Barr, 1963. *A neural net for consummatory behavior*. Working paper, Rand Corporation, RM-3393-PR, 4A.

E. W. Paxson and J. W. Smith, 1962. *A general neural net*. Working paper, Rand Corporation, RM-3406-PR, 5A.

F. Paycha, 1959. Medical diagnosis and cybernetics. *Mechanisation of thought processes* (D. V. Blake and A. M. Uttley, eds.); London: H.M. Stationery Office, Volume 2, 637–659, MA.

H. L. Pazer: see R. C. Meier.

R. Peabody: see J. S. Coleman.

C. C. Pegels, 1967. *Optimal plant structure and operation*. Doctoral dissertation, Purdue University, 3D.

C. S. Peirce, 1887. Logical machines. *American Journal of Psychology*, 1(1): 165–170, MA.

R. J. Pelletier: see J. D. Thompson.

R. Penchansky: see G. M. Kaufman.

R. E. Pendley: see D. L. Gottheil.

W. W. Penn, 1968. An antisubmarine warfare model for convoy protection. *IEEE Transactions on Systems Science and Cybernetics*, SSC-4(4): 413–418, 7D.

P. A. Perchonok and S. L. Levy, 1960. Application of digital simulation techniques to freeway on-ramp traffic operations. *Highway Research Board, Proceedings*, 39: 506–523, 7D.

W. C. Perkins, 1969. *A simulation analysis to evaluate the impact of the automatic stabilizers*. Working paper, Indiana University, 2D.

E. B. Perrin and M. C. Sheps, 1964. Human reproduction: a stochastic process. *Biometrics*, 20(1): 28–45, 8C.

E. B. Perrin and M. C. Sheps, 1965. A mathematical model for human fertility patterns. *Archives of Environmental Health*, 10(5): 694–698, 5C.

B. Persson: see J. C. Schoenman.

L. R. Peterson, 1967. Search and judgment in memory. *Concepts and the structure of memory* (B. Kleinmuntz, ed.); New York: Wiley, 153–180, 3C.

R. P. Peterson: see M. Mitchner.

A. C. R. Petit: see D. F. Boyd.

H. L. Peyrebrune, 1966. A comparison of precalculated-interchange assignment and an opportunity model traffic simulation. *Upstate New York Transportation Studies Notes*, 9: 6–8, 3C.

A. B. Pfaff: see M. Pfaff.

M. Pfaff, 1968. Experiments on an adaptive computer model of a distribution channel. *Digest of the second conference on applications of simulation* (A. Ockene, ed.); New York: Institute of Electrical and Electronic Engineers, Publication No. 68C60SIM, 179–188, 7D.

M. Pfaff, 1969. Simulation of complex organizational processes: design and analysis. *The design of computer simulation experiments* (T. H. Naylor, ed.); Durham: Duke University Press, Chapter 20, MS.

M. Pfaff and A. B. Pfaff, 1969. *Statistical analysis of simulations of human systems*. Working paper, Brookings Institution, MS.

J. Pfeiffer: see W. S. McCulloch.

J. Pfeiffer, 1952. This mouse is smarter than you are. *Popular Science Monthly*, 160(3): 99–101, 7A.

J. Pfeiffer, 1968. *New look at education*. Poughkeepsie: Odyssey, MG.

A. W. Phillips, 1950. Mechanical models in economic dynamics. *Economica*, 17(67): 283–305, 5D.

A. W. Phillips, 1954. Stabilisation policy in a closed economy. *Economic Journal*, 64(254): 290–323, 8D.

A. W. Phillips, 1957. Stabilisation policy and the time-forms of lagged responses. *Economic Journal*, 67(266): 265–277, 5D.

G. W. Pick: see H. J. Wootton.

A. M. Pierce, 1959. *A concise bibliography of the literature on artificial intelligence*. Working paper, U.S. Air Force Cambridge Research Center, PB-145105, MA.

W. P. Pierskalla, 1969. Analysis of a multistage inventory task: comments on a paper by Amnon Rapoport. *Behavioral Science*, 14(5): 378–389, 3C.

M. Pilisuk: see R. E. Overstreet.

Z. A. Piotrowski, 1965. Computer imitation of man. *American Journal of Clinical Hypnosis*, 8(1): 3–7, MA.

J. Pitrat, 1965. Machine simulation of intelligence. *International Journal of Computer Mathematics*, 1(2): 147–177, MA.

F. R. Pitts, 1962. Chorology revisited—computerwise. *Professional Geographer*, 14(6): 8–12, MD.

F. R. Pitts, 1963. Problems in computer simulation of diffusion. *The Regional Science Association, Papers and Proceedings, 11:* 111–119, MD.

F. R. Pitts, 1966. Scale and purpose in urban simulation models. *Research and education for regional and area development* (W. R. Maki and B. J. L. Berry, eds.); Ames: Iowa State University Press, 255–262, MD.

W. Pitts: see H. E. Tompkins.

Pittsburgh Area Transportation Study, 1963. *Final report, Volume 2: forecasts and plans.* Pittsburgh: Pittsburgh Area Transportation Study, 2C.

Pittsburgh Department of City Planning, 1962. *Data processing and simulation techniques.* Pittsburgh: Department of City Planning, MG.

T. Ploughman, W. Darnton, and W. Heuser, 1968. An assignment program to establish school attendance boundaries and forecast construction needs. *Socio-Economic Planning Sciences, 1*(3): 243–258, 6C.

S. V. Pollack: see T. D. Sterling.

C. H. Pollmar: see H. H. Goode.

G. Pompilj, 1968. Models for traffic in Rome. *Mathematical model building in economics and industry* (C.E.I.R.); New York: Hafner, 81–105, 5C.

I. D. Pool: A. R. Kessler.

I. D. Pool, 1962. *Simulmatics Media-Mix I: general description.* New York: The Simulmatics Corporation., 5C.

I. D. Pool, 1964. Simulating social systems. *International Science and Technology, 27:* 62–70, MG.

I. D. Pool, 1967. Computer simulations of total societies. *The study of total societies* (S. Z. Klausner, ed.); New York: Praeger, 45–65, MC.

I. D. Pool and R. P. Abelson, 1961. The Simulmatics project. *Public Opinion Quarterly, 25*(2): 167–183, 1C.

I. D. Pool and A. Bernstein, 1963. The simulation of human behavior—a primer and some possible applications. *American Behavioral Scientist, 6*(9): 83–85, MC.

I. D. Pool and A. R. Kessler, 1965. The Kaiser, the Tsar, and the computer: information processing in a crisis. *American Behavioral Scientist, 8*(9): 31–38, 7B.

I. D. Pool, R. P. Abelson, and S. L. Popkin, 1964. *Candidates, issues, and strategies.* Cambridge: MIT Press, revised edition in 1965, 1C.

I. D. Pool, R. P. Abelson, and S. L. Popkin, 1965. A postscript on the 1964 Election. *American Behavioral Scientist, 8*(9): 39–44, 1C.

I. D. Pool, J. F. Kramer, and H. L. Selesnick, 1966. Who is listening: evaluating audiences. *American Statistical Association, 1965 Proceedings of the Business and Economic Statistics Section:* 43–49, 5C.

D. M. Poore, 1969. Budgeting for changes in physical facilities and equipment. *Management action* (C. E. Weber and G. Peters, eds.); Scranton: International Textbook, 165–178, 1C.

J. Popkin: see L. R. Klein and see M. Liebenberg.

S. L. Popkin: see I. D. Pool.

S. L. Popkin, 1965. A model of a communication system. *American Behavioral Scientist, 8*(9): 8–11, 5C.

K. R. Popper, 1962. The machine argument. *Conjectures and refutations;* New York: Basic Books, 296–297, MA.

C. Porten: see S. W. Cragin, Jr.

A. Porter, 1960. The mechanical representation of processes of thought. *Memory, learning, and language* (W. Feindel, ed.); Toronto: University of Toronto Press, 35–54, MA.

R. C. Porter, 1965. A growth model forecast of faculty size and salaries in United States higher education. *Review of Economics and Statistics, 47*(2): 191–197, 2D.

R. G. Potter, Jr., and J. M. Sakoda, 1966. A computer model of family building based on expected values. *Demography, 3*(2): 450–461, 5C.

R. G. Potter, Jr., and J. M. Sakoda, 1967. Family planning and fecundity. *Population Studies, 20*(3): 311–328, 5C.

W. F. Pounds: see G. P. E. Clarkson.

M. F. J. Prachowny: see H. Tsurumi.

A. R. Pred, 1967. Postscript. *Innovation diffusion as a spatial process* (T. Hägerstrand); Chicago: University of Chicago Press, 299–324, MD.

R. L. Preger and K. C. Wehr, 1964. An electronic network which emulates conditioned reflex. *Fifth national symposium on human factors in electronics, Proceedings;* New York: Institute of Electrical and Electronic Engineers, 52–62, 5A.

L. E. Preston and N. R. Collins, 1966. *Studies in a simulated market.* Berkeley: University of California, 5D.

R. L. Pretty, 1966. The effect of right-turning vehicles on saturation flow through signalized intersections. *Australian Road Research Board Proceedings, 3*(1): 400–468, 7D.

R. L. Pretty, 1966. *Simulation of traffic in one and two-dimensional road layouts.* Doctoral dissertation, University of New South Wales, 5D.

R. L. Pretty and W. R. Blunden, 1964. On the computer simulation of a single channel queueing facility for a wide range of arrival and departure distributions. *Australian Road Research Board Proceedings, 2*(1): 248–259, MS.

A. E. Preyss, 1967. *A theory and model of human learning behavior in a manual control task.* Doctoral dissertation, Massachusettes Institute of Technology, 3C.

A. E. Preyss and J. L. Meiry, 1968. Stochastic modeling of human learning behavior. *IEEE Transactions on Man-Machine Systems, MMS-9*(2): 36–46, 3C.

K. H. Pribram: see G. A. Miller.

D. J. D. Price, 1965. Gods in black boxes. *Computers for the humanities?* (G. W. Pierson, ed.); New Haven: Yale University, 3–5, MG.

D. O. Price, 1959. A mathematical model of migration suitable for simulation on an electronic computer. *International Population Conference:* Wien: Im Selbstverlag, 665–673, 8C.

A. A. B. Pritsker: see R. A. Enlow.

A. A. B. Pritsker and P. J. Kiviat, 1969. Models and simulation. *Simulation with GASP II;* Englewood Cliffs, N.J.: Prentice-Hall, 1–7, MG.

A. A. B. Pritsker, R. C. Van Buskirk, and J. K. Wetherbee, 1959. Simulation to obtain a systems measure of an air duel environment. *IEEE Transactions on Computers, C-8*(1): 55–59, 7B.

P. M. Pruzan: see S. W. Cragin, Jr.

A. L. Pugh, III: see H. R. Hamilton, see L. F. McPherson, and see W. L. Swager.

E. L. Pugh, 1964. *Some examples of stochastic distortion, a Monte Carlo technique.* Working paper, System Development Corporation, SP-1584, MS.

E. L. Pugh, 1965. *A gradient technique of adaptive Monte Carlo.* Working paper, System Development Corporation, SP-1921/000/01, MS.

S. H. Putman: see H. W. Bruck.

S. H. Putman, 1963. *Industrial location model.* Working paper, Pittsburgh Department of City Planning, CRP Technical Bulletin 5, 5D.

S. H. Putman, 1966. Intraurban industrial location model design and implementation. *The Regional Science Association, Papers and Proceedings, 19:* 199–214, 6C.

S. H. Putman, 1967, Modeling and evaluating the indirect impacts of alternative Northeast Corridor transportation systems. *Highway Research Record, 180:* 81–93, 8D.

G. Pyatt, 1963. Industrial requirements for manpower in 1970. *British Association for Commercial and Industrial Education, Papers presented at the BACIE spring conference (Economic growth and manpower):* 27–37, 5D.

C. E. Pyers: see R. J. Bouchard and see K. E. Heanue.

C. E. Pyers, 1966. Evaluation of intervening opportunities trip distribution model. *Highway Research Record, 114:* 71–98, 3C.

H. Quastler, 1957. The complexity of biological computers. *IEEE Transactions on Computers, C-6*(3): 192–194, MA.

M. R. Quillian: see D. G. Bobrow.

M. R. Quillian, 1967. Word concepts: a theory and simulation of some basic semantic capabilities. *Behavioral Science, 12*(5): 410–430, 7A.

R. Quillian, 1962. A revised design for an understanding machine. *MT, Mechanical Translation and Computational Linguistics, 7*(1): 17–29, 8A.

K. Rainio, 1961. A stochastic model of social interaction. *Transactions of the Westermarck Society, 7:* 1–152, 5B.

K. Rainio, 1961. Stochastic process of social contacts. *Scandinavian Journal of Psychology, 2*(3): 113–128, 3B.

K. Rainio, 1962. A stochastic theory of social contacts: a laboratory study and an application to sociometry. *Transactions of the Westermarck Soicety, 8:* 1–103, 3B.

K. Rainio, 1965. Social interaction as a stochastic learning process. *European Journal of Sociology, 6*(1): 68–88, 3B.

K. Rainio, 1966. A study on sociometric group structure: an application of a stochastic theory of social interaction. *Sociological theories in progress* (J. Berger, M. Zelditch, Jr., and B. Anderson, eds.); New York: Houghton Mifflin, 102–123, 3B.

D. M. Ramsey: see J. A. Daly.

T. Rands: see D. Clark.

A. G. Rao: see J. R. Emshoff.

B. Raphael, 1964. A computer program which "understands". *Joint Computer Conference, Fall Proceedings, 26:* 577–589, 7A.

B. Raphael, 1964. *SIR: a computer program for semantic information retrieval.* Doctoral dissertation, Massachusetts Institute of Technology, 7A.

D. L. Raphael: see H. B. Gamble.

D. L. Raphael, 1967. Applications of complex behavioral models to regional and organizational analysis. *Journal of Industrial Engineering, 18*(1): 123–130, 2C.

D. L. Raphael, 1967. Applications of input-output methodology to microregions. *American Statistical Association, 1966 Proceedings of the Business and Economic Statistics Section:* 188–196, 2C.

Am. Rapoport, 1964. Sequential decision-making in a computer-controlled task. *Journal of Mathematical Psychology, 1*(2): 351–374, 3C.

Am. Rapoport, 1966. A study of a multistage decision making task with an unknown duration. *Human Factors, 8*(1): 54–61, 3C.

Am. Rapoport, 1966. A study of human control in a stochastic multistage decision task. *Behavioral Science, 11*(1): 18–32, 3C.

Am. Rapoport, 1967. Dynamic programming models for multistage decision-making tasks. *Journal of Mathematical Psychology*, *4*(1): 48–71, 3C.

Am. Rapoport, 1967. Variables affecting decisions in a multistage inventory task. *Behavioral Science*, *12*(3): 194–204, 3C.

Am. Rapoport, 1968. Choice behavior in a Markovian decision task. *Journal of Mathematical Psychology*, *5*(1): 163–181, 3C.

Am. Rapoport and A. Mowshowitz, 1966. Experimental studies of stochastic models for the Prisoner's Dilemma. *Behavioral Science*, *11*(6): 444–458, 3C.

An. Rapoport, 1954. Technological models of the nervous system. *Etc., A Review of General Semantics*, *11*(4): 272–283, MA.

An. Rapoport, 1962. An essay on mind. *Theories of the mind* (J. M. Scher, ed.); New York: Free Press, 271–304, MA.

An. Rapoport, 1964. *Strategy and conscience.* New York: Harper and Row, MD.

An. Rapoport and A. M. Chammah, 1965. *Prisoner's Dilemma.* Ann Arbor: University of Michigan Press, 3C.

An. Rapoport and P. Dale, 1966. Models for Prisoner's Dilemma. *Journal of Mathematical Psychology*, *3*(2): 269–286, 3D.

R. H. Rasche and H. T. Shapiro, 1968. The F.R.B.-M.I.T. econometric model. *American Economic Review, Papers and Proceedings*, *58*(2): 123–149, 1D.

N. Rashevsky, 1931. Learning as a property of physical systems. *Journal of General Psychology*, *5*(2): 207–229, MA.

N. Rashevsky, 1931. Possible brain mechanisms and their physical models. *Journal of General Psychology*, *5*(3): 368–406, MA.

N. Rashevsky, 1955. Is the concept of an organism as a machine a useful one? *The Scientific Monthly*, *80*(1): 32–35, MA.

P. N. Rastogi, 1969. Protracted military conflict and politico-economic stability. *SCi Simulation*, *12*(1): 23–36, 7D.

G. J. Rath: see K. W. Heathington.

E. A. Rawes, 1966. Media models and budget decisions. *Computers in advertising* (N. Rogers, ed.); London: The Institute of Practitioners in Advertising, 63–66, MC.

G. L. Reed: see J. W. Horn.

R. Reed, Jr., 1966. Simulation by Monte Carlo. *Tappi*, *49*(1): 28–32, MG.

P. A. Reese, 1968. *Steady state parameter estimation in computer simulated systems.* Working paper, Arizona State University, MS.

D. P. Reilly, 1967. *An analytical study of a Monte Carlo simulation program to solve the general queue length problem for several service stations.* Working paper, General Electric Re-Entry Systems Department, TIS-67SD204, MS.

K. D. Reilly, 1968. Digital computer simulation studies—studies of information networks. *Digest of the second conference on applications of simulation* (A. Ockene, ed.); New York: Institute of Electrical and Electronic Engineers, Publication No. 68C60SIM, 311–313, 7C.

W. Reinfield: see J. D. Carroll.

A. Reisman: see M. I. Taft.

J. Reitman, 1967. Simulation of a manufacturing system. *SCi Simulation*, *8*(6): 311–317, 7C.

W. R. Reitman, 1959. Heuristic programs, computer simulation, and higher mental processes. *Behavioral Science*, *4*(4): 330–335, MA.

W. R. Reitman, 1961. Information processing languages and heuristic programs: a new stage in the bead game. *First Bionics Symposium (Living prototypes—the key to new technology*, J. C. Robinette, ed.); Wright-Patterson AFB: Wright Air Development Division, TR 60-600, 409–417, MA.

A. Reisman and E. S. Buffa, 1964. A general model for production and operations systems. *Management Science*, *11*(1): 64–79, 8D.

R. F. Reiss, 1962. An abstract machine based on classical association psychology. *Joint Computer Conference, Spring Proceedings*, *21*: 53–70, 8A.

J. Reitman: see J. P. Carstens.

W. R. Reitman, 1961. Programming intelligent problem solvers. *IEEE Transactions on Man-Machine Systems*, *MMS-2*(1): 26–33, MA.

W. R. Reitman, 1963. Computer models of psychological processes and some implications for the theory and practice of education. *Needed research in the teaching of English* (E. R. Steinberg, ed.); Washington; U.S. Government Printing Office, 98–106, MA.

W. R. Reitman, 1963. Personality as a problem-solving coalition. *Computer simulation of personality* (S. S. Tomkins and S. Messick, eds.); New York: Wiley, 69–99, MA.

W. R. Reitman, 1964. Heuristic decision procedures, open constraints, and the structure of ill-defined problems. *Human judgments and optimality* (M. W. Shelly, II, and G. L. Bryan, eds.); New York: Wiley, 282–315, MA.

W. R. Reitman, 1965. *Cognition and thought.* New York: Wiley, 2A.

W. R. Reitman, R. B. Grove, and R. G. Shoup, 1964. Argus: an information-processing model of thinking. *Behavioral Science*, *9*(3): 270–281, 5A.

N. Rescher: see O. Helmer.

D. R. Rexworthy and D. W. W. King, 1960. Freeing city traffic. *New Scientist*, *7*(167): 197–199, 8C.

S. Y. Rhee, 1965. An urban traffic control simulator. *Second international symposium on the theory of road traffic flow, London 1963, Proceedings* (J. Almond, ed.); Paris: Organisation for Economic Co-operation and Development. 260–263, 7C.

R. I. Ribler, 1964. *System simulation: a conceptual approach.* Working paper, System Development Corporation, SP-1673, MG.

M. G. Richards and G. Williams, 1967. City of Worcester study techniques—2. Time function iteration. *Traffic Engineering & Control, 9*(3): 148–150 and 152, 3C.

M. G. Richards and G. Williams, 1967. City of Worcester study techniques—3. Gravity model and time function iteration. *Traffic Engineering & Control, 9*(4): 187–189, 3C.

D. Richardson: see T. Corlett.

R. Richardson: see A. P. Hare.

R. H. Richens, 1959. Tigris and Euphrates—a comparison between human and machine translation. *Mechanisation of thought processes* (D. V. Blake and A. M. Uttley, eds.); London: H.M. Stationery, Office, Volume 1, 281–302, MA.

E. Richman and S. Ehrenfeld, 1959. Industrial engineering techniques and operations research. *Journal of Industrial Engineering, 10*(6): 439–445, MG.

R. D. Richtmyer, 1958. *A non-random sampling method, based on congruences, for "Monte Carlo" problems.* Working paper, New York University Atomic Energy Commission Computing and Applied Mathematics Center, Report NYO-8674, MS.

J. C. Ridley: see M. C. Sheps.

J. C. Ridley, 1965. Recent natality trends in underdeveloped countries. *Public health and population change* (M. C. Sheps and J. C. Ridley, eds.); Pittsburgh: University of Pittsburgh Press, 143–171, 5C.

J. C. Ridley and M. C. Sheps, 1966. An analytic simulation model of human reproduction with demographic and biological components. *Population Studies, 19*(3): 297–310, 4C.

L. Rigsby: see J. S. Coleman.

N. W. Rives, Jr.: see J. M. Vernon.

B. H. P. Rivett, 1956. Operational research in the British coal industry. *Operations research for management, Volume II* (J. F. McCloskey and J. M. Coppinger, eds.); Baltimore: Johns Hopkins Press, 195–210, 5D.

B. H. P. Rivett, 1967. Why simulate? *Digital simulation in operational research* (S. H. Hollingdale, ed.); London: English Universities Press, 3–8, MG.

B. H. P. Rivett, 1968. *Simulation. Concepts of operational research;* London: Watts, 140–157, MG.

A. M. Rivlin: see G. H. Orcutt.

Road Research Laboratory, 1965. *Research on road traffic.* London: H.M. Stationery Office, MG.

R. Roark, 1960. A model of language extinction and formation. *Kroeber Anthropological Society Papers, 23*: 86–104, 6D.

E. B. Roberts: see H. R. Hamilton and see L. F. McPherson.

E. B. Roberts, 1959. Simulation techniques for understanding R and D management. *IEEE International Convention Record, 7*(10): 38–43, MD.

E. B. Roberts, 1962. Toward a new theory for research and development. *Industrial Management Review, 4*(1): 29–40, MD.

E. B. Roberts, 1963. Industrial dynamics and the design of management control systems. *Management Technology, 3*(2): 100–118. Reprinted in 1964 in *Management controls* (C. P. Bonini, R. K. Jaedicke, and H. M. Wagner, eds.); New York: McGraw-Hill, 102–126, 7D.

E. B. Roberts, 1964. *The dynamics of research and development.* New York: Harper and Row, 5D.

E. B. Roberts, 1964. New directions in industrial dynamics. *Industrial Management Review, 6*(1): 5–14, MD.

E. B. Roberts, 1964. Research and development policy-making. *Technology Review, 66*(8): 32–36, 7D.

E. B. Roberts, D. I. Abrams, and H. B. Weil, 1968. A systems study of policy formulation in a vertically-integrated firm. *Management Science, 14*(12): B-674–694, 5D.

E. M. Roberts: see H. R. Hamilton.

S. H. Robinovitz: see S. L. Coombs.

H. W. Robinson, 1962. The shape of advertising to come—1972. *The computer in advertising* (Central Media Bureau, eds.); New York: Association of National Advertisers, G1–G12, MC.

I. E. Robinson and D. F. Foster, 1968. The simulation of human systems. *Digest of the second conference on applications of simulation* (A. Ockene, ed.); New York: Institute of Electrical and Electronic Engineers, Publication No. 68C60SIM, 166–169, MA.

I. M. Robinson, 1964. A simulation model of the residential space market in San Francisco: a new tool for urban renewal planning and programming. *Second Annual Conference on Urban Planning Information Systems and Programs, Proceedings* (*Urban information and policy decisions,* C. D. Rogers, ed.), 97–117, 8C.

I. M. Robinson, H. B. Wolfe, and R. L. Barringer, 1965. A simulation model for renewal programming. *Journal of the American Institute of Planners, 31*(2): 126–134, 8C.

P. J. Robinson: see Y. Wind.

P. J. Robinson, 1958. Cases in simulation—a research aid as a management "demonstration piece". *Report of system simulation symposium* (D. G. Malcolm, ed.); New York: American Institute of Industrial Engineers, 47–58, MG.

P. J. Robinson, 1958. System simulation helps solve complex operations. *SAE Journal, 66*(2): 88–89, MG.

T. B. Roby, 1967. Computer simulation models for organization theory. *Methods of organizational research* (V. H. Vroom, ed.); Pittsburgh: University of Pittsburgh Press, 171–211, MD.

T. B. Roby and C. R. Budrose, 1965. Pattern recognition in groups: laboratory and simulation studies. *Journal of Personality and Social Psychology*, 2(5): 648–653, 3B.

T. J. Roby and R. S. Nickerson, 1964. Steps toward computer simulation of small group behavior. *DECUS Proceedings* (Digital Equipment Computer Users Society), *1963*: 139–181, 7B.

N. Rochester: see H. L. Gelernter and see H. E. Tompkins.

N. Rochester, J. H. Holland, L. H. Haibt, and W. L. Duda, 1956. Tests on a cell assembly theory of the action of the brain, using a large digital computer. *IEEE Transactions on Information Theory*, IT-2(3): S-80–93, 5A.

J. K. Rocks, 1967. Measuring American education. *The computer in American education* (D. D. Bushnell and D. W. Allen, eds.); New York: Wiley, 174–184, MD.

T. H. Rockwell, R. L. Ernest, and A. Hanken, 1968. A sensitivity analysis of empirically derived car-following models. *Transportation Research*, 2(4): 363–373, 2A.

R. Roda: see D. J. Duffy.

R. P. Roesser: see R. W. Snelsire.

A. Rogers, 1964. A stochastic analysis of the spatial dispersal of retail establishments. *A stochastic analysis of intraurban retail spatial structure;* doctoral dissertation, University of North Carolina at Chapel Hill, 192–225 and 270–273, 6C.

A. Rogers, 1966. Experiments with a matrix model of population growth and distribution. *Proceedings of the fourth international conference on operational research* (D. B. Hertz and J. Melese, eds.); New York: Wiley-Interscience, 490–496, 2C.

E. M. Rogers: see G. J. Hanneman and see J. D. Stanfield.

E. M. Rogers, 1969. Computer simulation of innovation diffusion in a peasant village. *Modernization among peasants*; New York: Holt, Rinehart and Winston, 343–359. This is the published version of *Computer simulation of innovation diffusion: an illustration from a Latin American village*, a 1965 working paper by J. D. Stanfield, J. A. Clark, N. Lin, and E. M. Rogers, 1D.

J. L. Rogers and A. S. Householder, 1953. "Can machines think?"—discussion. *Computers and Automation*, 2(9): 14–15, MA.

A. C. Rohloff: see A. A. Kuehn.

B. K. Rome: see S. C. Rome.

B. K. Rome and S. C. Rome, 1961. Leviathan—a simulation of behavioral systems to operate dynamically on a digital computer. *Information retrieval and machine translation* (A. Kent, ed.); New York: Interscience, Volume 2, 1181–1203, 8D.

B. K. Rome and S. C. Rome, 1964. Programming the bureaucratic computer. *IEEE Spectrum*, 1(12): 72–78 and 83–92, 7D.

B. K. Rome and S. C. Rome, 1966. Automated learning process (ALP). *Studies on behavior in organizations* (R. V. Bowers, ed.); Athens: University of Georgia Press, 312–347, 8C.

S. C. Rome: see B. K. Rome.

S. C. Rome and B. K. Rome, 1960. Formal representation of intentionally structured systems. *Information retrieval and machine translation* (A. Kent, ed.); New York: Interscience, Volume 1, 467–492, 8D.

S. C. Rome and B. K. Rome, 1961. The Leviathan technique for large-group analysis. *Behavioral Science*, 6(2): 148–152, 8D.

S. C. Rome and B. K. Rome, 1962. Computer simulation toward a theory of large organizations. *Computer applications in the behavioral sciences* (H. Borko, ed.); Englewood Cliffs, N.J.: Prentice-Hall, 522–555, 8D.

L. L. Roos, Jr. 1966. *Models of attitudes in a developing country—the Turkish case*. Doctoral dissertation, Massachusetts Institute of Technology, 3C.

L. L. Roos, Jr. 1969. *Urbanization and modernization—some computer-based experiments*. Working paper, Northwestern University, 3C.

A. O. Rorty, 1962. Slaves and machines. *Analysis*, 22(5): 118–120, MA.

M. O. Rosen: see C. C. Abt.

L. Rosenberg, 1967. Bernstein polynomials and Monte Carlo integration. *SIAM Journal on Numerical Analysis*, 4(4): 566–574, MS.

M. J. Rosenberg, 1963. Simulated man and the humanistic criticism. *Computer simulation of personality* (S. S. Tomkins and S. Messick, eds.); New York: Wiley, 113–124, MA.

F. Rosenblatt, 1958. The perceptron: a probabilistic model for information storage and organization in the brain. *Psychological Review*, 65(6): 386–408, 8A.

F. Rosenblatt, 1959. Two theorems of statistical separability in the perceptron. *Mechanisation of thought processes* (D. V. Blake and A. M. Uttley, eds.); London: H.M. Stationery Office, Volume 1, 421–456, MA.

F. Rosenblatt, 1960. Perceptron simulation experiments. *Proceedings of the IEEE*, 48(3): 301–309, 5A.

F. Rosenblatt, 1961. *Principles of neurodynamics*. Buffalo: Cornell Aeronautical Laboratory, 4A.

F. Rosenblatt, 1964. A model for experiential storage in neural networks. *Computer and information sciences* (J. T. Tou and R. H. Wilcox, eds.); Washington: Spartan, 16–66, 4A.

A. Rosenbloom: see D. L. Trautman.

L. Rosenburg: see B. Harris.

J. V. Rosenhead, 1968. Experimental simulation of a social system. *OR, Operational Research Quarterly*, 19(3): 289–298, 7C.

H. Rosenthal, 1965. Election simulation. *European Journal of Sociology*, 6(1): 21–42, MC.

H. Rosenthal, 1968. Voting and coalition models in election simulations. *Simulation in the study of politics* (W. D. Coplin, ed.); Chicago: Markham, 237–285, MD.

I. Rosenthal, 1954. The capacity of computers not to think. *Computers and Automation*, *3*(8): 28–29, MA.

D. W. Ross: see A. J. Lipinski.

J. Ross, 1961. *Human memory*. Doctoral dissertation, Princeton University, 8C.

T. Ross, 1933. Machines that think. *Scientific American*, *148*(4): 206–208, 6A.

T. Ross, 1938. The synthesis of intelligence—its implications. *Psychological Review*, *45*(2): 185–189, 6A.

R. W. Rothfusz: see D. P. Hattaway.

M. A. Rothman, A. M. Hilton, S. C. McLaughlin, E. T. Jaynes, and U. Neisser, 1963. Missing links in computer intelligence. *Science*, *140*(3563): 212–218, MA.

J. Rothstein: see H. E. Tompkins.

A. J. Rowe: see D. G. Malcolm.

A. J. Rowe, 1960. A research approach in management controls. *Management control systems* (D. G. Malcolm and A. J. Rowe, eds.); New York: Wiley, 273–291, 8D.

A. J. Rowe, 1961. Research problems in management controls. *Management Technology*, *1*(3): 6–15, MG.

A. J. Rowe, 1963. Simulation—a decision-aiding tool. *AIIE International Conference Proceedings*, 135–144, MG.

A. J. Rowe, 1965. Computer simulation—a solution technique for management problems. *Joint Computer Conference, Fall Proceedings*, *27*(1): 259–267, MG.

A. J. Rowe and J. R. Jackson, 1956. Research problems in production routing and scheduling. *Journal of Industrial Engineering*, *7*(3): 116–121, MG.

D. A. Rowe: see J. R. N. Stone.

W. D. Rowe, 1968. A model of bureaucratic growth using GPSS. *Digest of the second conference on applications of simulation* (A. Ockene, ed.); New York: Institute of Electrical and Electronic Engineers, Publication No. 68C60SIM, 173–175, 7D.

M. Rubinoff: see H. E. Tompkins.

E. R. Ruiter and P. W. Shuldiner, 1965. Operating costs at intersections obtained from the simulation of traffic flow. *Highway Research Record*, *89*: 26–36, 7C.

J. H. Russell, 1968. Progress function models and their deviations. *Journal of Industrial Engineering*, *19*(1): 5–10, 5C.

S. B. Russell, 1913. A practical device to simulate the working of nervous discharges. *Journal of Animal Behavior*, *3*(1): 15–35, 8A.

D. J. Rylander: see S. W. Cragin, Jr.

B. L. Ryle, 1961. Self-programming techniques in general purpose digital computers. *First Bionics Symposium* (*Living prototypes—the key to new technology*, J. C. Robinette, ed.); Wright-Patterson AFB: Wright Air Development Division, TR 60-600, 451–465, MA.

H. Sacks: see G. Werner.

W. Sadowski, 1965. The Monte Carlo method. *The theory of decision-making*; Oxford: Pergamon, 194–199, MC.

A. D. St. John, 1967. *Study of traffic phenomena through digital simulation.* Kansas City, Mo.: Midwest Research Institute, 2D.

J. M. Sakoda: see R. G. Potter, Jr.

S. I. Saleeb, 1967. *Logical design and associated computer studies for the hardware simulation of traffic dispersion.* Doctoral dissertation, University of Manchester, 7C.

S. I. Saleeb and M. G. Hartley, 1968. Simulation of traffic behaviour through a linked-pair of inter-sections. *Transportation Research*, *2*(1): 51–61, 7C.

D. M. Salmon: see A. J. Lipinski.

S. Saltzman, 1963. *On statistical models of the firm with an application.* Doctoral dissertation, Cornell University, 1B.

S. Saltzman, 1965. Survey of principle types of simulation models of the firm. *Association for Computing Machinery, Proceedings*, *20*: 469–475, MB.

P. J. Sandiford: see J. P. Jeanniot.

W. E. Sasser: see T. H. Naylor and see W. H. Wallace.

W. E. Sasser and T. H. Naylor, 1967. Computer simulation of economic systems . . . an example model. *SCi Simulation*, *8*(1): 21–32, MG.

K. Sato: see S. Ichimura.

B. W. Saunders, 1962. Design of manufacturing systems. *Production Engineer*, *41*(3): 130–139, MG.

R. M. Saunders: see O. J. M. Smith.

E. S. Savas, 1967. Computers in urban air pollution control systems. *Socio-Economic Planning Sciences*, *1*(2): 157–183, 8D.

E. S. Savas, 1969. Simulation and cost-effectiveness analysis of New York's emergency ambulance service. *Management Science*, *15*(12): B-608–627, 7C.

G. V. Savinov, 1962. Electric modelling of homeostatic systems. *Problems of cybernetics IV* (A. A. Lyapunov, R. Goodman, and A. D. Booth, eds.); London: Pergamon, 1173–1181, 7A.

J. D. Savvas: see W. F. Massy.

J. D. Savvas, 1963. The computer model method: a new tool for CPAs. *Journal of Accountancy*, *115*(6): 77–80, MG.

J. A. Sawyer: see N. K. Choudry.

K. M. Sayre: see F. J. Crosson.

K. M. Sayre, 1962. Human and mechanical recognition. *Methodos*, *14*(54): 27–40, MA.

K. M. Sayre, 1965. *Recognition*. Notre Dame, Indiana: University of Notre Dame Press, MA.

K. M. Sayre, 1967. Choice, decision, and the origin of information. *Philosophy and cybernetics* (F. J. Crosson and K. M. Sayre, eds.); Notre Dame, Indiana: University of Notre Dame Press, 71–97, MA.

K. M. Sayre, 1967. Philosophy and cybernetics. *Philosophy and cybernetics* (F. J. Crosson and K. M. Sayre, eds.); Notre Dame, Indiana: University of Notre Dame Press, 3–33, MA.

M. B. Schaffer, 1968. Lanchester models of guerrilla engagements. *Operations Research*, *16*(3): 457–488, 7B.

W. C. Schall, 1962. Industrial dynamics. *Instrumentation Technology*, *9*(9): 69–76, MD.

S. A. Scharff: see G. G. Hawley.

H. Scheilblechner: see A. P. Hare.

D. E. Schendel, J. O. Summers, and D. L. Weiss, 1968. Simulation and model testing. *Marketing and the new science of planning* (R. L. King, ed.); Chicago: American Marketing Association, 416–430, 2C.

G. R. Schink, 1968. *Estimation of forecast error in a dynamic and/or non-linear econometric model.* Working paper, University of Maryland, MS.

K. J. Schlager: see I. S. Lowry.

K. J. Schlager, 1964. How managers use industrial dynamics. *Industrial Management Review*, *6*(1): 21–29, 5D.

K. J. Schlager, 1964. *Productivity research through industrial systems simulation*. Madison: University of Wisconsin Center for Productivity Motivation, 5D.

K. J. Schlager, 1964. Simulation models in urban and regional planning. *Second Annual Conference on Urban Planning Information Systems and Programs, Proceedings (Urban information and policy decisions*, C. D. Rogers, ed.), 119–166, 5D.

K. J. Schlager, 1966. A recursive programming theory of the residential land development process. *Highway Research Record*, *126:* 24–32, 5D.

R. Schliewen: see M. N. Zald.

O. H. Schmitt: see H. E. Tompkins.

E. Schneider: see P. C. Mahalanobis.

J. C. Schoenman and B. Persson, 1966. *An analog of short-period economic change*. Stockholm: Almqvist and Wiksell, 2D.

R. E. Schofer and B. M. Levin, 1967. The urban transportation planning process. *Socio-Economic Planning Sciences*, *1*(2): 185–197, MD.

J. F. Schouten: see B. van der Pol.

W. E. Schrank and C. C. Holt, 1967. Critique of: "Verification of computer simulation models." *Management Science*, *14*(2): B-104–106, MS.

J. F. Schuh, 1965. *Principles of automation*. Eindhoven: Philips Technical Library, MA.

R. D. Schultz: see H. R. Hamilton.

G. Schussel, 1966. *Forecasting in the photographic industry*. Doctoral dissertation, Harvard University, 1C.

G. Schussel, 1967. Sales forecasting with the aid of a human behavior simulator. *Management Science*, *13*(10): B-593–611, 1C.

R. M. Schwarcz, 1967. Steps toward a model of linguistic performance: a preliminary sketch. *MT, Mechanical Translation and Computational Linguistics*, *10*(3): 39–52, 8A.

A. Schwartz: see D. D. Lamb.

H. Schwarz, 1963. Methods for determining trip distribution. *Traffic Engineering & Control*, *4*(11): 612–615, MC.

E. Scott: see M. Davidson.

E. Scott, 1959. *Simulation of social processes: a preliminary report of a survey of current research in the behavioral sciences*. Working paper, System Development Corporation, TM-435, MG.

R. L. Scott, 1959. *Monte Carlo method: a literature search*. Working paper, Atomic Energy Commission, Technical Information Service Extension, TID-3541, MC.

M. Scriven, 1953. The mechanical concept of mind. *Mind*, *62*(246): 230–240, MA.

M. J. Scriven: see M. Kochen.

T. A. Sebeok, 1963. The informational model of language: analog and digital coding in animal and human communication. *Natural language and the computer* (P. L. Garvin, ed.): New York: McGraw-Hill, 47–64, MA.

R. Seibel, 1961. Computer solutions to some noncomputational psychological problems. *Educational and Psychological Measurement*, *21*(1): 185–201, MA.

B. Seid: see L. Brotman.

W. D. Seider: see D. L. Katz.

D. R. Seidman, 1964. *Report on the activities allocation model*. Working paper, Penn Jersey Transportation Study, Paper 22, 8C.

D. R. Seidman, 1966. A decision-oriented model of urban growth. *Proceedings of the fourth international conference on operational research* (D. B. Hertz and J. Melese, eds.); New York: Wiley-Interscience, 480–489, 2C.

D. R. Seidman, 1966. The present and futures of urban land use models. *Fourth Annual Conference on Urban Planning Information Systems and Programs, Proceedings*, 119–128, 4D.

H. L. Selesnick: see I. D. Pool.

O. G. Selfridge: see M. L. Minsky.

O. G. Selfridge, 1956. Pattern recognition and learning. *Information theory* (C. Cherry, ed.); London: Butterworths, 345–353, MA.

J. W. Senders: see J. R. Carbonell.

S. D. Sessions, 1965. Sales/stock ratios: key to markdown timing. *New research in marketing* (L. E. Preston, ed.); Berkeley: University of California Institute of Business and Economic Research, 57–69, 5A.

P. Sevaldson: see R. M. Solow.

J. C. Shah: see W. P. Smith.

B. H. Shane: see H. J. Brightman.

C. Shanks, 1967. *Modelling and simulation of a psychiatric outpatient clinic.* Working paper, University of Saskatchewan, 2C.

C. E. Shannon with L. J. Savage, W. Pitts, R. W. Gerard, M. Mead, L. K. Frank, H. L. Teuber, J. H. Bigelow, H. Von Foerster, H. W. Brosin, and W. S. McCulloch, 1952. Presentation of a maze-solving machine. *Eighth Conference on cybernetics, Transactions (Cybernetics, H. Von Foerster, ed.); New York: Josiah Macy, Jr. Foundation, 173–180, 6A.

C. E. Shannon, 1953. Computers and automata. *Proceedings of the IEEE, 41*(10): 1234–1241, MA.

C. E. Shannon, 1955. Game playing machines. *Journal of the Franklin Institute, 260*(6): 447–453, 7A.

H. T. Shapiro: see J. F. Helliwell and see R. H. Rasche.

M. J. Shapiro: see C. H. Cherryholmes.

M. J. Shapiro, 1966. *The House and the federal role: a computer simulation of roll-call voting.* Doctoral dissertation, Northwestern University, 1D.

L. S. Shapley: see I. Mann.

A. E. Shaw and R. A. Mash, 1962. Computer analysis of traffic census. *Local Government Finance, 66*(7): 155–156, 7C.

G. S. Shaw and J. W. Abrams, 1966. Demand forecasting for airline scheduling. *Proceedings of the fourth international conference on operational research* (D. B. Hertz and J. Melese, eds.); New York: Wiley-Interscience, 444–457, 1C.

J. C. Shaw: see A. Newell.

J. R. Shelton, 1960. Solution methods for waiting line problems. *Journal of Industrial Engineering, 11*(4): 293–303, MC.

R. N. Shepard, 1964. Book review of E. A. Feigenbaum and J. Feldman, eds., "Computers and thought." *Behavioral Science, 9*(1): 57–65, MA.

M. C. Sheps: see E. B. Perrin and see J. C. Ridley.

M. C. Sheps, 1965. Applications of probability models to the study of patterns of human reproduction. *Public health and population change* (M. C. Sheps and J. C. Ridley, eds.); Pittsburgh: University of Pittsburgh Press, 307–332, MC.

M. C. Sheps, J. C. Ridley, and J. W. Lingner, 1966. Effects of selected factors on natality: quantitative estimation through simulation. *Simulation in Business and Public Health, Proceedings, 1:* 176–187, 5C.

T. B. Sheridan, W. M. Johnson, A. C. Bell, and J. G. Kreifeldt, 1964. Control models of creatures which look ahead. *Fifth national symposium on human factors in electronics, Proceedings;* New York: Institute of Electrical and Electronic Engineers, 229–240, 6A.

J. N. Sheth, 1967. A review of buyer behavior. *Management Science, 13*(12): B-718–756, MG.

Y. Shinkai: see S. Ichimura.

D. A. Sholl and A. M. Uttley, 1953. Pattern discrimination and the visual cortex. *Nature, 171*(4348): 387–388, MA.

J. H. Shortreed: see B. G. Hutchinson.

R. G. Shoup: see W. R. Reitman.

Y. A. Shreider, 1964. Fundamentals of the Monte Carlo method. *Method of statistical testing* (Y. A. Shreider, ed.); Amsterdam: Elsevier, 1–38. Also published in 1966 under the title *The Monte Carlo method;* London; Pergamon, 1–90, MS.

M. Shubik, 1958. Simulation of the firm. *Journal of Industrial Engineering, 9*(5): 390–392, MG.

M. Shubik, 1959. Simulation and the theory of the firm. *Contributions to scientific research in management;* Los Angeles: University of California, 69–78, MD.

M. Shubik, 1960. Bibliography on simulation, gaming, artificial intelligence and allied topics. *Journal of the American Statistical Association, 55*(292): 736–751, MA.

M. Shubik, 1960. Simulation of the industry and the firm. *American Economic Review, 50*(5): 908–919, MD.

M. Shubik, 1963. Simulation and gaming: their value to the study of pricing and other market variables. *Models of markets* (A. R. Oxenfeldt, ed.); New York: Columbia University Press, 307–338, MD.

M. Shubik, 1967. Simulation of socio-economic systems. *General Systems, 12:* 149–175, 7D.

M. Shubik, 1967. Transfer of technology and simulation studies. *The transfer of technology to developing countries* (Airlie House Conference, D L. Spencer and A. Woroniak, eds.); New York: Praeger, 119–140, MD.

P. W. Shuldiner: see E. R. Ruiter.

R. P. Shumate and J. R. Dirksen, 1965. A simulation system for study of traffic flow behavior. *Highway Research Record, 72:* 19–33, 5D.

H. N. Shycon and R. B. Maffei, 1960. Simulation—tool for better distribution. *Harvard Business Review, 36*(6): 65–75, 5C.

A. I. Siegel and J. J. Wolf, 1961. A technique for evaluating man-machine system designs. *Human Factors*, *3*(1): 18–28, 1C.

A. I. Siegel and J. J. Wolf, 1962. A model for digital simulation of two-operator man-machine systems. *Ergonomics*, *5*(4): 557–572, 5B.

A. I. Siegel and J. J. Wolf, 1963. Computer simulation of man-machine systems. *Unusual environments and human behavior* (N. M. Burns, R. M. Chambers, and E. Hendler, eds.); New York: Free Press, 61–86, 6B.

J. B. Siegfried: see M. L. Braunstein.

P. L. Simmons and R. F. Simmons, 1961. The simulation of cognitive processes: an annotated bibliography. *IEEE Transactions on Computers*, *C-10*(3): 462–483, MA.

P. L. Simmons and R. F. Simmons, 1962. The simulation of cognitive processes, II: an annotated bibliography. *IEEE Transactions on Computers*, *C-11*(4): 535–552, MA.

R. F. Simmons: see P. L. Simmons.

R. F. Simmons, 1962. Synthex: toward computer synthesis of human language behavior. *Computer applications in the behavioral sciences* (H. Borko, ed.); Englewood Cliffs, N.J.: Prentice-Hall, 360–393, MA.

R. F. Simmons, 1966. Automated language processing. *Annual review of information science and technology, Volume 1* (C. A. Cuadra, ed.); New York: Interscience, 137–169, MA.

R. F. Simmons, S. Klein, and K. McConlogue, 1962. Toward the synthesis of human language behavior. *Behavioral Science*, *7*(3): 402–407, 6C.

H. A. Simon: see G. W. Baylor, see G. P. E. Clarkson, see E. A. Feigenbaum, see L. W. Gregg, see C. C. Holt, see Y. Ijiri, see A. Newell, and see J. M. Paige.

H. A. Simon, 1961. Modeling human mental processes. *Joint Computer Conference, Western Proceedings*, *19*: 111–119, MA.

H. A. Simon, 1966. Political research: the decision-making framework. *Varieties of political theory* (D. Easton, ed.); Englewood Cliffs, N.J.: Prentice-Hall, 15–24, MA.

H. A. Simon, 1967. An information-processing explanation of some perceptual phenomena. *British Journal of Psychology*, *58*(1-2): 1–12, MA.

H. A. Simon, 1967. Motivational and emotional controls of cognition. *Psychological Review*, *74*(1): 29–39, MA.

H. A. Simon and M. Barenfeld, 1969. Information-processing analysis of perceptual processes in problem solving. *Psychological Review*, *76*(5): 473–483, 3A.

H. A. Simon and E. A. Feigenbaum, 1964. An information-processing theory of some effects of similarity, familiarization, and meaningfulness in verbal learning. *Journal of Verbal Learning and Verbal Behavior*, *3*(5): 385–396, 3C.

H. A. Simon and K. Kotovsky, 1953. Human acquisition of concepts for sequential patterns. *Psychological Review*, *70*(6): 534–546, 3C.

H. A. Simon and A. Newell, 1956. Models: their uses and limitations. *The state of the social sciences* (L. D. White, ed.); Chicago: University of Chicago Press, 66–83, MA.

H. A. Simon and A. Newell, 1958. Heuristic problem solving: the next advance in operations research. *Operations Research*, *6*(1): 1–10, MA.

H. A. Simon and A. Newell, 1961. Computer simulation of human thinking and problem solving. *Computers and Automation*, *10*(4): 18–26. Also published in *Datamation*, *7*(6): 18–20 and *7*(7): 35–37, 6A.

H. A. Simon and A. Newell, 1964. Information processing in computer and man. *American Scientist*, *52*(3): 281–300, MA.

H. A. Simon and A. Newell, 1965. Heuristic problem solving by computer. *Computer augmentation of human reasoning* (M. A. Sass and W. D. Wilkinson, eds.); Washington: Spartan, 25–35, MA.

H. A. Simon and P. A. Simon, 1962. Trial and error search in solving difficult problems: evidence from the game of chess. *Behavioral Science*, *7*(4): 425–429, 8A.

H. A. Simon and T. A. VanWormer, 1963. Some Monte Carlo estimates of the Yule distribution. *Behavioral Science*, *8*(3): 203–210, 3C.

P. A. Simon: see H. A. Simon.

J. D. Singer and H. Hinomoto, 1965. Inspecting for weapons production: a modest computer simulation. *Journal of Peace Research*, *2*(1): 18–38, 5D.

J. R. Singer, 1961. Electronic analog of the human recognition system. *Journal of the Optical Society of America*, *51*(1): 61–69, 6A.

J. Singh, 1966. *Great ideas in information theory, language and cybernetics*. New York: Dover, MA.

J. Singh, 1968. Physiological models and the computer. *Computer Studies in the Humanities and Verbal Behavior*, *1*(1): 21–30, MA.

R. Sisson: see M. Szekely.

R. L. Sisson, 1969. Computer simulation of a school system. *Computers and Automation*, *18*(3): 20–23, 5D.

W. Skogan: see K. Janda.

L. J. Slater, 1966. Computing the state of the economy. *Computer Journal*, *9*(1): 11–15, 7C.

D. P. Slevin: see H. I. Ansoff.

W. Sluckin: see R. Thomson.

W. Sluckin, 1954. *Minds and machines*. Harmondsworth, Middlesex: Penguin, MA.

R. D. Smallwood, 1967. Internal models and the human instrument monitor. *IEEE Transactions on Man-Machine Systems*, MMS-8(3): 181–187, 3C.

J. J. C. Smart, 1959. Professor Ziff on robots. *Analysis*, 19(5): 117–118, MA.

N. Smart, 1959. Robots incorporated. *Analysis*, 19(5): 119–120, MA.

R. J. Smeed, 1957. Traffic flow. *OR, Operational Research Quarterly*, 8(2): 115–123, 7D.

A. Smith: see J. A. C. Brown and see R. M. Solow.

J. Smith, 1968. *Computer simulation models*. New York: Hafner, MG.

J. E. K. Smith: see N. C. Waugh.

J. W. Smith: see E. W. Paxson.

D. J. M. Smith, 1953. Economic analogs. *Proceedings of the IEEE*, 41(10): 1514–1519, MD.

O. J. M. Smith and H. F. Erdley, 1952. An electronic analogue for an economic system. *Electrical Engineering*, 71(4): 362–366, 6D.

O. J. M. Smith and R. M. Saunders, 1951. Discussion of " Analogue computing techniques applied to economics." *AIEE Transactions*, 70(1): 562–563, 7D.

R. B. Smith: see W. N. McPhee.

R. B. Smith, 1968. *Examples of the interplay between survey research and computer simulations*. Columbus: Ohio State University, 2C.

R. B. Smith, 1969. Simulation models for accounting schemes. *American Behavioral Scientist*, 12(6): 21–30, 8D.

R. D. Smith: see E. P. Strong.

R. D. Smith, 1966. *Simulation of a psychological decision process*. Doctoral dissertation, Pennsylvania State University, 1A.

R. D. Smith and P. S. Greenlaw, 1967. Simulation of a psychological decision process in personnel selection. *Management Science*; 13(8): 8-409–419, 1A.

R. N. Smith: see E. P. King.

S. S. Smith: see H. J. Johnson.

W. G. Smith and M. B. Solomon, 1966. A simulation of hospital admission policy. *Communications of the ACM*, 9(5): 362–365, 4C.

W. P. Smith and J. C. Shah, 1964. Design and development of a manufacturing systems simulator. *Journal of Industrial Engineering*, 15(4): 214–220, 7D.

W. S. Smith, 1962. Synthesized travel desires. *Traffic Quarterly*, 16(2): 173–200, 3C.

Wilbur Smith and Associates, 1965. *Southeastern Virginia regional transportation study, Volume II: highway transportation plan and implementation program*. New Haven: Wilbur Smith and Associates, 5C.

Wilbur Smith and Associates, 1966. *Proposed Puget Sound crossing*. New Haven: Wilbur Smith and Associates, 5C.

J. Snatchko: see D. D. Lamb.

J. L. Snell: see J. G. Kemeny.

M. F. Snell and A. Norman, 1966. Plymouth and district land use/transportation survey—5. Analysis of the survey data. *Traffic Engineering & Control*, 8(3): 153–155, 6C.

R. W. Snelsire and R. P. Roesser, 1968. Computer learning through association. *Digest of the second conference on applications of simulation* (A. Ockene, ed.); New York: Institute of Electrical and Electronic Engineers, Publication No. 68C60SIM, 170–172, 5A.

V. P. Sochivko, 1964. Complex in data units in automatic control systems. *Cybernetics and electronic computer technology—USSR* (L. P. Krayzmer, ed., Gosenergoizdat, 1962); Washington: Joint Publications Research Service, JPRS No. 22799, 3–10, MA.

P. O. Soelberg: see K. J. Cohen.

M. B. Solomon: see W. G. Smith.

R. M. Solow, T. Barna, C. E. V. Leser, A. G. Carruthers, P. Sevaldson, L. Johansen, A. Smith, M. McManus, and J. R. N. Stone, 1964. Discussion on the paper by Richard Stone. *Econometric analysis for national economic planning* (P. E. Hart, G. Mills, and J. K. Whitaker, eds.); London: Butterworths, 96–104., MD.

T. Soltman: see D. D. Lamb.

V. Somenzi, 1956. Can induction be mechanized? *Information theory* (C. Cherry, ed.); London: Butterworths, 226–229, MA.

J. A. Sonquist, 1967. Simulating the research analyst. *Social Science Information*, 6(4): 207–215, 8C.

W. R. Soukup: see W. K. Holstein.

L. M. Spadaro, 1966. The heuristic value of simulation in economic and business research. *Simulation in Business and Public Health, Proceedings*, 1: 73–79, MG.

G. R. Sparks, 1968. A model of the mortgage market and residential construction activity. *American Statistical Association, 1967 Proceedings of the Business and Economic Statistics Section*: 77–83, 8D.

C. B. Speedy, 1962. Instruments for measuring and processing traffic data. *Australian Road Research Board, Proceedings*, 1(1): 318–336, MD.

D. L. Spencer and A. Woroniak, 1967. Summary: discussion of issues and controversies. *The transfer of technology to developing countries* (Airlie House Conference, D. L. Spencer and A. Woroniak, eds.); New York: Praeger, 185–209, MD.

M. H. Spencer, 1963. Computer models and simulations in business and economics. *MSU Business Topics*, 11(1): 21–32, MG.

M. H. Spencer, 1965. Simulation and symbolic models. *Computer technology—concepts for management* (C. A. Tasso, ed.); New York: Industrial Relations Counselors, Monograph number 25, 81–100, MG.

R. G. Spiegelman: see E. Duckstad.

R. G. Spiegelman and K. E. Duke, 1963. Projecting travel demand for urban transportation studies. *Traffic Quarterly, 17*(3): 355–374, 2C.

E. S. Spiegelthal, 1959. Computing educated guesses. *Joint Computer Conference, Western Proceedings, 15:* 70–73, MA.

R. J. Spilsbury: see J. O. Wisdom.

J. W. T. Spinks, 1960. An atomic automation. *Memory, learning, and language* (W. Feindel, ed.); Toronto: University of Toronto Press, 30–34, 7A.

M. H. Spiro, 1968. The impact of government procurements on employment in the aircraft industry. *Studies in economic stabilization* (A. Ando, E. C. Brown, and A. F. Friedlaender, eds.); Washington: Brookings Institution, 138–183, 2D.

R. L. Spitzer and J. Endicott, 1968. DIAGNO. *Archives of General Psychiatry, 18*(6): 746–756, 3C.

R. C. Sprague, 1963. Industrial dynamics: case example. *The encyclopedia of management* (C. Heyel, ed.); New York: Reinhold, 319–322, 7D.

C. H. Springer, R. E. Herlihy, and R. I. Beggs, 1965. Simulation. *Advanced methods and models;* Homewood, Ill.: Irwin, 173–201, MG.

R. C. Sprowls, 1962. Business simulation. *Computer applications in the behavioral sciences* (H. Borko, ed.); Englewood Cliffs, N. J.: Prentice-Hall, 556–573, 7B.

R. C. Sprowls, 1964. Simulation and management control. *Management controls* (C. P. Bonini, R. K. Jaedicke, and H. M. Wagner, eds.); New York: McGraw-Hill, 146–148, MG.

R. C. Sprowls and M. Asimow, 1962. A model of customer behavior for the Task Manufacturing Corporation. *Management Science, 8*(3): 311–324, 7C.

V. G. Sragovitch, 1964. Application of the Monte Carlo method to information theory. *Method of statistical testing* (Y. A. Shreider, ed.); Amsterdam: Elsevier, 156–195. Also published in 1966 under the title *The Monte Carlo method;* London: Pergamon, 216–256, MC.

Staff of The Electrical Experimenter, 1915. "Electrical dog" follows beam of light. *Science and Invention, 3*(2); 43, MA.

D. B. Stafford: see J. W. Horn.

R. A. Stafford, 1965. A learning network model. *Second cybernetic sciences symposium, Proceedings (Biophysics and cybernetic systems,* M. Maxfield, A. Callahan, and L. J. Fogel, eds.); Washington: Spartan), 81–87, 7A.

J. D. Stanfield: see G. J. Hanneman and see E. M. Rogers.

J. D. Stanfield, N. Lin, and E. M. Rogers, 1965. *Simulation of innovation diffusion.* Working paper, Michigan State University Department of Communication, 8D.

J. D. Stanfield, N. Lin, and E. M. Rogers, 1967. *Computer simulation of innovation diffusion in a peasant village.* Working paper, Michigan State University Department of Communication, 1D.

M. Stankard: see M. Szekely.

W. H. Starbuck: see J. M. Dutton.

W. H. Starbuck, 1961. Testing case-descriptive models. *Behavioral Science, 6*(3): 191–199, MS.

W. H. Starbuck and J. M. Dutton, 1971. The history of simulation models. *Computer simulation of human behavior* (J. M. Dutton and W. H. Starbuck, eds.); New York: Wiley, MG.

M. C. Stark, 1961. *Computer simulation of street traffic.* Washington: U.S. Department of Commerce, National Bureau of Standards Technical Note 119, 4D.

M. C. Stark, 1962. Computer simulation of traffic on nine blocks of a city street. *Highway Research Board Bulletin, 356:* 40–47, 7D.

M. C. Stark, 1964. Simulation of the arterial street. *Highway conference on the future of research and development in traffic surveillance, simulation, and control, Proceedings;* Washington: U.S. Department of Commerce, 144–151, 2D.

S. F. Stasch, 1966. *Simulation of diffusion of innovation: a conceptual approach.* Working paper, Northwestern University, MD.

S. F. Stasch, 1966. *Simulation of diffusion of innovation—of any value?* Working paper, Northwestern University, MS.

S. F. Stasch, 1968. *Disaggregative measures in validating simulations of social science phenomena.* Working paper, Northwestern University, MS.

S. F. Stasch, 1968. Sample size and chance in simulating the diffusion of innovation. *Marketing and the new science of planning* (R. L. King, ed.); Chicago: American Marketing Association, 360–365, MS.

S. F. Stasch, 1968. *Some aspects of multi-dimensional verification of simulations.* Working paper, Northwestern University, MS.

M. A. Steel, 1966. Traffic forecasting and assignment. *1966 British Joint Computer Conference:* 38–44, MC.

E. Stefferud, 1963. *The logic theory machine: a model heuristic program.* Working paper, Rand Corporation, RM-3731-CC, 7A.

V. Stefflre, 1965. Simulation of people's behavior towards new objects and events. *American Behavioral Scientist, 8*(9): 12–15, 8C.

W. A. Steger: see H. W. Bruck and see N. J. Douglas, Jr.

W. A. Steger, 1961. Simulation and tax analysis: a research proposal. *National Tax Journal, 14*(3): 286–301, 8D.

W. A. Steger, 1965. The Pittsburgh urban renewal simulation model. *Journal of the American Institute of Planners, 31*(2): 144–150, 8D.

W. A. Steger, 1965. Review of analytic techniques for the CRP. *Journal of the American Institute of Planners, 31*(2): 166–172, MG.

W. A. Steger, 1966. Analytic techniques to determine the needs and resources for urban renewal action. *IBM scientific computing symposium on simulation models and gaming. Proceedings*; White Plains, N.Y.; IBM Data Processing Division, 79–95, 5C.

W. A. Steger, 1966. The realities of simulation exercises for city planning. *Simulation in Business and Public Health, Proceedings, 1*: 189–203, MD.

W. A. Steger and N. J. Douglas, Jr., 1964. *Simulation model.* Working paper, Pittsburgh Department of City Planning, CRP Progress Report 5, 8D.

N. Steinberg and J. M. Agostini, 1966. Measuring the competitive effect of advertising on buying behavior with the "Marketing-Match" model. *ESOMAR Congress, 1966, Papers*; Copenhagen: European Society for Opinion Surveys and Market Research, Paper 3A, 5C.

N. Steinberg and J. M. Agostini, 1966. Predicting media schedule effectiveness by the "Media Planex" method. *ESOMAR Congress, 1966, Papers*; Copenhagen: European Society for Opinion Surveys and Market Research, Paper 4A, 5C.

H. O. Stekler, 1968. Forecasting with econometric models: an evaluation. *Econometrica, 36*(3): 437–463, MD.

H. O. Stekler, 1969. Econometric forecast errors: data revisions and judgmental elements. *American Statistical Association, 1968 Proceedings of the Business and Economic Statistics Section:* 290–294, 1D.

F. F. Stephan: see P. Kunstadter.

J. M. Stephens, 1929. A mechanical explanation of the law of effect. *American Journal of Psychology, 41*(3): 422–431, 6A.

T. D. Sterling and S. V. Pollack, 1965. Simulation. *Computers and the life sciences* (T. D. Sterling and S. V. Pollack, eds.); New York: Columbia University Press, 191–210, MG.

S. H. Sternberg, 1959. Application of four models to sequential dependence in human learning. *Studies in mathematical learning theory* (R. R. Bush and W. K. Estes, eds.); Stanford: Stanford University Press, 340–381, 3C.

S. H. Sternberg, 1963. Some aspects of the application and testing of learning models. *Handbook of mathematical psychology* (R. D. Luce, R. R. Bush, and E. Galanter, eds.); New York: Wiley, Volume 2, 89–116, MS.

B. H. Stevens: see J. D. Herbert.

M. E. Stevens, 1960. A machine model of recall. *Information processing* (International Federation for Information Processing, S. de Picciotto, ed.); Paris: UNESCO, 309–315, 6A.

D. J. Stewart: see F. H. George.

D. J. Stewart, 1967. Logical nets and organisms that learn. *Automation theory and learning systems* (D. J. Stewart, ed.); Washington: Thompson, 53–72, MA.

I. A. Stewart: see J. F. Helliwell.

C. J. Stokes and P. Mintz, 1965. How many clerks on a floor? *Journal of Marketing Research, 2*(4): 388–393, 7C.

J. R. N. Stone: see P. C. Mahalanobis and see R. M. Solow.

J. R. N. Stone, 1961. An econometric model of growth—the British economy in ten years time. *Discovery, 22*(5): 216–219, 8D.

J. R. N. Stone, 1962. A demonstration model for economic growth. *The Manchester School of Economic and Social Studies, 30*(1): 1–14, 8D.

J. R. N. Stone, 1963. A model of economic growth. *British Association for Commercial and Industrial Education, Papers presented at the BACIE spring conference (Economic growth and manpower):* 5–14, 5D.

J. R. N. Stone, 1964. British economic balances in 1970: a trial run on Rocket. *Econometric analysis for national economic planning* (P. E. Hart, G. Mills, and J. K. Whitaker, eds.); London: Butterworths, 65–95, 5D.

J. R. N. Stone, 1964. *A programme for growth, Volume 5: the model in its environment.* London: Chapman and Hall. Also published in 1965 under the title "The analysis of economic systems;" in *Study week on the econometric approach to development planning*; Chicago: Rand McNally, 3–88 (Pontificiae academiae scientiarum scripta varia 28), 5D.

J. R. N. Stone and A. Brown, 1962. *A programme for growth, Volume 1: a computable model of economic growth.* London: Chapman and Hall, 8D.

J. R. N. Stone and A. Brown, 1963. A programme for economic growth. *Data Processing, 5*(2): 72–77, 7D.

J. R. N. Stone and J. A. C. Brown, 1962. A long-term growth model for the British economy. *Europe's future in figures* (R. C. Geary, ed.); Amsterdam: North-Holland, 287–310, 5D.

J. R. N. Stone, A. Brown, and D. A. Rowe, 1964. Demand analysis and projections for Britain: 1900-1970—a study in method. *Europe's future consumption* (J. Sandee, ed.); Amsterdam: North-Holland, 200–225, 2C.

P. J. Stone: see R. F. Bales and see E. B. Hunt.

J. R. Stowers: see C. N. Swerdloff.

E. P. Strong and R. D. Smith, 1968. The computer and managerial control. *Management control models*; New York: Holt, Rinehart and Winston, 118–148, MG.

R. H. Strotz: see N. F. Morehouse.

R. H. Strotz, J. F. Calvert, and N. F. Morehouse, 1951. Analogue computing techniques applied to economics. *AIEE Transactions, 70*(1): 557–562, 5D.

R. H. Strotz, J. C. McAnulty, and J. B. Naines, 1953. Goodwin's nonlinear theory of the business cycle: an electro-analog solution. *Econometrica, 21*(3): 390–411, 5D.

W. H. Struble: see A. G. Beged Dov.

H. L. Stubbs: see R. E. Bach.

F. L. Stumpers, 1953. A bibliography of information theory (communication theory—cybernetics). *IEEE Transactions on Information Theory, PGIT-2*: 1–60, MA.

D. B. Suits, 1966. The economic outlook for 1966. *University of Michigan, Thirteenth Annual Conference on the Economic Outlook*: 1–22, 2D.

D. B. Suits, 1967. The economic outlook for 1967. *University of Michigan, Fourteenth Annual Conference on the Economic Outlook*: 1–27, 1D.

D. B. Suits, 1968. The economic outlook for 1968. *University of Michigan, Fifteenth Annual Conference on the Economic Outlook*: 1–31, 1D.

D. B. Suits, 1969. The economic outlook for 1969. *University of Michigan, Sixteenth Annual Conference on the Economic Outlook*: 1–26, 1D.

J. O. Summers: see D. E. Schendel.

F. H. Sumner: see R. L. Grimsdale.

P. Suppes: see R. D. Luce.

P. Suppes, 1969. Stimulus-response theory of automata and TOTE hierarchies: a reply to Arbib. *Psychological Review, 76*(5): 511–514, MA.

J. Surkis, G. R. Gordon, and N. Hauser, 1968. A simulation model of New York City police department's response system. *Digest of the second conference on applications of simulation* (A. Ockene, ed.); New York: Institute of Electrical and Electronic Engineers, Publication No. 68C60SIM, 218–221, 7D.

G. L. Sutherland: see G. W. Evans, II.

I. Sutherland: see W. R. Sutherland.

N. S. Sutherland, 1959. Stimulus analysing mechanisms. *Mechanisation of thought processes* (D. V. Blake and A. M. Uttley, eds.); London: H. M. Stationery Office, Volume 2, 557–601, MA.

W. R. Sutherland, M. G. Mugglin, and I. Sutherland, 1958. An electro-mechanical model of simple animals. *Computers and Automation, 7*(2): 6–8, 23–25, and 32, 4A.

L. L. Sutro, 1959. Emergency simulation of the duties of the President of the United States. *Joint Computer Conference, Western Proceedings, 15*: 314–323, MA.

A. Svoboda, 1963. Synthesis of logical systems of given activity. *IEEE Transactions on Computers, C-12*(6): 904–910, MS.

W. L. Swager, H. R. Hamilton, D. C. Sweet, S. E. Goldstone, N. M. Kamrany, and A. L. Pugh, III, 1964. *Estimating the economic impact of systems of works on the Susquehanna River basin through computer simulation.* Columbus, O.: Battelle Memorial Institute, MD.

C. E. Sweet, Jr.: see C. Ben.

D. C. Sweet: see H. R. Hamilton and see W. L. Swager.

C. N. Swerdloff and J. R. Stowers, 1966. A test of some first generation residential land use models. *Highway Research Record, 126*: 38–59. Reprinted in *Public Roads, 34*(5): 101–109, 1C.

S. Swerling: see P. G. Drew.

A. J. Syvertsen: see S. Kashin.

D. L. Székely, 1963. On the epistemology of the General Purpose Artificial Intelligence. *Cybernetica, 6*(2): 88–105, MA.

M. Szekely, M. Stankard, and R. Sisson, 1968. Design of a planning model for an urban school district. *Socio-Economic Planning Sciences, 1*(3): 231–242, 7D.

E. J. Taaffe, B. J. Garner, and M. H. Yeates, 1963. *The peripheral journey to work.* Evanston: Northwestern University Press, 3C.

M. I. Taft, 1966. *Toward a systems analysis approach to engineering education.* Doctoral dissertation, University of Southern California, 5C.

M. I. Taft and A. Reisman, 1967. Toward better curricula through computer selected sequencing of subject matter. *Management Science, 13*(11): 926–945, 5C.

C. C. Tappert, 1966. *On the neural modeling of speech processes.* Working paper, Cornell University Cognitive Systems Research Program, Report No. 9, 5A.

R. Tarjan, 1958. Neuronal automata. *Cybernetica, 1*(3): 189–196, MA.

J. D. Tarver, 1963. Computer programs for estimating and projecting county, city, and other local subdivisional populations. *Behavioral Science, 8*(2): 165–168, 5C.

M. Taube, 1961. *Computers and common sense.* New York: Columbia University Press, MA.

M. Taube, 1961. What good is bionics? *First Bionics Symposium (Living prototypes—the key to new technology*, J. C. Robinette, ed.); Wright-Patterson AFB: Wright Air Development Division, TR 60-600, 479–481, MA.

W. H. Taubert, 1968. A search decision rule for the aggregate scheduling problem. *Management Science, 14*(6): B-343–359, 7C.

P. Taubman: see M. Brown and see G. Fromm.

D. W. Taylor, 1960. Toward an information processing theory of motivation. *Nebraska symposium on motivation, 1960* (*Current theory and research in motivation*, M. R. Jones, ed.); Lincoln: University of Nebraska Press, Volume 8, 51–79, MA.

D. W. Taylor, 1963. Thinking. *Theories in contemporary psychology* (M. H. Marx, ed.); New York: Macmillan, 475–493, MA.

D. W. Taylor, 1965. Decision making and problem solving. *Handbook of organizations* (J. G. March, ed.); Chicago: Rand McNally, 48–86, MA.

D. W. Taylor, 1965. Simulation of human problem solving. *Computers for the humanities?* (G. W. Pierson, ed.); New Haven: Yale University, 137–141, MA.

E. M. Taylor: see A. W. McEachern.

G. P. Taylor, 1964. The computer in media planning. *Scientific Business*, 2(7): 287–294, MC.

J. G. Taylor, 1962. Philosophical implications. *The behavioral basis of perception*; New Haven: Yale University Press, 338–363, MA.

J. G. Taylor and J. A. Navarro, 1968. Simulation of a court system for the processing of criminal cases. *SCi Simulation*, 10(5): 235–240, 4C.

J. G. Taylor, J. A. Navarro, and R. H. Cohen, 1968. Simulation applied to a court system. *IEEE Transactions on Systems Science and Cybernetics*, SSC-4(4): 376–379, 4C.

J. L. Taylor: see J. E. Walsh.

J. L. Taylor, 1959. Development and application of a terminal-air-battle model. *Operations Research*, 7(6): 783–796, 7B.

T. H. Taylor, 1962. An introduction to the Monte Carlo method. *Naval Engineers Journal*, 74(1): 93–98, MC.

W. B. Taylor, 1957. A continuous model of a tank battle. *War gaming, Cosmagon, and Zigspiel* (No editor); Bethesda: Johns Hopkins University Operations Research Office, ORO-SP-12, AD-235892, 123–156, 7B.

W. K. Taylor, 1956. Electrical simulation of some nervous system functional activities. *Information theory* (C. Cherry, ed.); London: Butterworths, 314–327, 2A.

W. K. Taylor, 1959. Pattern recognition by means of automatic analogue apparatus. *Proceedings of the Institution of Electrical Engineers*, 106B(26): 198–209, 7A.

W. K. Taylor, 1962. A theory of cortical organization and learning. *IEEE Transactions on Information Theory*, IT-8(5): S-144–149, 5A.

W. K. Taylor, 1965. A model of learning mechanisms in the brain. *Progress in brain research, Volume 17: cybernetics of the nervous system* (N. Wiener and J. P. Schadé, eds.); Amsterdam: Elsevier, 369–397, 2A.

D. Teichroew, 1965. A history of distribution sampling prior to the era of the computer and its relevance to simulation. *Journal of the American Statistical Association*, 60(309): 27–49, MS.

A. J. Tella and P. A. Tinsley, 1968. The labor market and potential output of the FRB–MIT model: a preliminary report. *American Statistical Association, 1967 Proceedings of the Business and Economic Statistics Section*: 51–76, 2D.

B. Tencer: see E. P. Holland.

P. V. Teplitz: see M. D. Kilbridge.

R. A. Terry: see B. L. Capehart.

L. Tesler, H. Enea, and K. M. Colby, 1968. A directed graph representation for computer simulation of belief systems. *Mathematical Biosciences*, 2(1/2): 19–40, MA.

H. L. Teuber: see H. Von Foerster.

B. Thalberg, 1966. *A trade cycle analysis*. Lund: Studentlitteratur, 5D.

J. Thatcher: see J. W. Gyr.

H. Theil, 1965. Decision rules and simulation techniques in development planning. *Study week on the econometric approach to development planning*; Chicago: Rand McNally, 465–494 (Pontificiae academiae scientiarum scripta varia 28), 5D.

L. H. Thomas, 1953. A comparison of stochastic and direct methods for the solution of some special problems. *Operations Research*, 1(4): 181–186, MS.

R. E. Thomas and J. T. Tou, 1968. Evolution of heuristics by human operators in control systems. *IEEE Transactions on Systems Science and Cybernetics*, SSC-4(1): 60–71, 3C.

S. Thomas, 1965. Artificial intelligence. *Computers*; New York: Holt, Rinehart and Winston, 151–155, MA.

J. N. Thomasson, Jr., and P. H. Wright, 1967. Simulation of traffic at a two-way stop intersection. *Traffic Engineering*, 37(11): 39–45, 2D.

D. Thompson, 1965. Can a machine be conscious? *British Journal for the Philosophy of Science*, 16(61): 33–43, MA.

G. L. Thompson: see J. G. Kemeny.

H. E. Thompson, 1966. Sales forecasting errors and inventory fluctuations: random errors and random sales. *Management Science*, 12(5): 448–456, 7C.

J. D. Thompson: see R. B. Fetter.

J. D. Thompson and R. B. Fetter, 1963. The economics of the maternity service. *Yale Journal of Biology and Medicine*, 36(1): 91–103, 2C.

J. D. Thompson and R. B. Fetter, 1966. The application of simulation to hospital planning. *Simulation in Business and Public Health, Proceedings*, 1: 205–210, 3C.

J. D. Thompson, R. B. Fetter, C. S. McIntosh, and R. J. Pelletier, 1963. Predicting requirements for maternity facilities. *Hospitals*, *37*(4): 45–49 and 132, 3C.

J. D. Thompson, R. B. Fetter, C. S. McIntosh, and R. J. Pelletier, 1964 Computer simulation of the activity in a maternity suite. *Third international conference on operational research, Proceedings* (G. Kreweras and G. Morlat, eds.); London: English Universities Press, 213–222, 3C.

R. Thomson and W. Sluckin, 1953. Cybernetics and mental functioning. *British Journal for the Philosophy of Science*, *4*(14): 130–146, MA.

J. P. Thorne: see P. Bratley.

J. P. Thorne, P. Bratley, and H. Dewar, 1968. The syntactic analysis of English by machine. *Machine intelligence 3* (D. Michie, ed.); New York: American Elsevier, 281–309, 7A.

C. E. Tiedemann and C. S. Van Doren, 1964. *The diffusion of hybrid seed corn in Iowa: a spatial simulation model*. Working paper, Michigan State University Institute for Community Development and Services, Technical Bulletin B-44, 4D.

G. Tillinger, 1967. The methodology of computer simulation for economic systems. *Computer uses in the social sciences, Proceedings of the working conference*; Vienna: Institut für Höhere Studien und Wissenschaftliche Forschung Wien, MD.

E. H. Tinney: see R. H. Day.

P. A. Tinsley: see A. J. Tella.

K. D. Tocher, 1963. *The art of simulation*. Princeton: Van Nostrand, MS.

K. D. Tocher, 1966. The state of the art of simulation—a survey. *Proceedings of the fourth international conference on operational research* (D. B. Hertz and J. Melese, eds.); New York: Wiley-Interscience, 693–701, MG.

A. R. Tomazinis, 1962. A new method of trip distribution in an urban area. *Highway Research Board Bulletin*, *347*: 77–99, 3C.

A. R. Tomazinis, 1967. Modal split model in the Penn-Jersey Transportation Study area. *Highway Research Record*, *165*: 41–75, 2C.

A. R. Tomazinis and G. V. Wickstrom, 1962. Forming a comprehensive transportation flows model. *Highway Research Board Bulletin*, 347: 254–257, MC.

S. S. Tomkins, 1963. Simulations of personality: the interrelationships between affect, memory, thinking, perception, and action. *Computer simulation of personality* (S. S. Tomkins and S. Messick, eds.); New York: Wiley, 3–57, MA.

H. E. Tompkins, W. S. McCulloch, A. G. Oettinger, N. Rochester, D. H. Schmitt, M. E. Maron, E. L. Gruenberg, M. L. Minsky, J. Mauchly, M. Rubinoff, W. Pitts, and J. Rothstein, 1956. Symposium: the design of machines to simulate the behavior of the human brain. *IEEE Transactions on Computers*, *C-5*(4): 240–255, MA.

F. M. Tonge: see J. Feldman.

F. M. Tonge, 1961. *A heuristic program for assembly line balancing*. Englewood Cliffs, N. J.: Prentice-Hall, 7A.

F. M. Tonge, 1961. The use of heuristic programming in management science. *Management Science*, *7*(3): 231–237, MG.

G. C. Tootill: see S. H. Hollingdale.

W. S. Torgerson: see D. B. Yntema.

F. C. Toscano, 1965. *A generalized methodology for the simulation of transportation systems*. Doctoral dissertation, University of California at Los Angeles, 4C.

J. T. Tou: see R. E. Thomas.

J. T. Tou and K. S. Fu, 1965. Digital control concepts for nervous system synthesis and simulation. *Third international congress on cybernetics*; Namur, Belgium: Association Internationale de Cybernétique, 794–813, MA.

T. R. Trabasso: see M. P. Friedman.

T. R. Trabasso and G. H. Bower, 1966. Presolution dimensional shifts in concept identification: a test of the sampling with replacement axiom in all-or-none models. *Journal of Mathematical Psychology*, *3*(1): 163–173, 3C.

Traffic Research Corporation, 1963. *Review of existing land use forecasting techniques*. Working paper, Traffic Research Corporation; a second printing incorporating an additional appendix was published in 1964, MC.

D. L. Trautman: see J. H. Mathewson.

D. L. Trautman and J. H. Mathewson, 1954. Prognosis. *Analysis and simulation of vehicular traffic flow* (D. L. Trautman, H. Davis, J. Heilfron, E. C. Ho, J. H. Mathewson, and A. Rosenbloom); Los Angeles: University of California Institute of Transportation and Traffic Engineering, Research Report No. 20, 63–67, MG.

D. L. Trautman, J. Heilfron, E. C. Ho, H. Davis, and A. Rosenbloom, 1954. Reinforcing common-sense solutions. *Analysis and simulation of vehicular traffic flow* (D. L. Trautman, H. Davis, J. Heilfron, E. C. Ho, J. H. Mathewson, and A. Rosenbloom); Los Angeles: University of California Institute of Transportation and Traffic Engineering, Research Report No. 20, 9–18, MC.

L. E. Travis, 1962. *Observing how humans make mistakes to discover how to get computers to do likewise*. Working paper, System Development Corporation, SP–776, MS.

R. I. Triker: see D. Clark.

H. F. Trotter: see H. J. Arnold.

H. F. Trotter and J. W. Tukey, 1956. Conditional Monte Carlo for normal samples. *Symposium on Monte Carlo methods* (H. A. Meyer, ed.); New York: Wiley, 64–79, MS.

W. C. True: see H. H. Goode.

R. E. Trueman, 1968. *Application of some computer simulation techniques.* Working paper, San Fernando Valley State College, MC.

H. Tsurumi and M. F. J. Prachowny, 1968. *A four-sector growth model of the Canadian economy.* Working paper, Queen's University, 2D.

R. V. Tuason, 1965. *Experimental simulation on a predetermined marketing mix strategy.* Doctoral dissertation, Northwestern University, 5D.

Tucson Area Transportation Planning Agency, 1965. *Tucson area transportation study, Volume II: forecasts and the plan, 1965.* Tucson: Tucson Area Transportation Planning Agency, 2C.

J. W. Tukey: see H. J. Arnold and see H. F. Trotter.

J. W. Tukey, 1957. Antithesis or regression? *Cambridge Philosophical Society, Proceedings, 53*(4): 923–924. MS.

D. S. Tull: see P. E. Green.

A. M. Turing: see B. van der Pol.

A. M. Turing, 1950. Computing machinery and intelligence. *Mind, 59*(236): 433–460. Reprinted in 1956 under the title "Can a machine think?" in *The world of mathematics* (J. R. Newman, ed.); New York: Simon and Schuster, Volume 4, 2099–2123, MA.

A. Tustin, 1953. Economic regulation through control-system engineering. *Impact of Science on Society, 4*(2): 83–110, MD.

A. Tustin, 1953. *The mechanism of economic systems.* London: Heinemann, MD.

A. Tyree: see N. Keyfitz.

U. S. Defense Documentation Center, 1962. *Simulation of thought processes by computers.* Arlington, Va.: Armed Services Technical Information Agency, MA.

H. Ueno and S. Kinoshita, 1968. A simulation experiment for growth with a long- term model of Japan. *International Economic Review, 9*(1): 14–48, 1D.

L. Uhr: see M. Kochen and see C. Vossler.

L. Uhr, 1960. Intelligence in computers: the psychology of perception in people and in machines. *Behavioral Science, 5*(2): 177–182, MG.

L. Uhr, 1963. The development of perception and language: simulated models. *Computer simulation of personality* (S. S. Tomkins and S. Messick, eds.); New York: Wiley, 231–266, 6C.

L. Uhr, 1963. "Pattern recognition" computers as models for form perception. *Psychological Bulletin, 60* (1): 40–73, MA.

L. Uhr, 1965. Complex dynamic models of living organisms. *Computers in biomedical research* (R. W. Stacy and B. D. Waxman, eds.); New York: Academic Press, Volume 1, 15–31, MA.

L. Uhr, 1965. Pattern recognition. *Electronic information handling* (A. Kent and O. E. Taulbee, eds.); Washington: Spartan, 51–72, MA.

L. Uhr, 1966. Computer simulations of complex models. *Pattern recognition* (L. Uhr, ed.); New York: Wiley, 291–294, MA.

L. Uhr and G. Ingram, 1966. Language learning, continuous pattern recognition, and class formation. *Information processing 1965* (International Federation for Information Processing, W. A. Kalenich, ed.); Washington: Spartan, Volume 2, 333–334, 7A.

L. Uhr and C. Vossler, 1961. A pattern recognition program that generates, evaluates, and adjusts its own operators. *Joint Computer Conference, Western Proceedings, 19*: 555–569, 5A.

L. Uhr and C. Vossler, 1961. Recognition of speech by a computer program that was written to simulate a model for human visual pattern recognition. *Journal of the Acoustical Society of America, 33*(10): 1426, 7A.

L. Uhr and C. Vossler 1962. The search to recognize. *Symposium on optical character recognition* (G. L. Fisher, Jr., D. K. Pollock, B. Raddack, and M. E. Stevens, eds.); Washington: Spartan, 319–329, 5A.

L. Uhr and C. Vossler, 1963. A pattern recognition program that generates, evaluates, and adjusts its own operators. *Computers and thought* (E. A. Feigenbaum and J. Feldman, eds.); New York: McGraw-Hill, 251–268, 3A.

L. Uhr, C. Vossler, and J. Uleman, 1962. Pattern recognition over distortions, by human subjects and by a computer simulation of a model for human form perception. *Journal of Experimental Psychology, 63*(3): 227–234, 3C.

S. Ulam: see N. Metropolis.

S. Ulam, 1951, On the Monte Carlo method. *Proceedings of a second symposium on large-scale digital calculating machinery* (Harvard University Computation Laboratory); Cambridge: Harvard University Press, 207–212, MG.

S. M. Ulam, 1967. On general formulations of simulation and model construction. *Prospects for simulation and simulators of dynamic systems* (G. Shapiro and M. Rogers, eds.); New York: Spartan, 3–8, MG.

J. Uleman: see L. Uhr.

J. R. Ullmann, 1965. Some problems in artificial intelligence. *Progress in brain research, Volume 17: cybernetics of the nervous system* (N. Wiener and S. P. Schadé, eds.); Amsterdam: Elsevier, 102–117, 8A.

S. Urabe, 1966. Operations research activities on the Japanese National Railways. *Proceedings of the fourth international conference on operational research* (D. B. Hertz and J. Melese, eds.); New York: Wiley-Interscience, 359–362, 5C.

B. Urban: see G. E. Clark, Jr.

G. L. Urban: see D. B. Montgomery.

G. L. Urban, 1967. SPRINTER: a tool for new product decision makers. *Industrial Management Review,* *8*(2): 43–54, 5D.

G. L. Urban, 1968. Market responses models for the analysis of new products. *Marketing and the new science of planning* (R. L. King, ed.); Chicago: American Marketing Association, 105–111, MC.

W. R. Uttal, 1967. *Real-time computers.* New York: Harper & Row, MG.

A. M. Uttley: see D. A. Sholl and see B. van der Pol.

A. M. Uttley, 1953. Information, machines, and brains. *IEEE Transactions on Information Theory, PGIT-1*: 143–149 (Symposium on Information Theory, London, England, September 1950), MA.

A. M. Uttley, 1954. The classification of signals in the nervous system. *Electroencephalography and Clinical Neurophysiology, 6*(3): 479–494, 2A.

A. M. Uttley, 1956. Conditional probability machines and conditioned reflexes. *Automata studies* (C. E. Shannon and J. McCarthy, eds.); Princeton: Princeton University Press, 253–275, MA.

A. M. Uttley, 1956. Temporal and spatial patterns in a conditional probability machine. *Automata studies* (C. E. Shannon and J. McCarthy, eds.); Princeton: Princeton University Press, 277–285, MA.

A. M. Uttley, 1959. The design of conditional probability computers. *Information and Control, 2*(1): 1–24, 7A.

A. M. Uttley, 1962. Properties of plastic networks. *Biophysical Journal, 2*(2.2): 169–188, MA.

M. Valach: see J. Klír and see Z. Wünsch.

R. C. Van Buskirk: see A. A. B. Pritsker.

C. van de Panne: see J. A. C. Brown.

T. J. Vander Noot, 1966. *The simulation and extrapolation of population change: a case study, the population of the upper midwest.* Doctoral dissertation, University of Minnesota, 5C.

B. van der Pol, A. M. Turing, H. C. Calpine, D. M. MacKay, J. F. Schouten, A. A. Fairthorne, and A. M. Uttley, 1953. Discussion on Dr. A. M. Uttley's paper "Information, machines, and brains," *IEEE Transactions on Information Theory*, PGIT-1: 193–197 (Symposium on Information Theory, London, England, September 1950), MA.

C. S. Van Doren: see C. E. Tiedemann.

J. van Galen: see C. Levert.

R. L. Van Horn, 1969. The problem of validation. *The design of computer simulation experiments* (T. H. Naylor, ed.); Durham: Duke University Press, Chapter 11, MS.

R. M. Van Slyke, 1963. Monte Carlo methods and PERT problem. *Operations Research, 11*(5): 839–860, MS.

W. R. van Voorhis, 1956. Waiting-line theory as a management tool. *Operations Research, 4*(2): 221-231, MC.

T. A. VanWormer: see H. A. Simon.

T. A. VanWormer, 1963. *The Trimmer, a heuristic approach to the trim problem in the corrugated container industry.* Doctoral dissertation, Carnegie-Mellon University, 7A.

D. J. Veldman, 1967. Simulation. *Fortran programming for the behavioral sciences*; New York: Holt, Rinehart and Winston, 26–27, MG.

R. C. Vergin, 1966. Production scheduling under seasonal demand. *Journal of Industrial Engineering, 17*(5): 260–266, 7C.

J. M. Vernon: see T. H. Naylor.

J. M. Vernon, N. W. Rives, Jr., and T. H. Naylor, 1969. An econometric model of the tobacco industry. *Review of Economics and Statistics, 51*(2): 149–158, 2D.

R. Vichnèvetsky, 1967. Error analysis in the computer simulation of dynamic systems: variational aspects of the problem. *IEEE Transactions on Computers, C-16*(4): 403–411, MS.

H. G. von Cube: see N. A. Irwin.

H. von Falkenhausen, 1966. Traffic assignment by a stochastic model. *Proceedings of the fourth international conference on operational research* (D. B. Hertz and J. Melese, eds.); New York: Wiley-Interscience, 415–421, MC.

H. von Foerster, 1965. Memory without record. *The anatomy of memory* (Conference on learning, remembering and forgetting, Volume 1, D. P. Kimble, ed.); Palo Alto: Science and Behavior Books, 388–433, MA.

H. von Foerster, M. Mead, and H. L. Teuber, 1952. A note by the editors. *Eighth conference on cybernetics, Transactions* (*Cybernetics*, H. von Foerster, ed.); New York: Josiah Macy, Jr. Foundation, xi–xx, MA.

J. von Neumann, 1951. The general and logical theory of automata. *Cerebral mechanisms in behavior* (L. A. Jeffress, ed.); New York: Wiley, 1–31, MA.

J. von Neumann, 1958. *The computer and the brain.* New Haven: Yale University Press, MA.

A. M. Voorhees & Associates, 1963. *Waterbury area transportation study.* Washington: A. M. Voorhees & Associates, 2C.

A. M. Voorhees & Associates, 1964. *Multi-purpose centers for the Baltimore region: market potential.* Washington: A. M. Voorhees & Associates, 1C.

A. M. Voorhees & Associates, 1966. *A model for allocating economic activities into sub-areas in a state.* Working paper, A. M. Voorhees & Associates, 2D.

A. M. Voorhees & Associates, 1968. *Factors and trends in trip lengths.* Washington: National Cooperative Highway Research Program, Report 48, 7C.

C. Vossler: see L. Uhr.

C. Vossler and L. Uhr, 1962. A computer simulation of pattern perception and concept formation. *Second Bionics Symposium* (*Biological prototypes and synthetic systems, Volume 1,* E. E. Bernard and M. R. Kare, eds.); New York: Plenum, 233–243, 6C.

C. Vossler and L. Uhr, 1963. Computer simulations of a perceptual learning model for sensory pattern recognition, concept formation, and symbol transformation. *Information processing 1962* (International Federation for Information Processing, C. M. Popplewell, ed.); Amsterdam: North-Holland, 413–418, 3C.

F. A. Wagner, Jr.: see D. L. Gerlough.

F. Waldorf: see J. S. Coleman.

F. Waldorf and J. S. Coleman, 1971. Analysis and simulation of reference group processes. *Computer simulation of human behavior* (J. M. Dutton and W. H. Starbuck, eds.); New York: Wiley, 2D.

C. C. Walker, 1965. *A study of a family of complex systems—an approach to the investigation of organisms' behavior.* Doctoral dissertation, University of Illinois. 7A.

G. H. Walker, 1967. *A study on the simulation and optimization of a hypothetical total firm.* Doctoral dissertation, University of Texas, 7D.

S. H. Walker, 1956. Application of the Monte Carlo method in systems analysis. *American Institute of Industrial Engineers, Proceedings of the Annual National Conference,* 7(37): 1–12, MC.

A. Wallace, 1969. Linking the aggregate and industry levels—the econometric approach. *American Statistical Association, 1968 Proceedings of the Business and Economic Statistics Section*: 216–223, 5D.

G. F. Wallace: see G. W. Evans, II.

G. F. Wallace, 1967. The character of simulation. *Sci Simulation,* 8(5): 252–254, MG.

R. A. Wallace, 1952. The maze solving computer. *Association for Computing Machinery, Proceedings, Pittsburgh* (May): 119–125, 6A.

W. A. Wallace: see E. E. Kaczka.

W. A. Wallace, 1967. Computer simulation and law enforcement: an application to the automobile theft problem. *Law enforcement science and technology* (S. A. Yefsky, ed.); Washington: Thompson, Volume 1, 629–634, 5D.

W. H. Wallace: see T. H. Naylor.

W. H. Wallace, T. H. Naylor, and W. E. Sasser, 1968. An econometric model of the textile industry in the United States. *Review of Economics and Statistics,* 50(1): 13–22, 2D.

J. E. Walsh: see A. V. Gafarian and see J. B. Lathrop.

J. E. Walsh, 1956. Questionable usefulness of variance for measuring estimate accuracy in Monte Carlo importance sampling problems. *Symposium on Monte Carlo methods* (H. A. Meyer, ed.); New York: Wiley, 141–144, MS.

J. E. Walsh, 1963. Use of linearized nonlinear regression for simulations involving Monte Carlo. *Operations Research,* 11(2): 228–235, MS.

J. E. Walsh and J. L. Taylor, 1963. *Simulation of military logistics operation in an underdeveloped country.* Working paper, System Development Corporation, SP-1090/000/01, 8B.

M. J. Walsh: see L. J. Fogel.

J. R. Walter: see D. J. Clough.

W. G. Walter, 1950. An electro-mechanical "animal." *Discovery,* 11(3): 90–93. Reprinted in *Dialectica,* 4(3): 206–213, MA.

W. G. Walter, 1950. An imitation of life. *Scientific American,* 182(5): 42–45, 6A.

W. G. Walter, 1951. A machine that learns. *Scientific American,* 185(2): 60–63, 7A.

W. G. Walter, 1953. *The living brain.* New York: Norton, 4A.

W. G. Walter, 1953. Possible features of brain function and their imitation. *IEEE Transactions on Information Theory,* PGIT-1: 134–136 (Symposium on Information Theory, London, England, September 1950), 6A.

W. G. Walter, 1955. Studies on activity of the brain. *Tenth conference on cybernetics, Transactions* (*Cybernetics,* H. von Foerster, ed.); New York: Josiah Macy, Jr. Foundation, 19–31, MA.

A. Walton, 1930. Demonstrational and experimental devices. *American Journal of Psychology,* 42(1): 109–114, 7A.

J. R. Walton: see R. A. Douglas.

J. R. Walton and R. A. Douglas, 1962. A LaGrangian approach to traffic simulation on digital computers. *Highway Research Board Bulletin, 356*: 48–50, MD.

K. N. Waltz, 1968. Realities, assumptions, and simulations. *Simulation in the study of politics* (W. D. Coplin, ed.); Chicago: Markham, 105–111, MG.

J. H. Ward, Jr., 1961. Markov models and Monte Carlo techniques. *Educational and Psychological Measurement,* 21(1): 219–225, MC.

J. L. Ward: see J. R. Carbonell.

L. B. Ward: see G. K. Bennett.

J. G. Wardrop: see J. A. Hillier.

J. G. Wardrop, 1964. Practical applications of traffic theories. *Traffic Engineering & Control*, 5(10): 607–610, MC.

B. T. Warner, 1966. A model for total marketing. *Computers in advertising* (N. Rogers, ed.); London: The Institute of Practitioners in Advertising, 47–53, 5C.

H. C. Warner, Jr., 1965. *Decision-making in a savings and loan association: a simulation analysis.* Doctoral dissertation, University of Tennessee, 4D.

O. Wärneryd: see R. Malm.

P. Warnshuis, 1967. Simulation of two-way traffic on an isolated two-lane road. *Transportation Research*, 1(1): 75–83, 7C.

P. Warren: see D. C. Gazis and see C. Ohlin.

W. Wasow, 1951. On the mean duration of random walks. *Journal of Research of the National Bureau of Standards*, 46(6): 462–471, MS.

D. W. G. Wass: see J. H. H. Merriman.

W. D. Wätjen, 1965. Computer simulation of traffic behaviour through three signals. *Traffic Engineering & Control*, 6(10): 623–626, 6C.

J. B. Watt: see K. M. Colby.

D. G. Watts, 1969. Spectral analysis. *The design of computer simulation experiments* (T. H. Naylor, ed.); Durham: Duke University Press, Chapter 8, MS.

N. C. Waugh and J. E. K. Smith, 1962. A stochastic model for free recall. *Psychometrika*, 27(2): 141–154, 1C.

C. E. Webber: see J. A. Adams.

C. E. Weber: see C. G. Moore, Jr. and see B. L. Myers.

C. E. Weber, 1965. Intraorganizational decision processes influencing the EDP staff budget. *Management Science*, 12(4): B-69–93, 1B.

C. E. Weber and L. A. Welsch, 1967. A general model for sales planning. *Research toward the development of management thought* (M. P. Hottenstein and R. W. Millman, eds.); Academy of Management, 74–82, 1A.

W. L. Weber: see W. R. Dill.

F. V. Webster, 1958. *Traffic signal settings.* Harmondsworth, Middlesex: Road Research Laboratory, Paper 39, 7C.

K. C. Wehr: see R. L. Preger.

H. B. Weil: see E. B. Roberts.

R. L. Weil, 1966. The N-person Prisoner's Dilemma: some theory and a computer-oriented approach. *Behavioral Science*, 11(3): 227–234, 6B.

G. M. Weinberg, 1963. Systems research potentials using digital computers. *General Systems*, 8: 145–150, MG.

E. Weiner, 1966. A modal split model for southeastern Wisconsin. *Southeastern Wisconsin Regional Planning Commission, Technical Record*, 2(6): 1–56, 1C.

J. K. Weinstock, 1958. An inventory control solution by simulation. *Report of system simulation symposium* (D. G. Malcolm, ed.); New York: American Institute of Industrial Engineers, 65–71, 2C.

D. L. Weiss: see D. E. Schendel.

D. L. Weiss, 1962. Simulation of the packaged detergent industry. *Marketing precision and executive action* (C. H. Hindersman, ed.); Chicago: American Marketing Association, 152–161, 7B.

D. L. Weiss, 1964. Simulation for decision making in marketing. *Journal of Marketing*, 28(3): 45–50, MC.

G. H. Weiss: see D. C. Gazis.

P. Weiss, 1960. Love in a machine age. *Dimensions of mind* (S. Hook, ed.); New York: New York University Press, 193–197, MA.

S. F. Weiss: see F. S. Chapin, Jr. and see T. G. Donnelly.

H. Weitz, 1966. *Simulation models in marketing.* Yorktown Heights, N.Y.: IBM, Technical report 17–192, MD.

H. Weitz, 1967. The promise of simulation in marketing. *Journal of Marketing*, 31(3): 28–33. MG.

J. Weizenbaum, 1966. ELIZA—a computer program for the study of natural language communication between man and machine. *Communications of the ACM*, 9(1): 36–45, 6A.

J. Weizenbaum, 1968. Contextual understanding by computers. *Recognizing patterns* (P. A. Kolers and M. Eden, eds.); Cambridge: MIT Press, 170–193, 6A.

W. D. Wells, 1963. Computer simulation of consumer behavior. *Harvard Business Review*, 41(3): 93–98, MG.

L. A. Welsch: see C. E. Weber.

J. G. Wendel, 1957. Groups and conditional Monte Carlo. *Annals of Mathematical Statistics*, 28(4): 1048–1052, MS.

C. J. Wensrich: see R. Kraft.

G. Werner, B. L. Whitsel, and H. Sacks, 1969. Perceptual space of organisms and automata. *Simulation and modeling conference* (R. U. Benson, ed.); Pittsburgh: Pittsburgh chapters of ACM, IEEE-EC, and IEEE-SSC, and Midwest SCi, 185–191, MA.

J. T. Werner: see R. Werner.

R. Werner and J. T. Werner, 1969 *Bibliography of simulations: social systems and education.* La Jolla, California: Western Behavioral Sciences Institute, Contract OEC-1-7-071027-4273, MG.

K. Wertz: see T. H. Naylor.

S. A. West, 1968. *SMATSEL, a simulation of the decision processes in mate selection in Akiyama.* Working paper, Syracuse University Department of Anthropology, 2B.

L. Wester: see M. D. Kilbridge.

C. F. Westoff: see P. Kunstadter.

J. K. Wetherbee: see A. A. B. Pritsker.

F. H. Weymar, 1963. Industrial dynamics: interaction between the firm and its market. *Marketing and the computer* (W. Alderson and S. J. Shapiro, eds.); Englewood Cliffs, N. J.: Prentice-Hall, 260–276, 7D.

F. H. Weymar, 1968. *The dynamics of the world cocoa market*. Cambridge: MIT Press. 1D.

J. White: see R. McGinnis.

P. D. Whiting: see J. A. Hillier.

B. L. Whitsel: see G. Werner.

W. A. Wickelgren, 1962. A simulation program for concept attainment by conservative focusing. *Behavioral Science*, 7(2): 245–247, 7A.

G. V. Wickstrom: see A. R. Tomazinis.

N. Wiener, 1948. *Cybernetics*. New York: Wiley-MIT; second edition in 1961, MA.

N. Wiener, 1950. *The human use of human beings*. Boston: Houghton Mifflin, MA.

W. W. Wierwille and G. A. Gagné, 1966. Nonlinear and time-varying dynamical models of human operators in manual control systems. *Human Factors*, 8(2): 97–120, 3A.

J. D. Wiest, 1966. Heuristic programs for decision making. *Harvard Business Review*, 44(5): 129–143, MG.

L. M. Wiggins, 1966. The use of simulation to relate behavioral theory to social action. *Simulation in Business and Public Health, Proceedings*, 1: 217–220, MG.

N. Wiggins and P. J. Hoffman, 1968. Three models of clinical judgement. *Journal of Abnormal Psychology*, 73(1): 70–77, 3A.

C. W. Wightman: see J. C. Hay.

K. Wigley, 1968. *A program for growth, Volume 8: the demand for fuel, 1948-1975*. London: Chapman and Hall, 2D.

J. W. Wilcox: see L. F. McPherson.

R. B. Wilcox, 1964. Dynamic analysis and simulation of management control functions. *Automatic and remote control, applications and components* (International Federation of Automatic Control, V. Broida, ed.); London: Butterworths, 439–447, 7D.

E. E. Wilkes, 1967. Simulation by computer–a survey. *Australian computer conference, Proceedings of the third, Canberra, 16th May to 20th May, 1966* (G. N. Lance and T. Pearcey, eds.); Chippendale: Australian Trade Publications, 114–120, MG.

M. V. Wilkes, 1951. Can machines think? *Spectator*, 187(6424): 177–178, MA.

D. M. Wilkins, 1964. Computer simulation as a predictive method of fiscal planning for municipal government, *The cybernetic approach to urban analysis* (L.M. Swanson and G. O. Johnson, eds.); Los Angeles: University of Southern California, 150–157, MD.

R. Willey: see J. W. Gyr.

A. Williams: see J. D. Herniter.

B. O. B. Williams: see S. W. Cragin, Jr.

G. Williams: see M. G. Richards.

R. H. Williams, Jr., 1967. *A simulation study of a production scheduling problem in the carpet textile industry*. Doctoral dissertation, University of Alabama, 7A.

L. M. Wilson: see S. W. Cragin, Jr.

P. B. Wilson and D. C. Lach, 1967. Computer simulation developments in Canadian National Railways. *Second international symposium on the use of cybernetics on the railways* (P. B. Wilson and P. Rezac, eds.); Brussels: International Railway Congress Association, 176–182. Also published in 1968 in *Cybernetics and Electronics on the Railways*, 5(1): 44–50, 7C.

Y. Wind and P. J. Robinson, 1968. Simulating the industrial buying process. *Marketing and the new science of planning* (R. L. King, ed.); Chicago: American Marketing Association, 441–448, 7D.

J. W. L. Winder: see N. K. Choudry.

A. W. Winikoff, 1967. *Eye movements as an aid to protocol analysis of problem solving behavior*. Doctoral dissertation, Carnegie-Mellon University, MA.

C. B. Winsten: see M. Beckmann.

J. A. Winter, 1953. Thinking in men and machines. *Astounding Science Fiction*, 51(6): 146–160, MA.

J. O. Wisdom, 1951. The hypothesis of cybernetics. *British Journal for the Philosophy of Science*, 2(5): 1–24, MA.

J. O. Wisdom, R. J. Spilsbury, and D. M. MacKay, 1952. Symposium: mentality in machines. *Men and machines* (Aristotelian Society Supplementary Volume 26); London: Harrison, 1–86, MA.

D. A. Wismer, 1967. On the uses of industrial dynamic models. *Operations Research*, 14(4): 752–767, 7D.

M. Wohl, 1960. Simulation—its application to traffic engineering: Part I. *Traffic Engineering*, 30(11): 13–17 and 29, MG.

M. Wohl, 1960. Simulation—its application to traffic engineering: Part II. *Traffic Engineering*, 31(1): 19–25 and 56. 7D.

H. O. A. Wold: see P. C. Mahalanobis.

H. O. A. Wold, 1965. A graphic introduction to stochastic processes. *Bibliography on time series and stochastic processes* (H. O. A. Wold, ed.); Edinburgh: Oliver and Boyd, 7–76, MS.

J. J. Wolf: see A. I. Siegel.

H. Wolfe: see S. Barnoon.

H. B. Wolfe: see R. F. Meyer and see I. M. Robinson.

H. B. Wolfe, 1967. Model of San Francisco housing market. *Socio-Economic Planning Sciences, 1*(1): 71–95, 4D.

R. W. Wolff, 1965. Problems of statistical inference for birth and death queuing models. *Operations Research, 13*(3): 343–357, MS.

G. Wolford and G. H. Bower, 1969. Continuity theory revisited: rejected for the wrong reasons? *Psychological Review, 76*(5): 515–518, 2C.

J. Wolpert: see J. D. Herniter.

J. Wolpert, 1966. A regional simulation model of information diffusion. *Public Opinion Quarterly, 30*(4): 597–608, 1D.

S. Y. Wong, 1956. Traffic simulation with a digital computer. *Joint Computer Conference, Western Proceedings, 9*: 92–94, 7C.

T. H. Wonnacott: see T. H. Naylor and see J. P. Kleijnen.

W. W. Woodbury, 1951. Monte Carlo calculations. *Seminar on scientific computation, November, 1949, Proceedings* (IBM Applied Science Department and C. C. Hurd, eds.); New York: International Business Machines, 17–18, MC.

D. E. Wooldridge, 1963. *The machinery of the brain.* New York: McGraw-Hill, MA.

D. E. Wooldridge, 1968. *Mechanical man.* New York: McGraw-Hill, MA.

R. Wooldridge, 1962. Monte Carlo methods. *An introduction to computing*; London: Oxford University Press, 169–175, MC.

H. J. Wootton and B. V. Martin, 1966. Travel patterns in London 1962–1981. *Traffic Engineering & Control, 8*(4): 200–207, 7C.

H. J. Wootton and G. W. Pick, 1967. A model for trips generated by households. *Journal of Transport Economics and Policy, 1*(2): 137–153, 2C.

H. J. Wootton and G. W. Pick, 1967. Travel estimates from census data. *Traffic Engineering & Control, 9*(3): 142–145 and 152, 3C.

A. Woroniak: see D. L. Spencer.

R. D. Worrall, 1963. Simulation of traffic behavior on a digital computer. *Traffic Engineering & Control, 5*(2): 86–90 and 94, 2D.

P. M. Wortman, 1966. Representation and strategy in diagnostic problem solving. *Human Factors, 8*(1): 48–53, 8A.

J. B. Wright: see H. H. Goode.

P. H. Wright: see J. N. Thomasson, Jr.

Z. Wünsch and M. Valach, 1967. Attempt at experimental approach to some general problems of biocybernetical organization of the central nervous system. *Fourth international congress on cybernetics*; Namur, Belgium: Association Internationale de Cybernétique, 589–600. 4A.

J. K. Wyatt, 1964. What is simulation? *Data and Control, 2*(2): 20–21, MG.

W. H. Wynn, 1966. *An information-processing model of certain aspects of paired-associate learning.* Doctoral dissertation, Carnegie-Mellon University, 3C.

S. Yagil, 1963. Generation of input data for simulations. *IBM Systems Journal, 2*(September-December): 288–296, MS.

S. Yagil, 1968. Simulation of computer program distribution. *Digest of the second conference on applications of simulation* (A. Ockene, ed.); New York: Institute of Electrical and Electronic Engineers, Publication No. 68C60SIM, 249–253, 5C.

J. V. Yance, 1960. A model of price flexibility. *American Economic Review, 50*(3): 401–418, 2D.

N. V. Yarovitskii, 1966. Modeling of discrete systems on probabilistic automata. *Cybernetics, 2*(5): 27–33, MG.

M. H. Yeates: see E. J. Taaffe.

F. A. Yett: see J. F. Cogswell.

F. A. Yett, 1965. The simulation of management decisions for professional staff control. *Journal of Educational Measurement, 2*(1): 19–22, 7D.

V. H. Yngve, 1960. A model and an hypothesis for language structure. *Proceedings of the American Philosophical Society, 104*(5): 444–466, 8C.

V. H. Yngve, 1961. The depth hypothesis. *Structure of language and its mathematical aspects (Proceedings of symposia in applied mathematics, Volume 12,* R. Jakobson, ed.); Providence: American Mathematical Society, 130–138, 6A.

V. H. Yngve, 1966. Models of language users. *Seminar on computational linguistics* (A. W. Pratt, A. H. Roberts, and K. Lewis, eds.); Bethesda, Md.: National Institutes of Health, Public Health Service Publication 1716, 91–96, MA.

D. B. Yntema and L. Klem, 1965. Telling a computer how to evaluate multidimensional situations. *IEEE Transactions on Man-Machine Systems, MMS-6*(1): 3–13, 3A.

D. B. Yntema and W. S. Torgerson, 1961. Man-computer cooperation in decisions requiring common sense. *IEEE Transactions on Man-Machine Systems, MMS-2*(1): 20–26, MA.

W. P. Yohe: see J. M. Boughton.

G. F. Young: see G. T. Lathrop.

J. Z. Young, 1964. *A model of the brain.* London: Oxford University Press, MA.

J. Z. Young, 1966. *The memory system of the brain.* London: Oxford University Press. MA.

R. S. Yuill, 1964. *A simulation study of barrier effects in spatial diffusion problems.* Working paper, Northwestern University Department of Geography, Research Report No. 5, 4C.

J. A. Yurow, 1967. Analysis and computer simulation of the production and distribution systems of a tufted carpet mill. *Journal of Industrial Engineering, 18*(1): 135–140, 5D.

M. N. Zald and R. Schliewen, 1968. Ethno-methodology and simulation of organizational decision making. *Simulation in the study of politics* (W. D. Coplin, ed); Chicago: Markham, 227–233, MA.

S. Y. Zaslavskii, 1965. The structure of one type of associative net. *Cybernetics, 1*(3): 42–45, MA.

H. Zeigler: see M. A. Baer.

K. Zelin: see G. Gordon.

A. Zellner: see H. R. Hamilton.

A. Zellner, 1965. Estimation of parameters in simulation models of social systems. *Computer methods in the analysis of large-scale social systems* (J. M. Beshers, ed.); Cambridge: MIT-Harvard Joint Center for Urban Studies, 97–116, MS.

H. Zemanek, H. Kretz, and A. J. Angyan, 1961. A model for neurophysiological functions. *Information theory* (C. Cherry, ed.); London: Butterworths, 270–284, 4A.

P. Ziff, 1959. The feelings of robots. *Analysis, 19*(3): 64–68, MA.

J. R. Zimmerman: see D. L. Katz.

R. E. Zimmerman, 1956. A Monte Carlo model for military analysis. *Operations research for management, Volume* II (J. F. McCloskey and J. M. Coppinger, eds.); Baltimore: Johns Hopkins Press, 376–400, 7B.

R. E. Zimmerman, 1960. Simulation of tactical war games. *Operations research and systems engineering* (C. D. Flagle, W. H. Huggins, and R. H. Roy, eds.); Baltimore: Johns Hopkins Press, 711–762, 8D.

R. E. Zimmerman and J. F. Kraft, 1957. *CARMONETTE: a concept of tactical war games.* Working paper, Johns Hopkins University Operations Research Office, Staff Paper ORO-SP-33, AD-204089, 7B.

R. E. Zimmerman, G. Cramer, and E. Joseph, 1956. *Monte Carlo computer war gaming (U): a feasibility study.* Working paper, Johns Hopkins University Operations Research Office, Technical Memorandum ORO-T-325, AD-94459, 7B.

M. Zinn, 1965. *The use of computers in the media selection process.* Working paper, The Diebold Group, MC.

A. Zivian: see J. W. Gyr.

M. Zonis: see C. C. Abt.

M. Zymelman, 1963. *The cotton textile cycle: its nature and trend.* Washington: U. S. Department of Commerce, 2D.

M. Zymelman, 1965. A stabilization policy for the cotton textile cycle. *Management Science, 11*(5): 572–580, 2D.

M. Zymelman, 1968. Analog simulation of an elementary school system in a developing country—some policy implications. *Comparative Education Review, 12*(2): 149–158, 5D.

3

SIMULATION MODEL CONSTRUCTION

JOHN M. DUTTON

WARREN G. BRIGGS

INTRODUCTION

This paper defines descriptive computer simulation of human behavior and then describes the construction of such a simulation model. Although terms are defined briefly and the goals of the method are discussed, the main approach is to use examples whenever possible. Two straight-forward illustrations of behavior simulations are presented—the first, a deterministic model of an individual operating in an organizational environment, and the second, a probabilistic model carrying the flavor of interactions among people in a complex setting. Guidelines are offered for determining when simulation is appropriate and the paper concludes with a summary of the steps in a simulation study.

The literature offers various definitions of simulation. Most of these are in conflict because different writers refer to different object phenomena—like the proverbial nine blind men and the elephant. Some phenomenal objects are random; others are determined; some are inputs to a system; others are outputs, and still others are internal parts of the process. We simply propose that computer simulation is a representation of something. How something is represented is partly a function of what

it is, partly a function of convenience, and partly of the researcher's view of things.

People who question whether a simulation really duplicates what it represents fall into the trap of believing that "the symbol is the territory" [6]. A simulation obviously is not the real thing since, by definition, it cannot be. The researcher must not try to make the simulation look exactly like the real thing because if the simulation is as complicated as the real process it represents, it will be no more comprehensible than the real process is.

The computer simulation researcher needs to be particularly watchful of the complexity dilemma. If he hopes to understand complex behavior, he must construct complex models, but the more complex the model, the harder it is to understand. The power of the computer simulation is that it permits the researcher to build great verisimilitude into the model. But, as more than one user has realized while sadly contemplating his convoluted handiwork, he can easily construct a computer model that is *more* complicated than the real thing. Since science is to make things simpler, such results can be demoralizing as well as self-defeating.

Let us turn now to specific issues that arise in constructing a computer simulation of human behavior. Such issues include: finding a problem, representing an object phenomenon, choosing a method for explication, deciding what constitutes description and explanation, and achieving validation.

FINDING A PROBLEM

Simulation of behavior begins with the definition of a human problem—easier said than done. For though the path of science is lighted by good problems, such problems seldom drop like apples from a tree—they have to be picked and sorted. Sometimes the searcher gets hold of something, sometimes he doesn't. Newton was not only a bright guy, but also a lucky one.

So the effort doesn't *start* with a problem, but rather with a situation that looks interesting to study. Let's reach up and get one and find out what can be done with it. Suppose we found ourselves watching the following scene:

> We are observing a place called a "factory." What is that? Supposing the term is not familiar to us; it conveys no information. We decide to watch for a while to see if we can learn something. Watching from outside, we see movement to and from this place. People come and go, with movement concentrated at certain times. Materials are brought in, and different materials are taken away.
>
> It seems a curious place, this factory. What could be going on inside? We go in. There are many machines and people. Much movement is taking place; it is a hive of activity. Gradually we begin to see order and purpose in the events before us. We walk from one end of the factory to the other. We note that incoming materials are transformed by stages until they take the form of outgoing materials.
>
> The transformation is accomplished by a complicated interplay of men and machines. Some people tend machines, others move materials, others watch over events, and still others make records of what goes on and then pore over this information. We are close to one such record keeper. He is talking out loud to himself about what he is doing. His words seem like a set of arguments about his work. He says:
>
>> I'm supposed to keep track of the different types of material for this department.

> The rule book says each month I should look at the quantity on hand for each type of material. Each type has a minimum supply level. When the quantity is below this level, I'm supposed to order more. The rule book gives the new amount to order for each type of material.
>
>> But I've found I get in trouble if I follow the rule book exactly. Sometimes I end up with a lot of material we don't use. Other times we run short.
>
>> So I've added some rules of my own. When a material is moving slowly and we're not much under the minimum supply level, sometimes I don't order more. After all, there is a cushion built into the reorder level. On the other hand, if a material gets hot I've found I'd better order—even if the supply is not down to the minimum—or I will run out [2].

We look over the fellow's shoulder. We see the information in Table 1 written on his supply record. What problems could be stated about this situation? Do these problems have some importance or interest and, if so, would simulation provide a method for attacking them?

WHAT IS A SIMULATION OF BEHAVIOR?

The term "simulation of behavior" as used here may be defined more precisely in terms of the conditions it must satisfy. These conditions are that it:

(i) Examines a behavior process.

(ii) Gives a theory which describes and explains the process without ambiguity.[1]

(iii) Shows how the process is affected by its environment.

(iv) Be formulated in such a way that inferences about the process may be verified by observation.

The question of what constitutes a behavior process still remains to be clarified, however. Such a process has the following properties: It undergoes transformation through time. The

[1] The process itself may, however, contain ambiguity. If it does, a precise description of this ambiguity will be a necessary and acceptable part of the explanation.

TABLE 1 Supply Record Information and Actions of Supply Man During One Review Period

Supply item number	Past six month's usage					Last month	Supply record information					
							Amount on hand	Amount on order	Average monthly usage	Reorder level	Recommended order quantity	Action taken by supply man
1	308	260	271	240	305	251	800	0	253	750	750	None
2	450	470	530	520	551	530	1251	0	500	1200	1000	Order 1000
3	461	470	430	505	449	461	1010	0	450	1000	1250	None
4	980	1010	990	1050	1150	1300	2002	1000	1000	2500	3000	Order 2500
5	451	443	480	470	421	430	977	0	500	1000	1000	None
6	753	761	780	742	695	770	1470	0	760	1500	2000	Order 2000
7	2053	2200	1930	2550	2110	2090	6073	2000	2100	8000	10,000	None
8	650	623	585	610	570	550	1238	0	600	1250	4000	None
9	421	438	450	512	483	491	1053	500	400	1000	1500	Order 1000
10	360	371	328	355	339	361	1020	0	350	1000	1500	None

transformation depends partly on the initial state of the environment and the subsequent responses within the behavior process. The process may operate on its environment as well as being determined by it.

SIMULATION OF A MATERIAL CONTROL CLERK

Let's look at our factory material control clerk again, but this time from his viewpoint. Following the example of Fritz Roethlisberger, let's ask three questions. What is the situation asking of the person? What does the person bring to the situation? What is the resulting behavior process [11]?

What is the situation asking of the person? The clerk is asked to keep supply levels. At what level? Not too high and not too low. Too high means that he has flooded storage with unneeded material. We can infer that he realizes this is costly. But probably more importantly, he knows that lots of other people realize it too. Since he is a social animal, this may mean as much or more to him than abstract costs. On the other hand, too little supply can have equally dramatic consequences for his work situation. If he runs out of stock, he knows quite vividly that people leave his storeroom empty-handed and generally rather upset.

What human needs and expectation does the material control clerk bring to the situation? He aligns himself with the goals of the factory and the expectations of his associates at work. And, being an information processer, he uses these goals to measure his present situation and to respond. Gradually he adapts to it by finding rules, to maintain what he sees as a desirable state of affairs [3, 9].

Our simulation problem thus becomes the following: Let us determine the goals and rules the material control clerk uses to make his replenishment decisions. Then, let us construct a computer program that will apply these rules as the subject does, and thus reproduce his decisions. To do this, we must state the supply man's rules in the order he seems to use them.

A rule is something that is applied to a state of affairs; how it is applied depends on what state is observed. For example, we hear our stock clerk say, "Oh, it's twelve o'clock!" In

rule form what he means is: "When I observe it's noon, I should stop work and go to lunch." The clerk's going to lunch is conditional on his observing the hands of the clock at noon. In conditional form the statements are: If the clock shows noon, then go eat lunch. If not, continue working.

Such statements can be written in words, but it is more convenient to put them in the form of a flow diagram, which shows at a glance the chain of events and permits conditional branches to be represented easily. When the process contains many steps and branches that go back to previous steps, word descriptions become complicated.

Let's summarize our task. We shall attempt to represent the material supply man's behavior as (i) a set of goals, (ii) a set of possible states, and (iii) a set of rules to reduce the difference between a given state and the goals associated with that state [12]. We may now say the following about the material control clerk's goals, states, and rules:

(i)   His major goals with respect to supply levels are—
   Do not run out.
   Do not get flooded with material.
   Minimize cost of replenishment action.
(ii)   The states he encounters are—
   Level is low.
   Level is high.
   Level is satisfactory.
(iii)   His rules are—
   When level is low, order more material.
   When level is satisfactory or higher, do not order.

His process seems to be first to look at the level for a type of material, next to compare that level with the goal level, next to decide whether an order for more material is to be placed, and then, to go on to the next material. His behavior is "look," "process," "look," "process," . . . Figure 1 shows these major steps, in flow chart form, for each material.

Now all this may seem obvious because we've looked at what he does. But there are many *other* ways he could behave, had we cared to speculate. He might look at all the types of material and then process all the types. Or he might look at several. Or he might merely

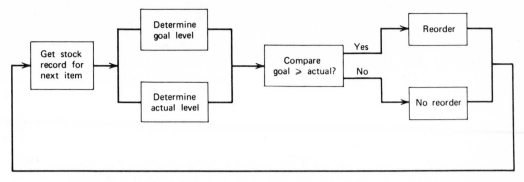

Figure 1 Material control clerk's major steps in deciding whether to order more material.

estimate quantities without looking at all. Or he might look at some, using these to estimate others. And so on *ad infinitum.*

In science, such detailed observation can save a lot of time. Theory can take you only so far. At some point, we must adjust the microscope and look at what is going on. When we look, we find our man does things in particular ways, and that our description is still far too general. The definitions of his goals, perceived states, and rules need sharpening. To construct a computer simulation program, we must make explicit comparisons between numbers. The numbers may represent symbols or quantities, but a computer can manipulate only numbers. Thus we need to assign numbers to both the symbolic and the numeric parts of his processes.

Let us begin by defining more precisely some of the terms in the flow chart (Figure 1). The clerk seems to begin analysis for each item by the obvious step of inspecting the level of material on hand. Less obvious is what goal he compares with this quantity. Perhaps we can infer something from what he says. He is aware of the rule to order when the level on hand falls below the reorder or goal level. Yet, he says he cannot follow this rule blindly, even though it is a useful beginning point to *compare the level on hand to the rule book reorder level.*

Although he now has a rough approximation of whether an order should be placed, we know this does not satisfy him. Subsequent steps are needed for each of two branches from the first comparison. Consider first the branch that finds current level below rule book reorder level. He

reports that he does not always order when this occurs, but that he also considers the recent rate of usage and the amount of the difference between the actual and the reorder levels. Moreover, it seems that at this point he would look at what he had on order, since this represents an expected addition to the actual supply. We hypothesize the following steps:

Look whether an amount is on order for this item.

If so, compare current and average usage rates.

If not, compare on hand to current rate of usage to find depletion date.

We decide to gather additional data to confirm or discredit our speculations. Thus we ask our clerk to submit to an experiment, wherein we hold out certain information our budding theory says the clerk will wish to have: (1) level on hand, (2) rule book reorder level, (3) current usage rate, (4) average usage rate, and (5) amount on order.

The experiment is designed to test two major conditions: (i) when level on hand exceeds rule book level and (ii) when rule book level exceeds level on hand. Ten trials are prepared for each condition, the clerk is instructed to follow his usual procedures and to request information when he needs it, and a record is kept of what information he requests and when. The results are given in Table 2.

We thus obtain added, experimental evidence for the previously hypothesized initial steps in his program, which measure the supply man's goals versus his current state, and can now

TABLE 2 Results of Controlled Experiment Performed by Clerk

| | Condition one Level on hand exceeds rule book level[a] | | | | | | Condition two Rule book level exceeds level on hand[a] | | | | |
| | Information requested | | | | | | Information requested | | | | |
Sequence of requests	(1)	(2)	(3)	(4)	(5)	Sequence of requests	(1)	(2)	(3)	(4)	(5)
1	10	0	0	0	0	1	10	0	0	0	0
2	0	10	0	0	0	2	0	10	0	0	0
3	0	0	10	0	0	3	0	0	0	0	10
4	0	0	0	10	0	4	0	0	0	0	0

[a] Table entries are frequencies of occurrence in 10 trials for each condition.

further interpret his behavior. The experimental results confirm a model with a first step comparison of level on hand with rule book reorder level. They also suggest that he goes beyond the rule book and adds criteria from his own experience in deciding whether to order. The experiment data also indicate other behavior such as that:

His procedure is highly invariant.

His program contains two major branches from the first step comparison of actual to rule book level.

Further information required by his program is conditional on which of the two branches is taken.

Similar interview data and experimental results permit still further specification of the offshoots growing from the two branches of the initial step, compare level on hand to rule book level. Finally, each branch terminates in one of the clerk's three observable actions: (i) do not order, (ii) order regular amount, and (iii) order less than regular amount. The following four conditional rules illustrate the supply man's behavior on one branch from the initial step:

When level on hand is below reorder level, an amount is on order, and usage is not up—do not order.

When level on hand is below reorder level, an amount is on order, and usage is up—order less than regular amount.

When level on hand is below reorder level, no amount is on order, and depletion date is not early—do not order.

When level on hand is below reorder level, no amount is on order, and depletion date is early—order regular amount.

The entire program may be verbalized in this manner. But a more efficient description is a flow chart and a computer program. Figure 2 gives a detailed flow chart and a FORTRAN source program for the supply clerk ordering decisions. This program and the foregoing show the clerk, at a gross behavior level, functioning as a buffer between demand and supply for material.

Our next step is to test the program against actual data. Figure 3 gives two comparisons of the program with actual data: first, a comparison of subject and program *outputs*; and, second, a record of the *internal* processes of the program as it encountered different material supply conditions, with its characteristic responses compared to the subject's.

The program does well on both comparisons. But it is now necessary to consider what constitutes a satisfactory computer simulation of human behavior. To be at least a satisfactory explanation of his behavior, the program's output should agree with the supply clerk's when operated on fresh data (first examined after the program was constructed).

Now assume that the program performs well on such fresh data. Can it now be said we have captured "the" theory for the supply man? No, it cannot.

On philosophical grounds, any theory is, by definition, incomplete [10]. But even so, other explanations may be more parsimonious or fundamental in their explanation than ours or may take into account conditions not considered in the present formulation. Whether other conditions should be included in the theory depends on two factors: (i) whether the objective is a *descriptive* or a *prescriptive* model and (ii) whether the additional conditions can be justified.

In a descriptive model the objective is to state how the behavior *does* occur given an *internal* criterion. In a prescriptive model, the objective is to state what behavior *should* occur to meet an *external* criterion, say, cost. Some studies have the first goal and others, the second. The present supply clerk model happens to have the first.

The justification factor applies to both descriptive and prescriptive studies, but in slightly

different ways. In descriptive models only necessary inferences and those most consistent with the evidence are made. We could make the descriptive model more complex, but only if by doing so we would improve the reliability or psychological content of the model and only if evidence were found for the added operations. Our goal was to represent the essentials of the stock clerk's behavior, and no more. For instance, we gave no consideration to whether the supply man might take the cost of a supply item into account. Furthermore our model took the average usage figure given and did not ask where it came from or how it might be modified; current usage was defined as last month's usage and no earlier patterns were examined.

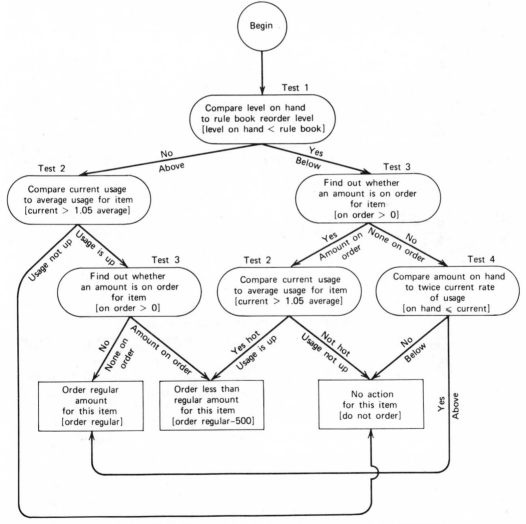

Figure 2 Supply clerk's decision rules for ordering more material. *Note:* Constants based on empirical data obtained from stock records and subject.

```
$10   1608*2*10**DUTTON*
$EXECUTE      PUFFT
PUFFT VERSION 11/01/67
      REAL NO,NOACT
      DIMENSION TEST1(10),TEST2(10),TEST3(10),TEST4(10),ACTION(10),
     1RECQTY(10),PACT(10)
      DATA YES,NO,NOACT,REDUCE,REGULR,BLANK/3HYES    ,3H NO    ,6HNO ACT,
     16HREDUCE,6FREGULR,6H *
      WRITE(6,44)
   44 FORMAT('1')
      DO 1 I=1,10
      TEST1(I) = BLANK
      TEST2(I) = BLANK
      TEST3(I) = BLANK
    1 TEST4(I) = BLANK
      DO 40 I=1,10
      READ(5,2)ITEM,USE6,ONHAND,ONORD,AVUSE,REORD,RECQTY(I),ACTION(I)
    2 FORMAT(I6,30X,6F6.0,2X,A6)
      IF(ONHAND.LT.REORD)GO TO 3
      TEST1(I)=NO
      IF(USE6.LT.(1.05*AVUSE))GO TO 20
      TEST2(I)=YES
      IF(ONORD)30,30,25
    3 TEST1(I)=YES
      IF(ONORD)5,5,4
    4 TEST3(I) = YES
      IF(USE6-(1.05*AVUSE))20,20,25
    5 TEST3(I)=NO
      IF(ONHAND-(2.*USE6))29,29,19
   20 TEST2(I)=NO
   21 QUANT =0
      PACT(I)=NOACT
      GO TO 40
   19 TEST4(I)=YES
      GO TO 21
   25 TEST2(I)=YES
      TEST3(I) = YES
      QUANT = RECQTY(I)-500.
      PACT(I)=REDUCE
      GO TO 40
   29 TEST4(I) = NO
   30 TEST3(I) = NO
      QUANT = RECQTY(I)
      PACT(I) = REGULR
   40 WRITE(6,41)ITEM,QUANT
   41 FORMAT(/' ACTION FOR ITEM',I4,' IS ORDER AMOUNT'F6.0)
      WRITE(6,42)(I,TEST1(I),TEST2(I),TEST3(I),TEST4(I),RECQTY(I),
     1ACTION(I),FACT(I),I=1,10)
   42 FORMAT('1'30X,'SUMMARY TABLE OF CONDITIONS ENCOUNTERED IN PROGRAM'
     X //' ITEM      ON HAND      CURRENT USAGE    AMOUNT        ON HAND'
     XABOVE     RECOMMENDED    SUPPLY MANS    PROGRAMS'/7X,           '
     XBELOW ON ORDER   ABOVE AVERAGE    ON ORDER     2 * CURRENT USAGE  ORD
     XER CUANTITY     ACTION        ACTION'//
     X(I4,9X,A6,10X,A6,7X,A6,10X,A6,11X,F6.0,8X,A6,6X,A6/))
      WRITE(6,43)
   43 FORMAT(  //'              *  TEST NOT NECESSARY'/'1')
      STOP
      END
```

→ **Figure 2 (continued)** Fortran source program for simulation model of supply clerk.

Figure 3 Output of simulation model of supply clerk compared with data.
↓

```
ACTION FOR ITEM    1 IS ORDER AMOUNT    0.
ACTION FOR ITEM    2 IS ORDER AMOUNT 1000.
ACTION FOR ITEM    3 IS ORDER AMOUNT    0.
ACTION FOR ITEM    4 IS ORDER AMOUNT 2500.
ACTION FOR ITEM    5 IS ORDER AMOUNT    0.
ACTION FOR ITEM    6 IS ORDER AMOUNT 2000.
ACTION FOR ITEM    7 IS ORDER AMOUNT    0.
ACTION FOR ITEM    8 IS ORDER AMOUNT    0.
ACTION FOR ITEM    9 IS ORDER AMOUNT 1000.
ACTION FOR ITEM   10 IS ORDER AMOUNT    0.
```

SUMMARY TABLE OF CONDITIONS ENCOUNTERED IN PROGRAM

ITEM	ON HAND BELOW ON ORDER	CURRENT USAGE ABOVE AVERAGE	AMOUNT ON ORDER	ON HAND ABOVE 2 * CURRENT USAGE	RECOMMENDED ORDER QUANTITY	SUPPLY MANS ACTION	PROGRAMS ACTION
1	NO	NO	*	*	750.	NO ACT	NO ACT
2	NO	YES	NO	*	1000.	REGULR	REGULR
3	NO	NO	*	*	1250.	NO ACT	NO ACT
4	YES	YES	YES	*	3000.	REDUCE	REDUCE
5	YES	*	NO	YES	1000.	NO ACT	NO ACT
6	YES	*	NO	NO	2000.	REGULR	REGULR
7	YES	NO	YES	*	10000.	NO ACT	NO ACT
8	YES	*	NO	YES	4000.	NO ACT	NO ACT
9	NO	YES	YES	*	1500.	REDUCE	REDUCE
10	NO	NO	*	*	1500.	NO ACT	NO ACT

          * TEST NOT NECESSARY

We omitted such elements because no evidence was obtained from historical records, interviews, or experiments to suggest that they were part of the supply man's behavior.

The justification of complexity in a prescriptive model does not depend, as in the descriptive model, on evidence or necessary inference but on how much complexity is necessary for the model to achieve the external criterion. If four costs contribute significantly to a total prescriptive cost criterion, the omission of one will be serious.

Both descriptive and prescriptive studies, however, have in common a sensitivity to one issue, the issue of marginal value versus marginal cost. Factors that add undue complication to the model or that involve heavy added research efforts, yielding little of descriptive or prescriptive usefulness, are questionable.

VARIETY VERSUS COMMONALITY ACROSS SIMULATION MODELS

Given the variety of explanations possible for the supply man's behavior, we might ask how likely it is that several independent researchers would agree. In this particular instance, we can compare the results of the work of 20 relatively naive, independent analysts on three criteria: (i) the analysts' apparent goals; (ii) the representation of the supply man's behavior; and (iii) inferences made about the supply man's goals and decision rules.

The analysts in this experiment were graduate

TABLE 3   Summary of the Work of 20 Analysts on the Supply Man's Behavior[a]

I. Apparent goals			
To understand supply man			70%[b]
To analyze value of supply man's rules for factory			35%
To infer character of demand environment			30%
To invent best possible supply rules			20%
II. Representation of supply man's behavior			
Serial process	75%	As few steps as possible	95%
Parallel process	20%	More steps than necessary	0%
Not clear	5%	Not clear	5%
	——		——
	100%		100%
III. What goals and rules were offered to explain supply man's decisions?			
A. Apparent goals:			
None apparent in program or discussion			70%
Low inventory but do not run out			30%
Minimum cost			5%
Minimum time spent on supply decisions			5%
B. Decision rules:			
Comparison of current and average usage			100%
Comparison of level on hand to reorder point			95%
Consideration of amount on order			30%
Usage time perspective: two months			40%
six months			35%
one month			15%
three months			5%

[a] Source: Data from computer programs written by 20 independent student analysts.
[b] Percentage figures may not total 100%, since choices are not mutually exclusive.

students in business administration. They were instructed to use the evidence given and to find a computer program that described how the supply clerk was making his decisions. Table 3 reveals that the objective of most of these student analysts was to represent the subject's viewpoint. But a sizable number, in addition, projected their own perceptions of his task.

The analysts could choose between a serial (sequential) or parallel (simultaneous) representation of the subject's behavior.[2] The summary shows, however, that the majority of models contained serial assumptions, which said the subject dealt with small pieces of his world one after the other.

The 20 analyst's programs also made common inferences regarding the supply man's operating goals and decision rules. As a result of two factors, the analysts devoted more attention to explicating the subject's decision rules than his goals: First, the available data on the subject's goals were relatively meagre and thus his rules were more easily inferred than were his constellation of goals. Second, when analysts took the objective of constructing a prescriptive (normative) model, their programs contained substituted goals. Of the goals assigned to the subject, the analysts preferred a combination of low supply level and depletion prevention supply conditions.

The high attention to inferred subject decision rules focused on four supply-level factors —major comparison measures, an adaptive buffer-level, range of historical usage values examined, and order quantities. On 85 percent of the occasions, comparison of current to average usage or level on hand versus reorder level occurred as a first or second step in the program. All but two programs incorporated an adaptive buffer-level rule. Fifty-five percent of the programs confined their view of current trends to the last 1 or 2 months and 85 percent modified the recommended order quantity by either 500 units or by selecting the reorder level amount (either rule fitted the data exactly).

We conclude that independent analysts arrive at similar results in descriptive simulation of a behavior process, even though many alternative representative models for the process can be constructed—a result that may indicate equal ignorance rather than equal insight, although at least it demonstrates that a variety of people, without extensive prior training in simulation,

can see something the same way. Thus the method can produce similar results across users, as a scientific method should.

DETERMINISTIC AND PROBABILISTIC PROPERTIES OF SIMULATION MODELS

Let's look at our model of the supply man objectively and reflect on its major properties. It focuses on a behavior process, something that occurs in a systematic and repeated way through time. The process is goal directed and rule ordered and appears to contribute to the maintenance of a symbiotic relationship between a member of an organization and his environment. The model tends to be organized around three types of behavior—input, process, and output. The general flow of behavior can be expressed thus:

Observe stimuli → Process stimuli
→ Produce a response

Such properties appear common to many simulation models of ongoing processes. It is not so much that simulation models have revealed such properties for the first time— although much of the literature on behavior has tended to ignore its systematic character—but rather that construction of a computer simulation model permits the researcher to state operational theory for the content of systematic, self-organized, and self-regulating behavior patterns.

One feature absent from our supply man model is the treatment of any part of his behavior as a chance or probabilistic event. Rather, all his behavior is seen as completely predictable or deterministic, once his decision rules and the supply records are known.

For at least two reasons, it is often interesting and desirable, however, *not* to represent all events in a simulation model as certain: First, some events that impinge on behavior may be random or probabilistic, and thus a *theoretical goal* of the model may be to represent behavior under such uncertain environmental or internal conditions. Second, it may be *convenient* to represent a process as a distribution of events, which occur with some probability. For example, events such as a baseball batter's being walked, striking out, or getting a hit depend on an

---

[2] Whereas the digital computer necessarily does one thing at a time, a program can be constructed to approximate a parallel process. For example, separate parallel processes can be represented, and such processes can then be incremented by a small amount either at random or in some prescribed order.

enormously complicated process of behavior, involving not only pitcher and hitter but other players, coaches, fans, the park, and the weather. In principle, such behavior may be largely deterministic, but to build a deterministic model completely explicating a baseball game would be enormously difficult, if not impossible. One of the authors has built a simulation model of baseball, and we reproduce it here to illustrate a *probabilistic* model of behavior.

BASEBALL-O-MATION—A Probabilistic Model of Behavior [1]

Introduction

The Great American Game of baseball can, from an objective viewpoint, be considered as a discrete, probabilistic process following rather specific rules. A myriad of statistics are gathered on major league play and, from these, some useful, relative frequencies can be deduced for application to a Monte Carlo simulation of the game.

A comprehensive computer simulation model for the play of many games between two particular teams estimates the most significant of these step-to-step probabilities. The model considers actual player and pitcher histories, adjusted for the particular situation of ballpark dimensions and also for the same or different handedness of batter and pitcher. A specific example is illustrated for simulated play between the Boston Red Sox and New York Yankees in Fenway Park. This simulation model, in spite of some simplifying assumptions, can be used for establishing relative likelihoods of either team winning, for evaluating the effect of different pitchers, or for examining player trades. It can also be used to evaluate different game strategies such as hit-and-run, bunts, stealing, batting orders, etc. This latter may be accomplished by simulating several sets of games between the same players, but using different strategies—a comparison not possible without simulation, since it is impossible to repeat a real game with only one thing changed, namely, the strategy being evaluated.

Simulating Uncertainty. Simulation is especially appropriate for problems that involve numerous probability calculations. Models conventionally represent the uncertainty of events by mathematical expression for probability distributions, such as the exponential distribution of time between calls for maintenance service. A great deal of realism can be built into a simulation model that considers un-

certainty as the historical relative frequency of a set of events.

The significant effect of uncertainty is sometimes overlooked when "best estimates" or averages instead of the full distribution are used. If the average time for a certain activity in the system is 10 minutes, it does not follow that only this average should be entered into the model. What about those instances that are absorbed into the average where the activity was performed in 5 minutes or 15 minutes? The practical consequence of such variability around an average can be readily observed. A barber shop set up to serve eight customers an hour will often have customers waiting, even though customers arrive at an average of only five an hour. In reality the number who do arrive in a particular hour may be more or less than the average, with unpleasant effects for barbers and customers alike.

A simulation model can include two basic kinds of uncertain elements: discrete probabilistic events and continuous probability distributions. Discrete probabilistic events are definite things that can happen, with assignable probabilities. For example, the uncertain outcome of a contract proposal might be the discrete events "win" or "lose," with assigned subjective probabilities of 0.60 and 0.40. The outcome might instead be a mathematical form for a discrete probability distribution, such as the binomial or the Poisson which would assign probabilities to 0, 1, 2, . . . orders, failures, customer calls, etc. As the name implies, continuous probability distributions describe uncertain values which are not integer numbers. Examples are time, length, cost, etc., which can be described by mathematical forms such as the exponential, Gamma or Normal distributions, or by subjective distributions of any shape. The so-called Monte Carlo technique is used in a simulation program to choose a particular value from either a discrete or continuous probability distribution.

Monte Carlo, as the term is used here, is a means of sampling at random from a given probability distribution. Most computers have a preprogrammed subroutine available to generate random numbers on command through a process that allows every number an equal chance of appearing—just as the famous roulette wheel at the Monte Carlo casino selects winners. This number is then used to sample the probability distribution included in the simulation model to obtain the specific outcome events.

The first step in using this technique is to array the events and the corresponding probabilities so that samples can be drawn with random numbers. The illustration in Figure 4 presents an example of one such array of data: The continuous probability distribution of the cost to complete a contract, plotted from a series of subjective probability estimates.

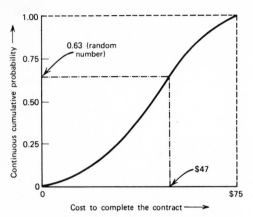

Figure 4 Continuous Probability Distribution Curve.

The next step in Monte Carlo sampling is to generate, or select, from a table a random number. This number is placed against the cumulative probability distribution, and the corresponding event or value is selected. Suppose the random number

found was 63 (defined as 0.63 on the probability scale). In the continuous probability distribution plot, we find that a cumulative probability of 0.63 corresponds to a contract cost outcome of $47.

Data on these probability distributions could be obtained from:

(i) A knowledge of the mechanical chance process (coin tossing).

(ii) Relative frequencies of past experience (defects in a process).

(iii) Subjective probability judgments (the cost to complete a contract).

Baseball as a Probabilistic Process

The Baseball-O-Mation model centers on the duel between pitcher and batter. Each duel leads to one of a number of alternative results. The model depicts the game of baseball as the accumulation of the consequences of a series of these duels. Development of the model involved several major stages. Player histories were required, a flow chart was prepared, a program was written, and, finally, the program was operated. These stages are described in more detail in the following paragraphs.

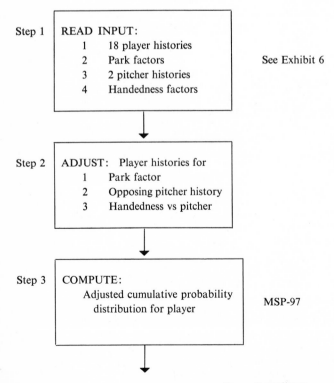

Figure 5 continues

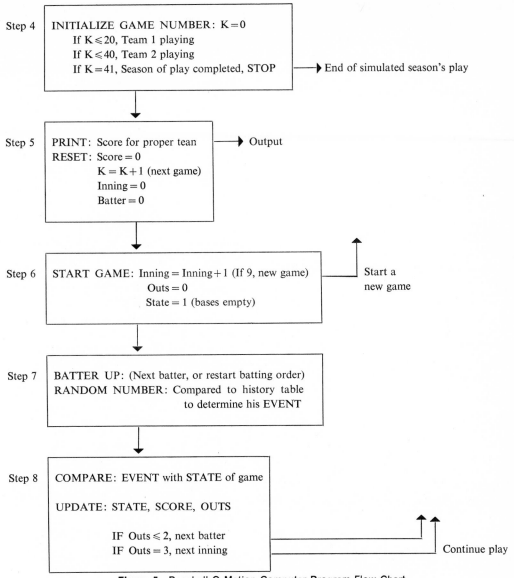

Step 4 | INITIALIZE GAME NUMBER: K = 0
If K ⩽ 20, Team 1 playing
If K ⩽ 40, Team 2 playing
If K = 41, Season of play completed, STOP → End of simulated season's play

Step 5 | PRINT: Score for proper team → Output
RESET: Score = 0
K = K + 1 (next game)
Inning = 0
Batter = 0

Step 6 | START GAME: Inning = Inning + 1 (If 9, new game) — Start a
Outs = 0   new game
State = 1 (bases empty)

Step 7 | BATTER UP: (Next batter, or restart batting order)
RANDOM NUMBER: Compared to history table
to determine his EVENT

Step 8 | COMPARE: EVENT with STATE of game

UPDATE: STATE, SCORE, OUTS

IF Outs ⩽ 2, next batter
IF Outs = 3, next inning   — Continue play

Figure 5 Baseball-O-Mation Computer Program Flow Chart.

Flow Charting

Once player histories are obtained, the next stage in programming Baseball-O-Mation is to develop a flow chart. Figure 5 presents the flow chart developed for a season of simulated baseball games between the Red Sox and the Yankees, together with selected parts of computer inputs, program statements and outputs. Eight major flow chart steps may be summarized as follows:

In Step 1, the program reads in the relevant data about the players and ballpark. A probability distribution for each player indicates the relative past frequency with which he has struck out, hit a home run, and so on. The possible outcome events of a player's appearance at the plate are defined below

as 11 significant events. The ardent sports fan can suggest more, but these are the most important. Figure 6 shows the player histories used for simulated play between the Yankees and Red Sox. For instance, the distribution for Mickey Mantle in terms of these events is shown overleaf.

In Step 2 the computer adjusts these historical probabilities by factors for the ballpark in which the game is being played, the opposing pitcher's performance record, and the relative "handedness" of pitcher versus batter.

Step 3 accumulates the adjusted relative frequencies from each player's history and reflects this information as a cumulative probability table.

Step 4 tells the computer how many games to

At-The-Plate Outcome Event Probability Table

Event	Unadjusted Probability[a] For Mantle	Cumulative Probability
1. Base on balls	.201	.201
2. Strike out	.173	.374
3. Out (not otherwise specified)	.218	.593
4. Sacrifice fly	.045	.637
5. Double play	.111	.748
6. Single (runner advances 1)	.047	.795
7. Single (runner advances 2)	.087	.882
8. Double (runner advances 2)	.023	.905
9. Double (runner advances 3)	.002	.907
10. Triple	.009	.916
11. Home run	.084	1.000
Total	1.000	—

[a] Adjustable for park, pitcher, and "handedness" factors.

play—here 20. The computer plays all the season's innings ($9 \times 20 = 180$ innings) for one team, printing the team's score every nine innings. It then repeats the same process for the second team. Comparative nine-inning scores indicate winners. (Tie scores stand.) An important assumption here is that the relative score does not affect future play.

Steps 5 and 6 initiate a particular game, update the number of innings, and print out the score.

Steps 7 and 8 describe the process by which each batter's event is selected and reflected in the progress of the game.

Program Logic

The next step in the development of the simulation program is to construct the game for computer play, that is to "pitch" to each player on each team, and then assess the results in terms of a box score. The logic employed to play the game is, of course, the very heart of the simulation. In simplified terms, the program logic consists of three parts, run in sequence, as follows:

(i) Generate a random number;
(ii) Determine the individual batter's event; and
(iii) Update the state of the game.

Each of these parts is explored in the following example.

Example: Mantle at the Pseudobat

It's the last of the ninth at Yankee Stadium. Score: Red Sox 1, Yankees 0! With two away and the bases loaded, Mickey Mantle steps to the plate. The program will now use his probability distribution to determine the next outcome event. Thus, Mantle's historical performance is about to be hit by a random number. The simulation program has stored this information in the computer as follows:

INNG 9, BATR 4, NØUT 2, NST 8,

or:

INNG 9 = current inning
BATR 4 = Mantle, in the batting order of the Yankees
NØUT 2 = current number of outs

C　　BASEBALL-Ø-MATIØN, INPUT DATA FØR RED SØX VS YANKEES

C　　BATTING ØRDER HISTØRY FØR BØSTØN RED SØX, 1961 DATA

C		E1	E2	E3	E4	E5	E6	E7	E8	E9	E10	E11**	HND	
RUNNELS	1.	.116	.077	.315	.063	.156	.075	.137	.042	'005	.007	.007	2.00	HIST1
BRESSØUND*	2.	.100	.134	.318	.063	.158	.064	.095	.032	.004	.007	.025	1.00	HIST1
YASTRZEMSKI	3.	.084	.152	.300	.063	.156	.059	.110	.044	.005	.010	.017	2.00	HIST1
PAGLIARØNI	4.	.132	.170	.285	.059	.145	.047	.086	.035	.004	.000	.037	1.00	HIST1
MALZØNE	5.	.074	.077	.346	.073	.182	.065	.122	.030	.003	.006	.022	1.00	HIST1
GEIGER	6.	.145	.151	.288	.058	.145	.048	.090	.031	.004	.010	.030	2.00	HIST1
HARDY	7.	.105	.167	.284	.059	.147	.056	.104	.056	.006	.006	.010	1.00	HIST1
SCHILLING	8.	.111	.104	.328	.066	.164	.064	.119	.031	.003	.003	.007	1.00	HIST1
CØNLEY	9.	.089	.282	.260	.055	.135	.043	.092	.034	.004	.000	.026	1.00	HIST1

* NØTE: "AVERAGE" PLAYER DATA USED FØR BRESSØUND SINCE INADEQUATE MAJØR LEAGUE DATA AVAILABLE

** EVENTS: SEE EXPLANATIØN GIVEN IN TEXT

Figure 6 continues

C BATTING ØRDER FØR NEW YØRK YANKEES, 1961 DATA

C		E1	E2	E3	E4	E5	E6	E7	E8	E9	E10	E11	HND**	
RICHARDSØN	1.	.050	.033	.388	.080	.200	.076	.138	.022	.002	.007	.004	1.00	HIST2
TRESH*	2.	.100	.134	.318	.063	.158	.064	.095	.032	.004	.007	.025	3.00	HIST2
MARIS	3.	.142	.097	.310	.063	.158	.040	.073	.021	.002	.006	.088	2.00	HIST2
MANTLE	4.	.201	.173	.218	.045	.111	.047	.087	.023	.002	.009	.084	3.00	HIST2
REED*	5.	.100	.134	.318	.063	.158	.064	.095	.032	.004	.007	.025	1.00	HIST2
HØWARD	6.	.064	.133	.281	.057	.141	.082	.152	.032	.004	.010	.044	1.00	HIST2
SKØWRØN	7.	.060	.180	.283	.070	.155	.057	.103	.034	.004	.007	.047	1.00	HIST2
BØYER	8.	.116	.149	.315	.064	.160	.047	.088	.030	.003	.009	.019	1.00	HIST2
ARRØYØ	9.	.034	.143	.290	.060	.150	.063	.116	.065	.007	.000	.000	2.00	HIST2

* NØTE: "AVERAGE" PLAYER DATA USED FØR TRESH AND REED SINCE INADEQUATE MAJØR LEAGUE DATA AVAILABLE

** HND CØDE: RIGHT 1.00; LEFT 2.00; SWITCH 3.00

Figure 6 Player History Table

NST 8 = state of the game, the code for bases loaded. (A total of eight different states define all ways of putting zero, one, two or three men on base).

Part 1: Generate a Random Number. A subroutine shown on the attached program listing (Figure 7) generates a three-digit random number and uses it to enter Part 2.

Part 2: Determine Individual Batter's Event. The computer stores a player history table (Figure 6), with all the players on one team stored in the first column, and the probabilities of each player's events (based on the individual batter's historical performance as updated for this ballpark and opposing pitcher) stored in the remaining columns across the table. Thus, the data on the Yankee batters would appear, in part, as follows:

The steps in the program establish Mickey Mantle's event by comparing the data in his row, 4, with the generated random numbers. Any random number from 01 to 201 would indicate that Mantle's event for this time at the plate would be a base-on-balls (Event 1). Similarly, a random number 202 to 374 would indicate a strikeout (Event 2), a random number 375 to 593 would indicate a sacrifice fly (Event 3), and so forth.

History Table of Player Performance

		Events[a] (designated "J")										
		1	2	3	4	5	6	7	8	9	10	11
	1 Richardson											
	2 Tresh											
Batting order	3 Maris											
Row numbers	4 Mantle	.201	.374	.593	.637	.748	.795	.882	.905	.907	.916	1.000
(desig- nated "I")	5 Reed											
	6 Howard											
	7 Skowron											
	8 Boyer											
	9 Arroyo											

[a] See earlier descriptions of event numbers.

The specific program steps that determine batter Mantle's event at this particularly critical moment (although the computer doesn't realize the implications of this very exciting game situation) are as follows:

Program Codes and Interpretations

DØ 59 J=2, 12: This establishes a "DØ" loop which does the indicated computations through statement number 59, for incremental values of J, from 2 to 12. J represents columns from the EVENT table shown earlier; 2 through 12 which correspond to Events 1 through 11, since the first column is the batter number.

IF(HIST(I, J)−X) 59, 60, 60: This "IF" statement transfers the program to different places, depending whether the number in parenthesis is −, 0, or +. The code HIST (I, J) indicates a row, I=4 here for Mantle's batting order, and a column, J, from the HISTory table of events. Each time through the DØ loop, J is increased by one as we move up in the cumulative probability of the events. X is the random number generated earlier. The DØ loop moves along steps of J until X is equal to, or larger than, the I, J HISTory table value. Then the IF statement throws the program out of the DØ loop to statement 60 which records the number of the

event, NEVT. For example, if X=.324, the DØ loop would stop at J=3, or NEVT=2 which indicates that Mantle strikes out.

IF(NEVT−2) 101, 102, 74: This IF statement branches the program to different next steps, depending on what NEVT the random number indicated. Thus, since Mantle struck out, NEVT=2, and (NEVT−2)=0, so the next step is at statement number 102.

102 NØUT=NØUT+1 GØ TØ 50: This simply increases the outs (already two, remember) by one, because of the above event; and then sends the program back to statement number 50.

50 IF(NØUT−3) 51, 401, 401: This is another IF statement. Since NØUT=3, we go to statement 401, which is another IF statement asking if this is the 9th inning, and if it is, ending the game and pointing out the fact that the Red Sox won, 1 to 0.

An illustrative part of the computer program (in FORGO for the MIT Sloan School's IBM 1620) for this simulation is shown in Figure 7. The output for 20 games of simulated play between the Red Sox and Yankees is shown in Figure 8, along with a statistical analysis of the significance of this simulation result regarding the likelihood of either team winning the next game.

```
C       START NEW INNING, ØR NEW GAME IF ØVER 9 INNINGS
    401 INNG = INNG + 1
        IF (INNG − 9) 410, 410, 402        (asks if game is over)
    410 NST = 1                            (bases empty⎫
        NØUT = 0                           (no outs     ⎬ at the start of a game)
     50 IF (NØUT − 3) 51, 401, 401
     51 I = I + 1                          (next batter)
        IF (I − 9) 55, 55, 52              (sees if batting order should start over)
     52 I = 1
C       RANDØM NUMBER VIA FØRGØ, REPLACE FØR FØRTRAN RUN
     55 X = IRAND                          ⎫
        X = X + 100000.                    ⎪
        V = X*347.                         ⎬(Special random number generator)
        IRAND = V                          ⎪
        W = IRAND                          ⎪
        X = W/100000.                      ⎭
        DØ 59 J = 2, 12                    ⎫
C       BATTER UP, NEVT = HIS ØUTCØME      ⎪(see attached explanation of the DØ loop—this step
        IF (HIST (I, J) − X) 59, 60, 60    ⎬relates the random number selected to the player's
     59 CØNTINUE                           ⎪event outcome, by comparison to that player's row in
     60 NEVT = J − 1                       ⎭the HISTORY table.)
C       NEVT UPDATES NST = STATE (MEN ØN BASE)
    500 IF (K − 1) 502, 501, 502
    501 PUNCH 5000, INNG, I, NØUT, NST, NEVT (punches card output of results of inning)
    502 CØNTINUE
```

Figure 7 continues

```
      IF (NEVT − 2) 101, 102, 74
   74 IF (NEVT − 4) 103, 104, 76
   76 IF (NEVT − 6) 105, 106, 78
   78 IF (NEVT − 8) 107, 108, 80
   80 IF (NEVT − 10) 109, 110, 111
  101 IF (NST − 2) 120, 121, 122
  120 NST = 2
      GØ TØ 50
  121 NST = 6
      GØ TØ 50
  122 IF (NST − 4) 123, 124, 125
  123 NST = 6
      GØ TØ 50
  124 NST = 5
      GØ TØ 50
  125 IF (NST − 8) 126, 127, 99
  126 NST = 8
      GØ TØ 50
  127 NST = 8
      NSCØ = NSCØ + 1 (score one run)
      GØ TØ 50
  102 NØUT = NØUT + 1 (increase number of outs)
      GØ TØ 50
  103 NØUT = NØUT + 1
      GØ TØ 50
  104 NØUT = NØUT + 1
  130 IF (NØUT − 3) 131, 50, 99
  131 IF (NST − 4) 50, 133, 134
  133 NST = 1
      GØ TØ 139
  134 IF (NST − 6) 135, 50, 136
  135 NST = 2
      GØ TØ 139
  136 IF (NST − 8) 137, 138, 99
  137 NST = 3
      GØ TØ 139
  138 NST = 6
      GØ TØ 139
  139 NSCØ = NSCØ + 1
      GØ TØ 50
  105 NØUT = NØUT + 1
  140 IF (NØUT − 3) 141, 50, 99
  141 IF (NST − 2) 50, 142, 143
  142 NST = 1
      GØ TØ 149
  143 IF (NST − 5) 50, 144, 145
  144 NST = 4
      GØ TØ 149
  145 IF (NST − 7) 144, 50, 144
  149 NØUT = NØUT + 1
      GØ TØ 50
  106 IF (NST − 2) 150, 151, 152
  150 NST = 2
```

(branches program to different statements, depending upon what event happened)

(defines the new state of the game; that is, the men-on-base)

STATE-ØF-GAME CØDES

Men on base

NST	1st	2nd	3rd
1	0	0	0
2	1	0	0
3	0	1	0
4	0	0	1
5	1	0	1
6	1	1	0
7	0	1	1
8	1	1	1

(Remainder of listing not shown)

Figure 7 Partial Listing of FORGO Program to Baseball-O-Mation.

C   RESULTS AND ANALYSIS ØF 20 GAMES ØF SIMULATED PLAY

C   FENWAY PARK FACTØRS

C   PITCHER, ARRØYØ (NEW YØRK)

C   PITCHER, CØNLEY (BØSTØN)

C SCØRES FØR RED SØX	C SCØRES FØR YANKEES
BØS GAME 0 SCØRE 0	NY GAME 0 SCØRE 0
BØS GAME 1 SCØRE 1	NY GAME 1 SCØRE 1
BØS GAME 2 SCØRE 1	NY GAME 2 SCØRE 3
BØS GAME 3 SCØRE 2	NY GAME 3 SCØRE 0
BØS GAME 4 SCØRE 4	NY GAME 4 SCØRE 6
BØS GAME 5 SCØRE 4	NY GAME 5 SCØRE 4
BØS GAME 6 SCØRE 2	NY GAME 6 SCØRE 14
BØS GAME 7 SCØRE 1	NY GAME 7 SCØRE 3
BØS GAME 8 SCØRE 2	NY GAME 8 SCØRE 4
BØS GAME 9 SCØRE 2	NY GAME 9 SCØRE 6
BØS GAME 10 SCØRE 0	NY GAME 10 SCØRE 3
BØS GAME 11 SCØRE 3	NY GAME 11 SCØRE 10
BØS GAME 12 SCØRE 1	NY GAME 12 SCØRE 6
BØS GAME 13 SCØRE 1	NY GAME 13 SCØRE 10
BØS GAME 14 SCØRE 3	NY GAME 14 SCØRE 7
BØS GAME 15 SCØRE 3	NY GAME 15 SCØRE 2
BØS GAME 16 SCØRE 4	NY GAME 16 SCØRE 4
BØS GAME 17 SCØRE 4	NY GAME 17 SCØRE 1
BØS GAME 18 SCØRE 3	NY GAME 18 SCØRE 2
BØS GAME 19 SCØRE 3	NY GAME 19 SCØRE 9
BØS GAME 20 SCØRE 8	NY GAME 20 SCØRE 3
AVE = 2.6 RUNS	AVE = 4.9 RUNS
$\sigma = 1.7$	$\sigma = 3.6$

WINNERS: YANKEES 12 GAMES

RED SØX 5 GAMES

TIED   3 GAMES

Mean difference $= 4.9 - 2.6 = 2.3$ runs

Variance $= 13.0 + 2.94 = 15.94$
$= (3.6)^2 + (1.7)^2$

Standard Deviation $= 4.0$ runs (of the *difference*)

Probability that the difference is greater than zero $= 0.717$

Thus, the Yankees have a 71.7% chance of winning in this situation

Figure 8 Results and Analysis of 20 Games of Simulated Play.

WHEN TO SIMULATE

When considering simulation, the first step is to consider the alternatives. Because one can always proceed in the fabrication of a computer model, simulation looks deceptively simple. Perhaps no other research strategy, however, poses as many philosophical and methodological questions:

When is simulation complete?

Is the computer program a theory?

How is such a theory manipulated?

Where can the theory be limited for simplified application?

How does one assess the generality of a simulation model?

How are the consequences of the model to be identified, except by exhaustive testing?

What are properties of a simulation model?

How may the model be compared to real-world data?

What is a necessary validation test?

What is a sufficient test?

The list of unanswered questions seems endless. Although many of these issues are involved in other study methods, they are not usually so ill defined.

Thus, the first rule in simulation is: examine the alternatives. Other research strategies may be more effective. A tight experimental design may deal with the central system variables in a more controlled way. Activity sampling may reveal major interactions of a complicated system, especially when combined with suitable statistical analysis. A formally constructed model may be more amenable to analysis and may permit clearer deductions. Even a field survey may better illuminate empirical relations between variables and suggest systematic features of a large system.

Sometimes, however, simulation is the best approach. When relations are nonlinear, when the system has interacting subsystems, and when many conditional responses exist, then simulation is a feasible and useful method.

Simulation seems especially useful as a means for understanding complicated processes. In these cases, simulation serves two purposes. First, it combines a variety of otherwise disparate elements into a single entity. When parts of a process may be observed and represented but the combined effect of the parts appears to defy formal definition, then simulation can be useful. Second, simulation can break down a complex problem into manageable parts. It is more than coincidental that so many simulators report: "No, I didn't simulate all I set out to, but I really understand that problem now, and I'm using other methods on parts of it. Moreover, the simulation suggested many new problems I hadn't considered."

A major portion of the value of a method lies in its capacity to help the researcher define problems. As a heuristic, simulation may have no peer. However, the method is slow—and expensive. Especially when real data are involved, simulation imposes both field and laboratory conditions on the research and also requires the care and feeding of a computer.

Any one of these technical factors is demanding; combined, they are formidable.

Circumstances, however, may prevent the use of conventional field or laboratory methods. For example, the system may change so gradually that field observation, over time, is precluded. When historical data are not available, time compressed in a computer model may be the most useful approach. Similarly, full-scale experiments with systems of human beings may be ruled out on humanitarian, political, or financial grounds. Simulation may be the study method to select in this case also.

To summarize:

In principle, nearly everything that can be accomplished by simulation can be accomplished by direct experimentation on the problem. In practice, however, it may be impossible or not feasible to experiment on the problem. How can the effects of alternative strategies in global war be tested, short of a holocaust? Can one really afford to change an operating system to "see what will happen"? An exploratory approach to solutions is clearly desirable, an approach using a representation of the system— a laboratory model, so to speak. Simulation can effectively provide such a model.

Compressing or expanding time, as necessary, the simulation concentrates on the essential workings of a system. Normally, simulation contributes to understanding of the system by indicating which factors are most critical in determining the system's output. A simulation provides dynamic flexibility for handling new, unexpected, and/or probabilistic situations. Above all, simulation permits the user to experiment—and to observe the results of the (simulated) change, while the rest of the modeled system remains constant. Simulation also provides information in a readily understandable format, information which can be acted on at no great cost in comparison to the cost of experimenting on the system itself.

Thus, the results of descriptive simulation serve at least three purposes. First, from such a study, better theories of human behavior may result. Of course, our supply man's decision making is only a tiny bit of all behavior, even of the supply man's total behavior. But behavioral data must always be accumulated bit by bit. Moreover, whether one must look at all the trees in the forest depends on the homogeneity of the forest. Do all supply men behave like ours? One suspects that in many ways they do.

A second use of descriptive models is to obtain ideas for improvement. Once we know our supply man's rules, we can test their organizational consequences under varying conditions of demand by employing the program as an experimental subject. These experiments may suggest marginal or even wholesale improvements in ordering procedures or they may reveal unsuspected properties of the model.

A third use of descriptive simulation is to reformulate the problem for an operations researcher. Our objective then might be to develop a formal set of procedures guaranteeing the best solution to the ordering problem when results are measured against one criterion—say, total cost. Simulation serves this goal by illustrating the variables with which a realistic optimizing method must deal.

The following is a summary of the requisites of simulation and the steps to be taken in constructing a simulation model [8].

SIMULATION REQUISITES

Simulation can be defined as a duplication of the essence of a system or activity, that is, the essential characteristics of the system. It should be emphasized that a simulation model is not reality and should not be expected to mirror it. Inevitably, the model will include some simplifying assumptions that are at variance with reality. In a sense, realism is not necessary. Rather, the model must capture, represent, and accurately express—by whatever means—the essential relationships among the elements of the system being *simulated*.

If the inputs, the operating rules, and the desired output of a system can be stated in numerical or formal logic symbols, the system can be simulated on a computer. The specific system elements included depends both on the objective (desired output) of the simulation and on what is known (or will be known) about the system in question. For example, perhaps detailed input–output behavior for all components of a system cannot be specified, but the input–output behavior of the overall system can be described. This information is often sufficient for achieving the desired goal. In this case, the simulation may be used for inductive study; that is, by knowing what comes out of the system, the simulator can empirically test hypothetical rules of behavior for the system elements. Inductive simulation might be used, for example, to study the behavior of individual customers when an overall market reaction is known.

Conversely, the behavior of individual system elements may be thoroughly understood, but the interrelationship of the elements—and consequently, the behavior of the system as a whole—may not be. Here, a simulation can help determine the nature of the composite output, in deductive fashion. For example, simulation may aid in synthesizing a new system of investment portfolio analysis when the performance of individual stocks relative to certain industries is known but when knowledge about the overall performance of the portfolio in the national economy is desired.

If sufficient realism can be obtained in sets of relatively simple equations, analytic models are, in general, less time-consuming and more directly productive of optimal results than are simulations. Therefore, when considering a possible application, one should have convincing evidence *not only* that simulation is potentially beneficial *but also* that it is better suited to the problem at hand than are other methods.

The variance between reality and the model may be found in the system's probabilistic transformations. A few discrete outcome states may be chosen as the outcome possibilities, when in fact the "real" outcomes resemble more closely a continuous distribution. Or averaged values may be employed to represent possible outcomes in a situation where averages do not tell the whole story. It may even be necessary to build omissions into the model because the computer on which the simulation is to be run is not large enough to handle a realistic model.

Are these assumptions or omissions of great consequence? This question must ultimately be answered in terms of the objectives of the simulation. It may be, for example, that a gross model will serve for making overall prediction, although such a model would describe inadequately the state of a particular point in the system at a given point in time.

The model designer should provide a comprehensive written statement of the simulation, including an explanation of all mathematical notations not otherwise clear. This statement should include a projection of the number of runs necessary to support various levels of confidence in the simulation results, as well as the estimated cost of a single run. A simulation incorporating elements of uncertainty is, after all, much like any sampling process, such as marketing research or quality control. The size of the sample depends on cost, the amount of additional information it provides, and the value of that information. These data are needed to project the time, cost, and benefits of the proposed simulation.

PLANNING THE SIMULATION STUDY

The steps in planning and carrying out a simulation normally are as follows:

(i) Study the operating realities of the system.

(ii) Determine the objectives of the simulation.

(iii) Collect relevant data and define relationships.

(iv) Develop and manually test the model.

(v) Program the model for a computer, test, and "debug."

(vi) Run the program.

(vii) Evaluate the results.

A thorough system analysis is critical to the development of an effective, economical simulation. A study of the problem may point the way to an analytic solution not previously imagined, thus avoiding the need for a simulation study. Analysis may also reveal previously overlooked conditions or relationships within the system that will suggest a simple, intuitive solution. In any case, system analysis will provide a clear understanding of the proposed simulation itself, its feasible objectives, and its constraints.

The analyst should consider both objectives and constraints in delineating the proposed scope, necessary detail, and estimated time, cost, and benefits of the simulation. Then decisions can be made about the specific outputs of the simulation, the resources to be made available, and the plan of attack.

THE FLOW DIAGRAM AND MODEL BUILDING

Once the objectives of the simulation have been established, the next step is to diagram the flow of information and events through the system. The flow diagram need show only the elements and flows of interest—that is, those that are pertinent to the problem, as defined.

When system analysis and initial flow diagramming have been completed, the analyst turns to development of the simulation model. Design of the model is preceded by a search for general data about system operations and by identification of all inputs and their transformations by the system that have significant effect on system outputs.

The simulation model may be modular (built up from large, self-contained subroutines or modules), atomistic (built up piece by piece, with the entire model being the only self-contained module), or a *combination* of the two constructions. The model may be static (with input the same from one run to the next) or dynamic (with input conditions changing over time); it may be designed to run for a second, a day, or a year or more; it may run in expanded time (as in simulation of an atomic explosion), real time (simulation of air defense tactics), or condensed time (simulation of several years of business operations).

The model should be reviewed before it is programmed to assess and to verify model elements, their relationships, and model outputs, and perhaps most important, to weigh costs against expected benefits.

COMPUTER PROGRAMMING

After design and manual test, the simulation model can be programmed for a digital computer. Essentially, programming is a three-step process involving:

(i) Conversion of relevant data to a form in which the machine can store and process it.

(ii) Establishment of the instructions or logic by which the computer will use the data.

(iii) Test or "debugging" of the translation and logic to ensure that the model represents the real world to the desired degree.

A brief description of the elements of an electronic digital computer and of the functions of each element may help in understanding computer programs and programming techniques. An electronic digital computer is made up of the following basic parts:

(i) *Memory.* The memory unit stores data and instructions until the calculating unit needs them. It also holds intermediate steps of the computation and information awaiting output. Computer memory devices include magnetic cores, discs, drums, and tapes. The time required to locate and retrieve data from the memory is known as "access time," and is usually expressed in milliseconds, microseconds, or nanoseconds—that is, thousandths, millionths, or billionths of a second.

(ii) *Calculating Unit.* This unit corresponds to the works of a mechanical calculator and performs similar functions, such as addition and multiplication, but does so in microseconds. The computer calculating unit has an additional feature, however, in the "logic" or branching function—that is, it will perform differently, depending on whether a number is positive or negative.

(iii) *Input and Output Devices.* These units include magnetic tapes, punched cards, typewriters, high-speed printers, graph plotters, and so forth. They are used to transfer data into the computer and to present results to the user.

(iv) *Control Unit.* The control unit manages the operation of the computer by means of a series of initial instructions. The instructions tell the machine when to bring in data, what calculations to perform, and how to present results.

PROGRAMMING AIDS

The series of initial instructions referred to above is the computer program. In effect, the program tells the control unit what to tell the other computer elements to do.

All digital computers deal entirely with and "converse" in binary codes. The machines accept numbers and symbols based on the decimal system, converting them internally, to the binary numbering system. The actual computations within the machine are done in the binary system, since these numbers (0 and 1) may be stored as an electrical state (on or off) or as a magnetic flux (magnetized or demagnetized) that can be read and manipulated by the computer.

The speeds and capacities of computers have increased dramatically since the introduction of electronic equipment and, more recently, of solid-state devices, but computer potential is often wasted because of the necessity for writing detailed programs to instruct the machines. Over the years, programming aids have been developed to make computer usage more efficient. The evolutionary stages are those of machine language, assembly language, and procedure-oriented language.

Machine-language statements were the earliest form of computer instructions. These instructions were expressed in imperative sentences, with one verb and one direct object, such as "add A," "subtract B," "store (at location) 1024." Each imperative instructed the computer to perform one distinct operation in its repertoire of perhaps several dozen operations, and it specified how this operation was to be performed.

At the start, these machine-language instructions were fed to the computer in strings of zeros and ones, that is, in binary numbers or "bits." Programs written in alphabetic characters and decimal numbers were manually transcribed into binary numbers. Perhaps the first major programming aid was the design of computers that could accept alphabetic letters and decimal numbers and convert them internally to the binary system.

Assembly-language programming relieved the programmer of the burden of writing programs in machine language. Through assembly programming, the locations of data or instructions were referred to by name or symbol, rather than by the numerical address used in machine language. Assembly language could be more easily followed by persons unfamiliar with a program; also, it increased coding accuracy and eliminated the need for detailed flow charts and coding comments. In addition, with assembly language the programmer could manipulate symbolic locations, or addresses.

The assembler converts the completed assembly language program into the machine language of the computer. Typically, the assembler analyzes all symbolic directions, converts them to machine instructions and addresses, and establishes the specified relationships between them.

Procedure-oriented languages were the next stage in the evolution of programming aids. These languages utilize "macroinstructions"— single instructions covering many steps in the actual computer operation. Macroinstructions allow common procedures to be filed in a "library." The programmer can then select a procedure and insert it in his program with only one instruction.

As in the case of assembly languages, another program stands between the procedure-oriented language and the computer. Called a compiler, this program is much more versatile than an assembler. In addition to performing the assembler's function of translating symbolic instructions and memory locations into machine language, the compiler expands the program by selecting the sets of machine-language instructions called for by the macro-instructions.

Three of the more widely known procedure-oriented languages are ALGOL, which concentrates on common arithmetic procedures; COBOL, which was designed for business purposes and includes common procedures for updating records, billing, and so on; and FORTRAN, which is more appropriate for scientific applications. Any of these languages may be used for a particular problem. But as with any task, each performs the job for which it was specifically designed more efficiently than do the others. A universal constraint, of course, is whether the available computer is able to translate the procedure-oriented language into its own language.

Several procedure-oriented languages have been devised specifically for simulation problems, for example SIMSCRIPT [7], DYNAMO [4], and the IBM GPSS (General Purpose Systems Simulator) [5]. These languages utilize macroinstructions. For example, SIMSCRIPT provides such commands as CREATE (a transaction); DESTROY (a transaction); FIND GREATEST (highest priority) TRANSACTION IN QUEUE.

The macroinstruction codes employed for simulation have been designed to be generally applicable. In the IBM GPSS, for example, the operating system to be simulated is described in special block diagrams; all the user needs to know is the rules by which the diagrams are constructed. The output can show traffic flow, queue lengths at particular points in the system, and other pertinent information. The GPSS will allow various statistical techniques to be introduced, complex logical decisions to be carried out, and interdependencies of variables, such as queue lengths, input rates, and processing time to be handled.

What the procedure-oriented macrolanguages gain in programming speed and ease, they sacrifice in compiler efficiency and, to some extent, in machine efficiency. The machine program written in procedure-oriented language may be longer, and thus more expensive to run, than other language programs. Or the longer program may strain computer memory capacity. Certain complex simulations programmed in, say, SIMSCRIPT could not be handled by the computers on which they are presently programmed. Larger units would be required. The lower costs of programming and debugging, however, could outweigh increases in running costs.

TIME, COST, AND BENEFITS

Will the simulation pay off? What are its advantages, and how do we recognize them? Against the effectiveness or benefits of the simulation, we must balance the costs of its development and operation, which include:

(i)   Analysis and model building.

(ii)   Participation of general and functional management.

(iii)   Programming and debugging.

(iv)   Clerical workers and key-punch operators.

(v)   Computer running time.

(vi)   Updating the simulation, if it is to be reused.

These costs will vary with the scope of the simulation study, the complexity of the system it is designed to emulate, the experience and skill of the analyst–management team concerned, the computer hardware available for use, the difficulty of programming, and the output required.

Reliable technical data on simulation costs are difficult to obtain, in part because of the indirect nature of many costs involved, and in part because cost underestimating is common. In general, analysis and programming time are the key factors.

Benefits of a simulation may also be difficult to predict or to quantify. But this uncertainty does not mean that simulation is useless in cases where only incomplete projections are available, since the nature of the technique is appropriate to applications of which the good results are not usually directly measurable.

REFERENCES

1. W. G. Briggs, 1960. *Baseball-o-mation, a simulation study*. Boston: Harbridge House. 2B.
2. K. J. Cohen, and F. Tonge, 1961. *A work problem in computer simulation*. Course note, Carnegie-Mellon University.
3. R. M. Cyert, and J. G. March, 1963. *A behavioral theory of the firm*. Englewood Cliffs, N.J.: Prentice-Hall. 2B.
4. J. W. Forrester, 1961. *Industrial dynamics*. Cambridge, Mass.: MIT Press. MD.
5. G. Gordon, 1961. *Preliminary manual for GPS—a general purpose systems simulator*. White Plains, N.Y.: IBM.
6. S. I. Hayakawa, 1949. *Language in thought and action*. New York.: Harcourt, Brace.
7. H. M. Markowitz, B. Hausner, and H. W. Karr, 1963. *SIMSCRIPT: a simulation programming language*. Englewood Cliffs, N.J.: Prentice-Hall.
8. T. H. Naylor, J. L. Balintfy, D. S. Burdick, and K. Chu, 1966. *Computer simulation techniques*. New York: Wiley. MG.
9. A. Newell, J. C. Shaw, and H. A. Simon, 1958. Elements of a theory of human problem solving. *Psychological Review, 65*(3): 151–166. MA.
10. K. R. Popper, 1959. *The logic of scientific discovery*. New York: Basic Books.
11. F. J. Roethlisberger, 1941. *Management and morale*. Cambridge: Harvard University Press.
12. H. A. Simon and A. Newell, 1956. Models: their uses and limitations. *The state of the social sciences* (L. D. White, ed.). Chicago: University of Chicago Press, 66–83. MA.

4

PROCESS MODELS AND STOCHASTIC THEORIES OF SIMPLE CONCEPT FORMATION

LEE W. GREGG

HERBERT A. SIMON

Psychologists who wish to formalize a theory today have two major alternatives: they may construct either a mathematical theory, usually stochastic, or an information-processing model in the form of a computer program. The work of Bower and Trabasso on concept attainment, carried out in the former mode, provides an opportunity to compare these two techniques in order to gain a deeper understanding of the contribution each can make to theory construction and testing [3]. This paper undertakes such a comparison, to test whether information-processing models can cast additional light on experiments that have already undergone sophisticated analysis in terms of stochastic learning theory.

THE BOWER–TRABASSO THEORY

In the first instance, we shall limit our discussion, as do Bower and Trabasso, to concept attainment experiments employing an N-dimensional stimulus with two possible values on each dimension, and having a single relevant

SOURCE: Reprinted from *Journal of Mathematical Psychology*, 4:246–276 (1967).

dimension (i.e., simple concepts). On each trial, an instance (positive or negative) is presented to the subject; he responds "Positive" or "Negative"; and he is reinforced by "Right" or "Wrong," as the case may be.

Bower and Trabasso's mathematical theory, devised to explain the results of their main experiments, may be described as follows [1, 3]:

1. On each trial the subject is in one of two states, K or $\bar{K}$. If he is in state K (he "knows" the correct concept), he will always make the correct response. If he is in state $\bar{K}$ (he "does not know" the correct concept), he will make an incorrect response with probability p.

2. After each correct response, the subject remains in his previous state. After an error, he shifts from state $\bar{K}$ to state K with probability π.

Bower and Trabasso derive mathematically a number of consequences from this theory: in particular, expected values and variances of a large number of statistics. They then proceed to show that in a substantial number of experiments, of which we shall discuss six in some detail, these expected values and variances are quite close to the sample statistics.

Estimates of the parameters p and π play a central role both in the analysis of the mathematical theory and in its fit to the empirical data. We will focus our attention, as do Bower and Trabasso, primarily on them. In this, we agree with Atkinson, *et al.* who say of this model [1, p. 69]:

The fundamental statistics of importance to the concept model are (1) stationarity and independency [of the estimates of p] prior to the last error and (2) the distribution of total errors or trial number of last error [determining π]. If these statistics conform to the predictions of the model, then we have found in practice that the remaining statistics accord well with predictions.

Once the subject has entered state K, he can no longer, according to the theory, make an error or return to state $\bar{K}$. Therefore we can be sure that the subject is in state $\bar{K}$ on every trial up to and including that on which he made his last error (and in state K on every subsequent

trial). Hence, pooling data for all subjects in state $\bar{K}$ for each trial, we can obtain independent estimates of p for each trial. The theory asserts that these are all estimates of the same population parameter, hence that the observed p should not vary significantly from trial to trial. In the experiments reported by Bower and Trabasso (except possibly Experiment 2 in Table 1, below), the observations confirm this prediction.

Since, whenever he makes an error, the subject has a probability, π, of moving from state $\bar{K}$ to state K, and since no errors will be made once state K is reached, the expected total number of errors will simply be $1/\pi$. The theory also asserts that π is constant from trial to trial, an assertion that implies that, on the average, the fraction of subjects still in state $\bar{K}$ who move to state K will not change over trials. Bower and Trabasso report little data on this point, commenting (p. 40) that:

TABLE 1   Experiments Analyzed in Bower and Trabasso (1964)

Experiment No.	Page Reference	Attributes		Relevant Attribute	Reversal	Number of Subjects[a]	Average Total Errors	Probability of Errors in $K(p)$
		Number	Type					
1	38–43	5	consonant strings	—	none	25	12.16	.523
2	61–65	3	geometrical 4 values paired	color	none	22	13.36	.493
3	66–69	4	"letter wheels"	particular letters	single	C 18 / R 18 / N 18	19.11 / 19.11 / 18.28	.491
4	72–74	6	geometrical	color	single	C 10 / R 10 / N 10	12.9 / 14.9 / 14.0	.500
5	77–79	5	geometrical	color	alternate errors	C 15 / R 15	8.0 / 7.81	
6	80–82	5	geometrical	color	*after* errors	(8 of 11 failed) 3	47.7	.499

[a] C, R, N stand for Control, Reversal, and Nonreversal, respectively. For details, see text and Bower and Trabasso [3], at the pages indicated in the second column.

No available data are sufficiently free of sampling error to permit quantitative decision between the [constant-π] assumption and the [increasing-π] assumption [when there are a large number of stimulus dimensions]. However, some of the results reported later in this paper contradict the notion that [π] changes appreciably over trials.

Bower and Trabasso use the reciprocal of the total number of errors to estimate π (or *average* π, if it changes), on the basis of the simple relation stated above.

We see that the whole of the rather formidable array of mathematical derivations in the Bower–Trabasso analysis can be summed up, for practical purposes, in the informal calculations we have just carried out. The only strong predictions of the theory (and, as we shall see, the only predictions with substantial psychological content) that are critically tested by the empirical data are the predictions of stationarity and independence of p from trial to trial.[1]

PROCESS DESCRIPTIONS

The mathematical theory of Bower and Trabasso is equivalent to the two numbered statements of the previous section, taken together with the ordinary laws of algebra and probability theory. The first statement determines the probability distribution of responses on each trial as a function of the subject's state; the second statement defines the conditions under which the state of the subject will change.

In a very aggregative sense, this theory can be regarded as a process model for the subject's behavior. The first statement describes, in terms of the probabilities of outcomes, a response process; the second, a learning process, also probabilistic. However, the theory states nothing about the subject's information processes that generate the probabilities. In this section we shall describe an alternative model of concept attainment that makes somewhat more detailed assumptions about these processes. Before we do, some methodological remarks about the credibility of theories are in order.

One point of view is that theories gain their

credibility solely from the accuracy of their predictions, account being taken of their parsimony in making these predictions. Each experiment is treated as an island unto itself, ignoring any knowledge about the world the experimenter might have had prior to making his predictions. From this point of view it is not relevant to ask how Bower and Trabasso came to write down their particular hypothetical description of the system. The only valid questions are whether the system's predictions are correct, and whether they are achieved parsimoniously. (We shall have more to say about parsimony later.)

There is another point of view on credibility, however: that the credibility of a theory depends on its plausibility as well as the accuracy of its predictions. This point of view, which has strong support in contemporary statistical decision theory, has been formalized along the following lines, based on Bayes' Theorem. Suppose that two alternative theories are under consideration, and that we wish to judge their relative credibility after certain empirical events (E) have occurred. Let $p(E|H_1)$ and $p(E|H_2)$, respectively be the probabilities that the *actually observed* events would have occurred if H_1 and H_2, respectively were the correct theory. We wish to compare $p(H_1|E)$ with $p(H_2|E)$—i.e., the relative probabilities that H_1 or H_2, respectively, are true, given E. Let $p(H_1)$ and $p(H_2)$, respectively be the probability of H_1 and H_2, respectively prior to the observations E. We may think of these probabilities as the "plausibilities" of the two theories on the basis of all facts known to us prior to the new observations. Then by Bayes' Theorem:

$$\frac{p(H_1|E)}{p(H_2|E)} = \frac{p(E|H_1)\,p(H_1)}{p(E|H_2)\,p(H_2)} \tag{1}$$

Thus, the credibility of each theory after the observation is quite as dependent on the plausibility, $p(H)$, of that theory, as upon the likelihood, $p(E|H)$, of its producing the observation.

In practice, theorists almost always behave in accordance with Bayes' Theorem: as though they thought the plausibility of their formalisms to be relevant to their credibility. An important argument for high prior plausibility of a theory

---

[1] This is not a criticism of the experiments, which were aimed primarily at testing the all-or-none hypothesis. For this hypothesis, the stationarity of p and π are the critical issues.

is to show that it follows (formally or informally) from assumptions that are plausible, i.e., assumptions that accord with prior knowledge. Bower and Trabasso do precisely this—they show informally that the stochastic theory we have outlined can be derived from plausible assumptions about the subject's information processing strategy [3]. There are a number of such discussions in their paper, the principal ones occurring on pages 39, 51, 81, 83–85, and 88–91. Since it will be relevant to our subsequent discussion, we quote the first of these at length:

The subject in a concept-identification experiment is viewed as testing out various hypotheses (strategies) about the solution of the problem. Each problem defines for the subject a population of hypotheses. The subject samples one of these hypotheses at random and makes the response dictated by the hypothesis. If his response is correct, he continues to use that hypothesis for the next trial; if his response is incorrect, then he resamples (with replacement) from the pool of hypotheses. . . .

Let us call the quoted statement a process model, P_0. The model P_0 lends plausibility to the stochastic theory, for it is obvious that, if we identify "subject is in state K" of the latter with "subject holds the correct hypothesis" of the former, then the stochastic theory can be derived from P_0. But the assumptions of P_0 agree with our previous experience of human behavior—that is what, no doubt, suggested them in the first place. The situation is depicted in Fig. 1.

It is of some interest to note that the stochastic theory is only slightly more economical of words than the process model. In fact, we stated the former in 65 words (excluding parentheses), Bower and Trabasso stated the latter in 77. On the other hand, the process model makes more and stronger predictions than the stochastic theory (lower dotted path in Fig. 1). We mention two of these as examples:

1. If there are $2N$ possible hypotheses, and if the correct hypothesis is determined in each experiment at random, with equal probability for each hypothesis, then it follows from P_0 that $\pi = 1/2N$.

2. If the subject, on each trial, verbalizes his hypothesis as well as his response, then he will change the verbalized hypothesis only if he made an error on the previous trial.

While the stochastic theory can be derived from P_0, the converse, as we have just seen, is not true. Indeed, it is easy to construct variants of P_0 from which the same stochastic theory is derivable. A simple variant would be to assume (local nonreplacement) that after each error, the subject selects a hypothesis at random from the possible hypotheses *excepting* the hypothesis he held on the previous trial. Call this variant P_1. A slightly more complex variant, which we shall call P_2, would be to assume (local consistency) that the subject selects a hypothesis from the subset of hypotheses that are consistent with the last instance presented to him. A still more complex variant, P_3, would assume

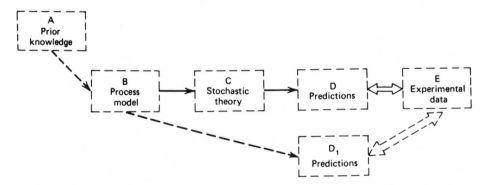

Figure 1 Theoretical structure (explicit and implicit) employed by Bower and Trabasso. Solid lines, and boxes enclosed by solid lines, depict the formal derivations and formal propositions, respectively. Broken lines, and boxes enclosed by broken lines, depict the informal derivations and propositions.

(global consistency) that the subject selects the new hypothesis randomly from the subset of hypotheses consistent with *all* the instances that have been presented to him. Moreover, in any of these sampling schemes, the different hypotheses might have unequal, instead of equal, probabilities of selection.

All four variant processing models, and others as well, imply the stochastic theory of Bower and Trabasso, or something almost indistinguishable from it. It follows that tests of that theory can contribute nothing to choosing among the variants—if the theory is consistent with the data, the actual behavior of the subject might correspond with any (or none) of the variant models.

This does not mean that the models are empirically indistinguishable or untestable. On the contrary, we have already seen that, if the experimenter chooses the correct concept and the instances at random, P_0 (replacement sampling) implies that $\pi = 1/2N$. By parallel reasoning, it is easy to see that P_1 (local nonreplacement sampling) implies $\pi = 1/(2N-1)$; while P_2 (local consistency) implies $\pi = 1/N$; and P_3 (global consistency) implies an increasing π, varying from $1/N$ after the first error to 1 after about $\log_2 N$ errors. Since, in all cases, the expected number of total errors is proportional to $1/\pi$, it should be easy to choose among these models except possibly between P_0 and P_1—between replacement and local non-replacement sampling.

FORMALIZATION OF THE PROCESS MODEL

We have seen that Bower and Trabasso gave *a priori* plausibility to their stochastic theory by deriving it informally from an informal process model. By making use of a simple programming language we can formalize the process model. We require some variables, a few constants, and some processes. Following the conventions of ALGOL names of variables, called identifiers, represent computer cells upon whose contents the usual arithmetic operations can be performed [6]. Additionally, the language incorporates the list processing features of IPL-V so that the contents of a cell may also refer to names of lists of symbols [7].

Variables

Instance: Its value is a *list* containing a value (e.g., "large," "square") for each of N attributes.

Attribute Structure: Its value is a *list* of pairs of values (e.g., "red-blue") for each of N attributes.

Correct Response: Its value is one of the two *constants:* "Positive," "Negative."

Correct Hypothesis: Its value is one of the $2N$ attribute values.

Current Hypothesis: Its value is one of the $2N$ attribute values.

Response: Its value is one of the two constants: "Positive," "Negative."

Reinforcement: Its value is one of the two constants: "Right," "Wrong."

New Hypothesis: Its value is one of the $2N$ attribute values.

List of Possible Hypotheses: Its value is the *list* of $2N$ attribute values.

Tally: Its value is a positive *integer*.

Constants

"Positive," "Negative," "Right," "Wrong"; the integers; K, the criterion of solution; and the symbols for the $2N$ attribute values.

Processes

The symbol "←" is read "is set equal to," and the symbol "∈," "is a member of." Processes numbered E1-E4 describe the experimenter's behaviors, and S1-S5 the subject's behaviors; while E0 is the "executive process," controlling their alternation. Where "random" is not otherwise qualified, it means "with equal probabilities."

E1: Do E3; then do E4.
   [E3 and E4 are defined below]
S1: If Current Hypothesis ∈ Instance,
   then Response ← "Positive,"
   else Response ← "Negative."
E2: If Response = Correct Response,
   then Reinforcement ← "Right,"
   else Reinforcement ← "Wrong."
S2: If Reinforcement = "Wrong,"
   then Current Hypothesis ← S5.
E3: Generate an instance by sampling randomly from each pair on Attribute Structure.
   Instance ← List of Attribute Values

E4: If Correct Hypotheses ∈ Instance,
    then Correct Response ← "Positive,"
    else Correct Response ← "Negative."
S5: Generate New Hypothesis by sampling
    randomly from List of Possible Hypotheses:
    Current Hypothesis ← New Hypothesis.
E0: Do E1, then S1, then E2;
    If Reinforcement = "Right,"
    then Tally ← Tally + 1,
    else Tally ← 0;
    If Tally = K,
    then halt;
    else do S2, then repeat E0.

On examination, this model will be recognized as a formalization of $P_0 \cdot P_1$ differs from it only in replacing S5 by $S5_1$.

S5$_1$: Generate New Hypothesis by sampling
    randomly from List of Possible Hypotheses;
    If New Hypothesis = Current
    Hypothesis,
    then sample again,
    else Current Hypothesis ← New
    Hypothesis.

A slightly more complex version, $S5_2$, corresponds to P_2:

S5$_2$: Generate New Hypothesis by sampling
    randomly from List of Possible Hypotheses;
    If New Hypothesis ∈ Instance,
    then sample again,
    else Current Hypothesis ← New
    Hypothesis.

Similarly, $S5_3$, corresponding to P_3, might have the following structure:

S5$_3$: Generate values from Instance, and
    remove each from List of Possible
    Hypotheses (if still on that List);
    Generate New Hypothesis by sampling
    randomly from List of Possible Hypotheses;
    Current Hypothesis ← New
    Hypothesis.

These are, of course, not the only possible process hypotheses for the subject's behavior. But they will serve to illustrate: (1) that the

process models can be formalized as fully as we please (i.e., we can formalize B of Fig. 1); (2) that these process models are empirically distinguishable (i.e., we can deduce direct connections between B and E of Fig. 1); (3) that they make stronger predictions of behavior than do the stochastic theories (including predictions about the subject's current hypothesis), and (4) that stochastic theories can be derived from them as formally as we please (i.e., we can formalize the relation of B to C in Fig. 1).

A CLOSER COMPARISON OF MODEL WITH THEORY

The relation between the stochastic theory and the process models can be stated even more precisely than it was in the previous section. For, we can formulate the stochastic theory in the same programming language as the process models; and, alternatively, we can extract a stochastic model from each of the process models that preserves all of its detail.

First, we give the process-language version of the stochastic theory:

M1: If State = "Learned,"
    then Reinforcement ← "Right,"
    else generate item randomly, with
    probabilities $(1-p)$ and p, from
    Reinforcement List, and
    Reinforcement ← Generator Output.
M2: If Reinforcement = "Wrong,"
    then generate item randomly, with
    probabilities π and $(1-\pi)$, from
    State List, and
    State ← Generator Output.
M0: Do M1,
    If Reinforcement = "Right,"
    then Tally ← Tally + 1,
    else Tally ← 0;
    If Tally = K,
    then halt;
    else do M2, then repeat M0.

Comparing this description with the earlier process models, we see that the new process M1 telescopes and simplifies the processes E1, S1, E2, E3, and E4 of the process model; while M2 telescopes S2 and S5.

Conversely, a Markov process corresponding

to the stochastic theory can be defined by considering the state of the subject after he has made a response, i.e., after execution of M1 and just before execution of M2. He is one of three possible states: Learned-Right (LR), Unlearned-Right (UR), and Unlearned-Wrong (UW).[2] The matrix of transition probabilities is:

$$
\begin{array}{c c c c}
 & \text{LR} & \text{UR} & \text{UW} \\
\text{LR} & \begin{bmatrix} 1 \\ 0 \\ \pi \end{bmatrix} & \begin{array}{c} 0 \\ (1-p) \\ (1-\pi)(1-p) \end{array} & \begin{array}{c} 0 \\ p \\ (1-\pi)p \end{bmatrix} \end{array} \\
\text{UR} \\
\text{UW}
\end{array}
$$

Now in similar fashion, we can define a set of states for the subject in the process model P_0 after he has made a response, i.e., after execution of E2 and just before execution of S2. Number the hypotheses 1 for the correct one, 2 for its alternative value on the same attribute, and $3, .., 2N$ for the remainder. Then the possible states are 1R, 2W, 3R, 3W, .., 2NR, 2NW—a total of 4N-2 states (since with hypothesis 1 the subject will necessarily make the correct response, and with hypothesis 2, the wrong one). The matrix of transition probabilities is:

	1R	⋯	iR	⋯	jR	⋯	2W	⋯	iW	⋯	jW	⋯
1R	1	⋯	0	⋯	0	⋯	0	⋯	0	⋯	0	⋯
⋮	·	⋯	·	⋯	·	⋯	·	⋯	·	⋯	·	⋯
	·	⋯	·	⋯	·	⋯	·	⋯	·	⋯	·	⋯
iR	0	⋯	$\frac{1}{2}$	⋯	0	⋯	0	⋯	$\frac{1}{2}$	⋯	0	⋯
⋮	·	⋯	·	⋯	·	⋯	·	⋯	·	⋯	·	⋯
	·	⋯	·	⋯	·	⋯	·	⋯	·	⋯	·	⋯
jR	0	⋯	0	⋯	$\frac{1}{2}$	⋯	0	⋯	0	⋯	$\frac{1}{2}$	⋯
⋮	·	⋯	·	⋯	·	⋯	·	⋯	·	⋯	·	⋯
	·	⋯	·	⋯	·	⋯	·	⋯	·	⋯	·	⋯
2W	$\frac{1}{2N}$	⋯	$\frac{1}{4N}$	⋯	$\frac{1}{4N}$	⋯	$\frac{1}{2N}$	⋯	$\frac{1}{4N}$	⋯	$\frac{1}{4N}$	⋯
⋮	·	⋯	·	⋯	·	⋯	·	⋯	·	⋯	·	⋯
	·	⋯	·	⋯	·	⋯	·	⋯	·	⋯	·	⋯
iW	$\frac{1}{2N}$	⋯	$\frac{1}{4N}$	⋯	$\frac{1}{4N}$	⋯	$\frac{1}{2N}$	⋯	$\frac{1}{4N}$	⋯	$\frac{1}{4N}$	⋯
⋮	·	⋯	·	⋯	·	⋯	·	⋯	·	⋯	·	⋯
	·	⋯	·	⋯	·	⋯	·	⋯	·	⋯	·	⋯
jW	$\frac{1}{2N}$	⋯	$\frac{1}{4N}$	⋯	$\frac{1}{4N}$	⋯	$\frac{1}{2N}$	⋯	$\frac{1}{4N}$	⋯	$\frac{1}{4N}$	⋯

where $k = (2N+1)$.

If the only behavior observed in this system is whether the response is "Right" or "Wrong," then all the states beyond 1R and 2W can be collapsed into a pair of states—call them AR and AW, respectively, and an aggregate matrix derived strictly from the previous one:

$$
\begin{array}{c c c c c}
 & \text{1R} & \text{AR} & \text{2W} & \text{AW} \\
\text{1R} & 1 & 0 & 0 & 0 \\
\text{AR} & 0 & \frac{1}{2} & 0 & \frac{1}{2} \\
\text{2W} & \frac{1}{2N} & \frac{(N-1)}{2N} & \frac{1}{2N} & \frac{(N-1)}{2N} \\
\text{AW} & \frac{1}{2N} & \frac{(N-1)}{2N} & \frac{1}{2N} & \frac{(N-1)}{2N}
\end{array}
$$

By a final step of aggregation, we can then aggregate the state AW, obtaining an approximation to the Bower–Trabasso matrix, with $\pi = 1/2N$ and $p = \frac{1}{2}$:

$$
\begin{array}{c c c c}
 & \text{1R} & \text{AR} & \text{W} \\
\text{1R} & 1 & 0 & 0 \\
\text{AR} & 0 & \frac{1}{2} & \frac{1}{2} \\
\text{W} & \frac{1}{2N} & \frac{(N-1)}{2N} & \frac{1}{2}
\end{array}
$$

[2] Bower and Trabasso call their theory a two-state process, but this refers only to the state of the subject before responding, not to the state of the entire system. See Bower and Trabasso [3, pp. 51–52].

Comparing this matrix with the one for the Bower–Trabasso theory, we see two differences, one large and one small. The big difference is that the Bower–Trabasso matrix has two free parameters, the new aggregate matrix has none—it predicts exact numerical values for π and p. The small difference is that the Bower–Trabasso matrix predicts no difference, prior to learning, between the probability of a right guess following a right guess and a right guess following a wrong guess, respectively. The matrix derived from P_0 predicts that the former probability will equal $\frac{1}{2}$, the latter $(N-1)/(2N-1)$.[3] This difference, of course, could be detected only in very large examples.

DERIVATION OF THEORY FOR MODIFIED EXPERIMENT

The process language description of the aggregated stochastic theory shows that the postulated aggregated processes intermingle the behaviors of E and S: M1 was derived from E1, S1, E2, E3, and E4 of the process model; while M2 was derived from S2 and S5. Hence there is no clear separation between those processes that define the experimental design, on the one hand, and those that define the subject's behavior on the other. If the experiment is altered in any respect, there is no direct way, in this representation, of deriving the corresponding changes in the process description or in the transition matrix.

Matters are quite different with the detailed model. For any change in the design of the experiment *which does not cause the subject to change his response strategy*, the process model can be used to predict outcomes simply by modifying the input constants and the experimenter processes to fit the new description of the experiment. This procedure does not introduce any new degrees of freedom into the assumptions about the subject's behavior, since the modifications are strictly determined by the conditions of the experiment.

For example, Bower and Trabasso describe an experiment in which, for one group of subjects after each Reinforcement of "Wrong," the value of Correct Hypothesis was reversed. To represent this experimental condition, we simply modify E2 to $E2_1$ as follows:

> $E2_1$: If (Response) = (Correct Response)
> then Reinforcement ← "Right,"
> else Reinforcement ← "Wrong,"
> and Correct Response ↔ Opposite Response;
> [where "↔" means
> "is interchanged with."]

In an even more trivial way, by changing the value of Attribute Structure, the number of stimulus dimensions or, for that matter, the number of values on each dimension, can be altered. Thus the experimental conditions can readily be replicated for all of the experiments described by Bower and Trabasso. Then, stochastic theories can be written for these new process models and, where feasible, more aggregative stochastic theories derived from them.

TESTING MODELS EMPIRICALLY

In Table 1 are listed six experiments described by Bower and Trabasso, yielding the data they use to support their theory. In each case they compute about a dozen statistics from the experimental data, and compare these with the corresponding statistics predicted by the theory after the free parameters have been estimated from the data. In a number of cases, they apply statistical tests to determine whether the differences between observed and predicted values can be attributed to chance.

The first two experiments and the controls in Experiments 3–5 correspond to the experimental conditions we have described previously. We shall speak of these as the "standard experiment." For each experiment, Bower and Trabasso examine the stationarity of p, estimate π from the observed data; then proceed to predict the remaining statistics.

Testability of the Models

There are, as we have seen, only two strong assumptions in the stochastic theory—if these

---

[3] If the subject has not learned, the *relative* probabilities of a correct and wrong response (from the third line of the table) will be $(N-1)/2N$ and $\frac{1}{2}$, respectively. Multiplying these by $2N/(2N-1)$, to normalize them so that they add to unity, we get the conditional probabilities $(N-1)/(2N-1)$ and $\frac{1}{2}[2N/(2N-1)]$, respectively.

are satisfied the rest of the data will pretty much follow. The first is, that so long as the subject does not hold the correct hypothesis, he will have a constant probability, p, of making an error. The data support this prediction well. Note that all variants of the process model make the much stronger prediction that p will be close to .5 (not eaxctly .5, as we have already shown). The data also bear out this much stronger prediction, which does not follow from the Bower–Trabasso theory.

The second assumption, and the more interesting one, is that π, the probability of hitting on the correct hypothesis is a constant. Again, the Bower–Trabasso theory does not predict the value of π, which the authors estimate directly from the data. Under the assumption, however, that the experimenter randomizes the choice of *correct hypothesis*, or that the subject selects hypotheses at random with equal probability, or both, we have already seen that the numerical value of π can be derived from any of the process models (although it will not be constant in P_3) and in general, will be different for each of the models; P_0, P_1, P_2, and P_3. Thus, it is possible to use the empirical data to choose among the process models.

This point is important, because it has genuine psychological import. The alternative assumptions, S5, $S5_1$, $S5_2$, and $S5_3$, respectively, about the subject's behavior place quite different loads on his memory, and in particular, on his short-term memory.

Under assumption S5, the subject need keep only his current hypothesis in short-term memory. Under assumption $S5_1$, he must retain the current hypothesis long enough to compare it with new hypotheses as he generates them; thus, for part of the time, he must hold two items in short-term memory.

Under assumption $S5_2$, the subject must also retain in memory the current instance, unless that instance is displayed by the experimenter during the entire duration of the trial. The amount of short-term memory required will vary with the number of attributes in the stimulus.

Finally, under assumption $S5_3$, the subject must, in addition to items mentioned previously, hold in memory the list of hypotheses not yet eliminated by previous instances. The length of this list will again depend on the number of stimulus dimensions. (It should be noted that these differences in assumption about memory requirements are explicit in the formal process models.)

Consideration of the psychological import of these assumptions, and especially their implications for short-term memory, calls attention to several aspects of experimental design whose significance is not apparent from the structure of the more abstract stochastic theory. We mention three of these:

First, it is important for the experimenter to vary the correct hypothesis across subjects, in order to wash out culturally or physiologically determined subject preferences for particular attributes. Without such randomization, π cannot be predicted (unless the additional assumption is made that the subjects' preferences are randomly and uniformly distributed). In the actual experiments the correct hypothesis was not randomized and hence, interpretation of the observed values of π is ambiguous for the Bower–Trabasso experiments, and these values have lessened utility for choosing among the alternative process models.

Second, the length of time that the instances are exposed for the subject, the consequent amount of opportunity for memorization, and the presence or absence of visual props holding information about current or previous instances of hypotheses all become critical in determining what the burden of short-term memory will be on the subject for the models incorporating S5, $S5_1$, $S5_2$, $S5_3$, respectively, and consequently, which of these processes the subject can or will employ.

Finally, other variables that affect the short-term memory requirements, and the differential salience of different stimulus dimensions, may also alter the strategies employed by subjects, hence the values of π. As we shall show in our discussion of Experiments 2 and 3, these variables may be important sources of noncomparability among experiments, and among the parameters of stochastic models describing their outcomes.

It can be seen that the predicted value of π will tend to be larger the greater the amount of information the subject retains in short-term memory, or has available to him in displayed information. There is no way in which these parameters can be represented formally in the stochastic theory, hence no way in which predictions of changed π resulting from changes in experimental design can be derived formally from the theory. These kinds of variables, on the other hand, are readily accommodated in process models—and can be accommodated formally by placing limits on the number of variables the subject can use.

Inconsistencies in Informal Derivations. Now let us consider Experiments 3–6, whose conditions deviate from the standard experiment. In order to predict what effects the changes in experimental design will have on the subject's behavior, Bower and Trabasso have to resort to informal argument, that is to say, to reasoning in terms of an implicit process model (B in Fig. 1) that is nowhere stated formally.

The difficulties to which such informal treatment can lead are illustrated by the analysis of Experiment 6, a pilot experiment. In order to explain why most subjects were unable to reach criterion on this experiment, Bower and Trabasso [3, pp. 80–82], in effect, assumed the process model with $S5_2$. (Models S5 and $S5_1$ both predict that the reversal will cause no difficulty for subjects in this experiment.) But if, for consistency, we also apply $S5_2$ in Experiment 4, we predict total errors of 6 or 7, while the observed value was 13 to 14.

Formalizing the process model would have made it obvious that no single one of the alternative processes we have defined will explain the data in both Experiments 6 and 4. Either a modified process model has to be introduced to remove the contradiction, or some essential difference must be found between the experiments to explain the subjects' use of different strategies. Let us sketch out some of the directions in which such an extension might lead.

None of these questions is raised by the stochastic theory, which is compatible with any and all of the process models. They arise only when an attempt is made to interpret the gross behavior of the subjects in terms of specific underlying psychological processes.

Abandoning the assumption of random, equiprobable selection of hypotheses would salvage $S5_2$ in Experiment 4, but only if color (the relevant dimension) has extremely low salience as compared with the other dimensions of the stimulus. For stimuli as simple and clear as those used in this experiment, this is not likely. For the moment, we put this possibility aside and retain the assumption of at least approximate equi-probability of sampling.

The entire situation is summarized in Table 2. In this table are recorded the actual average numbers of errors per subject for each experiment, and the predicted number for each experiment for each process model. Checks ($\surd$) designate those predictions that are close to the

TABLE 2   Predictions of Total Errors Four Models and Six Experiments[a]

Model	Experiment No. (From Table 1)								
	1	2	3		4		5		6
			C	R & N	C	R & N	C	R & N	
P_0	$10\surd$	6	8	8	$12\surd$	$12\surd$	$10\surd$	$10\surd$	10
P_1	$9\surd$	5	7	7	$11\surd$	$11\surd$	$9\surd$	$9\surd$	10
P_2	5	3	4	5	6	7	5?	5?	$\infty\surd$
P_3	2.1	1.4	2	2	2.3	2.3	2.1	2.1	$\infty\surd$
Actual Errors	12.2	13.4	19.1	18.7	12.9	14.5	8	7.8	48—∞

[a] The entries in the table are the average number of errors per subject predicted by each model for each experiment. The numbers followed by a check mark ($\surd$) are reasonably compatible with the actual data shown in the last line; the numbers followed by a question mark are conceivably consistent with the data; the remaining entries are incompatible with the data.

observed values, while question marks (?) designate two predictions that are perhaps "tolerable" if not close. The remaining predictions are certainly disconfirmed by the observations.

Consider first the subjects run under "standard conditions": 1, 2, 3C, 4C, and 5C. In three of these five cases (1, 4C, and 5C) the two models, P_0 and P_1, that assume that the subject uses little or no information about the specific content of the current or prior instances, predict well; in the other two cases (2 and 3C) they predict far too few errors. The models, P_2 and P_3, which assume more generous provision of short-term memory fail to predict correctly in all five cases. From the observations we conclude: (1) that subjects may behave as described in models P_0 or P_1, but certainly not as described in P_2 or P_3, and (2) that there must be some circumstances in Experiments 2 and 3C that are not reflected in any of the models.

Before we try to dispel all the mystery of the outcomes under standard conditions, let us turn to the remaining conditions, in which the experimenter, on one or more occasions in the course of the experiment, changed the correct hypothesis before the subject had learned it. Since we have combined the reversal and non-reversal variants of these conditions, we shall designate them as 3E, 4E, 5E, and 6. In the first three cases, the data for experimental subjects were substantially identical with data for the subjects in the corresponding control conditions; in the pilot experiment, 6, no control was run. Bower and Trabasso interpret the results, in Experiments 3–5, as confirming their theory. We now see that the results in Experiments 4 and 5 are consistent with models P_0 and P_1 (and 5 possibly with P_2), but that 3E is no more compatible than is 3C with *any* of the models, unless we modify them by assuming that the salience of the relevant attribute was much lower than the random sampling processes assume.

Detailed Analysis of Experiment 6. Next let us turn to Experiment 6. Bower and Trabasso explain at some length why the outcome of this experiment is just what should be expected. In their words [3, p. 80]:

"Although this procedure represents only a minor modification of that used in the prior reversal study [Experiment 5], analysis shows that the modifications are critical and that learning would be expected to be extremely slow."

The "analysis" to which they refer, and which they carry out on pp. 80–82, is not a formal derivation from the stochastic theory, but an informal derivation from a specific process model that differs from our P_2 only in supposing that the subject occasionally forgets part of the information he is holding in short-term memory. Specification of such a process model is, of course, the only basis on which the deviant results of Experiment 6 could be "expected," since in the stochastic theory there is no way of expressing this interaction of experimental conditions with the subject's behavior—hence no way of predicting the large increase in number of errors with the change in conditions, and the inability of most subjects to reach criterion.

On the other hand, Table 2 shows that, by combining strategy $S5_2$ for the subject with an appropriate formal description of the experimenter's strategy (replacing E2 by $E2_1$, to be precise), the inability of the subject to solve the problem can be deduced formally. Bower and Trabasso's explanation of Experiment 6 must be attributed wholly to the process model, whether used formally or informally, not to the stochastic theory.

Next, consider the relation of Experiment 6 to the other experiments. Experiment 6 (and *possibly* Experiment 5) is the only one that can be explained by models P_2 or P_3. The remaining experiments either require models P_0 or P_1, or are incompatible with all the models. Hence, unless some basis can be found for distinguishing Experiment 6 from the other experiments, the Bower–Trabasso analysis must be regarded as *ad hoc*. We shall not speculate as to what this basis might be. From the descriptions of the pilot experiment we detect no change in procedure that might reduce the load on short-term memory imposed by strategy $S5_2$, and hence the feasibility of the subject conforming to P_2. In the presence of such a change we would be inclined to propose the following:

STRATEGY SELECTION RULE. The subject will select the most efficient strategy that does not overburden his short-term memory (i.e., strategies, if feasible, will be preferred in the order $S5_3$, $S5_2$, $S5_1$, $S5$).

Assume, for example, that a stimulus of three or more dichotomous attributes is too large to be held in short-term memory along with the other variable information the subject requires (e.g., his current hypothesis, his response, the reinforcement). Then the subject would employ $S5_3$ only if all previous stimuli remain visible while he is choosing a new current hypothesis, and $S5_2$ only if the most recent stimulus remains visible during this period. With a slight extension of the process models, we could incorporate the strategy selection rule and short-term memory limits formally, and thereby seek to predict the outcomes of Experiments 1, 4C, 4R, 5C, 5R, and 6 within the framework of a single unambiguous model.[4]

The Anomalies in Experiments 2 and 3. This brings us back to the anomalous results of Experiments 2 and 3, where the subjects made far more errors than were predicted by any of the models. Notice that they made two or three times as many errors as would have been made by mode P_0, which is essentially a random device provided with a little bit of short-term memory.

When we examine Bower and Trabasso's descriptions of these experiments, we discover that the stimuli in these two experiments have complexities in their structures not shared by the stimuli in any of the other experiments. In Experiment 2, each attribute is 4-valued, and is transformed into a dichotomy by associating one response with a *pair* of values of the relevant attribute, the other response with the other pair of values. None of the process models would handle this situation without modifications.

In fact Bower and Trabasso also observe that their assumptions (i.e., the informal process model from which they derived the stochastic theory) do not fit the conditions in this experiment. In an Appendix [3, pp. 87–92], they develop an entirely new process model, and a

new stochastic theory derived from it, to give a better account of the data from this experiment. All of the interpretations in the body of their paper of Experiment 2 assume that π is the same for the 2-response and 4-response conditions, an assumption that does not follow from any of the process models, that does not fit the data well, and that is given up in their Appendix.

In Experiment 3, the stimulus letters are arranged in a "wheel," and the wheel orientations were randomly varied, since the experimenter intended only the letters as attribute values, and not their locations. Subjects may well have interpreted the situation differently and could have behaved as though there were several more dimensions present than the experimenter thought he had put there. For example, subjects may have concluded that the position in which a letter occurred (e.g., "T at bottom") was part of the concept.

Hence, while we have not formally extended the process models to account quantitatively for the errors in Experiments 2 and 3, it is easy to see why they should have been several times more numerous than predicted by models that took at face value the experimenter's abstract description of the stimulus. Clearly, the process models would need to be extended to include a perceptual "front end" to predict how the subject will encode for internal processing the actual stimulus configurations.[5]

Additional Tests of Process Models. Our discussion has shown that process models offer many advantages over more abstract stochastic theories for analyzing phenomena of the kind considered by Bower and Trabasso. They have a very important additional advantage, which we have not yet discussed, since its exploitation

---

[4] A control condition for Experiment 6 would have provided valuable additional information to test this hypothesis. The prediction would be that total errors would average five per subject.

[5] There is substantial evidence (including Experiment 3 here) that when the stimuli are complex, with "subtle" dimensions, differential salience of cues becomes very noticeable, and is moreover, subject to manipulation by pretraining [11]. Under these conditions the assumption in the subjects' strategies that all hypotheses are equi-probable is certainly incorrect. On the other hand, using simple and clearly-structured stimuli substantially the same as those in Experiments 4–6, the number of errors reported by Bourne and Haygood [2] are nearly those predicted by S5 (actual errors tend to exceed predicted, but usually not more than by 10%, rarely 20%).

calls for the collection of data that were not gathered in the Bower–Trabasso experiments. They make predictions not made by the stochastic theory (i.e., they provide direct formal connections between B and E of Fig. 1).

Using the process models only to make numerical predictions of π requires the sometimes questionable assumption of approximately equal salience of attributes. More important, it does not take advantage of the real predictive strength of the process models as compared with the stochastic theory. The process models predict not only the probability that the subject will make an error on each trial, but they also predict: (1) what specific response he will make, (2) what hypothesis he holds, and (3) what information he retains about previous instances and responses.

There seems to be no reason why the subject should not at least record his current hypothesis as well as his response. If it is objected that asking him for these additional behaviors will change the results, this is an objection that can readily be evaluated by a controlled experiment. Its *a priori* probability does not seem high to us.[6]

If these or equivalent data are recorded, the task of determining which (if any) model fits the behavior, for individual subjects as well as groups, becomes very much easier. To take just two examples, if a subject more than rarely stated a hypothesis (or gave a response) that was inconsistent with the previous instance, model P_2 and model P_3 clearly would not fit his behavior. And if he retained the same hypothesis after making an error, model P_0 would fit his behavior, but not P_1 or the others.

We can draw two main conclusions from our discussion of the empirical data. First, most of

the interesting psychological content in these experiments relates to subject strategies; that is, to matters on which the process models make definite assumptions (hence yield behavioral predictions), but on which the stochastic theory is silent. This is shown by Bower and Trabasso's informal use of process models as well as our more formal analysis. The stochastic theory is simply irrelevant to most of these issues, hence largely lacking in psychological content.

Second, to test process models effectively calls not only for manipulating conditions experimentally, as in the six experiments examined here, but also for obtaining more detailed behavioral data bearing directly on the hypotheses entertained by individual subjects on each trial. Gross performance data leave open—unnecessarily—too many questions about what the subjects actually are doing.

COMMENTS ON TESTING THEORIES STATISTICALLY

In the remaining two sections of this paper, we shall undertake to discuss the formal criteria for choosing among alternative theories, and then apply our conclusions to the choice between process models and abstract stochastic theories. The present section is mainly devoted to explaining why contemporary statistical theory gives us little help in the matter. The following section approaches the comparison of theories in terms of "degrees of falsifiability"— a concept most fully developed by Popper [8]. We shall see that the notion of falsifiability does, indeed, cast considerable light on the problem.

We shall first dispose of a rather specific statistical topic, then turn to a more general one. The former has to do with our reasons for considering only the stationarity and independence of p and the magnitude of π in comparing the predictions of the stochastic theory with the data. We have already quoted Atkinson *et al.* as taking the same point of view. Bower and Trabasso, although they compare for each of the experiments the predicted and observed values of a whole range of "fine-grained" statistics, seem to share this viewpoint also [3, p. 61]:

---

[6] Levine [5] has devised a method using blank (nonreinforcement) trials for determining from the responses what hypothesis the subject is using. Thus, even without using "introspective data," as subject reports of hypotheses are sometimes called, the strategy assumptions of the process models can be tested quite directly. They can also be tested, more weakly, without blank trials by analyzing the relation of responses to instances—strategy $S5_2$, for example, would definitely rule out certain "inconsistent" responses. Levine, using simple four-dimensional stimuli and self-paced trials, was able to demonstrate clearly that subjects in his experiment were using strategies somewhat "between" $S5_2$ and $S5_3$.

... most of the fine-grain statistics we have calculated are primarily sensitive to the existence of a stationary Bernouilli trials process prior to the last error. . . . Since this property characterizes a large portion of the sequence of responses obtained from a subject, we were actually trying to differentiate the models according to their assumptions about the remaining portion of the data. This is surely a losing strategy. . .

The Prediction of Standard Deviations

Let us make the point more explicit. Consider, for example, the errors made by a subject, all of which will occur while he is in state $\bar{K}$. Under a very wide range of assumptions, the distribution of these errors will be exactly or approximately geometric, with a standard deviation nearly equal to the mean.[7] That is what Bower and Trabasso predict for their experiments, and the observed standard deviations lie very close to the predicted ones.

Now this result might well seem puzzling, even if we were prepared to accept the basic ideas of the stochastic theory, for the following reason: As used for prediction, the theory assumes the same value of π for all the subjects—it makes no allowance for individual differences. Since there is every reason to suppose that individual differences in fact exist, why are not the actual standard deviations substantially larger than the predicted values? If V_T is the total variance in number of errors, V_B the "Bernoulli variance" from the assumption of constant probability, of shifting from state $\bar{K}$ to state K, and V_D the variance due to differences among subjects, then we should have approximately (since variances of mutually independent variables are additive, and these variables are nearly independent):

$$V_T = V_B + V_D \qquad (2)$$

But notice that, since standard deviations are square roots of variances, as long as V_D is not

---

[7] It is not at all uncommon to find in learning experiments that a very large part of the variance in the data can be explained by the assumption of pure guessing behavior prior to the trial on which the correct response is fixated. This result is often guaranteed by the experimenter (independently of whether the subject actually is behaving "randomly") when he randomizes stimulus sequences to avoid position preferences and the like. "Explaining" such data, then, is more a matter of verifying the laws of probability than testing psychological theories. See Simon [9, 10].

almost as large as V_B, the total standard deviation will remain very close to the Bernoulli standard deviation. Suppose, for example, that $\sigma_D = k\sigma_B$, so that $V_T = (1 + k^2)V_B$. Then:

$$\sigma_T = (1 + k^2)^{1/2} \sigma_B \qquad (3)$$

For $k = \frac{1}{2}$, this means that σ_T will only be about 11% larger than σ_B, for $(1 + k^2)^{1/2} = 1.11$. If $k = \frac{1}{4}$, $\sigma_T = 1.02\sigma_B$. Thus, if the intersubject standard deviation of π is even as much as one-half or one-quarter of its mean value, the augmentation of the variance will hardly be observable unless the samples are enormous.

We can be even more precise in showing how insensitive the statistics are to individual differences. In Experiment 5, summarized in Table 1, there were 16 subjects who started their criterion run on or before trial 5, in addition to the 10 subjects each in the C, R, and N conditions. For the data of these 46 subjects point predictions were made. Bower and Trabasso have this to say [3, p. 75]:

For these predictions, $p = .50$ and $\pi = .087$. The predictions are very accurate. Especially impressive are the predictions of the variance of total errors and the variance of the trial of the last error.

Now the only way that individual differences can enter into the formalized mathematical theory is through variation in p or π. Since π, as we have seen, can take on a range of values depending on the psychological assumptions about processing, we give the expression for the variance of total errors assuming a rectangular distribution of π.[8]

Given the geometric distribution for total errors with parameter,

$$g(T, \pi) = \pi(1 - \pi)^{T-1}, \qquad 0 < \pi < 1 \quad (4)$$

Let

$$\varphi(\pi) = \frac{1}{\pi_2 - \pi_1} = \frac{1}{\Delta}, \qquad \pi_1 < \pi < \pi_2 \quad (5)$$

be the rectangular distribution for π over the range π_1-π_2. Then the joint distribution is

---

[8] We wish to thank Professor Tarow Indow, Keio University, who developed these equations and has kindly consented to our using them.

$$F(T) = \frac{1}{\pi_2 - \pi_1} \int_{\pi_1}^{\pi_2} \pi (1-\pi)^{T-1} \, d\pi \qquad (6)$$

$$= \frac{1}{(\pi_2 - \pi_1) T(T+1)}$$

$$\left[-(1+T\pi)(1-\pi)^T \right]_{\pi_1}^{\pi_2} \qquad (7)$$

The expected value for total errors becomes

$$E(T) = \sum_{T-1}^{\infty} TF(T)$$

$$= \frac{1}{\pi_2 - \pi_1} \left[\sum_{T-1}^{\infty} \frac{-(1+T\pi)}{(T+1)} (1-\pi)^T \right]_{\pi_1}^{\pi_2} \qquad (8)$$

$$= \frac{1}{\pi_2 - \pi_1} \ln \frac{\pi_2}{\pi_1} \qquad (9)$$

and the variance is

$$\sigma^2(T) = \frac{2}{\pi_1 \pi_2} - E(T) - [E(T)]^2 \qquad (10)$$

In the limit, these expressions are the same as the Eq. 14 of Bower and Trabasso [3, p. 52].

$$\lim_{C_2 \to C_1} E(T) = \frac{1}{\Delta} \ln \left(1 + \frac{\Delta}{\pi_1} \right)$$

$$= \frac{1}{\Delta} \left(\frac{\Delta}{\pi_1} - \frac{\Delta^2}{\pi_1} + \cdots \right) = \frac{1}{\pi_1} \qquad (11)$$

where $\pi_2 = \pi_1 + \Delta$,

$$\lim_{\pi_2 \to \pi_1} \sigma^2(T) = \frac{1 - \pi_1}{\pi_1{}^2} \qquad (12)$$

Returning now to the specific example when $\pi = .0873$. Then, the limiting value of

$$E(T) = \frac{1}{.0873} = 11.45 \qquad (13)$$

and the limiting value of

$$\sigma(T) = [\sigma^2(T)]^{1/2} = \frac{1}{\pi}(1-\pi)^{1/2}$$

$$= E(T)(1-\pi)^{1/2} = 11.45 \, (0.9127)^{1/2}$$

$$= 10.96 \qquad (14)$$

These are the point estimates, when π is estimated from the observed value of 11.45 mean errors obtained from the data of the 46 subjects.

Now, doubling and halving the mean value of .087, we assume a distribution of π extending over a four-to-one range, with $\pi_1 = .0453$ and $\pi_2 = .174$. Substituting these values into Eqs. 9 and 10 yields

$$E(T) = \frac{1}{(.174) - (.0435)} \ln \frac{.174}{.0435} = 10.60 \quad (15)$$

$$\sigma^2(T) = \frac{2}{(.174)(.0435)} - 10.6 - (10.6)^2$$

$$= 146 \qquad (16)$$

and the estimate of the standard deviation of total errors becomes

$$\sigma(T) = (146)^{1/2} = 12.08 \qquad (17)$$

Compared with the value of 10.96, this is an increase of only 10% in σ, due to the assumed individual differences, for a fourfold range in variation of the learning parameter. For these large individual differences the increase in variance is barely detectable.

Prediction of the Other "Fine-Grain" Statistics

By similar arguments we can show that almost all of the "fine-grain" statistics reflect mainly the random component introduced into the experiment by the experimenter, through the initial guess behavior of the subject. Hence, the statistics are insensitive to individual differences, or, for that matter, to any other psychological aspects of the subject's behavior that might be expected to affect the statistics.

To demonstrate this, we compare in Table 3 actual and predicted statistics for one of Bower and Trabasso's experiments with the statistics of an unbiased coin flipped a number of times equal to the average number of learning trials of the experimental subjects. It can be seen that the coin-flipping statistics fit the observations about as well as do the statistics from the stochastic theory. The only difference, of course, between the pure guessing model and the stochastic learning model is that the former terminates the series of trials at a predetermined point, while termination in the latter is itself a random phenomenon with an exponential distribution over trials. Hence this demonstration does not show that the stochastic theory is wrong, merely that it has minimal psychological content.

Statistical Tests of Extreme Hypotheses

We turn next to the more general question of how to evaluate the deviations between predictions and observations—how to decide whether they are small enough to ignore or

TABLE 3   Comparison of Stochastic Theory with Pure Guessing Model

	Pure Guessing	Observed[a]	Predicted (Stochastic)[a]
Total errors	20.97	20.85	20.85
Errors before first success	1.00	1.01	.99
σ	1.41	1.39	1.37
Errors before second success	2.00	2.17	2.05
σ	2.00	2.29	7.07
Trial of last error	40.94	40.94	40.94
Successes between adjacent errors	1.00	1.04	1.04
σ	1.41	1.42	1.45
Probability of error following error	.50	.46	.48
Alternation of success and failure	21.47	22.04	21.06
Runs of errors R	10.48	11.23	10.72
Runs of k errors, r_1	5.24	6.33	5.54
r_2	2.62	2.52	2.68
r_3	1.31	1.20	1.30
r_4	.66	.52	.62
Error pairs C_1	10.00	9.56	10.11
C_2	9.75	9.67	9.86
C_3	9.50	9.12	9.63
C_4	9.25	9.20	9.40
C_5	9.00	8.75	9.17

[a] The "Observed" and "Predicted" Data are from Bower and Trabasso's first reversal experiment [3, p. 73, Table II], the "Pure Guessing" predictions are explained in the text.

large enough to invalidate the theory. Bower and Trabasso follow common practice in this matter: they treat the stochastic theory as a null hypothesis, and use such statistics as chi-square or the Kolmogorov–Smirnov statistic to find the probability that observations as deviant as the actual ones could have arisen by chance.

It is generally agreed today among mathematical statisticians that this procedure is wholly inadmissible. We will not repeat the argument at length, since it has been put forth several times in the statistical and psychological literature. A well-known statement was published by Grant [4]. When a mathematical theory is taken as the null-hypothesis, the testing procedure has two unpleasant characteristics: (1) the poorer the data (small samples or

"noisy" data), and the weaker the power of the test, the more likely is the hypothesis to be accepted; and (2) the better the data, and the more powerful the test, the more likely the rejection even of a hypothesis that is an excellent first approximation (say, within a few per cent) to the "true" theory, e.g., the $1/2N$ hypothesis. Use of distribution-free statistics, like the Kolmogorov–Smirnov, is particularly objectionable under these circumstances, since such statistics almost invariably have low power. All that can be said for them is that they are unlikely to reject a theory that is even roughly correct. Using only such weak tests, a student in the sophomore physics laboratory might be unable to "disprove" Galileo's law of falling bodies, which he could more likely do with chi-square and reasonably precise apparatus. As others have suggested, the best way to deal with this dilemma is to dispense with significance tests entirely.

This, properly, is what Bower and Trabasso do, making only a formal bow in the direction of tests of significance, and placing their main reliance on finding "critical" experiments that separate alternative hypotheses radically. But this brings us back to the discussion of the previous section, for the variant predictions in the critical experiments come, as we have seen, not from the stochastic theory but from the informal, and only partially stated, process models that stand behind the theory.

ON THE CHOICE OF THEORIES

There is general agreement on at least one criterion for rejecting a theory: if it fails badly in its empirical predictions it should be repaired or discarded. What constitutes a "bad" fit is, as we have just seen, a debatable question.

A long interval of days, months, or years often intervenes between the moment when a theory is first conceived and the moment when it can definitively be rejected or accepted (the latter, of course, only until a better theory comes along). To guide our behavior during this interval, we need not only criteria for accepting and rejecting theories, but also criteria to tell whether to "entertain" theories. As a matter of fact, much of the debate about the relative merits of different theories is debate not about which theory to *accept* (since the evidence is inconclusive), but debate about which theory or theories to *entertain*.

Falsifiability

Universality and Precision. There is a connection between the criteria for accepting and rejecting theories and the criteria for entertaining them. Popper [8, Ch. 6] after a careful analysis of these criteria, concludes that the best reason for entertaining a theory is that it is testable (more accurately "falsifiable")—i.e., that it makes strong predictions that are readily capable of being refuted by evidence if the theory is, in fact, false. Putting the matter more vividly, you can't get into much trouble

proposing a theory, however fantastic on its face, if there are numerous opportunities to demonstrate its ridiculousness empirically.

Let us, following Popper, restate the criterion in a number of other forms, to show that it really agrees with common sense and common belief on the matter. Ignoring whatever we may know about the facts of the matter, consider the two following theories:

T1.   All heavenly bodies move in circles.

T2.   All planets move in ellipses.

Theory T1 is decidedly stronger than theory T2, on two grounds: (1) in applying to all heavenly bodies, and not just planets, it is the more *universal*; (2) in specifying circles, which are special cases of ellipses, it is more *precise*. The falsifiers of T2 are a subclass of the falsifiers of T1; any observation that would falsify T2 (e.g., observation of a planet not moving in an ellipse) would also falsify T1, but not conversely. Since in a theory it is desirable to obtain the maximum of prediction from the minimum of assumptions, the more universal and precise a theory, hence the more falsifiable, the better.

The greater precision of T1, as compared with T2, may be viewed in a slightly different way. Suppose all the bodies we are observing move in a plane in Euclidean space. Then, since three points determine a circle, there is a possibility of disconfirming T1 with as few as four observations of the position of a heavenly body. Since five points determine an ellipse, T2 could never be disconfirmed with fewer than six observations of a planet. Thus, a theory is stronger the fewer the free parameters at our disposal in fitting it to data. Precision, in the context of curve fitting, varies inversely with numbers of degrees of freedom. Again, the intuitive criteria we apply in judging the "plausibility" of theories lead us to prefer the stronger theory.

Simplicity. Another consideration leads to exactly the same conclusion [8, Ch. 7]. "Simple" theories are generally thought preferable to "complex" theories. A number of reasons have been put forth for preferring simplicity, but the most convincing is that a simple theory is not as easily bent, twisted, or molded into fitting data as is a complex theory. This is merely a variant form of the argument for fewer rather than more degrees of freedom—i.e., for the more precise rather than the less precise theory.

Of course, no matter how two theories may compare in precision or universality, we will always prefer one that fits the empirical evidence to one that is falsified by the evidence. Hence, in the case of two theories related as T1 and T2, we will entertain the weaker, T2, only if the stronger, T1, is falsified.

Application of the Criteria. It is often objected to process models in general, and computer simulation models in particular, that they are too "flexible," hence weak and not falsifiable. They have, it is argued, too many degrees of freedom so that, by simple adjustment of parameters, they can be made to fit the data no matter how the data come out.

This impression seems to arise from the fact that simplicity is sometimes equated with parsimony, and that process models, when compared with mathematical theories, have the appearance of being decidedly garrulous and not parsimonious at all. For example, Bower and Trabasso's stochastic theory appears to be based on only two equations containing two parameters; while a computer program that is a literal translation of model P_0 contains about 200 instructions in IPL-V, a list processing programming language, in addition to a substantial amount of input data to specify the stimulus structure.

Appearances in this case are decidedly deceptive. A large part of the program and data in the process model are required to make explicit things that are only implicit—but of necessity assumed—in the stochastic theory. Our earlier comparison of the formalized descriptions of the models with the program implementing the theory shows that the differences in parsimony are more apparent than real as soon as both formulations are held to the same standards of explicitness.

Far more crucial than the number of words it takes to state a theory are the criteria for measuring its falsifiability. We have shown in detail that in terms of these criteria, the process models are stronger (more precise) theories than the stochastic theory, since the latter can be deduced (at least approximately) from P_0 and several of its variants. Hence, any observation that would falsify the stochastic theory would falsify the process models. Hence, until the process models are falsified by data, they are the preferable ones to entertain.

Flexibility. There still remains a slight aura of paradox about this conclusion, for we have demonstrated at least one kind of flexibility in the process models: we have shown how, by modifying S5, we could fit a number of different experimental outcomes. Yet all of these variants are (approximately) consistent with the stochastic theory. Hence, the process models (1) appear to offer more points of adjustment, and (2) appear to be easy to change to avoid falsification (though not to a greater extent than is admitted by the vagueness of the stochastic theory).

The paradox disappears if we are careful to distinguish between parameters available within a *single* theory, on the one hand, and alternative theories within a *class* of theories, on the other. The process models do not contain any free parameters. (The stimulus structure is not a free parameter, since this is dictated by the nature of the actual stimulus, defined in the experimental design.) If one of them is falsified by experimental data, the only recourse is to replace it by a different process model—another theory.

On the other hand, the stochastic theory contains two free parameters, which can be used to fit the observed values of p and π. This is precisely why the single stochastic theory is consistent with the whole set of process models, and hence is weaker than they are. Furthermore, if it is impossible to fit the data with the two free parameters, recourse may be had to the same expedient that is admitted by the process models: to change the theory. If a one-element theory does not fit, perhaps a two-element theory will, or a theory modified in some other way. This is, quite properly, the procedure that Bower and Trabasso adopt in their Appendix in order to provide a better explanation for the data of Experiment 2. They construct a new informal process model, and then derive from it a new stochastic theory that fits the data better than does the theory in the body of their paper.[9]

Formally, it is very difficult and perhaps impossible to distinguish between parameter-fitting and replacing a theory with a different but similar one. Thus it would not be formally wrong to regard a process like S5 as a "parameter" to be fitted, and the whole class of process models as a single one-parameter theory. But if we play this game, we must play it symmetrically: we can equally well view the stochastic theory as a particular member of a wider class of *n*-parameter theories, in which all but two of the parameters have zero as their particular value.

More important, we do not have to play the game at all. If we prefer strong theories to weak, then the precision of each individual process model is a definite asset. It gives us many opportunities to falsify the model. (And many additional opportunities not available for the stochastic theory, if we observe the subject's choices of hypotheses and his specific responses.) Second, because the model specifies the experimental instructions as well as the subject's strategy, it gives (without introducing free parameters) a full range of predictions over many experimental conditions. Third, if it turns out, as it has with the data we have examined, that no one of the models fits all of the data, we may be able to strengthen the theory again by incorporating several of the models in it, but adding also a process that determines the conditions under which the strategies of each model will be evoked. We have sketched out how this might be done in the case at hand. If all of the submodels in the composite are con-

sistent with the stochastic theory then, at worst, the composite model will be as strong as the stochastic theory, and almost always considerably stronger, for in any *particular experiment* it will make specific predictions without using any free parameters.

We add one comment of a more pragmatic kind. Persons who claim that it is "easy" to modify a process model, because of its garrulousness, to fit experimental data simply have never tried. The usual result of modifying a computer program, for any reason, is that the program behaves nonsensically. A program that is put together at random will give every evidence of being a random device—until it stops entirely or loops. Hence, modifying a program to fit particular discrepant observations without destroying the fit elsewhere is a good deal harder than estimating parameters, and probably at least as hard as modifying a mathematical theory by introducing new degrees of freedom via new parameters. Even if we give the theorist wide privileges of "fitting" them, process models in the form of computer programs are highly falsifiable—and most of the time demonstrably false.

CONCLUSION

In this paper we have used a concept attainment experiment previously studied in considerable detail by Bower and Trabasso in order to compare stochastic theories, on the one hand, with process models formalized as computer simulation programs, on the other.

We have constructed a class of process models from which the stochastic theory proposed by Bower and Trabasso can be derived. We have demonstrated how the stochastic theory can be translated into a very aggregative process model; and we have demonstrated how one of the process models can be expressed as a stochastic theory, and that stochastic theory, in turn, aggregated, until the Bower–Trabasso theory is obtained in close approximation.

We have shown that Bower and Trabasso in fact make use of informal process models, closely related to the ones we have formalized, in carrying out their analysis; and that the analysis could not have been carried out without them, or some equivalent. They use these

---

[9] Trabasso and Bower [12] adopt the same strategy again to explain the data of some of their cue reversal experiments. Apparently they explore a number of (informal) process models before accepting one as the basis for their revised stochastic theory, for they comment (p. 169): "This rule is the only one we have been able to devise which is consistent with the results of our prior experiments on presolution reversals." The new model involves specific, and rather elaborate assumptions about the information the subject holds in short-term memory while executing the strategy we have called S5. As in their other experiments, Bower and Trabasso use none of the detailed information about each subject's individual choices that would provide much stronger tests of the model than the statistical aggregates actually used.

informal models (a) to provide grounds of plausibility for the stochastic theories, (b) to make predictions of detail not encompassed in the stochastic theories, and (c) to make predictions for new experimental conditions to which the stochastic theories do not apply. Formalizing the process models makes it easy to detect where Bower and Trabasso were led into unconscious inconsistencies while applying process assumptions (in particular, assumptions about subject's strategies) to specific experiments.

We have reviewed the statistical evidence for the validity of the stochastic theories, and have shown that the accurate predictions of fine-grain statistics that have been achieved with them must be interpreted as validations of the laws of probability rather than of the psychological assumptions of the theories, and that the classical tests of statistical significance cannot properly be applied to testing theories of this kind.

Finally, we have discussed the criteria that might be used in choosing between relatively detailed process models, on the one hand, and highly aggregated stochastic theories, on the other, as vehicles for explaining concept attainment. We have shown that, in the case at hand, the process models are to be preferred as being stronger and more readily falsified than the stochastic theories. The process models are more universal, in permitting predictions over a wider range of experimental situations without introducing new, *ad hoc*, assumptions. They are more precise, in making more definite predictions, and predictions about many aspects of the subjects' behavior that have been abstracted away in the stochastic theories. They are simpler and more parsimonious, in allowing fewer degrees of freedom to fit them to the data.

The distinction between process models and stochastic theories is, of course, a matter of degree—we have shown that the stochastic theory can be treated as a very gross process model, but one with only modest psychological content. The process models that have been described here are themselves relatively uncomplicated, not so much because they abstract from the subject's behavior (although they certainly do not contain any detailed assumptions about his microprocesses), as because the class of situations they were designed to handle is extremely simple. Perhaps one of their most promising characteristics is that they can gradually be expanded to handle wider ranges of situations, and handle them in detail, without damaging their efficacy in simple situations. In this way they provide a means, not previously available, for gradually integrating our theoretical models over wider and wider ranges of behaviors until that happy day arrives when we shall have a theory of the whole cognitive man.

REFERENCES

1. R. C. Atkinson, G. H. Bower, and E. J. Crothers, 1965. *An introduction to mathematical learning theory.* New York: Wiley.
2. L. E. Bourne, Jr., and R. C. Haygood, 1959. The role of stimulus redundancy in concept identification. *Journal of Experimental Psychology, 58*(3): 232–238.
3. G. H. Bower, and T. R. Trabasso, 1964. Concept identification. *Studies in mathematical psychology* (R. C. Atkinson, ed.); Stanford: Stanford University Press, 32–94.
4. D. A. Grant, 1962. Testing the null hypothesis and the strategy and tactics of investigating theoretical models. *Psychological Review, 69*(1): 54–61.
5. M. Levine, 1966. Hypothesis behavior by humans during discrimination learning. *Journal of Experimental Psychology, 71*(3): 331–338.
6. D. D. McCracken, 1962. *A guide to ALGOL programming.* New York: Wiley.
7. A. Newell, ed., 1961. *Information processing language-V manual.* Englewood Cliffs, N.J.: Prentice-Hall; second edition in 1964.
8. K. R. Popper, 1959. *The logic of scientific discovery.* New York: Basic Books.
9. H. A. Simon, 1957. Amounts of fixation and discovery in maze learning behavior. *Psychometrika, 22*(3): 261–268.
10. H. A. Simon, 1962. A note on mathematical models for learning. *Psychometrika, 27*(4): 417–418.
11. T. R. Trabasso, 1963. Stimulus emphasis and all-or-none learning in concept identification. *Journal of Experimental Psychology, 65*(4): 398–406.
12. T. R. Trabasso, and G. H. Bower, 1966. Presolution dimensional shifts in concept identification: a test of the sampling with replacement axiom in all-or-none models. *Journal of Mathematical Psychology, 3*(1): 163–173. 3C.

PART II

INDIVIDUALS

The papers in this section describe aspects of the behavior of single human beings. Smith and Greenlaw, and Dutton and Starbuck each studied only one person. Newell and Simon; Feldman, Laughery, and Gregg; and Cyert, March, and Moore each studied more than one individual while their models were being developed, but their models are designed to fit and are tested against the unique behaviors of unique people.

Interestingly, these studies comprise the strongest group of studies in this book from the viewpoint of validation effort, and they also represent the most radical innovation that simulation has brought to social science research. We have classified all six studies as belonging to type 1,[1] and this is the only one of the four case-study sections we were able to fill with type 1 studies. At the same time, these studies depart from the mainstreams of social science in at least three ways:

1. First, they assume that self-reports of conscious thought provide useful and valid information about the structure of thought. When psychology was born in the late nineteenth century, introspection was considered the primary research method; but even then,

"direct introspection—observation of a process which is still running its course—is . . . entirely worthless" because "I cannot enjoy and examine my enjoyment at one and the same time."[2] In 1924 John Watson argued: "As a result of this major assumption that there is such a thing as consciousness and that we can analyze it by introspection, we find as many analyses as there are individual psychologists. There is no way of experimentally attacking and solving psychological problems and standardizing methods" [4, p. 6]. The behaviorist revolution Watson led produced fairly general acceptance of the notions that introspective evidence was nonobjective, unreplicatable, superficial (because thinking is primarily subvocal), and irrelevant (because "we could still think in some sort of way even if we had no words" [4, p. 214].

On similar grounds, introspective evidence has been rejected throughout the social sciences. Historians and political scientists have been cautious about accepting decision makers' public explanations of their decisions; anthropologists and sociologists have argued that behavior is strongly shaped by traditions and norms which are so deeply imbedded in culture that members of the culture are unconscious of them; economists and many kinds of social engineers have argued that actual decision

---

[1] The strong prior evaluation of the Newell and Simon study is based on the Logic Theorist, a precursor of GPS, rather than on the content of this article alone.

[2] The quotations are from page 33 of E. B. Titchener, 1896, *An outline of psychology* [2].

processes can be discounted as imperfect realizations of the decision maker's rational intent. Disciplines like psychiatry and abnormal psychology have attended seriously to introspective evidence, but have qualified their attention by stating that conscious thought is an erroneous and superficial indicator of more basic, unconscious thought.

2. Second, these studies assume that an individual human is worthy of study, whereas the social sciences as a whole have rejected the study of individuals. For example, psychologists have nearly always studied artificial aggregates created by summing the behaviors of many individuals, and the psychological subspecialty of "individual differences" is devoted to describing the frequencies of various behaviors across large subject groups. The common attitude on single individuals is they are not sufficiently general to be interesting; they are special cases having relevance to the studied individual alone. The proper domain of the research scientist is general theory, which describes many individuals simultaneously, and this general theory can best be obtained by studying many individuals simultaneously. There are psychologists who debate this view— Joseph Wood Krutch, Jean Piaget, and B. F. Skinner being examples—but they are clearly exceptions to a disciplinary pattern.

Of course, historians and political scientists study individuals, but they do so because the specific individuals have significantly affected social events, not because of an interest in the individual as a worthy object of scientific study. Economists and sociologists almost universally define individual behavior out of their disciplines. The only systematic exceptions to this general pattern have been the psychiatrists who sought unique cures for unique illnesses, and it is probably significant that psychiatrists identify more strongly with the medical than with the social sciences.

3. Third, these studies assume that individual behavior can be predicted. One reason social scientists have avoided the study of individuals is that they believe individual behavior is inherently erratic, random, and unpredictable. Another reason is the belief that individual behaviors are inherently much more complex and difficult to model than aggregate behaviors, which average out the idiosyncratic characteristics of individuals. Consider, for example, the psychological theories of learning. These are formulated as stochastic processes that assume large portions of the observed behaviors are random and that imply only smooth, general trends are predictable. To ascertain the smooth trends, one must have several observations of each trial in the learning sequence, but these repeated observations cannot be obtained from a single subject because his previous experiences affect his later actions. Thus the smooth trend can be obtained only by repeating the study with many different people each of whom has had no previous experience in the task. Essentially similar rationales prevail in other branches of psychology, sociology, economics, anthropology, and the social engineering sciences.

As useful background reading for this section, we recommend E. R. Guthrie and G. P. Horton's 1946 study *Cats in a puzzle box* [1] and E. C. Tolman's 1948 article "Cognitive maps in rats and men" [3]. The debate between Guthrie and Tolman crystallizes one of the basic properties of these models and presents one of the major issues such models will have to meet in the future.

The reader may wish to consider the following studies as alternatives or supplements to the ones included here.

TYPE 1 STUDIES

L. D. Barbosa, 1961. *Studies on traffic flow models.*
M. L. Braunstein, and O. F. Coleman, 1967. An information-processing model of the aircraft accident investigator.
J. Feldman, 1959. *An analysis of predictive behavior in a two-choice situation.*
L. W. Gregg, 1967. Internal representations of sequential concepts.
E. B. Hunt, and C. I. Hovland, 1961. Programming a model of human concept formulation.
E. G. Hurst, Jr., and A. B. McNamara, 1967. Heuristic scheduling in a woolen mill.

J. W. Loughary, D. D. Friesen, and R. Hurst, 1966. Autocoun: a computer-based automated
   counseling system.
C G. Moore, Jr., and C. E. Weber, 1969. Buyer decisions and simulated buyer decisions.
B. L. Myers, and C. E. Weber, 1969. Purchase planning for department store buyers.
C. E. Weber, and L. A. Welsch, 1967. A general model for sales planning.

TYPE 2 STUDIES

P. D. Fox, and C. H. Kriebel, 1967. An empirical study of scheduling decision behavior.
M. Kabrisky, 1966. *A proposed model for visual information processing in the human brain.*
C. G. Moore, Jr., and C. E. Weber, 1969. A comparison of the planning of sales by two department
   store buyers.
W. R. Reitman, 1965. *Cognition and thought.*
T. H. Rockwell, R. L. Ernest, and A. Hanken, 1968. A sensitivity analysis of empirically derived
   car-following models.
W. K. Taylor, 1956. Electrical simulation of some nervous system functional activities:
W. K. Taylor, 1965. A model of learning mechanisms in the brain.
A. M. Uttley, 1954. The classification of signals in the nervous system.

TYPE 3 STUDIES

J. R. Carbonell, J. L. Ward, and J. W. Senders, 1968. A queueing model of visual sampling: experimental
   validation.
C. R. Corner, 1965. *Simulation of human thought.*
G. W. Dickson, 1965. *Decision making in purchasing.*
E. A. Feigenbaum, 1959. *An information processing theory of verbal learning.*
E. A. Feigenbaum, and H. A. Simon, 1963. Elementary perceiver and memorizer: review of experiments.
N. V. Findler, 1966. An information processing theory of human decision making under uncertainty
   and risk.
L. J. Fogel, A. J. Owens, and M. J. Walsh, 1964. On the evolution of artificial intelligence.
E. B. Hunt, 1963. Simulation and analytic models of memory.
J. C. Myers, 1968. *Project Seal: simulation experiment in adaptive learning.*
J. M. Paige, and H. A. Simon, 1966. Cognitive processes in solving algebra word problems.
H. A. Simon, and M. Barenfeld, 1969. Information-processing analysis of perceptual processes in
   problem solving.
L. Uhr, and C. Vossler, 1963. A pattern recognition program that generates, evaluates, and adjusts
   its own operators.
W. W. Wierwille, and G. A. Gagné, 1966. Nonlinear and time-varying dynamical models of human
   operators in manual control systems.
N. Wiggins, and P. J. Hoffman, 1968. Three models of clinical judgment.
D. B. Yntema, and L. Klem, 1965. Telling a computer how to evaluate multidimensional situations.

REFERENCES

1. E. R. Guthrie, and G. P. Horton, 1946. *Cats in a puzzle box.* New York: Rinehart.
2. E. B. Titchener, 1896. *An outline of psychology.* New York: Macmillan.
3. E. C. Tolman, 1948. Cognitive maps in rats and men. *Psychological Review, 55*(4): 189–208.
4. J. B. Watson, 1925. *Behaviorism.* New York: Norton.

5

SIMULATION OF HUMAN THOUGHT

ALLEN NEWELL

HERBERT A. SIMON

INTRODUCTION

This paper is concerned with the psychology of human thinking. It sets forth a theory to explain how some humans try to solve some simple formal problems. The research from which the theory emerged[1] is intimately related to the field of information processing and the construction of intelligent automata, and the theory is expressed in the form of a computer program. The rapid technical advances in the art of programming digital computers to do sophisticated tasks have made such a theory feasible.

It is often argued that a careful line must be drawn between the attempt to accomplish with machines the same tasks that humans perform, and the attempt to simulate the processes humans actually use to accomplish these tasks. The program discussed in the paper, GPS (General Problem Solver), maximally confuses the two approaches—with mutual benefit. GPS has previously been described as an attempt to

build a problem-solving program [4, 5], and in our own research it remains a major vehicle for exploring the area of artificial intelligence. Simultaneously, variants of GPS provide simulations of human behavior. It is this latter aspect—the use of GPS as a theory of human problem solving—that we want to focus on here, with special attention to the relation between the theory and the data.

THE ROLE OF SIMULATION IN PSYCHOLOGY

The path of scientific investigation in any field of knowledge records a response to two opposing pulls. On the one side, a powerful attraction is exerted by "good problems"—questions whose answers would represent fundamental advances in theory or would provide the basis for important applications. On the other side, strong pulls are exerted by "good techniques"—tools of observation and analysis that have proved to be incisive and reliable. The fortunate periods in a science are those in which these two pulls do not paralyze inquiry by their opposition but cooperate to draw research into fruitful channels.

When this happy condition is not substantially satisfied, science is threatened by schism. Some investigators will insist on working on

SOURCE: This paper is a composite of "The Simulation of Human Thought," "GPS, A Program That Simulates Human Thought," and "Computer Simulation of Human Thinking."

[1] We would like to express our indebtedness to J. C. Shaw, who has been our colleague in most of our research into complex information processes, including the GPS program which forms the basis of this paper.

important problems with methods that are insufficiently powerful and that lack rigor; others will insist on tackling problems that are easily handled with the available tools, however unimportant those problems may be.

Stress arising from the mismatch of ends and means is seldom completely absent from any science; examples could be provided from contemporary biology, meteorology, or mathematics. But it has been blatantly apparent in the science of psychology. At the beginning of this century the prevailing thesis in psychology was associationism. It was an atomistic doctrine, which postulated a theory of hard little elements, either sensations or ideas, that became hooked or associated together without modification. It was a mechanistic doctrine, with simple fixed laws of continuity in time and space to account for the formation of new associations. Those were its assumptions. Behavior proceeded by the stream of associations: each association produced its successors, and acquired new attachments with the sensations arriving from the environment.

In the first decade of the century a reaction developed to this doctrine through the work of the Würzburg school. Rejecting the notion of a completely self-determining stream of associations, it introduced the task (Aufgabe) as a necessary factor in describing the process of thinking. The task gave direction to thought. A noteworthy innovation of the Würzburg school was the use of systematic introspection to shed light on the thinking process and the contents of consciousness. The result was a blend of mechanics and phenomenalism, which gave rise in turn to two divergent antitheses: behaviorism and the Gestalt movement.

The behavioristic reaction insisted that introspection was a highly unstable, subjective procedure, whose futility was amply demonstrated in the controversy on imageless thought. Behaviorism reformulated the task of psychology as one of explaining the response of organisms as a function of the stimuli impinging on them and measuring both objectively. However, behaviorism accepted, and indeed reinforced, the mechanistic assumption that the connections between stimulus and response were formed and maintained as simple, determinate functions of the environment.

The Gestalt reaction took an opposite turn. It rejected the mechanistic nature of the associationist doctrine but maintained the value of phenomenal observation. In many ways it continued the Würzburg school's insistence that thinking is more than association—thinking has direction given to it by the task or by the set of the subject. Gestalt psychology elaborated this doctrine in genuinely new ways in terms of holistic principles of organization.

Behaviorism and the acceptance of the norms of the natural sciences in psychology greatly restricted for a generation or more the range of behavioral phenomena with which the psychologist, as scientist, was willing to concern himself. Unless an aspect of behavior could be examined in the laboratory and could be recorded and measured in an entirely objective fashion, it was not, in the prevailing view, a proper subject of study.

There has been considerable relaxation of this austerity in the past decade, although not without misgiving and apology. A leading text on experimental psychology, for example, in introducing the topics of problem-solving, insight, thinking, and language behavior, observes:

These topics have often been omitted from textbooks in the past—perhaps because of some subtle aura of "mentalism." Historically, of course, thought and meaning were the central problems for psychology. The wide circle that American psychologists have been making through behaviorism seems to be bringing them back again to the same core of the science, but perhaps they are returning with more precise techniques and a more objective point of view than would otherwise have been attained [7].

There is no need to document in detail this resurgence in psychology of concern with the central topic of thinking. This subject had been kept alive during the heyday of behaviorism by a number of outstanding men—the names of Köhler, Tolman, Wertheimer, Bartlett, Duncker, and Maier come at once to mind—who refused to allow fixed canons of rigor to bar them from studying the relevant and the significant. In turn, their work provided foundations on which the more recent investigators—Luchins-Heidbreder, Harlow, deGroot, Guetzkow, and Bruner, to mention some examples—have built. Those who regard thinking as the core of psychological inquiry and who urge a return to concern with it, do not want to turn the clock back. The behaviorists and operationalists are, of course, right in demanding objectivity, clarity, and rigor. Relatively few psychologists are satisfied with the vagueness of Gestalt language and with explanation at the level it permits. Few are satisfied with the eclectic language of James, and many find excessive vagueness and ambiguity in the "mediation" hypotheses of his middle-of-the-road descendants.

The task is not simply to restore thinking to the center of the psychological stage; it is to study thinking with as much methodological sophistication as we demand for simpler phenomena. Consequently, the increasing attention to thought processes does not merely reaffirm their importance but it reflects a growing belief that the techniques of psychological inquiry have become adequate, at least to some degree, to the subject matter. Whether the belief was fully justified a decade ago, when the resurgence began, is a moot question. The main thesis of this paper is that the belief is justified now—that the technological advances that are necessary to permit a theory of thinking to be formulated and tested have occurred.

To understand complex phenomena we must have powerful tools of inquiry—tools for observing facts and tools for reasoning from complicated premises to their consequences. The invention of the telescope and of calculus played crucial roles at one stage in the history of physics, and the invention of the cyclotron and of quantum mechanics at a later stage. New observing instruments made visible the previously invisible phenomena that had to be known if the theory was to advance. New analytic instruments made comprehensible the facts revealed by the telescope and cyclotron, which otherwise would have been inscrutable. A science of complex phenomena needs powerful machines for observing and powerful tools for reasoning.

The phenomena of human thinking are more complex than the phenomena that physics studies. In some respects the former are easier to observe than the latter—human verbal behavior is present and audible, neither submicroscopic nor as distant as the stars. (To be sure, we do not have instruments for observing cerebral events that are nearly as revealing as the instruments of physics.) But observable or not, human behavior has not been easy to interpret. We have had great difficulties in building successful theories to explain it.

Until a decade ago, the only instruments that we had for building theories about human behavior were the tools we borrowed and adapted from the natural sciences: operationalism and classical mathematics. And so inadequate are the tools to the task that a highly respected psychologist offered in earnest the doctrine that we must build a science without a theory—surely a doctrine of desperation.

With the advent of the modern digital computer and the emergence of the concept of a program, the situation altered radically. The computer was invented as a machine to do arithmetic rapidly. But as matters turned out, a machine to do arithmetic was a machine that could manipulate symbols. It was natural to ask whether such a machine could perform some of the more general symbol-manipulating processes required for thinking and problem solving as well as the very specialized processes required for arithmetic. The answer, as we shall see, is "yes." There is now substantial evidence, which we shall review, that a digital computer, appropriately programmed, can carry out complex patterns of processes that parallel exceedingly closely the processes observable in human subjects who are thinking.

But the significance of the computer does not lie solely in its ability to exhibit humanoid behavior. It lies even more in the fact that we can specify with complete rigor the system of processes that make the computer exhibit this behavior—we can write a program that constitutes a theory of the computer's behavior in literally the same sense that the equations of Newtonian dynamics constitute a theory of the motions of the solar system. The genuinely new analytic instrument available for explaining human behavior is the program.

Thinking is to be explained by writing a program for a thinking process. If the program is complicated—as it usually is—so that it is hard to predict what behavior it will produce, we code the program for a computer. Then we compare the behavior of the computer so programmed with the behavior of a human subject performing the same tasks. Thus, the programming language provides a precise language for expressing theories of mental processes; the computer provides a powerful machine for grinding out the specific behavioral consequences of the theories and for comparing these consequences in detail—sentence by sentence—with the verbal behavior of human subjects.

The methodology provides a powerful test of the sufficiency of the theories. If a program is vague or incomplete, the computer will not operate—it will not do what we assert it will do. Conversely, if we are able to write a program that, realized on a computer, simulates human behavior closely, we can assert that we have discovered a set of mechanisms at least sufficient to account for the behavior. No dark corners are left in which vitalism or mysticism can lurk—nor even the vagueness of "mediational" hypotheses.

These are large claims. It is time to present the evidence for them. We can only do this, however, after stating a little more fully what we mean by an explanation of behavior and how a computer program can constitute an explanation of the processes of human thinking and problem solving.

WHAT IS AN EXPLANATION?

To explain a phenomenon means to show how it inevitably results from the actions and interactions of precisely specified mechanisms that are in some sense "simpler" than the phenomenon itself. Thus, a chemical reaction is explained by reducing it to the interactions of atoms having specified properties. A spinal reflex is explained by reducing it to a sequence of neural and synaptic processes.

For complex phenomena there may be, and usually are, several levels of explanation; we do not explain the phenomena at once in terms of the simplest mechanisms but reduce them to these simplest mechanisms through several stages of explanation. We explain digestion by reducing it to chemical events; we explain the chemical reactions in terms of atomic processes; we explain the atomic processes in terms of the interactions of subatomic particles.

Every flea has its little fleas, and the scientist's view accepts no level of explanation as "ultimate."

Programs explain behavior in terms of an intermediate level of mechanism, simpler than the behavior itself but more complex than neural events. The intermediate mechanisms provide a theory of the behavior and also a starting point for the next stage of reduction—either to neural events or to still another level of mechanism above the neurological.

Concretely, human thinking is to be explained in terms of precisely specified simple mechanisms called elementary information processes. Elementary information processes are organized into complex processes—thinking, problem-solving, verbal behavior—by programs. Programs are long, branching sequences of elementary processes. In the course of behavior, at each branch point, a particular continuation is selected and followed conditionally on the outcome of a simple test (itself an elementary information process) of the identity or difference of a pair of symbols.

In summary, the study and explanation of complex human behavior is to proceed as follows:

1. Behavior is to be explained by specifying programs that will, in fact, produce the behavior. These programs consist of systems of elementary information processes.

2. Elementary processes are to be explained by showing how they can be reduced to known physiological processes in the central nervous system and its appendages.

Since we are concerned here with only the first of these two tasks of explanation—the reduction of behavior to information processes—what guarantee exists against introducing vitalism by the back door? What is to prevent one of the elementary processes from harboring some kind of elan vital? Since explanation at the second level has not been carried out, we cannot guarantee directly that the human nervous system contains mechanisms capable of performing each of the elementary information processes. But we can insist that there exists some mechanism—a mechanism that can be explained completely at the level of physics—capable of performing all these processes. We can demand that the processes and the programs constructed of them be realized in a digital computer. If the computer executes the processes and, in executing them, simulates human thinking, then no vitalistic mystery can be hidden in the postulates.

We are not talking of a crude analogy between the nervous system and computer "hardware." The inside of a computer does not look like a brain any more than it looks like a missile when it is calculating its trajectory. There is every reason to suppose that simple information processes are performed by quite different mechanisms in computer and brain, and we shall sometime want to know what the brain mechanisms are as we now know the mechanisms of the computer. However, once we have devised mechanisms in a computer for performing elementary information processes that appear very similar to those performed by the brain (albeit by quite different mechanisms at the next lower level), we can construct an explanation of thinking in terms of these information processes that is equally valid for a computer so programmed and for the brain.

PROGRAMS AS EXPLANATIONS

We have described a program as a conditionally branching sequence of elementary information processes. To explain a behavior path by a program is quite analogous to explaining the path of a planetary system by a system of differential equations. The differential equations determine what will happen next (during the next "infinitesimal" interval of time) as a function of the exact state of the system at the beginning of the interval. The program determines what the mechanism will do next as a function of its exact state at the moment—this state being dependent, in turn, on the previous history of the system and its current environment.

How is the "right" program discovered—the one that explains the behavior? In the same way that the correct theory is found for any phenomena. One recipe is this: tape-record some human subjects who are thinking aloud while solving problems (make observations of the phenomena); try to write a computer program that you think will simulate the human protocols (formulate some differential equations); realize the program on a computer, and determine what behavior path it would follow when confronted with the same problems as the human subjects (integrate the equations numerically); compare the simulated with the actual behavior (compare the predictions with the data); modify the program on the basis of the discrepancies that are discovered (modify the equations). Repeat until you are satisfied with the fit.

A number of investigators have independently proposed this general path to the explanation of higher mental processes, and its origins can be traced back at least to Ach and the Wurzburg School. In recent times, perhaps the most explicit examples are to be found in deGroot's investigation of the thought processes of chess players [2] and in *A Study of Thinking* by Bruner and his associates [1]. Bruner uses the term strategy, borrowed from the mathematical theory of games, for what we have called a "program." What the digital computer and the techniques of programming add is the machinery that gives us hope of following this path, not merely in principle and in general, but in fact and in detail.

COMPUTER SIMULATION OF A PROGRAM

The methodology outlined above requires that a computer simulate the sequence of verbal utterances of a human subject (or other symbolic behavior, such as button pushing). It is easy to understand how this can be done once we recognize that computers fundamentally have nothing to do with numbers. It is only by historical accident that we perceive computers as mechanisms for manipulating numerical symbols. They are, in fact, extremely general devices for manipulating symbols of any kind; and the elementary processes required to simulate human thinking could be performed by a computer that had no special capacity for rapid arithmetic—that could do no more than simple counting. The programs we shall describe make no essential use of the computer's arithmetic processes.

What processes can a general-purpose computer perform? Some of the crucial ones are these:

1. It can read a symbol—transform a symbol presented to its input mechanisms into a different representation of that symbol in its internal storage (transform a pattern of holes on a punched card into a pattern of magnetism in core storage). The relation between the external and internal representation is quite flexible, almost arbitrary, and can be altered by the program.

2. It can move a symbol—reproduce in a storage location a symbol that is present in another storage location, with or without a change in the form of representation.

3. It can generate a symbol—create and store a pattern in one of its modes of internal representation.

4. It can compare two symbols, executing one program step if they are identical, but a different one if they are not.

5. It can associate two symbols, allowing access to one symbol (the associated symbol) when the other is given.

Programs can be written that combine these simple processes into processes that are slightly more complex. For example, a computer can be programmed to manipulate a series of symbols as a list, so that it can perform such operations as: "Put this symbol at the end of that list," or "Find a symbol on this list which is identical with that symbol." Such list structures, and the processes for operating on them, have many resemblances to human memory and association.

Finally, still more complex programs can be composed that enable a computer to respond to instructions like: "Solve the problems on the following list," "Print out the steps of the proof, giving the justification for each step," "Print out the processes used at each step of the problem-solving process: the methods, what is being noticed and attended to, what plans are formed, what subproblems are created." When this last stage has been reached, the trace that the computer prints out while it is attempting to solve the problem can be compared, line by line, with the tape recording of the human thinking-aloud protocol. If the stream of words produced by the two processes is almost the same, then the computer program that produced the trace is an explanation of the thought process

of the human subject in every significant sense of the word.

TESTING PROGRAMS AS THEORIES

The phrase "almost the same" glides over the whole problem of goodness of fit. Unfortunately, existing statistical theory offers no solution to the problem in the situation we have described, nor can we propose any simple answer. A rough and ready answer is that the evidence provided by five minutes of thinking aloud and the corresponding trace is so voluminous as to scarcely leave room for doubt whether a first approximation has been achieved or not. This is a subjective answer, and we should like to discuss a slightly more objective, though weaker one:

"Turing's Test"

No two human subjects solving the same problem will have the same program or produce the same protocol. Hence, any single program can only be a precise theory of the behavior of a single subject. There must be, however, close qualitative similarities among the programs and protocols of appropriately selected classes of subjects—if not, then it is meaningless to speak of a theory of human problem solving. Suppose that we mix ten traces of computer programs and ten human protocols in an urn. Suppose that a properly qualified human observer is unable to separate, with more than chance success, the protocols produced by the computer programs from those produced by the humans. Then we shall say that the programs that produced the computer traces pass Turing's test [2] and provide a satisfactory explanation of the human protocols.

Turing's test can be applied in stronger or weaker forms. Comparison of the move chosen by a chess program with the moves

[2] A test of this sort was first proposed by A. M. Turing in a discussion of whether a machine could think [8]. Given two communication channels (say teletypes), one connected to a human, the other to a machine, a human interrogator was to identify which channel was the machine's. Active questioning was allowed, and the machine's problem was to fool the interrogator, despite the best efforts of the human on the other channel (who it was assumed would side with the interrogator) to reveal his identity.

chosen by human players in the same position would be a weak test. The program might have chosen its move by quite a different process from that used by the humans. For the task environment itself defines what are appropriate behaviors, and any mechanism capable of behaving adaptively in the environment might be expected to exhibit about the same external behavior. Similarity of function does not guarantee similarity of structure, or of process.

However, if data are gathered by the thinking-aloud technique or by other means that indicate the processes used to select the behavior, it may and usually will be possible to distinguish different ways of arriving at the result. If the program makes the same analysis as the humans, notices the same features of the board, overlooks the same traps, then we shall infer, and properly, that down to some level of detail, the program provides an explanation of the human processes. The more minute and detailed the comparison between program and behavior, the greater will be the opportunities for detecting differences between the predicted and actual behaviors.

This method of theory building and testing meets the problem of induction no better and no worse than other methods. There never is, and can never be, a guarantee that some other theory will not explain the data equally well or better. As in other sciences, it will be time to face this problem when someone actually proposes an alternative theory that explains the data equally well and in comparable detail. Meanwhile, the validity of programs as theories can be tested in stronger and stronger form by pushing the level of detail of matching down toward the level of elementary information processes.

THE GENERAL PROBLEM SOLVER

To give substance to these generalities, we shall examine the General Problem Solver [4, 6]. The General Problem Solver was devised to simulate the behavior of some specific human subjects solving problems in symbolic logic in a task situation devised by O. K. Moore and Scarvia Anderson [3]. Some 30 thinking-aloud protocols for these tasks have been recorded in the laboratory at Carnegie Tech. Comparison of these with data obtained for 64 subjects by Moore without requiring the subjects to think aloud indicates that there are no substantial differences in process under the two conditions.[3]

GPS, as we shall call the program, is called "general" because it is not limited to the task for which it was originally devised. Hand simulation indicates it can also solve the Whitehead and Russell logic problems, do trigonometric identities, perform formal integration and differentiation, and, with a small extension to the program, solve algebraic equations. As will be seen, there is reason to hope that it can be extended to an even wider range of tasks.

Before comparing GPS in detail with human behavior, we should like to observe that it does solve problems. Hence its program constitutes a system of mechanisms, constructed from elementary information processes, that is a sufficient system for performing certain tasks that humans perform. However much it may prove necessary to modify the details of the program for close human simulation, in its present form it constitutes an unequivocal demonstration that a mechanism can solve problems by functional reasoning.

In simplest terms, GPS is a program for reasoning about means and ends. It grew out of our observation that the protocols of laboratory subjects contained many statements of the following sorts: "So in all these now I have notes as to exactly what I can do with them." (Paraphrase: "Here are some means at my disposal, what ends will they serve?") "I'm looking at the idea of reversing these two things now . . . then I'd have a similar group at the beginning." (Paraphrase: "If I use means X, I will achieve Y.") "I'm looking for a way, now, to get rid of that symbol." ("What is the means to achieve this end?") "And now I'd use Rule 1." ("I'll apply means X.")

Closer scrutiny of the protocols reveals that the vast majority of the statements in them fall within this general framework. Simulating the behavior of these subjects requires a program that can handle problems in this kind of functional language. Further, the functional language makes no reference to the specific

---

[3] Professor Moore kindly provided us with the full data on his subjects prior to publication.

subject matter of the problem—in this instance symbolic logic. The program must be organized to separate its general problem-solving procedures from the application of these to a specific task. GPS is such a program.

The adjective "general" does not imply that GPS can reason about all or most kinds of problems; or that it will simulate all or most human problem-solving activity. It simply means that the program contains no reference to the task content, and hence is usable for tasks other than the one for which it was devised.

GPS operates on problems that can be formulated in terms of objects and operators. An operator is something that can be applied to certain objects to produce different objects (as a saw applied to logs produces boards). The objects can be described by the features they possess (boards have flat parallel sides), and by the differences between pairs of objects (a 2- × 4-inch board is thicker than a 1- × 4-inch board). Operators may be restricted to apply to only certain kinds of objects (nails are used on wood, not steel); and there may be operators applied to several objects as inputs, producing one or more objects as output (joining four beams to produce a frame).

Various problems can be formulated in a task environment containing objects and operators: to find how to transform one object into another; to find an object with specified features; to modify an object so that a specified operator can be applied to it; and so on. In the task environment confronting our laboratory subjects, the objects were symbolic logic expressions (which the subjects were told were messages in code). The operators were 12 rules of logic for transforming one or two input expressions into an output expression. Figure 1 gives these rules. For example, by Rule 1 an expression of the form $(A \cdot B)$ could be transformed into $(B \cdot A)$, thus reversing the order of the symbols. The problems given the subjects were to "recode," using the rules, one or more given logic expressions into a different logic expression. One problem, for example, was to transform $R \cdot (-P \supset Q)$ into $(Q \lor P) \cdot R$.

A statement like: "I'm looking for a way, now, to get rid of that horseshoe" expresses a goal. The goal in this instance is to eliminate

a difference (the "horseshoe" in the original expression versus the "wedge" in the desired expression) between one object and another. The goals that the subjects mention in their protocols take a variety of forms. We have incorporated three types of goals that account for the vast majority of goals statements, in the present version of GPS. They are:

Goal Type No. 1 Find a way to transform object a into object b (i.e., a sequence of operators to accomplish the transformation). Objects are formed by building up expressions from letters $(P, Q, R, \ldots)$ and connectives . (dot), $\lor$ (wedge), $\supset$ (horseshoe), and $-$ (tilde). Examples are P, $-Q$, $P \lor Q$, $-(R \supset S) \cdot -P$; $--P$ is equivalent to P throughout.

Twelve rules exist for transforming expressions (where A, B, and C may be any expressions or subexpressions):

R1. $A \cdot B \to B \cdot A$
   $A \lor B \to BA$
R2. $A \supset B \to -B \supset -A$
R3. $A \cdot A \leftrightarrow A$
   $A \lor A \leftrightarrow A$
R4. $A \cdot (B \cdot C) \leftrightarrow (A \cdot B) \cdot C$
   $A \lor (B \lor C) \leftrightarrow (A \lor B)C$
R5. $A \lor B \leftrightarrow -(-A \cdot -B)$
R6. $A \supset B \leftrightarrow -A \lor B$
R7. $A \cdot (B \lor C) \leftrightarrow (A \cdot B) \lor (A \cdot C)$
   $A \lor (B \cdot C) \leftrightarrow (A \lor B) \cdot (A \lor C)$
R8. $A \cdot B \to A$ Applies to main
   $A \cdot A \to B$ expression only.
R9. $A \to A \lor X$ Applies to main
                           expression only.
R10. $\left.\begin{matrix} A \\ B \end{matrix}\right\} \to A \cdot B$ A and B are two main expressions.
R11. $\left.\begin{matrix} A \\ A \supset B \end{matrix}\right\} \to B$ A and $A \supset B$ are two main expressions.
R12. $\left.\begin{matrix} A \supset B \\ B \supset C \end{matrix}\right\} \to A \supset C$ $A \supset B$ and $B \supset C$ are two main expressions.

Figure 1 Rules for Transforming Logic Expressions

Goal Type No. 2 Apply operator q to object a (or to an object obtained from a by transformations).

Goal Type No. 3 Reduce the difference, d, between object a and object b by modifying a.

The problems initially given the subjects established transform goals; "getting rid of the horseshoe" expresses a reduce goal; "And now I'd use Rule 1" states an apply goal.

To attain a goal, consideration of the goal must evoke in the problem solver some idea of one or more means that might be relevant. The subject, for example, who says "I'm looking for a way, now, to get rid of that horseshoe," follows this statement with, "Ah . . . here it is, Rule 6. So I'd apply Rule 6 to the second part of what we have up there." Applying Rule 6 (see Figure 1) has been evoked as a method for getting rid of horseshoes.

Thus, the evoking process is represented in GPS by associating with each type of goal one or more methods for attaining a goal of that type. These are shown in Figure 2. Method No. 1, associated with Transform goals, consists of: (a) matching the objects a and b to find a difference, d, between them; (b) setting up the Type No. 3 subgoal of reducing d, which if successful produces a new transformed object, c; (c) setting up the Type No. 1 subgoal of transforming c into b. If this last goal is achieved, the original Transform goal is achieved. The match in step (a) tests for the more important differences (in terms of some priority list) first.

Method No. 2, for achieving an Apply goal, consists of: (a) determining if the operator can be applied by setting up a Type No. 1 goal for transforming a into the input form of the operator q [which we call $C(q)$]; (b) if successful, the output object is produced from the output form of q [$P(q)$].

Method No. 3, for achieving a Reduce goal, consists of: (a) searching for an operator that is relevant to reducing the difference, d; (b) if one is found, setting up the Type No. 2 goal of applying the operator, which if attained produces the modified object.

To see how GPS goes about applying these goal types and methods to the solution of problems, consider a concrete example. We shall use the problem mentioned earlier: to "recode" the expression, L_1, $R \cdot (-P \supset Q)$ into the expression L_0, $(Q \lor P) \cdot R$. As we go along we shall explain the recoding rules as far as is necessary to understand the example.

GPS begins by establishing the Type No. 1 goal of transforming L_1 into L_0. Among the information processes available to it—built up from the elementary processes, are a number of tests for the possible differences among pairs of expressions, for example:

1. A test whether the same or different variables (letters) appear in the two expressions;
2. A test whether each variable occurs the same or a different number of times;
3. A test whether a variable or group occurs in the same or in a different position;
4. A test whether a pair of connectives $(\cdot, \lor, \supset)$ is the same or different.

And so on. The tests may be applied to whole expressions or to corresponding parts of expressions [e.g., $(-P \supset Q)$ and $(Q \lor P)$].

Method No. 1 applies these tests in order. It discovers a difference in position of the R's in L_1 and L_0, and establishes the Type No. 3 goal of reducing this difference. For each difference, it has available a list of operators that are possibly relevant to removing a difference of that kind. (These lists can be constructed by GPS itself by examining the set of available operators.) In this case, it discovers that Rule 1, which transforms an expression of form $(A \cdot B)$ or $(A \lor B)$ into an expression of form $(B \cdot A)$ or $(B \lor A)$, respectively, affects differences in position. Consequently, it establishes the Type No. 2 subgoal of applying Rule 1 to L_1. This can be done by identifying R with A and $(-P \supset Q)$ with B in the rule, thus producing L_2, $(-P \supset Q) \cdot R$ as the output expression.

This done, the original goal now sets up the new subgoal of transforming L_2 into L_0. Repeating the cycle, a difference in connectives is found between the left-hand sides of L_2 and L_0, respectively; a rule, R_c is found that changes connectives by transforming $(-A \supset B)$ into $(A \lor B)$, and hence that transforms $(-P \supset Q) \cdot R$ into L_3, $(P \lor Q) \cdot R$.

A third repetition of the basic cycle discovers the difference in position between $(P \lor Q)$ in L_3 and $(Q \lor P)$ in L_0, and applies R_1 to remove the difference. Finally, GPS discovers that the product of this transformation is identical with L_3, and declares the problem solved. We may summarize the steps as follows:

Step	Expression	Justification for Step
L_1	$R \cdot (-P \supset Q)$	Given
L_2	$(-P \supset Q) \cdot R$	Rule 1
L_3	$(P \lor Q) \cdot R$	Rule 6 inside parenthesis
L_0	$(Q \lor P) \cdot R$	Rule 1 inside parenthesis

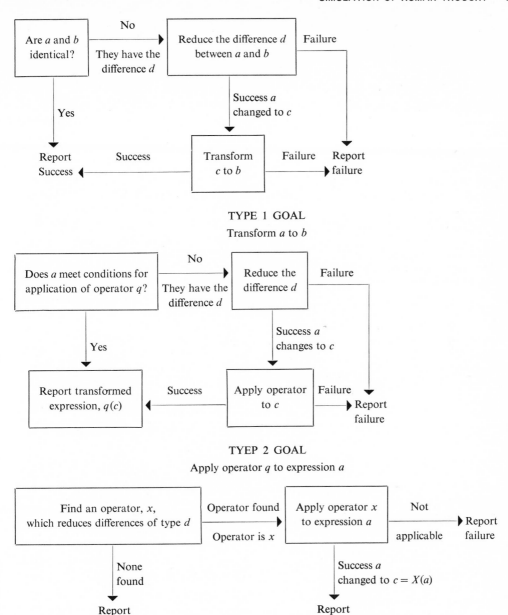

TYPE 1 GOAL

Transform *a* to *b*

TYEP 2 GOAL

Apply operator *q* to expression *a*

TYPE 3 GOAL

Reduce the difference *d* between *a* and *b*

Figure 2 Methods Associated with **GPS** Goals.

A COMPARISON WITH HUMAN BEHAVIOR

Granted that GPS can solve this problem, and many that are a good deal more difficult, why do we suppose that the processes of GPS resemble in any way the processes a human would use in solving the same problem? Let us compare GPS's processes, as just narrated, with the content of the protocol of a human subject solving the same problem. We shall let the reader judge whether the two processes are or are not closely similar. (Neither the particular problem nor the human protocol we shall examine was used in devising GPS.)

Line	Simulation	Protocol
1	L_0: $(Q \vee P) \cdot R$	(Expression to be obtained)[a]
2	L_1: $R \cdot (-P \supset Q)$	(Expression given at start)
3	Goal 0: Transforms L_1 and L_0	(Goal set by experimenter)
4	Match gives position difference (Δp)	I'm looking at the idea of reversing these two things now.
5	Goal 1: Reduce Δp between L_1 and L_0	(Thinking about reversing what?)
6	Search list of rules	The R's. . . .
7	Goal 2: Apply R_1 to L_1	
8	Match: R_1 applicable	
9	Test rule functions: reduces Δp	then I'd have a similar group at the beginning
10	no others	but that seems to be. . . .
11	Set to execute R_1 when analysis complete	I could easily leave something like that 'til the end,
12	Goal 3: Transform right L_1 into left L_0	except then I'll. . . .
13	Match gives position difference (Δp)	
14	Goal 4: Reduce Δp between right L_1 and left L_0	
15	Search list of rules	
16	Goal 5: Apply R_1 to right L_1	
17	Match: R_1 fails, right L_1 has $\supset$ (Δc)	(Applying what rule?)
18	Goal 6: Apply R_2 to right L_1	Applying . . . for instance, 2.
19	Match: R_2 applicable	
20	Test rule functions: reduces Δp,	
21	but introduces unwanted— (Δs)	That would require a sign change.
22	Reject goal	(Try to keep talking, if you can.)
23	Goal 7: Apply R_3 to right L_1	Well . . . then I look down at Rule 3
24	Match: R_2 not applicable	and that doesn't look any too practical
25	Goal 8: Apply R_4 to L_1	Now 4 looks interesting.
26	Match: R_4 not applicable[b]	It's got three parts similar to that . . . and . . .
27		there are dots so the connective . . . seems to work easily enough,
28	Test rule functions: doesn't reduce Δp	but there's no switching of order.
29	Reject goal	
30	Goals 9 to 13: Apply R_5 to R_9 to L_1	
31	All goals fail on match	
32	or test of function.	
33	Search rules again, but don't reject	I need that P and a Q changed
34	without attacking subproblem	so . . .
35	Goal 14: Apply R_1 to right L_1	
36	Match: R_1 fails, right L_1 has $\supset$ (Δc)	I've got a horseshoe there. That doesn't seem
37	Test rule functions: reduces Δp, no others	practical any place through here.
38	Set to execute R_1, if applicable	
39	Goal 15: Reduce Δc between right L_1 and R_1	I'm looking for a way now, to get rid of that horseshoe.
40	Search list of rules, for rule with $\supset$	
41	that reduces Δc.	
42	Goal 16: Apply R_6 to right L_1	Ah . . . here it is, Rule 6.
43	Match: R_6 applicable	
44	Test rule functions: reduces Δc	
45	reduces Δs	
46	Set to execute R_6 when analysis complete	

Figure 3 continues

Line	Simulation	Protocol
47	Goal 17: Transform right	
48	L_1 after reducing Δp, Δc, Δs, into left L_0	
49	Match: transformed right	
50	L_1 identical with left L_0	
51	Goal achieved, and analysis complete	
52	Execute R_6 on the right L_1 (from line 46)	So I'd apply Rule 6 to the second part of what
53		we have up there.
54		(Want to do that?)
55		Yeah.
56	L_2: $R \cdot (P \vee Q)$	(OK, to line 1 you apply R_6. Line 2 is $R \cdot (P \vee Q)$
57	Execute R_1 on right L_2 (from line 38)	And now I'd use Rule 1.
58		(Rule 1 on what part? You can use it with the
		entire expression or with the right part.)
59		I'd use it in both places.
60		(Well, we'll do them one at a time . . . which do
61		you want first?)
62		Well, do it with P and Q.
63		
64	L_3: $R \cdot (Q \vee P)$	[$R \cdot (Q \vee P)$. Now the entire expression?]
65	Execute R_1 on L_3 (from line 11)	Yeah
66	L_4: $(Q \vee P) \cdot R$	[On line 3, Rule 1 . . . you'd get $(Q \vee p) \cdot R$]
67	Match: L_4 identical with L_0	And . . . that's it. (That's it all right, OK . . .
		that wasn't too hard.)

[a] Statements in parentheses are experimenter's statements and explanatory comments. All other statements are the subject's.

[b] But the subject mistakenly thinks R_4 is applicable; therefore tests its functions.

Figure 3 Comparison of trace with human protocol.

In the right-hand half of Figure 3 we reproduce, word for word, the human protocol, omitting only some introductory paragraphs. In the left-hand half we reproduce the trace (hand simulated) of a program that, we believe, approximates closely the processes of the subject's thinking. This program is not identical with the one we described for GPS, but incorporates some modifications to fit it to the empirical data. Basically, however, the objects, operators, differences, goal types, and methods that appear in this trace are those of GPS.

Scanning down the protocol, we see that the subject sets up the goal of transforming L_1 into L_0, notices the difference in order of terms in the two expressions, and considers reversing them (lines 4–9). Simultaneously, the program is establishing the same goal (Goal 0), noticing the same difference (line 4), discovering that Rule 1 reduces this difference (line 9), and fixating the idea of applying Rule 1 when the analysis is complete. (This distinction between

overt and covert action is one of the modifications introduced.)

Next, the subject scans down the list of rules —there is explicit evidence that he looks at Rules 2, 3, and 4—rejecting each because it doesn't apply (Rule 3), would introduce a new difference ("That would require a sign change"), or doesn't perform the function of switching the P and Q (Rule 4). Simultaneously, the program is establishing the goal of reducing the difference in order of P and Q (Goal 4), scanning the list of rules, and rejecting them for the same reasons.

Next, the subject observes that the horseshoe creates difficulty in changing the P and Q (lines 36–37), and erects the goal of eliminating the horseshoe, discovering that Rule 6 will do this (line 42). He applies Rule 6, then Rule 1 to the right-hand subexpression, then Rule 1 to the whole expression, and observes that he has solved the problem. Simultaneously, the program undertakes a second search for a rule that will reverse P and Q (lines 33–34), but now tackles as a subproblem getting an otherwise relevant rule to be applicable. Considering Rule 1, it establishes the subgoal (Goal 15) of changing the horseshoe to a wedge, finds Rule 6, checks whether this will solve the problem, then executes Rules 6, 1, and 1 (on the whole expression) in that order.

A SECOND COMPARISON WITH HUMAN BEHAVIOR

We shall now consider a somewhat more complicated problem, and look in greater detail at the correspondence between the GPS trace and the subject's protocol. An engineering student is asked to transform the expression

$$(R \supset -P) \cdot (-R \supset Q)$$

into the expression $-(-Q \cdot P)$. The subject has practiced applying the rules, but he has previously done only one other problem like this. His sequence of reasoning on the problem as a whole and the initial section of his protocol are given in Figure 4.

The first portion of the GPS trace is shown in Figure 5. GPS's initial problem is to transform $L1$ into $L0$. Matching $L1$ to $L0$ reveals that there are R's in $L1$ and no R's in $L0$. This difference leads to the formulation of a reduce goal,

Course of solution:

1.	$(R \supset -P) \cdot (-R \supset Q)$	$-(-Q \cdot P)$

2.	$(-R \vee -P) \cdot (R \vee Q)$	Rule 6 applied to left and right of 1.
3.	$(-R \vee -P) \cdot (-R \supset Q)$	Rule 6 applied to left of 1.
4.	$R \supset -P$	Rule 8 applied to 1.
5.	$-R \vee -P$	Rule 6 applied to 4.
6.	$-R \supset Q$	Rule 8 applied to 1.
7.	$R \vee Q$	Rule 6 applied to 6.
8.	$(-R \vee -P) \cdot (R \vee Q)$	Rule 10 applied to 5 and 7.
9.	$P \supset -R$	Rule 2 applied to 4.
10.	$-Q \supset R$	Rule 2 applied to 6.
11.	$P \supset Q$	Rule 12 applied to 6 and 9.
12.	$-P \vee Q$	Rule 6 applied to 11.
13.	$-(P \cdot -Q)$	Rule 5 applied to 12.
14.	$-(-Q \cdot P)$	Rule 1 applied to 13. QED.

Protocol on first part of problem:

"Well, looking at the left-hand side of the equation, first we want to eliminate one of the sides by using Rule 8. It appears too complicated to work with first. Now—no,—no, I can't do that because I will be eliminating either the Q or the P in that total expression. I won't do that at first. Now I'm looking for a way to get rid of the horseshoe inside the two brackets that appear on the left and right sides of the equation. And I don't see it. Yeh, if you apply Rule 6 to both sides of the equation, from there I'm going to see if I can apply Rule 7."

Experimeter writes: 2nd. $(-R \vee -P) \cdot (R \vee Q)$
"I can almost apply Rule 7, but one R needs a tilde. So I'll have to look for another rule. I'm going to see if I can change that R to a tilde R. As a matter of fact, I should have used Rule 6 on only the left-hand side of the equation. So use Rule 6, but only on the left-hand side."

Experimenter writes: 3rd. $(-R \vee -P) \cdot (-R \supset Q)$
"Now I'll apply Rule 7 as it is expressed. Both—excuse me, excuse me, it can't be done because of the horseshoe. So—now I'm looking—scanning the rules here for a second, and seeing if I can change the R to $-R$ in the second equation, but I don't see any way of doing it." (Sigh.) "I'm just sort of lost for a second."

Figure 4 Subject on Problem D1.

L0 $-(-Q \cdot P)$
L1 $(R \supset -P) \cdot (-R \supset Q)$

GOAL 1 TRANSFORM L1 INTO L0
      GOAL 2 DELETE R FROM L1
            GOAL 3 APPLY R8 TO L1
                  PRODUCES L2 $R \supset -P$

      GOAL 4 TRANSFORM L2 INTO L0
            GOAL 5 ADD Q TO L2
            REJECT

    GOAL 2
            GOAL 6 APPLY R8 TO L1
                  PRODUCES L3 $-R \supset Q$

GOAL 7 TRANSFORM L3 INTO L0
      GOAL 8 ADD P TO L3
            REJECT

GOAL 2
      GOAL 9 APPLY R7 TO L1
            GOAL 10 CHANGE CONNECTIVE TO $\vee$ IN LEFT L1
                  GOAL 11 APPLY R6 TO LEFT L1
                        PRODUCES L4 $(-R \vee -P) \cdot (-R \supset Q)$

            GOAL 12 APPLY R7 TO L4
                  GOAL 13 CHANGE CONNECTIVE TO $\vee$ IN RIGHT L4
                      GOAL 14 APPLY R6 TO RIGHT L4
                          PRODUCES L5 $(-R \vee -P) \cdot (R \vee Q)$

            GOAL 15 APPLY R7 TO L5
                  GOAL 16 CHANGE SIGN OF LEFT RIGHT L5
                      GOAL 17 APPLY R6 TO RIGHT L5
                          PRODUCES L6 $(-R \vee -P) \cdot (-R \supset Q)$

            GOAL 18 APPLY R7 TO L6
                  GOAL 19 CHANGE CONNECTIVE TO $\vee$
                      IN RIGHT L6
                      REJECT

                GOAL 16
                  NOTHING MORE

            GOAL 13
              NOTHING MORE

        GOAL 10
          NOTHING MORE

Figure 5 Trace of GPS on First Part of Problem D1.

which for readability has been given its functional name, *Delete*. The attempt to reach this goal leads to a search for rules which finds Rule 8. Since there are two forms of Rule 8, both of which are admissible, GPS chooses the first. (Variants of rules are not indicated, but can be inferred easily from the trace.) Since Rule 8 is applicable, a new object, *L2*, is produced. Following the method for transform goals, at the next step a new goal has been generated: to transform *L2* into *L0*. This in turn leads to another reduce goal: to restore a *Q* to *L2*. But this goal is rejected by the evaluation, since adding a term is more difficult than deleting a term. GPS then returns to Goal 2 and seeks another rule that will delete terms. This time it finds the other form of Rule 8 and goes through a similar excursion, ending with the rejection of Goal 8 altogether.

Returning again to Goal 2 to find another rule for deleting terms, GPS obtains Rule 7. It selects the variant $(A \lor B) \cdot (A \lor C) \to A \lor (B \cdot C)$, since only this one both decreases terms and has a dot as its main connective. Rule 7 is not immediately applicable; GPS first discovers that there is a difference of connective in the left subexpression, and then that there is one in the right subexpression. In both cases it finds and applies Rule 6 to change the connective from horseshoe to wedge, obtaining successively *L4* and *L5*. But the new expression reveals a difference in sign, which leads again to Rule 6—that is, to the same rule as before, but perceived as accomplishing a different function. Rule 6 produces *L6*, which happens to be identical with *L4* although GPS does not notice the identity here. This leads, in Goal 19, to the difference in connective being redetected; whereupon the goal is finally rejected as representing no progress over Goal 13. Further attempts to find alternative ways to change signs or connectives fail to yield anything. This ends the episode.

We now have a highly detailed trace of what GPS did. What can we find in the subject's protocol that either confirms or refutes the assertion that this program is a detailed model of the symbol manipulations the subject is carrying out? What sort of correspondence can we expect? The program does not provide us with an English-language output that can be put into one-to-one correspondence with the words of the subject. We have not even given GPS a goal to "do the task and talk at the same time," which would be a necessary reformulation if we were to attempt a correspondence in such detail. On the other hand, the trace, backed up by our knowledge of how it was generated, does provide a complete record of all the task content that was considered by GPS and the order in which it was taken up. Hence, we should expect to find every feature of the protocol that concerns the task mirrored in an essential way in the program trace. The converse is not true, since many things concerning the task surely occurred without the subject's commenting on them (or even being aware of them). Thus, our test of correspondence is one-sided but exacting. Let us start with the first sentence of the subject's protocol:

"Well, looking at the left-hand side of the equation, first we want to eliminate one of the sides by using Rule 8."

We see here a desire to decrease *L1* or eliminate something from it, and the selection of Rule 8 as the means to do this. This stands in direct correspondence with Goals 1, 2, and 3 of the trace. Let us skip to the third and fourth sentences: "Now—no,—no, I can't do that because I will be eliminating either the *Q* or the *P* in that total expression. I won't do that at first."

We see here a direct expression of the covert application of Rule 8, the subsequent comparison of the resulting expression with *L0*, and the rejection of this course of action because it deletes a letter that is required in the final expression. It would be hard to find a set of words that expressed these ideas more clearly. Conversely, if the mechanism of the program (or something essentially similar to it) were not operating, it would be hard to explain why the subject uttered the remarks that he did.

One discrepancy is quite clear. The subject handled both forms of Rule 8 together, at least as far as his comment is concerned. GPS, on the other hand, took a separate cycle of consideration for each form. Possibly the subject followed the program covertly and simply reported the two results together. However, we would feel that the fit was better if GPS had proceeded something as follows:

GOAL 2 DELETE R FROM L1
    GOAL 3 APPLY R8 TO L1
        PRODUCES L2 R $\supset$ $-$P OR $-$R $\supset$ Q

GOAL 4 TRANSFORM L2 INTO L0
    GOAL 5 ADD Q TO R $\supset$ $-$P OR ADD P TO $-$R $\supset$ Q
        REJECT

We shall consider further evidence on this point later. Let us return to the second sentence, which we skipped over:

It appears too complicated to work with first.

Nothing in the program is in simple correspondence with this statement, though it is easy to imagine some possible explanations. For example, this could merely be an expression of the matching—of the fact that $L1$ is such a big expression that the subject cannot absorb all its detail. There is not enough data locally to determine what part of the trace should correspond to this statement, so the sentence must stand as an unexplained element of the subject's behavior. Now let us consider the next few sentences of the protocol:

Now I'm looking for a way to get rid of the horseshoe inside the two brackets that appear on the left and right side of the equation and I don't see it. Yeh, if you apply Rule 6 to both sides of the equation, from there I'm going to see if I can apply Rule 7.

This is in direct correspondence with Goals 9

to 14 of the trace. The comment at the end makes it clear that applying Rule 7 is the main concern and that changing connectives is required in order to accomplish this. Further, the protocol shows clearly that Rule 6 was selected as the means. All three rule selections provide some confirmation that preliminary test for feasibility was made by the subject—as by GPS—in the reduce goal method. If there was not selection on the main connective, why wasn't Rule 5 selected instead of Rule 6? Or why wasn't the $(A \cdot B) \vee (A \cdot C) \rightarrow A \cdot (B \vee C)$ form of Rule 7 selected? However, there is a discrepancy between trace and protocol, for the subject handles both applications of Rule 6 simultaneously (and apparently was also handling the two differences simultaneously); whereas GPS handles them consequentially. This is similar to the discrepancy noted earlier in handling Rule 8. Since we now have two examples of parallel processing, it is likely that there is a real difference on this score. Again, we would feel better if GPS proceeded somewhat as follows:

GOAL 9 APPLY R7 TO L1
    GOAL 10 CHANGE CONNECTIVE TO $\vee$ IN LEFT L1 AND RIGHT L1
        GOAL 11 APPLY R6 TO LEFT L1 AND RIGHT L1
            PRODUCES L5 ($-$R $\vee$ $-$P)$\cdot$(R $\vee$ Q)

A common feature of both of these discrepancies is that forming the compound expressions does not complicate the methods in any essential way. Thus, in the case involving Rule 8, the two results stem from the same input form and require only the single match. In the case involving Rule 7, a single search was made for a rule and the rule was applied to both parts simultaneously, as if only a single unit was involved.

There are two aspects in which the protocol provides information that the program is not equipped to explain. First, the subject handled

the application of Rule 8 covertly and commanded the experimenter to make the applications of Rule 6 on the board. The version of GPS used here did not make any distinction between internal and external actions. To this extent it fails to be an adequate model. The overt-covert distinction has consequences that run throughout a problem, since expressions on the blackboard have very different memory characteristics from expressions generated only in the head. Second, this version of GPS does not simulate the search process sufficiently well to provide a correspondent to "And I don't see it. Yeh, . . .". This requires providing a facsimile of the rule sheet and distinguishing search on the sheet from searches in the memory. The next few sentences read:

I can almost apply Rule 7, but one R needs a tilde. So I'll have to look for another rule. I'm going to see if I can change that R to a tilde R.

Again the trace and the protocol agree on the difference that is seen. They also agree that this difference was not attended to earlier, even though it was present. Some fine structure of the data also agrees with the trace. The right-hand R is taken as having the difference (R to $-R$) rather than the left-hand one, although either is possible. This preference arises in the program (and presumably in the subject) from the language habit of working from left to right. It is not without consequences, however, since it determines whether the subject goes to work on the left side or the right side of the expression; hence, it can affect the entire course of events for quite a while. Similarly, in the Rule-8 episode the subject apparently worked from left to right and from top to bottom in order to arrive at "Q or P" rather than "P or Q." This may seem like concern with excessively detailed features of the protocol, yet those details support the contention that what is going on inside the human system is quite akin to the symbol manipulations going inside GPS. The next portion of the protocol is:

As a matter of fact, I should have used Rule 6 on only the left-hand side of the equation. So use 6, but only on the left-hand side.

Here we have a strong departure from the GPS trace, although, curiously enough, the trace and the protocol end up at the same spot, $(-R \lor -P) \cdot (-R \supset Q)$. Both the subject and GPS found Rule 6 as the appropriate one to change signs. At this point GPS simply applied the rule to the current expression; whereas the subject went back and corrected the previous application. Nothing exists in the program that corresponds to this. The most direct explanation is that the application of Rule 6 in the inverse direction is perceived by the subject as undoing the previous application of Rule 6. After following out this line of reasoning, he

then takes the simpler (and less foolish-appearing) alternative, which is to correct the original action.

The final segment of the protocol reads:

Now I'll apply Rule 7 as it is expressed. Both—excuse me, excuse me, it can't be done because of the horseshoe. So—now I'm looking—scanning the rules here for a second, and seeing if I can change the R to $-R$ in the second equation, but I don't see any way of doing it (Sigh). I'm just sort of lost for a second.

The trace and the protocol are again in good agreement. This is one of the few self-correcting errors we have encountered. The protocol records the futile search for additional operators to affect the differences of sign and connective, always with negative results. The final comment of mild despair can be interpreted as reflecting the impact of several successive failures.

Let us take stock of the agreements and disagreements between the trace and the protocol. The program provides a complete explanation of the subject's task behavior with five exceptions of varying degrees of seriousness. There are two aspects in which GPS is unprepared to simulate the subject's behavior: in distinguishing between the internal and external worlds, and in an adequate representation of the spaces in which the search for rules takes place. Both of these are generalized deficiencies that can be remedied. It will remain to be seen how well GPS can then explain data about these aspects of behavior. The subject handles certain sets of items in parallel by using compound expressions; whereas GPS handles all items one at a time. In the example examined here, no striking differences in problem solving occur as a result, but larger discrepancies could arise under other conditions. It is fairly clear how GPS could be extended to incorporate this feature.

There are two cases in which nothing corresponds in the program to some clear task-oriented behavior in the protocol. One of these, the early comment about "complication," seems to be mostly a case of insufficient information. The program is making numerous comparisons and evaluations that could give rise to comments of the type in question. Thus this error does not seem too serious. The other case, involving the "should have . . ." passage, does seem serious. It clearly implies a mechanism (maybe a whole set of them) that is not in GPS. Adding the mechanism required to handle this one passage could significantly increase the total capabilities of the program. For example, there might be no reasonable way to accomplish this except to provide GPS with a little continuous hindsight about its past actions.

HOW EFFECTIVE IS GPS?

In testing whether this program provides a good theory or explanation of the behavior of the human subject, we can raise two kinds of questions:

(a) How much did we have to modify GPS to construct a program that would fit this subject's protocol?

(b) How good is the fit of the modified program to the protocol?

In the next paragraphs we shall discuss some of the methodological issues that are imbedded in these questions. We are, of course, considering a test of simulation that is much stronger than Turing's test, and perhaps the reader can be persuaded from the evidence thus far that GPS and its variants will pass Turing's test.

Fitting a General Program to Specific Behavior

The form the theory takes is a program—in this case, GPS. But, as in the natural sciences, the theory is more appropriately expressed as a class of programs to be particularized and applied to concrete situations by specifying parameter values, initial conditions, and boundary conditions. For example, one subject may attach higher priorities to a difference in variables, another to a difference in connectives. GPS is fitted to these subjects' behavior by modifying the program to represent the difference in priorities—this is precisely what we did in constructing the example shown in Figure 3.

As in all fitting of theory to data, we must watch our degrees of freedom. If we are allowed to introduce a parameter change or a

new mechanism for each bit of behavior to be explained, we will have explained nothing. The program must be a parsimonious description of the mechanisms generating the behavior. Let us point out—to be sure the reader understands—that the trace is the output of the program, and not modifiable at will. Any change in the program affects the trace in a number of places. A change to reduce one discrepancy—say the apparently more exhaustive initial search of the list of rules mentioned above—is likely to introduce new discrepancies. In the case in point, we were unable to find any simple change in the program that would remove this particular discrepancy and yet leave the rest of the fit as good as it is.

Comparing a Trace with Behavior

The computer does not yet speak fluent idiomatic English, hence we cannot compare the trace with the subject's protocol literally word for word. The trace says: "GOAL 1: REDUCE ΔP BETWEEN L_1 AND L_0." The subject says: "I'm looking at the idea of reversing these two things now." The trace says: GOAL 6: APPLY R_3 TO L_1." The subject says: ". . . then I look down at Rule 3." Instead of having the computer speak English, we could hope for a code (in the psychologist's sense of the word) that would reduce the human conversation to "problem-solving content." Again, techniques are currently lacking for doing this, but perhaps we can agree that a large amount of the content of the subject's remarks is captured in the computer's "phrases."

Further, the trace describes the information processes uniformly down to a specified level of detail, while the protocol fluctuates greatly in its explicitness—sometimes providing more detail, but usually much less. Thus in our search example, it is certainly possible that the subject scanned the entire set of rules, but simply failed to mention them after the first few. This kind of mismatch is probably inevitable, at least in the present state of our knowledge. The most we can aim for is a trace that avoids sins of omission and contradiction, although it may sometimes speak when the subject remains silent.

We do not mean that the level of detail in the protocol is arbitrary—in fact, we suspect that it is very much related to the mechanisms and functions of consciousness in problem solving and learning. The distinction between conscious and unconscious does not appear in the present GPS mechanisms, and hence cannot be reflected in a nonarbitrary way in the trace.

The exhibits presented here provide a sample of the work that has been done in comparing GPS, and variants of it, with the problem-solving behavior of human subjects. Relatively little simulation has been carried out to date—it is a painstaking activity. Our most intensive empirical study thus far has been a simulation of behavior covering a period of 30 minutes. The following conclusions, from this intensive study, and from less-detailed examination of about 20 other protocols seems reasonably certain:

1. Measured in terms of time and numbers of words, virtually all the behavior of subjects falls within the general framework of means-end analysis. The three goal types we have described account for at least three-fourths of the subjects' goals, and the additional goal types for which we find evidence are close relatives to those we have mentioned.

2. The three methods we have described represent the vast majority of the methods applied to these problems. One additional exceedingly important method—planning—has been incorporated in GPS [4], but limits on time prevent us from discussing it here. Planning appears in several different forms in the protocols, but in all of them it serves the function of temporarily omitting details in order to see if the main line of reasoning will yield a solution.

3. There are evidences that the programs of the subjects change—that they learn—in the course of problem solving. For example, initially they have to scan the rules, one by one, to find an applicable rule; later, once they create the goal of reducing a specified difference, they choose almost instantaneously a rule that is relevant to that particular difference. No clear distinction between learning and problem solving appears. Some of the learning takes place—and is used—in the course of attempting a single problem (one-half hour). In fact, the

GPS network of goals and subgoals constitutes a "learning about the problem," so that on successive phases of the solution, the subject behaves very differently. Conversely, some of the learning occurs as the result of specific problem-solving activity devoted to learning.

CONCLUSION

In this paper we have described a method for the study of human problem solving and other higher mental processes, have given examples of an application of the method, and have indicated the theory of human problem solving that emerges.

The method consists in constructing a theory of central processes in the form of a program, or class of programs, demonstrating the sufficiency of the theory to produce problem-solving behavior by realizing it in a computer, and testing the theory against human processes by comparing the trace generated by the program with the protocol of a human subject.

The application consisted in constructing a general problem-solving program, capable of solving problems in logic and other domains, demonstrating that a computer so programmed could solve problems, and comparing its processes with those of human subjects in a problem situation designed by O. K. Moore.

The theory of human problem solving consists in a program, constructed of elementary information processes, for reasoning in terms of goals and methods for attaining those goals. Perhaps the most striking characteristic of this program is that it selects the paths it explores by first determining the functions that have to be performed, and then by finding courses of action relevant to those functions. In this and other ways it reflects (and incorporates in determinate mechanisms) the "insightfulness" and "directedness" that has so often been observed as a salient characteristic of human problem solving. In terms of today's nomenclature in psychology, one could describe it as a "mediational" theory that encompasses "Gestalt" processes. Its novelty is that it is definite and that, at least in one problem area, it works.

It is easy to point to difficulties and unfinished tasks. Systematic methods for fitting programs to protocols and testing goodness of fit are nonexistent. The "General" Problem Solver is still highly specific compared with the humans it simulates. The construction and testing of learning programs has hardly begun. Only the most rudimentary programs for simulating "simple" human processes have been written, and these have not been tested. There is little information for selecting the correct set of elementary processes; and even less for connecting them with neural mechanisms.

In spite of this imposing agenda of unfinished business, we wish to record our conviction that it is no longer necessary to talk about the theory of higher mental processes in the future tense. There now exist tools sharp enough to cut into the tough skin of the problem, and these tools have already produced a rigorous, detailed explanation of a significant area of human symbolic behavior.

REFERENCES

1. J. S. Bruner, J. J. Goodnow, and G. A. Austin, 1956. *A study of thinking*. New York: Wiley.
2. A. D. DeGroot, 1946. *Thought and choice in chess*. Amsterdam: North-Holland; English translation published in 1965 by Mouton.
3. O. K. Moore, and S. B. Anderson, 1954. Modern logic and tasks for experiments on problem solving behavior. *Journal of Psychology*, *38*(1): 151–160.
4. A. Newell, J. C. Shaw, and H. A. Simon, 1959. A report on a general problem-solving program for a computer. *Computers and Automation*, *8*(7): 10–17. Reprinted in 1960 under the title "Report on a general problem-solving program" in *Information processing* (International Federation for Information Processing, S.de Picciotto, ed.); Paris: UNESCO, 256–264. 5A.
5. A. Newell, J. C. Shaw, and H. A. Simon, 1960. A variety of intelligent learning in a General Problem Solver. *Self-organizing systems* (M. C. Yovits and S. Cameron, eds.); New York: Pergamon, 153–189. 7A.
6. A. Newell, J. C. Shaw, and H. A. Simon, 1962. The processes of creative thinking. *Contemporary approaches to creative thinking* (H. E. Gruber, G. Terrell, and M. Wertheimer, eds.); New York: Atherton, 63–119. 6A.
7. C. E. Osgood, 1953. *Method and theory in experimental psychology*. New York: Oxford University Press.
8. A. M. Turing, 1950. Computing machinery and intelligence. *Mind*, *59*(236): 433–460. Reprinted in 1956 under the title "Can a machine think?" in *The world of mathematics* (J. R. Newman, ed.); New York: Simon and Schuster, Volume 4, 2099–2123. MA.

6

SIMULATION OF BEHAVIOR IN THE BINARY CHOICE EXPERIMENT

JULIAN FELDMAN

INTRODUCTION

Modern, high-speed digital computers have been used to simulate large, complex systems in order to facilitate the study of these systems. One of these systems that has been studied with the aid of computer simulation is man. The present report describes another addition to the growing list of efforts to study human thinking processes by simulating these processes on a computer. The research summarized here has been concerned with simulating the behavior of individual subjects in the binary choice experiment [3]. The first section contains a description of the experiment. An overview of the model is given in the second section. The model for a particular subject is described in some detail in the third section.

THE BINARY CHOICE EXPERIMENT

In the binary choice experiment, the subject is asked to predict which of two events, E_1 or E_2, will occur on each of a series of trials. After the subject makes a prediction, he is told which event actually occurred. The sequence of events is usually determined by some random mechanism, e.g., a table of random numbers. One and only one event occurs on each trial.

SOURCE: Reprinted from *Proceedings of the Western Joint Computer Conference*, 19: 133–144 (1961).

The events may be flashes of light or symbols on a deck of cards. The subject is usually asked to make as many correct predictions as he can.

In the research reported here, the experiment described in the preceding paragraph was modified by asking the subject to "think aloud" —to give his reasons for making a prediction as well as the prediction itself. The subject's remarks were recorded. The subject was instructed to "think aloud" in order to obtain more information on the processing that the subject was doing. This technique has been used in some of the classical investigations of problem-solving behavior [2, 5] and in other computer simulation studies of thinking [1, 7]. A comparison of the behavior of subjects in the binary choice experiment who did "think aloud" with the behavior of subjects who did not "think aloud" did not reveal any major differences [3]. The events in the present experiment were the symbols "plus" and "check." "Check" occurred on 142 of 200 trials and "plus" on the remaining 58 trials. The symbols were recorded on a numbered deck of 3-inch $\times$ 5-inch cards. After the subject made his prediction for trial t, he was shown card t which contained a "plus" or "check." While the subject was predicting the event of trial t, he could only see the event of trial t-1. A transcription of the tape recording of the remarks of subject DH and the experimenter, the author, in an hour-long binary choice experiment is presented in the Appendix. In the Appendix and the rest of this report, the symbols "plus" and "check" are represented by "P" and "C" respectively. The transcription will be referred to as a protocol.

THE BASIC MODEL

To simulate the behavior of an individual subject in the binary choice experiment, a model of the subject's behavior must be formulated as a computer program. If the program is then allowed to predict the same event series as the subject has predicted, the behavior of the program—the predictions and the reasons—can be compared to the behavior of the subject. If the program's behavior is a reasonable facsimile of the subject's behavior, the program is at least a sufficient explanation of the subject's behavior. The level of explanation is really determined by the subject's statements. No attempt is made to go beyond these to more basic processes, e.g., neurological or chemical, of human behavior. Thus, the model is an attempt to specify the relationship between the reasons or hypotheses that the subject offers for his predictions and the preceding hypotheses, predictions, and events. The subject is depicted as actively proposing hypotheses about the structure of the event series. These hypotheses are tested by using them to predict events. If the prediction of the event is correct, the hypothesis is usually retained. If the prediction of the event is wrong, a new hypothesis is generally proposed.

THE MODEL FOR DH

The model for each subject is based on a detailed examination of the protocol and some conjectures about human behavior. Perhaps the best thing to do at this point is to describe in some detail a model for the subject, DH, whose protocol appears in the Appendix.

The Hypotheses

This model proposes two types of hypotheses about the event series. The first type of hy-

pothesis is a pattern of events. The model has a repertoire of nine patterns:

> progression of C's
> progression of P's
> single alternation
> 2 C's and 1 P
> 1 C   and 2 P's
> 2 P's and 2 C's
> 3 P's and 3 C's
> 4 P's and 4 C's
> 4 P's and 3 C's

The model can propose that the event series is behaving according to one of these patterns and use the pattern hypothesis to predict the event of a given trial, t. The predictions of the first two patterns—progression of C's and progression of P's—for trial t are independent of the events preceding trial t. The predictions of the other patterns (the alternation patterns) are dependent on these preceding events. Thus, if the subject proposes the pattern "single alternation" for trial t and the event of trial $t-1$ was a C, the prediction for trial t is a P. In order to facilitate the determination of the prediction of an alternation pattern for trial t, the patterns are coded as sorting nets. For example, the pattern "2 C's and 1 P" is represented in the following fashion:

> Is event $t-1$ a C?
>   No—Predict C for trial t.
>   Yes—Is event $t-2$ a C?
>   No—Predict C for trial t.
>   Yes—Predict P for trial t.

The second type of hypothesis that the model can propose is an antipattern or guess-opposite hypothesis. For example, the model can propose that the event of trial t will be the opposite of that predicted by a given pattern. This type of hypothesis is the model's representation of the notion of "gambler's fallacy"—the reason people predict "tails" after a coin falls "heads" seven times in a row.

The most general form of hypothesis has two components: a pattern component and a guess-opposite component. The prediction of the hypothesis is obtained by finding the prediction of the pattern component. If the hypothesis has a guess-opposite component, then the prediction of the hypothesis is the opposite of the pattern prediction. If the hypothesis does not have a guess-opposite component, then the prediction of the hypothesis is the prediction of the pattern component. Thus, while the prediction of the pattern hypothesis "progression of C's" is always a C, the prediction of the hypothesis "guess-opposite-progression-of-C's" is always a P.

The Basic Cycle

The basic cycle of the model is as follows: The model uses an hypothesis to predict the event of trial t. The event is then presented. The model in Phase One "explains" the event of trial t with an explanation hypothesis. In Phase Two a prediction hypothesis for trial t + 1 is formed. The model uses this prediction hypothesis to predict trial t + 1. The event of trial t + 1 is presented, and the cycle continues.

Phase One

The basic motivation for this phase of the model is that the model must "explain" each event. An acceptable explanation is an hypothesis that could have predicted the event. The processing of Phase One is represented in the flow chart of Figure 1.

The processing to determine the explanation hypothesis for trial t begins by testing whether the pattern component of the prediction hypothesis for trial t could have predicted the event of trial t correctly. If the pattern component could have predicted correctly, the pattern component is the explanation hypothesis. If the pattern component could not have predicted correctly, the pattern-change mechanism is evoked. Thus if the prediction hypothesis for trial t contained only a pattern component and the hypothesis predicted correctly, the explanation hypothesis for trial t is the prediction hypothesis for trial t. If the prediction hypothesis for trial t contained a guess-opposite component and the hypothesis predicted correctly, the pattern-change mechanism is evoked because the pattern component could not have predicted the event correctly by itself. If the prediction hypothesis for trial t was a guess-opposite hypothesis and it predicted incorrectly, the pattern component of the prediction-hypothesis becomes the explanation hypothesis for trial t. The motivation here is really quite simple although the explanation may sound involved. If, in this binary situation, the hypothesis that a pattern will change leads to an incorrect prediction, the pattern must have persisted; and the pattern is an acceptable explanation of the event. If the hypothesis that a pattern will change leads to a correct prediction, the pattern obviously did not persist; and the possibility of a new pattern is considered.

The pattern-change mechanism is evoked on trial t if the pattern component of the prediction hypothesis for trial t is unable to predict the event of trial t. The pattern-change mechanism consists of two parts. The first part evokes

A. COULD THE PATTERN COMPONENT OF THE PREDICTION-HYPOTHESIS FOR TRIAL T HAVE PREDICTED THE EVENT OF TRIAL T CORRECTLY?

    B. YES — EXPLANATION-HYPOTHESIS FOR TRIAL T IS THE PATTERN COMPONENT OF THE PREDICTION-HYPOTHESIS FOR TRIAL T.

    C. NO — EVOKE PATTERNS THAT COULD HAVE PREDICTED THE EVENTS OF TRIALS T AND T−1 CORRECTLY. THE PATTERN OF THE PREDICTION-HYPOTHESIS FOR TRIAL T IS EVOKED IF IT COULD HAVE PREDICTED CORRECTLY THE EVENTS OF TRIAL T−1, T−2, AND T−3.

    D. SELECT FROM THE SET OF EVOKED PATTERNS THAT PATTERN THAT HAS BEEN SELECTED MOST OFTEN ON PRECEDING TRIALS.

    E. IS THE SELECTED PATTERN THE PATTERN COMPONENT OF THE PREDICTION-HYPOTHESIS FOR TRIAL T?

        F. YES — EXPLANATION-HYPOTHESIS FOR TRIAL T IS THROW ME OFF THE SELECTED PATTERN.

        G. NO — EXPLANATION-HYPOTHESIS FOR TRIAL T IS THE SELECTED PATTERN.

Figure 1 Phase One of Binary Choice Model for DH.

H. DID THE PREDICTION-HYPOTHESIS FOR TRIAL T CONTAIN A GUESS-OPPOSITE COMPONENT?

  I. YES — DID THE PREDICTION-HYPOTHESIS FOR TRIAL T PREDICT THE EVENT OF TRIAL T CORRECTLY?

    J. YES — PREDICTION-HYPOTHESIS FOR TRIAL T+1 IS GUESS-OPPOSITE THE PATTERN COMPONENT OF THE EXPLANATION-HYPOTHESIS FOR TRIAL T.

    K. NO — DID THE PREDICTION HYPOTHESIS FOR TRIALS T−1 AND T−2 CONTAIN GUESS-OPPOSITE COMPONENTS AND WERE THE PREDICTIONS OF THE EVENTS OF THESE TRIALS CORRECT?

      L. YES — PREDICTION-HYPOTHESIS FOR TRIAL T+1 IS GUESS-OPPOSITE THE EXPLANATION-HYPOTHESIS FOR TRIAL T.

      M. NO — PREDICTION-HYPOTHESIS FOR TRIAL T+1 IS THE EXPLANATION-HYPOTHESIS FOR TRIAL T.

  N. WILL THE EXPLANATION-HYPOTHESIS FOR TRIAL T CONTINUE? (SEE TEXT FOR AN EXPLANATION OF THIS TEST.)

    O. YES — PREDICTION-HYPOTHESIS FOR TRIAL T+1 IS THE EXPLANATION-HYPOTHESIS FOR TRIAL T.

    P. NO — PREDICTION-HYPOTHESIS FOR TRIAL T+1 IS GUESS-OPPOSITE THE EXPLANATION-HYPOTHESIS FOR TRIAL T.

Q. PREDICT EVENT FOR TRIAL T+1.

Figure 2 Phase Two of Binary Choice Model for DH.

a subset of the nine patterns listed above. The second part of the pattern-change mechanism selects a single pattern out of the evoked set. A pattern is evoked, i.e., considered as a possible explanation of the event of trial t, if the pattern can predict the events of trials t and t−1. The pattern of the prediction hypothesis for trial t, i.e., the pattern that cannot predict event t, is included in the evoked set if it can predict events t−1, t−2, and t−3. Of the patterns that are evoked, the pattern that has been selected most often on prior trials is selected as the pattern component of the explanation hypothesis. If the pattern component of the prediction hypothesis for trial t is selected, then the explanation hypothesis is an antipattern hypothesis which is the model's interpretation of the subject's hypothesis "you have thrown me off the pattern" (cf. trial 9 of the protocol in the Appendix). The model interprets event t as an attempt to "throw me off" when the following three conditions are met: (1) the pattern is unable to predict the event of trial t; (2) the pattern is able to predict at least the three consecutive events of trials t−1, t−2, and t−3; and (3) the pattern is also the most frequently selected of those patterns that are evoked.

Phase Two

While Phase One is concerned mainly with the processing of the pattern component of the hypothesis, Phase Two is concerned with the processing of the guess-opposite component. Phase Two is represented in the flow chart of Figure 2.

If the prediction hypothesis for trial t contained a guess-opposite component, the guess-opposite component is processed in a fashion quite analogous to the processing of the pattern component in Phase One. If the antipattern prediction hypothesis for trial t predicted the event of trial t correctly, the guess-opposite component is retained, and the prediction hypothesis for trial t+1 is guess-opposite-the-pattern-of-the-explanation-hypothesis. If the antipattern prediction hypothesis for trial t predicted the event of trial t incorrectly, the guess-opposite component is considered for retention in a fashion analogous to the "throw-me-off" consideration for patterns. If the prediction hypotheses for trial t−1 and t−2 had guess-opposite components and these hypotheses predicted correctly, then the guess-opposite component is retained for the prediction hypothesis of trial t+1. If these conditions are not fulfilled, the guess-opposite component is dropped; and the prediction hypothesis for trial $t+1$ is the explanation hypothesis for trial t.

If the prediction hypothesis for trial t did not contain a guess-opposite component, the model considers whether or not the guess-opposite component should be introduced on trial $t+1$. The model makes this decision on the basis of its past experience. It determines the number of consecutive events including and preceding the event of trial t that can be predicted by the explanation hypothesis for trial t. This number will be called N_1. Then the model searches its memory backward from the last trial included in N_1 to find a trial for which the explanation hypothesis was the same as the explanation hypothesis for trial t. Then the model determines the number of contiguous events including, preceding, and following this prior occurrence of the explanation hypothesis of trial t that can be predicted by this hypothesis. This number will be called N_2. If $N_2 = N_1$, the model decides that the explanation hypothesis for trial t will not be the prediction-hypothesis for trial $t+1$. The prediction hypothesis for trial $t+1$ becomes guess-opposite-the-explanation-hypothesis for trial t. If $N_2 > N_1$, the model decides that the explanation hypothesis for trial t will be the prediction hypothesis for trial $t+1$. If $N_1 > N_2$, the model decides that this prior occurrence of the explanation hypothesis for trial t is really not pertinent and continues to search its memory for an occurrence of the explanation hypothesis where $N_2 \geq N_1$. If no such occurrence can be found, the prediction hypothesis for trial $t+1$ is the explanation hypothesis for trial t.

PREDICTING WITH THE MODELS

Models of individual behavior like the one described for DH can be used to predict the same series of binary events that the subject was asked to predict. The predictions and hypotheses of the model—the model's protocol—can then be compared to the subject's protocol. The model does not speak idiomatic English, and so the comparison is made between the machine's protocol and a suitably coded version of the subject's protocol.

The model's protocol can be generated by presenting the model with the events in the same way the subject was presented with the events in the binary choice experiment; or the computer can take the experimenter's role, too, if suitable precautions are taken to prevent the model from peeking. However, this straightforward method of simulating the subject's behavior raises difficulties. These difficulties are identical to those of getting a chess or checker program to play a book game [6, 8]. Because the decision of the chess or checker program at move m depends on its decisions at the preceding moves, $m-1$, $m-2$, . . . , such a program, when it is playing a book game, must be "set back on the track" if its move deviates from the book move. The program and the book must have the same history if the program is to have a fair chance to make the same decision as that made in the book game. This "setting back on the track" may involve resetting a large number of parameters as well as changing the move itself. Elsewhere, I have called this "setting-back-on-the-track" technique *conditional prediction*. The prediction of the model is conditional on the preceding decisions of the model being the same as those of the subject it is trying to predict [4].

The application of the conditional prediction technique to binary choice models such as the one described above for the subject DH involves (1) comparing the program's behavior and the subject's behavior at every possible point, (2) recording the differences between the behaviors, and (3) imposing the subject's decision on the model where necessary. A type of monitor system is imposed on the program to perform these functions. The model for DH with the conditional prediction system controls is represented in Figures 3 and 4. An example will help clarify these figures. In Figure 3, after each decision by the model to keep the pattern of the prediction hypothesis for trial t for the explanation hypothesis for trial t (B), this decision is compared to the subject's decision (1). If the model's decision was different from that of the subject, control is transferred to the pattern-change mechanism (3 trials). If the model's decision was the same as that of the subject, control is transferred to another part of the monitor (117 trials). Figures 3 and 4 only

A. COULD THE PATTERN COMPONENT OF THE PREDICTION-HYPOTHESIS
    FOR TRIAL T HAVE PREDICTED THE EVENT OF TRIAL T CORRECTLY?

  B. YES — EXPLANATION-HYPOTHESIS FOR TRIAL T IS THE PATTERN
      COMPONENT OF THE PREDICTION-HYPOTHESIS FOR TRIAL T.
*   1. DID SUBJECT'S EXPLANATION-HYPOTHESIS
*   FOR TRIAL T CONTAIN PATTERN COMPONENT
*   OF THE PREDICTION-HYPOTHESIS FOR TRIAL T?   120
*   YES — GO TO 6.   117
*   NO — ERROR — FAILURE TO EVOKE PATTERN-
*   CHANGE MECHANISM. GO TO C.   3

  C. NO — EVOKE PATTERNS THAT COULD HAVE PREDICTED THE EVENTS
      OF TRIALS T AND T−1 CORRECTLY. THE PATTERN OF THE
      PREDICTION-HYPOTHESIS FOR TRIAL T IS EVOKED IF IT COULD
      HAVE PREDICTED CORRECTLY THE EVENTS OF TRIALS T−1, T−2,
      AND T−3.
*   2. WAS THE PATTERN OF THE SUBJECT'S EXPLANATION-
*   HYPOTHESIS FOR TRIAL T EVOKED?   78
*   YES — GO TO D.   61
*   NO — ERROR — FAILURE TO EVOKE PATTERN.
*   ADD SUBJECT'S PATTERN TO EVOKED SET
        AND CONTINUE.   17

  D. SELECT FROM THE SET OF EVOKED PATTERNS THAT PATTERN THAT
      HAS BEEN SELECTED MOST OFTEN ON PRECEDING TRIALS.
*   3. WAS THE PATTERN OF THE SUBJECT'S EXPLA-
*   NATION-HYPOTHESIS FOR TRIAL T SELECTED?   78
*   YES — GO TO E.   64
*   NO — ERROR — FAILURE TO SELECT PATTERN.
*   REPLACE INCORRECT PATTERN WITH SUBJECT'S
*   PATTERN AND CONTINUE.   14

  E. IS THE SELECTED PATTERN THE PATTERN COMPONENT OF THE
      PREDICTION-HYPOTHESIS FOR TRIAL T?

  F. YES — EXPLANATION-HYPOTHESIS FOR TRIAL T IS THROW ME OFF
      THE SELECTED PATTERN.
*   4. DID SUBJECT'S EXPLANATION-HYPOTHESIS
*   FOR TRIAL T CONTAIN THROW-ME-OFF?   27
*   YES — GO TO H.   26
*   NO — ERROR — INCORRECT EVOCATION OF
*   THROW-ME-OFF. DELETE THROW-ME-OFF
*   AND GO TO H.   1

  G. NO — EXPLANATION-HYPOTHESIS FOR TRIAL T IS THE
      SELECTED PATTERN.
*   5. DID SUBJECT'S EXPLANATION-HYPOTHESIS
*   FOR TRIAL T CONTAIN THROW-ME-OFF?   51
*   YES — ERROR — FAILURE TO EVOKE THROW-ME-
*   OFF, INSERT THROW-ME-OFF AND GO TO H.   3
*   NO — GO TO H.   48
*   6. DID SUBJECT'S EXPLANATION-HYPOTHESIS
*   FOR TRIAL T CONTAIN THROW-ME-OFF?   117
*   YES — ERROR — FAILURE TO EVOKE THROW-ME-
*   OFF. INSERT THROW-ME-OFF AND GO TO H.   3
*   NO — GO TO H.   114

Figure 3 Summary of Behavior of Phase One of Binary Choice Model for DH
Adapted for Conditional Prediction.

contain the results for 195 trials because the model began at trial 6.

CONCLUSIONS

Deficiencies of the Models

The model for DH and the similar models that have been constructed to simulate the behavior of two other subjects in the binary choice experiment [3] are deficient in several respects. First of all, the comparison of the behavior of the model to that behavior of the subject from which the model was developed is, of course, not a very good test of the model. This type of comparison only yields some indication of the adequacy of the model and its components. Comparison of the behavior of the model to sequences of behavior of the subject not used in constructing the model awaits correction of some of the deficiencies mentioned below.

The segment of the model which has the highest number of errors relative to the number of times it is used is the guess-opposite segment (see Figure 4). The subject certainly exhibits this type of behavior, but the model does not very often predict "guess opposite" when the subject does.

The pattern-change segment has a better error record, but it raises another issue. This segment is actually a selection device. A pattern is selected from the list of patterns that the subject uses. A more elegant pattern-change mechanism would generate a pattern out of the

H. DID THE PREDICTION-HYPOTHESIS FOR TRIAL T CONTAIN A GUESS-OPPOSITE COMPONENT?

    I. YES — DID THE PREDICTION-HYPOTHESIS FOR TRIAL T PREDICT THE EVENT OF TRIAL T CORRECTLY?

        J. YES — PREDICTION-HYPOTHESIS FOR TRIAL T+1 IS GUESS-OPPOSITE THE PATTERN COMPONENT OF THE EXPLANATION-HYPOTHESIS FOR TRIAL T.

            * 7. DID SUBJECT'S PREDICTION-HYPOTHESIS
            *   FOR TRIAL T+1 CONTAIN GUESS-OPPOSITE
            *   COMPONENT?   6
            *   YES — GO TO 12.   5
            *   NO — ERROR — INCORRECT RETENTION OF
            *   GUESS-OPPOSITE COMPONENT. DELETE
            *   GUESS-OPPOSITE AND GO TO 12.   1

        K. NO — DID THE PREDICTION HYPOTHESIS FOR TRIALS T−1 AND T−2 CONTAIN GUESS-OPPOSITE COMPONENTS AND WERE THE PREDICTIONS OF THE EVENTS OF THESE TRIALS CORRECT?

        L. YES — PREDICTION-HYPOTHESIS FOR TRIAL T+1 IS GUESS-OPPOSITE THE EXPLANATION-HYPOTHESIS FOR TRIAL T.

            * 8. DID SUBJECT'S PREDICTION-HYPOTHESIS
            *   FOR TRIAL T+1 CONTAIN GUESS-OPPOSITE
            *   COMPONENT?   2
            *   YES — GO TO 12.   2
             *   NO — ERROR — INCORRECT RETENTION OF
            *   GUESS-OPPOSITE COMPONENT, DELETE
            *   GUESS-OPPOSITE AND GO TO 12.   0

        M. NO — PREDICTION-HYPOTHESIS FOR TRIAL T+1 IS THE EXPLANATION-HYPOTHESIS FOR TRIAL T.

            * 9. DID SUBJECT'S PREDICTION-HYPOTHESIS
            *   FOR TRIAL T+1 CONTAIN GUESS-OPPOSITE
            *   COMPONENT?   12
             *   YES — ERROR — FAILURE TO KEEP GUESS-
            *   OPPOSITE COMPONENT. INSERT GUESS-
            *   OPPOSITE AND GO TO 12.   1
            *   NO — GO TO 12.   11

Figure 4 continues

N. WILL THE EXPLANATION-HYPOTHESIS FOR TRIAL T CONTINUE?
(SEE TEXT FOR AN EXPLANATION OF THIS TEST.)

   O. YES — PREDICTION-HYPOTHESIS FOR TRIAL T+1 IS THE
EXPLANATION-HYPOTHESIS FOR TRIAL T.

                     *10. DID SUBJECT'S PREDICTION-HYPOTHESIS
                     *   FOR TRIAL T+1 CONTAIN GUESS-OPPOSITE
                     *   COMPONENT?   136
                     *   YES — ERROR — FAILURE TO EVOKE GUESS-
                     *   OPPOSITE COMPONENT. INSERT GUESS-
                     *   OPPOSITE AND GO TO 12.   10
                     *   NO — GO TO 12.   126

   P. NO — PREDICTION-HYPOTHESIS FOR TRIAL T+1 IS GUESS-
OPPOSITE THE EXPLANATION-HYPOTHESIS FOR TRIAL T.

                     *11. DID SUBJECT'S PREDICTION-HYPOTHESIS
                     *   FOR TRIAL T+1 CONTAIN GUESS-OPPOSITE
                     *   COMPONENT?   39
                     *   YES — GO TO 12.   2
                     *   NO — ERROR — INCORRECT SELECTION OF
                     *   GUESS-OPPOSITE. DELETE GUESS-OPPOSITE
                     *   AND CONTINUE.   37
                     *12. WAS PATTERN OF SUBJECT'S EXPLANATION-
                     *   HYPOTHESIS FOR TRIAL T THE SAME AS
                     *   THE PATTERN OF THE SUBJECT'S PREDICTION-
                     *   HYPOTHESIS FOR TRIAL T+1?   195
                     *   YES — GO TO Q.   192
                     *   NO — ERROR — FAILURE TO CHANGE PATTERN.
                     *   INSERT SUBJECT'S PATTERN IN PREDICTION-
                     *   HYPOTHESIS FOR TRIAL T+1 AND CONTINUE.   3

Q. PREDICT EVENT FOR TRIAL T+1.

                     *13. DID SUBJECT PREDICT SAME EVENT?   195
                     *   YES — GO TO A.   193
                     *   NO — ERROR — INCORRECT PREDICTION.
                     *   CORRECT AND GO TO A.   2

Figure 4 Summary of Behavior of Phase Two of Binary Choice Model for DH
Adapted for Conditional Prediction.

preceding sequence of events and some basic concepts. One of these concepts might be that patterns with equal numbers of P's and C's are preferred to alternation patterns with unequal numbers of P's and C's, all other things being equal.

The models have no mechanisms for making perceptual errors—"seeing" one symbol when another has occurred. Examination of the protocol of DH (Appendix) indicates that he does sometimes think that a C is a P (e.g., trial 196).

The models do not have a sufficiently rich repertoire of hypotheses. Subjects entertain more types of hypotheses about the event series than the two types, pattern and antipattern

used in the model for DH. Some subjects entertain more sophisticated hypotheses. For example, one subject was able to detect the fact that a series of events was randomized in blocks of ten trials, i.e., the series had 7 P's and 3 C's in each block of ten trials.

Some evidence also exists that when suitably motivated by money, some subjects in a binary choice experiment will predict the most frequent event on each trial. Models for these subjects require statements of the conditions under which subjects abandon testing other hypotheses or at least abandon testing hypotheses by using them to predict events. Hypotheses could still be considered and tested without using them to predict events.

Contributions of the Models

The consequences of computer simulation for the study of human behavior have been discussed at some length in several places, and I have made a limited statement of my views on this matter in another place [4]. It will suffice then to discuss some of the implications of the work reported here for our understanding of behavior. The computer models of binary choice behavior are relatively simple computer programs; however, they are relatively complex psychological models. A widely accepted view of binary choice behavior has been the idea of verbal conditioning embodied in the stochastic learning model. In its simplest form, this model says the subject's probability of predicting E_1 or E_2 in the binary choice experiment is an exponentially weighted moving average over preceding events. The verbal conditioning model is hardly consistent with the hypothesis-testing behavior exhibited by DH and a dozen other subjects for whom I have protocols. Protocols of group behavior in the binary choice experiment made available to me by David G. Hays are also consistent with the general idea of hypothesis-testing. Other inadequacies of the verbal conditioning model and evidence for hypothesis-testing models have been discussed elsewhere [3].

The computer has provided the exponents of hypothesis-testing models of behavior with the means for studying and testing these complex models. Oversimplified explanations of human behavior can no longer be justified on the grounds that the means for studying complex models do not exist. Hopefully, the use of computers to simulate human behavior can extend man's intellect by helping him study his own behavior.

APPENDIX: PROTOCOL OF SUBJECT DH[1]

(All right, now I'll read the instructions to you. I'm going to show you a series of symbols. They will either be a P symbol or a C symbol. Before each word I'll give the signal NOW. When you hear the signal NOW, tell me what symbol you expect will occur on the next trial

[1] The statements in parentheses are those of the experimenter.

and why you selected that symbol. That's the purpose of the tape recorder. Take your time. After you have given me your guess, I will show you the correct symbol. Your goal is to anticipate each word as accurately as you can. Please . . . Well, do you have any questions?) Primarily, I just guess whether it'll be a P or a C. (That's it.) But this explaining why I think so. It can be little more than—I think it'll be this, I guess, I have a feeling. How more involved can it be than that? (Well, whatever reasons you have. If those are the only reasons that occur to you as you go thru this, those will be the only reasons. Maybe they won't. OK, we'll try a few and then if you have any questions . . .)

(Now what do you expect the first symbol will be?) P. (OK, the 1st symbol is a C.)
(OK, now what do you expect the 2d symbol will be?) It'll be a P. (Why?) It's pictured in my mind. (OK, the 2d symbol is a C.)
I'll say a C. (Why?) Primarily this time because I'm trying to outguess you. (OK, the 3d symbol is a C.)
(What do you say for the 4th symbol?) I'll say C again. (Why?) This time I feel it'll be a C. (The 4th symbol is a C. When you give your answer, if you say, "I think the 5th one will be something," it'll be easier to check the tape against the answer sheet.)
(What do you think the 5th one will be?) The 5th one will be a P. (Why is that?) I feel it'll be a P, that's all. (The 5th one is a C.)
(What do you think the 6th one will be?) The 6th one will be a C because you've been giving me C's all along, and I don't think this progression will end. (The 6th one is a C.)
(What do you think the 7th one will be?) The 7th one will be a C because I don't think the progression will be broken. (OK, the 7th one was a C.)
The 8th one will be a C for the same reason. You won't break the progression. (OK, the 8th one is a P.)
(What do you think the 9th one will be?) The 9th one will be a C. (Why is that?) I think that you just gave me the P to throw me off and you'll continue the progression. (The 9th one is a C. Oh, one thing, can you see these cards?) Yes. (Can you see me writing?) No, I can't. (OK.) I'm not looking. (Well, you can look at these cards. I want you to see I'm not picking these out of my head. This set has been predetermined.)

All right. This one will be a P. The 10th one will be a P. (Why is that?) I feel that the progression will start to mix up now. (The 10th one is a C.)

(What do you think the 11th one will be?) The 11th one will be a C. You're continuing the progression. (The 11th one is a C.)

(What do you think the 12th one will be?) The 12th one will be a C because you're continuing the progression. (The 12th one is a P.)

The 13th one will be a C. The 12th one was a P. You were trying to throw me off. The progression will continue. (The 13th one is a P.)

The 14th one will be a P. You're beginning a new progression with P's. (The 14th one is a P.)

The 15th one will be a P. You're still continuing the progression. (The 15th one is a P.)

(What about the 16th one?) The 16th one will be C. . . . to throw me off now. (The 16th one is a C.)

The 17th one will be a C. You're going to see if I'll revert to the progression of P's. (The 17th one is a C.)

The 18th one will be a P. You're going to break this progression of C's. (The 18th one is a C.)

The 19th one will be a P. You're going to get off this progression of C's. (The 19th one is a P.)

The 20th one will be a P. You're going to try to throw me off trying to make me think that all— think you're going back to the other progression which I'm confused about now. I don't remember what the last one was—C, I believe. (The 20th one is a P.)

The 21st one will be a C. You won't continue with the progression of P's. (The 21st one is a P.)

The 22d one is a C. You're doing this so that I might think the P progression will continue. (The 22d one is a C.)

The 23d one will be a C. You're trying to make me think that the next one will be a P—going back to the old progression. (The 23d one is a C.)

The 24th one will be a C. You're going to continue the progression of C's. (The 24th one was a C.)

The 25th one is a C. You're still going to continue the progression of C's. (The 25th one is a C.)

The 26th one is still a C. You'll continue the progression. (The 26th one is a C.)

The 27th one is a P. You'll break the progression now. (The 27th one is a C.)

The 28th one will be a P. You're going to break the progression now. (The 28th one is a C.)

The 29th one is a C. You're continuing the progression. (The 29th one is a C.)

The 30th is a C. You'll still continue the progression. (The 30th one is a C.)

The 31st one will be a C. You'll continue the progression. (The 31st one is a C.)

The 32d is a C. You'll still continue the progression (The 32d is a P.)

The 33d is a C. You gave me a P last time to throw me off. (The 33d is a C.)

The 34th is a C. You'll continue the progression. (The 34th is a C.)

The 35th is a P. You're going to throw me off the progression. (The 35th is a C.)

The 36th is a C. You'll continue the progression. (The 36th is a C.)

The 37th is a C. You'll continue the progression. (The 37th is a C.)

The 38th is a C. You'll continue the progression. (The 38th is a C.)

The 39th is a C. You'll continue the progression. (The 39th is a C.)

The 40th is a C. You'll continue the progression. (The 40th is a C.)

The 41st is a C. You'll continue the progression. (The 41st is a C.)

The 42d is a C. You'll continue the progression. (The 42d is a C.)

The 43d is a C. You'll still continue the progression. (The 43d is a C.)

The 44th is a C. You'll still continue the progression. (The 44th is a C.)

The 45th is a C. You'll still continue the progression. (The 45th is a C.)

The 46th is a C. You'll still continue the progression. (The 46th is a C.)

The 47th will be a P. You'll now break the progression. (The 47th is a C.)

The 48th will be a C. You'll go back to the old progression. (The 48th is a C.)

The 49th is a C. You'll continue the progression. (The 49th is a C.)

The 50th is a C. You'll continue the progression. (The 50th is a P.)

The 51st will be a C. You gave me the P to throw me off. (The 51st is a P.)

The 52d is a P. You've begun a progression of P's. (The 52d is a C.)

The 53d is a P. You gave me a C to throw me off. (The 53d is a C.)

The 54th is a C. You'll continue the progression of C's. (The 54th is a C.)

The 55th is a C. You'll still continue the progression. (The 55th is a C.)

The 56th is a C. You'll continue the progression. (The 56th is a P.)

57 is a P. The P will throw me off the progression thinking you had tried to throw me off the C progression with your last P. (57 you said was a P?) P. (57 was a C.)

58 is a C. You began a progression of C's. (58 is a P.)

59 is a C. You're still trying to throw me off with the C's. (59 is a P.)

60 will be a P. You're beginning a progression of P's. (60 is a C.)

61 is a P. You're zigzagging between P's and C's. (61 is a P.)

62 is a C. You'll continue the oscillation. (62 is a C.)

63 is a C—rather 63 is a P because of the oscillation pattern. (63 is a P.)

64 is a C because of the oscillation pattern. (64 is a C.)

65 is a P because of the oscillation pattern. (65 is a C.)

66 is a C. You've begun a progression of C's. (66 is a P.)

67 will be a C. You're oscillating again. (67 is a C.)

68 is a C. You're having a different type of oscillation—2 C's between a P. (68 is a P.)

69 is a C. You're oscillating with C's and P's. (69 is a C.)

70 will be a P. It's the alternate symbol. (70 is a P.)

71 will be a C because of the oscillation sequence. (71 is a C.)

72 will be a P because of the oscillation sequence (72 is a C.)

73 will be a C. You've begun a new progression of C's. (73 is a C.)

74 is a C. You're continuing the progression. (74 is a C.)

75 is a C. You're still continuing with the progression. (75 is a C.)

76 is still a C. You're continuing with the progression. (76 is a C.)

77 is a C. You're still continuing with the progression. (77 is a C.)

78 is a C. The progression is continuing. (78 is a P.)

79 is a C. The P is to throw me off. The progression continues. (79 is a C.)

80 is a C. The pregression will continue. (80 is a C.)

81 is a C. The progression continues. (81 is a P.)

82 will be a C. You're alternating now with C's and P's. (82 is a P.)

83 is a P. You've begun a progression of P's. (83 is a C.)

84 will be a C. The P's were given to throw me off. (84 is a P.)

85 will be a P. You've begun a new alternating sequence. (85 is a P.)

86 will be a C. You're following with a C and 2 P's. Another C will come. (86 is a C.)

87 will be a P. You'll follow the same sequence. (87 is a C.)

88 will be a P. You've begun a sequence of 2 C's and a P. (88 is a C.)

89 is a C. You've begun a new progression of C's. (89 is a C.)

90 is a C. You'll continue the progression. (90 is a C.)

91 is a C. The progression continues. (91 is a C.)

92 is a C. The progression continues. (92 is a P.)

93 is a P. The P's given to me previously to make me think that the progression was being broken and that you would revert to it after the P. The next one will be a P. (93 is a C.)

94 will be a C. You've gone back to the C progression. (94 you say now is a C.) 94 is a C. (OK, 94 is a C.)

95 is a C. You've begun a progression of C's. (95 is a P.)

96 will be a C. You're alternating now with C's and P's. (96 is a P.)

97 is a C. You've begun a progression of a C and 2 P's. (97 is a P.)

98 is a P. You've begun a progression of P's. (98 is a C.)

99 is a C. You've begun a progression of 3 P's and 3 C's. You've already had the 3 P's. 98 (sic) will be a C. (That was . . . 99 is going to be a C. You said. 99 is a C.)

(What's 100?) 100 will be a C. It follows the progression. (100 is a C.)

101 will still be a C. Continue the progression of 3 P's and 3 C's. (101 is a C.)

102 will be a C. You've begun a progression of C's. (102 is a C.)

103 is a C. You'll continue the progression of C's. (103 is a C.)

104 is a C. You'll continue with the progression. (104 is a C.)

105 will be a C. You'll continue the progression. (105 is a C.)

106 will be a P. You'll break the progression now. (106 was a C.)

107 will be a C. You'll continue the progression. (107 was a P.)

108 will be a C. You gave me the P to throw me off. The progression will continue. (108 is a C.)

109 will be a C. You'll continue the progression. (109 was a P.)

110 will be a C. You're alternating with C's and P's. (110 is a C.)

111 will be a P. You'll continue the alternation. (111 was a P.)

112 will be a C. You'll continue the alternation. (112 was a P.)

113 will be a C. You've begun a progression of a C and 2 P's. (113 is a P.)

114 will be a P. You've begun a progression of P's. (114 is a P.)

115 will be a P. You'll continue the progression. (115 is a C.)

116 will be a P. The C was given to throw me off. (116 is a C.)

117 is a C. You've begun a progression of 4 P's and 4 C's. (117 is a P.)

118 will be a P. The progression has changed from 4 P's and 4 C's to 4 P's and 3 C's. (118 is a C.)

119 will be a P. You're alternating with C's and P's. (119 is a C.)

120 will be a C. You're continuing the progression. (120 is a P.)

121 will be a P. You have a progression of 2 C's and 2 P's. (121 is a P.)

122 will be a C. You'll continue this progression of 2 and 2. (122 is a C.)

123 will be a C. You're continuing the progression. (Of what?) Of 2 C's and 2 P's. (123 is a C.)

124 will be a C. You've begun a progression of C's. (124 is a C.)

124 (sic) will be a C. You're continuing the progression. (125 is a C.)

126 will be a C. You're continuing the progression. (126 is a P.)

127 will be a C. You gave me the P to throw me off. (127 is a P.)

128 will be a P. You've begun a progression of P's. (128 is a C.)

129 will be a C. You've begun a progression of 2 P's and 2 C's. (129 was a C.)

130 will be a C. You've begun a progression of C's. (130 is a P.)

131 will be a P. You're continuing the progression of 2 P's and 2 C's. (131 is a C.)

132 will be a P. You're alternating the signs now. (132 is a C.)

133 will be a C. You've begun a sequence of C's. (133 is a C.)

134 will be a C. You're continuing the sequence. (134 is a C.)

135 is a C. You're continuing with the progression. (135 is a P.)

136 will be a P. You've begun . . . you're trying to throw me off now with a 2d P. Think there would be only one P. (136 is a C.)

137 is a C. You're going to continue with the progression of C's. (137 is a C.)

138 is a C. You'll continue the progression. (138 is a C.)

139 is a C. You'll continue the progression. (139 is a P.)

140 is a C. The P was given to throw me off. (140 is a P.)

141 is a C. You gave me the 2 C's (sic) for the same reason as the previous time you had given me the 2 C's 'er 2 P's . . . (141 is a C.)

142 is a C. You'll continue with the progression. (142 is a C.)

143 is a C. You'll continue with the progression. (143 is a C.)

144 is a C. You'll continue with the progression. (144 is a C.)

145 is a P. You'll break the progression. (145 is a C.)

146 is a C. You'll continue the progression. (146 is a C.)

147 is a C. You'll continue the progression. (147 is a C.)

148 is a C. You'll continue the progression. (148 is a C.)

149 is a C. You'll continue the progression. (149 is a C.)

150 is a C. You'll still continue the progression. (150 is a C.)

151 is a C. You'll still continue the progression. (151 is a C.)

152 will be a P. You'll break the progression. (152 is a C.)

153 is a C. You'll continue the progression. (153 is a P.)

154 is a C. You've broken the progression and you'll revert to it now. (154 is a C.)

155 is a C. You'll continue the progression. (155 is a P.)

156 is a C. You're alternating with P's and C's. (156 is a C.)

157 is a C. The alternation of P's and C's was to throw me off the progression of C's. The C progression will continue. (157 is a P.)

158 is a C. You're still going back to C sequence. (158 is a C.)

159 is a C. You're still going to continue this sequence. (159 is a P.)

160 is a C. You have an alternating sequence of P's and C's. (160 is a C.)

161 will be a P. You'll continue to alternate. (161 is a P.)

162 will be a C. You'll continue this oscillation. (162 is a P.)

163 will be a C. You'll continue the alternation. (163 is a C.)

164 will be a P. You'll continue the alternation. (164 is a C.)

165 will be a P. You'll go back to the alternation. (165 is a C.)

166 will be a C. You've begun a sequence of C's. (166 is a C.)

167 will be a C. You've begun a sequence of C's. (167 is a P.)

168 will be a P. You've begun a sequence of 2 C's and 2 P's. (168 is a C.)

169 is a C. The previous P's were given to throw me off. You'll continue the sequence of C's. (169 is a C.)

170 will be a C. You'll continue the sequence. (170 is a P.)

171 will be a P. You'll begin a sequence of P's. (171 is a P.)

172 will be a C. You'll revert to the C's. (172 is a C.)

173 will be a C. You're alternating with 2 P's and 2 C's. (173 is a P.)

174 will be a C. The alternation is a C and a P. (174 is a C.)

175 will be a P. You'll continue this alternation. (175 is a C.)

176 will be a C. You've begun a sequence of C's. (176 is a P.)

177 will be a C. You'll continue with the progression of C's. (177 is a P.)

178 will be a C. You've begun a progression of 2 P's and 2 C's. (What did you say 178 was?) A C. (178 is a C.)

179 will be a C. You'll continue with another C to complete the sequence of 2 P's and 2 C's. (179 is a C.)

180 will be a P. You'll continue this sequence. (180 is a C.)

181 is a C. You've begun a sequence of C's. (181 is a C.)

182 is a C. You'll continue the sequence. (182 is a C.)

183 is a C. You'll continue the sequence. (183 is a P).

184 will be a C. The P was given to throw me off. (184 is a C.)

185 is a C. You'll continue the sequence of C's. (185 is a C.)

186 will be a C. You'll continue the sequence. (186 is a C.)

187 will be a C. You'll continue the sequence. (187 is a C.)

188 is a C. You'll continue the sequence. (188 is a C.)

189 is a C. You'll continue the sequence. (189 is a P.)

190 will be a C. The P was given to throw me off. (190 is a C.)

191 will be a C. The double P (sic) was given to throw me off a little more. (191 is a C.)

192 is a C. You've . . . been giving me a sequence of 2 P's and 2 C's. (192 is a C.)

192 (sic) is a P. You're continuing the sequence of 2 P's and 2 C's. (193 is a C.)

194 is a C. You've begun a sequence of C's. (194 is a C.)

195 is a C. You'll continue the sequence. (195 is a P.)

196 will be a P. You have a sequence here of inserting 2 P's. (196 is a C.)

197 is a C. The P was given to throw me off. (197 is a C.)

198 will be a C. You'll continue the sequence. (198 is a C.)

199 is a C. You'll continue the sequence. (199 is a C.)

200 will be a C. You'll continue the sequence. (200 is a C.)

REFERENCES

1. G. P. E. Clarkson, and H. A. Simon, 1960. Simulation of individual and group behavior. *American Economic Review, 50*(5): 920–932. MA.
2. K. Duncker, 1945. On problem solving. *Psychological Monographs, 58*(5): 1–112.
3. J. Feldman, 1959. *An analysis of predictive behavior in a two-choice situation.* Doctoral dissertation, Carnegie-Mellon University. 1A.
4. J. Feldman, 1962. Computer simulation of cognitive processes. *Computer applications in the behavioral sciences* (H. Borko, ed.); Englewood Cliffs, N.J.: Prentice-Hall, 336–359. MA.
5. E. Heidbreder, 1924. An experimental study of thinking. *Archives of Psychology, 11*(73): 1–175.
6. A. Newell, J. C. Shaw, and H. A. Simon, 1959. *Report on the play of chess player I-5 of a book game of Morphy vs. Duke Karl of Brunswick and Count Isouard.* Pittsburgh: Carnegie-Mellon University, CIP-21. MA.
7. A. Newell, and H. A. Simon, 1961. The simulation of human thought. *Current trends in psychological theory*; Pittsburgh: University of Pittsburgh Press, 152–179. 1A.
8. A. L. Samuel, 1959. Some studies in machine learning using the game of checkers. *IBM Journal of Research and Development, 3*(3): 210–229.

7

SIMULATION OF HUMAN PROBLEM-SOLVING BEHAVIOR

KENNETH R. LAUGHERY
LEE W. GREGG

To date, the technique of computer simulation of cognitive processes, especially those processes related to human behavior in problem-solving tasks, has been described primarily in terms of the content of a few constructed programs. Two closely related program structures have been published that attempt to define information-processing behavior for the class of tasks where the selection of a fixed number of allowable operations comprises the complete solution of the problem [7, 8]. Such tasks include proving theorems in logic and choosing moves in chess play. A system has been described by Hunt and Hovland [5] that will handle the organization of positive and negative instances into conjunctive, relational, or disjunctive concepts—the classic concept attainment task in which values of attributes of the stimulus materials (their color, form, and number) provide the informational elements for comparison. A third simulation model was developed for serial acquisition of motor or verbal responses under a correction method of presentation. The purpose of the present report is to describe the manner in which one proceeds from a set of behavioral data to a computer program that will serve as a model of the behavior. The data

SOURCE: Reprinted from *Psychometrika*, 27(3): 265–282 (1962).

to be presented is a selected sample (not intended to be representative) of a larger body of data collected from many Ss in the context of the last task mentioned above. Its function is merely to provide examples of the various analysis techniques as they are described.

As in the formulation of every theory, the development of a computer model represents a series of inferences based on observations. The nature of these inferences and the form into which they are conceptually molded are governed by certain initial assumptions: (i) what we choose to call a fact or observation, and (ii) what we consider to be the defining causal relations between these facts. Modern psychology theory, for example, typically treats group means—averages based on many trials, many responses, or many Ss—as the appropriate "facts" on which lawful relationships must be based. The imputed relations between individual observations of a dependent variable are frequently ignored or are ascribed to random or error variables. Hullian theory [4], Thurstone's discriminable dispersion [9], and the basic equations of test theory [3] are based on such assumptions. Stochastic models of learning [1] can exist only because of these assumptions.

In contrast, a computer simulation model is

TABLE 1   Search Behavior—Subject 1 (S1)

Setting	Protocol
	Well, I guess the thing to do now is to try to find the next correct one and see what I can figure out from there.
LRRR	I'll reverse that.
RLLL	I'm moving from left to right just eliminating the various possibilities of 3–1 patterns.
LRLL	I'll reverse that.
RLRR	For some reason I don't think this is a 3–1 pattern.
	Why? (asked by E)
LLRL	Because it hasn't clicked so far.
LLLR	
RRRL	Now I've eliminated the 3–1 patterns. Now I'm going to try all four in one direction.
RRRR	Reverse of that.
LLLL	Now I'm going to try the 2–2 pattern.
LLRR	Now I'm going to reverse the direction of the pairs.
RRLL	Now I'm going to use different combinations of 2's facing toward the right. The means and the extremes now—with the means facing toward the left.
RLLR	Now with the extremes facing toward the left and the means toward the Right.
LRRL	Now I'm going to try a 2–2 pattern with 1 and 3 facing the same direction and 2 and 4 facing the same direction.
LRLR	Now I'll reverse the direction.
RLRL[a]	

[a] Correct setting.

completely deterministic with respect to the causal relationships linking the observations it attempts to reproduce. What are these observations? Table 1 and Table 2 are samples of two individual Ss' (S1 and S2) behaviors in a problem-solving task. The symbols L's and R's

TABLE 2   Search Behavior—Subject 2 (S2)

Setting	Protocol
	Well, I'm going to turn all the switches to the left and then I'm going to start at one end and try both positions for each switch in combination until I get the right one. I'm going to change this switch (the one on the right) and leave the other three the same. If that doesn't—I'll try the second from the right in both positions with this furtherest on the right in both positions in each case. Then get all the possible combinations.
LLLL	Now I'll change the position of the far right switch.
LLLR	
	Now I'll change the third from the left.
LLRR	
	Now I'm changing the far right to try the combination.
LLRL	
	Now I'll try—switching the second from the left.
LRRL	
	The far right—
LRRR	
LRLR	
LRLL	
	Now I'll continue the far left switch
RRLL	
RRLR	
RRRR	
RRRL	
	I'm trying all the possible combinations—I think
RLRL	
RLRR	
RLLR[a]	

[a] Correct setting.

under the column headed "Setting" refer to the positions of four switches mounted on a panel in front of S. The phrases and sentences on the right are things S said as he manipulated the switches to produce the settings. These motor and verbal responses are the data—about two minutes' worth for each S. The goal is to explain these data—to do so by means of a theory that will not only account for the fragment presented in the tables but also for S's performance over the entire problem and other similar problems as well.

The deterministic assumption leads us to postulate a set of subprocesses (organized in the form of a computer program) that will generate the behavior exhibited by S, response by response. Since all of the subprocesses perform symbolic manipulations according to prescribed rules (none of which allows for the existence of random variation), any successful program necessarily defines a lawful, orderly relation between the successive responses. We think of these subprocesses as information processes comprising a complex information processing system isomorphic, at the processing level of description, to that of our human S. Note that the computer program (not the computer itself) fully embodies the "theory."

By the "information-processing level of description," we mean that the cognitive acts of the individual are reduced to specific mechanisms that operate upon the ideational content and produce outputs that guide continual behavior. These mechanisms are more simple than the phenomena which they are purported to explain. Explanation takes the form of showing how such specific mechanisms combine in particular ways so that the more complex phenomena are inevitable results. Although reductionism in psychology typically connotes a physiological level of description, the reduction that results from the computer simulation technique is to a more elementary behavioral level rather than to a physiological one. And it is behavior, cognitive and motor, that the existing embryonic models explain.

The power of the simulation technique is that it enables the theorist to see the behavioral results of the application of the model to a task. In general, this would not be possible in any other way, since the interactions of the elementary information processes become so complex that the amount of time required to trace through the branching network soon becomes prohibitive.

The sets of statements that comprise the program define processes that take symbols as input and produce new symbols as output. The symbols represent the task environment, the switches, their positions, the environmental consequences of S's responses, and the like. The symbols also include the knowledge and information that S brings to the task, as well as that gained by S during the performance of the task.

THE PROBLEM-SOLVING TASK

In this study, S is seated in front of a panel on which four switches are mounted horizontally, as shown in Figure 1. Above these switches is a button, and above the button is a light. Each switch has two positions—left and right. Some combination of lefts and rights of these four switches—a setting—will allow the light to come on when the button is pushed. A sequence of different settings is used to establish a problem. The level of difficulty can be varied by the pattern of switch positions within the sequence, which can be made more or less regular.

O — light
⊙ — button
*S*1   *S*2   *S*3   *S*4

Figure 1   Panel arrangement.

S's task is to be able to make the light come on every time he pushes the button (this is the definition of the solution). S is informed that the sequence may follow some pattern (in which case he may be able to find a rule that will generate the sequence) or that the combinations may be random and he will have to memorize the sequence.

Two kinds of data are collected. First, the position of each switch is recorded each time S pushes the button, or tests if the combination is correct. Second, S is asked to verbalize his ideas as he works through the problem. He is asked to "think aloud."

ANALYSIS OF BEHAVIORS

In a simulation study of this kind, the initial phases of the data analysis are (i) to identify the way Ss represent the environment, (ii) to describe general categories of behavior, and (iii) to identify, within the more general behavior categories, the rules or heuristics which interact with the environmental representation to make up the behavioral processes.

REPRESENTING THE ENVIRONMENT

The first step is to identify the manner in which S internally represents the environment. If a computer program is to simulate human behavior, it must have available an environment to act upon. This step can be accomplished by examining S's protocol for specific references to the environment.

Many things are implied in the term "representing the environment." A first consideration is the elements or parts of the environment that S selects as relevant to the task—the elements toward which he directs his attention. Protocols from a number of Ss indicate that the relevant items in the present task are: the individual switches and their values or positions, the light (on or off), and the button.

In addition to determining which elements S considers relevant, it is important to notice the names or labels that S attaches to them. Tables 1 and 2 present examples of two subjects referring to the same parts of the environment with completely different labels. S1's statement "Now I'm going to try a 2-2 pattern with 1 and 3 facing the same direction, and 2 and 4 facing the same direction," in conjunction with other similar statements, indicates that he was labeling the switches 1, 2, 3, and 4 from left to right, respectively (each switch was assigned a particular name). Unlike S1, S2 did not have a name for each switch; instead, he referred to the various switches by their positions from the left or right end of the panel. Statements such as "Now I'll change the position of the far right switch" and "Now I'll change the third from the left" in Table 2 are evidence for this conclusion. Furthermore, S2 often referred to the same switch by relating it to *different* sides of the panel at different times, viz., "the second from the right" and "the third from the left" (Table 2). Both statements refer to the switch that S1 called "3."

In all cases for all Ss, the values of the four switches were labeled "left" and "right." Statements such as "opposite of what it was before" were often encountered; but such references are really concerned with relationships and not with names of objects or values.

The manner in which S forms relationships between objects in the environment will be an important factor in determining the way he will operate upon the environment. These relationships may take the form of grouping, recoding, etc., of various elements at a point in time or may relate the same object at different times. An example of the former (grouping, recoding, etc.) in this task is the way the Ss recoded the four individual switches into various configurations or settings. In Table 1, S1 refers to "3-1," "2-2," and "four-in-one-direction" patterns—meaning the relative number of switches having different values (e.g., a 3-1 would have three switches to the left and one to the right, or three to the right and one to the left). These terms include a group of settings, and within a group are names for individual configurations. Examples within the 2-2 patterns: individual configurations are referred to as "the means and the extremes" and "the two on the left and the two on the right." Hence, relationships between the environmental elements are noted in terms of groups of switches and groups of settings.

Relationships are noted between the same elements at different points in time. Statements such as "opposite of what it was before" (mentioned above) and "same as before" were very common, and imply definite relationships over the passage of time. In their verbalizations, Ss seldom referred to the button or the light. These elements were usually implied in statements such as "I'll test if that is correct—it's wrong," with S interpreting the button as "test," and the light (the outcome of the test) as "right" or "wrong."

It is interesting to note that in the protocols collected from a large number of Ss in this task, none of them refers to the experimenter as a relevant part of the environment. Feldman [2], in a simulation study of binary choice behavior, found that S often made such statements as "You (E) were trying to throw me off," meaning that S believed his hypothesis was correct but that E was trying to trick him.

IDENTIFICATION OF BEHAVIOR CATEGORIES

The second step in handling the data is to map out qualitatively different kinds of behavior that S exhibits. This is done by reading through the transcriptions of S's protocol with a view toward identifying major recurrent classes of behavior. In general, the description of these recurrent themes can be couched in terms of S's goals, i.e., what he says he is trying to do.

Early in performance of the sequential task, we find statements like "I'm just throwing the switches at random to see if I can get the light to come on" or "Just looking now for a correct one." As the particular S (quoted above) worked on the second setting during the first trial of his first problem (finally succeeding), he said, "There it is! With three to the right and one to the left. Now—ah—I suppose I have to remember this for the next time . . . three to the right and one to the left." And after a long interval of silence, E says, "It's these periods of silence that I really want to know about." S replied, "You mean what I'm thinking? Well, now I'm trying to think—trying to fit some way in—where maybe three of them are one way and the next . . . maybe it moves down to this one that's off. You know what I mean?"

Believe it or not, E did know what S was trying to say even though his statements at this early stage of the problem-solving experience were vague and incoherent. Here, S was "trying to fit" the idea of sequence of settings RRRL, RRLR, RLRR, LRRR to the problem. This sequence was a hypothesis about the solution, and S was about to test if it was correct. (Many of the words and labels S uses have meaning only in the context provided by a knowledge of the responses that are made in setting switches.) In a later problem, the same S begins work with a statement similar to his first comment. He says, "Well again—we'll just start by random. See what happens." He elaborates by giving his definition of "random," i.e., "trial and error with the system I used before." That "random system" takes the form of a systematic search, starting with three switches in the direction "to the right," and a single switch "to the left." His method of searching to "see what happens" is precisely one of the earliest ideas about sequences of settings in which three (settings) are one way, and one, the other way, that he had thought of as a possible solution to the first problem.

It is the fact of recurring statements of "trying to" or "attempting to" or "wanting to" that leads to the formulation of behavioral modes in terms of S's goals. What he says, coupled with what he does, as he reaches fairly well-defined landmarks within the problem situation leads to the identification of rather broad behavioral patterns. These define the framework within which the specific information processes are built.

From the above sample of statements from S's protocol, it is apparent that searching, remembering, and testing an idea or hypothesis concerning the problem sequence (in whole or in part), as modes of cognitive behavior, occur very early. Specifically, the definitions of these "modes" and their goals are as follows.

1. *Search.* S's goal in this mode is simply to find a combination of switch positions that will make the light go on when the button is pushed.

2. *Remembering.* S tries to recall specifically (on the basis of prior learning) the next correct setting.

3. *Hypothesis Testing.* S's goal is to test to see if any of the hypotheses that he has available will serve to generate all or part of the problem sequence.

4. *Hypothesis Generation.* S attempts to generate new hypotheses on the basis of what he has learned about the problem thus far.

Most of what follows is an attempt to describe the search behavior of the Ss whose data are presented on Tables 1 and 2.

PROCESS RULES FOR S1'S SEARCH BEHAVIOR

In the identification of process rules, the motor responses can be treated as the inputs and outputs (the settings before and after the rule is applied). By examining the differences between the inputs and outputs and giving close attention to S's verbal reports, it is often possible to identify the nature of the rules. Usually, but not always, it is necessary to examine a sequence of differences in order to discover which rule(s) is being applied, i.e., the rule is more easily identified when viewed in the context of a variety of inputs and outputs.

The data presented in Table 1 occurred at the beginning of a random problem after S1 had solved three earlier problems where the solutions could be described in the form of simple rules.

S1 usually enters the search mode under one of two conditions: (i) at the beginning of the problem, and (ii) at those times (and there may be several) when he is making little progress in finding a solution and feels that he needs more information. Evidence for this can be seen in Table 1 (the first comment under Protocol) where S1 says "Well, I guess the thing to do now is to try to find the next correct one and see what I can figure out from this."

S1's perception of the switch patterns is characterized by his naming various "forms" that ignore the actual values of the switches—left or right. He says, "I'm . . . just eliminating the various possibilities of 3-1 patterns." He tries the patterns of each form in a particular order: the 3-1 patterns, then the 4-0, then the 2-2's.

The way in which he actually makes changes in the switch settings is governed by four rules.

First Rule. The rule that has the highest priority is one that produces an opposite setting. Notice S1's statements, "I'll reverse that." To produce an opposite setting means that S must manipulate all four of the individual switches.

Second Rule. This rule is based on what S1 calls "moving from left to right." In the 3-1 form, the changes are made so that the switch that is different from the other three is displaced one to the right. Here, too, we notice that the actual values of the switches (left or right) are not referred to by S1 and do not appear to be important to the changes that are made.

Third Rule. This rule uses the idea of a major symbol. A major symbol is the direction, right or left, that appears most frequently in a particular setting. For the 4-0 and 3-1 forms, the value is obvious. For the 2-2 settings, however, an arbitrary decision is called for. By defining the major symbol as the value of the switch on the left, we are able to match consistently what S1 does; namely, S1 keeps the major symbol the same when producing a new setting whether of the same form or of a different form. Notice that the higher priority of the opposite rule overrides this one, so that the first change is from LRRR to RLLL. Then the rule "moving across" (the switch that is different moves one place to the right), but with major symbol kept the same, produces the new setting LRLL.

Fourth Rule. This rule specifies the three distinct patterns that the subject (in this case S1) names for the 2-2 form. The list defines the order in which patterns are tried. As before, the "opposite rule" and the "major symbol rule" make it possible to produce the specific settings. The distinct patterns are:

1. "The two on the left and the two on the right."
2. "The means and the extremes."
3. "One and three, and two and four."

PROCESS RULES FOR S2'S SEARCH BEHAVIOR

Like S1, S2 enters the search mode at the beginning of each new problem and at those times when little progress is being made toward a solution. The data in Table 2 occurred at the beginning of S2's second problem, where the solution consisted of simply applying the rule "same" after finding the first correct setting, RLLR. Because he tried the same sequence in the first problem (but found the correct one much sooner), it can be concluded that this search procedure was available to S2 from the beginning—he did not learn it in the task situation. Furthermore, the sequence of configurations within search was constant for S2 over a series of problems, whereas S1 altered the order in which the different forms were attempted as a function of what he had learned about the current problem and previous problems. Although these procedural differences exist, it is nevertheless true that at the level at which the definitions have been stated for the various modes, S1 and S2 were seeking the same goal in the search mode. Evidence for this is a number of statements made by S2 just before trying sequences like those in Table 2: "I'm going to start back in the sequence again and see if I can see any relationships," and "I'm going to try all possible combinations again."

Close examination of S2's search behavior reveals three basic facts about the procedure. First, a "base setting"—LLLL—was always used as a starting point. S1's concept of a major symbol had no relevance here, because the base was independent of any prior activity. A second factor is that S2 made only one switch throw in going from one setting to the next, a procedure that is maximally efficient with respect to number of manipulations. S1, however, made no apparent attempt to maximize along this dimension, and could not have done so within the various forms. Finally, as was noted in S1's 3-1 sequence, a "direction of movement" is apparent in S2's search. The general pattern of changes (one at a time) takes place from right to left. Another S in using a similar procedure described it as "moving across and filling in."

An additional point regarding the search procedures of these two Ss is that both eliminated all 16 possible configurations without repeating. This is certainly consistent with the goal of finding the next correct setting as *quickly* and *efficiently* as possible.

PROCESS REPRESENTATION

Flow Charts

Flow charts are prepared for specific modes based on segments of the data like that of Tables 1 and 2. The rules identified from the analysis of the sequence of settings and the reasons stated by S determine the structure of the flow charts. Such structures show how the rules interact to produce the sequence of behaviors. For example, Figure 2 is the flow chart for the 3-1 form for S1's search. In it the rules are incorporated as processes that determine the particular sequence of 3-1 settings. Figure 3 is the flow chart for S2's search behavior.

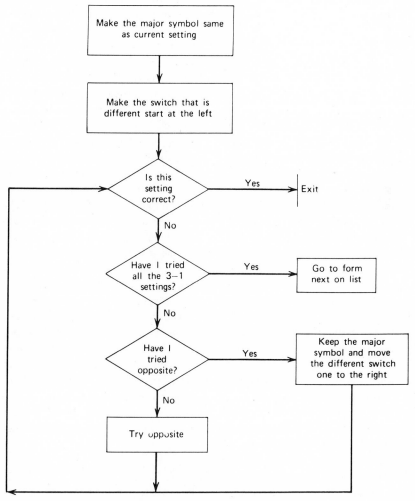

Figure 2   3-1 form flow chart.

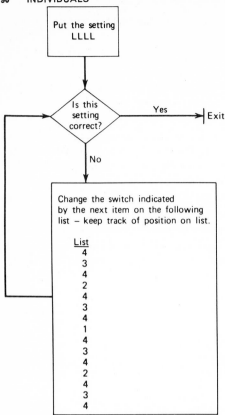

Figure 3 Search procedure used by S2.

Actually, each block of the flow chart is a process that has inputs and produces outputs. The inputs and outputs are symbols that represent objects and relationships between objects as we interpret S's perception of them. In this way, S's representations of switches, the rules for manipulating switches, the ordered lists of changes and forms, and the like, are made available to the computer.

Psychological vs. Non-psychological Processes

Some of the processes (those based on the rules) have psychological significance; others do not. This distinction is crucial in the simulation approach. A psychologically significant process is one that transforms its input to its output in a way that parallels the processes employed by S. A process that is not psychologically significant is one that generates the desired output from the input, but does so with no pretense of representing S's processes.

The reason for having these two kinds of processes is twofold. First, there are occasions

when one is simply unable at that time to identify what the subject is doing in going from a given input to an output. Because our program is deterministic, a way must exist for getting by this hurdle. The procedure is to construct a process (completely experimenter-made) that will produce the desired results. A second situation is when the process has been identified, but the lack of adequate programming techniques makes it difficult but not impossible (the computer is capable but the programmer is not) to write the desired process in the form of a program.

Examples of processes that are and are not psychologically significant are shown in Figures 2 and 3, respectively. The flow chart for S1's behavior in generating the settings in the 3-1 form includes the major symbol, movement from left to right, the switch that is different, and the opposite processes. These processes are the same as those verbalized and employed by S1. When programmed and executed on the computer, they are capable of taking the same inputs and producing the same outputs as S1 does in the problem-solving task.

Although the procedure described by the flow chart for S2's search is also capable of taking the same inputs and producing the same outputs as S2, the processes described by the diagram are not directly analogous to those verbalized and used by S2. As previously stated, S2 employed a set of rules that included ideas such as "direction of movement" and "change one switch each time." The method employed by the program consists of a list of switch names which, when taken one at a time, define a sequence of changes that match those produced by S2.

The goal, of course, is to construct a program in which all processes are psychologically significant. The first limitation—where one is unable to identify the process—will be overcome as the behavior is better understood. The programming problem can be expected to improve with experience on the part of the programmer and more adequate "languages" for stating processes.

CONSTRUCTING THE MODEL

In order to put the processes in the form of a computer program, a language especially designed for this kind of work is used. The language is an information-processing language (IPL-V) developed by Newell et al. [6]. It lends itself to this kind of work because of the way it handles inputs and outputs. It will manipulate symbols in the machine without regard to their arithmetic representation. Processes can be named and can be subsequently executed by a single program statement. Moreover, recursive features make it possible to execute a process one part of which is the process itself. In the IPL-V language, the information (representation of the environment) and the rules for operating upon this information are expressed as lists. Two kinds of lists are employed—data lists and program lists. The data lists are used to represent the information. For example, a setting is represented by the following list:

List Name

L

L

R

L

Each element on a list represents a switch, and the value of that element (L or R) is the position of the switch. This list corresponds to the setting LLRL.

The rules are expressed as program lists, where each element in the list corresponds to an operation in the series of operations required to effect the rule. The program lists when applied to the data lists constitute a process.

The program is a hierarchical structure—rules (program lists) are capable of executing other rules, and these "subrules" can execute other "sub-subrules," and so on. For example, the highest-order program list would determine when the computer was behaving in the various modes; the program lists for search would determine when the various forms were to be tried; and the program for a 3-1 form would determine the major symbol, direction of movement, etc.

It may appear that the processes are unrelated—one set of rules operating upon a series of data lists (information), then another set of rules operating upon a different set of data lists, etc. Such is not the case. The information and the rules for manipulating this information are, in some sense, independent. The same data lists can serve as input to various program lists which, in turn, produce a different output. Thus, it is the invariant data list structures that act as the unifying element and cause the processes to result in a lawful flow of behavior.

TESTING THE MODEL

Having identified the processes and constructed the program, we reach the point where we test our theory by computer simulation. The program is executed on a computer and the machine's performance is compared with S's behavior. In order to provide an adequate test, the behavior with which the computer output is compared must, of course, be different from the behavior which served as a basis for the model's construction.

Because the computer model is completely deterministic, it is possible to compare more than just the motor responses (settings). Every response produced by the model is the result of some rule (or set of rules) being applied to a specific input (the "reason"). It is a relatively easy task to make the computer display these reasons in addition to the responses. These "computer protocols" can then be compared with S's reasons which result in an additional test. Because the model predicts both the responses and the reasons, three types of errors can be distinguished.

1. The response is correct but the reason is wrong.
2. The response is wrong but the reason is correct.
3. Both the response and the reason are wrong.

Tables 3 and 4 present the results of the simulations corresponding to the particular segments of search behavior that were observed in Tables 1 and 2 respectively. A fair amount of success has been achieved to date in simulating the search behavior of S1 and S2 in other problems, This is, however, only a small part of the entire working program which will, for these Ss, handle shifts from one mode to another and simulate quite well the order and nature of the hypotheses attempted within the hypothesis-testing mode. The entire program is roughly 2,000 instructions, of which 300 are unique to

TABLE 3 Machine Behavior—Simulation of Subject 1

Setting	Protocol
	Go to search. Try 3–1 pattern, moving from left to right—the major symbol is right.
LRRR	
	Try opposite.
RLLL	
	Have I tried all 3–1 patterns—no—I move on to the next one—the major symbol is the same as the major symbol in the last one.
LRLL	
	Try opposite.
RLRR	
	Have I tried all 3–1 patterns—no—I move on to the next one—the major symbol is the same as the major symbol in the last one.
RRLR	
	Try opposite.
LLRL	
	Have I tried all 3–1 patterns—no—I move on to the next one—the major symbol is the same as the major symbol in the last one.
LLLR	
	Try opposite.
RRRL	
	Have I tried all 3–1 patterns—yes—it is not a 3–1 pattern. The next pattern to try is a 4–0. Create the 4–0 pattern that keeps the major symbol the same.
RRRR	
	Try opposite.
LLLL	
	It's not a 4–0 pattern. The next pattern to try is a 2–2. Make the two on the left different from the 2 on the right. Keep major symbol the same.
LLRR	
	Try opposite.
RRLL	
	Try another combination of 2–2 patterns—try "means and extremes." Keep major symbol the same.
RLLR	
	Try opposite.
LRRL	
	Try another combination of 2–2 patterns. Try "every other one."
LRLR	
	Try opposite.
RLRL[a]	

[a] Correct setting.

TABLE 4 Machine Behavior—Simulation of Subject 2

Setting	Protocol
	Go to search. Try all possible patterns by changing one switch for each new pattern. Change switches in the order they appear on List #1. Start with setting LLLL.
LLLL	
	Change switch 4.
LLLR	
	Change switch 3.
LLRR	
	Change switch 4.
LLRL	
	Change switch 2.
LRRL	
	Change switch 4.
LRRR	
	Change switch 3.
LRLR	
	Change switch 4.
LRLL	
	Change switch 1.
RRLL	
	Change switch 4.
RRLR	
	Change switch 3.
RRRR	
	Change switch 4.
RRRL	
	Change switch 2.
RLRL	
	Change switch 4.
RLRR	
	Change switch 3.
RLLR[a]	

[a] Correct setting.

the search mode. There are perhaps 500 additional instructions used in search that are also used in other modes. The program is a closed information-processing system that will solve problems in much the same way S solved the same problems. At present, it will generate a limited class of new hypotheses insufficient to match S's behavior on certain problems.

CONCLUSIONS

This paper has attempted to describe some general procedures that have been successful in going from a set of behavioral data to a computer model of the behavior. The data analysis consists of three phases: (i) identifying S's environmental representation, (ii) discovering general behavior categories, and (iii) identifying, within these categories, the rules which interact with the environmental representation to make up behavioral processes. The processes can be expressed as flow charts which, in turn, serve as a guide in constructing the program (model). When producing flow charts, one often finds it necessary to construct non-psychological processes which do not parallel those employed by S but are necessary to make the program work. The model is tested by executing the program on a computer and comparing the machine's performance with S's behavior.

What makes this approach profitable? If the simulation required a separate rule for each response or if the processes that have been created for the Ss whose data have been presented applied only to themselves (or only to those Ss in solving a particular problem), then this work would seem fruitless indeed. But, it is now possible to see a great deal of redundancy, not just in S's behavior but rather in the application of basic processes that have been discovered in this and other cognitive tasks.

While it is true that in the analysis one looks for reasonably stable behavioral sequences first, the fruitfulness of the work lies not in reproducing these but in discovering generally applicable processes that use different inputs and yield different outputs to generate complex streams of behavior. The fact is that certain basic processes occur over and over to produce different sequences of behavior. The processes are derived from just a limited set of rules. For example, the rule "try opposite" appears as a part of many hypotheses in the test-hypothesis mode; and many times, where not sure of his memory, S will try the opposite of a setting that he thought he had remembered during the remembering mode.

The concept of "direction" is an example of a basic process that was critical to the search behavior of both S1 and S2. It was also observed in the solution hypothesis (cited earlier) that produced the sequence RRRL, RRLR, RLRR, LRRR. The basic processes "same," "different," and "direction" are all evident in the hypothesis-generation mode. Time after time, Ss referred to similarities and differences as well as patterns based upon a direction of movement when generating a new hypothesis from a sequence of settings.

This work is distinguished by the level of analysis (its ideographic nature and the detail to which the individual's responses are attended) in contrast to the more molar, nomothetic relationships that have been featured in recent behavioral history. The processes we have discovered are constructs; these processes are hypothetical when viewed as information-processing entities, but as surely tied to input/output relationships as any previously defined intervening variable.

REFERENCES

1. R. R. Bush, and W. K. Estes, eds., 1959. *Studies in mathematical learning theory.* Stanford: Stanford University Press.
2. J. Feldman, 1961. Simulation of behavior in the binary choice experiment. *Joint Computer Conference, Western Proceedings, 19*: 133–144. 1A.
3. H. Gulliksen, 1950. *Theory of mental tests.* New York: Wiley.
4. C. L. Hull, 1943. *Principles of behavior.* New York: Appleton-Century-Crofts.
5. E. B. Hunt, and C. I. Hovland, 1961. Programming a model of human concept formulation. *Joint Computer Conference, Western Proceedings, 19*: 145–155. 1A.
6. A. Newell, ed., 1961. *Information processing language-V manual.* Englewood Cliffs, N.J.: Prentice-Hall; second edition in 1964.
7. A. Newell, J. C. Shaw, and H. A. Simon, 1958. Chess-playing programs and the problem of complexity. *IBM Journal of Research and Development, 2*(4): 320–335. 8A.
8. A. Newell, J. C. Shaw, and H. A. Simon, 1958. Elements of a theory of human problem solving. *Psychological Review, 65*(3): 151–166. MA.
9. L. L. Thurstone, 1927. A law of comparative judgment. *Psychological Review, 34*(4): 273–286.

8

PRICE AND OUTPUT DETERMINATION IN A RETAIL DEPARTMENT STORE

RICHARD M. CYERT
JAMES G. MARCH
CHARLES G. MOORE, Jr.

In Chapter 6 of *A Behavioral Theory of the Firm*, we outlined the general form of a theory of decision making in a complex organization [2]. Here we propose to apply this general model to a specific organization and a specific set of decisions. In order to make the application, it will be necessary to elaborate considerably the abstract model. However, we believe that the elaboration is a special instance of the more general theory, that it is possible to use the model as a base for the simulation of the decision process in a specific case, and that the predictions generated by the elaborated model bear a close relation to actual observed behavior.

The organization chosen for intensive study is one department in a large retail department store. The firm involved is part of an oligopolistic market consisting (for most purposes) of three large downtown stores. Each of the firms involved also operates one or more suburban stores, but the focus of this study is the downtown market (where each store makes most of

SOURCE: An edited reprint of Chapter 7 of R. M. Cyert and J. G. March, 1963, *A Behavioral Theory of the Firm*.

its sales). The firm is organized into several merchandising groups, each of which has several departments. The firm, in total, has more than 100 major departments. We have studied, with varying degrees of intensity, the price and output decisions in about a dozen of the firm's departments. From these dozen we have chosen one for intensive investigation, and the specific model reported here is literally a model of decision making in that specific department. In our judgment, the decision processes we report for this department could be generalized with trivial changes to other departments in the same merchandising group and could be generalized with relatively modest changes to most other departments outside the immediate group. Because of the great similarity in operation among department stores, we believe the model represents many aspects of decision making in retail department stores.

We present the model at two levels of specificity. In the first section we outline the decision process in the organization in rather general terms. In the second section we elaborate some of the decision rules in order to provide specific, explicit predictions of decisions.

GENERAL VIEW OF PRICE AND OUTPUT DETERMINATION IN A RETAIL DEPARTMENT STORE

An organization makes relatively independent price and output decisions. There are loose connections between the two decision areas, but for the most part decisions are made with reference to different goals and different stimuli. Although we will want to elaborate the goals of the organization somewhat when we turn to specific decision rules, we can describe two general goals that the department pursues: (1) *a sales objective;* the department expects (and is expected by the firm) to achieve an annual sales objective; (2) *a mark-up objective;* the department attempts to realize a specified average mark-up on the goods sold. Organizational decision making occurs in response to problems (or perceived potential problems) with respect to one or the other of these goals. In this sense it is clear that the behavior of the department is problem-oriented and conforms to the general problem-solving decision model suggested earlier.

Sales Goal

The general flow chart for decision making with respect to the sales goal is indicated in Figure 1. The organization forms sales "estimates" that are consistent with its sales goal and develops a routine ordering plan for

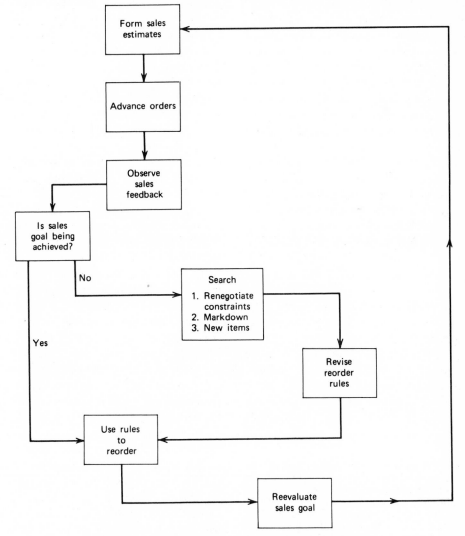

Figure 1 General form of reaction to sales goal indicators.

advance orders.[1] These orders are designed to avoid overcommitment, pending feedback on sales. As feedback on sales is provided, results are checked against the sales objective. If the objective is being achieved, reorders are made according to standard rules. This is the usual route of decisions, and we will elaborate it further below.

Suppose, however, that the sales goal is not being achieved. Under such circumstances a series of steps is taken. First, the department attempts to change its environment by negotiating revised agreements with either its suppliers or other parts of its own firm or both. Within the firm, it seeks a change in the promotional budget that will provide greater promotional resources for the goods sold by the department. Outside the firm, the department seeks price concessions from manufacturers that will permit a reduction in retail price. If either of these attempts to relax external constraints is successful, reorders are made according to appropriately revised rules.

Second, the department considers a routine mark-down to stimulate sales generally and to make room for new items in the inventory. As we will indicate below, the department ordinarily has a pool of stock available for mark-downs and expects to have to reduce the mark-up in this way on some of the goods sold. It will attempt to stimulate all sales by taking some of these anticipated mark-downs. Once again, if the tactic is successful in stimulating sales, reorders are made according to slightly revised rules.

Third, the department searches for new items that can be sold at relatively low prices (but with standard mark-up). Most commonly such items are found when domestic suppliers are eliminating lines or are in financial trouble. A second major source is in foreign markets.

In general, the department continues to search for solutions to its sales problems until it finds them. If the search procedures are successful, all

goes well. In the long run, however, it may find a solution in another way. The feedback on sales not only triggers action, but also leads to the re-evaluation of the sales goal. In the face of persistent failure to achieve the sales goal, the goal adjusts downward. With persistent success it adjusts upward.

Mark-up Goal

The flow chart in Figure 2 outlines the departmental reaction with respect to the mark-up goal. The reactions are analogous to those shown in Figure 1, but have a somewhat different impact. On the basis of the mark-up goal (and standard industry practice), price lines and planned mark-up are established. Feedback on realized mark-up is received. If it is consistent with the goal, no action is taken and standard decision rules are maintained.

If the mark-up goal is not being achieved, the department searches for ways in which it can raise mark-up. Basically, the search focuses on procedures for altering the product mix of the department by increasing the proportion of high mark-up items sold. For example, the department searches for items that are exclusive, for items that can be obtained from regular suppliers below standard cost, and for items from abroad. Where some of the same search efforts led to price reduction (and maintenance of mark-up) when stimulated by failure on the sales goal, here they lead to maintenance of price and increase in mark-up. At the same time, the organization directs its major promotional efforts toward items on which high mark-ups can be realized. In some instances, the department has a reservoir of solutions to mark-up problems (e.g., pressure selling of high mark-up items). Such solutions are generally reserved for problem solving and are not viewed as appropriate long-run solutions. Finally, as in the case of the sales goal, the mark-up goal adjusts to experience gradually.

We think the general processes reflected in Figures 1 and 2 correctly represent the decision process in the firm under examination. They do not, however, yield specific, precise predictions. Detailed models of the major price and output decisions need to be developed and compared with results from the organization studied. This task is undertaken in the next sections.

---

[1] This statement may not portray the process accurately. During the period we observed it was not possible to determine the interactions between the sales estimates and the goals. They always tended to be consistent with each other but it was difficult to determine the extent to which an implicit goal of "equal or exceed last year's sales" influenced the estimates.

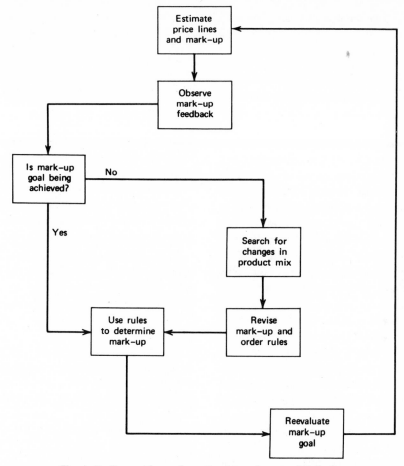

Figure 2 General form of reaction to mark-up goal indicators.

DETAILS OF OUTPUT DETERMINATION

The concept of output is not obviously relevant to a department store. In fact, if our major interest were in retail organizations, we would not describe any decisions as being output decisions. However, we are interested more generally in business firms, and we wish to identify a decision variable in the retail setting that has the same general attributes as the output decision in a production organization. A department store does not produce goods; it buys goods for resale. Consequently, orders and the process of making order decisions comprise the output determination of the firm. As the manufacturing firm adds to inventory by production, the retail firm adds to inventory by ordering.

As we have already suggested, the output decision is essentially a decision based on feed-back from sales experience. No explicit calculation of the probable behavior of competitors is made, and although expectations with respect to sales are formed, every effort is made to avoid depending on any kind of long-run forecast. Output decisions are designed to satisfy two major goals. These are (1) to limit mark-downs to an acceptable level and (2) to maintain inventory at a reasonable level.

The firm divides output decisions into two classes—advance (initial) orders and reorders. Each is dependent on a different set of variables and performs a different function. Advance orders allow the firm (and its suppliers) to avoid uncertainty by providing contractual commitments. They also account for the bulk of the total orders. Reorders are only a small part of the total orders, but they provide virtually all the variance in total orders. Insofar as the output decision is viewed primarily as a decision with respect to total output, reorders are much more important than advance orders in fixing the absolute level.

Advance Orders

Advance orders represent the base output of the department. The size of the advance order depends on two things: one is the estimated sales, the other a simple estimate of the variance in sales. In a general way, the apparent motivation with respect to advance orders is to set the commitment at such a level that the base output alone will be greater than sales only if extreme estimation errors have been made. Thus, refinements in estimation are not attempted and simple estimating procedures are used, modified somewhat by special organizational needs only remotely related to the issue of accuracy.

The estimation of sales. The store operates on a six-month planning period. The individual department estimates dollar sales expected during the next six months. At the same time, sales are estimated on a monthly basis for each product class over the six-month period. Since the accuracy of the estimate is not especially critical (at least within rather broad limits) for the total output decision, we consider the organizational setting in which the estimate is made in order to understand the decision rules. A low forecast, within limits, carries no penalties. The forecast cannot, however, be so low relative to past history that it is rejected (as being unrealistic) by top management. Limits on the high side are specified by two penalties for making a forecast that is not achieved. First, achievement of forecasts is one of the secondary criteria for judging the performance of the department. Although the department cannot significantly affect the sales goal by underestimation, it can to a limited extent soften criticism (for failure) by anticipating it. Second, an overestimate will result in overallocation of funds. If the department is unable to use the funds, it is subject to criticism. As a result, the sales estimate tends to be biased downward.

The primary data used in estimating sales are the dollar sales (at retail prices) for the corresponding period in the preceding year. Although the data are commonly adjusted slightly for "unique" events, the adjustments are not

significant. The following naive rule predicts the estimates with substantial accuracy.[2]

Rule 1. The estimate for the next six months is equal to the total of the corresponding six months of the previous year minus one-half of the sales achieved during the last month of the previous six-month period.

From the point of view of output decisions, the more critical estimates are those for the individual months. The monthly figures are used directly in determining advance orders for the individual seasons. The estimation procedure for a specific product class is as follows:

Rule 2. *For the months of February, March, and April.* Use the weekly sales of the seven weeks before Easter of the previous year as the estimate of the seven weeks before Easter of this year. In the same way, extend the sales of last year for the weeks before and after the season to the corresponding weeks of this year.

Rule 3. *For the months of August and September.* The same basic procedure as in Rule 2 is followed, with the date of the public schools' opening replacing the position of Easter. The opening dates of county and parochial schools also are significant. If these dates are far enough apart, the peak will be reduced, but the estimate for the two months will still represent the total sales of the corresponding two months of the previous year.

Rule 4. *For the months of May, June, October, November, and December.* Estimated sales for this year equal last year's actual sales.

Rule 5. *For the months of January and July.* Estimated sales for this year equal one-half of last year's actual sales rounded to the nearest $100.

This set of simple rules provides an estimate of sales that is tightly linked to the experience of the immediately previous year with a slight downward adjustment (i.e., in Rule 5).

The Seasonal Advance Order Fraction. The department distinguishes four seasons—Easter, Summer, Fall, and Holiday. The seasons, in fact, do not account exhaustively for all months, but they account for most of the total sales.

---

[2] We do not mean to imply that the department consciously uses such a rule. Although the rule was inferred from a study of actual behavior, the head of the department did not describe his estimation rule in these terms.

Estimates of sales are established on the basis of the monthly estimates. These estimates do not necessarily include all months in the season. The following estimation rules are used:

Easter: Cumulate sales for the seven weeks before Easter.

Summer: Cumulate sales for April, May, June, and one-half of July.

Fall: Cumulate sales for one-half of July, August, and September.

Holiday: Cumulate sales for October, November, and December.

These cumulations give a seasonal sales estimate for use in establishing advance orders. Once such an estimate is made, some fraction of the estimated sales is ordered.

Advance orders generally offer some concrete advantages to the department. Greater selection is possible (some goods may not be available later), and some side payments may be offered by the producer (e.g., credit terms, extra services). The department exploits these advantages by ordering a substantial fraction of its anticipated sales in advance, but an attempt is made to limit the advance order fraction to an output that would be sold even under an extreme downward shift in demand.

The size of the advance order fraction is the result of learning on the part of the organization and reflects the differences among the seasons in sales variability and the degree of seasonal specialization of the items. The greater the susceptibility of seasonal sales to exogenous variables (e.g., weather), the lower the fraction. The more specialized the merchandise sold during a season (i.e., the greater the difficulty of carrying it over to another season), the lower the fraction. At the time we observed the organization, the fraction (estimated from interviews and analysis of data) and the timing of advance orders for each of the seasons were as follows:

Seasons	% of Estimated Sales Placed in Advanced Orders	Time Order Made
Easter	50	Jan. 15–20
Summer	60	March 10–15
Fall	75	May 20–25
Holiday	65	Sept. 20–25

In general we expect this simple model to predict quite well, diverging only when the department makes *ad hoc* adjustments. Our observations lead us to believe this will not happen frequently.

Reorders

For all practical purposes, reorders control the output of the department. As the word implies, a reorder is an order for merchandise made on the basis of feedback from inventory and sales. Because of lead-time problems, much of the feedback is based on early season sales information. Thus, the timing of a reorder depends on the length of time to the peak sales period as compared with the manufacturing lead-time required.

Reorder Rules. Reorders are based on a re-estimate of probable sales. Data on current sales are used in a simple way to adjust "normal" sales. The reorder program specifies reorders for a given type of product class as a result of a simple algebraic adjustment.

Let T = the total period of the season

τ = the period of the season covered by the analysis

$S_{i\tau}$ = this year's sales of product class i over τ

$S'_{i\tau}$ = last year's sales of product class i over τ

$S'_{i(T-\tau)}$ = last year's sales of product class i over $T-\tau$

I_i = available stock of i at time of analysis including stock ordered

M_i = minimum amount of stock of i desired at all times

$O_{i(T-\tau)}$ = reorder estimate

Then,

$$O_{i(T-\tau)} = \left[\frac{S_{i\tau}}{S'_{i\tau}} \cdot S'_{j(T-\tau)} + M_i \right] - I_i$$

If $O_{i(T-\tau)} \leqslant 0$ no reorders will be made. In addition, orders already placed may be canceled, prices may be lowered, or other measures taken to reduce the presumed overstocking. Such an analysis would be made for each product class. The figure that results is tentative, subject to minor modifications in the light of anticipated special events.

Open-to-Buy Constraint

The firm constrains the enthusiasms of its departments by maintaining a number of controls on output decisions. One of the more conspicuous controls is the "open-to-buy." The open-to-buy is, in effect, the capital made available to each department for purchases. The open-to-buy for any month is calculated from the following equation:

$$B_\tau = (I^*_{\tau+1} - I_\tau) + S^*_\tau$$

where B_τ = open-to-buy for month τ

$I^*_{\tau+1}$ = expected inventory (based on seasonal plans) for beginning of month $(\tau+1)$

I_τ = actual inventory at beginning of month τ

S^*_τ = expected sales

The department starts each month with this calculated amount (B_τ) minus any advance orders that have already been charged against the month. Any surplus or deficit from the preceding month will increase or decrease the current account, as will cancellation of back orders or stock price changes.

Although the open-to-buy is a constraint in output determination, it can be violated. As long as the preceding rules are followed and the environment stays more or less stable, the open-to-buy will rarely be exceeded. From this point of view, the open-to-buy is simply a long-run control device enforcing the standard reorder procedure and alerting higher levels in the organization to significant deviations from such procedure. However, the constraint is flexible. It is possible for a department to have a negative open-to-buy (up to a limit of approximately average monthly sales). Negative values for the open-to-buy are tolerated when they can be justified in terms of special reasons for optimistic sales expectations.

The open-to-buy, thus, is less a constraint than a signal—to both higher management and the department—indicating a possible need for some sort of remedial action.

DETAILS OF PRICE DETERMINATION

The firm recognizes three different pricing situations: *normal*, *sales*, and *mark-down* pricing.

The first two situations occur at regularly planned times. The third is a contingent situation, produced by failure or anticipated failure with respect to organizational goals. In each pricing situation the basic procedure is the same, the application of a mark-up to a cost to determine an appropriate price (subject to some rounding to provide convenient prices).

The bulk of sales occur at prices set by either normal or sales pricing procedures. Mark-down pricing is one of the main strategies considered when search is stimulated. During the time period we observed, the demand was strong enough to permit fairly consistent achievement of the department's pricing goal—an average realized mark-up in the neighborhood of 40 per cent. As a result, we did not observe actual situations in which the pressure to reduce prices stemming from inventory feedback conflicted with the pressure to maintain or raise mark-up stemming from over-all mark-up feedback.

Normal Pricing

Normal pricing is used when new output is accepted by the department for sale. As we have already observed, the problem of pricing is simplified considerably by the practice of price lining. In effect, the retail price is determined first and then output that can be priced (with the appropriate mark-up) at that price is obtained. Since manufacturers are aware of the standard price lines, their products are also standardized at appropriate costs.

For each product group in the firm there is a normal mark-up. Like the seasonal advance order fraction, mark-up is probably subject to long-run learning. For example, it varies in a general way from product group to product group according to the apparent risks involved, the costs of promotion or handling, the extent of competition, and the price elasticity. However, in any short run the normal mark-up is remarkably stable. The statement is frequently made in the industry that mark-ups have remained the same for the last 40 or 50 years.

Standard Items. In the department under study, normal mark-up is 40 per cent. By industry practice, standard costs (wholesale prices) ordinarily end in $.75. By firm policy, standard prices (retail prices) ordinarily end in $.95. Thus, all but two of the price levels are in accord with the following rule:

Divide each cost by 0.6 (1—mark-up) and move the result to the nearest $.95.

The results of this rule and the effective mark-ups are shown in Table 1.

TABLE 1   Standard Prices

Standard Costs ($)	Standard Price ($)	Effective Mark-Up (%)
3.00	5.00	40.0
3.75	5.95	37.0
4.75	7.95	40.2
5.50	8.95	38.5
6.75	10.95	38.3
7.75	12.95	40.1
8.75	14.95	41.5
10.75	17.95	40.0
11.75	19.95	41.0
13.75	22.95	40.0
14.75	25.00	41.0
18.75	29.95	37.4

Exclusive items. In some cases, the department obtains items that are not made available to competition. For such products and especially where quality is difficult to measure, the prices are set higher than the standard. The pricing rule is as follows:

When merchandise is received on an exclusive basis, calculate the standard price from the cost, then use the next highest price on the standard schedule.

Import Items. Presumably because they are frequently exclusive items, because of somewhat greater risks associated with foreign suppliers, and because of the generally lower costs of items of foreign manufacture for equal quality, the department increases the mark-up for imported items. For the product class studied the standard accepted mark-up is 50 per cent greater than normal mark-up (which gives a target mark-up of 60 per cent). This leads to the following rule for pricing imports:

Divide the cost by 0.4 (i.e., 1—mark-up) and move the result to the nearest standard price. If this necessitates a change of more than $.50, create a new price at the nearest appropriate ending (that is, $.95 or $.00).

Regular Sale Pricing

We can distinguish two situations in which normal pricing is not used; one is during the regular sales held by the firm a few times during the year, the other when the department concludes that a mark-down is needed to stimulate purchases or to reduce inventory levels. In this section we consider the first case. As in the case of normal pricing, sales pricing depends on a series of relatively simple rules. In almost all cases sales pricing is a direct function of either the normal price (i.e., there is a standard sales reduction in price) or the cost (i.e., there is a sales mark-up rule). Both the figures on reduction and the sales mark-up are conventional, subject perhaps to long-run learning but invariant during our observations. The general pricing rules for sales operate within a series of constraints that serve to enforce minor changes either to ensure consistency within the pricing (e.g., maintain price differentials between items, maintain price consistency across departments), or to provide attractive price endings (e.g., do not use standard price endings, if feasible use an "alliterative" price).

General Constraints. The department prices for sales within a set of five policy constraints. These constraints have not changed in recent years and are viewed by the organization as basic firm policy. They are subject to review rarely.

1. If normal price falls at one of the following lines, the corresponding sale price will be used:

Normal Price ($)	Sale Price ($)
1.00	0.85
1.95	1.65
2.50	2.10
2.95	2.45
3.50	2.90
3.95	3.30
4.95	3.90
5.00	3.90

2. For all other merchandise, there must be a reduction of *at least* 15 per cent on items retailing regularly for $3.00 or less and *at least* $16\frac{2}{3}$ per cent on higher-priced items.

3. All sales prices must end with 0 or 5.

4. No sale retails are allowed to fall on price lines normal for the product group concerned.

5. Whenever there is a choice between an ending of 0.85 and 0.90, the latter ending will prevail.

Departmental Decision Rules. Subject to the general policy constraints, the department is allowed a relatively free hand. Since the policy constraints do not uniquely define sales pricing, it is necessary to determine the departmental decision rules. These rules are indicated in detail in the flow charts in Figures 3 and 4.

Mark-down Pricing

In our earlier discussions of organizational decision making, we suggested that a general model of pricing and output determination must distinguish between the ordinary procedures (that account for most of the decisions made) and the special search procedures that are triggered by special circumstances. We have already seen how such procedures enter into the determination of output in the present case.

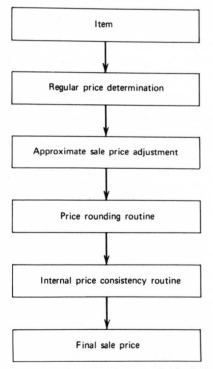

Figure 3   Major subroutines of sale pricing decision.

We turn now to search and "emergency" behavior on the price side. Price is the major adaptive device open to the department in its efforts to meet its mark-up goal, maintain sales, maintain inventory control, and in general meet the demands of other parts of the organization. We have already indicated how an increase in mark-up (e.g., on imports and special items) is used by the department. We turn now to mark-downs.

The department has two decisions to make on mark-downs: when, and how much? In a general sense, the answer to the first question—the question of timing—is simple. The organization reduces price when feedback indicates an unsatisfactory sales or inventory position. The indicators include the inventory records, sales records, physical inventory, reports on competitive prices, and the open-to-buy report. Mark-downs because of product properties (e.g., defects) are of secondary importance. With respect to the amount of mark-down, the organization has a set of standard rules. These have developed over time in such a way that their rationale can only be inferred in most cases, but a general characteristic of the rules is the avoidance of pricing below cost except as a last resort.

Timing of Mark-Downs. Occasions for mark-downs are primarily determined by feedback on sales performance. There are three general overstock situations that account for the majority of the mark-downs:

1. *Normal remnants.* These are the odd sizes, less popular colors, and less favored styles remaining from the total assortment of an item that sold satisfactorily during the season.

2. *Overstocked merchandise.* This category includes items that have experienced a satisfactory sales rate but about which the buyer was overly optimistic in his orders. As a result, the season ends with a significant inventory that is well balanced and includes many acceptable items.

3. *Unaccepted merchandise.* This category represents merchandise that has had unsatisfactory sales. The sales personnel try to determine during the season whether the lack of

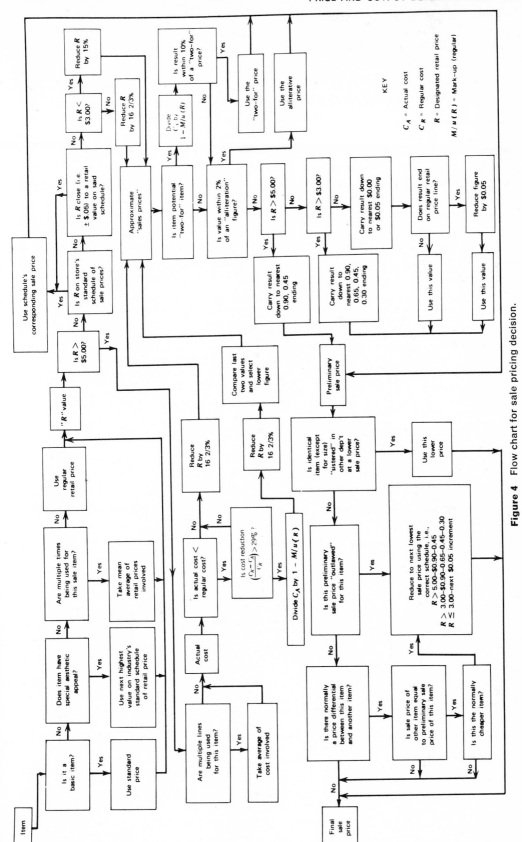

Figure 4 Flow chart for sale pricing decision.

acceptance is due to overpricing or to poor style, color, and so forth. The distinction is usually made by determining whether the item has been ignored. If it has, the latter causes are usually inferred. If the item gets attention but low sales, the inference is that the price is wrong.

In addition, there are a number of quantitatively less important reasons for considering mark-downs. For example, the firm will meet competition on price (if a check indicates the competitor's price is not a mistake). If a customer seeks an adjustment because of defects in the merchandise, a mark-down will be taken. If special sale merchandise is depleted during a sale, regular merchandise will be reduced in price to fill the demand. If wholesale cost is

reduced during the season, price will be reduced correspondingly. In nonreturnable merchandise is substandard on arrival, it will be reduced.

Most of the merchandise that becomes excess (especially for the reasons outlined above) will be mentally transferred to an "availability pool." When a specific opportunity arises or when certain conditions develop that necessitate a mark-down, items are drawn out of this pool and marked down for the occasion involved. Store-wide clearances are scheduled by the merchandise manager on nonrecurring dates throughout the year (except during the pre-Fourth-of-July period and the after-Christmas period) to provide all departments with an opportunity to clear out their excess stocks.

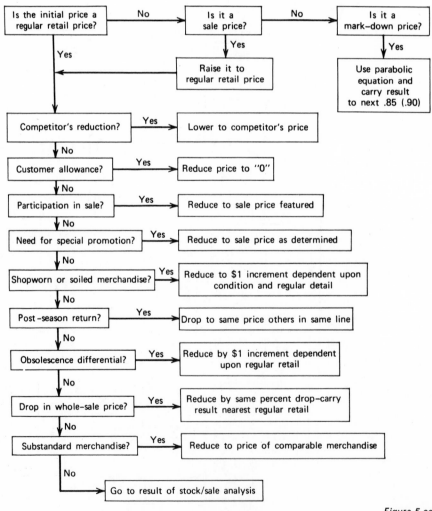

Figure 5 continues

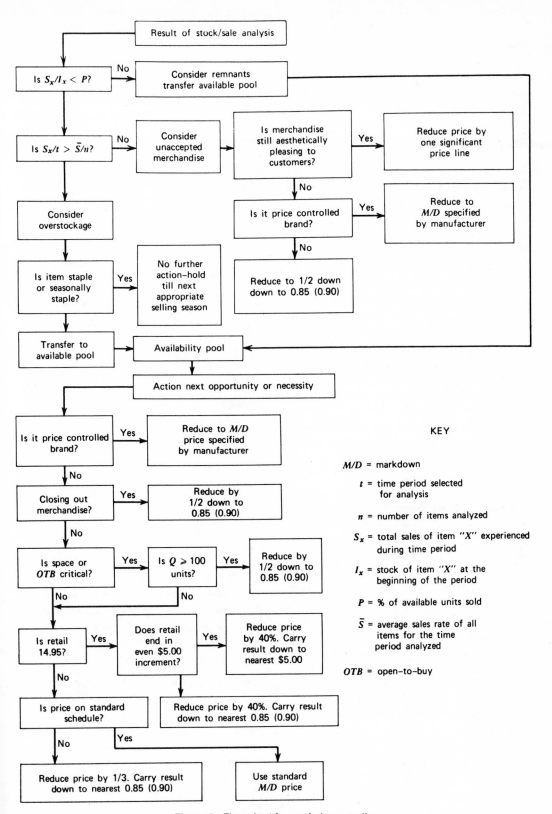

Figure 5   Flow chart for mark-down routine.

However, there may be times during the year when the department cannot wait for the next scheduled clearance for reasons of limited space or limited funds. If, for example, the department is expecting a shipment of new merchandise at a time when display and storage facilities are inadequate to accommodate the new shipment, it is necessary to reduce inventory by means of mark-downs.

The department may take mark-downs when its open-to-buy is unsatisfactory. (Whenever the open-to-buy falls to the −$15,000 level, it would be judged to be in unsatisfactory condition.) The department will not necessarily take mark-downs as the principal means of rectifying this state of affairs *per se* but will attempt instead to cancel merchandise on order or to charge back merchandise already received. These steps will not be taken if the department expects relief from an increased sales rate within the immediate future or if the present average mark-up is low. However, if the department has an urgent need to purchase additional merchandise and the open-to-buy at the time is in the red to the extent that the division merchandise manager will not approve any additional orders, the department will then take mark-downs for the amount necessary to permit the desired purchase to take place.

Amount of Mark-Down. The complete model for predicting actual mark-down prices is given in Figure 5. The general rule for first mark-downs is to reduce the retail price by $\frac{1}{3}$ and carry the result down to the nearest mark-down ending (i.e., to the nearest $.85). There are some exceptions. Where the ending constraint forces too great a deviation from the $\frac{1}{3}$ rule (e.g., where the regular price is $5.00 or less), *ad hoc* procedures are occasionally adopted. On higher-priced items, a 40 per cent mark-down is taken. On a few items manufacturers maintain price control. Occasionally, items represent a closeout of a manufacturer's line and a greater mark-down is taken.

Although the department did not seem to follow any specific explicit rule with second or greater mark-downs, the higher the first mark-down value the greater tended to be the reduction to the succeeding mark-down price.

In fact, this relationship seemed to follow the top half of the parabolic curve

$$Y^2 = 5(X-2)$$

where Y = succeeding mark-down price
      X = initial mark-down price

Accordingly, the following empirically derived rule seems to work well with second or higher mark-downs:

Insert the value of the initial mark-down price in the parabolic formula and carry the result *down* to the nearest $.85 ($.90).

As a description of process, this rule is obviously deficient. However, in view of the limited number of cases involved and the inability of the department to articulate the rules, we have used this rough surrogate.

TESTS OF THE DETAILED MODELS

We have tried to develop a model that would yield testable predictions, but there are two major limits on such a goal. First, we have not been completely successful in defining a model that will make precise predictions in every decision area. Second, where we have been successful in developing a model, we are constrained by the availability of data. The value of data for the purpose of testing models has not always been controlling in data-retention decisions by the firm. Despite these limits, we have been able to develop models for the major price and output decisions and to subject all but one of the major components of those models to some empirical test.

Output Determination

The output determination model consists of three segments—sales estimate, advance orders, and reorders. In each of the tests described below, the data used are new and are not the data with which the model was developed.

Sales Estimation. The sales estimation model is composed of the rule for estimating sales for the six-month period and the rules for the estimation of the sales of individual months. The data available were for a two-year period so that the test is far from conclusive. However, there is no reason to believe that the model would not be valid for a larger sample of data. The first part of the model, the estimation of total sales for a six-month period, predicts the total within 5 per cent in each of the four test instances. With the set of monthly rules, we can predict about 95 per cent of the monthly sales estimates within 5 per cent. There is no question that the predictive power could be increased still further by additional refinement of the rules. However, at this point it does not seem desirable to expend resources in that direction.

Advance Orders. This segment of the model and the sales estimation segment are related as we have shown previously. Therefore, discrepancies between predicted and actual data are difficult to allocate precisely between the two segments although we have some clues from the above testing. Unfortunately, the firm does not keep its records of advance orders any length of time so no extensive test of the model was possible. We were able to accumulate only four instances in which the predictions of the model could be compared with the actual figures.

Season	Predicted Advance Orders	Actual Advance Orders
1	18,050	16,453
2	26,550	24,278
3	36,200	35,922
4	43,000	35,648

Reorders. This segment is one that it is most important to test. The fact is, however, that the data on reorders are not kept in a systematic fashion, and we have not been able to make any kind of test.

Price Determination

Much more adequate data are available for the pricing models. In each case the model was tested and performed adequately.

Mark-up. In order to test the ability of the model to predict the price decisions that will be made by the buyer on new merchandise, an unrestricted random sample of 197 invoices was drawn. The cost data and classification of the item were given as inputs to the computer

model. The output was in the form of a predicted price. Since the sample consisted of items that had already been priced, it was possible to make a comparison of the predicted price with the actual price.

The definition of a correct prediction was made as stringent as possible. Unless the predicted price matched the actual price to the exact penny, the prediction was classified as incorrect. The results of the test were encouraging; of the 197 predicted prices, 188 were correct and 9 were incorrect. Thus 95 per cent of the predictions were correct. An investigation of the incorrect predictions showed that with minor modifications the model could be made to handle the deviant cases. However, at this point it was felt that the predictive power was good enough so that a further expenditure of resources in this direction was not justified.

Sale Pricing. In order to test the model, a random sample of 58 sales items was selected from the available records. For each item the appropriate information as determined by the model was used as an input to the computer. The output was in the form of a price that was a prediction of the price that would be set by the buyer. Again we used the criterion that to be correct the predicted price must match the actual price to the penny. Out of the 58 predictions made by the model, 56 (or 96 per cent) were correct.

Mark-Downs. In testing this part of the model the basic data were taken from "mark-down slips," the primary document of this firm. Naturally such slips do not show the information that would enable us to categorize the items for use in the model. It was necessary, therefore, to use direct methods such as the interrogation of the buyer and sales personnel to get the information necessary to classify the items so that the model could be tested. All of the data used were from the previous six-month period. It would be possible on a current basis to get the information that would enable the model to make the classifications itself as part of the pricing process.

The test for a correct prediction was as before —correspondence to the penny of the predicted and the actual price. A total sample of 159 items was selected and predictions made of the markdown price for each item. Of the 159 prices predicted, 140 were correct predictions by our criterion and 19 were wrong. This gives a record of 88 per cent correct—the poorest of the three models. Though this model does not do as well as the other two, its record is, in our view, adequate.

SUMMARY

The tests that have been made of the model tend to support it. Clearly some of the tests are inadequate because of the paucity of the data. Also, we have not attempted to build alternative models and compare predictive ability. Undoubtedly, alternative models can be built and can be made to predict well. However, we have been interested in building a model that embodies the actual decision-making process. . . . We do not believe a radically different model can be built that captures the actual decision process and predicts as well. Because our objective is to understand the actual process, we have not attempted to minimize the number of assumptions, the number of variables, or the number of inputs to the model.

The department store model is a specific application of a general model. . . . The evidence supports the specific model and thereby presents corroborative evidence for the general model. We would not argue that the evidence is conclusive. It is not. It is, however, consistent with the model. The model lends itself to further elaboration and testing—and the world is full of firms for further empirical study.

REFERENCES

1. R. M. Cyert, and J. G. March, 1963. *A behavioral theory of the firm.* Englewood Cliffs, N.J.: Prentice-Hall. 2B.

9

SIMULATION OF A PSYCHOLOGICAL DECISION PROCESS IN PERSONNEL SELECTION[1]

ROBERT D. SMITH
PAUL S. GREENLAW

A basic problem facing all organizations is that of personnel selection. Currently, many organizations are utilizing information derived from psychological tests along with other data to guide them in their personnel selection decisions. Tests have been designed to measure an applicant's aptitude, skills, vocational interests, and such "personality" characteristics as impulsiveness, submissiveness, responsibility, etc. Some of these tests are quite well accepted, while the value of others is more controversial [1, 5, 12].

The interpretation of psychological data often poses a fairly complex decision problem. Such is frequently the case when an organization utilizes a battery of tests, each measuring one or more psychological dimensions, to test applicants for any one of several different jobs, each with different skill and personality require-

SOURCE: Reprinted from *Management Science*, *18*: B–409–419 (1967).

[1] The authors wish to acknowledge the assistance provided in this research by Mr. Charles K. Rudman, Mrs. Tonia Klein, Dr. Philip T. Launer, and Dr. Sal A. Pizzurro, of the Klein Institute for Aptitude Testing, Inc.

ments. In this type of analysis, many test scores have meaning only when examined in light of: (1) other scores in the battery, and (2) the requirements of a specific job for which the individual is applying. Further, those interpreting these data are often called on not only to recommend whether or not the applicant should be hired, but also to develop a written description of each applicant's psychological characteristics.

In this type of decision-making, the interpreter is faced with an ill-structured problem which is not amenable to solution by algorithmic techniques. In recent years, considerable research has been devoted to developing computerized simulations of the human thought processes involved in dealing with such problems. For instance, Clarkson [3, 4] has simulated the thought processes of a trust investment officer in making portfolio selection decisions; Tonge [13] has developed a computer program for assembly line balancing; and Kleinmuntz [8, 9] has developed decision rules for the interpretation of a single psychological test, the MMPI. These studies—often referred to as heuristic programs—have been based on the following assumptions:

1. Humans, in making decisions, break down complex problems into numerous simpler but interrelated sub-problems.

2. Individuals also develop and follow with some degree of consistency, decision rules—which can be identified and isolated—to handle these sub-problems, and that consequently,

3. Complex thought processes can be represented by networks of relatively simple decision branches, reflecting these rules.

In the present study, a computer simulation was developed of the thought processes of a psychologist as he interpreted various data about job applicants being considered for employment. This model was designed to output, as did the pyschologist, both: (1) interpretive comments about each applicant, and (2) a recommendation as to whether or not the applicant should be employed. This research was aimed at both developing a descriptive model of the human thought processes involved in this type of analysis, and exploring the possibility of utilizing computerized interpretive simulations as prescriptive models for personnel selection.

THE DECISION PROBLEM UNDER CONSIDERATION

Selected for study was a psychologist employed by a large consulting firm specializing in personnel selection, as he analyzed data regarding certain individuals being considered for jobs with client firms. All applicants being analyzed were females under consideration for clerical and clerical-administrative positions such as billing clerk, statistical clerk, and executive secretary. These individuals had been subjected to initial screening by the client firms prior to being tested.

In making his analysis of each applicant, the psychologist had three basic types of informational inputs at his disposal.

First were nineteen test scores from the following test battery:

1. The Otis Mental Ability Test [10].

2. The Gordon Personal Profile [7], which measures four personality characteristics: as-

cendancy, responsibility, emotional stability, and sociability.

3. The Gordon Personal Inventory [6], designed to measure the individual's cautiousness, intellectual curiosity, personal relations, and vigor.

4. The Washburne Social Adjustment Inventory [14], which provides both a measure of seven specific personality characteristics, including truthfulness, and an overall measure of social adjustment.

5. The Short Employment Tests [2], measuring verbal, numerical and general clerical skills.

Second, the psychologist had information as to the applicant's age and number of years of previous relevant job experience, and whether the individual was: (1) applying for a job with the firm, or (2) a present employee being considered for a promotion.

Finally, the interpreter was provided by the client firm with an indication as to the relative importance of each of six job requirement variables for the specific position for which the individual was being considered. These job variables were: ability to process numerical data, vocabulary and verbal fluency, accuracy, speed, ability to work under time pressure, and all-round administrative ability.

The psychologist's task was to analyze each of the above inputs, and their interrelationships, and to provide the client firm with both: (1) a written description of the applicant's skills, ability and personality characteristics as related to the requirements of the job under consideration, and (2) his recommendation regarding the advisability of hiring (or promoting) the individual. Analysis revealed that the psychologist's recommendations fell into one of four categories: hire (or promote); hire or promote, but only as a fair risk; reject; or check the applicant's background further. The further background check recommendation was made primarily when an applicant's score on the Washburne truthfulness factor was low, giving an indication that the individual may not have been honest in the personality tests in the battery and/or in providing information on the firm's application blank. A schematic diagram summarizing this decision process is provided in Figure 1.

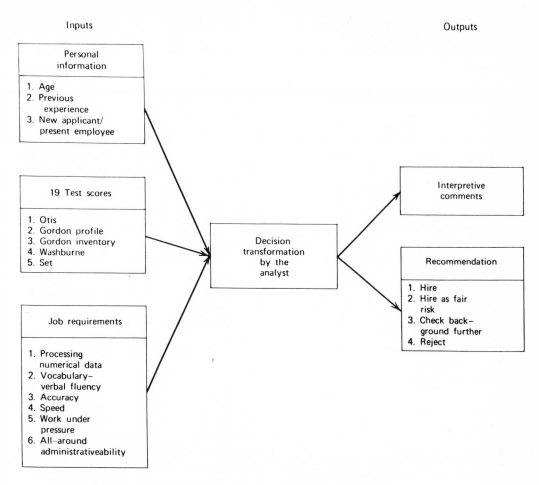

Figure 1 The decision problem under consideration.

CONDUCTING THE RESEARCH

Three basic steps were involved in conducting the research: (1) data collection; (2) developing and programming the model; and (3) analyzing the results generated by the model. We will now discuss each of these steps.

Data Collection

Data upon which the model was to be built were collected in two ways. First, the decision problem was discussed with members of the consulting firm, and all manuals available relative to the psychological tests utilized were analyzed. Second, the protocol method was utilized as a means of examining the thought processes of the particular psychologist chosen for the study. That is, the psychologist was asked to verbalize his thoughts as he analyzed the selection problem, and these verbalizations were recorded on tape, to be transcribed later into written form for analysis. These verbalizations were examined in two distinct ways. First, the psychologist was asked to discuss each of the numerous input variables and their interrelationships, and to indicate how they influenced both his written interpretations and hiring recommendations. Second, he was asked to analyze sixteen cases from the files of the firm and to verbalize each step in his analysis. Following are edited excerpts from one such verbalization:

Here is a woman age 50 being considered for the position of *Branch Office Clerk*. This is a job involving *general office work*, a *relatively routine office job*. No analysis of complex problems is involved. Her *score on the general intelligence test indicates* that she is *above average in intelligence*. She also has a score *just above average for intellectual curiosity* which means that although she is of above average intelligence she's *not likely to feel unchallenged in her job*. Consequently, we say that she is *readily trainable, mentally alert, and a bright woman*. Her *intelligence test* performance is *all the more healthy* since she is *age 50* and in our experience we find that as people approach their later maturity, they tend to slow down on time tests. Next question, of course, is whether she has specific *ability for handling general office work*. Consequently I must *look at her performance* in the *clerical area*. Now she is at the *32nd percentile*. So *immediately* I must raise the question—"*What is this performance due to ?*" Is it *slowness* on the test or *lack of accuracy ?* I find that there is *nothing wrong with accuracy*. She just didn't cover too much ground. All I would say is that although *she moves slow when it comes to handling clerical problems*, her accuracy is quite good.

The italicized words and phrases in the above protocol were those considered as reflections of basic decision rules followed by the interpreter; and the transcriptions of all protocol tapes were so underscored to facilitate the development of the model.

Development of the Model

Constructing a model of complex thought processes involves the breaking down of these processes into simple elements. In the construction of our model, a network of simple branching statements was developed, each representing a decision rule employed by the psychologist. Since the output desired from the model was to include interpretive comments as well as a selection recommendation, two decisions had to be made in designing each branch in the program. These were: (1) what interpretive comments, if any, were to be printed out, and (2) to which other branches in the decision process would the model go next. At some branches, no interpretive comments were considered necessary. The IF, GO TO branch illustrated in Figure 2, for example, simply provided for classifying the applicant on the basis of the range into which her clerical

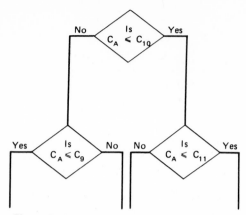

Figure 2 Branch with no interpretive comments.

ability test score fell; interpretive comments regarding this variable were reserved until later in the program after other related variables had also been examined. An example of a case in which interpretive comments were included is the IF, PRINT and GO TO branch illustrated in Figure 3. All applicants channeled up to this branch had failed to score well on "goal orientation," and this branch differentiates applicants simply scoring somewhat below average from those scoring quite poorly on this factor. In its completed form, the model network consisted of approximately 300 IF and GO TO statements and 150 PRINT statements, and was programmed for the IBM 7074 computer. On this particular system, between one and two seconds of computer time are required for the processing of each applicant.

Analysis of the Simulation Results

The final step in the research was that of the measurement and analysis of the outputs obtained from the simulation model. Some researchers who have developed simulations of thought processes have verified their results by comparing decisions made by the computer with those made humanly, given the same input data [3, 4]. This type of verification indicates the degree to which the model arrives at the same solutions to decision problems as does the human. Since this study was designed to provide not only final selection recommendations, but also numerous interpretive comments supporting each recommendation, it was necessary to examine both types of outputs.

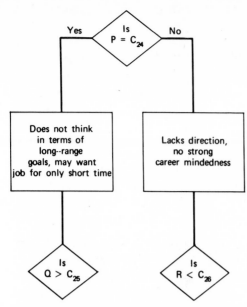

Figure 3 Branch with interpretive comments.[2]

As a means of first determining the degree to which the model generated the same selection recommendations as had the analyst, all input data for each of the 16 cases from which the protocol was derived were fed into the model. In all 16 cases, the model provided the same employment recommendation as had the psychologist. Of these, six were to hire; three to hire as a fair risk; one to obtain a further background check; and six to reject. Then, as a more

[2] The numerically subscripted c's in Figures 2 and 3 represent parameters in the model.

valid test of the model, eight new cases which had been interpreted by the psychologist since the protocol had been obtained, and which had not been used in the development of the model, were presented to the computer. In seven of these eight cases, the model provided the same employment recommendation as that which had been arrived at by the human analyst. The results of this test are illustrated in Figure 4.

These data were then analyzed statistically to answer the following question: "If the model were randomly classifying applicants into each of the four possible categories, what would be the probability of reaching agreement between the model and human, purely by chance, as good or better than that actually obtained?" Multinomial analysis was utilized to determine the probability of obtaining at least seven out of eight identical selections, assuming that the computer randomly assigned applicants to each of the four categories 25% of the time. Such a probability is approximately .0004.[3] With such

[3] This figure was arrived at as follows. The multinomial probability $[P_b(r) = C_r^n p^r q^{n-r}]$ of obtaining agreement between the model and human in seven out of eight cases, assuming that the model randomly assigns $\frac{1}{4}$ of the cases to each of the four recommendation categories, is: $(C_7^8)\ (\frac{1}{4})^7\ (\frac{3}{4})^1$ or, .000366. The probability of agreement in all eight cases is: $(C_8^8)\ (\frac{1}{4})^8\ (\frac{3}{4})^0$ or, .0000153. Summing these two probability figures gives .000381. It should also be noted that the probability of the model and human reaching agreement on any *single* case, assuming the model to be a random classifier, will

Human Recommendations	Model Recommendations				
	Hire	Hire as Fair Risk	Background Check	Reject	Total
Hire	3	0	0	0	3
Hire as Fair Risk	0	2	1	0	3
Background Check	0	0	0	0	0
Reject	0	0	0	2	2
Total	3	2	1	2	8

Figure 4 Human and model recommendations.

APPLICANT IS ABOVE AVERAGE IN INTELLIGENCE, WOULD CALL HER VERY
    BRIGHT AND MENTALLY ALERT
APPLICANT POSSESSES GOOD CLERICAL ABILITIES
IS NOT ACCURATE WHEN WORKING WITH NUMBERS
APPLICANT IS VERY PROFICIENT IN EXPRESSING HERSELF VERBALLY
APPLICANT IS CONTENT
GOAL ORIENTED
SOMEWHAT BELOW AVERAGE IN SOCIAL ADJUSTMENT, MAY TEND TOWARD
    THE SHY SIDE
PUTS FIRST THINGS FIRST
IS SENSITIVE TO FEELINGS AND PROBLEMS OF OTHER PEOPLE
HAS SELF-CONTROL, SHOULD BE ABLE TO MAKE AND EXECUTE PLANS
WILL NOT TAKE THE LEAD IN GROUP SITUATIONS
PASSIVE, LACKS SELF-CONFIDENCE
OVERLY DEPENDENT
PERSEVERING, DETERMINED AND RELIABLE
HOWEVER, BASED UPON SPECIFIED JOB REQUIREMENTS, IT APPEARS THAT
THIS APPLICANT MAY BE HIRED WITHOUT SERIOUS RESERVATIONS.

Figure 5 Computer output for one applicant.

a small probability, the hypothesis that the computer was simply a "random classifier" was rejected.

The next step in the analysis of results was that of examining the interpretive comments outputted by the model. An illustration of one complete set of such comments is provided in Figure 5. As the reader will note, this language is not as polished as one would expect from a human interpretation. Additional polish could have been provided for (e.g., more connecting words and phrases), but this would have required using more storage locations. Determining the degree to which such model-generated comments were in agreement with the humanly made ones, given the same input data, involved considerably more subjective judgment than had testing for agreement on the selection recommendations. This was because the phraseology of computerized comments was generally somewhat different than the human phraseology; and the semantic question had to be asked: "Was the psychological *meaning* of the

words utilized by the model and the human substantially the same or not?"

In attempting to answer this question, the complete computer output from six cases was presented to the psychologist upon whose thought processes the model had been developed, for further analysis.[4] He was asked to compare the computer output with the interpretive comments he had originally made, and to answer the following questions:

1. How many of the interpretive comments possessed substantially the same meaning as had his own?

2. How many of the comments were "incorrect" when compared with his own analysis?

3. How many comments which he had included in his own analysis were *omitted* in the computer report?

always be $\frac{1}{4}$, *regardless* of the probability of the analyst's assigning cases to any particular category. For example, should the analyst recommend hiring 100% of the time, the probability is that a random classifier's hire recommendations would be in agreement 25% of the time; or should the analyst recommend 50% hires and 50% rejects, the probability of agreement on hires and rejects would be (.50) (.25) or, 12.5% in each case—for a total probability of agreement of 25%.

[4] The psychologist was asked to analyze only six cases because of his heavy work load at the time. We should also note that one technical limitation of the computer program was that, once certain unfavorable test scores had been found, it would branch immediately to the reject recommendation and provide no interpretive comments relative to those scores not yet examined. The psychologist, on the other hand, would provide a more comprehensive set of interpretive comments in such cases. For this reason, none of the cases in which the computer branched early in the program to "reject" were utilized in this analysis. The computer model could, of course, be reprogrammed to provide for more complete interpretations in such cases.

4. How many psychologically valid comments, if any, were included in the simulated interpretation which *he* had omitted in his own analysis?

The results of this comparative analysis are summarized in Figure 6.

As a further means of obtaining a judgment as to the "correctness" of the computer interpretations, another psychologist with the consulting firm, who was quite familiar with the interpretive methods used by the psychologist under study, was asked to examine some of the output data. He was given all input data from the sixteen protocol cases, and the computer interpretations generated for each case; but was not shown the interpretive reports originally made by the protocol analyst. He was then asked to judge whether each interpretive comment was psychologically sound or not. Altogether, the sixteen cases contained a total of 290 interpretive comments, of which 273 were judged sound. These judgments, of course, did not provide any indication of the degree to which the model successfully simulated the protocol analyst's thought processes. The fact

that 94% of the comments made by the computer were considered sound, however, does suggest that the simulated interpretations were highly congruent with the psychological thinking of the firm, at least as so perceived by the evaluator.

DISCUSSION

The focus of this study has been upon the thought processes of a psychologist analyzing data in making interpretations and recommendations for personnel selection. The results obtained indicate that the psychologist broke down his problem into smaller sub-problems and consistently followed relatively simple decision rules in their resolutions. Additionally, analysis of the protocol indicated that he tended to follow a similar *sequencing* of these rules in the analysis of each case. For example, in all sixteen cases the analyst first checked the requirements of the job for which the applicant was being considered; then noted the individual's age and years of previous relevant experience; and next examined the applicant's mental ability score.

Applicant	Total Number of Comments in Simulated Report	Number of Comments in Simulated Report Included also in Human Analysis	Number of "Incorrect" Comments in Simulated Report	Number of Comments Omitted in Simulated Report, but Included in Human Analysis	Number of Comments Included in Simulated Report not Included in Human Analysis
1	27	23	0	1	4
2	29	24	2	1	3
3	30	28	1	1	1
4	23	19	3	1	1
5	36	30	4	0	2
6	28	24	1	1	3
Total	173	148	11	5	14

Figure 6 Human and model interpretive comments.

There were probably at least two major reasons for the development of these sequential patterns by the analyst. First, the examination of certain bits of information prior to that of others sometimes permitted a reduction in the time required for analysis. For example, one decision rule followed by the analyst was as follows: "If the applicant's 'truthfulness' score on the Washburne Social Adjustment Inventory is low, give little attention to her scores on both the Gordon Personal Profile and Personal Inventory." By examining the truthfulness score prior to the Gordon scores, the psychologist eliminated the unnecessary task of detailed Gordon analysis in all those cases in which applicants' truthfulness scores were low. Second, the psychologist's fairly consistent decision-rule sequencing served as a standing plan which provided him with relief from the task of making certain decisions. That is, through the development of sequencing rules the psychologist was able to simplify his decision making by transforming problems of the type "after data bit x has been examined, *decide on* which bit of data to examine next," to ones of the type: "After x has been examined, go to y if interpretation a has occurred, but go to z if b has occurred"; etc. (paraphrased from [11, p. 313]).

Our research also suggests the feasibility of utilizing computerized interpretive programs as prescriptive models for personnel selection in organizations. Such utilization might provide several contributions to personnel decision making. First, interpretations can be made much more quickly by the computer than by humans. Such added speed would be of special value in certain cases, e.g., when a firm is opening a new plant in a particular location and is faced with the problem of quickly screening large numbers of job applicants. Second, computerized programs might significantly reduce the costs involved in personnel selection. In our research, for example, the cost of computer time averaged less than 5¢ per interpretation, whereas each interpretation if rendered by a professional psychologist might cost a firm up to $50. Computerized interpretation would, of course, be economically justified only if a sufficient number of applicants were being processed so that the present value of the savings from all future interpretations would exceed the initial investment cost of developing the program. Computerized programs may also provide better and more consistent decision making. In some large firms, for example, selection recommendations are made in several geographically decentralized divisions by different individuals with varying degrees of psychological expertise. In such cases, utilization of a common program derived from the mental processes of the "most expert" interpreter(s) in the firm should lead to both better and more consistent recommendations being made throughout the firm. In addition, some of the decision rules followed by the expert interpreter might be improved upon by experimenting with the parameters in the model simulating his thought processes. Improvement of human decision rules by experimentation in such a manner was accomplished by Kleinmuntz in his MMPI program [8, p. 14].

If computerized interpretive models are to be utilized *effectively*, validation of the decision processes being simulated would, of course, be required, i.e., it must be established that the decision rules being followed are effecting "good" selection decisions. Such validation was beyond the scope of the present study. Also, our research was limited to the analysis of applicants for clerical and clerical-administrative positions. Whether interpretive models based on the simulation of processes involved in the often more complex task of analyzing data on applicants for managerial and professional positions can serve effectively to prescribe organizational behavior has, to our knowledge, not yet been demonstrated.

REFERENCES

1. L. E. Albright, J. R. Glennon, and W. J. Smith, 1963. *The use of psychological tests in industry*. Cleveland: Howard Allen.
2. G. K. Bennett, and M. Gelink, 1965. *Short employment tests*. New York: Psychological Corporation.
3. G. P. E. Clarkson, 1962. *Portfolio selection: a simulation of trust investment*. Englewood Cliffs, N.J.: Prentice-Hall. 8A.

4. G. P. E. Clarkson, and A. H. Meltzer, 1960. Portfolio selection: a heuristic approach. *Journal of Finance*, *15*(4): 465–480. 8A.
5. E. E. Ghiselli, and R. P. Barthol, 1953. The validity of personality inventories in the selection of employees. *Journal of Applied Psychology*, *37*(1): 18–20.
6. L. V. Gordon, 1963. *Gordon personal inventory*. New York: Harcourt, Brace and World.
7. L. V. Gordon, 1963. *Gordon personal profile*. New York: Harcourt, Brace and World.
8. B. Kleinmuntz, 1964. MMPI decision rules for the identification of college maladjustment: a digital computer approach. *Psychological Monographs*, *77*(14): 1–22. 5A.
9. B. Kleinmuntz, 1963. Profile analysis revisited: a heuristic approach. *Journal of Counseling Psychology*, *10*(4): 315–321. 5A.
10. A. S. Otis, 1928. *Manual of directions for the Otis self-administering tests of mental ability*. New York: Harcourt, Brace and World.
11. M. D. Richards, and P. S. Greenlaw, 1966. *Management decision making*. Homewood, Ill.: Irwin.
12. E. S. Stanton, 1964. Psychological testing in industry: a critical evaluation. *Personnel Journal*, *43*(1): 27–32.
13. F. M. Tonge, 1961. *A heuristic program for assembly line balancing*. Englewood Cliffs, N.J.: Prentice-Hall. 7A.
14. J. N. Washburne, 1940. *Manual for interpretation of the Washburne social adjustment inventory*. New York: Harcourt, Brace and World.

10

FINDING CHARLIE'S RUN-TIME ESTIMATOR[1]

JOHN M. DUTTON
WILLIAM H. STARBUCK

This paper is about one section of a simulation program. The program simulates Charlie, a real man who works in a real factory. As production scheduler, his job is to specify the sequence in which customer orders are produced in the plant.

The whole Charlie is an intricate and often contradictory human being. But we are concerned here with but a fragment of Charlie. We shall describe him as an information-processing system, and one whose relevant characteristics are completely defined by the task of creating schedules.

Charlie is not a subject chosen at random. First, he has survived an organizational selection process. The job he holds has a high rate of turnover. It is psychologically demanding and unforgiving of errors of commission or omission. Some scheduler job turnover is due to promotion, but most reflects failure to achieve results. Second, we interviewed six schedulers and selected Charlie because he was apparently successful in a complicated plant, because he was cooperative, and because he was articulate. Thus we do not represent Charlie as being an average scheduler. Rather we believe he is above

average in his grasp of the problems with which he is confronted on the job and in his ability to cope with these problems for the factory's benefit. Finally, we chose Charlie because his processes were stable. He had been on the job four years. Our simulation is a model of performance, not learning. Thus we sought a subject whose scheduling processes were not apt to be changing rapidly.

WHY OUR INTEREST

The overall scope of our research about Charlie is fairly broad. In one respect, we do not care about Charlie at all. We want to understand how his factory fits into its market and its parent corporation, and how the people in the factory organize their problem-solving activities. But after some months of study, we concluded that it would not be too drastic a distortion to proceed on the premise that Charlie is the most influential person in his plant. Formally he is quite far down the organizational hierarchy, but his job is considered central in the sense that he is involved in or told about almost every event that affects the plant's operations. Furthermore, the things Charlie did were interesting in their own right.

Two of the reasons for our interest in

[1] We acknowledge the assistance on this project provided by Carter L. Franklin, II, and Bruce J. Klein.

Charlie's problem solving are relevant here. First, Charlie regularly solves two tandem, two-dimensional cutting problems. He assigns orders to one or the other of two cutting machines and specifies how the machines should be operated to maximize profits. This is a difficult cluster of problems. There have been several operations research studies of two-dimensional cutting problems, and so far as we can tell, none has improved on or even equalled the quality of Charlie's performance. His solutions are essentially optimal by the simple criteria that the operations research studies have used, and he considers many subtle criteria that the operations research studies have so far ignored.

Second, Charlie is an extremely complex structure. One reason operations research studies of this problem have not been overwhelmingly successful is that the problem is uncomputably large. The number of alternative production schedules is not literally infinite, but the number is so large that it would be impractical to enumerate all possible schedules on even the fastest electronic computer. Moreover, a schedule cannot be evaluated by a single, simple criterion. And the composite criterion contains many conditional terms, many nonlinear terms, and many local optima.

Considering how complex Charlie's problems are, it is hardly surprising that he himself is a complex information-processing system. Indeed, his cognitive structure is approximately as sophisticated and elaborate as that of a skilled chess player. Whereas the chess player memorizes sequences of moves made in previous games, Charlie memorizes the performance characteristics of the plant under various operating conditions. As we shall see shortly, some of his numerical tables include thousands of entries. Whereas the chess player plans strategy in terms of the positions and capabilities of up to 32 chessmen, Charlie schedules in terms of the statuses and requirements of up to 24 manufacturing operations. Whereas the chess player plans up to 8 moves into the future, choosing among probable sequences of moves, Charlie schedules as many as 10 orders simultaneously, choosing among alternative sequences of order clusters.

To a greater extent than the chess player,

however, Charlie is confronted with time-linked uncertainty. He can predict production rates, but he cannot depend strongly on his predictions because each of the hundreds of operations occurring in the plant at any time is subject to random disturbances. He can predict the proportions of today's orders that will be available at various times during the day, but he cannot predict the content of the customers' orders. Each order received may call for major revisions in the production schedule, by making a more efficient schedule feasible or by making infeasible the schedule that would otherwise have been most efficient. Because customers make changes in their original orders, orders already fitted into schedules must be deleted. Thus the further into the future Charlie tries to plan, the more likely it is that his plans will prove infeasible or inefficient, and he must constantly weigh the risks of solving his problems too soon against the risks of waiting too long.

Waiting too long is the most serious error Charlie can make. All the work done in the factory is specified by Charlie's schedules. If the plant is not kept supplied with schedules, it shuts down; and when several hundred factory people are put out of work, for even a few minutes, the reasons best be impressive.

From Charlie's viewpoint the plant is not a producer but a consumer—a consumer of his schedules. His descriptions of stress-filled moments evoke the image of a ravenous machine that devours fabric faster than he can supply it. Charlie rarely attends to orders for which manufacturing operations have been partially or totally completed. He sees himself as a producer of work backlog, and he treats backlog as though it is an inventory that deteriorates with age. Therefore, the important orders are those in the backlog of work to be done. Each schedule he creates is an increment to the backlog inventory; each job of work done in the factory depletes the backlog inventory. Because the arrival of new orders can devaluate the backlog that Charlie has already created, low average backlog is a measure of his scheduling skill.

Charlie behaves as if he had a set of goals, pefined as a desired state of affairs within the plant. The increase or decrease of scheduling

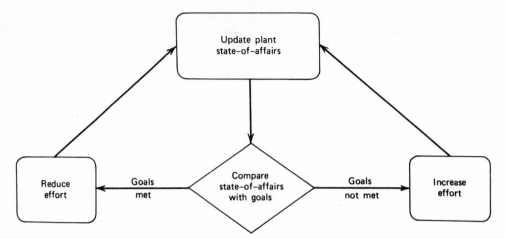

Figure 1   Charlie's goal-directed behavior.

effort is contingent on the evaluation of the plant's current state. Charlie's goal orientation is generally depicted in Figure 1.

Considered in the current state of affairs is an estimate of the backlog of scheduled orders. Thus, it is important for Charlie to know what time of day each machine will run out of work, so he can have a new production schedule ready shortly before it is needed. He must be able to look at the schedule on the factory floor and, knowing what orders are now being processed, predict when all of the orders will have been processed. He must also be able to predict how many hours of work each new schedule represents so that, given his estimate of when work on the new schedule will begin, he can predict when the next new schedule will be needed.

Our concern in this paper is Charlie's method for making such predictions: the procedure by which he computes the production time for a group of orders given the sequence in which the orders will be processed. Run-time estimates are not the most important part of Charlie's job, and the estimation procedure is by no means the most complicated piece of information processing he performs. But run-time estimation illustrates the research methods we have used to uncover Charlie's problem-solving techniques, and it is sufficiently intricate to illustrate some of the properties of complex human thought.

To understand how Charlie estimates run time, it is necessary to know some characteristics of the production process he controls. The

next section gives a brief description of the technology, then we turn to analysis of Charlie's run-time estimator itself.

FABRICATOR TECHNOLOGY

The run-time estimates on which we shall focus are *fabricator* times. Fabrication is the first stage of production in Charlie's plant, and fabricator times are especially interesting for two reasons. First, fabrication is the most complex operation in the plant, making run-time estimation a sophisticated art. Charlie's run-time estimation methods for simpler manufacturing operations are correspondingly simpler. Second, fabrication is the most indispensable operation in the factory. Every order begins with fabrication, whereas the performance of subsequent operations is contingent on the specifications of individual orders.

A fabricator is schematically diagrammed in Figure 2. In the first stage, raw materials are drawn from spindles and hoppers and are combined into a fabric. The fabric is produced in a strip of defined width and, for all practical purposes, infinite length. Charlie's fabricator schedule specifies the fabric width, and the machine crew controls width by varying the number of spindles used. Assuming the machine's mode of operation does not have to be changed and no mechanical breakdowns occur, fabric could flow out of the first stage endlessly. There would be only occasional slowdowns when depleted spindles are replaced.

However, the fabricator's mode of operation must be changed rather frequently to accommodate the needs of different customers, and the vast majority of spindle changes are made while the fabricator is stopped for other setups.

The second stage of the fabricator cuts the fabric into strips. The cutting devices are called rippers, and they may be set-up to cut at virtually any group of positions across the fabric. The number of rippers used and their positions are specified in the fabricator schedule, but the widths of the ripped strips are ultimately determined by the dimensional specifications of individual orders. That is, each customer order includes specifications for the cutting to be done on the fabricator, and it is part of Charlie's job to decide what width of fabric to produce and how the total width should be ripped in order to minimize cutting waste and to maximize the total output of the fabricator. Ordinarily, the solution involves cutting more than one order simultaneously.

Ripper setups are both time-consuming and frequent. There are three banks of rippers. One

bank is used for cutting, and the other two banks are available for setting up future cutting patterns. If all of the orders are large, there will be enough time during the use of one cutting pattern to prepare for the next, and the only downtime for the fabricator as a whole is the time required to switch from one ripper bank to another. Nevertheless, the fabricator must be stopped each time the ripper banks are switched, and the consequent lost production time is significant. Moreover, orders are not always large enough to permit ripper setups to be prepared while the fabricator is operating, and in such cases the fabricator must be stopped while the rippers are positioned.

The final stage of the fabricator is a crosscut section that chops the ripped fabric into rectangular blanks. However, the technology for crosscut setups is much more sophisticated than the technology for ripper setups, and the crosscut changes make a negligible contribution to the total setup time.

The plant can produce an extremely large number of different fabric types. Figure 3 indicates the range of alternatives. Fabric can

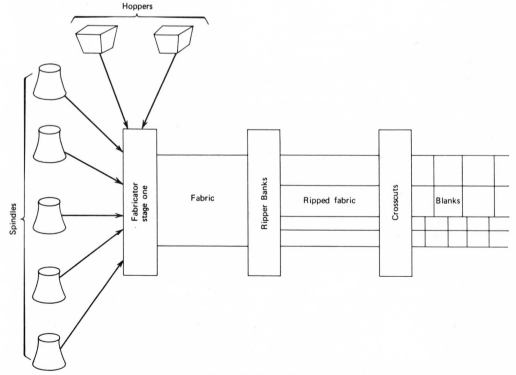

Figure 2 Fabricating.

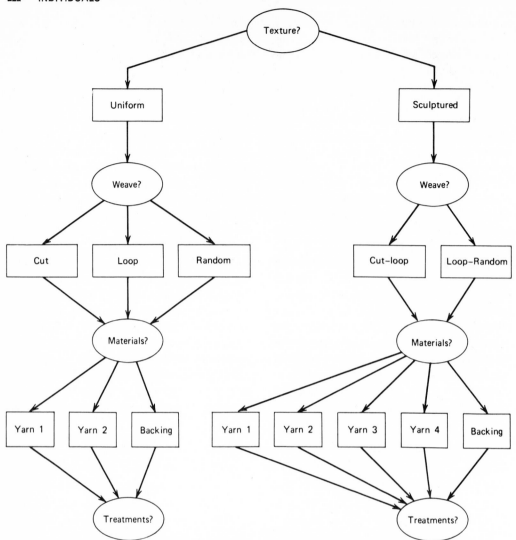

Figure 3   Fabric-type variables. The special fabricator produces uniform texture, random weave fabric only.

be woven in two textures: uniform and sculptured. Uniform texture fabric can be woven in three different weaves—cut, loop, or random—and from a large selection of yarns. Similarly, sculptured texture fabric can be woven with either of two weaves—cut-loop or loop-random—and because four yarns are used instead of two, it can be woven in an even larger variety of compositions. Finally, any of several special treatments can be applied while the fabric is being woven. Of course, the kinds of yarns used and the ways they are combined affect the fabricator's speed.

It happens that Charlie's plant receives a large proportion of orders for uniform texture,

random weave (UTRW) fabric. Therefore the plant has two fabricators, a general fabricator that can produce any fabric in the product line and a special fabricator that produces only UTRW fabric. The capacity of the special fabricator is slightly less than the average daily requirements for UTRW fabric, though, and it is normal to produce some UTRW on the general fabricator.

CHARLIE'S ESTIMATION PROCESS

The first agenda item in our research project was to identify the problem. We first saw the run-time estimation problem while sitting at

Charlie's knee. For the better part of a year, we observed Charlie in his job at the plant, seated beside his desk and following him around the factory floor. For a continuous period of about one month, we collected extensive data on the flows of information to and from Charlie: data on what information he received and when, on what he did with this information and when, and on how he spent his time during an in-plant working day. We also built up a file of the routine, formally sanctioned documents concerning Charlie's job over several months. In short, we sought concrete data from which we could infer how Charlie's work world looked *to Charlie*.

It was soon evident that Charlie sees himself as a producer of backlog and sees the plant as a consumer of backlog, and that he measures backlog in hours of production. When he arrives in the morning, his first act is to conduct a plant survey. He takes inventory of the work backlog at each manufacturing operation and converts the physical measures of inventory into hours of work ahead, making statements like: "Number 3 cutting machine will run out of work at 2:30." Each time Charlie completes a schedule, he translates it into hours of work and updates his mental image of the machine backlogs.

Although he is concerned with every operation in the factory, Charlie devotes nearly all of his time to scheduling the two fabricators. There are several reasons for this focus of concentration. First, the basic scheduling rule for operations downstream of the fabricators is "first in, first out." Thus control over the sequence of orders leaving the fabricators tends to be control over the sequence of orders at every operation downstream. Second, the individual department foremen spend much of their time routing orders through their departments. They check to see what orders will shortly be ready for their machines; they expedite orders that are behind schedule and delay orders that are ahead of schedule; they alert other foremen to orders that are nearly ready for transfer, and the entire group of foremen assembles about twice each day to discuss special problems. Third, the fabricators are extremely expensive, high-volume machines. They are manned by large crews of men; they

represent large capital investments; they produce a large portion of the plant's waste. Inefficient fabricator scheduling would have serious consequences for profit. Finally, fabricator scheduling is an intellectually challenging task. Charlie derives real pleasure from generating elegant solutions to the problems he encounters, and he is conscious that few people would have the mental skill and wealth of experience necessary to produce elegant solutions. Certainly, the two fabricators must be scheduled jointly by someone who is aware of the downstream consequences of his decisions.

Thus Charlie maintains close contact with the current operating status of the fabricators. Besides his morning survey of the entire plant, he surveys the fabricator backlog at least once each day and often two or three times. He normally generates two schedules each day for each fabricator, one in the late morning and another in the late afternoon—and he may make several more small additions or deletions to the schedules posted on the factory floor. In total, he is likely to estimate fabricator run times between 6 and 20 times each day. A typical work day in terms of fabricator backlog is shown in Figure 4.

Having decided to look carefully at Charlie's run-time estimator, we set out to identify the major variables that he considers when making an estimate. The plant itself was a poor context in which to gather that information. Charlie at work is a busy man and can afford to devote little time to run-time estimation. Moreover, his plant activities are often interrupted by requests from other people. Our questions would simply have added to his burden, and induced fragmentary and ill-considered answers. So we took Charlie to the university where he could make several dozen estimates in a few hours, could talk aloud while he was working, and could explain what he was doing and why. There we tape-recorded Charlie's comments, and later listened to what he said, and debated why. We learned that Charlie is aware of long-run average fabricator rates by work type. He said:

Over a long period of time uniform texture (UT) work will average 1500 to 1800 yards per hour, while sculptured texture (ST) work will go at 1000 to 1200 yards.

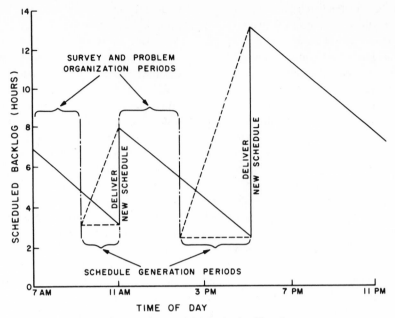

Figure 4 A typical fabricator backlog day.

But we also learned that Charlie does not rely on these averages to estimate run time. He breaks a complete schedule into conceptual segments, all orders within a segment having the same texture and weave. Thus the uniform texture, cut weave orders comprise one segment, and the uniform texture, loop weave orders comprise another segment. All orders running on the special fabricator comprise a single segment because they are all uniform texture, random weave. Charlie estimates a run time for each schedule segment. Then the total run time is obtained by adding (a) the separate run times of all the segments and (b) the changeover times for converting the general fabricator from one weave or texture to the next.

We also learned that Charlie thinks in terms of fabricator speed rather than in terms of fabricator time. Obviously, the numbers added in the computation just described are time estimates. Charlie does think in terms of time when he accumulates segment run times into a total schedule run time. But this accumulation is the very last step in his estimation process. His basic conceptual tool for estimating the run time of a single segment is the fabricator speed. He characterizes each schedule segment by its "length," the total lineal yardage of fabric created for that segment. Then he estimates the fabricator speed, in yards per hour, when

producing the kinds of fabric appearing in that segment. Segment run time is computed by dividing length by speed

$$\text{Time} = \frac{\text{Length}}{\text{Speed}}$$

The computation of segment length is simple and straight-forward: the lineal yardage for each cutting pattern—each setup of rippers and crosscuts—appears in a column on the schedule document, and Charlie adds these pattern lengths on a desk calculator. All of the art of run-time estimation lies in estimation of fabricator speeds, and speed is a fairly complicated function of the fabric and cutting-pattern characteristics.

Charlie explained that no one had taught him to estimate speeds, and he had no formulas to apply.

When I first came to work here, I was told what the average speeds were. But these averages are not dependable. The work may go much quicker or much slower than the averages.

I developed my own set of rules governed by past performance. These rules consider the items we've discussed here. None of this was passed on to me.

In fact, Charlie knows more about fabricator speed than anyone else in the plant, including the fabricator crews. The reasons lie partly in the content of the firm's union labor contract, but mostly in the rudimentary nature of the plant's information system. Each fabricator crew submits a list, at the end of its working shift, of the orders processed during that shift. Only the total volume of work over the eight hours is stated, no details about the running times of individual orders. Since many orders of widely varying types are fabricated during a shift, there is little hope of distinguishing among the variables that affect performance.

Charlie had strong incentive to understand and predict fabricator performance, so he systematically observed the fabricators in operation, interviewed the fabricator crewmen, and compared actual run times with his predictions. Over the years he had been in his job, he gradually built up a mass of information about fabricator speeds, organized this information in his memory, and developed a mental

procedure for retrieving the information relevant to a specific estimate. None of Charlie's lore was written down.

The gross structure of his speed estimating procedure is look, process, look, process, look, . . . He looks at the schedule document, extracts one item of information, processes this item mentally, and returns to the schedule document for a new item. The items he looks at and the sequence in which he looks at them are extremely stable—essentially independent of the schedule content—and by the time Charlie has completed the sequence of items, he has estimated the fabricator speed.

We were able to infer quite a bit of Charlie's information-processing sequence from our tape recordings of his comments. Then we drew up a tentative list of factors that Charlie seemed in one way or another to attend to in estimating run time. These factors are given in Figure 5.

Factor Number	Factor Name	Description of Factor	Possible Range of Values Encountered in Run-Time Estimation
1	Fabricators	One general and one special fabricator	1–2
2	Schedule increment	Length of new fabricator schedule in yards	15–24,000
3	Types of work	Major fabric types	1–5
4	Raw materials	Composition of work in terms of strength, resistance, and appearance specifications	1–500
5	Fabric widths	Number of spindles used	21–45
6	Number of fabric width changes	Number of spindle changes required to produce the work backlog	0–30
7	Customer order characteristics	A variety of changes in the characteristics of individual customer orders which might add set-up time, including: ripper changes, cross-cut changes, and fabric treatment changes	1–50
	Speed of production	Rate of production for work backlog in yards/hour	600–2400
	Production time	Hours backlog estimated	30 minutes to 24 hours

Figure 5   Tentative list of factors perceived by subject in backlog estimation, with ranges of values encountered.

Though we learned much from Charlie's running comments, we could not satisfy ourselves as to the exact content of Charlie's information - processing sequence. Charlie wanted to cooperate, but he was not used to making explicit what he did. "I just do this work automatically, without thinking about it." Thus, too many comments were fragmentary or ambiguous. Sometimes Charlie seemed to omit comments, or to begin a comment on one theme and end it on another. One explanation for his behavior appeared to be more satisfactory than the others, but the evidence to support it was far from overwhelming.

We decided to try a new method to encourage Charlie to make direct descriptive statements about his own behavior. The essential requirement, we thought, was the establishment of some symbolic conventions by which Charlie could say what he was doing and we could understand what he meant. To impose these symbolic conventions on his verbal behavior appeared impractical; it might take much training and would almost certainly interfere with the free commentary he was already making. We decided on the use of a graphic event recorder.

The event recorder consisted of a box fitted with ten buttons which were electrically connected to pens in a multichannel event recorder.[2] Each pen was activated by one, and only one, button. The apparatus was con-

structed so that all event pens were mutually exclusive; that is, only one event pen could be depressed at a time. The plan was that the subject would indicate the beginning of a new activity by pressing the button associated with that activity.

The event recorder experiments were carried out as follows. On the basis of Charlie's comments while making run-time estimates, we identified six acts that we thought described his procedure:

> Note texture and weave.
> Count ripper set-ups.
> Count spindle changes.
> Estimate speed.
> Estimate total length.
> Estimate run-time.

To this list, we added two acts that we had no reason to believe were relevant:

> Count materials changes.
> Estimate average rip length.

Average rip length is the average lineal yardage per ripper setup, that is, total segment length divided by the number of ripper setups in the segment. Our assumption was that Charlie would ignore these two activity alternatives. The eight acts were then assigned to the first eight event recorder buttons in the sequence shown in Figure 6. Buttons nine and ten were used for residual action descriptions in case we had missed something.

A number of backlog schedules were prepared from historical data. The subject was told the general objectives of the experiment, was shown

---

[2] Equipment consisted of an Esterline-Angus Model A620X, ink type, 20-channel event recorder, together with a custom-built button panel.

Pushbutton	Initial Description by Experimenters	Final Description After Charlie's Revisions
1	Note texture and weave	Note texture and weave
2	Count materials changes	Examine material composition
3	Count ripper setups	Estimate ripper setups
4	Count spindle changes	Count fabric width changes
5	Estimate speed	Estimate speed
6	Estimate average rip length	Estimate average rip length
7	Estimate total length	Add rip lengths
8	Estimate run time	Divide length by speed
9	Ask for more information	Ask for more information
10	Perform other activity	Perform other activity

Figure 6 Event recorder list.

the event recorder, and was then given the following specific instructions:

In this experiment we are going to use a different procedure. Notice, in front of you is a console with a series of buttons on it. We are going to use this apparatus to see if we can find out more about how you estimate backlog.

Notice each button has a label. Each label is supposed to represent something you may do when you estimate backlog. Some of these you may actually use and some you may not. We may have the right activities listed and we may not. We want you to help us find out.

We will proceed as follows. The experimenter is holding a number of actual backlog schedules. He is going to ask you to estimate these schedules one by one. He is not going to give you the schedules. But he will give you any information you ask for. But you must ask for information by pushing one of the buttons on the console. If button seems not labelled as it should be, say so, and a label which seems right to you will be made up.

With these instructions, a panel of labels with which the subject was comfortable was developed. Once this was accomplished, the subject was given a further series of schedules. Every fourth schedule was held by the experimenter; the remainder were placed in front of the subject. The subject was instructed to call out the numbers and names of the activities he employed and to say out loud what he was doing for the record. Excerpts from the taped records of the initial experiments were as follows:

Subject: "Number 7: Add production quantities. The total is 9000 yards.

"Number 4: Number of raw material changes. That is 3.

"Number 2: Changes in ripper setups. That is approximately 10.

"Number 6: Estimate average rip length. That is 1000 yards.

"You know, I think I need to know something that's not on here. I need to know the composition of this raw material. I don't see any button for this."

Experimenter: "You are right. There is none. Let's revise button #2. Alright?"

Subject: "I'll write 'material composition' down for the button #2 label, OK?"

Experimenter: "Fine, do that."

The paper tapes from the event recorder were collected and used to produce data on the sequence of buttons pushed and the time required to perform each activity.

This sounds complicated. But Charlie had no difficulty in doing it. In the first place, he was thoroughly accustomed to giving us a running commentary. He had many hours of experience in doing so, scattered over literally years of collaboration. In the second place, he was more or less accustomed to pushing buttons while he worked. A desk calculator and a typewriter are always in front of him on his desk, and he uses them frequently and familiarly. After about two hours of practice, Charlie was pushing the event recorder buttons automatically and by position, without looking at them.

The two-hour practice period helped to acquaint Charlie with the experimental procedure, but much of the time was spent revising the labels on the pushbuttons. Charlie suggested activity descriptions that were more explicit than those we had chosen. For example, he pointed out that "estimate run time" was a straightforward division operation and that "estimate total length" amounted to adding up the lengths of fabric cut with each ripper setup. He kindly avoided using the word "pretentious." Charlie also changed the content of some of the activity descriptions. He said the number of materials changes was irrelevant; he wanted to know what specific materials would be used. He ignored spindle changes as such, but he wanted to know how many times the fabric width was to be changed. He observed:

As a general rule, I hardly ever count ripper setups. What I'll do is just look at it; just glance at it. As far as actually counting, no, I never count.

Can we put one in there and say *estimate*? In other words, not count them. Because I do look at them. So, in a sense, it is counting them. But I'm not counting. You just look at the set-ups. If you've got a lot, you know you're going to run slower. If you've got one, you're going to run faster. They're just average.

By the end of the practice period, Charlie was using all of the first eight pushbuttons on the event recorder, as shown in Figure 6, and was ignoring the last two buttons altogether. The next day, he made 96 run-time estimates using the recording apparatus, and he followed a very clearly defined activity sequence in making each estimate. The frequencies with which Charlie performed each activity are given in Figure 7. The only departures from complete consistency were: (a) eight times he counted width changes before examining the materials list, (b) eight times he failed to count the width changes, and (c) five times he did not estimate the number of ripper setups.

We were surprised by the consistency of the activity sequence. So was Charlie. Near the end of the experiment, he said:

You know, I *do* follow a definite procedure in this estimation of run time. And what I do is much clearer to me now. I'm sure I'm doing it just as I do all the time in the plant. There is a very set pattern to this, isn't there? The sequence on all of these estimates is the same.

However, the important surprises for us lay in the content of the activity sequence. Charlie ignored spindle changes. Of course, the great majority of spindle changes are made while the fabricator is stopped for ripper setups, but Charlie ignored the spindle changes that did not coincide with ripper setups as well. He took

account of the characteristics of the yarns employed as raw materials. We had not expected him to make such precise calculations, or put another way, we had not expected raw materials to make much difference in the fabricator speed. Charlie sometimes omitted the counts of width changes and ripper setups, and he consistently performed the activity we had predicted he would ignore: estimate average rip length.

With the advantage of hindsight, we decided that Charlie sometimes did not count width changes simply because width changes are irrelevant to his speed estimates. Width changes always coincide with ripper setups, and width decreases take less time than ripper changes. A width increase may take more time than a ripper change, because an increase requires cleaning of parts of the machinery. For that reason, fabric width is increased only a few times a day, the pattern being one large increase to a wide width followed by several small decreases to successively narrower widths. Thus it is conceivable that Charlie would make allowance for some, but not all, width changes. However, we doubt that he does so.

Activity Number	Push-button	Description	Chosen								Omitted
			1st	2nd	3rd	4th	5th	6th	7th	8th	
1	1	Note texture and weave	96								
2	7	Add rip lengths (compute total length)		96							
3	2	Examine material composition			88	8					
4	4	Count fabric width changes			8	80					8
5	3	Estimate ripper setups					91				5
6	6	Estimate average rip length						96			
7	5	Estimate speed							96		
8	8	Divide length by speed								96	
Others	9, 10										96
None						8	5				

Figure 7 The activity sequence.

We have two pieces of evidence for this viewpoint in addition to the eight omissions of pushbutton four. First, Charlie described the activity as "count fabric width changes." Although the total number of width changes is not a reliable estimator of the number of width increases, width *increases* are at least as easy to observe on the schedule document as are width *changes*. Presumably Charlie had the option of describing the activity as "count fabric width increases." He is an articulate and perceptive man. Second, our statistical analyses of Charlie's speed estimates, using both experimental data and data collected on the job, have never turned up discernible width-change or width-increase effects. We have concluded that, although Charlie may well take the number of width changes into account, the consequences of this accounting are too weak and erratic for us to measure.

We have also inferred that Charlie omitted "estimate ripper setups" because of irrelevance, but a different kind of irrelevance. Initially, we found these omissions and his consistent inclusions of "estimate average rip length" the most surprising and perplexing characteristics of his activity sequence. The rippers are changed virtually every time the cutting pattern is changed, and because the fabricator has to be brought to a dead stop, ripper setups account for much of the fabricator downtime. A run-time estimate that ignores ripper setups should be inaccurate indeed. So we had expected Charlie to make an accurate count of the number of ripper setups, and possibly to distinguish ripper setups that could be mostly completed while the fabricator was running from setups that could not. Conversely, we had thought average rip length was a wholly subsidiary statistic that Charlie calculated for fun sometimes but put to no practical use.

After some reflection, we realized that we had reversed the importance of the two statistics. Because Charlie knew the total length, average rip length conveyed the same information as the number of ripper setups. One can be used to compute the other:

$$\text{Ripper setups} = \frac{\text{Total length}}{\text{Average rip length}}$$

In fact, Charlie can come up with a pretty accurate estimate of average rip length after quickly running his eyes down the list of rip lengths shown on a schedule. His estimates of the number of ripper setups, after a similarly brief scan, are less accurate, exhibiting twice as much percentage error. So far as we have been able to determine, he uses his estimate of ripper setups as a rough check on his estimate of average rip length, but depends on the latter rather than the former. "Estimate ripper setups" is strictly a redundant activity.

This is not to suggest that Charlie estimates average rip length and then divides into the total length to compute the number of setups. Quite the opposite. He does not think in terms of setups or setup times at all. He thinks in terms of average fabricator speed, allowing for setup times, and thinks of speed as a property that depends on average rip length.

$$\text{Speed} = f \text{ (average rip length)}$$

Of course, speed also depends on texture, weave, and the yarns used. Average rip length only characterizes the setup requirements of a schedule. Charlie's overall characterization of run-time estimation is given in the following comment written after the experiment (italics added):

When the total length increases and the ripper setups decrease, the speed increases. Of course, when the material becomes heavier, the speed will be reduced and vice-versa.

When trying to estimate the amount of time that a schedule will take, there are several factors to be considered. These determining factors are as follows: texture, weave, ripper setups, the approximate average rip length per ripper setup, and special runs. The estimation of total running time is based on calculation or memory or sometimes both. I automatically know the run speeds of certain materials of long-run lengths, but when the amount of ripper setups increases, *then I have to calculate the total length and note the average rip length of all of the ripper setups,* and from this information, I will make an educated estimate of the total amount of time to run the entire schedule.

THE STRUCTURE OF CHARLIE'S SPEED TABLE

Our attack on the activity "estimate speed" began with the premise that Charlie had in his head something like an algebraic formula. Not necessarily a formula he could write down, but a systematic computation procedure, at any rate, which generated a speed given texture, weave, materials, and average rip length. For example, we conjectured as follows: Activity one starts this computation by selecting an initial speed estimate corresponding to a specific texture and weave combination, typical materials, and typical average rip length. The initial speed estimate would be one of five numbers, since only five combinations of weave and texture are possible. Then activity three modifies the initial estimate by taking into account the materials actually used, while still assuming typical average rip length. Finally the speed estimate is modified to account for the actual average rip length. If the modification procedures are properly designed, accurate speed estimates can be obtained from conceptually simple calculations.

The preceding conjecture may be elegant, but it has loopholes. Why, for instance, does "add rip lengths" appear in the middle of the calculation process even though total length is presumed to have no effect on speed? For most of the schedules that Charlie encounters, average rip length has stronger effects on speed than weave, texture, or materials; why does the computation not start with average rip length and then modify for texture, weave, and materials?

We gradually were disabused of the idea that Charlie has a computation procedure for speed and were convinced that he obtains his speed estimates by a table look-up. That is, Charlie has memorized the associations between speed and the schedule characteristics, and he looks up speeds in his memory in somewhat the way one looks up telephone numbers in a directory. In our interviews, Charlie talked as if the existence of a computation procedure was a novel idea, intriguing to contemplate but difficult to conceive of. He thinks of the speeds in his table as discrete numbers distilled from a long series of unique experiences. Although he can interpolate and extrapolate these numbers—implying that the stored speeds must be specific examples from a systematic family of numbers—he distrusts the interpolated values and speaks of them as hypotheses to be tested

in application. The stored values are so much more reliable that they might be a different kind of information altogether. In fact, Charlie can recount, for a large proportion of his table entries, specific remembered situations in which the circumstance was encountered and the speed observed. The only speeds that he does not so document, apparently, are those appropriate to situations arising almost daily.

The existence of Charlie's speed table is awesome to contemplate. In some ranges, he distinguishes speed in increments of 25 yards per hour. If his table had that density across the entire range of speeds and for all possible combinations of texture, weave, and materials, it would contain 15,000 to 20,000 entries.

Obviously, Charlie has not memorized 20,000 table entries. He distinguishes speed in increments of 25 yards per hour only in the most frequently encountered speed ranges for the most frequently encountered textures, weaves, and materials. Other speed ranges increment by 50 yards per hour, and most of the table increments by 100 yards per hour. Moreover, most of the possible combinations of texture, weave, and materials do not appear in the table, either because they represent illogical product configurations or because they are not bought by the customers Charlie's plant serves.

Yet, by even the most conservative estimates, the table must include 2000 entries; and the most probable size seems to be about 5000 entries. We quickly decided that it would be impractical to try to extract a literal duplicate of the table from Charlie. It would take an enormous amount of time, and the results would be of little interest.

On the other hand, there is interest in the abstract content of Charlie's speed table. It is the invention of one, fairly bright human being who has analyzed and organized his years of experience and put his learning into accessible form. One wonders how logical and rational the result might be. In principle, the table entries should form a pattern. Charlie's statements like

When the total length increases and the ripper setups decrease, the speed increases. Of course, when the material becomes heavier, the speed will be reduced and vice-versa.

imply that he sees a pattern. The underlying discipline of the fabricating machinery implies both that there should be a pattern and that the pattern should have certain properties. But saying the table entries should form a pattern is hardly the same thing as saying they do. Nonsystematic variations in the fabricating process may have obscured the systematic variations. Charlie had no procedural help from his organization. The formally recorded observations of the process aggregate many different effects, and even a single schedule includes several segments. Charlie cannot design schedules to yield run-time information; he has to schedule orders as the customers place them.

We initiated a series of experiments designed to explore the structure of Charlie's speed tables. The theory behind the experiments was simple: total production time for one ripper setting is equal to setup time for the rip plus processing time per yard times the number of yards ripped.

Our first experiment presented Charlie with a series of schedules in which every order was for UTRW fabric and every order utilized the same raw materials. Unrealistic, but not impossibly unrealistic, because the special fabricator schedules involve only UTRW fabric and because the specified raw materials were ones that a significant portion of the real orders specify. The schedules in the first experiment

differed in total length and in the numbers of ripper setups, spindle changes, fabric width changes, and crosscut setups. Then a second experiment was conducted in which the schedule segments differed in texture and weave, and UTRW segments were assigned to both the special and the general fabricators. The schedule characteristics varied in the first experiment were also varied in the second, so there were only two unrealistic aspects of Charlie's task: every order still specified the same raw materials, and run-time estimates were made for each schedule segment separately. Finally a third experiment varied the raw materials. Not every possible configuration of raw materials was presented. There are just too many possibilities. The configurations regularly encountered in the plant were explored thoroughly; a sample of the irregularly encountered configurations was included; and a few configurations of extreme type were presented. In addition to materials, all of the schedule characteristics varied in the second experiment were varied in the third. The entire series of experiments took many hours spread over several weeks. Charlie made some of the estimates at the university, some at work, and some at his home. The total experimental design is summarized in Figure 8.

| | | | Number of Different Values Assigned to the Independent Factor in Each Experiment | | | |
| | Description of Independent Factor | | Series I | Series II | | Series III |
v			Exp. A	Exp. B	Exp. C	Exp. D
1	F	Fabricators	1	2	2	2
2	P	Fabric types (texture and weave)	1	4	5	5
3	M	Number of raw material compositions	1	2	5	65
4	W_1	Spindle changes: Measure 1	5	4	4	1
5	W_2	Spindle changes: Measure 2	4	*	*	*
6	R_1	Ripper setups: Measure 1	4	4	3	1
7	R_2	Ripper setups: Measure 2	10	10	*	*
8	R_3	Ripper setups: Measure 3	4	10	*	*
9	L	Length of schedule segment	5	5	3	3
10	N	Number of trials	35	96	140	306

Total trials   577

* Omitted

Figure 8   Summary of design of series of three major Charlie run-time experiments.

We shall not attempt to describe here our entire analytic process. By the time we were done, Charlie had made 577 run-time estimates —roughly the number of estimates made during two months of factory work—and 53 statistical calculations were performed to estimate the magnitudes of the effects of various schedule characteristics and to evaluate alternative theoretical formulations. (See Appendix A for summary statistics.) What we found was:

1. Charlie's speed estimates for UTRW segments are the same for both the special fabricator and the general fabricator.

2. The only setups affecting Charlie's estimates are ripper setups. His speeds ignore fabric width changes, spindle changes, and crosscut changes except in so far as they can be subsumed into the ripper changes.

3. The ripper setup times implicit in Charlie's estimates do not vary significantly with fabric weave, but do vary with fabric texture. Sculptured fabric setups are treated as if they take longer than uniform fabric setups.

4. The implicit setup times are about six minutes for uniform fabric and ten minutes for sculptured fabric. These setup figures could not be substantiated in any rigorous way because

stopwatch data could not be obtained. But casual observation of a few ripper changes gave estimates close to those above.

5. Processing time per lineal yard of fabric varies with texture, weave, and materials. We found, however, that this variation could be adequately represented in terms of a single variable: the weight of a square yard of fabric. Weight can be calculated in a straightforward manner once one knows the weights of the yarns and the geometry implied by the texture and weave, but Charlie himself does not make such calculations. He does not know the geometric coefficients that the calculation requires (we obtained them from a distant industrial research laboratory) and he has no record of the weights of various fabrics.

6. According to Charlie's speed estimates, processing time per lineal yard ranges from 12 to 36 seconds, depending on the kind of fabric in process. The implicit processing times for specific fabrics are about 20 percent longer than manufacturer's specifications for the fabricators. But neither fabricator is new, and the wage-incentive plan imposes an upper limit on machine crew earnings.

The final algebraic equation developed is:

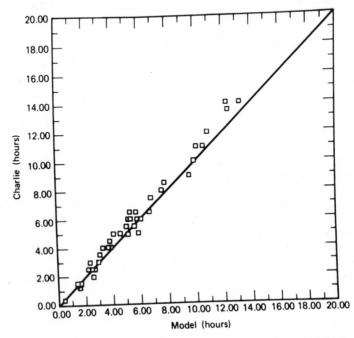

Figure 9 Plot of actual versus predicted run-time values for special fabricator schedules.

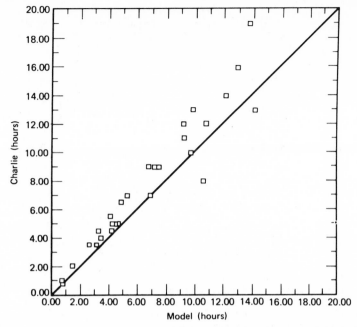

Figure 10   Plot of actual versus predicted run-time values for general fabricator schedules.

$$T = \alpha R + (\beta + \gamma W) \cdot L$$

where T = total run time for the schedule segment

R = number of ripper setups

W = weight per square yard of fabric

L = length (lineal yardage)

α = time per setup, and

$\beta + \gamma W$ = time per yard of production

With unweighted regressions, the correlations between this equation and Charlie's estimates are .9937 for uniform texture schedules and .9935 for sculptured texture schedules. However, Charlie thinks in terms of speed rather than time, so his behavior can be more realistically represented by regressions in which the data are weighted by the factor L^2/T^4. For such weighted regressions, the correlations with Charlie's estimates are .9866 for uniform texture schedules and .9856 for sculptured texture schedules. The approximate average error in the run time was 4 minutes for uniform schedules and 7 minutes for sculptured. Considering the fact that Charlie always rounds his estimates— he never states run time more accurately than the nearest 15 minutes, and long run times are stated to the nearest hour—we think these correlations are remarkable.

At this point, having what we believed was an acceptable model of Charlie's estimation procedure, we compared the performance of the model with his in-plant, run-time estimates. A three-week sample of actual schedules and time estimates had been collected before the run-time experiments were performed. These schedules were coded and a computer program was written to test the model.

The fit for the special fabricator, shown in Figure 9, was rewarding. Only 6 of 41 estimates fell more than two standard deviations from the theoretical values, and all these 6 cases were short schedules whose actual values fell close to the predicted limits. Charlie's tendency to round upward would account for 5 of the 6 cases, although this judgment is tenuous because his rounding introduces noise.

But the fit for the general fabricator schedules was disappointing. Of 30 predictions, 11 fell outside the two standard deviations range, and the model consistently predicted lower run times than did Charlie, as shown in Figure 10. The average error was one and one-quarter hours. Obviously, the model for the general fabricator contained a glaring error.

Analysis of the content of the general fabricator schedules revealed several facts.

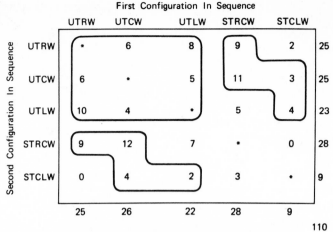

Figure 11 Summary of frequency of six types of changeover in weave and texture for the general fabricator for a six-week period.

Uniform texture, one weave to another	39
Sculptured to uniform texture (common weave)	27
Uniform to sculptured texture (common weave)	27
Sculptured to uniform texture (no common weave)	7
Uniform to sculptured texture (no common weave)	7
Sculptured texture, one weave to another	3

Total general fabricator changeovers for six weeks   110

First, in designing the run-time experiments the times required to change the general fabricator from one weave to another, and from uniform to sculptured texture, were overlooked. Second, we failed to recognize the sequences of changeover between weave and texture that Charlie prefers. Third, all the consequences that follow from assigning small amounts of UTRW work to the general fabricator were not perceived.

Changeovers are heavily concentrated into three of six possible sequences, as given in Figure 11. The six sequences constrain Charlie.

He might prefer always to use a common weave when moving from uniform to sculptured work. But the special fabricator accepts only UTRW work. When such work is in short supply, Charlie may be unable to assign UTRW work to the general fabricator to obtain a desired changeover sequence. Hence Charlie may sometimes find costly changeover unavoidable. But the data in Figure 11 indicate that Charlie avoids certain changeover sequences, and especially those going directly from one sculptured configuration to another.

$$Y = \text{Charlie} - \text{Model} = \beta_1(UT_i \text{ to } UT_j) + \beta_2[UT_i \text{ to } ST_k(CW)]$$
$$\text{Cases} = 30$$
$$R = .6795$$
$$R^2 = .4617$$
$$SE = 1.3372$$

Variable Entered	R^2	Entering F Value	Coefficient	Standard Deviation
UT_i to $ST_k(CW)$	.4029	19.5	1.28	0.34
UT_i to UT_j	.4617	3.0	0.55	0.31

Figure 12 Summary of regression analysis of difference between predicted and actual run times for general fabricator.

We decided to try to explain the difference between our predicted times and Charlie's actual times in terms of the three most common changeovers: *UT* to *UT*, *ST* to *UT(CW)*, and *UT* to *ST(CW)*. The results, summarized in Figure 12, show that two general fabricator changeovers, *UT* to *UT* and *UT* to *ST(CW)*, explain nearly 70 percent of the differences between Charlie and the model. The *UT* to *UT* allowance is one and one-quarter hours and the *UT* to *ST* allowance is one-half hour. The other four factors showed low levels of statistical significance.

Now we believed we had an explanation for much of the poor fit between the actual and predicted values for the general fabricator. Application of changeover allowances left only 5 of the 30 estimates more than two standard deviations from the theory, and generally improved the correspondence between theoretical and actual, as shown in Figure 13.

CONCLUSION

We think we understand how Charlie estimates run time. More importantly, we think we understand the rational basis of his estimation procedure. His estimates are accurately predicted by the equation

$$T = \alpha R + (\beta + \gamma W) \cdot L \qquad (1)$$

and the coefficients in the equation—α, β, and γ —have reasonable values.

Of course, Charlie does not perceive himself as using equation (1). He sees his behavior as:

$$T = L/S \qquad (2A)$$

$$S = f(A, \text{texture, weave, materials}) \qquad (2B)$$

where

S = speed
A = average rip length

However, applying the identity $L = AR$, we can compute Equation 2B from Equations 1 and 2A

$$S = \cfrac{1}{\cfrac{\alpha}{A} + \beta + \gamma W} \qquad (2C)$$

and infer that Equation 2C describes Charlie's speed table.

Thus Charlie uses two nonlinear relations, one of which is pretty complicated, to generate one simple linear relation.

We think there are at least three reasons that he uses the more circuitous method. First, he perceives run time as a function of average

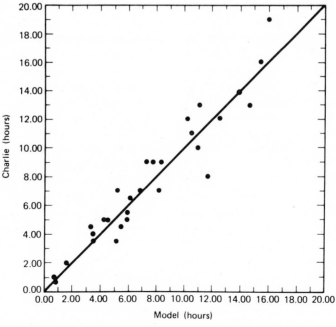

Figure 13 Plot of actual versus predicted run-time values for general fabricator schedules using modified model.

speed, not as a sum of setup times and process times. Equation 2A is more than an algebraic relation; it is his basic orientation toward the run-time problem. And once Equation 2A is adopted as a frame of reference, the curvature inherent in Equation 2A makes curvature in Equation 2B inescapable. In this respect, Charlie is the victim of his organization's tradition. Formal performance reports on the fabricators—whether reports on one work crew during one shift, reports prepared daily or weekly for the plant management, or reports by corporate headquarters on the comparative standings of different plants—are stated in terms of speed. The other people in the company, whether on the plant floor or in the corporate board room, always discuss fabricator performance in terms of speed. And that includes the man who introduced Charlie to his job. It was not by chance Charlie said: "When I first came to work here, I was told what the average speeds were."

Second, Charlie really does not see Equation 2B as the kind of relation that can or should be stated in an algebraic form. Equation 2B is a table. Perhaps it is a table because the relations it describes have curvature and their translation into algebraic form is difficult. Perhaps it is a table because the entries were learned at different times and are based on different amounts of evidence. Perhaps it is a table because new information can be added to a table in bits and pieces without affecting all the old information. Whatever the reason, so long as (2B) is a table Charlie cannot combine (2B) with (2A) and derive a single equation like (1). He cannot discover a new formulation of the run-time problem until he discovers a new formulation of the information he uses in his estimates.

Third, remember Charlie works under time pressure. It is quite plausible that calculating (1) would take Charlie longer (especially on the many familiar configurations of average rip length, texture, weave, and materials) than using the table look-up implied by (2A) and (2B). Charlie likes fast methods.

By some criteria Charlie's approach would be termed roundabout. Yet, the circuitousness of Charlie's procedure and the fact that he stores speeds in tabular form just heightens our amazement over the consistency of his estimates and the crisp logic of his method.

If Charlie's perceptions of fabricator performance are erroneous, they are erroneous in an unbelievably systematic fashion, and the systematic error has survived thousands of tests against market-dictated orders. We have looked at a man performing an intricate job with only the guidance of his own experience, and we have seen him conquer distorted perceptions and environmental idiosyncrasies to create a rational problem-solving technique.

APPENDIX:
STATISTICAL ANALYSES OF CHARLIE'S RUN-TIMES

Two computer programs were used: (1) the "WRAP" weighted regression analysis program; and (2) the "BIMD 2R" UCLA Biomedical stepwise regression program. Each program possessed desired features: WRAP permitted observations to be weighted; BIMD 2R permitted use of a zero intercept. In all, 53 different regressions were carried out using these programs.

The first goal was to determine how much each of the basic schedule characteristics influenced the run-time estimates. The data used were from experiment A, in which fabricator, texture, weave, and raw material composition were held constant. Analysis showed that (for a given fabricator, product type, and raw material composition) nearly all the variance in run time could be accounted for with two variables: backlog length and number of ripper setups. These effects may be seen in Exhibit A-1.

On the basis of the experiment A data, it seemed that the run-time model should be simplified to include only length (L) and setups (R). This result generalized to the case where texture and weave also varied. Exhibit A-2 shows the results of regressions using data from both experiments A and B.

The second goal was to discover the effects of product type and raw material composition, using data from experiments A, B, and C. The analysis summarized in Exhibit A-3 showed that product type and composition significantly affected run time.

The third goal was to discover an efficient continuous measure of product type and raw material composition. The compression of product type and composition was essential to the development of a general model; separate measures for each combination of product type and raw material composition would result in a table of perhaps 2500 coefficients. Moreover, it was philosophically desirable to reduce these variables to one or two scalar vectors.

After giving some thought to the theoretical relation of fabricator speed to texture, weave, and raw materials, we concluded that the physical mass of product was the primary determinant of speed. Mass depended both on the densities of the yarns used and on the amounts of yarn per square yard of product. The latter is determined by texture and weave. Exhibit A-4 shows the results obtained by treating the data from experiments A, B, and C according to this formulation.

The final goal was to determine whether run-time estimates were different for the two fabricators, except in so far as the orders produced were different. The experiments had intentionally included similar schedules for each of the fabricators, and Exhibit A-5 shows the results of treating the fabricators identically. Comparison of Exhibits A-4 and A-5 indicates that pooling the uniform weave estimates only slightly reduced the multiple correlation and greatly reduced the standard error.

The regression analyses showed that ripper setup times were significantly longer for sculptured weave schedules than for uniform weave schedules. This difference agreed with Charlie's generalizations about run time, with his protocols, and with the event recorder data. And when all experimental data were combined in a single regression, the result was an increase in standard error and a decrease in multiple correlation. Therefore, the distinction between uniform and sculptured work was retained.

The remaining regressions were devoted to obtaining better estimates of the coefficients. An unweighted regression assumes the dependent variable is homoscedastically distributed about the regression line. In the present instance, this amounts to assuming that the likelihood of a deviation from the regression line depends on the *time error*. But Charlie does not estimate time. He estimates speed and calculates time from his speed estimate. Thus, it seems more reasonable to assume that the likelihood of a deviation from the regression line depends on the *speed error*. Regressions with speed as the dependent variable are not convenient because of the nonlinearity of the speed function (Equation 2C in the text). Therefore, we retained time as the dependent variable, but weighted the observations in proportion to L^2/T^4, approximating a nonlinear regression with speed as the dependent variable.

The algebraic reasoning behind this approximation was as follows. Assume the speed, S, is normally distributed with mean μ_S and standard deviation σ.

$$f(S) = \frac{1}{\sqrt{2\pi}\sigma} \exp\left[-\frac{1}{2}\left(\frac{S-\mu_S}{\sigma}\right)^2\right]$$

Since $T = L/S$, the absolute value of dS/dT is L/T^2, and:

$$f(T) = \frac{1}{\sqrt{2\pi}\sigma}\frac{L}{T^2} \exp\left[-\frac{1}{2}\left(\frac{L/T-\mu_S}{\sigma}\right)^2\right]$$

$$f(T) = \frac{1}{\sqrt{2\pi}\kappa} \exp\left[-\frac{1}{2}\left(\frac{T-L/\mu_S}{KL/(T\mu_S)}\right)^2\right]$$

where

$$K = \sigma\frac{T^2}{L}$$

Assume the expected value of T, μ_T, is length divided by the expected value of speed.

$$f(T) = \frac{1}{\sqrt{2\pi}\kappa} \exp\left[-\frac{1}{2}\left(\frac{T-\mu_T}{K\mu_T/T}\right)^2\right]$$

For any single observation, T is an estimator of μ_T, and the ratio μ_T/T is approximately unity. Thus $f(T)$ is approximately a Heteroscedastic Normal with the "variance" equal to $\sigma^2 T^4/L^2$. The observations are weighted in inverse proportion to this variance, σ^2 being an irrelevant constant [1, 2].

Exhibit A-6 shows the results of the weighted regressions. The standard error for uniform texture schedules is slightly increased over the value obtained by unweighted regression; the standard error for sculptured texture schedules is greatly reduced.

EXHIBIT A-1.   Summary of Regression Analysis #5: Uniform Texture, Random Weave, One Raw Material Composition

Model Run Time $= T =$

$$\beta_1 W + \beta_2 R_1 + \beta_3 R_2 + \beta_4 R_3 + \beta_5 L + \beta_6 W^2 + \beta_7 R_1^2 + \beta_8 R_2^2 + \beta_9 R_3^2 + \beta_{10} L^2 + \beta_{11} \log L$$

Cases = 70	$\bar{T} = 2.759$
$R = .9990$	$\sigma_i = 3.492$
$R^2 = .9980$	Standard Error of Estimate (SEE) = .1687

Variable Entered	R	Entering F Value	Coefficient	Standard Deviation
L	.9938	5549.5	.00005	.00000
R_1	.9985	209.9	.02927	.07992
$(R_1)^2$	.9988	17.9	.00158	.00575
$(L)^2$	.9989	2.0	.00000	.00000
$\log L$	.9989	2.5	.01315	.02196
W	.9989	1.2	.09533	.03556
$(W)^2$	.9990	3.5	$-.00838$	.00348
R_3	.9990	0.7	$-.09309$	.06585
$(R_3)^2$	.9990	1.2	.00866	.00678
R_2	.9990	0.6	.06958	.09186
$(R_1)^2$	.9990	0.7	.00158	.00575

EXHIBIT A-2. Summary of Regression Analyses #9, #14, #15, #16 and #17: All Textures and All Weaves, One Raw Material Composition

$$T = \beta_1 W_1 + \beta_2 R_1 + \beta_3 R_3 + \beta_4 L + \beta_5 W_2 + \beta_6 L^2$$

	#9 UTRW Uniform Texture, Random Weave			#14 UTCW Uniform Texture, Cut Weave			#15 UTLW Uniform Texture, Loop Weave			#16 STCLW Sculptured Texture, Cut-Loop Weave			#17 STLRW Sculptured Texture, Loop-Random Weave		
Cases	70			48			48			48			48		
R	.9989			.9991			.9762			.9977			.9879		
R^2	.9978			.9982			.9530			.9953			.9759		
SEE	.1703			.1801			.7386			.3441			.7834		
Variable Entered	Entering F Value	Coefficient	Standard Deviation	Entering F Value	Coefficient	Standard Deviation	Entering F Value	Coefficient	Standard Deviation	Entering F Value	Coefficient	Standard Deviation	Entering F Value	Coefficient	Standard Deviation
L	5549.5	.5340	.0247	2836.3	.5064	.0386	622.2	.4202	.1495	1911.4	.7384	.0573	704.6	.4031	.1505
R_1	209.9	.0739	.0097	211.2	.1237	.0114	20.1	.0792	.0449	144.8	.1112	.0215	47.8	.1400	.0480
R_3	6.3	.0404	.0128	1.1	.0146	.0143	1.0	.0505	.0580	1.5	.0331	.0273	4.7	.1252	.0623
L^2	7.9	.0058	.0018	0.5	.0018	.0024	0.0	.0016	.0100	0.0	−.0006	.0053	0.0	−.0022	.0106
W_2	4.7	−.0637	.0223	17.7	.1623	.0391	0.0	−.0178	.1564	1.7	−.0738	.0712	5.2	.3740	.1602
W_1	3.2	−.0219	.0121	4.3	.0521	.0242	0.6	.0336	.0999	6.7	.0565	.0269	1.0	.1028	.1023

EXHIBIT A-3. Summary of Regression Analysis #21: All Textures, All Weaves, Five Raw Material Compositions

$$T = \beta_1 R_1 + \beta_2 UTCW_1 + \beta_3 UTCW_2 + \beta_4 UTCW_3 + \beta_5 UTCW_4 + \beta_6 UTCW_5$$
$$+ \beta_7 UTLW_1 + \qquad \cdot \qquad \cdot \qquad \cdot \qquad + \beta_{11} UTLW_5$$
$$+ \beta_{12} UTRW_1 + \qquad \cdot \qquad \cdot \qquad \cdot \qquad + \beta_{16} UTRW_5$$
$$+ \beta_{17} STCLW_1 + \qquad \cdot \qquad \cdot \qquad \cdot \qquad + \beta_{21} STCLW_5$$
$$+ \beta_{22} STCRW_1 + \qquad \cdot \qquad \cdot \qquad \cdot \qquad + \beta_{26} STCRW_5$$

Cases = 542 $R = .9954$

SEE = .4579 $R^2 = .9908$

Raw Material Composition (M)		*F Values, Coefficients, and Standard Deviations for Each of Five Raw Material Compositions and Five Combinations of Texture and Weave*				
		UTCW	UTLW	UTRW	STCLW	STCRW
1	F	1122	952	946	1580	1966
	$\beta_2-\beta_6$	.6700	.6171	.6152	.7953	.8870
	SD	.0200	.0200	.0200	.0200	.0200
2	F	1104	794	1034	1790	1565
	$\beta_7-\beta_{11}$	.6648	.5639	.6367	.8464	.7915
	SD	.0200	.0200	.0197	.0200	.0200
3	F	688	483	506	998	944
	$\beta_{12}-\beta_{16}$	.5249	.4399	.4501	.6320	.6146
	SD	.0200	.0200	.0200	.0200	.0200
4	F	1195	1121	940	2437	2539
	$\beta_{17}-\beta_{21}$	.6915	.6699	.6135	.9875	1.0079
	SD	.0200	.0200	.0200	.0200	.0200
5	F	1920	1041	1992	3225	3016
	$\beta_{22}-\beta_{26}$	.5964	.4391	.5291	.7728	.7473
	SD	.0136	.0136	.0118	.0136	.0136

EXHIBIT A-4. Summary of Regression Analyses #38 through #40: All Textures; All Weaves; Sixty-Five, Raw-Material Compositions

$T = \alpha R + \beta L + \gamma L \cdot M^*$ where M^* is weight per square yard of fabric.

	General Fabricator						Special Fabricator		
	Uniform Texture			Sculptured Texture			Uniform Texture		
Cases	270			280			604		
R	.9972			.9935			.9938		
R²	.9944			.9871			.9876		
SEE	.1002			.5460			.3499		
Variable Entered	F Value To Remove	Coefficient	Standard Deviation	F Value To Remove	Coefficient	Standard Deviation	F Value To Remove	Coefficient	Standard Deviation
R	53	.08929	.01226	284	.17291	.01025	382	.09763	.00499
L	68	.01378	.00167	4	.00868	.00413	242	.02797	.00180
L·M*	524	.00027	.00001	282	.00026	.00002	317	.00021	.00001

EXHIBIT A-5. Summary of Regression Analysis #41: Combining All Uniform-Texture, Random-Weave Work For Both Fabricators

Model Run Time $= T = L/S = \alpha R + \beta L + \gamma L \cdot M^*$

Cases = 874   R = .9937
SEE = .0303   R² = .9874

Variable Entered	R²	Entering F Value	Coefficient	Standard Deviation
L·M*	.9715	29,803	.00021	.00001
R	.9831	596	.10460	.00417
L	.9874	296	.02548	.00148

EXHIBIT A-6. Summary of Regression Analyses #46 and #47: Weighted Observations, All Uniform and All Sculptured Work

$$T = \alpha R + \beta L + \gamma L \cdot M^*$$

Regression Weight $= L^2/T^4$

Overall Values	All Uniform Work			All Sculptured Work		
Cases	874			280		
R	.9866			.9856		
R^2	.9734			.9714		
SEE	.0804			.1346		
Variable	Coefficient	SD	F Ratio	Coefficient	SD	F Ratio
Constant	−.00275	.00546	25	−.09362	.01317	50
R	.09652	.00336	821	.15364	.00847	328
L	.02240	.00125	320	.02382	.00414	33
$L \cdot M^*$	.02173	.00088	605	.01957	.00166	137

REFERENCES

1. F. N. David, and J. Neyman, 1938. Extension of the Markoff theorem on least squares. *Statistical Research Memoirs*, 2: 105–116.
2. W. H. Starbuck, 1965. *The heteroscedastic normal*. Lafayette, Ind.: Purdue University, Institute paper No. 106.

PART III

INDIVIDUALS WHO INTERACT

As the second chapter pointed out, there have been relatively few studies describing interaction between individuals (category B). Consequently, this category was redefined to include studies of individuals (category A) or hypothetical "average" individuals (categories C or D) in which the model included a forecast of another human's behavior, a mutual adjustment process, or systematic exchanges of information with others. Such preinteractive models are represented here by Weber's study, which otherwise would fall in category A, by Overstreet's study, which otherwise would fall in category C, and by the studies of Kilbridge and Wester, and Kaczka and Kirk, which otherwise would fall in category D. Only two of the included studies can fairly be said to represent interaction between identifiable individuals, and there is ambiguity in the classification of these. Both the Cyert, Feigenbaum, and March study and the Crecine study could be classified in category D if one chose to read them that way.

The lack of category B studies is not a phenomenon we predicted in advance, and is rather inconsistent with both the interests of social scientists and the comparative advantages of computer simulation. Interpersonal interaction is a much more ubiquitous interest of social scientists than is individual thinking: interaction is the predominant concern of social psychologists; processes of bargaining and influence are recurrent topics in anthropology,

political science, economics, labor relations, peace research, and mathematics; and even economists, who generally restrict themselves to aggregate phenomena, analyze duopoly and oligopoly interactions. Models of interaction are difficult to formulate verbally and mathematically because Alice's behavior depends on Betty's behavior, because Alice and Betty may perceive the situation differently, and because there is likely to be a difference between what Alice intends to say and what Betty hears Alice saying. Computer simulation is probably the only method now available for representing interaction realistically.

However, the lack of interaction studies is a fact, and given the fact, one can see plausible explanations for it.

1. The study of interaction between individuals is subject to at least two of the liabilities afflicting the study of individuals: one must believe that individuals are worth studying, and one must believe that individual behavior is predictable. Should one want a model that explains why behavior occurs as well as what behavior occurs, he is confronted by the third liability as well: dependence on introspective evidence.

2. Assuming that a well-developed interaction model should operate at approximately the same level of detail as the individual models presented in the preceding section, the study of

interaction is more difficult than the study of individuals. First, one must model at least twice as many individuals, and each submodel is likely to be distinct from the others. Second, most human interaction occurs in natural language, and unless one is quite selective about the kind of interaction he studies, he is likely to be sidetracked by problems of language processing. Note that the six studies included here either leave the communication process implicit (Kilbridge and Wester, and Kaczka and Kirk) or describe communication that occurs through a numeric code. Third, it is more difficult to obtain data: subjects are reluctant to expose thought processes having social implications, and unless one excludes face-to-face communication, obtaining introspective evidence during the course of the interaction either destroys the interaction process or seriously distorts it.

3. Social psychology, the discipline having nominal responsibility for the study of interaction between individuals, is basically atheoretic. The usual response to an experimental finding is the design of another experiment, rather than elaboration of a theoretical paradigm, and the theories that have been developed emphasize simplicity rather than accuracy. In common with other branches of experimental psychology, social psychology searches for the smooth, general trends observable in aggregate data, but in contrast to most experimental psychology, social psychology relies almost exclusively on ordinal, greater-than evaluations, which are only useful for and restrict future development to qualitative theories.

Interaction research in political science, labor relations, and anthropology either has followed the social psychological pattern or has developed descriptions of real-world interaction behavior that are even less tightly related to theories. Economists and mathematicians began and have remained at the other extreme: elaborate theoretical formulations that are not systematically related to empirical evidence. Two obvious examples are duopoly theory and game theory.

There is very little advantage in developing a simulation model unless one wants a comparatively rich and complex theory and wants to make a supraqualitative comparison between the theory's implications and observations of reality. Verbal and mathematical models are quicker and more fruitful than simulation models as long as the models are simple enough to yield to analytical treatment, and quite drastic abstractions to obtain simplicity are feasible when the accuracy of the model's implications is only a qualitative measurement.

The reader may wish to consider the following studies as alternatives to the ones included here. We especially recommend T. W. Carroll's *SINDI 2* (which is, unfortunately, a book-length mimeo).

TYPE 1 STUDIES

T. W. Carroll, 1969. *SINDI 2: simulation of innovation diffusion in a rural community of Brazil.*
R. M. Coe, 1964. Conflict, interference, and aggression: computer simulation of a social process.
J. P. Crecine, 1969. *Governmental problem solving: a computer simulation of municipal budgeting.*
D. Gerwin, 1969. *Budgeting public funds.*
S. Saltzman, 1963. *On statistical models of the firm with an application.*

TYPE 2 STUDIES

H. J. Brightman, E. E. Kaczka, and B. H. Shane, 1969. *A simulation model of individual behavior in a work group.* Paper 69–821–1.
T. W. Carroll, and G. J. Hanneman, 1968. Two models of innovation diffusion.
J. T. Gullahorn, and J. E. Gullahorn, 1964. Computer simulation of human interaction in small groups.
S. A. West, 1968. *SMATSEL, a simulation of the decision processes in mate selection in Akiyama.*

TYPE 3 STUDIES

H. J. Brightman, E. E. Kaczka, and B. H. Shane, 1969. *A simulation model of individual behavior in a work group.* Paper 69–822–2.

R. Boguslaw, and R. H. Davis, 1969. Social process modeling: a comparison of a live and computerized simulation.

J. R. Emshoff, R. W. Blanning, and A. G. Rao, 1966. *A behavioral model of the prisoner's dilemma.*

G. H. Haines, Jr., 1961. The rote marketer.

A. P. Hare, R. Richardson, and H. Scheilblechner, 1968. *Computer simulation of small group decisions.*

M. L. Levin, 1970. *A simulation of the flow of influence in social systems.*

W. S. Marshall, 1967. Simulating communication network experiments.

K. Rainio, 1962. A stochastic theory of social contacts: a laboratory study and an application to sociometry.

K. Rainio, 1965. Social interaction as a stochastic learning process.

T. B. Roby, and C. R. Budrose, 1965. Pattern recognition in groups: laboratory and simulation studies.

11

MODELS IN A BEHAVIORAL THEORY OF THE FIRM

RICHARD M. CYERT
EDWARD A. FEIGENBAUM
JAMES G. MARCH[1]

Recent attempts to develop a behavioral theory of the firm have focused particularly on the internal characteristics of a business firm as a decision-making organization. They have used the rough framework of both the theory of competitive pricing and the modern efforts to extend that theory to situations of imperfect competition such as the case of oligopoly and duopoly where only a few, or possibly only two, firms supply a given market. They have, however, gone further in introducing as an important part of the theory the process by which business organizations make decisions. Since business firms are organizations, it has seemed reasonable a priori to assume that a theory of business behavior ought not to treat them as individual decision-makers [1, 2, 3, 4, 5, 6, 7, 8, 12, 14, 17].

Two major obstacles to the acceptance of such a theory of pricing are obvious. First, it must be shown that the theory is at least as good as other existing theories in its ability to predict firm behavior [11, pp. 14–15]. Convincing

demonstrations on either side of this point are not available. In our judgment, a major portion of the effort in the next decade of research on pricing should be directed to answering this question (or to making it irrelevant). But we do not propose to discuss the point in detail here. Second, a way must be found to deal with the complex theory implicit in the decision-making process approach. A major problem perceived by those sympathetic to a behavioral theory has been the lack of a methodology suitable for handling the kinds of complexities that seemed to be needed [13]. It is to this problem and to the development of a specific model to which we address ourselves in this paper.

We show that a relatively complex model of the firm as a decision-making organization can be developed and used to yield economically relevant and testable predictions of business behavior. The methodology involved is computer simulation. The model is one of a specific type of duopoly. As a rough test of reasonableness, we compare the predictions of the model with actual data. Our hope is that the model will illustrate the promise of simulation as a technique of model building in economic theory and the behavioral sciences in general and at the

SOURCE: Reprinted from *Behavioral Science*, 4: 81–95 (1959).
[1] The authors owe a considerable debt to a large group of colleagues and students for their comments on the general approach and specific models presented here.

same time demonstrate a general method for examining many of the concepts previously discussed in more abstract terms.

THE DECISION-MAKING PROCESS

Recent theories of organizational behavior have emphasized several important characteristics of the decision-making process that are dealt with awkwardly in the theory of the firm. First, organizational decisions depend on information, estimates, and expectations that ordinarily differ appreciably from reality. These organizational perceptions are influenced by some characteristics of the organization and its procedures. The procedures provide concrete estimates—if not necessarily accurate ones [7]. Second, organizations consider only a limited number of decision alternatives. The set of alternatives considered depends on some features of organizational structure and on the locus of search responsibility in the organization. This dependence seems to be particularly conspicuous in such planning processes as budgeting and price-output determination [1]. Finally, organizations vary with respect to the amount of resources they devote to organizational goals on the one hand and suborganizational and individual goals on the other. In particular, conflict and partial conflict of interests is a feature of most organizations and under some conditions organizations develop substantial internal slack susceptible to reduction under external pressure [8].

The concept of organizational or internal slack is used to describe a situation within an organization in which individual energies potentially utilizable for the achievement of organizational goals are permitted to be diverted. The form of the slack may vary from a labor force not working at its full capability to overly large departmental budgets. The extent and regularity with which the organization meets its goals, especially the profit goal, will affect the amount of internal slack.

Our objective is to show how the general attributes of decision-making, some of which have been described above, can be introduced into a behavioral theory of the firm. Although our elaboration is an obvious abstraction of the details of procedures used in a complex organization, each of the processes specified can serve as headings for a further set of subprocesses. We have specified a decision process that involves nine distinct steps:

(1) *Forecast competitors' behavior.* The fact that firms assume something about the reactions of their rivals is, of course, incorporated in any theory of oligopoly. Our approach is to build into the model some propositions about the ways in which organizations gain, analyze, and communicate information on competitors. The concept of organizational learning, a process by which expectations of competitors' behavior are modified on the basis of experience, is a major element in this formulation.

(2) *Forecast demand.* We have attempted to build a model that can encompass descriptions of the process by which the demand curve (the relationship between the price of the product and the quantity which can be sold at that price) is estimated in the firm. In this manner, we are able to introduce organizational biases in estimation and allow for differences among firms in the way in which they adjust their current estimates on the basis of experience.

(3) *Estimate costs.* We do not assume, as in the theory of the firm of economics, that the firm has achieved the optimum combination of resources and the lowest cost per unit of output for any given size plant. We believe it is necessary to introduce the factors that actually affect the firm's costs, estimated as well as achieved.

(4) *Specify objectives.* As has been noted above, organizational "objectives" may enter at two distinct points and perform two quite distinct functions. First, in this step they consist in goals the organization wishes to achieve and which it uses to determine whether it has at least one viable plan [see step (5)]. There is no requirement that the objectives be co-measureable since they enter as separate constraints all of which "must" be satisfied. Thus, we expect to be able to include profit goals, share of the market goals, production goals, etc. [15]. Second, the objectives may be used as decision criteria in step (9). As will become clear below, the fact that objectives serve this twin function rather than the single (decision-rule) function commonly assigned to them is of major importance to the theory.

The order of steps (1), (2), (3), and (4) is irrelevant in the present formulation. We assume that a firm performs such computations more or less simultaneously and that all are substantially completed before any further action is taken. Since the subsequent steps are all contingent, the order in which they are performed may have considerable effect on the decisions reached. This is particularly true with respect to the order of steps (6), (7), and (8). Thus, one of the structural characteristics of a specific model is the order of the steps.

(5) *Evaluate plan.* On the basis of the estimates of (1), (2), and (3) alternatives are examined to see whether there is at least one alternative that satisfies the objectives defined by (4). If there is, we transfer immediately to (9) and a decision. If there is not, however, we go on to step (6). This evaluation represents a key step in the planning process that is ignored in a model that uses objectives solely as the decision rule. Certain organizational phenomena (e.g., organizational slack) increase in importance because of the contingent consequences of this step.

(6) *Re-examine costs.* We specify that the failure to find a viable plan initially results in the re-examination of estimates. Although we list the re-examination of costs first here, the order is dependent on some features of the organization and will vary from firm to firm.[2] An important feature of organizations is the extent to which a firm is able to "discover" under the pressure of unsatisfactory preliminary plans "cost savings" that could not be found otherwise. In fact, we believe it is only under such pressure that firms begin to approach an optimum combination of resources. With the revised estimate of costs, step (5) occurs again. If an acceptable plan is possible with the new estimates, the decision rule is applied. Otherwise, step (7).

(7) *Re-examine demand.* As in the case of cost, demand is reviewed to see whether a somewhat more favorable demand picture cannot be obtained. This might reflect simple optimism or a consideration of new methods for influencing demand (e.g., an additional advertising effort). In either case, we expect organizations to revise demand estimates under some conditions and different organizations to revise them in different ways. Evaluation (5) occurs again with the revised estimates.

(8) *Re-examine objectives.* Where plans are unfavorable, we expect a tendency to revise objectives downward. The rate and extent of change we can attempt to predict. As before, evaluation (5) is made with the revised objectives.

(9) *Select alternative.* The organization requires a mechanism (a) for generating alternatives to consider and (b) for choosing among those generated. The method by which alternatives are generated is of considerable importance since it affects the order in which they are evaluated. Typically, the procedures involved place a high premium on alternatives that are "similar" to alternatives chosen in the recent past by the firm or by other firms of which it is aware. If alternatives are generated strictly sequentially, the choice phase is quite simple: choose the first alternative that falls in the estimate space, that is the set of positions determined by the estimated demand and estimated cost curves. If more than one alternative is generated at a time, a more complicated choice process is required. For example, at this point maximization rules may be applied to select from among the evoked alternatives. In addition, this step defines a decision rule for the situation in which there are no acceptable alternatives (even after all re-examination of estimates).

There are two important observations to be made about a theory having these general characteristics. First, as we increase the emphasis on describing in some detail the actual process by which the firm makes price and output decisions, we decrease the relevance of one of the major debates in the theory of the firm. Whether the firm maximizes, "satisfices,"[3] or just tries to survive is not the main issue (if indeed it is an issue at all). The emphasis on the process of making decisions in an organization obviates the need for the simple decision rules

---

[2] Although we have identified these re-evaluations in terms of strict sequence, an alternative interpretation can be made in terms of intensity of search.

[3] "The key to the simplification of the choice process in both cases is the replacement of the goal of *maximizing* with the goal of *satisficing*, of finding a course of action that is 'good enough'" [16].

and simple models implicit in much of that controversy.

The second point is a related one. Conventional mathematics is a somewhat awkward tool for developing the implications of a theory such as the one described here. It is no accident, therefore, that interest in detailed process models has grown with the development of the digital computer. Computer simulation is well suited to the complexities that are introduced when internal firm variables are utilized in the theory. The significance of simulation for business behavior has been explored vigorously in the so-called "business games" developed as business training devices; their potential for economic theory is at least as great.

A SPECIFIC DUOPOLY MODEL

The theoretical framework we have outlined in the preceding section can be viewed as an executive program for organizational decisions. That is, we conceive of any large scale oligopolistic business organization as pusuing the steps indicated. A change in decision must (within the theory) be explained in terms of some change in one of the processes specified. As we have noted above, such a conception of the theory seems to suggest a computer-simulation model rather than treatment in mathematical form [9]. The rationale, of course, remains the same. We wish to explore the implications of the model.

The intention has been to construct a plausible set of estimation and decision rules for different types of organizations, and to simulate on a computer the behavior of these firms over time. When we attempt to develop models exhibiting the process characteristics we have discussed above, it becomes clear that our knowledge of how actual firms do, in fact, estimate demand, cost, etc., is discouragingly small. We know with reasonable confidence some of the things that many firms do but at a number of points in the model we can make only educated guesses. Moreover, what knowledge we have (or think we have) tends to be qualitative in nature in situations where it would be desirable to be quantitative.

Because of these considerations, the models of firms with which we will deal here should be viewed as tentative approximations. They contain substantial elements of arbitrariness and unrealistic characterizations. For example, we believe that each of the models as it stands almost certainly exaggerates the computational precision of organizational decision-making. In general, we have not attempted to introduce all of the revisions we consider likely at this time primarily because we wish to examine whether some major revisions produce results which reasonably approximate observed phenomena.

The model is developed for a duopoly situation. The product is homogeneous and, therefore, only one price exists in the market. The major decision that each of the two firms makes is an output decision. In making this decision the firm must estimate the market price for varying outputs. When the output is sold, however, the actual selling price will be determined by the market. No discrepancy between output and sales is assumed, and thus no inventory problem exists in the model.

We assume a duopoly composed of an ex-monopolist and a firm developed by former members of the established firm. We shall call the latter, "the splinter," and the former, "the ex-monopolist" or, for brevity, "monopolist." Such a specific case is taken so that some rough assumptions can be made about appropriate functions for the various processes in the model. The assumptions are gross; but it is only through some such rough model that a start can be made. To demonstrate that the model as a whole has some reasonable empirical base, we will compare certain outcomes of the model with data from the *can industry*, where approximately the same initial conditions hold.

We can describe the specific model at several levels of detail. In Table 1 the skeleton of the model is indicated—the "flow diagrams" of the decision-making process. This will permit a quick comparison of the two firms. In the remainder of this section of the paper we will attempt to provide somewhat greater detail (and rationale) for the specific decision and estimating rules used.[4]

The decision-making process postulated by the theory begins with a "forecast" phase (in which competitor's reaction, demand, and costs

---

[4] The computer program, developed in the IT language for the IBM 650 computer, can be obtained from the authors.

TABLE 1   Process Model for Output Decision of Firm

1. Forecast: Competitor's reactions	Compute conjectural variation term for period t as a function of actual reactions observed in the past
2. Forecast: Demand	Keep slope of perceived demand curve constant but pass it through the last realized point in the market
3. Estimate: Average unit costs	Cost curve for this period is the same as for last period. If profit goal has been achieved two successive times, average unit costs increase
4. Specify objectives: Profit goal	Specify profit goal as a function of the actual profits achieved over past periods
5. Evaluate: Examine Alternatives	Evaluate alternatives within the estimate space. If an alternative which meets goal is available, go to (9). If not, got to (6)
6. Re-examine: Cost estimate	Search yields a cost reduction. Go to (5). If after evaluation there, decision can be made, go to (9). If not, go to (7)
7. Re-examine: Demand estimate	Estimate of demand increased after search. Go to (5). If after evaluation, decision can be made, go to (9). If not, go to (8)
8. Re-examine: Profit goal	Reduce profit goal to a level consistent with best alternative in the estimate space as modified after (6) and (7)
9. Decide: Set output	Selection of alternative in original estimate space to meet original goal, in modified estimate space to meet original goal, or in modified estimate space to meet lowered goal

are estimated) and a goal specification phase (in which a profit goal is established). An evaluation phase follows, in which an effort is made to find the "best" alternative given the forecasts. If this "best" alternative is inconsistent with the profit goal, a re-examination phase ensues, in which an effort is made to revise cost and demand estimates. If re-examination fails to yield a new best alternative consistent with the profit goal, the immediate profit goal is abandoned in favor of "doing the best possible under the circumstances." The specific details of the models follow this framework.

Forecasting a Competitor's behavior

The model being analyzed in the paper assumes two firms in the market (a duopoly). As a result one of the significant variables in the decision on the quantity of output to produce

for each firm becomes an estimate of the rival firm's output. For example, assume the monopolist in period (t) is considering a change in output from period $(t-1)$. At the same time the monopolist makes an estimate of the change the splinter will make. At the end of period t the monopolist can look back and determine the amount of change the splinter made in relation to his own change. The ratio of changes can be expressed as follows:

$$V_{m,t} = \frac{Q_{s,t} - Q_{s,t-1}}{Q_{m,t} - Q_{m,t-1}}$$

where $V_{m,t} =$ the change in the splinter's output during period t as a percentage of the monopolist's output change during period t.

$Q_{s,t} - Q_{s,t-1} =$ the actual change in the splinter's output during period t.

$Q_{m,t} - Q_{m,t-1} =$ the actual change in the monopolist's output during period t.

In the same way we have for the splinter the following:

$$V_{s,t} = \frac{Q_{m,t} - Q_{m,t-1}}{Q_{s,t} - Q_{s,t-1}} = \frac{1}{V_{m,t}}$$

The Ex-Monopolist. When the monopolist in period t is planning his output, he must make an estimate of his rival's output, as noted above. In order to make this estimate we assume that the monopolist first makes an estimate of the percentage change in the splinter's output in relation to his own change, that is, an estimate of $V_{m,t}$. We have assumed that the monopolist will make this estimate on the basis of the splinter's behavior over the past three time periods. More specifically we have assumed that the monopolist's estimate is based on a weighted average, as follows:

$$\begin{aligned} V'_{m,t} = \; & V_{m,t-1} \\ & + 1/7\,[4(V_{m,t-1} - V_{m,t-2}) \\ & + 2(V_{m,t-2} - V_{m,t-3}) \\ & + (V_{m,t-3} - V_{m,t-4})] \end{aligned}$$

where $V'_{m,t}$ = the monopolist's estimate of the change in the splinter's output during period t as a percentage of the monopolist's output change during period t, that is, an estimate of $V_{m,t}$.

Note that $(V'_{m,t}) \cdot (Q_{m,t} - Q_{m,t-1})$ is the monopolist's estimate of the splinter's change in output, $Q_{s,t} - Q_{s,t-1}$.

The Splinter. We would expect the splinter firm to be more responsive to recent shifts in its competitor's behavior and less attentive to ancient history than the monopolist, both because it is more inclined to consider the monopolist a key part of its environment and because it will generally have less computational capacity as an organization to process and update the information necessary to deal with more complicated rules. Our assumption is that the splinter will simply use the information from the last two periods. Thus $V'_{s,t} = V_{s,t-1} + (V_{s,t-1} - V_{s,t-2}).$[5] In the same manner as above $(V'_{s,t}) \cdot (Q_{s,t} - Q_{s,t-1})$ is the splinter's estimate of the monopolist's change in output, $Q_{m,t} - Q_{m,t-1}$.

Forecasting Demand

We assume that the actual market demand curve is linear. That is, we assume the market price to be a linear function of the total output offered by the two firms together. We also assume that the firms forecast a linear market demand curve (quite different, perhaps, from the actual demand curve). There has been considerable discussion in the economics literature of the frequent discrepancy between the "imagined" demand curve and the actual demand curve [17], and it is this concept that is incorporated in the model. The values of the parameters of the "imagined" demand curve are based on rough inferences from the nature of the firms involved.

The Ex-Monopolist. We assume that, because of its past history of dominance and monopoly, the ex-monopolist will be over-pessimistic with respect to the quantity which it can sell at lower prices, i.e., we assume the initial perception of the demand curve will have a somewhat greater slope than the actual market demand curve. On the assumption that information about actual demand is used to improve its estimate, we assume that the ex-monopolist changes its demand estimate on the basis of experience in the market. The firm assumes that its estimate of the slope of the demand curve is correct and it "repositions" its previous estimate to pass through the observed demand point.

The Splinter. We posit that the splinter firm will initially be optimistic with respect to the quantity which it can sell at low prices. That is, the initial slope (absolute value) of its demand curve will be somewhat less than that of the actual market demand curve. Secondly, we assume that initially the splinter firm perceives demand as increasing over time. Thus, until demand shows a down turn, the splinter firm estimates its demand to be 5% greater than that found by repositioning its perceived demand through the last point observed in the market-place.

Estimating Costs

In the process for forecasting and realizing costs, we do not make the assumption that the

[5] Obviously we do not maintain that the form and parameters of these "learning" functions are empirically validated. The functions are somewhat arbitrary but we hope not unreasonable.

firm has achieved optimum costs. We assume, rather, that the firm has a simplified estimate of its average cost curve, that is, the curve expressing cost as a function of output. It is horizontal over most of the range of possible outputs; at high and low outputs (relative to capacity) costs are perceived to be somewhat higher.

Further, we make the assumption that these cost estimates are "self-confirming," i.e., the estimated costs will, in fact, become the actual per-unit cost [8]. The concept of organizational slack as it affects costs is introduced at this point. Average unit cost for the present period is estimated to be the same as last period, but if the profit goal of the firm has been achieved for two consecutive time periods, then costs are estimated to be 5% higher than "last time."

The specific values for costs are arbitrary. The general shape of the cost curves has been discussed in detail in the literature and studied empirically [10]. The concept of organization slack has some important implications for the theory of the firm and has been defined earlier.

The Ex-Monopolist. The monopolist's initial average unit cost is assumed to be $800 per unit in the range of outputs from 10% to 90% of capacity. Below 10% and above 90% the initial average unit cost is assumed to be $900.

The Splinter. It is assumed that the competitor will have somewhat lower initial costs. This is because its plant and equipment will tend to be newer and its production methods more modern, Specifically, initial average costs are $760 in the range of outputs from 10% to 90% of capacity. Below 10% and above 90% costs are assumed to average $870 per unit produced.

Specifying Objectives

The multiplicity of organizational objectives is a fact with which we hope to deal in later revisions of the present models. For the present, however, we have limited ourselves to a single objective defined in terms of profit. In this model the function of the profit objective is to restrict or encourage search as well as to determine the decision. If given the estimates of competitors, demand, and cost, there exists a production level that will provide a profit that is satisfactory, we assume the firm will adopt such

a course. If there is more than one satisfactory alternative, the firm will adopt that quantity level that maximizes profit. Whether even such a restricted maximization procedure is appropriate is a subject for further research.

The Ex-Monopolist. We assume that the monopolist, because of its size, its substantial computational ability, and its established procedures for dealing with a stable rather than a highly unstable environment, will tend to maintain a relatively stable profit objective. We assume that the objective will be the moving average of the realized profit over the last ten time periods. Initially, of course, the monopolist will seek to maintain the profit level achieved during its monopoly.

The Splinter. The splinter firm will presumably be (for reasons indicated earlier) inclined to consider a somewhat shorter period of past experience. We assume that the profit objective of the splinter will be the average of experienced profit over the past five time periods and that the initial profit objective will be linked to the experience of the monopolist and the relative capacities of the two. Thus, we specify that the initial profit objectives of the two firms will be proportional to their initial capacities.

Re-examination of Costs

We assume that when the original forecasts define a satisfactory plan there will be no further examination of them. If, however, such a plan is not obtained, we assume an effort to achieve a satisfactory plan in the first instance by reviewing estimates and finally by revising objectives. We assume that cost estimates are reviewed before demand estimates and that the latter are only re-examined if a satisfactory plan cannot be developed by the revision of the former. The re-evaluation of costs is a search for methods of accomplishing objectives at lower cost than appeared possible under less pressure. We believe this ability to revise estimates when forced to do so is characteristic of organizational decision-making. It is, of course, closely related to the organizational slack concept previously introduced. In general, we have argued that an organization can ordinarily find possible cost reductions if forced to do so and that the amount of the reductions will be a function of the amount of slack in the organization.

It is assumed that the re-examination of costs under the pressure of trying to meet objectives enables each of the organizations to move in the direction of the "real" minimum cost point. For purposes of this model it is assumed that both firms reduce costs 10% of the difference between their estimated average unit costs and the "real" minimum.

Re-examination of Demand

The re-evaluation of demand serves the same function as the re-evaluation of costs above. In the present models it occurs only if the re-evaluation of costs is not adequate to define an acceptable plan. It consists in revising upward the expectations of market demand. The reasoning is that some new alternative is selected which the firm believes will increase its demand. The new approach may be changed

advertising procedure, a scheme to work salesmen harder, or some other alternative which leads the firm to an increase in optimism. In any event, it is felt the more experienced firm will take a slightly less sanguine view of what is possible. As in the case of estimating demand, we assume that all firms persist in seeing a linear demand curve and that no changes are made in the perceived slope of that curve.

The Ex-Monopolist. As a result of the re-examination of demand estimates, it is assumed that this firm revises its estimates of demand upward by 10%.

The Splinter. The assumption here is that the upward revision of demand is 15%.

Re-examination of Objectives

Because our decision rule is one that maximizes among the available alternatives and our rule for specifying objectives depends only on

TABLE 2   Initial and Structural Conditions for Models Exhibited in Table 3

Initial Market Demand (unknown to firms)	$p = 2000 - q$
Initial Perception of Demand Schedule by Ex-Monopolist	$p = 2200 - 3q$
Initial Perception of Demand Schedule by Splinter	$p = 1800 - q$
Ex-Monopolist's Average Unit Cost $\begin{cases} .1q_{MAX,M} < q_M < .9q_{MAX,M} \\ q_M > .9, q_M < .1 \end{cases}$	800 900
Splinter Average Unit Cost $\begin{cases} .1q_{MAX,s} < q_s < .9q_{MAX,s} \\ q_s > .9, q_s < .1 \end{cases}$	760 870
"Real" Minimum Average Unit Cost	700
Ex-Monopolist's Capacity	400
Splinter's Capacity	50
Market Quantity	233
Market Price	1500
Ex-Monopolist's Profit Goal	163,100
Splinter's Profit Goal	20,387
Conjectural Variations ($V'_{m,t}$ and $V'_{s,t}$)	All zero initially
Splinter's over-optimism of demand in forecast phase	5%
% Splinter raises demand forecast upon re-examination	15%
% Ex-Monopolist raises demand forecast upon re-examination	10%
Cost Reduction achieved in M's and S's search for lower costs	10% of costs above "real" minimum average unit cost
% Costs rise attributable to increase in "internal slack"	5%
% Actual Demand schedule shifts to right each time period	8%
Constraint on changing output from that of the last period	$\pm 25\%$
% of capacity at which firm must be producing before it may expand (subject to other conditions)	90%
% change in capacity, when expansion occurs	20%

outcomes, the re-evaluation of objectives does not, in fact, enter into our present models in a way that influences behavior. The procedure can be interpreted as adjusting aspirations to the "best possible under the circumstances." If our decision rule were different or if we made (as we might prefer in future revisions) objectives at one time period a function of both outcomes and previous objectives, the re-evaluation of objectives would become important to the decision process.

Decision

We have specified that the organization will follow traditional economic rules for maximization with respect to its perception of costs, demand, and competitor's behavior. The specific alternatives selected, of course, depend on the point at which this step is invoked (i.e., how many re-evaluation steps are used before an acceptable plan is identified). The output decision is constrained in two ways: (1) A firm cannot produce, in any time period, beyond its present capacity. Both models allow for change

in plant capacity over time. The process by which capacity changes is the same for both firms. If profit goals have been met for two successive periods and production is above 90% of capacity, then capacity increases 20%. (2) A firm cannot change its output from one time period to the next more than ± 25%. The rationale behind the latter assumption is that neither large cutbacks nor large advances in production are possible in the very short run, there being large organization problems connected with either.

The various initial conditions specified above are summarized in Table 2, along with the other initial conditions required to program the models.

RESULTS OF THE DUOPOLY MODEL

We have now described a decision-making model of a large ex-monopolist and a splinter competitor. In order to present some detail of the behavior that is generated by the interacting models, we have reproduced in Table 3 the values of the critical variables on each of the

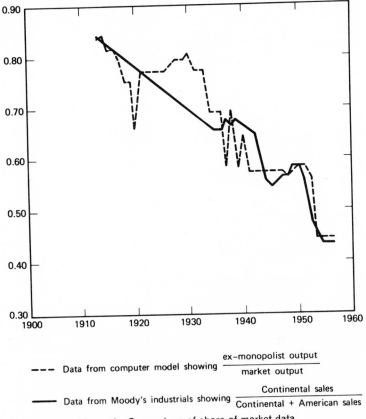

--- Data from computer model showing $\dfrac{\text{ex-monopolist output}}{\text{market output}}$

—— Data from Moody's industrials showing $\dfrac{\text{Continental sales}}{\text{Continental + American sales}}$

Figure 1 Comparison of share of market data.

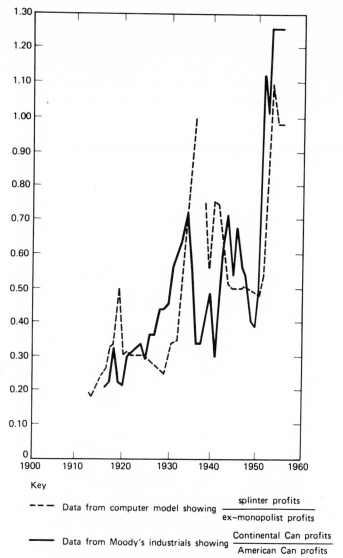

Key

– – – Data from computer model showing $\dfrac{\text{splinter profits}}{\text{ex–monopolist profits}}$

───── Data from Moody's industrials showing $\dfrac{\text{Continental Can profits}}{\text{American Can profits}}$

Figure 2 Comparison of profit-ratio data.

major decision and output factors.[6] By following this chart over time, one can determine the time path of such variables as cost, conjectural variation, and output for both of the firms. More than any one thing, a careful study of this table will give a feeling for the major characteristics of the behavioral theory we have described.

In addition, we have compared the share of market and profit ratio results with actual data generated from the competition between

American Can Company and its splinter competitor, Continental Can Company, over the period from 1913 to 1956. These comparisons are indicated in Figures 1 and 2.[7] In general, we feel that the fit of the behavioral model to the data is rather surprisingly good, although we do not regard this fit as validating the approach.[8]

[6] Market demand was varied in the following way: (1) The slope of the demand curve was held constant. (2) At each time period the intercept, I_t, was set equal to aI_{t-1}. The value of "a" was 1.08 for periods 1–16, .90 for periods 17–20, 1.00 for periods 21–26, and 1.08 for periods 27–43.

[7] One of the parameters in the model is the length of time involved in a single cycle. In comparing the output of the model with the American-Continental data, this parameter was set at 12 months.

[8] It should be clear that the validity of the approach presented in this paper is not conclusively demonstrated by the goodness of fit to the can industry data. We have indicated that under the appropriate assumptions, models of firm decision processes can be specified that yield predictions

It should be noted that the results in period XLV do not necessarily represent an equilibrium position. By allowing the firms to continue to make decisions, changes in output as well as changes in share of market would result. One of the reasons for the expected change is the demand curve is shifting upward. Another, and more interesting reason, is that no changes have been made within the organizations. In particular, the splinter firm by period XLV is a mature firm, but the model has it behaving as a new, young firm. One of our future aims is to build in the effect on organization, and hence on decision-making, of growth and maturity of the organization.

---

approximating some observed results. However, the situation is one in which there are ample degrees of freedom in the specification of parameters to enable a number of time series to be approximated. Although in this case we have reduced the number of free parameters substantially by specifying most of them a priori, the problems of identification faced by any complex model are faced by this one and will have to be solved. The general methodology for testing models that take the form of computer programs remains to be developed.

An examination of Table 3 indicates that the re-examination phase of the decision-making process was not used frequently by either firm. This characteristic is the result of a demand function that is increasing over most of the periods.

Whether this stems also from an inadequacy in the model's description of organizational goal-setting or is a characteristic of the real world of business decision-making is a question that can be answered only by empirical research.

DISCUSSION

One of the primary points that has been stressed here is the importance of the decision-making process for the theory of the firm. The implication of this position is that the decisions studied by conventional theory can be better understood when variables relating to the internal operation of a business firm are added to the theory. Accordingly, we would hope that such a theory would not only lead to improved prediction on the usual questions but would

TABLE 3   Values of Selected Variables at 2-Period Intervals

	I	III	V	VII	IX	XI	XIII	XV
Market								
Price	1,420	1,710	2,196	2,763	3,283	3,927	4,430	4,942
Output	290	311	262	205	209	195	303	466
Ex-Monopolist								
Aspiration Level	163,100	165,671	169,631	176,800	173,221	178,385	203,693	246,746
Conjectual Variations	0	0	.74	−22.4	1.09	.74	.26	.35
Costs (A.U.C.)	826	813	881	944	1,041	1,106	1,219	1,344
Output	240	251	206	153	161	150	233	363
Number of Re-examination Steps	2	0	0	3	0	0	0	0
Competitor								
Aspiration Level	20,387	27,107	31,448	39,763	46,218	39,684	54,245	79,090
Conjectural Variations	0	0	9.2	−1.78	−6.58	8.72	3.39	3.96
Costs (A.U.C.)	760	798	865	954	1,023	1,057	1,166	1,285
Output	50	60	56	52	48	45	70	103
Number of Re-examination Steps	0	0	0	3	3	0	0	0
Profit Ratio								
Competitors Profits ÷ Monopolists Profits	.19	.21	.26	.34	.30	.30	.30	.28
Share of Market								
Competitors Output ÷ Total Output	.17	.19	.21	.25	.23	.23	.23	.2?

TABLE 3 (continued)

	XVII	XIX	XXI	XXIII	XXV	XXVII	XXIX	XXXI
Market								
Price	5,425	3,722	2,785	2,573	2,229	1,719	2,286	2,970
Output	713	914	855	534	360	335	250	140
Ex-Monopolist								
Aspiration Level	319,561	348,006	247,445	182,580	157,664	148,648	154,010	158,120
Conjectural Variations	.28	.30	−.38	.05	.64	−1.07	28.4	−1.40
Costs (A.U.C.)	1,482	1,634	1,801	1,986	2,085	1,710	1,609	1,436
Output	566	703	658	369	207	193	143	80
Number of Re-examination Steps	0	0	0	0	1	3	0	3
Competitor								
Aspiration Level	113,595	121,973	86,083	60,742	37,977	19,272	28,402	37,123
Conjectural Variations	4.76	3.91	6.3	−17.1	2.21	−.32	2.43	50.7
Costs (A.U.C.)	1,417	1,562	1,623	1,790	1,853	1,821	1,608	1,669
Output	147	211	197	165	153	142	107	60
Number of Re-examination Steps	0	0	0	3	0	1	0	0
Profit Ratio								
Competitor's Profit ÷ Monopolist's Profit	.26	.30	.34	.68	.98	.74	.75	.64
Share of Market								
Competitor's Output ÷ Total Output	.21	.23	.23	.31	.43	.42	.43	.43

	XXXIII	XXXV	XXXVII	XXXIX	XLI	XLIII	XLV	
Market								
Price	3,355	3,742	4,099	4,546	5,463	6,730	7,294	
Output	218	340	529	735	777	727	1,126	
Ex-Monopolist								
Aspiration Level	159,060	179,859	203,892	239,045	280,940	260,501	340,745	
Conjectural Variations	.85	.95	.96	.65	3.77	1.91	1.35	
Costs (A.U.C.)	1,363	1,502	1,656	1,826	2,013	2,071	2,283	
Output	125	195	303	432	342	320	500	
Number of Re-examination Steps	0	0	0	0	0	0	0	
Competitor								
Aspiration Level	38,627	53,005	77,001	109,136	164,566	266,512	396,911	
Conjectural Variations	1.32	1.31	1.32	2.3	−.8	3.16	.79	
Costs (A.U.C.)	1,840	2,029	2,237	2,466	2,719	2,771	3,055	
Output	93	145	226	303	435	407	626	
Number of Re-examination Steps	0	0	0	0	0	0	0	0
Profit Ratio								
Competitor's Profit ÷ Monopolist's Profit	.49	.49	.49	.47	.90	.97	.95	
Share of Market								
Competitor's Output ÷ Total Output	.43	.43	.43	.41	.56	.56	.56	

also facilitate the investigation of other important problems, e.g., allocation of resources within the firm.

The theory we have used differs from conventional theory in six important respects: (1) The models are built on a description of the decision-making process. That is, they specify organizations that evaluate competitors, costs, and demand in the light of their own objectives and (if necessary) re-examine each of these to arrive at a decision. (2) The models depend on a theory of search as well as a theory of choice. They specify under what conditions search will be intensified (e.g., when a satisfactory alternative is not available). They also specify the direction in which search is undertaken. In general, we predict that a firm will look first for new alternatives or new information in the area it views as most under its control. Thus, in the present models we have made the specific prediction that cost estimates will be re-examined first, demand estimates second, and organizational objectives third. (3) The models describe organizations in which objectives change over time as a result of experience. Goals are not taken as given initially and fixed thereafter. They change as the organization observes its success (or lack of it) in the market. In these models the profit objective at a given time is an average of achieved profit over a number of past periods. The number of past periods considered by the firm varies from firm to firm. (4) Similarly, the models describe organizations that adjust forecasts on the basis of experience. Organizational learning occurs as a result of observations of actual competitors' behavior, actual market demand, and actual costs. Each of the organizations we have used readjusts its perceptions on the basis of such learning. The learning rules used are quite simple. This is both because simple rules are easier to handle than complex rules and because we expect the true rules to be susceptible to close approximation by simple ones. (5) The models introduce organizational biases in making estimates. For a variety of reasons we expect some organizations to be more conservative with respect to cost estimates than other organizations, some organizations to be more optimistic with respect to demand than others, some organizations to be more attentive

to and perceptive of changes in competitors' plans than others. As we develop more detailed submodels of the estimation process, these factors will be increasingly obvious. In the present models we have not attempted to develop such submodels but have simply predicted the outcome of the estimation process in different firms. (6) The models all introduce features of "organizational slack." That is, we expect that over a period of time during which an organization is achieving its goals a certain amount of the resources of the organization are funneled into the satisfaction of individual and subgroup objectives. This slack then becomes a reservoir of potential economies when satisfactory plans are more difficult to develop.

In order to deal with these revisions, the models have been written explicitly as computer programs. Such treatment has two major values. First, simulation permits the introduction of process variables. The language of the computer is such that many of the phenomena of business behavior that do not fit into classical models can be considered without excessive artificiality. Entering naturally into the model are cost and demand perceptions within the firm in relation to such factors as age of firm, organizational structure, background of executives, and phase of the business cycle; information handling within the firm and its relation to the communication structure, training, and reward system in the organization; and the effects of organizational success and failure on organizational goals and organizational slack.

Secondly, simulation easily generates data on the time path of outputs, prices, etc. For that large class of economic problems in which equilibrium theory is either irrelevant or relatively uninteresting, computer methodology provides a major alternative to the mathematics of comparative statics.

At the same time the models highlight our need for more empirical observations of organizational decision-making. Each of the major steps outlined in the program defines an area for research on business behavior. How do organizations predict the behavior of competitors? How do they estimate demand and costs? What determines organizational planning objectives? In the models we have specified we have introduced empirical assumptions for such things as organizational learning and changes in organizational aspiration levels. We have ignored several factors we consider quite important (e.g., informational biases stemming from variations in the communication structure). In the final development of the model these relationships must be defined from observable characteristics of business organizations.

We see three major directions for further research. First, we would hope that further attempts will be made to compare the results of the models with observable data. In these studies it will be possible to change such variables as have been indicated above and others that appear to be important in the model. Second, we need a great deal of work in actual organizations identifying the decision procedures used in such things as output decisions. Field research on organizations has frequently been extremely time-consuming and costly relative to the results it has produced, but we believe that research focused on the questions raised by the model is both necessary and feasible. Third, there is room for substantial basic research in the laboratory on human decision-making under the conditions found in business organizations. Many of the major propositions in organization theory depend on evidence generated by studies in the laboratory and many of the mechanisms with which we have dealt can be profitably introduced into controlled experiments.

REFERENCES

1 R. M. Alt, 1949. The internal organization of the firm and price formation: an illustrative case. *Quarterly Journal of Economics, 63*(1): 92–110.
2. D. W. Bushaw, and R. W. Clower, 1957. Toward a generalized theory of price determination and a unified theory of price and quantity determination. *Introduction to mathematical economics*; Homewood, Ill.: Irwin, 176–190.
3. E. H. Chamberlin, 1946. Duopoly and oligopoly. *The theory of monopolistic competition*; Cambridge, Mass.: Harvard University Press, fifth edition, 30–55.
4. E. H. Chamberlin, 1946. Selling costs vs. production costs. *The theory of monopolistic competition*; Cambridge, Mass.: Harvard University Press, fifth edition, 117–129.
5. E. H. Chamberlin, 1946. Selling costs and the theory of value: group equilibrium. *The theory of monopolistic competition*; Cambridge, Mass.: Harvard University Press, fifth edition, 149–171.
6. W. W. Cooper, 1951. A proposal for extending the theory of the firm. *Quarterly Journal of Economics, 65*(1): 87–109.
7. R. M. Cyert, and J. G. March, 1955. Organizational structure and pricing behavior in an oligopolistic market. *American Economic Review, 45*(1): 129–139.
8. R. M. Cyert, and J. G. March, 1956. Organizational factors in the theory of oligopoly. *Quarterly Journal of Economics, 70*(1): 44–64.
9. R. M. Cyert, H. A. Simon, and D. B. Trow, 1956. Observation of a business decision. *Journal of Business, 29*(4): 237–248.
10. J. Dean, 1951. Findings of empirical studies on cost. *Managerial economics*; New York: Prentice-Hall, 292–296.
11. M. Friedman, 1953. *Essays in positive economics*. Chicago: University of Chicago Press.
12. R. A. Gordon, 1948. Short-period price determination in theory and practice. *American Economic Review, 38*(3): 265–288.
13. T. C. Koopmans, 1957. Implications of tool developments for future research. *Three essays on the state of economic science*; New York: McGraw-Hill, 208–217.
14. A. G. Papandreou, 1952. Some basic problems in the theory of the firm. *A survey of contemporary economics* (B. F. Haley, ed.); Homewood, Ill.: Irwin, Volume 2, 183–219.
15. H. A. Simon, 1955. A behavioral model of rational choice. *Quarterly Journal of Economics, 69*(1): 99–118.
16. H. A. Simon, 1957. *Models of man*. New York: Wiley.
17. S. Weintraub, 1942. Monopoly equilibrium and anticipated demand. *Journal of Political Economy, 50*(3): 427–434.

12

SIMULATION MODELS OF THE PRISONER'S DILEMMA GAME

R. EDWARD OVERSTREET

INTRODUCTION[1]

The Prisoner's Dilemma is a two-person, non-zero-sum game that has interested social scientists considerably in recent years. A non-zero-sum game is one in which the gain of one of the players is not necessarily the loss of the other; the sum of the two players' payoffs varies as a function of the strategies played. Each player must choose one of two alternatives, C or D, and his decision is made without knowing what the other player will choose. The players do not communicate verbally. A payoff matrix, like Figure 1, determines the payoffs to the players. The players know the payoffs, and have an opportunity to study the matrix before making the choice. The entries in each cell of the matrix are the payoffs to the players; the first amount is the payoff to player 1, the second to player 2. For example, if player 1 chooses C and player 2 chooses D, player 1 receives nothing and player 2 receives 5¢.

In the Prisoner's Dilemma game, the players face the following dilemma. If player 1 chooses C, he will make either 3¢ or nothing, depending on player 2's choice. If player 1 chooses D, however, he will make either 5¢ or 1¢. If player 2 chooses C, player 1 can make 5¢ instead of 3¢ by choosing D. If player 2 chooses D, player 1 can make 1¢ instead of nothing by choosing D. Thus, regardless of what player 2 chooses, player 1 will make more if he chooses D. By the same reasoning, player 2 should choose D. The game looks the same to player 2 as it does to player 1, and regardless of what player 1 chooses, player 2 will make more by choosing D.

Both players will maximize their payoffs by choosing D. D maximizes the minimum possible payoff to a player, and it maximizes the maximum possible payoff to a player. But if both players choose D, they will each receive 1¢, whereas if both players chose C, they would each receive 3¢. That is the dilemma. Choosing C involves risk. If a player chooses C, he takes the chance of receiving nothing when his opponent chooses D. C is a good choice only when the player knows his opponent will also choose C; but when a player knows his opponent will choose C, his own best choice becomes D—which gives him 5¢ instead of 3¢.

		Player 2's choice	
		C	D
Player 1's choice	C	3¢,3¢	0¢,5¢
	D	5¢,0¢	1¢,1¢

Figure 1 Payoff matrix for typical 2×2 Prisoner's Dilemma game.

[1] The author wishes to express gratitude to Dr. Marc Pilisuk for allowing the use of his experimental data and for advice on the construction and testing of several of the models.

For this reason, C is called the "cooperative" strategy, and D is called the "defection" or "noncooperative" strategy.

The Prisoner's Dilemma game can be compared with an arms race between two nations. Both nations are spending large sums of money to arm themselves against each other. It would be better for both countries if they did not arm themselves and used the money for more constructive purposes. However, if one country disarmed while the other remained armed, the disarmed country would be at the other's mercy, and would be worse off than if it had remained armed. In terms of the payoff matrix of the game, making weapons corresponds to choice D; disarming corresponds to choice C; and an arms race corresponds to both players choosing D.

When used as an experimental setting, the Prisoner's Dilemma is usually a multitrial game rather than a one-trial game. The experiment consists of a sequence of trials. Each player makes his choice at the beginning of each trial, without knowing what his opponent will choose. When both choices are recorded, the players are told what their opponents chose, and are told what their payoffs are. The game is then repeated exactly as before. After ten to twenty such repetitions, the players usually "lock in," or adopt regular patterns of behavior like con-

tinually choosing C or continually choosing D.

Another modification of the game is the use of more than two choice alternatives. For example, the subjects may be offered six alternatives, ranging from complete cooperation to complete defection, so that they can choose degrees of cooperation or noncooperation, instead of having to make an all-or-nothing choice. A payoff matrix from a game of this kind is presented in Figure 2. Multiple choice games are used in the experiments and simulations presented below.

STUDIES OF THE PRISONER'S DILEMMA

The Prisoner's Dilemma has been investigated both theoretically and experimentally. Luce and Raiffa [4] devoted a chapter to the Prisoner's Dilemma. Rapoport and Chammah [9] thoroughly discussed the game and presented a number of theoretical models of subject behavior, including stochastic learning models, Markov chain models, and various dynamic models. Computer simulation plays a fairly important part in the theoretical work. For instance, Rapoport and Chammah simulated various models and used these simulations to study model implications. Different values of the models' parameters were used to generate

		Partner's choice					
		0	1	2	3	4	5
Subject's choice	0	5,5	3,6	1,7	$-1,8$	$-3,9$	$-5,10$
	1	6,3	4,4	2,5	0,6	$-2,7$	$-4,8$
	2	7,1	5,2	3,3	1,4	$-1,5$	$+3,6$
	3	8,-1	6,0	4,1	2,2	0,3	$-2,4$
	4	9,-3	7,-2	5,-1	3,0	1,1	$-1,2$
	5	10,-5	8,-4	6,-3	4,-2	2,-1	0,0

Figure 2 Payoff matrix for experiments 6P and 6NP. Choice of zero is total cooperation; choice of 5 is total defection. Entries are read as follows: 1st entry is payoff to subject, 2nd to his partner.

artificial choice sequences similar to those obtained in experiments with human subjects.

An extensive literature exists on experimental work. Rapoport and Orwant [10] reviewed the early experimental work on the Prisoner's Dilemma and other games. Recent studies have examined the effects of such variables as: sex of the players; false feedback from the "other player"; asking subjects to predict what their opponents will choose on the next trial; and requiring that subjects make their choices *gradually* in steps, rather than all at once, and allowing them to observe what their partners are doing at a specific point in the decision process [1, 6, 8, 9].

Simulation models are frequently employed to generate artificial data, in order that the properties of the models may be examined. The comparison of model predictions for individual subjects with the actual experimental choices by these subjects, however, is apparently never done. In simulation studies, the accepted practice seems to be to generate artificial data, to compute some descriptive statistic from it—

such as the mean rate of cooperation across subjects—and to compare this statistic with one obtained from an experiment with many human subjects [2]. Such a process does not simulate individual behavior but simulates a population of individuals, which is an entirely different thing. No published study has attempted to simulate the behavior of individual subjects rather than group statistics.

This paper tests simulations, based on individual inputs for each subject, which generate *individual* predictions for individual subjects on a trial-by-trial basis.

SEVEN MODELS

Seven simulation models of individuals playing the Prisoner's Dilemma game will be tested against the behavior of actual experimental subjects. The models fall into two general types: (1) simulation models that were derived mostly from theoretical analyses, without recourse to experimental data; and (2) simulation models derived solely from examination

Notation:

$S(n)$—subject's choice on trial n
$P(n)$—partner's choice on trial n
$SP(n)$—subject's payoff on trial n
$PP(n)$—partner's payoff on trial n
GT—greater than
GE—greater than or equal to
LT—less than
LE—less than or equal to
$=$—equal to

Terminology:

Gesture—	$S(n\text{-}1)$ is a gesture if: $S(n\text{-}1)\ LT\ S(n\text{-}2)$
	and $S(n\text{-}1)\ LE\ P(n\text{-}2)-5$
Stab—	$S(n\text{-}1)$ is a stab if: $S(n\text{-}1)\ GT\ S(n\text{-}2)$
	and $S(n\text{-}1)\ GE\ P(n\text{-}2)+5$
Response—	$S(n\text{-}1)$ is a response if: $S(n\text{-}1)\ LE\ P(n\text{-}2)$
	and $S(n\text{-}2)\ GT\ P(n\text{-}2)$
Retaliation—	$S(n\text{-}1)$ is a retaliation if: $S(n\text{-}1)\ GE\ P(n\text{-}2)$
	and $S(n\text{-}2)\ LT\ P(n\text{-}2)$
Compet lockin—	trial n is a compet lockin if $S(n) = P(n) = 20$
Coop lockin—	trial n is a coop lockin if $S(n) = P(n) = 0$

This version of Grip is for the 21-choice game. Several of the contingencies have been combined here when they yield the same predictions, for economy of presentation. Also, a few contingencies have been excluded due to a lack of any data in Experiment *6NP* to confirm or disconfirm their predictions.

Figure 3 Main flow chart for Grip.

of experimental data. The *Grip* model is an example of the latter; the *New-Math* model is a combination of the two types; and the other five models are theoretical in origin.

1. Grip

Grip is a contingency model constructed by a hand examination of raw data.[2] Among the models reported here, it alone was developed exclusively using the techniques of computer simulation.

Small samples of raw data were examined in an attempt to discover regularities in subject behavior. Data were taken from a subset of the subjects who participated in the 21-choice experiment described below. Seven broad categories were established to describe the nature of the interaction between players during trial $n-1$. Data falling within each category were examined to see if the behavior that occurred on trial n could be predicted with any regularity. For this purpose, it was often necessary to establish subcategories within the seven main categories. The process yielded a flow chart containing 68 different categories, or contingencies. Ten important contingency categories are shown in Figure 3.

IF $P(n\text{-}1) = 0$ go to 100
IF $S(n\text{-}1) = 0$ go to 300
IF $S(n\text{-}1)$ was a gesture   go to 400
IF $P(n\text{-}1)$ was a gesture   go to 6
IF $S(n\text{-}1)$ was a stab   go to 900
IF $P(n\text{-}1)$ was a stab   go to 1000
IF $S(n\text{-}1)$ was a response or retaliation   go to 1500
IF $P(n\text{-}1)$ was a response or retaliation   go to 1400
IF $SP(n\text{-}1)\ LT\ 0$ go to 1300
IF $PP(n\text{-}1)\ LT\ 0$ $S(n) = S(n\text{-}1) - 2$
go to 1100

Figure 3a The main choice points of the model. See Figure 3b for the remainder of the model.

2. Naive

The Naive model is the simplest one; it predicts that the choices on the next trial will be the same as they were on the last. It has been observed in many areas of science, for instance in meteorology, that such a model frequently yields accurate short-term predictions, so this Naive model was included as a check on the accuracy of the other models.

[2] A more complete discussion of the Grip model and its properties is available in an unpublished manuscript, "Simulation Models of Sequential Choices in the Prisoner's Dilemma," by R. Edward Overstreet and Marc Pilisuk [5]. The paper reported the results of the testing of the Grip Choice, Probability, Naive, and Chance models, with data from the 21-choice game, and it concluded that for 5 of the contingencies of the Grip model, Grip predicted significantly better than all the other models. However, the present study indicated, when the 6-choice-game, nonprediction data were examined, that Grip did not predict significantly better than any other model except Chance, in these 5 contingencies. Hence, the conclusions that were reached in the earlier paper were not replicated, and must be regarded with circumspection.

3. Probability

The Probability model is a multiple-choice modification of a linear learning model developed for the two-choice game by Herniter, Williams, and Wolpert [2]. It assumes that subjects will choose alternatives for which they have been rewarded, and they will avoid alternatives that have lost them money. The model consists of two equations:

$$P_{i,n} = P_{i,n-1}(1 - K_{i,n-1}) \tag{1}$$

$$P_{i,n} = P_{i,n-1} + K_{i,n-1}(1 - P_{i,n-1}) \tag{2}$$

$P_{i,n}$ = the probability of defection by
  subject i on trial n.

$K_{i,n} = \pi_{i,n}/\alpha$

$\pi_{i,n}$ = the absolute value of subject i's
  payoff on trial n.

α = a constant reflecting the importance
  assigned by the subjects to
  monetary payoffs.

α is positive and greater than the maximum absolute value in the payoff matrix, so $K_{i,n}$ is

100   IF $S(n\text{-}1) = 0$ go to 101

            Go to 200

101   IF $S(n\text{-}1)$ was a stab   go to 131

            $S(n) = 0$

131   IF $n\,LE\,10$ $S(n) = 0$

            IF trials $n\text{-}1$, $n\text{-}2$, or $n\text{-}3$ were coop lockins,

                    $S(n)$ is stochastic, $S(n) = 0$, probability 2/3

                                   $S(n) = 20$, probability 1/3

            IF trials $n\text{-}1$, $n\text{-}2$, $n\text{-}3$, and $n\text{-}4$ were all coop lockins, $S(n) = 20$

            $S(n) = 0$

200   IF $S(n\text{-}2) = 20$ go to 220

            IF $S(n\text{-}2) = 0$ go to 230

            IF $S(n\text{-}1) = 20$ $S(n) = 15$

            $S(n) = S(n\text{-}1) - 2$

220   IF $P(n\text{-}2) = 20$ go to 221

            $S(n) = S(n\text{-}1) - 3$

221   IF $S(n\text{-}1) = 20$ $S(n) = 20$

            $S(n) = S(n\text{-}1)$

230   IF $P(n\text{-}2)$ was stab, $S(n) = P(n\text{-}1)$

            $S(n) = 0$

300   IF $S(1) = 0$ and $n\,LE\,10$ go to 310

3002   IF $n = 3$ go to 303

303   IF $n\text{-}2$ or $n\text{-}3$ was a coop lockin go to 340

            If there have been two or more consecutive compet-lockin trials, go to 350

3001   IF $n = 3$ go to 370

            IF $P(n\text{-}1)\,GT\,P(n\text{-}2)\,GT\,P(n\text{-}3)$ $S(n) = 0$

            Go to 370

310   IF $n = 2$ or $n = 3$ $S(n) = 0$

            IF $n\,GT\,10$ go to 3002

            $S(n) = P(n\text{-}1) - 5$

320   IF $P(n\text{-}1)\,GE\,5$ and $n\text{-}2$ was a coop lockin   go to 370

            IF $P(n\text{-}2)\,GE\,5$ or $S(n\text{-}2)\,GE\,5$, and $n\text{-}3$ was a coop lockin   go to 370

            $S(n) = 0$

340   IF $S(n\text{-}2) = 20$ $S(n) = 20$

            $S(n) = 0$

350   IF $P(n\text{-}1) = 20$ $S(n) = 20$

            Go to 3001

370   IF $P(n\text{-}1)\,LT\,5$ $S(n) = 1$

            IF P has stabbed S in the past and S did not retaliate following the stab, $S(n) = 20$

            IF $S(n\text{-}1) = S(n\text{-}2) = S(n\text{-}3) = 0$ $S(n) = 20$

            $S(n) = 0$

400   IF $P(n\text{-}1)$ was a response or a retaliation   go to 410

            IF $P(n\text{-}1) = 20$ $S(n) = 20$

            IF $P(n\text{-}1)$ was a gesture $S(n) = S(n\text{-}1) - 2$

            $S(n) = P(n\text{-}1)$

410   IF $S(n\text{-}1) = P(n\text{-}1)$ go to 411

            IF $P(n\text{-}1) - S(n\text{-}1)\,LE\,5$ $S(n) = S(n\text{-}1) - 1$

            $S(n) = P(n\text{-}1)$

411   IF $P(n\text{-}2)\,GT\,P(n\text{-}1)$ $S(n) = S(n\text{-}1) - 5$

            $S(n) = S(n\text{-}1)$

6   IF $S(n\text{-}1)$ was a stab $S(n) = S(n\text{-}1) - 1$

            Go to 700

Figure 3b continues

700   IF $S(n\text{-}1)$ was a retaliation   go to 710
       $S(n) = S(n\text{-}1)$
  710 IF $S(n\text{-}1) = 20$ $S(n) = 20$
       IF $P(n\text{-}1) = P(n\text{-}3) = P(n\text{-}5)$ and $P(n\text{-}2)\ GT\ P(n\text{-}3)$ and $P(n\text{-}2)\ GT\ P(n\text{-}1)$ $S(n) = S(n\text{-}1)$
       $S(n) = S(n\text{-}1) - 2$
900   IF $P(n\text{-}1)$ was a stab $S(n) = S(n\text{-}1)$
       IF $P(n\text{-}2) = 0$ and $S(n\text{-}1)\ GE\ 10$ $S(n) = S(n\text{-}1)$
       $S(n) = S(n\text{-}1) - 2$
1000   IF $P(n\text{-}1) - S(n\text{-}1)\ LT\ 10$ $S(n) = S(n\text{-}1)$
       $S(n) = 20$
1500   IF $P(n\text{-}2) = S(n\text{-}1)$ $S(n) = S(n\text{-}1)$
       IF $S(n\text{-}1)$ was a retaliation $S(n) = S(n\text{-}1)$
       IF $SP(n\text{-}1)\ LT\ 0$ $S(n) = P(n\text{-}1)$
       IF $P(n\text{-}2) = P(n\text{-}1)$ $S(n) = S(n\text{-}1)$
       $S(n) = P(n\text{-}1) - 1$
1400   IF $P(n\text{-}2) - S(n\text{-}1)$ $S(n) = S(n\text{-}1)$
       IF $P(n\text{-}1)$ was a retaliation   go to 1410
       $S(n) = S(n\text{-}1) - 1$
  1410 IF $SP(n\text{-}1)\ LT\ 0$ $S(n) = P(n\text{-}1)$
       $S(n) = S(n\text{-}1)$
1300   IF $P(n\text{-}1) = 20$ and $n\text{-}2$ was a compet lockin, as well as $n\text{-}3$, $n\text{-}4$, and $n\text{-}5$, $S(n) = S(n\text{-}1) + 1$
       $S(n) = P(n\text{-}1)$
1100   IF $n\text{-}1$ was compet lockin   go to 1110
       IF $P(n\text{-}1) = S(n\text{-}1) \neq 20$ go to 1120
  1121 IF $P(n\text{-}1)\ GT\ S(n\text{-}1)$ and $P(n\text{-}2)\ GT\ S(n\text{-}2)$

$$\text{OR } S(n\text{-}1)\ GT\ P(n\text{-}1) \text{ and } S(n\text{-}2)\ GT\ P(n\text{-}2)\quad S(n) = \frac{S(n\text{-}1) + P(n\text{-}1)}{2}$$

       $S(n) = S(n\text{-}1)$
  1110 IF $P(j) = 20$ for $j = n\text{-}1, \ldots, n\text{-}k$, and $n\text{-}1$ was a compet lockin, $S(n) = 20$
       IF $n\text{-}1$, $n\text{-}2$, and $n\text{-}3$ were compet lockins, go to 1112
       $S(n) = 20$
  1112 $S(n)$ is a stochastic variable, with the following values:

$S(n)$	Probability
20	.88
19	.05
18	.01
17	.01
16	.01
15	.01
10	.02
0	.01

  1120 IF $n = 3$ go to 1121
       IF $S(n\text{-}1)\ LT\ S(n\text{-}2)$ OR $P(n\text{-}1)\ LT\ P(n\text{-}2)$ *and* $S(n\text{-}2)\ LT\ S(n\text{-}3)$ $S(n) = S(n\text{-}1) - 1$
       IF $S(n\text{-}1)\ LT\ S(n\text{-}2)$ OR $P(n\text{-}1)\ LT\ P(n\text{-}2)$ $S(n) = S(n\text{-}1)$
       Go to 1121

Figure 3b   Secondary choice points.

between zero and one. Equation 2 is used if both subjects had positive payoffs, if both had negative payoffs, or if both had zero payoffs on trial $n-1$. Equation 1 is used if one subject had a positive payoff and one had a negative payoff.

The model is generalized to games with more than two alternatives by (a) identifying the alternatives numerically, using zero for complete cooperation and L for complete defection, and then (b) choosing the alternative $LP_{i,n}$, the product being rounded to the nearest integer. Thus, alternative zero is chosen when $P_{i,n}$ is near zero; alternative one is chosen when $P_{i,n}$ is near $1/L$; alternative two when $P_{i,n}$ is near $2/L$; and alternative L when $P_{i,n}$ is near one.

The Probability model is initialized by choosing values for $P_{i,1}$ and α. Tests against experimental data suggested that the best values for these parameters were $P_{i,1} = 1$ and $\alpha = 120\%$ of the maximum payoff, so these values were used in the tests below.

4. Choice

The Choice model is a refinement of the Probability model. The Probability model can, with the next-trial-prediction test, correct its errors only partially. For example, if the Probability model predicts that a subject will completely cooperate on trial n, and he actually defected on trial n, then the model corrects for this error only partially in predicting trial $n+1$. It uses the actual payoffs on trial n. But $P_{i,n}$ is given by the equations of the model, and not by the fact that the subject defected—which implies that $P_{i,n}$ is close to one. The other models make complete correction of their errors, because they utilize only actual data from trial $n-1$ and do not rely on computations of the model for any input data. The Probability model is thus at a disadvantage compared to these other models.

The Choice model is an attempt to reduce the sensitivity of the Probability model to error perpetuation. Since the choice alternatives are numbered from zero to L, $P_{i,n}$ can be estimated from the subject's actual choice on trial $n-1$, instead of being carried forward from the previous prediction. In particular, the Choice model uses Equations 1 and 2 with

$$P_{i,n-1} = \frac{X_{n-1}}{L}$$

where X_{n-1} is the number of the alternative actually chosen on trial $n-1$. In all other respects, the Choice and Probability models are identical.

5. Old Math

This model is the classical game-theoretic model which assumes that the subject will choose the alternative that maximizes his expected payoff. The two parameters of the model are: (1) how the subject estimates his expected payoff, and (2) how far into the future he looks in considering his expected payoff—does he maximize his expected payoff for the next trial or its sum over the next ten trials?

Since the subject's payoff is a function of both his own choice and of that of his opponent, before the subject can estimate his expected payoff, he must have some hypothesis about what his opponent will do on the next trial. The Old-Math model assumes that this hypothesis specifies a single alternative: "I think my opponent will choose alternative three on the next trial." It is not assumed that the subject is sophisticated enough to form some sort of expected probability distribution over the entire set of alternatives open to his opponent. The subject assigns the entire mass of his probability function to one alternative. This assumption is made for simplicity, and could, of course, be relaxed.

The problem for the simulation becomes: How does the subject arrive at his estimate of what his opponent will do? As will be shown, there are data on what subjects expect their opponents to choose, although there is no perfect explanation for these expectations. The Old-Math model is tested using two different assumptions about the prediction process. One assumption is that $P_{j,n} = P_{j,n-1}$ where j indicates the opponent (the Naive model). The other assumption is that $P_{j,n}$ is predicted by the Choice model.

The second issue in the model is how far-sighted the subject is when computing his expected payoff. In the Prisoner's Dilemma, it is always to the subject's advantage to choose total defection regardless of what he thinks his opponent will choose, provided that he is interested only in his payoff on trial n. Furthermore, if he assumes that $P_{j,n-1} = P_{j,n} = P_{j,n+1} = \cdots = P_{j,n+k}$, even if the subject "looks" k trials into the future in computing his expected payoff, it is still to the subject's advantage to choose total defection. The subject is assuming that his opponent will continue to choose the same alternative no matter what. However, if the subject assumes $P_{j,n}$ is determined by a nonconstant relation like Equations 1 and 2, he will expect his opponent to retaliate on trial $n+1$ against a total defection on trial n, and it is not necessarily to his advantage to choose total defection. Thus, unless subject i estimates his opponent's choice $P_{j,n} = P_{j,n-1}$, it may make a difference whether he is interested only in his payoff on trial n or in his *total* payoff over the next k trials. The Old-Math model is tested accordingly, varying k from 1 to 15.

When k is greater than one, the Old-Math model assumes that the subject predicts his opponent's reactions to the choices on trial n, and predicts his own reactions to his opponent's reactions. The model assumes that the subject predicts his own reactions in the same fashion as he predicts his partner's reactions. Thus, the Old-Math model represents a subject who himself predicts his own *and* his opponent's future behavior in order to determine his best choice for trial n. It is not suggested that subjects actually go through this process consciously, but that subjects act approximately in this manner, or as if they were doing this.

6. New Math

When the expected payoff is computed only for the next trial, expected payoff maximization always leads to complete defection. However, subjects typically do not choose total defection on every trial. This suggests they are not maximizing their expected payoffs on the next trial. They could be estimating expected payoffs over k trials, a hypothesis tested by the Old-Math model. Or they could be maximizing not at all, a hypothesis partially tested by the other models. Or they could be maximizing something other than expected payoffs. The New-Math model is one realization of a theory in which the subject maximizes something other than his own monetary payoff. It is conceived that subjects are concerned with maximizing

not only their own payoffs, but also the joint payoff to the *pair*. That is, it may be that subjects are somewhat altruistic and want to maximize some joint function of their own payoffs and those of their opponents. This goal seems especially plausible when both subjects in a pair have not been "hurt" by profits at one another's expense, permitting a mutual interest to develop in the welfare of the pair as a whole.

Assume that a subject is concerned with maximizing a function

$$\Phi = (1-a)\pi_1 + a(\pi_1 + \pi_2)$$

where: $0 \leqslant a \leqslant 1$; π_1 is the subject's own payoff; and π_2 is his opponent's payoff. Φ is a weighted sum of the subject's payoff and the pair's payoff, and it can also be written $\Phi = \pi_1 + a\pi_2$. When a is zero, the subject is interested only in his own payoff, and when a is unity, he is interested only in the joint payoff to the pair. He never values payoff to his opponent more highly than payoff to himself‘ and he never places a positive valuation on his opponent's losses.

The model further assumes that a is a function of the previous interaction between the subjects. There are infinite different functions that might relate a to previous experiences, but the New-Math model assumes:

$$a_n = K_{i,n} + (1 - K_{i,n}) a_{n-1} \qquad (3)$$

$$a_n = (1 - K_{i,n}) a_{n-1} \qquad (4)$$

where $K_{i,n}$ has the same meaning as in Equations 1 and 2. Equation 4 is used after one subject received a positive payoff and the other subject received a negative payoff, and Equation 3 is employed otherwise. Thus, when both subjects are more or less "in the same boat"—both making money or both losing it—their altruism increases with $\pi_{i,n}$. When one subject is making money and the other is losing it, both subjects become less altruistic.

As with the Old-Math model, two additional parameters must be specified: (1) how the subject predicts what his opponent will do, and (2) how far into the future the subject looks to calculate his (and his opponent's) expected payoff. These two parameters are treated in the New-Math model exactly as they are treated in the Old-Math model.

7. Chance

The final model serves as a null criterion against which to compare the other models. It assumes that subjects choose among alternatives completely at random and with each alternative being equally likely.

METHODS OF TESTING

The seven models were programmed for a computer, and the models' choices were compared to the choices of subjects from three experiments. The three experiments are described in Table 1. Three kinds of tests were applied, but only one of these tests will be used to report results here, for reasons outlined below.

One approach to simulation testing is to give the model the subject's actual behavior during the first two or three trials, and then to ask the model to generate a prediction for the rest of the trial sequence. Since errors made in the prediction of trial $n-1$ are not corrected before a prediction is made for trial n, the technique might be called "long-run prediction." Two measures of "long-run prediction" accuracy were used in this study. First, the mean choice over all subjects and trials was computed and compared with the experimental mean. Second, the predicted choices over the final five trials were compared with the actual choices made.

However, there are serious problems with "long-run prediction," which render both tests unsatisfactory. The first problem is perpetuation and multiplication of errors. If the simulation model makes an error in the early or middle part of the sequence, it will use this error as input data for generating the rest of the sequence. Since the seven models presented here predict trial n from trial $n-1$, a small error early in the prediction sequence can produce large errors in the final results. Clearly, this is both a harsh and an inaccurate test of a model. The second problem may be specific to the data used in this research. The subjects' choices on trial k were correlated with those on trial j for all j and k. The resulting correlation matrix demonstrated that the choices on the first two trials were not significantly correlated with choices on any other trials, whereas choices on *all other* trials were significantly intercorrelated. This result casts doubt on the meaning or significance of results obtained by simulation when only the first two trials are taken as input.

In spite of these problems, the two "long-run prediction" measures were computed for each of the three experiments and for each of the seven models, and the models were rank ordered for accuracy—six rank orders. Accuracy measures were also computed for the "next-trial prediction" method (which will be described below), yielding three more rank orderings of the models. The nine rank orderings

TABLE 1   Data

Experiment	21	6NP	6P
Sources [6, 7]	Pilisuk, Potter, Rapaport, and Winter	Pilisuk and Skolnick	Pilisuk and Skolnick
Number of choice alternatives	21	6	6
Number of pairs of subjects	64 Male	24 Male 24 Female	24 Male 24 Female
Number of trials played by each pair	55	25	25
Did subject's report the choices they expected their opponents to make on the next trial?	No	No	Yes

TABLE 2 Significant Differences in the Accuracy Figures

Comparing an accuracy figure from experiment A with one from experiment B,		the difference must be at least Δ to be significant at the 95% level
Experiment A	Experiment B	Δ
21	21	2.34%
6NP or 6P	6NP or 6P	5.78%
6NP or 6P	21	4.42%

were compared by Kendall's coefficient of concordance, and the result ($W = .784, p < .001$) indicated that the rankings were highly intercorrelated. The two rank orderings from the "long-run prediction" tests were summed, and the rank orders of the sums were identical with the rank orders from the "next-trial prediction" method—identical for each of the three experiments. Thus, there is little to be lost by ignoring the "long-run prediction" tests, and only the

"next-trial prediction" test will be considered hereafter.

The "next-trial prediction" method operates as follows: The computer is given the actual choices on trial $n-1$ and the predictions of the opponent's behavior, where appropriate and available. This information is used to predict the choice on trial n according to each of the models, and the prediction is compared with the actual choice on trial n. The error is recorded as a tally in an error distribution. For example, a prediction that is three points too high is tallied in the $+3$ interval of the distribution. The computer then "forgets" its prediction for trial n, retaining only the error measurement, and uses the actual choices and predictions during trial n to generate predictions for trial $n+1$. This process is carried out for all trials in the sequence except for the first two. As a result, 6784 predictions were generated for experiment 21 and 1104 predictions were generated for experiments 6NP and 6P each, and the resulting error distributions were printed out.

Ideally, the three error distributions would be Normal, have means near zero, and have small standard deviations. The actual distributions are not Normal, however. For all models except

TABLE 3 Accuracy Figures. Not-significant differences indicated by brackets

Experiment 21		Experiment 6NP		Experiment 6P	
Model	Accuracy %	Model	Accuracy %	Model	Accuracy %
Grip	86.3	Naive	87.6	Grip	Not tested
Naive	84.5	Grip	83.9	Naive	79.8
Choice	84.3	Choice	83.0	Choice	77.2
New-Math[a]	78.7	New-Math[a]	80.9	New-Math[a]	71.2
Probability	78.2	Probability	74.4	Probability	69.8
Old-Math	47.5	Old-Math	53.2	Old-Math[b]	65.7
Chance	22.0	Chance	27.2	Chance	25.1

[a] Figures for New-Math model were obtained by assuming that subjects use the Choice model to predict their opponents' behavior. If the Naive model is used instead, the accuracy of New-Math increases somewhat (see Table 5).

[b] Old-Math is a considerably more accurate predictor in 6P than in either 21 or 6NP. The reason for this is that Old-Math accurately predicts total defection, and subjects in 6P chose total defection more frequently than did the subjects in 21 and 6NP.

TABLE 4   Accuracy Figures for Differing Values of a and k in the New-Math Models. Data from experiment *6NP* are used, so accuracy differences greater than 5.78% are significant

	$k = 1$	$k = 2$	$k = 5$	$k = 10$	$k = 15$	$k =$ to end of sequence
New-Math with $a =$ .00	80.9	78.8	74.4	74.3	74.6	71.8
$a =$ .08	81.0					
$a =$ .16	81.0					
$a =$ .25	78.6	78.2	74.2	73.5	74.3	71.3
$a =$ .50	65.4	66.1	66.7	68.2	68.9	65.5
$a =$ .75	57.7	56.5	55.4	57.4	56.9	53.2
$a = 1.00$	52.6	52.7	52.0	52.0	52.1	49.3
Old-Math	53.2	54.3	49.8	49.8	49.8	48.7

the Chance model, the error distributions exhibit marked kurtosis in containing abnormally large amounts of data at the tails of the distributions. Accordingly Normal distribution statistics are not employed in this paper, and nonparametric techniques are used instead. The *accuracy figure* for each model is defined as the proportion of data occurring within the intervals 0 ± 1 for the *6NP* and *6P* experiments and 0 ± 4 for experiment *21*. For the Grip, New-Math, Naive, and Choice models, most of the distributions had modes at zero, and the accuracy figures were between 70% and 80%. If the distributions were Normal, this would correspond to distributions with means of zero and with standard deviations of about 5% of the scale length. Thus, these four might be classified as "good" models.

Differences between accuracy figures are distributed according to the Kolmogorov-Smirnoff two-sample test. Differences significant at the 95% level are given in Table 2.

RESULTS

The accuracy figures for the seven models, tested on all three experiments, are given in Table 3.

The Chance model is significantly less accurate than all others; and of the remaining models, the Old-Math model is significantly worse than the others. The best models are Grip, Choice, and Naive. The New-Math and Probability models are of intermediate accuracy, with the New-Math model being significantly more accurate than the Probability model only in the *6NP* experiment.

Of special interest are some findings regarding the New-Math and Old-Math models. Table 4 shows that both models predict best under the assumption that subjects only consider their expected payoffs one trial into the future. Further, for the New-Math model, the optimal initial level of a is between 0 and .25, indicating that there is little initial inclination toward altruism. The New-Math model predicts significantly better than the Old-Math model for nearly all values of a and k; the Old-Math model is slightly better when $a = 1$ and $k = 1$ or 2. Table 5 shows that the New-Math model is most accurate when α, from Equations 3 and 4, is 120% of the largest payoff in the matrix. A similar result was obtained for the α from Equations 1 and 2, using the Probability and Choice models. Table 5 also shows that the Naive model produces higher accuracy than the

TABLE 5   Accuracy Figures for Differing Values of α and for Four Predictions of Opponent's Reaction in the Old-Math and New-Math Models. $k=1$; data from 6NP[a]

		Model Used to Predict Opponent's Next Choice		
	Choice	Naive	Average of Last Five Trials	Average of Last Three Trials
New-Math with				
$\alpha = 1.2$	80.9	82.4	—	—
$\alpha = 2.4$	76.8	76.5	76.6	76.6
$\alpha = 3.6$	75.2	76.2	73.6	73.6
$\alpha = 4.8$	71.1	73.4	70.2	69.9
$\alpha = 6.0$	67.5	70.3	66.6	66.5
$\alpha = 7.2$	64.0	66.7	63.2	63.6
Old-Math	53.2	53.2	53.2	53.2

[a] The maximum possible payoff in 6NP was 10. Since the maximum possible payoff in 21 was 40, α was taken to be 50 in the experiment 21 calculations and to be 12 in the experiment 6NP and 6P calculations.

Choice model or than two averaging predictors; however, none of these differences across models is statistically significant.

Experiment 6P obtained the subject's predictions of their opponent's next choices. When these actual predictions were substituted for hypothetical predictions in the New-Math model, accuracy increased by an insignificant amount from 71.2 to 73.2.[3] The actual predictions were compared with three hypothetical prediction rules. The significantly higher accuracy of the Naive model, as shown in Table 6,

TABLE 6   Accuracy Figures for Subjects' Predictions of their Opponents' Next Choices

Model	Accuracy %
Naive	83.5
Choice	74.3
Average of the Last Five Choices	71.0

implies that subjects entertain very simple notions about how their opponents will react

[3] The above accuracy figures are based on data from experiment 6P, and the calculation assumed $\alpha = 12$ and $k=1$.

to the previous trial. This result also brings into serious question the findings of Table 4, regarding how far into the future subjects look under the New-Math model. If subjects assume that their opponents will not change their behavior at all, making this assumption for trials beyond trial $n+1$, then it would make no difference whether a subject looks one trial into the future or 15 trials into the future.

Finally, the New-Math model predicts male behavior in experiment 6P significantly more accurately than female behavior, 75.9% to 69.7%. The Old-Math model predicts the behavior of both sexes with equal accuracy. The Choice model predicts males better than females, though not significantly so.

DISCUSSION

Two main points develop from the results reported in this paper. The first point is that the New-Math model is clearly superior to the Old-Math model in predicting subject behavior; the New-Math model was significantly better at the 95% level on all measures. It has long been known that a model of expected payoff maximization does not adequately explain subject behavior in the Prisoner's Dilemma, given that subjects maximize only the payoff on the next trial. Table 4 shows that the Old-Math model is inadequate even assuming that subjects calculate their payoffs far into the future.

The New-Math model maximizes Φ, and Φ can be interpreted as a utility function involving an externality. Much of the previous work in game theory assumed that expected utility was independent of the expected payoff to the other subject. If this assumption is replaced with one in which the utility function involves the payoff to the opponent, the maximization principle and other findings of classical game theory may not be as inapplicable to the Prisoner's Dilemma and other nonzero-sum games as had been thought. The New-Math model is really only a modification of expected payoff maximization, so it is applicable to many games, including n-person games and games with side payments. Other models presented in this paper may not possess this generality. It is difficult, for example, to see how the Grip model could be applied with much success to an n-person game with side payments. This generality gives the New-Math model more value than might be assigned on the basis of the accuracy figures in Table 3.

The second point is that the four best models —Naive, Grip, Choice, and New Math—are so similar in their accuracy that one cannot state that one model is the "best" model of subject behavior. The researcher can never prove the optimality of one model to the exclusion of all other possible models. In this instance, however, one cannot even prove the optimality of *any* of the seven models to the exclusion of the other six.

The failure of Grip, Choice, and New Math to perform better than Naive is disturbing. Naive is clearly an unacceptable model, since it implies that subjects will never change their behavior—which is simply not true. The failure of the other models to predict better than Naive may indicate that the others are simply not very good models.

One possible source of the difficulty may be that all the models predict that the subject will choose a certain alternative, with a probability of *one*. Better accuracy should be obtained with Choice and New Math if their predictions were made in the form of *probability distributions* over the entire set of alternatives, with the probability distributed over more than one

alternative. If Choice and New Math were so modified, their accuracy might become significantly better than the accuracy of Naive, which necessarily assigns the entire probability mass to one alternative. For a further discussion of models that use probabilistic, instead of algebraic, predictions, see Luce [3].

It may be that another measure of simulation model behavior would produce more consistent differences between the models. Although expecting a model to project behavior over a long period of time, without error correction, is a heavy burden, one might employ a test method in which the model simulated five trials into the future. After five trials, the prediction would be compared with the actual data; the error would be corrected; and a new prediction would begin. But the author expects that the accuracy figures for all models would decrease with this method in comparison to results from the "next-trial prediction" method, and that differences between the four best models would still not be significant. These expectations arise because the five-trial technique is a mixture of the "next-trial prediction" and "long-run prediction" methods. The latter method yielded less accurate predictions than the former, and was unable to produce any significant differences between the four best models.

Only two other alternatives are apparent. One might examine the models to see if they generate mutually exclusive predictions for certain circumstances in the Prisoner's Dilemma. Attempts by the author to find such circumstances have thus far failed. The other alternative is to apply the various models to n-person games, to zero-sum games, to games with side payments, to infinite games, and so on, and then to proclaim "best" that model which accounts most accurately for subject behavior in the greatest variety of game situations. It seems that little is to be gained by further testing of these models with data from the Prisoner's Dilemma.

SUMMARY

Seven different models of subject behavior in the Prisoner's Dilemma game are described, including: a tomorrow-will-be-like-today model; a random-choice model; a contingency model; two modifications of a linear learning model; an expected-payoff maximization model; and a maximization model which assumes that the subjects maximize a weighted sum of their own and their opponents' payoffs. The four best models do not appear to differ meaningfully in accuracy, although they are developed from widely different assumptions about subject behavior. However, the random-choice model and the payoff maximization model are clearly less accurate than the others. That the Naive model performs as well as the other models implies either that the other models are inadequate or that the method of testing the models is inadequate.

REFERENCES

1. S. M. Halpin, and M. Pilisuk, 1967. *Prediction and choice in the Prisoner's Dilemma.* Lafayette, Ind.: Purdue University, Institute paper No. 174.
2. J. D. Herniter, A. Williams, and J. Wolpert, 1967. Learning to cooperate. *Peace Research Society, Papers,* 7: 67–82. 6D.
3. R. D. Luce, 1959. *Individual choice behavior.* New York: Wiley.
4. R. D. Luce, and H. Raiffa, 1957. *Games and decisions.* New York: Wiley.
5. R. E. Overstreet, and M. Pilisuk, 1967. *Simulation models of sequential choices in the Prisoner's Dilemma.* Working paper, Purdue University. 3B.
6. M. Pilisuk, and P. Skolnick, 1968. Inducing trust: a test of the Osgood proposal. *Journal of Personality and Social Psychology,* 8(2): 121–133.
7. M. Pilisuk, P. Potter, A. Rapoport, and J. A. Winter, 1965. War hawks and peace doves: alternate resolutions of experimental conflicts. *Journal of Conflict Resolution,* 9(4): 491–508.
8. M. Pilisuk, J. A. Winter, R. Chapman, and N. Haas, 1967. Honesty, deceit, and timing in the display of intentions. *Behavioral Science,* 12(3): 205–215.
9. An. Rapoport, and A. M. Chammah, 1965. *Prisoner's Dilemma.* Ann Arbor: University of Michigan Press. 3C.
10. An. Rapoport, and C. Orwant, 1962. Experimental games: a review. *Behavioral Science,* 7(1): 1–37.

13

AN ECONOMIC MODEL FOR THE DIVISION OF LABOR

MAURICE KILBRIDGE
LEON WESTER

The industrial or technical division of labor, as distinguished from the social division of labor, is the rational division of work among persons and machines within a particular enterprise. It has as its object an increase in the productivity of labor and machines, and its extent at any time and place is a function of the extent and stability of the market, the product, and methods employed.

Although the technical division of labor is the most obvious characteristic of the modern factory system, it is an ancient and natural phenomenon that far predates the industrial revolution. The great ancient civilizations of the Mediterranean world fostered factory systems for the mass production of some consumer goods in which extensive division of labor was undoubtedly practiced. Xenophon provides evidence of such division of labor in Greece of the fourth century B.C.

In large cities—there are places even where one man earns a living by only stitching shoes, another by cutting them out, another by sewing the uppers together, while there is another who performs none of of these operations but only assembles the parts [5].

Similar workshops, usually depending on slave labor, are known to have existed in Ancient

Egypt and Imperial Rome for the production of bedsteads, knives, shields, pots and pans and other cheap goods in quantity.

In medieval times it was not uncommon for the larger manors to operate factories for the production of both civil and military goods on a divided-labor basis. The workers, who were mostly serfs not required on the land, performed specialized tasks, the work being divided into a sequence of operations. The products were used mostly within the manor, but sometimes were sold in local markets, giving rise to conflicts with guild producers. Arthur Salz tells us that the spread of the technical division of labor "was artificially delayed by the guild system. The guilds' restriction upon the enlargement of handicraft enterprises and the increase of labor productivity checked technical specialization as practiced on the great estates and effected instead a dismemberment of production into independent enterprises" [7].

During the Renaissance there was a famous arsenal at Venice where war goods from small arms to ships were turned out by highly divided labor using mass production techniques. In reading the diary of a Spanish visitor to the arsenal we find a description of what may well have been the first progressive assembly line. He writes:

SOURCE: Reprinted from *Management Science, 12*: B-255–269 (1966).

And as one enters the gate there is a great street on either hand with the sea in the middle, and on one side are windows opening out of the houses of the arsenal, and the same on the other side, and out came a galley towed by a boat, and from the windows they handed out to them, from one the cordage, from another the bread, from another the arms, and from another the balistas and mortars, and so from all sides everything which was required, and when the galley had reached the end of the street all the men required were on board, together with the complement of oars, and she was equipped from end to end. In this manner there came out ten galleys, fully armed, between the hours of three and nine [6].

These galleys had a length of 160 feet, a beam of 19 feet and depth of nine feet. They mounted nine cannons and had a fighting contingent of 45 swordsmen. A crew of 171, of whom 150 were oarsmen, manned the ship under the control of ten officers. In addition to 50 oars there were two masts and sails.[1] These were the largest fighting galleys of their day, and we are told by the Spanish visitor that they came off the provisioning line at the rate of ten ships in six hours, or thirty-six minutes per ship, a rate achieved through extensive division of labor.

Under the cottage industry or household economy system of the eighteenth century the technical division of labor became a significant and widespread phenomenon. In the textile trade, for example, whole villages specialized in a single function. Thus there were spinning villages and weaving villages and other villages where cloth was only dyed and finished. And within the cottages the division was carried further. The typical hand weaver employed his entire family in subdivided tasks of preparing the yarn and finishing the cloth. The cottage shoemaker, surrounded by his family and perhaps a journeyman and an apprentice or two, divided the work into specialties so that each person produced only parts and the master assembled them into the finished shoe.

In the first years of the industrial revolution, before the extensive use of machinery and centralized power, manual factories existed throughout England, factories in which the

---

[1] Description of a Model of a Typical XVII Century Venetian Galley, Museum of Science and Industry, Chicago, Illinois. Donated by the Italian Government.

work was done mostly by hand. They produced common consumer items such as pins, buttons, shoes, household utensils, hand tools, cloth, and equestrian and marine supplies. In these factories the division of labor was carried to an extent not seen before and seldom seen since. The most famous account of these factories is that by Adam Smith who describes pin making in the 1770's.

One man draws out the wire, another straightens it, a third cuts it, a fourth points it, a fifth grinds it at the top for receiving the head; to make the head requires two or three distinct operations; to put it on, is a peculiar business, to whiten the pins is another; it is even a trade by itself to put them into the paper; and the important business of making a pin is, in this manner, divided into about eighteen distinct operations, which, in some manufactories, are all performed by distinct hands, though in others the same man will sometimes perform two or three of them [8].

Minute division of labor of this degree is rarely found in modern factories, mostly because of the development of machinery to replace men in the performance of very simple tasks. Thus, the making of pins, for example, has run the full cycle of fabrication, from complete manufacture by one craftsman, through the phase described by Smith of highly divided manual labor, to today's automatic pin-making machine, several of which are operated by one man. The notable exception to this trend, as we shall see, is not in fabrication, but in the assembly line, where highly divided manual labor remains the mode of operation in even the most advanced industries.

COST CRITERIA IN THE DIVISION OF LABOR

The division of labor has prevailed through the years as industrial managers consciously applied the economic "law of the division of labour—that in every industry the productivity of labour increases proportionately with the extension of labour" [1]. The trouble with this "law," of course, is that it is one-directional and states no economic limit to the extension of the division of labor. Yet there must be a point at which, in any particular situation, the further division of labor induces diseconomies. When the market is large enough to support the division of labor beyond this point, as is the case today in many consumer-goods industries, another principle is needed to define the economic limit. In these cases, as will be shown, the product and the manufacturing methods determine the costs and benefits of the division of labor and delimit its economic extent.

Four kinds of costs will be shown to inhere in the division of labor: imbalance-of-work cost, nonproductive-work cost, learning cost and the wage cost of skill. In general, the imbalance of work and nonproductive work tend to increase with the division of labor, while the cost of learning and the wage cost of skill tend to decrease. The minimum total of these four defines the least-cost division of labor.

The imbalance-of-work cost results from the imperfect divisibility of productive tasks. In extending the division of labor, productive operations, which by nature are not perfectly divisible, must be subdivided into smaller and smaller tasks, and these sub-tasks assigned to separate workers so that each worker has approximately the same amount of work to do in a given time. For any given kind of work the imbalance-of-work cost rises with the division of labor. The cost is zero when one man performs the entire task, and it rises steadily with subdivision of work until the point is reached where it is technically impossible to divide the task further.

Non-productive work induced by the division of labor takes the form of handling of product from worker to worker, time spent in starting and stopping work on each unit of product, and the increased communications and control necessitated by the interdependence of functions. Generally speaking, for any given kind of work, the cost of associated non-productive work increases with the division of labor. It is least, but not zero, when the entire assembly is performed by one man, and generally reaches its highest point when the division of labor is carried to the extreme.

Learning cost has three components: the pace-achievable cost, initial-learning cost and recurring-learning cost. The pace-achievable cost is not intrinsically related to learning cost, but is included here for ease of analysis. It considers the relationship between length of task and the degree of dexterity, and hence work pace, achievable for a given kind of work. Generally speaking, except for extremely short tasks, the work pace that can be achieved by the individual is a function of the length of task. Within limits, the shorter the task the faster the potential work pace. Any achievable work pace slower than the fastest possible achievable pace represents a cost associated with the division of work. Initial-learning cost is the cost of the period of skill acquisition when the beginner in the work is producing less than a practiced worker. This cost, quite naturally, decreases with the division of labor. Recurring-learning cost is the continued cost of initial learning due to employee turnover. For any given turnover rate, it also tends to decrease with the division of labor. The three components of learning cost behave in much the same fashion; all decrease with further division of labor, and hence their total also decreases.

The wage cost of skill relates the division of labor to the deskilling of work. As tasks become more specialized, the range of skills required to perform each is narrowed, and workers of general skill are no longer required. With extensive division of labor, relatively unskilled workers can be assigned the fragmented tasks and the general skill of the craftsman passes to the system and the engineers who organize it. With a decline in skill requirements a corresponding decline in wages is normally experienced. The wage cost of skill therefore declines with extension of the division of labor.

In the analysis that follows an economic model will be developed that relates the above costs to the extent of the division of labor. Noneconomic factors are not considered. This is not to ignore the problem of the possible psychological costs of highly specialized and repetitive tasks, but to admit that we have, as yet, no way of measuring the consequences of worker alienation, if, indeed, such alienation is a consequence of specialization. Only immediate and tangible costs are included in the analysis. Possible long-run morale-related costs are not included. The best or optimum division of labor will thus be defined as that which yields the lowest direct labor cost of production per unit, when this labor cost is composed of the four partial costs identified above.

THE DIVISION OF LABOR
IN ASSEMBLY WORK

The nature and extent of the division of labor in some industrial activities is dictated by the machinery and equipment employed in them. In many mechanized and automated processes the technology determines the assignment of work, the worker being involved in the process only in the performance of those tasks that have not successfully been incorporated in the machine. His work is a composite of residual functions. The division of labor conforms to the machine.

In other industrial activities, however, where manual labor predominates, and only small tools are employed, the situation is reversed. Instead of the worker being an adjunct of the machine, the tool is an adjunct of the worker. Such is the case in assembly work which is essentially manual. Assembly work represents the largest segment of industrial activity in which the choice of the division of labor can be made virtually without restrictions of technology. For this reason the economic extent of the division of labor is studied here in the context of assembly work.

The division of labor in assembly is facilitated by the conveyor line. Workers are stationed along the line on which the frame of the product being assembled moves. The total job is broken into elements of work and assigned in approximately equal shares to the workers on the line. Each operator adds his share of work as the product passes him. The measure of the division of labor is the amount of time the product spends at each operator's work station.[2] This period is commonly called the "cycle time." The problem of the economic extent of the division of labor, then, is to determine the optimum cycle time, or that which yields the lowest unit direct labor cost of assembly. In the model that follows it is assumed that the market will absorb any volume of assembled product and thus that the relevant cost factors are those previously

described that are intrinsic to the division of labor.

There is an ultimate limit to the division of assembly work imposed by the nature of the work itself, a point being eventually reached at which further division is not feasible. This is the point of the irreducible work element, which for technical reasons cannot be subdivided. A work element, for the purpose of this paper, is defined as an indivisible unit of work which cannot be rationally subdivided. That is, it cannot be split between two operators. The largest such work element in the assembly job will be assumed[3] to set the lower limit of feasible cycle times. The upper limit is the total assembly work done as a one-man operation. Between these limits, and typically quite close to the lower one, industry chooses its cycle times.

Although in practice the choice of cycle times is more frequently based on intuition than analysis, it is made with a high degree of conformity among industries. In a survey conducted by the authors it was found that most companies, when the volume of sales was high and consistent, chose cycle times of about one minute. In the consumer electronics industry typical assembly cycles range from 0.5 to 1.5 minutes, in the major appliance industry from 0.8 to 2.0 minutes, and in automotive from 1.0 to 1.5 minutes. This high degree of conformity leads one to ask if industrial managers have perhaps instinctively hit upon one minute as the optimum division of labor in assembly.

For purposes of this analysis the simplifying assumption will be made that the range of assembly cycle times, that is, the range within which the division of labor is analyzed here, will not be sufficient to influence the wage cost of skill. This is typically true in the case of progressive assembly lines. The job grade of assembly-line worker, for a given kind of work, usually carries a single wage rate in any one company and does not vary with changes in length of cycle time.

The remaining three costs (imbalance of work, nonproductive work and learning cost) do vary

---

[2] For purposes of this paper, the simplifying assumption is made that each work station is manned by one and only one operator. In practice, an operator may, during short production runs, man more than one station; and on lines making large products (automobiles, for example) work stations are frequently manned by several operators.

[3] This assumption does not always hold in practice. It is possible to assign two operators to work in parallel on alternate units of product, each performing only the largest irreducible element. In this way, the lower limit is halved for all other stations on the line.

with changes in cycle time, even at the minutest division of labor. The mode of analysis will be to find the functional relationship between cycle time and dollar cost for each of these three component costs separately, and then to combine them in a total cost function that can be minimized to yield the least-cost, or optimum cycle time.

The three cost functions are now discussed, starting with imbalance-of-work cost.

IMBALANCE-OF-WORK COST[4]

In the context of progressive assembly imbalance-of-work time is the amount of idle time on the line due to the imperfect division of work between operators. In practice those operators having shorter work assignments will seldom stand idle at the end of each cycle, but will work continuously at a slower pace. The effect, measured in terms of labor cost, however, is the same as if they were idle part of the time and working at a faster pace the rest of the time.

The degree or per cent of imbalance of work is the ratio between the average idle time for each operator and the largest assignment time for any operator. (The largest assignment time, of maximum operator's time is, by definition, the cycle time.) Stated otherwise, the per cent of imbalance of work is the ratio between the total idle time induced by the division of labor and the total time spent by the product in moving from the beginning to the end of the line. It is calculated by the formula:

Imbalance of Work (%)

$$= \frac{\text{Max. Op's Time} - \text{Ave. Op's Time}}{\text{Max. Operator's Time}} \times 100 \qquad (1)$$

The nature of the work and the production facilities used influence the degree of imbalance of work because they determine the distribution of the work element times and the extent of restrictions to achieving good balance. But for any specific product and work method, the imbalance of work among the operators on the line is a function of only the cycle time, or the extent of the division of labor. Other things equal, for a given division of labor, good

[4] The content of this section is discussed more fully in [4].

balance of work is more easily achieved when the work consists of many small elements rather than a few large elements.

The second characteristic of assembly work that influences the degree of balance attainable is the nature of the restrictions imposed on the ordering of work elements. When there are no restrictions of the commutability of the work elements, that is, on the ordering or time sequence in which they can be performed, the work can be more completely equalized among operators. This is so because of the freedom of choice in assigning elements of work among the assemblers.

At the other extreme, where each element of work must be performed at one and only one point in a time sequence, there is no freedom of choice in the assignment of work elements and the problem of equalizing the work among the assemblers is more difficult. Between these extremes is found most assembly work.

Three types of restrictions are discussed in the literature [4]: (1) restrictions on the time sequencing of the assembly of components or piece parts, (2) restrictions imposed by fixed facilities or machines on the assembly line, (3) restrictions of position, where position refers to the position of the object being assembled with relation to the operator or operators.

To study the relationship between the division of labor and imbalance of work, data were gathered for a variety of assembly situations. For each kind of work curves were plotted of the imbalance experienced as a function of the cycle time used. The equations of all curves were of the form

$$\% \text{ Imbalance} = a/CT^b \qquad (2)$$

where imbalance means the per cent of imbalance of work and CT is the cycle time. The values of the parameters a and b depend on the nature of the work and the balancing restrictions. For the wiring and soldering of radio and television chassis, data gathered in one company for 108 chassis lines yielded the equation

$$\% \text{ Imbalance} = 4.62/CT^{.60} \qquad (3)$$

This is the kind of work that will be used for purposes of illustrating the selection of the least-cost division of assembly labor later in this paper.

COST OF NON-PRODUCTIVE WORK[5]

The second kind of cost inherent in the division of labor is the cost of associated non-productive work induced by the division of labor. In the context of assembly-line work this takes the form of handling of product and tools, and operator movement to and from the work position. Product handling involves putting the product on and off the line, positioning it, and moving it between stations (when this is done by hand as on manual conveyor lines). Tool handling includes picking up and putting aside all hand tools and small instruments of production.

Return-to-position time is the time required for an operator to return, after finishing work on a unit of product, to his original work position to start the next unit. In the case of standing assembly the operators may walk some distance along the line while performing their work. In seated assembly time is spent swinging the upper body from one unit to the next and in searching for the starting point of the next assembly cycle. This time is in addition to that required to move from one component to another within the same unit of product and therefore must be considered a time-cost associated with the division of work.

The fourth and last kind of non-productive-time cost is that of station-size allowance. This is time given to compensate the assembly worker for the increased distance he must move or reach to pick up and bring into position the piece parts he assembles. As the cycle time and the variety of tasks done by each operator increases, so does the number of different components used at each station. As the storage area required to hold these components gets larger, the average reach and move distance to get components also increases.

The above kinds of non-productive work can be sorted out from the productive work, and calculated as a per cent of total work. It has been shown [2] that the per cent of non-productive work is a function of the division of labor, and is largest for very short cycles. The nature of the function depends on the product being assembled, the assembly tools and

fixtures, and whether a powered or non-powered conveyor is used. Since the function differs somewhat with each situation, no general algebraic expression for it can be given. For the wiring and soldering of radio and television chassis on a power-driven belt conveyor line, the specific work chosen to illustrate the selection of the least-cost assembly cycle, the relationship between the division of labor and associated non-productive work is given by the curve of Figure 1.

LEARNING COST[6]

This is the cost involved in the assembly workers' learning to perform their tasks at an acceptably fast pace. In this context "learning" becomes "group learning," since all operators on the line must progress at the same rate. Where model changes are frequent and employee turnover is high the cost of learning may represent a considerable part of direct labor cost.

Learning cost will depend, of course, on other factors in addition to the length of task, but only task length is considered here. Also, the nature of the assembly work and the volume of the production run are assumed known, and wage rates are held constant and uniform for the assembly group. This can be done without loss of generality and will be seen to approximate closely the typical short-run industrial situation.

The division of labor influences learning cost in three ways, through: (1) the pace ultimately attained, (2) the initial learning time, and (3) the recurring learning cost. As mentioned earlier in this paper, the pace ultimately attained is not strictly related to learning, but is included in the learning cost analysis for convenience. Empirical data indicate that the work pace ultimately attainable for a given kind of assembly is a function of the task length, or cycle time. The ultimate pace is slowest for very short and very long tasks and fastest for tasks of intermediate length.

When the task is very short a restricted motion pattern is repeated continuously. Observations indicate that this induces cramping and muscle fatigue, inhibiting the worker's ability to maintain a uniformly fast pace. As the task

[5] The content of this section is discussed more fully in [2].

[6] The content of this section is discussed more fully in [3].

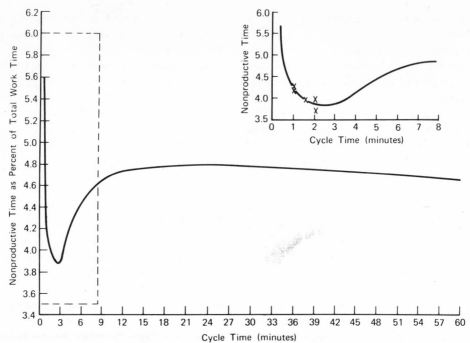

Figure 1 Nonproductive time as percent of total work time for various assembly cycle lengths on powered conveyor lines.

length increases and the motion pattern becomes diversified simple muscle fatigue declines. Beyond a point, however, a counter-vailing influence tends to reduce the pace attainable. Forgetting, fumbling, loss of motor skill and rechecking time increase, resulting in a slowing of pace. A task of intermediate length avoids the penalties of both extremes. The operator can develop a touch system, constant, unchanging rhythm, and a smooth continuous work pattern that is not too restricted and yet well defined, resulting in a high level of speed and skill.

This phenomenon is not to be confused with initial learning, which will be taken up later. The gist of the above is that when the job is well learned and productivity has leveled off, there will be, for a given kind of work, a difference in the pace attained depending on the length of task. There is an ideal task length or cycle time corresponding to fastest ultimate pace achievable and all other task lengths result in slower pace. It has been shown [3] that if Σ is the total work content of the assembly job in minutes, w is the hourly wage rate, $p(l)$ is the pace attainable[7] at task length l, and $p(l^{\sim})$ is the fastest ultimate pace attainable (at the ideal

task length $l^{\sim}$), then the extra labor cost of assembly, C_1, due to the difference in pace attainable between task lengths l and $l^{\sim}$ is given by

$$C_1 = nw[100/p(l) - 100/p(l^{\sim})]\,l/60 \qquad (4)$$

where[8] $n = [\Sigma/l]$, the number of line operators.

The second way in which task length influences learning cost is through its effect on initial learning time. This is the time it takes a group of assembly operators to learn to do, at ultimate pace, a specific new task that belongs to the general class of tasks in which they are experienced. It is the practice effect only and does not apply to the training of unskilled workers.

In the article previously mentioned [3] it has been shown that, other things being equal, for a given kind of work, initial learning time is a function of task length. Plotting productivity against repetitions of the cycle results in a one-parameter family of power curves. From these functions the cost of initial learning can be calculated. In short, if m is the number of units

[7] $p(l)$ and $p(l^{\sim})$ are pure numbers, without units, ranging, in practice, from about 40 to about 140.

[8] This notation means that n must be an integer equal to Σ/l, or the next larger integer.

in the production run, n is the number of operators, w is the hourly wage rate, and l is the task length, the average unit cost of initial learning for the entire line is

$$C_2 = (nwl/m)\left[\sum_{r=0}^{r_a} 1/f(r,l) - (r_a+1)/p(l)\right] \quad (5)$$

where r is number of repetitions performed and r_a is the least number of repetitions for which ultimate pace is attained. In (5) $p(l)$ is taken from (4) and $f(r,l)$ is the power function associating productivity with repetitions of the cycle of length l.

The third component of learning cost is known as recurring learning. Because of employee turnover and transfers learning costs continue, even after the line has reached ultimate pace. When replacement workers are added to the line the company sustains a learning cost. Either the entire line slows to the pace of the replacement worker, or a special operator is put with the replacement worker at his station. In the latter case, which is the customary solution, the two workers together meet the pace of the line until the replacement worker is able to keep up alone. The analysis here is based on the assumption that a special operator is added and the line does not slow down. The recurring learning cost is therefore the wages of special operators while assisting replacement operators to reach the pace of the line. It is a function of the task length and the points in the production run at which replacements are made.

Recurring learning is analyzed with reference to the family of curves $f(r,l)$ of equation (5). A replacement operator learns as an individual until he overtakes the pace of the group. To develop a statement of recurring learning it is thus necessary to express analytically the time it takes the average replacement operator to overtake the group pace, considering the pace of the group when he starts and the respective group and individual learning curves. If the replacement operator starts work at the Ith (initial) repetition of the cycle, and overtakes the pace of the line at the Fth (final) repetition, the unit cost of recurring learning has been shown to be

$$C_3 = (I/Q)\lambda nlw \sum_{r=I-1}^{F-1} 1/f(r,l) \quad (6)$$

where Q is annual production, λ is annual turnover rate, and n, l, w, $f(r,l)$ have the same meaning as in (5). The total learning cost per unit is then $(4)+(5)+(6)$, or

$$C = nlw\left\{(5/3[1/p(l) - 1/p(l^\sim)]\right.$$

$$+ (1/m)\left[\sum_{r=0}^{r_a} 1/f(r,l) - (r_a+1)/p(l)\right]$$

$$\left. + (\lambda/Q)\sum_{r=I-1}^{F-1} 1/f(r,l)\right\} \quad (7)$$

APPLICATION OF THE MODEL

To test the above analysis of the costs of the division of labor in a typical industrial situation, data were collected on 108 chassis assembly lines in a radio and television manufacturing plant located in the Chicago area. Three components of direct-labor costs were considered: imbalance-of-work-cost, cost of non-productive work, and learning cost. The wage cost of skill was ignored since the range of cycle times used in the study was not sufficient to influence wage rates.

The computations were based on a total work content time of 90 minutes per unit of product, a wage rate of $2.00 per hour, and a turnover rate of 50 per cent per annum. It was also assumed that the plant was in operation 250 days per year, working one daily shift of 450 minutes. The cost computations were performed for cycle timesof 0.5, 1.0, 1.5, 2.0, 2.5, 3.0 and 3.5 minutes, and for production runs of 200 to 10,000 units in increments of 200 units, of 10,000 to 50,000 units in increments of 400 units, and of 50,000 to 100,000 units in increments of 1,000 units. The unit cost of imbalance was calculated from equation (3), the unit cost of non-productive work was derived from Figure 1, and the total learning cost per unit was determined from learning curves and equation (7). The calculations were performed on an IBM 7090 digital computer.[9]

Table 1 is a summary of the results obtained. It can be seen that the lowest direct labor cost of assembly occurs for a cycle time of:

[9] Appreciation is expressed to Miss Adrienne J. Lipson of IIT Research Institute for writing the computer program.

TABLE 1 Total Unit Cost of Three Intrinsic Factors for Various Cycle Times in the Consumer Electronics Industry (Wiring and Soldering of Radio and Television Chassis on a Powered Conveyor Line)

Cycle Time in Minutes	0.5	1.0	1.5	2.0	2.5	3.0	3.5
Cost[a] due to imbalance	0.2241	0.1478	0.1159	0.0975	0.0853	0.0765	0.0697
Cost due to nonproductive time	0.1536	0.1344	0.1280	0.1232	0.1216	0.1232	0.1280
Cost due to learning ($m = 200$)[b]	5.1095	6.7584	8.1026	10.1728	11.3302	12.3727	15.0298
Total Cost in $	5.4872 (Min.)	7.0406	8.3465	10.3935	11.5371	12.5724	15.2275
Cost due to imbalance	0.2241	0.1478	0.1159	0.0975	0.0853	0.0765	0.0697
Cost due to nonproductive time	0.1536	0.1344	0.1280	0.1232	0.1216	0.1232	0.1280
Cost due to learning ($m = 2,000$)	0.5145	0.6840	0.8491	1.1019	1.3535	1.5971	1.9464
Total Cost in $	0.8922 (Min.)	0.9662	1.0930	1.3226	1.5604	1.7968	2.1441
Cost due to imbalance	0.2241	0.1478	0.1159	0.0975	0.0853	0.0765	0.0697
Cost due to nonproductive time	0.1536	0.1344	0.1280	0.1232	0.1216	0.1232	0.1280
Cost due to learning ($m = 3,600$)	0.2876	0.3840	0.4909	0.6539	0.8609	1.0649	1.3003
Total Cost in $	0.6653 (Min.)	0.6662	0.7348	0.8746	1.0678	1.2646	1.4980
Cost due to imbalance	0.2241	0.1478	0.1159	0.0975	0.0853	0.0765	0.0697
Cost due to nonproductive time	0.1536	0.1344	0.1280	0.1232	0.1216	0.1232	0.1280
Cost due to learning ($m = 3,800$)	0.2727	0.3643	0.4674	0.6245	0.8284	1.0299	1.2578
Total Cost in $	0.6504	0.6465 (Min.)	0.7113	0.8452	1.0353	1.2296	1.4555
Cost due to imbalance	0.2241	0.1478	0.1159	0.0975	0.0853	0.0765	0.0697
Cost due to nonproductive time	0.1536	0.1344	0.1280	0.1232	0.1216	0.1232	0.1280
Cost due to learning ($m = 36,000$)	0.0323	0.0466	0.0880	0.1500	0.3066	0.4663	0.5734
Total Cost in $	0.4100	0.3288 (Min.)	0.3319	0.3707	0.5135	0.6660	0.7711

TABLE 1 (continued)

Cycle Time in Minutes	0.5	1.0	1.5	2.0	2.5	3.0	3.5
Cost due to imbalance	0.2241	0.1478	0.1159	0.0975	0.0853	0.0765	0.0697
Cost due to nonproductive time	0.1536	0.1344	0.1280	0.1232	0.1216	0.1232	0.1280
Cost due to learning ($m = 62,000$)	0.0204	0.0308	0.0692	0.1265	0.2808	0.4384	0.5396
Total Cost in $	0.3981	0.3130 (Min.)	0.3131	0.3472	0.4877	0.6381	0.7373
Cost due to imbalance	0.2241	0.1478	0.1159	0.0975	0.0853	0.0765	0.0697
Cost due to nonproductive time	0.1536	0.1344	0.1280	0.1232	0.1216	0.1232	0.1280
Cost due to learning ($m = 63,000$)	0.0201	0.0305	0.0688	0.1260	0.2802	0.4378	0.5388
Total Cost in $	0.3978	0.3127	0.3127 (Min.)	0.3467	0.4871	0.6375	0.7365
Cost due to imbalance	0.2241	0.1478	0.1159	0.0975	0.0853	0.0765	0.0697
Cost due to nonproductive time	0.1536	0.1344	0.1280	0.1232	0.1216	0.1232	0.1280
Cost due to learning ($m = 85,000$)	0.0160	0.0249	0.0621	0.1177	0.2711	0.4280	0.5269
Total Cost in $	0.3937	0.3071	0.3060 (Min.)	0.3384	0.4780	0.6277	0.7246
Cost due to imbalance	0.2241	0.1478	0.1159	0.0975	0.0853	0.0765	0.0697
Cost due to nonproductive time	0.1536	0.1344	0.1280	0.1232	0.1216	0.1232	0.1280
Cost due to learning ($m = 100,000$)	0.0141	0.0226	0.0593	0.1142	0.2672	0.4237	0.5217
Total Cost in $	0.3918	0.3048	0.3032 (Min.)	0.3349	0.4741	0.6234	0.7194

[a] All costs are in dollars per unit assembled.
[b] m is the number of units in the production run.

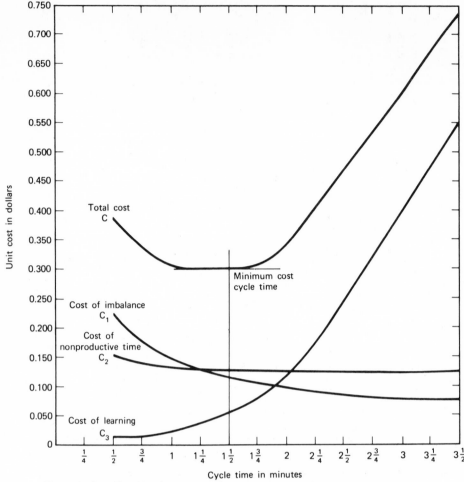

Figure 2 Partial and total cost curves for production run of 100,000 units. (Data taken from Table 1.)

0.5 minutes or less when the production run is less than 3700 units;

approximately 1.0 minute when the production run is between 3700 and 62,500 units;

approximately 1.5 minutes when the production run exceeds 62,500.

Figure 2 shows the partial and total cost curves for a production run of 100,000 units. The data are taken from Table 1. It is easily seen that C_1, the cost of imbalance of work, and C_2, the cost of non-productive time, decrease with a lengthening of work cycle. The cost of learning, C_3, however, increases rapidly with longer cycle times. The total cost, C, is minimum at about a 1.5 minute cycle time. The total cost curve is very flat bottomed, however, and variations in cycle time of ± 0.5 minutes have little effect on cost.

Table 1 shows that for volumes of between 3000 and 100,000, a range that covers the typical production run of radio and television chassis, a one minute cycle time is either optimum, or within 1.6 mills per unit of being optimum. Production managers in this industry, who almost universally favor a one minute cycle time, appear to have chosen instinctively the best division of labor. One wonders if the same is true in the automotive industry, where the work is quite different, but where a one minute cycle time is also favored for final assembly lines. A study similar to the one reported here would have to be undertaken to answer this question.

For any given cycle time the total direct labor cost of assembly decreases with an increase in the volume of production. At a one minute cycle time, for example, the assembly cost drops from $7.04 per unit at a volume of 200 units to $0.30 per unit at a volume of 100,000 units. This cost reduction is not unexpected, although the magnitude of the decline is surprising. Since the costs of imbalance and non-productive time do not vary with the size of production run, the reduction is due entirely to spreading the learning cost over greater volume. The advantage of high volume production in reducing indirect or fixed costs per unit has always been known, but its great influence on reducing direct labor cost has, we suspect, not been fully appreciated.

The table contains one surprise—the optimum division of labor increases with the volume of production run. This is contrary to the view generally held since the days of Adam Smith that the division of labor is a function of the size of the market. The implication of this view is that larger volumes of production justify more extensive division of labor. Exactly the opposite is true in the case presented here. Indirect costs have not been taken into consideration, of course, and it is possible that their inclusion would alter the final results. As far as direct labor costs are concerned, however, the results are clear and unequivocal.

This paper presents only a first effort in a mode of analysis not previously applied to a study of the division of labor. Similar studies must be made of other industries and products before generalization is attempted. The analysis should also be extended to machine as well as assembly work. Indirect costs must also be brought into the analysis. Only then will it be possible to develop a general theory of the economic extent of the division of labor.

REFERENCES

1. C. Bücher, 1901. *Industrial evolution*. New York: Holt.
2. M. D. Kilbridge, 1961. Non-productive work as a factor in the economic division of labor. *Journal of Industrial Engineering*, *12*(3): 155–159.
3. M. D. Kilbridge, 1962. A model for industrial learning costs. *Management Science*, *8*(4): 516–527.
4. M. D. Kilbridge, and L. Wester, 1961. The balance delay problem. *Management Science*, *8*(1): 69–84.
5. F. Klemm, 1959. *A history of Western technology*. New York: Scribner.
6. F. C. Lane, 1934. *Venetian ships and shipbuilders of the renaissance*. Baltimore: John Hopkins Press.
7. A. Salz, 1934. Specialization. *Encyclopaedia of the social sciences* (E.R.A. Seligman, ed.); New York: Macmillan, Volume 14, 279–285.
8. A. Smith, 1776. On the division of labor. *An inquiry into the nature and causes of the wealth of nations*; London: Strahan and Cadell, Book 1, Chapter 1.

14

MANAGERIAL CLIMATE, WORK GROUPS, AND ORGANIZATIONAL PERFORMANCE

EUGENE E. KACZKA

ROY V. KIRK

Several investigators of organizational behavior [1, 11, 12, 15] have indicated that one of the major shortcomings of research on organizations is that the studies in this area are not well integrated. Cyert and March [8], in the development of a behavioral theory of the firm, and Bonini [3], in his simulation of information and decision systems in the firm, have integrated some of the findings of organizational research with economic theory; however, their models ignore the characteristics and effects of work groups. This omission or simplication appears to be based on the argument that work groups have a negligible influence on the performance of industrial organizations.

Likert [13] has integrated a large amount of survey data on the effects of the relationship of management with its work force. The empirical evidence indicates that managerial climate affects the behavior of industrial work groups; therefore, Likert and Seashore [14] hypothesized that managerial climate has a significant effect on the performance of industrial organizations, but it still must be established that the be-

havior of work groups has a significant effect on the performance of industrial organizations. In strikes, work groups do, indeed, affect organizational performance; but if work groups have an effect on organizational performance in the day-to-day operations, then a behavioral theory of the firm should take this into account.

The hypothesis that managerial climate affects organizational performance would be difficult to test in an industrial context by a field study [14]. Besides being costly and impractical, the experiment would be confounded by the dynamics of the environment and the effects of uncontrolled internal variables. The present study attempted a computer simulation to investigate the general question posed by Likert and Seashore: Does a managerial climate that is *employee-oriented* result in a higher level of organizational performance than a managerial climate that is *task-oriented*? More generally, the study was designed to investigate three problems: (1) the effect of work groups, under various conditions of managerial climate on the performance of the firm, (2) the integration of work group behavior with the behavioral theory of the firm, and (3) the feasibility of

SOURCE: Reprinted from *Administrative Science Quarterly*, *12*: 253–272 (1967).

experimental simulation through the use of a digital computer in socio-psychological studies.

APPROACH

The approach of this study was (1) to develop a computer simulation model of a firm incorporating the behavior of management and work groups, and (2) to study the behavior of the model within an experimental design that stressed the effects of work groups on the performance of the firm.

The nature of the research question dictated that the model of the firm include elements representing industrial work groups, lower management, middle management, and top management. These elements were linked by information systems and procedures that simulated real systems and procedures as nearly as possible. The behavior of these elements was based on published empirical data and observations of ongoing business operations. Economic decision behavior in the model was based on the behavioral theory of the firm, and the behavior of work groups in the model was based on data gathered by the Institute for Social Research at Ann Arbor. The model also incorporated a representation of the market in order to treat the firm as an economic entity. For experimental purposes, the model was constructed in a form that permitted changes in the parameters constituting the managerial climate; this permitted ready adaptation to computerization.

Experimentation with the model involved changing parameters that represented some of the dimensions of managerial climate. Although the number of dimensions that could have been investigated was quite large, the number actually examined had to be limited to make the study manageable. The dimensions chosen for analysis constituted a judgment sample using the following guidelines: (1) they were suggested by Likert and Seashore; (2) management could, to some degree, control them; (3) data were available that permitted the establishment of bounds on the experimental changes made in them.

Five dimensions of managerial climate were selected for analysis:

1. *Grievance behavior.* The percentage of grievances submitted settled by foremen and superintendents.

2. *Cost emphasis.* The weight given to cost performance by superintendents in the evaluation of foremen, and the percentage of deviation of actual costs from budgeted costs that management regarded as tolerable.

3. *Leadership style.* The percentage of working time devoted to employee-oriented leadership by foremen and by superintendents.

4. *Congruence of leadership style.* The differences between leadership styles employed by foremen and by superintendents.

5. *Attitudes of industrial engineering departments.* The percentage of tight work standards loosened or the percentage of loose standards tightened by the industrial engineering department.

Each of these experimental dimensions was assigned two extreme levels on the continuum of managerial climate from employee-oriented to task-oriented.

A factorial experimental design was selected, because in the study of complex systems, this type of design permits the experimenter to evaluate the combined effect of two or more variables when varied simultaneously; that is, information obtained from a factorial experiment is more comprehensive than that gained from a series of single-factor experiments, and interaction effects can be evaluated [7, 21]. Moreover a factorial design is statistically efficient, yielding minimum variance estimates.

The performance of the model firm was measured by six criterion variables:

1. *Profit.* Since tax considerations were excluded, this was the gross profit per period.

2. *Sales.* To measure sales effectiveness, the normal seasonal and cyclical demand shifts were removed from the actual sales; thus, the variable treated was sales in excess of seasonal and cyclical changes.

3. *Ratio of sales to inventory.* This quantity was simply the ratio of the sales revenue in period t to value of the inventory on hand at the end of period $t-l$.

4. *Unit cost.* This measure was defined as the total cost per period divided by the number of units produced per period.

5. *Group pressure.* This quantity was the aggregate of the work pressures felt by each of the work groups. Pressure was defined as the difference between the group production norms in period t and the production scheduled in period t.[1]

6. *Group cohesion.* The cohesion indices for each of the groups averaged in each period to provide this aggregate measure.[2]

The first four measures are frequently used in standard financial analysis of business performance [17]. The last two measures are extensively used in sociological and psychological studies [13]. In addition, the waste performance of the work groups and management's administrative expenses, although not directly measured, could be indirectly evaluated.

[1] This definition is derived from the work of V. E. Buck, "Job Pressures on Managers, Sources, Subjects, and Correlates" [6].

[2] This is an index number which is used as a measure of "the total field of forces which act upon members to remain in the group." The definition is taken from L. Festinger, S. Schacter, and K. Back [10]. The initial values these indices assume are derived from data presented in S. E. Seashore [18].

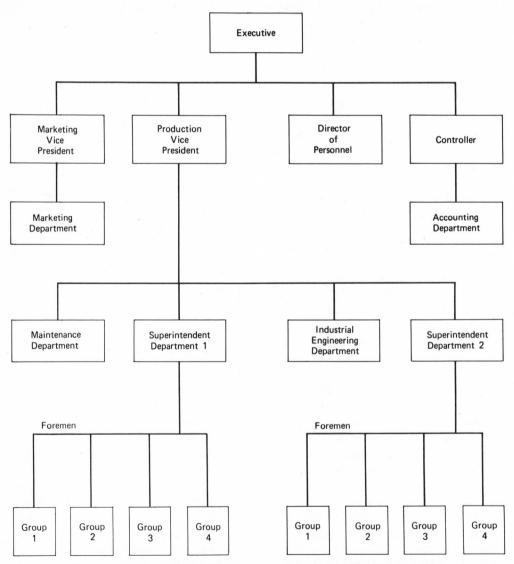

Figure 1 Company organization chart. (The executive may be a single decision maker or a group vested with the power to make the executive decisions of the firm.)

MODEL

Overall Structure of Model

An actual firm was used as a basis for the organizational structure of the hypothetical firm (see Figure 1). The structure of the model firm, which consisted of an information system, a decision system, and the characteristics of the various organizational members, was made as nearly like the structure of the actual firm as possible.[3] The independent research findings of several sociologists and psychologists were used in developing the characteristics, behaviors, and decision rules of the work groups and their superiors. The consistency of the research findings employed in developing the model of work groups and foremen was checked with the techniques of logical circuit design. The portion of the model dealing with top management and the staff was derived from the models of Cyert and March [8], and Bonini [3].

Generally accepted accounting practices were used as the guidelines for the accounting system in the model, and data from actual firms were used in specifying the values assumed by the accounting parameters. The description of the response of the market to the various actions taken by the firm was derived from the work of Tull [20]; Brown, Hulswit, and Kettelle [5]; and Boulding [4]. Each element in the model received specific kinds of information through formal and informal channels. Based upon this information, the current status of the element, and what had been learned from past actions, an explicit set of decisions was made which generated information sent to other elements of the firm. This process was repeated several times in each of the simulated time periods. Thus, the effect of any element on the performance of the model firm is the result of a large number of interrelated, time-lagged decisions. Table 1 summarizes the content of the model and the behavior of model elements. An outline of relationships among some of the more important elements in the model is as follows:

[3] For a more detailed description of the model relating the various constructs to the findings of specific studies, see E. E. Kaczka [11]. Copies of the listing of the simulation program may be obtained from Eugene E. Kaczka.

Relationships Among Elements

Executive Committee. The executive committee evaluates, quarterly, the internal and external results of its actions and takes measures which it feels are appropriate to the realization of its goals. It may change marketing strategies, exert pressures on individuals, or even revise budgets and goals.

Marketing Vice-President. The marketing vice-president seeks to achieve his sales goals first by prompting additional sales effort in his own department, secondly, by recommending marketing strategy changes to the executive committee, and finally, by adjusting his own goals. His behavior is sensitive to recent market information as well as to the pressures exerted by the executive committee and the production vice-president.

Production Vice-President. The production vice-president is concerned with maintaining satisfactory production and inventory levels, and controlling production costs. He tries to realize these goals by influencing the behavior of his peers, his immediate subordinates, and his staff. Furthermore, the importance of the various goals is not fixed, but responds to internal and external changes. As goal priorities change, trade-offs may be made. For example, should he desire above-average production levels, he may tolerate larger variances from budgeted costs in hopes of promoting the realization of his production goal. The particular actions he takes or the trade-offs he makes are, of course, dependent upon the pressures exerted upon him by the executive committee.

Director of Personnel and the Industrial Engineering Department. The director of personnel and the industrial engineering department jointly review and evaluate grievances. Their actions are dependent upon the pressures exerted by the production vice-president. The industrial engineering department's treatment of work standards is similarly affected. The disposition of grievances and the revision of work standards directly affect the behavior of the work groups.

TABLE 1 Summary of Content of Model

Position	Functions, Decisions and Actions	Factors Influencing Actions	Information Received	Information Transmitted
Executive or executive committee	1. Establish profit goal. 2. Set product price. 3. Set level of promotional expenditures. 4. Finalize cost expectations. 5. Influence level of sales effort. 6. Influence behavior of subordinates and advisors.	1. Degree success in achieving goals. 2. Current market information. 3. Current accounting data. 4. Internal recommendations. 5. Market trends. 6. Cost trends.	1. Actual sales. 2. Sales forecasts. 3. Requests for price and promotional changes. 4. Income statements. 5. Tentative budgets. 6. Estimated effects of price and promotional changes.	1. Current price. 2. Marketing goals. 3. Cost expectations. 4. Informal appraisal of performance of subordinates. 5. Disposition of recommendations.
Marketing vice-president	1. Prepare sales forecasts. 2. Recommend price changes. 3. Recommend promotional expenditures. 4. Influence marketing and administrative costs. 5. Influence level of sales effort.	1. Sales performance relative to sales goals. 2. Current market trends. 3. Pressures from superiors and peers. 4. Cost performance relative to budget.	1. Actual sales. 2. Current marketing administrative expenses. 3. Price and promotional changes. 4. Evaluations of sales effort.	1. Sales forecasts. 2. Price and promotional recommendations. 3. Desired level of sales effort. 4. Informal pressures on subordinates.
Production vice-president	1. Establish production and inventory policies. 2. Set specific production levels. 3. Influence performance of subordinates and peers. 4. Influence administrative costs.	1. Recent cost performance of subordinates. 2. Pressures exerted by executive committee. 3. Current levels of production. 4. Existing and projected inventory levels. 5. Actual and forecast sales.	1. Current inventory levels. 2. Sales forecasts. 3. Executive committee's evaluation of his performance. 4. Current costs generated by departments supervised. 5. Trends in production costs.	1. Production schedules. 2. Projected inventory levels. 3. Informal appraisal of subordinates. 4. Pressure on marketing vice-president.
Controller (accounting department)	1. Maintain accounting records. 2. Prepare budgets. 3. Review and adjust budget rates. 4. Pay work force.	1. Cost variances. 2. Production activities. 3. Pressures from executive committee. 4. Cost trends.	1. Production scheduled. 2. Sales forecast. 3. Production rates realized.	1. Budgetary data. 2. Current costs. 3. Status of inventories.

TABLE 1 (continued)

Position	Functions, Decisions and Actions	Factors Influencing Actions	Information Received	Information Transmitted
Director of personnel	1. Review and evaluate grievances with industrial engineering department.	1. Current attitudes of production vice-president and superintendents. 2. Grievance history of the group giving rise to the grievance.	1. Grievances. 2. Production scheduled.	1. Disposition of grievances.
Industrial engineering department	1. Cooperate with director of personnel in handling grievances. 2. Review and adjust work standards.	1. Cost history of relevant group. 2. Recommendations of superintendents. 3. Pressure exerted by production vice-president regarding costs. 4. Age of work standard.	1. Accounting records. 2. Production scheduled. 3. Informal pressures and recommendations from superintendents and production vice-president.	1. Work standard revisions.
Maintenance department	1. Maintain equipment and facilities.	1. Recent production levels.	1. Production schedules.	1. Costs incurred.
Department superintendent	1. Supervise performance of foremen. 2. Control costs of administering his department. 3. Review and evaluate grievances. 4. Influence actions of industrial engineering department. 5. Influence leadership behavior of his foremen.	1. Costs generated by foremen supervised. 2. Grievance histories of work groups. 3. Current levels of production scheduled. 4. Pressures exerted by superiors. 5. His leadership style. 6. Performance of other department.	1. Production schedules. 2. Reports of costs. 3. Grievances. 4. Informal appraisal of performance by production vice-president. 5. Reports of unusual levels of overtime.	1. Production schedules. 2. Grievance dispositions. 3. Evaluations of the performance of his foremen. 4. Pressures for improved performance. 5. His own leadership style.

TABLE 1 (*continued*)

Position	Functions, Decisions and Actions	Factors Influencing Actions	Information Received	Information Transmitted
Foreman	1. Influence manufacturing costs. 2. Supervise productive efforts. 3. Process grievances. 4. Adjust time spent in direct contact with work groups. 5. Engage in fractional bargaining. 6. Adjust leadership style.	1. Current levels of production scheduled. 2. Reports on his cost performance. 3. His own estimate of reasonable production levels. 4. Leadership style of his superintendent. 5. His estimate of appropriate leadership behavior. 6. Pressure exerted by the superintendent.	1. Production schedules. 2. Grievances. 3. Informal pressures from his superintendent. 4. Leadership style employed by his superintendent.	1. Production schedules. 2. Pressure on work group. 3. Grievances. 4. Rewards. 5. Punishments. 6. Informal evaluation of his work group's performance.
Work group	1. Manufacture product. 2. Evolve production norms. 3. Generate grievances. 4. Bargain with foreman. 5. Adjust cohesive behavior. 6. Influence direct and indirect production costs.	1. Characteristics of work performed. 2. Perceived influence of foremen with superiors. 3. Relative pay rate. 4. Leadership style of foremen. 5. Relative grievance success. 6. Pressures exerted by superiors. 7. Duration of pressures. 8. Actions of industrial engineering department. 9. Punishment-reward behavior of foremen. 10. Level of fractional bargaining of their foremen. 11. Their own cohesiveness.	1. Production schedules. 2. Disposition of grievances. 3. Changes in level of supervision. 4. Response of management. 5. Work standard revisions. 6. Pressures exerted by foremen.	1. Grievances. 2. Production rates. 3. Costs realized.

Department Superintendents. The primary goals of a department superintendent are the realization of production schedules, satisfactory cost performance, and the reduction of pressures. To achieve these goals, he attempts to influence the industrial engineering department, the foremen he supervises, and the work groups of the foremen. The actions taken depend on his own performance, the performance of the other superintendents, and the levels of production currently scheduled. His evaluation of each foreman, which is a function of the leadership style of the foreman, the cost performance of the section the foreman supervises, and the grievance activity of the foreman's section, is reflected in his disposition of grievances and in the pressures he exerts on the foreman.

Foremen. The foreman responds to pressures from above and below. His efforts to reduce these pressures are also affected by his section's cost performance and current levels of production. They take the form of changes in leadership style, punishment-reward behavior, direct supervision, and fractional bargaining. The vigor with which he pursues cost and production goals is affected by his own estimates of reasonable production levels.

Work Groups. Each of the work groups is concerned with the maintenance or improvement of its position in the organizational hierarchy, and with the reduction of pressures. The work groups possess characteristics that are affected by the nature of the work they perform and are reflected in their pay rates, grievance activities, production norms, and levels of cohesion.[4] In response to changes in status measures or in pressures, they evolve production norms, affect direct and indirect production costs, engage in social activities, and generate grievances. Their actions are affected by their position in the work force, their relationship with their foreman, their estimate of his influence with the superintendent, and the degree of success achieved in their previous collective actions.

[4] These characteristics are largely derived from the findings of L. R. Sayles [16], and Seashore [18].

RESULTS

Table 2 summarizes the results of the experimentation on the means of the criterion variables.[5] The following notation is used in referring to the experimental variations performed on the model: A, grievance behavior, B, cost emphasis, C, leadership style, D, congruence of leadership style, E, attitude of the industrial engineering department.

Some of the more interesting findings were:

1. *Employee-oriented grievance attitude:* Very little effect on the performance criteria.

2. *Low emphasis on cost:* Average level of profits lower; ratio of sales revenue to inventory value lower; unit costs and average level of group cohesion at higher average levels.

3. *Employee-oriented leadership style:* High average levels of profits; high ratio of sales revenue to inventory value; average levels unit costs, group cohesion, and group pressure significantly lower.

4. *Low congruence in leadership style:* Higher average levels of profits; higher ratio of sales revenue to inventory value; significantly lower average of group cohesion and group pressure.

5. *Attitude of industrial engineering department tending toward loose, stable work standards:* Higher average level of profits; lower average level in unit costs.

6. *Employee-oriented attitude towards grievances together with low cost emphasis or an industrial engineering department attitude favoring, loose, stable work standards:* Lower level of group cohesion.

7. *Low emphasis on cost and low congruence of leadership style:* Lower levels of group cohesion and group pressure; lower profits; higher unit costs; lower group pressure.

8. *Low emphasis on cost and attitude of industrial engineering department tending toward loose, stable work standards:* Profits higher and sales efficiency lower.

9. *Employee-oriented leadership style and low congruence of leadership style:* Higher average

[5] This table shows only one of the analyses performed on the criterion variables. The variances and the trends were also studied and are discussed in Kaczka [11]. To check the stability of the model, several long-term and short-term analyses were conducted. The results indicated a very high degree of stability.

TABLE 2   Significant Effects on Means of Criterion Variables

Experimental Variation[a]	Profits/1000	Sales Efficiency	Sales Revenue to Inventory Value		Group Cohesion	Group Pressure
B	-10.195^b	—	$-.06812^c$	$.1506^b$	2.010^b	—
C	7.046^b	—	$.06410^c$	$-.1163^b$	-5.637^b	$-.0941^b$
D	5.925^b	—	$.06548^c$	$-.0881^b$	-2.362^b	$-.0217^b$
E	1.183^c	—	—	$-.0302^b$	—	—
AB	—	—	—	—	-1.148^b	—
AE	—	—	—	—	-1.205^c	—
BC	—	—	—	—	-2.069^b	$-.0458^b$
BD	-1.592^b	—	—	$.0246^b$	1.194^d	$-.0165^c$
BE	1.080^c	$-.00306^c$	—	$-.0197^c$	—	—
CD	3.498^b	—	$.06939^c$	$-.0598^b$	—	$-.0240^b$
DE	$-.886^d$	—	—	—	—	—
Block	—	$-.00709^b$	—	—	—	—

[a] A, grievance behavior; B, cost emphasis; C, leadership style; D, congruence of leadership style; E, attitude of industrial engineering department. The main effect is defined as the difference between the average response at the employee-oriented level and the average response at the task-oriented level; i.e., $A_1 - A_0$. For A and B, the interaction effect of AB is defined as the difference between the effect of changing from A at the task-oriented level to A at the employee-oriented level with B at the task-oriented level and B at the employee-oriented level. For more details see O. L. Davies [9].
[b] Level of significance is .01.
[c] Level of significance is .05.
[d] Level of significance is .10.

level in the ratio of sales revenue to inventory value; lower average level of group pressures.

10. *Low congruence of leadership style and an industrial engineering department favoring loose but stable work standards:* Low average level of profits.

[6] Two findings bear comparison with Bonini's [3]. Bonini found that a tight industrial engineering department reduced cost and price, but profits were not changed significantly, since there was also a large decrease in sales. This study found that a loose industrial engineering department decreased unit costs and increased profits. Part of this difference may be attributed to a related factor, cost emphasis, which is treated separately in this study. A low emphasis on costs results in high costs and low profits. In this study, the combined effect of high emphasis on costs and a tight industrial engineering department yields lower unit costs, a slightly higher sales, and higher profits. Thus, the effects on unit costs are similar. Bonini also observed that high variability in the environment had a positive effect on sales. This is similar to the effect observed when firms were initially faced with declining sales. Under this condition, sales efficiency was higher. It is important to remember there are several differences between this model and Bonini's. The most obvious are that this model explicitly incorporated work groups, and dealt only broadly with the marketing function. Bonini did not incorporate work groups but developed, more extensively, the sales aspect of his model firm.

11. *Rising demand initially:* Sales efficiency lower.[6]

IMPLICATIONS FOR MANAGERIAL CLIMATE

As measured by both economic and socio-psychological criteria, the results indicate that performance of the business firm is significantly affected by managerial climate; however, an employee-oriented managerial climate does not lead to higher levels of performance in all cases. In fact, low emphasis on costs has a marked negative effect on profits and a marked positive effect on unit costs. Thus, employee-oriented cost emphasis leads to a lower level of organizational performance. An employee-oriented attitude towards grievances has very little effect on organizational performance.

There are, however, several employee-oriented factors and interactions of factors that do result in higher levels of organizational performance. Employee-oriented leadership and low congruence of leadership style both result in higher profits, lower unit costs, and a higher ratio of sales revenue to inventory. An industrial engineering department tending toward loose, but stable work standards results in higher profits and lower unit costs. The largest interaction effects on unit cost, profit, and ratio of sales to inventory result from the employee-oriented leadership style and low leadership style congruence. Most of the findings indicate that an employee-oriented managerial climate can result in higher levels of organizational performance as measured by economic criteria.

The socio-psychological measures indicate that employee-oriented managerial climate tends to yield lower levels of pressure and group cohesion. For example, employee-oriented leadership style and high congruence of leadership style both result in low group pressure and low group cohesion. However, low emphasis on cost appears to have no effect on group pressure, but results in a higher level of group cohesion.

As pressure is defined in this study, negative values indicate higher production norms and, therefore, high levels of organizational performance. Seashore's study indicates that high group cohesion is not directly related to the level of production norms, but to the ability of a work group to enforce its norms [18]. In other words, if cohesion is high, the variability in production about the production norm is low and vice versa. In this study, the cases yielding high production norms tended to yield low group cohesion.

These findings indicate that a potent mechanism in the model has the following form:

1. Some forms of employee-oriented behavior, such as leadership style, lead to an increase in the level of production norms.

2. Higher production norms lead to lower unit costs, which in turn result in higher profits, and because of the lower inventory value, in a higher ratio of sales to inventory.

3. Higher production norms result in lower group pressure, which in turn contributes to lower group cohesion.

In the cases of low emphasis on cost, the lower performance does not appear to result solely from lower production norms. It seems that decreased sensitivity to cost allows administrative expenses and overhead costs to increase. Such increases are tolerated because of the looser definition of efficiency under low-cost emphasis.

LIMITATIONS AND CONCLUSIONS

Limitations

There are several limitations to the findings, implications, and conclusions of this study. Not all aspects of the business firm were included in the model used; strong emphasis was placed on production functions of the firm. Not all of the dimensions of the managerial climate were investigated, nor were all the criteria suggested by Likert and Seashore studied.

The model used was a synthesis of empirical data from actual firms, published empirical research reports, and derivations from the Cyert and March model and the Bonini model. Validation of the model rested on the fact that the model is based on real-world phenomena as described by specific empirical studies; however, no attempts were made to replicate and predict the actual behavior of a specific firm.

There was also the limitation imposed by the form of data available for this research. Some of the data were not in the precise quantitative form that would have been most useful. Furthermore, the available research studies often investigated only the linear relationships between variables; therefore, the fidelity of the approximation varied over the range of values that the independent variables might assume.

Within the bounds of these limitations, there are significant conclusions that can be drawn from this study.

Work Group Effects

The work groups in the model do respond to differences in managerial climate, and in turn the response of the work groups does have significant effects on the performance of the business organization.

Work groups affect the performance of the firm, as measured by specific economic criteria, by changes in their production norms, their cohesion, and their waste performance.[7] These influences alter the variability of the productive

---

[7] This is referred to as the variable portion of overhead in the model. It is an aggregate measure of such factors as scrap loss and the work-rework ratio.

effort and the levels of direct and indirect costs. Their behavior changes unit costs which, in turn, affect profits and the ratio of sales to inventory.

Under managerial climates in which the leadership style is employee-oriented, or in which the congruence of leadership style is low, unit costs are low and profits are high. The low levels of group pressure under these conditions indicate high production norms; therefore, the higher levels of organizational performance in these cases can be attributed to the behavior of work groups. In cases where the cost emphasis is low, unit costs are high and profits are low. The difference in cost emphasis appears to have no effect on group pressure. If group pressure were high, it would indicate that the high unit costs were affected by low production norms. Instead, it appears that the higher unit costs can be attributed to the higher levels of administrative expense of the superintendents and production vice-president, and to the poor waste performance of work groups tolerated under low emphasis on cost. Thus, in this case, although the work groups may have some effect on organizational performance, some of the effect should be assigned to the less efficient performance of the management of the organization.

A similar argument can be made about the effects of an industrial engineering department favoring loose, stable work standards. Since group norms do not appear to be affected, low unit costs and higher profits may be attributed to a combination of better waste performance and lower levels of administrative costs.

The interaction of low emphasis on cost with employee-oriented leadership style and with low congruence of leadership style produces high production norms. In these cases, however, high norms are overshadowed by poorer waste performance and higher administrative costs. In the first case there is no material effect on unit costs; in the second case, unit costs are higher and profits are lower. Therefore, the claims of higher organizational performance as a result of effects of low emphasis on cost and employee-oriented leadership behavior on work groups should be tempered by consideration of their effects on managerial performance.

On the whole, the results indicate that the behavior of work groups has a significant effect on the performance of industrial organizations. Furthermore, the estimate of the effects of work groups is a conservative one. This study does not consider turnover, changes in product quality, labor negotiations, and strikes. Were such factors considered, one would expect the effects of work groups on the performance of industrial organizations to be even greater than those observed. For example, poor labor relations and a lowering of product quality could result in a decrease in customer loyalty. This in turn would result in lower sales and, very likely, lower profits.

Work Group Behavior and the Behavioral Theory of the Firm

The general objective of behavioral theorists in their studies of the firm is to extend classical economic theory to include organizational and behavioral concepts. For example, Bonini's work extended the work of Barnard and Simon and stressed decision making as the basic element in organizational behavior [2, 3, 19]. His model of the firm included such organizational concepts as hierarchy, authority, influence, and, also incorporated the concepts of pressure and organizational slack used by Cyert and March [8].

This research study goes beyond Bonini's study in adding empirically based details about the behavior of work groups. The link between the work groups and the executive levels of management was provided by the middle and lower levels of management. It was felt that this extension was justified, if work groups exert significant effects on the economic performance of business organizations. Failure to consider the behavior of work groups implies either that work groups do not affect the performance of organizations or that such behavior is not pertinent to the factors being studied.

The results of this study indicate that work groups do exert a significant effect on the economic performance of the business firm. As a result, the decision-making behavior in the organization may be influenced by the behavior of work groups. The findings seem to justify extending the behavioral theory of the firm to the level of work groups. At the very least, they indicate that further investigation into the integration of the behavioral theory of the firm and the behavior of industrial work groups is warranted.

Computer Simulation and Socio-Psychological Experimentation

This study demonstrates the feasibility of computer simulation for socio-psychological experimentation. Here, simulation was employed in the investigation of a specific hypothesis; however, the advancement made by this study in the area of socio-psychological experimentation is limited. Part of the limitation of this study is due to the type of problem studied. Socio-psychological systems are very complex. As a result, the data and the specification of the relationships between variables often lack the precision desired in a computer simulation. The amount of programming effort needed to conduct a simulation is a constraint, even with the advances that have been made in simulation languages. For the present, at least, the application of computer simulation to the study of socio-psychological problems will not lead to complete prediction and replication of real-world phenomena, but will be restricted to modest, feasible goals. The goal of this study was both modest and feasible and required: (1) a statistically rigorous research design, (2) a model that incorporated empirically derived phenomena, and (3) a computer program that represented the behavior of a business organization. Each of these requirements was satisfied.

Conclusions on the Central Question

Likert and Seashore argue that a managerial climate that is employee-oriented rather than task-oriented will yield a higher level of organizational performance. They indicated that it would be necessary to eliminate the effects of market trends and technological innovation to test this hypothesis. The model employed in this study was constructed to meet these requirements. Furthermore, the structure and content of the model was based, as much as possible, on the published empirical reports of the Institute for Social Research, the empirical basis of much of the Likert and Seashore study, although the model did not consider all the effects they suggested.

In general, the results tend to support the Likert and Seashore hypothesis. Several of the dimensions of managerial climate and interactions of these dimensions yielded higher levels of organizational performance under employee orientation than were realized under task orientation. The notable exception was low emphasis on cost, which yielded poorer performance.

In summary, the most efficient levels of performance result when concern for cost performance is combined into concern for the employees of the organization.

REFERENCES

1. R. F. Bales, 1959. Small-group theory and research. *Sociology today* (R. K. Merton, L. Broom, and L. S. Cottrell, eds.); New York: Basic Books, 293–305.
2. C. I. Barnard, 1938. *The functions of the executive.* Cambridge, Mass.: Harvard University Press.
3. C. P. Bonini, 1963. *Simulation of information and decision systems in the firm.* Englewood Cliffs, N.J.: Prentice-Hall, second edition in 1967 by Markham Publishing of Chicago. 5B.
4. K. E. Boulding, 1955. *Economic analysis.* New York: Harper, third edition.
5. A. A. Brown, F. T. Hulswit, and J. D. Kettelle, 1956. A study of sales operations. *Operations Research, 4*(3): 296–308.
6. V. E. Buck, 1963. *Job pressures on managers: sources, subjects, and correlates.* Doctoral dissertation, Cornell University.
7. W. G. Cochran and G. M. Cox, 1950. *Experimental designs.* New York: Wiley, second edition in 1957.
8. R. M. Cyert, and J. G. March, 1963. *A behavioral theory of the firm.* Englewood Cliffs, N.J.: Prentice-Hall. 2B.
9. O. L. Davis (ed.), 1956. *The design and analysis of industrial experiments.* New York: Hafner.
10. L. Festinger, S. Schachter, and K. Back, 1950. *Social pressures in informal groups.* New York: Harper.
11. E. E. Kaczka, 1966. *The impact of some dimensions of managerial climate on the performance of industrial organizations.* Doctoral dissertation, Rensselaer Polytechnic Institute. 2B.
12. H. J. Leavitt, and B. M. Bass, 1964. Organizational psychology. *Annual Review of Psychology, 15*: 371–398.
13. R. Likert, 1961. *New patterns of management.* New York: McGraw-Hill.

REFERENCES continued

14. R. Likert, and S. E. Seashore, 1963. Making cost control work. *Harvard Business Review, 41*(6): 96–108.
15. A. J. Lott, and B. E. Lott, 1965. Group cohesiveness as interpersonal attraction: a review of relationships with antecedent and consequent variables. *Psychological Bulletin, 64*(4): 259–309.
16. L. R. Sayles, 1958. *Behavior of industrial work groups.* New York: Wiley.
17. E. Schwartz, 1962. Financing current operations, Part I. *Corporation finance:* New York: St. Martin's, 232–250.
18. S. E. Seashore, 1954. *Group cohesiveness in the industrial work group.* Ann Arbor, Mich.: Institute for Social Research.
19. H. A. Simon, 1957. *Administrative behavior.* New York: Macmillan, second edition.
20. D. S. Tull, 1965. The carry-over effects of advertising. *Journal of Marketing, 29*(2): 46–53.
21. B. J. Winer, 1962. *Statistical principles in experimental design.* New York: McGraw-Hill.

15

INTRAORGANIZATIONAL DECISION PROCESSES INFLUENCING THE EDP STAFF BUDGET

C. EDWARD WEBER[1]

INTRODUCTION

The paper reports the results of a field study and suggests implications for a behavioral theory of the firm. *The Behavioral Theory of the Firm* and related works provide a conceptual framework for analyzing management decision making [3, 5, 7, 11, 12]. Within this framework, managing can be viewed as a process involving the interaction of the decision strategies of the members of the organization; and a strategy can be defined as a set of constraints, rules or relations among variables that govern the sequence of responses to information [1, 8, 9].[2]

Budgeting, the primary orientation of the paper, is hypothesized in *The Behavioral Theory of the Firm* to be part of the more general process of setting goals [3, pp. 26–38]. The firm

SOURCE: Reprinted from *Management Science*, *12*: B-69–92 (1965).

[1]The author is indebted to James G. March for his comments thoughout the study. Many useful suggestions were made by my colleagues, and able assistance was given by Walter McGhee and P. K. B. Nayar.

[2]Herbert Simon, for example, defines strategy as a detailed prescription that governs the sequence of responses of a system to a complex task environment [9, p. 6]. In a paper, "Deliberation and Judgment," [1, p. 49] C. West Churchman defines personal logic as the process by which the information processor transforms inputs into decisions.

is considered to be a coalition in which members bargain about policy commitments; and, then they use the budgeting process to bargain about the specific content of the commitments. Policy matters, it is argued, are exceedingly complex and defy exact definition in advance of implementation.

Major aspects of a behavioral theory of the firm, accordingly, are that the budgeting of resources is the outcome of the interaction of the decision strategies of several individuals and that this interaction can be characterized as a bargaining process. However, there are few field studies which address themselves to the content and interaction of decision strategies in ongoing business firms.[3]

The field study reported here is intended to contribute to a behavioral theory of the firm in several ways. First, it shows the constraints entering into the strategies of managers in a specific situation. Secondly, the analysis of these strategies suggests how organization goals are woven into the decisions of individual managers; and, thirdly, the analysis suggests the character of the interaction of decision strategies. I found

[3] For examples of two field studies, one by R. M. Cyert, J. G. March and C. G. Moore [3, Chapter 7], and the other by G. P. E. Clarkson [2].

less bargaining in the field situation than the above aspects of the behavioral theory of the firm would lead me to expect. There were conflict and "politics," but these appeared to be due to differences in judgments about goal expectations of others, especially superiors.

The field study focused on several managers whose strategies influenced the budgeted size and composition of the staff of an electronic data processing department in a company. Two of the managers were directly responsible for proposing the salary budget of the electronic data processing department (EDP), but their decisions were influenced by the goal statement of their superiors, by the "demand for service" from their most dynamic user, and by corporate staff members who had formal advisory positions.[4]

Method of Analysis

Five computer decision models were developed to describe the strategies of the managers studied. To test the models, simulated decisions were used to predict actual decisions; and comparisons were made between the predicted and actual decisions.

The analysis of budgeting and related strategies in an ongoing organization can be approached in different ways. My approach was to formulate hypotheses about the strategies from interviews, to construct models from the hypotheses, and then to test the models with different data. The models assert that certain data are the inputs for the decision strategies and that decisions are reached on the basis of these inputs and on the basis of specific relations between the inputs and the decisions.

Computer programs have the value of allowing one to describe decision strategies more rigorously and to test these descriptions more systematically. Ambiguity in the results of a field study is difficult to avoid in any event, but the ambiguity can be reduced by the effort to translate prose descriptions or schematic representations of behavior into computer program statements. Essentially, this is a reduction in the ambiguity of the hypotheses proposed by the researcher. Various interpretations still remain

of what relationships were observed, but this is the nature of field study where one can make limited observations of complex open systems. The reported research is no exception; but I submit that, despite the "curve fitting," systematic field study provides insight for theory construction and added confidence for the design of laboratory experiments.

Approximately 50 interviews were conducted with the persons involved in the budget and related processes. These interviews were conducted to develop the computer programs and to obtain data for simulation. In addition, questionnaires were used to obtain other data for simulation.

It was necessary to use past decisions in the study. Since decisions on budgets are made only once a year in the company, the time required to wait for future decisions was too great to accumulate such data. Widespread, reassignments of personnel which were made after the collection of past data, further complicated the problem of follow-up.

Separate computer programs were developed for the decision strategies of the participants. Five programs were written in total. These programs had to be developed and tested as separate entities because the interviews were confidential. To test the programs as an integrated model would have required that I ask directed questions about situations described by the other participants, and this would have revealed sources of information.

Although the confidential nature of the data made it more appropriate that the decision strategies of the participants be written and tested as separate programs, integration of the strategies may bring out the character of their interaction more clearly. To do this, hypotheses were gleaned from the interviews on how the programs of the participants were related to each other.

The five models are described in the next section, along with suggested hypotheses for their connections to each other. In the following section, data for testing the models are summarized. As indicated above, comparisons were made between predicted decisions and actual decisions. In the final section, the characteristics of the interaction of the strategies and other implications are discussed.

---

[4] Goss [6] provides an example in another context of how control is exercised through formal advisory positions.

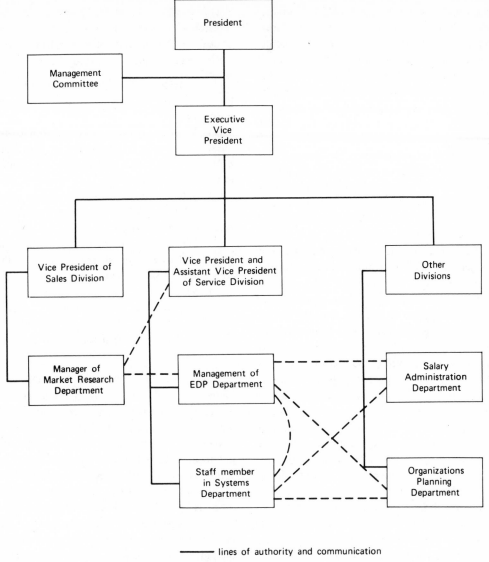

lines of authority and communication

— — — lines of communication

Figure 1 Organization.

MODELS OF DECISION STRATEGIES

Models were developed for the decision strategies of the following participants:

1. Manager of market research;
2. Management of EDP (electronic data processing department);
3. Staff member of systems department; and
4. Superior of EDP management.

The organizational structure of these managers and others whose judgments they considered is shown in Figure 1.

The market research department was the largest user of electronic data processing services outside of accounting and absorbed 30% of EDP's processing time. The manager of market research reported to the vice president of the sales division. In the course of implementing the projects of his department, he communicated with EDP management and their superiors.

The management of EDP (Figure 1) consisted of the supervisor of EDP and his manager who was also responsible for other kinds of administrative service departments. They worked as a team, making decisions on what projects were to be done by EDP and what staff budgets to propose for EDP. In the process of making their decisions, the supervisor gathered routine and technical information and his manager maintained liaison with other departments. The manager over the EDP supervisor reported to the assistant vice president of the service division.

In the systems department, the strategy of a senior staff member was studied. He, of course, reported to the manager of the systems department; and the manager of the systems department reported to the assistant vice president of the service division.

The superior of EDP management as shown in Figure 1 was the assistant vicepresident of the service division. Although he was also the superior of the manager of the systems department, the assistant vice president of the service division is referred to simply as the superior of EDP management in the paper because this was the role he played in the decision processes under consideration. The assistant vice president of the service division appeared to be the internal operating head of the division, while his superior, the vice president, appeared to handle certain external company relations and to participate in the deliberations of the management committee. The vice president appeared to interpret company policies discussed by the management committee to his subordinates. It is important to note that the manager of market research also participated in management committee deliberations.

Model I: Manager of Market Research

The work done by market research involved the analysis of information and ranged from elaborate, routine and repetitive projects to high priority "one-shot" projects. The manager of market research received project suggestions from the chairman of the board, the president, the executive vice president, the management of the sales department, his own department and companies with which they dealt. Market research, for example, estimated the demand for new products, analyzed information gathered by company salesmen, and appraised the feasibility of plant locations.

The model for the manager of market research was developed to simulate a sequence of decisions on initiating projects. His decisions which were simulated included the following:

(1)   Whether market research should undertake specific project proposals for the analysis of information;

(2)   Whether market research should request assistance in the processing of data from EDP in the event that market research decided to undertake a project;

(3)   Whether market research should press its request if EDP did not agree to give assistance when requested initially;

(4)   What, if any, alternative method should be selected to accomplish the project if EDP continued to reject their request;

(5)   Whether to ask EDP to modify its decision to postpone the completion of a report in the event that EDP agreed to undertake a project and later felt that the agreed deadline should be extended.

These decisions influenced the EDP staff budget (Model III). It is hypothesized in Model III that EDP management would make a judgment on the need to expand service in developing its proposed budget, and this judgment appeared to depend upon the interaction between market research and EDP in the scheduling of projects. There were, of course, other users of EDP's services, but their requirements were stable and did not enter into the budget decisions of EDP management. In effect, the interaction between EDP and market research created political pressures which EDP management did not choose to ignore.

Figure 2 represents the computer model of the strategy which the manager of market research appeared to use in order to initiate projects. The flow diagram is a condensation of the complete program and is intended only to convey the major constraints in the manager's strategy. The complete programs are available to the reader who wishes to pursue the analysis in greater depth. Not all of the types of decisions outlined above are explicitly shown in this chart, but they are implicit in its structure.

The market research manager's strategy consisted of a sequence of constraints, and his choice depended upon whether a specific

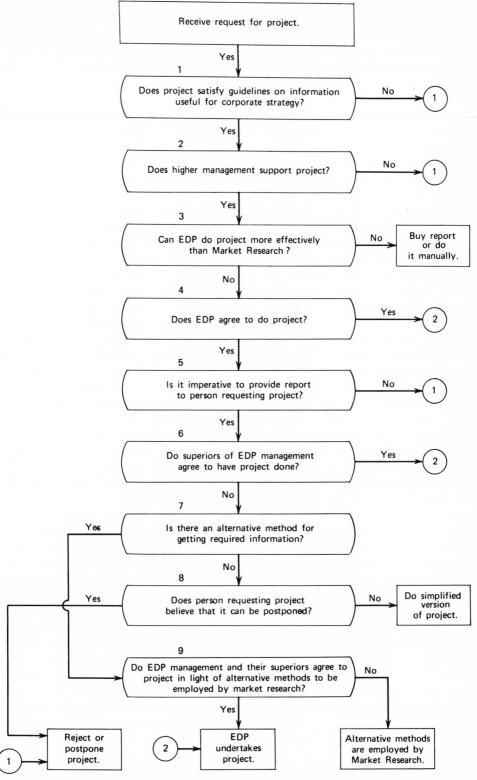

Figure 2   Model I: Manager of market research project initiation strategy.

project satisfied these constraints. This can be readily observed in Figure 2 by scanning it from top to bottom, without tracing through the flow of the arrows. The constraints and other elements in the strategy are numbered and are referred to as No. 1, No. 2, etc. in the paper.

The constraints entering into his strategy were of two types. One type is related to the technical feasibility of the project while the other type is related to his judgments of the objectives of other managers, especially superiors.[5] Both types of constraints were found in the decision strategies of the other participants as well.

Hopefully, the flow charts can convey the decision strategies without an extensive description accompanying them; but it may be helpful to describe the first one in some detail. The first major constraint (Figure 2, No. 1) considered by the manager of market research involved the usefulness of the information for corporate strategy. The usefulness of the information was evaluated in terms of four overlapping guides. Information was considered to be useful if it pertained to the productivity of salesmen, pricing, competitive position, and sales volume. Another guideline implicit in No. 1 and included in the program was the availability of the data to carry out the project. Whether a proposal satisfied one or more of these guidelines contained in No. 1 was a judgment by the manager of market research which entered into the program as in input. In general, the research was an endeavor to simulate how the managers combined or weighed their many technical and political judgments to reach a decision rather than an endeavor to simulate the judgments themselves.

If the project satisfied constraint No. 1, then it was considered in terms of its likely support from higher management (sales vice president, executive vice president, president, and/or chairman of the board). In considering this constraint (Figure 2, No. 2), the manager of market research took into account several guidelines. One consideration was whether he had resources to commit to the proposal. Another was whether higher management was willing to

commit resources to the proposal if he did not have the resources. He did not commit his own resources or request authorization to commit other resources to the proposal before taking into account potential conflict between the proposal and the current objectives of the company. The manager of market research made this judgment after sounding out higher management and possibly individuals from organizations outside the company. For example, one proposal, which was to request the collection of information by a customer, raised the question of whether the request would harm relations with this customer.

The next constraint (Figure 2, No. 3) was the judgment by the manager of market research on whether EDP could do the project more effectively than his own department. Here, a consideration was the cost of purchasing the report and the cost of doing it manually compared to using data processing equipment. Another consideration was whether the project was too big for EDP.

The manager of market research asked EDP to undertake the processing of data if he judged that EDP could do it more effectively than his own department. His strategy then depended upon the response of EDP management to his request (Figure 2, No. 4). If EDP management rejected his request or asked him to postpone it, the manager of market research made a judgment on the necessity of providing the information (No. 5). The judgment involved sounding out the person originally requesting the information from market research.

The manager of market research took his request to the assistant vice president and then to the vice president of the service division if he judged it imperative to provide the report. Information that they rejected the request (Figure 2, No. 6) caused the manager of market research to consider alternative ways (No. 7) of processing information for the project. These alternatives included having the project done on equipment located in divisions of the company not responsible for this type of work, having the project done by an outside agency, and enlarging his own staff to undertake the project. It is important to note that he did not directly undertake an alternative method of processing the information but simply proposed such

[5] The concept of organizational objectives as constraints in the strategy of the decision maker is elaborated by Simon [10].

action. He, then, waited for a response from EDP (No. 9). EDP management and their superiors might offer to process the information when alternative methods were proposed as shown in Figure 2. They apparently had an interest in maintaining their position as the department which serviced the divisions located at company headquarters. The way in which they responded to requests and suggestions from the manager of market research is shown in later flow charts.

The strategy used by the manager of market research to reach his decisions on his requests that EDP management modify its postponement of the report deadline is not shown in Figure 2. However, the constraints entering into this decision were similar to those shown in Figure 2.

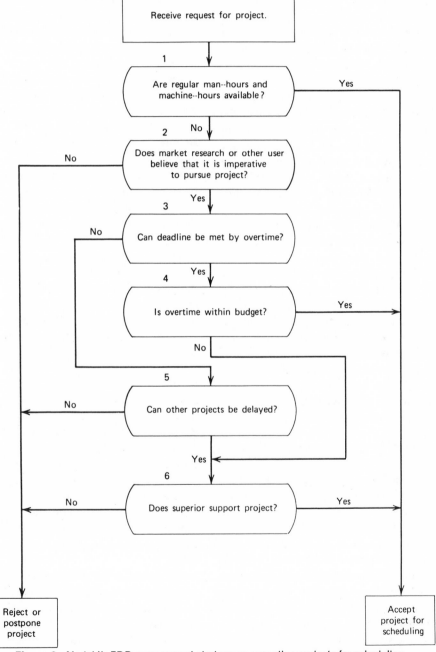

Figure 3   Model II: EDP management strategy on accepting projects for scheduling.

Model II. EDP Management—Scheduling

Model II represents the decision strategy of EDP management in considering requests from the manager of market research and other users. At the time of the study, however, only market research was requesting additional data processing service.

Figure 3 shows the major constraints included in the model. The decision strategy for accepting or rejecting projects seems to be straightforward. Projects were accepted if slack existed (Figure 3, Nos. 1, 3 and 4). Even if slack did not exist, projects could be accepted. This depended, first, on whether ongoing projects could be postponed (No. 5). Processing payroll, for example, was a project that could not be postponed. Secondly, it depended on whether the superior of EDP management was judged to support the project (No. 6). EDP management apparently made this judgment after sounding out their superiors. Again, we find that the constraints were about either technical matters or the objectives of superiors.

One might expect that agreement would be reached easily between market research and EDP since the participants were oriented towards the same considerations, but such was not the case. The objectives were apparently interpreted differently by the participants in the early stages of the decision process, and the interpretations apparently converged only later. Possible explanations are discussed in the section on implications. It is interesting to note, however, that the deliberations of the management committee appeared to be the common source of these interpretations.

Model III. EDP Management—Budgeting Strategy

EDP management proposed a staff budget at the end of the third quarter of the year for the following year. The proposed budget showed the number of persons for each of 13 job grades. The critical decisions in constructing the staff budget were the number of persons to propose in each of the 13 grades. In making these decisions, EDP management weighed the feasibility of specific proposals for changing the existing composition and size of staff. Model III describes the strategy which EDP management apparently employed in deciding the size and composition of its staff budget, and the constraints for this strategy are shown in Figure 4. There are four major aspects of EDP management's strategy described by this model. First, there are constraints set by the objectives which EDP management was expected to meet in their budget. Secondly, there is a list of proposals for modifying the size and composition of the staff, and there are accompanying rules for the search or recall of these proposals. Thirdly, there are technical and "political" constraints used to evaluate proposed changes; and fourthly, there are rules for calculating the budget.

The first aspect described by Model III involves the constraints set by the objectives which EDP management was expected to meet in their budget (Figure 4, No. 1). These constraints consisted of the need to expand staff in order to meet requests for service and the need to reduce cost. EDP made judgments on the appropriate values to be taken by these constraints, and these judgments entered into their decision strategy (and the model) to determine their approach to revising the staff budget. As indicated above, such judgments were inputs for the model and set the values of the constraints since the purposes of the research were to determine the constraints in the decision strategies and to determine the relations among these strategies. The judgments were obtained by interviews and questionnaires.

The constraint on whether there was an imperative need to expand service (No. 1) seemed to result from conflictual interaction between EDP management and the manager of market research over the scheduling of projects. Their strategies for scheduling projects are shown in Figures 2 and 3 and are described above. The constraint on whether there was an imperative need to reduce cost (No. 1) seemed to result from communications with the superior of EDP management. The superior's strategy is shown in Figure 5 and is described below.

The second aspect of Model III is the list of proposals for modifying the size and composition of the staff with the accompanying search rules (Figure 4, No. 2). These proposals were received from systems over the course of the year and were held for review during the

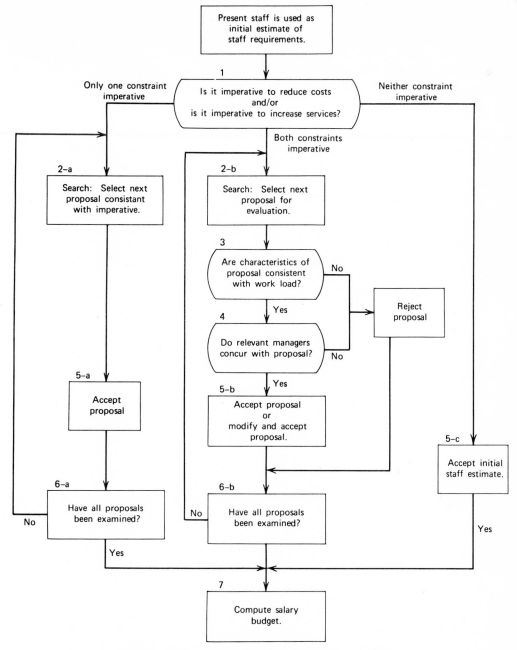

Figure 4   Model III: EDP management budgeting strategy.

budget period. The proposals called for specific changes in the number of persons associated with specific grades. It is important to emphasize that the proposals were *not* designed to meet the constraints to expand service and/or reduce cost but to meet specific changes in the organization of the work. These constraints (No. 1) set the climate in which the proposals

were evaluated. A proposal, for example, might be to transfer certain work from EDP to other locations and to reduce certain grades by specific amounts. Another example, might be to increase the number in the higher grades by specific amounts and to reduce the number in lower grades by specific amounts because of the installation of a larger computer. The search or recall of proposals from the list of proposals was apparently straightforward. All proposals were considered if there were conflicting constraints to expand service and to reduce cost; and only proposals consistent with these constraints were recalled for consideration if the constraints were not in conflict.

The third aspect described in Figure 4 is the set of technical and political constraints (Nos. 3 and 4) used to evaluate specific proposals where the constraints (No. 1) to expand service and to reduce cost were not consistent. This situation prevailed in the years studied, and EDP management faced the problem of resolving the conflict. Their strategy was apparently to relax the constraints on cost and service (No. 1) and to test for consensus (No. 4) on all available proposals. In effect, they by-passed a means-end analysis and tested for agreement on specific changes [7].

Proposals could call for an expansion, contraction, or no change (e.g., "conduct a study"). One proposal, for example, was to reduce the staff by given numbers in specified grades because of a transfer of work from EDP to other departments in the company. Another proposal was to expand staff by a specified amount because of the addition of certain work. Both kinds of proposals could be and were reviewed for the same budget, and both could be and were incorporated into the staff estimate if they satisfied the constraints summarized in Nos. 3 and 4. The characteristics of the proposal had to be consistent with the work load or changing complexity of the work (No. 3) for the proposal to be acceptable. For example, a proposed reduction in staff would need to be accompanied by a specific reduction in assigned work; or an upgrading of staff would need to be accompanied by new activities related to the

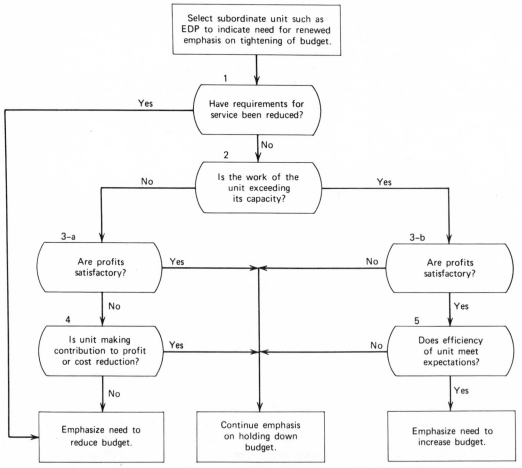

Figure 5 Model IV-a: Superior of EDP management emphasis on tightening subordinates' budgets.

operation of a larger computer. The relevant managers had to concur with the proposal (No. 4) for it to be acceptable. The managers whose consensus was relevant depended upon the characteristics of the proposal and could include the superiors of EDP management, managers of user departments, systems staff, salary administration staff, and organization planning staff.

The fourth aspect is about the rules for calculating the budget. The present staff is used as the initial estimate of staff requirements in making the calculations. Any proposed changes which are accepted, or modified and accepted, are used to modify the initial estimate (No. 5). For example, proposed reductions in staff are halved under specified circumstances before being accepted. Total salaries are computed in the model by multiplying the number in a grade by the midpoint of the salary range of the grade and by summing the salaries across all grades (No. 7).

In sum, EDP management sought to propose a budget which reflected company objectives as these objectives were communicated by other participants to EDP management and were interpreted by EDP management.

Model IV. Superior of EDP Management

Model IV was developed for the following types of decisions made by the superior of EDP management:

(1) Whether to emphasize the tightening of subordinate units' budgets; and

(2) Whether to support proposals to change the size and mix of EDP staff.

These decisions relate to Model III on EDP management's strategy in proposing a staff budget. The decisions about the emphasis on tightening the budget (Model IV) are associated with the constraint in Model III on the need to reduce cost. The exact connection was seemingly the result of the judgment of EDP management on what the superior said and the context in which it was said. The decisions of the superior on supporting specific proposals (Model IV) were related to the constraint in Model III on the need for consensus among specified managers.

The major constraints contained in Model IV are shown in Figures 5 and 6. The constraints relate to the superior's judgment on the profit position of the company and on the overload and efficiency of the subordinate unit. The basis for his judgment on the profit position of the company was apparently the deliberation of the management committee.

Model V: System's Staff Member

The decisions included in Model V are the following:

(1) Whether to make a specific proposal on the size and organization of EDP staff; and

(2) Whether to support proposals for which EDP management is checking for consensus.

The strategy for the first type of decision is shown in Figure 7. The strategy for the second is similar to that of the first type and is not shown. The first type of decision relates to how proposals get on the list of proposals in Model III, while the second relates to the check for consensus in the same model.

As indicated earlier, the timing of decisions by systems to recommend changes was sporadic and was not confined to the same quarter of the year during which the budget was prepared. Systems was apparently the primary source of proposals for staff changes, and it was a source that sometimes generated ideas independently from EDP management.

Model V includes two occasions for which the staff member from systems considered changes in the size or mix of EDP staff, and these are shown at the top of Figure 7. The staff member considered making recommendations either if his department felt that there was a need for such a change or if it received a request to make recommendations. Both types of occasions implied a responsiveness of systems to the objectives of higher management. The felt need arose when system's own projects were being impeded by an inadequate organization or lack of staff in EDP. These were projects which systems had been requested to design by higher management and to whose success systems was committed. Requests to make recommendations came when there was a change in the mix of projects for programming and processing data.

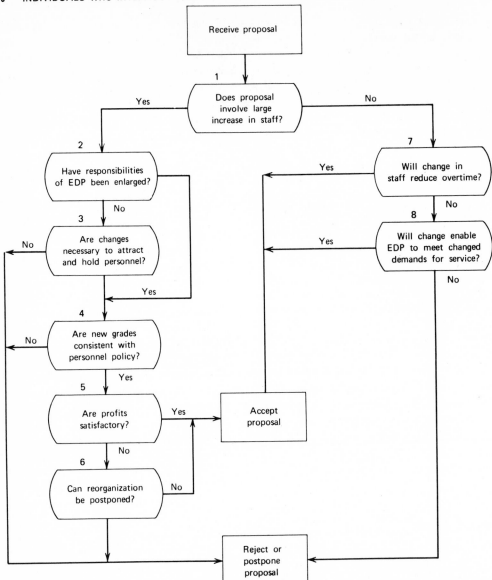

Figure 6 Model IV-b: Superior of EDP management review of proposals to change EDP staff budget.

If the staff member of systems decided to make recommendations to EDP management, he developed a proposal for changing the organization of EDP (Figure 7, No. 3). The development of the proposal is enclosed in a broken line to indicate that this stage of the decision process is not included in the model. The proposals are treated as inputs for the model.

The major constraints for reviewing proposals are shown in Figure 7. The constraints are technical feasibility, consistency with personnel policy, and acceptability to other organizational units (Nos. 1, 2, 5 and 6). Again, we can

observe the same type of "touching base" as was observed in the budget process and with the same results. In making their decisions, the participants took each others' attitudes into account. There seems to be a mutual exploration undertaken whenever it is necessary to determine how proposed changes relate to the corporate objectives.

SIMULATION RESULTS

The models were developed on the basis of information from one year and tested on the basis of information from the two previous years. Testing the models, as indicated above, involved the use of simulated decisions to predict actual decisions, and the comparison of the predicted and actual decisions.

Information for testing the models was obtained from budgets, memoranda on budget guidelines, and questionnaires. Questionnaires were very heavily relied upon for testing because the greater part of the information hypothesized to be required for decision was not recorded. For example, Model II asserted that

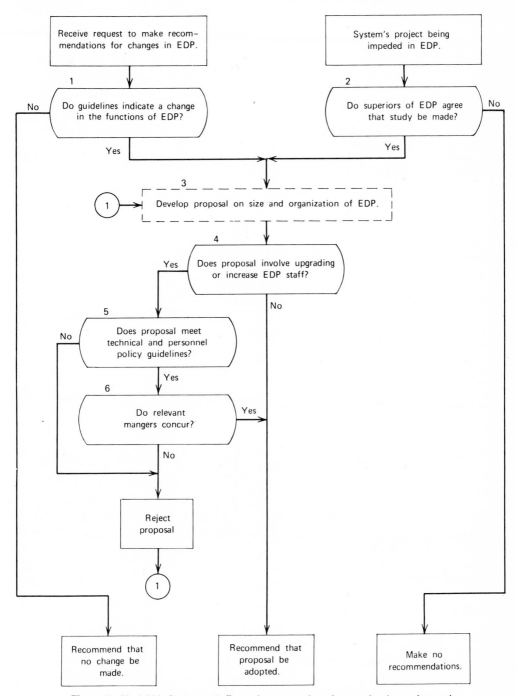

Figure 7   Model V: Systems staff member proposing changes in size and organization of EDP staff.

TABLE 1   Frequency with Which Predicted and Actual Decisions Were the Same and Frequency with Which They Were Different

Type of Decision	Number of Decisions in the Two Years for Which Models Were Tested		
	Predicted same as Actual	Predicted not same as Actual	Total
Model I: Manager of Market Research			
1. Decisions on undertaking proposals for analysis of information	13	1	14
2. Decisions on requesting assistance from EDP	8	1	9
3. Decisions on pressing request if EDP did not agree to give assistance	3	0	3
4. Selection of alternative methods if EDP, again, rejects requests	5	4	9
5. Decisions on requesting EDP to modify its postponement of report deadline	2	0	2
Total	31	6	37
Model II: EDP Management			
1. Decisions on accepting projects for scheduling	9	3	12
Total	9	3	12
Model III: EDP Management			
1. Decisions on feasibility of proposals for changing staff budgets	5	0	5
2. Decisions on number of staff by job classes proposed in the budgets	24	2	26
Total	29	2	31
Model IV: Superior of EDP Management			
1. Decisions about emphasis to place on the tightening of subordinate units' budgets	2	3	5
2. Decisions about whether to approve proposals to increase EDP salary budgets	4	1	5
Total	6	4	10
Model V: Systems Staff Member			
1. Decisions on size and organization of EDP staff	6	1	7
2. Decisions on whether to support proposals	3	0	3
Total	9	1	10

projects were accepted automatically if running time and manpower were available, but there were no records of manpower and running time. The information had to be obtained by questionnaire. Eleven different questionnaires were used to obtain the needed information. The questions were randomly ordered to reduce influencing the responses by a "logical" sequence. One of the questionnaires is shown in the Appendix.

The comparison of predicted and actual decisions for the two years for which the models were tested is summarized in Table 1. The table shows, for each type of decision, the number of predicted and actual decisions which were the same and the number of decisions which were not the same.

The comparison in Table 1 reveals that the predicted results were the same as the actual results for the predominate number of situations for some models and for a non-significant number of situations for other models.[6] I returned to the company to interview the managers in question and to examine the relevant documents for each instance in which the predicted results diverged from the actual results. An endeavor was made to reconstruct in each instance how the actual decision was made and to compare this with the simulated strategy. The differences where the divergence seems significant are examined in the remaining part of this section.

Model I predicted the actual decisions in almost every instance, except for the fourth type of decision (Table 1). In type 4 decision, the manager of market research was hypothesized to select *one* among alternative methods of processing data (e.g. enlarge his own staff) if

---

[6] One test of the significance of the observed results is to use the normal approximation to the binomial distribution with $\mu = \hat{p} = .50$ and $\sigma\hat{p} = \sqrt{\bar{p}\bar{q}/n}$ where p' is the observed proportion of the total decisions correctly chosen by the model. Using this test with a two-tail confidence interval and assuming the .05 level, Models I, III, and V yield significant results; while Models II and IV yield non-significant results. The same results are obtained when the binomial distribution is used directly instead of the normal approximation. There are methodological questions in testing these models statistically. For example, the above test assumes that the types of decisions within a particular model are independent, but this does not seem to be the case. The most serious question is how one weighs the evidence obtained from the interviews to construct the models against the sample displayed in Table 1 to test the models. The sample must be small because of the nature of the decision process. Statistical decision theory could, perhaps, be used if the interviewer were willing to attach probability statements to the hypotheses developed from the interviews. Perhaps consideration should be given to this possibility; but not in a situation as complex as the one contained in the study.

EDP would not undertake the work. In fact, he divided the work among the several alternatives in the four instances for which the predicted results differed from the actual results. In two of these four instances, he compromised with EDP management; and divided the work between EDP and another method such as contracting it out. The model assumed that at least one method was adequate for accomplishing the work, but this apparently was not correct. An interesting question is why testing for adequacy and combining methods did not occur earlier in the decision strategy. An earlier effort in this direction would have avoided extensive conflict. I submit that an earlier effort was not possible because of the participants' mutual expectation that EDP would undertake all such work. The constraints on EDP prevented them from meeting this expectation, and the conflict was necessary perhaps to make compromises among methods a legitimate solution.

Model II predicted only nine of the twelve instances correctly (Table 1). The three instances of incorrect predictions were actually situations in which the model was unable to make predictions. A hypothesis in the model was that EDP management would be certain about whether their superior supported the project and whether manpower was available during regular time. Uncertainty existed, however, in the three situations; and the model was not designed to process such inputs.

For Model III, the predicted results were the same as the actual results for a predominant number of situations (Table 1). The two discrepancies which did occur seemed to be attributable to clerical errors in the actual process. For Model IV, in contrast, the predicted and actual decisions (type 1) were the same in only two of the five instances. In one of the three incorrect predictions, the actual decision was to expand the department's budget because of an anticipated increase in work; but the model considered an overload only when it had already occurred. The model did not include *anticipated* changes because no data existed to support its inclusion during the time in which the model was being constructed. The other two incorrect predictions involved situations where the superior was uncertain about the values to be assigned to his constraints. The model was not designed to cope with this ambiguity. This divergence between predicted and actual results was similar to the one uncovered in Model II. Finally, the results for Model V included only one instance in which the predicted decision was not the same as the actual. In this one instance, the staff member relaxed the constraint of requiring consensus for the proposal.

IMPLICATIONS

In the paper, the major constraints in the models were described, and some general relations among the models were suggested. Data for testing the models were summarized; but, as pointed out above, it was not feasible to test the relations among the models.

The constraints and their interrelations which were apparently operative in the situation have implications for the behavioral theory of the firm and managerial effectiveness. These implications relate to characteristics of the constraints, the information used, and the decisions made.

Characteristics of Constraints

The managers' decision strategies contain constraints which seem to have several dominant characteristics. These include the following:

(1) Responsiveness by the participants to organizational goals;

(2) Attention by the participants to cues from other participants; and

(3) Assignment of different weights to the importance of the cues.

The first characteristic is the responsiveness by the participants to statements of organizational goals. The chief executive and his management committee stated apparently whether projected profits were satisfactory, whether special emphasis should be placed upon cost reduction to obtain satisfactory profit and whether sales strategy should be changed. The changes in sales strategy involved innovation in the use of information. The new uses were technically feasible because of data processing technology. Changes in sales strategy resulted in added work for EDP; and the need to expand and

reorganize the staff. It appears on the basis of the decision models that the participants accepted the statements on goals by top management as the relevant criteria for making their choices.

The participants did not directly bring to bear personal goals, contrary to my expectations. The individuals had personal values, of course; but these values did not seem to be immediately relevant for the decisions which were studied. In other words, the participants did not appear to create values or norms for the organization, but they may have accepted the values of others "in exchange" for career advancement and other rewards [4, pp. 3–67; 8].

The second characteristic is attention by the participants to cues from other participants. Responsiveness is insufficient for explaining the decision process. Why did the participants "touch base" with each other? Why did they not know the nature of the goal statements without touching base? Various explanations can be put forward. For example, it can be argued that the participants did not want to "rock the boat"; or it can be argued that they use this as a means to resolve conflicting goals or expectations about performance which were placed upon them by their superiors; or it can be argued that they were imitating similar behavior by their superiors.

Each of these explanations is plausible, but they relate to more fundamental phenomena. The goal statements did not appear to be operational, and the participants had to learn how a specific proposal related to profit, cost and service. As one of the participants said:

I think it is everyone's objective to reduce cost and only spend money (service) where it will pay for itself by providing tools to manage and increase profit. The problem is distinguishing between service that will result in greater profit and service that is just an increase in cost. It is too simple to say that one group wants to reduce cost and another group wants service.

The participants, as a group, did not perceive a direct way to "calculate" the profitability of a proposal; but they perceived this to be a matter for subjective judgment. They sought to learn the meaning of the goals of the enterprise by probing the appropriateness of a concrete action or proposal. They sought to discover how the other participants interpreted goal statements. The participants attended to cues from the other participants to appraise the proposal.

"Touching base" is a way of learning the operational meaning of the goal statements. It is a way of transforming non-operational goals into operational goals.

Presumably, the participants would cease to be attentive after awhile if the proposals were repetitive. The proposals were not repetitive for the most part, however, because they arose out of the newly introduced sales strategy.

The third characteristic is the assignment of different weights to the importance of cues from different sources. Greater weight seems to be given to cues within divisions of the company than between them and to be given to cues from superiors than from lateral participants. These different weights appear in the decision models in several ways. A negative attitude by certain participants would lead to dropping a proposal, while a negative attitude by others would only lead to its modification. In some stages of the decision process, choices were made without consulting all of the participants. Finally, the requirement for consensus gave veto power to participants within an organizational unit since they were not the ones initiating the change.

Two explanations seem plausible for the different weights, and evidence existed for both. The authority structure provided a reason for assigning greater weight to cues from within the organizational division than to those from other divisions. The superior seemed to have extensive influence over the career advancement of subordinates, and one would expect that cues from the superior would be attended to very closely under this circumstance. Also cues from others reporting to a common superior would be attended to since these persons are more likely to be cognizant of the attitudes of the common superior than those outside the division.

The frequency of communication is another explanation for the greater weight given to some cues. One may expect to find more occasions for communicating with other participants within an organizational unit than with those in another organizational unit. Indeed, there appeared to be no ongoing mechanism for communicating between divisions except at the top level of the hierarchy. Communication between participants in different divisions at the lower levels of the hierarchy appeared to be sporadic and to be evoked by disagreements over the scheduling of projects.

The models are, of course, a simplification of the situation and are perhaps an oversimplification, and the data were limited for testing them. The information or cues received by participants is assumed to be known with certainty in the models; but, in reality, a participant may not be able to judge the position of another participant with certainty. The models also assume that the participants would have the required information. Sometimes, the assumptions did not correspond to the situation, and some of the failures to simulate the situation seemed to result from this lack of correspondence. My impression is that the constraints were ignored usually when the information or cues were not available, and the choice would be made on the available information. However, the lack of information or cues was not always ignored, and then its lack seemed to result in a decision not to act or to take a negative action.

Characteristics of Information Decisions

The decisions seem to have two general characteristics. One is whether they involve disagreement or agreement. Disagreement can arise during the scheduling of projects or whenever one of the participants seeks consensus on a proposal.

The second characteristic is the relation of the decisions to the growth of EDP staff. For example, market research may press to have EDP undertake additional work, and the senior staff member in systems may approve proposals involving the expansion of EDP staff.

On the information side, two characteristics also seem to be pervasive: profit and innovation. Whether profit is satisfactory characterizes the information required by many of the constraints either directly or indirectly. The participants either directly interpreted the statements of the chief executive and his management committee or looked for support and agreement from those who made such interpretations.

The proposals to process data are items of information which obviously are essential for the strategies of the participants, and these proposals can be characterized by the company's commitments to innovation. The stimulus for those proposals was apparently a commitment of the chief executive and his management committee to a new sales strategy. This sales strategy involved innovation in the use of information technology. Their previous sales strategy used information which resulted from the routinized processing of standardized data. The new sales strategy used additional kinds of information. The additional information, itself, was not specified; but only the general purposes of the information were specified. It was the responsibility of the management to innovate informational projects. Although innovation in the use of information was associated with sales strategy, it could be associated with any decision strategy, such as production scheduling, capital budgeting, and so forth. The essential notion is a commitment to innovation in the use of information.

Implications on the relations among the characteristics of the information and decisions are summarized in Figure 8. Let us assume that the combination occurs which is represented in the upper left box of Figure 8.[7] This combi-

[7] This assumption is not intended to suggest that profit and innovation in sales are independent of each other but that they can characterize a situation separately or together.

nation is unsatisfactory profit and no innovation. The models would suggest that there would be no requests from market research to EDP for the undertaking of data processing projects since such projects would not facilitate company sales strategy. No alternatives to increase the size of EDP would be proposed since there would be no felt need by systems or the superior EDP management for the expansion of EDP. Proposals would be made to decrease the staff of EDP if the existing functions were making no tangible contribution to profit (as perceived by the superior of EDP management) or if there were a decrease in the functions of EDP (as perceived by systems). In the budget process, there would be a demand to cut cost if EDP were making no tangible contribution to profit (as perceived by superior of EDP management). In this situation, any proposal by systems to reduce staff would be accepted. If the superior of EDP management perceived that the department were making a tangible contribution to profit, there would be neither an imperative to reduce cost nor expand service; and the current budget would be maintained. At no point in the decision process would there be disagreement among the participants, and the staff would remain the same or decline.

The combination of satisfactory profits and no innovation is represented in the upper right box of Figure 8. The lack of commitment to innovation would again result in no requests by market research for new data processing projects to be undertaken by EDP; and there

	Unsatisfactory Profit	Satisfactory Profit
No innovation in use made of information technology	Agreement. Static or declining staff.	Agreement. Static staff.
Innovation in use made of information technology	Conflict. Small upward adjustment and major growth postponed.	Agreement. Growth reflects rate of innovation.

Figure 8 Summary of relations among information and decision characteristics.

would be no demand for the increased use of EDP services. No proposals to change the size of EDP staff would be proposed by systems since neither the superior of EDP management nor systems would be prompted to look into the efficiency of EDP and since the work activities of EDP would not be increasing. Under these conditions, there would be no imperative to reduce costs or to expand service; and the current budget would be proposed for next year. Accordingly, there would be no disagreement among the participants and the size of the staff would not change.

Innovation and unsatisfactory profits are represented in the lower left box in Chart 8. Under these conditions, market research would propose that new data processing projects be undertaken by EDP. EDP management would schedule these projects until they reached their budget constraints. After the budget limit was reached, EDP management would continue to schedule projects, which they perceived as achieving the objectives of top management, until the limits of their capacity were reached. Otherwise they would refuse. Since project proposals were received from lateral units, there was no automatic connection established between the proposals and the objectives of top management. The need to learn the operational meaning of these objectives by trial and error would mean that some projects would be refused that met these objectives. These projects would then be referred to the superior of EDP management by market research in an endeavor to have the projects scheduled. These projects would be scheduled if it became apparent in discussions with the superior of EDP management that they met the objectives of the chief executive and his management committee. Accordingly, there would be disagreement over the scheduling of projects and delay in the expansion of the work of EDP.

This expansion, however, would eventually occur and would bring about a need to expand EDP staff. The increasing EDP work load would bring about the realization by systems that there was a need to expand and/or upgrade EDP. Systems, however, would be slow to make proposals to EDP management because their superior would delay approval of any proposals because of the unsatisfactory profit. In con-

structing its budget, EDP management would be faced with inconsistency between the constraints of expanding service and reducing costs. They would relax these constraints and search for consensus on all existing proposals to change the size of the staff. There would be approval for small upward adjustments, but the superior of EDP management would postpone approval of any major changes. Accordingly, there would be disagreement throughout the decision process and only small upward adjustments would be allowed.

Innovation and satisfactory profits are represented in the lower right box on Chart 8. Under these conditions, market research would make proposals for data processing projects to EDP. These projects would be scheduled by EDP management until EDP's capacity was reached. The expansion of EDP work would result in the proposals to expand EDP staff. Systems would be able to make these proposals without delay. They would touch base and obtain approval quickly because profits were satisfactory. In the budget process, the constraint on the performance of EDP management would be to expand service. Accordingly, all legitimate proposals involving an increase and/or upgrading in the staff would be incorporated into the proposed budget. Throughout the decision process there would be no disagreement among the participants on the need to schedule projects or on the expansion of the staff. The growth of the staff would reflect the amount of data processing requested by market research.

In sum, major growth is inferred from the decision strategies only when innovation occurs and profits are satisfactory. The size of the staff is static or increases at a very small rate, it is argued, although profits are satisfactory if no innovation occurs. This is contrary to the traditional empire building hypothesis. The explanation for the lack of empire building may be in the manner in which slack is conserved. In the behavioral theory of the firm, it is purported that organizational units build up slack when profits are satisfactory. A major reason for doing this is the need to meet contingencies that could hamper the manager's responsiveness to organizational goals. The slack-building hypothesis leaves the question unsettled on *the form* in which slack is conserved. The manager can be more effective, perhaps, if he chooses a form that allows flexibility in its use (e.g. "overtime"). This flexibility implies that the funds are relatively uncommitted, and this reduces the manager's ability to defend his slack against "budget officers," etc. The manager may respond by making a relatively permanent commitment of his slack, and adding to the staff is a form of conserving slack which is relatively permanent. Accordingly, empire building may be a response to inappropriate budget procedures which were apparently absent with respect to the participants of the study. In support of this observation, it was noted in the study that funds were budgeted in forms which left them uncommitted.

APPENDIX:

A SAMPLE QUESTIONNAIRE FOR MODEL II

1. Briefly describe project.

2. Was this one of the following:
     regularly scheduled project
     newly proposed repetitive project
     project for reprogramming to new equipment
     special request?

3. Did you have occasion to reconsider project?

	YES	NO	UNCERTAIN OR NOT RELEVANT
1. Was project scheduled to meet completion date requested by sponsor?			
2. Did sponsor of project believe that imperative to do project?			
3. Did sponsor of project request that project be discontinued?			
4. Was manpower (key punchers, operators, programers) available during regular time?			
5. Could sufficient manpower and running time for this project be obtained by delaying currently scheduled programming for other projects?			
6. Was overtime within budget constraints if needed to schedule project?			
7. Was project scheduled to be done at date later than completion date requested by sponsor?			
8. Did you discontinue project?			
9. Was running time available on equipment?			
10. Did you delay currently scheduled programming for other projects and schedule this project?			
11. Was overtime sufficient to provide the needed running time and manpower?			
12. Did you request project be postponed or redesigned?			
13. Were project requirements small for manpower and running time on equipment?			
14. Did superior believe that imperative to do project?			

REFERENCES

1. C. W. Churchman, and H. B. Eisenberg, 1964. Deliberation and judgment. *Human judgments and optimality* (M. W. Shelly, II, and G. L. Bryan, eds.); New York: Wiley, 45–53.
2. G. P. E. Clarkson, 1963. A model of trust investment behavior. *A behavioral theory of the firm* (R. M. Cyert and J. G. March); Englewood Cliffs, N.J.: Prentice-Hall, 253–267. 8A.
3. R. M. Cyert, and J. G. March, 1963. *A behavioral theory of the firm.* Englewood Cliffs, N.J.: Prentice-Hall. 2B.
4. A. Etzioni, 1961. *A comparative analysis of complex organizations.* New York: Free Press.
5. A. G. Frank, 1959. Goal ambiguity and conflicting standards. *Human Organization, 17*(4): 8–13.
6. M. E. Goss, 1961. Influence and authority among physicians in an outpatient clinic. *American Sociological Review, 26*(1): 39–50.
7. C. E. Lindblom, 1959. The science of "muddling through". *Public Administration Review, 19*(2): 79–88.
8. J. G. March, and H. A. Simon, 1958. *Organizations.* New York: Wiley.
9. H. A. Simon, 1960. *The new science of management decision.* New York: Harper.
10. H. A. Simon, 1964. On the concept of organizational goal. *Administrative Science Quarterly, 9*(1): 1–22.
11. Ja. D. Thompson, and A. Tuden, 1959. Strategies, structures, and processes of organizational decision. *Comparative studies in administration* (J. D. Thompson, P. B. Hammond, R. W. Hawkes, B. H. Junker, and A. Tuden, eds.); Pittsburgh: University of Pittsburgh Press, 195–216.
12. O. E. Williamson, 1963. Managerial discretion and business behavior. *American Economic Review, 53*(5): 1032–1057.

16

A COMPUTER SIMULATION MODEL OF MUNICIPAL BUDGETING[1]

JOHN P. CRECINE

An increasing awareness of the importance of urban governmental activities draws attention to municipal expenditures and to the municipal operating budget. Little effort has been directed toward the question of how municipalities allocate resources. The work reported here represents an attempt to develop a positive theory of municipal resource allocation for large metropolitan communities and to subject this theory to empirical tests. Cleveland, Detroit, and Pittsburgh are used as data points.

1. A POSITIVE, EMPIRICAL THEORY OF MUNICIPAL BUDGETING

The model is stated in the form of a computer program. The nature of the budgetary decision process suggests such an approach. Even a superficial examination of the municipal resource allocation procedure indicates that it is the result of a *sequence* of decisions—departmental requests, mayor's executive budget, and final council appropriations. A computer program is really a collection of *instructions* executed in a *specific* sequence. If a computer

SOURCE: Reprinted from *Management Science, 13*: 786–815 (1967).

[1] Based on a paper presented at the 1966 Midwest Political Science Association Meeting, Chicago, Illinois. A much more detailed discussion of the work presented here will be found in [3].

program is to be an appropriate way to describe the budgetary process, the individual rules ought to be stable over time and executed in a specific sequence (be part of a "stable" structure). Fortunately, there are some compelling reasons why this should be so.

One obvious reason why programmed decisions tend to deal with repetitive problems, and *vice versa*, is that "if a particular problem recurs often enough, a routine procedure will usually be worked out for solving it." Certainly the municipal budget is a recurrent problem (yearly). Evidence is growing that recurrent, complex problems are solved by individuals by breaking the global problem into a series of less complex ones, and then solving the simplified problems sequentially.

In particular, the problem-solving behavior of individuals has been described using a computer program, for a trust investment officer by Clarkson [2], a department store buyer by Cyert, March, and Moore [4], and laboratory subjects solving simple problems [10, 11] and chess players by Newell and Simon [9].

1.1. Computer Simulation of Municipal Budgeting

A simulation of the budgetary process must describe the behavior of many individuals—

department budget officers, budget officials in the mayor's office, and the council. There is no reason to think that the hundred or so actors involved in the formal budgetary decision system will be any more difficult to "program" or simulate than *single individuals*, however. The difficulty, if any, arises from the number of decisions and decision makers in our model, and the quantity of data to be analyzed.[2]

Simulation as a Research Tool. "Simulation is a technique for building theories that reproduce part or all of the output of a behaving system [2, p. 16]." In addition, some simulation models have the goal of reproducing not only final results but intermediate outputs as well. This is the task to which the model addresses itself. The attempt to reproduce output and procedures is in the form of a computer program representing the structural form of the decision process (sequence of decisions), the functional form of the individual decision rules (individual equations representing actual decision rules), and the decision parameters (values of "constants" or empirically determined variables embedded in the structure and functional relations of the model).

2. OVERVIEW OF MUNICIPAL BUDGETING

The entire decision process can usefully be thought of as an organized means for the decision maker to deal with the potential complexity of the budgetary problem. The most prominent feature of the "original" problem in

terms of its contribution to complexity is an externally imposed constraint of a balanced budget[3]—by requiring that, *at some level of generality*, all budget items be considered simultaneously.

2.1. Problem Perception

Before proceeding, we should note that the "problem we are referring to is the budgetary problem as seen by the actual decision makers (department officials, mayor and mayor's staff, and council members). It is quite clear (from interviews) that the decision makers *do not* see the problem as one of optimally balancing community resources, allocating funds among functions to achieve overall community goals, and the like. The problem is generally "seen" by department heads as one of submitting a budget request that (1) assures the department of funds to carry on existing programs as part of a continuing attack on existing problems, (2) is acceptable to the mayor's office, and (3) provides for a reasonable share of any increase in the city's total budget, enabling the department to attack new problems (if any). The mayor's problem is largely one of recommending a budget that (1) is balanced, (2) at least maintains existing service levels, (3) provides for increases in city employee wages if at all possible, and (4) avoids tax increases (especially property tax increases, in the belief that increased property taxes cause business and industry to move from the city, reducing the municipal tax base). If, after achieving some of the above objectives, the mayor has "extra" funds, they will be used to sponsor programs or projects the mayor has on his "agenda," or to grant a portion of departments' supplemental requests.

The "problem" for the council is to review the mayor's budget recommendations and check for "obvious" errors and omissions. Because of the complexity and detail in the mayor's budget and lack of council staff, the council's options are limited largely to approving the mayor's budget. The requirement of a balanced budget means that a change in one expenditure category, for instance, implies a balancing change in other account categories,

---

[2] The implications of the "magnitude of the problem" are many. First, it should be fairly obvious that each actor in our simulation model will be described in a simpler manner than the individual problem solvers in most of the works cited above. Secondly, assumptions will have to be made which will detract from the overall accuracy (i.e., completeness) of the model. For example, it will be necessary to assume that each department head in the system behaves according to the same decisional model, with only parameters changing. It is obviously not practical or reasonable to interview all department heads and all parties involved in the budgetary process. Behavioral rules attributed by others to our decision makers will have to be incorporated in the model without individual verifications. The reasonableness and "accuracy" of these necessary "short cuts" will, of course, be measured empirically when the model is tested.

[3] Required in the city charter, articles of incorporation, or by State Legislature.

administrative units, or revenues—i.e., one change in the budget (by council) implies many changes which the council has neither the time nor staff to consider.

2.2. Partitioning the Problem into Manageable Subproblems

One of the ways municipal decision makers deal with the *potential* complexity of the municipal resource allocation problem is through their necessarily simplified perception of the problem as discussed above. Other simplifying heuristics observed were:

1. The operating budget is treated separately from the capital budget as a generally independent problem. The only behavioral connection between the operating and capital budgets is the "logical" elaboration of capital budgeting decisions in the operating budget.[4]

2. The budget is formulated within a system of administrative units (departments and bureaus) and account categories (salaries, supplies and expenses, equipment, etc.) that is extremely stable from year to year. This partial structuring of the problem "allows" most of the decision makers to treat the appropriation question for one account category in one administrative unit as a (sub-) problem, separate from the overall resource allocation problem. Thus, the overall problem is transformed into a series of smaller problems of determining appropriations for individual departments.

3. The revenue estimates are generally separate from expenditure estimates. That is, estimates of yields from a given tax are treated independently from expenditures. While, on occasion, tax rates may be adjusted somewhat on the basis of preliminary calculations of *total expenditure estimates*, in order to balance the budget, tax *yield estimates* are seldom manipulated to achieve a balance.

4. The structure of the decision process

---

[4] The "legitimate" claim on operating funds by the capital budget is reflected in the following, found in the Mayor's Message accompanying the 1965 Pittsburgh Budget:
"A big item in the Lands and Buildings request pertains to the opening and operation of the new Public Safety Center next Spring. . . . There is a non-recurring expenditure of $150,000 for new furniture . . . and $91,000 is sought for maintenance personnel."

itself represents a division of labor between department heads, the mayor's office, and the council—reflecting not only the administrative hierarchy, but a set of simplifying heuristics for making a complex problem manageable.

5. Finally, an additional simplifying policy is found in all cities investigated. The presence of a uniform wage policy which maintains relative positions of employees within a city-wide civil service pay scale, eliminates the potentially complex problem of deciding wage rates on an individual basis while attempting to maintain "similar-pay-for-similar-jobs" standards.[5]

2.3. Governing by Precedent

Perhaps the overriding feature of the mayor's budgetary "problem" is the balanced budget requirement. *If* the mayor took even the majority of items in the budget under serious consideration, his task would be enormous. The requirement of a *balanced* budget *could* mean that not only would the mayor have to consider every budget item, but he would have to consider each item relative to all other items. Somehow the entire level of police expenditures would have to be justified in light of the implied preemption of health department services, public works, fire department expenditures, etc. Obviously the mayor does not have either the staff, cognitive abilities, or time to undertake such a study—even if the necessary knowledge and information existed.

Instead, as we have seen above, the mayor perceives this year's budget problem as basically similar to last year's with a slight change in resources available (new revenue estimates) for dealing with a continuing set of municipal problems (police and fire protection, urban renewal, public works, transportation) augmented by a small number of newly emerging problems and a small number of partial solutions to old problems. In this context, a "logical" way to proceed in solving the complex budgeting problem is to take "last year's solution" (current appropriations) to the problem and modify it in light of *changes* in available resources and shifts in municipal problems to obtain "this year's solution." This,

---

[5] On occasion, uniformed policemen and firemen's salaries are treated separately from the others.

of course, means that the budget is a slowly changing thing, consisting of a series of "marginal changes" from previous budgets.[6] Only small portions of the budget are reconsidered from year to year and consequently, once an item is in the budget, its mere existence becomes its "reason for being" in succeeding budgets.

[6] These notions are very similar to those of "disjointed incrementalism" [1, 7].

This "government by precedent" is an integral part of most positive models of decision making in the literature. Cyert and March's *A Behavioral Theory of the Firm* describes the usage of previous solutions and solution procedures to solve new problems and is largely a model of *incremental* adaptations of economic organizations to their internal and external environment [4, p. 104]. Braybrooke and Lindblom argue that "precedent" is justi-

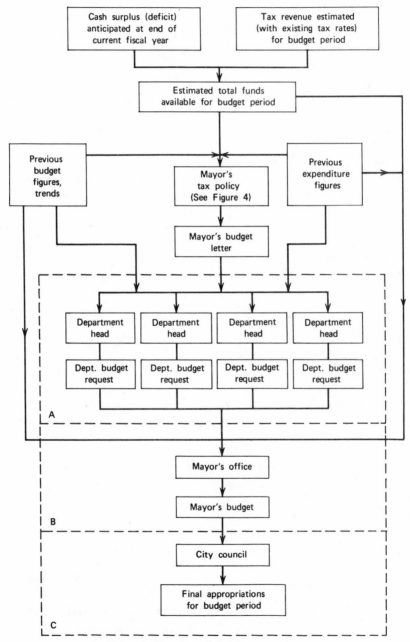

Figure 1 Overview of decision procedures.

fied and defensible as a "rational" decision strategy [1, pp. 225–245]. Wildavsky emphasizes the role of "precedent" as an "aid to calculation" in the Federal budgetary process [13, pp. 13–18, 58–59].

2.4. Openness of Public Decisions

A basic property of decision making in the public sector (vs. the private) is the realization that both decisions and decision procedures are always subject (at least potentially) to public scrutiny. Decisions in the public sector would tend to be more "defensible" than corresponding ones in the private sector and each particular decision (budget item) in a decision system (entire budget) ought to be able to stand on its own "merits." In addition, decision *procedures* are also subject to public question. We would argue that the openness of public decisions reinforces the use of rather straightforward methods of partitioning the budgetary problem, the use of *precedent* as a defensible[7] decision strategy, and encourages the use of simpler, easier-to-understand decision procedures than might otherwise be found.

3. FORMAL MODEL OF MUNICIPAL BUDGETING

In the context of the problem complexity and devices used to deal with that complexity, we now turn to an analysis of the model's behavioral characteristics. An overview of the model is found in Figure 1. Inasmuch as the model can be broken down into three reasonably independent submodels (the existence of these submodels illustrates the use of partitioning and division of labor in dealing with complexity), we will discuss each submodel separately.

3.1. Scope of Model

The formal, computer model explicitly considers three decision processes—departmental requests as formulated by the various department heads in city government, mayor's budget for council consideration, and the final appropriations as approved by city council. These three processes are indicated by areas A, B, and C in Figure 1. The outputs of the departmental-request submodel are inputs to the mayor's budget submodel and outputs of the mayor's submodel are inputs to the council appropriations submodel.

The outputs of each submodel correspond quite closely in number and level of detail with the outputs (or decisions) found in the municipal budgetary process. In the model, each department included in the general fund or operating budget has requests for appropriations for each of 2 to 5 standard account categories—depending on the city involved. For example, the model produces at each of the 3 stages of the decision process, the dollar estimates for the City Planning Department shown below.

Cleveland		Detroit		Pittsburgh	
Personnel Services	} X	Administrative Salaries	} X	Administrative Salaries	} X
Materials, Supplies,		Non-Adm. Salaries		Non-Adm. Salaries	} Y
Expenses, Equipment,		Materials, Supplies and	} Y	Materials, Supplies and	} W
Repairs and Improve-	} Y	Expenses		Expenses	
ment		Equipment and Repairs	} Z	Equipment	} U
				Maintenance	} Z

44 to 64 departments and administrative units are involved in the cities examined, with each unit having estimates for 2–5 accounts. Between 128 and 220 decisions are produced at each of the three stages of the model, for each year in the study, in each of the three cities examined.

[7] We would also argue that, in general, the need for "defensible" decisions leads to more conservative decisions in the public sector than in the private.

At this point, one might legitimately ask two important questions:

1. Why are accounts categorized in the manner indicated?

2. Why is "dollars" the unit of resource allocation rather than men, number of street lights, etc.?

Both questions are "crucial" ones for a normative theory of budgeting. In a positive theory, however, the answers are rather straight-forward—and essentially identical. People interviewed in all three cities think and talk in terms of "dollars"; they differentiate (at least in interviews) expenditures in terms of the same categories used in their city's accounting system. Apparently, dollar amounts provide the relevant reference points for dealing with the conceptual framework provided by the city's accounting system[8] and provide the basis for the participants' cognitive maps of the process.

3.2. DEPT. Submodel

ROLE. The role of the department head is similar to that of the agency or bureau chief in the Federal government as described in the Wildavsky study [13, pp. 8–21]. His objective is to obtain the largest possible amount of funds for his department and his purposes. Just as "'Washington is filled' . . . 'with dedicated men and women who feel that government funds should be spent for one purpose or another,'"[9] so are municipal governments. In general, department heads, through experience and the process of socialization into their positions, and by "learning" that their request is likely to be cut by the mayor's office or council, tend to ask for more than they "expect" to get. This "padding" of the budget is one part of a system of mutual expectations and roles. Department heads are expected to ask for more than they really "need," the mayor's office is expected to cut these requests in order to balance the budget.

CONTEXT. The decisions we are speaking of set the limit on spending for the coming fiscal year. They are limits on manpower, supplies, material, and equipment. They are not program budgets in the sense that exact activity mixes are included in the municipal budget. In a sense, what we are talking about is an intermediate decision. This decision provides the constraints under which decisions about particular activities that a department will undertake must be made. The setting of *levels*

of expenditures is just one part of the department head's continuing problems. Within a given expenditure ceiling, many different activity mixes can be utilized. "Low ceilings, in short, can still permit several rooms [12, p. 414]."

DEPT. Model Characteristics. The role of the mayor's budget letter and the budget forms sent to the department head is a clear one. Together with the time schedule for submission of the completed budget forms, these items have the effect of structuring the department head's problem for him. Budget forms are typically sent to department heads less than two months in advance of the presentation of the completed budget to council. The department head usually has about one month before his completed request forms are due in the mayor's office.

The importance of the time deadline should not be underestimated. In that there is no moratorium on the department head's problems, budget compilation represents an additional workload. In the context of a myriad of nonbudgetary problems and duties, most department heads are more than willing to accept the problem structure provided by the budget forms. To do otherwise would not only involve creating an alternative structure, but would place the "burden of proof" on the department head as far as justifying the alternative to the mayor's office.

Just how is the problem presented to the department head so as to pre-structure it for him?

BUDGET FORM. Budget forms seem to be nearly one of the physical constants of the universe [13, p. 59]. They are laid out at the top of the facing page.

By structuring the department head's problem, the forms "bias" the outcome or decision in two ways:

1. They provide a great deal of incentive for the department head to formulate his requests within the confines of the existing set of accounts.

2. They provide for an automatic comparison between "next year's" request, and "this

---

[8] A legitimate question would be, "Why was a city's accounting system designed around a particular set of account categories?" This, however interesting and important, is beyond the scope of the study.

[9] A quote of President John F. Kennedy, [12, p. 414.].

	Expenditures Last Year	Appropriations This Year	Next Year's Request
Standard Account 1	$54321.00	$57400.00	?
Itemization of 1	—	—	
Standard Account 2	$43219.00	$45600.00	?
Itemization of 2			
⋮			
Standard Account N	$100.00	$120.00	?
Itemization of N			

year's" appropriation—which automatically determines that "this year's" appropriation provides one criterion or reference point for "next year's" request.

The Mayor's budget letter always contains instructions which reinforce the structuring of the problem provided by budget forms—to provide a ". . . written explanation for any change in individual code accounts," "(e)xperience for the years 1962 and 1963 is shown . . . to assist you in estimating your needs for 1965," "(u)nder the heading 'Explanation of Increases and Decreases' must be explained the factors . . . which make up the increase or decrease over or under," "the current budget allowance is shown above on this form."

The level of detail in line items has its influence on the department head's decision process also. (In one city studied, one of the line items listed a $3.00 current appropriation for "Mothballs.") In general, each item broken out in the budget (each line item) "forces" one historical comparison and, hence, represents one more constraint the department request must satisfy. In the face of an increasing number of constraints (increasing as budget detail increases), it is not so surprising that the department head resorts to simpler decision rules to handle this potentially difficult problem. In addition, we would predict that the more detailed the budget (in terms of line items), because of the structure of the budget forms, the less change in requests (and appropriations) from year to year.

The need for effective budgetary control in the mayor's office, made more difficult by the presence of a small staff[10] (small in relation to a similar organization in the private sector), is met by a large number of simple, historical comparisons and has, in many instances, resulted in a burdensome amount of detail—responded to by busy department heads with little change in budget behavior from year to year.

The "tone" of the letter accompanying the budget forms has the effect of providing an arbitrary ceiling on the department's request (Figure 2, item 5). If the department total exceeds the "ceiling," the overage is generally submitted as a "supplemental" request (Figure 2, items 7 and 8). In addition, changes in salary *rates* through raises or promotions are submitted as a supplemental request (or not at all). Supplemental requests are accompanied with a detailed explanation and are treated separately by the mayor's office—and are always on the "agenda" when the department head meets with the mayor's office to discuss his requests.

So far, we have discussed only the constraints a department head must satisfy and the procedures he must follow. There is, obviously, some room for maneuvering. Many of the department head's "calculations" involve figuring "what will go" with the mayor's office.[11] This calculation involves using current appropri-

[10] For instance, in the City of Pittsburgh, no more than four people examine the entire budget in great detail. Of these four, at least one is faced with the purely physical task of putting the budget together, checking, and compiling city totals.

[11] Similar to Wildavsky's observations of department heads at the large end of the budgetary funnel [13, pp. 25–31.] and Sorensen's at the small end of the federal decision funnel [12, p. 414.].

1. Budget letter and Budget Forms received from mayor containing: a. current appropriations for all account categories in the department; b. current total appropriation; c. previous year's expenditures in various account categories; d. estimate of allowable increase over current appropriations implied from the "tone" of the mayor's budget letter.

2. Trend of departmental appropriations—direction and magnitude of recent changes in amounts of appropriations in departmental account categories.

3. Department, using information from 1. and 2., formulates a "reasonable request" for funds in its existing account categories, using current appropriations as a "base" or reference point and adjusting this estimate according to whether there was an increase in appropriations last year (for some accounts, an increase for the current year means a decrease for next year—equipment—, for others, an increase for the current year indicates another increase next year), and the difference between last year's expenditures and appropriations.

4. Using "reasonable requests" calculated in 3., a preliminary department total request is calculated.

5. Is the total department request outside the guidelines set by the mayor's office (implied from the "tone" of the mayor's budget letter)?

no / yes

6. Check to see if there are any increases in salary accounts over current appropriations

7. All department requests in all categories are adjusted so that any increase (proposed) over current appropriations is submitted as a supplemental request. Go to 6. to check for salary increases.

no increase / increase

8. Make regular request equal current appropriations and put increase in as supplemental request.

9. Calculate total of regular departmental request.

10. Send regular requests and departmental total to mayor's office along with supplemental requests.

Figure 2. General DEPT. Request Decision Process[a]

[a] For a more detailed flowchart of the DEPT. Submodel and a listing of the FORTRAN II computer program, see [3].

ations as a base and adjusting this amount for recent appropriation trends, discrepancies between appropriations and corresponding expenditures, and the like (Figure 2, item 3). The results of this "calculation" are then tested to see if they satisfy the constraints discussed above. Preliminary decisions are then adjusted until constraints are satisfied, and the final request is entered on the standard budget forms and sent to the mayor's office for consideration.

Behavior Not Included in Formal DEPT. Model. A quick look at the DEPT. model would indicate that (at least according to our theory) department budgetary behavior varies from department to department only by the relative weights assigned to previous appropriations, trends, and expenditures by the various department heads (Figure 2, item 3). Furthermore, it is contended (by the model) that these relative weights are stable over time. Missing from the formal model are notions of non-regular innovation (or change) by department administrators and notions of the department as a mechanism for responding to particular kinds of complaints from the citizenry—in short, the department is conceived of as explicitly responding to only the mayor's pressure. Also missing are changes in the budget requests as logical elaborations of other policy commitments—implied increases in operating budget because of capital budgeting considerations, changes in intergovernmental support for services (the classic problem in this category involves the highly volatile state-local split of welfare payments), transfer of activities to (and from) other governing units (transfer of hospital system to State or county, etc.), and changes in activity level and scope because of funds obtained from sources (Urban Renewal planning and demonstration grants, the Federal Anti-Poverty Program, etc.) other than the general fund. Our model does not preclude innovative behavior, however. It merely states that innovation (if any) takes place within a regularly changing budget ceiling. It could be argued that a system of weights attached to current appropriations, trends, etc., that leads to relatively large, regular request increases represents a greater potential for innovation than do those leading to smaller increases (or decreases)—providing, of course, that a portion of the request is granted. On the other hand, it could be argued that the presence of a budget ceiling in the face of changing citizenry needs and pressures (precipitating a change in department goals and program needs) forces a department head to "innovate" to survive. Cyert and March, citing the work of Mansfield [8], side with the former concept of innovation rather than the latter. They argue that the presence of "organizational slack" (evidenced

by budgetary increases) ". . . provides a source of funds for innovations that would not be approved in the face of scarcity but that have strong subunit support." Major technological innovations, it is argued, are not problem-oriented innovations [4, p. 279]. At any rate, our model does not restrict certain kinds of innovation-producing behavior. The model is, however, unable to predict or recognize the acceptance of "major" innovations (major changes in expenditure and appropriations).

The other "charge" the model is open to is that it fails to deal with "outside" influences at all. This is particularly true if by departmental responses to pressure one assumes that total (for the department) external pressure and influence is a thing that varies a good deal from year to year and that mechanisms for responding to that pressure would lead to irregular budget decisions reflecting this variation. If, however, one assumes that each department has, over the years, "made its peace" not only with the mayor's office, but with the extra-governmental environment, then the pressure response mechanisms (i.e., constant responses to constant pressures) would also be reflected in the system of weights, above. The model does not exclude a pressure-response kind of budgetary behavior, but has a good deal to say about the nature and context of the response (and pressure). The reasonableness of our characterization of "innovation" and "pressure" is reflected in the model residuals.

3.3. MAYORS Budget Recommendation Model

ROLE. The function of the mayor's office relative to the budget is to fulfill the legal obligation of submitting a balanced budget to the city council for its consideration. The key word, of course, is "balanced." Most of the problem solving activity and behavior in the mayor's office revolves around attempts to eliminate a deficit or reduce a surplus. Like most other organizations, subunit requests (stated needs) almost always exceed available resources. So, *vis-à-vis* the departments, the mayor's office's role is that of an economizer, cutting departmental requests to the "bare minimum" in lean years and keeping the cost of government "under control" when revenues are more plentiful.

Characteristics of the MAYOR's Model. The decision process in the mayor's office can usefully be thought of as a search for a solution to the balanced-budget problem. In a sense, the mayor has guaranteed the existence of a solution through use of budget guidelines set up in his letter of instruction to department heads. Approximately four months before the final budget is due for council passage, the mayor obtains preliminary revenue estimates from people in city government and from an outside source. Armed with a rough estimate of money available for expenditure in the next budget period, current appropriations, and a knowledge of "required" and predetermined budgetary changes for the coming year, the mayor is able to make a rough guess of the total allowable increase or decrease over current appropriations. From this figure, an estimate of the "allowable" percent increase (or decrease) is made and transmitted to department heads *via* the budget letter. (Only the output from this part of the process is explicitly included in our model—"tone of mayor's letter.") In most instances, then, the "sum" of the budget requests reaching the mayor's office represents a "nearly" (within 10%) balanced budget.

The revenue estimate enters into the process at this point as an independent constraint to be satisfied. On very few occasions are revenue or tax *rates* changed to bring the budget into balance. In the municipalities investigated, there was no evidence of any altering of tax *yields* to balance the budget.[12] Almost all tax rate increases are tied to general wage increases. Our formal model does not include the part of

the decision process evoked when the revenue constraint becomes so restrictive (or loose) as to necessitate a change in tax rates. (See Figure 4.) Tax rate decisions are made prior to sending the budget letter to department heads and are considered as given from that point on.

Just as the budget forms and account categories structure the problem for the department head, they also structure it for the mayor's office (Figure 3, items 1 and 3). The legal requirement of a balanced budget also helps structure the problem for the mayor's office and partially determines its role behavior. Together the system of accounts and balanced budget requirements specify the cognitive map of the decision situation for mayor's office participants.

Preliminary Screening of Requests. As budget requests are received from departments by the mayor's office, they are screened individually (Figure 3, item 4). The screening process reflects particular biases and relationships between the mayor's office and individual department heads (and departments). "Department heads are dealt with differently during the (budget) hearings. Some department heads can be depended on for an honest budget request. Others have a history of being less-than-realistic in their budgets."[13] Different perceptions of different departments are reflected in both model structure and model parameters (Figure 3, item 4). The interaction of perceptions and role (to cut requests) describes the preliminary screening process.

Basically, if the department request for a given account category is less than current appropriations, a preliminary, automatic acceptance of the request is made. If the request is larger than current appropriations, a request evaluation procedure is evoked that "calculates" or subjectively determines preliminary appropriation figures (Figure 3, item 4). A particular department can evoke one of four subjective evaluation procedures. The procedure evoked represents the cognitive map used by the mayor's office in dealing with that department.

The four basic procedures consist of two which arrive at a preliminary appropriation figure by making marginal adjustments in the

---

[12] One exception to the general rule that there is no alteration of the revenue yield estimates (revenue side) to achieve balance with expenditures, was found. For a couple of years in Detroit (1960–1962), part of the cost of government operations was financed through "overly optimistic" revenue estimates which ultimately resulted in operating deficits. Those deficits (technically illegal) were then refinanced, with debt service charges for this refinancing showing up in subsequent operating budgets as deductions from revenue available for general fund expenditures. This brief "operating practice" was quickly discontinued by a new city administration. The magnitude of the effect of this practice on the planning process (budget formation) is unclear and is not incorporated in the formal model. The effects were reflected as larger deviations of model estimates from actual decisions during particular years in the City of Detroit.

[13] November, 1964 interview with chief budget officer in one of the three sample cities. Name withheld on request.

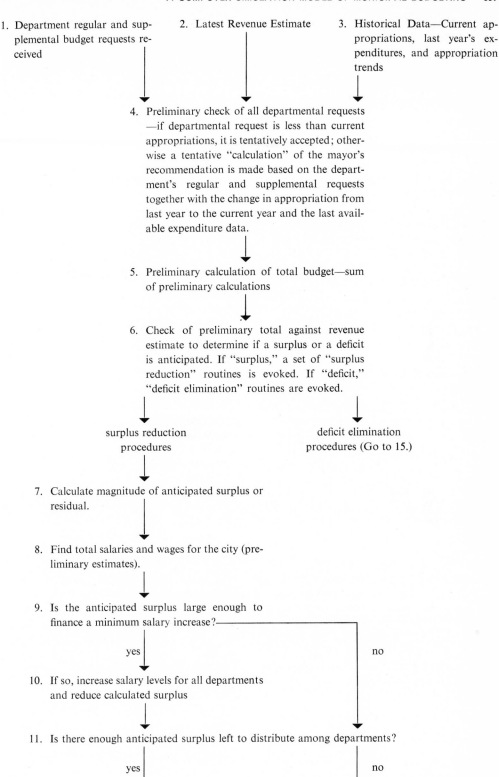

1. Department regular and supplemental budget requests received

2. Latest Revenue Estimate

3. Historical Data—Current appropriations, last year's expenditures, and appropriation trends

4. Preliminary check of all departmental requests —if departmental request is less than current appropriations, it is tentatively accepted; otherwise a tentative "calculation" of the mayor's recommendation is made based on the department's regular and supplemental requests together with the change in appropriation from last year to the current year and the last available expenditure data.

5. Preliminary calculation of total budget—sum of preliminary calculations

6. Check of preliminary total against revenue estimate to determine if a surplus or a deficit is anticipated. If "surplus," a set of "surplus reduction" routines is evoked. If "deficit," "deficit elimination" routines are evoked.

surplus reduction procedures

deficit elimination procedures (Go to 15.)

7. Calculate magnitude of anticipated surplus or residual.

8. Find total salaries and wages for the city (preliminary estimates).

9. Is the anticipated surplus large enough to finance a minimum salary increase?

yes   no

10. If so, increase salary levels for all departments and reduce calculated surplus

11. Is there enough anticipated surplus left to distribute among departments?

yes   no

Figure 3 continues overleaf

12. Consider the highest priority, non-salary account category (that has not yet been considered) starting with general expense accounts and ending with equipment and maintenance accounts.

Prepare final budget recommendations (Go to 26.)

13. Increase the budget recommendation for the account category under consideration for all departments (until the surplus is exhausted) by granting a portion of each department's supplemental request. When (and if) money runs out, prepare final budget recommendations.

money runs out
(Go to 26.)

14. Move to next highest priority account category and go to 12. If all categories have been considered, prepare final budget recommendations (Go to 26.).

Deficit elimination procedures

15. Consider accounts in reverse order of their priority (consider equipment and maintenance first, salaries last.).

16. Check, department by department, to see if the preliminary budget estimate (mayor's) for the account category under consideration is within the limits (% of current appropriations) implied in the mayor's budget letter to departments.

within limits | outside limits

17. If within limits, no change in preliminary budget estimate

18. Decrease preliminary estimate of budget so that it falls within mayor's limits.

19. Repeat 16.–18. until deficit is eliminated or departments have all been considered.

deficit eliminated | all departments considered

Prepare final budget recommendation (Go to 26.).

20. Consider next lowest priority account (Go to 16.), unless all account categories have been examined.

all account categories checked, for all departments | next lowest priority account (Go to 16.)

Figure 3 continues.

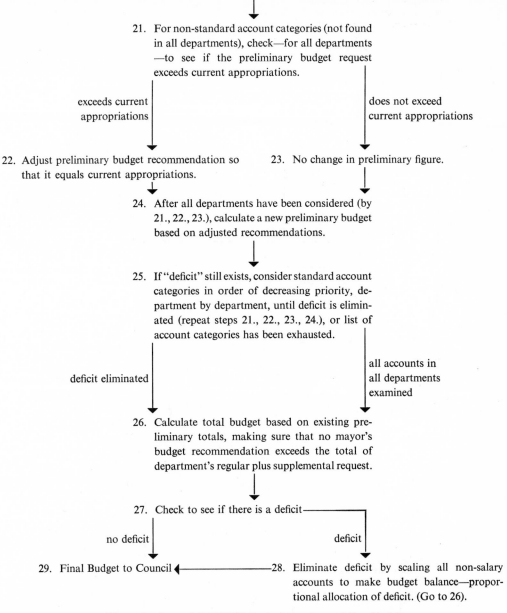

21. For non-standard account categories (not found in all departments), check—for all departments—to see if the preliminary budget request exceeds current appropriations.

exceeds current appropriations

does not exceed current appropriations

22. Adjust preliminary budget recommendation so that it equals current appropriations.

23. No change in preliminary figure.

24. After all departments have been considered (by 21., 22., 23.), calculate a new preliminary budget based on adjusted recommendations.

25. If "deficit" still exists, consider standard account categories in order of decreasing priority, department by department, until deficit is eliminated (repeat steps 21., 22., 23., 24.), or list of account categories has been exhausted.

deficit eliminated

all accounts in all departments examined

26. Calculate total budget based on existing preliminary totals, making sure that no mayor's budget recommendation exceeds the total of department's regular plus supplemental request.

27. Check to see if there is a deficit

no deficit

deficit

29. Final Budget to Council ◄————— 28. Eliminate deficit by scaling all non-salary accounts to make budget balance—proportional allocation of deficit. (Go to 26).

Figure 3   General MAYOR'S Budget Recommendation Model[a]

[a] For a more detailed flowchart of the MAYORS Submodel and a listing of the FORTRAN II computer program, see [3].

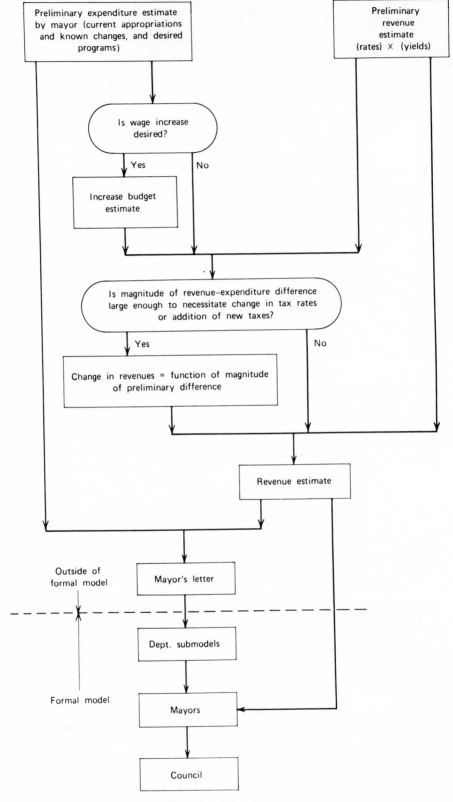

Figure 4 Mayor's tax decision process.

departments request figures—representing departments that submit "honest" or "realistic" budget estimates—and two which make adjustments in current appropriations to arrive at preliminary recommendation figures—representing less "realistic" or "honest" departments. The choice of procedures and parameter values was made on the basis of empirical tests using regression models. The four models used were:

(i) Department head's request respected and adjusted by his supplemental request and current trends.

(ii) Department head's request ignored, and current appropriations adjusted to reflect recent trends and over or underspending in the past.

(iii) Department head's request used as a basis for calculation and changes in it are based on the magnitude of the requested change in appropriations, supplemental requests, and past change in appropriations.

(iv) Department request ignored and change from current appropriations based on previous changes and magnitude of underspending or overspending in the past.

The values of the estimated parameters represent the relative weights given to variables in the particular model by decision makers in the mayor's office.

From the preliminary screening of requests outlined above (Figure 3, item 4), a preliminary budget total is compiled (Figure 3, item 5).

The next step in the process is to balance the preliminary budget. The "directives" issued by the Mayor's Office in the budget letter to department heads may be viewed as devices for guaranteeing that the budget will be "nearly" balanced. All alterations in regular departmental requests are aimed at balancing the budget. "Balancing techniques" are:

1.   Raise tax rates or add a new tax to eliminate anticipated deficit.

2.   Cut "lower priority" account categories (maintenance, equipment) to bring expenditures into line with revenues.

3.   Grant some supplemental requests to reduce anticipated surplus.

4.   Eliminate an "undesirable" tax or reduce tax rates to reduce anticipated surplus.

In general, strategies 1 and 4 are used when the anticipated discrepancy between revenues and expenditures is high, while techniques 2 and 3 are used if revenues and expenditures are reasonably close. The general tendency is to move toward a balance between revenues and expenditures by changing either revenue *or* expenditure, but not both. Only "techniques" 2 and 3 are a formal part of the model.

Surplus Elimination Procedures. If a surplus is anticipated, several standard spending alternatives are considered in order of their priority:

1.   General salary increase (Figure 3, items 8 to 10).

2.   Grant portion of supplemental requests (Figure 3, items 11 to 14):

    a. general expense accounts (Figure 3, item 12);

    b. equipment accounts;

    c. maintenance accounts.

Although the formal model only includes the above alternatives, others are clearly evoked. It can be said with reasonable assurance, though, that the first alternative considered is a general salary increase whenever a surplus is anticipated.

The model is also "incomplete" in the sense that some departmental priority list obviously exists in the granting of supplemental requests. Thus, the sequence in which departments are considered (the order of departments in Figure 3, items 11 and 13) is important under a revenue constraint. The model's assumption that departments are considered in the order of their account numbers is a poor one, but not enough department request data existed to establish any other reasonable priority list.[14] An analysis of the model residuals, however, failed to reveal any discernible pattern (or "list").[15] A priority list of account categories does exist though, and is shared by departments, the mayor's offices, and council. The

[14] It should be noted that a substantial portion of the department-priority phenomena is accounted for in the preliminary screening of requests.

[15] In deficit-elimination years, an underestimate would be expected for departments with low account numbers (in the computer-coded data) and an overestimate would be expected for departments with high account numbers. The opposite expectations would exist for surplus-elimination years. This phenomenon was not observed.

salience of wage and salary accounts is readily discernible through interviews.

Deficit Elimination Routines. If, instead of an anticipated surplus after preliminary screening of requests, a potential deficit appears (the usual case), routines are evoked to eliminate the deficit. One routine not evoked in the formal model, but one of the alternatives evoked in practice, is the routine that says "raise taxes."

The alternatives are evoked in the following order.

(a) Check preliminary recommendations (lower priority accounts first) to see if they are within limits on increases[16]—bring all preliminary recommendations within limits.

(b) Eliminate all recommended increases over current appropriations in non-salary items, considering low priority accounts first.

(c) Uniform reduction of all non-salary accounts to eliminate deficit, if all else has failed.

The order in which alternatives are considered represents a priority list for the alternatives (in order of their decreasing desirability) and a search routine evoked by the problem of an anticipated deficit (Figure 3, item 15).

The order-of-account sanctity for the mayor's office is identical to that of the department. This shared preference ordering[17] is as follows:

1. administrative salaries,
2. non-administrative salaries and wages,
3. operating expenses, supplies, materials, etc.,
4. equipment,
5. maintenance,

with maintenance and equipment the first accounts to be cut (and the last to be considered for an increase in the surplus elimination routines) and salaries the last. This deficit elimination procedure is executed only as long as a "deficit" exists. The first acceptable alternative (balanced budget) found is adopted and search activity is halted.

One item that is never reduced from current appropriations in the usual sense is salaries and wages. The salary and wage accounts are

[16] The limit is roughly equivalent to the limit indicated in the mayor's letter to department heads.
[17] Shared also with the council.

different from other accounts in that they represent commitments to individuals currently employed. There are no mass layoffs, etc., rather, a freeze is placed on the filling of positions vacated by retirement, resignation, and death and scheduled step-raises and salary increments are deferred.

Finally, either by reducing the surplus or by eliminating a deficit, the mayor's office arrives at a balanced budget.

Behavior Not Included in Formal MAYORS Model. Perhaps the most prominent omission of problem-solving behavior is the lack of a priority list for departments. The model assumes that the priority list is ordered the same way as the account numbers. The overall importance of this faulty assumption is, of course, an empirical question. An analysis of model residuals suggests this was not important or was reflected in estimated parameter values.

The entire budgetary process model we have constructed hypothesizes a stable decision structure between cities, and a stable decision structure over time within cities. Stability in decision structure between cities is "explainable" through problem similarity. Stability within cities reflects stable sets of relationships existing between positions and roles through processes of learning, reinforcement, and socialization. This assumption of stability and uniform socialization is predicated on the assumption that only a relatively few occupants of government positions change in a given period of time. The obvious exception to this situation occurs when an administration is defeated at the polls. This results in a complete reordering of position occupants and relationships. The gradual socialization, learning process will no longer hold. So, we expected and found the largest systematic model errors in those years immediately following the start of a new administration.

Another kind of behavior not included in the model is the kind reflecting the mayor's response to external (to the government) pressure and constraints. Again, as in the DEPT. models, the MAYORS model does not preclude a mayoralty response to requests for services from "powerful" interest groups or

TABLE 1   Sample of Municipal Account Complexity

Department of Public Works

1963 Code		Departmental Estimates 1964	Appropriation Year 1963	Expenditures Year 1962	Increase or Decrease '64 over '63
Acct. No.	Title of Account				
Division of Incineration					
1687	Miscellaneous Services				
B-5	Recharge Fire Extinguishers	$50.00	$—	$89.26	$—
B-5	Extermination Service	200.00	—	—	—
B-8	Towel Rental	25.00	—	.26	—
B-9	Supper Money	100.00	—	—	—
B-13	Freight and Express Charges	89.00	—	—	—
B-17	Public Property and Property Damage Insurance	125.00	—	—	—
B-18	Water Cooler Rental	390.00	—	390.00	—
B-18	Power Shovel Rental	12,960.00	—	14,880.00	—
B-18	Truck Rental for Incinerator and Bell Farm	3,765.00	—	2,295.00	—
B-20	Waste Disposal Permits	50.00	—	50.00	—
B-20	Demurrage on Oxygen and Acetylene Tanks	170.00	—	200.40	—
B-20	Services, N.O.C.	275.00	—	—	—
B-21	Test Boring, Survey and Report, for Landfills	1,000.00	—	—	—
Totals		$19,199.00	$18,199.00	$17,904.92	$1,000.00

individuals. It only postulates that the response is *within* the budget constraint for the department involved. The model, as constructed, implies that either the "response-to-pressure" is systematic and regular over the years (implying a stable system of "pressure" or "influence" in the community) and is reflected in the model parameters, or it does not enter the part of the budgetary process represented by our model at all. The only case where external "influence" could be conceived of as imposing a decisional constraint is in the revenue estimate. Most systematic "pressure" from the business community concentrates on keeping tax rates constant, and not on particular expenditure items.

The importance of these conscious omissions are reflected in the empirical tests of the model.

3.4. Characteristics of the COUNCIL Model

The role of the city council is a limited one. The primary reason is more one of cognitive

and informational constraints than lack of interest. The city budget is a complex document when it reaches the council. The level of detail makes it virtually impossible to consider all or even a majority of items independently. An example of this complexity is the Mayor's budget for the Pittsburgh Department of Public Works, the Division of Incineration, Miscellaneous Services Accounts found in Table 1. It illustrates the kind of document the council must deal with.

The council is asked to deal with the budget at this level of detail. The sheer volume of information to be processed limits the ability of a council, without its own budget staff, to consider the budget in a sophisticated or complex manner.

Perhaps a more important computational constraint is the balanced budget requirement. If there is no slack in the budget the mayor presents to council (Figure 5, item 8), then any increase the council makes in any account

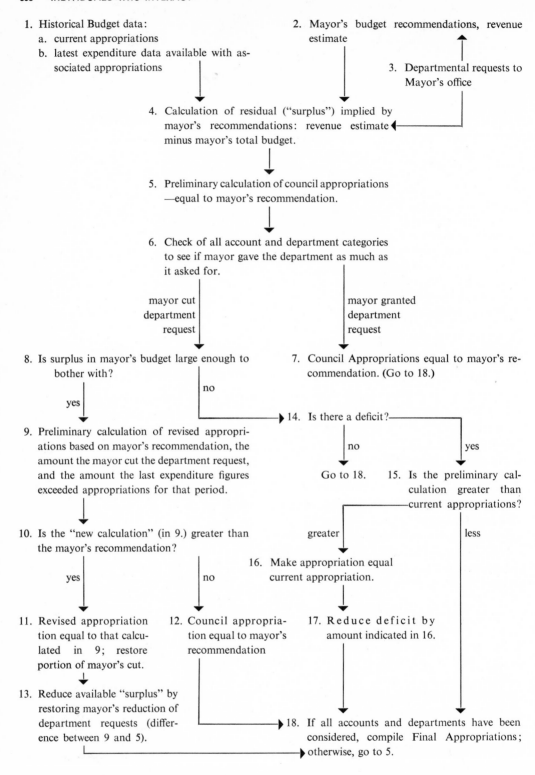

Figure 5   General COUNCIL Appropriation Model[a]

---

[a] For a more detailed flowchart of the COUNCIL Submodel and a listing of the FORTRAN II computer program, see [3].

category must be balanced with a corresponding decrease in another account or with tax increase. So, in the presence of a revenue constraint, the council cannot consider elements of the budget independently as is done in Congress. Davis, Dempster, and Wildavsky found that Congressional budgetary behavior could be described extremely well using a series of linear decision rules [5]. Behavior of this nature would not be possible if it were required that the sum of the changes in budgets made by Congress add to zero—i.e., the budget must add up to an amount predetermined by the President. Congressmen and Congressional committees also have staffs, councilmen do not.

Another reason for the limited effect of the council on the budget reflects the nature of the "pressures" they face. All interest groups, neighborhood organizations, department heads, etc. feel that some department's budget should be increased. The pressures transmitted to council concerning the operating budget are of one kind—those advocating increases in the mayor's recommendations. The other side of the argument—curtailment of government activities—is seldom, if ever, presented to council. This countervailing influence enters the decision process not at the council level, but generally through the mayor's office and in particular, through the mayor's revenue estimate.

Given the above limitations, the council is "forced" to use the mayor's decisions as the reference points for their decisions. The constraints—"pressure," informational, and computational—coupled with a recommended budget with no slack to allocate (not enough difference between estimated revenues and recommended expenditures "to be bothered with") makes it extremely difficult for council to veto[18] or change the mayor's budget significantly.

Overview. Generalizing, the entire model is one of a systematic, bureaucratic administrative decision process. The stability of the decision system is portrayed as evolving from the restrictive revenue environment, an assumed continuity in the actors manning the system,

---

[18] Occasionally the council will defeat a proposed new tax—income tax in Cleveland, tax for meat inspectors in Detroit—but seldom will it defeat expenditure recommendations.

and an implied stable or non-existent "community power network." The interaction of problem complexity and need for decision, combined with the lack of extra-governmental reference points or standards, produces a decision system which uses historical experience and precedent as its operating standards; a system which handles interest conflicts (high service rates, low taxes) by largely ignoring divergent viewpoints and using feasibility as the prime decision criterion; a system which handles complexity by fragmenting and simplifying the problem. By assuming (implicitly) that "this year's problem" is nearly identical to "last year's," "this year's solution" will be nearly identical to "last year's." It is a system that structures a complex problem, formulates alternatives and makes choices using simple decision rules.

4. MODEL TESTS

The formal model of the budgetary process was subjected to many forms of empirical tests. Basically the model was used to generate budget decisions for six years in Pittsburgh (1960–1965), seven years in Detroit (1958–1959 to 1964–1965), and ten years in Cleveland (1956–1965). Model results were then compared with the observed budgetary decisions in the cities.

Three primary goodness-of-fit indicators were used: "modified-r^2" statistics, a comparison of the relative predictability of the simulation model with three naive models, and a regression of observed budgetary decisions on model predictions.

We can view the linear regression, r^2-statistic as a measure of the relative precision of the linear hypothesis *vs.* the alternative hypothesis that the dependent variable is randomly distributed about its mean:

$$r^2 = 1.0$$
$$- \frac{\sum (\text{observed} - \text{regression prediction})^2}{\sum (\text{observed} - \text{mean of observed})^2}$$

By substituting "model estimate" for "regression prediction" and more reasonable alternative hypotheses for "mean of observed," modified-r^2

statistics were constructed,[19] and calculated for each year in each city. The model performed satisfactorily on these measures.

Three alternative, naive models were also tested and compared with the simulation model:

1. Constant-increase model

$$B_{i,t} = (1.0 + \alpha_i) B_{i,t-1}$$

2. Constant-share-of-the-budget-total model

$$B_{i,t} = \beta_i \left(\sum_{j=1}^{n} B_{j,t} \right)$$

3. Constant-share-of-the-budget-increase model

$$B_{i,t} - B_{i,t-1} = \delta_i \left[\left(\sum_{j=1}^{n} B_{j,t} \right) - \left(\sum_{j=1}^{n} B_{j,t-1} \right) \right]$$

where

$B_{i,t}$ = budget for account i, year t
n = total accounts in city general fund budget
$\alpha_i, \beta_i, \delta_i$ = empirically estimated parameters (regression coefficients).

The simulation model results were then compared with the naive model predictions. Choices between our simulation model and each of the naive models were then made using two statistics suggested by Hunt.[20] In nearly every case, the simulation model "performed" better on both choice measures. It should be noted, however, that the constant-share-of-the-budget-total model also predicted quite well.

[19] The "more reasonable" alternative hypotheses used were: "This year's budget for a particular standard account in a given administrative unit equals
a. Last year's budget for that item, or
b. the average, over the study period, for that item."
[20] The statistics used [6, pp. 40–44.] were:
Min Σ [(estimated—observed)²/(estimated)], and
Min Σ [(estimated—observed)²/(observed)].

Finally, the following relationship was tested:

[Model Estimate of Appropriations]
    = a[Observed Appropriations] + b

For an unbiased model that predicts perfectly, the expected value of "a" is 1.0 and the expected value of "b" is 0.0. The results for model tests, where inputs were updated at the beginning of each budget year, are found in Table 2.

The true test of goodness-of-fit, however, is the ability of the model to describe the actual budgetary decision process. From all indications, our model does this quite well.

We found a change in goodness-of-fit associated with a change in administration in Detroit, but not in Pittsburgh or Cleveland. This was to be expected, since the "change-overs" in Cleveland and Pittsburgh represented a change only in the person occupying the mayor's position and represented a kind of hand-picked replacement by the incumbent party (the departing mayors moved on to higher political office). This indicates that, in Cleveland and Pittsburgh, the mayors underwent a process of socialization. No perceivable differences in goodness-of-fit were associated with increasing or decreasing revenues, indicating our surplus and deficit elimination routines were equally valid.

5. ANALYSIS OF MODEL RESIDUALS

In general, there are two kinds of "budgetary" change.

1. Those changes resulting from the continuation and elaboration of existing policies, and

2. Those changes resulting from shifts in municipal policies.

TABLE 2   Regression of Observed Decisions on Model Predictions

City	a	Std. error of "a"	b	r^2	n
Cleveland	.977	.001	− $5282	.9980	999
Detroit (excluding Welfare Dept.)	.984	.005	$7281	.9772	918
Pittsburgh	.991	.002	− $28	.9975	1002

Our model is clearly one describing changes of the first kind. It is a model of the standard procedures which result in particular forms of marginal adjustments in resource allocation from year to year.

The model does not describe changes of the second kind—significant shifts in municipal policies. The model, however, by filtering out (i.e., "predicting" or "explaining," in the statistical sense) incremental changes, draws attention to those items ("unexplained") in the budget that are not marginal adjustments or elaborations of previous policies.

By focusing on the "unexplained" changes in resource allocation, we can discover a great deal about the budgetary process as a change process. "Unexplained" changes include:

1. Incremental changes whose cumulative effect results in a "non-incremental" change.
2. Non-incremental policy shifts.[21]
3. Significant changes in policy, not reflected in the budget.

It should be noted that not all large changes are "changes resulting from shifts in municipal policies," and not all small changes are "changes resulting from the continuation and elaboration of existing policies." For example, a significant policy shift may result from the decision to handle the city's welfare load through the welfare department, rather than have the program administered by the county or the state for a fee. The total budget cost may be nearly the same, so this "significant" change may never be reflected in the operating budget. On the other hand, suppose the city decides to build an office building of their own to house a number of departments, rather than rent office space. Once the building has been completed, several years after the initial decision, a large change is noted in the budget—a change our formal model is not equipped to handle. This change, representing an increase in personnel and building maintenance expenses and large

decreases in rental expenses for the departments affected does not represent a significant shift in policy, however. It is merely an elaboration of a long-existing policy (resulting from the decision to build rather than rent). The original decision to build represents a significant "policy shift," however, and anticipated operating budget changes may or may not have been an important part of this capital decision. Our point is that for purposes of analyzing the 1966 operating budgetary process, the items resulting from previous capital decisions represent "automatic" changes in appropriations.

Model deviations[22] were classified by their perceived "cause." Four types of "causes" appear reasonable:

1. Change in External Environment
   a. Intergovernmental transactions
      (i) State and Federal subsidies and regulations
      (ii) Transfer of functions involving other governments
   b. Catastrophic event, emergency, crises, etc.—reaction to focus of public attention

2. Changes in Internal Environment
   a. New administration (new actors in system of interrelationships)
   b. Change in departments or functions
      (i) Transfers of activities—change in organizational structure
      (ii) Changes in programs, functions

3. Lack of Model Information
   a. Implications of capital budgeting decisions
   b. Additional revenue sources discovered
   c. Change in system of accounts
   d. Other

[21] The use of the term "innovation" has been consciously avoided because of lack of a generally-agreed-upon, operational definition of the concept. Rather, "policy shift" will be our theoretical construct. An allocation decision represents a "policy shift" when either through cumulative effects of small changes or immediate effects, it brings about a "significant" reallocation of resources between account categories.

[22] In each city, for each year, the five deviations largest in magnitude and the five largest percentage deviations were examined. In each city, for each year, the five deviations largest in (absolute) magnitude and the five largest percentage deviations were examined. "Causes" were associated with individual deviations on the basis of published information. It should be noted that, in nearly every case, the "reason" for the deviation was found in the Mayor's Budget Message to the Council. In other words, the actual devision system identified nearly the same set of unusual decisions as did our model. This, perhaps, is a more significant indication of goodness of fit than the many statistical measures calculated [3, Section 6].

4. Unexplained, Miscellaneous, and Other
   a. Model coding errors and missing data
   b. "Improper" accounting procedures (Detroit only—capital items included in operating budget, 1958–1959 to 1961–1962)
   c. Increased work load (or decreased)
   d. Other, unexplained

Those "causes" that represent "policy shifts" would be:
1.a.(ii) Transfers of functions involving other governments
1.b.   "Catastrophic event," emergency, etc.
2.a.   New administration
2.b.(i) Transfers of activities—organizational change
2.b.(ii) New programs, functions
3.b.   Additional revenue sources discovered
"Policy elaborations" would correspond to:
1.a.(i) State and Federal subsidies and regulations
3.a.   Implications of capital decisions.
3.c.   Change in system of accounts
3.d.   Other information not part of allocation (timing of elections) process
4.c.   Increased workload

5.1. Results

An analysis of model residuals revealed some consistent patterns of change in Cleveland, Detroit, and Pittsburgh. Two principal patterns were noted, only one of which could be described as a "policy shift." One class of revealed "unprogrammed" changes represented changes dictated by the external environment. These were largely due to changes in levels of "earmarked" revenues (especially in Cleveland) and the terms of negotiated contracts (in both Cleveland and Pittsburgh). The other area of change, representing a kind of "policy shift," was observed in those problem areas and activities where Federal funding and involvement was greatest.

The presence of citizenry demands, needs, etc. does not appear to be related to "policy shifts" in any systematic way. This is probably due to the presence of "needs," demands, etc. for additional services in *all* areas of municipal activity, none of which can be fully "satisfied" given revenue conditions.

6. SUMMARY

Traditional studies of public finance and governmental decision making, by trying to couple economic, political, and population characteristics to municipal expenditure items, attempt to identify those forces that determine the direction of budgetary drift. Their (implicit) contention is that the "role" of governmental decision makers is that of a translator of environmental characteristics into expenditure items.

By emphasizing the "short-run," we have stressed internal characteristics of the "Government" decision process and the relationship between current and historical decisions. In Figure 6, our findings are that in the short-run, items 5 and 6 are the most significant. By studying the budgetary phenomena over time, others have emphasized items 1, 2, 3, and 4 almost to the exclusion of 5. The question now remains—do our short-run findings apply in the long run? Our model described a somewhat "drifting" budgetary process. Do long-run "pressures" determine the overall direction of that drift?

6.1. Causes of Model Drift

Model drift could be biased by external constraints. "Expenditures" would be "allowed" to drift "only so far" without being corrected. They would then be brought back into line with "national standards," party or pressure group demands, population needs or tastes, etc. If, in fact, this were the case, evidence of the use of correcting mechanisms should exist in our model deviations because of the lack of provisions for the mechanisms in our model.

6.2. "Observed" Environmental Corrections in Drift

In Detroit, corrections in drift (model deviations) seemed to consist of establishing new departments in the urban renewal area, adjusting appropriations to correspond with State and user revenue changes, and one adjustment in Police and Fire salaries resulting from a Public Administration Survey report (that could be interpreted as a correction in drift to correspond to some national operating standard).

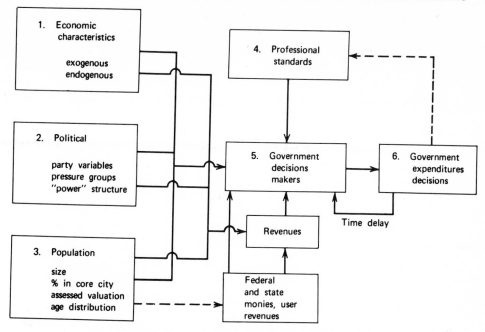

Figure 6 Environmental factors in municipal change.

Cleveland's drift corrections consisted of new departments in the urban renewal area, adjustments in appropriations because of changes in State and user revenue contributions and costs of negotiated contracts, and special wage increases for Police and Fire (corresponding to "national" rates?).

Pittsburgh appears much the same, with changes in State revenue contributions, the terms of negotiated service contracts (street lighting), and the emergence of city activities in areas of Federal program involvement accounting for most of the environmental corrections in model drift.

It appears from an analysis of our residuals over time that environmental corrections:

1. Are seldom (if ever) evoked directly to bring specific expenditure items "into line," *or*
2. Are filtered through the revenue constraint (see Figure 6), blurring the "cause" of increased (decreased) revenues and blunting possible direct impact on specific budget items.

In any event, environmental corrections appear to be more related to revenue changes than expenditure changes. Hence, their *impact* on expenditures appears to be a blurred one that is excised through the administrative allocation

and decision process rather than through any direct "expenditure-correction" mechanism.

Some *direct* environmental corrections were observed however. Negotiated contracts and changes in "ear-marked" revenue (State and user) provided some clear "corrections." The existence of Federal monies for municipal programs also appears to have "caused" a change in the "budgetary drift."

What seems to emerge from this study is an opportunity model of budgetary change. The broad "pattern of drift" is accelerated or depressed due to changes in general revenues. The "drift" in specific expenditures items changes in response to changes in "ear-marked" revenues or the terms of negotiated contracts. Rapid spurts of growth are observed in those areas where the city has the *opportunity* to expand activities because of the presence of revenues (Federal funds), rather than in areas having rapid changes or spurts in "needs." This also could be due to the fact that "needs" do not change in "spurts" either.

From a normative standpoint, the drifting *general fund* budget has some appeal. If, in fact, we are *able* to specify desired changes in municipal expenditures as a function of environmental changes, the "system" (if we have a Darwinian view of the world) would tend to place these expenditures *outside* of the general fund. The funding of activities where we *can* "logically" connect environmental changes (demands, ability to pay, etc.) to expenditure (or activity) changes, is common. The extreme case results in a "private" good where "supply equals demand" and level of activity is determined by the price mechanism. Somewhere in between lie the public power and utility companies where price roughly equals cost of goods sold and supply (activity level) equals "demand." Public transportation com-

panies, hospitals, community colleges, etc. all have a system of user taxes where the municipal government provides a partial subsidy. Generally, only activities where user-tax financing is not feasible or undesirable receive a full municipal subsidy and hence are "eligible" for inclusion into the general fund. *It should not be surprising, then, that in the absence of a system of standard costs or ways of determining activity levels* (characteristics of general fund activities) *the decision systems exhibit drifting, opportunistic characteristics.*

REFERENCES

1. D. Braybrooke, and C. E. Lindblom, 1963. *A strategy of decision.* New York: Free Press.
2. G. P. E. Clarkson, 1962. *Portfolio selection: a simulation of trust investment.* Englewood Cliffs, N.J.: Prentice-Hall. 8A.
3. J. P. Crecine, 1969. *Governmental problem solving: a computer simulation of municipal budgeting.* Chicago: Rand McNally. 1B.
4. R. M. Cyert, and J. G. March, 1963. *A behavioral theory of the firm.* Englewood Cliffs, N.J.: Prentice-Hall. 2B.
5. O. A. Davis, M. A. H. Dempster, and A. B. Wildavsky, 1966. On the process of budgeting: an empirical study of Congressional appropriations. *Papers on non-market decision making* (G. Tullock, ed.); Charlottesville: University of Virginia, 63–132.
6. E. B. Hunt, 1965. The evaluation of somewhat parallel models. *Mathematical explorations in behavioral science* (F. Massarik and P. Ratoosh, eds.); Homewood, Ill.: Irwin, 37–55. MS.
7. C. E. Lindblom, 1959. The science of "muddling through." *Public Administration Review, 19*(2): 79–88.
8. E. Mansfield, 1961. Technical change and the rate of imitation. *Econometrica, 29*(4): 741–766.
9. A. Newell, J. C. Shaw, and H. A. Simon, 1958. Chess-playing programs and the problem of complexity. *IBM Journal of Research and Development, 2*(4): 320–335. 8A.
10. A. Newell, and H. A. Simon, 1961. GPS, a program that simulates human thought. *Lernende Automaten* (H. Billing, ed.); Munich: R. Oldenbourg KG, 109–124. 1A.
11. A. Newell, and H. A. Simon, 1963. Computers in psychology. *Handbook of mathematical psychology* (R. D. Luce, R. R. Bush, and E. Galanter, eds.); New York: Wiley, Volume 1, 361–428. MA.
12. T. C. Sorensen, 1965. *Kennedy.* Scranton: Harper and Row.
13. A. B. Wildavsky, 1964. *The politics of the budgetary process.* Boston: Little Brown.

PART IV

INDIVIDUALS WHO
AGGREGATE

The studies in this section add individuals together to obtain an aggregate. Gullahorn and Gullahorn simulate the 148 respondents to a questionnaire. Pool, Abelson, and Popkin forecast votes in the 1960 presidential election. Fetter and Thompson send several thousand mothers through a maternity ward.[1] Ben, Bouchard, and Sweet reproduce the travel patterns in Sioux Falls, South Dakota. Swerdloff and Stowers compare five methods for forecasting the residential development of Greensboro, North Carolina. And Schussel predicts the orders placed by 24 retailers for Polaroid film.

As the introduction to the studies of individuals pointed out, a focus on aggregate behavior tends to simplify one's model. The erratic and idiosyncratic behaviors of individuals can be represented by distributions of random variables around average behavior patterns, and the average behavior patterns themselves can be represented by smooth, easily expressed trends. In part, this simplicity is an automatic, logically derivable consequence of the addition operation. For example, the Central Limit Theorem says that if one adds together a large number of statistically independent random variables, each having a different and unknown statistical distribution, the sum will have a normal distribution and can be subjected to formal statistical analyses. But the formal properties of aggregation are much less significant than are the properties of the model-builder's viewpoint. A focus on aggregate behavior is a perceptual orientation rather than an inevitable property of the real world. One sets out to discover smooth, easily expressed trends, and because that is what one is looking for, the erratic and idiosyncratic becomes random. Seeing randomness, one is in turn free to ignore the processes that create the random behavior and free to develop and act on logical implications of randomness such as the Central Limit Theorem. If the process has worked effectively, one has vastly reduced the complexity of the modeled situation, has emphasized the important and essential, and has invented analytic tools that are appropriate to his needs.[2]

[1] It is debatable whether the Fetter and Thompson study represents human behavior. Like many studies that we excluded from the bibliography, this one treats humans as inanimate occupants of a queueing system. However, we decided to consider this study as a simulation of human behavior because (a) having babies in a hospital is a uniquely human activity and (b) the occupancy periods implicitly represent decisions by doctors and patients about problems having numerous feasible solutions.

[2] The reader may find helpful Andre Nataf's 1968 article "Aggregation" [1].

The existing simulation models of aggregate behavior have generally achieved an extreme and stark simplicity. Linear difference systems such as Markoff processes are often the most complex functional relations used; not a few aggregate models comprise just one polynomial equation; and many other aggregate models are cascades of Poisson or multinomial lotteries. In addition, because this section excludes interactive models, interdependence among the aggregated individuals occurs only through mutual-occupancy constraints such as one finds in queueing models, and the simplicity of nature is reinforced by selection.

One result is that these aggregate models make more extensive use of the computer's speed and large size than do other simulation models. The programs are data processors as opposed to information processors. Another result is that these models can take greater advantage of special-purpose software and sophisticated methodological techniques. Languages like SIMSCRIPT and GPSS, while offering more general applicability, appear to have been designed with aggregate models in mind. And the vast majority of systematic methodology studies (category MS) have been oriented to simple, aggregate models.

However, the availability of appropriate software and sophisticated methods has not induced their adoption. Only a small portion of the model-builders have used simulation languages and virtually none have attempted to implement such techniques as antithetic variates or importance sampling. The nonadoption of simulation languages may be the result of rational calculations to the effect that the benefits such languages offer are more than offset by the costs of learning a new language or by the difficulties of communicating the coded programs to noninitiates. But it is difficult to construct a parallel argument that rational calculation has prevented the recognition of available methodological studies. The most plausible explanation is ignorance. Particularly in studies of individuals who aggregate, computer simulation is adopted as a pragmatic solution to a massive computation problem, and the machine is perceived as an oversized desk calculator that can complete an enormous number of elementary arithmetic operations within a reasonable time span. The model-builder does not think of simulation as a distinct methodology possessing a useful body of literature, and since he does not search for relevant literature, he does not read it. Of course, the product is acceptable; simulation is too new for methodological standards to have disseminated throughout social science, and the consumers of simulation studies are as unaware as the producers.

According to established social science norms, the methodological indifference of aggregate simulation is deplorable: studies should be methodologically pristine even if pristineness requires that one study unimportant problems rather than important problems, and studies should use standardized statistics even if the model does not satisfy the assumptions underlying the statistical tests. Obviously, standards of cleanliness and uniformity must be established and enforced. Until they are, model-builders will look upon simulations as a methodological short-circuit that frees them to work on important or interesting, but intractable, problems; different simulation studies will follow whatever procedures the model-builders themselves understand and find convincing; and the readers of simulation studies will have to decide on a study-by-study basis whether they understand and are persuaded by the procedures used.

In addition to the six studies included here, the reader may wish to consider the following.

TYPE 1 STUDIES

R. J. Bouchard, and C. E. Pyers, 1965. Use of gravity model for describing urban travel.
F. S. Chapin, Jr., and S. F. Weiss, 1968. A probabilistic model for residential growth.
Connecticut Highway Department, 1961. *Hartford area traffic study report, Volume I.*
J. Feldman, F. Tonge, and H. Kanter, 1963. Empirical explorations of a hypothesis-testing model of binary choice behavior.
G. R. Funkhouser, 1968. *A general mathematical model of information diffusion.*

W. G. Hansen, 1962. Evaluation of gravity model trip distribution procedures.
J. D. Herniter, V. J. Cook, and B. Norek, 1969. *Microsimulation of purchase behavior for new and established products.*
S. Kashin, A. J. Syvertsen, and M. L. Landsman, 1968. *The Queens-Long Island traffic demand model.*
Los Angeles Regional Transportation Study, 1963. *Volume I: base year report 1960.*
Louisiana Department of Highways, 1962. *New Orleans metropolitan area transportation study, 1960–1980, Volume II—outlook for the future.*
J. W. Morrison, Jr., and C. R. Moores, 1962. *The application of analog computers to traffic intersection problems.*
G. H. Orcutt, M. Greenberger, J. Korbel, and A. M. Rivlin, 1961. *Microanalysis of socioeconomic systems.*
D. M. Poore, 1969. Budgeting for changes in physical facilities and equipment.
G. S. Shaw, and J. W. Abrams, 1966. Demand forecasting for airline scheduling.
A. I. Siegel, and J. J. Wolf, 1961. A technique for evaluating man-machine system designs.
A. M. Voorhees & Associates, 1964. *Multi-purpose centers for the Baltimore region: market potential.*
N. C. Waugh, and J. E. K. Smith, 1962. A stochastic model for free recall.
E. Weiner, 1966. A modal split model for southeastern Wisconsin.

TYPE 2 STUDIES

R. P. Abelson, and A. Bernstein, 1963. A computer simulation model of community referendum controversies.
E. M. L. Beale, and P. A. B. Hughes, 1966. A computer assessment of media schedules.
S. R. Broadbent, 1965. *Computer Assessment of Media, the LPE media model.*
R. P. Browning, 1968. Hypotheses about political recruitment: a partially data-based computer simulation.
M. Cole, 1965. Search behavior: a correction procedure for three-choice probability learning.
DeLeuw, Cather & Associates, 1966. *Peninsula area transportation study, Commonwealth of Virginia, Volume I: Survey findings and data projections.*
D. J. Duffy, N. Hauser, and R. Roda, 1967. A computer simulation model of a police communication system.
H. B. Gamble, and D. L. Raphael, 1965. *A microregional analysis of Clinton County, Pennsylvania, Volume I.*
H. B. Gamble, and D. L. Raphael, 1966. *A microregional analysis of Clinton County, Pennsylvania, Volume II.*
D. H. Gensch, 1969. A computer simulation model for selecting advertising schedules.
G. Gordon, and K. Zelin, 1968. *A simulation study of emergency ambulance service in New York City.*
W. Helly, 1961. Simulation of bottlenecks in single-lane traffic flow.
W. A. Gunn, 1964. Airline system simulation.
B. Harris, J. Nathanson, and L. Rosenburg, 1966 *Research on an equilibrium model of metropolitan housing and locational choice, interim report.*
M. G. Howat, 1965. *A digital computer simulation of driver overtaking, following and passing.*
N. H. Jennings, and J. H. Dickins, 1958. Computer simulation of peak hour operations in a bus terminal.
T. R. Lakshmanan, and W. G. Hansen, 1965. Market potential model and its application to a regional planning problem.
D. D. Lamb, E. Dickman, L. S. Friedman, T. Soltman, R. Byrne, J. Snatchko, R. Karg, R. Arnold, A. Schwartz, A. Colker, and K. Arnold, 1969. *An urban-regional model of small area change for southeastern Michigan.*
A. M. Lee, and P. A. Longton, 1959. Queueing processes associated with airline passenger check-in.
J. F. Morrall, M. P. Ness, and B. G. Hutchinson, 1968. Traffic prediction models for central business district planning.
Niagara Frontier Transportation Study, 1966. *Final report, Volume two: travel.*
Pittsburgh Area Transportation Study, 1963. *Final report, Volume 2: forecasts and plans.*
A. Rogers, 1966. Experiments with a matrix model of population growth and distribution.
D. E. Schendel, J. O. Summers, and D. L. Weiss, 1968. Simulation and model testing.
C. Shanks, 1967. *Modelling and simulation of a psychiatric outpatient clinic.*
R. B. Smith, 1968. *Examples of the interplay between survey research and computer simulations.*
R. G. Spiegelman, and K. E. Duke, 1963. Projecting travel demand for urban transportation studies.
J. R. N. Stone, A. Brown, and D. A. Rowe, 1964. Demand analysis and projections for Britain: 1900–1970—a study in method.
A. R. Tomazinis, 1967. Modal split model in the Penn-Jersey Transportation Study area.
Tucson Area Transportation Planning Agency, 1965. *Tucson area transportation study. Volume II: forecasts and the plan, 1965.*
A. M. Voorhees & Associates, 1963. *Waterbury area transportation study.*
G. Wolford, and G. H. Bower, 1969. Continuity theory revisited: rejected for the wrong reasons?
H. J. Wootton, and G. W. Pick, 1967. A model for trips generated by households.

TYPE 3 STUDIES

J. A. Adams, and C. E. Webber, 1963. A Monte Carlo model of tracking behavior.

R. C. Atkinson, 1961. The observing response in discrimination learning.

B. Benjamin, W. P. Jolly, and J. Maitland, 1960. Operational research and advertising: theories of response.

D. Brand, B. Barber, and M. Jacobs, 1967. Technique for relating transportation improvements and urban development patterns.

A. S. Bregman and D. W. Chambers, 1966. All-or-none learning of attributes.

W. H. Brockman, 1966. *A stimulus conditioning learning model and its application to pattern recognition.*

G. E. Brokke, and W. L. Mertz, 1958. Evaluating trip forecasting methods with an electronic computer.

R. R. Bush, E. H. Galanter, and R. D. Luce, 1959. Tests of the "beta model."

R. R. Bush, and F. Mosteller, 1959. A comparison of eight models.

J. F. Cogswell, R. L. Egbert, D. G. Marsh, and F. A. Yett, 1965. Construction and use of the school simulation vehicle.

B. P. Cohen, 1963. *Conflict and conformity.*

J. S. Coleman, E. Heau, R. Peabody, and L. Rigsby, 1964. Computers and election analysis: the "New York Times" project.

R. L. Day, 1965. Simulation of consumer preference.

W. B. Denton, 1965. *An information processing model of human concept learning.*

J. Feldman, and J. F. Hanna, 1966. The structure of responses to a sequence of binary events.

J. Fidler, 1967. Commercial activity location model.

M. P. Friedman, T. R. Trabasso, and L. Mosberg, 1967. Tests of a mixed model for paired-associates learning with overlapping stimuli.

D. L. Gerlough, and F. A. Wagner, Jr., 1965. Simulation of traffic in a large network of signalized intersections.

G. H. Haines, Jr., 1968. The use of alternative models on a set of consumer data.

K. E. Heanue, and C. E. Pyers, 1966. A comparative evaluation of trip distribution procedures.

C. E. Helm, 1965. Simulation models for psychometric theories.

D. M. Hill, D. Brand, and W. B. Hansen, 1966. Prototype development of statistical land-use prediction model for Greater Boston region.

D. L. Hintzman, 1968. Explorations with a discrimination net model for paired-associate learning.

E. B. Hunt, J. Marin, and P. J. Stone, 1966. *Experiments in induction.*

H. Hyrenius, I. Holmberg, and M. Carlsson, 1967. *Demographic models: DM3.*

N. A. Irwin, and H. G. von Cube, 1962. Capacity restraint in multi-travel mode assignment programs.

R. C. Joyner, 1968. Computer simulation of concept learning by individuals in a minimum social situation.

J. H. Kell, 1960. A theory of traffic flow on urban streets.

T. R. Lakshmanan, and W. G. Hansen, 1965. A retail market potential model.

H. J. Leonard, and W. B. Delano, 1965. Distribution model for short and long distance travel.

W. F. Massy, and R. E. Frank, 1965. The study of consumer purchase sequences using factor analysis and simulation.

R. L. Morrill, 1965. The Negro ghetto: problems and alternatives.

L. R. Peterson, 1967. Search and judgment in memory.

A. E. Preyss, and J. L. Meiry, 1968. Stochastic modeling of human learning behavior.

Am. Rapoport, 1964. Sequential decision-making in a computer-controlled task.

Am. Rapoport, 1968. Choice behavior in a Markovian decision task.

Am. Rapoport, 1967. Dynamic programming models for multistage decision-making tasks.

Am. Rapoport, and A. Mowshowitz, 1966. Experimental studies of stochastic models for the Prisoner's Dilemma.

An. Rapoport, and A. M. Chammah, 1965. *Prisoner's Dilemma.*

M. G. Richards, and G. Williams, 1967. City of Worcester study techniques—2. Time function iteration.

M. G. Richards, and G. Williams, 1967. City of Worcester study techniques—3. Gravity model and time function iteration.

L. L. Roos, Jr., 1969. *Urbanization and modernization—some computer-based experiments.*

H. A. Simon, and T. A. VanWormer, 1963. Some Monte Carlo estimates of the Yule distribution.

H. A. Simon, and K. Kotovsky, 1963. Human acquisition of concepts for sequential patterns.

H. A. Simon, and E. A. Feigenbaum, 1964. An information-processing theory of some effects of similarity, familiarization, and meaningfulness in verbal learning.

R. D. Smallwood, 1967. Internal models and the human instrument monitor.

W. S. Smith, 1962. Synthesized travel desires.

R. L. Spitzer, and J. Endicott, 1968. DIAGNO.

S. H. Sternberg, 1959. Application of four models to sequential dependence in human learning.

E. J. Taaffe, B. J. Garner, and M. H. Yeates, 1963. *The peripheral journey to work.*

R. E. Thomas, and J. T. Tou, 1968. Evolution of heuristics by human operators in control systems.

T. R. Trabasso, and G. H. Bower, 1966. Presolution dimensional shifts in concept identification: a test of the sampling with replacement axiom in all-or-none models.

L. Uhr, C. Vossler, and J. Uleman, 1962. Pattern recognition over distortions, by human subjects and by a computer simulation of a model for human form perception.

C. Vossler, and L. Uhr, 1963. Computer simulations of a perceptual learning model for sensory pattern recognition, concept formation, and symbol transformation.

W. H. Wynn, 1966. *An information-processing model of certain aspects of paired-associate learning.*

REFERENCE

1. A. Nataf, 1968. Aggregation. *International encyclopedia of the social sciences* (D. L. Sills, ed.); New York: Macmillan, Volume 1, 162–168.

17

COMPUTER SIMULATION OF ROLE CONFLICT RESOLUTION

JOHN T. GULLAHORN
JEANNE E. GULLAHORN[1]

The present paper discusses experiments involving computer simulation of three role conflict situations. The first experiment is described in detail, and progress is reported on two additional experiments undertaken to test the generality of the original model.

A ROLE CONFLICT FIELD STUDY

The senior author's field research on role conflict among labor union leaders posed a situation involving two roles—a union chief stewardship and a responsible position in the company-sponsored employees' club [2]. The questionnaire page and responses are shown in Table 1. An attempt was made to establish the respondent's moral commitment to each role.

SOURCE: This paper is a composite of "Some Computer Applications in Social Science" (*American Sociological Review*, 1965, *30*: 353–365) and System Development Corporation paper SP-2261/000/00, November 1965.
[1] Wayne A. Olin, a graduate student in sociology at Michigan State University and a Summer Student Associate at System Development Corporation in 1965, worked with us during the tenure of his Student Associateship. We are indebted to him for a number of provocative ideas. We also express continuing gratitude to S. S. Shaffer of System Development Corporation for his patient assistance with technical problems.

Then moral and practical sanctions for each position were introduced and systematically varied by qualifying pressures from three reference groups. The respondent was invited to withdraw from one role or the other or, as an alternative, to "retain both positions." This third course was plainly labeled a decision of desperation, for he was told, "You really haven't time to do both jobs well." Responses in the middle column are thus a rough index of unresolved felt role conflict.

Union members responding to the questionnaire expressed a stronger commitment to the chief stewardship than to the employees' club position. Under the eight combinations of reference group pressures, almost twice as many (43 percent) would resign from the employees' club office as would give up the chief stewardship (22 percent).

Three reference groups exerted pressures on the respondents, and all three introduced consistent differences in response. The greatest shift came from yielding to persons represented by the respondent in his capacity as chief steward. The union executive committee was no more influential than management. Table 2 presents the percentage who would resign from each position under each source and direction of pressure.

TABLE 1 Union Stewardship *vs.* Employees' Club Office Dilemma:
Percentage Distribution of Questionnaire Responses by Union Members

Assume that you are an officer of the Employees' Club, which is largely supported by the company. You believe strongly in the union and attend meetings regularly. Your fellow workers have chosen you to be their Chief Steward, and you wonder whether you should resign from the club office so that you can devote your time to the job of Chief Steward. *You really haven't time to do both jobs well.* You feel responsible for the continued success of a program which you have started for the club, and at the same time you feel obligated to do a good job as Chief Steward.

In each of the following situations, please check the appropriate space to indicate the action you would be most likely to take.	I would be most likely to do the following		
	Resign from club office	Retain both positions	Resign from position of chief steward
An officer of the company tells you that if you continue your good work in the Employees' Club it may lead to a management position. What if—			
1. Both the union Executive Committee and the people you represent as Chief Steward want you to keep the club office.	19	44	37
2. The executive committee wants you to keep the club office—the people you represent want you to serve as steward.	42	36	22
3. The executive committee wants you to serve as steward —the people you represent want you to keep the club office.	29	39	32
4. Both the executive committee and the people you represent want you to serve as steward.	61	24	15
Your work as Chief Steward will give you more chance to make a favorable showing before management than will the club office. What if—			
5. Both the executive committee and the people you represent want you to keep the club office.	30	40	30
6. The executive committee wants you to keep the club office—the people you represent want you to serve as steward.	55	32	13
7. The executive committee wants you to serve as steward —the people you represent want you to keep the club office.	39	39	22
8. Both the executive committee and the people you represent want you to serve as steward.	71	22	7
$N = 148$; Average percentages	43	35	22

If a person feels more strongly committed to one of two competing roles, then role conflict will increase as reference group pressures build up in favor of the other role. For respondents who favored retaining the chief stewardship, increasing pressures toward retaining the club office should increase the intensity of felt role conflict. The possibility that unresolved role conflict produces an increasing tendency to view the situation unrealistically, to attempt more than one can accomplish, was tested in the field study by offering the respondents an

TABLE 2   Percent Who Would Resign

	From Employees' Club Office Under Pressure to Keep:			From Union Chief Stewardship Under Pressure to Keep:		
Source of Pressure	Union Steward- ship	Club Office	Difference	Union Steward- ship	Club Office	Difference
Persons represented	57	29	28	14	30	16
Executive committee	50	37	13	19	25	6
Management	49	38	11	18	26	8

opportunity to reject either of the roles or to retain both although they would not have time to do both jobs well. We expected increased pressures in favor of the employees' club to cause a higher percentage to choose the "retain both positions" category.

Interviews with union members as well as observations of meetings suggested the following rank order of the three reference groups' power: (1) persons represented; (2) the executive committee; (3) management.[2] On the basis of these expectations, we predicted the rank orderings of responses shown in Table 3. We expected item number 1 to produce the highest number of responses in the "retain both positions" category because all three reference groups favor the employees' club office, and this office was the generally less desirable one according to personal preferences. We expected a coalition of pressures from persons represented and the executive committee in favor of

[2] Actually, as indicated in Table 2, the latter two groups did not differ essentially in this questionnaire situation.

TABLE 3   Predicted and Observed Rank Orderings of Questionnaire Items: Percentages Who Would

Item No.[a]	Groups Favoring Employees' Club:	Resign from Club Office Rank Ordering		Retain Both Positions Rank Ordering		Resign from Stewardship Rank Ordering	
		Predicted	Observed	Predicted	Observed	Predicted	Observed
1.	All three groups	8	8	1	1	1	1
5.	Persons represented and executive committee	7	6	2	2	2	3
3.	Persons represented and management	6	7	3	4	3	2
7.	Persons represented	5	5	4	3	4	4
2.	Executive committee and management	4	4	5	5	5	5
6.	Executive committee	3	3	6	6	6	7
4.	Management	2	2	7	7	7	6
8.	None	1	1	8	8	8	8
	Spearman Rank Order Correlations	$r_s = .98$	$(p < .01)$	$r_s = .98$	$(p < .01)$	$r_s = .95$	$(p < .01)$

[a] Item numbers refer to Table 1. Rank in this table is based on the amount of pressure exerted by reference groups to retain the club office.

the club office (item 5) to be ranked second in intensity of induced role conflict, as reflected in decisions to retain both positions; a combination of pressures from persons represented and management (item 3) to be third, and so on. Comparison of our predicted rank ordering with that observed in the questionnaire response frequencies indicates that the data support our expectations (Table 3).

THE SIMULATION STUDY

On the basis of the field research, and also on the basis of George Homans' theory of elementary social behavior and Herbert Simon's treatise on decision making [5], we developed hypotheses about the information processing involved in role conflict resolution [3]. We decided to employ computer simulation to explore the logical implications of these hypotheses.

In computer modeling one must develop a symbolic representation of both the experimental situation and the theoretical system. Neither task is trivial. Researchers simulating human chess play, for example, must develop a means of representing the chess board, the pieces, and the operating rules concerning legal moves. As a separate and additional problem, they must program hypotheses concerning human strategies in playing. Similarly, in simulating the behavior of labor union members participating in our survey, it was necessary to represent the information in the questionnaire items and the administration of the questionnaire. Then we proceeded to write computer routines detailing our hypotheses about the information processing that culminated in a questionnaire response. Figure 1 flow-charts the program adapting our computer model, HOMUNCULUS, for role conflict resolution.[3]

The executive routine selects a simulated respondent to "answer" the questionnaire (Figure 1, Box 1). In the role-conflict situation, a labor-union member is rewarded by role behavior in a selected position as well as by approval from relevant reference groups. He has a history of reinforcement from activities

[3] A description of the full model appears in John T. Gullahorn and Jeanne E. Gullahorn [4].

involving both the employees' club and the local union. Since the reward value of each of these activities varies among members, the program assigns to each simulated respondent an individual set of reward values for the club office and the chief stewardship, using a random number generator (Box 2). The average value of the numbers generated by this Monte Carlo technique equals the averages from the observed data from labor union members—that is, 43 points for the chief stewardship and 22 points for the employees' club office.[4]

Interview data indicated that a few union members made their decisions without detailed assessment of reference group pressures when the perceived reward value of one or both statuses was so high that the respondent was unwilling to sacrifice it. In simulating these short-cut decisions (Boxes 3 to 8 in Figure 1), we assign as cutoff points 81 percent of the possible maximum value for the chief stewardship position and 93 percent of the possible maximum value for the employees' club office. These figures correspond to the data presented in Table 1: even with all reference group pressures aligned in favor of the employee's club, 19 percent still resigned from it in favor of the chief stewardship; and with all pressures favoring the chief stewardship, 7 percent nonetheless rejected it in favor of the employees' club office. Thus, when a synthetic respondent's assigned value for one and only one of the positions exceeds the cutoff point, he is made to resign from the other position without further processing. If his values for both positions exceed the cutoff points, he selects the middle course and resigns from neither, because the net profit from choosing one alternative is lower than the value of either position.

Our model follows Homans' definition of cost and profit: the cost of an activity is the

[4] Monte Carlo techniques are not inherent in simulation models. Indeed, HOMUNCULUS is generally a deterministic computer model. In the present situation we did not have data indicating individual values for relevant parameters; therefore we resorted to a Monte Carlo procedure to generate random values over a range that seemed reasonable on the basis of interview and other data from the field study.

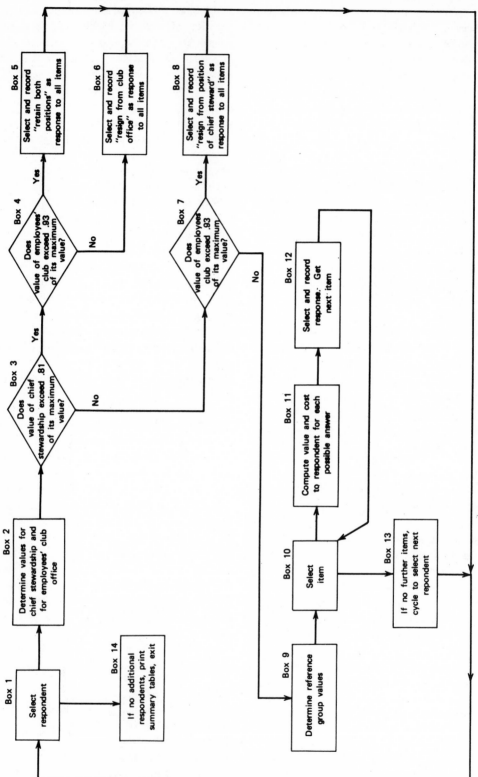

Figure 1   Flow diagram for simulation of role conflict resolution.

value of an alternative forgone in pursuing the activity [5]. The cost of selecting one role is the value of the rejected role. The net social profit of an activity is simply its reward value minus its cost [5].

Only a small proportion of our simulated respondents make shortcut decisions. For the majority, the choice depends on the individual's sensitivity to pressure from each of the three reference groups. Assuming that the simulated respondents—like real union members—have past histories involving interaction with each group, we used a Monte Carlo method to generate random numbers and assigned these as individual values for each group. The average values of the numbers so generated equal the observed sensitivities to pressures represented by the "Difference" columns of Table 2.

After reference groups have been given their values (Box 9), the first item from the questionnaire is presented to the simulated subject (Box 10) for processing (Box 11) leading to selection of a response (Box 12). Using the values for each position and for sensitivity to each reference group's pressure, the program computes both the reward and the cost of each possible course of action. The simulated respondent selects the alternative yielding the

greatest profit. After all items have been answered and the choices recorded, the program returns to the executive routine, which selects the next respondent and repeats the process.

We hypothesized that as role conflict increased, respondents increasingly would choose to retain both positions. In our initial formulation, we considered selection of the "retain both positions" alternative a choice by default resulting from inability to decide between the conflicting roles. This hypothesis is not inconsistent with Homans' theory, the basis for HOMUNCULUS. The personal cost of foregoing the expected rewards from either position may be so high as to preclude the respondent's realizing a profit from favoring one role at the expense of the other. Therefore, we predicted that the respondent would choose the desperate alternative of retaining both positions, without actively considering the potential rewards and costs ensuing from such a course of action.

An alternative formulation is also consistent with Homans' theory, however. Rather than making the decision by default, the respondent resolves his dilemma by comparing the expected social profit of this choice with the expected profits from a decision in favor of

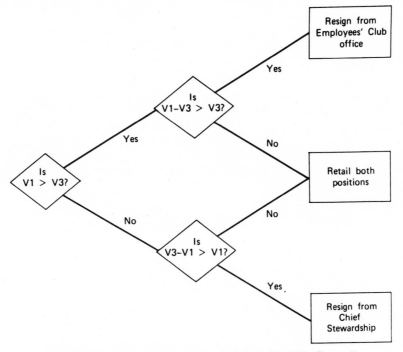

Figure 2 Flow diagram for decision by default (Box 11 in Figure 1).

either one of the positions, selecting the most profitable of the three courses of action.

Our survey data supported our prediction that as pressures mounted in favor of the less-favored position, respondents increasingly would decide to retain both roles rather than choose between them (Table 3). But we could not assess the adequacy of either of our hypotheses regarding decision strategies through conventional methods of analysis. In programming a sequence of computer instructions, however, we could state precisely the information processing of each strategy; and simulation runs generated the logical outcomes of each strategy.

Figure 2 on the previous page summarizes our hypothesis that retaining both positions is a decision by default. Such a decision occurs when the expected profit from the favored position is less than the reward value of the less-valued position. As the data in Table 4 indicate, rank orderings of the frequencies of responses to items by simulated respondents agree with the observed item rank orderings from union members as well as with the theoretically predicted item rank orderings. However, Table 5 shows that the percentage distribution of choices by simulated respondents differs significantly from that by union members on seven of the eight individual items.

TABLE 4 Union Stewardship *vs.* Employees' Club Office Dilemma: Results of Computer Simulations Involving Different Decision-Making Strategies

	Resign from Club Office	Retain both Positions	Resign from Stewardship
Simulation Based on Decision-By-Default Strategy:			
Correlations between			
computer and theory	1.00	.74	.95
computer and people	.98	.76	· 1.00
Simulated respondents—percentages	42	45	13
Simulation Based on Profit Evaluation for All Three Response Options:			
Correlations between			
computer and theory	1.00	.98	.95
computer and people	1.00	.95	1.00
Simulated respondents—percentages	40	43	17
Simulation Based on Profit Evaluation for All Three Response Options Plus Consonance and Integrity Considerations:			
Correlations between			
computer and theory	.98	.98	.95
computer and people	1.00	.95	1.00
Simulated respondents—percentages	42	36	22
Data from Survey Participants:			
Correlations between			
theory and people	.98	.98	.95
Labor union respondents—percentages	43	35	22

TABLE 5 Percentage Distribution of Responses From Simulated Respondents in Terms of Three Decision-Making Hypotheses

Item No.	Hypothesis 1: Decision by Default			Hypothesis 2: Compute Profit for Each Response			Hypothesis 3: Hypothesis 2 Plus Consonance and Integrity Values		
	Resign office	Retain both	Resign as steward	Resign office	Retain both	Resign as steward	Resign office	Retain both	Resign as steward
1.	21	46	33	16	51	33	20	46	34
2.	42	50	8[a]	41	45	14[a]	45	35	20
3.	27	51	22[a]	20	50	30[a]	23	44	33
4.	57	39	4[a]	62	31	7[a]	63	24	13
5.	26	55	19[a]	20	54	26[a]	23	47	30
6.	54	42	4[a]	58	35	7[a]	61	28	11
7.	37	53	10[a]	33	50	17[a]	36	40	24
8.	69	27	4[a]	70	25	5	70	19	11

[a] Comparisons were made between the computer-simulated subjects' responses to each item and the responses of labor union members to the item (as reported in Table 1). For each set of three responses marked with an a, X^2 with 2 degrees of freedom > 5.991 ($p < .05$).

Fig. 3 (p. 358) summarizes the processing involved when each respondent computes the social profit from all three decision alternatives before choosing among them. (Consonance and integrity values—which we shall discuss presently—were not involved in the simulation of the simple social profit strategy. Consequently, for example, $V1 = U1$.) As indicated in Tables 4 and 5, the computer output corresponds very closely to both the theoretical item rank orderings and the observed rank orderings, but the distribution of choices by simulated respondents differs significantly from that of union members on six of the eight individual items. We conclude, therefore, that the social profit hypothesis is more adequate, in general, than the decision-by-default hypothesis, but some aspects of the decision process are still neglected in the social profit model.

To explain one of Gerard's small group experiments [1], Homans postulated four important influences on individual behavior: personal preference, social approval, cognitive consonance, and personal integrity. With these, he provided a cogent analysis of data that Gerard could not explain [5]. In the runs described thus far, our computer model incorporated only two of these influences on decision making—personal preference and social

approval (the sensitivity to reference group pressures). Using Homans' framework, we can postulate that cognitive consonance will lead a respondent to increase the value of his preferred choice if reference group pressures support it. On the other hand, maintenance of personal integrity will make him reluctant to yield to pressure.

Consonance scores for each simulated individual are determined as follows. The respondent's personal valuation for the chief stewardship is added to his personal valuation for the club office. The absolute difference between these two scores is then subtracted from their sum to obtain: $MaxVal = S1 + S3 - |S1 - S3|$. The consonance score is a random number between zero and MaxVal.[5] Using this method to compute the score, we assume that the importance to an individual of having others agree with him decreases as the two roles have increasingly different personal values to him. Consequently, if he favors the chief stewardship over the employees' club office only slightly, reference group support is more likely to be decisive.

We have assumed, as Homans does, that a cost is incurred in lost personal integrity when

[5] *Editors' note*: If $S1 > S3$, $0 \leqslant Score \leqslant 2 \cdot S3$. If $S3 > S1$, $0 \leqslant Score \leqslant 2 \cdot S1$.

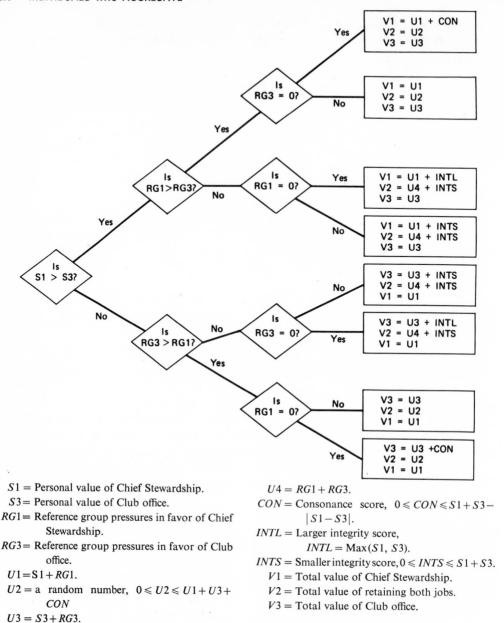

Figure 3 Flow diagram for respondent computation of social profit from all three decisions.

$S1$ = Personal value of Chief Stewardship.

$S3$ = Personal value of Club office.

$RG1$ = Reference group pressures in favor of Chief Stewardship.

$RG3$ = Reference group pressures in favor of Club office.

$U1 = S1 + RG1$.

$U2$ = a random number, $0 \leqslant U2 \leqslant U1 + U3 + CON$

$U3 = S3 + RG3$.

$U4 = RG1 + RG3$.

CON = Consonance score, $0 \leqslant CON \leqslant S1 + S3 - |S1 - S3|$.

$INTL$ = Larger integrity score,

$INTL = \text{Max}(S1, S3)$.

$INTS$ = Smaller integrity score, $0 \leqslant INTS \leqslant S1 + S3$.

$V1$ = Total value of Chief Stewardship.

$V2$ = Total value of retaining both jobs.

$V3$ = Total value of Club office.

one changes a decision because of pressure rather than conviction. When all relevant reference groups oppose an individual's personal choice, maximum pressure is exerted on him to agree with everybody, and maintenance of integrity has its highest value. If most of the pressure exerted by others opposes a person's choice, but if some groups support him, yielding involves a smaller loss of integrity. Having some support for either decision, one will not necessarily be surrendering just because of pressure.

Scores representing the value of maintaining integrity are computed as follows. When all reference groups oppose an individual's personal preference, integrity values are added to both his evaluation of his favored role and his evaluation of retaining both positions. Assuming that the greatest value for integrity follows from not yielding at all, we add a high increment to that decision, resulting in the doubling of the value of the respondent's favored alternative. Since some value accrues when a respondent's integrity is not completely compromised—when he retains the position he values most, and also keeps the positions urged by reference groups—then a smaller increment is made to the alternative of keeping both positions. This smaller integrity score is a random number between zero and $S1 + S3$. When over half, but not all, of the reference group pressure opposes the respondent's preference, the integrity increment both for his personal preference and for retaining both positions is a random number between zero and $Max(S_1, S_3)$. Note that although "all reference group pressures" will usually mean pressures from all three groups, this is not necessarily the case; one or even two of the groups may be exerting no pressure.

The methods of including cognitive consonance and personal integrity in the computer program are indicated in Figure 3. Incorporating these additional influences on rewards and costs produces the computer-generated results summarized in Tables 4 and 5. Table 4 shows the close correspondence in the rank-order correlations. Table 5 shows that the computer-generated responses and labor union members' decisions do not differ significantly on any of the eight individual questionnaire items. Data from both the computer-simulated respondents and the human respondents support our theoretical predictions, and this version of the model produces data that are remarkably close to living persons' responses, even in the variations from predictions.

TWO FURTHER APPLICATIONS

To test the generality of the role conflict resolution model, we have begun simulating decision making in two other situations that were presented in the original survey. One of these, a union trial dilemma is shown in Table 6. It manipulates familiar pressures in role conflict research: universalistic value orientations to social obligations versus particularistic value orientations to friendship expectations. Three types of pressures are systematically varied in favoring either of two extreme courses of action—expelling one's best friend, who is found guilty of antiunion activities, or being lenient. Unlike the conflict between the stewardship and club positions, in this situation there is no suggestion that the middle course—suspending the culprit—might be unsatisfactory.

In one simulation, we used the social-profit criterion incorporating only evaluations of personal preference and social approval. As shown in Table 7, the generated results produced a satisfactory correspondence between rank orderings of items by simulated and actual respondents only for the extreme response options. The relative frequencies of choices in the "suspend" category differed considerably; rho was only .51. Furthermore, individual item distributions for simulated respondents differed significantly from actual survey data. A second simulation that included consonance and integrity considerations brought the rank orderings of all three response categories into closer correspondence with observed results. However, individual item distributions still diverge.

One possibility is that our representation of this situation is at fault. At the time the field work was done, we assumed that a reference group's pressure for leniency would be construed by the respondents as a pressure for the most lenient option—the imposition of a fine. It now appears that respondents strongly favoring expulsion may interpret leniency pressures as a recommendation to suspend rather than to fine. The latter alternative is dissonant with their own preferences and their valuations of the reference group. We are planning to test the consequences of this formulation, but we see here an example of how computer modeling can aid and refine field research. Had the computer simulation been available at the time of the original field study, it would have been used to pretest the questionnaire, and the wording of these ambiguous items would have been modified before the survey was conducted.

The third survey situation concerns a union officer who is offered a promotion into management—a promotion that would require his resigning from the union. As shown in Table 8, three pressures are again varied in this situation,

TABLE 6   Union Trial Dilemma: Percentage Distribution of Questionnaire Responses by Union Members

Assume that charges have been brought against one of your best friends for *serious* antiunion activities. He had been one of the best and most loyal organizers while the union was getting under way. *You are a member of the trial board* appointed to investigate the charges and recommend action. Your friend pleads guilty as charged.

In each of the following situations, please check the appropriate space to indicate the action you would be most likely to take	When the trial board meets I would probably vote as follows and urge others to do the same		
	Expel from local	Suspend for a month	Fine or not punish
Suppose that you know your friend will continue acting the same way, and his action will make union–company cooperation impossible unless he is expelled. What if—			
1. Your family thinks you ought to defend your friend—the executive board recommends leniency.	31	37	32
2. Your family thinks you ought to defend your friend—the executive board recommends that you expel him.	45	35	20
3. Your family thinks you ought to expel him—the executive board recommends leniency.	26	41	33
4. Both your family and the executive board think you ought to expel him.	53	28	19
Suppose that a company official tells you he fears the man will become a martyr if punished, and this will injure union–company cooperation. What if—			
5. Your family thinks you ought to defend your friend—the executive board recommends leniency.	21	35	44
6. Your family thinks you ought to defend your family—the executive board recommends that you expel him.	36	35	29
7. Your family thinks you ought to expel him—the executive board recommends leniency.	20	41	39
8. Both your family and the executive board think you ought to expel him.	49	28	23
$N = 148$; Average percentages:	35	35	30

and the respondent is given four choices: definitely accepting the promotion, probably accepting it, probably rejecting it, or definitely rejecting it.

Herbert Simon has raised an important issue concerning decision making: Do people usually optimize, or do they usually "satisfice"? Economic man has long been portrayed as maximizing his gain by taking the best of all alternative choices open to him. Simon believes that a decision maker generally satisfices: he "looks for a course of action that is satisfactory or 'good enough'" [6]. In simulating the promotion dilemma, we wanted a program incorporating optimizing decision rules and one incorporating satisficing rules, so that we could contrast the results from the two.

Constructing a computer routine that maximizes is straightforward enough; the simulated respondent merely considers the rewards and costs of each alternative and selects the one yielding the greatest profit. Satisficing requires further elaboration. Criteria for "good enough" must be established, and a sequence must be determined in which the alternatives are to be examined. Our computer routine assigns a "threshold of acceptability"—a random number that ranges from zero to an upper limit which is the sum of the personal value of accepting, the value of rejecting, and the value of approval from the reference groups. The simulated subject selects a response to evaluate by a weighted random choice. If the value of the response exceeds the threshold, he accepts it. Otherwise, he tries another response. He continues until he finds an acceptable response or has checked them all. If no response meets the acceptable level of profit for a satisficing choice, he selects a response by the optimizing procedure.

Table 9 reports the consequences of following each of the two decision-making strategies. For the optimizing procedure, the rank-order correlation between living and synthetic subjects is adequate only for the extreme categories of "definitely accept" or "definitely reject"; in the intermediate categories the correspondence

between simulated and actual responses is poor. For the satisficing criterion on the other hand, the rank-order correlations for three of the response categories are significant, and the fourth category shows a decided improvement. Simulated respondents still differ from real union members in response frequencies for individual items, however, so we are not satisfied with the performance of the present model.

Actually, results to date are encouraging. The first experiment replicated the field survey more closely than we had anticipated. The second and third experiments involve more complex situations, and the theory is not sufficiently refined to account for selection of the less extreme responses. The model predicts responses in extreme response categories adequately, and its handling of the intermediate categories is improved. If we reduce the categories to two, accept or reject, the model produces results having a rank-order correlation of .99 and an improved item response distribution; but we

TABLE 7 Union Trial Dilemma: Results of Computer Simulations Involving Different Decision-Making Strategies

	Expel from Local	Suspend for a Month	Fine or No Punishment
Simulation Based on Profit Evaluation for All Three Response Options:			
Correlations[a] between computer and people	.93	.51	.98
Simulated respondents—percentages	28	48	24
Simulation Based on Profit Evaluation for All Three Response Options Plus Consonance and Integrity Considerations:			
Correlations[a] between computer and people	.88	.96	.95
Simulated respondents—percentages	23	57	20
Data from Survey Participants:			
Labor union respondents—percentages	35	35	30

[a] Spearman rank-order correlation coefficients.

TABLE 8   Promotion Dilemma: Percentage Distribution of Questionnaire
Responses by Union Members

Assume that an officer of your local has come to the attention of management and has been offered a promotion
to a managerial job which would make it necessary for him to resign from the union.

	What should the union officer do?			
In each of the following situations please check in the appropriate space whether you think the union officer should accept or reject this offer of promotion	Definitely accept the promotion	Probably accept the promotion	Probably reject the promotion	Definitely reject the promotion
Suppose that the man thinks he will progress to a high management position, and—				
1. Both his closest friends and his wife urge him to accept the promotion.	71	11	1	17
2. His closest friends urge him to accept the promotion—his wife wants him to refuse the promotion.	31	29	21	19
3. His closest friends urge him to refuse the promotion—his wife wants him to accept the promotion.	38	40	6	16
4. Both his closest friends and his wife urge him to refuse the promotion.	22	16	28	34
Suppose that the man thinks he was offered the promotion to buy him off because he has been a thorn in management's side, and—				
5. Both his closest friends and his wife urge him to accept the promotion.	20	12	21	47
6. His closest friends urge him to accept the promotion—his wife wants him to refuse the promotion.	10	13	25	52
7. His closest friends urge him to refuse the promotion—his wife wants him to accept the promotion.	12	20	26	42
8. Both his closest friends and his wife urge him to refuse the promotion.	9	8	13	70
$N = 148$; Average percentages:	26	19	18	37

do not want to throw away data by collapsing categories. Perhaps additional considerations will have to be introduced in the decision-making routines. In general, however, we prefer to keep the conceptual framework as simple as possible; we shall not introduce new concepts unless further analysis indicates that our present repertoire is insufficient.

CONCLUSION

In this brief outline of our current research, we have tried to indicate some of the problems and potential merits of the computer as a tool for theory development and verification. Develop-

ing an adequate representation of a real-life situation—be it a chess game, a questionnaire survey, or a small group experiment—is a complex programming venture. Formulating hypotheses as computer instructions forces one to detail exactly what variables are to be processed and how they are to interact; ambiguities in one's verbal theory become painfully apparent. Modularizing the program into relatively self-contained subroutines facilitates the testing of alternative formulations. For instance, the routines flow-charted in Figure 2 and 3 were easily incorporated into the over-all program depicted in Figure 1—without major system changes.

Although the cost is high in translating from verbal formulation to symbolic representation, a profit results when we find ourselves able to set theoretical processes in motion and to generate data that are the logical results of the hypotheses. Comparisons with studies of humans then provides opportunities for testing the validity of the programmed theory.

TABLE 9 Promotion Dilemma: Results of Computer Simulations Involving Different Decision-Making Strategies

	Definitely Accept	Probably Accept	Probably Reject	Definitely Reject
Simulation Based on Optimizing Strategy:				
Correlations[a] between computer and people	.93	.49	.43	.82
Simulated respondents—percentages	36	3	3	58
Simulation Based on Satisficing Strategy:				
Correlations[a] between computer and people	1.00	.64	.73	.95
Simulated respondents—percentages	27	13	12	48
Data from Survey Participants:				
Labor union respondents—percentages	26	19	18	37

[a] Spearman rank order correlation coefficients.

REFERENCES

1. H. B. Gerard, 1954. The anchorage of opinions in face-to-face groups. *Human Relations*, 7(3): 313–325.
2. J. T. Gullahorn, 1956. Measuring role conflict. *American Journal of Sociology*, 61(4): 299–303.
3. J. T. Gullahorn, and J. E. Gullahorn, 1963. Role conflict and its resolution. *Sociological Quarterly*, 4(1): 32–48.
4. J. T. Gullahorn, and J. E. Gullahorn, 1964. Computer simulation of human interaction in small groups. *Joint Computer Conference, Spring Proceedings*, 25: 103–113. Reprinted in *SCi Simulation*, 4(1): 50–61. 2B.
5. G. C. Homans, 1961. *Social Behavior*. New York: Harcourt, Brace and World.
6. H. A. Simon, 1957. *Administrative behavior*. New York: Macmillan, second edition.

18

VOTER RESPONSES TO CANDIDATES, ISSUES, AND STRATEGIES IN THE 1960 PRESIDENTIAL ELECTION[1]

ITHIEL DESOLA POOL
ROBERT P. ABELSON
SAMUEL L. POPKIN

THE IDEAS BEHIND THE PROJECT

Computer simulation was put to its first political use during the Presidential campaign of 1960. The simulation involved a novel technique for processing public opinion data, and was also a field test of some theories of opinion formation.

By early 1959, McPhee had developed a simulation of electoral behavior, designed to trace long political waves in the four-year election cycle.[1] These waves occur as new age groups enter the voting population and older voting groups die out. Useful as it might be for its purposes, McPhee's model was not one that would answer the action questions a candidate might ask during a campaign.[2]

An action model should focus on items about which:

a. A candidate has genuine strategic alternatives;

b. The behavioral sciences have some relevant theories;

c. The necessary data exist.

SOURCE: This paper is an edited extract from I. D. Pool, R. P. Abelson, and S. L. Popkin, 1964: *Candidates, issues, and strategies*, except that the conclusion is taken from I. D. Pool and R. P. Abelson, 1961: The Simulmatics project.

[1] Much of McPhee's early work has since been published in his (1963) *Formal Theories of Mass Behavior* [10]. Also see Coleman, 1964: *Introduction to Mathematical Sociology* [6] and his 1961: Analysis of Social Structures and Simulation of Social Processes with Electronic Computers [5].

[2] It should be noted, however, that in subsequent months the McPhee model was adopted by IBM and CBS and totally reinterpreted. The time periods were scaled down from years to weeks and the simulation was used with substantial success to analyze the Wisconsin primaries (see W. McPhee [10]).

James Coleman also developed a campaign simulation which he used in Baltimore (J. Coleman and Waldorf [7]).

Both the McPhee and Coleman simulations were designed to be used in conjunction with a special field survey. They were designed to explore the processes of voter decision making. They would be of more interest than our simulation to a social psychologist. They were not, however, designed for action research by a national party.

And campaign issues meet those criteria. A candidate can choose the issues on which he stands. Should be speak out on civil rights, or about communism and national defense, or about conservation and natural resources? Social milieu and party are much more important than issues in determining a voter's decision [2, 4]. The candidate's image and personality may also be more important. But these are things about which the candidate can do little. He controls the issues he talks about.

Issues and how the voters respond to them are also topics that social scientists know something about. Both theories and data about them exist. The data are in public opinion poll archives. The theories deal with a human tendency to maintain a subjective consistency in orientation to the world.

The theory of cross pressures was formulated by Lazarsfeld, Berelson, and others in studies of the election campaigns of 1940 and 1948. The theory starts with the familiar observation that party affiliation is statistically related to certain social variables. In the North, rural people, upper-income people, Protestants, and (at that period) older people tend to be Republicans. Urban people, poor people, Catholics, Jews, and (at that period) Negroes and young people tend to be Democrats. In the South, being rural and thus to a greater extent part of the old South increases the chance that one is a Democrat; Southern Republicans are found mostly in the cities.

Such correlations arise in various ways. In part they are reflections of tradition. But tradition is not just a matter of an individual's habit. It is even more a matter of group reinforcement. Berelson, Lazarsfeld, and McPhee found that only 33 percent of Democrats in Elmira, New York, said that among their three closest friends there was a Republican; only 20 percent of Republicans said that among their three closest friends was a Democrat. In each case the voter's image of the world was an overwhelmingly balanced one. Small-town people know small town people and tend to vote Republican. Rich people know rich people, and tend to vote Republican. Catholics know Catholics and tend to vote Democratic.

However, when social milieu and political views are out of balance, adjustment processes may be set in motion. The voter may compromise his views toward those of his friends, or attempt to convince his friends of the merit of his own views. Failing this, he may manage to misperceive his friends' views, or he may try to find new friends whose views are more congenial. Of the three adjustive processes— social influence, misperception, and social locomotion—it seems likely that the first is most common when a few people with strong views interact with many people with weak views; the second is most likely when people with moderately strong views interact socially but do not often discuss politics; and the third is most likely when people with moderately strong views interact socially and discuss politics, but find themselves within a fluid enough social network to change their friendship circles.[3]

There is, in any case, a minority for whom consistency of influence does not prevail. Such people are under cross pressure. The lifelong Democrat who is a rich, rural, Protestant is under cross pressure. So is the rich urban Catholic. The latter's coreligionists press him toward the group's traditional Democratic affiliation. His wealthy business colleagues press him to a Republican one. We can also think about cross pressures arising from issue attitudes. The Vermont farmer who is approaching 65 and strongly in favor of Medicare may find himself torn between normal Republican affiliations and a Democratic issue stand. A big-city industrial laborer who thinks domestic Communists have infiltrated the government and who does not want Negroes living near him may find himself under cross pressure between his labor interests and his other views.

What do we know about men under cross pressure? The Lazarsfeld-Berelson studies present several hypotheses.

1. It is among the people under cross pressure that we find the individuals who change their minds from election to election and within the campaign period.

2. However, even among these people most end up voting for their traditional party. While

---

[3] All three balancing mechanisms, but most especially friendship changes, were observed in experimentally created social groups by Newcomb [12].

some resolve the conflict by switching, more of them resolve it by such other means as misperceiving where their party stands (that is, a Democrat may accept as fact his platform's ceremonial tributes to balanced budgets).

3. Some people under cross pressure resolve their conflict by withdrawing cathexis from politics. Men under cross pressure are less interested in the campaign, and a higher proportion of them become nonvoters.

4. People under cross pressure make up their minds late in the campaign. People under unified pressures are apt to have their minds made up from the beginning.

These statements about election campaigns are consistent with the more general formulations of balance theory [1, 3]. Consider balance among three objects, one of them a cognizing human being P, and the other two the objects X and Y of which P is cognizant. P can feel positively, negatively, or neutrally toward X and toward Y, and he can believe assertions about the relation of X and Y. Suppose that P feels positively toward X and Y; the situation would be balanced only if he also believes X and Y are positive toward each other. The statement "my friend favors the Democratic candidate," if said by a Democrat, asserts a balanced situation. If said by a Republican, it represents an imbalance. Balance theory predicts that when imbalance exists there is some tendency to restore balance. This may happen by a change in some belief (the above hypothesis 1 about voting), or by misperceptions (hypothesis 2), or by withdrawing attention from the subject (hypothesis 3), or in other ways.

The theories of cross pressure and balance were a natural basis for an election simulation. However, theories without data will not permit a predictive simulation. Essential to our operation was the existence of a vast file of old public opinion survey cards which could provide measurements of the attitudes of different groups in the population toward relevant issues. The main poll archive is the Roper Public Opinion Research Center in Williamstown, which made feasible the project described here. The Williamstown Center agreed to the use of their archives on two conditions: first, all basic data were to be made

available to the Center so the Republican Party would have an equal opportunity to use them; second, all results could be published after the election.

The first step in the project was to identify all polls anticipating the elections of 1952, 1954, 1956, and 1958. Preelection polls on the 1960 contest were added when they became available. We selected those polls that contained standard identification data on region, city size, sex, race, socioeconomic status, party, and religion. Further, we restricted our attention to polls that asked about vote intention and about a substantial number of preselected issues such as civil rights, foreign affairs, and social legislation. From 1952 to 1958 we found 50 usable surveys covering 100,000 respondents. Fifteen polls anticipating the 1960 elections were added to this number, and the 65 surveys represented over 130,000 interviews.

THE HISTORY OF THE PROJECT

A key figure in the initiation and carrying out of the project was Mr. Edward Greenfield, a New York businessman actively engaged in Democratic politics. The Simulmatics Corporation was organized in 1959 with Mr. Greenfield as President. Although the project was fundamental scientific research, it was clear that universities should not accept financing from politically motivated sources or permit a university project to play an active role in supplying campaign advice to one party.

By June of 1960 a report on the Negro vote in the North was prepared. It was a sample of what might be done by the Simulmatics process. On August 11, the Kennedy campaign asked the Corporation to prepare three reports, on the image of Kennedy, on the image of Nixon, and on foreign policy as a campaign issue. These three reports were to be delivered in two weeks, and along with them, we were to conduct a national sample survey that would bring the Simulmatics data up to date.

The survey confirmed the published Gallup finding that Nixon was well in the lead, and it made us aware that women were responsible for Nixon's lead. It also persuaded us that voters were focusing on foreign policy at that point in the campaign. The relationship between such current intelligence and a simulation model developed out of historical data is analogous to the relationship between current weather information and a climatological model. One can predict tomorrow's weather best if one has not only current information but also historical information into which current reports can be fitted.

The introduction of the survey results was possible only because of prior preparation. The survey was ordered on a Thursday, the field interviewing took place between Saturday and the following Thursday, by Friday morning all cards had been punched, and by Friday night the preprogramed analysis had been run and preliminary results were given to the National Committee. The swiftness of the entire operation is, of course, a testimony to the advantages of a high-speed computer system.[4] And the possibility of such turnabout times opens up new opportunities for action research in the social sciences.

When we planned the project, we anticipated active campaign work from the beginning of the summer until about September 15. How far the investment was justified by the two weeks of work actually done is a question that we find impossible to assess. The answer depends on how much impact the reports had on the campaign. They were seen by perhaps 15 key decision makers, but they were read intelligently. President Kennedy was an avid and able user of political research. He not only understood enough to trust research; he understood enough to know when and in what respects to distrust it. He could ask the right questions and could distinguish between findings and implications.

The question most often asked us is how influential were our reports? Neither we, nor the users, nor even John F. Kennedy if he were alive, could give a certain answer. When a policy maker reaches a decision, he knows what conscious factors enter into it. But he seldom knows which conversations that he has had or words that he has read were responsible for initially injecting those ideas into his head, or

reinforcing them, or turning them into final convictions. In a Presidential campaign there are only a limited number of policy alternatives and there are myriad voices arguing for each of them. Our own contribution was to bolster by evidence one set of alternatives. With one exception, they were the alternatives that the candidate ended up choosing. We believe that fact showed his sagacity; we know it was not due to a simple cause–effect relationship between our data and his action.

ORGANIZING THE DATA

The data consisted of questionnaires from 65 national surveys, covering 130,000 individuals.

Such massive data required substantial innovations in analytic procedures. The study was an experiment in research with abundant libraries of survey data. To gain the advantages that could accrue from using 130,000 cases, we had to simplify and to standardize what would otherwise have been an unmanageable mass.

The data were reduced to a 480×52 matrix. The number 480 represented types of voters, defined by socioeconomic characteristics. One voter type might be "Eastern, metropolitan, lower income, white, Catholic, female Democrats." Another might be "Southern, rural, upper income, white, Protestant, male Independents." The number 52 represented "issue clusters," political characteristics on which the voter type would have a distribution. Most of these were political issues, such as foreign aid, the United Nations, and McCarthyism. Other so-called issue clusters included such indicators of public opinion as "Which party is better for people like you?", vote intention, and nonvoting.

One can picture the 480×52 matrix as containing four numbers in each cell. The first number stated the total number of persons within a voter type who had been interrogated on that particular item. The other three numbers trichotomized those respondents into the percentages pro, anti, and undecided.

We first assembled such a matrix for each biennial election separately. The number of surveys for each election period were:

---

[4] Nonetheless, such intense pressure is not an optimum condition for research work. Clerical errors inevitably occurred. It was our good fortune that none of those we have found since have caused us to alter any conclusions.

TABLE 1 Definition of the 480 Voter-Types[a]

In each of 4 regions: South, East, Midwest, West

By Sex, Religion, Ethnicity

7 SES and City-Size Levels	Protestant Males			Protestant Females			Catholic Males			Catholic Females			Jews			Negroes		
1. A Urban	R	D	I	R	D	I	R	D	I	R	D	I	R	D	I	R	D	I
2. A+B Town	R	D	I	R	D	I	R	D	I	R	D	I						
3. A+B Rural	R	D	I	R	D	I	R	D	I	R	D	I						
4. B Urban	R	D	I	R	D	I	R	D	I	R	D	I	R	D	I	R	D	I
5. C Urban	R	D	I	R	D	I	R	D	I	R	D	I						
6. C Town	R	D	I	R	D	I	R	D	I	R	D	I						
7. C Rural	R	D	I	R	D	I	R	D	I	R	D	I						

96 cells   4 ×   = 384 cells

In 1 region: Border

	Protestant Males			Protestant Females			Catholic Males			Catholic Females			Jews			Negroes		
1+2+3 combined	R	D	I	R	D	I	R	D	I	R	D	I	R	D	I	R	D	I
4+5+6+7 combined	R	D	I	R	D	I	R	D	I	R	D	I	R	D	I	R	D	I

36 cells   1 ×   = 36 cells

TABLE 1   Definition of the 480 Voter-Types—*Continued*

	Rep.	Dem.	Ind.
1. Protestants without SES rating in non-labor-force families	R	D	I
2. Catholics without SES rating in non-labor-force families	R	D	I
3. Persons of no religion	R	D	I
4. Persons of other religion	R	D	I

Add, in all 5 regions

5 × 12 cells = 60 cells

480 cells

a Key: R means Republican; D means Democratic; I means Independent.
A means professional, executive, and managerial occupations; B means white-collar occupations; C means blue-collar occupations.
Urban refers to metropolitan areas exceeding 100,000 population; town refers to communities between 5,000 and 100,000; rural refers to places under 5,000.

1952	16
1954	15
1956	5
1958	14
1960	15 (up to January 1960)

The first four basic matrices were compiled by Spring 1960 and were cumulated together to form a four-period master matrix. Most of the work during the 1960 campaign was done on the four-period master matrix. In addition, in the summer of 1960 we were receiving 1959 surveys and making up the 1960 matrix. The idea was to work with a five-period master and, if we had worked into September, we would have done so. In the years following 1960, we have often used the five-period master, and the reports to follow will indicate whether the four-period or five-period master is used.

Three questions arise about this operation: How did we select the surveys we used? How did we come to define the 480 voter-types in the way we did? How did we define the 52 issues?

We specified the following requirements for a survey:

1. It had to use a national cross section or probability sample.

2. It had to be an election poll, asking the respondent how he intended to vote. It also had to have some additional political questions: how the individual had voted in the past, had he voted or did he intend to vote, and so on. Not all of the latter items were required on all surveys, but we were interested only in surveys with a certain minimum richness.

3. The surveys had to contain questions about the issues we had listed as potentially important. Although no survey contained information on more than a few such issues, we were interested only in surveys with questions on at least four or five issues.

4. The face-sheet data on the survey had to cover all of the items necessary to classify respondents into one or another of the 480 voter types into which we were distributing respondents. The types are indicated in Table 1. It will be noted that states were divided into five regions.

The regional division of states was:

East: Maine, New Hampshire, Vermont, Massachusetts, Rhode Isalnd, Connecticut, New York, New Jersey, Pennsylvania

South: Virginia, North Carolina, South Carolina, Georgia, Florida, Alabama, Mississippi, Arkansas, Louisiana, Oklahoma, Texas

Midwest: Ohio, Michigan, Indiana, Illinois, Wisconsin, Minnesota, Iowa, Missouri, North Dakota, South Dakota, Nebraska, Kansas

West: Montana, Arizona, Colorado, Idaho, Wyoming, Utah, Nevada, New Mexico, California, Oregon, Washington

Border: Maryland, Delaware, West Virginia, Kentucky, Tennessee

Hawaii and Alaska were omitted because they were not included in the surveys.

A decision had to be made as to how many types we could effectively use and which variables were most predictive. We decided to have about 500 types, since 100,000 cases divided into 500 types would give an average of 200 cases per type. Attitudes considered in as few as 10 surveys would then be measured by an average of 40 cases per type.

If we had felt free to use one more variable, it would have been age. Young voters behave differently from old, partly because of age, but even more because they grew up in a different era. But to have added three levels of age would have given us 1440 types, with many types having only a handful of cases to represent them. Education is highly enough correlated with socioeconomic status that it would have added little predictive power. Since we were forced to drop age and education as type-defining variables, we treated them instead as issues 51 and 52. That is, we recorded for each type the numbers of people who were young and old and the numbers with high and low education.

We use the word issue very loosely to describe 52 sets of survey results. A list of the issue names can be found in Table 2, and a few of the so-called issues deal with such matters as past vote, nonvoting, and other behaviors not well described by the word issue.

TABLE 2   The Fifty-Two Issue Clusters

1. Attitude Toward Truman
2. Anti-McCarthyism
3. Attitude Toward Nixon
4. Anti-Nixon Voting
5. Attitude Toward Eisenhower
6. Attitude Toward Stevenson
7. Symington versus Nixon
8. Kennedy versus Nixon
9. Pro-Negotiationism
10. Defend Europe
11. Sympathetic to Europe
12. Neo-Fascist
13. Withdraw Troop Commitments
14. Anti-Catholic
15. Pro-Labor
16. New Deal Philosophy
17. Civil Rights
18. Anti-Administration
19. Congressional Votes
20. Which Party for Prosperity
21. Which Party for Personal Finances
22. Which Party Best in Crisis
23. Best Party for People Like Self
24. Normal Presidential Vote
25. Congress versus Ike
26. Stevenson versus Eisenhower (1952)
27. Stevenson versus Eisenhower (1956)
28. Union Membership
29. Fear of War
30. Concern with Rising Prices
31. Concern over Wages, Unemployment
32. Foreign Policy Knowledge
33. Salience of Civil Rights
34. Interest in Elections
35. Nonvoting
36. Extreme Nonvoting
37. Voting Intent Record
38. Ike Vote but Democratic for Congress
39. Which Party Best for Peace
40. World Situation Complacency
41. Meet with Soviets
42. Red China Policy
43. Attitude Toward English, French
44. Attitude Toward Asian Neutrals
45. Attitude Toward Israel
46. Defense Commitments
47. Disarm H-Bomb
48. Preparedness
49. Attitude Toward U.N.
50. Attitude Toward Foreign Aid
51. Age
52. Education

The first step in organizing our data was to identify questions that seemed to bear on the 52 issue clusters we had listed as relevant. But there are problems to this procedure. Even if one finds numerous surveys dealing with a common issue, they do not all ask the same questions. Take as an example the matter of civil rights. One survey might ask "Are you in favor of the Supreme Court's decision on school integration?" Another might ask "Do you favor a Fair Employment Practices Commission (FEPC)?" On another the question might be "Should the schools in Little Rock be integrated now?" Each question has one answer that can be characterized as pro-civil rights, another that can be characterized as anti-civil rights, and other answers that are indeterminate and nonresponsive. But: (1) How can one know that different questions really deal with the same attitude? (2) Even if they do, don't they cut that latent attitude at different points on the scale?

On a single survey we could establish the fact that two or more questions measure a single attitude by correlating them across individuals. Between surveys we could do the same thing by correlating across groups. However, we did not use the 480 voter types because the number of individuals in a type who replied to any single question would have been much too small. For correlating single questions across voter types, we had to use a restricted number of larger types. We settled on 15 macrotypes.

We actually used a double criterion of latent attitude equivalents. First, we required that each question distribute in the same way across the 15 macrotypes. Second, questions were treated as dealing with the same topic only if we subjectively felt them to be so.

It may be asked why we used a subjective criterion. We could have intercorrelated all questions with all other questions, and by factor analysis grouped those that intercorrelated highly. For certain purposes that would have been the thing to do. However, for our purposes it seemed essential to define issues in ways close to the substance of current politics. For example, responses to a question on school integration might correlate highly with responses to a question on atomic testing. This would prove interesting things about the structure of political attitudes, but it would be hard to use a cluster containing such substantively diverse material in advising a candidate on the preparation of his speeches.

Even when we have established that different questions tap the same underlying attitudes, the cutting points may be different. If the items form a Guttman scale, those who give an affirmative answer to one question may encompass all those who give an affirmative answer to a second question, but also some of those who say no on the second question. Fewer people in the United States favor an FEPC than are ready to accept school integration. Though both questions tap the same latent attitude, the latter does so in a milder form.

If the sampling on two surveys is uniform, then the fact that different questions are used to tap a single attitude is no problem. Compare attitudes of two respondent types, I and II, the first of which is twice as numerous as the second. Barring random variations, each sample will have twice as many persons of type I as of type II. Suppose on each sample we used a different measure of a single latent attitude: our operational index of that latent attitude remains the proportion of affirmative replies even though these are replies to different questions. While such a combined measure is far more complex and less intuitive than a simple percentage of affirmative replies, it is no different in principle from any index based on several questions occurring within a single questionnaire.

FORTY-EIGHT SYNTHETIC STATES WITHOUT LOCAL POLITICS

In the data bank, five geographic regions of the United States were one variable by which voter types were defined. American politics are regional. But in some respects they are even more localized than that.

Presidential elections are determined by states. It is not enough to guess the Democratic percentage in the Northeast; one needs to estimate which way New York will go. A favorite game all through a campaign is adding up electoral college estimates state by state.

One benefit from the large number of interviews used was the possibility of approximating state-by-state results. A single national survey—even a large one—has too few cases to permit any significant analysis of state politics. The same would have been true, even for our

voluminous data, if we had attempted a state-by-state analysis in a simple way. We had about 2000 interviews per state, but in a small state, there might have been no more than 300 or 400 interviews. On an issue cluster that occurred in one-tenth of the surveys, there would be too few cases for effective analysis. We therefore created synthetic states.

By an elaborate analysis of census, poll, and voting data, we estimated the number of persons of each voter type in each state. Since *region* was one defining characteristic for the 480 voter types, there were at most 108 voter types in any state. It was assumed that a voter of a given type would be identical regardless of the state from which he came. A synthetic state therefore consisted of a weighted average of the voter types in that state, the weighting being proportional to the numbers of such persons in that state.

We do not assert that the assumptions on which this synthesis is based are true. They are partly false. The interesting question intellectually is how good were the results obtained. The test is how well state-by-state predictions correspond to reality. To the extent that they do, the essential differences between states are in distributions of types rather than in other geographic differences such as political history.[5]

SIMULATING THE 1960 CAMPAIGN

The Problem Posed

In August 1960, when we were called on to use the assembled system, the most pressing question facing the Democratic high command was how to handle the religious issue. Kennedy had handled it in Wisconsin and West Virginia by public attacks on bigotry. In both cases he was successful, and he had gone on to win the nomination in a splurge of optimism. Then suddenly, the bottom seemed to fall out. The polls began showing Nixon well ahead and everywhere anti-Catholic activities, statements, and literature began to appear.

[5] The accuracy of syntheses of states is critically dependent on appropriate regional definitions. The states where the simulation was most notably off included Arizona, Nevada, New Mexico, Idaho, and Colorado, states mostly of small population, and states which we attempted to treat as Western. The assumption that the Mountain area was uniform with the West was misleading.

The strategic alternatives were a policy of minimizing attention to the religious issue by discussing it as little as possible and a policy of publicly attacking those who introduced the issue into the campaign. The latter tended to draw Kennedy's religion into the limelight. Every attack on those who injected the religious issue brought it even more into focus.

The Formulas Chosen

When faced with a question about a hypothetical future, the next step in a simulation is to formulate subjectively, but with as much detail and precision as possible, what one believes will be true under the alternative being simulated. One may draw on theory, experience, common sense, guesswork, or any other source. One must, however, formulate quite rigorously the principles that will become operative. The simulation does not provide these insights. It works out their implications in a large system.

The notions we had about the impact of the religious issue were expressed in a series of equations. The equations represent a campaign in which only two forces play a role: one, past voting inclinations, and the other, attitudes toward a Catholic in the White House.

The basic mechanism in the simulation was a fairly straightforward application of the cross-pressure findings of earlier studies. We grouped the 480 voter types into 9 subsets arising from a 3×3 classification on religion and party: Protestants, Catholics, and Others; Republicans, Democrats, and Independents. The two main groups under cross pressure were those marked with an X in Table 3, the Protestant Democrats and the Catholic Republicans.

TABLE 3   Cross-Pressure Patterns

	Republicans	Democrats	Independents
Protestants	(1)	X (2)	(2)
Catholics	X (4)	(3)	(3)
Others	(4)	(5)	(5)

For each of the nine situations, we predicted how voters would behave. Some of the situations seemed similar so we ended up with only five separate sets of predictive equations. We shall go through these in order. The relevant equations are indicated by the numbers in Table 3.

1. Protestant Republicans. They were not under cross pressure. Since our data bank revealed no substantial dislike of Nixon as an individual among such voters, we did not expect their 1960 vote to differ substantially from their 1956 vote. Thus we wrote two equations

[1]
$$V_k = P_{56}(1 - P_{35})$$
$$V_n = Q_{56}(1 - P_{35})$$

The Kennedy percentage (V_k) in any voter type would be the percentage of persons in that voter type who indicated a preference for Stevenson in 1956 (P_{56}) reduced by the nonvoting record of that voter type ($1 - P_{35}$). The equation for the Nixon percentage (V_n) was the same, except that it used the 1956 Eisenhower supporters (Q_{56}).

2. Protestant Democrats and Protestant Independents. First, we decided that, barring the religious issue, Congressional vote intentions would be a better index of the Protestant Democrats' 1960 vote than would their 1956 vote. Too many of them defected to Eisenhower in 1956 for us to believe that 1956 was a good indicator of normal behavior. A better predictor would be how the Protestant Democrat had voted for Congress, modified by any anti-Catholic sentiment he might have.

The most obvious equation was one that subtracted from the Congressional vote a proportion of those voters who expressed anti-Catholic sentiments.[6] However, those Democrats who were anti-Catholic might be the ones who in practice voted Republican anyway. Our system could not give us that information for each respondent. One respondent might have been polled about his vote intentions, and

---

[6] The typical question that went into this cluster was "If your party nominated an otherwise well-qualified man for President, but he happened to be a Catholic, would you vote for him?"

another man, on a different survey, might have been polled on whether he would vote for a Catholic for President. We had to find one or more surveys on which both questions appeared, and we found that the ratio ad/bc in Table 4 averaged about .6. With that information we could estimate how many of the anti-Catholics were hopeless cases anyhow (that is, had gone Republican for Congress) and how many would be net losses only in a campaign dominated by the religious issue.[7]

TABLE 4 Correlation Table for Estimating Impact of Religious Issue on a Democratic Voter Type

Congressional Vote Intentions	Attitude on the Religious Issue	
	Anti-Catholic	Not Anti-Catholic
Democratic	a	b
Republican	c	d

Finally, we took account of the previously established finding that voters under cross pressure stay home on election day more often than voters whose pressures are consistent, and we doubled the historically established non-voting index for these types.

[7] Interissue correlations were a serious problem. We met the problem in part by having as many as 480 types, each defined by a number of major variables. The types were socially quite homogeneous, and many demographic variables were being controlled for. In addition, there was a way, when it seemed important, roughly to estimate within-type correlations for most pairs of variables.

Since we were working with a large collection of data, there was a fairly high probability that we could find one survey at least, on which questions had been asked which were components of each of the two indices that we wished to correlate. Having found a single survey with questions on both issues, we could run correlations within voting types. These correlations were individually worthless since the number of cases for any one correlation would be trivial. There were two options. One was to aggregate voter types. The other was to disregard the significance of the individual correlations. All we were interested in was an estimate of their average.

With appropriate compromise between these two options, it becomes possible to arrive at a rough estimate of the typical correlation within the voter types. We could assign values to the cells of the contingency table whose marginals we already knew and whose correlation coefficient we now have estimated.

Thus we arrived at equations

$$V_k = (P_{58} - a)(1 - 2P_{35})$$

[2]

$$V_n = (Q_{58} + a)(1 - 2P_{35})$$

The estimate of anti-Catholics (that is, persons in cell a in Table 4) was arrived at by:

$$P_{14} = \text{percent anti-Catholic.}$$

$a + b = P_{58}$ = percent of the voter type who had indicated a Democratic Congressional vote intention.

$c + d = Q_{58}$ = percent of the voter type who had indicated a Republican Congressional vote intention.

$$a + c = P_{14}(P_{58} + Q_{58})$$
$$\frac{ad}{bc} = .6$$

$$.4a^2 + [Q_{58} + .6P_{58} - .4P_{14}(P_{58} + Q_{58})]a$$
$$= .6P_{58}P_{14}(P_{58} + Q_{58})$$

Independents are not under cross pressure if they are true Independents. But few Independents are truly independent; they have propensities one way or the other. One might doubt the applicability of the equation for Independents on the basis of the large nonvoting factor applied to party Democrats, but Independents are less interested in politics and vote less.

3. Catholic Democrats and Independents. These are again groups who would feel no cross pressure. We expected their basic vote propensity for 1960 to be indexed better by their Congressional vote than by their 1956 Eisenhower-Stevenson vote. However, if the religious issue were maximally salient (and that is what we were simulating), they would be even more solidly Democratic than they were when voting for Representatives. We had no issue cluster dealing with pro-Catholicism by Catholics, only one dealing with anti-Catholicism. So we guessed that one third of the vote among Catholic Democrats and Independents, which the Democrats normally lost, would come back to them in the Kennedy campaign. This is the relationship expressed by the first

TABLE 5   Numbers of Potential Voters in Different Cross-Pressure Situations

	Republicans	Democrats	Independents	Total
Protestant	22.9%	25.2%	13.9%	62.0%
Catholic	5.0%	12.3%	6.0%	23.3%
Other	3.0%	7.5%	4.2%	14.7%
Total	30.9%	45.0%	24.1%	100.0%

term of the next two equations. The second term is the turnout correction.

$$[3] \qquad V_k = \left(P_{58} + \frac{Q_{58}}{3} \right)(1 - P_{35})$$

$$V_n = \frac{2Q_{58}}{3}(1 - P_{35})$$

4. Catholic and Other Republicans. A Catholic Republican would be under cross pressure. So would a Jewish or Negro Republican, since he would sense bigotry as an attack on him.

At first glance, the next equation seems to have the cross-pressured Catholic Republicans acting like the Catholic Democrats. Again, we postulated that one third of those who voted for Republican Congressional candidates would swing over to the Democrats in the simulated environment. But the one-third shift for type 3 above is among a small group: Democrats who had favored a Republican for Congress. Here the one-third shift is among a large group: Republicans who voted Republican. Since most voters resolve their cross pressures by staying with their party, a one-third shift is a big shift.

According to previous studies, cross-pressured voters also vote less. They stay home. It is not clear that this is true, but we initially assumed it. We furthermore assumed that those for Nixon would stay home more than those for Kennedy, since Nixon supporters would perceive their vote as an act of alliance with the bigots against themselves. We raised the nonvoting factors by 2 and 3, respectively.

$$[4] \qquad V_k = \left(P_{58} + \frac{Q_{58}}{3} \right)(1 - 2P_{35})$$

$$V_n = \frac{2Q_{58}}{3}(1 - 3P_{35})$$

5. Negro and Jewish Democrats and Independents. The remaining groups are not large. Table 5 shows the percentage of voters in each situation. But formulating the appropriate equations for Negro and Jewish Democrats and Independents was highly problematic.[8]

We decided to treat them as under cross pressure. Negro and Jewish Democrats who resented anti-Catholicism would be pressed in the direction they would follow anyhow and could be disregarded. Those who were anti-Catholic would be under cross pressure. So we introduced into the equations the same sort of mechanism that we used for Protestant Democrats. For Negro and Jewish Independents the situation was even fuzzier. Although it was clear that some part of these voter types should be treated as under cross pressure between normally Democratic inclinations (despite their independence) and their religious biases, it was not clear what election to use in assessing their Democratic inclinations. We hedged by averaging 1956 and 1958 figures.

Finally, we estimated turnout for these groups to be poor, since Independents never turn out well and Negroes are extensively disenfranchised.

$$.4a^2 + \tfrac{1}{2}[Q_{56} + Q_{58} + .6P_{56} + .6P_{58} \\ - .4P_{14}(P_{56} + P_{58} + Q_{56} + Q_{58})]a$$

$$= \frac{.6}{4}(P_{56} + P_{58})P_{14}(P_{56} + P_{58} + Q_{56} + Q_{58})$$

[8] Strictly, what we are here calling "Negro and Jewish" should be labeled "Other." It is a residual category containing all persons not classified as Protestants or Catholics. But this means Negroes (for whom we disregarded religion) and Jews, because other-religion and no-religion voter types are negligible.

[5] $$V_k = \left(\frac{P_{58}+P_{56}}{2} - a\right)(1-2P_{35})$$

$$V_n = \left(\frac{Q_{58}+Q_{56}}{2} + a\right)(1-2P_{35})$$

The Outcome of the Simulation

Using common sense and social science theory, we thus estimated how different types of voters would respond to a campaign focused on the religious issue. The computer applied these equations to the information recorded in the data bank, and computed averages for each of 48 states.

The report we made to the Democratic National Committee was limited to the North, because a Democratic vote would not necessarily be a Kennedy vote in the South. The outcome was a ranking of 32 states ranging from the one in which Kennedy would do best to the one in which he would do worst. The ranking was:

1.	Rhode Island	17.	Pennsylvania
2.	Massachusetts	18.	Nevada
3.	New Mexico	19.	Washington
4.	Connecticut	20.	New Hampshire
5.	New York	21.	Wyoming
6.	Illinois	22.	Oregon
7.	New Jersey	23.	North Dakota
8.	California	24.	Nebraska
9.	Arizona	25.	Indiana
10.	Michigan	26.	South Dakota
11.	Wisconsin	27.	Vermont
12.	Colorado	28.	Iowa
13.	Ohio	29.	Kansas
14.	Montana	30.	Utah
15.	Minnesota	31.	Idaho
16.	Missouri	32.	Maine

The product-moment correlation over states between the simulated Kennedy index (not strictly speaking a percent of the vote) and the actual Kennedy vote in the election was .82. And this satisfying result was based on political data gathered before November 1958. Surveys on the 1960 election were not incorporated into this analysis.

The most relevant comparison is with the Kennedy–Nixon polls taken in late 1958. The correlation between the state-by-state result of these polls and the actual outcome is but .53,

as compared to .82 for the simulation. The simulation, in short, portrayed trends that actually took place between the time the data were collected and election day two years later. By election day the polls were doing very well indeed; their final predictions were very close to the national result. But one had to simulate processes of change in order to get good predictions out of the earlier polls.

This does not mean that what we did in 1960 we could equally well have done in 1958. Although our data were all available in 1958, one essential fact was missing at that time: what scenario to simulate. Many scenarios were possible for 1960, and most were simulable. It was only when the events were close at hand, however, that a realistic scenario could be chosen.

TESTING THE ASSUMPTIONS

A complex model can predict real-world outcomes correctly and yet can be wrong in many details. It may predict accurately because the main effects are correctly represented, and yet it may contain many irrelevancies. One always must question the details of a complex model, even if it passes the test of good prediction.

Sensitivity testing is one of the more important uses of computer simulation. One often designs a computer model not for the purpose of predicting but for the purpose of gaining an understanding of the process represented. By varying each of the parameters of the model one can see which ones make a difference and which ones do not. Some variables may account for much of the variance, some may account for little. To explore the sensitivity of the prediction to each parameter is one way of understanding what is taking place. We shall now examine two variables in our equations, religion and voter turnout, and see what would have happened if each had been a little bit different.

Religion

Intuitively, the most interesting variable in our simulation was anti-Catholicism. The simulation was designed to explore its effects. But the good prediction does not prove that anti-Catholicism was an important factor in the election outcome. Our simulation took a normal vote base—basically the Congressional vote—and modified it by religious factors. If perchance the Congressional vote base correlated with the 1960 outcome and religious bias had a uniform effect in every state, we would get a good prediction despite the triviality of the religious issue.

Was that the case? To find out we must see how well the simulation would have predicted without the religious factor. Was the correlation between the simulation and the real outcome as high for a simulation that did not include the religious factor as for one that did include it? The answer is "no." The simulation is highly sensitive to religion.

We document this conclusion first by seeing what happens if we disregard anti-Catholicism. Elimination of anti-Catholicism from our equations would have lowered the correlation with the November results from .82 to .62 which is only about 60 percent as good.[9]

The religious issue cut both ways. Not only did some Protestants reject Kennedy but also some Catholic Republicans swung to him. We have seen the net result was highly sensitive to the Protestant bias factor. Now let us see how sensitive it was to Catholic shifts.

The original simulation assumed that one-third of all Catholics who would otherwise have voted Republican would swing to Kennedy.

[9] The variance accounted for is the square of the correlation coefficient, that is, about .66 and .38, respectively.

That was an arbitrary figure arrived at by guess, and it is legitimate to enquire whether our guess was a reasonable one. Instead of testing what would have happened if we had dropped the Catholic shift altogether, we set it at each value from 0.1 to 1.0. In short, we ask not only what would have happened if .333 of Catholic Republican voters shifted, but also what would have happened if one-tenth did, two-tenths did, more, or all did. Figure 1 shows the result with the four-period data matrix used in the original simulation. The correlation is quite stable for all values of the "C-shift," but the dispersion (the square root of the mean-square error) varies markedly, achieving .038 when it is assumed that 70 percent of Catholic Republicans shifted to Kennedy. This figure seems much too high intuitively, and below we discuss a modification producing a more reasonable "C-shift."

Figure 2 carries the sensitivity analysis one step further. It illustrates what happens when we simultaneously vary the "C-shift" and anti-Catholicism. How good a correlation do we get, for example, if we drop them both and simply use the party base as a prediction? The correlation is about .5 or less than 40 perntceas good as the original simulation.

We can assume no anti-Catholicism and still get a good correlation if we also assume that 80 to 100 percent of all Republican Catholics voted for Kennedy. But that pair of assumptions produces an average deviation between 8 and

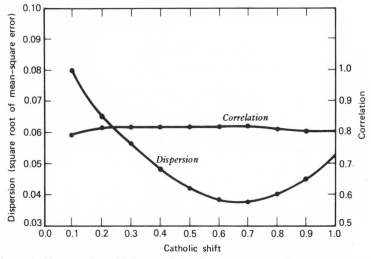

Figure 1 How good would the simulation have been with different values of the Catholic shift (using the 4-period master)?

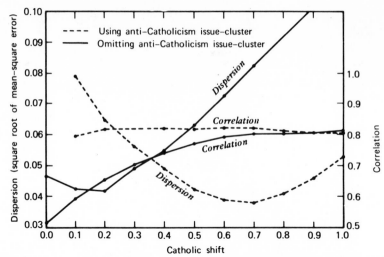

Figure 2 The effect of anti-Catholicism and the Catholic shift simultaneously compared (using the 4-period master).

12 percentage points. It separates states with large Catholic populations from those with small ones well enough to produce a close correlation of predicted to actual, but it does it in a way that denies to Nixon many of the votes he got.

Clearly no simulation that omits anti-Catholicism is better than the original simulation. Nor is there any giving a good prediction which fails to recognize that a large Catholic shift took place.

The Catholic shift worked in the same way on the five-period data bank. Figure 3 compares the four- and five-period simulations. Although the correlations are essentially the same, the five-period simulation has much lower dispersions for Catholic shifts below .6. The five-period data bank contains more poll replies on the 1958 election, which the Democrats won, and is less influenced by the Eisenhower bandwagon of 1952 and 1956. Consequently, it achieves a good prediction with a Catholic shift of only .5—a much more plausible value than the .7 we found with the four-period data bank.

Millions of non-Catholics who would otherwise have voted Democratic could not bring themselves to vote for a Catholic. Our model says roughly that one out of five Protestant Democrats or Protestant Independents who

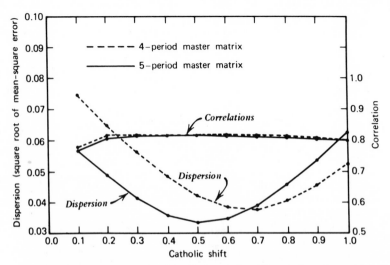

Figure 3 Comparison of results with 4-period and 5-period master matrix.

would otherwise have voted Democratic bolted because of the religious issue. The actual number of bolters varied with the voter type and was determined by the proportion who replied on surveys that they would not want to vote for a Catholic.

What our model tends to show is that the poll question was a good one. The model suggests that the number of people who overcame the social inhibitions to admitting prejudice to a polltaker was about the same as the number who overcame the political inhibitions to bolting their party for reasons of bias.

The proportion among Protestant voters who expressed reluctance to vote for a Catholic varied as indicated in Table 6. On the basis of their Congressional voting, 49.9 percent of all Protestants nationally and 59.2 percent in the 32 Northern states would have voted Republican anyhow. But among the rest, a net loss of around one-fifth was suffered by Kennedy because of religion. The apparent gross number of Democratic defectors who thought religion was a reason for their action was still larger, but some of these voters would have defected anyhow on other grounds. They had done so already in elections in which the religious issue did not arise. Other defectors among Democrats would be offset by the return to the party of Protestant Democrats who had been voting Republican.

TABLE 6 Percentage of Protestants Who Objected to Voting for a Catholic for President

Rural	34.8%
Town	34.8%
Urban	31.8%
A + B SES	36.1%
C SES	30.9%
Democrats	25.6%
Republicans	46.7%
Independents	30.0%
Total	34.4%

Offsetting the loss of Protestant votes for Kennedy was a strong swing to him by Catholics. There had been a massive defection to Eisenhower and against Stevenson by Catholics in 1956. Fully 35 percent of Catholic Demo-

crats voted Republican in that year. Kennedy recovered these Catholic defectors and more. Taking Congressional voting as a base for estimating normal party vote, about 40 percent of the Republican Catholics switched to Kennedy. There are 2.5 times as many Protestants as Catholics, but the Catholic shift was more pronounced. If our model is right, the Protestants who shifted because of the religious issue outnumber the Catholics who did so by 1,500,000. Kennedy gained 2,800,000, and lost 4,300,000 votes. Seven million voters out of 68,000,000 defected because of religion.[10]

There has been much debate as to which candidate gained by the religious issue. The simulation gives an interesting answer. The shift cost Kennedy 1.5 million votes, or 2.3 percent of the total, but gained him 22 electoral votes. Bunching of the Catholic shift in large, closely fought, industrial states, and the location of much of the Protestant shift in Southern states gave Kennedy an electoral vote advantage despite a popular vote disadvantage. By our calculations, Kennedy lost by the religious issue the following states that he otherwise would have won:

	Electoral Votes
Kentucky	10
Tennessee	11
Florida	10
Virginia	12
Oklahoma	8
Montana	4
Idaho	4
Utah	4
California	32
Oregon	6
Washington	9
	110

[10] Using polls, the Survey Research Center estimated that 10.8 percent of the voters, 7,350,000, switched on the religious issue, Kennedy's net loss being 2.2 percent, that is, 1,500,000 (Converse, Campbell, W. Miller, and Stokes [8]). This is a remarkable concurrence of results by different methods, with different data, from different periods, S.R.C's from the campaign period itself, ours from years before.

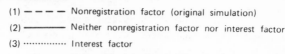

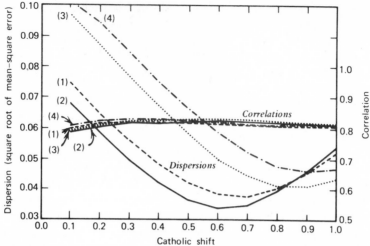

Figure 4 Effect of turnout corrections using data from 4-period master matrix.

He won the following states that he would otherwise have lost:

Connecticut	8
New York	45
New Jersey	16
Pennsylvania	32
Illinois	27
New Mexico	4
	———
	132

Voter Turnout

The simulation suggests that the turnout pattern for the 1960 election was substantially different from that in 1952 and 1956. It seems that the Democratic turnout was much higher than usual, probably as high as for Republicans.

The equations in the original simulation all involved a term that was either $(1 - P_{35})$, $(1 - 2P_{35})$, or $(1 - 3P_{35})$. P_{35} is the percentage who said they normally did not vote, and the weighting factor, 1, 2, or 3, was determined by the amount of cross pressure the voter type was assumed to be under. We could estimate turnout by the issue cluster concerning nonregistration, or we could estimate turnout by the issue cluster dealing with interest in the election. We could estimate turnout by both nonregistration and interest, or we could use

neither factor and assume turnout equal for all groups.

Figure 4 graphs the four alternative uses of turnout information. It indicates that the best alternative was to use no turnout information at all. Although the correlation coefficients are the same in all cases, any use of turnout information increased the average error substantially by lowering the Democratic vote.[11] Omitting any turnout factor resulted in a slightly higher Catholic vote because working class groups, who are heavily Catholic, vote less regularly than the average. That in turn results in the best prediction being found at a slightly lower C-shift, .6, than in the simulations with a turnout factor included.

Finally, Figure 5 shows that using the five-period data bank and omitting any turnout correction gives still better and more reasonable results. With the usual correlation of over .8, we get a dispersion of only about 3 percent with a Catholic shift of .5 or even .4.

The failure of a turnout correction to improve the results is a nontrivial finding. It directly contradicts a major theory that we and others

---

[11] Besides the multiple weights on nonvoting used in the original simulation the simulations were also tried weighting every group's vote by $(1 - P_{35})$. The results were very much the same as for multiple weighting.

have used and accepted: the proposition that persons under cross pressure vote less than others.

In the classic study by Berelson, Lazarsfeld, and McPhee of 1948 voting in Elmira, New York [2] persons faced with cross pressures were found to become less interested in politics. The finding fits general psychological propositions about human behavior. But it does not fit the 1960 national election data.[12]

We are forced to conclude that nonvoting is not necessarily a function of cross pressure. Sometimes it is and sometimes it is not. Apparently there are unidentified intervening variables for which we must now search, and we can only speculate about what those variables are. In 1948 when the Elmira study was done, there was a remarkable amount of abstentionism. Dewey, as a personality, alienated many Republicans, but Truman did not attract them either. Many Democrats were repelled by an image of "Communism and corruption" that the Republicans has been trying to plaster on

[12] It must be mentioned to the credit of William McPhee, one of the authors of *Voting* and one of our colleagues in the initiation of the Simulmatics project, that in 1959 when we were setting up our model he expressed the view that his book had been wrong on this point. He warned against relying on this mechanism in the model. Pool declined to be guided by McPhee's doubts and incorporated the nonvoting mechanism into the equations in accordance with cross-pressure theory.

the Truman administration, but Dewey did not attract them. Democrats driven from their party or Republicans from theirs had no place to go and no positive cause to serve by switching. Perhaps cross pressure meant staying home in 1948, because cross pressure was alienation.

In 1960, bigoted Protestant Democrats and Catholic Republicans were under cross pressure, and the pressures suggested purposeful action. The bigot who felt that the country would be endangered by a Catholic was much more motivated than the man who just lacked respect for both Dewey and Truman. The bigot had to vote to achieve his clear purpose. The Republican Catholic was not being pushed away from Nixon by dislike of him. He was attracted by Nixon, and he was attracted by the image of Kennedy as a man of his own kind and by the need to protect his people against the attacks of the bigots. He was being pulled to a vote, not pushed from one.

In the jargon of psychological theories of conflict [9, 11], one would say that 1948 represented an "avoidance-avoidance" conflict for cross-pressured voters, whereas 1960 represented an "approach-approach" conflict. Conflict theory predicts that the subject in an "avoidance-avoidance" conflict will avoid the choice if possible, whereas in an "approach-approach" conflict he will be motivated to consider both alternatives until a choice is

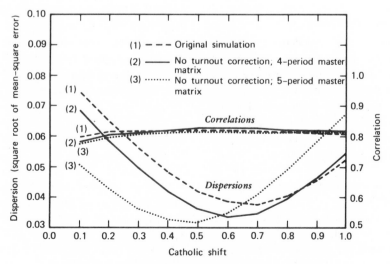

Figure 5 Effect of data-base and turnout corrections.

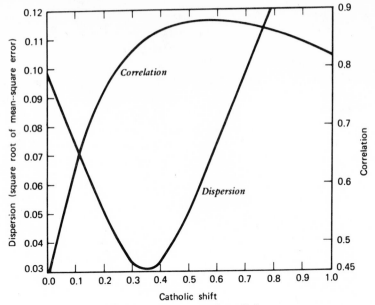

Figure 6 "Lucky guess" prediction.

finally made. It seems clear that the 1960 Catholic Republican was faced with an approach-approach conflict, but the situation for the anti-Catholic Protestant Democrat is not really quite so clear. A strong bigot would have found a Republican vote attractive; milder anti-Catholicism would emphasize avoidance of a Kennedy vote rather than approach toward a Nixon vote. One alternative, which we did not test, would have been an asymmetric turnout correction that kept anti-Catholic Protestant Democrats away from the polls but propelled Catholic Republicans toward them.

"Lucky Guess" Prediction

A "lucky guess" prediction derived from the 1956 Stevenson vote and the number of Catholics in each state would have achieved better results than the simulation if the appropriate guess could have been arrived at by intuition. One simply takes the 1956 Stevenson percentage for each state and adds to it a fraction of the Catholic percentage of each state. As shown in Figure 6, a lucky guess of .35 would have given a dispersion of .03 and a correlation of .85.

Since the Democrats normally get about 60 percent of the Catholic vote, a 35 percent shift would give 95 percent of the Catholic vote to the Democrats. Thus, the lucky guess is not so much a model of what happened as it is a post-factum discovery of numerical coincidences. However, the numbers do suggest something. In the South, the continuity from 1956 implies that Eisenhower, Stevenson, and anti-Catholicism were all epiphenomena: each managed to symbolize more real loyalties and discontents that were keeping some Southerners in the Democratic Party and driving some others out. So too, in the country as a whole, votes in 1960 and votes in 1956 followed much the same pattern aside from religious realignments. The Democrats whom the Ike charisma attracted and the ones whom the religious issue drove away were—barring the religious variable—people having the same social characteristics. The lucky guess model sets us to asking to what extent the Ike charisma and anti-Catholicism were also epiphenomena rather than causes.

THE BEST-FIT SIMULATION

We may use simulation in still another way—postdiction to analyze what actually did happen in 1960. We improve the model until it corresponds as closely as it can to reality. Then what goes on inside the model may be suspected to represent what was going on in reality.

There is, of course, no trick to figuring out in retrospect a set of parameter values that gives a good prediction. The point of doing so is not to crow about how good the match is, for we pick the parameters to achieve that match. The point is that a model that matches the real world may indicate what was happening in the real world.

This raises a crucial question for any simulation study: How can the model ever be validated? A complex model can never be validated by any single observation. The more independent variables there are in a model the more dependent variables the model must predict before it can inspire confidence. And the more items it predicts correctly, the greater the likelihood that the model is in a one-to-one relation to reality.

For example, it is no test of an election model that it happens to pick the winner of a Presidential contest. A number of methods, ranging from following the gambling odds to sheer luck, have at least a 50–50 chance of doing that. It is a much more rigorous test to require that the model produce a prediction for a distribution over 48 states. If it passes that test, the chance that the model is only coincidentally related to reality is relatively small. Additional tests would be whether the model correctly predicts men versus women, Negroes versus whites, rich versus poor, and so on. With every successive test a model passes, we gain confidence that its dynamics are those of the real world.

That is why we are interested in postdicting with the best model using mechanisms that it is plausible to believe are the real ones. And so we took the 1960 model, shifted the parameters to pick the best-fit values, examined where the predictions were still poor, introduced other variables, and wound up with a model about as good as the variables and data would permit.

This best-fit simulation used the same equations as our 1960 one with the following exceptions:

1. We dropped the turnout correction that had added nothing to the accuracy of our prediction.

2. We used the five-period master deck of data.

3. We assumed a shift to Kennedy of .4 of Catholics who otherwise would have voted Republican. A .3 shift is almost as good, and

better by some criteria, so this departure from the .33 used in 1960 is not really significant.

4. We introduced a new shift in the Southern states only: 10 percent of Negroes who would otherwise have voted for Nixon voted for Kennedy, and 10 percent of whites who would otherwise have voted for Kennedy voted for Nixon.

The last correction recognized that our previous simulation overstated Kennedy strength in the South. There was more working against Kennedy in the South than anti-Catholicism. States rights, civil rights, conservatism, and race were adding to white Democratic defections, and white defections were partially offset by the growing Southern Negro vote.

Table 7 presents the postdicted and actual vote in each of the 48 continental states.

How close is that postdiction? For the country as a whole it gives Kennedy 322 electoral votes, 8 more than he actually won on the continent. The mean deviation of the postdicted percentage vote from the actual is but 0.9 percent in the 32 Northern states, and but 0.6 percent for the country as a whole.

But to pick parameters retrospectively to fit the country as a whole is easy. The first true test of the model is whether it places the individual states in their proper relationship. One test of that is the correlation across states between the postdiction and the actual results. This is the test we dared accept in 1960. The best-fit simulation does no better on the Northern states than our 1960 simulation, but it brings the Southern states into line to some degree.

	Product Moment Coefficient of Correlation Across States Between Simulation and November Outcome
32 Northern States	.81
48 States	.70

The correlation tells us that about two-thirds of the variation between states in the North and about one-half of the variation across the country are explained by this best-fit simulation.

TABLE 7 Best-Fit Simulation

State	Predicted	Actual
Louisiana	.66	.64
Texas	.61	.51
Rhode Island	.59	.64
Oklahoma	.57	.41
Delaware	.57	.51
Florida	.57	.48
Arkansas	.56	.54
Virginia	.56	.47
Alabama	.56	.58
Massachusetts	.56	.60
North Carolina	.56	.52
Mississippi	.56	.60
South Carolina	.55	.51
Georgia	.55	.63
Maryland	.55	.54
New Mexico	.54	.50
New York	.54	.53
Connecticut	.54	.54
Kentucky	.52	.46
California	.52	.50
New Jersey	.52	.50
Illinois	.51	.50
West Virginia	.51	.53
Arizona	.51	.45
Tennessee	.50	.46
Wisconsin	.49	.48
Michigan	.49	.51
Colorado	.48	.46
Montana	.47	.49
Ohio	.47	.47
Minnesota	.47	.51
Pennsylvania	.46	.51
Washington	.46	.49
Nevada	.46	.51
Missouri	.45	.51
Wyoming	.45	.45
New Hampshire	.45	.47
Oregon	.45	.47
North Dakota	.44	.45
Nebraska	.43	.38
Indiana	.43	.45
South Dakota	.43	.42
Vermont	.42	.41
Utah	.42	.45
Iowa	.42	.43
Kansas	.42	.39
Idaho	.41	.46
Maine	.39	.43

A still more rigorous test can be applied, namely the deviation of the simulation from the election results. (If we were exactly 5 percent high in every state, the correlation would be 1.0, or perfect, while the average deviation would be 5 percentage points.) This is a criterion we declined to try to satisfy in 1960, but which in retrospect we see was achievable. Both the median absolute deviation and the root mean square deviation were reasonably small and smaller in the North.

	Median Percentage Points of Difference Between Kennedy Vote in Simulation and in Election (Percent)	Root Mean Square of Differences Between Percentage for Kennedy in Simulation and Election (Percent)
32 Northern States	2.1	3.2
48 States	2.5	4.7

The model reproduces enough of what was different about states to account fairly well for results state by state.

Thanks to the Gallup Poll, a few more tests can be applied. Did the simulation postdict the votes of men versus women correctly, of Negroes versus whites, of Catholics versus Protestants, of upper- versus lower-income people? Such comparisons cannot be made between the simulated and actual returns because the actual vote is not recorded by voter type. Comparison can be made between the simulation (based on poll figures up to and including 1959) and Gallup Poll figures from the fall of 1960. Since both these measures are random variables, differences may occur because the simulation is off, or because poll results contained some margin of error, or both.

The late Gallup Poll results are a good measure of group votes. The late October-early November surveys predicted the election with an overall, across-the-board error of but one-half percent. This is not really prediction because the poll does not attempt to anticipate how people will change. Rather, the late surveys report voter decisions after the voters have made up their minds. Error arises because the report is based on a sample, rather than on the total population. The Gallup Poll was probably accurate both at the beginning of August, when it reported Nixon 6 points in the lead, an in October-November, when the overall poll figure could be checked against the real vote. But neither figure was a prediction.

Table 8 makes the comparisons.

TABLE 8 Kennedy Percentage of the Two-Party Vote

	As Postdicted by Best-Fit Simulation (Percent)	As Reported by Gallup Poll[a] (Percent)
Men	52	52
Women	49	49
Nonwhite	66	68
Whites	51	49
Catholics	80	78[b]
Protestants	39	38[b]
Jews	71	81
Metropolitan	58	60
Town	48	45
Rural	47	46
C; Manual Workers	61	60
A + B	44	43
Republican	14	5
Democrat	80	84
Independent	48	43

[a] *The Boston Globe*, January 27, 1964. The fact that the largest deviations are in party affiliation is interesting and revealing. People do not change their sex, or domicile, or occupation when they decide how to vote. They may, however, change their conception of their party affiliation to make it consonant with their vote intention. Apparently some persons did so, which may account for the very small numbers of Republicans for Kennedy and Democrats for Nixon in the Gallup Poll results.

[b] An independent poll reported by the Survey Research Center in an unpublished paper found the Kennedy vote to have been 81 percent among Catholics, 37 percent among Protestants, confirming the Gallup Poll and our simulation.

CONCLUSION

The test of any new method of research is successful use. The outcome of the present study gives reason to hope that computer simulation may indeed open up the possibility of using survey data in ways far more complex than has been customary in the past. The political "pros" who commissioned this abstruse study were daring men to gamble on the use of a new and untried technique in the heat of a campaign. The researchers who undertook this job faced a rigorous test, for they undertook to do both basic and applied research at once. The study relied on social science theories and data to represent the complexity of actual human behavior to a degree that would permit the explicit presentation of the consequences of policy alternatives.

This kind of research could not have been conducted ten years ago. Three new elements have entered the picture to make it possible: first, a body of sociological and psychological theories about voting and other decisions; second, a vast mine of empirical survey data now for the first time available in an archive; third, the existence of high-speed computers with large memories. The social science theories allow us to specify with some confidence what processes will come to work in a decision situation. The backlog of survey data permits us to estimate the parameters of these processes with fair precision and great detail for each small element of our national population. The computer makes possible the handling of this mine of data. More important still, it makes possible the precise carrying out of long and complex chains of reasoning about the interactions among the different processes. In summary, we believe that conditions now exist for use of survey data in research far more ambitious than social scientists are' used to. If it is possible to reproduce, through computer simulation, much of the complexity of a whole society going through processes of change, and to do so rapidly, then the opportunities to put social science to work are vastly increased. It is our belief that this, which was put to a test by the campaign research reported here, is now possible.

REFERENCES

1. R. P. Abelson, and M. J. Rosenberg, 1958. Symbolic psycho-logic: a model of attitudinal cognition. *Behavioral Science*, 3(1): 1–13.
2. B. R. Berelson, P. F. Lazarsfeld, and W. N. McPhee, 1954. *Voting*. Chicago: University of Chicago Press.
3. R. Brown, 1962. Models of attitude change. *New directions in psychology, Volume I* (R. Brown et al.); New York: Holt, Rinehart, and Winston, 1–85.
4. A. Campbell, P. E. Converse, W. E. Miller, and D. E. Stokes, 1960. *The American voter*. New York: Wiley.
5. J. S. Coleman, 1961. Analysis of social structures and simulation of social processes with electronic computers. *Educational and Psychological Measurement*, 21(1): 203–218. MD.
6. J. S. Coleman, 1964. *Introduction to mathematical sociology*. New York: Free Press.
7. J. S. Coleman, and F. Waldorf, 1962. *Study of a voting system with computer techniques.* Working paper, Johns Hopkins University. 4D.
8. P. E. Converse, A. Campbell, W. E. Miller, and D. E. Stokes, 1961. Stability and change in 1960: a reinstating election. *American Political Science Review*, 55(2): 269–280.
9. K. Lewin, 1935. The psychological situations of reward and punishment. *A dynamic theory of personality;* New York: McGraw-Hill, 114–170.
10. W. N. McPhee, 1963. *Formal theories of mass behavior*. New York: Free Press.
11. N. E. Miller, 1944. Experimental studies of conflict. *Personality and the behavior disorders* (J. McV. Hunt, ed.); New York: Ronald, Volume I, 431–465.
12. T. M. Newcomb, 1961. *The acquaintance process*. New York: Holt, Rinehart, and Winston.

19

SIMULATION OF A HOSPITAL SUBSYSTEM: THE MATERNITY SERVICE

ROBERT B. FETTER
JOHN D. THOMPSON

The work reported here applies computer simulation to the design and utilization of a hospital facility.[1] Major effort has been devoted to constructing simulation models that describe various hospital subsystems. The models comprise a laboratory in which questions of interest to hospital administrators may be attacked experimentally, and our long-run goal is a comprehensive laboratory that will test a large variety of hypotheses about hospital design, organization, and operation.

In a larger sense, we are attempting to add to general knowledge concerning the applicability of simulation models in management problems. Although such models have been widely used, systematic knowledge enabling one to use them efficiently is not in sight. A great deal of attention has been paid to model construction, some to model validation, but very little to the tactical problems of generating information valuable to decision makers [3]. The problems of predicting the technical and economic consequences of a change in operating policies via a simulation model are formidable. Yet our work gives us

SOURCE: An edited composite of R. B. Fetter and J. D. Thompson, 1965: The simulation of hospital systems; and J. D. Thompson and R. B. Fetter, 1963: The economics of the maternity service.
[1] We acknowledge the contributions of Richard B. Egen in programming and experimentation.

considerable hope that we have at least the rudiments of a useful laboratory.

Three models of hospital subsystems have been completely developed and are currently in use experimentally. The models describe the maternity suite, an outpatient clinic, and a surgical pavilion. This paper summarizes our work on the maternity suite.

THE ECONOMICS OF THE MATERNITY SERVICE

The relationship between the size of a hospital, as measured by its average daily census, and the percentage occupancy of its beds has fascinated students in hospital planning and administration for many years. Extension of this relationship to include the cost of operating reveals its importance. If, indeed, the size of small hospitals results in low percentage occupancy and in high operating costs, the relationship is not only fascinating but a basic determinant of hospital economics.

One of the first major discussions of this relationship appeared in *Hospital Care in the United States* where C. H. Hamilton described the lower occupancy in smaller hospitals and advanced a theory to explain it [2]. When Dr. Hamilton stated, "Both statistical theory and study of individual hospital data indicate that the extreme limit of occupied beds will not be greater or less than the average daily census plus or minus approximately four times the square root of the average daily census," he implicitly assumed the daily census followed a Poisson distribution. For a Poisson distribution the mean equals the variance, and the above formula puts the limits of occupancy at four standard deviations from the mean.

If we accept the Poisson distribution of daily census, we accept suppositions but weakly demonstrated by the Commission and considered rather shaky in the light of present practice. The Poisson distribution assumes that every admission is a random occurrence, independent of every other admission. This ignores scheduled admissions and waiting lists for non-emergency elective admissions. Further all patients' lengths of stay are assumed to follow a single, negative exponential distribution. This also does not withstand examination.

If a Poisson distribution is used to predict bed needs, the result is ultraconservative. The extreme limit of four standard deviations from the average would imply a service failure probability much less than 0.001. The formula $c + 4\sqrt{c}$ implies that 80 percent occupancy is not reached until 300 to 400 beds are used. Such mathematical projection does illustrate that smaller institutions tend to have lower occupancy than larger institutions, but it is in no way predictive in situations for which only population characteristics are known.

Hospitals are probably mixed systems, responding in part to random demands and in part to schedulable demands. Such a theory would explain the differences in occupancy between various clinical services in a hospital. Obstetrics probably is more "random" than medicine, which is more "random" than surgery. Expected occupancy levels would vary inversely with this degree of randomness.[2]

---

[2] The basis for this conceptual model of the hospital was advanced less exactly in a paper covering the first aspects of this investigation: Thompson. Avant, and Spiker [4]. Blumberg [1] clarified the approach in isolating the probable different inputs to each "distinctive patient facility." While this latter paper was primarily concerned with predicting bed needs, the possible economic implications of various inputs were also mentioned.

The character of the prediction problem may be observed if one attempts analysis using past experience. Table 1 divides the 33 hospitals offering obstetrical services in Connecticut into three groups according to the number of obstetrical discharges. Group I has over 2000 discharges a year; Group II discharges from 1000 to 2000 obstetrical patients a year; and Group III has under 1000 discharges a year.

The fifth column of Table 1 shows that average occupancy in the three groups varies from 70.6 percent in Group I and 59.9 percent in Group II to 43.6 percent in Group III. Table 2 shows the number of hospitals in each group above and below the median percent occupancy (62.3%).

Fisher's Exact Test reveals that average occupancy is significantly lower in Group III than in Group II or Group I, and significantly lower in Group II than in Group I. The size of a maternity service would seem, at first comparison, to affect the percentage of occupancy.

There are two factors other than size that may contribute to these differences in occupancy: the average length of stay and the supply of beds relative to the demand. The first of these is included in the fourth column of Table 1, and though the average length of stay varies from 2.8 days to 6.3 days, there is no significant difference in the average lengths of stay among the hospital groups. When occupancy is corrected for length of stay, there are still significant occupancy differences between Group I and Group II and between Group I and Group III; only the significant difference between Group II and Group III disappears.

With the data available, it is almost impossible to measure the supply of beds relative to the demand, much less to predict the facilities required for any level of service. Information of this kind could only be obtained by counting the days when all the beds were occupied, and even these figures would not allow effective prediction of facility economics. Other measurements of utilization, such as discharges, are affected by the percent occupancy—the factor to be isolated—and the average length of stay—the factor already considered. However, we can determine whether the size of each maternity service equals its average census plus three times the square root of its average census. A

TABLE 1   Maternity Service Statistics from 33 Hospitals

Hospital	Discharges	Patient Days	Average Days Stay	Percent Occupancy	Average Beds in Com-plement	Beds Required Using $3\sqrt{A.C.}$	Direct Cost of Routine Services (Dollars)	Net Gain or Loss (Dollars)
Group I Hospitals—over 2000 Discharges per Year								
I-1	6275	30,758	4.902	73.3	115	112	5.20	(1.80)
I-2	5503	25,356	4.608	73.9	94	94	6.10	4.20
I-3	3592	14,165	3.760	66.9	58	57	4.33	12.79
I-4	3503	16,676	3.943	68.2	67	66	7.44	(2.35)
I-5	3292	13,039	3.961	74.4	48	54	8.60	3.82
I-6	2685	12,058	4.491	62.3	53	50	6.36	(.05)
I-7	2671	12,011	4.497	71.5	46	50	7.13	(1.84)
I-8	2406	10,727	4.458	77.3	38	50	5.91	2.04
I-9	2289	9,047	3.952	63.6	39	40	7.22	(2.31)
I-10	2158	10,608	4.916	72.7	40	45	5.46	1.07
Weighted Averages			4.493	70.6			6.22	1.51
Group II Hospitals—from 1000 to 2000 Discharges per Year								
II-1	1949	8,969	4.602	53.4	46	39	4.71	(1.50)
II-2	1778	6,771	3.808	64.0	29	31	8.51	1.95
II-3	1775	7,022	3.956	66.3	29	32	7.67	3.10
II-4	1725	7,751	4.493	75.8	29	35	8.08	4.14
II-5	.1685	6,759	4.011	50.0	37	31	4.32	(.99)
II-6	1609	6,229	3.871	71.1	24	29	6.32	1.47
II-7	1472	6,416	4.359	53.3	33	30	8.39	(4.26)
II-8	1393	8,282	5.945	54.0	42	37	6.99	(5.31)
II-9	1360	6,914	5.084	65.3	29	32	7.05	(3.44)
II-10	1300	8,155	6.273	79.8	28	37	8.42	(2.36)
II-11	1210	5,058	4.180	57.7	24	25	4.51	3.88
II-12	1161	4,764	4.103	42.1	31	24	9.12	(6.82)
Weighted Averages			4.512	59.9			6.97	(.86)
Group III Hospitals—Under 1000 Discharges per Year								
III-1	987	4,057	4.107	42.7	26	21	12.68	(13.45)
III-2	906	3,989	4.403	42.9	25	21	6.40	(4.01)
III-3	903	3,426	3.794	40.8	23	19	10.62	(6.82)
III-4	806	3,468	4.303	52.8	18	19	11.40	(4.12)
III-5	764	2.113	2.766	57.9	10	13	12.71	(7.00)
III-6	639	2,814	4.404	77.1	10	16	9.14	.36
III-7	570	2,528	4.345	49.5	14	15	9.09	(7.76)
III-8	458	1,790	3.908	40.1	12	12	6.13	(4.74)
III-9	396	1,689	4.265	46.3	10	11	18.51	(18.08)
III-10	338	1,491	4.411	40.8	10	10	5.66	(5.57)
III-11	329	1,344	4.085	26.3	14	9	13.67	(21.66)
Weighted Averages			3.856	43.6			10.55	(7.97)

TABLE 2 Distribution of Individual Hospitals by Group—Above and Below Median Occupancy Rate (62.3% in Hospital I-6)

	Group I	Group II	Group III	Total
Occupancy above 62.3%	9	6	1	16
Occupancy below 62.3%	0	6	10	16
	9	12	11	32

breakdown of the three groups by this criterion is contained in Table 3, and the groups do not differ significantly in meeting the criterion. In fact, the criterion fits the capacities fairly well: 25 of the hospitals have capacities within 5 beds of the criterion figure, and the net bed difference between the projected and actual for the entire state is but − 13 against a total of 1150 maternity beds.

Thus there are indications from actual data that the size of the maternity service influences the percent occupancy, although average length of stay and the supply of beds relative to demand were not held exactly constant in fixing this relationship.

COMPUTER SIMULATION OF THE MATERNITY SERVICE

One way of holding these two factors constant is to simulate the maternity service under varying numbers of admissions. The development and validation of this simulation model was reported previously [5].

What is required is a prediction of the occupancy distribution for any set of population characteristics and any number of beds. As a demonstration, a distribution based on Hospital I-2 for 1961 was postulated, and the rate was increased and decreased while preserving the relative properties of the original distribution. The service time distributions for the various facilities were taken from actual records. The number of beds and the number of labor, delivery, and postpartum facilities were made large enough so that jamming would not occur, so the output shows the service given by any structure of facilities. For example, by determining the number of beds for which the service level is 95 percent,[3] the relationship between size of population served and facilities required can be demonstrated. Cost and efficiency can then be plotted as a function of admissions rate.

[3] This means that 95 percent of the patients can be accommodated by this number of beds. The remaining 5 percent could be cared for through flexible facilities or through advancing the time of discharge for patients ready to leave the hospital.

TABLE 3 Number of Hospitals in Each Group with a Capacity Greater than or Less than the Average Census plus Three Times the Square Root of the Average Census

	Group I	Group II	Group III	Total
Capacity greater than the criterion	4	5	4	13
Capacity equals the criterion	1	0	2	3
Capacity less than the criterion	5	7	5	17
	10	12	11	33

TABLE 4 Facilities Required for Maternity Service

Admissions per Year	90% Service		95% Service		99% Service					
	Beds	Beds per 100 Patients per Year	Beds	Beds per 100 Patients per Year	Beds	Beds per 100 Patients per Year	Rooms			
							Labor Rooms	Postpartum Rooms	Caesarean Rooms	Delivery Rooms
580	13	2.24	14	2.42	17	2.93	2	1	1	1
1693	33	1.94	35	2.07	40	2.36	4	1	1	2
2771	51	1.84	54	1.95	60	2.17	5	2	1	2
3874	70	1.81	73	1.88	80	2.06	7	2	1	3
5000	89	1.78	93	1.86	102	2.04	8	2	1	3
5506	98	1.78	102	1.85	110	2.00	8	3	1	3
6106	110	1.80	114	1.86	122	2.00	9	3	1	4
7229	124	1.72	128	1.76	135	1.87	10	3	1	4
8161	145	1.78	150	1.84	160	1.96	12	3	2	4
9424	165	1.75	170	1.82	180	1.91	13	4	2	5

The results of the simulation runs are contained in Table 4, and the relationship between size and occupancy, as expressed by the beds required to serve 100 patients in a year, is graphed in Figure 1. The difference between the simulation and actual experience gives some interesting technical and economic information concerning maternity operations. We can see from Figure 1 that bed investment costs per 100 patients level off at 4000 admissions per year, but become increasingly higher below this level. The number of labor, delivery, and post partum facilities, shown in Table 4, give even greater investment requirements for the lower admission rates. Conversely, we discern the point at which size ceases to pay off in terms of lowered investment cost per patient.

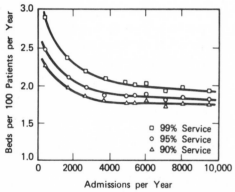

Figure 1　Relationship between beds required and size of maternity service for three service levels.

SIZE OF SERVICE AND OPERATING COSTS

Operating costs are difficult to isolate, but it can be inferred from available data that direct costs are more than proportionally higher for mater-

nity suites serving small populations. The measurement used in evaluating the cost of various services is the direct cost of routine services. This cost, as reported in Connecticut, is the cleanest figure obtainable—uninfluenced by interest charges, overhead allocations, or varying patterns of utilization. Furthermore, it correlates $+.957$ with hours of bedside care, implying that direct costs of routine services reflect the labor costs of the maternity unit.

The average direct cost of routine services for the 33 hospitals is $6.94 per patient day. The average is $6.22 for Group I hospitals, $6.97 for Group II hospitals, and $10.55 for Group III. So Group III hospitals cost 69.6 percent more than those in Group I. When these costs are analyzed by individual hospitals, as was done for occupancy, Table 5 results. Differences by group are not as marked as in some of the previous charts, but there is a significant difference between the costs of Group I and Group III. This evidence, coupled with the differences in average group costs, warrants the conclusion that size of unit affects not only investment costs but the direct cost of operating as well.

Total per diem costs contain too many components to reflect the economic relationships between size, occupancy, and costs. However, total costs and revenue can be used to indicate the magnitude of the problem. The corrected average total cost per patient day for the 33 hospitals is approximately $37.77, and the average income per patient day is $37.46, indicating a loss of $0.31 a patient day. Group I hospitals profited at $1.51 a patient day, while Groups II and III lost money at the rate of $0.86 and $7.97 a day, respectively. When each hospital's experience is compared with the median loss, as in Table 6, the familiar pattern of differ-

TABLE 5　Distribution of Individual Hospitals by Group—Above and Below Median Direct Cost of Routine Services ($7.22 in Hospital I-9)

	Group I	Group II	Group III	Total
Direct cost of routine services:				
Above $7.22	2	6	8	16
Below $7.22	7	6	3	16
	9	12	11	32

TABLE 6   Distribution of Individual Hospitals by Group—Above and Below Median Loss ($2.31 in Hospital I-9)

	Group I	Group II	Group III	Total
Loss above $2.31	1	5	10	16
Loss below $2.31	8	7	1	16
	9	12	11	32

ences between the groups again emerges. It would appear that not only do the smaller hospitals cost more, but they are less able to recover their costs than are the larger hospitals.

A REVISED SIMULATION PROGRAM

The original maternity service program was abandoned and a new one written using SIMSCRIPT. The original program was cumbersome to use; it was not general enough to deal with some policy questions of interest; and it consumed an inordinate amount of computer time. The new program is quite general and relatively economical. The program uses the SIMSCRIPT time file where the events defined by us are described briefly below.

START. This event is caused by an input card. It sets up: the time length of run, the number of cases to be run, the facilities available, the initial numbers of scheduled patients (caesareans and/or induced labor) and regular patients, and the time at which the system is to be considered initiated.

SCHED causes the input of induced labor cases at policy-determined times during the day, with an upper limit on the number allowed at each input. Selected days of the week can be excluded, for example, Saturday and Sunday.

ELECT defines processing times for induced labor cases and calls subroutine ROOM. ROOM determines whether the appropriate facility is available, and if so, calls subroutine ALLOC. ALLOC creates an event notice signaling the end of each process stage, making the facility available again. If a facility is not available, ROOM assigns the patient to a queue.

PATSC performs the same function as ELECT for caesareans, and PATIN performs these for regular patients.

EPROC accumulates statistics relative to facilities and patients when a patient leaves a facility and either enters another type of facility or leaves the hospital.

ANALY computes the output reports at the end of each run.

RLBAC resets all tabulations to zero, allowing one to initiate the system in a nonempty state.

An option of importance is provided in subroutine ALLOC. As a patient is moved through the system, credit for time spent in queues may be deducted from processing times. The program may be run with this feature "on" in order to indicate the true extent of alternative actions required as the facilities become crowded. However, in assessing the value of alternative amounts of facilities, it may be desirable to run with this feature "off" and thus observe theoretical queues.

EXPERIMENTS WITH THE NEW MODEL

The model was validated in the same manner as was our previous model. Data accumulated at Grace-New Haven Community Hospital were used as input. For a period of 30 days, the actual activity in the maternity suite was recorded, including those occupancy statistics that are computed by the model. The model was then used to simulate the situation, and various statistics were computed and compared to the actual experience.

Initially, differences were observed that appeared to us significant. In order to resolve the tactical issues involved, an experiment was devised in which sample size, initiating period, and random number seed were varied systematically. The Latin Square that resulted is shown in Table 7. A statistic of great importance is the estimated standard deviation of the occupancy distribution, and as can be seen, the variation in this estimate is quite large. An analysis of variance showed random number seed to be the only significant source of variability, although one would hypothesize that sample size would be most important. Replicating the experiment with several random number seeds and pooling the results showed us that sample size was indeed the significant source of variation, and occupancy statistics were those expected on the basis of our observations.

After this initial difficulty with the random-number generator, we concluded that results are relatively insensitive to different initiating periods of more than 20 days, but relatively sensitive to sample size. The minimum sample size is 3000 patients, and stable estimates of critical parameters (e.g., the variance of the distribution of bed utilization probabilities) are obtained only after 5000 patients have been processed. However, processing times on an IBM 7094 are less than 20 seconds per 1000 patients, giving reasonable costs of analysis even for the required sample sizes.

Table 8 shows typical occupancy statistics for the hospital and for the model. Comparisons as shown were made to check the model's repro-

duction of the process it purports to describe. No claims to validity for other processes, even other maternity-suite processes, can be made. However, the process is rather stable, regardless of actual environment.

Two analyses using the model are outlined opposite.

Effect of Increase in Admissions Rate

Table 9 shows the effect of increasing the load on a 25-bed hospital from 1130 patients per year to 1320 and then to 1660. Although the labor and delivery facilities are capable of handling 1660 patients, the 25 beds will soon reach a critical load at which the service level will decrease sharply. The increase from 1320 to 1660 patients is sufficient to drive the service level down from above 0.99 to 0.92, thus making the facility seriously deficient. Limited experimentation should be undertaken in situations of this kind to plot facility requirements at selected service levels, and the information could be used to guide the hospital administration's long-range planning.

Effect of Induced Labor Cases

The second case illustrates the effect of a change in policy concerning the admission of

TABLE 7   Output Statistics of Simulator with Variation in Sample Size, Initiating Period, and Random Number Seed

Sample Size	1000			2000			3000		
Random Number Seed	1	57319	283	1	57319	283	1	57319	283
Initiating Period (Days)	20	30	40	40	20	30	30	40	20
Beds									
Mean number	73.4	74.8	74.5	73.0	73.5	69.9	72.1	74.2	69.4
Standard deviation	8.64	8.35	11.14	8.75	9.25	11.14	8.95	10.94	10.99
Labor Rooms									
Mean number	4.29	4.40	4.54	4.33	4.38	4.26	4.22	4.37	4.23
Standard deviation	2.34	2.05	2.23	2.28	2.22	2.27	2.17	2.29	2.28
Delivery rooms									
Mean number	.49	.49	.48	.47	.49	.45	.48	.48	.45
Standard deviation	.73	.71	.69	.71	.70	.68	.71	.70	.68
Mean time in labor	5.87	5.46	5.88	5.78	5.63	5.85	5.67	5.66	5.85
Mean time in delivery	.88	.85	.85	.85	.87	.85	.86	.86	.86
Mean time in postpartum	1.39	1.29	1.29	1.37	1.31	1.28	1.34	1.32	1.32
Mean time in bedroom	4.62	4.58	4.60	4.62	4.59	4.60	4.63	4.59	4.60

TABLE 8   Comparison of Occupancy Statistics—Hospital vs. Model

	Proportion of Time Given Number of Rooms Was Occupied over 308 Days			
	Postpartum		Delivery	
No. of Rooms	Hospital	Model	Hospital	Model
0	0.4788	0.4510	0.6118	0.6209
1	0.3410	0.3496	0.2983	0.2882
2	0.1264	0.1460	0.0802	0.0759
3	0.0385	0.0423	0.0069	0.0130
4	0.0129	0.0097	0.0024	0.0018
5	0.0024	0.0012	0.0004	0.0002
6	0.0000	0.0002		
Mean	0.7809	0.8147	0.4912	0.4873
Std. dev.	0.862	0.916	0.499	0.501

induced labor cases. The study hospital with no induced labor admissions serves as the base for comparison. The policy adopted for the experiment allows admission twice a day, five days a week, with a maximum of seven patients per admission. Data on processing times were obtained from a hospital similar to the study hospital except for this policy.

As can be seen in Table 10, the utilization of labor facilities increases and bed utilization seems to decrease. However, this apparent decrease is attributable to bias introduced by the random number sequence and is not significant as a function of the policy change. The most striking feature is the stability in beds required to give the same service. The standard deviation of bed occupancy remains virtually unchanged at 9.52 for 10 percent and 20 percent induced labor cases. Table 11 shows the numbers of each facility required to give the indicated service. One additional labor room would be needed to accommodate the change in policy.

The hospital administration is now in a position to consider whether the advantages from instituting the policy are worth the price to be paid—one labor room and perhaps a slight decrease in service level.

In another simulation run, the policy was altered to smooth the flow of induced labor cases. They were scheduled six times a day, five days a week, with the overall rate held at 20 percent. As a result, average occupancy is unchanged, but the standard deviation of bed occupancy decreases to 9.05, and one bed could be eliminated at the same service level. It can be strongly concluded that scheduling is an important aspect of the policy. One or two admission times per day with 10 percent induced labor cases might increase bed requirements, whereas more admission times per day with fewer patients per admission can have an important smoothing effect.

DISCUSSION

Much of what is concluded here is suspected by some people, and probably has been verified in practice by a few. However, it illustrates the use to which this model may be put, and more importantly, it demonstrates that an objective tool is available for testing hypotheses about maternity service design and operation.

The first and most obvious application lies in the area of planning. Thirteen of the 33 hospitals in Connecticut are situated in 6 cities, 5 cities having 2 hospitals and 1 city having 3 hospitals. When these multiple hospital towns are compared with our estimates of economically feasible services, some startling results emerge. In one city, there was a Group II hospital with a 37-bed maternity unit of an economically marginal size, but the service had to be provided. A

TABLE 9   Effect of Increasing Load Facility Utilization

Facilities Available	Patients/Year											
	1130				1320 (Present Load)				1660			
	Utilization	Mean No. Used	Std. Dev. of Usage		Utilization	Mean No. Used	Std. Dev. of Usage		Utilization	Mean No. Used	Std. Dev. of Usage
Labor (5 beds)	0.1763	0.8816	0.9486		0.2042	1.0210	1.0215		0.2596	1.2982	1.1249
Reg. del. (2 rooms)	0.0572	0.1144	0.3371		0.0683	0.1365	0.3695		0.0869	0.1738	0.4150
Caesarean del. (1 room)	0.0196	0.0196	0.1387		0.0220	0.0220	0.1467		0.0240	0.0240	0.1532
Postpartum (5 beds)	0.0313	0.1567	0.4002		0.0369	0.1844	0.4351		0.0463	0.2316	0.4870
Beds (25 beds)	0.5107	12.7671	3.4956		0.5929	14.8222	3.7391		0.7359	18.3978	3.7707
Beds required for given	0.90	21 beds				23 beds				> 25 beds	
service level	0.95	19 beds				21 beds				> 25 beds	
	0.90	17 beds				20 beds				24 beds	

TABLE 10 Comparison of Occupancy Statistics for Various Proportions of Induced Labor Cases

Percent of Patients Who Elect Induced Labor

Number of Units Provided	0%			10%			20%		
	Utilization	Mean No. Used	Std. Dev. of Usage	Utilization	Mean No. Used	Std. Dev. of Usage	Utilization	Mean No. Used	Std. Dev. of Usage
Labor	0.2953	4.4298	2.3783	0.3112	4.6682	2.3784	0.3276	4.9135	2.3784
Reg. del.	0.0975	0.4873	0.8396	0.1083	0.5417	0.8406	0.1227	0.6136	0.8409
Caesarean del.	0.0771[a]	0.0771	0.2972	0.0647[a]	0.0647	0.2105	0.0586[a]	0.0586	0.2103
Postpartum del.	0.0543	0.8147	0.8411	0.0559	0.8391	0.8412	0.0574	0.8605	0.8413
Beds	0.7450	74.4971	9.5139	0.7324	73.2363	9.5215	0.7281	72.8117	9.5191

[a] Differences not significant

TABLE 11   Facility Requirements for Induced Labor Policy

Facility Type	Required Service Level	No. of Units Required at Given Percent Elections		
		0%	10%	20%
Labor	0.99	10 (0.986)[a]	11 (0.988)	11 (0.991)
Reg. del.	0.99	3 (0.998)	3 (0.996)	3 (0.995)
Caesarean del.	0.99	1	1	1
Postpartum del.	0.99	3 (0.989)	3 (0.987)	3 (0.987)
Beds	0.99	96	96	96
Beds	0.95	89	89	89

[a] The number in parentheses is the estimated service level.

second hospital was built in this town with a 10-bed unit, and as a consequence, the 10-bed unit is operating at 77 percent occupancy while the 37-bed unit is operating at 50 percent occupancy. It would have been far more economical to concentrate all the maternity beds in one unit and the simulator would have allowed the evaluation of these alternatives.

In another section of the state, there are three hospitals within seven miles of each other. Each discharges approximately 1300 patients a year from their maternity services, and the services contain a total of 99 beds. Table 12 compares the simulated facility requirements for three services processing 1300 to 1400 deliveries a year with the facilities required for a single service processing 3900 to 4200 admissions a year. Not only

can substantial personnel savings be anticipated by operating one unit instead of three, but fewer beds serving a larger population would result in higher occupancy. The delivery suite requirements for the single unit are significantly less than for the three. The service given by these alternatives is at the same level, and perhaps if costs had been stated in these terms, different facilities would have been constructed.

But what of hospitals which must have small obstetrical services because they are the only hospital in the community? Is there any way to free their obstetrical services from random demand, low occupancy, and high costs? The artificial isolation of obstetrical beds from the beds in other services not only results in low service occupancy, but may result in surgical

TABLE 12   Comparison of Requirements for One Centralized vs. Three Decentralized Maternity Services

	Beds	Labor rooms	Post-partum rooms	Caesarean rooms	Delivery rooms
Required for 1300 to 1400 admissions per year	30	3	1	1	2
	30	3	1	1	2
	30	3	1	1	2
Total facilities for three separate maternity units	90	9	3	3	6
Required for 3900 to 4200 admissions per year	75	7	2	1	3

waiting lists, because empty obstetrical beds are not used for surgical patients. If such isolation is required for medical reasons, the cost is one the community must bear. If, however, isolation is being maintained because of out-moded regulations, this study demonstrates the cost of such regulations. Is it not time to inquire into the medical reasons for maternity isolation? A mixed input, part random and part scheduled, could raise the percentage occupancy of maternity beds, and in these days of increasing hospital costs, it is necessary to consider every alternative that might decrease cost per patient day.

Computer models can and should play an important role in hospital administration. The benefits for both planning and operations could be significant. Contributions to investment and policy problems have been demonstrated, and additional contributions can be made if the approach is used by those responsible for the design of health services.

REFERENCES

1. M. S. Blumberg, 1961. "DPF concept" helps predict bed needs. *Modern Hospital*, 97(6): 75–81.
2. Commission on Hospital Care, 1947. *Hospital care in the United States*. New York: The Commonwealth Fund.
3. R. W. Conway, 1963. Some tactical problems in digital simulation. *Management Science*, 10(1): 47–61. MS.
4. J. D. Thompson, O. W. Avant, and E. D. Spiker, 1960. How queuing theory works for the hospital. *Modern Hospital*, 94(3): 75–78.
5. J. D. Thompson, R. B. Fetter, C. S. McIntosh and R. J. Pelletier, 1963. Predicting requirements for maternity facilities. *Hospitals*, 37(4): 45–49 and 132. 3C.

20

AN EVALUATION OF SIMPLIFIED PROCEDURES FOR DETERMINING TRAVEL PATTERNS IN A SMALL URBAN AREA

CONSTANTINE BEN

RICHARD J. BOUCHARD

CLYDE E. SWEET, JR.

Since the early 1940s transportation planning studies have been conducted in urban areas throughout the country in an increasingly comprehensive manner. In most of these areas basic data on travel patterns, social and economic characteristics of trip makers, and the uses of land have been collected, and the type and extent of transportation facilities have been determined. The interrelationships between these various kinds of data have in turn been analyzed to the point that today several theories on urban travel are emerging. These theories are in the form of traffic models, or equations, composed of the various parameters which influence the generation and distribution of urban trips as well as the routes which these trips will traverse. One of the most widely used theories on urban travel is the gravity model theory which utilizes a gravitational concept to describe the distribution ot trips between various parts of an urban area.

With the advent of travel models, the theory has been advanced that the need for basic data

SOURCE: Reprinted from *Highway Research Record*, *88*: 137–170 (1965).

on travel patterns may be less now than before these models were developed. In the past four years, interest has grown in the use of small sample home interview data for calibrating traffic models, particularly the gravity model, in urban areas. For example, the Hartford Area Traffic Study [1] collected travel data from only 200, or 0.1 percent, of the dwelling units within the study area. The Southeast Area Traffic Study [6] collected such data from 1384 or 2.0 percent of the dwelling units within its study area. Several other studies [10, 17] have used similar sampling rates. Although theories have been advanced concerning travel patterns and the desirability of reducing the amount of travel data to be collected, little has been done to quantify their accuracy and validity.

This research had two principal objectives. The first was to examine the ability of a calibrated gravity model to reproduce the trip distribution patterns in a particular small urban area. To achieve this objective, full use was made of comprehensive origin-destination survey data in calibrating the gravity model for the urban area under study. The ability of this calibrated gravity model to simulate the area's trip distribution patterns was then investigated by comparing the gravity model movements against movements from the O-D survey.

The second objective was to evaluate simplified procedures for calibrating a gravity model trip distribution formula for the same urban area. Instead of calibrating with all the available data, only that trip information available from the external cordon survey and from a subsample of the original home interview survey was used. Simplified procedures were used to determine productions and attractions from detailed socio-economic data. The ability of this calibrated gravity model to simulate the area's travel patterns was then investigated by comparing the resultant gravity model movements against the movements obtained from the standard O-D survey of the area.

The small urban area selected for this research was Sioux Falls, S. Dak. (population, 62,000). In 1956, a comprehensive home interview O-D survey was conducted in 12.5 percent of the area's nearly 20,000 dwelling units [15],

the rate recommended by the U.S. Bureau of Public Roads [3] for urban areas of this size. The standard external cordon and truck and taxi surveys [15] were also conducted, as were surveys of the land use and the type and extent of the area's transportation facilities. Unpublished data on the capacity and level of service characteristics of Sioux Falls transportation facilities, retail sales figures by zone, and certain employment and labor force statistics were supplied by the South Dakota Department of Highways. Also available were the results of a 1960 parking survey [14]. The study area was divided into 74 traffic zones with 10 external stations. For summary and general analysis, these zones and stations were combined into 28 districts (Figure 1).

GRAVITY MODEL THEORY

The gravity model theory, its mathematical statement, and the five parameters for calculating trip interchanges from this statement have been discussed in detail by Bouchard and Pyers

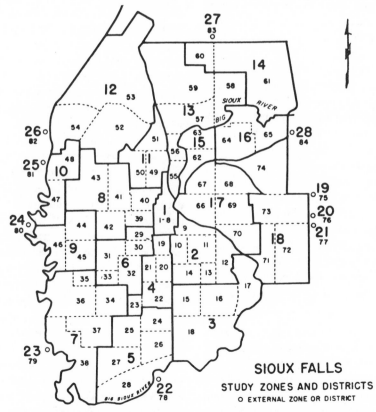

Figure 1 Zonal and district boundaries, Sioux Falls, S. Dak., study area, 1956.

[2, p. 2]. However, the results of the present study indicate that there is no need for the application of the zone-to-zone adjustment factors, $K_{(i-j)}$, in the case of Sioux Falls. The need for these factors seems to be more pronounced in large urban areas where the range in various social and economic conditions of the residents is large.

TESTING THE GRAVITY MODEL THEORY FOR A SMALL URBAN AREA

This phase of the research deals with calibrating a gravity model from data obtained in the Sioux Falls O-D survey and testing the ability of this calibrated model to simulate the travel patterns found in the O-D survey. The steps involved in this phase were identical to those which have been completely documented in two recent publications by the U.S. Bureau of Public Roads [4, 5]. These were essentially:

1. Processing basic data on the area's travel patterns and transportation facilities to provide three of the basic inputs to the gravity model formula, i.e., zonal trip production and attraction values and the spatial separation between zones;

2. Developing travel time factors, $F_{(t_{i-j})}$, to express the effect of spatial separation on trip interchange between zones;

3. Balancing zonal attraction factors, A_j, to assure that the trips attracted to each zone by the gravity model formula were in close agreement with those shown by the O-D survey data;

4. Examining these estimated trip interchanges to determine the need for adjustments to reflect various factors not directly accounted for in the model; and

5. Comparing the final gravity model trip interchanges with those from the home interview survey to test the ability of the model to simulate the 1956 travel patterns in the Sioux Falls area.

For this research, the total daily vehicular trips with either origins or destinations in the study area were used. Excluded from the study were trips which had neither their origins nor their destinations within the cordon (through trips) and all transit trips. The trips were strati-

fied into the following categories: (a) home-based auto-driver work trips, (b) home-based auto-driver nonwork trips, and (c) nonhome-based vehicular trips.

The measure of spatial separation between zones (t_{i-j}) was composed of the off-peak minimum path driving time between zones plus the terminal time in the production and attraction zones connected with the trip. Terminal times were added to driving times at both ends of the trip to allow for differences in parking and walking times in the zones as caused by differences in congestion and available parking facilities.

Basic Data

All information from the home interview, external cordon, and truck and taxi surveys had previously been verified, coded and punched in cards. This information was made compatible as to meaning and location on the cards. The records were edited to insure that all pertinent information had been recorded correctly, and the edited records were then separated into the three trip purpose categories previously described. A table of zone-to-zone movements was then prepared for each trip purpose category. Each trip record was examined and all trips from each zone of production to every zone of attraction were accumulated. During this accumulation process the total number of trips produced by and attracted to each zone in the study area was also determined. These zonal trip production and attraction values were used to calculate trip interchanges with the gravity model formula. The zone-to-zone movements were subsequently used in testing the ability of the gravity model to simulate the 1956 travel patterns in Sioux Falls.

The data from the transportation facilities inventory had to be processed in the same way. This allowed the computation of the spatial separation between zones. Interzonal driving times were obtained from a description of the major street system in the area using a standard tree-building computer program. Intrazonal driving times were determined from an examination of the speeds on the highway facilities in each zone of the study area. Terminal times in each zone were determined by analyzing the results of the 1960 parking survey [14], which

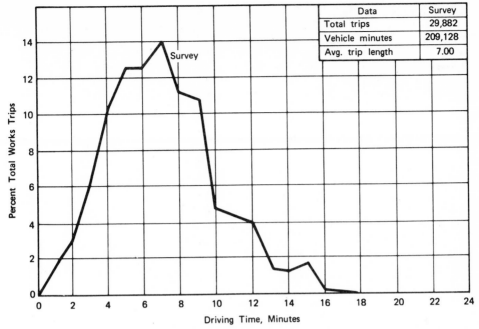

Figure 2 Trip length frequency distribution, home-based auto-driver work trips, Sioux Falls, 1956.

indicated to some extent the congestion and available parking facilities in each zone; central business district (CBD) zones were allocated 3 min and all other zones were allocated 1 min of terminal time.

Developing Travel Time Factors

The best set of travel time factors associated with each trip purpose was determined through a process of trial and adjustment. To determine travel time factors by this procedure, information is needed which reflects the effect of trip length on trip making. A useful summary of such information was obtained by determining the number and percent of trips for every minute of driving time for each trip purpose category. From the data on travel patterns, information was available on interzonal trips, and from the data on transportation facilities on driving times between zones. The trip length frequency distribution was obtained by combining the number of trips between each zone with the minimum path travel times between the zone pair, and repeating this process for all possible zone pairs. The resulting curve for work trips is shown in Figure 2. Table 1 summarizes this pertinent information for all trip purpose categories.

TABLE 1 Distribution of Vehicular Trips by Purpose, Sioux Falls, 1956

Purpose	No. of Trips	Veh-Min of Travel	Avg. Trip Length
Home-based work	29,882	209,128	7.00
Home-based nonwork	65,759	404,749	6.15
Nonhome-based	63,280	360,736	5.70
Total	158,921	974,613	6.13

The procedure used was to assume a set of travel time factors for each trip purpose and to calculate trip interchanges using the gravity model formula, zonal trip productions and attractions and zonal separation information, obtained as previously described. The initial estimate of trip interchanges was then combined with the minimum time paths to obtain an estimated trip length frequency distribution for each trip purpose category. A comparison of the actual and the estimated trip length frequency distributions and the average trip length figures indicated close agreement. However, the discrepancies between the actual and the estimated

TABLE 2 Travel Time Factor Adjustment process, Work Trips

Driving Time	Percent Trips (Actual)	Travel Time Factor 1	Percent Trips (Est. No. 1)	Adj. Travel Time Factor[a]	Travel Time Factor 2[b]
1	1.68	162	1.24	219	220
2	2.93	152	2.12	210	210
3	6.09	142	4.88	177	185
4	10.28	132	10.32	131	150
5	12.61	122	13.49	114	125
6	12.57	112	13.62	103	110
7	13.91	102	13.26	107	100
8	11.22	092	11.26	92	085
9	·10.91	082	11.42	78	079
10	4.20	072	6.04	50	067
11	4.40	062	5.33	51	061
12	3.98	052	3.52	59	057
13	1.53	042	1.56	41	050
14	1.34	032	1.09	39	048
15	1.70	022	0.74	51	045
16	0.04	012	0.08	06	010
17	0.01	0	0.04	0	002
18	0	0	0	0	0
19	0	0	0	0	0
20	0	0	0	0	0

[a] From $\dfrac{\% \text{ trips (actual)}}{\% \text{ trips (est. No. 1)}} \times$ travel time factor 1.

[b] From Figure 3.

figures were larger than desired by the research staff (± 3 percent on average trip length with the frequency curves closely paralleling each other). Consequently, a revised gravity model estimate was made.

To make a revised estimate, new sets of travel time factors were calculated for each trip purpose category. The percentage of survey trips occurring during each minute of driving time was divided by the percentage of gravity model trips occurring during the same time increment, and the results of this division were multiplied by the initial factor. An example of this procedure is given in Table 2. These new factors were then plotted on log-log graph paper for the appropriate 1-min intervals for each trip purpose category, as shown in Figure 3. A line of best fit was drawn (by judgment) through the plotted points to obtain a smooth curve for travel time factors (Figure 3).

These new sets of travel time factors were

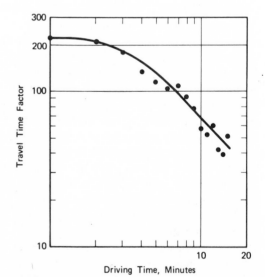

Figure 3 Determining revised travel-time factors, work trips.

then used in the same manner as in Calibration 1 to obtain a new estimate of trip interchanges with the model. New estimated trip length frequency curves, person hours of travel, and average trip length figures were developed and compared with the survey data. This comparison indicated that the gravity model estimates were within the established criteria. Consequently, the second estimate of travel time factors was judged to describe adequately the effect of spatial separation on trip interchange between zones in Sioux Falls. These final travel time factors are given for each trip purpose in Table 3.

TABLE 3   Final Travel Time Factors by Trip Purpose, Sioux Falls, 1956

Driving Time	Work	Nonwork	Nonhome-Based
1	220	280	300
2	210	260	270
3	185	220	210
4	150	160	120
5	125	130	100
6	110	090	080
7	100	085	070
8	085	070	060
9	079	060	055
10	067	050	044
11	061	039	038
12	057	035	032
13	050	027	030
14	048	025	026
15	045	021	023
16	010	016	014
17	002	000	005
18	000	000	000
19	000	000	000
20	000	000	000

Adjustment of Zonal Trip Attractions

The number of trips distributed by the gravity model to any given zone does not generally equal that shown by the O-D surveys as actually attracted to the zone, because the gravity model formula does not have any built-in adjustment to insure such results. This variation in zonal attractions is a difficulty inherent in all currently available trip distribution techniques. Therefore, the trip attractions (A_j) for each zone were adjusted to bring the number of trips assigned to a given zone into balance with

the trip attraction of that zone as determined by the survey.

Prior to balancing attractions, the estimated trip attractions resulting from Calibration 2 were compared with the actual attractions as shown by the survey to determine the differences. The two items of information for each zone were plotted for each trip purpose. An example for work trips is shown in Figure 4. A technique developed by Brokke and Sosslau [13] was used to judge the adequacy of the estimated figures. This earlier work established a reasonable approximation of the error that can be expected to result from O-D surveys of various sample rates, depending on the volume of trips measured. Curves developed to show the error in the survey volumes in terms of the root-mean-square (RMS) error, which is similar to the standard deviation, have been shown by Smith [12, Figure 3]. Two-thirds of the time (68.2 percent) the error in the origin-destination survey data, for a particular sample rate and volume group, will fall within one RMS error. Over 95 percent of the time, the recorded volumes will be within two RMS errors, and so forth. To determine the reliability (the degree of acceptability of the gravity model estimates) of the number of trips attracted to each zone in the study area, the RMS error for each volume group for the 12.5 percent sample rate was plotted as shown in Figure 4 and the points were connected by the dashed lines. If two-thirds of the points fall within these dashed lines, no adjustments are required. However, if less than two-thirds fall within these lines, all zonal attraction values should be adjusted. An examination of the results shown in Figure 4 indicated that the variations were small and entirely within the limits just described. The other two trip purposes showed similar results. Nevertheless, for purposes of this research, the zonal attraction values for each trip purpose were adjusted to obtain a more realistic measure of the error in the actual distribution of the trips. The adjustment was made by dividing the zonal trip attraction from the O-D survey by the trips attracted to each zone as developed by the gravity model and then multiplying the result by the original zonal trip attraction factor developed from the O-D survey. The amount of adjustment required for each trip purpose was relatively

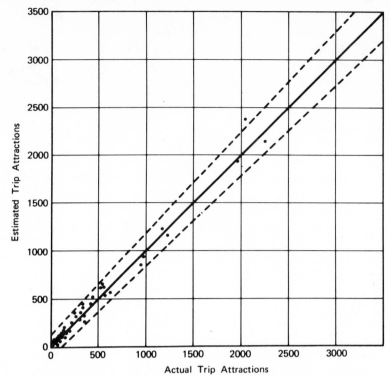

Figure 4 Comparison of work-trip attractions, Calibration 2, Sioux Falls, 1956.

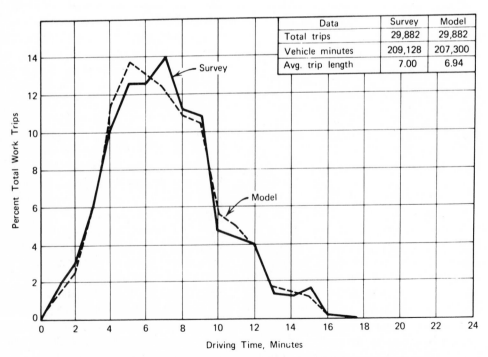

Data	Survey	Model
Total trips	29,882	29,882
Vehicle minutes	209,128	207,300
Avg. trip length	7.00	6.94

Figure 5 Trip-length frequency distribution, home-based auto-driver work trips, Sioux Falls, 1956.

small. In most zones the adjustment was less than 10 percent and in no case was the adjustment greater than 20 percent. There was no discernible pattern in the required adjustment.

The gravity model interchanges were then recalculated using the adjusted zonal attraction values. The slight differences in this information between Calibrations 2 and 3 indicated that the zonal attraction factor adjustment had very little effect on the variation. Part of this, of course, can be explained on the basis of the rather small adjustments which were required to balance the zonal adjustment factors for each trip purpose. The results of this third and final calibration in terms of the trip length frequency distribution and the average trip length for work trips are shown in Figure 5.

To investigate the effect of the zonal attraction factor adjustment on actual trip interchanges, the district-to-district movements were examined for both the second and third calibrations. District-to-district movements, rather than zone-to-zone movements were used in this analysis to obtain a more meaningful accumu-

lation of trips. The results of this analysis for work trips, shown in Figure 6, were quite similar for the other two trip purposes although the dispersion was somewhat more pronounced. However, in no case was the dispersion greater than 15 percent. An examination of this information indicated that the attraction adjustment procedure had only a small effect on trip interchanges.

Checking Model for Geographical Bias

In using the gravity model, several researchers have discovered the need for various adjustment factors to account for special conditions within an urban area which affect travel patterns but are not accounted for in the model. For example, a recent study in Washington, D.C., indicated that the Potomac River had some influence on trip distribution patterns [2]. A study in New Orleans, La., indicated similar problems connected with river crossings [11]. A study in Hartford, Conn., indicated that toll bridges crossing the Connecticut River also had an effect on travel patterns [1]. In each of these

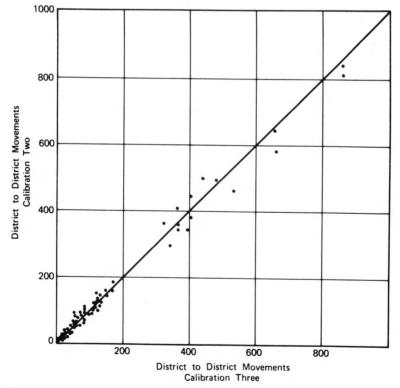

Figure 6 Comparison of district-to-district movements, home-based auto-driver work trips, Sioux Falls, 1956.

cases, the effects of these conditions were indicated to the gravity model by time penalties on
those portions of the transportation system for
which discrepancies in the model were observed.
In addition, some studies have indicated geographical bias caused by factors other than
topographical barriers. For example, the
Washington, D.C., study showed the need for
adjustment factors to account for a rather
unique relationship existing in that area. Before
incorporating the adjustment factors into the
gravity model formula, the estimated trip interchanges were significantly biased in that the
model did not adequately account for the fact
that medium income blue collar workers
residing in certain parts of the Washington area

had no job opportunities within the central parts
of the area. If work trips had been further stratified, perhaps the need for adjustment factors
would have been reduced.

Several tests were conducted on the results of
Calibration 3 to determine the need for adjustment factors such as those just described. One of
these tests involved the Big Sioux River which
bisects the Sioux Falls area as shown in Figure 1.
For those trips crossing the Big Sioux River, the
total trip interchanges as shown by the home
interview survey were compared directly with
the results of the gravity model. In addition,
both of these items were compared with volume
counts taken on all the bridges crossing this
river. As indicated in Table 4, there is a very

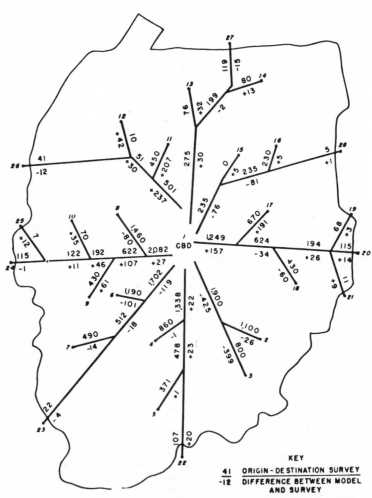

Figure 7 Corridor analysis, actual versus estimated home-based, auto-driver work
trips to CBD, Sioux Falls, 1956.

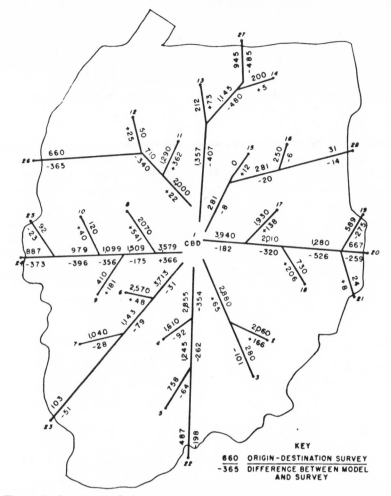

Figure 8 Corridor analysis, actual versus estimated home-based, auto-driver nonwork trips to CBD, Sioux Falls, 1956.

KEY
660 ORIGIN-DESTINATION SURVEY
-365 DIFFERENCE BETWEEN MODEL AND SURVEY

TABLE 4 Comparison of Total Vehicular Trips Crossing Big Sioux River, Sioux Falls, 1956

Facility	Trips (No.)		
	Vol. Count	O-D Survey	Gravity Model
Cherry Rock Av.	1,511	1,640	1,660
Cliff Ave., S.	9,132	8,420	9,444
Tenth St.	14,842	16,296	16,648
Eighth St.	8,606	6,612	6,080
Sixth St.	3,864	2,900	3,576
McClellan St.	3,069	2,596	2,032
Cliff Ave., N.	4,699	4,156	3,904
Totals	45,723	42,620	43,344
Percent from Vol. Count	—	−6.8	−5.2
Percent from O-D Survey	+7.3	—	+1.7

close agreement between these three sources of information; this indicates that the Big Sioux River is no barrier to travel.

Another test for geographical bias was conducted for trips to the CBD of Sioux Falls. Trips from each district to the CBD, by trip purpose, as shown in Calibration 3 of the gravity model were compared directly with the same information from the O-D survey. These results are shown in Figures 7, 8, and 9. An analysis of these figures indicates that no significant bias is present in the model and, furthermore, the gravity model estimates are close to the O-D survey.

Final Results

The total trips resulting from the final calibration of the gravity model and from the O-D survey were assigned to the transportation network. An examination of the results of these two assignments was made by comparing the number of trips crossing a very comprehensive series of screenlines. Figure 10 shows this comprehensive series of screenlines and also identifies each screenline. Table 5 compares the actual and estimated trips crossing each of these screenlines. An examination of the absolute and the percent differences between the actual and the estimated screenline crossings indicated only four differences larger than 10 percent and none which have absolute volume discrepancies large enough to affect design considerations.

One final test was made to determine the statistical significance of the differences between the gravity model estimates and the O-D survey data. The results of this test are given in Table 6. When these results were compared with the O-D survey error [13], the gravity model estimates had almost the same degree of reliability as the O-D survey data.

The tests and comparisons shown in this section of the report indicate that the calibrated three purpose gravity model adequately simulates the trip distribution patterns shown by the O-D survey. Nevertheless, it is desirable to have a measure of the differences in the results which would have been obtained for lesser and higher degrees of trip stratification than the three purposes used in this research. To date, little has been done to investigate these differences. The analysis to be outlined is not conclusive, but it does shed considerable light on the subject.

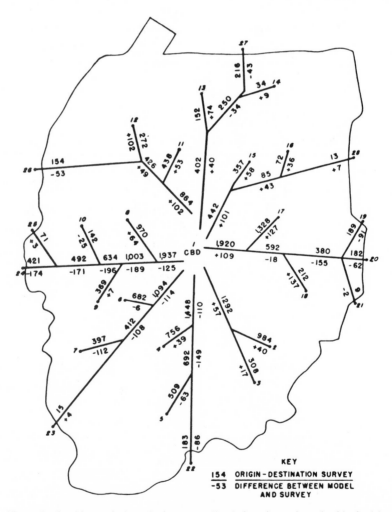

KEY

154 ORIGIN-DESTINATION SURVEY
-53 DIFFERENCE BETWEEN MODEL AND SURVEY

Figure 9 Corridor analysis, actual versus estimated nonhome-based vehicular trips to CBD, Sioux Falls, 1956.

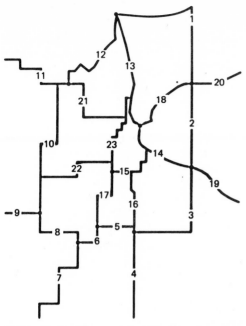

Figure 10 Location and identification of comprehensive series of screenlines, Sioux Falls, 1956.

The analysis procedure was as follows. Gravity models were calibrated for the following trip purpose stratifications:

1. One purpose model—total vehicular trips; and
2. Six purpose model—home-based auto-driver work trips, home-based auto-driver shop trips, home-based auto-driver miscellaneous trips, home-based auto-driver social-recreation trips, nonhome-based vehicular trips, and truck and taxi trips.

The same techniques and the same number of calibration runs were made in these two models as were made in calibrating the three purpose model. The same tests were also performed on these models as on the three purpose model with about the same degree of accuracy. Table 5 gives the absolute and percentage differences between the model and survey trips crossing the comprehensive series of screenlines (Figure 10) for one purpose, three purpose, and six purpose

TABLE 5   Total Trips Crossing Screenlines, Sioux Falls, 1956

		One Purpose Model		Three Purpose Model		Six Purpose Model	
Screenline No.	O-D Survey Vol.	Vol.	Diff. from O-D (%)	Vol.	Diff. from O-D (%)	Vol.	Diff. from O-D (%)
1	7,952	6,996	−12.0	7,344	−7.6	7,440	−6.4
2	21,012	20,580	−2.1	20,460	−2.6	20,552	−2.2
3	13,516	14,216	+5.2	13,900	+2.8	13,222	−2.2
4	11,384	12,344	+8.4	12,060	+5.9	11,956	+4.2
5	9,744	9,332	−4.2	9,252	−5.0	9.336	−5.0
6	8,784	9,500	−8.2	9,392	+6.9	9,444	+7.5
7	6,280	6,788	+8.1	6,824	+8.7	6,852	+9.1
8	6,568	6,984	+6.3	7,032	+7.1	7,152	+8.9
9	2,264	2,772	+22.4	2,676	+18.2	2,648	+17.0
10	17,448	17,808	+2.1	17,592	+0.8	17,668	+1.3
11	5,868	6,468	+10.2	6,532	+11.3	6,704	+14.2
12	5,592	6,484	+16.0	6,412	+14.7	6,392	+14.3
13	13,656	13,660	0.0	14,840	+8.7	13,924	+2.0
14	22,908	25,096	+9.6	23,040	+0.6	22,720	−0.8
15	33,220	31,400	−5.5	32,144	−3.2	34,005	+2.4
16	10,032	10,736	+7.0	10,012	−0.2	10,120	+0.8
17	13,424	14,016	−4.4	13,760	+2.5	14,012	+4.4
18	9,724	10,324	+6.2	10,276	+5.7	10,424	+7.2
19	10,060	11,352	+12.8	11,044	+9.8	11,092	+10.3
20	5,332	5,240	−1.7	5,420	+1.6	5,556	+4.2
21	8,496	9,056	+6.6	9,136	+7.5	9,200	+8.3
22	13,332	14,612	+9.6	14,504	+8.8	14,672	+10.0
23	41,500	40,660	−2.0	41,852	+0.8	39,995	−3.6

TABLE 6 Comparisons of District-to-District Movements[a]

Volume Group	O-D Survey Trip Mean	O-D Survey Trip Freq.	RMS Error Abs.	RMS Error Percent
(a) Home-Based Auto-Driver Work Trips				
0– 99	21	400	17	80.95
100– 199	133	40	47	35.34
200– 299	259	13	87	33.59
300– 499	402	13	85	21.14
500–1,499	920	8	166	18.04
(b) Home-Based Auto-Driver Nonwork Trips				
0– 99	27	423	24	88.89
100– 199	136	53	83	61.03
200– 299	239	28	87	36.40
300– 499	380	22	112	29.47
500– 999	728	22	231	31.73
1,000–2,999	1,711	9	276	16.13
(c) Nonhome-Based Auto-Driver Trips				
0– 99	25	473	22	88.00
100– 199	144	62	63	43.75
200– 299	241	30	100	41.49
300– 499	385	33	101	26.23
500– 999	773	9	119	15.39
1,000–4,999	1,695	9	263	15.52

[a] 1956 O-D survey data vs gravity model estimates, relative difference measured in terms of percent RMS error:

$$\text{Percent RMS error} = 100 \left(\frac{\sqrt{\Sigma(d)^2}}{n/\bar{x}} \right)$$

where
d = difference between surveyed and estimated,
n = number of district-to-district movements, and
$\bar{x}$ = mean of surveyed trips.

models. Results indicate that the three purpose model is better than the one purpose model, but the increased accuracy obtained with a six purpose model is only slightly greater than with a three purpose model.

USE OF SIMPLIFIED PROCEDURES FOR DETERMINING TRIP DISTRIBUTION PATTERNS IN A SMALL URBAN AREA

The previous phase of this research illustrated that the gravity model formula can be used to simulate trip distribution patterns in a small urban area when comprehensive home interview data are available for use in developing the model to fit the area's travel patterns. The research reported in this section examines the feasibility of reducing the amount of data necessary to develop the gravity model. Since in developing the gravity model for Sioux Falls, no significant geographical bias was observed, it was not necessary to make use of all the data available for the area. This led to an exploration of smaller samples of data for calibrating the gravity model. This phase of the research was accomplished in the following steps.

1. The minimum sample size of home interview survey required to provide the information necessary to develop the gravity model formula for Sioux Falls was determined. Since the previous phase of this research illustrated that information on zonal trip production and attraction and a trip length frequency distri-

TABLE 7 Comparison of Total Trip Productions for Various Sample Sizes, Southeast Area Traffic Study, 1962

Trip Purpose	1,384 Sample[a] Sample Trips	1,384 Sample[a] Percent Total Trips	1,384 Sample[a] Diff. (%)	592 Sample[b] Ex-panded Trips	592 Sample[b] Percent Total Trips	592 Sample[b] Diff. (%)	153 Sample[c] Ex-panded Trips	153 Sample[c] Percent Total Trips	153 Sample[c] Diff. (%)[d]
Home-based work	2,067	32.9	0	2,006	30.9	−3.0	1,936	32.6	−6.3
Other home-based	3,218	51.3	0	3,446	53.1	+7.1	3,139	52.9	−2.5
Nonhome-based	990	15.8	0	1,040	16.0	+5.1	859	14.5	−13.2
Total	6,275	100.0	0	6,492	100.0	+3.5	5,934	100.0	−5.4

[a] Sample rate, 2.4 percent.
[b] Sample rate, 1.1 percent.
[c] Sample rate, 0.3 percent.
[d] Percent difference from 2.4 percent sample.

bution of trips, by trip purpose, was all that was required for a gravity model calibration, the small sample data must provide sufficient information to develop these parameters. This step involved an analysis of subsample data from several urban areas and the development of curves that could be used to determine the relative error which would occur for different size samples.

2. Zonal trip production and trip attraction values for each trip purpose were estimated using the total trips expanded from the small sample, their split among the various purposes, and certain social and economic characteristics of each individual zone. Zonal trip production and attraction values were developed in this manner because they are not available from small sample data, and they were compared directly with the data from a comprehensive O-D survey to determine the reliability of the techniques used.

3. Trip interchanges for each trip purpose were determined using the results of the previous two steps and the gravity model formula. The synthetic trip distribution patterns were then compared directly with the O-D survey results.

Determining Overall Travel Characteristics from Small Sample

It has been reported by studies using small sample home interview surveys that the data collected in such surveys are adequate for calibrating a gravity model [1, 6]. Those using small sample home interview surveys in the past have reported that the resulting data can be used to develop the total number of trips in the area, as well as the percentage of trips for each of the several trip purposes and travel mode categories. Furthermore, they indicated that these data gave sufficient information concerning the length of urban trips, an important parameter in the development of travel models.

There is some evidence available to substantiate these reports. For example, a recent study by the Connecticut Highway Department compared the total universe of trips as well as the percentages of trips for each of three trip purposes for subsamples of 153 and 592 home interviews. These subsamples were drawn from an original field sample of 1384 home interviews taken in the Southeast Area Traffic Study. Some of the results of this study, given in Table 7, indicate that samples as low as 600 interviews may give approximately the same results for

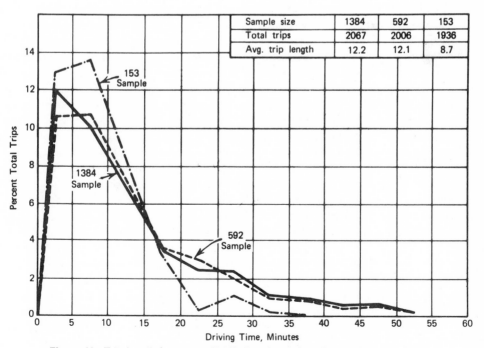

Sample size	1384	592	153
Total trips	2067	2006	1936
Avg. trip length	12.2	12.1	8.7

Figure 11 Trip-length frequency distribution, home-based, auto-driver work trips, southeast Connecticut, 1960.

TABLE 8   Comparison of Total Trip Productions for Selected Sample Sizes, North Carolina Research Project N, 1963

Trip Purpose	1457 Sample			742 Sample			196 Sample		
	Sample	Percent Total Trips	Diff. (%)[a]	Ex-panded Trips	Percent Total Trips	Diff. (%)[a]	Ex-panded Trips	Percent Total Trips	Diff. (%)[a]
Home-based work	26,207	38.9	0	25,781	38.6	−1.6	26,080	39.0	−0.5
Other home-based	27,760	41.2	0	27,887	41.7	+0.5	27,101	40.5	−2.4
Nonhome-based	13,437	19.9	0	13,194	19.7	−1.8	13,720	20.5	−2.1
Total	67.404	100.0	0	66,862	100.0	−0.8	66,901	100.0	−0.8

Trip Purpose	383 Sample			248 Sample			192 Sample		
	Ex-panded Trips	Percent Total Trips	Diff. (%)[a]	Ex-panded Trips	Percent Total Trips	Diff. (%)[a]	Ex-panded Trips	Percent Total Trips	Diff. (%)[a]
Home-based work	24,382	38.5	−7.0	25,920	40.0	−1.1	27,498	39.3	+4.9
Other home-based	27,983	44.2	+0.8	27,896	43.0	+0.5	26,637	38.1	−4.0
Nonhome-based	10,991	17.3	−18.2	11,053	17.0	−17.7	15,802	22.6	+17.6
Total	63,356	100.0	−6.0	64,869	100.0	−3.8	69,937	100.0	+3.8

[a] Percent difference from total sample.

total trips by trip purpose as the 1384 interviews originally made in the field. The 1384 sample, used as a base, is small and it must be realized that it contains inherent sampling error. This same study also compared the trip length frequency distributions and average trip lengths for the same trip purposes and sample sizes. The results for work trips (Figure 11) show that the trip length frequency distributions and mean trip lengths are very similar for the 1384 and 592 sample sizes, with the 592 interviews being about as adequate as the 1384 interviews. The same data for the 153 samples show significant error.

A recent study in North Carolina [9] compared the total trips and trip percentages for three trip purposes for subsamples of 192, 196, 248, 383, and 742 home interviews drawn from an original field sample of 1457 home interviews taken in Fayetteville, N.C. Some of the results of this study (Table 8) indicate that samples as low as 600 might give approximately the same results for total trips by purpose as the 1457 original interviews. This study also compared the trip length frequency distributions (Figure

12) and mean trip lengths. These figures were very similar for the 1457 and 742 sample sizes. A sample size greater than 383 was necessary for an adequate mean trip length reproduction.

A similar study, recently completed by the Urban Planning Division of the U.S. Bureau of Public Roads, examined the variation in total trips, purpose split, average trip lengths, and trip length frequency distributions for sub-samples of 2021 and 404 interviews. These subsamples were from an original field survey of 16,169 home interviews taken during the Pittsburgh Area Transportation Study. Table 9 gives the total sample figures and the results of the comparisons of total trips and purpose split for each subsample. Figure 13 illustrates the trip length frequency distributions and the mean trip length figures for one of the six purposes in each of the sample rates tested. This information indicates that small samples yield adequate data on these overall travel characteristics, but the minimum sample rate shown by the Pittsburgh study appears to be around 2000 interviews, as compared with about 600 interviews in the

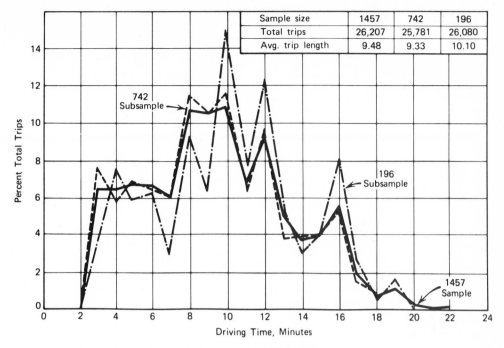

Sample size	1457	742	196
Total trips	26,207	25,781	26,080
Avg. trip length	9.48	9.33	10.10

Figure 12 Selected trip-length frequency distributions, home-based, auto-driver work trips, North Carolina study, 1963.

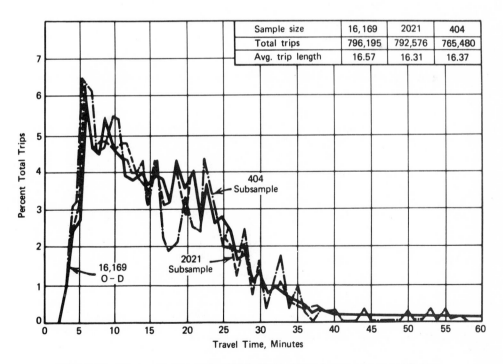

Sample size	16,169	2021	404
Total trips	796,195	792,576	765,480
Avg. trip length	16.57	16.31	16.37

Figure 13 Trip-length frequency distributions, home-based person work trips, Pittsburgh, Pa., 1958.

TABLE 9 Comparison of Total Trip Productions for Various Sample Sizes, Pittsburgh, Pa., 1958

Trip Purpose	16,169 Sample[a]			2021 Sample[b]			404 Sample[c]		
	Sample	Percent Total Trips	Diff. (%)[d]	Ex-panded Trips	Percent Total Trips	Diff. (%)[d]	Ex-panded Trips	Percent Total Trips	Diff. (%)[d]
Home-based work	796,195	34.1	0	792,576	33.9	−0.5	765,480	33.3	−3.9
Home-based other	425,074	18.2	0	440,784	18.8	3.7	436,920	19.0	2.8
Home-based soc-rec.	288,047	12.3	0	293,752	12.6	2.0	311,280	13.5	8.1
Home-based shop	286,883	12.3	0	276,416	11.8	−3.6	289,640	12.6	1.0
Home-based school	232,875	10.0	0	218,264	9.3	−6.3	191,920	8.4	−17.6
Nonhome-based	306,915	13.1	0	318,688	13.6	3.8	303,520	13.2	−1.1

[a] Sample rate, 4.0 percent.
[b] Sample rate, 0.5 percent.
[c] Sample rate, 0.1 percent.
[d] Percent difference from 4 percent sample.

Connecticut and North Carolina studies. The Pittsburgh analysis used person trips, whereas the other two studies used auto-driver trips. The results appear consistent since the Pittsburgh analysis stratified trips six ways and the Connecticut and North Carolina analyses used only three trip stratifications.

Several subsamples of the Sioux Falls home interview data were also examined for their ability to yield accurate figures on total trip productions, average trip lengths, and trip length frequency distributions by trip purpose. The results of these analyses for 599 and 199 dwelling unit subsamples and the original 2399 field samples appear in Table 10 and Figures 14, 15, and 16. These results reinforce the findings of the previously mentioned studies which indicate that samples as small in number as 600 can be used to determine the overall average characteristics of travel in a small urban area, when three trip stratifications are used.

The results for the Sioux Falls analytical sub-

TABLE 10 Comparison of Total Trip Production for Various Sample Sizes, Sioux Falls, 1956[a]

Auto-Driver Trip Purpose	2399 Sample[b]			599 Sample[c]			199 Sample[d]		
	Sample	Percent Total Trips	Diff. (%)[e]	Ex-panded Trips	Percent Total Trips	Diff. (%)[e]	Ex-panded Trips	Percent Total Trips	Diff. (%)[e]
Home-based work	25,161	24.2	0	26,564	24.4	5.6	26,292	26.4	4.5
Home-based nonwork	50,782	48.9	0	53,848	49.4	6.0	47,232	47.4	−7.0
Nonhome-based	27,924	26.9	0	28,516	26.2	2.1	26,040	26.2	−6.8
Total	103,867	100.0	0	108,744	100.0	4.6	101,496	100.0	−2.4

[a] These figures are from internal home interview person trip data only and do not include information available from the truck, taxi, and external cordon survey. Auto-driver trip data from both of these sources were used in developing trip interchanges synthetically as described in text and given in Table 12.
[b] Sample rate, 12.5 percent.
[c] Sample rate, 3.1 percent.
[d] Sample rate, 1.0 percent.
[e] Percent difference from 12.5 percent sample.

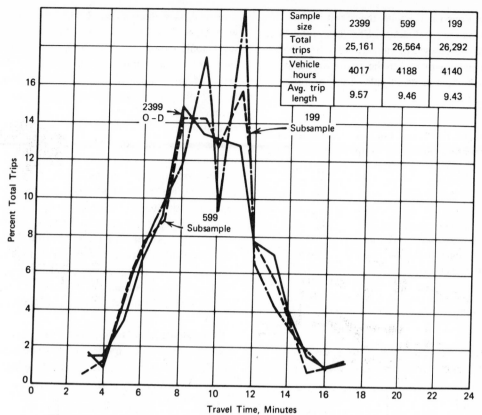

	Sample size	2399	599	199
	Total trips	25,161	26,564	26,292
	Vehicle hours	4017	4188	4140
	Avg. trip length	9.57	9.46	9.43

Figure 14   Trip-length frequency distributions, home-based, auto-driver work trips, Sioux Falls, 1956.

samples were analyzed to see if general curves could be developed to approximate the error which would occur in mean trip length and total trips by trip purpose and trips per dwelling unit for various sample sizes. The curves which were developed from the relationship between the standard deviation of the mean and the square root of sample size are shown in Figures 17 and 18. They give the expected error which would occur in the indicated parameters for various sample sizes, based on the known variance in the trip data.

A statistical analysis of the ability of small samples to adequately estimate trip production and average trip length characteristics in the Pittsburgh, Pa., study area has also been made. The results of this analysis, shown in Figures 19 and 20, indicate the reliability of small sample home interview surveys in determining the overall travel characteristics of an urban area.

The research discussed in the next section of this report is based entirely on the sample size analyses. It utilizes the results of the 599 sub-

sample of the Sioux Falls home interview survey and the standard external cordon survey in calibrating a synthetic gravity model.

Determining Zonal Trip Production and Attraction Values

As stated earlier, two of the basic parameters required to estimate trip interchanges by the gravity model formula are the number of trips produced by each zone and the number of trips attracted to each zone for each trip purpose category. This information cannot be obtained directly from a small sample home interview. Consequently, some assumption has to be made as to how the total number of trip productions and trip attractions distribute themselves on a zonal basis.

The assumptions made and procedures used to obtain zonal trip production and attraction values in this research are very similar to previously reported synthetic procedures [1, 17]. These procedures make use of detailed socioeconomic data in developing productions and attractions for use with the gravity model trip distribution technique. For example, labor force can be used to indicate work trip production, employment can be used for work trip attraction, and retail sales for nonwork trip attraction.

TABLE 11 Total Internal Vehicular Trip Production Rates by Trip Purpose, Sioux Falls, 1956[a]

Trip Purpose	Trips per Car
Home-based work trips	1.36
Home-based nonwork trips	2.84
Nonhome-based trips	2.98
Total vehicular trips	7.18

[a] Information included in this table includes travel data from both the 599 home interview sample and the truck and taxi surveys.

Table 11 indicates that there was a total of 7.18 trips made for every car owned by the persons who were interviewed; 1.36 of these were work trips, 2.84 were nonwork trips, and 2.98 were nonhome-based trips. By applying these rates to the total number of automobiles in the area, a total number of trips, by trip purpose, can be obtained. The total number of automobiles in the study area can be obtained from several sources such as census data (only for the census year), state, county, or city auto registration records, or special surveys. In this study the information was obtained from the 1956 comprehensive home interview survey. The resulting estimates of total trip production for each trip purpose are given in Table 12. Since total trip productions for the entire study area must equal total trip attractions for the entire study area in each trip purpose category, estimates of total trip attractions are also available from this procedure and are given in Table 12.

Home-Based Auto-Driver Work Trips. As one might suspect, work trips are closely associated with labor force and employment; these were

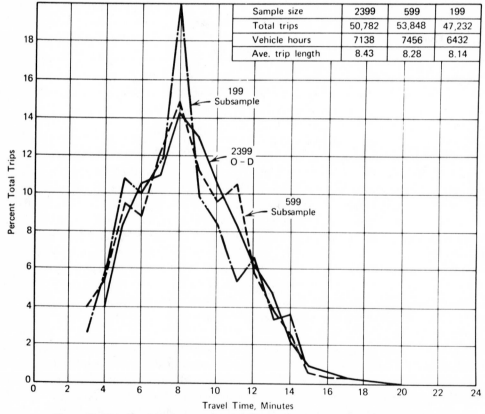

Sample size	2399	599	199
Total trips	50,782	53,848	47,232
Vehicle hours	7138	7456	6432
Ave. trip length	8.43	8.28	8.14

Figure 15 Trip-length frequency distributions, home-based, nonwork trips, Sioux Falls, 1956.

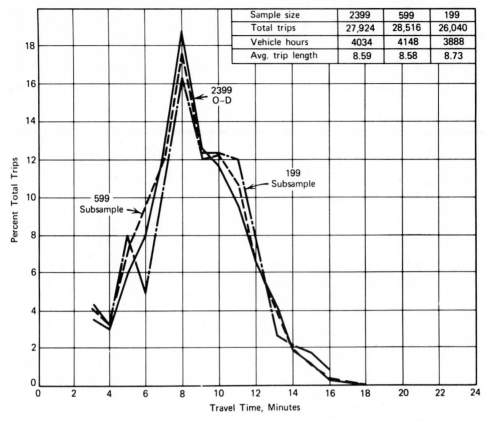

Sample size	2399	599	199
Total trips	27,924	28,516	26,040
Vehicle hours	4034	4148	3888
Avg. trip length	8.59	8.58	8.73

Figure 16 Trip-length frequency distributions, nonhome-based trips, Sioux Falls, 1956.

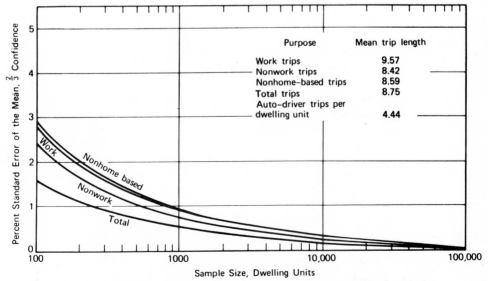

Purpose	Mean trip length
Work trips	9.57
Nonwork trips	8.42
Nonhome–based trips	8.59
Total trips	8.75
Auto–driver trips per dwelling unit	4.44

Figure 17 Percent standard error of mean trip length versus sample size in dwelling units, Sioux Falls, 1956.

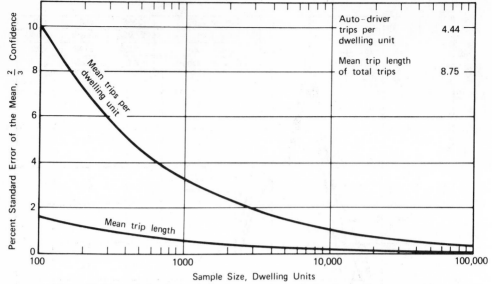

Figure 18 Percent standard error versus sample size in dwelling units for mean trip length and trips per dwelling unit, Sioux Falls, 1956.

the basic socio-economic data used to determine zonal production and attraction values for this trip purpose.

Zonal Trip Productions. These values for the 74 internal zones for this trip purpose were derived from zonal information on the labor force. Labor force data are generally available from sources such as census reports, labor statistics, and reports. In this research, the information for each zone was taken from data available for Sioux Falls. From studies in other areas [1, 17], it has been found that there are about 0.80 daily work trips produced (one-way) for each person in the labor force. This figure differs from 1.0 work trips (one-way) because

some persons in the labor force are unemployed, on vacation, walk to work, etc. An examination of the survey data in the Sioux Falls area indicated similar trip rates. Consequently, to determine the total number of work trip productions by auto and transit in each zone, the labor force in each internal zone was first multiplied by 0.80.

To determine transit usage, the information given in Table 13 was used. This information was developed from survey data in Chicago, Ill. By entering this table with the zonal information on car ownership and net residential density, an index of transit usage is obtained. The resulting zonal indices were then totaled and equated to the work trip transit usage for the Sioux Falls study as determined from the small sample home

TABLE 12 Total Vehicular Trip Productions and Attractions by Trip Purpose, Sioux Falls, 1956

	Productions			Attractions		
Trip Purpose	Internal[a]	External[b]	Total	Internal[a]	External[b]	Total
Work	27,475	2,175	29,650	28,212	1,438	29,650
Nonwork	57,219	8,010	65,229	60,123	5,106	65,229
Nonhome-based	59,966	4,956	64,922	59,847	5,075	64,922
Total	144,660	15,141	159,801	148,182	11,619	159,801

[a] These figures obtained by multiplying trip rates given in Table 11 by total cars owned by residents of study area.
[b] These figures from standard external cordon survey.

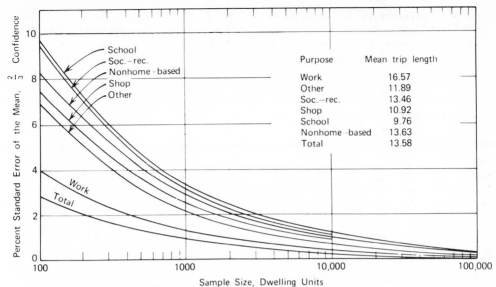

Figure 19   Percent standard error of mean trip length versus sample size in dwelling units, Pittsburgh, Pa., 1958.

interview survey. A correction factor was developed which, when applied to the previously developed indices, would yield figures on zonal work trip transit usage; these figures, when totaled, would agree with that shown for the total study area by the small sample. The application of this correction factor was based on the assumption that a three-dimensional plot of the characteristics of variation in transit usage would maintain the same form and shape from one city to another. This correction factor for Sioux Falls was 0.5, and when applied to the zonal indices, it brought the total estimated work transit trips into agreement with the total from the small sample. The number of person work trips made by auto for each zone was then obtained by subtracting these transit work trips from the total person work trips for each zone. To correct for car occupancy and to arrive at auto-driver work trips, the information from

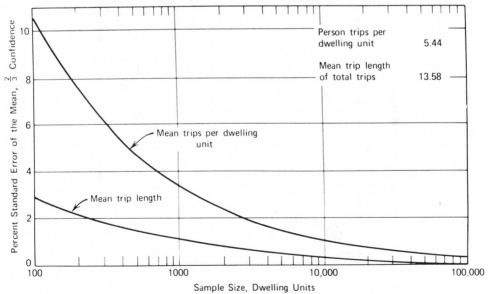

Figure 20   Percent standard error versus sample size in dwelling units for mean trip length and trips per dwelling unit, Pittsburgh, Pa., 1958.

TABLE 13 Percentage of All Work Trips Made by Transit (17)

	Work Trips by Transit (%)					
	Net Land per Family					
Cars per 1000 Persons	10,000 Sq Ft	5000 Sq Ft	2500 Sq Ft	1200 Sq Ft	600 Sq Ft	300 Sq Ft
500	5	7	11	19	33	65
450	7	9	13	21	35	67
400	9	11	15	23	37	69
350	11	13	17	25	39	71
300	13	15	19	27	41	73
275	14	16	20	28	42	74
250	15	17	21	29	43	75
225	16	18	22	30	44	76
200	17	19	23	31	45	77
175	18	20	24	32	46	78
150	19	21	25	33	47	79
125	20	22	26	34	48	80

Table 14 was applied to the total automobile work trips previously developed for each zone. Table 14 shows the relationship between car ownership and car occupancy, as developed from data in the Chicago area. Assuming that the relationship between car occupancy and car ownership is relatively stable from urban area to

TABLE 14 Relationship Between Car Occupancy and Car Ownership for Total Work Trips (17)

Cars per 1000 Persons	Persons per Car
500	1.20
450	1.23
400	1.27
350	1.30
300	1.33
250	1.40
200	1.46
150	1.52
100	1.65

urban area, the information in Table 14 is also usable in Sioux Falls.

For each of the 10 external stations in Sioux Falls, the number of automobile work trips produced by each station was estimated as a percentage of the adjusted total trips for all purposes recorded at all stations during a standard external cordon survey. The adjusted total trips for all stations were obtained by deducting the through trips from the total external station trips and analyzing the remaining trips. The adjusted total station trips consisted of auto and taxi trips between the external stations and the

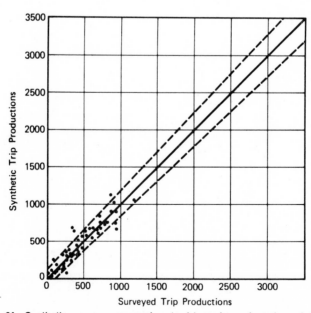

Figure 21 Synthetic versus surveyed auto-driver, home-based work-trip productions, Sioux Falls, 1956.

zones. The percentage of automobile work trips produced by the 10 external stations was determined to be 20 percent of this adjusted external station volume.

To determine the accuracy of these procedures, the auto-driver work trip productions estimated for each zone were compared with those shown by the 1956 comprehensive O-D survey. The results are shown in Figure 21. These comparisons were also analyzed using the RMS error criteria described earlier, and the analysis indicated very close agreement between the actual and the estimated values. The limits of one RMS error are shown as dashed lines in Figure 21.

Zonal Trip Attractions. These values for each of the 74 internal zones were developed from zonal employment information. Information on the number of people employed in each zone was available from employment statistics and also from information collected in a special survey by the Sioux Falls Chamber of Commerce. From an analysis of the data, it was determined that each employee in Sioux Falls attracted about 0.83 person work trips per day. The remaining employees were not recorded as making work trips because of illness, vacations, and walk to work trips. Consequently, to obtain an estimate of the total person work trips attracted to each zone, zonal employment figures were multiplied by 0.83. Corrections were then made for transit usage and car occupancy by using the information in Tables 13 and 14, as previously described for work trip productions, to arrive at auto-driver work trip attractions. In addition to these two corrections, a control figure for work trips to the CBD was also applied. Essentially, the estimated auto-driver work trips to the CBD were factored to meet the number indicated by the small sample and the external survey. All non-CBD zones were then factored in a similar manner so that the total auto-driver work trips remained the same.

For each of the 10 external stations, auto-driver work trip attractions were determined in the same manner as external station auto-driver work trip productions. The percentage of total station auto-driver trips (minus through trips) which were attracted by the external stations was determined to be 6.0 percent.

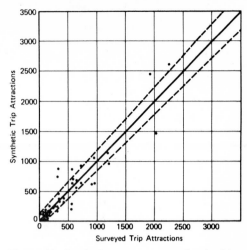

Figure 22 Synthetic versus surveyed auto-driver, home-based work-trip attractions, Sioux Falls, 1956.

To determine the accuracy of these procedures, the auto-driver work trip attractions estimated for each zone were compared with those shown by the 1956 comprehensive O-D survey. The results are shown in Figure 22. These comparisons were analyzed in the same manner as the work trip productions and the analysis indicated very close agreement between the actual and the estimated values.

Home-Based Auto-Driver Nonwork Trips. Zonal trip productions for the 74 internal zones for this purpose of trip were derived from zonal data on car ownership obtained from the O-D survey. As previously pointed out, however, car ownership data are also generally available from several other sources. Table 11 indicates that there are 2.84 home-based auto-driver nonwork trips per car. This figure was applied to the number of cars owned by the residents of each of the internal zones to determine trip production values for this trip purpose. For the 10 external stations, the nonwork trip productions were obtained in the same manner as described for external station auto-driver work trip productions. Nonwork trip productions were determined to be 30 percent of the total station volume. To test the accuracy of these procedures, the auto-driver nonwork trip productions estimated for each zone were compared with those shown by the 1956 comprehensive O-D survey. The results are shown in Figure 23.

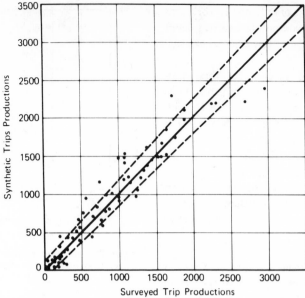

Figure 23 Synthetic versus surveyed auto-driver, home-based nonwork trip productions, Sioux Falls, 1956.

These comparisons were analyzed and the results indicated very close agreement between the actual and the estimated values.

Zonal trip attractions for the 74 internal zones for this trip purpose were derived from zonal data on population and retail sales. By dividing the total internal auto-driver nonwork trip attractions into the total population of the area, the population per attraction for this purpose was obtained. By repeating this process for the total retail sales in the area, the unit of sales per attraction was also obtained. By dividing the larger of these rates (population) by the smaller (retail sales) it was found that 1.69 units of retail sales were required to attract each nonwork trip, whereas 1.00 units of population were required to attract each nonwork trip. By using this technique a weighting factor equal to population + 1.69 × retail sales was established as an indicator of the auto-driver nonwork trip attractions in each zone. Consequently, the total number of attractions for this purpose were prorated to the zones using this weighting factor. As in the case of the auto-driver work trip attractions, nonwork trip attractions were factored to insure that the CBD attraction values are equal to those shown by the small sample survey data. The non-CBD attractions were then adjusted accordingly to keep the total

attractions the same as shown by the small sample.

For the 10 external stations, trip attractions for this trip purpose were obtained in the same manner as described for external station auto-driver work trip productions. The percentage of total station auto-driver trips (minus the through trips) which were nonwork trips was determined to be 20 percent.

To test the accuracy of these procedures, the auto-driver nonwork trip attractions estimated for each zone were compared with those shown by the 1956 comprehensive O-D survey. The results, shown in Figure 24, were analyzed and indicated reasonable agreement between the actual and estimated values.

Nonhome-Based Auto-Driver Trips. Several studies have reported that auto-driver nonhome-based trip production is associated with car ownership [1, 17]. Because by definition the trip productions are equal to trip origins and trip attractions are equal to trip destinations for nonhome-based trips, production and attraction values should be equal on a zonal basis as well as on a study area basis. Since origins should closely agree with destinations on a zonal basis during the 24-hr day, productions must also agree closely with attractions. This information was used in determining zonal trip productions and attractions for nonhome-based auto-driver trips in this research project. Zonal trip productions and attractions for the 74 internal zones for this trip purpose were derived from zonal data on car ownership, which in this research was obtained from the origin-destination survey. Table 11 indicates that there are 2.98 nonhome-based vehicular trips per car. This figure was applied to the number of cars owned in each internal zone to determine trip production values for this trip purpose.

For the 10 external stations, trip productions and attractions were obtained in the same manner as described for external station auto-driver work productions. The percentages which were nonhome-based auto-driver productions and attractions were determined to be 18.5 and 19.0, respectively.

To test the accuracy of these procedures, the auto-driver nonhome-based trip productions and attractions estimated for each zone were compared with those shown by the 1956 comprehensive O-D survey. An analysis of the results shown in Figures 25 and 26 indicated rather poor agreement between the actual and estimated values. An examination of the internal nonhome-based trip productions and attractions from other studies showed similar agreement for these values.

Determining Trip Distribution Pattern

The previously described procedures provided zonal trip production and attraction values for each of the trip purpose categories. However, before interchanges can be calculated using the gravity model formula, some measure of spatial separation between the zones must be developed. For the purpose of this phase of the research, the minimum path driving times between zones, the intrazonal times, and the terminal times used were as developed for the previous phase of this work. In addition, some measure of the effect of this spatial separation on trip interchange between zones, $F_{(t_{i-j})}$, is also required. In this phase of the research, full use was made of the travel time factors already developed for each trip purpose during the previous phase of the research. This was done because the trip length frequency curves for the 599 subsample were so similar to those for the total sample which was used to develop the travel time factors. The values of these factors are shown in Table 3.

With all the required parameters available, the gravity model calculations were made to obtain a synthetic trip distribution pattern. This pattern was then compared to the O-D survey data to determine the accuracy and, consequently, the ability of the simplified procedures described in this report to supply the necessary

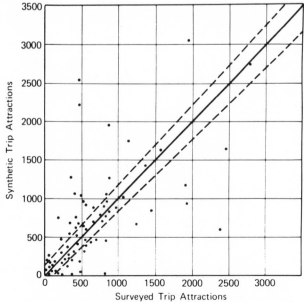

Figure 24 Synthetic versus surveyed auto-driver, home-based nonwork trip attractions, Sioux Falls, 1956.

information for adequately simulating trip distribution patterns. Several tests were involved in the comparisons.

First, the synthetic trip length frequency distributions and average trip lengths were compared with those from the O-D survey for each trip purpose category. The results for work trips are shown in Figure 27; the other two

purposes also exhibit very close agreement. The results of this test indicated that the decision to use the travel time factors from the previous phase of this research was a correct one. If an initial set of travel time factors had been assumed and the normal trial and adjustment process utilized, the final result would have been travel time factors identical to those shown in Table 3.

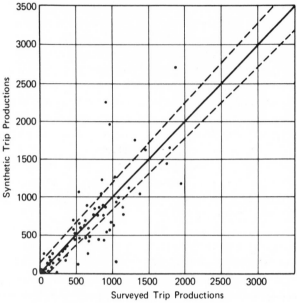

Figure 25 Synthetic versus surveyed nonhome-based vehicular trip productions, Sioux Falls, 1956.

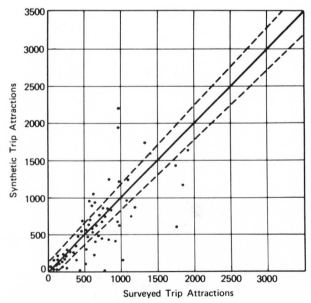

Figure 26 Synthetic versus surveyed nonhome-based vehicular trip attractions, Sioux Falls, 1956.

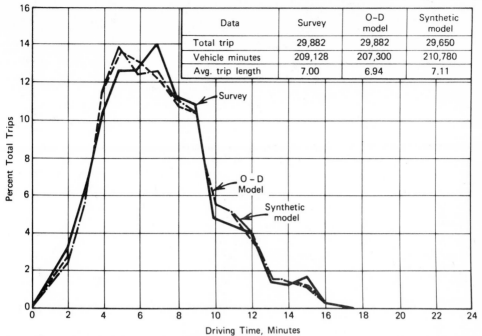

Data	Survey	O–D model	Synthetic model
Total trip	29,882	29,882	29,650
Vehicle minutes	209,128	207,300	210,780
Avg. trip length	7.00	6.94	7.11

Figure 27   Trip-length frequency distributions, home-based, auto-driver work trips, Sioux Falls, 1956.

Tests were made comparing the trips attracted to each zone by the gravity model with those shown by the synthetic procedures for each trip purpose. The results for all purposes indicated an accuracy within one RMS error. Figure 28 shows the results for nonwork trips which had the largest scatter.

TABLE 15   Comparison of Total Vehicular Trips Crossing Big Sioux River, Sioux Falls, 1956

Facility	Vol. Count	O-D Survey	Syn. Gravity Model
Cherry Rock Ave.	1,511	1,640	1,512
Cliff Ave., S.	9,132	8,420	9,208
Tenth St.	14,842	16,296	16,832
Eighth St.	8,606	6,612	6,752
Sixth St.	3,864	2,900	4,564
McClellan St.	3,069	2,596	1,972
Cliff Ave., N.	4,699	4,156	2,048
Totals	45,723	42,620	42,888
Percent Diff. from Vol. Count		−6.8	−6.2
Percent Diff. from O-D Survey	+7.3		+0.6

Another test was made of the number of synthetic trips crossing the Big Sioux River. These figures were compared with those from the O-D survey and again, the differences were small (Table 15).

Synthetic trips to the CBD, for each trip purpose, were also compared with the same movements from the total sample. The results for work trips (Figure 29), indicate that there is no geographical bias present in the synthetic interchanges and that the discrepancies between the two sets of information are quite small.

Synthetic trip interchanges for total trips were then assigned to the minimum path driving time network. The expanded trips from the full O-D sample were also assigned. These two sources of information were then compared by analyzing the differences over the comprehensive series of screenline crossings shown in Figure 10. The results of the comparisons are given in Table 16.

Finally, a statistical comparison of the actual and the estimated trips was made for each trip purpose (Table 17). An analysis of the comparisons indicated acceptable results for all purposes when compared with similar studies [7, 8, 11] and with the comparisons resulting from the first phase of this research (Table 6).

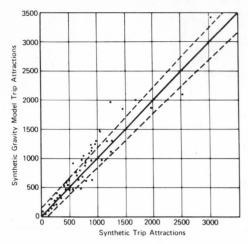

Figure 28 Synthetic versus synthetic gravity model home-based, auto-driver nonwork trip attractions, Sioux Falls, 1956.

TABLE 16 Total Trips Crossing Screenlines, Sioux Falls, 1956

Screenline No.	O-D Survey Vol.	Syn. Gravity Model Vol.	Diff. from O-D (%)
1	7,952	7,280	−8.5
2	21,012	21,120	+0.5
3	13,516	13,224	−2.2
4	11,384	10,428	−8.4
5	9,744	8,516	−12.6
6	8,784	8,440	−3.9
7	6,280	6,520	+3.8
8	6,568	6,100	−7.1
9	2,264	1,980	−12.5
10	17,448	18,420	+5.6
11	5,868	4,836	−17.6
12	5,592	3,872	−30.8
13	13,656	15,280	+10.6
14	22,908	23,584	+2.9
15	33,220	33,204	0.0
16	10,032	10,996	+9.6
17	13,424	14,220	+5.9
18	9,724	12,200	+25.5
19	10,060	10,720	+6.6
20	5,332	5,476	+2.7
21	8,496	8,364	−1.5
22	13,332	14,192	+6.5
23	41,500	41,468	−0.1

TABLE 17 Comparisons of District-to-District Movements[a]

Volume Group	O-D Survey Trip Mean	O-D Survey Trip Freq.	RMS Error Abs.	RMS Error Percent
(a) Home-Based Auto-Driver Work Trips				
0– 99	21	400	20	95.24
100– 199	133	40	58	43.61
200– 299	259	13	119	45.95
300– 499	402	13	98	24.38
500–1499	920	8	186	20.22
(b) Home-Based Auto-Driver Nonwork Trips				
0– 99	27	423	28	103.70
100– 199	136	53	83	61.03
200– 299	239	28	103	43.10
300– 499	380	22	166	43.68
500– 999	728	22	282	38.74
1000–2999	1,711	9	343	20.05
(c) Nonhome-Based Auto-Driver Trips				
0– 99	25	473	24	96.00
100– 199	144	62	82	56.94
200– 299	241	30	122	50.62
300– 499	385	33	157	40.78
500– 999	773	9	289	37.39
1000–3999	1,311	8	457	34.86

[a] 1956 O-D survey data vs synthetic gravity model estimates, relative difference measured in terms of percent RMS error (see footnote to Table 6).

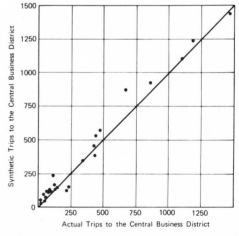

Figure 29 Actual versus synthetic model nonhome-based vehicular trips to CBD, Sioux Falls, 1956.

SUMMARY AND CONCLUSIONS

The application of the gravity model theory in a particular small urban area was investigated and, because it was the theory of the gravity model which was being tested, the model was developed using all of the travel information normally collected during a comprehensive O-D survey obtained by using the dwelling unit sample size recommended in the Public Roads Home Interview Manual [3]. The home interview survey provided the data on trip production, trip attraction, and trip length distribution needed for developing the model, as well as information on the zonal trip interchanges used to test the gravity model results.

A three purpose gravity model was calibrated following the procedures outlined in this paper but more fully detailed previously [15]. The calibrated gravity model was then thoroughly tested against the O-D trip distributions and volume counts. These tests revealed that the gravity model formulation adequately simulated trip distribution patterns for the Sioux Falls area.

Having determined that the three purpose model was adequate, when based on the data from the full O-D survey, we then investigated the question of reducing the O-D survey sample necessary to develop the model. To determine the appropriate sample sizes to investigate, the results of studies of small samples in other cities were collected and analyzed. Comparisons were made with the full field sample, by trip purpose, of total trips, average trip lengths, and trip length frequency distributions for each of several subsamples. From the tests made in Sioux Falls and from an analysis of other studies, it was determined that about 600 home interview samples in combination with the standard external cordon survey provided adequate data for obtaining, by purpose, total trips, trip length frequency distributions, and average trip lengths.

Since a small sample does not yield stable data on zonal trip productions and attractions by trip purpose, these items of information must be obtained by other techniques. Synthetic procedures based on detailed socio-economic data were used for this purpose. The results of the synthetic procedures were compared to the O-D survey productions and attractions, and the procedures were shown to be satisfactory for computing productions and attractions for Sioux Falls.

Finally, the synthetic productions and attractions were combined with the travel time factors that reflected the 599 home interview sample to determine a trip distribution pattern for each trip purpose. The results were compared with the O-D survey distribution and the patterns agreed closely.

With these separate analyses completed, the following conclusions appear warranted:

1. The gravity model formula provided an adequate framework for determining trip distribution patterns for Sioux Falls.

2. A three purpose trip stratification of home-based work, nonwork, and nonhome-based trips was sufficient in the small urban area.

3. For Sioux Falls, a 599 home interview sample used in combination with detailed socio-economic data and the standard truck, taxi, and external cordon surveys provided sufficient data for a three purpose gravity model calibration. Sioux Falls is a self-contained urban area with a single center and no strong travel linkages to other urban areas. This city does not exhibit any social or economic factors which might have a significant effect on travel patterns, and which might require adjustments to the gravity model trip distributions. The findings for Sioux Falls may not apply to cities exhibiting different characteristics.

4. The synthetic procedures used in this research to compute zonal trip productions and attractions are satisfactory for this small urban area when used in combination with detailed socio-economic data and with limited travel data from a small sample survey.

Further research should be conducted to determine if the findings for this small urban area can have wider application.

REFERENCES

1. C. F. Barnes, Jr., 1961. Integrating land use and traffic forecasting. *Highway Research Board Bulletin, 279*: 1–13.
2. R. J. Bouchard, and C. E. Pyers, 1965. Use of gravity model for describing urban travel. *Highway Research Record, 88*: 1–43. 1C.
3. Bureau of Public Roads, 1954. *Manual of procedures for home interview traffic study.* Washington: Bureau of Public Roads, revised edition.
4. Bureau of Public Roads, 1963. *Calibrating and testing a gravity model for any size urban area.* Washington: Bureau of Public Roads. MC.
5. Bureau of Public Roads, 1963. *Calibrating and testing a gravity model with a small computer.* Washington: Bureau of Public Roads. MC.
6. Connecticut Development Commission and Connecticut Highway Department, 1962. *The Connecticut interregional land use/transportation program, a program of integrated planning for long-range land use and transportation development of the State of Connecticut, prospectus.* Working paper, Connecticut Interregional Planning Program. 8C.
7. E. Duckstad K. E. Duke, R. G. Spiegelman, B. Lefkowitz and A. Painter, 1962. Economic population and trip projections. *City-county highway plan for San Mateo County*; San Jose: G. S. Nolte and Associates, 92–114, 2C.
8. K. E. Heanue, L. B. Hamner, and R. M. Hall, 1965. Adequacy of clustered home interview sampling for calibrating a gravity model trip distribution formula. *Highway Research Record, 88*: 116–136.
9. J. W. Horn, D. B. Stafford, D. R. Hinson and G. L. Reed, 1964. *An investigation to correlate synthetic land use origin and destination techniques to field conducted origin and destination surveys, final report.* Raleigh: University of North Carolina at Raleigh Highway Research Program. MS.
10. Los Angeles Regional Transportation Study, 1963. *Volume I: base year report 1960.* Los Angeles: Los Angeles Regional Transportation Study. 1C.
11. Louisiana Department of Highways, 1962. *New Orleans metropolitan area transportation study, 1960–1980, Volume II—outlook for the future.* Baton Rouge: Louisiana Department of Highways Traffic and Planning Section. 1C.
12. B. L. Smith, 1965. Gravity model theory applied to a small city using a small sample of origin-destination data. *Highway Research Record, 88*: 85–115.
13. A. B. Sosslau, and G. E. Brokke, 1960. Appraisal of sample size based on Phoenix O-D survey data. *Highway Research Board Bulletin, 253*: 114–127.
14. South Dakota Department of Highways, 1960. *Parking survey, Sioux Falls central business district.* Pierre: South Dakota Department of Highways Research and Planning Division.
15. South Dakota Department of Highways, 1956. *Sioux Falls origin and destination traffic study, 1956.* Pierre: South Dakota Department of Highways Research and Planning Division.
16. A. M. Voorhees, 1959. Use of mathematical models in estimating travel. *Proceedings of the American Society of Civil Engineers, Journal of the Highway Division, 85*(HW4): 129–141.
17. R. H. Wiant, 1961. A simplified method for forecasting urban traffic. *Highway Research Board Bulletin, 279*: 128–145.

21

A TEST OF SOME FIRST GENERATION RESIDENTIAL LAND USE MODELS

CARL N. SWERDLOFF
JOSEPH R. STOWERS

This paper reports on a comparative evaluation of five operational residential land use forecasting techniques, four of which have been previously used in urban transportation planning studies. These techniques are representative of the earliest of efforts in the development of operational urban activity simulation models and continue to serve, either in their original or in modified form, a great number of transportation planning organizations. Urban activity simulation models currently under development, while in most cases considerably more complex and, hopefully, more accurate, in many instances draw upon notions and fundamental concepts which either originated with or were adapted to these early techniques. Improvements being introduced in these later, second generation models include more complex statistical estimating procedures, the stratification of residential locators into several distinct groups, and the incorporation of behavioral relationships in the model formulation. These newer techniques may require several years of research, evaluation, and refinement before they become fully operational. Meanwhile, the

SOURCE: Reprinted from *Highway Research Record*, *126*: 38–59 (1966).

less sophisticated approaches evaluated in this report should continue to be useful to smaller metropolitan areas lacking the resources for developmental research.

The primary objective of this project was to compare the relative accuracy of these approaches through a series of ex post facto tests, holding all conditions constant except the interrelationships among variables, so that differences in "forecasts" would be a function only of inherent differences in models.

There is a temptation to interpret a study of this nature as a contest of sorts and to turn to a table of results for the proclaimed "winner." Any such evaluation of the results is unwarranted for several reasons. First, the contestants are not all of the same class. Some are more truly "forecasts," and some are merely data fitting problems. The latter involve fitting different numbers of parameters. More information is used in some than in others. Perhaps most important, the results represent a sample of one, out of a rather large universe of possible test conditions. Entirely different results might occur in other cities, at other time periods, by other forecasters, working with other data problems.

GENERAL PROCEDURES

The five residential land use forecasting procedures are each variants of work done by others. The only innovations introduced here are the authors' simplifications and modifications to suit peculiar test conditions—apologies are made to the progenitors of these models for possible misrepresentations of their original work. In any realistic planning application, more care would necessarily be given to the particular forecasting tool used. Trends would be more carefully analyzed, the forecasters would be more familiar with the area, and output of models would be scrutinized in detail and modified as judgment indicated. In contrast, the authors have applied the models coldly and crudely, accepting the immediate output in an attempt to make objective comparisons.

The techniques used were (a) the density-saturation gradient method, (b) accessibility model, (c) regression, and (d and e) two intervening opportunity models.

The density - saturation gradient method (DSGM) is a simplification of the approach used by the Chicago Area Transportation Study [6, 7]. Of the five techniques, the DSGM is least computer oriented, more demanding of subjective inputs, and therefore least suitable for objective comparison with other approaches, particularly when the forecasters are not intimately familiar with the area. The method is based essentially on the regularity of the decline in density and percent saturation with distance from the CBD, and the stability of these relationships through time.

The simple accessibility model is based upon the concept formulated by Walter Hansen [8, 9]. Growth in a particular area is hypothesized to be related to two factors: the accessibility of the area to some regional activity distribution, and the amount of land available in the area for development. The accessibility of an area is an index representing the closeness of the area to all other activity in the region. All areas compete for the aggregate growth and share in proportion to their comparative accessibility positions weighted by their capability to accommodate development as measured by vacant, usable land.

The third method used in this study, multiple linear regression, is a popular approach because of its operational simplicity and ability to handle several variables [1, 4, 5]. The proportion of total regional growth which locates in a particular area is assumed to be related to the magnitude of a number of variables which in some manner are measures of geographic desirability as viewed by those making the locational decision. The procedure is to determine those factors, and their weights, which in linear combination can be related to the amount of growth which has been observed to take place over a past time period. These factors (called independent variables) and their weights (regression coefficients), in linear combination (the regression equation) can then be applied to the individual analysis areas to forecast the magnitude of growth (the dependent variable).

Although more commonly applied to the problem of trip distribution, the intervening opportunities models can be used in simulating the distribution of urban activity. Two separate and distinct formulations were applied in this study, both based upon the general notion that the probability that an opportunity is accepted decreases as some function of the number of opportunities ranked closer to a central distributing point. The Stouffer formulation was originally applied to intra-urban migration [13]. A related formulation has more recently been investigated as a trip distribution technique [15]. Schneider's formulation was originally applied to trip distribution [3] and is currently being used in distributing urban activity [10, 11].

The test area used in this study was Greensboro, North Carolina. This city was chosen for a number of reasons. First and most important, a rather extensive information file on a small area basis for two time periods (1948 and 1960) was available. Secondly, it was felt that Greensboro was representative of the kind and size city for which forecasting techniques of the kind being examined would still be most appropriate after the development of more sophisticated models in the largest metropolitan areas.

The data for the study came from two major sources. The data obtained from the University of North Carolina contained a wide variety of information for the Greensboro area coded to

3,980 grid cells, each one 1000 ft square, for a circular area of about 7-mi radius. These data included quantitative measures of land use, population, residential density, proximity to various activities and to the CBD, and certain environmental measures [2]. With certain exceptions, these data were available at the grid level for two time periods, 1948 and 1960.

The data supplied by Alan M. Voorhees and Associates included 1960 population, employment, accessibility to shopping, and accessibility to employment, for each of about 250 zones. These latter accessibility measures were computed from zone-to-zone traveltimes over the highway network.

A number of problems were encountered in combining the data from these two sources in a form suitable for testing of the models. Principal among these were the following.

1. *The aggregation of grids to zones.* Since it was felt desirable to work at a level of aggregation more typical of transportation studies, it was necessary to define new zone boundaries following grid lines approximating the irregular old zone boundaries. No important error was introduced since only accessibility scores from the original zone file were used in subsequent analyses—all extensive quantities used were grid aggregates.

2. *Estimation of 1948 dwelling units.* Consideration of all data sources and the purpose of the study led to the decision to use dwelling units as the item to be predicted. However, 1948 dwelling unit data were not directly available. Estimates were made and various checks applied by using 1948 land area, a 1948 USGS map for suburban areas, 1950 census block statistics for the central city (changes were not large for the inner area from 1948–1960), and the 1960 land area and dwelling unit densities.

3. *Estimation of accessibility measures for 1960 for certain zones at the fringe.* The area covered by the zone file did not extend to the boundaries of the grid coverage area in all directions. Rather than eliminate this area entirely, estimates of accessibility measures were made for about one-half of the outer ring of zones by examining contours of iso-accessibility lines, which follow fairly regular patterns in the fringe area.

MODEL DESCRIPTION AND METHODOLOGY

Density-Saturation Gradient Method

The DSGM is the least formally structured forecasting procedure of the five. No formal theoretical statements or mathematical hypotheses are required, although the staff of the Chicago Area Transportation Study have presented excellent conceptual explanations of their empirical findings and rationale for their projections [7]. This theoretical development, however, is not essential to the purpose of this paper.

Before discussion of the actual application of the DSGM to the Greensboro area, mention should be made of certain reservations which existed prior to the testing. The only known previous application of this approach was for the Chicago area. There was some initial fear that the regularities in activity distribution about the central place, which is axiomatic to the method, would not be manifest for a city of the size of Greensboro. The declines in density and percent capacity result from the operation of the competitive land market, a mechanism which might not exert the dominating influence upon spatial organization in a city of Greensboro's size. It will be seen that these fears were unwarranted, and that in fact the distribution of residential activity was markedly structured about the CBD.

Two semi-independent forecasts were made using the DSGM in order to determine the sensitivity of the results to variations in the critical assumptions made. A principal distinction was that the first trial was made using air-line distance from the high value corner (HVC) as the key spatial variable, whereas traveltime to the HVC was used in the second trial. (The HVC is a point representative of the hypothetical activity center of the CBD).

Figure 1 shows the relationship between 1948 dwelling unit density and air-line distance from the HVC. Each point on this plot represents the gross residential density (street area included) for a ring around the HVC. Each ring is defined by the boundaries of all zones whose centroids fall within $\pm\frac{1}{2}$ mile of the nominal distance of the ring from the HVC with the exception of the

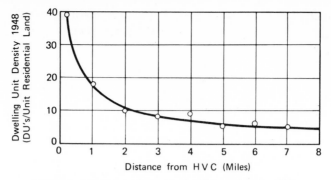

Figure 1 Dwelling unit density by distance bands, 1948.

first or CBD ring. The plot indicates a surprisingly regular decline in residential densities with distance from downtown in Greensboro in 1948. This was encouraging since the reliability of the DSGM depends greatly on the strength and stability of this relationship.

The method depends equally upon the relationship between distance and percent saturation. To compute the latter, residential capacity must be defined. Mathematically capacity is defined as existing dwelling units plus the product of vacant available, suitable land, and expected residential density. A decision had to be made at this juncture as to the density values to be used in the computation. Theoretically this should be the anticipated average density at which all future residential development will occur. These values should be developed from an intensive analysis of trends in residential density patterns and zoning policies. For purposes of this study, however, future densities for each zone were assumed to be those given by the smooth hand-fitted curve of Figure 1. Prior to the acceptance of this single curve for the density gradient, gradients were plotted for each of five sectors. Although these plots exhibited less regular relationships, no significant variation between sectors was noted.

Vacant, suitable land for residential development was estimated by subtracting marginal land and land zoned for nonresidential uses from 1948 nonurban land. A systematic, but subjective procedure was used in the treatment of zoning: land was weighted by factors ranging from 0 for grids zoned only for industry to 1.0 for grids zoned only for residential use; land in grids zoned for mixed uses and other nonindustrial uses was weighted subjectively on a scale from zero to unity.

Having future residential development densities and vacant available land, it was possible next to compute both the residential saturations, in dwelling units and existing percent saturation, for each distance ring from the HVC. The latter values, resulting from the division of saturation into 1948 dwelling units, were then used to construct the percent saturation gradient. Figure 2 conforms very well with the plot expected for an urban area. The rather distinct and sharp transition between the 3½- and 4½-mi points indicates a transition from the area of urban character into the predominantly rural portions of the study region. The almost negligible slope of the curve beyond the 4½-mi point is indicative of agricultural development and the absence of any strong competition for location with reference to central Greensboro.

The next step involved the 1960 projection of the percent saturation curve, also shown in Figure 2. (Percent saturation gradients by sector for 1948 were also plotted; however, as in the case of the density gradient, there was some additional scatteration of points, but no basis for using sector-specific gradients.) This is the most critical and subjective step in the forecasting process, the only restraint on the projected curve being that the area under the new curve must account for the projected regional growth. The number of dwelling units in the study area grew from a 1948 total of 27,191 to 41,250 in 1960 or a growth of 52 percent. One can proceed in almost an infinite number of ways insofar as establishing an acceptable projection of the percent saturation gradient. It was, however, found useful to first develop a feeling for the overall scale of the problem, that is, the area under the final curve which would be commensurate with the required final regional population. As a first approximation to the 1960 gradient each ordinate value was raised a distance equivalent to 52 percent of the 1948 value. The resultant curve then approximated the forecast condition under the assumption of uniform growth over the entire region. The following general criteria were then introduced to modify the naive first approximation of the shape of the gradient in 1960:

1.   The bulk of the residential growth would occur in the 2-, 3-, and 4-mi rings.

2.   The inner ring would suffer a slight decline.

3.   The shape of the gradient would tend to bow out in the 1- to 3-mi range.

4.   The sharp transition in slope of the 1948 saturation gradient observed at about the 4- to 5-mi point would become less abrupt in 1960.

5.   The areas 5 miles and beyond would show some exurban growth, but the general flat slope would remain.

Relatively few attempts were necessary to arrive at a solution which was of satisfactory shape and which conformed with the actual 1948–1960 increase in total dwelling units.

Multiplying the appropriate ordinate value from the forecast percent saturation gradient (Figure 2) by the ring saturation quantities established the forecast dwelling unit totals by analysis ring.

The projected growth of each ring was distributed to zones in a two-step process

following the logic of CATS. The allocation to districts (defined by ring-sector boundaries) was handicapped by a lack of historical data. Ideally the trends in land use composition and growth rates between sectors should be studied in detail. For trial one, however, the simple assumption was made that sectors would share growth in proportion to available residential capacity.

The final distribution to zones was based on a systematic, but subjective linear weighting of the following factors:

1.   Distance to convenience shopping,

2.   Available residential capacity,

3.   Distance to the major street system,

4.   Percent of industrial development in the zone, and

5.   Percent of residential development in the zone.

Trial two, which was conducted independently of trial one, differed from the above procedure in two principal ways:

1.   Traveltime to the HVC was substituted for airline distance as the major independent variable. Zones were aggregated into 1-min interval rings for all analyses.

2.   Ring growth was allocated to sectors (i.e., the district-level forecast) in proportion to the product of each sector's available residential capacity and the number of existing (1948) dwelling units.

Otherwise, the process followed that of trial one, including the method of estimating density

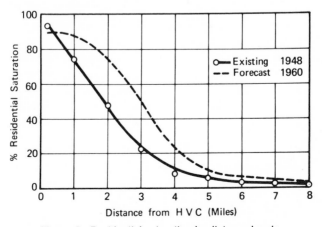

Figure 2   Residential saturation by distance bands.

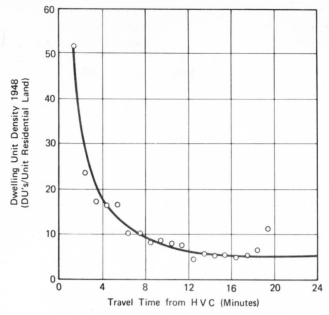

Figure 3 Dwelling unit density by time bands, 1948.

and holding capacity, the sector definitions, and the allocation of growth from districts to zones.

Figure 3 shows the dwelling unit density gradient as determined from the ring analysis for trial two. As expected the same general shape is observed as for trial one. Figure 4 shows both the percent saturation curve calculated for the 1948 base period, and the forecast of the 1960 percent saturation curve. The shape of the latter gradient is quite similar to that for trial one except for a slight decrease in the growth allocated to the inner rings, resulting in a lessening of the bowing effect and a reduction in the slope of the gradient in the intermediate areas.

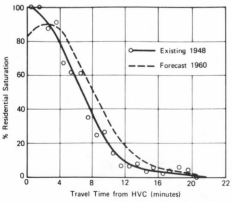

Figure 4 Residential saturation by time bands.

Accessibility Model

The generalized form of the accessibility model is as follows:

$$G_i = G_t \frac{A_i^a V_i}{\sum_i A_i^a V_i}$$

where

G_i = the forecast growth for zone i;

G_t = total regional growth = $\sum_i G_i$;

A_i = accessibility index for zone i;

V_i = vacant available land in zone i; and

a = empirically determined exponent.

The computation of the accessibility index traditionally is as follows:

$$A_i = \sum_j \frac{E_j}{T_{ij}^b}$$

where

E_j = a measure of activity in zone j (total employment used in this study);

T_{ij} = traveltime from zone i to zone j; and

b = an empirically determined exponent.

However, "friction factors" developed in the gravity model calibration by Alan M. Voorhees and Associates were actually used in the computation of accessibility:

$$A_i = \sum_j E_j F_{ij}$$

where F_{ij} is the friction of time separation of zones T_{ij} minutes apart. The F_{ij} values are approximately proportional to the actual number of trips T_{ij} minutes long per trip-end in each pair of zones T_{ij} minutes apart. In practice the computation of F_{ij} is considerably complicated by a desire to have the F_{ij} values form a smooth monotonic relation to T_{ij} yet maintain approximate equality between the resulting mean trip length and the actual mean trip length.

With the above definition of the model only one parameter, a, need be estimated to make the forecast. Two options were open:

1. Make a judgment of the value of a from previous work in other cities, and forecast 1960 zonal growth to have an independent test of the model; or
2. Fit a "best" value for a using the actual 1948–1960 changes in dwelling units.

Both options were actually used. For option 1 a value of 2 was assumed for a. (Hansen found that a value of about 2.7 was optimal for Washington, D. C.; the presumption that accessibility would have less influence in shaping growth in a smaller city is substantiated by the subsequent results in fitting values for a.) Methods used in fitting a to the 1948–1960 data are described in the Appendix.

Regression

For several reasons it was felt desirable to express the dependent variable of the multiple regression formulation as some function of the 1948–1960 growth rather than as some function of the absolute amount of cumulative development at a single point in time. The latter option was open, and has been used by others [2, 12]; however, it was rejected to maintain comparability with the dependent variables of the other models, as well as to conform to standard practice in transportation planning models. As has been pointed out by the Traffic Research Corporation [16], there is good reason to expect greater accuracy for relatively short-range forecasts when predicting increments of growth.

Using change in dwelling units, or some function thereof, as the dependent variable, it was not possible with the available data to produce an independent forecast to check against the 1960 data. The equation parameters had to be estimated from the full 1948–1960 data files. Hence, accuracy results are shown in the next section only for a fitted model, and not for a forecast, in contrast to the other 4 methods. Dwelling unit data for a third point in time would be required to examine the forecasting reliability of the calibrated regression equation.

The usual regression approach differs from the other models used in this study in two additional important ways:

1. Many, rather than one or two independent variables may be incorporated, and
2. Variables are related to growth only in linearly weighted combinations, although variables may be transformed prior to regression.

The latter restraint is imposed by the use of a standard regression program (the BIMD 34 stepwise multiple regression program developed by the UCLA Bio Medical Center for the IBM 7090/7094 was used in this work). Of course nonlinear regression equations may be developed, but different normal equations must be solved and standard regression programs may not be used.

Numerous equations were developed, each involving the testing of various hypotheses regarding the functional relationships between variables. A total of 44 independent variables plus certain selected nonlinear transformations were examined in all, including:

1. Measures of zone size and amount of land in different uses;
2. Accessibility to employment;
3. Time and distance to HVC;
4. Zonal employment, total and by major type;
5. Densities for 1948;
6. Vacant available land;
7. Zoning protection;
8. Land value; and
9. Proportions of total land and developed land in each major use.

Four definitions of the dependent variable were tested:

1. Increase in dwelling units (DU):
2. Log DU;
3. DU per unit of available land (DU/L); and
4. Log [DU/L].

The logarithmic transformations were employed to test certain hypotheses regarding exponential relationships, as for example, are expressed in the accessibility model. The growth-per-unit-of-available-land transformations were employed in an attempt to remove all measures of zone size from the equations, and thereby, to avoid the possibility of distorted relationships due to the pecularities of area definitions.

The final equation accepted after comparing the accuracy and reasonableness of all trials was

$$Y = -2.3 + 0.061X_1 + 0.00066X_2 \\ + 1.1X_3 - 0.11X_4 - 0.0073X_5$$

where

Y = logarithm of growth in dwelling units 1948–1960 per unit vacant land;

X_1 = zoning protection, 1948;

X_2 = percent of total land area in residential use, 1948;

X_3 = logarithm of accessibility to employment, 1960;

X_4 = dwelling unit density, 1948; and

X_5 = percent of total use land in industrial use, 1948.

The coefficient of correlation is 0.61. Table 1 contains the t and beta (β) values (standardized regression coefficient) for each of the independent variables in the equation. All regression coefficients are significantly different from zero with 95 percent confidence. Having the greatest β value, the transformed accessibility variable is shown to exhibit the most influence upon the estimate of the dependent variable. Percent of urban land which is in industrial use has the lowest β values and, therefore, contributes least to the total equation estimate.

TABLE 1 Relative Significance and Explanatory Power of Variables in Regression Equation

Independent Variable	t	β
Log accessibility to employment, 1960	4.30	0.321
Zoning code, 1948	2.89	0.213
Percent of total land residential, 1948	2.70	0.187
Dwelling unit density, 1948	−3.28	−0.177
Percent of urban land industrial, 1948	−2.98	−0.159

The zoning code was a value from 0 to 9, where a higher value indicated zoning control closer to single family residential only, and lower value marginal-to-no zoning control. The positive relationship then indicates the positive environmental influence of strict residential zoning policy. The positive contribution of accessibility to work areas is self-explanatory. Also, the positive contribution of percent of total area devoted to residential development is interpreted as a measure of residential clustering. The tendency for slow growth or even decline in the residential stock of the close in, old city areas, coupled with the rapid increase in the fringe and newly settled locations accounts for the negative coefficient for dwelling unit density. The negative contribution of percent industrial land is indicative of the restraint on new residential development in areas immediately adjacent to industrial areas.

Because the estimation was couched in both logarithmic and intensity units, several operational difficulties were introduced. The estimating equation was incapable of either accepting negative values for the dependent variable or estimating decline in any zone. All zones which suffered dwelling unit decline over the calibration period were approximated to have shown no change. An additional problem was encountered for several zones which experienced dwelling unit growth, but which had no vacant land available in 1948. Without some adjustment the growth intensity value becomes infinite. These few cases were handled by substituting large arbitrary values of growth intensity. Finally, there is no built-in provision, as there is for other models, to assure that the accumulated zonal estimates obtained from the regression equation solution will equal the actual total regional growth. All regression estimates had to be factored up to sum to the actual regional growth.

Two Intervening Opportunity Models

Although the two opportunity models tested are based on quite different initial assumptions and take on dissimilar mathematical form, nevertheless, both can be reduced to a simple general hypothesis. In the context of this problem, the probability that a suitable residential opportunity (a unit of available capacity) is accepted for development is hypothesized to be a monotonically decreasing function of the number of intervening opportunities, opportunities being ranked by time from the HVC.

Some improvement in these models could undoubtedly be made by allocating increments of growth from more than one point, perhaps from all major centers of employment in proportion to the amount of employment in each center. This would make the test of the intervening opportunities models more comparable to the accessibility model procedure.

Stouffer Formulation. The Stouffer model may be defined in the following manner:

$$g_p = \frac{kO_p}{O}$$

where

g_p = number of dwelling units forecast to be located in a particular area p;

O_p = opportunities in interval p;

O = total number of opportunities from central distribution point through interval p; and

k = constant of proportionality to assure that the total number of dwellings located equals the actual total growth.

As stated, the Stouffer formulation can be applied without the need for assuming any parameter values. However, it is an operational requirement that the study area be structured into a number of discrete geographic units which are then ranked from a central distribution point, the HVC in this case. One method of aggregating areas, which Strodtbeck has shown to have some appealing properties, is to delineate a small number of rings containing approximately equal numbers of opportunities [14]. For the initial application of the Stouffer model to the allocation of residential growth, the Greensboro study area was divided into 10 rings, each of which was composed of a whole number of zones and an approximately equal number of opportunities. Zones were assigned to rings according to their ranking in time from the HVC.

It was then possible to determine g_p, the forecast number of dwellings in ring p by direct substitution in the formula. The ring forecasts

were then proportioned among the constituent zones on the basis of opportunities.

For an explanation of the fitting of the Stouffer equation to 1948–1960 data the equation must be converted into its continuous differential form as follows:

$$d(G_P) = \frac{kd(O)}{O}$$

By integrating

$$G_P = k \ln O + C$$

where

G_P = the total number of dwellings allocated to all opportunities from the central point up to and including opportunity interval p;

$d(G_P)$ = dwellings allocated to opportunity interval p;

$d(O)$ = opportunities in interval p; and

C = constant of integration.

This equation plots as a straight line of slope k where the ordinate, total allocated dwellings, is in linear form and the abscissa, total accumulated opportunities, is a logarithmic scale. As a test of the appropriateness of the Stouffer formulation in describing the spatial distribution of residential growth in Greensboro, the actual accumulated zonal dwelling unit growth 1948–1960 was plotted against accumulated 1948 opportunities, the zones being ranked by traveltime to the HVC. If the Stouffer model is valid the resulting plot should follow a straight line. It was immediately obvious that a single straight line could not be adequately fitted to the points, but rather that two distinct straight lines were necessary (Figure 5). After hand fitting the two lines, 1960 growth estimates were made to the individual zones from the straight lines and the error computed. These results and those computed from the initial, non-calibrated test of the Stouffer formula are discussed later with results of the other four models.

Schneider Formulation. As applied to the distribution of residential activity, the Schneider model takes the following form:

$$d(G_p) = g_t[e^{-\ell O} - e^{-\ell(O + O_p)}]$$

where

G_p = total number of dwellings in opportunity interval from the central point up to interval p.

g_t = total growth to be allocated;

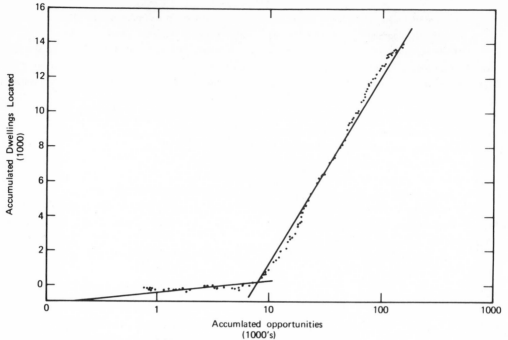

Figure 5 Test of Stouffer's formulation.

ℓ = model parameter expressing the probability of an opportunity being accepted for location;

O = total number of opportunities ranked from the central point up to interval p;

O_p = opportunities in interval p.

As a necessary condition for applying the model the parameter ℓ must be stipulated. For the first trial of the model for a 1960 forecast without benefit of the 1948–1960 data, ℓ was estimated from the assumption that the actual dwelling unit increase within the study boundaries was 99 percent of the aggregate Greensboro oriented growth. (The theoretical model is based on a distribution to an unbounded area; application to a finite area requires specification of the number of accepted opportunities being outside the boundary, or equivalently, the percentage accepted up to the boundary.) The ℓ resulting from this assumption was 12.76×10^{-6}.

For an explanation of the fitting of the Schneider formulation to 1948–1960 data, the formula can be restated after integration as

$$G_p = g_t[1 - e^{-\ell O}]$$

Subtracting g_t from both sides and rearranging,

$$g_t - G_p = g_t e^{-\ell O}$$

or

$$\ln(g_t - G_p) = \ln g_t - \ell O$$

This relationship plots as a straight line where the ordinate, $(g_t - G_p)$, is in logarithmic scale and the abscissca, total accumulated opportunities from the central point (O), is in linear scale. The slope is ℓ and the intercept g_t.

If the Schneider formulation effectively replicates the spatial distribution of residential growth in Greensboro then plotting the actual quantity $(g_t - G_p)$ versus accumulated opportunities (O), in semilogarithmic forms, should yield a straight line (Figure 6).

As with the Stouffer formulation, the Greensboro data appear to exhibit two distinct straight line segments, rather than one, as required by the initial model formulation. The zones comprising the transition area between the two straight line segments (Figure 6) are the same ones as those at the juncture of the two line segments for the Stouffer formulation (Figure 5). The slopes of the fitted lines can be loosely compared to the short and long trip ℓ's which have become standard practice in applying the Schneider formula as a trip distribution model. The slope for the central city line segment is 1.707×10^{-6}, and that for the outer, suburban area is 10.9×10^{-6}.

The distribution of residential growth in Greensboro from 1948 to 1960 did not adequately conform to either of the intervening opportunities formulations over the complete range of opportunities. It is noteworthy, however, that the data plot as two straight lines in both Figures 5 and 6. It was also pointed out that the transition points in the vicinity of the intersection of the fitted straight lines in both figures were the same data points representing the same zones. Although a detailed examination of these zones has not been attempted it does appear that they approximate a transition ring in Greensboro which separates the "inner city," marginal growth area from the suburban, rapid expansion area. This band encircles the HVC at a radius of $1\frac{1}{2}$ to 2 miles. For a city the size of Greensboro, which in 1948, exhibited a leveling off in the percent saturation gradient at $3\frac{1}{2}$ to $4\frac{1}{2}$ miles from the HVC, the area circumscribed by this transition band probably was characteristic of similar areas in most cities— old and perhaps showing signs of blight with little available residential capacity.

The inner area straight line slopes drawn to the two plots are both very close to the horizontal. In contrast, there are quite steep slopes for the plots representing suburban areas. A hypothetical locator viewing the opportunity surface from the HVC in accordance with either of the two plots apparently assesses himself a greater penalty in passing up suburban opportunities as opposed to inner-city ones. That is, the inner-city opportunities are a less desirable subset of the total as evidenced by the significantly lower slope on the plots, hence a lower probability of accepting individual opportunities. One may conjecture that location choices from the inner-city opportunity subset are responsive more to the individual living qualities of the opportunities other than its accessibility, which may be extended to the notion that the inner-city opportunities are viewed more or less as of homogeneous access in opposition to the suburban subset where opportunity access is of greater import in the locational choice.

Of interest from a purely forecasting viewpoint is the question of the stability of the

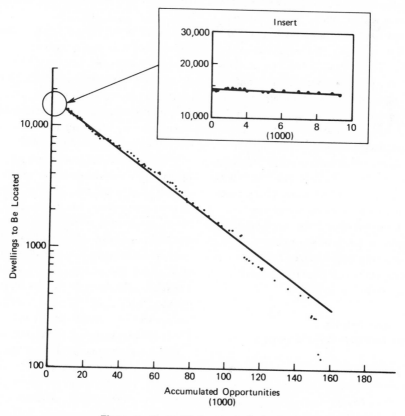

Figure 6 Test of Schneider's formulation.

TABLE 2 Error Sum of Squares for All Trials[a]

| Method | Zone | Districts | | Rings | | Sector |
		By Distance Ring	By Time Ring	By Distance	By Time	
DSGM						
Trial I	2.33	6.97	—	8.36	—	9.69
Trial II	2.41	—	4.43	—	4.07	3.02
Accessibility model						
Forecast	1.80	4.16	2.84	3.25	2.33	4.58
Fitted	1.79	3.98	2.76	2.18	1.99	4.46
Regression (fitted)	1.85	4.71	3.14	5.16	2.84	3.71
Stouffer model						
Forecast	2.21	6.45	4.22	5.57	3.48	11.25
Fitted	1.91	4.72	3.07	2.42	1.46	8.84
Schneider model						
Forecast	2.07	6.16	4.13	4.10	3.38	13.92
Fitted	1.95	4.65	3.08	1.91	1.65	10.18
Naive model	2.20	7.66	5.22	20.64	10.54	16.18

Levels of Aggregation spans the six right columns; *Districts* spans "By Distance Ring" and "By Time Ring"; *Rings* spans "By Distance" and "By Time".

[a] All values have been multiplied by 10^{-6}.

handfitted lines in Figures 5 and 6. Do the slopes remain more or less constant over time and how does the transition area behave in relation to the total opportunity surface? One may speculate, for example, that the straight line relationships fitted to the data will hold over time and that the diffusion in residential location observed in the past is merely a reflection of the diffusion in the opportunity surface; that is, a physical dispersion outwards occasioned by the filling in of less distant areas, rather than of an alteration in the location function. On the other hand, it is possible that over time the slopes of the plots may be flattening out which is symptomatic of a society less restrained by the impedance of travel. Clearly, answers to speculations of this nature are required before one can estimate the applicability of the fitted lines to forecasting to a future time point.

PERFORMANCE AND INTERPRETATION OF RESULTS

Performance

The single accuracy measure which was calculated for all trial forecasts was the sum of squares of dwelling unit forecasting error. These measures were computed at four levels of geographic aggregation: sector, ring, district, and zone, for all trials. A sixth forecast was made using the naive assumption of equal growth for all zones. The error sum of squares computed under this assumption, which will be referred to as the naive model, is $(n-1)$ times the variance in actual zonal residential growth. It will serve as a benchmark in evaluating the results of the five techniques listed.

Table 2 gives the computed error sum of squares for all of the forecasts and calibrations at each level of aggregation. For sake of complete comparisons, the results of zone level forecasts for each of the models (not for the DSGM) have been aggregated to districts and rings defined both by time and distance from the HVC. Trial one of the DSGM was based on analysis at the level of district as defined by distance from the HVC; therefore results are not shown for districts as defined by time to HVC, and vice versa for trial two of the DSGM.

The sums of squares of differences between estimated and actual are analogous to "unexplained" variances of a statistical model. However, since valid statistical inferences obviously cannot be drawn, this terminology should not be used. The error measurements of Table 2 do provide an index which can be used to compare results in any single column, that is, for the same level of aggregation. Comparisons between columns are meaningless, since different numbers of areas and different variances from mean growth rates are involved at different levels of aggregation.

To provide some degree of comparison between levels of aggregation, as well as between forecast techniques, Table 3 gives the ratio of each error to that for the naive model.

There are rather poor results at the zone level for all five methods. In some instances the naive model, assuming equal growth for all zones, actually exceeds the level of accuracy of forecasts. The particularly discouraging results of the DSGM at the zone level are evidence of poor choice of criteria by the authors in distributing growth from districts to zones. As pointed out earlier, this method requires historical data that were not available and requires intimate familiarity with the area,

which the authors lacked. The technique itself should not be blamed.

Undoubtedly, a substantial amount of the error at such a fine level of detail as the zone can be attributed to inaccuracies in data—assumptions made in certain estimates, incompatibility of merged files, differences in definitions between time periods, etc. However, other factors are contributory. The average zone contained only 109 dwelling units in 1948 and increased 56 to 165 by 1960. These values are far too small to hope for reliable predictions with any model. Obviously, differences between zones at this level are largely due to random variations not explainable by models. The districts represent a more reasonable level of detail at which to examine and compare accuracies. For the sake of comparison with transportation study practices, the average district (defined by distance rings) used in this study could be expected to have about 8000 person trip-ends in 1948 (about 660 dwelling units with 3.2 persons per dwelling and 4 trip-ends produced per person).

TABLE 3 Ratio of All Errors to Naive Model Error

| | | Levels of Aggregation | | | | |
| | | Districts | | Rings | | |
Method	Zone	By Distance Ring	By Time Ring	By Distance	By Time	Sector
DSGM						
Trial I	1.06	0.91	—	0.41	—	0.60
Trial II	1.10	—	0.85	—	0.39	0.19
Accessibility model						
Forecast	0.82	0.54	0.54	0.16	0.22	0.28
Fitted	0.81	0.52	0.53	0.11	0.19	0.28
Regression (fitted)	0.84	0.62	0.60	0.25	0.27	0.23
Stouffer model						
Forecast	1.01	0.84	0.81	0.27	0.33	0.70
Fitted	0.87	0.62	0.59	0.12	0.14	0.54
Schneider model						
Forecast	0.94	0.80	0.79	0.20	0.32	0.86
Fitted	0.89	0.61	0.59	0.09	0.15	0.63
Naive model	1.0	1.0	1.0	1.0	1.0	1.0

TABLE 4   Comparison of Errors to Size of Forecast Values, Accessibility
Model Forecast

Levels of Aggregation	RMSE $\sqrt{\dfrac{s \cdot s}{n}}$	Average 1960 DU (per areal unit)	Average Growth 1948–1960	Number of Areas
Zone	85	165	56	249
District[a]	381	1006	342	41
Rings[a]	600	4580	1560	9

[a]By distance.

Table 4 shows the relative accuracy of the accessibility model forecast at various levels in comparison to the size of the values being forecast. In this table the root-mean-square-error (RMSE) is used as the measure of error, since it can be compared with the magnitude of the forecast values: about two-thirds of the errors fall within RMSE values.

The RSME is roughly half of the average 1960 dwelling units per zone, and about a third of the average 1960 dwelling units per district. Of course, these accuracies must be viewed in relation to the overall growth rate of 52 percent. Intuitively one would expect that the ratios of the RMSE's to the 1960 values might be nearly cut in half if the overall growth rate was half as large.

The accessibility model performed substantially better than other unfitted models at most levels of aggregation (Table 3); but the fitted Stouffer and Schneider models were quite comparable to the fitted accessibility model. Somewhat surprisingly, the addition of several other explanatory variables in linear regression form did not improve the accuracy.

Results at the sector level are of interest because of the implications for forecasting radial corridor movements. Here the intervening opportunity models yield comparatively poor results, perhaps because they were not made sensitive to the distribution of employment, as were the accessibility model and regression equation.

Trial one of the DSGM assumed relative growth by sectors in proportion to available capacity—a weak assumption judging by comparison with the error of trial two. The importance of residential character in attracting additional growth apparently holds at all levels—between sectors as demonstrated by comparison of the two DSGM trials, and as a factor at the zone level as demonstrated by the statistical significance of that factor in the regression analysis.

Examination of Actual Patterns of Growth

All forecasts of 1960 density were based on the assumption that development in any zone would occur at the density indicated by a smooth line drawn through the 1948 density vs

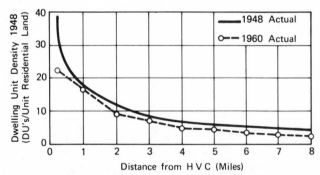

Figure 7 Dwelling unit density by distance bands.

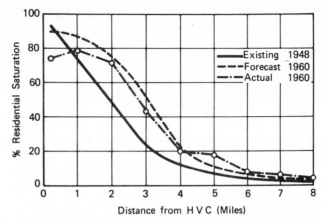

Figure 8 Percent residential saturation by distance bands.

distance (or time) from the HVC. Figure 7 compares the actual 1960 density-distance gradient with that for 1948. There appears to have been a rather uniform amount of decrease in density at all distances, except for the core area where the decrease was substantial. This obviously accounts for some error in the forecasts which required estimates of 1960 density (DSGM and the opportunity models), especially in the core area.

The actual 1960 and 1948 percent saturation gradients are compared in Figure 8, along with the forecast curve used for trial one of the density-saturation gradient method. Not surprisingly, the actual 1960 curve does not follow as smooth a curve as for 1948, since the plot represents percentage of 1948 capacity rather than 1960 capacity. The most significant errors in the forecast appear to be due to the unexpectedly large decline in the core and the amount of

growth that occurred in relatively remote portions of the area, ring 5 and 6. However, the general shape of the forecast curve is appropriate.

Figure 9 shows the same comparisons for the results of the accessibility and regression models. The agreement with the actual 1960 gradient is quite good, except for the obvious inability of these techniques, as used in this study, to predict decreases in the core.

In an attempt to picture how the residential density structure of the study region changed, Figure 10 was drawn. Using the data for total dwelling units and residential land area from the distance to HVC ring analysis, cumulative percent of total regional dwellings was plotted against cumulative percent total residential land area on a ring aggregate basis, proceeding outwards from the core ring. The plots for the actual conditions in 1948 and 1960 are shown. If smooth curves were drawn the slope at any

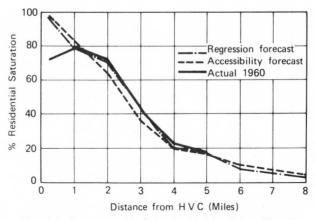

Figure 9 Percent residential saturation by distance bands.

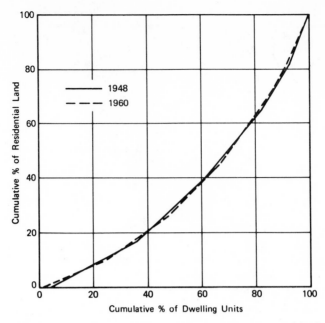

Figure 10 Cumulative dwelling versus cumulative residential land.

point would represent the inverse of density for the marginal dwelling unit. A diagonal line drawn on Figure 10 would represent uniform residential density for the entire study area. The bowing of each of the curves below the diagonal indicates the decline in density as one proceeds outwards from the HVC. If densities in the inner area were to decline along with an increase in the dwelling unit densities in the outer rings, the region as a whole would be approaching a state of uniform density, and the curve would shift toward the diagonal. On the other hand, if the difference between inner and outer area densities were to increase substantially, then there would be a shifting of the plot down and to the right. Understanding that the plots in Figure 10 represent an overall increase from 1948 to 1960 of 52 percent, the rather minute change in the density structure of the study area as described by these plots is outstanding.

Although the two plots (Figure 10) appear to coincide almost exactly, they should not be misread as indicating no change in the geographic distribution of dwelling units from 1948 to 1960. Each of the data points representing a distance ring has shifted downward and to the left from its 1948 position to 1960. That is, inasmuch as the majority of residential growth occurred in the suburban rings, the dwelling

stock of the inner rings in 1960 represents a smaller proportion of the total region stock than in 1948 and also utilizes a smaller proportion of total residential land; hence, the shifting of the data points downward and to the left.

An interesting question is whether similar plots for other urban areas exhibit this same constancy as found in Greensboro. If this is found to be so, such plots could be quite helpful in residential forecasts.

CONCLUSIONS

1. Simple, nonbehavioral residential land use forecasting models, which do not discriminate between the locational patterns of different types of households, are sufficiently accurate to be recommended for use in relatively small metropolitan areas of 100,000 population or larger. The Greensboro area's spatial structure and pattern of growth clearly demonstrates a degree of organization warranting analytical treatment in the planning process.

2. Land use forecasting with simple first generation models produced reasonably accurate results for levels of geographic aggregation where the average areal unit contained a population of about 2000 persons. Efforts to forecast growth for much smaller areas may

prove unjustified. At zone levels of about 300 population, these models appeared to offer little or no assistance in forecasting.

3. Differences in accuracy among the five forecasting methods are not large enough to warrant a strong recommendation for any single one in preference to others. Any of the methods would appear to be preferable to forecasting without the benefit of analytical techniques.

4. The simple accessibility model yielded the most accurate forecast of all methods used without benefit of calibration to time series data, for this one test. Errors in fitting were relatively insensitive to small changes in the exponent of accessibility.

5. None of the multiple linear regression models tested offered improvement over two-variable fitted models despite the fact that five or more factors were included in the regression equations.

6. Multiple regression models possess certain drawbacks. If the dependent variable is ex-pressed as an extensive quantity (e.g., increase in dwelling units) then measured relationships with independent variables are influenced by pecularities of area definition and size, and may not conform satisfactorily with logical hy-potheses regarding the land development process. Nonlinear transformations on the dependent variable such as logarithms or fractional power functions are unsatisfactory because the usual least squares criterion tends to bias the parameter estimates to produce good fits to small values and poor fits to large values. Expression of the dependent variable as an intensive quantity (e.g., dwelling unit increase per unit area) may be the most satisfactory operational solution except that relationships which are actually nonlinear may not be properly represented. Perhaps this might be handled by treating certain independent vari-ables as sets of dummy variables.

7. Although the two intervening opportunity models performed satisfactorily as used in this study, some evidence pointed to the possibility of improvement by allocating growth from all major centers of employment rather than from just a single point, the CBD. In addition, each

of the two models implies a different straight line plot on different semilogarithmic coordi-nates which did not hold true for Greensboro over the entire study area. Apparently the hypotheses are valid, but separate functions may be necessary for the built up, inner-city area, and the developing suburban area.

8. The forecasting approach used by CATS differed from the other models in important respects. It forces the analyst to become intimately familiar with the study area before attempting to forecast. This is probably the strongest feature to recommend it. The graphical analyses that the method is based on represent excellent descriptions of the key spatial relation-ships of a metropolitan area—even for relatively small areas. The methods of analysis are useful tools regardless of the forecasting technique used. They can serve as checks on the reason-ableness of forecasts made by less subjective models.

However, as applied in this study, the method is time-consuming, requiring considerable hand work and far more data manipulation. The method is less adaptable to the computer, and hence would be cumbersome for testing of alternative land use policies, or for recursive use in combination with other submodels.

9. The five techniques examined admittedly are far from representative of the extent of current land use forecasting research. They do represent the initial attempts and as such lack the sophistication and elegance of later thinking. These are descriptive models in that they do not involve themselves with the behavior of decision-makers; nor do they possess any real theoretical content. It is highly probable that the key to increased forecasting accuracy for small sub-areas lies in the ability of the analyst to simulate the decision process of subpopulations of the region.

ACKNOWLEDGMENTS

The authors wish to express their gratitude to both Professor F. S. Chapin, Jr., of the Uni-versity of North Carolina and to A. M. Voorhees of Alan M. Voorhees and Associates for making available the data utilized in this study.

APPENDIX:

CALIBRATION OF ACCESSIBILITY MODEL

Two procedures were used in the attempt to estimate the optimal exponent of accessibility: linear regression on transformed variables and an iterative, nonlinear least squares fit of the untransformed dependent variable.

Linear Regression on Transformed Variables

Three transformed versions of the standard accessibility model were tested:

$$\log G_i = \log a + b \log V_i + c \log A_i \quad (1)$$

which, in nonlogarithmic form is

$$G_i = aV_i^b A_i^c;$$

$$\log \left(\frac{G_i}{V_i}\right) = \log a + b \log A_i \quad (2)$$

or in nonlogarithmic form

$$G_i = aV_i A_i^b;$$

$$\log G_i - \log V_i = \log a + b \log A_i \quad (3)$$

which is the same as Equation 2 in nonlog form.

The nonlogarithmic forms of Equations 2 and 3 are essentially equivalent to the standard form of the model as stated in the body of this report. They would be identical if the normal equations contained the condition that

$$a = \frac{G_T}{\sum_i V_i A_i^b}$$

Since a standard regression program was used, this condition may be violated, and equation estimates must be factored to sum to actual total growth. This holds for all three of the transformed versions of the model.

Equation 1 also expresses vacant land as a power function in contrast to its linear form in the standard formula.

The basic problem, however, is that the least squares criterion is different for each version (the minimization of unexplained variance in the dependent variable) since the dependent variable is different for each. None is the correct criterion. The log transform tends to produce a bias toward better fits for small values of the untransformed dependent variable. Table 5 summarizes the results of the three versions.

TABLE 5   Results of Three Versions of Linear Regression on Transformed Accessibility Model

Item	Eq. 1	Eq. 2	Eq. 3
Accessibility			
exponent (b)	3.52	1.63	2.29
Log a	−8.0	−3.2	−4.9
Vacant land			
exponent (c)	1.51	1	1
Sums of squares of			
error ($\times 10^6$)	2.21	1.89	1.78

The fairly wide variation in the accessibility exponent, as well as in the error term leads one to be suspicious of regression on transformed dependent variables.

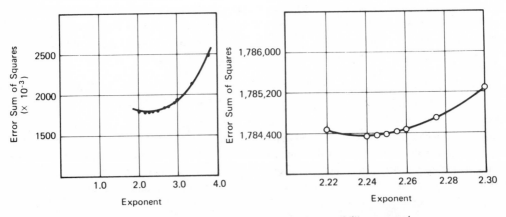

Figure 11   Accessibility model error versus accessibility exponent.

Nonlinear Least Squares Fit of Exponent

A routine was programmed to iterate toward the true least squares solution for the standard accessibility model

$$G_i = G_T \frac{A_i V_i^b}{\sum_i A_i V_i^b}$$

Figure 11 shows the results in the form of a plot of the sums of squares of error vs a range of exponents. A smooth curve with a minimum at $b = 2.24$ is apparent.

It is interesting to compare these results with the b value of 2.7 reported by Hansen for Washington, D.C. One might expect this value to increase with the size of the city.

REFERENCES

1. Baltimore Regional Planning Council, 1963. *A projection of planning factors for land use and transportation*. Baltimore: Maryland State Planning Department, Technical Report No. 9.
2. F. S. Chapin, Jr., and S. F. Weiss, 1962. *Factors influencing land development*. Chapel Hill: University of North Carolina Institute for Research in Social Science. 8C.
3. Chicago Area Transportation Study, 1960. Estimated land use in 1980. *Final report, Volume II: data projections*; Chicago: Chicago Area Transportation Study, 16–33.
4. Connecticut Highway Department, 1961. *Hartford area traffic study report, Volume I*. Hartford: Connecticut Highway Department, fourth printing. 1C.
5. C. H. Graves, 1965. Two multiple regression models of small-area population change. *Highway Research Record, 102*: 42–53.
6. J. R. Hamburg, 1959. Land use projection for predicting future traffic. *Highway Research Board Bulletin, 224*: 72–84.
7. J. R. Hamburg, and R. H. Sharkey, 1961. *Land use forecast*. Working paper, Chicago Area Transportation Study, Report 3.2.6.10.
8. W. G. Hansen, 1959. How accessibility shapes land use. *Journal of the American Institute of Planners, 25*(2): 73–76.
9. W. G. Hansen, 1960. Land use forecasting for transportation planning. *Highway Research Board Bulletin, 253*: 145–151. MC.
10. G. T. Lathrop, and J. R. Hamburg, 1965. An opportunity-accessibility model for allocating regional growth. *Journal of the American Institute of Planners, 31*(2): 95–103. 7D.
11. G. T. Lathrop, J. R. Hamburg, and G. F. Young, 1965. Opportunity-accessibility model for allocating regional growth. *Highway Research Record, 102*: 54–66. 5C.
12. I. S. Lowry, 1964. *A model of metropolis*. Working paper, Rand Corporation, RM-4035-RC. 1D.
13. S. A. Stouffer, 1940. Intervening opportunities: a theory relating mobility and distance. *American Sociological Review, 5*(6): 845–867.
14. F. L. Strodtbeck, 1949. Equal opportunity intervals: a contribution to the method of intervening opportunity analysis *American Sociological Review, 14*(4): 490–497.
15. A. R. Tomazinis, 1962. A new method of trip distribution in an urban area. *Highway Research Board Bulletin, 347*: 77–99. 3C.
16. Traffic Research Corporation, 1963. *Review of existing land use forecasting techniques*. Working paper; Traffic Research Corporation; a second printing incorporating an additional appendix was published in 1964. MC.

22

SALES FORECASTING WITH THE AID OF A HUMAN BEHAVIOR SIMULATOR[1]

GEORGE E. SCHUSSEL

The purpose of this article is to report the results of research that was done using simulation of human behavior characteristics as an aid in forecasting. The objective of the research was to test the feasibility of simulating the decision behavior of a large, non-homogeneous sample of people and to test the usefulness to a firm of simulating the external environment in which the firm operated. It was felt that the only valid way to test these points was to construct the simulation in such a manner that it would be used for forecasting. The heart of the research work consisted of a simulation model that was constructed of the film reordering techniques of thirty-three photographic dealers. The simulation was constructed to aid a manufacturer in determining the orders for film that would be placed at his warehouse by these dealers. Due to historical experience, the manufacturer had a good idea of what the retail sales of his various film types were, however, he had difficulty in forecasting his own sales because of the perversity in the way that

SOURCE: Reprinted from *Management Science, 13*: B-593–611 (1967).
[1] This article is based on G. E. Schussel, 1966, *Forecasting in the Photographic Industry: Testing a Simulation Model*, Unpublished dissertation, Harvard University [3].

the dealers reordered film. Because the film product of the manufacturer was very perishable, forecasting sales became an extremely important input to the production scheduling decision.

Even though the manufacturer felt that he could forecast retail sales fairly accurately, his past attempts at converting the forecasts of retail sales into the forecasts of company sales had proved very inaccurate. From this problem came the idea of interviewing dealers and constructing a simulation model of their behavior which would take a forecast of retail sales as input and convert this forecast into a forecast of orders placed at the warehouse.

The basic information for the simulation of dealer behavior was derived from detailed field interviewing of the thirty-three dealers in the study. Retail sales forecasts were obtained from company executives.[2]

In order to test the efficacy of the simulation

[2] To eliminate confusion in the remainder of this article, "retail demand" will mean the amount of film sales requested by customers of the dealers; "sales" will refer to the actual sales made by the dealers. The quantity "sales" is always less than or equal to "retail demand" because of film stock-out conditions. The word "orders" refers to sales of film by the manufacturer to the dealer.

model and to establish a bound on the accuracy of the model, it was necessary to devise a testing procedure for the model. This test consisted of determining the actual retail sales for the group of stores over a fifteen-week period and using these actual sales as input for the simulation model. The output of orders from these dealers was available for the fifteen-week period and with the true sales as input, the basic accuracy of the simulation model was testable. Weekly inventory counting at each store in the study, plus the record of shipments made from the manufacturer were sufficient to determine the actual weekly retail sales over the period of the study.

Several different methods of generating sales forecasts were used in conjunction with the simulation to forecast orders for the fifteen-week period. Also, in addition to the forecasts, several other order forecasts were obtained by more conventional means. These other forecasts also served to test the usefulness of the simulation model as a forecast aid. From the results of the study, it was concluded that simulation of the human decision processes of a large non-homogeneous group is possible. The simulation model performed well when actual retail sales were used as input. It was also concluded that using the simulation in conjunction with forecasted retail sales was the most accurate of the various methods which were examined of forecasting orders to the manufacturer. Three executives had been asked simultaneously to forecast retail sales of, and direct orders from, two dealer samples which were made up from the thirty-three dealers in the study. One sample consisted of nine large volume dealers and the other was made up of the remaining twenty-four smaller volume dealers. In every forecasted case (six) the combination of forecasted sales and simulation of dealer behavior proved more accurate than the direct forecast of orders, even though the executives included in the study were less familiar with forecasting retail sales than orders. General conclusions about the usefulness of this type of procedure for forecasting are made at the end of this article.

The fact that unsophisticated retailers seem to have a sufficiently systematic set of procedures to permit simulation by a computer model is encouraging because it may permit the use of the sales forecasting technique presented in this article by other firms which market products through retail dealers. The only new technique that this article presents involves the use of the simulation as the transfer function between a forecast of retail sales and a forecast of wholesale orders. The necessity of a sales forecast was not alleviated by the use of the simulation model. The use of this technique, however, may permit some firms to achieve more accurate and more easily performed forecasts than the more inaccurate forecasts which are now made.

The Polaroid Corporation of Cambridge, Massachusetts cooperated in making the research reported here possible. During the time that the research was being done, Polaroid manufactured five types of film which so dominated Polaroid's retail consumer film sales that they could have been considered the entire Polaroid film line. The five types of film had different sales backgrounds in the sense that they had been in the market widely varying lengths of time. At the beginning of the study, film type 1 had been available in the market place for eleven years, while types 4 and 5 had only been sold one and one-half years. Type 2 had been in the market place seven years, while type 3 had been available for two years. Film types 1 through 3 were used by an older type of Polaroid camera which was no longer made, and therefore the sales of these film types were decreasing over time. Film types 4 and 5 were used by the standard production Polaroid cameras and just three months prior to the inception of the study, two new cameras had been brought out which used these film types. The sales of film types 4 and 5 were therefore growing relatively rapidly. Because of the substantial differences of time in the market and the fact that they were in different stages of their life cycles, the five film types helped to generalize the study with respect to product history. This generality is important because it permits more confidence in the success that might be expected by adopting this article's methodology to firms who wish to forecast sales for products other than film.

METHODOLOGIES

Four methods were used in the study to forecast dealer orders to the manufacturer. One of these methods was a direct forecast of dealer orders without any intermediate analytical steps, while the other three methods required intermediate analysis before arriving at a completed forecast for orders. These forecast methodologies were essentially parallel approaches to the same problem. The one important difference among the methods is that a direct approach to forecasting orders does not require any other forecast as an input. The two-step forecasts involving the simulation model require the input of a retail sales forecast. The simulation model then acts as a transfer function on this sales forecast.

First Method—Regression on Past Orders

The first approach to forecasting dealer orders was a conventional statistical approach that used the regression technique for forecasting. The input data for this method consisted of the past total monthly quantities of each type of film ordered by the dealers in each sample for two and one-half years. (The manufacturer sold five types of film to the dealers.) These order figures were seasonally adjusted on a monthly basis. The method used was the standard "ratio to moving average" technique [1]. Least squares regression lines with time as the independent variable and orders dependent, were then obtained. A total of ten regression equations were determined, one for each film type in each sample. These regression equations were then used for forecasting with new values for the time variable. An example is:

$$\text{Orders} = 1458.118 - 9.2274 \text{ time}$$

which was the regression equation for film type 1 in the nine-dealer sample. Time is equal to 1 for January, 1963, and is incremented by 1 for every month thereafter, e.g., time is 30 for June 1965 and therefore "orders" has a predicted value of 1181. These resulting figures were then multiplied by the monthly seasonal factors to obtain the forecasted orders. These forecasts were single points, not distributions as some of the other forecasts were.

Second Method—Simulation on Regression Sales Forecast

The regression method outlined above was also used to forecast historical retail sales figures. These forecasts of retail sales figures

were then input as point forecasts for the simulation model.

As mentioned before, the simulation technique for order forecasting required retail sales forecasts for input, and the regression sales forecast was one method used for generating these sales forecasts.

Third Method—Executive Forecast of Orders

As an alternative to the regression forecast of retail sales, three executives at Polaroid were asked to forecast retail sales and wholesale orders from the two samples of dealers for the fifteen-week study period. The retail sales forecast was used as part of the input for method 4, and the executives' wholesale order forecasts constituted the "third method." These forecasts were obtained by showing the three executives relevant data on the past sales and orders of the study dealers and asking them to use this information, in addition to their own opinions of future trends, to determine the sales and order forecasts.

Fourth Method—Simulation on Executive Sales Forecasts

The effectiveness of the simulation model was to be primarily tested by comparing the accuracy of the forecasted order output from the simulation model to the forecast of orders made by the company executives. This fourth method used the executive retail sales forecasts as input for the simulation model. The output from this method could be compared with the executives' order forecasts since both the executives and simulation model had the executives' sales forecasts for input. This fourth forecasting model, like the second, used the simulation model.

After the executives had had an opportunity to study historical sales and order data on the two dealer samples, they were individually asked questions about the future sales and orders of the two dealer samples. When they were questioned about sales, five-point probability distributions of expected sales for the first five-week period in the study were obtained. Questions concerning the rest of the study period (the remaining ten weeks) were then asked, conditioned on hypothetical outcomes for this first period. The second period forecasts were therefore conditional on the results of the first period and were handled thusly in the simulation model. The cumulative probability distributions for the first period (five weeks) and the distributions for the second period (ten weeks) were later used in conjunction with a random number generator to generate demand for the simulation.

The output order forecasts from the simulation were probabilistic in nature and were described by a mean and standard deviation. The distributional nature of the forecast output by method 4 was due to two factors. First of all, the input sales forecasts were distributional; and second, because of the use of Monte Carlo techniques, the simulation model itself was inherently probabilistic.

Simulation Test—Simulation of Orders Using Actual Sales

A fifth type of "order forecast" was used to test the accuracy of the simulation model. This test consisted of putting known dealer sales for the fifteen-week period into the simulation model and comparing the model's output of orders with the actual orders that were received by Polaroid.

The actual sales of the dealers were obtained by taking weekly inventories at each store for a period of fifteen weeks (16 inventory takings). This information, plus the record of dealer shipments from the Polaroid warehouse, was adequate for determining the weekly sales of the dealers. Other factors, such as loans of film between dealers, were covered in questions at the end of each inventory taking.

The simulation model, acting as a transfer function, then converted these sales figures into order figures to Polaroid. The inherent accuracy limits on the simulation model were then evaluated by comparing these "forecasted orders" with the actual ones that were received.

INTERVIEW RESULTS

Inventories and Ordering

The purpose of carrying an inventory is to have a readily available stock of goods to sell. Although all merchants carry inventories of the products they sell and regularly order to build up their inventories, many different types of systems are used by retailers to maintain their inventories.

The first requirement of keeping an inventory is to have some method of knowing when the inventory has fallen to a point where a reorder is necessary. Among the dealers in the study, this was done in one of two ways. The first involved a periodic inventory taking at intervals such as one week or a month. The stock in every item being reviewed by the store was counted and those that were below a desired level were reordered. The other basic type of system can be called the constant reviewing system. Every time that an item was sold, the person doing the selling noticed how much of that item was left in inventory. When this amount reached a specified low point, it was then reordered. In practice, this type of review was usually just a quick visual survey when the item was removed from the shelf.

The advantage of the periodic review is that in practice it is usually a more reliable method. The only person who needs to be aware of the reorder point is the person who reviews the counting of the items. Also, because most of the counting is done at one time, the ordering can be done at one time. The disadvantage of this periodic counting of inventory is that unless a unit control system is used, it requires the investment of time and effort by someone to go around and do the counting. The constant review system requires noticing how much of an item is left after each sale and this usually can be accomplished without making a large additional investment of time or effort. Although, in theory, the constant review system can supply better information than the periodic inventory, in practice this was not true for the dealers in the study. This was because no stores were found where everyone knew the reorder points of all the types of film carried and conscientiously wrote down the items that were below their reorder points.

Instead of ordering only when an item was below its reorder point, certain stores ordered up to desired inventory levels all of the products supplied by a manufacturer when they ordered anything from him. In this case, the necessity for ordering one item served as the "trigger" for other items to be ordered.

After the decision to place an order with a manufacturer was made, the typical dealer next decided the quantity to order in each item. Often the amount ordered varied seasonally, being greater when retail sales were larger. Here again, the seasonality varied from dealer to dealer. Some dealers had what could be called a "desired inventory level" which they ordered up to. Typically, this was an estimated month's sales of an item. Therefore, in busy seasons, the desired inventory level was higher.

As opposed to the desired level concept, some dealers liked to reorder in constant quantities. For example, because it is factory packaged in cartons of fifty, Polaroid film is conveniently ordered in multiples of fifty. Constant quantity reordering required more orders in a busy season but did not require explicit estimates of sales or desired levels to be made.

The day of the month also had an effect on some dealers. By ordering as far away from the payment due day as possible, the dealer could effectively have the manufacturer finance part of his inventory. In theory, this should be much more important for ordering from a manufacturer whose products represent a large volume for a dealer. This was borne out in the interviewing. Dealers who purchased and sold relatively large quantities of Polaroid products were more apt to take advantage of the billing dates. Four of the nine dealers in the large volume sample and four of the twenty-four in the small volume sample paid attention to the day of the month before ordering.

Four camera stores and five discount stores were in the sample of nine large dealers. The twenty-four dealer sample was comprised of eleven camera stores, five department stores, two discount stores, two drug stores, two jewelry stores, one Army-Navy store, and one book store. The ordering and inventory systems varied considerably among the diverse store types and also among different stores within any particular type. It proved impossible to make generalizations about ordering systems used by the various store types, with the following two exceptions:

1. *Department store camera departments* used the most explicit planning in ordering. Most department stores kept records of previous year's sales and used these in addition to present trends for determining order quantities.

2. *Drug stores* used the constant review trigger level type of system. It would be almost prohibitive for a drug store to count periodically all of the stock of the many thousands of items it carries.

Retailers also made decisions about how often to place orders. The dealers who ordered more frequently required more of a time investment in counting, making up and submitting their orders. Also, since more shipments were required for the same volume of film, the average shipping cost, as a percentage of total cost of goods, was higher. However, the dealers who maintained a small inventory with frequent reorders lost no more sales because of stock-outs than those who maintained a large inventory with infrequent reorders. The added cost of more frequent orders was balanced off by being able to maintain a lower inventory level. Because of faster inventory turnovers, the probability of having out-of-date film was less for those dealers who frequently reordered.

Dealer Differences

The dealers in this study were placed into two separate samples so that the orders placed by the larger dealers would not swamp the ordering of the small dealers. The nine dealers in the large volume sample averaged slightly over 10,000 rolls and packs of Polaroid film sold in 1964; the largest dealer sold 20,000 and the smallest dealer sold 5,000. The twenty-four dealers in the small volume sample average 1,500 units in sales in 1964; the largest sold slightly under 4,000 rolls and packs and the smallest sold 340. With the exception of the store size in terms of sales volume, the most important distinguishing characteristics of the dealers are listed below.

1. *Having a periodic review, and how often they had it.* Three dealers counted their stock twice a month, four counted it once a month, and twenty-one of the thirty-three sample dealers did not use a periodic review.

2. *Ordering constant amounts of film versus having a desired inventory level; and the values of these amounts.* Twelve dealers conceived of the ordering process as one of bringing stock up to a certain desired level; the other twenty-one

dealers thought of it more in terms of ordering fixed amounts. The actual values varied from as few as ten units to as many as 400.

3. *Average delay from the time the decision to place an order is made to the delivery of this order.* For twenty-one of the dealers, the delay was one week; for the other twelve, it was two weeks. This delay included the store delays for processing outgoing orders and the incoming shipments.

4. *Types of film carried.* Twenty-five of the dealers carried all types of film in the study. Five did not carry Type 3; two did not carry Type 1; and one dealer did not carry either Type 1 or Type 3.

5. *Regular and emergency order trigger levels on film.* These figures varied substantially with the size and type of dealer, ranging from zero to 200 units as the trigger level.

6. *Batching orders, i.e., whether a dealer reviews and possibly adds to his orders items which are not below their trigger level.* The idea of batching orders arises because it is very simple to add other items to an order which is being placed with a manufacturer. The order is considered a batched one only if it contains some items which would not have been ordered had not an order been placed with the manufacturer at this time. By this definition, fourteen dealers batched their orders; while nineteen did not.

7. *Ordering so as to take advantage of the manufacturer's billing dates, thereby gaining an extra two weeks to a month of financing on film inventories.*[3] Eight dealers tried to take advantage of the billing dates; twenty-five paid no attention to billing dates as far as Polaroid was concerned.

8. *Percentage of total sales made to industrial accounts.* This percentage varied widely among the different film types handled by dealers. Some dealers had no industrial sales of any types, while others sold as much as 80% of their Type 1 film to industrial users.

---

[3] Polaroid's payment policy was that payment for any order placed between the 25th of one month and the 10th of the consecutive month is not due until the 10th of the following month. For example, payment for an order placed on May 28 is not due until July 10. Any order placed between the 11th and 24th of the month has payment due the 10th of the following month.

There were many other distinguishing characteristics among stores in the study (store type, sales volume, number of employees, etc.). These factors are related to the ones mentioned above. For example, a store with a large sales volume will tend to have high trigger levels and reorder amounts. However, in the researcher's opinion, these other distinguishing characteristics did not present any meaningful differences with respect to ordering patterns that could not be handled by quantitative descriptions of the above points. In fact, very few consistent clues to ordering behavior were discovered by examination of these more visible characteristics.

The information that was derived from the interviews was used to first conceptualize and then construct the model representation of the manner in which retailers order film. This model explicitly covered all of the above mentioned differences among the dealers and constructed a logical framework for these differences. The model was first quantified into flow charts and then programmed into source code so that it could be simulated. This simulation was a single, conceptual representation of the ordering behavior of all of the interviewed dealers. The individual dealer differences were handled in the model by tests at appropriate points which defined a unique path through the model.

SIMULATION MODEL

Programming

The simulation model was programmed in FORTRAN and run on the IBM 7094 at the Harvard Computing Center. The total programming to accomplish the simulation was divided into two jobs. The first program (the demand program) took the basic input data and generated specific consumer demand for each film type for each dealer in each period. The second program, which was the heart of the simulation, took the demand and simulated the dealer decision behavior.

Demand Generator

In addition to some secondary chores, the primary purpose of the first program (demand generator) was to take the general sales forecasts made by the executives and break down these forecasts into specific demands for each dealer, for all five film types and for each week. The basic inputs for this program were:

1.   An expectation of the way that retail sales would vary over the fifteen-week period.

2.   Factors that assigned what percentages of the entire forecast were to be given to each dealer and each film type. The record of past orders to Polaroid for 1964 was the criterion used to determine these percentages.

3.   The total forecast distribution of sales for each film type in the period under consideration.

The program first generated a figure for the total demand by using the cumulative probability distribution curve for forecasted sales in conjunction with the random number supplied by the random number generator. The actual conversion from random number to sales figure was done by means of a cumulative probability curve. The theory for this is rather simple and is explained in [2].

Main Program

The dealer logic chart Figure 1 is a representation of the part of the simulation model that emulated the dealer's logic in making his reorder decision. This dealer logic was part of the main program. The main program took the output of the first program, the individual dealer demand, and generated the final order pattern to Polaroid.

Much of the programming in the main program was devoted to bookkeeping and other secondary chores. The dealer logic itself, however, is rather important and is partially described below.

Dealer Logic

The first thing that the program did for each cycle through the model was to add the film orders received by the dealer during that period because of orders placed during previous periods.

The retail demand was next presented and if the dealer had enough film to cover all of his demands, sales equal to the demand were made. If not enough film was available, sales were made up to the level of film in stock.

The trigger level order routine was next entered. All dealers, whether or not they had a trigger level type of reorder system, had a low point trigger which could cause them to order stock. If orders were never placed other than at periodic intervals, then this trigger was considered to be negative.

With "status" defined as the amount of film on hand plus that on order, the program next tested whether the status was greater than the desired inventory level of the dealer. If it was not, a probabilistic order factor was calculated. This factor was an interpretation of the trigger level questions that were asked of the dealers. The interpretation was that this factor was the percentage "chance" that the dealer would want to place an order if he noticed that a film type was below its trigger level. This percentage "chance" was calculated by linearly interpolating or extrapolating from two known points. These two points were two levels of film where it was assumed the correct corresponding "chance" was known and could be derived from the following conceptualization of the dealers' decision process. The amount of film that was the answer to the trigger level question on the research questionnaire was assumed to be the point at which there was a 50% chance that the dealer would want to place an order. At zero units of film, it was assumed that there was a 100% chance that the dealer would want to place an order. Any amount of film in stock plus that on order corresponded to a "chance" that could be calculated by linearly interpolating or extrapolating from these two points. For example if the trigger level was twenty rolls on hand and on order, then the factor was .75 for ten rolls, .5 for twenty rolls and .25 for thirty rolls.

Initially, the researcher did not have the above model in mind when he asked the dealers the trigger level questions. However, after a few interviews, the researcher noticed that about one-half of the inventory levels of all combinations of dealers and film types were below the amounts the dealer had given as trigger levels. Observation of the inventory levels of the rest of the dealers led to the above model.

Next, a second probabilistic factor was calculated independently of the first. This second factor was time related and could be interpreted as the probability that the dealer would notice that his film stock has reached a reorder point. Dealers tended to order more before a holiday and this factor reflected this point. In addition,

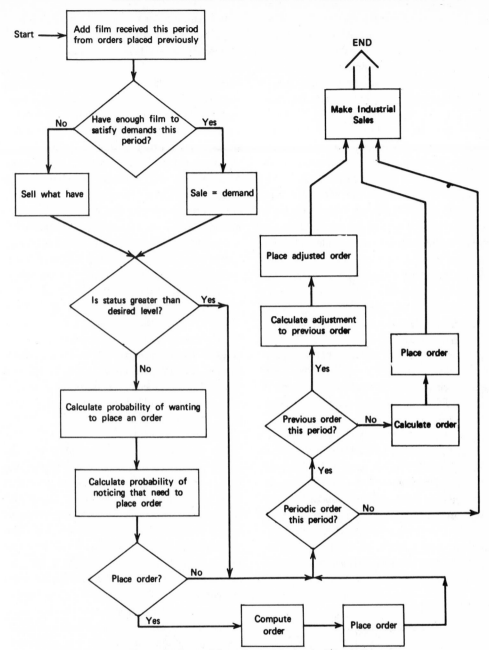

Figure 1 General flow chart of dealer decision logic.

some dealers paid attention to the payment due date so that they could get added financing on their inventories. More than one dealer was encountered who would not place an order from around the 20th to the 24th of the month.

Therefore, there were two time probabilistic factors, one for the dealer who watched the cutoff date and one for the dealer who did not. The proper factor was selected and multiplied by the first probabilistic factor. The rationale

for this was that the probability that an order would be placed was equal to the product of the probability that the dealer would notice he needed to order times the probability that he would want to order if he noticed he needed to. A random number was generated and if this number was less than the product of the probability factors, the order was placed.

The actual order placed next depended on whether the dealer was a "desired inventory level" or a "constant order" dealer. The difference was noticed in the interviews, where it was ascertained that some dealers conceived of the ordering process as a bringing of stock up to a predetermined point, and others simply put in an order of a constant given amount (such as fifty) of a type when they were below trigger.

Before the trigger level routine was left, a test was made to determine whether this dealer batched his orders. A dealer who batched his orders was simply one who reviewed all of his Polaroid film stock for ordering when he had to reorder one type. If the dealer did not batch his orders, the trigger level order routine was cycled for all of the film types. However, if he did batch orders and an order for one type of film had been placed, then the trigger level routine was left and the batch routine was entered.

This batch routine used secondary trigger levels and secondary desired inventory levels. If an order had already been placed for one type of film, the likelihood was increased that the dealer would include others that were below their desired levels although still above the primary trigger levels. Therefore the secondary trigger levels were higher than the primary trigger levels. When this type of secondary order was placed, however, the amount ordered was usually less than would have been the case if the film had been ordered because of being below the primary trigger. Accordingly, the secondary desired levels were always lower than the primary desired levels. Perhaps this section might be made clearer by a numerical example. Assume the primary and secondary trigger and desired levels to be as follows:

TABLE 1   Inventory Levels

	Film Types				
	1	2	3	4	5
Primary Trigger Level	10	15	10	20	15
Secondary Trigger Level	20	20	20	30	25
Secondary Desired Level	40	60	25	70	60
Primary Desired Level	50	75	30	90	75

If the inventory levels of the dealer were 5, 18, 12, 85, and 31 and the level of the first film type succeeded in triggering an order, then the desired order would be for 45, 42, 13, 0, and 0 units of film. Because Polaroid film can only be ordered in multiples of ten the actual order would be rounded to 50, 40, 10, 0, and 0 units of film. If, because of the random nature of the triggering device, the first film type had not succeeded in triggering the order, then no order would have been placed because no other film type is below its primary trigger. Therefore, for batched stores where a primary order had been placed, the batch routine added an order for any film whose status was below the secondary trigger level.

If no primary order was placed, or one was placed but the store was one that did not batch order, the trigger level routine was exited from. The next section of program took care of finishing out the primary trigger order for the dealer. It could have been possible that a level was lower than the trigger and yet, because of the random number that was generated, no order for that particular film type had been placed. If an order had been placed in the primary trigger routine, it is only reasonable to expect that any other film that was below its primary trigger would have been added, even if the dealer didn't batch orders. A subsequent section in the program took care of this.

The next section of the program was the periodic review section. The logic in placing the trigger level orders first was that in the stores using the periodic order concept the trigger level was an emergency order level which took precedence over regular periodic orders. Once the program had progressed to the periodic review section, a test was made to see if a periodic review was scheduled by the dealer during the current period. If the dealer did not have a review scheduled for the current period or if this dealer did not use the periodic review concept, the whole section was skipped.

If the store did have a periodic order review during this period, the next test was for whether an order had already been placed because of a trigger. If no order had been placed, the periodic review was then effected. The order was calculated according to the constant order or the desired level policy and it was placed. If an order had been placed, the next test was for whether all of the film types had been ordered. If they had been, the program proceeded to the next section. If some film types had not been ordered during this period, the program entered a section which calculated a supplemental order section, if necessary, to the one that had already been placed.

The supplemental section was necessary because if a dealer regularly ordered only at periodic intervals and a partial order had already been calculated for him in this period, the model had interpreted this partial order as an "emergency" order to fill in the dealer's stock until the next regular reordering period. Since the model now became aware that this was the regular ordering period, the amounts formulated as an "emergency" order for this period were converted into the regular amounts that would have been ordered in a regular periodic order. The supplemental section made this conversion. Since all of this happened in one time period, the "emergency" order and supplemental order showed up as one order.

The program took care of a dealer's industrial sales after the periodic review section was over. These industrial sales were different from ordinary sales in that they were usually made to a small number of customers who called relatively infrequently and ordered relatively large amounts of film at one time.

The rest of the program consisted of certain bookkeeping operations, output, and the statistical section which computed the basic statistics on sales and orders that were of interest.

The main part of the program was cycled through four different cycle indexes: the number of dealers, the number of periods (15), the number of executives (3), and the number of simulation cycles. Because of their interactions, the five film types were taken care of interdependently on each cycle. The other four factors, however, operated independently and therefore could be handled by cycling. From the innermost to the outermost, the central part of the program was cycled for all dealers, then all periods, then the executives, and finally the simulation cycles (which, along with random numbers, introduced the distribution aspect to the outcomes).

The final output from the simulation was a single page giving the mean and standard deviation of the total orders placed with Polaroid for each of the three five-week periods in the study. In addition, the value of the total sales experienced by the dealers at retail was given. There were many other things besides sales and orders that could be calculated from this program: average inventory levels, fluctuations in inventory, lost sales due to stockouts, etc. However, these were not of immediate interest to the object of the research and therefore the only printouts concerned the above points.

RESULTS

Some of the forecast methods used in the research required forecast distributions on sales as part of their input. These methods and the other methods that used the simulation model as a transfer function generated output forecasts of orders that were distributions instead of point forecasts. These distributions were the result of the probabilistic nature of the reordering mechanism embodied in the simulation model and the distributional input for those forecasts that had such input. The results presented below do not discuss the distributional nature of these forecasts; instead, they treat the mean of these forecasts as certainty equivalents. This is a simplification that is only strictly valid for problems with quadratic losses. The reader who is interested in an analysis of the meaning and importance of the output distributions is referred to the thesis footnoted by the title.

Measurement Statistics

Each forecast method generated two cases of fifteen forecasts: one forecast for each of three five-week periods, five types of film, and two samples. In order to determine which of the forecast methods is "best" we must derive a summary statistic that reflects, somehow, the accuracy of the forecast. This statistic can and should be derived from the economic environment in which the forecasts are used. The effectiveness of the forecast can be judged only in terms of the losses that will be incurred because of errors in the forecasts. Therefore, any statistic that is used devoid of derivation from a cost structure will not necessarily guarantee the correct choice of which is the "best" forecast method. This important point is often overlooked because of the ease of using well-known classical statistics. However, one major advantage of the simulation methodology is that it permits us to model specific real world cost structures and develop specialized statistics where necessary.

The derivation of two summary statistics is presented below. The assumptions which are made do not have to be met exactly for these statistics to be applicable. If one forecast method is best as judged by each of several different statistics that were derived from different assumptions, then we can feel fairly confident about its superiority under general circumstances.

If one of the forecast methods generated forecasts that were always somewhere between every other method's forecasts and the true value, we could definitely say that this method was superior under all reasonable evaluation statistics. Unfortunately, this is not the case for any of the methods used.

For the derivation, it is assumed that the costs associated with any forecasted outcome, corresponding action, and actual outcome can be estimated. It is also assumed that we have a method which tells us what the optimal action is for each forecast and that the forecast errors are not compensating. With this information, we can simply itemize the cost associated with every forecast plan and total them. The method giving the lowest cost is "best." For example, assume actions have been taken on the second method's forecast for film type 1 in period I. Assume Polaroid sales were forecasted at 620 while in actuality they were 750. The difference between the money cost to the company resulting from incorrect action based on the forecast of 620, as opposed to the correct action based on a forecast of 750 can be called $x_{1,1}$. The summation of the x's over all three periods and five film types would serve as a summary statistic that satisfies the condition of reflecting the associated cost structure. This statistic, or any linear transformation of it, is the proper statistic to be used for ranking the methods.

Absolute Deviation

It is interesting to look at the assumptions embodied by the use of classical statistics, such as absolute deviation and squared deviation. This is now done and the forecasts by the various methods are ranked according to these measures. Assume the following conditions:

1. Costs associated with the action corresponding to a forecast that is too large are equal to the costs associated with a forecast that is too small by the same amount.
2. The cost of any particular forecast error is the same for all types of film.
3. Errors in different periods or film types cannot cancel each other out. They are not compensating in the sense that over-production in one period or type cannot be used to counteract under-production in another period or type.
4. Losses are strictly proportional to the magnitude of the forecast error. This condition is commonly known as "linear losses."

With these assumptions, the proper ranking statistic is absolute deviation summed over the fifteen forecasts corresponding to each film type and period. The first condition implies symmetry and permits the absolute value of over and under deviations to be merely added. The second condition is necessary to permit additivity across the five film types. The third condition eliminates interdependencies among the fifteen figures so that minimization of the pieces will provide minimization of the whole. Looked at in another way, the third condition is also necessary for additivity. The fourth condition states that these deviations or a common linear transformation of them are the figures that should be added.

Squared Deviation

The use of the sum of squared deviations as a ranking statistic results from the same set of assumptions listed above except for number 4. This assumption is replaced by a statement of the form that losses are proportional to the magnitude of the square of the forecast error. As the error becomes larger the losses become larger more rapidly than linearly proportional losses.

Ranking of the outputs of the forecast methods according to sum of absolute deviations and sum of squared deviations are presented in Tables 2 and 3. Any inference made from this ranking is strictly valid only for the assumptions outlined; however, informally we can infer that the methods with the smaller figures are generally superior. It should also be

TABLE 2   Ranking of Forecast Methods

Forecast Method	Sum of Absolute Deviations
Sample of 24 Stores	
(1) Simulation on actual sales	1997
(2) Simulation on First's forecast of sales	2293
(3) Simulation of Second's forecast of sales	2620
(4) Simulation on Third's forecast of sales	2803
(5) Regression forecast of orders	2940
(6) Third's forecast of orders	3010
(7) First's forecast of orders	3340
(8) Second's forecast of orders	3560
(9) Simulation on regression forecast of sales	4652
Sample of 9 Stores	
(1) Simulation on actual sales	1836
(2) Simulation on Second's forecast of sales	5008
(3) Simulation on regression forecast of sales	5414
(4) Second's forecast of orders	5870
(5) Simulation on Third's forecast of sales	5899
(6) Regression forecast of orders	6100
(7) Simulation on First's forecast of sales	6176
(8) Third's forecast of orders	7020
(9) First's forecast of orders	7860

TABLE 3   Ranking of Forecast Methods

Forecast Method	Sum of Squared Deviations
Sample of 24 Stores	
(1) Simulation on actual sales	513,157
(2) Simulation on First's forecast of sales	558,061
(3) Simulation on Second's forecast of sales	713,810
(4) Regression forecast of orders	800,600
(5) Simulation on Third's forecast of sales	827,319
(6) Third's forecast of orders	1,075,300
(7) First's forecast of orders	1,256,200
(8) Second's forecast of orders	1,476,800
(9) Simulation on regression forecast of sales	2,501,398
Sample of 9 Stores	
(1) Simulation on actual sales	342,158
(2) Simulation on Second's forecast of sales	3,068,170
(3) Simulation on First's forecast of sales	3,719,958
(4) Second's forecast of orders	3,787,100
(5) Regression forecast of orders	3,995,400
(6) Simulation on regression forecast of sales	4,338,180
(7) Simulation on Third's forecast of sales	4,727,055
(8) Third's forecast of orders	4,919,800
(9) First's forecast of orders	8,407,600

noted that no use was made of the fact that some methods generated distributions instead of point forecasts; only the means of these forecasts were used.

It is not the purpose of this article to explore the problems associated with measurement statistics. However, it should be mentioned that as we move away from the above mentioned assumptions, the analysis of certain points can become difficult. If assumption 3 is reversed so that errors are compensating, then it is possible that a method which produced very poor forecasts for specific films and specific periods could, by chance, produce an overall excellent series of forecasts. This, however, is a statistical problem and not a problem associated with the forecast methods.

Method Evaluations

Certain facts stand out from a study of the rankings. The first is that the simulation model was able to generate the best order output when actual sales were used as "forecasted sales." This was to be expected, and had the simulation not done this, the validity of the model would have been in doubt. The effectiveness of this test of the simulation is especially noticeable in the nine dealer sample.

If the manufacturer is interested in forecasting his own orders from retailers, he would also be interested in the accuracy of the order forecasts from this model. A statistic reflecting the basic accuracy obtainable from the simulation is the average error percentage of the order output for each sample when actual sales were used as input. The mean error percentage of the simulation model's output in this case was 14.1% for the twenty-four dealer sample and 5.5% for the nine dealer sample. If the two samples are combined on a base weighted according to total orders, the average output error is 8.1%. Total orders in all film types amounted to 14,140 units from the twenty-four dealer sample and 32,060 units from the nine dealer sample.

A final and important point about the rankings in Tables 2 and 3 is that in all four cases, two samples and two statistics, every executive's sales forecast operated on by the simulation was superior to the straight forecast of orders made by the same executive. This is probably the most important single outcome of the study and is discussed further in the following section.

CONCLUSIONS

Most of the ordering systems used by the retailers in this study were informal variants of trigger level and constant review systems. A hope that there would be visible store characteristics, which would aid in the determination of the type of ordering system used, was not borne out. Few conclusions could be drawn about the type of reorder system that a store used from characteristics such as store type, location, and sales volume. Similar stores (e.g., camera stores in the same general location with approximately the same sales volume in Polaroid film and other items) were found that used different inventory systems, kept different types of records, and reordered at different intervals. As mentioned before, drug stores primarily used trigger level systems in ordering film, while department stores primarily used periodic reviews, along with records of previous sales of the items, as a basis for ordering.

A basic reason for this lack of uniformity in the ordering habits of similar stores is that in most cases, both periodic review and trigger level ordering systems with different reorder frequencies can accomplish essentially the same purpose for a retailer. Moreover, the amount of inefficiency that is introduced into the overall management of a small business by having an inventory that is not exactly optimal is not great enough to significantly influence the retailer's success. The result is a wide diversity of systems among comparable stores. It is therefore the opinion of this researcher that studies which attempt to correlate product ordering with some visible store characteristics either will not be successful or will be successful only because they propose a clever or novel way of looking at the problem.

In most cases, it would probably not be valid to try to force another product into the specific reordering model for Polaroid film used in this thesis. The most outstanding characteristic of simulation as a tool of analysis is that it is the most specific, non-generalizable form of analysis available. For example, if one tried to use the simulation to help in forecasting orders of Kodak film it could be possible that the interactions in the ordering process among the large number of different film types made by Kodak would be such that this model would not work very well. The theoretical interactions could be of the same form, but the large number of different types and the way that errors propagate might make useless for Kodak the simulation constructed for this thesis. Therefore, it is possible that the specific model derived for this thesis cannot be generalized even to other film producers.

Even though the simulation could do a good job of emulating the dealer ordering mechanism, it would be of little value if there was no way of forecasting sales. The fact that the model can create an order output that is close to the actual (when the actual sales are used) is primarily interesting in the sense that a bound is determined on how good one can expect the results from the model to be. More interesting is how well the simulation model performs on available forecasts. On this point, the model used in this research did well, even though it had no influence on the sales forecasts that were the basic inputs for the simulation runs.

The fact that all of the executives' sales forecasts used in combination with the computer simulation were superior to the direct order forecasts is especially impressive when it is realized that these executives were more used to forecasting orders than sales. The reason that the simulation yielded such improvements was that it reflected the cyclical nature of the order. If more effort could have been put into the forecast, better results probably would have been forthcoming. Since the simulation was only a transfer function, it could not produce a good order forecast from a poor sales forecast.

Considering all of the results that were derived from the research on both samples of dealers, it appears that a behavioral simulation model of the type constructed can be useful in the analysis and prediction of retailer behavior. More generally, we can state that a behavioral simulation model can be useful for analysis or forecasting in marketing problems where one tries to simulate the external environment of the firm. Whether the simulation approach is the correct one in terms of cost justification depends on the specific problem area.

Unsophisticated retailers seem to have a sufficiently systematic set of procedures to permit simulation of these procedures by a computer model. This is not such a surprising conclusion, since we would expect successful dealers to have a rationale for their actions. Those that do not have rational (not necessarily sophisticated) patterns of business behavior probably have gone out of business. For many products, these procedures may be determined by interviewing retailers. There is nothing particularly unusual about film that would lead us to believe that we can successfully model the reordering of film and not of other products.

There were many particular characteristics, both of the market place and of the particular product line, that led to the model developed in this research. However, these were not requisite characteristics for developing a simulation model of the reordering process. For example, if film were heavily promoted, a section in the simulation model could have taken this into account. By definition, if one wishes to simulate a process, he must model the special characteristics of that process. Just because another process does not possess those characteristics does not mean that it cannot be modeled likewise. It does mean that the model constructed for the first case probably will not fit the second.

A simulation model can be useful for under-standing a process quite apart from the prediction of that process. In the process of constructing the model, the researcher developed an understanding of the way in which dealers operated in reordering film. In an industrial situation, such an understanding could be brought to bear on problems that the simulation model did not handle explicitly.

A simulation model of the type that was constructed for this research could also be useful in experimentation leading to a better understanding of the market environment. One variable could be varied while the rest are held constant, and variations in the output could then be compared with the changes in the input variable, so that a better understanding of the environment can be obtained. For example, a step function of sales could be arbitrarily introduced, so that the resulting ordering pattern could be studied. Sensitivity tests would also be possible. If a change in corporate policy affecting dealer ordering was being contemplated, this change could be programmed into the model and the effect on the forecasting of orders generated by the model could be studied. This type of information would be valuable in corporate decisions.

Because the primary purpose of this research was to examine the ordering process which acts as a transfer function between retail sales and wholesale orders, little attention was paid to factors not immediately relevant to this transfer function. An example of this was the type of regression analysis that was used—a strictly standard regression. Little thought was given to novel ways of forecasting sales because this could validly constitute another topic of research. It is obvious, however, that any improvements that can be made in retail sales forecasting would tie in directly with the results of this study. In fact, the results of the research suggest that the transfer function between the retail sales and wholesale orders is tractable and that further work should be done in the area of forecasting retail sales.

REFERENCES

1. F. C. Mills, 1955. *Statistical methods.* New York: Holt, third edition.
2. R. Schlaifer, 1959. *Probability and statistics for business decisions.* New York: McGraw-Hill.
3. G. Schussel, 1966. *Forecasting in the photographic industry.* Unpublished dissertation, Harvard University. 1C.

PART V

INDIVIDUALS WHO AGGREGATE AND INTERACT

The studies in this section represent interaction as well as aggregation. Since interaction involves forecasting, feedback, and multiple decision units, one expects these models to be more complex and more difficult to analyze than the models of the previous section. On the whole, the expectation is confirmed, but the differences between the two categories are hardly clear-cut. Many of the models of individuals who aggregate and interact are less complicated than many of the models of individuals who aggregate. Evidently, model-builders differ in the extent to which they perceive complexity, and these individual differences blur or erase the distinctions between models deriving from the represented phenomena. The reader should compare the voting model of McPhee, Ferguson, and Smith with the model of Pool, Abelson, and Popkin, and should compare the attitude model of Waldorf and Coleman with the model of Gullahorn and Gullahorn.

Unfortunately, the studies by McPhee, Ferguson, and Smith and by Waldorf and Coleman are the only studies in this section not related to macroeconomics. Zymelman simulates, on an analog computer, the price and output fluctuations in the cotton textile industry.

Desai simulates the world market for tin. And both Liebenberg, Hirsch, and Popkin and deLeeuw and Gramlich simulate short-run changes in the United States' economy.

The emphasis on macroeconomics results from the editors' concern for empirical validation. Except in macroeconomics, the category D studies have depended on loose, qualitative observations of the real world to justify the models' assumptions or to establish the plausibility of the models' outputs. In this respect, the contrast between categories C and D is quite striking, and one can infer that this difference results from the difference in model complexity. A more complex model implies more effort in programming and analysis; if the total effort put into one study is substantially fixed, more programming and analysis implies less data gathering. A more complex model also implies that the model-builder is more conscious of the real world's complexity and of the model's distorting abstractions, and willingness to validate and test probably decreases as a model-builder becomes more skeptical of his model's realism. Thus, the category D models could be more realistic, in general, than the category C models, and yet the builders of category D models could be less willing to demonstrate that realism.

The macroeconomic models are atypical in at least two respects. First, the model-builders display a strong orientation toward policy applications. They seek models which policy makers will trust and use, and therefore they estimate the empirical accuracy of each model component (equation) and then estimate the accuracy of the entire model in a demonstrative forecast. The result is a very high, average standard of empirical validation. Second, the macroeconomic models are based on a long, developmental history. Although the availability of computers accelerated the rate at which econometric models were built and induced the creation of more detailed and complex models, economists have been constructing mathematical, empirically estimated models throughout the twentieth century, and have also been constructing direct ancestors of these simulation models since the 1930s. One product of this long history is that the macroeconomic models are concisely described; the model-builders assume that readers will be familiar with previous formulations and with much of the logical analysis underpinning new formulations. Another product is that the models are elaborate, the simplest and most abstract formulations having been explored long ago. And still another product is that the individual equations of the models are relatively accurate, the model-builders having the advantage of knowing what functional relations have succeeded or failed previously.

Because the large macroeconomic models are so large and complex, the economists are having to wrestle with methodological problems that most other simulators have either avoided or ignored.

1.   Interaction and feedback imply that some of the modeled relations are simultaneous equations that must be solved in parallel. If there are many simultaneous equations and the equations are individually nonlinear, the model-builder is confronted by an absence of solution algorithms, and even an absence of algorithms for determining whether a solution exists.

2.   Simultaneous equations also imply that unknown parameters estimated one-equation-at-a-time are likely to be biased. Yet techniques for simultaneous parameter estimation are well-developed only for systems of linear equations, because only linear systems guarantee that the error terms have unique optima.

3.   When a model contains numerous nonlinear equations, each of which only approximates reality, the errors in individual equations cascade through the system in elusive and surprising ways. The result is that an assemblage of individually accurate equations may behave inaccurately and inexplicably inaccurately.

It is fortunate that some econometricians have begun to work on these problems because strategies for solving them are among simulation's high priority needs. Since linear systems can be efficiently represented by mathematical models, to restrict simulation models to linear formulations is to forgo one of the computer's comparative advantages; it seems inevitable that future simulation models will increasingly stress complex, nonlinear formulations. Yet it is futile to invent models that are too complex to solve or to analyze, and until powerful and appropriate methods of solution and analysis are created, an increasing number of complex models is likely to produce an increasing number of frustrated and disillusioned model-builders. The analytic tools will have to be ready when model-builders begin to feel the need for them.

The reader may want to consider the following articles in addition to the ones included in this section.

TYPE 1 STUDIES

I. Adelman, 1963. Long cycles—a simulation experiment.
A. E. Amstutz, 1967. *Computer simulation of competitive market response.*
T. E. Anderson, E. A. Kidd, and K. R. Laughery, 1968. *Urban intersection study—Volume II: a computer simulation model of driver behavior at intersections.*
R. J. Ball, 1967. Economic model building for control.
M. Brown, and P. Taubman, 1962. A forecasting model of federal purchases of goods and services.

C. H. Cherryholmes, and M. J. Shapiro, 1969. *Representatives and roll calls.*
K. J. Cohen, 1960. *Computer models of the shoe, leather, hide sequence.*
J. S. Duesenberry, O. Eckstein, and G. Fromm, 1960. A simulation of the United States economy in recession.
J. W. Elliott, 1967. *A computerized macroeconomic forecasting system.*
M. K. Evans, 1969. *An econometric model of the French economy.*
M. K. Evans, and L. R. Klein, 1967. *The Wharton econometric forecasting model.*
H. Galper, and E. Gramlich, 1968. A technique for forecasting defense expenditures.
G. J. Hanneman, and T. W. Carroll, 1969. *SINDI 1: simulation of information diffusion in a peasant community.*
J. F. Helliwell, L. H. Officer, H. T. Shapiro, and I. A. Stewart, 1968. *RDX1—a quarterly model of the Canadian economy.*
L. R. Klein, 1964. A postwar quarterly model: description and applications.
L. R. Klein, and J. Popkin, 1961. An econometric analysis of the postwar relationship between inventory fluctuations and changes in aggregate economic activity.
K. R. Laughery, and E. A. Kidd, 1968. *Urban intersection study—Volume I: summary report.*
W. L. L'Esperance, G. Nestel, and D. Fromm, 1969. Predictions and policy analysis with an econometric model of a state.
I. S. Lowry, 1964. *A model of metropolis.*
R. L. Morrill, 1965. Migration and the spread and growth of urban settlement.
T. H. Naylor, W. H. Wallace, and W. E. Sasser, 1967. A computer simulation model of the textile industry.
R. H. Rasche, and H. T. Shapiro, 1968. The F.R.B.–M.I.T. econometric model.
E. M. Rogers, 1969. Computer simulation of innovation diffusion in a peasant village.
H. O. Stekler, 1969. Econometric forecast errors: data revisions and judgmental elements.
D. B. Suits, 1967. The economic outlook for 1967.
D. B. Suits, 1968. The economic outlook for 1968.
D. B. Suits, 1969. The economic outlook for 1969.
H. Ueno, and S. Kinoshita, 1968. A simulation experiment for growth with a long-term model of Japan.
F. H. Weymer, 1968. *The dynamics of the world cocoa market.*
J. Wolpert, 1966. A regional simulation model of information diffusion.

TYPE 2 STUDIES

W. H. L. Anderson, and J. Cornwall, 1961. Problems of growth policy.
Bay Area Simulation Study, 1968. *Jobs, people and land.*
J. M. Boughton, and T. H. Naylor, 1968. *Simulation experiments with a monetary policy model.*
D. E. Boyce, and S. E. Goldstone, 1966. A regional economic simulation model for urban transportation planning.
J. J. Browne, and J. J. Kelly, 1968. Simulation of elevator system for world's tallest buildings.
N. K. Choudry, Y. Kotowitz, J. A. Sawyer, and J. W. L. Winder, 1968. *An annual econometric model of the Canadian economy, 1928–1966.*
J. Cornwall, 1959. Economic implications of the Klein-Goldberger model.
R. J. Crom, and W. R. Maki, 1965. A dynamic model of a simulated livestock-meat economy.
R. F. Dawson, and H. L. Michael, 1966. Analysis of on-ramp capacities by Monte Carlo simulation.
G. Fromm, 1969. Utility theory and the analysis of simulation output data.
H. Galper, 1968. The timing of federal expenditure impacts.
H. Galper, 1969. The impacts of the Vietnam War on defense spending: a simulation approach.
G. R. Green, 1968. *Multiplier paths and business cycles: a simulation approach.*
H. R. Hamilton, S. E. Goldstone, J. W. Milliman, A. L. Pugh, III, E. B. Roberts, and A. Zellner, 1969. *Systems simulation for regional analysis.*
L. R. Howard, and D. D. Eberhardt, 1967. Airline simulation for analysis of commercial airline markets.
D. S. Huang, and M. D. McCarthy, 1967. Simulation of the home mortgage market in the late sixties.
S. H. Hymans, 1970. The trade-off between unemployment and inflation: theory and measurement.
G. Fromm, and P. Taubman, 1968. *Policy simulations with an econometric model.*
J. H. Kell, 1964. Simulation of the intersection.
R. M. Lewis, and H. L. Michael, 1963. Simulation of traffic flow to obtain volume warrants for intersection control.
T. C. Liu, 1963. An exploratory quarterly econometric model of effective demand in the postwar U.S. economy.
C. S. Mayer, 1964. *Interviewing costs in survey research.*
A. L. Nagar, 1966. *Stochastic simulation of the Brookings econometric model.*
W. T. Newlyn, 1950. The Phillips/Newlyn hydraulic model.
J. H. Niedercorn, and J. F. Kain, 1963. An econometric model of metropolitan development.
H. Pack, 1968. Formula flexibility: a quantitative appraisal.
W. C. Perkins, 1969. *A simulation analysis to evaluate the impact of the automatic stabilizers.*
R. C. Porter, 1965. A growth model forecast of faculty size and salaries in United States higher education.
A. D. St. John, 1967. *Study of traffic phenomena through digital simulation.*

J. C. Schoenman, and B. Persson, 1966. *An analog of short-period economic change.*
M. H. Spiro, 1968. The impact of government procurements on employment in the aircraft industry.
M. C. Stark, 1964. Simulation of the arterial street.
D. B. Suits, 1966. The economic outlook for 1966.
A. J. Tella, and P. A. Tinsley, 1968. The labor market and potential output of the FRB–MIT model: a preliminary report.
J. N. Thomasson, Jr., and P. H. Wright, 1967. Simulation of traffic at a two-way stop intersection.
H. Tsurumi, and M. F. J. Prachowny, 1968. *A four-sector growth model of the Canadian economy.*
J. M. Vernon, N. W. Rives, Jr., and T. H. Naylor, 1969. An econometric model of the tobacco industry.
A. M. Voorhees & Associates, 1966. *A model for allocating economic activities into sub-areas in a state.*
W. H. Wallace, T. H. Naylor, and W. E. Sasser, 1968. An econometric model of the textile industry in the United States.
K. Wigley, 1968. *A programme for growth, Volume 8: the demand for fuel, 1948–1975.*
J. Wolpert, 1967. A regional simulation model of information diffusion.
R. D. Worrall, 1963. Simulation of traffic behaviour on a digital computer.
J. V. Yance, 1960. A model of price flexibility.

TYPE 3 STUDIES

M. S. Alba, 1967. *Microanalysis of the socio-dynamics of diffusion of innovation: a simulation study.*
A. Ando, and F. Modigliani, 1969. Econometric analysis of stabilization policies.
E. R. Arzac, 1967. The dynamic characteristics of Chow's model: a simulation study.
R. J. Ball, and T. Burns, 1968. An econometric approach to short-run analysis of the U.K. economy, 1955–66.
L. W. Bowden, 1965. *Diffusion of the decision to irrigate: simulation of the spread of a new resource management practice in the Colorado northern high plains.*
J. E. Cohen, 1966. *A model of simple competition.*
R. A. Douglas, and J. R. Walton, 1962. *The simulation on a digital computer of rural highway configurations and the movement of traffic, Final report.*
T. Hägerstrand, 1965. A Monte Carlo approach to diffusion.
N. O. Jørgensen, 1961. Determination of the capacity of road intersections by model testing.
J. H. Kell, 1963. Results of computer simulation studies as related to traffic signal operation.
K. Mori, 1966. Simulation analysis of fluctuations and growth of the Japanese economy: 1955–1960.
R. L. Morrill, 1963. The development of spatial distributions of towns in Sweden: an historical-predictive approach.
C. C. Pegels, 1967. *Optimal plant structure and operation.*
An. Rapoport, and P. Dale, 1966. Models for Prisoner's Dilemma.

23

A MODEL FOR SIMULATING VOTING SYSTEMS

WILLIAM N. McPHEE
JOHN FERGUSON
ROBERT B. SMITH

I. INTRODUCTION

This paper describes a model that promises to be a convenient instrument for solving an old difficulty. Assume one is given detailed research knowledge about the individual behavior involved in some mass situation, for example, professional research knowledge on how people vote in Western democracies. How does one proceed from such knowledge at the microscopic level to some macroscopic picture of how, when it is all put together, the aggregate system works? For example, how do significant properties of electoral systems emerge from various combinations of individual processes and different institutional arrangements?

As an example of one such aggregate, the American electoral system displays remarkable capacities of reequilibration after disturbance, having oscillated back and forth around a 50–50 division between the two parties for more than a century. The reasons for this are not made apparent, however, by mere projection up to the requisite magnitudes from a sample of individual voters, politicians, and laws—even though

SOURCE: An edited composite of W. N. McPhee and R. B. Smith, 1962: A Model for analyzing voting systems, and W. N. McPhee, 1961: Note on a campaign simulator.

the whole is the consequence of these parts in some complex sense. The complexity is the problem. Many mass phenomena involve unknown problems in compounding the known facts about individuals and their nonadditive interactions, yet compounding is necessary to reach the socially significant implications in the aggregate.

The difficulty in certain social fields is curiously upside down, however, from the relations between observation and theory in most science. What is required is not the usual "downward" penetration—that is, given the total behavior of a system at the molar level, the breaking down of this whole analytically to the microscopic level. Rather, we are given analytic knowledge at the level of the micro units, and we wish to proceed "upward" to the system level. It is a synthetic problem. The dynamic behavior of the aggregates is the unknown in the problem, even though it consists of logical consequences of what is known or assumed about individuals.

With such problems in mind, a simple model of individual voting behavior has been constructed. It lends itself to rapid logical manipulation of sizable numbers of units (voters) arranged in complicated structures (communities) through long sequences of processes (eras or generations). These manipulations help to analyze problems in electoral dynamics of a complexity too great to be easily understood by more conventional verbal and mathematical methods.

Computer Simulation. Although the present instrument was created as an entirely substantive project, prior to knowledge of machinery for manipulating it, it deals with large problems whose implications are difficult to discover without an automatic computer. The model represents events in a very literal sense. Thousands of concrete voters are represented, and each carries out the processes of the model in detail. For example, its social-discussion process might be represented more elegantly by probability equations summarizing their effect. But here, voters influencing one another actually do come into a central place in the machine. Their specific preferences are concretely compared. Each may go through detailed processes representing a form of social influence of the other on him.

Since a computer is serial, however, it has the inconvenience for simulation of social processes that the rest of the voting community must wait while each person acts. If extremely detailed processes were involved here for every individual voter, it would be a long wait, to say the least, to process a sample community over a generation with presently available equipment. So, it is a fortunate accident of the history of this model that it was originally designed without knowledge of information-processing theories. Its processes are close to mathematical ideas in their simplicity and often use numerical short-cuts. In this intermediate character, the present work resembles that of Balderston and Hoggatt [1]. They simulate directly in computer operations a market with each of almost 200 wholesalers, retailers, and suppliers concretely making decisions, actually communicating with one another, and so on. The complexity is far greater than could be handled mathematically, but of necessity it is much simplified from what would be possible in representing one such decision maker.

The General Plan. It is useful to begin by asking: What are the most important findings to come out of modern studies about voting decisions during election campaigns?[1] Ironically, the crucial discovery is that most votes are not really fresh decisions made during the given election campaign. In established party systems found in the Western world today, votes are fashioned over many elections. Starting from youth, there is a gradual process of political socialization or "politicization," whose eventual product typically is a more or less habitual allegiance to one party [9]. The individual's enduring partisanship is implemented in the given election when he chooses whether to continue that party preference or to make an exception.

The model utilizes this knowledge in the problem formulation itself, choosing as the most significant subject matter the long-term process of political socialization, rather than the single campaign or election prediction. In this elongation, there is a resemblance to learning models. Successive elections are like successive learning trials, and like the learning theorists, we are primarily interested not in the single trial but in the cumulative effect over a political era or generation. We are interested in sufficiently long and complex sequences to modify the system's capacities and propensities in ways not obvious in the elementary processes at one time. The events of each election are probably more adequately represented than are the psychological processes of rats on each trial in a learning model. Yet because the psychological processes of single rats on single learning trials are unknown, whereas the processes of voting communities in an election well-known, the oversimplification here will be more evident.

Three processes are represented: (1) response to external political stimuli, (2) mutual influence of individuals within the immediate social environment of one another, and (3) the learning over time of the habit of partisanship. How these act to produce successive modifications in the voter is diagrammed in Figure 1.

---

[1] Reference here is chiefly to the so-called panel studies initiated by Lazarsfeld and Berelson in 1940 and elaborated by others in now more than a dozen election studies in this country, the British Commonwealth, and Western European elections. The present model was the direct result of trying to find processes that would reproduce the inventory of findings through 1954 compiled by B. R. Berelson, P. F. Lazarsfeld, and W. N. McPhee [4].

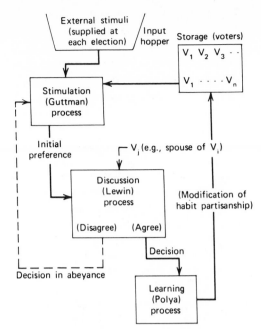

Figure 1 Flow chart of the model.

First, the model takes from the input hopper an injection of political stimuli for the period since the last election. These are used in a Stimulation Process. Each voter is stimulated, and emerges with an initial preference of greater or lesser degree for one party in the current campaign. This preference is something like a first impression, the kind we get from casual reading of the newspapers prior to serious thought and discussion.

Later, most voters enter the subroutine in the middle of the diagram, labeled Discussion Process. Here each voter encounters another voter, a spouse or friend, with whom he exchanges views. If his friend's impressions match his own, his initial preference will tend to be strengthened into a decision. If his friend disagrees, the voter will return to the stimulation process for further exposure to external stimuli, which may then either confirm or alter his initial preference.

The output of the discussion process is a voting decision which becomes the input to the subroutine labeled Learning Process. This process resembles, not a conventional learning theory, but a simpler model used elsewhere to represent the progressive development of disease and similar self-intensifying phenomena. What is growing here, over many elections, is the

partisan bias that makes most people habitual Republicans or Democrats.

The data output can be voluminous and highly varied. For, this is a completely observable system; any combination of the hundreds of thousands of operations per problem can be monitored.

II. THE DETAILS

In the following exposition, the properties of the voters will be introduced as they come into play, as input or output, in the processes of the model.

The Stimulation Process

P or Partisanship. What we call party loyalty or partisanship is represented by index numbers. In most uses, these are interpreted as if they represented probabilities of voting for the parties, say, Democrat or Republican. These P dispositions are defined for a given election from the outcome of past ones. But they must be set to some initial state for the first election so that the system may be started externally. In the two-party version, for example, if an individual has the partisanship values (.2,.6) at a particular time, he then has a 20 percent chance of voting for one major party, a 60 percent chance of voting for its opposite, and a 20 percent chance of nonvoting.

As in the real world, each individual's partisanship values may increase or decrease over time. In fact, the time paths of development of these partisan dispositions are a central concern in much current work.

G or Grouping. In the real world, each voter may be classified in certain groupings or stratifications of the population to which politicians make differential appeals. Consequently, each is identified with a G symbol, representing his membership in a voter category. A given G category in the model may be interpreted as workers, or southerners, or some more abstract type, as the analyst's problem dictates. Indeed, it could be a personality category, if political appeals affect personalities differentially.

The G symbols determine to what distribution of political stimuli the voter will be exposed. They channel to the appropriate voters as many as eight different sources of stimulation during the given election. This enables the theorist using the model to arrange for different appeals to be made by a party to distinct strata in the population.

The Stimulation Process. With these essential ingredients in mind, we can outline the process in which they are used. The stimulation process is designed to permit maximum flexibility with inputs of stimulus patterns to G groups. Every user of the model can give his own substantive interpretation to these patterns. Interpretations need conform only to the basic idea that distributions of stronger or weaker stimuli will operate such that the weaker the voter's disposition for the party, the stronger will be the external stimulus needed to yield a choice.

Voters are exposed to a now-developing campaign, whose events are represented by changing stimuli. The central idea is that an appeal or news event is a distribution of stimuli. Actually, this is a familiar fact of life in other guises. Suppose we wish to test in a survey the strength of appeal of a given argument for a given cause. This requires some scale of gradation, as along the top of Figure 2, on which a

person indicates how compelling he perceives this argument to be. Over many people, answers are dispersed as at the bottom of Figure 2. Thus, "the" appeal of an argument is actually many appeals, a distribution. For reasons made evident below, this is a perceptual dispersion.

Although the connection between the two is ordinarily not drawn, there is an idea in survey analysis that illustrates what is meant by the effect of an appeal. Consider how poll analysts predict turnout. They make an index locating people along a scale of disposition to vote. Then they establish a cutting point, above which the sample is treated as representative of voters, below of nonvoters. This is the same as giving the former probability 1 and the latter probability 0 of responding. Pollers know this is a simplification and that there is a sequence of increasing probabilities of voting as one proceeds up the scale. Call this sequence a response function.

The response function, while it probably increases monotonically with increasing partisanship disposition, is obviously conditional on the stimulus situation. If the appeal is great, for example, a Roosevelt or Eisenhower on the

Scale for rating the appeal of an argument:

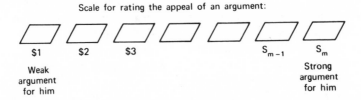

Proportion of people perceiving such strength of appeal:

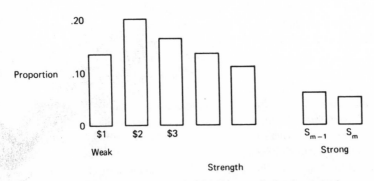

Figure 2   Rating the appeal of an argument.

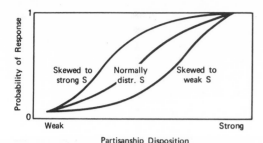

Figure 3 Response functions.

ticket, then "fair-weather friends" of the party come out in unusual numbers. The response curve bulges up at low and intermediate disposition levels, where voting is ordinarily undependable. Whereas in a dull contest, the curve is concave; only the diehards with high disposition levels respond with high probability. Lazarsfeld calls these different functions, evoked by different stimulus items, trace lines. But for present purposes they are best referred to as conditional response functions, that is, functions of the partisanship disposition but in a way that is conditional on the stimulus situation. Figure 3 gives idealized examples of response functions. The stimulation process connects the two problems above. It takes as input appeals that are distributions of stimuli varying in their perceived cogency. Then the "impressions" that a voter gains from these stimuli are functions of the basic disposition. The voter's basic disposition is always controlling, but the stimulus situation changes the form of the response curve in favorable or unfavorable ways.

The mechanism that elicits a response for each voter was designed without any explicit statistical connection in mind. Its assumption is that in Guttman scales [8]: The weaker the person's disposition, the stronger the attraction needed to elicit a "yes" impression. The stronger the disposition, the weaker the attraction needed, and thus the more likely a single stimulus will be acceptable.

Interest. It is useful now to explain an output of the stimulation process. Consider a voter of .7 partisanship for the Democrats who, by sampling in the stimulation process, receives a symbol of strength .6 from the Democrats this year. With partisanship of .7 he merely needed to draw any stimulation symbol greater than .3

to have said "yes" to the Democratic choice. That the actual symbol had the strength of .6, and was greater than the minimum needed, would be irrelevant.

However, the strength of the symbol has meaning. The user of the model has set up a distribution of higher or lower probabilities of strong stimuli. So high stimulus numbers define a new concept: excess stimulation. The rather strong Democratic partisan who needed only something more than .3, but got a .6 symbol, has an excess stimulation of .3.

The concept here is like the notion of an "indifference" curve in economic theory. A price or offer above the curve is accepted, one below is not. In this model, the indifference appeal is a stimulus exactly equal to $1 - P$; for example, if the probability of voting Democratic is 0.7, the indifference stimulus is 0.3. Stimuli greater than this indifference point are interpreted as creating positive interest in proportion to the excess.

The excess is recorded by the model and used in social discussion processes as the degree of interest in discussing one's beliefs and trying to convince others. It is also interpreted in the learning process as the "impact" of this campaign on this voter, for purposes of weighing this experience in his longer-term formation of partisanship.

Choice or Intention. An interest is produced originally for both parties, since a voter is stimulated by both. Usually, interest in one party is positive and interest in the others is negative. Only the positive one is used. Yet under conditions of strong stimulation from two parties—for example, in the major duel between Roosevelt and Willkie—both interests could be positive for some voter with inclinations to vote for both candidates. In that event, the model takes the higher of the two interests as dominant. This is entered as the voter's interest, and the party involved is recorded as the voter's choice.

After the first stage of stimulation, this choice is interpreted as only a first impression or intention. Later, after other processes that may or may not change it, the surviving choice on election day is recorded as the final decision.

The Learning Process

Interest and choice are the inputs to a simple learning-like process that, at the conclusion of this election, generates the next election's P's or partisan probabilities. Although this takes place last, it is discussed here while its inputs are fresh in mind.

One of the most noncommittal assumptions that could be made about long-run partisanship is a simple persistence forecast, the assumption that frequencies of voting for the parties remain constant for short historical periods, even though votes turn over. A roughly equivalent assumption for individuals would be that a voter's future probability will be his frequency of voting over some recent past period. A Social Science Research Council Committee found this assumption to be about as accurate as the public opinion polls.[2]

It is useful for exposition to see how one might implement this simple assumption. The computer would keep for each voter a tally of how many times he votes Democratic, how many times nonvoting, and how many times Republican. After each election, the machine would divide to find the proportion of votes to date for the Democrats and would make this historical proportion the voter's partisan probability for the Democrats. A new Republican P would be calculated in the same way, and the total for both parties plus nonvoting would equal 1.00.

The idea that probability equals frequency would seem to be a know-nothing assumption. Actually, it involves major theoretic commitments. Consider the case of a young voter with little voting experience. Concretely, suppose he has voted once for each of the two parties and failed to vote once, so that his tallies are 1,1,1. The result for the next election is a .33 probability for each of the three alternatives. Now, suppose this young voter votes Democratic in the next election. His tally for that party is 2, and the probability of voting Democratic increases from .33 to .50.

Consider the same choice made by the same voter after he is a mature person with 21 elections gone by. If these votes had been equally divided by thirds as in the example of the young voter, the probability would again be .33 for each party. But now a new vote for the Democrats would increase the ratio from .33 to only .36. This is a minor increase of .03 in comparison to the same event at a younger age, when the increase was .17. Thus, the assumption implies among other things, that the less the cumulative experience, the more influence any new experience will have. This result, of course, is just what we want in the case of voting, judging by all research evidence.

Consider another implication of the assumption. It will operate to increase the chances in future elections of repeating the choices that survive discussion and reconsideration in the current election. A vote for a given party makes future votes for it still more probable. The result is a progressive process, the more it happens, the more likely it is to happen (although not deterministically because of random elements in stimulation or changes in the stimulus situation). The process is logically identical with G. Polya's urn models worked out to represent progressive phenomena, say, in the contagion of infectious disease.[3] Feller, Friedman, and Coleman [5, 6, 7] report models having much the same logical consequences as Polya's, but we call it a Polya process.

The use of such a process here, to gradually build up partisan bias through the years, is a summarizing interpretation of a variety of voting studies [4]. Among the mechanisms having this consequence are: the selective exposure to arguments and perceptual distortions that follow a commitment; the effect of rationalizing one's preference to others; the social rewards that reinforce most such choices; and the voter's increasing antagonism to the opposite party following its attacks on his own candidate choices. Such mechanisms are not incorporated directly, nor is there any psychological learning process in the model. It is merely that the mechanisms' statistical consequences are all in the progressive direction simulated.

[2] F. Mosteller et al. [11]. Also Lee Benson has shown that, from the Civil War to the 1890s the frequencies of voting for the two parties remained virtually unchanged in almost all small election districts in a test state [2, 3].

[3] For concreteness, Polya visualizes sampling with replacement from an urn of different colored balls. Each time a color is chosen, an additional ball of that color is added to the urn.

Weight by Interest. Numerical quantities used in any such process are arbitrary until experience is available on how the process behaves in relation to real data, but important modifications of the simplified assumption remove some of the arbitrariness and improve realism. First, instead of keeping a tally of one unit for each choice and assuming that new probabilities are the frequency of all past choices weighted equally, it is better to give the tally unit a variable weight. A good weight is the excess stimulation previously interpreted as interest. Thus, the model tallies the voter's final interest in the cumulative total for the party he chose, and the probability for the next time is the past frequency of voting for each party weighted by the degree of interest at that time.

Interest varies sensitively with the strength of external stimulation. So, the weight given this election in future elections will be in proportion to something like the impact (excess stimulation over minimum thresholds) of the campaign stimuli. Presidential elections, with the substantially stronger stimuli required to produce high turnout, will have more weight than Congressional elections. Especially strong appeals aimed at particular groups (high stimulus symbols for specific G's, or by interpretation, events especially affecting those groups' self-interests), will have weighty effects on those groups' future partisanship.

Also implied is that votes for the other, habitually not-preferred party have less weight in long-term learning. For where P is low, even strong stimuli produce little excess. This low weighting of unusual choices results in reproducing the empirically real tendency for voters to fall back into older patterns after temporarily successful disturbances, for example, Democrats' choices of Eisenhower in 1952. Appeals must be sustained over a number of elections, as Democratic stimuli were sustained in the New Deal–Fair Deal era, to accomplish significant switching of partisanship. Since for nonvoters the negative interest is tallied analogously, apathy is self-reinforcing unless social forces intervene.

Forgetting. A second modification of the simplified assumption also makes the model more realistic. It is an arithmetical shortcut used in place of a forgetting process. If there were no forgetting in real political systems over many decades, the older voters would be basing their judgments on so much accumulated experience that events of the current era would have almost no weight. The assumption approximated is the following: forgetting of an election choice is proportionate to the number of elections since then. The shortcut computation is performed by multiplying the summed tallies of votes (weighted by interest) by a constant less than 1, for example .85. Since an old election choice has been reduced many times, it is of low current weight.

The Discussion Process

The middle of the three main routines can now be presented. It is best explained in connection with Figure 4.

Social influence is a switching operation that changes the articulation between the other processes. The model is seen from the standpoint of one person, Ego, who initiates influence. A second person, Alter, is the recipient of influence. Who the Alter is for this Ego is determined by the user, who specifies sociometric ties in the form of cross-references. Each Ego has at most one Alter.

Assume both voters have been initially stimulated, and Ego enters the discussion process.

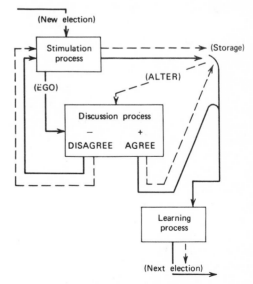

Figure 4 Two persons interacting.
——————— EGO, who initiates
– – – – – ALTER, to whom initiated

The program examines the interest of both Alter and Ego to determine whether they are jointly interested enough in this election to discuss it. Rather arbitrarily, the model lets discussion take place if the average of the two interests is above the indifference point for voting. The summation implies that either could bring up the topic. If both are interested, discussion is likely; if neither, it is unlikely. But a much interested person can talk politics with a slightly uninterested nonvoter.

If the two do talk politics, their initial intentions are compared to determine agreement. If they disagree, both are sent back to the stimulation process. There they may develop new choices and new degrees of interest—although the new intention will often be the same as the old. The new choices, upon restimulation, depend on the voter's own internal dispositions and on the external stimuli to which his group is being exposed—exactly as in the initial stimulation. Then both return to storage with this new provisional choice. Later, some other voter might initiate to Ego, and Alter might initiate to someone else.

If the two voters had agreed, the initial choices would have been retained, and the two voters returned to storage. The socially supported choice is not subjected to new stimulation and will tend to survive as the decision on election day. In mature stages of the process, sociometric cliques tend toward homogeneity; the voter is likely to be agreed with and his initial preference is likely to survive until election day.

A person who is confirmed on the wisdom of his choice by associates who agree with him will be affected by that particular preference because his choice will survive on election day and permanently affect his future dispositions. In effect, friends and associates act to reinforce in the learning sense of selecting behavior to encourage. By this process, stable dispositions will be learned out of what can at first be random responses.

When there is disagreement, however, no explicit inhibition is administered. All that happens is further exposure to stimulation. In effect, the final decision is held in abeyance, a half-conscious counterpart of giving further consideration to the choice. The theory in this case is a variant of Kurt Lewin's "social reality" idea. Unsure of the correct choice (objective reality), voters test their preferences against friends' impressions (social reality). If the test does not confirm the social validity of their impressions, they again check with objective reality (the stimulation process). It is a cross-checking of objective by social, and social by objective, stimuli.

This process was chosen because its consequences include many known empirically. For example, whether a changed choice emerges in place of the first one, will depend on the strength of the person's convictions. Repeating the stimulation process brings his P partisanships back into play, and if his partisanship is strong for the party of his initial choice, the odds are he will make that choice again. However, a person with weak disposition toward the party he originally chose will be unlikely to come up with the same choice. In accord with evidence from voting studies, influence changes the votes of persons who are weakly partisan.

The flavor of social determinism that has accompanied research on social influence in politics is here remedied. If political stimuli strongly favor the party of original choice, the person repeating the stimulation process will tend to come up again with that same choice. In fact, the person who attempted to influence him is more likely to be the victim. Thus, the reality of external events strengthens the hand of one side or the other, and the political stimuli the user has chosen to represent some historical situation have ramifications throughout the model.

An attractive feature of the discussion process, on at least intuitive grounds, is that the voter makes up his own mind. Nothing is transferred from one voter to the other, as in diffusion ideas taken from chemistry, and no forces are exerted, as in notation from physics. No decision is reached that is not convincing to the voter himself. In cases of agreement, he retains a decision he made himself. In disagreement, he makes up his own mind again, and if that represents a change, his own new impressions confirm the prior judgment of his intimates.

What then is the effect of influence? To see it simply, consider a situation in which two alternatives are chosen at random with equal chance.

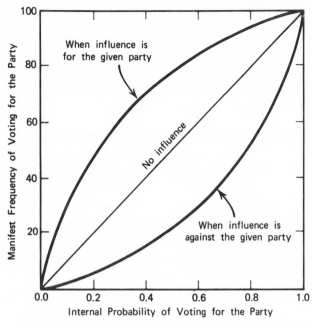

Figure 5   Voting probabilities conditional of social influence.

But assume one of these will be unacceptable to a person whose judgment one trusts. So, if that choice turns up, let it be rechecked by taking another look, namely, drawing another sample of the stimuli. Let that second draw be retained, whatever. The advisor's choice had a 50 percent chance randomly, and it gets a 1/2 chance of replacing the other alternative on the second draw. The probability is .50 plus 1/2 times .50, or .75, that the advisor's choice will win out.

Figure 5 shows how the frequencies are affected by different probabilities of voting for a party. The diagonal gives vote frequencies expected (vertical) for people with different internal probabilities for the given party (horizontal). The lower frequency is that manifested in the face of influence against this party: the upper frequency is that manifested when influence is for this party. Contrary influence is most effective when dispositions are weak; favorable influence when dispositions are moderate.

Decision Rule. When all voters are processed, and no further discussions can occur, what is cast as a final vote and learned for future partisanship is the surviving choice of each voter. In the simple example above, it would be the outcome of the second passage through the stimulation process. In practice, it might involve

still more discussion because of the action of other voters.

The model has the simplicity of classic democratic theory and the arbitrariness of its modern implementation in elections. The former depended on discussion to crystallize the alternative viewpoints and their free competition to determine the surviving decision. The latter sets an arbitrary date for cloture, often before ordinary people will have had much discussion among themselves.

Data Conventions

Children. The model will "raise" its own future voters. Although not crucial for adult problems, social influence will significantly affect future voters introduced into the system before legal age. One reason is that the young will not have built up strong partisan dispositions. When influenced to reconsider, the young are less likely to come up with the same choices again. The parent or other influencer can easily get new choices to select among, in reinforcement, by causing the younger voters to reconsider. More important, for the young the recording of a socially encouraged choice makes a significant increment in the partisanship calculation.

With a decade or so of selective encouragement of choices, the encouraged choice becomes internally self-maintaining. For, each choice makes its own repetition more likely, and in time a durable bias is built up. Social influences may now be removed from the individual's experience, but his voting choice persists in a gyroscopelike manner.

At what age children are introduced to the system, with what sociometric relations to parents and peers, and with what initial states of partisanship, and so on, are at the discretion of the model's user.[4] The model is very sensitive to these initial conditions, however, and experience is as yet unavailable on how widely they can be made to vary without violating the spirit of other internal processes.

Sociometric Nets. Similarly, sociometric configurations are left outside the theory proper because these are the variables and structural situations the analyst is likely to want to manipulate independently. At present, the scheme provides space for only one associate. Yet each voter is tied into two relatively independent net segments—the net of the Alter, and the net of one or more Egos for whom the voter is Alter. The given voter is thus grounded socially in at least one network, and some are grounded in many different net segments. Since the model treats these relationships as intimate, continuous associations, it is doubtful that a much larger number of ties would be realistic.

III. EXPERIMENTS WITH AN ELECTION CAMPAIGN[5]

In 1960, the model was used to study voter shifts during the final month of the Wisconsin

[4] Voters representing children are given very small numbers representing past experience. These are used to calculate partisanships for the first election and thereafter accumulate with real choices. In the first decade, the parent is used for "friend." Then the children are simply entered into the system a decade or so before voting age. They are allowed to make choices like everybody else, they are influenced by their parents by the same process adults use to influence each other; and they learn according to the succession of events. Indeed, all processes work as well for socializing as for adult decision making. After a decade or so of such incubation, the children are taken out of the machine and their sociometric ties are changed from parents to peers (friends and spouses). Then, with all other information intact as accumulated, they are reintroduced into the machine as voters for participation in adult problems.

[5] Charles Higby of the University of Wisconsin was helpful in these tests.

presidential primary between Humphrey, Kennedy, and Nixon. Since it was legal to cross over into either primary, without registration, we treated it as a three-way race.

Since the model was designed to explain long-run phenomena and one cycle of calculations represented a complete campaign, analysis of a single campaign was approached with trepidation. It was necessary to interpret a calculation cycle as the reaction to one appeal within the campaign, and because of time contraints, it was not possible to readjust the model parameters to this interpretation. Thus, the model's predictions were expected to exaggerate the voter shifts that actually occurred, but to be qualitatively correct.

The tests were made possible by data kindly supplied by Elmo Roper, Inc., who modified some of their customary procedures in a survey for Columbia Broadcasting System. Each survey respondent was represented in the model as a voter, and assigned to one of twenty homogeneous demographic groups. A group's distribution of reactions to a campaign appeal (Figure 2) was inferred from a prior survey when members of the group were asked to rate how the given appeal struck them as an argument for the given cause. Different response functions for each candidate (Figure 3) were inferred by latent structure analysis of responses to the survey made one month before the election.[6]

This replica of the electorate was set in motion toward future states of affairs, with opinions changing as a function of discussion and learning and subsequent campaign appeals. Assumptions about campaign appeals other than those that actually occurred were introduced to analyze the different dynamic possibilities of the original situation.

A crude test of the model would be for it to move closer to the actual voting behavior of precincts than the survey. The model would pass this test well, but only by choosing its stimuli in the light of the outcome: weak Nixon and select-

[6] The two-class model as described by P. F. Lazarsfeld [10]. Murray Gendell tested this model against subsequent turnout in a panel study of the 1950 election; the correspondence was not systematically bad. Our results in 1956 and 1960 tests were not significantly different from poll predictions based on the same data.

ed strong Humphrey appeals to go with the generally strong Kennedy appeals. The chief change during the final month was a disappearance of 25–30 percent of the intended Republican vote. Roper made the survey prior to the main campaigning. Nixon was uncontested and did not campaign, and Republican voters dropped from about 40 percent to under 30 percent of the total vote.

Figures 6 and 7 illustrate a test problem which, in principle, could have been analyzed before the election because it was plainly impending. It is the question:

What would happen if the Democratic contest were heated up by using Humphrey's and Kennedy's strongest appeals, while simultaneously weakening Nixon as an attraction? That is, if we relax one of the three forces in a previously taut situation, which of the other two would benefit?

This was simulated for all candidates in all twenty population groups simultaneously.

Figure 6 illustrates the best situation for the underdog, Humphrey. His strongest group was composed of farmers in the northwest half of the state, and the issue Kennedy and Humphrey are stressing in this model run is Humphrey's best, his farm appeal. Along the bottom of the figure is shown Nixon's percentage of the three-

way vote, and the vertical shows Humphrey's percentage. A point defines these two votes, and their difference from 100 percent is the Kennedy vote. The arrows represent changes in the vote division as reported by the model.

Under the circumstances of Figure 6, Humphrey runs away with the vote. The upper arrow moves dramatically to the upper left, which is high for Humphrey and low for Kennedy and Nixon. These ideal circumstances were partly realized for Humphrey in this group of voters in the actual election. The X's show precinct votes in the official election for all relevant precincts identified by an analysis carried out by historian Lee Benson. The X precincts suggest a response much like the model's: Nixon's hold on the normally Republican groups was relaxed, and Humphrey benefited.

Why didn't Humphrey forge ahead, then, when the Nixon vote relaxed?

The upper arrow and the X precincts concern Protestants only. The lower arrow and the 0 precincts represent Catholics, and the latter went to Kennedy even under the circumstances of Figure 6. In virtually all groups all over the state, the model and the precincts showed much the same.

A more serious problem for Humphrey is illustrated in Figure 7 which concerns middle-

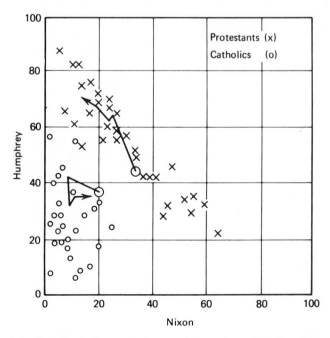

Figure 6 Humphrey's farm appeal among farmers in northwestern Wisconsin.

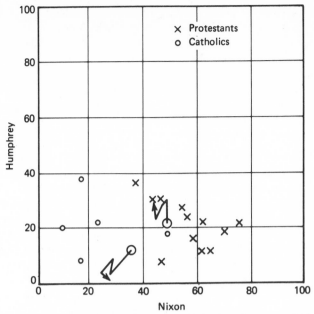

Figure 7   Humphrey's farm appeal among middle-class townspeople in north-western Wisconsin.

class townspeople. They are similar to farmers except that, like most other Republican groups in the state, they did not have an immediate stake in the farm problem. Among such people, the farm issue, and indeed most Humphrey appeals, tended not to go anywhere. The non-farm Protestants were mostly traditional Republican types, and they held for Nixon. Both model arrows and precincts stayed to the low right center.

In a greater or (usually) lesser degree all over the state, Humphrey was in a squeeze between Kennedy and Nixon. With Kennedy holding much of the Catholic vote and getting more with each appeal, Humphrey's potential was in the Protestant vote. But most of that is nor-

mally Republican, and the presence of Nixon on the ballot tied down the main bloc of protestant votes. The only major exceptions were farmers and, to a lesser degree, urban lower-income Protestants.

Weakening the Nixon appeal released a high proportion of Republican Catholics for Kennedy and a low proportion of Republican Protestants for Humphrey. But since Republican Protestants are more numerous than Republican Catholics, Kennedy and Humphrey gained almost equal numbers of votes, and the cross over left the statewide ratio between Kennedy and Humphrey nearly unchanged. Therefore, a lot of dynamics went nowhere, a result that is, if disappointing, realistic.

REFERENCES

1. F. E. Balderston, and A. C. Hoggatt, 1962. *Simulation of market processes.* Berkeley: University of California. 7D.
2. L. Benson, 1957. Research problems in American political historiography. *Common frontiers of the social sciences* (M. Komarovsky, ed.); Glencoe, Ill.: Free Press, 113–183.
3. L. Benson, 1961. *The concept of Jacksonian democracy.* Princeton: Princeton University Press.
4. B. R. Berelson, P. F. Lazarsfeld, and W. N. McPhee, 1954. *Voting.* Chicago: University of Chicago Press.
5. J. S. Coleman, 1961. Analysis of social structures and simulation of social processes with electronic computers. *Educational and Psychological Measurement, 21*(1): 203–218. MD.
6. W. Feller, 1957. *An introduction to probability theory and its applications.* New York: Wiley, Volume 1, second edition.

7. B. Friedman, 1949. A simple urn model. *Communications on Pure and Applied Mathematics,*
   2(1): 59–70.
8. L. Guttman, 1950. The basis for Scalogram analysis. *Measurement and prediction* (S. A. Stouffer,
   L. Guttman, E. A. Suchman, P. F. Lazarsfeld, S. A. Star, and J. A. Clausen); Princeton: Princeton
   University Press, 60–90.
9. H. H. Hyman, 1959. *Political socialization.* Glencoe, Ill.: Free Press.
10. P. F. Lazarsfeld, 1950. The logical and mathematical foundation of latent structure analysis.
    Measurement and prediction (S. A. Stouffer, L. Guttman, E. A. Suchman, P. F. Lazarsfeld, S. A. Star,
    and J. A. Clausen) Princeton: Princeton University Press, 362–412.
11. F. Mosteller, P. J. McCarthy, E. S. Marks, and D. B. Truman, 1949 *The pre-election polls of 1948.*
    New York: Social Science Research Council.

24

A STABILIZATION POLICY FOR THE COTTON TEXTILE CYCLE

MANUEL ZYMELMAN[1]

The cotton gray goods industry provides an example of a market as close to the classical concept of pure competition as can be found in modern day life.

This market is subject to periodic fluctuations [2, 3, 4, 5, 6, 7]. In spite of the recognition of the wasteful and damaging effects of wide swings in employment, prices, and profits, very little has been done to stabilize these fluctuations.

Some proposed policies such as shortening the work week, tantamount to a policy of restricted supply, and those of price stabilization are not operational. This is because private interest may conflict with the interest of the industry as a whole, and the atomization of the industry does not lend itself to collusive action.

Nevertheless, due to the particular market structure of the industry as described below, it was found that a production policy whose implementation does not involve collusion nor a clash between private profit incentive and industry gains, can help stabilize the fluctuations of the cotton textile cycle.

SOURCE: Reprinted from *Management Science*, 11: 572–580 (1965).
[1] I wish to thank Dr. Peter Hansen for his help in solving the technical difficulties that a construction of an electronic model entails. This work is based on a comprehensive study of the textile industry undertaken under the auspices of the Department of commerce. Parts of this study were published in [7].

This article deals with such a stabilization policy. This policy was tried in a simulated experiment of a behavioral model of the cotton textile gray goods market with an analog computer.

The gray goods market is composed of about three-hundred producers who spin and weave raw cotton into "gray" (i.e., not dyed or finished) cotton cloth. Some of these firms specialize in either spinning yarn or weaving, but the trend has been toward integration.

There are also many buyers—mostly converters who buy gray cloth from the mills, have the cloth finished, and then re-sell it to firms that cut it for use in garments and other products. In the case of mills that include finishing plants, the converting department functions essentially as an independent converter.

While the profit of the mill is a function of mill margins (i.e., the spread between production costs and prices of gray cloth), the converter's profit is a residual—the difference between the cost of gray goods he buys plus the costs of finishing, and the price he receives for finished cloth.

The converter has no control over production. He must assess the market—buy gray goods when prices are low and sell finished goods when prices are high. His customers expect rapid delivery so he must carry considerable inventory. Yet he dare not over-accumulate inventories lest he be caught in a squeeze of falling prices. Excessive inventories in such a situation could ruin him.

There are about 1200 converters (including those who convert man-made fibers). They comprise one of the few aggressively competitive industries left in the economy. Even the physical market place fits in with the type of competitive markets described in the classroom. Much of it is compressed into a one-half square mile area in New York. Communication is extremely efficient.

Gray goods prices are determined by the bargaining power of the mill (see appendix). When inventories start to accumulate at the mills the mills' bargaining power weakens. In contrast, an increase in unfilled orders strengthens the mills' bargaining position. In dealing with a mill, the converter is a price-taker. He orders a certain quantity of cloth at the price quoted by the mill.

The converter's decision to order from the mill is based on three factors:

(a) Demand of the cutter for finished cloth. This is the only exogenous input in this model. The cutter does not speculate in cloth. He does not hold it in anticipation of price rises nor withhold purchases in times of price decline. His purchases are a derived demand and fluctuate seasonally.

(b) The converter's price expectations. The converter speculates in the gray goods market. When prices are rising he steps up his purchases anticipating further price rise. In periods of lower prices, he will hold off purchases in anticipation of further declines.

(c) The converter's inventory needs. Minimum inventories are required for normal conduct of business. When inventory drops below this minimum, the converter tends to replenish his stock regardless of the existing trend in prices. On the other hand, when inventory accumulates and reaches higher levels than those he can afford, the converter tries to reduce inventories. The upper limit of his inventory is a function of the cost of carrying

inventories, credit standing, and other financial influences.

Typically, the mill delivers about three months after it receives an order from a converter. Delivery must normally be made from inventory because it takes a mill about six months after an order is received to actually produce cloth. (See Appendix.)

Mathematically the model can be expressed as follows:

$$Dcut_t = f(t)$$
$$Dconv_t = Dcut_t + Dsp_t + Dinv_t$$
$$Dsp_t = K_2(P_t - P_{t-1})$$
$$Dinv_t = \alpha(Imin - Iconv_t)^+$$
$$\qquad - \beta(Iconv_t - Imax)^+$$
$$\text{where } (x)^+ = \max(0, x)$$

$$P_t = K_1\left(\frac{U.O.}{Im}\right)_{t-3} + a$$
$$Q_t = Dconv_{t-6}$$
$$U.O._t = U.O._{t0} + \int_0^t (Dconv - S)\, d\tau$$

$$Im_t = Im_{t0} + \int_0^t (Q - S)\, d\tau$$

$$Iconv_t = Iconv_{t0} + \int_0^t (S - Dcut)\, d\tau$$

$Dcut$ = Demand of cutter
$Dconv$ = Demand of converter
Dsp = Speculative demand
$Dinv$ = Demand dependent on the level of converter's inventory
Q = Mill production
P = Price
$U.O.$ = Unfilled Orders at the mill
S = Shipments from mill to converter
Im = Inventory at the mill
$Iconv$ = Inventory at the converter
t = Time in months

α, β = Speed of converter's reaction to inventory levels

a, K_1, K_2 = Coefficients

$Imin, Imax$
$\qquad$ = Lower and upper limits of converter's inventory

SIMULATION OF THE MODEL

In order to be able to assess the effect of different policies we used simulation techniques with an analog computer. The advantages of an analog computer in this case reside in its flexibility and time saving properties. While a digital computer is more accurate, has greater capacity, and is therefore better suited for a system with a large number of equations, the preparatory steps consume large amounts of time and the results are harder to visualize. In our case to find a general policy, accuracy is not an important factor. The model is relatively small, and the oscilloscope can present up to eight variables simultaneously. This permits us to observe the effect of a change in the value of a parameter, or a change in policies on the whole system. These changes can be effected by simply turning a knob or making a connection in the circuit.

The preceding mathematical equations for the model can be represented by the circuit shown in Figure 1.

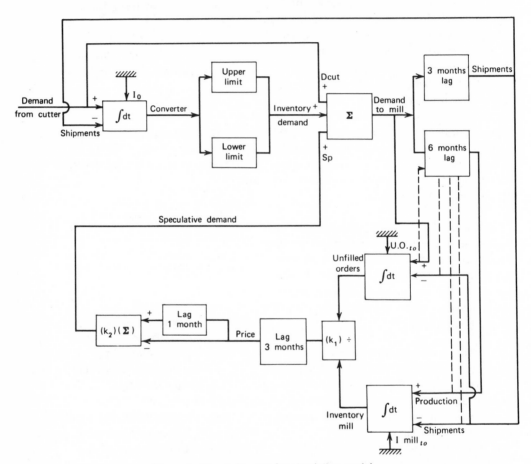

Figure 1. Circuit diagram for simulation model.

The time shape of the different variables can be seen in Photograph 1 taken, by a special method, from the oscilloscope of the analog computer. The horizontal axis measures time and the vertical axis the value of the different variables. By shifting the origin of the vertical scale we can simultaneously observe up to 8 variables.

Once the electronic model behaves similarly to actual market performance, different policies can be tried.[2] Mill management is particularly

[2] The movements of the variables resemble fluctuations of the available data (see chart of time series in appendix). In our case the only available data are prices, production, mill inventories and unfilled orders. Since lags between prices and unfilled order/inventories, and lags between production and demand are built-in features of the model, they cannot be used as proof for the validity of the model.

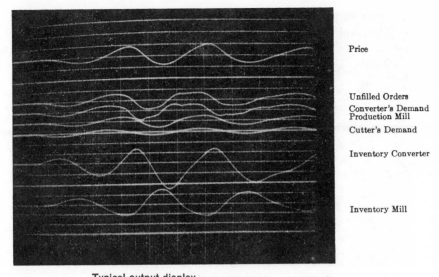

Price

Unfilled Orders
Converter's Demand
Production Mill
Cutter's Demand

Inventory Converter

Inventory Mill

Typical output display.
Photograph 1   Every horizontal division represents 1 year—total length of the oscilloscope represents 10 years.

concerned with the amplification of impulses the system receives from exogenous variables. That is, a small variation in the demand for cloth from the cutter causes large fluctuations in inventories, production, and prices.

By analyzing the loops of the electronic circuit, we can see a possibility of dampening fluctuations by narrowing the range of price fluctuations. But this policy is not practical. The market structure prevents it. The mill cannot control the exogenous demand of the cutter or the converter, nor can it control prices because the market is competitive. The only variable that the mill can control is the production decision.

By definition

$$P = K_1 \frac{U.O.}{Im} + a$$

and

$$\Delta P = K_1 \frac{\Delta U.O.}{Im} - \frac{U.O.}{Im^2} K_1 \Delta Im$$

$$+ O\left(|\Delta U.O.| + |\Delta Im|\right)$$

ignoring infinitesimals of higher order, and

However, the negative correlation between production and inventory of the mill is a result of the experiment and does correspond to reality. The same can be said about the amplitude of the fluctuations as per cent of the mean value of inventories, production, and prices. The amplitude is greater in inventories than in production, and the fluctuations of prices are the smallest compared with production and inventories. This is also a fact that resembles reality.

assuming that there is a price level acceptable to the mill

$$P = K_1 \frac{\overline{U.O.}}{\overline{Im}} + a$$

$$\frac{d\Delta P}{dt} = \frac{K_1}{\overline{Im}} \left[\frac{d\Delta U.O.}{dt} - \frac{\overline{U.O.}}{\overline{Im}} \frac{d\Delta Im}{dt} \right] \quad (1)$$

$$\frac{d\Delta U.O.}{dt} = \Delta O - \Delta S \quad \text{and}$$

$$\frac{d\Delta Im}{dt} = \Delta Q - \Delta S$$

Replacing in (1) we have

$$\frac{d\Delta P}{dt} = \frac{K_1}{\overline{Im}} \left[(\Delta O - \Delta S) - \frac{\overline{U.O.}}{\overline{Im}} (\Delta Q - \Delta S) \right]$$

$$= K_3 [(\Delta O - \Delta S) - K_4 (\Delta Q - \Delta S)]$$

$$= E \quad (2)$$

where

ΔO = Change in orders
ΔS = Change in shipments
ΔQ = Change in production
K_3, K_4 = Constants

To dampen the fluctuations of the market, expression (2) must be minimized. If we feed back E to the production decision function (dotted line in the circuit diagram) the system becomes stabilized. Photograph 2 shows the path followed by the different variables when the amplitude of the fluctuations of the exogenous input (demand of the cutter) were increased twofold. Photograph 3 shows the same situation

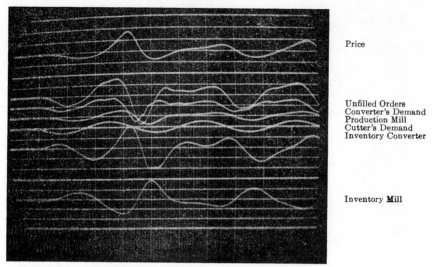

Price

Unfilled Orders
Converter's Demand
Production Mill
Cutter's Demand
Inventory Converter

Inventory Mill

Photograph 2 Responses to exogenous fluctuations.

after the feedback was introduced.

What is the practical meaning of this?

Production policies actually pursued by mills take into account only incoming orders from converters, and quantity produced is

$$Q_t = D\text{conv}_{t-6}$$

With the new policy the decision to produce takes into account also changes in inventories and changes in unfilled orders, and quantity produced now is

$$Q_t = D\text{conv}_{t-6}$$

$$+ K_3 \left[(\Delta O - \Delta S) - \frac{\overline{U.O.}}{\overline{Im}} (\Delta Q - \Delta S) \right]$$

In other words: When mills schedule production, they should not only pay attention to incoming orders but also to changes in existing unfilled orders and changes in inventories. Moreover, when mills decide to increase or decrease production relative to the flow of incoming orders, they should consider the ratio of unfilled orders to inventories. Since historically this relationship has been always greater than one, it follows that more attention should be given to changes in inventories than to changes in unfilled orders.

By following this policy the single firm can accomplish the same objective of stabilization of prices and production without collusion or price fixing.

APPENDIX

This article is the result of an extensive study made for the Textile and Clothing Division. Business and Defense Services Administration of the Department of Commerce. The American Cotton Manufacturers Institute provided statistical data consisting of monthly figures of mill production, inventories, prices and unfilled orders from 1948 to 1960. Behavioristic assumptions of the model are based on more than 100 personal interviews with converters, mill management, garment manufacturers, union officials, textile consultants and, especially, the officials and staff members of textile associations.

Determination of the Parameters

The behavioral assumption that prices are determined by the bargaining power of the mill is corroborated by statistical analysis: linear correlation of prices lagged by three months and the ratio of unfilled orders to inventory was .89.

Prices lagged by three months

$$= K_1 \frac{\text{unfilled orders}}{\text{inventory}} + a$$

"a" represents costs and is expressed in cents/yard

K_1 is also expressed in cents/yard

Monthly demand of the converter was calculated

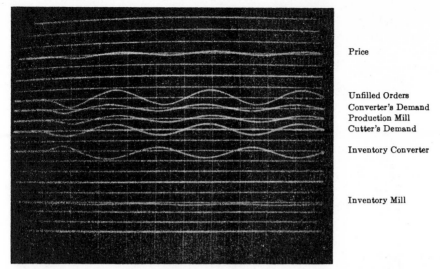

Price

Unfilled Orders
Converter's Demand
Production Mill
Cutter's Demand

Inventory Converter

Inventory Mill

Photograph 3 Responses to extreme exogenous fluctuations when corrective feedback is added.

from the formula:

$$\text{Demand}_n = P_n - (I_n - I_{n-1})$$
$$+ (\text{U.O.}_n - \text{U.O.}_{n-1})$$

$P_n = $ Monthly production in period n

$I_n = $ Inventory held at the mill at the end of period n

$\text{U.O.}_n = $ Unfilled orders at the end of period n

The correlation between the series of converter's demand as calculated above and production of the mill is .88 when production lags by 7 months. In our model a 6-month lag is used because it corresponds more closely with the information received from interviews.

To assess the magnitude of the coefficient K_2—amount of yards demanded per unit of change in price per month—we calculated the regression line between first differences of price and deviation from trend of converter's demand. This value is only approximate because fluctuations around a trend are not only due to price changes but also reflect changes in inventories. However, this procedure is useful. It determines an order of magnitude and, thus, limits the number of choices for experimental values.

There are no data available for the cutter's demand, the exogenous input of the model. We calculated its order of magnitude by averaging production of the mill over the last two cycles. We assumed that the cutter is the ultimate recipient of the mill's production. The input

experimented with was sinusoidal: $y = m + b \sin \alpha t$, with m the mean value of the average production as calculated above.

Initial values for inventories and unfilled orders of the mill were calculated by averaging the monthly values of these variables over the last two cycles. There are no time series available of inventories held by converters. We estimated their initial value as 80% of initial values of inventories held at the mill. This estimate was arrived at by averaging data published by the Bureau of the Census for the only year available [1] and comparing with mill data.

There are no data available for the values of the upper and lower limits of converters' inventories. We tried values ranging from 125 to 175 per cent for the upper limit and 50 to 75 per cent for the lower limit.

A similar approach was followed in estimating the coefficients α and β that measure how fast the converter reacts to changes that carry inventories above his maximum limit or below his minimum limit. In the final experiment, a value of .5 was used for both α and β becuase this corresponds roughly with qualitative statements obtained from interviews.

Data for the run portrayed in Photograph 1 includes:

D cutter $= 500 + 50$ million yards/month;
Period $= 3$ years

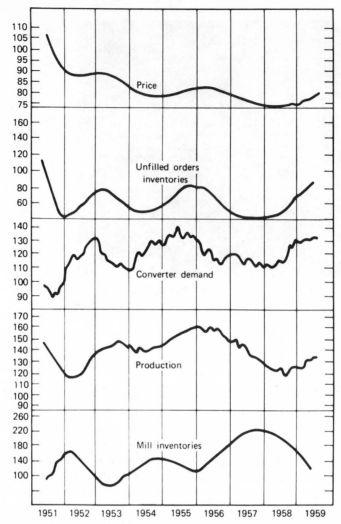

Cotton textile indexes, 1951–1959 (based on 12-month moving averages (1947–1949 = 100). Source: Data supplied by the American Cotton Manufacturers Institute.

Initial Inventory of Converter = 400 million yards

Unfilled Orders Mill = 1,300 million yards

Inventory of Mill = 500 million yards

K_1 = 1.277 cents/yard

K_2 = 100 million yards/cent/month

$\alpha = \beta = .5$/month

REFERENCES

1. Bureau of the Census, 1960. *Current Industrial Reports*, Series M22A (60–9) Washington: U.S. Department of Commerce.
2. T. J. Davis, 1958. *Cycles and trends in textiles.* Washington: U.S. Government Printing Office.
3. B. G. Hickman, Jr., 1951. *Cyclical fluctuations in the cotton textile industry.* Doctoral dissertation, University of California at Berkeley.
4. W. H. Miernyk, and M. Zymelman, 1961. *Inventories in the textile cycle.* Washington: U.S. Government Printing Office.
5. T. M. Stanback, Jr., 1954. *Short run instability in the cotton broadwoven goods industry.* Doctoral dissertation, Duke University.
6. T. M. Stanback, Jr., 1958. The textile cycle: characteristics and contributing factors. *Southern Economic Journal*, 25(2): 174–188.
7. M. Zymelman, 1963. *The cotton textile cycle: its nature and trend.* Washington: U.S. Department of Commerce. 2D.

25

AN ECONOMETRIC MODEL OF THE WORLD TIN ECONOMY, 1948-1961

MEGHNAD DESAI[1]

INTRODUCTION

The instability of the prices of primary products and the consequent effects on the incomes of primary producers have been a subject of prolonged debate. Interest in this problem arose for the first time in postwar years when economists put forth proposals to avert a repetition of the interwar situation, when prices of primary products fell drastically and cartels and restrictive producers' agreements had to be resorted to in order to contain the effects of business cycles. The purpose of this study is to analyze the problems of price stabilization in the context of a single commodity—tin. After a brief description of the nature of the world tin economy, we shall present our estimates of a simultaneous equation model purporting to explain the structure of the world tin economy. In explaining the major variables—consumption, output, and price—we shall try to link them with

macroeconomic "business cycle" variables.

In the last section, an attempt will be made to explore the policy implications of our model. We shall use the technique of simulation to explore the policy measures a stabilizing authority can use to confine the fluctuations of tin prices and of producers' revenues within a specified range. Our results show, for example, that the traditional weapons used by the International Tin Council since 1956, namely, buffer stocks and output control, are adequate; but the buffer stock has to be of much larger size than that at present. We can show, therefore, that there is a policy that can help avert the adverse effects of cyclical changes in demand on the prices of primary products.

PART ONE

Tin is a typical primary product. Its consumption is confined mainly to industrially developed countries—the United States, Canada, and Western Europe—and more than 90 per cent of its output comes from predominantly "poor" countries like Malaya, Bolivia, Indonesia, China, Thailand, Nigeria, and Burma. Thus, the market for tin is purely international. Tin is also, therefore, specially suitable for a study of transmission of fluctuations from developed to underdeveloped countries.

Tin has mainly metallurgical rather than

SOURCE: Reprinted from *Econometrica, 34*: 105–134 (1966).

[1] This is a part of a Ph.D. dissertation submitted by the author to the Graduate School of Arts and Sciences, University of Pennsylvania, Philadelphia. It is a pleasure to acknowledge the continued and patient help received from Professor L. R. Klein. The author also acknowledges the help of Dr. F. G. Adams, Paul Taubman, and K. Krishnamurty, as well as that of the *Econometrica* referee and Professor Malinvaud, who suggested a number of improvements in the final draft.

chemical uses. It is always used in alloy form. The main alloy of tin is tinplate, out of which tin cans are made. Tinplate is a sheet of steel with a thin coating of tin. This accounts for nearly two-fifths of total consumption of tin in the United States and other developed countries. There has been a downward trend in the tin content of tinplate in the United States as well as Europe, but this has not threatened the primary place of tinplate among tin alloys.

There are several other tin alloys—tin-lead, tin-zinc, and tin-copper—which are more familiarly known as solder, babbitt, bronze, brass, etc. [4]. These alloys have a wide variety of uses. The main uses are for filling out seams in motorcar bodies, gas meters, roller blinds, telephones, motorcar radiators, electric light bulbs, condenser tubes, rings, heavy-duty bearings, etc. Due to this multiplicity, it was thought useful to classify tin consumption into two main classes—tin for tinplate (T_1) and tin for nontinplate uses (T_2).

The United States has been the most important single consumer of tin. In the postwar period, due to rapid technical substitution of the other metals for tin, there has been a relative as well as an absolute decline in U.S. tin consumption (see Table 1). U.S. tin consumption has also been cyclically more unstable in the postwar periods than the consumption in other regions. These and an additional factor led to the decision to isolate U.S. tin consumption from world consumption. The additional factor was the importance in the United States of recovered or secondary tin. This accounted for nearly 30 per cent of the total tin consumption in the United States during the postwar period. We grouped total world consumption into three separate parts: U.S. tin consumption, tin consumption by Canada and the countries of the Organization for European Economic Cooperation (OEEC), and tin consumption by the rest of the world.

Malaya, Bolivia, and Nigeria have been the main producers of tin in the postwar period, if we exclude China. Tin mining is characterized by multiplicity of number and variability in size of units. Most of the large mines in Malaya and Nigeria are owned by British interests. The structure of ownership was observed to be closely integrated and formed very nearly a cartel. This cartel was essentially the same as was

TABLE 1 Regional Distribution of Tin Consumption 1948–1961 (long tons)

	1948	1949	1950	1951	1952	1953	1954
U.S.	59,863	47,164	71,012	56,883	45,321	53,959	54,427
Canada and Europe	49,326	44,987	55,686	56,594	59,330	51,614	57,148
Rest of Free World	15,311	16,779	19,407	19,603	19,874	20,527	22,475
China and Eastern European Countries	4,500	5,070	5,895	6,920	7,474	7,900	8,350
Total	129,000	114,000	152,000	140,000	132,000	134,000	143,000

	1955	1956	1957	1958	1959	1960	1961
U.S.	59,828	60,470	54,429	47,998	45,833	51,028	49,695
Canada and Europe	61,349	63,072	64,035	60,901	74,193	83,209	80,568
Rest of Free World	22,820	26,448	25,034	29,096	32,824	31,763	35,537
China and Eastern European Countries	10,003	10,010	11,500	12,010	12,090	14,000	14,200
Total	154,000	160,000	155,000	150,000	165,000	180,000	180,000

SOURCE: ITC *Yearbook*, 1956, 1960, 1961, *passim* [5, 6, 7].

observed by several students of the tin economy in the interwar period, except for the fact that mines in Bolivia and Indonesia were nationalized in the postwar period, thus weakening the hold of the cartel. The methods used in mining also vary a great deal in capital intensity, the main ones being gravel pumping, hydraulicking, dredging, and open-cart mining.

Tin refining, on the other hand, is dominated by a small number of large units. There is one smelter in Malaya and one in Singapore. There is one smelter each in the United Kingdom, Belgium, Netherlands, and the United States. The U.S. smelter was very active during World War II, but in the postwar years its smelting output has declined. There are close interconnections between the companies that own the other five smelters. The ownership of smelters and holding interests in mining are closely knit with a system of interlinking directorates.

The high degree of vertical integration has played a major role in various price stabilization schemes. The early efforts to stabilize the price of tin during the interwar period were mainly producers' schemes, and a frequent criticism of the International Tin Agreement of 1956 is that, in spite of the formal inclusion of consumer countries as members, the Agreement retains a heavy producers' bias. It is necessary to go into the history of past schemes to understand the policy background of the current Agreement.

Immediately following the end of World War I, the tin industry was faced with surplus stocks. The recession of 1921–1922 only compounded the problem. An agreement was signed by the governments of Malaya and the Dutch East Indies in February, 1921, to take the supplies off the market. It was decided not to release the supplies until prices reached £240 per ton instead of the prevailing level of £168 per ton. The Bandoeng Pool bought nearly 20,000 tons in 1921 and did not dispose of it until April, 1923. From April, 1923, to December, 1924, the entire stock was disposed of at the rate of 5 per cent a month. The price in December, 1923, was £239. The gradual release of stocks disguised a situation of potential excess demand until the end of 1924. The years 1925 and 1926 witnessed high prices and a substantial inflow of venture capital. Remote and high-cost areas were explored, mining

techniques became more capital intensive, and fixed costs increased.

The increased output capacity threatened a situation of excess supply, and as early as 1927, schemes were proposed to maintain the price of tin at £300 per ton. A number of voluntary control schemes were tried during 1929 and early 1930. When the price of tin had fallen from £221 per ton in March, 1929, to £175 per ton in February, 1930, the Tin Producers' Association decided to adopt a compulsory control scheme.

The International Tin Control Scheme (ITCS) of 1931 was an international producers' agreement with compulsory legislative backing. Consuming countries were not represented. The announced objective was to establish "a fair and reasonable equilibrium" between output and consumption. Since no similar action was taken during the 1925–1928 period when prices were rising, one must conclude that the objective of equilibrium was heavily weighted in one direction. Bolivia, British Malaya, Nigeria, and Dutch East Indies were signatories to the agreement. The main weapon was restriction of output with reference to an allocated quota that was based on the 1929 output. Within the year 1931, output cutback was increased from 23 per cent of the quota in the beginning of the year to an average of 35 per cent for June–December, 1931. In addition to the agreement, an International Tin Pool was formed, financed by a private holding company, Anglo-Oriental Corporation, and the Dutch East Indies government. The objective was to take excess supplies off the market until the price reached the £150 per ton level. The Pool in December, 1931, had 21,000 tons in its stock.

Prices improved slightly in 1932. In December, 1931, the price of tin was £139 per ton; by December, 1932, this had reached £150 per ton. This was accomplished by increasing the output cutback from 44 to 56 per cent of the 1929 output in June, 1932, and to 67 per cent from July, 1932, to the end of 1933. The price in 1933 stood at an average of £195, and by December, 1933, it was £228 per ton. The International Tin Pool disposed of its supplies during the period, November, 1933, to January, 1934.

The ITCS was renewed for a period of four years in 1934. Prices were rising and visible stocks were declining, but the output cutback was reduced only slightly to 60 per cent of the 1929 output. In addition, a buffer stock was formed to withhold supplies. The scheme drew a lot of criticism due to the buffer-stock measure, especially in the United States. There was a feeling that prices were being pegged too high. The average price during 1935 was £226 per ton, and by December, 1936, it was £236 per ton. Output restriction was reduced to 10 per cent by March, 1936.

The last interwar scheme (1937–1941) was an improvement upon earlier schemes and was the model for the postwar agreement. Output quotas were continued, but in June, 1938, due to the recession, a buffer-stock scheme came into operation. It was based on contributions by producer countries to the buffer stock up to a total of 10,000 tons. Also, it was specified for the first time that an attempt would be made to fix the price between £200 per ton and £230 per ton. At the time when the range was fixed, the price stood at £188 per ton. Output restriction in the first half of 1939 raised the price from an average of £215 per ton to £230 per ton in August, 1939. The outbreak of war solved the problem of the industry. Between the end of August, 1939, and the end of September, 1939, the price of tin rose from £274.4 per ton to £397.6 per ton. In December, 1939, it stood at £285.6 per ton. By this time, the agreement had become nearly inoperative.

Continuous output restriction with a view to raising the price of tin was the chief characteristic of the schemes during 1931–1941. In action designed to "stabilize" the price, there was a marked asymmetry in the sense that there were no rules proposed for action during a period of excess demand. The emergence of the U.S. as a major buyer during the war and after the war for the first time brought on the scene a major consumer country with neither financial nor holding interests in tin production. This led to some modification of proposed control schemes in the postwar period. The U.S. government proposed that the buffer stock should be designed so as to be able to buy tin when prices were too low and sell it when prices threatened to rise too much. It suggested a maximum size of 30,000 tons with a stipulation that at least 15,000 tons should be retained to counter high prices. The producer countries had

different views about the function of a tin agreement. They proposed a buffer stock of 15,000 tons and a minimum price of £880 per ton, as contrasted to the U.S. proposal of £520 per ton. The producers did not have any clear proposal about the action of buffer stock in high-price ranges.

The postwar negotiations began in 1948 but it was a long time before agreement was reached. There was excess production during the years 1948—1953, but almost all of it was absorbed by the U.S. strategic stockpile (see Table 2). The onset of the Korean War further reduced the urgency of action. It was only toward the end of the Korean War and after the cessation of the U.S. strategic stockpile purchases that agreement was reached. Prices had begun to fall from the high level reached during 1951 and 1952, and producer countries were reconciled to a buffer stock of 25,000 tons. The agreement was made final in December, 1953, but did not come into operation until July, 1956. The decision by the new U.S.

TABLE 2   World Consumption and Output of Tin 1948–1961

(000 of tons)

	World Consumption[a]	World Output[a]	Additions to U.S. Strategic Stockpile[b]
1948	124.5	146.7	21.9
1949	108.9	157.8	45.7
1950	146.1	162.0	42.3
1951	133.1	163.2	1.2
1952	124.5	165.6	58.4
1953	126.1	170.7	30.62
1954	134.7	169.5	(1st half)
1955	144.0	169.0	
1956	150.0	167.0	
1957	143.5	164.0	
1958	138.0	116.0	
1959	152.9	120.0	
1960	166.0	136.0	
1961	165.8	137.0	

[a] Excluding USSR, China, and Eastern European Countries.
[b] Estimated. *Source*: U.S. Congress, Senate Committee on Interior and Insular Affairs: Stockpile and Accessibility of Strategic and Critical Raw Materials for the United States in Times of War, Hearings before the Special Subcommittee in Minerals, Materials, and Fuel Economics (Washington: U.S. Govt. Printing Office, 1954) Part I, pp. 182–3.

Administration not to join the agreement led to certain immediate changes in the final draft as soon as the agreement came into operation.

The buffer stock was 15,000 tons and the minimum price was increased from £640 per ton to £730 per ton. The agreement specified a lower range of prices when the Buffer Stock Manager was obliged to buy tin and an upper range when the Buffer Stock Manager was obliged to sell tin and a middle range when no activity was advised. If prices fell too low, output restriction was prescribed, but no action was prescribed for consumer countries for periods of high prices. The producers were permitted to contribute to the buffer stock in cash equivalent of 10,000 tons at the minimum price.

The machinery of the agreement broke down once during 1958 when prices fell below the floor price, and, even after increasing the buffer stock contributions, the operations of buying had to be suspended due to lack of funds. Output restriction in the form of export control was resorted to. In April, 1961, prices rose above the ceiling due to continued output restriction during 1958–1960, and the Buffer Stock Manager exhausted his tin supplies. In spite of these setbacks, the agreement was renewed for another five years in July, 1961.

Continued output restriction during 1958–1960 led to an impairment of output capacity, and high prices have prevailed during the years since July, 1961. The minimum price was raised to £790 per ton in the second agreement.

We make use of the policy experience of the agreement in our simulation experiments. The agreement has seen price stabilizing as a producers' problem and a problem of preventing low prices, but we shall try to add a new feature to the two weapons of output restriction and buffer stock. We allow sales out of consumer countries' stocks, expecially the U.S. stockpile, to assure that price does not go beyond the ceiling price. Our simulation experiment indicated that, given no control over the forces that determine the demand for tin, a buffer stock of 35,000 tons in addition to a policy of export control would assure price stability. This, as we can see, is much closer to the size that the U.S. delegation proposed in the postwar negotiations than the size that the producers proposed and that the agreement accepted.

PART TWO

In this section we shall present our estimates of the structural equations which are designed to explain the forces behind tin consumption, output, and prices. Our sample consists of 14 annual observations over the period 1948–1961. All of the variables, except the macroeconomic ones, and the dummy variables were in physical terms and were converted to index numbers (1953 = 100). The small size of the sample necessitated the use of many dummy variables since we did not have enough observations to group separately according to the presence or absence of a special circumstance. The symbols and the units of data are explained in the Appendix.

As we said above, total tin consumption was divided into three regions. For the U.S., as well as Canada and the OEEC, we tried to study tin used for tinplate (T_1) and tin used for non-tinplate (T_2) separately. Since the U.S. is the single most important consumer, we shall discuss the equations estimated for the U.S. in detail. The equations for the other region were patterned mainly after the U.S. Our model puts greater emphasis on tin consumption. Thus, out of the total 18 equations in our model (including identities), 15 pertain to consumption, and 3 suffice for output, stocks, and price. This was also because of the fact that output behavior did not exhibit significant differences from country to country.

U.S. Tin for Tinplate

The main single use of tinplate is for food and beverage cans. Other minor uses are for utensils, motorcar bodies, and for export. More than 80 per cent is accounted for by food and beverage cans. Our first equation relates tin used for tinplate to total tinplate output in the U.S., both in physical terms and converted to index numbers. The main feature of tin consumption for tinplate purposes in the U.S. is the declining tin content of tinplate. A trend variable was introduced to explain that:

$$T_1 = 33.7813 + 0.8889 TP - 3.3389 t$$
$$(.1269) \qquad (.5099)$$
$$(\bar{R}^2 = .7892, \ \bar{S}^2 = 16.54) \quad (1)$$

Figures in parentheses are standard errors. No price variable was used in this equation because the price of tin as well as the price of possible substitutes like aluminum were tried in alternative formulations but were found to be statistically nonsignificant. This price inelasticity of demand for tin has been noted in previous studies [9]. The declining tin content has been mainly a result of increasing adoption of the electroyltic method of manufacturing tinplate in place of the hot-dipped method. This proportion of electrolytic tinplate to total tinplate output has behaved very similarly to a straight upward trend in the postwar years, and hence, a simple time trend sufficed for our purposes. The use of a time trend creates problems for extrapolation. These problems were faced in simulation of the model and will be discussed in their appropriate place.

$$TP - X = -38.1050 + 1.3178\,MF$$
$$(.1149)$$
$$- 14.8300\,\text{Strike}_t + 7.6343\,\text{Strike}_{t-1}$$
$$(3.5917) \qquad\qquad (3.6194)$$
$$(\bar{R}^2 = .9169, \bar{S}^2 = 21.70) \quad (2)$$

$TP - X$ stands for tinplate output excluding exports of tinplate. MF is output of manufactured food. Strike is a dummy variable for steel strike. Tinplate output is reduced during years when there is a long steel strike, but the canning companies only draw down their stocks of tinplate. In the period following the strike, there is a twofold demand to be met—tinplate for regular production of cans as well as for building up depleted stocks. This is the reason why a dummy variable has been introduced for Strike lagged as well as for Strike.

The third equation in the US T_1 subsystem is the following:

$$MF = 62.5000 + 0.3885\,Cf + 2.2143\,t$$
$$(.3209) \qquad (.4278)$$
$$(\bar{R}^2 = .9898, \bar{S}^2 = 1.46) \quad (3)$$

Cf is consumer expenditure on food in 1954 dollars,[2] and t is a simple time-trend variable. To these three equations we add an identity:

$$TP = (TP - X) + X \qquad (4)$$

where X stands for tinplate exports.

<hr>

[2] One could go on to explain Cf by gross national product, but it is sufficient for our purpose to assume Cf to be exogenous to our system.

U.S. Tin for Nontinplate

We have already described above the many uses to which the different alloys of tin are put. To take account of this, we made a composite Index of Industrial Production for seven products which appeared to be the main users of these tin alloys. The products were: (1) blast furnaces and steel works, (2) ferrous castings and forgings, (3) nonferrous shapes and castings, (4) stamping tools, (5) TV and radio sets, (6) motor vehicle parts, and (7) metal-working machinery. The individual series in each of these products were taken from Federal Reserve Board Index of Industrial Production, and these were combined together using their weights as given in the FRB Index and then converted to a 1953 base.[3] The equation for tin for nontinplate was:

$$T_2 = 40.9300 + 0.8261\,CI - 2.3821\,t$$
$$(.2267) \qquad (.6380)$$
$$(\bar{R}^2 = .4823, \bar{S}^2 = 71.29) \quad (5)$$

T_2 was in physical units converted to the 1953 base; CI stands for the composite index; t is again a time trend. The time trend was used to account for technical substitution against tin in the alloys.

$$CI = 18.3700 + .3557\,DE + 1.0800\,GDPI$$
$$(.1175) \qquad (.1921)$$
$$(\bar{R}^2 = .8012, \bar{S}^2 = 20.20) \quad (6)$$

DE stands for defense expenditure in billions of 1954 dollars, and $GDPI$ is gross domestic private investment in billions of 1954 dollars. Since CI included many capital goods items, it was thought appropriate to use these variables.

Secondary Tin

We have already mentioned the importance of secondary or recovered tin in the U.S. (see Table 3). This is never used for tinplate but always for other alloys. Secondary tin is recovered from tinplate scrap, lead base scrap, and copper base scrap. For scrap, we used the data on consumption of purchased scrap by smelters, refineries, brass mills, and foundries which are collected by the Bureau of Mines and

<hr>

[3] It would be more sensible to weight tin-using industrial products by their unit-tin consumption, but such data were not readily available.

published in [10]. These scrap data were combined into a single scrap series using the following weights based on the pattern of usage in 1953:

Copper-base scrap	.4479
Lead-base scrap	.3129
Tinplate scrap	.2392
	————
	1.0000

(Source: ITC *Statistical Yearbook*, 1961 [7].)

We found a gap between figures for output of secondary tin and consumption of secondary tin from year to year. A part of this gap was accounted for by recovered tin in imported tin base alloys. Therefore, we formulated the following relationship:

$$US\,T_s^c = T_s \text{ output} + T_s^m \qquad (7)$$

T_s^c stands for secondary tin consumption; T_s for output for secondary tin output; and T_s^m for tin in imported tin base alloys.

T_s output $= -19.3901$
$$+\ 0.1236 \text{ Scrap} + 16.1644 \text{ War}$$
$$(.0296) \qquad\qquad (4.1231)$$
$$(\bar{R}^2 = .7377,\ \bar{S}^2 = 38.20) \quad (8)$$

The data for scrap are in thousands of weighted tons. War is a dummy variable for years of Korean War. It took a value of 1 for 1950, 1951, and 1952 and 0 everywhere else. This was included to emphasize the greater economy exercised in use of tin and the higher efficiency in recovery processes.

TABLE 3 Secondary Tin Consumption in U.S. as per cent of T_2

1948	52.76	1955	54.15
1949	59.87	1956	54.00
1950	48.83	1957	56.04
1951	55.00	1958	57.14
1952	65.51	1959	60.89
1953	59.02	1960	62.63
1954	57.53	1961	60.66

SOURCE: *Commodity Yearbook*, 1962.

Canada and the OEEC

Our detailed analysis of U.S. consumption has already given us guidelines on the variables to be used for other regions. For Canada and Western

Europe, we could not bring out the downward movement in tin content of tinplate as well as nontinplate uses. This was due to a strong upward trend in all the variables which created problems of multicollinearity. We also could not construct a composite index similar to that for the U.S. since we did not have continuous detailed data. Secondary tin is also not very important for this region and was therefore neglected. Thus, the equations were as follows:

$$T_1 = 63.2310 + 0.4272\,TP$$
$$(.0533)$$
$$(\bar{R}^2 = .8167,\ \bar{S}^2 = 84.59) \quad (9)$$

$$TP = -115.4700 + 2.3467\,MF$$
$$(.1456)$$
$$(\bar{R}^2 = .9485,\ \bar{S}^2 = 109.46) \quad (10)$$

$$MF = -29.9357 + 2.3493\,FVM_{t-\frac{1}{4}}$$
$$(.1609)$$
$$(\bar{R}^2 = .9462,\ \bar{S}^2 = 23.04) \quad (11)$$

$FVM_{t-\frac{1}{4}}$ is fruit, vegetables, and meat output lagged one quarter. Other variables have the same definitions as before.

$$T_2 = 62.8742$$
$$+\ 0.3964\,MP + 32.3478 \text{ Stockpile}$$
$$(.0935) \qquad\quad (7.2111)$$
$$(\bar{R}^2 = .9042,\ \bar{S}^2 = 59.77) \quad (12)$$

$$MP = -8.7357 + 2.6440\,GDPI$$
$$(.0812)$$
$$(\bar{R}^2 = .9887,\ \bar{S}^2 = 13.15) \quad (13)$$

MP stands for metal products index. The stockpile variable is a dummy variable that takes on a value of 1 in 1959, 1960, and 1961. This was introduced to account for a sudden increase in West Germany's consumption of tin from 9,804 tons in 1958 to 16,850 tons in 1959, 27,745 tons in 1960, and 25,801 tons in 1961. This was found to be uncorrelated with the trend in tinplate output or output of metal products of West Germany. The reason behind this commercial stockpile was thought to be a desire to protect possible German interests in British and Belgium tin mining and smelting companies during a period of low prices. The data are too scanty, however, to be able to either uphold or reject this speculation.

$GDPI$ was gross domestic private investment in Canada and Western European countries in billions of 1954 U.S. dollars.

Rest of the World

Tin consumption by the rest of the world is not explained in our model in any detail. We treated it as a simple upward trend:

$$RWT = 13.246 + 1.4481 \, t$$
$$(.0973)$$
$$(\bar{R}^2 = .9401, \ \bar{S}^2 = 2.16) \quad (14)$$

RWT does not include tin consumption by the USSR, Eastern Europe, and China. The variable is in physical units in thousands of tons.

This completes our analysis of world tin consumption. We have seen that the price of tin does not appear as an independent variable in any one of the equations. The consumption of tin is linked ultimately to macroeconomic variables like consumption expenditure on food, investment, and defense expenditure. We can bring together demands of these various regions into total world demand now:

World Demand
$$= US \, T_1 + US \, T_2 - T_s^c$$
$$+ \text{OEEC and Canada} \, T_1$$
$$+ \text{OEEC and Canada} \, T_2 + RWT$$
$$+ \text{US strategic stockpile} \quad (15)$$

Output of Tin

Output of tin did not vary much from year to year during 1948–1957. From 1958 to 1961 it showed a downward shift mainly due to export control imposed by the International Tin Council. We tried several alternative relationships for output. Introduction of current price, lagged price, current stock level, or lagged stock level were all found to be of not much help since all these variables were statistically nonsignificant. We finally adopted a simple relationship for output:

World Output
$$= 70.7359 + 0.2578 \, \text{Output}_{t-1}$$
$$(.1392)$$
$$- .1744 \, \text{Export Control}$$
$$(.0418)$$
$$(\bar{R}^2 = .7076, \ \bar{S}^2 = 32.52) \quad (16)$$

Output was in physical units and was then converted to index numbers (1953 = 100). Export Control was a dummy variable with a slight difference. Instead of putting in the value of 1 for years in which there was export control, we put in the total exportable quantities for each year as fixed by the ITC. This was 93,000 tons in 1958, 98,000 tons in 1959, and 110,000 tons in 1960. We put in 93 for 1958, 98 for 1959, and 110 for 1960. The coefficient of the export control variable is therefore a product of the negative shift in output due to the presence of export control and positive effect due to growing relaxation of export restriction.

One can also see in the output equation the fairly large constant term. This gives us an idea of the inflexibility of output from year to year.

Price of Tin

Since neither consumption nor output was found to be responsive to price, price was assumed to be determined by difference between output and consumption. The level of tin stocks was introduced as a variable representing the history of output consumption imbalance. Again, several alternative formulations of the relation of price to excess supply were tried, and the following was finally chosen:

$$\text{Price} = 139.3600$$
$$+ 30.7316 \, \text{War} - 0.3542 \frac{\text{Stocks}}{\text{Demand}_{t-1}}$$
$$(5.5569) \qquad (.0734)$$
$$(\bar{R}^2 = .7561, \ \bar{S}^2 = 74.28) \quad (17)$$

Price of tin refers to the average price of a ton of standard tin on the London Metal Exchange in pounds for any year. This was also converted to index numbers. War is a dummy variable for the Korean War as already explained in connection with Equation 8 above. Demand denotes world demand, and Stocks refers to world stocks, excluding strategic stockpiles. These too were in index number form. The stocks variable was explained as:

$$\text{Stocks}_t = \text{Stocks}_{t-1} + \text{Output}_t - \text{Demand}_t$$
$$(18)$$

As can be seen from the equations above, our model departs considerably from the usual structure of market models. By the usual structure of market models, we mean the following type of three-equation model:

$$D_t = D(P_t)$$
$$S_t = S(P_t) \qquad (I)$$
$$D_t = S_t$$

Our model can be represented as contrasted to the one above as follows:

$$D_t = D(Y_t)$$
$$S_t = S(S_{t-1})$$
$$P_t = P\left(\frac{\text{Stocks}_{t-1}}{D_t}\right) \qquad \text{(II)}$$

$$\text{Stocks}_t = \text{Stocks}_{t-1} + S_t - D_t$$

The property of the model that immediately strikes us when we present the model in this way is the recursive nature of System II. If we assume Y_t to represent the exogenous macroeconomic variable, the system above has a unidirectional causal sequence. We tried to test, therefore, if our model was recursive.

We do not need to discuss in detail the properties of recursive systems. We shall just mention the two well-known conditions that a system of equations must satisfy in order to be recursive [8].

1. A triangular matrix of coefficients of endogenous variables—the β matrix.
2. A diagonal Σ matrix of variance and covariance of error terms in the structural equations.

Our β matrix is presented in Table 4. This is an 18×18 matrix for the following 18 endogenous variables: U.S.—T_1, TP, MF, T_2, CI, T_s^c, T_s Output, $TP-X$; OEEC and Canada—T_1, TP, MF, T_2, MP; Rest of the World—RWT, World Demand, World Output, Price, and Stocks. The Γ matrix of coefficients of predetermined variables is also presented in Table 5 for the following 18 predetermined variables: t, War, Strike, Strike$_{t-1}$, Output, Export Control, Stocks$_{t-1}$, Stockpile, US $GDPI$, US Cf, US DE, OEEC $GDPI$, $FVM_{t-\frac{1}{4}}$, Scrap, U.S. Strategic Stockpile, T_s^m, X, $(S/D)_{t-1}$. We can see that the β matrix is fully triangular. The first of our two conditions is therefore satisfied.

Our Σ matrix (see Table 6) is 14×14 since we have 14 stochastic equations in our model. For a 14×14 symmetric matrix, we have to test the hypothesis of zero-covariance for 91 off-diagonal elements. We calculated the simple correlations between u_i and u_j and found that 85 out of the 91 $R^2 u_i u_j$ were not significantly different from zero. We could not, however,

conclude that the Σ matrix was completely diagonal. It appeared nearly decomposable as follows:

	A	B
A	zero correlations $u_i u_j$	zero correlations $u_i u_j$
B		nonzero correlations $u_i u_j$

The nonzero elements in the southeastern element were six. They involved the following error terms:[4]

$$u_2 u_7, \ u_6 u_8, \ u_2 u_{10}, \ u_3 u_{12}, \ u_4 u_{12}, \ u_5 u_{13}$$

In all, there are 10 error terms of 10 equations involved in the above six elements. Out of these equations, 3, 5, 6, 12, and 13 use only predetermined variables. The remaining five equations, 2, 4, 7, 8, and 10, were reestimated using a modified version of two-stage least squares. In each equation where an endogenous variable was used as an independent variable (e.g., MF in the $(TP-X)$ equation) instead of the observed values of the endogenous variable, its computed values from another equation (e.g., the MF equation) were used. This procedure was used by Barger and Klein in their quarterly model of U.S. Economy [2].

Our final set of equations was therefore as follows:

United States

$$T_1 = 33.7813 + .8889 \, TP - 3.3389 \, t$$
$$\qquad\qquad (.1269) \qquad (.5099)$$
$$\qquad\qquad (\bar{R}^2 = .7892, \ \bar{S}^2 = 16.54) \quad (1)$$

$$TP - X = -39.2293 + 1.3276 \, MF$$
$$\qquad\qquad\qquad (.1114)$$
$$\qquad - 14.0516 \, \text{Strike} + 7.2064 \, \text{Strike}_{t-1}$$
$$\qquad\quad (3.4496) \qquad\qquad (3.5072)$$
$$\qquad\qquad (\bar{R}^2 = .9228, \ \bar{S}^2 = 20.22) \quad (2)$$

---

[4] The numbering of equations here is slightly different from that in our complete system, since the identities are dropped. Equations 4, 7, 15, and 17 were excluded. The new ordering is as follows: US T_1, 1; $TP-X$, 2; MF, 3; T_2, 4; CI, 5; T_s Output, 6; OEEC T_1, 7; TP, 8; MF, 9; T_2, 10; MP, 11; RWT, 12; World Output, 13; and Price, 14.

TABLE 4 β Matrix of Endogenous Coefficients

	Stocks	Demand	U.S. T_1	TP	$TP-X$	MF	T_2	CI	T_s^c	T_s	Output	OEEC T_1	TP	MF	T_2	MP	RWT	Output	Price
Stocks	1.00	−1.00																	
Demand		1.00																	
US T_1			1.00	.8889 (.1269)															
TP				1.00															
$TP-X$				1.00	1.00	1.3178 (.1149)													
MF						1.00													
T_2							1.00	.8261 (.2267)											
CI								1.00											
T_s^c									1.00										
T_s Output										1.00	1.00								
OEEC T_1												1.00	.4275 (.0533)						
TP													1.00	2.3467 (.1456)					
MF														1.00					
T_2															1.00	.3964 (.0935)			
MP																1.00			
RWT																	1.00		
Output																		1.00	
Price																			1.00

TABLE 5 Γ Matrix—Coefficients

	t	War	Strike	Strike$_{t-1}$	Output$_{t-1}$	Export Control	Stocks$_{s-1}$	Stock-pile	US GDPI	US Cf
Stocks	0						1.00			
Demand	0									
US T_1	−3.3389 (.5099)									
TP	0									
$TP-X$	0		−14.8300 (3.5917)	+7.6343 (3.6194)						
MF	2.2143 (.6380)									0.3885 (.3209)
T_2	−2.3821 (.4278)									
CI	0								1.0800 (.1921)	
T_s^c	0									
T_s Output	0	16.1644 (4.1231)								
OEEC T_1	0									
TP	0									
MF	0									
T_2	0							32.3478 (7.2111)		
MP	0									
RWT	2.2038 (.6380)									
Output	0				0.2578 (.1392)	−0.1744 (.0418)				
Price	0	30.7316 (5.6569)								

$$MF = 62.5000 + .3885\,Cf + 2.2143\,t$$
$$(.3209) \qquad (.4278)$$
$$(\bar{R}^2 = .9898,\ \bar{S}^2 = 1.46) \quad (3)$$

$$TP = (TP-X) + X \quad (4)$$

$$T_2 = 13.1285 + 1.1695\,CI - 3.2341\,t$$
$$(.1063) \qquad (.7742)$$
$$(\bar{R}^2 = .5776,\ \bar{S}^2 = 73.7975) \quad (5)$$

$$CI = 18.3700 + .3557\,DE + 1.0800\,GDPI$$
$$(.1175) \qquad (.1921)$$
$$(\bar{R}^2 = .8012,\ \bar{S}^2 = 20.20) \quad (6)$$

$$T_s^c = T_s \text{ Output} + T_s^m \quad (7)$$

$$T_s \text{ Output} = -19.3901 + .1236\,\text{Scrap}$$
$$(.0296)$$
$$+ 16.1644\,\text{War}$$
$$(4.1231)$$
$$(\bar{R}^2 = .7377,\ \bar{S}^2 = 38.20) \quad (8)$$

OECC and Canada

$$T_1 = 65.3286 + .4126\,TP$$
$$(.0789)$$
$$(\bar{R}^2 = .6863,\ \bar{S}^2 = 168.52) \quad (9)$$

of Predetermined Variables

US DE	OEEC GDPI	$FVM_{t-\frac{1}{2}}$	Scrap	Strat. Stockpl.	T_s^m	X	$(S/D)_{t-1}$	α_0	$\bar{R}^2$	$\bar{S}^2$
								0		
				1.00				0		
								33.7813	.7892	16.54
					1.00			0		
								−38.1050	.9169	21.70
								62.5000	.9898	1.46
								40.9300	.4823	71.29
0.3557 (.1175)								18.3700	.8012	20.20
						1.00		0		
			0.1236 (.0296)					−19.3901	.7377	38.20
								63.2310	.8167	84.59
								−115.4700	.9485	109.46
		2.3493 (.1609)						−29.9357	.9462	23.04
								62.8742	.9042	59.77
	2.6440 (.0812)							−8.7357	.9887	13.15
								16.858	.9758	1.95
								70.7359	.7076	32.52
							−0.3542 (.0734)	139.3600	.7561	74.28

$$TP = -115.3714 + 2.3459\,MF$$
$$(.2196)$$
$$(\bar{R}^2 = .9034,\ \bar{S}^2 = 237.58)\quad(10)$$

$$MF = -29.9357 + 2.3493\,FVM_{t-\frac{1}{2}}$$
$$(.1609)$$
$$(\bar{R}^2 = .9462,\ \bar{S}^2 = 23.04)\quad(11)$$

$$T_2 = 64.3142 + .3945\,MP + 32.7530\ \text{Stockpile}$$
$$(.1003)\qquad\quad(7.6956)$$
$$(\bar{R}^2 = .9053,\ \bar{S}^2 = 66.57)\quad(12)$$

$$MP = -8.7357 + 2.6440\,GDPI$$
$$(.0812)$$
$$(\bar{R}^2 = .9887,\ \bar{S}^2 = 13.15)\quad(13)$$

Rest of the World

$$RWT = 13.246 + 1.4481\,t$$
$$(.0974)$$
$$(\bar{R}^2 = .9401,\ \bar{S}^2 = 2.16)\quad(14)$$

World

World Demand

$$= US\,T_1 + US\,T_2 - US\,T_s^c$$
$$+\ \text{OEEC and Canada } T_1$$
$$+\ \text{OEEC and Canada } T_2 + RWT$$
$$+\ \text{US strategic stockpile}\qquad(15)$$

TABLE 6 Σ Matrix Empirical Correlations Among $\hat{u}_i$, $\hat{u}_j$. Confidence Limit $R^2 = .2830$

	u_1	u_2	u_3	u_4	u_5	u_6	u_7	u_8	u_9	u_{10}	u_{11}	u_{12}	u_{13}	u_{14}
u_1	1.00	.0003	.1179	.1918	.0061	.0221	.0225	.0087	.0003	.0172	.0154	.0284	.0016	.0515
u_2		1.00	.1551	.1856	neg.	.0180	.6794	.0018	.0707	.2891	.0170	.0200	.0040	.2522
u_3			1.00	.0099	.0006	.0502	.1071	.1761	.0472	.1022	neg.	.3477	.0013	.2410
u_4				1.00	.0772	.0501	.0073	.1050	.0003	.0008	.0012	.3519	.0606	.0734
u_5					1.00	.0968	.0035	.0838	.0567	.0701	.1191	.1078	.2864	.0629
u_6						1.00	.0877	.4445	.0197	.0026	.0380	.1730	neg.	.2304
u_7							1.00	.0043	.0634	.1887	.0453	.1009	.0684	.1695
u_8								1.00	neg.	.0653	.1257	.2674	.0716	.0909
u_9									1.00	.0084	.1660	.0024	.2249	.0606
u_{10}										1.00	.0128	.0012	.1255	neg.
u_{11}											1.00	neg.	.1696	.0143
u_{12}												1.00	.1615	.1811
u_{13}													1.00	.0180
u_{14}														1.00

World Output

$$= 70.7359 + .2578 \text{ Output}_{t-1}$$
$$(.1392)$$
$$- .1744 \text{ Export Control}$$
$$(.0418)$$
$$(\bar{R}^2 = .7076, \ \bar{S}^2 = 32.52) \quad (16)$$

$$\text{Price} = 139.3600$$
$$+ 30.7316 \text{ War} - .3542 \left(\frac{\text{Stocks}}{\text{Demand}}\right)_{t-1}$$
$$(5.6569) \qquad (0.734)$$
$$(\bar{R}^2 = .7561, \ \bar{S}^2 = 74.28) \quad (17)$$

$$\text{Stocks}_t = \text{Stocks}_{t-1} + \text{Output}_t$$
$$- \text{Demand}_t \quad (18)$$

If we compare the coefficient estimates obtained by modified least squares with those obtained by direct least squares, we can note a close similarity between the two. In the equations for $TP-X$, OEEC T_1, OEEC TP, and OEEC T_2 the coefficients are very close. Only in the US T_2 equation, we observe a substantial change. The coefficient of CI as estimated by direct least squares was 0.8261 and that estimated by modified least squares is 1.1695. The same is true of the coefficient of t which changed from -2.3821 to -3.2341. The standard errors in both cases were proportionately smaller for modified least squares than for direct least squares.

This completes our exposition of the structure of the model. We can now go on to the results of simulation studies in the next section.

PART THREE

In this section we shall discuss the result of some simulation runs performed on our model in order to test the effectiveness of alternative proposals. The method used was identical to the one described by Adelman and Adelman [1]. We introduced shocks of both Type I and Type II. Shocks of Type I are added to the trend extrapolated values of exogenous variables in the system. This is to assure that our simulated series of exogenous variable values incorporates most of the statistical fluctuations observed in the historical series. Shocks of Type II try to make use of the random error term present in each of the non-definitional equations. Econometric models are highly simplified versions of

a realistic situation. Most of the coefficients are sample estimates of population parameters and as such are subject to a margin of error. These various reasons make it necessary to introduce random error terms in behavioral equations, and it is our purpose to try to incorporate them in our simulated system so as to bring it closer to a realistic situation. Our simulation run extended over 25 years. The main assumption in the experiment is that the deviations of values of exogenous variables from their trend values have a Gaussian distribution with zero mean and with standard deviation which is approximated by $\bar{S}$, as measured by a regression of the exogenous variable on the time trend. For purposes of simulation, we suppressed all the dummy variables in our model. The six exogenous variables which were used in our simulation experiment are the following: US $GDPI$, US DE, US Cf, OEEC and Canada $GDPI$, OEEC and Canada $FVM_{t-\frac{1}{4}}$, and US Scrap, besides a simple trend variable, t. The results of regressions of the first five of these variables against the trend variable are shown in Table 7. US Scrap did not exhibit any significant trend, and all deviations, therefore, were assumed to be deviations from the mean value.

TABLE 7 Linear Trend Equations for Exogenous Variables

	Constant Term	t	$\bar{R}^2$
US $GDPI$	47.5176	0.9338 (.3899)	.3232
US DE	23.7399	1.4521 (.6450)	.2972
US Cf	57.4613	1.3785 (.0466)	.9842
OEEC & Canada $GDPI$	25.6154	2.9126 (.0470)	.9639
OEEC & Canada $FVM_{t-\frac{1}{4}}$	243.385	1.8745 (.1822)	.8832

(Figures in parentheses are standard errors.)

The reduced-forms equations for each of the main endogenous variables were the following:

$$US\,T_1 = 73.1223 + .4551\,Cf - .7451\,t$$
$$+ u_1 + 8.889\,u_2 + 1.1714\,u_3 \qquad (1)$$

$$US\,T_2 = 56.1055 + .2938\,DE + .8922\,GDPI$$
$$- 2.3821\,t + u_4 + .8251\,u_5 \qquad (2)$$

$$T_s\ \text{output} = -19.3901 + .1236\ \text{Scrap} + u_6 \qquad (3)$$

OEEC and Canada T_1

$$= -16.1643 + 2.3569\,FVM_{t-\frac{1}{2}} + u_7$$
$$+ .4275\,u_8 + 1.0032\,u_9 \qquad (4)$$

$$OEEC\,T_2 = 59.4114 + 1.0481\,GDPI + u_{10}$$
$$+ .3964\,u_{11} \qquad (5)$$

$$RWT = 13.246 + 1.4481\,t + u_{12} \qquad (6)$$

$$\text{Output} = 70.7350 + .2578\ \text{Output}_{t-1} + u_{13} \quad (7)$$

The generation of simulated values for the exogenous variables was done as follows. The normal curve of error was divided into 25 equal parts up to three standard deviations. For each equal part, the n/σ value was read from a table, and this was multiplied by $\bar{S}$ to obtain the n values or deviations from the trend. A fresh picking of 25 random numbers from 00 to 24 was made from a table of random numbers for

each exogenous variable. The order in which the number appeared determined the years for which the particular n value would be added. For the 13 error terms, similar experiments were performed.

As in the case of the Adelman-Adelman experiment, using shocks of Type II gave us better results than shocks of Type I. Shocking exogenous variables alone, in the absence of dummy variables and error terms, gave us almost no fluctuations in the endogenous variables. Figure 1 shows the simulated values of output and total consumption under shocks of Type I (Simulation II) and under shocks of Type I as well as shocks of Type II (Simulation IIA).

Our simulation experiments were performed under three alternative assumptions:

I. The system as it was estimated with no modifying assumptions.

II. The system with no downward trend in US T_1 and US T_2 but a downward trend in OEEC and Canada T_1 and T_2 with a lower asymptote.

III. The system with a downward trend in US T_1 and T_2 as well as a downward trend in OEEC and Canada with lower asymptotes.

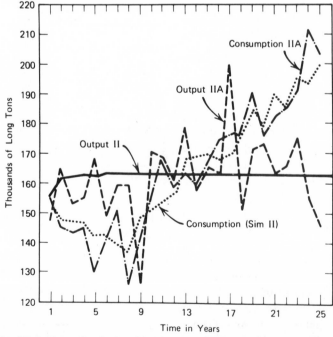

Figure 1 Simulated values of output and total consumption under Type I and Type II shocks.

TABLE 8   Simulation II—Quantities in Long Tons. Index Nos. 1953=100

US T_1	US T_2	T_s^c	OEEC T_1	OEEC T_2	RWT	D_t	Output	ΔS	S_t	S_t Index	D_t Index	S_t/D_t	P_{t+1}
30191	46028	21483	28929	35831	34578	154074	147830	−6244	74953	78.89	98.32	80.24	110.94
31557	49429	25949	21839	31917	37478	146271	162724	+16453	91406	96.21	93.34	103.07	102.85
31458	42926	22735	22785	32129	36800	143363	152483	+9120	100526	105.81	91.49	115.65	98.40
34397	39239	21852	23406	29341	40194	144725	155455	+10730	111256	117.11	92.36	126.79	94.45
29676	37209	27892	22009	28086	41298	130386	167382	+36996	148252	156.05	83.21	187.53	72.94
33989	46296	24644	18501	24840	40441	139423	149172	+9749	158001	166.31	88.97	186.92	73.15
36343	44215	28941	25052	23383	49628	149680	159650	+9970	167971	176.81	95.52	185.10	73.80
35411	17869	33540	23429	23999	44878	127717	158739	+31022	198993	209.46	81.50	257.00	48.33
37712	44020	24523	21847	24181	45846	140066	125684	+14382	213375	224.60	89.38	251.28	50.36
37894	43423	20069	22632	26380	49271	155077	169760	+14683	228058	240.05	98.96	242.57	53.44
38278	48784	28044	26055	26099	50944	170091	168485	−1606	226452	238.36	108.55	219.59	61.58
41617	43839	28044	23935	24731	52661	158739	160655	+1916	228368	240.38	101.30	237.29	55.31
42689	46607	−28000	26151	26629	49708	163784	178048	+14264	242632	255.39	104.52	244.35	52.81
43308	39941	24654	24678	28841	47818	159932	157740	−2192	240440	253.09	102.06	247.98	51.53
42929	38598	27324	26737	28731	57350	167021	165300	−1721	238719	251.28	106.59	235.74	55.86
43214	45069	25926	27452	29251	55190	174250	163385	−10865	227854	239.84	111.20	215.68	62.97
48389	42621	28845	27055	30874	56024	176118	198356	+22238	250092	263.25	112.39	234.23	56.40
46448	32854	24356	27953	32126	59972	174997	151275	−23722	226370	238.28	111.68	213.36	63.79
44765	41289	19095	28986	31212	61734	188891	171127	−17764	208606	219.58	120.54	182.16	74.84
47720	27244	27195	30859	32106	65114	175848	172766	−3082	205524	216.33	112.22	192.77	71.08
46541	36274	25690	28429	34394	62655	182603	162020	−20583	184941	194.67	116.53	167.05	80.19
49278	29170	23215	30201	34109	65375	184918	166301	−18617	166324	175.07	118.01	148.35	86.82
48453	30551	23509	31721	37097	66284	190597	174860	−15737	150587	158.51	121.63	130.32	93.20
48587	47314	25705	35046	36103	68496	209841	156647	−53194	97393	102.51	133.91	76.55	112.25
49548	39860	28306	35890	37110	68836	202938	145993	−56945	40448	42.58	129.51	32.88	127.71

TABLE 9 Simulated Values of Exogenous Variables

	US $GDPI^a$	US DE^a	US CF^a	OEEC $GDPI^a$	OEEC $FVM_{t-\frac{1}{4}}$	US Scrap^a
1	64.7285	49.4798	77.3468	72.50	75.62	839.96
2	72.0484	45.8399	78.5667	68.23	73.82	949.62
3	61.4286	39.7899	79.7650	76.70	75.10	816.54
4	63.5185	49.8798	83.9052	76.08	79.21	877.08
5	59.8087	50.9699	84.2184	83.16	79.99	894.79
6	68.7484	49.9499	84.2143	82.33	79.71	900.50
7	60.6886	62.8699	86.4617	88.13	89.27	973.04
8	51.7089	56.4199	86.3512	89.70	87.73	883.37
9	70.9584	59.4999	88.0995	91.53	87.92	918.78
10	65.3486	55.2501	88.8559	102.35	91.39	863.95
11	71.6684	62.8399	88.2223	99.47	92.95	925.63
12	75.6584	57.5298	94.0863	99.04	93.00	940.49
13	80.4082	58.2599	94.6788	102.97	95.83	797.12
14	80.0882	65.4900	98.7650	107.77	98.94	906.22
15	79.1782	63.9298	86.5995	108.50	101.83	912.50
16	72.3184	68.7899	98.2196	112.18	102.28	933.06
17	81.9181	62.9699	99.7315	116.24	101.95	1066.15
18	69.7185	69.4699	100.5296	121.47	106.00	870.80
19	76.9083	74.9999	102.5391	118.50	106.35	723.43
20	75.6184	78.8899	104.6892	121.93	111.88	992.46
21	81.6182	72.2000	105.5954	129.42	110.81	856.52
22	77.2683	77.9297	106.9451	123.65	108.68	849.09
23	79.5082	76.0012	105.7855	137.37	113.20	829.67
24	73.4084	83.6098	107.5030	137.12	118.98	889.08
25	83.9382	91.2697	111.8811	138.86	119.32	959.91
$\sigma y, t^d$	5.4406	3.6331	1.0816	2.2847	1.6093	57.12

a Billions of US 54 dollars.
b Millions of tons.
c Thousands of tons.
d σ y,t is the variance of residuals estimated from the linear trend equation for each of the variables (see Table 7).

Case I proved explosive. The historical downward trend in tin content of tinplate and in T_2 in OEEC and Canada was not brought out in our original structure, and hence, the strong upward trend in demand for tin in OEEC and Canada and Rest of the World led to an exhaustion of stocks of tin in the eighth year of simulation. If we added an estimated 349,000 tons of U.S. stockpile to world stocks, all stocks were exhausted in the nineteenth year, and since price was determined by the lagged stocks-demand ratio, price showed continuous upward movement.

This led us to make separate estimates of declining tin content of tinplate in both the U.S. and OEEC and Canada. The tin content of tinplate and the tin content of all metal products in the case of T_2 were separately analyzed. The equations were as follows:

$$\text{US}\frac{T_1}{TP} = 0.0126$$

$$-\underset{(.000013)}{.00006898}\ \frac{\text{electrolytic tinplate}}{\text{total tinplate}} \times 100$$

$$(\bar{R}^2 = .6577)$$

The dependent variable was in physical terms. We had the advantage that the independent variable had an upper asymptote at 100, unlike a simple trend variable. This helped us to fix the lower unit of tin content of tinplate as given by the highest value of the independent variable. It was found that the value of tin content of tinplate thus obtained was already reached in 1961 in the U.S.; hence, no further decline in tin content was assumed. For the OEEC and Canada, we tried similar methods. We did not have information on an electrolytic tinplate output in all of the OEEC countries. We tried a simple linear trend equation:

$$\text{OEEC and Canada } \frac{T_1}{TP} = .0171 - .0005566\,t$$

$$\frac{T_2}{MP} = 1.3190 - .0480\,t$$

The lower limit for OEEC and Canadian tin content was fixed at the same level as that attained by the U.S. in 1961. This was reached in the seventh year of simulation. The lower limit of T_2/MP in OEEC and Canada as of T_2/CI in the U.S. for 1961 was also reached in the seventh year.

All of our further experiments for policy purposes in the tin economy were then built around Assumption II—no technical substitution in US T_1 and T_2 beyond the values attained in 1961 and technical substitution in OEEC and Canada with a lower limit which was reached by the seventh year. Simulation experiments under Assumption III, as listed above, proved to be too pessimistic in resulting price solutions and were not pursued much further. Tables 8 and 9 outline the solution of Assumption II in detail.

Given the "free" solution of the structure under Assumption II, the following alternative policy variables were tried. The aims in all of these experiments were (a) to limit fluctuations of the price of tin between £730 and £950 and (b) to maximize gross revenue,[5] world output times world price, and minimize its fluctuations from year to year.

II.A. Keep stock of tin at the 1961 level of 81,197 tons throughout. The price will then fluctuate only due to fluctuations in demand. All extra output would be bought out by a buffer stock at the flow price of £730 per ton and sold at the going price if output fell short of demand.

This plan proved highly successful in maintaining stability and high average gross revenue but was very costly. The buffer stock has to buy tin from year 2 to year 12 and also in year 16 to maintain stocks at a constant level. The cost is more than recovered by the end of the period, but at one moment £11 million are required.

[5] One should really be maximizing net revenue rather than gross revenue, but the information on cost conditions is unavailable.

II.B. This and subsequent plans use output restriction as well as buffer stock purchase and sale. When in any year t output exceeds demand, the ITC tries in year $t+1$ to limit output to a level equal to last year's demand. Thus, the demand for year t is put in as output of year $t+1$. This goes on until output in any year falls short of demand. When this happens, output restriction is abandoned until again excess output appears on the scene. When a large excess demand appears which cannot be met by private stocks, U.S. strategic stockpiles would be used. (The use of stockpile is not unrealistic since, in recent years, such arrangements are being worked out between the ITC and the U.S. government.)

II.C. In addition to II.B, a buffer stock of 20,000 tons or cash equivalent is maintained.

II.D. In addition to II.B, a buffer stock of 35,000 tons or cash equivalent is maintained.

II.B does not perform as well as II.A (see Table 10). Output control, by itself, is not sufficient to maintain price stability. II.C yields higher average revenue and less variance of revenue than II.B. But in both II.B and II.C, the attempt to maintain price between £730 and £950 fails. From years 6 to 11, price in both cases falls below the lower limit. The buffer stock of 20,000 tons in II.C proves inadequate as it did during the First International Tin Agreement. The buffer stock is exhausted in the fifth year of simulation in II.C. But the improvement of II.C above II.B as far as revenue concerned shows that buffer stock does strengthen the output control weapon. II.D shows,

TABLE 10 Mean Annual Revenue and Its Variance Under Alternative Stabilization Plans

(million pounds)

Plan	Mean annual revenue	Variance of revenue
II	87.8504	520.3138
II.A	132.4566	449.9163
II.B	120.5421	530.7428
II.C	126.6868	505.9456
II.D	131.1318	494.8998

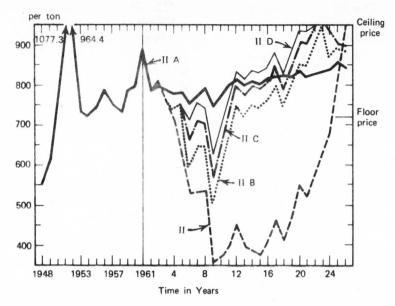

Figure 2 Price paths in five simulation experiments.

however, what a better sized buffer stock could do. Its size is 35,000 tons, and II.D does as well as II.A with comparatively smaller cost. Price goes down below the floor price in only three years, as compared to six years under II.B and II.C. The cost of the buffer stock is £2.55 million as compared to £11 million of II.A. (See Figure 2 for a graphic presentation of price paths in the five simulation experiments.)

We can derive the following conclusions from our policy experiments:

1. Noninterference with the price of tin and the output of tin as in Plan II gives us the worst results.

2. A combination of a crude output control with a large-sized buffer stock can be sufficient

to assure virtual stability of prices and high revenue.

It is interesting to note that a buffer stock of 35,000 tons for the First International Tin Agreement was originally proposed by the U.S. delegation during preliminary negotiations, but the producing countries apparently favored a much smaller buffer stock on grounds of cost.

We have ignored most of the variables that may temporarily disturb prices; for example, a U.S. steel strike. We could also try many more alternative assumptions about behavior of demand. But our purpose was to demonstrate the uses to which simulation can be put for analyzing problems of policy in the context of a commodity market as has already been done in the context of macroeconomic policy [3].

TABLE 11   Basic Data on Endogenous and Predetermined Variables, 1948–1961

Year	World Output[a]	US T_1	US T_2	Price	Stocks[a]	US TP	US MF
	tons	tons	tons	£ per ton	tons	tons	
1948	86.18	100.64	109.21	75.37	146.53	79.88	89
1949	92.65	94.60	78.56	82.79	142.53	77.80	91
1950	95.59	113.64	126.95	101.76	121.37	95.76	93
1951	95.59	97.87	105.98	147.23	97.16	92.87	95
1952	97.05	87.26	94.13	131.80	104.74	84.75	99
1953	100.00	100.00	100.00	100.00	100.00	100.00	100
1954	99.41	104.53	92.18	98.32	76.63	100.83	103
1955	98.81	105.95	105.48	101.15	75.68	107.13	107
1956	97.65	109.63	102.99	107.65	71.68	113.83	111
1957	95.88	101.37	93.35	103.16	92.74	113.84	111
1958	68.23	92.44	80.17	100.44	99.79	106.99	113
1959	70.00	80.00	96.51	107.34	104.95	95.13	118
1960	80.00	105.44	86.36	108.87	91.68	122.94	121
1961	80.59	97.54	87.69	121.44	85.47	117.34	125
Base year value[b]	170,000.00	31,970.00	53,670.00	731.70	95,000.00	4,269,543.00	[c]

Year	US $TP-X$	Scrap	Ts Output	World Demand	RWT	Canada and OEEC TP	Canada and OEEC T_1
	tons	thousands of weighted tons	tons	tons	thousand tons	tons	tons
1948	73.81	962.17	97.44	91.67	153.11	67	76
1949	73.01	755.45	80.55	97.02	167.79	77	87
1950	94.13	952.64	114.77	118.04	194.07	95	112
1951	89.61	923.20	111.39	85.78	196.03	101	115
1952	83.26	879.32	104.35	115.67	198.74	109	122
1953	100.00	942.42	100.00	100.00	205.27	100	100
1954	97.76	884.82	94.89	86.26	224.75	119	114
1955	103.05	949.79	102.68	92.95	228.20	137	125
1956	112.82	935.20	106.66	97.21	264.48	148	137
1957	113.21	875.21	87.90	93.56	250.34	167	144
1958	112.13	818.43	82.61	90.52	290.96	165	134
1959	100.11	917.87	85.86	98.42	328.24	195	145
1960	127.10	895.81	79.89	109.03	317.63	215	153
1961	124.41	834.68	76.33	100.85	355.37	205	136
Base year value[b]	3,889,270.00		27,602.00	164,600.00			18,498

(Continued on next page)

TABLE 11 *(continued)*

Year	Canada and OEEC *MF*	Canada and OEEC T_2	Canada and OEEC *MP*	US *CI*	*t*	OEEC $FVM_{t-\frac{1}{2}}$ million tons	US strategic stockpile thousand tons
	tons						
1948	75	78	66	76.91	1	45.552	21.5
1949	83	87	74	67.51	2	46.905	45.7
1950	86	106	82	86.99	3	48.797	42.3
1951	90	107	93	92.37	4	57.311	1.2
1952	93	111	96	87.24	5	52.999	58.4
1953	100	100	100	100.00	6	57.659	30.6
1954	104	109	110	83.69	7	59.932	—d
1955	110	115	124	104.07	8	60.239	—
1956	115	113	132	98.70	9	59.791	—
1957	121	113	137	96.78	10	61.736	—
1958	124	110	140	76.35	11	61.633	—
1959	128	143	149	92.29	12	69.478	—
1960	133	166	162	97.12	13	69.056	—
1961	135	167	170	93.85	14	70.879	—
Base year value[b]		33,116					

[a] 1947 figures for "world output" and "world stocks" are 63.33 and 144.21, respectively.
[b] Physical units converted to index numbers (1953 = 100).
[c] Blanks indicate column figures already converted to index numbers.
[d] Dashes indicate zero.
SOURCES: Figures for US *MF* from International Tin Council, *Statistical Yearbook*, 1961 [7]. Figures for OEEC and Canada from *OEEC General Statistics* and *Business Statistics*, 1961.

APPENDIX

List of Variables

Endogenous

U.S.

1. T_1	Consumption of tin for tinplate in long tons converted to index numbers (1953 = 100).
2. *TP*	Output of tinplate in tons converted to index number (1953 = 100).
3. *TP−X*	Output of tinplate, excluding exports, in tons converted to index numbers (1953 = 100).
4. *MF*	Output of manufactured food industries as published in *Business Statistics, 1961* converted to index numbers (1953 = 100).
5. T_2	Consumption of tin including secondary tin for uses other than tinplate production in long tons converted to index numbers (1953 = 100).
6. *CI*	Composite Index of Industrial Production combining seven individual output series using their weights as published in *FRB Index of Industrial Production* converted to 1953 base.
7. T_s^c	Consumption of secondary tin in long tons converted to index numbers (1953 = 100).
8. T_s Output	Output of secondary tin in long tons converted to index numbers (1953 = 100).

OEEC and Canada

9. T_1	Same as 1 above.
10. *TP*	Same as 2 above.

11. *MF*	Same as 4 above; source, *OEEC General Statistics*.
12. T_2	Same as 5 above.
13. *MP*	Index of metal products output as given in *OEEC General Statistics*.
14. RWT	Consumption of tin by rest of the world, excluding USSR, Eastern European countries, and China, in long tons.
15. World Demand	Total world consumption of tin including US strategic stockpile.
16. World Output	World mining output of tin, excluding output of China, in long tons converted to index numbers (1953 = 100).
17. Price	Average annual price per long ton of standard tin as quoted on the London Metal Exchange in pound sterling converted to index numbers (1953 = 100).
18. Stocks	World stocks of tin ore and tin metal including tin in transit.

Predetermined

19. Output$_{t-1}$	Same as 16 above lagged one year.
20. Stocks$_{t-1}$	Same as 18 above lagged one year.
21. *t*	Time trend, value of 1 in 1948.
22. War	Dummy variable for Korean War value of 1 for 1950, 1951, and 1952; 0 everywhere else.
23. Strike	US steel strike. Dummy variable having a value of 1 in 1952, 1959; 0 everywhere else.
24. Strike$_{t-1}$	Same as 23, having value of 1 in 1953, 1960; 0 everwhere else.
25. *Cf* (US)	Consumer expenditure on food in billions of 1954 dollars.
26. *GDPI* (US)	Gross domestic private investment in billions of 1954 dollars.
27. *DE* (US)	Defense purchase of goods and services in billions of 1954 dollars.
28. $FVM_{t-\frac{1}{4}}$ (OEEC and Canada)	Output of fruit, vegetable, and meat in millions of tons from September of previous year to August of current year.
29. *GDPI* (OEEC and Canada)	Defined same as 26 above.
30. Stockpile	A dummy variable for possible West German private stockpile of tin; 1 in 1959, 1960, and 1961; 0 everywhere else.
31. US strategic stockpile	Additions to US strategic stockpile. For source, see Table 2.
32. Export Control	Maximum permissible quantity of exports of tin as fixed by ITC in thousands of long tons; 93 in 1958, 98 in 1959, and 110 in 1960; 0 everywhere else.
33. T_s^m	Secondary tin contained in imported tin-base alloys.
34. Scrap	A weighted total of copper-base, lead-base, and tin-base scrap in thousands of tons.
35. *X*	Tinplate exports of the U.S.

REFERENCES

1. I. Adelman, and F. L. Adelman, 1959. The dynamic properties of the Klein-Goldberger model. *Econometrica*, 27(4): 596–625. 1D.
2. H. Barger, and L. R. Klein, 1954. A quarterly model for the United States economy. *Journal of the American Statistical Association*, 49(267): 413–437.
3. J. S. Duesenberry, O. Eckstein, and G. Fromm, 1960. A simulation of the United States economy in recession. *Econometrica*, 28(4): 749–809. 1D.
4. E. S. Hedges, ed., 1960. *Tin and its alloys*. London: Arnold.
5. International Tin Council: *Statistical Yearbook*, 1956, London: International Tin Council, 1956.
6. International Tin Council: *Statistical Yearbook*, 1960, London: International Tin Council, 1960.
7. International Tin Council: *Statistical Yearbook*, 1961. London: International Tin Council, 1961.
8. L. R. Klein, 1953. *A textbook of econometrics*. Evanston, Ill.: Row, Peterson.
9. K. E. Knorr, 1945. *Tin under control*. Stanford: Stanford University.
10. N. J. Langer, ed., 1961. *Metal statistics 1961*. New York: American Metal Market.

26

ANALYSIS AND SIMULATION OF REFERENCE GROUP PROCESSES

FRANK WALDORF
JAMES S. COLEMAN

INTRODUCTION

One consistent theme throughout the history of social psychology concerns the tendency of persons to shape their attitudes and behavior after others in their immediate social environment. This theme has been followed under a number of labels including "social influence processes," "reference groups," and "social reality." The process that these labels signify manifests itself in a simple way: individuals change their attitudes to be consistent with certain other individuals in their environment.

To a sociologist, this process becomes particularly interesting when it is embedded in a structured system of individuals, for then there are indirect effects at the level of the system itself, as the influence "flows" through the various channels in the system.

This paper describes work, using an electronic computer, which examines these processes of influence as they operate in a loosely structured social system. The research consists of two parts, the second flowing directly from the first. The first part is an analysis that asks two related questions: (a) Does the existence of friendships imply a movement toward attitude consistency? and (b) Does attitude consistency contribute significantly to the maintenance of friendship?

The results of the analysis are in the form of frequencies of change based on the history of each person and his friend.

As an example, let us take the desire to attend college. The analysis asks if the desire to attend college affects friendship, that is, are students who want to attend college more likely to maintain friendships with others who want to go to college than with others who do not want to go? The analysis also asks if a person's friendship with another who wants to go to college increases his chances of wanting to go to college.

The second part of this work is a synthesis of the total system as it moves forward in time. In the first part, we look at the individual components of the system. Now we put the components back together, recreating the system. Then we put the system into motion and see how these processes affect the system as a whole.

When we carry forward the example of going to college into the synthesis, we can examine the effect these two processes would have over time in a given high school, first on attitudes toward college attendance, and second, on networks of friendship.

Taken together, the results of the analysis feed into the synthesis as data. The analysis gives frequencies of various attitudes based on ego and alter history. The synthesis takes these frequencies as probabilities and predicts future attitudes based on past histories.

This preface has been designed to give an overview of the strategy employed in this project. The remainder of the paper will discuss first the raw data, then the analysis and its results, and finally the simulation and its results.

THE DATA

Let us say just a brief word about our input data. In the academic year 1958–1959, a group at the University of Chicago conducted two surveys at ten different high schools in Illinois. The schools surveyed were chosen because of the wide variation in their pupils' socioeconomic condition. The questionnaires contained two types of questions:

34. What fellows here in school do you go around with most often? (Give both first and last names.)

76. Do you drink beer?
   4............yes, regularly
   5............yes, occasionally
   6............no

The first type was designed to determine the social network, like the second part of question 34, which asked, "What fellows (or in the case of girls, "What girls") here in school do you go around with most often?" The second type of question was designed to determine attitudes. The first questionnaire of 160 questions was administered in the fall. In the second questionnaire, administered in the spring, there were many repeated questions in order to get a measure of change in attitude or friendship from fall to spring. It was such questions that we used in our analysis.

THE ANALYSIS

Program

In performing the computer analysis, we raised two questions: (1) If any person, A, is friendly with person B, over a period of time, will the attitude of B affect the attitude of A? and

(2) Will it affect A's continued friendship with B? For purposes of illustration, let us take a simple issue that can be answered by either an attitude of "yes" or "no," like the question, "Do you drink beer?" For purposes of simplicity we will ignore the "yes, occasionally" answer which was processed in the actual computer experiments we performed. Over a period of time, there are the three general kinds of possibilities diagrammed in Figure 1. The first possibility is that A can change his attitude to conform with B's. The reverse might also occur, with B adopting A's attitude. A second possibility is a stalemate. Neither A nor B changes his attitude. The third possibility is that A may turn from B to a friend whose attitude is more compatible, such as person C.

	TIME 1	TIME 2
	A (No)	A (Yes)
First possibility: A changes attitude	looks to	still looks to
	B (Yes)	B (Yes)
	A (No)	A (No)
Second possibility: stalemate	looks to	still looks to
	B (Yes)	B (Yes)
	A (No)	A (No)
Third possibility: A changes friend	looks to	looks to
	B (Yes)	C (No)

Figure 1 Three possible consequences of inconsistent attitudes.

So far we have spoken only of movements toward compatibility. Figure 2 shows that in all, there are 16 possible combinations of attitudes for ego and alter as we move from Time 1 to Time 2. Some of these combinations, it should be noted, are movements *away* from compatibility of attitudes. To take an extreme example, in cell 41, A changes from "no" to "yes" while B is changing from "yes" to "no." The results of the analysis are obtained by comparing the frequency of changes toward compatibility with the frequency of changes away from compatibility.

		B (Alter)			
Time 1 ↓ Time 2		1 Yes ↓ No	2 Yes ↓ Yes	3 No ↓ No	4 No ↓ Yes
	1 Yes ↓ No	11	12	13	14
	2 Yes ↓ Yes	21	22	23	24
A (Ego)	3 No ↓ No	31	32	33	34
	4 No ↓ Yes	41	42	43	44

Figure 2   Sixteen combinations of attitude change by ego and alter.

The computer program operated as follows in the analyses: The sixteen configurations of attitudes can be rearranged as indicated in Figure 3. The computer takes each person in a given school as an ego and adds to one of these sixteen cells depending on the history of alter and ego. For instance, if alter had answered "no", in both time periods, that is, in both fall and spring questionnaires, and ego answered "no" on both questionnaires, the program would increment by one the counter with the letter R in it. If alter had answered "no" in the fall and "yes" in the spring, while ego had answered "yes" both times, it would add one to the counter marked with the letter S. When we finish counting for all egos, all lines in the array would look something like the line marked with the letter T. For simplicity, we have omitted numbers from other lines.

The first part of our analysis asks "Does friendship affect attitude?" If friendship does affect attitude, we would expect a movement toward compatibility. In terms of the counters before us, we would expect the sum of these two counters (31 and 32), divided by the sum of these four (31, 32, 41, 42) to be smaller than the sum of these two (33 and 34) over the sum of these four (33, 34, 43, 44). Look at the fall attitudes of ego and alter. In the lower two lines,

alter and ego had the same fall attitude. In the upper two lines, they had opposite fall attitudes. If friendship affects attitude, there should be a higher percentage of "no" answers in the second two lines than in the first two lines.

Results

We carried out such an analysis on four schools, two questions in each school. For each question there were three possible answers instead of two. If the effects under study were in fact operative, one of the three percentages would be greater than the other two; but this condition will occur by chance one third of the time. Therefore, to have positive results, that is, to be able to say that friendship does have an effect on attitude, the proportion of correct prediction must be better than .333.

Table 1 indicates the effects of friendship on attitudes. On the question "Do you smoke?" boys alone were tested. Out of 12 comparions 8 turned out as predicted, which would have occurred not more than 2 times out of 100 by chance. This indicates that friendship did have an effect on smoking habits for boys.

On the question "What would you like to be remembered as in this school?" only 5 out of 12 comparisons were as predicted for boys and 9

		COUNTERS		PROBABILITIES	

If Alter Changed *and* Thus	At Time 1 Ego Was	*then*	Count Here if at Time 2 Ego Was	*and*	Probability of Ego Attitude at Time 3 is
			Yes | No		P (yes) | P (no)
Yes → No	No		$_{41}30$ | $_{31}20$ T		0.6 | 0.4 T'
Yes → Yes	No		$_{42}$ | $_{32}$		
No → No	No		$_{43}$ | $_{33}$ R		
No → Yes	No		$_{44}$ | $_{34}$		
Yes → No	Yes		$_{21}$ | $_{11}$		
Yes → Yes	Yes		$_{22}$ | $_{12}$		
No → No	Yes		$_{23}$ | $_{13}$		
No → Yes	Yes		$_{24}$ S | $_{14}$		

Figure 3   Counters and probabilities.

TABLE 1   Effects of Friendship on Attitudes

Do you smoke?

	Boys	
	Actual	Chance
Comparisons as predicted	8	4
Total comparisons	12	12
	$P \simeq .02$	

How do you want to be remembered?

	Boys		Girls	
	Actual	Chance	Actual	Chance
Comparisons as predicted	5	4	9	4
Total comparisons	12	12	12	12
	$P \simeq .33$		$P < .01$	

TABLE 2   Effects of Attitudes on Friendship

Do you smoke?

	Boys	
	Actual	Chance
Comparisons as predicted	4	5
Total comparisons	15	15
	P > .50	

How do you want to be remembered?

	Boys		Girls	
	Actual	Chance	Actual	Chance
Comparisons as predicted	7	5	6	4
Total comparisons	15	15	12	12
	P ≃ .18		P ≃ .12	

out of 12 for girls. The result for boys would have occurred by chance alone 33 times out of 100, but for girls, the probability of a chance occurrence was less than 1 in 100. This provides little or no evidence that friendship affected boys' attitudes about how they wanted to be remembered in school. However, friendship among girls apparently did affect their attitudes on this question.

Much less in line with prediction were the results to our second major question in the analysis Does attitude affect friendship? As diagrammed in Figure 4, the program looked at the fall attitude of alter and ego, and counted whether the ego changed friends in the spring. For instance, if ego and alter both had a fall attitude of "yes" but ego changed friends in the spring, the program would count in counter N. In general, we would expect the probability of changing friends to be higher where fall attitudes were incompatible.

Comparing chance expectation to the actual results of our computer experiments shows little if any effect. See Table 2. On the question of smoking (boys alone were tested), 4 out of 15 comparisons turned out as predicted, which would have occurred by chance more than 50 times out of 100. On the question of being remembered, 7 out of 15 comparisons were as

Fall Attitudes		Friendships		
Alter	Ego	Changed friend	Didn't change	
No	No			1
No	Yes			2
Yes	No			3
Yes	Yes	N		4

Program keeps one set of counters and one of probabilities.

Figure 4   Does attitude consistency help maintain friendship?

predicted for boys and 6 out of 12 for girls. The results for boys could have occurred by chance alone 18 times in 100; and for girls the probability of a chance occurrence was 12 in 100.

At least one of the reasons these results show little or no effect is the method used to locate the friend for each person. To the sociometric question we used, "What fellows here in school do you go around with most often?"—there were up to ten answers recorded. The likelihood of a person putting down his friends in the same order fall and spring is not high. Instead of searching the whole list of ten friends, to see if an ego maintained his friendship, the program arbitrarily took the first name both fall and spring as the only friend. Therefore, our program finds more changes of friend than probably existed in reality.

THE SIMULATION

Program

Once we have made the analysis, we can proceed with a synthesis. We have looked at the system on the individual level, noting the frequency of various attitude changes. Now we set our system in motion and watch how the system as a whole changes over a period of time. The analysis can be manipulated to give us the following situation. We know ego and alter attitudes at Time 1 and alter attitude at Time 2. If we know the probabilities for ego attitude when ego and alter have this particular history of attitudes, we can decide what ego attitude will be for Time 2. To make the simulation move in time, we say arbitrarily that the predicted attitude will be ego's attitude at Time 3. Hence we can go through a school and predict attitudes for each student based on his own attitude at Time 1 and his friend's attitudes at Times 1 and 2.

But where do we obtain the probabilities? By returning to the configuration of counters shown in Figure 3, we see that each counter was filled on the basis of alter attitude at Times 1 and 2 and ego attitude at Time 1. Since an ego with that history can be only "yes" or "no" at Time 3, the probabilities across a given row must add up to 1.0. Note how the "30" and "20" of line T are converted into the 0.6 and 0.4 of line T'. Hence the program can create a set of probabilities as based on ego and alter history, which then allows it to take each student in a school and predict his attitude in the new time period, Time 3.

A complication

At this point, perhaps it would be wise to make note of a complication that we have avoided up to this time. As we noted at the outset, a person could keep his same friend or he could choose a new one. Our discussion so far has referred only

to egos that keep the same alter. But what if our ego changes alter? Then the program uses the procedure in Figure 5 to create what we have called a "composite alter." In the fall, A chooses B. B's fall attitude becomes the fall attitude of the composite alter. In the spring, A chooses C. C's spring attitude becomes the spring attitude of the composite alter. In the analysis, the program treated a composite alter the same as a real alter. For the synthesis, the program keeps a separate set of probabilities for people who change friends and uses the correct probability for a given ego, depending on his changing or keeping his friend. Hence, instead of 16 probabilities, the program really operates with 32.

TIME 1 Fall	TIME 2 Spring
A chooses B.	A chooses C.
Alter's attitude is B's attitude.	Alter's attitude is C's attitude.

Figure 5   Making a composite alter.

For simplicity, we have explained our program with a question with two possible answers. With such questions the computer must calculate 32 probabilities. When the possible answers to the attitude question increase, the complexity of the problem is increased by a power of 4. In our actual computer experiments, we have used questions that have either 3 possible answers or have been arbitrarily reduced to that. Hence, the actual program manipulates 162 probabilities. We hesitated to expand our program to include 4-dimensional questions because it would have been necessary to calculate 512 probabilities.

Results

In order to present our results, we asked the program for two kinds of proportions. The first kind of proportion was based on the ego's previous attitudes. We then treated this proportion like a transition probability in a stochastic process, to calculate future distributions. The results of this calculation are shown on the graphs below by the continuous line, and is what we call *psychologically expected*, that is, expected on the basis of individual history without social influence. For each time cycle, an ego's attitude was also predicted on the basis of his own and his friend's attitudes. This *socially predicted* proportion is illustrated on the graphs by X's or pluses.

For those of you who like your probabilities to add up to 1.0, or your percentages to add up to 99.99 percent, let me note that we have omitted one part of the three-part answer to save visual confusion. All our illustrations are taken from School 9, a large suburban school in northern Illinois.

Figure 6 graphs the results on the question, "Do you smoke?" addressed to boys. We see that as time progresses, the percentage of regular smokers rises more quickly by the social than by the psychological process. Correspondingly, the percentage of "no" answers drops more quickly in the social than in the psychological process. Thus the effect of friendship on smoking behavior at the individual level, which was evident in the analysis, had consequences also for the system: it accelerated the trend toward greater smoking.

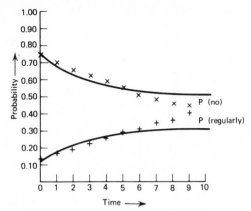

Figure 6   Do you smoke? Boys only.
+ Yes, regularly
Yes, occasionally—not graphed
× No
− Psychologically expected

Figure 7 graphs the results on the other attitude question examined in the analysis above: "What would you like to be remembered as here at school?" For girls the possible answers were "student," "leader in activities," and "most

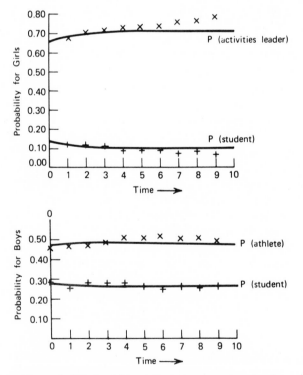

Figure 7   What would you like to be remembered as?
+ Student
× Activities leader or athlete
Most popular—not graphed
− Psychologically expected

popular." For boys, possible answers were "student," "athlete," and "most popular." For girls, the increase of "activities leader" as a choice seems to be strongly accelerated by the social process; the percentage desiring to be student drops more rapidly as a result of the social interaction.

Unfortunately, many of our simulation results look very much like the answer given by the program for the boys in School 9 on this question. The social and psychological lines seem to parallel each other very closely, indicating that the social process has little effect on the change of attitude.

Another question is included in the simulation for School 9, though the analytical comparisons are not included in the earlier section of the paper. The question concerns drinking beer, and the results are graphed in Figure 8. The boy or girl could respond that he drinks beer not at all, only occasionally, or regularly. By the psychological process alone, there is an increase in beer drinking among both girls and boys. For girls, the social process appears to accelerate the psychological one, increasing beer drinking more rapidly than would be predicted on the basis of individual changes alone. For boys, however, no effect is apparent.

One use we plan to make of this program is to locate the socially relevant issues in a school. In other words, if the social processes diverge radically from the purely psychological ones on a particular issue, we are inclined to conclude that this issue is a subject of social importance in this school. By listing the areas of opinion that are important in a given school, we shall be able to describe the social and attitudinal climate of the school.

The analysis and simulation presented above are only a beginning in the detailed study of the interplay of attitudes and friendships in a school. We present them principally to illustrate an approach that we feel will be of great value in the study of complex systems: a combination of analysis and simulation to study the behavior of the system.

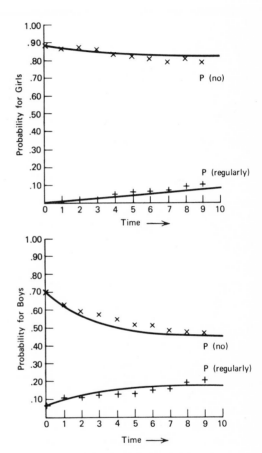

Figure 8 Do you drink beer?
+ Yes, regularly
Yes, occasionally—not graphed
× No
− Psychologically expected

27

A QUARTERLY ECONOMETRIC MODEL OF THE UNITED STATES: A PROGRESS REPORT

MAURICE LIEBENBERG
ALBERT A. HIRSCH
JOEL POPKIN

In recent years economists have made increased use of a relatively new tool for analyzing the behavior of the overall economy—the econometric model. This kind of model—of which there are now a considerable number—attempts to depict in a set of equations the essential quantitative relationships that determine the behavior of such magnitudes as output, income, employment, and prices. Econometric models have been used for forecasting, estimating the quantitative impact of alternative Government policies, and testing various hypotheses about the nature of the business cycle.

This article presents a quarterly model of the U.S. economy that has been developed by the Office of Business Economics. It is a variant of one constructed under the direction of Professor Lawrence R. Klein at the Wharton School of Finance and Commerce of the University of Pennsylvania. The original model, consisting of 34 equations, was designed primarily as a forecasting instrument. [2, 7, 8]. In the model's further development at OBE, this characteristic has been maintained.

SOURCE: Reprinted from *Survey of Current Business* 46 (5): 13–39 (1966).

It should be made quite clear that this article is a progress report on work that must be regarded as experimental. Forecasting business activity is hazardous whatever technique is used and the econometric technique is no exception. This article is published with the intention of fostering the progress of research in this field; no predictions of the future will be presented.

The first part of this article deals with the nature of econometric models. The second describes the OBE model. The third reports the results of tests that show how well the model has depicted the behavior of the U.S. economy since the Korean war.

ECONOMETRIC MODELS

The characteristics of an econometric model and the steps involved in its construction and use will be explained by reference to a simplified version of actual models. The following set of six equations constitutes a complete model, although hardly a realistic one, and will serve to illustrate the main points.

$$C_t = \alpha_0 + \alpha_1 Y_t + \alpha_2 C_{t-1} + u_{1t} \qquad (1)$$
$$I_t = \beta_0 + \beta_1 P_t - \beta_2 K_{t-1} + u_{2t} \qquad (2)$$
$$W_t = \gamma_0 + \gamma_1 Y_t + \gamma_{2t} + u_{3t} \qquad (3)$$
$$Y_t = C_t + I_t + G_t \qquad (4)$$
$$P_t = Y_t - W_t \qquad (5)$$
$$K_t = K_{t-1} + I_t \qquad (6)$$

The variables included in the above equations are defined as:

C = Consumption

Y = Income (net product)

W = Wage income

P = Nonwage income

I = Net investment

K = Net capital stock at end of period

t = time

G = Government expenditures on goods and services

u_1, u_2, u_3 = disturbance terms

The subscript t refers to a given time period; $t-1$ to the previous period.

The first equation states that consumption in the current period depends on the same period's income and on consumption in the previous period. Net investment, represented in Equation 2, is determined by nonwage income earned in the current period and by the net capital stock available at the end of the previous period. Wages, in Equation 3, are related to income and time. The latter stands for factors that are not further specified and that affect the economic variables gradually and persistently. The remaining three equations, called identities, are definitional statements and are needed to complete the model. Total income (or net product) is defined in Equation 4 as the sum of consumption, net investment, and government expenditures. (The items that in the real world constitute differences between net income and product are omitted.) Nonwage income is the difference between total income and wage income (Equation 5), and the net capital stock at the end of the current period is equal to the last period's stock plus current net investment (Equation 6).

The first three equations contain, besides explanatory variables on the right-hand side, the variables u_1, u_2, and u_3 respectively. These terms, called disturbance terms, are included in explicit recognition of the fact that the other variables

cannot fully explain movements of the dependent variables on the left-hand side. Assuming that no significant variables have been omitted, the disturbance terms can be regarded as reflecting random elements representing the net effect of a host of unknown and unpredictable factors. Ideally they are small so that the remaining ("systematic") part of each equation accounts for most of the movements in the dependent variable. The last three equations, because they hold by definition, contain no disturbance terms.

The following section explains how the equations of a model are constructed. A later section shows how they are solved and how a model is used.

Constructing the Model

As a basis for an econometric model the investigator must, first of all, establish a conceptual framework that sets forth the way in which he believes the economy to work. In the example, for instance, there are three components of final demand—consumption, investment, and government expenditures—that are determined by different sets of factors. Total demand, made up of three components, calls forth production of an equal amount; this implies that there are no resource limitations. On the income side, it is assumed that wages are systematically explained while nonwage income is residually determined.

Such a framework does not, of course, fix the exact character of the model. There is wide latitude left with respect to the particular form a model may take. For instance, it may be highly aggregative, containing only a few variables and equations, like the illustrative example, or it may be very disaggregative, containing many.[1] The choice depends in part on how much the model builder wishes to explain and upon how much detail he thinks is needed to make a model perform reasonably well. Models also vary with respect to the length of the unit time period; in practice, this period has varied from a quarter to a year.

There is also considerable latitude at the next step of model building—the formulation of the

---

[1] Recently developed models vary in size from a five equation model [4], to the very large Brookings-SSRC model, which has over 300 equations in the complete version [3].

component equations. In the example, the first three equations represent the kind over which the model builder has discretion, for they embody hypotheses regarding economic behavior; the identities arise naturally as logical requirements for completeness.

The investigator selects equations as a result of testing various economic hypotheses on empirical data. More specifically, he uses regression methods in determining how well the hypotheses fit the data for some selected time period. In the process, he obtains estimates of the parameters, that is, values of the α's, β's, and γ's. Equations embodying given hypotheses may be entertained during the fitting and testing stage only to be subsequently discarded because they explain the historical data poorly. Others may be discarded even if they fit such data well, because they do not provide adequate predictability when tested beyond the period of fitting.

The testing of hypotheses with actual economic magnitudes and the selection of a workable set of equations are the most important tasks of the model builder. He must decide not only which variables are to be included in each equation but also what form the variables are to take. Together, these two decisions constitute what is called *specification*. For instance, in the example, the consumption equation might have contained, instead of total income, W and P as separate variables. In specifying equations, the model builder is normally guided by economic theory institutional knowledge of the economy, and results obtained by other research workers. But there remains a wide area of freedom for exercising ingenuity which is reflected in different specifications among different models for equations explaining the same dependent variable. The task of specification is never really finished since new research may suggest other relevant variables and new forms. Revised specification may also be called for because of basic changes in the economy that make the old equations inapplicable.

Using the Model

After the equations have been decided upon and the parameters estimated, the model can be tested as a whole and applied. This means solving the set of equations for values of the unknown or *endogenous* variables. First, values of the inputs

to the model are obtained. These inputs are all those variables assumed to be known at the time the model is to be processed; in the case of the illustrative model, these are the prior period's consumption and capital stock, time, and government expenditures. These variables are referred to as *predetermined*, and they include both lagged values of endogenous variables and other magnitudes, such as time and government expenditures, designated as *exogenous*. Variables are regarded as exogenous if they are believed to be determined essentially outside the economic system. However, certain other variables may be treated as exogenous if they cannot be adequately predicted by regression equations or if making them endogenous would require a substantially enlarged model.

After the predetermined values have been introduced into the equations, the entire set is solved simultaneously, and the outputs—the endogenous variables—are obtained. In the example, there are six independent equations and six unknowns, the current endogenous variables C_t, Y_t, I_t, W_t, P_t, and K_t. Thus, the model is complete and can be solved. The disturbance terms are also unknowns, but are assumed to be zero in accordance with their statistically expected value. Clearly, the values determined for each unknown depend on both the magnitude of the inputs and the coefficients (the estimates of the α's, β's, and γ's).

When the model is used for forecasting purposes, it is apparent that in addition to the lagged values, projections of all the exogenous variables must be included as inputs. In the illustrative model, there are only two such variables, time and government expenditures. Only the latter, of course, is not known with certainty. With all predetermined values introduced, a solution is obtained for the first of the future time periods. Forecasts beyond the first period are made by further projections of exogenous variables and the use of needed outputs of earlier solutions as lagged endogenous variables. In the simple model, C_t and K_t obtained in the first period become C_{t-1} and K_{t-1} with respect to the next. Successive solutions trace out a path over time for all the endogenous variables.

Although this article focuses on the use of econometric models for forecasting purposes, the policy use of a model is illustrated here. In the simple model, there is only one variable that can be regarded as an instrument of government policy, namely government expenditures. It is necessary only to introduce into the model an alternative contemplated value for such expenditures under the assumed new policy and to solve the model under the changed conditions. The difference in the model's behavior under the two assumed values of government expenditures represents the effect of the proposed change.

By slightly enlarging the model, it is possible to illustrate another policy use. If the first equation is modified by substituting disposable income—income minus taxes—for total income and including an additional equation for taxes, the system is again complete with seven equations and seven unknowns. The model could then be used to examine the probable effects of a proposed change in tax rates. This would involve changing the parameters of the tax equation to conform with the proposed changes in rates and solving the model using the alternative tax functions.

The Working of a Simple Model

At this stage, an attempt will be made to describe verbally how the illustrative model would work if it were used to forecast the effects of a given increase in government expenditures. In the case of simple models, such a verbal account is possible, and it helps nonmathematicians to understand the essence of econometric models. In the case of models as complex as the OBE model that will be described, a verbal account is not possible.

1. The assumed increase in government expenditures will result in an increase in product (income) (Equation 4). This, in turn, will result in an increase in consumption (Equation 1), and this, in turn, in an increase in product (income) (Equation 4), and so on, all within the same time period.

2. The assumed increase in government expenditures will also result in an increase in the profit component of income (Equations 4 and 5), and this will stimulate investment (Equation 2). Next, the increase in investment will affect production, income, and its profits component, and this will in turn stimulate investment (see the

same equations). A profit-investment interaction will be in progress, similar to the income-consumption interaction sketched in paragraph 1.

3. The increases in investment, by raising income, will also contribute to the income-consumption interaction described in paragraph 1; and the income-consumption interaction will contribute to the profit-investment interaction described in paragraph 2.

Thus, the initial increase in government expenditures will result in a cumulative upward movement in production and income and their components—consumption and investment and wages and profits. How far this cumulative movement will proceed depends on the spending behavior of consumers and investors. The higher the additional spending out of additional income, the larger the total effect of the initial increase in government expenditures. However it can be shown that the upward movement will always reach a limit provided not all the additional income is spent.

This exhausts the effects of the increase in government spending on economic activity in the same period. However there are additional effects in the next period.

4. In that period, consumption will increase further, reflecting the dependence of current consumption on prior-period consumption (Equation 1), and this will in turn tend to stimulate aggregate economic activity and its components in a manner very similar to that already sketched for the prior period.

5. However, another force will be working in the opposite direction: Investment during the prior period will have increased the capital stock, and this will reduce investment during the current period (Equation 2). This will tend to bring about a cumulative downward movement in economic activity and its components.

Whether, how soon, and where the system will finally settle in response to the increase in government expenditures will depend on the tialini state of the economy and the particular behavior patterns reflected in the equations. If the system does settle down to a unique income value, one may regard the effect of the additional government expenditure as the resulting (ultimate) change in output. The ratio of the change in output to the initial change in expenditure is called the *long-run multiplier*.[2] If the ratio is computed on the basis of the first period effect only, it is called the *impact multiplier*. In a later section of this article, the impact multiplier for the OBE model will be given.

The above explanation of how the model works within a period illustrates the economic meaning of simultaneity. Mathematically, this is reflected in the fact that none of the equations can be used alone to solve for the left-hand variable; the system must be solved as a whole.

It would be possible by different specifications of equations to remove the simultaneous character of the simple models. We could, for example, substitute Y_{t-1} for Y_t in the first equation. Consumption would then depend exclusively upon lagged variables. In that case, the equation could be solved in isolation from the others since all values on the right would be known.

If the time period t is short enough, say a week, the substitution of lagged income for current income is not unreasonable; decisions to spend this week may well depend on last week's income and not on the current week's. When the time period is much longer—a quarter or more, as it is in almost all models—unidirectional causality becomes doubtful. That is, income earned within the quarter can clearly affect expenditures within the same period, so that causation runs in both directions. Such interdependence also applies to other variables and points up the importance of simultaneity in a realistic characterization of economic behavior.

Forecasting Errors

Needless to say, econometric models do not produce perfect forecasts of the future. There are several reasons for this. First, errors can be made in the projections of the exogenous variables. In our simple example, for instance, government expenditures may turn out to be different from

[2] In some contexts, the multiplier is confined to the effects on output of changes in exogenous variables operating through the consumption-income interrelationship. In this article, the use of the term is extended to include effects on output through the entire model. It should also be noted that a model does not have a single value for the multiplier. Different exogenous elements may have different effects. Thus, an assumed change in transfer payments would have a smaller effect on output than an equal change in purchases.

those that had been projected. Second, the data to which the equations are fitted usually contain errors; these will affect the estimates of the parameters. Incidentally, errors in the data will also result in a somewhat false standard against which errors of prediction are measured.

These two sources of error should be distinguished from those that occur in the construction and solution of the model and that would lead to faulty forecasts even if the exogenous variables and the data were perfect. To focus on these "model" errors, it is useful to regard an econometric model as a device that translates given inputs—the predetermined variables—into certain outputs, and to inquire into the reasons why this translation process may go wrong.

One reason for a model's failure to serve as a perfect translator stems from the fact that no conceivable set of equations can take full account of all the causal factors that influence given variables. We have already referred to the disturbance terms, which reflect the factors not taken into account in the systematic parts of the equations. Although the assumption is made that the expected value of the disturbance terms is zero, in any given instance the actual value may be either positive or negative. This will result in differences between predicted and actual values.

A second type of error also is due to the disturbances; their presence tends to obscure underlying relationships, thus resulting in imprecise estimates of parameters. In other words, the parameter estimates are subject to sampling error because any given set of observations has associated with it a unique set of disturbances that would, in general, be different if the same structure underlay another set of observations.

Third, the various behavioral equations may not correctly specify the underlying economic relationships. In terms of our simple model, for instance, consumption may depend not only on current income and lagged consumption but also on, say, liquid assets held by consumers. This is likely to result in incorrect estimates of parameters and also in nonrandom residuals.

A final class of errors that may be distinguished stems from shortcomings in our methods of statistical inference. For instance, when two or more variables on the right-hand side of an equation tend to move closely together, it is difficult to calculate their separate effects on the left-hand term. This again affects the parameter estimates. Also in this class is the problem of bias in the parameter estimates when the equations are part of a simultaneous system. (Appendix B contains a description of the methods used to cope with this problem in the present model.)

The reader might infer from the above listing that econometric models are beset with errors. This is far from true, as the subsequent discussion of the performance of the OBE model will show. The econometric approach is comparable in validity to alternative approaches—for instance, the "judgmental" method, which may also use econometric methods but which does not rely on an explicit set of simultaneous equations, or the "economic indicators" approach originally developed by the National Bureau of Economic Research. The particular promise of the econometric method stems from the fact that it provides explicit formulations of the cause-effect relationships in the economy which can be communicated and which are open to inspection and testing. In addition, compared with methods confined to predicting only directional change, the method has the clear advantage of quantification.

A DESCRIPTION OF THE OBE MODEL

The equations of the model presently in use at OBE are shown in Appendix A. This model represents the current stage in a process of development that began with the Wharton School model referred to in the introduction.

The original model, with only slight modification and with prices assumed exogenous, was tested at OBE over a fairly long period. During this period, certain changes were made.[3] The

[3] Some of the changes led to fairly important modifications of the original version, while others entailed relatively minor respecification. The most fundamental changes were the substitution of an explicit short-term labor demand function for an implicit relationship involving a production function, the introduction of an explicit equation for the overall price deflator, the substitution of a different equation for corporate profits, the further disaggregation of consumer durables, the introduction of an equation for housing starts, and the incorporation of a variable statistical discrepancy in the income-product identity.

model presented in this article incorporates all changes made up to the time of this writing. As research progresses and as changes in the economy warrant, further modifications will be made.

In its present form, the model consists of 48 equations including identities. This section briefly describes the equations of the model and points out the principal mechanisms that merge the different parts into an interdependent system.

Categories of Equations

The model may conveniently be divided into six groups of equations: those explaining (1) components of GNP, (2) prices and wage rates, (3) labor force and employment-related magnitudes, (4) income components, (5) monetary variables, and (6) miscellaneous variables needed to round out the model. Each of these blocks of equations will be discussed briefly.

Components of GNP. Four equations explain personal consumption expenditures in 1958 dollars. These equations pertain to expenditures for autos and parts, other consumer durables, nondurables, and services other than housing. Housing services are projected exogenously. Each of the consumption components is made a function of disposable personal income, deflated by an appropriate price deflator, and of other relevant variables. Among the latter, lagged consumption, reflecting time taken to adjust consumption to changing income levels, figures prominently in the nondurables and services equations. Other relevant variables include the ratio of nonwage to wage income—which is introduced to allow for an income distribution effect—population, and deflated liquid assets held by households at the end of the preceding quarter.

Gross private domestic investment in 1958 dollars is estimated in three components: residential structures, fixed nonresidential investment, and the change in business inventories. For the residential component, an equation is included to predict the number of private nonfarm single-family housing units started during the quarter.[4] Multifamily starts, which have

[4] This equation is a modified version of the one developed for total private housing starts by S. J. Maisel [10]. The rationale for the modified equation is discussed by Albert A. Hirsch [6].

become quantitatively significant only in recent years, are added exogenously because a satisfactory equation for them has not yet been developed. Expenditures on new nonfarm housing construction are obtained by multiplying the predicted starts by cost per unit started, expressed in 1958 dollars; this product is phased out over time by using a pattern developed by the Census Bureau. The total residential structures component is obtained by adding "additions and alterations" and investment in farm residential structures as exogenous variables.

Investment in nonresidential structures and producers' durable equipment depends primarily on businessmen's quarterly anticipations of plant and equipment expenditures reported in the OBE–SEC survey, converted into 1958 dollars. First anticipations—projections usually made 6 months in advance—are used in the equation. In addition to this variable, the equation contains some others, reflecting the factors that may cause actual investment to differ from anticipated investment. Such equations are frequently called realization equations.

The use of anticipatory data in a model, when such data are shown to be reliable, may be definitely advantageous for forecasting. However, the use of such data limits the time period over which forecasts can be made. For more extended forecasts, it would be necessary to substitute an equation reflecting the basic determinants of actual investment outlays for the equation containing the anticipatory data. Alternatively, supplementary equations designed to predict investment anticipations could be introduced.

For purposes other than forecasting, equations containing exogenous anticipatory variables are generally unsatisfactory. For instance, if one wishes to test the effects of alternative tax policies, the use in the model of exogenous investment anticipations is an obstacle, because it is not possible to determine the effect of the alternative policies on the anticipations.

Inventory investment is explained by total sales of private GNP to final markets, the prior period's inventory investment, durable manufacturers' unfilled orders, and total inventories on hand at the beginning of the period, all in 1958 dollars. The last variable, appearing with a negative coefficient introduces a cycle-producing element into the model, as growth of inventories in the current period tends to dampen inventory investment in subsequent periods.

Imports (in 1958 dollars) are estimated by two equations, one for finished goods and services and the other for crude materials and foodstuffs. The first is similar to the consumption functions in that it includes disposable income deflated by the implicit price deflator for imports and the ratio of nonwage to wage income. The materials and foodstuffs equation contains lagged private GNP divided by the import deflator.

Exports and government purchases of goods and services—both exogenous variables—complete the accounting for GNP.

Price and Wage Rate Equations. Price indexes are needed to derive current-dollar estimates of GNP components and for other purposes, such as deflating disposable income or output in the various equations. Most indexes represent the appropriate implicit GNP deflators.

The equation for the price deflator for private GNP is a function of the average unit wage cost of private output for the current quarter and two previous ones, and of the two-quarter change in private final sales. The latter variable is made dependent upon capacity utilization in order to reflect increased sensitivity of prices to demand pressures when output is near capacity.

Three component deflators—those for consumer nonauto durables, nondurables, and fixed nonresidential investment—are made functions of the change in the overall price deflator and their own lagged values. Two other deflators—for consumer services and for residential structures—are made functions of the average wage rate. Deflators for autos and parts and for imports are exogenous.

The average (private sector) wage rate, which is estimated in the form of a percentage change over the previous four quarters, is related to the state of the labor market as measured by the unemployment rate during the intervening period, and to two factors that have a major role in collective bargaining decisions: changes in consumer prices and corporate profits. The relative wage change one year earlier—the change from eight to four quarters earlier—is also introduced. This term appears with a negative sign, suggesting that current wage changes are moderated by prior wage changes.

Labor Force and Employment Equations. The labor force has increased secularly, both in absolute terms and as a proportion of the working-age population. It is also somewhat responsive to cyclical variations in employment. The labor force equation incorporates all of these elements. The dependent variable is expressed as a participation rate, and the explanatory variables are the proportion of the working-age population employed and a time trend.

Man-hours of labor employed are estimated in an equation reflecting both secular and cyclical variations in productivity [13]. The secular variable is capacity output, which determines man-hour requirements at full capacity. Two other variables serve to adjust man-hours from full capacity to actual levels of production. One represents an intermediate adjustment of man-hours to an output level equal to a moving average of recently experienced output levels, called "planned" output. The other is a shortrun adjustment to account for the difference between actual and planned output. Secular changes in man-hour requirements due to technological change, the growth of the stock of capital, and other factors are introduced by making two of the coefficients in the equations dependent upon time. For purely statistical reasons the equation was estimated by first dividing through by capacity output.

Private employment is derived by dividing the estimate of total man-hours by an index of average weekly hours worked. The equation for average hours worked contains the variables "capacity utilization" and "time" to reflect cyclical and secular movements.

Income Equations. Income components represented by separate equations are: wages and salaries (including other labor income), nonwage personal income (consisting of proprietors' income, rental income of persons, dividends, and personal interest income), corporate profits (including the inventory valuation adjustment), and dividends.

Private wages and salaries are obtained as the product of private man-hours and the wage rate (including other labor income); government employee compensation is estimated exogenously. The equation for corporate profits reflects the fact that profits are the excess of sales revenues over costs. Thus, corporate profits are made to vary positively with corporate sales and negatively with the ratio of the money wage rate to the overall price deflator, man-hours per unit of output, and the ratio of capacity to actual output. The last variable serves as a proxy for unit fixed costs.

Nonwage personal income less dividends is made a function of corporate profits and time. Corporate profits are introduced to reflect some association between the entrepreneurial income component and profits. The time trend is largely associated with the secular behavior of the other elements. Dividends are related to their value in the previous period and are also made to vary with current corporate profits.

Disposable personal income is obtained by adding total transfer payments to wage and nonwage incomes and subtracting personal tax and nontax payments and personal contributions for social insurance. Transfers other than unemployment compensation are exogenous.

Monetary Equations. The model contains a small group of equations pertaining to monetary magnitudes. The short-term interest rate is made a function of excess reserves in the prior period and of the current rediscount rate. Both are exogenous to the model. The long-term rate is, in turn, made a function of the short-term rate and its own lagged value. The long-term rate is used in the equations for the FHA mortgage yield and for household liquid assets. The latter is also made to depend upon personal consumption expenditures to reflect transactions demand for money.

Miscellaneous Equations. Finally, there are some equations that are not conveniently categorized. These are equations for new orders, unfilled orders, shipments, depreciation, unemployment compensation, personal tax and nontax payments, indirect business taxes, corporate tax liability, capacity output, and a number of identities required to complete the structure. Only brief mention will be made here of the more important functions.

New orders placed with manufacturers of durable goods are estimated by relating them to corporate profits. New orders, in turn, enter into the equation for shipments of these goods. The timing relationship between orders and shipments is variable and depends on the size of the lagged ratios of backlogs of unfilled orders to shipments.[5] Unfilled orders, which are required also in the inventory investment and nonauto durables price deflator equations, are obtained from lagged unfilled orders and the difference between new orders and shipments. The new and unfilled orders, shipments, and corporate profits variables in the above relationships are deflated by an index of wholesale prices for durable goods.

Private output at capacity levels, used in a number of equations, is given by a production function relating output to labor and capital and an exponential trend to reflect technological advance. The equation has the Cobb-Douglas form and uses fixed nonresidential capital stock and 97 percent of the civilian labor force less government employment as measures of available capital and labor respectively.

The equation for personal tax and nontax payments is a simple relation between such payments and the sum of wage and salary and personal nonwage income. Indirect business taxes are related to final sales of private GNP and to time.

Of the many identities in the model, the one relating the income and product sides of the national income and product account deserves brief mention. In addition to income and product flows, this statement contains the reconciliation items, which include the statistical discrepancy. In the present model, the discrepancy is not assumed at some predetermined value but is allowed to vary within certain limits imposed on its movement and level.[6]

The Model as an Interdependent System

The foregoing description of the equations does not make clear the interdependent character of the system. As noted in the discussion of interdependencies in the simple illustrative

model, it is impossible to give an effective verbal account of the interdependence in a model consisting of many equations. However, with the aid of the flow chart (Figure 1), which depicts a simplified version of OBE's model, some idea may be obtained of the main interrelationships.

The rectangular boxes in the center of the chart represent, in condensed form, the main current endogenous variables in the model—the variables for which a simultaneous solution is sought. The rounded boxes to the left and right of the vertical dashed lines represent, respectively, the more important, exogenous and lagged endogenous variables.

The important simplifications to note are: Compensation of government employees (GNP originating in government) is assumed to be zero. Consumption, investment, and import components have been aggregated into single variables. Component price deflators are represented by one box. Corporate profits and personal nonwage income are consolidated into one nonlabor income variable, which is treated residually in the simplified version although not in the full model. Some relationships, such as those that determine unfilled orders, liquid assets, and housing starts, are not shown. The time variable, which appears in several equations, is left out, as are relatively minor explanatory variables. Finally, reconciliation items between national income and product are neglected.

The lines connecting the boxes of the chart reveal the direct dependencies among variables. The arrows indicate the cause-effect direction of these dependencies. In the chart, no distinction is made between behavioral equations and identities.

Some of the interrelationships in the system can now be traced. It is useful to point out first the linkage between product and income in the model. The boxes representing the GNP components at the right of the endogenous portion of the chart plus government purchases and exports make up total GNP. By deflating the latter (see the line connecting the implicit GNP deflator with the line emanating from GNP), GNP in 1958 dollars is obtained. The main linkage to the income side of the accounts is shown by the line leading from GNP in 1958 dollars to the box for man-hours and the box for weekly hours. One important link thus occurs

---

[5] The equation used for shipments has the same form as that used by Joel Popkin in "The Relationship Between New Orders and Shipments [11].

[6] See Appendix C for the reasons for this treatment and an account of the constraints imposed.

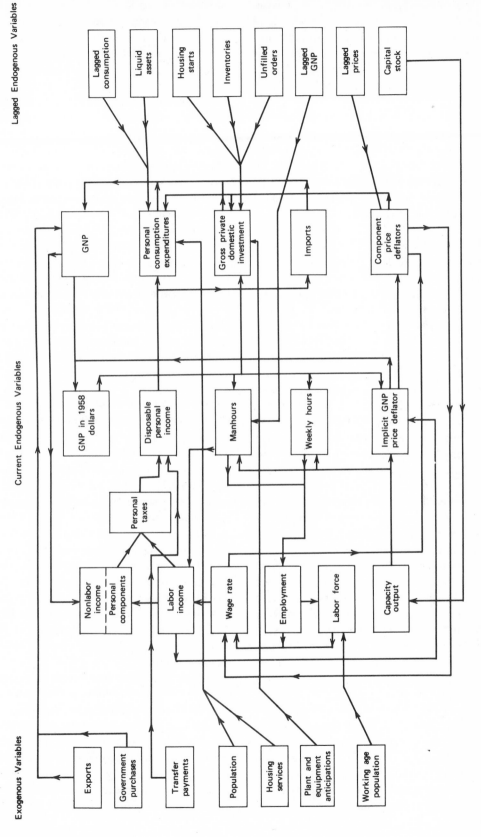

Figure 1 Condensed flow diagram. Source: U.S. Department of Commerce, Office of Business Economics.

via employment variables. The nest of boxes concerned with employment and with the wage rate determines labor income. As was indicated earlier, nonlabor income is determined residually in this simplified version of the model, that is, as the difference between GNP and labor income.

The feedback from income to product can also be delineated. As expected, the main linkage is revealed via the chain "income-taxes-disposable income-consumer expenditures." This chain can easily be followed in the chart.

The way in which prices are determined in the model can also be set forth. It is best seen by tracing the lines that lead into the implicit price deflator box. One such path emanates from GNP in 1958 dollars, another from labor income, and a third from capacity output. The first two of these flows combine to influence prices by changing unit labor costs. The first and third variables indicate the effect of capacity pressures on prices.

The description of the model given previously indicated that component prices are made functions of the overall implicit price deflator and, in some instances, of the wage rate. The main influence on component prices stems from the former—the box immediately adjacent—but it can also be seen that a line emanates from the wage rate and from lagged prices.

A number of other relationships can be followed in the chart. For example the relationships among the boxes concerned with employment and related variables can be traced. Employment is derived from man-hours and average weekly hours: To show this, a line from weekly hours joins one from man-hours and leads to employment. The wage rate is affected by unemployment—the difference between labor force and employment—and by prices. Thus, lines flow to the wage rate box from employment, labor force, and the component price deflators.

The reader will note that, with the exception of the rounded boxes representing the predetermined variables, which lie at the extreme right and left of the chart, all boxes have arrows entering them as well as emanating from them. This reveals the simultaneous character of the system and makes it possible to trace paths which are closed—that is, paths from any endogenous variable through other endogenous

variables and back to the original variable. There are many such closed paths—or loops—in the system. The income-product loop is seen to be the main element of simultaneity. Another important loop is that involving wages and prices.

The earlier discussion of the illustrative model introduced the concepts of long-run and impact multipliers. These ratios constitute important characteristics of specific models. In the present model, the multiplier is not a constant but depends to some degree on the levels of some variables. A test for a recent period yielded an impact multiplier on purchases of approximately 1.8. This means that if government purchases were to be changed by $1.0 billion, the effect on output in the same quarter would be $1.8 billion. Owing to the feedbacks via lagged endogenous variables, the cumulative effect would be larger in subsequent quarters. No figure is given here for the long-run multiplier because the present model neglects effects of changes in exogenous variables on the plant and equipment anticipations variable—an omission that would lead to an underestimate of long-run effects.

TESTING THE MODEL

Whether a model is to be used for forecasting or for studying policy or business cycles, the criterion of acceptability must be the accuracy of the predictions it produces. In policy studies, in which interest focuses on quantitative differences in economic behavior resulting from alternative policy actions, it is necessary, as was noted earlier, to take all major policy instruments into account and to derive endogenously as many as possible of the nonpolicy variables. This may result in some loss of forecasting accuracy. But even in policy applications, forecasting accuracy must be reasonably good if one is to have confidence that the dynamic structure of the economy has been adequately captured by the set of equations.

This section presents three sets of results: (1) a quantitative analysis of the overall behavior of the model during the entire period 1953 through 1965; (2) an examination of the model's performance in predicting cyclical turning points; and (3) a detailed presentation of the model's performance for 1965, a year that lies outside the period over which the equations were fitted.

These results do not represent forecasts in the

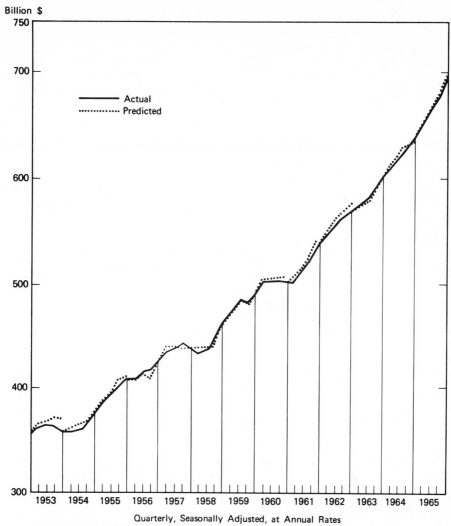

Figure 2 Predicted versus actual GNP, 1953–1965. Note: Each four-quarter sequence of forecasts starts from actual GNP in the fourth quarter of the preceding year. Source: U.S. Department of Commerce, Office of Business Economics.

usual sense of prediction of events before they occur. They are, rather, *ex-post* forecasts in which exogenous variables are assigned their actual values. Lagged endogenous variables, however, are those generated by the model as current endogenous variables of prior quarters. While such tests are not strictly pertinent to an actual forecasting situation, they have the advantage of eliminating errors made in projecting the exogenous variables. Obviously, in judging the validity of a model, errors due to wrong assumptions about the exogenous variables are not relevant.

There is, however, a sense in which tests for the period prior to 1965 are not fully adequate. Since

this is the period to which the equations of the model were fitted, it is somewhat uncertain whether the basic structure of economic behavior was captured or whether the equations reflect special factors unique to the period. There is the further point that the structure of the economy may have changed since the period over which the equations were fitted. The only conclusive test of forecasting accuracy is whether a model continues to perform satisfactorily beyond the period from which it was derived. This limitation, however, does not imply that *ex-post* forecasts are of no value. Adequate performance over the fitted period is at least a necessary condition for acceptance; a model that performs poorly over the fitting period is not likely to be a good fore-casting tool.

It is important to note in this connection that apart from the tests of the individual equations discussed earlier, the model requires testing as a whole. Even if the separate equations fit well, have statistically significant coefficients, and are theoretically reasonable, the model as a whole may still perform unsatisfactorily. This may be because the simultaneous solution of the entire system and the use of an earlier period's outputs as later inputs may cause errors.

Model Performance, 1953–65

To test the model's quantitative performance, *ex-post* forecasts of economic activity were made for each of the 13 years 1953 through 1965. In each case, the model was run for the four quarters of the year using the fourth quarter of the previous year as the jumpoff point. Known values of exogenous variables were used throughout. All lagged endogenous variables arising from quarters within the year were those yielded by the model rather than actual values. Thus, the results provide a test of how accurately the model generates a sequence of outputs from an initial starting point.

Major results of the tests are shown in Tables 1, 2, and 3 and in Figure 2. Table 1 gives predicted and actual values of GNP in current dollars by quarter and by year. The last two pairs of lines show predicted and

TABLE 1   Predicted and Actual Gross National Product, 1953–65 (Billions of dollars seasonally adjusted at annual rates)

	Current Dollar Totals												
	1953	1954	1955	1956	1957	1958	1959	1960	1961	1962	1963	1964	1965
1st Quarter													
Predicted	366.6	362.5	385.1	408.9	442.3	439.8	473.5	505.7	510.7	548.6	573.8	613.9	658.1
Actual	364.2	360.7	386.2	410.6	436.9	434.7	474.0	503.0	503.6	547.8	577.0	614.0	657.6
2nd Quarter													
Predicted	369.2	366.2	395.0	416.1	443.5	442.6	485.6	506.1	518.3	560.5	581.0	628.3	670.5
Actual	367.5	360.4	394.5	416.2	439.9	438.3	486.9	504.7	514.9	557.2	583.1	624.2	668.8
3rd Quarter													
Predicted	373.9	369.1	407.1	415.3	439.4	445.0	483.6	506.6	529.9	568.7	592.3	636.5	683.3
Actual	365.8	364.7	402.5	420.6	446.3	451.4	484.0	504.2	524.2	564.4	593.1	634.8	681.3
4th Quarter													
Predicted	372.6	374.4	412.2	427.4	439.9	459.2	487.4	508.7	543.3	575.8	604.8	638.1	697.7
Actual	360.8	373.4	408.8	429.5	441.5	464.4	490.5	503.3	537.7	572.0	603.6	641.1	697.2
Year													
Predicted	370.6	368.0	399.8	416.9	441.3	446.6	482.5	506.8	525.6	563.5	588.0	629.2	677.4
Actual	364.6	364.8	398.0	419.2	441.1	447.3	483.6	503.8	520.1	560.3	589.2	628.7	676.3
	Year-to-Year Changes												
	(Billions of current dollars)												
Predicted	25.1	3.4	35.0	18.9	22.1	5.5	35.2	23.2	21.8	43.4	27.7	40.0	48.7
Actual	19.1	0.2	33.2	21.2	21.9	6.2	36.3	20.2	16.3	40.2	28.9	39.5	47.6
	(Billions of 1958 dollars)												
Predicted	21.4	−0.9	34.0	7.6	10.6	−4.2	31.5	14.9	14.2	34.3	17.1	27.1	29.3
Actual	17.7	−5.8	31.0	8.0	6.5	−5.2	28.6	11.9	9.5	32.7	20.0	27.6	32.0

SOURCE: U.S. Department of Commerce, Office of Business Economics.

actual year-to-year changes in current- and constant-dollar GNP. Table 2 lists the errors in predicting current-dollar GNP and its major components, disposable personal income, real GNP, and the implicit price deflator for GNP. Errors are defined as predicted minus actual values. Table 3 presents summary statistics on errors for the same items. The chart shows predicted and actual GNP; each four-quarter forecast is shown as starting from its prior fourth quarter actual GNP jumpoff.

General time path. Table 1 and Figure 2 show that the model performed quite well over the period. For 9 of the 13 years, the error in predicting GNP for the year was $3.0 billion or less. As shown in Table 3, the average absolute error (obtained by disregarding the signs of the individual errors) for all 13 forecasts was $2.3 billion. The average absolute error for constant-dollar GNP was $2.9 billion. As the bottom line in Table 1 shows, the model predicted the declines in constant-dollar GNP in both 1954 and 1958.

These results are highly summary and conceal strengths and weaknesses in predicting quarterly economic behavior as well as the behavior of individual components. Table 3 shows, for example, that (average absolute) errors are not, in general, uniform throughout the year. For current-dollar GNP, the error tends to increase with the distance from the jumpoff quarter, although the pattern is not completely consistent. The error made in fourth quarter predictions, for example, was $3.7 billion, as compared with $2.5 billion for the first quarter. This is not surprising, since successive quarterly forecasts embody whatever errors were made in prior periods' components, and these enter as inputs in later periods.

In some instances, relatively small errors in GNP for the year as a whole reflect offsetting positive and negative errors made in the individual quarters. For 1957 as a whole, for example, predicted GNP differed from actual GNP by only $0.2 billion, because an overestimate of $4.5 billion for the first half of the year was virtually offset by an underestimate for the second half.

Quarterly errors in current-dollar GNP ranged from a low of—$6.9 billion (third quarter of 1957) to a high of $11.8 billion (fourth quarter of 1953); errors in constant-dollar GNP ranged

from—$7.2 billion (fourth quarter of 1965) to $8.8 billion (second quarter of 1954). However, the summary measures given in Table 3 show that such large errors were exceptional.

Absolute Errors in Components. Comparatively small errors in total GNP may also reflect larger but partly offsetting errors in the components, as can be seen from Table 2. In general, however, errors in components were also moderate.

The largest errors occurred in consumption expenditures. Average absolute errors in this component were about the same as for total GNP. One might well expect this since consumption expenditures account for about two-thirds of GNP and usually for a large proportion of its changes.

Errors in predicting residential construction, fixed nonresidential investment, and net exports were relatively small. (Errors in net exports reflect errors in imports since exports are exogenous.) Average absolute errors in each of these items for all quarters and years were less than $1.0 billion.

On the average, errors in inventory change were somewhat larger than those in the last three items mentioned but less than those in consumption expenditures. Errors in inventory change were often relatively large, but it should be remembered that inventory change is the most volatile element in GNP.

Price behavior was perhaps the poorest aspect of the model results. Average absolute errors in the implicit GNP deflator were 0.3 points for each of the first two quarters, or only somewhat less than the average quarterly increase in the actual deflator; for the third and fourth quarters, the errors were larger. However, the equation system is such that errors in the price index and in real output tend in opposite directions; thus, current-dollar GNP does not bear the full brunt of errors in price.

Evidence of Bias. There is evidence that errors of prediction in the model are not entirely random. For the period as a whole, there was a slight tendency to overestimate GNP. This is indicated by positive average errors (obtained by netting positive and negative errors), shown in the second column of table 3 for each quarter and for the year as a whole; somewhat larger average

TABLE 2   Quarterly and Annual
(Billions of current dollars seasonally adjusted

	1953					1954				
	1Q	2Q	3Q	4Q	Year	1Q	2Q	3Q	4Q	Year
Gross national product	2.4	1.7	8.1	11.8	6.0	1.8	5.8	4.4	1.0	3.2
Personal consumption expenditures	.5	3.2	7.2	11.9	5.6	2.9	2.9	2.3	1.2	2.3
Residential structures	−.8	−1.0	−.3	0	−.6	−.2	−.5	−.9	−.7	−.5
Fixed investment, nonresidential	.9	−.8	−.4	.1	0	.6	1.5	1.0	1.3	1.2
Change in business inventories	2.0	.8	2.6	2.0	1.9	−.5	1.8	2.6	−.4	.9
Net exports	.0	−.5	−.9	−2.1	−.9	−1.1	.3	−.6	−.7	−.5
Disposable personal income	−.3	.7	5.9	9.2	3.9	1.4	4.9	4.9	3.8	3.8
GNP in constant (1958) dollars	2.0	.7	7.4	4.7	3.7	5.0	8.8	5.6	.2	4.9
Implicit price deflator for GNP (1958 = 100)	.1	.2	.4	1.7	.7	−.6	−.5	−.1	.2	−.3

	1958					1959				
	1Q	2Q	3Q	4Q	Year	1Q	2Q	3Q	4Q	Year
Gross national product	5.1	4.3	−6.4	−5.2	−.7	−0.5	−1.3	−0.4	−3.1	−1.1
Personal consumption expenditures	1.6	1.8	−1.9	−.3	.3	−1.7	−2.6	−4.2	−4.9	−3.3
Residential structures	.3	−.4	−2.8	−3.3	−1.6	−.1	.6	1.0	1.0	.7
Fixed investment, nonresidential	.4	−.1	−.3	.3	.1	−.1	−1.4	−.3	−.5	−.6
Change in business inventories	2.7	2.7	−1.8	−2.9	.2	1.1	.9	1.5	−.1	1.0
Net exports	.2	.1	.4	1.1	.4	.3	1.2	1.5	1.3	1.1
Disposable personal income	1.3	1.7	−5.4	−2.9	−1.3	−.7	−1.7	.3	−.3	−.6
GNP in constant (1958) dollars	7.4	5.3	−4.9	−3.8	1.0	2.3	2.5	4.8	1.9	2.9
Implicit price deflator for GNP (1958 = 100)	−.4	−.2	−.3	−.3	−.4	−.5	−.7	−1.1	−1.0	−.8

	1963					1964				
	1Q	2Q	3Q	4Q	Year	1Q	2Q	3Q	4Q	Year
Gross national product	−3.2	−2.1	−0.8	1.2	−1.2	−0.1	4.1	1.7	−3.0	0.5
Personal consumption expenditures	−2.7	−.2	.4	5.2	.7	.7	3.2	.4	.7	1.3
Residential structures	−.7	−.4	.4	−.4	−.3	−.6	.2	.5	.0	.1
Fixed investment, nonresidential	.6	−.3	.3	.3	.2	−1.6	−.2	−.9	−2.5	−1.3
Change in business inventories	−.2	−1.2	−2.1	−3.5	−1.7	1.7	1.0	1.8	−2.2	.4
Net exports	−.1	.2	.1	−.3	.1	−.3	−.2	.0	1.0	.1
Disposable personal income	−2.8	−1.4	.0	1.0	−.8	1.2	2.5	1.3	−2.5	.7
GNP in constant (1958) dollars	−2.1	−1.6	−4.2	−3.8	−2.9	−.6	.0	−.5	−.9	−.5
Implicit price deflator for GNP (1958 = 100)	−.2	−.1	.7	.9	.4	.1	.7	.3	−.3	.1

NOTE: Error equals predicted minus actual.

Prediction Errors: Selected Items, 1953–65

at annual rates, unless not applicable)

	1955					1956					1957			
1Q	2Q	3Q	4Q	Year	1Q	2Q	3Q	4Q	Year	1Q	2Q	3Q	4Q	Year
−1.1	0.6	4.6	3.4	1.8	−1.7	−0.1	−5.3	−2.1	−2.3	5.4	3.6	−6.9	−1.6	0.2
−1.2	.6	4.2	4.6	2.0	.3	1.3	−1.8	1.0	.2	.2	1.4	−4.3	−3.4	−1.5
−.1	.2	.6	1.4	.5	−1.3	−2.0	−1.7	−1.0	−1.5	1.7	.7	−.4	−.4	.4
.3	0	−.8	−1.2	−.5	−.4	1.7	.6	.7	.7	.6	.2	−1.8	−1.6	−.7
−.5	−.3	.6	−1.4	−.4	−.8	−1.2	−3.3	−2.7	−2.0	1.9	1.1	−1.4	2.7	1.1
.4	.1	−.1	.2	.2	.5	.1	.9	−.1	.3	.9	.4	.9	.9	.8
.7	1.8	3.0	4.2	2.3	−1.1	−.6	−4.0	−3.6	−2.3	1.2	.7	−5.9	−2.8	−1.7
.5	1.5	6.2	3.8	3.0	.5	.9	−3.1	.2	−.4	5.7	5.6	.1	5.2	4.1
−.3	−.2	−.2	0	−.2	−.5	−.2	−.5	−.5	−.4	−.1	−.4	−1.5	−1.5	−.9

	1960					1961					1962			
1Q	2Q	3Q	4Q	Year	1Q	2Q	3Q	4Q	Year	1Q	2Q	3Q	4Q	Year
2.7	1.4	2.4	5.4	3.0	7.1	3.4	5.7	5.6	5.5	0.8	3.3	4.3	3.8	3.2
4.0	−.6	1.7	2.7	2.0	5.4	4.6	5.3	4.5	4.9	−.3	2.8	3.1	4.0	2.3
−1.3	−.7	−.4	−.4	−.6	−.4	.4	.9	.3	.3	−.2	−.6	−.3	−.1	−.3
−.3	.3	1.1	.4	.4	−.1	−.2	−.2	.7	.2	.8	−.7	−.7	.4	−.1
.2	1.8	.4	4.5	1.7	3.3	−.7	−.4	.4	.7	.1	1.4	2.2	−.1	1.0
.3	.6	−.3	−1.8	−.3	−1.1	−1.1	.1	−.2	−.5	.3	.5	.1	−.2	.2
1.7	−1.3	−.7	2.5	.6	3.0	.6	1.1	.2	1.3	.7	1.3	3.8	6.0	2.9
1.9	1.2	2.6	6.1	3.0	6.1	2.4	4.0	6.6	4.7	1.8	2.6	2.6	−.2	1.6
.2	.1	.0	−.2	.0	.2	.1	.3	−.3	.1	−.2	.2	.3	.8	.3

	1965			
1Q	2Q	3Q	4Q	Year
0.5	1.7	1.8	0.5	1.1
2.9	−.4	1.9	3.0	1.9
−.9	−.6	−.2	−.8	−.6
−1.3	.2	−1.2	−.5	−.7
−.5	.5	−.6	−3.1	−.9
.5	2.1	2.0	1.9	1.6
1.5	.4	3.2	4.1	2.3
−1.5	−.5	−1.7	−7.2	−2.7
.4	.4	.6	1.3	.7

SOURCE: U. S. Department of Commerce, Office of Business Economics.

TABLE 3 Summary Measures of Quarterly and Annual Prediction Errors for Selected Items, 1953–65

(Billions of current dollars seasonally adjusted at annual rates, unless not applicable)

	Average absolute error	Average error	Range Low	Range High		Average absolute error	Average error	Range Low	Range High
					Change in business inventories:				
					1Q	1.2	.8	−.8	3.3
					2Q	1.2	.7	−1.2	2.7
					3Q	1.6	.2	−3.3	2.6
					4Q	2.0	−.5	−3.5	4.5
Gross national					Year	1.1	.3	−2.0	1.9
product:									
1Q	2.5	1.5	−3.2	7.1	Net exports:				
2Q	2.6	2.0	−2.1	5.8	1Q	.5	.1	−1.1	.9
3Q	4.1	1.0	−6.9	8.1	2Q	.6	.3	−1.1	2.1
4Q	3.7	1.4	−5.2	11.8	3Q	.6	.3	−.9	2.0
Year	2.3	1.5	−2.3	6.0	4Q	.9	.1	−2.1	1.9
					Year	.5	.2	−.9	1.6
Personal consumption expenditures:					Disposable personal income:				
1Q	1.9	1.0	−2.7	5.4	1Q	1.4	.6	−2.8	3.0
2Q	2.0	1.4	−2.6	4.6	2Q	1.5	.7	−1.7	4.9
3Q	3.0	1.1	−4.3	7.2	3Q	3.0	.6	−5.9	5.9
4Q	3.6	2.3	−4.9	11.9	4Q	3.3	1.4	−3.6	9.2
Year	2.2	1.4	−3.3	5.6	Year	1.9	.9	−2.3	3.9
Residential structures:					GNP in constant (1958) dollars:				
1Q	.7	−.4	−1.3	1.7	1Q	2.9	2.2	−2.1	7.4
2Q	.6	−.3	−2.0	.7	2Q	2.6	2.3	−1.6	8.8
3Q	.8	−.3	−2.8	1.0	3Q	3.7	1.5	−4.9	7.4
4Q	.8	−.3	−3.3	1.4	4Q	3.4	1.0	−7.2	6.6
Year	.6	−.3	−1.6	.7	Year	2.9	1.7	−2.9	4.9
Fixed investment, nonresidential:					Implicit price deflator for GNP (1958 = 100)				
1Q	.6	.0	−1.6	.9	1Q	.3	−.1	−.6	.4
2Q	.6	.0	−1.4	1.7	2Q	.3	.0	−.7	.7
3Q	.7	−.3	−1.8	1.1	3Q	.5	−.1	−1.5	.7
4Q	.8	−.2	−2.5	1.3	4Q	.7	.1	−1.5	1.7
Year	.5	−.1	−1.3	1.2	Year	.4	−.1	−.9	.7

SOURCE: U.S. Department of Commerce, Office of Business Economics.

errors are observed for real than for current-dollar GNP.

The tendency to overestimate GNP reflected primarily a similar tendency in personal consumption expenditures. Table 2 shows that positive errors in consumption were generally associated with positive errors in disposable income—an important determinant of consumption. However, such errors were not perfectly correlated. Furthermore, disposable income exhibited smaller average errors than did consumption.

Average errors in GNP components other than consumption were all less than $1.0 billion and in most cases less than $0.5 billion, indicating little or no bias in estimating these components. Despite sizable average absolute errors in the implicit GNP deflator, there was no apparent bias in estimating it.

Business Cycle Turning Points

Tests of a model's performance in predicting business cycle turning points are clearly important in an overall appraisal. Success in making such predictions strongly suggests that critical dynamic elements in the economy have been taken into account in the set of equations. Failure to pass such tests reflects adversely on a model's reliability, at least for periods when economic activity is undergoing changes in direction.

Such tests can be applied with varying degrees of rigor. A stringent criterion of success is the requirement that all turning points be estimated with precise timing. This test is particularly rigorous when actual changes in direction are slight. An alternative criterion is that forecasts show a directional change in the neighborhood of the actual turning point. Although considerably less rigorous, such a criterion still permits appraisal of the model's usefulness since a somewhat mistimed signal of change is clearly better than no signal at all.

In this section, the behavior of the model in predicting constant-dollar GNP at its six cyclical turning points during the 1953–61 period is examined. Three separate four-quarter forecasts were made preceding each turning point. The first used as a jumpoff the quarter three periods before the actual reversal; the second and third started, respectively, from two quarters and one quarter before the reversal. Thus, there were in all 18 forecasts, 9 for upturns and 9 for downturns.[7]

Figure 3 presents the forecasts of both constant-dollar and current-dollar GNP for each of the turning points. The discussion focuses on constant-dollar GNP because it is the most comprehensive measure of real economic activity.

[7] The forecast three quarters before the 1958 upturn jumps off from the peak quarter in 1957 and thus is also a forecast made one quarter in advance of the downturn that followed.

Summary of Turning Point Behavior. The rigorous criterion of exactly coincident timing was met by the model only infrequently. Three of the nine forecasts of downturns were precisely timed—one made two quarters and two made one quarter in advance. None of the forecasts made three quarters ahead manifested precise timing. In recoveries, timing was accurate only when the forecast was made one quarter before the actual upturn; prediction was accurate in two of the three cases. The results at both peaks and troughs suggest that precision is increased when the jumpoff quarter is close to the actual turning point.

The performance of the model was very good when the criterion was relaxed to require only that it predict a turning point in the neighborhood of the actual turning point—for instance, one quarter on either side. Figure 3 shows that all but 3 of the 18 forecasts met this criterion. The exceptions were forecasts made three quarters before directional changes occurred.

The foregoing summary was concerned solely with the extent to which turning points were successfully predicted. The following section is a brief analysis of the model's behavior with particular reference to individual cycles.

Performance in Individual Cycles. Perhaps the best performance at cyclical turning points was in the 1957–58 period. Forecasts two and three quarters before the fourth quarter 1957 decline showed a contraction in activity in the third quarter. The forecast made one quarter before the actual turning point predicted it correctly. All three of these forecasts warned of a substantial decline in constant-dollar GNP, similar to that which actually occurred.

Beginning two quarters ahead, the model also predicted the 1958 upturn and to some extent its strength. Of particular interest is the forecast made two quarters before the upturn began. It shows a continuation in the decline of real GNP for one more quarter, followed by a leveling off prior to recovery. The forecast one quarter before the upturn correctly predicted the recovery.

On balance, the behavior of the model in the mild recession of 1960–61 was not as good as in the 1957–58 recession. The model performed as well, if not better, in predicting the downturn,

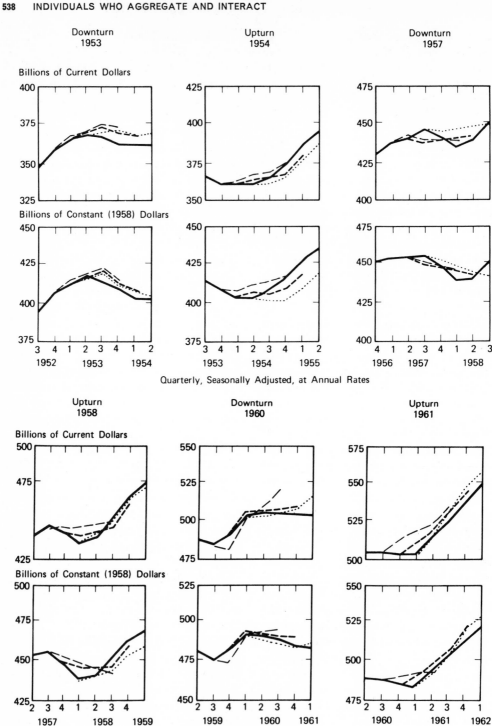

Figure 3 Current and constant dollar GNP at cyclical turning points, 1953–1961: Predicted versus actual. Source: U.S. Department of Commerce, Office of Business Economics.

Actual ——————
Three quarters ahead — — — — —
Two quarters ahead – – – – – ⎫ Predicted
One quarter ahead   ·············· ⎭

but was markedly less successful in predicting the upturn.

With respect to the 1960 downturn, the forecast made three quarters earlier started from the third quarter of 1959. This quarter was dominated by the contractionary influence of a strike in the steel industry. The model predicted a continued decline for one quarter, a sharp advance for one quarter, and much smaller advances for the two quarters in which actual constant-dollar GNP was edging down from its peak. The forecast made two quarters before the downturn gave early warning of the exact quarter in which it would start. The forecast made one quarter before the downturn was timed correctly and the predicted decline was about the right size. In addition, this forecast indicated the ensuing upturn, but placed it in the first quarter of 1961, when actual constant-dollar GNP fell only slightly further to reach its trough for that recession.

The prediction made three quarters before the upturn was quite inaccurate, forecasting the recovery two quarters before it actually occurred. The forecast made one quarter later also gave a premature signal. The forecast made at the trough correctly indicated recovery. However, in view of the failure of the two preceding forecasts to materialize, it could easily have been discounted as another premature signal.

The forecasts for the 1953–54 period, particularly for the recovery, were least satisfactory though still relatively useful. All forecasts, including the one made three quarters ahead, showed a recession but in each case one quarter later than it actually occurred. Despite the timing error, the persistency with which the model suggested a recession made the forecasts of value. During the recession, two premature signals of recovery were obtained, although the second one suggested it would be abortive. A continuation of the decline in constant-dollar GNP was forecast at the trough.

Forecast for 1965

As was pointed out earlier, the forecast for 1965, since it is outside the period to which the equations were fitted, is a more adequate test of the model's performance than are the forecasts made for 1953–64. Moreover, 1965 presented something of a challenge to econometric models

because special account had to be taken of a number of unusual events.

A dock strike occurred early in the first quarter reducing the volume of imports and exports. At the same time, production of autos picked up sharply following the auto strikes in late 1964. Steel producers and users continued to accumulate inventories in anticipation of a steel strike. During the third quarter of the year, excise taxes on a number of consumer goods—mainly consumer durables—were removed, lowering prices paid by consumers. Apart from the further reduction in income tax rates in 1965, personal tax payments dropped from the somewhat inflated levels of the first half, which were associated with the underwithholding of taxes in 1964.

Fortunately, an econometric model is sufficiently flexible to make allowances for special factors of the kind just described. In an actual forecasting situation, such factors must, of course, be anticipated and quantified along with the usual exogenous variables. In testing the model over a past period, as with the OBE model, the task is made easier by the existence of *ex-post* information regarding the special factors. But most special elements cannot be isolated with precision even in retrospect. For example, in the present instance available data do not clearly indicate how much inventory buildup was due to the anticipation of a strike and how much was "normal." It is usually possible, however, to prepare at least a crude estimate of the special factors.[8]

[8] Specifically, the following adjustments were made: To allow for abnormal auto purchases in the first quarter, a "dummy" variable—which is included in the auto equation to take care of strike situations—was assigned a value of one, adding $1.9 billion more to consumer purchases than the equation would otherwise have yielded. Similarly, $2.0 billion was temporarily added to inventories to allow for unusual steel and auto inventory buildup. An estimated reduction in imports during the first quarter and a subsequent makeup in the second, associated with the dock strike, were similarly incorporated.

Amounts of $2.5 billion, $3.0 billion, and $0.5 billion were added to the personal tax function for the first, second, and third quarters respectively. The implicit price deflators for "other" durables and total private output were reduced after the second quarter by 1.7 and 0.3 points respectively, on the assumption that the reductions in excise taxes were fully passed on to consumers; indirect business taxes were reduced by $1.6 billion.

TABLE 4 Predicted and Actual Gross National Product and Components, Income and Reconciliation Items, and Selected Supplementary Items, 1965

(Billions of dollars seasonally adjusted at annual rates, unless not applicable)

	1964 4th Qtr. Actual	1st Quarter Predicted	1st Quarter Actual	1st Quarter Difference	2d Quarter Predicted	2d Quarter Actual	2d Quarter Difference	3d Quarter Predicted	3d Quarter Actual	3d Quarter Difference	4th Quarter Predicted	4th Quarter Actual	4th Quarter Difference	Year Predicted	Year Actual	Year Difference
Gross national product	641.1	658.1	657.6	0.5	670.5	668.8	1.7	683.3	681.5	1.8	697.7	697.2	0.5	677.4	676.3	1.1
Personal consumption expenditures	405.9	419.8	416.9	2.9	424.1	424.5	-.4	434.4	432.5	1.9	444.0	441.0	3.0	430.6	428.7	1.9
Automobiles and parts	24.8	29.9	30.3	-.4	28.2	29.3	-1.1	29.2	30.3	-1.1	30.1	30.1	.0	29.4	30.0	-.6
Durable goods other than automobiles and parts	33.1	34.5	34.3	.2	35.0	34.2	.8	36.1	35.0	1.1	38.0	36.3	1.7	35.9	35.0	.9
Nondurable goods	180.9	185.0	182.8	2.2	187.5	187.9	-.4	191.9	190.5	1.4	195.3	195.0	.3	189.9	189.0	.9
Services	167.1	170.4	169.5	.9	173.4	173.1	.3	177.2	176.7	.5	180.6	179.6	1.0	175.4	174.7	.7
Gross private domestic investment	97.7	100.7	103.4	-2.7	102.9	102.8	.1	104.2	106.2	-2.0	105.9	110.3	-4.4	103.4	105.7	-2.3
Fixed investment, nonresidential	63.5	65.6	66.9	-1.3	68.6	68.4	.2	69.7	70.9	-1.2	72.5	73.0	-.5	69.1	69.8	-.7
Residential structures	26.7	26.8	27.7	-.9	27.4	28.0	-.6	27.5	27.7	-.2	26.4	27.2	-.8	27.0	27.6	-.6
Change in business inventories	7.5	8.3	8.8	-.5	6.9	6.4	.5	7.0	7.6	-.6	7.0	10.1	-3.1	7.3	8.2	-.9
Net exports of goods and services	8.9	6.5	6.0	.5	10.1	8.0	2.1	9.4	7.4	2.0	8.8	6.9	1.9	8.7	7.1	1.6
Exports*	38.4	34.7	34.7	.0	40.4	40.4	.0	40.1	40.1	.0	40.8	40.8	.0	39.0	39.0	.0
Imports	29.5	28.2	28.6	-.4	30.3	32.4	-2.1	30.7	32.7	-2.0	32.0	33.9	-1.9	30.3	31.9	-1.6
Government purchases of goods and services*	128.6	131.3	131.3	.0	133.5	133.5	.0	135.4	135.4	.0	139.0	139.0	.0	134.8	134.8	.0
Gross national product	641.1	658.1	657.6	.5	670.5	668.8	1.7	683.3	681.5	1.8	697.7	697.2	.5	677.4	676.3	1.1
Less: Capital consumption allowances*	56.9	57.7	57.7	.0	58.3	58.3	.0	59.1	59.1	.0	59.8	59.8	.0	58.7	58.7	.0
Indirect business tax and nontax liability	59.3	60.9	61.5	-.6	62.5	61.4	1.1	62.2	62.0	.2	63.5	62.9	.6	62.3	62.0	.3
Business transfer payments*	2.4	2.3	2.3	.0	2.3	2.3	.0	2.3	2.3	.0	2.3	2.3	.0	2.3	2.3	.0
Statistical discrepancy	-2.2	-1.2	-3.1	1.9	-.3	-1.4	1.1	.5	1.4	-.9	1.0	2.4	-1.4	.0	-.2	.2

	1	2	3	4	5	6	7	8	9	10	11	12	13	14	15	16
Plus: Subsidies less current surplus of government enterprises*	1.5	1.4	1.4	.0	1.3	1.3	.0	1.2	1.2	.0	1.1	1.1	.0	1.2	1.2	.0
Equals: National income	526.3	539.8	540.6	-.8	549.0	549.5	-.5	560.4	557.9	2.5	572.2	570.8	1.4	555.4	554.7	.7
Less: Corporate profits and inventory valuation adjustment	64.9	69.0	71.7	-2.7	70.8	72.0	-1.2	72.3	73.5	-1.2	72.2	75.2	-3.0	71.1	73.1	-2.0
Contributions for social insurance*	28.4	28.9	28.9	.0	29.2	29.2	.0	29.6	29.6	.0	30.2	30.2	.0	29.5	29.5	.0
Wage accruals less disbursements*	-.1	.0	.0	.0	.0	.0	.0	.0	.0	.0	.0	.0	.0	.0	.0	.0
Plus: State unemployment insurance benefits	2.4	2.2	2.4	-.2	2.0	2.2	-.2	2.0	2.2	-.2	2.0	2.0	.0	2.0	2.2	-.2
Business and other government transfer payments to persons*	34.4	35.9	35.9	.0	35.2	35.2	.0	39.0	39.0	.0	37.6	37.6	.0	36.9	36.9	.0
Interest paid by government (net) and by consumers	19.5	19.9	19.9	.0	20.4	20.4	.0	20.8	20.8	.0	21.1	21.1	.0	20.6	20.6	.0
Dividends	17.7	18.2	18.0	.2	18.7	18.6	.1	19.2	19.2	.0	19.7	19.9	-.2	19.0	18.9	.1
Equals: Personal income	507.1	518.1	516.2	1.9	525.4	524.7	.7	539.5	536.0	3.5	550.3	546.0	4.3	533.3	530.7	2.6
Less: Personal tax and nontax payments	60.7	65.2	64.8	.4	66.5	66.2	.3	65.1	64.8	.3	65.9	65.7	.2	65.7	65.4	.3
Equals: Disposable personal income	446.4	452.9	451.4	1.5	458.9	458.5	.4	474.4	471.2	3.2	484.4	480.3	4.1	467.6	465.3	2.3
Less: Personal consumption expenditures	405.9	419.8	416.9	2.9	424.1	424.5	-.4	434.4	432.5	1.9	444.0	441.0	3.0	430.6	428.7	1.9
Interest paid by consumers*	10.4	10.6	10.6	.0	11.0	11.0	.0	11.3	11.3	.0	11.6	11.6	.0	11.1	11.1	.0
Personal transfer payments to foreigners*	.6	.6	.6	.0	.6	.6	.0	.6	.6	.0	.6	.6	.0	.6	.6	.0
Equals: Personal saving	29.5	21.9	23.3	-1.4	23.2	22.4	.8	28.1	26.8	1.3	28.2	27.1	1.1	25.4	24.9	.5
Saving rate (percent)	6.6	4.8	5.2	-.3	5.1	4.9	.2	5.9	5.7	.2	5.8	5.6	.2	5.4	5.4	.0
Gross national product in constant (1958) dollars	584.7	596.2	597.7	-1.5	603.0	603.5	-.5	611.2	613.0	-1.8	617.2	624.4	-7.2	606.9	609.6	-2.7
Implicit price deflator for GNP (1958 = 100)	109.6	110.4	110.0	.4	111.2	110.8	.4	111.8	111.2	.6	113.0	111.7	1.3	111.6	110.9	.7
Civilian labor force (millions of persons)	74.5	74.9	75.0	-.1	75.2	75.5	-.3	75.5	75.8	-.3	75.8	76.1	-.3	75.4	75.6	-.2
Employment (millions of persons)	70.7	71.4	71.3	.1	72.0	71.9	.1	72.3	72.4	-.1	72.5	72.9	-.4	72.1	72.2	-.1
Unemployment (millions of persons)	3.8	3.5	3.6	-.1	3.3	3.6	-.3	3.2	3.4	-.2	3.3	3.2	.1	3.3	3.4	-.1
Unemployment rate (percent)	5.1	4.6	4.8	-.2	4.3	4.7	-.4	4.2	4.4	-.2	4.4	4.2	.2	4.4	4.6	-.2

* Exogenous variables.

SOURCE: U.S. Department of Commerce, Office of Business Economics and U.S. Department of Labor, Bureau of Labor Statistics.

TABLE 5   Predicted and Actual Values for Endogenous Variables, 1965[a]

	1964 4th Qtr. Actual	1st Quarter			2d Quarter			3d Quarter			4th Quarter			Year		
		Predicted	Actual	Difference	Predicted	Actual	Difference	Predicted	Actual	Difference	Predicted	Actual	Difference	Predicted	Actual	Difference
Gross national product components, billions of 1958 dollars:																
Personal consumption expenditures																
Automobiles and parts	24.8	29.6	30.2	−0.6	28.0	29.1	−1.1	29.4	30.7	−1.3	30.5	30.4	0.1	29.4	30.1	−0.7
Durable goods other than automobiles and parts	33.1	34.4	34.3	.1	34.8	34.3	.5	36.3	35.7	.6	38.0	37.5	.5	35.9	35.4	.5
Nondurable goods	171.8	174.6	173.2	1.4	175.8	176.4	−.6	179.2	177.8	1.4	181.0	181.0	.0	177.6	177.1	.5
Services, excluding housing	90.5	91.9	90.8	1.1	92.2	91.9	.3	93.4	92.9	.5	94.3	93.6	.7	93.0	92.3	.7
Fixed investment, nonresidential	59.6	61.0	62.5	−1.5	63.2	63.7	−.5	63.6	66.0	−2.4	65.6	67.6	−2.0	63.4	65.0	−1.6
Residential structures, nonfarm	23.0	23.3	23.8	−.5	23.6	23.9	−.3	23.4	23.2	.2	22.3	22.6	−.3	23.2	23.3	−.1
Change in business inventories	7.1	7.7	8.6	−.9	6.4	6.2	.2	6.5	7.2	−.7	6.5	9.8	−3.3	6.8	7.9	−1.1
Imports of crude materials and foodstuffs	5.8	5.3	5.0	.3	5.3	5.8	−.5	5.3	5.0	.3	5.4	6.0	−.6	5.3	5.4	−.1
Imports of other goods and services	23.2	22.2	22.8	−.6	24.7	26.1	−1.4	25.0	27.1	−2.1	26.0	26.9	−.9	24.5	25.7	−1.2
Gross private output, excluding housing services	478.4	488.8	490.4	−1.5	494.1	494.7	−.6	500.8	502.3	−1.5	504.8	512.0	−7.2	497.1	499.8	−2.7
Gross private output at capacity	552.0	558.7	559.0	−.3	565.4	567.0	−1.6	569.4	571.3	−1.9	577.2	579.3	−2.1	567.7	569.2	−1.5
Implicit price deflators (1958 = 100):																
Personal consumption expenditures	107.7	108.1	108.0	.1	108.9	108.7	.2	109.1	109.0	.1	109.6	109.3	.3	108.9	108.8	.1
Durable goods other than automobiles and parts	100.0	100.3	100.0	.3	100.8	99.7	1.1	99.4	98.0	1.4	100.0	97.1	2.9	100.1	98.7	1.4
Nondurable goods	105.3	105.9	105.5	.4	106.7	106.5	.2	107.1	107.2	−.1	107.9	107.7	.2	106.9	106.7	.2
Services, excluding housing	116.8	117.1	117.6	−.5	118.6	118.7	−.1	119.8	119.9	−.1	120.7	120.6	.1	119.0	119.2	−.2
Fixed investment, nonresidential	106.6	107.5	107.0	.5	108.6	107.3	1.3	109.6	107.4	2.2	110.6	108.0	2.6	109.1	107.4	1.7
Residential structures, nonfarm	113.6	112.6	114.2	−1.6	113.5	115.1	−1.6	114.5	117.1	−2.6	115.7	117.9	−2.2	114.1	116.1	−2.0
Gross private output, excluding housing services	107.7	108.5	108.0	.5	109.4	108.9	.5	109.9	109.2	.7	110.8	109.4	1.4	109.6	108.9	.7

Income and related items, billions of dollars:																
Nonwage personal income	123.3	124.7	124.4	.3	126.8	128.5	−1.7	128.4	130.7	−2.3	128.9	133.0	−4.1	127.2	129.2	−2.0
Wage and salary disbursements and other labor income	359.7	368.2	366.4	1.8	374.5	371.7	2.8	383.1	377.4	5.7	395.2	387.0	8.2	380.2	375.6	4.6
Profits tax liability	28.1	28.5	29.5	−1.0	29.2	29.8	−.6	29.8	30.1	−.3	29.8	31.1	−1.3	29.3	30.1	−.8
Undistributed profits and inventory valuation adjustment	19.1	22.9	24.2	−1.3	22.5	23.6	−1.1	22.1	24.2	−2.1	20.8	24.2	−3.4	22.1	24.1	−2.0
State unemployment insurance benefits	2.4	2.2	2.4	−.2	2.0	2.2	−.2	2.0	2.2	−2.	2.0	2.0	.0	2.0	2.2	−.2
Wage rate, hours worked and output per manhour, private sector:																
Annual wage rate, thousands of dollars	5.626	5.683	5.643	.040	5.771	5.727	.044	5.881	5.765	.116	5.967	5.781	.186	5.826	5.729	.097
Index of weekly hours worked, 1957–59 = 100	.988	.990	.993	−.003	.988	.988	.000	.989	.988	.001	.989	.990	−.001	.989	.990	−.001
Index of output (excluding housing services) per man-hour, 1957–59 = 100	1.203	1.219	1.222	−.003	1.224	1.227	−.003	1.242	1.244	−.002	1.235	1.251	−.016	1.230	1.236	−.006
Monetary variables:																
Interest rate, 4–6 month commercial paper, percent	4.06	4.47	4.30	.17	4.47	4.38	.09	4.49	4.38	.11	4.66	4.47	.19	4.52	4.38	.14
Yield, corporate bonds (Moody's) percent	4.58	4.66	4.56	.10	4.73	4.58	.15	4.79	4.66	.13	4.86	4.77	.09	4.76	4.64	.12
Mortgage yield, secondary market, FHA-insured new homes, percent	5.45	5.47	5.45	.02	5.50	5.45	.05	5.53	5.45	.08	5.57	5.49	.08	5.52	5.46	.06
Liquid assets of households, billions of dollars	323.8	329.7	332.9	−3.2	334.6	338.9	−4.3	345.7	348.5	−2.8	355.9	359.0	−3.1	341.5	344.8	−3.3
Miscellaneous:																
Net stock of fixed investment, nonresidential, billions of 1958 dollars	468.1	472.8	472.7	.1	478.0	478.0	.0	483.0	483.7	−.7	488.4	489.4	−1.0	480.6	481.0	−.4
Durable manufacturers' new orders per quarter, billions of 1957–59 dollars	58.1	61.6	62.1	−.5	63.2	62.1	1.1	64.5	63.5	1.0	64.3	65.4	−1.1	63.4	63.3	.1
Durable manufacturers' shipments per quarter, billions of 1957–59 dollars	56.8	56.8	60.1	−3.3	58.8	59.9	−1.1	60.4	61.6	−1.2	62.7	62.4	.3	59.7	61.0	−1.3
Durable manufacturers' unfilled orders, end of quarter, billions of 1957–59 dollars	52.4	56.7	53.8	2.9	60.5	55.5	5.0	64.1	57.2	6.9	68.0	60.2	7.8	62.3	56.7	5.6
Private nonfarm housing starts, thousands of units	1532.0	1501.5	1450.0	51.5	1488.9	1524.0	−35.1	1422.3	1431.0	−8.7	1415.5	1537.7	−122.2	1457.0	1485.7	−28.7

NOTE: All data not specifically noted are at seasonally adjusted annual rates.

[a] Items shown in Table 4 are not repeated here.

SOURCE: U.S. Department of Commerce, Office of Business Economics and Bureau of the Census; U.S. Department of Labor, Bureau of Labor Statistics; Board of Governors, Federal Reserve System.

It may be noted in this connection that the 1953–64 forecasts discussed previously were not adjusted for special factors other than through the use of the "dummy" variables appearing in the auto and inventory equations and through allowance for changes in taxes.

Tables 4 and 5 present in full detail the outputs of the model by quarter and for the year as a whole, together with corresponding actual values and errors of prediction. Table 4 presents GNP and its components in current dollars, income and reconciliation items, and certain supplementary items including labor force and employment data. Table 5 gives endogenous variables not shown in Table 4.

1965 Performance. The model closely depicted the degree and pattern of economic expansion during the year. It yielded a GNP of $677.4 billion for the year as a whole, or $1.1 billion above the actual level. This represents an error of 2.3 percent in predicting the change in GNP from 1964, the actual change being $47.6 billion. The error in predicting the change from the fourth quarter 1964 to the fourth quarter 1965 was only $0.5 billion. As shown in Figure 4, the model results gave a good depiction of the general pattern of quarterly GNP changes over the course of the year. This pattern was characterized by large changes for the first and final quarters and somewhat more moderate gains for the intervening periods. The major components did not do quite as well on either an annual or a quarterly basis.

Table 4 shows that GNP was slightly overestimated for each quarter of the year, as has been the tendency since the Korean war. This reflects mainly a pattern of overestimating personal consumption expenditures. Not all consumption components were overestimated, auto purchases being the notable exception. Errors in individual investment components, though usually negative, were relatively small, except for the underestimate of inventory change in the fourth quarter, when actual inventories rose by an exceptional $10.1 billion.

Personal income was overestimated, particularly in the third and fourth quarters. Positive errors centered in wage income and are attributable to an increasingly overestimated wage rate. Positive errors in wages were partly offset by

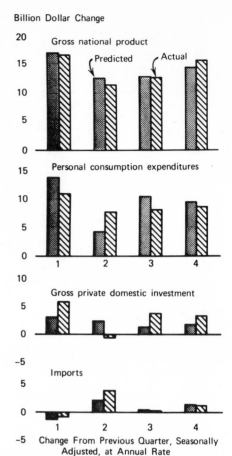

Figure 4

Predicted versus actual quarterly changes in GNP and major components, 1965. Source: U.S. Department of Commerce, Office of Business Economics.

underestimates of nonwage personal income. Predicted corporate profits (including inventory valuation adjustment), which in the model are inversely related to the wage rate, were also below actual levels.

GNP in 1958 dollars, unlike current-dollar GNP, was slightly underestimated for the first three quarters of the year and substantially so— by $7.2 billion—for the fourth quarter. This reflects excessive price increases predicted by the model. The implicit GNP price deflator determined by the model was consistently higher than the actual, and markedly so by the fourth quarter. As shown in forecasts for earlier years, prices have been difficult to predict, though not always for the same reasons. In the present case, excessive price gains yielded by the model are clearly associated with over-estimation of the wage rate.

Because the price results were not very

TABLE 6 Predicted and Actual Major Forecast Items, 1965: Exogenous and Endogenous Price Versions

(Billions of dollars seasonally adjusted at annual rates, unless not applicable)

	1964—4th Qtr.	1Q Prices Exogenous	1Q Prices Endogenous	1Q Actual	2Q Prices Exogenous	2Q Prices Endogenous	2Q Actual	3Q Prices Exogenous	3Q Prices Endogenous	3Q Actual	4Q Prices Exogenous	4Q Prices Endogenous	4Q Actual	Year Prices Exogenous	Year Prices Endogenous	Year Actual
Gross national product	641.1	659.0	658.1	657.6	670.9	670.5	668.8	683.6	683.3	681.5	700.3	697.7	697.2	678.4	677.4	676.3
Personal consumption expenditures	405.9	419.9	419.8	416.9	424.1	424.1	424.5	435.0	434.4	432.5	446.1	444.0	441.0	431.3	430.6	428.7
Residential structures	26.7	27.2	26.8	27.7	27.7	27.4	28.0	28.0	27.5	27.7	26.8	26.4	27.2	27.4	27.0	27.6
Fixed investment, nonresidential	63.5	65.3	65.6	66.9	68.1	68.6	68.4	68.3	69.7	70.9	71.2	72.5	73.0	68.2	69.1	69.8
Change in business inventories	7.5	8.8	8.3	8.8	7.4	6.9	6.4	7.6	7.0	7.6	8.5	7.0	10.1	8.1	7.3	8.2
Net exports of goods and services	8.9	6.4	6.5	6.0	10.1	10.1	8.0	9.3	9.4	7.4	8.7	8.8	6.9	8.5	8.7	7.1
Disposable personal income	446.4	453.5	452.9	451.4	459.3	458.9	458.5	475.0	474.4	471.2	487.4	484.4	480.3	468.8	467.6	465.3
Gross national product (1958 dollars)	584.7	599.1	596.2	597.7	605.4	603.0	603.5	615.0	611.2	613.0	626.6	617.2	624.4	611.5	606.9	609.6
Implicit price deflator for GNP (1958 = 100)	109.6	110.0	110.4	110.0	110.8	111.2	110.8	111.2	111.8	111.2	111.7	113.0	111.7	110.9	111.6	110.9
Civilian labor force, millions of persons	74.5	74.9	74.9	75.0	75.3	75.2	75.5	75.6	75.5	75.8	75.9	75.8	76.1	75.4	75.4	75.6
Employment, millions of persons	70.7	71.6	71.4	71.3	72.1	72.0	71.9	72.4	72.3	72.4	72.9	72.5	72.9	72.2	72.1	72.2
Unemployment, millions of persons	3.8	3.4	3.5	3.6	3.2	3.3	3.6	3.1	3.2	3.4	3.0	3.3	3.2	3.2	3.3	3.4
Unemployment rate, percent	5.1	4.5	4.6	4.8	4.3	4.3	4.7	4.2	4.2	4.4	4.0	4.4	4.2	4.2	4.4	4.6

source: U.S. Department of Commerce, Office of Business Economics and U.S. Department of Labor, Bureau of Labor Statistics.

satisfactory, another forecast was made with actual price deflators replacing those predicted by the equations. Since in this version prices were assumed to be exogenous, the model was reduced in scope to predicting real quantities on the product side.

Table 6 shows the main results for this alternative forecast. Interestingly, the behavior of current-dollar GNP and its major components was little affected during the first three quarters by making prices exogenous. However, GNP in 1958 dollars was estimated above the actual level in each quarter in this version. In the fourth quarter, current-dollar GNP was $2.6 billion higher than before; that is, additional real output more than offset the reduction in price level.

In both versions of the forecast, the unemployment rate approximated the sharp decline that took place over the year. In the full version, the rate did not fall quite to the actual fourth quarter level, while in the exogenous price version it dropped below. The lower unemployment rate in the exogenous price version reflects a larger gain in employment—virtually the same as the actual increase—associated with the greater rise in real output. In both cases, expansion of the labor force was somewhat underestimated.

It seems fair to say that this particular forecast has been improved by making prices exogenous. Whether this would be generally the case in actual *ex-ante* forecasting depends, of course, on how well independent price projections can be made.

FURTHER RESEARCH

The inadequacies of wage and price determination in the model point up the need to improve the specifications of the wage and price functions. This is a major challenge facing all econometric model builders. Apart from this, further work is required in several areas to improve the OBE model. These areas include the monetary equations, the equations for inventories, man-hours, and imports. In addition, a number of the present equations show evidence of nonrandom residuals, suggesting the need for improved specifications.

Beyond this, the usefulness of the OBE model would be increased by further adapting it for policy purposes. This, as has been noted, entails the introduction of more policy variables and also the provision of endogenous explanations for as many nonpolicy variables as possible. In this connection, the major task ahead is the development of an endogenous function for fixed investment.

APPENDIX A:

ESTIMATED EQUATIONS

Numbers in parentheses under coefficients are standard errors of the coefficients. Key to variables and other abbreviations follows equations.

I. GNP Component Equations

(1) Personal consumption expenditures, automobiles and parts

$$C_a = -134.0 - 11.0 \frac{p_a}{p_c} + .104 \frac{Y-T}{p_c} + 129.0(h_w)_{-1} + 1.85d_a;$$
$$\quad (.14) \quad (6.4) \quad (.006) \quad (19.4) \quad (.30)$$

$$TSLS, \bar{R}^2 = .91, \bar{S} = 1.0, D.W. = 1.25.$$

(2) Personal consumption expenditures, durables other than automobiles and parts

$$C_{od} = 28.0 + .060 \frac{Y-T}{p_{od}} - 65.2 \frac{P}{W} + .060 \left(\frac{L_h}{p_{od}}\right)_{-1}^{dev};$$
$$\quad (.07) \quad (.002) \quad (15.2) \quad (.008)$$

$$TSLS, \bar{R}^2 = .98, \bar{S} = .5, D.W. = .88.$$

(3) Personal consumption expenditures, nondurables

$$C_n = 31.1 + .252 \frac{Y-T}{P_n} + .210 \frac{1}{8} \sum_{i=-1}^{-8} (C_n)_i;$$
$$(.15) \quad (.025) \qquad (.083)$$

$$TSLS, \bar{R}^2 = .995, \bar{S} = 1.0, D.W. = 1.23.$$

(4) Personal consumption expenditures, services (except housing)

$$C_s = -44.2 + .069 \frac{Y-T}{P_s} + .476 \frac{1}{8} \sum_{i=-1}^{-8} (C_s)_i + .347N;$$
$$(.06) \quad (.015) \qquad (.161) \qquad\qquad (.118)$$

$$TSLS, \bar{R}^2 = .998, \bar{S} = .5, D.W. = 1.13.$$

(5) One-family housing starts, private nonfarm[1]

$$HS_s = -768 + .622(HS_s)_{-1} - .113(HS_s)_{-3} - 43.9(r_m)_{-1} + 1530 \left(\frac{R_h}{q_h}\right)_{-1} - .0216V_{-2}^{dev};$$
$$(7.9) \quad (.137) \qquad\qquad (.081) \qquad\qquad (13.9) \qquad (486) \qquad\qquad (.0235)$$

$$OLS, \bar{R}^2 = .92, \bar{S} = 54.5, D.W. = 1.96.$$

(6) Residential structures, nonfarm

$$I_h = -.14 + .001022 \left[.41 \left(\frac{C_h}{q_h} HS\right) + .49 \left(\frac{C_h}{q_h} HS\right)_{-1} + .10 \left(\frac{C_h}{q_h} HS\right)_{-2} \right]$$
$$(1.06) \quad (.000060)$$

$$- .19d_1 + .0d_2 + .38d_3 + I_{hr};$$
$$(.21) \quad\ (.23) \quad\ (.24)$$

$$OLS, \bar{R}^2 = .93, \bar{S} = .4, D.W. = 1.36.$$

(7) Fixed investment, nonresidential

$$I_p = 11.0 + .804I_p^e + .108(\Delta X)_{-1} + .524(I_p^a - I_p^e)_{-2} + .163t + .14C_a;$$
$$(1.5) \quad (.045) \quad (.026) \qquad\quad (.126) \qquad\qquad (.012)$$

$$OLS, \bar{R}^2 = .96, \bar{S} = 1.0, D.W. = 1.25.$$

(8) Change in business inventories

$$I_i = 49.9 + .232(X - I_i - C_s) + .363(I_i)_{-1} - .354 \sum_{j=-\infty}^{-1} (I_i)_j + .215(U_d)_{-1} + .72t + 4.34d_i;$$
$$(0.2) \quad (.044) \qquad\qquad\qquad (.084) \qquad (.053) \qquad\qquad\quad (.064) \qquad\quad (.18) \quad (.86)$$

$$TSLS, \bar{R}^2 = .81, \bar{S} = 1.6, D.W. = 2.04.$$

(9) Imports other than crude materials and foodstuffs

$$F_{if} = 15.5 + .0573 \frac{Y-T}{P_i} - 49.4 \frac{P}{W};$$
$$(0.1) \quad (.0026) \qquad\quad (17.0)$$

$$TSLS, \bar{R}^2 = .97, \bar{S} = .6, D.W. = .60.$$

(10) Imports of crude materials and foodstuffs

$$F_{im} = 3.94 + .0027 \left(\frac{pX}{p_i}\right)_{-1};$$
$$(.03) \quad (.0005)$$

$$OLS, \bar{R}^2 = .35, \bar{S} = .2, D.W. = 1.18.$$

[1] Prior to 1961 the average Treasury bill yield, lagged two, three, and four quarters, is used in place of $(r_m)_{-1}$ with coefficient of -84.8.

II. Price and Wage Rate Equations

(11) Implicit price deflator, gross private output, except housing services

$$p = \underset{(.0006)}{.226} + \underset{(.076)}{1.305} \frac{1}{3} \sum_{i=0}^{-2} \left(\frac{W - W_g}{X}\right)_i + \underset{(.00042)}{.00208} \left(\frac{X}{X_c}\right)^{9.2} \sum_{j=0}^{-1} \Delta(X - I_i)_j + \underset{(.00018)}{.00113t};$$

$$TSLS, \; \bar{R}^2 = .996, \; \bar{S} = .004, \; D.W. = .99.$$

(12) Implicit price deflator, personal consumption expenditures, durables other than automobiles and parts

$$p_{od} = - \underset{(.0004)}{.095} + \underset{(.18)}{.77\Delta p} + \underset{(.04)}{1.08(p_{od})_{-1}} + \underset{(.000045)}{.000154(U_d)_{-1}};$$

$$TSLS, \; \bar{R}^2 = .96, \; \bar{S} = .003, \; D.W. = 1.39$$

(13) Implicit price deflator, personal consumption expenditures, nondurables

$$p_n = - \underset{(.0005)}{.019} + \underset{(.18)}{.95\Delta p} + \underset{(.012)}{1.016(p_n)_{-1}};$$

$$TSLS, \; \bar{R}^2 = .99, \; \bar{S} = .003, \; D.W. = 1.86.$$

(14) Implicit price deflator, personal consumption expenditures, services (except housing)

$$p_s = - \underset{(.002)}{.118} + \underset{(.004)}{.155w} + \underset{(.41)}{1.56} \frac{C_s}{C'};$$

$$TSLS, \; \bar{R}^2 = .99, \; \bar{S} = .010, \; D.W. = .28.$$

(15) Implicit price deflator, residential structures, nonfarm

$$q_h = \underset{(.002)}{.491} + \underset{(.003)}{.115w};$$

$$TSLS, \; \bar{R}^2 = .97, \; \bar{S} = .011, \; D.W. = .73.$$

(16) Implicit price deflator, fixed investment, nonresidential

$$q_p = \underset{(.0006)}{.023} + \underset{(.23)}{1.39\Delta p} + \underset{(.008)}{.976(q_p)_{-1}};$$

$$TSLS, \; \bar{R}^2 = .997, \; \bar{S} = .004, \; D.W. = 1.83.$$

(17) Wage rate (private sector)

$$\frac{w - w_{-4}}{w_{-4}} = - \underset{(.002)}{.015} + \underset{(.0016)}{.0106} \left[\sum_{i=0}^{-3} \left(\frac{N_L - N_w - N_e}{N_L}\right)_i \right]^{-1}$$

$$+ \underset{(.293)}{.877} \sum_{i=0}^{-3} \left(\frac{p_c - p_{c-1}}{p_{c-1}}\right)_i + \underset{(.00047)}{.00128(p_c - p_{c-4})} - \underset{(.119)}{.311} \frac{w_{-4} - w_{-8}}{w_{-8}};$$

$$TSLS, \; \bar{R}^2 = .57, \; \bar{S} = .012, \; D.W. = .77.$$

III. Employment, Weekly Hours, and Labor Force Equations

(18) Average weekly hours (employees)

$$h_w = \underset{(.0005)}{.821} + \underset{(.018)}{.223}\,\frac{X}{X_c} - \underset{(.00004)}{.00041t};$$

$$TSLS,\ \bar{R}^2 = .92,\ \bar{S} = .003,\ D.W. = 1.71.$$

(19) Man-hours per unit of capacity output

$$\frac{h(N_w - N_g + N_e)}{X_c} = \underset{(.0002)}{.1684} - \underset{(.00008)}{.00109t} + [\underset{(.013)}{.125} - \underset{(.00059)}{.00148t}]\frac{X^* - X_c}{X_c}$$

$$+ \underset{(.0121)}{.0579}\,\frac{X - X^*}{X_c};\ X^* = \frac{1}{6}(3X_{-1} + 2X_{-2} + X_{-3});$$

$$TSLS,\ \bar{R}^2 = .99,\ \bar{S} = .00105,\ D.W. = .51.$$

(20) Civilian labor force

$$\frac{N_L}{N'} = \underset{(.0030)}{.5753} + \underset{(.126)}{.183}\,\frac{N_w + N_e}{N'} + \underset{(.00023)}{.00047t} + .83\,(\hat{u}_{N_L})_{-1};$$

$$TSLS(TN),\ \bar{R}^2 = .13,\ \bar{S} = .0035,\ D.W. = 1.85.$$

IV. Nonwage Income Components Equations

(21) Nonwage personal income

$$P = 55.6 + \underset{(.062)}{.149}P_c + \underset{(.035)}{.794}t + DIV;$$
$$(.2)$$

$$TSLS,\ \bar{R}^2 = .98,\ \bar{S} = 1.6,\ D.W. = .66.$$

(22) Corporate profits and inventory valuation adjustment

$$P_c = \underset{(.2)}{215.0} + \underset{(.053)}{.275}\left[\frac{CGP}{pX}\right]pX - \underset{(11.4)}{19.4}\,\frac{w}{p} - \underset{(140)}{550}\,\frac{h(N_w - N_g + N_e)}{X} - \underset{(7.6)}{40.0}\,\frac{X_c}{X} - D_{ac};$$

$$OLS,\ \bar{R}^2 = .99,\ \bar{S} = 1.5,\ D.W. = .59.$$

(23) Dividends

$$DIV = - \underset{(.038)}{.576} + \underset{(.0102)}{.0418}P_c + \underset{(.033)}{.897}DIV_{-1};$$

$$TSLS,\ \bar{R}^2 = .99,\ \bar{S} = .2,\ D.W. = 2.72.$$

V. Monetary Equations

(24) Interest rate (short-term), 4–6 month commercial paper

$$r_s = \underset{(.03)}{1.06} - \underset{(.102)}{.214}R_{-1} + \underset{(.087)}{.977}r_d;$$

$$OLS,\ \bar{R}^2 = .92,\ \bar{S} = .24.\ D.W. = .80.$$

(25) Yield, corporate bonds (Moody's)

$$r_L = .243 + .082r_s + .885(r_L)_{-1};$$
$$(.017) \quad (.030) \qquad (.039)$$

$$TSLS, \bar{R}^2 = .96, \bar{S} = .11, D.W. = 1.45.$$

(26) Mortgage yield, FHA-insured new homes

$$r_m = .591 + .198r_L + .739(r_m)_{-1};$$
$$(.015) \quad (.070) \qquad (.077)$$

$$TSLS, \bar{R}^2 = .96, \bar{S} = .10, D.W. = .97.$$

(27) Liquid assets of households

$$L_h = -154 + 1.084p_c(C' + C_r) + 152\frac{1}{(50)^{r_L}} + .85(\hat{u}_{L_h})_{-1};$$
$$(2.4) \quad (.047) \qquad\qquad\qquad (50)^{r_L}$$

$$TSLS(TN), \bar{R}^2 = .93, \bar{S} = 2.4, D.W. = 1.98.$$

VI. Miscellaneous Equations

(28) Capital consumption allowances, constant dollars (fixed nonresidential capital stock)

$$D_p = -4.89 + .0340(K_p)_{-1};$$
$$(.04) \quad (.0010)$$

$$OLS, \bar{R}^2 = .96, \bar{S} = .2, D.W. = .15.$$

(29) Gross private output at capacity[2]

$$X_c = 3.734(10)^{.00223t}[(K_p)_{-1}]^{.305}[.97(N_L - N_g)]^{.695}$$

(30) Personal tax and nontax payments[3]

$$T_p = a_0 + a_1 Y$$

(31) Corporate profits tax liability[13]

$$T_c = b_0 + b_1 P_c$$

(32) Indirect business tax and nontax liability

$$T_i = -9.39 + .125_p(X - I_i) + .112t;$$
$$(.10) \quad (.011) \qquad\qquad (.050)$$

$$TSLS, \bar{R}^2 = .995, \bar{S} = .7, D.W. = .36.$$

(33) State unemployment insurance benefits

$$TR_u = -1.60 + 1.11(N_L - N_w - N_e);$$
$$(.05) \quad (.06)$$

$$TSLS, \bar{R}^2 = .88, \bar{S} = .3, D.W. = .66.$$

---

[2] For explanation of how equation is estimated, see Appendix B.
[3] Coefficients are determined on basis of recent tax behavior and modified when required to comply with changes in the tax laws.

(34) New orders, manufacturers' durables

$$O_d = -1.10 + .955 \frac{P_c}{p_{wd}} \; ;$$
$$ (.33) \quad (.052)$$

$$TSLS, \ \bar{R}^2 = .87, \ \bar{S} = 2.3, \ D.W. = 1.12.$$

(35) Shipments, manufacturers' durables

$$S_d = 13.8 + .917\Delta(O_d)_{-1} - .202\Delta\left(\frac{U_d}{S_d}O_d\right)_{-1} + .715(O_d)_{-2};$$
$$ (.3) \quad (.142) \qquad\qquad (.076) \qquad\qquad\quad (.048)$$

$$OLS, \ \bar{R}^2 = .84, \ \bar{S} = 1.8, \ D.W. = 1.33.$$

(36) Unfilled orders, manufacturers' durables

$$U_d = -.38 + .92(O_d - S_d) + (U_d)_{-1};$$
$$ (.11) \quad (.04)$$

$$OLS, \ \bar{R}^2 = .93, \ \bar{S} = .8, \ D.W. = 1.32.$$

VII. Identities

$$(37) \qquad h = \frac{h_w(N_w - N_g) + h_e N_e}{N_w - N_g + N_e}$$

$$(38) \qquad HS = HS_s + HS_m$$

$$(39) \quad p_a C_a + p_{od} C_{od} + p_n C_n + p_s C_s + p_r C_r + q_h I_h$$
$$+ I_{hf} + q_p I_p + pI_i + e_i - p_i(F_{if} + F_{im}) + F_e + G = GNP$$

$$(40) \qquad GNP = pX + W_g + p_r C_r$$

$$(41) \quad W + P + P_c - DIV - i_c - i_g + T_b + TR_b + D_{ac}$$
$$+ D_{anc} + T_i - S_g + SD = GNP; \quad |SD| \leqslant 4.0, \quad |SD - SD_{-1}| \leqslant 1.0$$

$$(42) \qquad Y = W + P$$

$$(43) \qquad T = T_p - TR_u - TR_o + T_e$$

$$(44) \qquad w = \frac{W - W_g}{h_w(N_w = N_g)}$$

$$(45) \qquad p_c = \frac{p_a C_a + p_{od} C_{od} + p_n C_n + p_s C_s + p_r C_r}{C' + C_r}$$

$$(46) \qquad C' = C_a + C_{od} + C_n + C_s$$

$$(47) \qquad S_p = Y - T - p_c(C' + C_r) - i_c - TR_f$$

$$(48) \qquad S_c = P_c - T_c - DIV$$

$$(49) \qquad K_p = (K_p)_{-1} + .25I_p - D_p$$

Key to Abbreviations

(All variables except interest rates are seasonally adjusted. All components of the national income and product accounts are at annual rates; other flow variables are at quarterly rates unless otherwise noted. Variables preceded by * are exogenous.)

C'	Personal consumption expenditures, except housing services, billions of 1958 dollars.
C_a	Personal consumption expenditures, automobiles and parts, billions of 1958 dollars.
$*c_h$	Average cost per new private nonfarm housing unit started, in thousands of dollars.
CGP	Corporate gross product, billions of dollars (ratio CGP/pX is assumed exogenous).
C_n	Personal consumption expenditures, nondurables, billions of 1958 dollars.
C_{od}	Personal consumption expenditures, durables other than automobiles and parts, billions of 1958 dollars.
$*C_r$	Personal consumption expenditures, housing, billions of 1958 dollars.
C_s	Personal consumption expenditures, services (except housing), billions of 1958 dollars.
d_1, d_2, d_3	Seasonal dummy variables, housing expenditures equation; d = 1 in quarter corresponding to subscript, 0 otherwise.
$*d_a$	Dummy variable for auto equation (-1 during strike quarter; $+1$ following strike quarter; $+1$ in 1955 to reflect abrupt credit and taste changes; 0 otherwise).
$*d_i$	Dummy variable for inventory equation (-1 during strike quarter; $+1$ before and after strike; 0 otherwise).
$*D_{ac}$	Capital consumption allowances, corporate sector.
$*D_{anc}$	Capital consumption allowances, noncorporate sector.
dev	Deviation from least squares linear trend.
DIV	Dividends, billions of dollars.
D_p	Capital consumption allowances, constant dollars, fixed nonresidential capital stock, quarterly rate, billions of 1958 dollars.
e_i	Discrepancy in jumpoff quarter between change in business inventories in current dollars and pI_i.
$*F_e$	Exports, billions of dollars.
F_{if}	Imports other than crude materials and foodstuffs, billions of 1958 dollars.
F_{im}	Imports of crude materials and foodstuffs, billions of 1958 dollars.
$*G$	Government purchases of goods and services, billions of dollars.
GNP	Gross national product, billions of dollars.
h	Average weekly hours index, private sector (1957–59 = 1.000).
$*h_e$	Average weekly hours index, self-employed (1957–59 = 1.000).
h_w	Average weekly hours index, private employees (1957–59 = 1.000).
HS	Private nonfarm housing starts, in thousands at annual rate.
$*HS_m$	Number of new 2 or more family units started, in thousands at annual rate.
HS_s	Number of new single-family units started, in thousands at annual rate.
$*i_c$	Interest paid by consumers, billions of dollars.
$*i_g$	Net interest paid by government, billions of dollars.
I_h	Residential structures, nonfarm, billions of 1958 dollars.
$*I_{hf}$	Residential structures, farm, billions of 1958 dollars.
$*I_{hr}$	Residential construction expenditures on other than new units (additions and alterations, etc.), billions of 1958 dollars.
I_i	Change in business inventories, billions of 1958 dollars.
I_p	Fixed investment, nonresidential, billions of 1958 dollars.
I_p^a	Actual plant and equipment outlays in billions of dollars deflated by q_p.
$*I_p^e$	Anticipated plant and equipment outlays; first anticipations in billions of dollars deflated q_{p-2}.
K_p	End of quarter net stock of plant and equipment, billions of 1958 dollars.

L_h	End of quarter liquid assets held by households (currency + demand and bank savings deposits + savings and loan shares), in billions of dollars.
$*N$	Total population in millions.
$*N'$	Population, ages 18–64 in millions.
$*N_e$	Self-employed, millions.
$*N_g$	Civilian government employment, millions.
N_L	Civilian labor force, millions.
N_w	Civilian wage and salary employment, millions.
O_d	Durable manufacturers' new orders, billions of dollars deflated by p_{wd}.
p	Implicit price deflator, gross private output, except housing services (1958 = 1.000).
P	Nonwage personal income (sum of proprietors' income, rental income of persons, dividends, and personal interest income), billions of dollars.
$*p_a$	Implicit price deflator, personal consumption expenditures, automobiles and parts (1958 = 1.000).
p_c	Implicit price deflator, personal consumption expenditures (1958 = 1.000).
$*p_i$	Implicit price deflator, imports (1958 = 1.000).
p_n	Implicit price deflator, personal consumption expenditures, nondurables (1958 = 1.000).
p_{od}	Implicit price deflator, personal consumption expenditures, durables other than automobiles and parts (1958 = 1.000).
$*p_r$	Implicit price deflator, personal consumption expenditures, housing (1958 = 1.000).
p_s	Implicit price deflator, personal consumption expenditures, services (except housing) (1958 = 1.000).
$*p_{wd}$	Wholesale price index, durable goods (1957–59 = 1.00).
P_c	Corporate profits and inventory valuation adjustment, billions of dollars.
q_h	Implicit price deflator, residential structures, nonfarm (1958 = 1.000).
q_p	Implicit price deflator, fixed investment, nonresidential (1958 = 1.000).
$*R$	End of quarter excess reserves as percent of total reserves.
$*r_d$	Federal Reserve average discount rate (percent).
R_h	BLS consumer rent index (1957–59 = 1.000).
r_L	Percent yield, corporate bonds (Moody's).
r_m	Percent yield, secondary market, FHA-insured new homes.
r_s	Rate, 4–6 month commercial paper (percent).
S_c	Undistributed profits and inventory valuation adjustment, billions of dollars.
S_d	Manufacturers' shipments, durable goods, billions of dollars deflated by p_{wd}.
SD	Statistical discrepancy, billions of dollars.
$*S_g$	Subsidies less current surplus of government enterprises, billions of dollars.
S_p	Personal saving, billions of dollars.
t	Time in quarters (1953 − I = 1.0).
$*T_b$	Employer contributions for social insurance, billions of dollars.
T_c	Profits tax liability, billions of dollars.
$*T_e$	Personal contributions for social insurance, billions of dollars.
$\mathbf{T}_i$	Indirect business tax and nontax liability, billions of dollars.
T_p	Personal tax and nontax payments, billions of dollars.
$*TR_b$	Business transfer payments, billions of dollars.
$*TR_f$	Personal transfer payments to foreigners, billions of dollars.
$*TR_o$	Transfer payments to persons, except State unemployment insurance benefits, billions of dollars.
TR_u	State unemployment insurance benefits, billions of dollars.
U_d	Unfilled manufacturers' orders, durable goods at end of quarter, billions of dollars, deflated by p_{wd}.
$(\hat{u}_{L_h})_{-1}$	Estimate of lagged disturbance, liquid assets equation.

$(\hat{u}_{N_L})_{-1}$	Estimate of lagged disturbance, labor force equation.
V	Number of vacant nonfarm housing units, end of quarter, in thousands.
w	Annual wage rate, private sector, in thousands of dollars.
W	Wage and salary disbursements and other labor income, billions of dollars.
$*W_g$	Government compensation, billions of dollars.
X	Gross private output, except housing services, billions of 1958 dollars.
X^*	Planned private output, billions of 1958 dollars.
X_c	Gross private output at capacity, billions of 1958 dollars.
$Y\!-\!T$	Disposable personal income, billions of dollars.
OLS	Ordinary least-squares estimate.
$TSLS$	Two-stage least-squares estimate.
TN	Equation is estimated using Theil-Nagar transformation of variables.[4]
$D.W.$	Durbin-Watson statistic: Test for serial correlation of residuals.
$\bar{R}^2$	Adjusted coefficient of determination.
$\bar{S}$	Adjusted standard error of estimate.

[4] See H. Theil and A. L. Nagar [12].

APPENDIX B

METHOD USED TO OBTAIN

ESTIMATES OF PARAMETERS

With a few exceptions, the two-stage least-squares (TSLS) method was used to obtain estimates of the parameters in the equations of the model. Among the various methods available to obtain consistent estimates in an interdependent simultaneous system, this is by far the simplest to apply and has been shown in past studies to yield acceptable results.

The application of TSLS to obtain parameter estimates for the present model differs in one important respect from the more usual way the method is used. The customary procedure has been to obtain the first-stage computed values by regressing all "right-side" endogenous variables on all predetermined variables in the system or on some selected subset of them. In the present instance, because of the large number of predetermined variables relative to the number of observations, the computed values were obtained by regressing the endogenous variables on leading principal components of the predetermined set.[5] In brief, principal components are certain linear combinations of the variables in the predetermined set which capture in condensed form the essential information contained in the full array. The method was adopted

[5] See, for example, T. W. Anderson [1, pp. 272 281], and T. Kloek and L. B. M. Mennes [9].

primarily for convenience and to avoid computational difficulties associated with large systems that have strong correlations among the predetermined variables. It was found that 10 principal components were sufficient and all but exhausted the information contained in the full set. Thus, all first-stage regressions were based on the set of derived variables, 10 in number.

Specific mention should be made of the method used to obtain parameter estimates for capacity output given by equation (29). The parameter estimates were obtained indirectly as follows:

(1) A linear homogeneous Cobb-Douglas production function was first fitted, using actual private output, man-hours employed, and utilized capital approximated by multiplying the Wharton School Index of capacity utilization by total capital. The computed elasticities were used in the next step.

(2) The difference

$$\log X_c' - a \log K \\ - (1-a) \log [.97 \, (N_L - N_g)]$$

was then regressed on time, where $X_c' = \dfrac{X}{WSI}$.

(3) The constant term and the coefficient for time from (2) and the elasticities from (1) were incorporated into Equation (29). Values computed from this equation for X_c rather than X_c' are used to define capacity output. The usual supplementary statistics are not shown for this equation.

The above procedure was adopted to remove the unrealistic fluctuations in capacity output obtained by direct application of the Wharton School Index. The fluctuations arise primarily because of the inapplicability, in a strict sense, of the index, which is based on indexes of industrial production, to a GNP concept of total private output. Although this procedure removes the fluctuations, it does not correct for possible bias in the estimate of capacity level.

APPENDIX C:

TREATMENT OF THE STATISTICAL DISCREPANCY IN THE MODEL

In designing econometric models, it has been customary to include equations to account for all but one income item—usually corporate profits—which is then determined residually through the constraint, found in the national income and product accounts, that income plus reconciliation items equal product. This implies that values for the usual reconciliation items, including the statistical discrepancy, must be introduced. In general, the discrepancy is set at the previous period's or some other predetermined level.

This procedure has the serious drawback that the residual item must bear the brunt of errors made elsewhere in the model—errors that are by no means necessarily offsetting. To alleviate this difficulty, the present model uses a different approach. Behavioral equations initially determine *all* income elements, including corporate profits. Then, in order to avoid overdetermination implied by adding the income-product identity (there being then more equations than unknowns), the statistical discrepancy is defined as a new variable, rather than assuming a preassigned value. This makes the discrepancy, rather than an income component, the residual.

Clearly, the discrepancy cannot be allowed to vary without limit since the essential identity between income and product must hold. Thus, two constraints are introduced to limit the behavior of the discrepancy: (1) Its level is constrained to vary within the approximate historically observed range, from − $4.0 billion to + $4.0 billion, and (2) its maximum allowable quarterly change is set at $1.0 billion. Move-ments of the discrepancy beyond either of these limits give rise to an excess that must be eliminated.

The method of elimination is as follows: Adjustments are made on certain income-determining equations, namely those for the wage rate, man-hours, corporate profits, and personal nonwage income, by shifting the constant terms in these equations by amounts sufficient to eliminate the excess discrepancy when the model is again solved.

These adjustments have two effects. First, they serve to reconcile income and product by spreading the excess residual element among the major income components rather than concentrating it in profits. Second, because of feedbacks to spending primarily via disposable income, the levels of income and product are adjusted to the point where they are consistent with both the necessary income-product identity (within the above-stated discrepancy limit) and the requirements of the model.

The relative amounts of adjustment introduced into the four equations are somewhat arbitrary; they were determined so that the resulting income increment or decrement would be distributed among wages, corporate profits, and personal nonwage income in amounts based partly on the relative sizes of these components, and partly on the residual character of corporate profits and entrepreneurial income. Equal weight was attached to the wage rate and to man-hours in affecting wage payments.

The decision to confine adjustments exclusively to income items was not arbitrary. It was based on examination of the multipliers implied by the given system of equations. This examination showed that errors made on the product side of the accounts tend to bring about similar errors on the income side in both magnitude and direction. Errors on the income side, however, do not affect product commensurately, and they therefore tend to affect the statistical discrepancy. Thus, the procedure adopted is based mainly on what is expedient to bring about a desired change in the statistical discrepancy. However, apart from expediency, it appears quite likely that the income equations are more precarious, which also suggests the adoption of the adjustment procedure, at least on a provisional basis.

APPENDIX D:

METHOD USED TO SOLVE

THE MODEL[6]

Examination of the model equations shows that many of them are nonlinear in endogenous variables. Given such a system, the usual methods of matrix inversion for the solution of a set of linear equations cannot be applied, and an alternative method must be employed.

The particular method used to solve the model was originally suggested by Professor Klein and consists, essentially, in the separation of the equations of the system into two parts. The first step in the solution is to introduce provisional values for a select set of variables in one of the parts—values from the previous period are satisfactory for this purpose. The variables selected are such as to remove the nonlinearities in the set so that a linear solution method can be applied to obtain provisional values for the remaining unknowns. These values are then introduced into the second part, which can then also be solved as a linear set. The solution yields revised values for the variables initially introduced into the first set. After a number of iterations (usually five to seven), the process converges to a solution for the entire set of equations.

Solution is assumed complete when two successive iterations yield values of the endogenous variables that differ by no more than 0.05 percent. This ensures that all variables are computed correctly to the degree of precision given by the corresponding data. Because of the treatment accorded to the statistical discrepancy

[6] Solutions were carried out on an IBM 7094 computer by means of a program called OMNITAB [5].

(see Appendix C), the iteration procedure is carried out twice for each quarter in which the discrepancy does not fall within the prescribed limits.

APPENDIX E:

CONSTANT AND TIME TREND

ADJUSTMENTS

In most of the equations of the model there is evidence of serial correlation of residuals. This indicates either imperfections in specification or auto-correlated errors of measurement in the data. To minimize forecasting errors resulting from serial correlation, it is reasonable to adjust the intercept or constant term of each equation showing such correlation so that the computed value of the dependent variable coincides with the last observed value or with the average of recently observed values.

In simulating with the model, wherever serial correlation was believed to be present, constants were adjusted as just described. Either the value of the last quarter (prior to forecast) or average values of the last four quarters were used depending on whether serial correlation was deemed to be strong or moderate. For equations estimated with the Theil-Nagar transformation, this procedure was superseded by appropriate explicit treatment of the lagged residual.

In applying the model beyond the sample period, it is also appropriate to examine residuals in equations containing trend terms to see if there has been a shift in the trend. Thus, in making the 1965 forecast, a trend correction was applied to the man-hours equation because of an apparent drift of the residuals over the recent period prior to 1965.

REFERENCES

1. T. W. Anderson, 1958. Principal components. *An introduction to multivariate statistical analysis*; New York: Wiley, 272–287.
2. E. F. Denison, F. Modigliani, and L. R. Klein, 1964. Comments (on L. R. Klein's "A postwar quarterly model"). *Models of income determination* (National Bureau of Economic Research); Princeton: Princeton University Press, 36–57. MD.
3. J. S. Duesenberry, G. Fromm, L. R. Klein, and E. Kuh, eds., 1965. *The Brookings quarterly econometric model of the United States*. Chicago: Rand McNally.
4. I. Friend, and P. Taubman, 1964. A short-term forecasting model. *Review of Economics and Statistics*, 46(3): 229–236.

REFERENCES continued

5. J. Hilsenrath, G. G. Ziegler, C. G. Messina, P. J. Walsh, and R. J. Herbold, 1966. *OMNITAB: a computer program for statistical and numerical analysis.* Washington: U.S. Government Printing Office, National Bureau of Standards Handbook 101.
6. A. A. Hirsch, 1964. *Predicting housing starts: Professor Maisel's model modified.* Working paper, U.S. Department of Commerce, Staff Working Paper in Economics and Statistics No. 5.
7. L. R. Klein, and J. Popkin, 1961. An econometric analysis of the postwar relationship between inventory fluctuations and changes in aggregate economic activity. *Inventory fluctuations and economic stabilization* (U.S. Congress, Joint Economic Committee); Washington: U.S. Government Printing Office, Part III., 69–89. 1D.
8. L. R. Klein, 1964. A postwar quarterly model: description and applications. *Models of income determination* (National Bureau of Economic Research); Princeton: Princeton University Press, 11–36. 1D.
9. T. Kloek, and L. B. M. Mennes, 1960. Simultaneous equations estimation based on principal components of predetermined variables. *Econometrica, 28*(1): 45–61.
10. S. J. Maisel, 1963. A theory of fluctuations in residential construction starts. *American Economic Review, 53*(3): 359–383.
11. J. Popkin, 1965. The relationship between new orders and shipments: an analysis of the machinery and equipment industries. *Survey of Current Business, 45*(3): 24–32.
12. H. Theil, and A. L. Nagar, 1961. Testing the independence of regression disturbances. *Journal of the American Statistical Association, 56*(296): 793–806.
13. T. A. Wilson, and O. Eckstein, 1964. Short-run productivity behavior in U.S. manufacturing. *Review of Economics and Statistics, 46*(1): 41–54.

28

STAFF ECONOMIC STUDY: THE FEDERAL RESERVE-MIT ECONOMETRIC MODEL

FRANK DE LEEUW

EDWARD GRAMLICH

A group of economists at the Massachusetts Institute of Technology and at the Board of Governors of the Federal Reserve System have been working together on a new quarterly econometric model of the United States.[1] This paper is the first report of some of the preliminary results of the model.

Since the number of econometric models of the United States can no longer be counted on the fingers of even two hands, it is natural to

SOURCE: Reprinted from *Federal Reserve Bulletin*, *54* (1): 11–40 (1968).

[1] The MIT group was under the direction of Franco Modigliani and Albert Ando, and included varying proportions of the time of Charles Bischoff, Dwight Jaffe, Morris Norman, Robert Rasche, Harold Shapiro, Gordon Sparks, and Richard Sutch.

The Federal Reserve group currently includes, besides the authors, Enid Miller, Helen Popkin, Alfred Tella, and Peter Tinsley, again with varying proportions of working time. Patric Hendershott was until recently a member of the group.

Views expressed in the paper are those of its authors. All the colleagues listed have helped shape these views but have not edited or corrected this paper.

As in all staff economic studies, the authors are responsible for the analyses and conclusions set forth and the views expressed are not necessarily those of the Board of Governors, the Federal Reserve Banks, or members of their staffs.

wonder why we are adding one more to the list. In this instance the major purpose is to be able to say more than existing models about the effects of monetary policy instruments—both in themselves and in comparison with other policy instruments. No existing model has as its major purpose the quantification of monetary policy and its effect on the economy. As a consequence even those which do contain some treatment of monetary instruments and effects suffer from puzzling results either in their financial sectors or in the response to financial variables in other sectors—results which their proprietors would surely investigate further were the models to be used to say something about monetary developments on a current basis. We have tried to avoid these difficulties by concentrating most of our efforts on the treatment of financial markets and on the links between financial markets and markets for goods and services.

A few comments on some of the differences between the Federal Reserve-MIT and other models may clarify this last point. In the financial sector, the general structure of our equations is similar to some other recent models, but our estimates of the lags are quite different. By experimenting with alternative formulations applied to data through 1965 and testing the results against data for 1966 and early 1967, we have tentatively concluded that lags in the demand for money are shorter than many recent estimates, and that the transitory impact effect of open-market operations on interest rates (as contrasted to longer-run effects) is smaller than a number of other models imply. The financial sector also differs from some others by including the market for bank commercial loans as an integral part of the determination of money stock and interest rates, and by including a fairly broad range of interest rates.

In the investment sector, the plant and equipment equations (due to Charles Bischoff) are derived from the neoclassical theory of the business firm, but with allowance for lags in forming expectations, lags between orders and shipments, technological change, and the possibility that substitution between capital goods and other factors of production may be feasible to a much greater degree when new equipment or plant is being ordered than after it has been installed. Interest rates and tax rates enter these equations in the way in which the theory of the firm—after modification for the complications just listed—suggests they should affect returns on investment projects.

The equations for housing distinguish between builders and owners of houses on the one hand, and users of dwelling space on the other. It is in the equation describing decisions by the former group to change the inventory of houses under construction that current and recent interest rates enter with a powerful effect. Nevertheless, our model fails to predict the full extent of the decline in housing starts in 1966, and further work to try to determine whether we are understating the effects of monetary policy on housing is high on our future agenda.

Expenditures and taxes of State and local governments are endogenous in our model, in contrast to any other model of our acquaintance. The equations emphasize the interdependence of spending and taxing decisions, with an important interest rate effect on State and local construction expenditures and a smaller, but still noticeable, effect on the proportion of current expenditures financed by taxes.

Finally, in our consumption equations we have attempted to distinguish the services yielded by stocks of durable goods from expenditures on durable goods which are a part of consumer spending in the national accounts. The sum of the services of durable goods and expenditures on nondurables and services is the consumption variable that we relate to current and past income, whereas the allocation of the sum among its components depends on relative prices, existing stocks, and other variables. One result of this formulation is a small effect of interest rates on the allocation of total consumption (in our sense) and hence on consumer expenditures on durable goods.

These are some of the distinguishing features of our model. The preliminary results suggest that both monetary and fiscal policies have powerful effects on the economy, though monetary policy operates with a longer lag. We also find that the response of money income to both monetary and fiscal policy changes is stronger than that implied by other large-scale econometric models.

At this point in our work, however, we would like to emphasize the tentative nature of any conclusions derived from the model. Not all of the key equations predict well, and the number of observations outside our sample period on which to base an evaluation is still fairly small. In fitting the model, we have made very extensive use of recent improvements in techniques for estimating lag distributions. But with respect to simultaneous equations difficulties, our efforts so far have been largely confined to using a simultaneous estimation technique or transforming an equation to neutralize the bias only in those cases where we felt the problem was especially likely to be important. Putting the model together in its present form has made us aware of some unexpected system characteristics which need to be examined in more detail. We hope that those who use and read about the model will not simply note and store away its major findings but will suggest alternative specifications that we should consider.

* * *

This first report describes the performance and interaction of three large blocks of equations in the model. The first section deals with the financial block—supply and demand equations for financial claims and their dynamics. The second section deals with the fixed-investment block, covering housing, plant and equipment, and the behavior of State and local governments. The third section deals with the consumption-inventory block, and covers income shares, imports, and Federal personal taxes as well as consumption and inventory investment. Each of these sections includes a general description of the block of equations, results of dynamic prediction tests (that is, predictions which generate their own lagged values as they go along), and results of simulations illustrating the behavior of the block. An appendix lists and briefly describes the individual equations of the blocks. The emphasis on the performance of blocks of equations means that there are only brief references to the theoretical hypotheses and the detailed estimation work underlying individual equations. Papers by those who were directly responsible for individual equations will fill these gaps.

The final section of the paper deals with the three blocks combined. It presents prediction results and simulation experiments. A few miscellaneous tax and income share equations are introduced for the first time in this section. Still to be added is the price (supply equation) and labor market block, on which we are presently at work. The simulations of the final section treat prices and wage rates as exogenous, but since our price-wage sector will show a fair degree of price and wage rigidity in the short run under conditions of moderate slack in labor and product markets, the simulations of the final section do indicate roughly the estimates of the effects of monetary policy which are emerging from our efforts so far.

I. THE FINANCIAL BLOCK

The first block of equations describes the behavior of financial markets, given GNP and its components on the one hand and a number of Federal Reserve policy-determined variables on the other. In this, as in other models of financial behavior, the quantity supplied of an open-market operations variable—for this model, unborrowed bank reserves—is ex-

ogenous and the identity relating it to deposits, reserve requirements, and bank free reserves (Equation 1 on p. 576) is a central equation of the block. Demand equations for the various uses of reserves (Equations 2 through 4) depend on interest rates and other variables—most importantly, GNP and its components—with interest rates rising or falling in the short-run to bring quantities demanded into balance with the exogenous supply.

As changes in interest rates affect investment, the short-run interest rate effects of changes in monetary policy variables are reduced and the effects on income increased. Our main goal, partly reached in Section IV of this paper, is to explain these effects on income; but in the financial block we shall take GNP and its components as exogenous and consider solely the equations dealing with supplies and demands in financial markets.

Demand equations for demand deposits, time deposits, and free reserves—the three uses of unborrowed reserves—all include the lagged stock of the dependent variable as one of the explanatory variables. The presence of a lagged stock term makes deposits and free reserves adjust only gradually to changes in their determinants, and therefore implies large temporary jumps in interest rates in order to clear markets in response to a change in unborrowed reserves or reserve requirements. It is difficult to understand why the adjustment in deposits and reserves implied by the introduction of lagged stocks should be as gradual as it usually turns out to be in studies of the demand for money or of bank behavior. In our model adjustments are somewhat faster than in a number of other recent models, and the implied temporary jumps in interest rates are not so large. The simulations described below indicate just how large they are; the estimation and testing procedure which led to this result is outlined in the appendix.

Banks are assumed to accommodate short-run changes in loan demand by their business customers partly by changing their free reserve position. Other bank earning assets are not assumed to have this direct effect on reserve behavior, with the result that the composition of bank credit has a short-run effect on interest rates in the model. The main influence on changes in bank commercial loans is business inventory investment.

The various interest rates in the financial sector are closely interrelated. A number of equations explain the slower-moving rates largely as complex distributed lags of the more volatile short-term rates or of the corporate bond rate which in turn depends on short-term rates. The dividend yield on common stocks is one of these slower-moving rates; our equation does not explain a high portion of its variance, but does connect it with the corporate rate and thereby relates at least some of the variation in stock prices to developments in other financial markets.

The dividend yield equation also contains terms measuring the past rate of growth of dividends as a proxy for expected capital gains. Apart from these terms, variables reflecting price expectations are absent from the model. It is very difficult to detect such influences in data for this economy during the last two decades, although price expectation effects are clearly present in economies with larger and more variable inflationary spurts.

Dynamic Predictions

Predictions of the financial sector during 1966 and early 1967 are fairly successful. Table 1 shows prediction results based on a dynamic simulation (that is, one generating its own lagged values as it goes along) of the sector starting in the third quarter of 1965. The model successfully predicts the unusually large increases and then declines in interest rates. It does not predict the absolute decline in demand deposit holdings which took place in 1966, but it does predict a very marked slowdown in their rate of growth. Since 1966 and 1967 were outside the sample period used to fit the model, these results are decidedly encouraging. However, the fact that we selected from among several sets tested those equations which performed best in 1966 and early 1967 certainly

TABLE 1   Dynamic Predictions, Financial Block

Item	1965		1966				1967
	Q III	Q IV	Q I	Q II	Q III	Q IV	Q I
	(In per cent)						
Treasury Bill rate:							
Actual	3.86	4.16	4.60	4.58	5.03	5.20	4.52
Predicted	3.40	4.24	4.51	4.98	5.21	5.13	4.48
Corporate Aaa bond rate:							
Actual	4.50	4.61	4.81	5.00	5.32	5.38	5.12
Predicted	4.60	4.82	5.02	5.20	5.35	5.42	5.35
Mortgage rate:							
Actual	5.76	5.78	5.85	6.03	6.17	6.39	6.34
Predicted	5.74	5.82	5.97	6.14	6.30	6.42	6.46
	(In billions of dollars)						
Demand deposits:							
Actual	128.9	131.1	133.3	132.8	132.2	131.6	133.5
Predicted	129.3	131.0	132.1	132.6	133.0	134.1	135.8
Time deposits:							
Actual	142.6	147.5	150.5	155.5	158.1	160.4	167.4
Predicted	141.7	145.8	150.2	153.7	156.9	160.4	164.7
Free reserves:							
Actual	−.15	−.02	−.26	−.36	−.40	−.09	+.21
Predicted	−.17	+.04	−.10	−.27	−.46	−.40	+.02

NOTE: Financial dollar amounts are all averages of the 2 months surrounding the end of quarter; for example, fourth quarter is average of December and January.

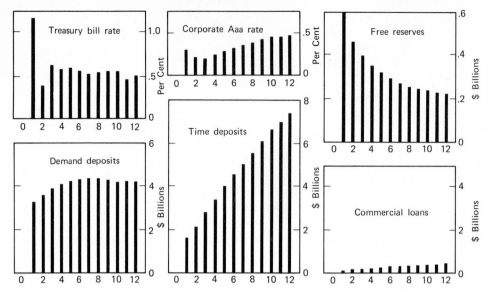

Figure 1 Effects of a step increase of $1 billion in unborrowed reserves, financial block. Dynamic simulation, initial conditions of 1963 QI.

biases the prediction tests in our favor. It will be some time before we are able to say with confidence how well these equations perform outside the sample period.

As in other sectors of the model, predictions based on one period simulation (that is, using actual values of all lagged variables) are much more accurate than the dynamic predictions in Table 1. Since the model is intended to be of use for evaluating alternative policies over several quarters, however, dynamic predictions are a more relevant test.

Simulation Results

To keep the present paper to manageable size, we present only two simulation results for the financial sector, one tracing out the effects over time of a step increase in unborrowed reserves, and the other tracing out the effects of a step increase in GNP. Simulations of other monetary policy variables in the model—required reserve ratios, the discount rate, and the ceiling rate on bank time deposits—will be the subject of a future presentation.

The unborrowed reserve simulation, illustrated in Figure 1, shows the differences between (a) solution values for the model beginning in 1963 QI with unborrowed reserves $1 billion above actual values and (b) solution values for the model beginning in 1963 QI with actual

unborrowed reserves.[2] All other variables exogenous to the financial block are held at actual values for both sets of solution values but in both sets, lagged values of endogenous variables are generated by the model as the solutions progress from quarter to quarter. All the simulation results in the paper follow the same pattern—differences between two sets of dynamic solution values starting in 1963-QI and holding at actual levels all exogenous variables except the one which is the subject of the simulation.

The familiar whiplash effect of open-market operations on interest rates—the large initial impact followed by a smaller permanent effect—is visible in Figure 1, but in much milder form than in a number of other financial models. The impact effect is due to lags in the demand for money and free reserves, and its mildness in Figure 1 is due to the shorter lags in the present model than in some others. For the corporate rate, the initial impact effect is even smaller than the longer-run effect.

Demand deposits soon approach a change

---

[2] For the starting point of the simulations, we wanted a fairly recent quarter without abnormal pressures in credit or goods market and preferably with enough slack capacity so that the absence of a price-wage sector would not greatly affect simulation results for the rest of the model. The first quarter of 1963 fills all of these requirements.

about four times the change in unborrowed reserves. This multiple is smaller than the reciprocal of the average reserve requirement against demand deposits for two reasons. First of all, free reserves absorb some of the change in unborrowed reserves—a large fraction initially, and a small fraction even after a lag because of the decline in the bill rate relative to the discount rate, which has not changed. Second, some of the increase in reserves is required to back the increase in time deposits which takes place over a long period because market rates of interest fall relative to the time deposit rate. The fact that not all banks are members of the Federal Reserve System affects the multiple in the opposite direction from the free reserve and time deposit effects.

The second simulation of the financial block deals with a step increase of $10 billion in GNP. It is necessary to make an assumption about how much of the increase goes into inventory investment in order to solve the commercial loan demand equation; the assumption we use is that $4 billion of the $10 billion goes into inventory investment the first quarter, $3 billion of the $10 billion in the second quarter, and so on down to zero in the fifth and succeeding quarters.

The results, depicted in Figure 2, indicate that, according to our model, income changes have important and fairly prompt effects on financial markets. Interest rates on Treasury bills are driven up sharply, and the corporate bond rate responds after a short lag. The effect on demand deposits builds up to nearly a billion dollars, then falls off as higher interest rates curb the demand for money. The effect on time deposits, as before, develops much more slowly.

II. THE INVESTMENT BLOCK

The investment block of the model consists of components of final demand which are often considered autonomous in simple income-expenditure systems; namely, housing, producers' equipment and structures, and the expenditures and taxes of State and local governments. All of these items are relatively insensitive to the current quarter's income and relatively sensitive to interest rates and relative prices.

The equations for producers' durable equipment and for nonresidential structures (both due to Charles Bischoff) allow interest rates, tax regulations, and relative prices all to affect expenditures through their effect on desired capital-output ratios, in the way suggested by the neoclassical theory of the firm. The empirical fitting of these equations is sufficiently flexible to allow for long lags in adjustment, certain kinds of technological change, and different weights for the corporate bond rate and the dividend-price ratio in measuring the cost of capital.

The fitting also allows for the possibility that

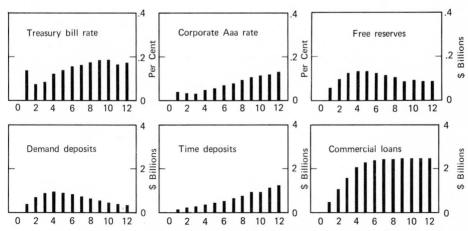

Figure 2   Effects of a step increase of $1 billion in GNP, financial block. Dynamic simulation, initial conditions of 1963 QI.

capital goods and other factors of production may be much more readily substitutable at the time new capital is being ordered than after it has been installed. For producers' equipment, a "putty-clay" model, in which factor substitution is possible only up until the time of placing orders, turns out to fit the data better than a model in which capital intensity can be altered after—as well as before—installation. One implication of the putty-clay formulation is that a permanent change in interest rates affects investment gradually over the entire time-span needed to replace the existing capital stock rather than in a more concentrated period. For structures, in contrast to producers' equipment, a model allowing for substitution after as well as before installation turns out to fit the data better than a putty-clay model.

Bischoff's equations have other interesting features. With respect to tax laws, they measure the present value of depreciation deductions under various laws, the investment tax credit, and even the effect of the 1964 Long Amendment which changed the tax treatment of equipment eligible for the investment credit. With respect to all cost variables, these equations allow for an elasticity of substitution different from one. For producers' equipment, the central demand variable is not final expenditures but new orders. Orders are translated into expenditures through a variable-weight distributed lag. A technique developed by Peter Tinsley is used to estimate the way the lag lengthens in periods of supply bottlenecks (as measured by a high ratio of unfilled orders to expenditures) and shortens when the bottlenecks disappear.

The housing sector of the model, which follows the work of Gordon Sparks, distinguishes between houses as providing a stream of services for those who live in them and houses as profitable investments for those who own them. The rental price index clears the housing service market. After a lag this rental price rises with real income and population and falls with the supply of houses. In another relationship, the same rental price is the numerator of the investment rate of return on houses, the denominator being the price deflator for houses. This relationship, involving long lags, relates the rate of return on houses

to the rate of interest on mortages. The rate of return does not adjust by the full amount of the change in the mortgage rate, implying that houses and mortgages are not perfect complements.

Builders are assumed to respond to investment demand. If this demand is high, as measured by the investment rate of return on houses relative to mortgage rates, builders carry high levels of inventory under construction, and housing starts and expenditures are high. On the other hand, if mortgage rates are high, housing inventory and starts are low.

The housing sector estimated in this way has interesting dynamic properties. In the long run the mortgage rate and the investment return on houses should be approximately in balance, and housing inventories and expenditures should not be greatly affected by the level of mortgage rates. But in the short- and medium-run, the fact that a change in mortgage rates is only slowly transmitted to a change in the rate of return on houses means that a rise in mortgage rates can have strong depressing effects on housing expenditures.

The housing sector may underestimate the influence of some basic variables on housing expenditures. Income, population, and the stock of houses are all forced to operate through the rental market, and it may be that imperfections in the measured rental price index unduly weaken the effects of these variables. Similarly, it may be that the mortgage rate does not capture all relevant dimensions of the ease or tightness of credit, especially in periods such as 1966 when nonbank financial institutions experienced a marked reduction in deposit inflows. We plan to examine both of these possibilities in more detail and eventually hope to develop a more elaborate treatment of nonbank financial intermediaries and the credit side of the housing market.

The equations explaining the behavior of State and local governments have as their basis the constraint against borrowing on current account faced by these institutions. This constraint introduces strong interdependence of spending and tax decisions for States and localities. Tax revenues are affected by expenditure needs, and expenditures are in turn affected by taxes.

For reasons relating to the simultaneous equations bias, the expenditure equations have been solved directly for their reduced form. Thus expenditures depend on such variables as Federal grants-in-aid, income, interest rates, population, the proportion of the population of school age, and prices. Taxes are affected by the current expenditures that have to be revenue financed together with income, with the proportion of revenue-financing depending on interest rates.

Dynamic Predictions

The investment block was solved dynamically for the six-quarter period from 1965 QIII to 1966 QIV. Most of the equations have been fit through the end of 1965, and since these equations are generally highly dependent on interest rates, 1966 predictions would be of special interest.

The results of the dynamic predictions are given in Table 2. Rather than present actual and calculated values for every variable in the block,

Table 2 only shows the important summary variables for each type of spending. Thus the equation for expenditures on housing summarizes the performance of the entire housing market, and so forth.

To review the results briefly, the housing sector predicts actual housing expenditures well until 1966 QIII, when the decline in actual expenditures was much greater than that shown by our model. Our predictions turn down at the right point, but they do not fall nearly enough. Possibly a model allowing for nonprice credit rationing would improve the housing predictions for late 1966.

Actual expenditures for producers' durables did not turn down until early 1967; but here, in contrast to the housing equations, our predictions understate expenditures by turning down two quarters too soon.

The experience for the other equations is much better. Predicted expenditures for nonresidential structures are low throughout the period, but by the end of the period the model is

TABLE 2 Dynamic Predictions, Investment Block (In billions of dollars)

| Item | 1965 | | 1966 | | | |
	QIII	QIV	QI	QII	QIII	QIV
Residential construction:						
Actual	26.4	26.2	26.5	25.3	23.2	20.4
Predicted	26.5	26.4	26.0	25.4	24.7	23.8
Producers' durable equipment:						
Actual	46.8	48.3	50.0	51.2	53.1	55.1
Predicted	46.6	48.8	50.6	51.0	50.8	50.8
Nonresidential construction:						
Actual	25.1	27.3	28.3	27.5	28.2	27.7
Predicted	24.6	25.2	25.8	26.5	27.0	27.3
State and local government expenditures:						
Actual	70.4	72.5	74.3	76.2	78.1	80.2
Predicted	70.5	72.3	74.5	76.3	78.0	80.0
Surplus of State and local governments:						
Actual	1.5	1.1	2.4	2.9	3.3	3.0
Predicted	2.5	2.7	3.2	3.2	3.3	3.2
Total residential and nonresidential construction and producers' durable equipment						
Actual	98.3	101.8	104.8	104.0	104.5	103.2
Predicted	97.7	100.4	102.4	102.9	102.5	101.9

performing appreciably better than in the beginning. Predicted purchases by State and local governments are extremely accurate throughout the period, as are even the predictions of the entire budget surplus which includes errors for all purchase, tax, and transfer equations.

The last item of the table summarizes the performance of the investment block, by listing the actual and predicted values for expenditures on housing, producers' durables, and structures, which make up gross private domestic fixed investment. Because the errors in housing and producers' durables offset each other, the total gross investment error is relatively small, averaging somewhat less than $1.5 billion.

Simulations of Behavior of Block

Two basic simulation runs for the investment block trace out the effects of changes in income and the effects of changes in interest rates. As in the financial block, simulation results are differences between a dynamic solution using either higher-than-actual income or higher-than-actual interest rates and a dynamic solution using actual income and interest rates, both solutions starting in 1963 QI. The income simulation inserted a $10 billion step increase in GNP—GNP was put $10 billion above its actual level in each quarter—with appropriate responses in other income variables but no

change from actual interest rates; while the interest-rate simulation inserted a percentage point increase in the corporate bond rate with appropriate responses in other interest rates but no departure from actual income.

The results for the 12 quarters after the change are presented in Figures 3 and 4. The housing sector behaves very much as described above. There is almost no effect of income on housing expenditures, attributable to the fact that the income elasticity of the rent index is very low. Yet there is a very sharp effect of interest rates. This effect reaches its peak of $2.8 billion six quarters after the interest rate change, and then gradually recedes to zero as the mortgage rate and the rate of return on houses come into balance.

Expenditures for producers' durables also behave as the putty-clay model implies. They respond almost immediately to income and then recede to zero as the desired capital-output ratio is restored. But because of the fixed-factor proportions of installed equipment, the response to interest rates shows a very gradual decline which still has not reached its peak after 3 years.

Lags in the structures equation are very long. The underlying model implies that at some point the response either to income or interest rates will reach a peak, and then fall towards zero. As Figures 3 and 4 indicate, the expenditure response still has not reached its maximum 3 years after the initial change. Yet it

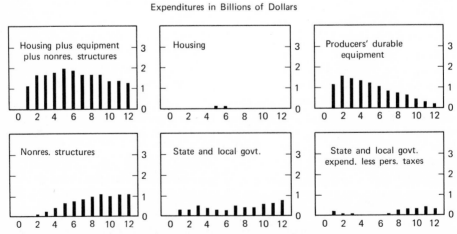

Expenditures in Billions of Dollars

Figure 3   Effects of a step increase in GNP of $10 billion, investment block. Dynamic simulation, initial conditions of 1963 QI.

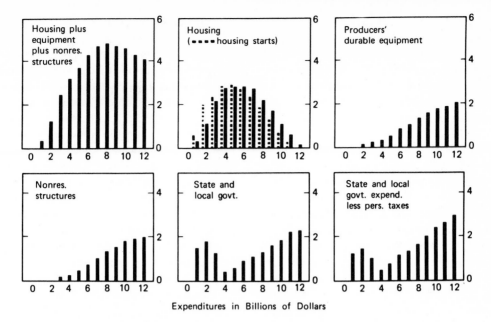

Figure 4   Effects of a step increase in the corporate bond rate of 1 per cent, investment block. Dynamic simulation, initial conditions of 1963 QI.

is interesting to note that in this case, as opposed to equipment, the lag patterns are similar for income and interest rates.

The purchases made by State and local governments respond fairly rapidly both to income and to interest rates. In the income simulation the budget surplus increases because revenues increase even more than purchases. But for the revenue items that matter—excluding the effect on indirect taxes, which do not feed back to the model to a significant extent—the response is slightly less than the expenditure response, such that States and localities are a slight destabilizing force in the determination of aggregate demand as long as interest rates are held constant.

In the interest rate simulation the initial bulge in the State and local expenditure effect is due to a large postponement effect for wages and salaries, and the long-run effect is due to the delayed response of construction expenditures—which behave in a manner similar to producers' structures. The budget surplus increases more than expenditures decrease in this simulation because high interest rates result in decreased borrowing or in increased tax financing of the expenditures already being made.

III. THE CONSUMPTION-INVENTORY BLOCK

The third block of equations describes the behavior of consumption, inventory investment, imports, personal income, and taxes and includes the identity adding up the components of GNP. These variables are all tied very closely to the level of, or changes in, current income, and would be considered endogenous in even the simplest income-expenditure system. The multiplier sector would be an appropriate title for this block.

The multiplier implicit in the present model is more complicated than the simple textbook concept. One important reason is that we distinguish between the national accounts version of consumption, which includes expenditures on consumer durables, and our own version, which instead includes the flow of services—as best we can estimate it—from these durables. Following many other students of consumption,[3] we assume our concept has a stable relation to current and past income. This concept of consumption shows smaller variations than the national accounts total since an additional dollar spent on consumer

[3] For example, Milton Friedman [5] and Albert Ando and Franco Modigliani [2].

durables raises our consumption by less than a dollar now and by a positive amount in subsequent quarters, rather than by a full dollar now and nothing in subsequent quarters. One implication of this view of consumption is that expenditures on durable goods are quite sensitive to changes in income, because large changes in expenditures are necessary in order to keep our version of consumption in its desired relationship with income.

The allocation of consumption between nondurables and services on the one hand and the services of durable goods on the other depends on relative prices, existing stocks of durables, recent income changes, and to a minor extent interest rates. These forces have all been constrained so that if they increase one component of consumption, they decrease one or more others by an exactly offsetting amount.

A second important reason for a complex multiplier is the inventory investment equation. Our model allows the different components of final demand to affect inventories by different amounts—implying different inventory-sales ratios—and with different lags—implying different periods of production or different ways of

forming sales expectations. One prominent example of the differing lags which has received much attention lately is defense spending [6]; in our equation defense spending has an effect on inventories *before* the final expenditures are recorded in the national accounts. Our equation also features a faster speed of adjustment, and therefore a larger accelerator effect, than most other models.

The rest of the block is fairly standard. In the absence of an elaborate treatment of income distribution through the price and wage block, we have a simple equation which relates personal income net of exogenous transfer payments to current and past GNP. Personal income taxes on a liability basis depend on personal income, exemptions, and the average tax rate in equations based on the work of Ando and Brown. As they recommend, the model uses a tax accrual disposable income concept rather than the cash version used in the national accounts [1].

Dynamic Predictions

Dynamic predictions for the consumption-inventory block beginning in 1965 QIII are

TABLE 3 Dynamic Predictions, Consumption-Inventory Block (In billions of dollars)

	1965			1966		
Item	QIII	QIV	QI	QII	QIII	QIV
GNP level:						
Actual	690.0	708.4	725.9	736.7	748.8	762.1
Predicted	691.8	712.8	729.8	739.5	752.1	763.3
GNP changes:						
Actual	14.6	18.4	17.5	10.8	12.1	13.3
Predicted	16.4	21.0	17.1	9.6	12.7	11.1
Disposbale income:						
Actual	479.2	489.1	498.1	505.5	514.9	524.5
Predicted	479.0	489.3	499.7	506.9	516.1	525.1
Consumer expenditures:						
Actual	436.4	447.8	458.2	461.6	470.1	473.8
Predicted	441.6	451.4	461.5	468.1	476.6	483.6
Inventory investment:						
Actual	7.9	8.7	9.6	14.4	12.0	19.0
Predicted	5.4	10.1	10.8	10.8	7.6	9.3
Imports:						
Actual	32.9	34.4	36.0	37.1	39.0	39.7
Predicted	33.6	35.1	36.5	37.3	38.0	38.6

quite successful. The main exogenous variables on which the predictions depend are fixed investment, exports, and various receipts and expenditures of Federal, State, and local governments. Given actual values of these variables, the model makes only small errors in predicting the course of GNP (see Table 3).

The principal change in the behavior of GNP during the period was the slowdown in quarterly changes starting in the second quarter of 1966. This the model captures at precisely the correct time. A secondary change in the behavior of GNP was the rise in the fourth quarter of 1966 due to extraordinarily high levels of inventory investment. This change the model does not capture, greatly understating inventory investment at the end of 1966.

The understatement of inventory investment in the second and fourth quarters of 1966 is offset in part by an overstatement of consumption expenditures. In part, this offset is a lucky accident. In part, however, it is what we would expect from examining the inventory equation of the model. Consumption expenditures in the current quarter have an involuntary, negative effect on inventory investment so that an error in predicting current consumption leads to a partially offsetting error in predicting inventory investment in the same quarter.

Policy Simulations

Simulations which are most helpful in illustrating the dynamics of this block of equations are those showing how a maintained increase in government or fixed investment spending, or a change in tax rates or transfer payments, multiply into changes in GNP. Before those simulations of the whole block, however, it may be helpful to illustrate the behavior of the consumption equations alone in response to a step increase in disposable income.

Table 4 below traces out the pattern of consumption on the one hand and consumer expenditures on the other in response to a maintained increase of $1 billion in disposable income. Total consumption follows the behavior of Equation 11, rising by 37.3 per cent of the income change in the first quarter, then rising by smaller increments, and after 3 years

reaching 94 per cent of the income change. A portion of this increased consumption goes into the services of durable goods. In order for the services of durable goods to rise, it is necessary for expenditures on durable goods to rise by an accelerated amount at first, then as stocks rise, to fall back gradually toward the new level of consumption. Total consumer expenditures therefore increase initially by 67.5 per cent of the change in disposable income, continue rising until they actually exceed 100 per cent of the income change for a few quarters, and then decline towards 94 per cent.

TABLE 4   Effects of a $1 Billion Step Increase in Disposable Income

(In billions of dollars)

Quarter	Consumption	Consumer expenditures
1	.37	.68
2	.46	.75
3	.54	.82
4	.61	.88
5	.67	.93
6	.73	.97
7	.78	1.01
8	.83	1.04
9	.86	1.05
10	.89	1.06
11	.92	1.07
12	.93	1.07
13	.94	1.06
14	.94	1.04
15	.94	1.02
16	.94	.99

Turning now to the complete consumption-inventory block, we trace out first the effects of a step increase of two percentage points in the aggregate Federal personal income tax rate. As in the simulations of the financial and investment blocks, all variables exogenous to this sector except the tax rate were put at their actual values during 1963-64 while the tax rate was raised by 0.02 above its actual value during each quarter. An increase of two percentage points is roughly a 10 per cent increase, since the actual rate was between 0.20 and 0.23 during the period. It represented a little over $4 billion dollars in tax revenue at actual levels of income

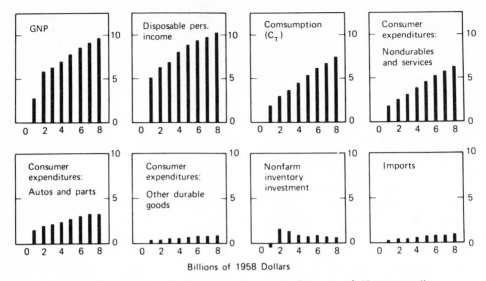

Billions of 1958 Dollars

Figure 5 Effects of a step increase in the personal tax rate of .02, consumption-inventory block. Dynamic simulation, initial conditions of 1963 QI.

during the period. But that dollar amount, like many of the dollar amounts in these simulations, depends on the general size of the economy during the simulation period.

The GNP effects of the policy change are shown in Figure 5 in constant dollars. They begin with two big steps and continue with six much smaller ones. Using $4.15 billion as the initial revenue value of the tax change, we can derive GNP multipliers which begin at 0.7 and 1.4 in the first two quarters, and then rise slowly to 2.4 after eight quarters. Disposable income is affected by more than GNP, with the margin between the two declining over time. Most of the change in GNP is due to changes in the components of consumer expenditures; import and inventory effects are quite small. Inventory investment is increased slightly in the first quarter, reflecting unanticipated declines in consumer expenditures; in the second quarter it is decreased by a somewhat greater amount, reflecting the accelerator effects of the decline in consumer spending; and thereafter it is decreased by declining amounts.

The second policy change we trace through this block is a maintained increase of $5 billion in defense spending—that is, a level of defense spending $5 billion above actual levels starting in the first quarter of 1963, with other variables exogenous to this sector held at actual levels. Figure 6 sets out the results. Since the $5 billion

is in current prices, results for this simulation are also presented in current dollars, in contrast to the results of the tax rate change simulation.

The GNP effects of the rise in defense spending begin before the rise is actually recorded as a final expenditure, since inventory investment depends in part on next quarter's defense expenditures. This initial effect is a small one. however, amounting to less than half of the rise in defense spending. Large effects begin in quarter 1 and increase by generally declining amounts thereafter. GNP multipliers are 1.5 in quarter 1, 1.7 in quarter 2, and small increases thereafter up to 2.4 in quarter 8. Effects on consumption are less important in this simulation than they were in the tax change, for the initial shock to the system only gradually spreads to disposable income in this simulation; whereas it has its full initial impact on disposable income in the tax change case. Import and inventory effects again are small.

Comparison of the tax and the defense expenditure multipliers brings out some interesting characteristics of this block. In the long run, the expenditure multiplier is slightly larger than the multiplier of a lump-sum tax change because of the leakage into personal saving. In the eight-quarter simulations depicted in Figures 5 and 6, however the expenditure multiplier is larger than the tax multiplier only in the first few quarters, and slightly smaller thereafter. One reason for this similarity is that in the medium run the response of consumer spending to changes in income is quite large, even exceeding one in some quarters. A second reason is that the tax simulation is a simulation of a *rate* change, not a lump-sum change, and therefore has effects which grow as the economy grows. A final reason is that the inventory effects of a change in exogenous spending are bunched around the time of the expenditure, whereas the inventory effects of a tax change are spread over a long period when consumer expenditures are changing.

IV. THE THREE BLOCKS COMBINED

We now combine the three blocks already described—the financial block, the investment block, and the consumption-inventory block—into a single group of simultaneous equations. The principal exogenous variables which ultimately drive the system are: population and other demographic variables; Federal Government expenditures and tax rates; monetary policy variables; exports; and wages and prices (except for rents and the price of houses, which are explained in the investment block). A fourth block containing price (supply) equations and labor market equations, now under development, will remove prices and wages from the exogenous list.

The simulations in this section illustrate how the first three blocks interact. We have run some simulations (not shown below) including preliminary price and labor market equations,[4] which suggest that except in conditions of high resource utilization, the major results for the three blocks will continue to hold for the entire model.

Dynamic Predictions

Dynamic predictions starting in 1965 QII for the three blocks combined are not as good as predictions for individual blocks, but they are nevertheless decidedly encouraging. For GNP, as Table 5 shows, the model predicts the marked slowdown in growth which begins in 1966 QII. It fails to predict the slight pickup in growth in the fourth quarter, but that pickup was short-lived, and it is likely that the model would be on track again in 1967 QI.

A rise in interest rates of something like the right magnitude is predicted, though there is a large error in the bill rate prediction for 1966 QII. Whether the three blocks together predict the decline in interest rates in 1967 QI, as the financial block alone did, we will not know until we finish collecting 1967 data for all three blocks. The demand deposit predictions fail to

[4] Some of these equations are described in Alfred Tella and Peter Tinsley [8].

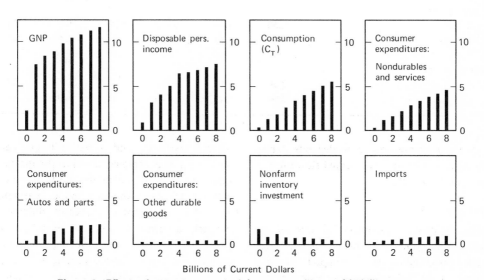

Figure 6 Effects of a step increase in defense expenditures of $5 billion, consumption-inventory block. Dynamic simulation, initial conditions of 1963 QI.

TABLE 5   Dynamic Predictions, Three Blocks Combined

Item	1965 QIII	1965 QIV	1966 QI	1966 QII	1966 QIII	1966 QIV
	(In billions of dollars)					
GNP level:						
Actual	690.0	708.4	725.9	736.7	748.8	762.1
Calculated	690.7	709.4	725.4	736.1	745.6	753.1
GNP changes:						
Actual	14.6	18.4	17.5	10.8	12.1	13.3
Calculated	15.3	18.7	16.0	10.7	9.5	7.4
Consumer expenditures:						
Actual	436.4	447.8	458.2	461.6	470.1	473.8
Calculated	441.1	450.3	460.1	466.7	473.8	479.7
Residential construction: ≤						
Actual	26.4	26.2	26.5	25.3	23.2	20.4
Calculated	26.6	26.3	25.7	25.1	24.2	23.3
Producers' equipment and nonresidential structures:						
Actual	71.9	75.8	78.3	78.7	81.3	82.8
Calculated	71.2	74.2	76.3	77.1	76.9	76.4
Inventory investment:						
Actual	7.9	8.7	9.6	14.4	12.0	19.0
Calculated	5.4	9.8	10.4	10.6	7.0	6.6
Demand deposits:						
Actual	128.9	131.1	133.3	132.8	132.2	131.6
Calculated	129.1	130.8	132.2	132.3	132.5	132.8
	(In per cent)					
Corporate bond yield:						
Actual	4.50	4.61	4.81	5.00	5.32	5.38
Calculated	4.65	4.84	4.95	5.29	5.39	5.51
Treasury bill rate:						
Actual	3.86	4.16	4.60	4.58	5.03	5.20
Calculated	3.60	4.26	4.22	5.42	5.16	5.47

catch the absolute decline in deposits during 1966, but they do show a marked slowdown in their rate of growth.

Simulation Results

The simulation experiments of this section trace out the effects of three policy changes already investigated for individual blocks—namely, a $1 billion step increase in unborrowed reserves, a $5 billion step increase in defense spending, and a 0.02 (10 per cent) increase in the personal tax rate. In the near future we plan to simulate the effects of a much wider range of government policy variables. As before, the results represent differences between a dynamic solution including the policy change and one excluding the policy change, with both solutions starting in 1963 QI.

For the unborrowed reserve simulation (Figure 7), effects on fixed investment (partly due to lower interest rates and partly due to higher income) build up gradually to a little more than $3 billion. Effects on GNP are small in the first few quarters; they accelerate as the increase in fixed investment has its multiplier influence, and then decelerate as fixed investment reaches a peak. At the end of the 3 years GNP has increased by more than $11 billion, which implies a somewhat higher multiplier for un-borrowed reserves than is shown by most other models (see Table 6). This simulation says, then, that monetary policy is ultimately quite power-ful but that the lags are long. To that extent, these tentative results suggest that monetary policy is difficult to use as a stabilization device. The powerful impact of a policy change will not come into play until one year hence, when it is inevitably more difficult to predict the needs of stabilization policy.

Both fiscal policy simulations tell different stories (see Figures 8 and 9). As in the con-sumption-inventory block, changes in defense spending operate faster than income tax changes, which depend on the delayed res-ponse of consumption. Also it remains true that the medium-term (2- to 3-year) multiplier for income taxes is higher than that for defense spending. This result follows from the fact that the medium-term consumer expenditure propensity is greater than one (see Section III), and from the fact that the income

tax multiplier has not yet entered the reversal range that occurs when actual stocks of capital and consumer durables approach their target levels.

It is interesting to observe the behavior of fixed investment in these simulations. In both cases the income change induces more invest-ment than the stabilizing interest rate change shuts off, and fixed investment reinforces the multiplier action. This property contradicts the argument that the induced rise in interest rates will restrict fixed investment enough to offset part of the initial expenditure change.

The simulations indicate that fiscal policy suffers less from the lag problems that plague monetary policy. Both multipliers, especially that for purchases, approach their maximum levels rapidly, and are responsible for strong effects on GNP less than half a year after the policy change. The lag problems that may interfere with the effectiveness of fiscal measures are lags between recognition of the need for action and actual changes in tax rates or expenditures, not lags in the economy's response to the policy changes.

Comparison of Multipliers of Alternative Models

A brief comparison of our 3-year multipliers with those estimated by a few other models are given in Table 6.

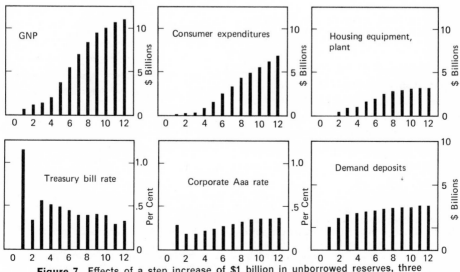

Figure 7 Effects of a step increase of $1 billion in unborrowed reserves, three blocks combined. Dynamic simulation, initial conditions of 1963 QI.

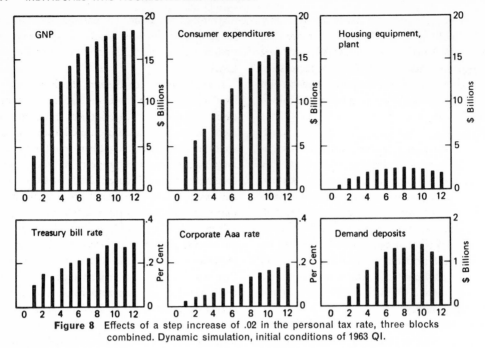

Figure 8   Effects of a step increase of .02 in the personal tax rate, three blocks combined. Dynamic simulation, initial conditions of 1963 QI.

TABLE 6   Comparison of 3-Year Multipliers of Different Models

Model	Un-borrowed reserves	Defense spending	Personal tax cut
Federal Reserve—			
MIT model	11.2	3.2	4.2
Brookings model [6]	8.2	2.7	1.2
Wharton School model [3]	2.9	2.9	2.4
Michigan model[a]	n.a.	2.5	1.7

[a] Unpublished results of the University of Michigan model supplied by Daniel B. Suits.

The table indicates that all of our multipliers are higher than those for other models. The difference is due primarily to the fact that our version of consumption gives rise to a much higher medium-run consumer propensity to spend than is shown by other models. The same factor accounts for our higher personal tax multiplier.[5]

[5] Our multiple tax multiplier seems to be unusually high relative to our expenditure multiplier in Table 6. Although this result is partly explained by the greater-than-one medium-run expenditure propensity mentioned above, the major share of the explanation lies in the time period chosen as the basis of the multiplier calculation. Had we presented

V. CONCLUSION

It is apparent from the limited number of policy simulations conducted that our model finds monetary policy to be quite powerful —much more so than is found in other econometric models. Future refinements of our model, of which an examination of the financial intermediary-credit rationing process in the mortgage market is a basic one, could increase the relative power that we attribute to monetary policy and might shorten the lags.

These findings follow strictly from our best specification of the way in which monetary policy affects the economy. They are not caused by simple expedients such as throwing in the money supply whenever nothing else works. Although we emphasize that our conclusions are tentative and caution against using

2-year results, the expenditure and tax multipliers would have been quite similar. The same is true of longer-run 5- to 7-year multipliers. It is only in the 3- and 4-year range, when the expenditure multiplier has begun to decline from its maximum value while the tax multiplier has not, that the unusual result of Table 6 obtains.

We should like to emphasize here also that these findings are preliminary. It may be that further experimentation with consumption will lead to different functional forms, statistical estimates, and multiplier calculations.

them as a basis for generalizations about stabilization policy, we think it significant that a more intensive examination of monetary policy than is usual in econometric models finds monetary factors to be more important than they are usually found to be.

APPENDIX :

FINANCIAL BLOCK

The central supply identity of the financial block (Equation 1) relates unborrowed reserves, taken as exogenous, to three endogenous uses of reserves—reserves against private demand deposits, reserves against time deposits, and free reserves—and one exogenous use—Federal Government demand deposits. The open-market variable which the Federal Reserve System controls to the last dollar is not unborrowed reserves but its own portfolio of government securities. Yet changes in the two are closely related, and there is no doubt that the System can, and often does, consciously offset movements in the other elements in its balance sheet so as to influence unborrowed reserves.

The next three equations (Equations 2 to 4) explain demands for the three endogenous components of unborrowed reserves. Bank holdings of free reserves—excess reserves minus borrowing from the Federal Reserve System—are thought of as an inventory held because of uncertainty about changes in deposits and in loans to regular customers which affect banks' reserve positions. The target amount of free reserves depends on the Treasury bill rate, representing earnings foregone on other assets, and the discount rate, representing the cost of raising reserves. Actual levels of free reserves depend not only on target amounts but also on changes in the balance-sheet items against which free reserves are a buffer stock; that is, on movements in deposits or—for the banking system as a whole—unborrowed reserves and on movements in commercial loans. Demands for demand deposits and time deposits (Equations 3 and 4) depend on GNP and interest rates, variables which are suggested by either an inventory or a portfolio theory approach to the public's financial behavior.

Several varieties of statistical difficulty complicate the estimation of Equations 2 to 4. There are simultaneous equations problems, bias problems in the coefficient of the lagged dependent variable, and, in the case of the time deposit yield, measurement error problems. In view of these difficulties, the three equations

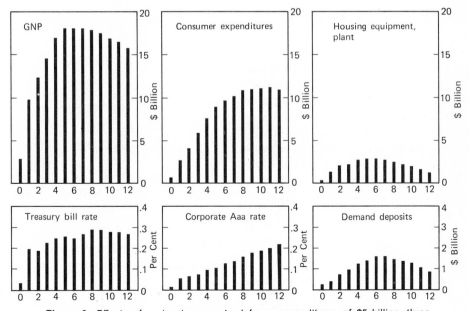

Figure 9 Effects of a step increase in defense expenditures of $5 billion, three blocks combined. Dynamic simulation, initial conditions of 1963 QI.

were each estimated in two ways, once with quantities as the dependent variable and once with interest rates as dependent.[1] There are reasons for believing that coefficients estimated in these alternative ways should bracket "true" coefficients with respect to these difficulties. A number of alternative combinations of quantity and interest rate versions of the equations were used to predict the extremely large movements in financial variables during 1966 and early 1967—the equations were fit through 1965. The results were not a clear-cut victory for any one set of estimates; the best combination on many grounds, and the one used in this presentation, is the quantity version of the free reserves and time deposit equations and the interest-rate version of the demand deposit equation (Equation 3: it has been solved for the quantity for listing here).

Equation 5 explains business borrowing in the form of commercial loans. The public's demand for currency is not an integral part of the model as it now stands; interest rates and consumer expenditures affect currency holdings, but there is no feedback from currency. There would be a feedback if currency plus unborrowed reserves were the open-market variable of the model; and a currency equation is included in the model (Equation 6) in order to make possible simulation experiments with this alternative policy variable.

Interest rates appear in all of the Equations 2 through 6, and it is increases or declines in these rates which, in the short run, make commercial banks and the public willing to hold exactly those quantities of deposits and free reserves which use up the unborrowed reserves supplied by the Federal Reserve.

The remaining equations of the model—Equations 7 through 12—describe interrelations among various interest rates. Equation 7 is a term-structure relationship based on the work of Modigliani and Sutch, and derived ultimately from the expectations hypothesis combined with the hypothesis that expectations about interest rates are a combination of extrapolative

elements (with respect to recent changes) and regressive elements (with respect to longer-term changes). Equation 8 is a supply equation for time deposits, relating the yield at which banks are willing to accept time deposits to other rates, portfolio composition, and the exogenous ceiling rates set by the regulatory authorities. Equations 9, 10, and 11 are simply empirical relationships among interest rates. Experiments with a full-scale mortgage market in place of Equation 11 were not far enough along to use in the present version of the model, but we are continuing work on an expanded mortgage-housing treatment.

The final equation of the financial sector deals with the yield on common stocks, which is related to corporate bond rates and past rates of growth of dividends, along lines suggested by Modigliani and Miller. Stock market yields are thus endogenous to our model, responding to other long-term rates of interest with coefficients which sum to a little less than one. The standard error of this equation is quite large, indicating that much of the quarter-to-quarter change in stock market yields is unexplained by the variables in our equation. However, the equation does indicate a strong link to other financial markets.

Equations

1. Reserve identity

$$RU = (RF + .074\,S_1 - .005\,S_2 + .051\,S_3 - .121\,S_4)$$
$$+ R_{EQD} \cdot k_D \cdot DD + R_{EQD} \cdot DD_{GM}$$
$$+ R_{EQT} \cdot k_T \cdot DT + e_{RF}$$

2. Demand for free reserves

$$\Delta RF = -.232 + .081\,S_2 + .025\,S_3 + .197\,S_4$$
$$+ .463(\Delta RU + RREL) + .180\,R_{DIS}$$
$$- .127\,R_{TB} - .078\,\Delta CL - .289\,RF_{-1}$$

3. Demand for demand deposits (ln R_{CP} + ln R_{TD} was the dependent variable).

$$\ln DD = -.3453 - .0718 \ln R_{CP} - .0718 \ln R_{TD}$$
$$+ .3333 \ln Y + .6667 \ln DD_{-1}$$
$$+ .840\,\hat{u}_{-1}$$

---

[1] In the interest rate versions, dependent variables were: an average of R_{CP} and R_{TD} in the demand deposit equation, R_{TD} in the time deposit equation, and the differential R_{TB}-R_{DIS} in the free reserve equation.

4. Demand for time deposits

$$DT/Y = .01386 + .00941\,R_{TD} - .00158\,R_{TB}$$
$$- .00348\,R_C + .8953\,(DT/Y)_{-1}$$
$$- .1477\,(\Delta Y/Y_{-1})$$

5. Demand for commercial loans

$$\Delta CL = .1167\,E_I - .450\,\Delta R_{CL} + .544\,\Delta CL_{-1}$$

6. Demand for currency

$$\ln CURR = -.3382 - .035\ln R_{TD} + .157\ln C_P$$
$$+ .843\ln CURR_{-1} + .758\,\hat{u}_{-1}$$

7. Term structure

$$R_C = 1.1225 + .337\,R_{CP} + \sum_{i=1}^{18} w_i\,R_{CP_{-i}}$$

$w_1 = -.024$	$w_7 = .064$	$w_{13} = .023$
$w_2 = .015$	$w_8 = .059$	$w_{14} = .018$
$w_3 = .041$	$w_9 = .052$	$w_{15} = .015$
$w_4 = .057$	$w_{10} = .044$	$w_{16} = .012$
$w_5 = .065$	$w_{11} = .036$	$w_{17} = .009$
$w_6 = .067$	$w_{12} = .029$	$w_{18} = .005$
	$\Sigma w_i = .587$	

8. Supply of time deposits

$$R_{TD} = -.362 + .390\left(\frac{CL}{DD+DT}\right)$$

$$+ .800\left(\frac{CL}{DD+DT}\right)_{-1}$$

$$+ .390\left(\frac{CL}{DD+DT}\right)_{-2}$$

$$+ .008\,(R_C+R_{C_{-1}}) + .463\,R_{MAX}$$
$$- .360\,R_{MAX_{-1}} + .869\,R_{TD_{-1}}$$

9. Commercial paper rate

$$R_{CP} = .5775 + .7234\,R_{TB} + .3178\,R_{TB_{-1}}$$
$$- .2469\,D_{UCD}$$

10. Commercial loan rate

$$R_{CL} = .448\,R_C + .160\,R_{CP} + .341\,R_{CL_{-1}} + .762$$

11. Mortgage rate

$$\Delta R_M = .078\,\Delta R_{CP} + .362\,\Delta R_{C_{-1}} + .417\,\Delta R_{M_{-1}}$$

12. Stock market yield

$$R_D = \sum_{i=0}^{4} w_i\,R_{C_{-i}} - \sum_{i=4}^{14} w'_i\left[\frac{\Delta Y_{CD_{-i}}}{Y_{CD_{-i-1}}}\right] + .9452\,\hat{u}_{-1}$$

$w_0 = .0294$	$w'_4 = .49$	$w'_{10} = .89$
$w_1 = .1608$	$w'_5 = .82$	$w'_{11} = .79$
$w_2 = .2235$	$w'_6 = 1.03$	$w'_{12} = .52$
$w_3 = .2176$	$w'_7 = 1.12$	$w'_{13} = .32$
$w_4 = .1431$	$w'_8 = 1.11$	$w'_{14} = .14$
$\Sigma w_i = .7744$	$w'_9 = 1.03$	$\Sigma w'_i = 8.26$

Glossary

* indicates exogenous to financial block.

Interest rates, in per cent

R_{CL}	bank business loans
R_C	Aaa seasoned corporate bonds (Moody's)
R_{CP}	4–6 month commercial paper
R_D	dividend yield on common stock (Moody's)
*R_{DIS}	discount rate, N. Y. Federal Reserve Bank
R_M	new conventional mortgages, FHLBB
R_{TB}	3-month Treasury bills
R_{TD}	bank time and savings deposits (including CD's)
*R_{MAX}	ceiling rate on bank time deposits

Amounts, in billions of dollars (seasonally adjusted, except RF and RREL)

CL	bank commercial loans
*C_P	consumer expenditures (annual rates)
$CURR$	currency
DD	demand deposits
*DD_{GM}	government demand deposits at member banks
*e_{RF}	error in reserve identity (statistical discrepancy)
*E_I	inventory investment (annual rates)
RF	free reserves, not seasonally adjusted
*$RREL$	reserves released through reserve requirement changes
*RU	unborrowed reserves
DT	time deposits
*Y_{CD}	dividend payments (annual rates)
*Y	GNP (annual rates)
*D_{UCD}	CD dummy (1 after 1962)

Ratios (between zero and one)

$*k_D$ proportion of demand deposits at member banks; seasonally adjusted

$*k_T$ proportion of time deposits at member banks; seasonally adjusted

$*R_{EQD}$ weighted average reserve requirement ratio against member bank demand deposits

$*R_{EQT}$ reserve requirement ratio against member bank time deposits

NOTES—$\hat{u}_{t-1}$ in this and the following blocks indicates that the variables were transformed into the semi-first-difference form

$$x_t - bx_{t-1}$$

before estimation, where b is the coefficient of $\hat{u}_{t-1}$. S_1 through S_4 are seasonal dummy variables.

Financial dollar amounts are all averages of the 2 months surrounding end of quarter; for example, fourth quarter is average of December and January.

INVESTMENT BLOCK

Equations 3 and 4 give expressions for the rate of return at which future earnings should be discounted, both for producers' durables and for structures. These rates of return are functions of the dividend-price ratio, the industrial bond yield, corporate tax rates, and the desired long-run debt-equity ratio. The parameters are estimated in nonlinear fashion together with the investment functions.

Equations 5 and 6 use these rates of return to derive expressions for the imputed rent which must be earned by a new machine to make its purchase worthwhile. Along with rates of return, the implicit rental also depends on the price of capital equipment, the rate of depreciation, and various features of the tax law—the investment credit, the present value of depreciation deductions under various laws, and tax rates.

The desired capital-output ratios for equipment and structures are given in Equations 7 and 8. Their ratios depend on the price of output, the imputed rent, and a trend factor reflecting technological change. The exponents of the relative price terms are the elasticities of substitution between factors, which are again estimated in a nonlinear fashion.

The important equations of the business fixed investment sector are 9 and 14, which explain respectively the new orders of producers' durable equipment and the actual purchases of structures. Both of these equations represent desired capital in real terms as a distributed lag function of the product of real output and the desired capital-output ratio. For structures, the dynamics of this lag are complicated by the presence of the lagged capital stock (Equation 15). For producers' durables, the dynamics are even further complicated by a separate distributed lag between orders and expenditures (Equation 10). This lag depends on the orders-shipments ratio, with supply bottlenecks, as represented by a high ratio, postponing the lag. The orders-shipments relationships are described in Equations 11 to 13.

For the housing sector, Equation 19 explains the rental price. This price then determines the price of houses by Equation 20. Equation 20 imposes the requirement that in the long run the net return on investment in houses is brought into equilibrium with mortgage rates. There should be a variable approximating capital gains in the net rate of return equation, but we have not yet been able to find one which works well.

Equation 17 explains housing inventory under construction. This equation assumes that builders are influenced only by rates of return on houses and mortgage rates. As mentioned in the text, it may not give enough importance to other variables.

The remaining equations close up the housing sector. Equation 16 defines the variable we use to approximate the inventory of (unsold) houses under construction. The weights in the equation are based on construction and sales statistics, along with an assumption about the effect on housing starts of a sold but unstarted house. The equation is used to solve for real housing starts in value terms. Equation 18 then gives expenditures as a distributed lag on starts, with a constant and time trend to pick up the coverage difference (additions and alterations). Equation 21 uses expenditures to calculate the real stock of housing and feedback into determination of the rent index.

Equations 24 to 27 explain the purchases and transfer payments of State and local governments. These values, along with Equation 31 and identity 23, are the total net expenditures which go into tax Equations 28 to 30 and 32. Of this total, all but construction needs to be revenue-financed, and the construction ratios in the tax equations are a way of adjusting for this difference. It would have been difficult to proceed otherwise because grants-in-aid would have had to be allocated between construction and all other. The income variable used in the State and local sector, defined in Equation 22, is net of Federal taxes and plus Federal transfers.

Equations

A. Investment in Plant and Equipment

Gross business product identity

1. $Y_B = Y - C_N - E_{FW} - E_{SW} - Y_F$

Cost of capital relationships

2. $R_{CBI} = -.0133 + .9325 R_C + .0635 R_D$
$+ .0045 \, \text{time} + .8512 \, \hat{u}_{-1}$

3. $R_E = (1 - \alpha_2 t_c)(-1.30 + .6290 R_{CBI}$
$+ .2160 R_D)$

4. $R_S = (1 - \alpha_2 t_c)(-1.833 + .0264 R_{CBI}$
$+ .7258 R_D)$

Identities defining current dollar rent per unit of new investment

5a. for 1948–63

$$P_{QE} = \frac{P_{PD}(.01 \, R_E + \alpha_3)(1 - t_c z_e - z_k + z_k t_c z_e)}{1 - t_c}$$

5b. for 1964–66

$$P_{QE} = \frac{P_{PD}(.01 \, R_E + \alpha_3)(1 - t_c z_e - z_k)}{1 - t_c}$$

6. $P_{QS} = \dfrac{P_{PS}(.01 \, R_S + \alpha_4)(1 - t_c z_s)}{1 - t_c}$

Identities defining equilibrium capital-output ratio

7. $V_E = \left(\dfrac{P_B}{P_{QE}}\right)^{.877} e^{.00081 \, (\text{time} - 42.5)}$

8. $V_S = \left(\dfrac{P_B}{P_{QS}}\right)^{.450} e^{-.00295 \, (\text{time} - 42.5)}$

Demands for orders and expenditures, producers' durable equipment

9. $\dfrac{O_{PD}}{P_{PD}} = \displaystyle\sum_{i=0}^{16} \dfrac{w_i V_{E_{-i-1}} Y_{B_{-i}}}{P_{B_{-i}}} + \sum_{i=1}^{17} \dfrac{w'_i V_{E_{-i}} Y_{B_{-i}}}{P_{B_{-i}}}$

w_0 =	.0502	w'_1 =	−.0495
w_1 =	.0422	w'_2 =	−.0401
w_2 =	.0339	w'_3 =	−.0310
w_3 =	.0256	w'_4 =	−.0223
w_4 =	.0174	w'_5 =	−.0141
w_5 =	.0095	w'_6 =	−.0064
w_6 =	.0022	w'_7 =	.0006
w_7 =	−.0045	w'_8 =	.0068
w_8 =	−.0105	w'_9 =	.0120
w_9 =	−.0154	w'_{10} =	.0163
w_{10} =	−.0192	w'_{11} =	.0194
w_{11} =	−.0217	w'_{12} =	.0212
w_{12} =	−.0228	w'_{13} =	.0217
w_{13} =	−.0222	w'_{14} =	.0208
w_{14} =	−.0198	w'_{15} =	.0182
w_{15} =	−.0154	w'_{16} =	.0140
w_{16} =	−.0088	w'_{17} =	.0079
Σw_i =	.0207	$\Sigma w'_i$ =	−.0045

10. $\dfrac{E_{PD}}{P_{PD}} = \displaystyle\sum_{i=0}^{5} w_i \left(\dfrac{O_{PD}}{P_{PD}}\right)_{-i}$

$+ \displaystyle\sum_{i=0}^{5} w_i \left(\dfrac{O_{PD}}{P_{PD}}\right)_{-i} \left(\dfrac{O_{UME}}{E_{ME}}\right)_{-i-1}$

w_0 =	.6475	w'_0 =	−.3575
w_1 =	.2555	w'_1 =	−.0724
w_2 =	.0598	w'_2 =	.1061
w_3 =	−.0018	w'_3 =	.1781
w_4 =	.0090	w'_4 =	.1431
w_5 =	.0302	w'_5 =	.0022
Σw_i =	1.0002	$\Sigma w'_i$ =	−.0004

11. $O_{UME} = O_{UME-1} + .25(O_{ME} - E_{ME})$

12. $O_{ME} = 6.0640 + .9665 \, O_{PD} - .0289 \, \text{time}$

13. $E_{ME} = 8.2212 + .8554 \, E_{PD} + .0041 \, \text{time}$

Demand for nonresidential structures

14. $\dfrac{E_{PS}}{P_{PS}} = \displaystyle\sum_{i=1}^{16} \dfrac{w_i V_{S_{-i}} Y_{B_{-i}}}{P_{B_{-i}}} - .2710\, K_{SR}$

w_1	= .0038	w_{10}	= .0025
w_2	= .0051	w_{11}	= .0021
w_3	= .0056	w_{12}	= .0019
w_4	= .0057	w_{13}	= .0017
w_5	= .0053	w_{14}	= .0015
w_6	= .0048	w_{15}	= .0013
w_7	= .0042	w_{16}	= .0008
w_8	= .0035	Σw_i	= .0528
w_9	= .0030		

Identity defining stock of nonresidential structures

15. $K_{SR} = \left(1 - \dfrac{\alpha_4}{4}\right) K_{SR_{-1}} + .25 \left(\dfrac{E_{PS}}{P_{PS}}\right)_{-1}$

B. Housing Sector

Housing inventory, starts, and expenditures

16. $K_{HIR} = \displaystyle\sum_{i=0}^{3} w_i \left(\dfrac{H_S}{P_H}\right)_{-i}$

w_0	= .55	w_3	= .03
w_1	= .47	Σw_i	= 1.20
w_2	= .15		

17. $\Delta K_{HIR} = \displaystyle\sum_{i=0}^{7} w_i (\Delta R_M)_{-i} + \sum_{i=0}^{7} w_i \left(\Delta \dfrac{P_R}{P_H}\right)_{-i}$

$\qquad\qquad + .5170\, \hat{u}_{-1}$

w_0	= $-.3584$	w_0'	= 1.76
w_1	= $-.2771$	w_1'	= 3.06
w_2	= $-.2062$	w_2'	= 3.92
w_3	= $-.1458$	w_3'	= 4.35
w_4	= $-.0958$	w_4'	= 4.35
w_5	= $-.0562$	w_5'	= 3.91
w_6	= $-.0270$	w_6'	= 3.04
w_7	= $-.0083$	w_7'	= 1.74
Σw_i	= -1.1748	$\Sigma w_i'$	= 26.13

18. $E_H = 2.9658 + \displaystyle\sum_{i=0}^{2} w_i H_{S-i} + .0408\, \text{time}$

$\qquad\qquad + .7109\, \hat{u}_{-1}$

w_0	= 1.8541	w_2	= .5079
w_1	= 1.8271	Σw_i	= 4.1891

Rent and house prices

19. $\Delta \ln P_R = .5972 - .0957 \ln \dfrac{K_{HR}}{N}$

$\qquad + .0207 \ln \dfrac{Y_D}{P_c N} - .0782 \ln \dfrac{P_{R-1}}{P_c}$

$\qquad - .2031\, \hat{u}_{-1}$

20. $\Delta \left(\dfrac{P_R}{P_H}\right) = -.0037 + \displaystyle\sum_{i=1}^{12} w_i (\Delta R_M)_{-i}$

$\qquad\qquad + .2545\, \hat{u}_{-1}$

w_1	= .0102	w_8	= .0060
w_2	= .0099	w_9	= .0050
w_3	= .0095	w_{10}	= .0039
w_4	= .0090	w_{11}	= .0027
w_5	= .0084	w_{12}	= .0014
w_6	= .0077	Σw_i	= .0806
w_7	= .0069		

Identity defining housing stock

21. $K_{HR} = .994\, K_{HR_{-1}} + .25 \dfrac{E_H}{P_H}$

C. State and Local Governments

Expenditures

22. $Y_S = Y - T_{FP} - T_{FC} - T_{FI} - T_{FS} - T_{FE}$
$\qquad - e_T + G_{FP} + G_{FU} + G_{FS} + INT_F$

23. $E_{ST} = E_{SW} + E_{SC} + E_{SO} + G_{SP}$
$\qquad\qquad + INT_S - T_{SS} - G_{FG}$

24. $\dfrac{E_{SC}}{NP_G} = .302 + \displaystyle\sum_{i=0}^{11} w_i \left(\dfrac{Y_S}{NP_G}\right)_{-i}$

$\qquad + \displaystyle\sum_{i=0}^{11} w_i' \left(\dfrac{Y_S}{NP_G}\right)_{-i} (R_C)_{-i}$

$\qquad + \displaystyle\sum_{i=0}^{1} w_i'' \left(\dfrac{G_{FG}}{NP_G}\right)_{-i}$

$\qquad + \displaystyle\sum_{i=0}^{1} w_i''' \left(\dfrac{P_S}{P_G}\right)_{-i} \left(\dfrac{Y_S}{NP_G}\right)_{-i}$

$\qquad + .1744 \left(\dfrac{N_{20}}{N}\right) \left(\dfrac{Y_S}{NP_G}\right)$

$w_0 = -.0428$ $w_3' = -.0003$

$w_1 = -.0273$ $w_4' = -.0003$

$w_2 = -.0150$ $w_5' = -.0004$

$w_3 = -.0053$ $w_6' = -.0004$

$w_4 = .0016$ $w_7' = -.0005$

$w_5 = .0062$ $w_8' = -.0005$

$w_6 = .0089$ $w_9' = -.0004$

$w_7 = .0100$ $w_{10}' = -.0003$

$w_8 = .0096$ $w_{11}' = -.0002$

$w_9 = .0081$ $\Sigma w_i' = -.0050$

$w_{10} = .0057$ $w_0'' = .2924$

$w_{11} = .0030$ $w_1'' = .0986$

$\Sigma w_i = -.0372$ $\Sigma w_i'' = .3910$

$w_0' = -.0006$ $w_0''' = -.0198$

$w_1' = -.0006$ $w_1''' = .0340$

$w_2' = -.0005$ $\Sigma w_i''' = .0142$

25. $$\frac{E_{SO}}{NP_G} = 4.394 - .0272 \frac{Y_S}{NP_G}$$

$$- .0104 \left(\frac{P_S}{P_G}\right)\left(\frac{Y_S}{NP_G}\right)$$

$$+ .1334 \left(\frac{N_{20}}{N}\right)\left(\frac{Y_S}{NP_G}\right)$$

$$- .0006 R_C \left(\frac{Y_S}{NP_G}\right)$$

$$+ \sum_{i=0}^{1} w_i \left(\frac{G_{FG}}{NP_G}\right)_{-i}$$

$w_0 = .1970$ $w_1 = .1679$ $\Sigma w_i = .3649$

26. $$\frac{E_{SW}}{NP_G} = 32.722 + .3086 \frac{G_{FG}}{NP_G}$$

$$+ .0835 \left(\frac{P_S}{P_G}\right)\left(\frac{Y_S}{NP_G}\right)$$

$$+ .1298 \left(\frac{N_{20}}{N}\right)\left(\frac{Y_S}{NP_G}\right)$$

$$+ \sum_{i=0}^{1} w_i \left(\frac{Y_S}{NP_G}\right)_{-i}$$

$$+ \sum_{i=0}^{3} w_i (R_C)_{-i} \left(\frac{Y_S}{NP_G}\right)_{-i}$$

$w_0 = -.0762$ $w_1' = -.0002$

$w_1 = -.0277$ $w_2' = .0016$

$\Sigma w_i = -.1039$ $w_3' = .0021$

$w_0' = -.0017$ $\Sigma w_i' = .0018$

27. $$\frac{G_{SP}}{NP_G} = 8.041 + .1074 \frac{G_{FG}}{NP_G}$$

$$- .0104 \left(\frac{L_E+L_A}{N}\right)\left(\frac{Y_S}{NP_G}\right)$$

$$+ \sum_{i=0}^{1} w_i \left(\frac{Y_S}{NP_G}\right)_{-i}$$

$$+ \sum_{i=0}^{1} w_i' (R_C)_{-i} \left(\frac{Y_S}{NP_G}\right)_{-i}$$

$w_0 = .0219$ $w_0' = -.0004$

$w_1 = -.0126$ $w_1' = .0007$

$\Sigma w_i = .0093$ $\Sigma w_i' = .0003$

Taxes and profits of government enterprises

28. $$\frac{T_{SP}}{N} = -37.671 + .0258 \frac{Y_H}{N} + .2470 \frac{E_{ST}}{N}$$

$$- .0053 (R_C)\left(\frac{E_{ST}}{N}\right)$$

$$- .5358 \left(\frac{E_{SC}}{E_{ST}+G_{FG}}\right)\left(\frac{E_{ST}}{N}\right)$$

29. $$\frac{T_{SI}}{N} = -14.944 + \sum_{i=0}^{1} w_i \left(\frac{Y_S}{N}\right)_{-i}$$

$$+ \sum_{i=0}^{1} w_i' \left(\frac{E_{ST}}{N}\right)_{-i}$$

$$- .0053 (R_C)\left(\frac{E_{ST}}{N}\right)$$

$$- 1.2280 \left(\frac{E_{SC}}{E_{ST}+G_{FG}}\right)\left(\frac{E_{ST}}{N}\right)$$

$w_0 = -.0014$ $w_0' = .7684$

$w_1 = .0277$ $w_1' = .1149$

$\Sigma w_i = .0263$ $\Sigma w_i' = .8833$

30. $T_{SC} = -.418 + .0177 Y_C + .0365 E_{ST}$

$$- .0514 \left(\frac{E_{SC}}{E_{ST}+G_{FG}}\right) E_{ST}$$

$$- .0010 R_C E_{ST}$$

31. $T_{SS} = .0900 + .1110 E_{SW}$

32. $G_{SS} = -.301 + \sum_{i=0}^{1} w_i(Y_S)_{-i} + .0859\,E_{ST}$

$$- .1520\left(\frac{E_{SC}}{E_{ST}+G_{FG}}\right)(E_{ST})$$

$$- .0033\,(R_C)(E_{ST})$$

$w_0 = -.0038 \qquad w_1 = .0064 \qquad \Sigma w_i = .0026$

Glossary

* indicates exogenous to investment block.

Investment in plant and equipment

Y_B	gross business products, current dollars
$*Y$	GNP, current dollars
$*C_{NW}$	output originating in households, current dollars
$*E_{FW}$	Federal compensation of employees, current dollars
E_{SW}	State and local compensation of employees, current dollars
$*Y_F$	output originating abroad, current dollars
$*R_{CBI}$	Moody's industrial bond yield, per cent
$*R_D$	Moody's industrial dividend-price ratio for common stocks, per cent
R_C	Moody's Aaa corporate bond rate, per cent
R_E	cost of capital, equipment, per cent
R_S	cost of capital, structures, per cent
P_{QE}	current dollar rent, equipment, decimal
P_{QS}	current dollar rent, structures, decimal
$*P_{PD}$	price deflator, producers' durable equipment, decimal
$*P_{PS}$	price deflator, producers' structures, decimal
P_B	price deflator, gross business product, decimal
V_E	equilibrium capital-output ratio, equipment
V_S	equilibrium capital-output ratio, structures
O_{PD}	orders for producers' durable equipment, current dollars
E_{PD}	expenditures on producers' durable equipment, current dollars

O_{ME}	orders for machinery and equipment, current dollars
E_{ME}	shipments of machinery and equipment, current dollars
O_{UME}	stock of unfilled orders for machinery and equipment, current dollars
E_{PS}	expenditures on producers' structures, current dollars
K_{SR}	capital stock of producers' structures, 1958 dollars
$*$time	1 in 1948 QI, increments by one every quarter
$*t_c$	corporate tax rate, decimal
$*z_k$	rate of tax credit for investment in producers' durable equipment, decimal
$*z_e$	present value of depreciation deduction per dollar of new producers' durable equipment, decimal
$*z_s$	present value of depreciation deduction per dollar of new producers' durable structures, decimal
$*\alpha_2$	desired proportion of debt in corporate capital structures, $= .2$, 1948–66
$*\alpha_3$	annual rate of depreciation of producers' durable equipment, $= .16$, 1948–66
$*\alpha_4$	annual rate of depreciation of producers' structures, $= .06$, 1948–66
e	base of natural logarithm
$\hat{u}_{-1}$	previous period error term

Housing

E_H	expenditures for residential construction, current dollars
H_S	housing starts times average value per start, current dollars quarterly rates
K_{HR}	stock of houses, 1958 dollars
K_{HIR}	housing inventory under construction, 1958 dollars
P_R	rental price component of consumer price index, decimal
P_H	housing price deflator in the national income accounts, decimal
$*P_C$	consumer expenditure price deflator, national income accounts, decimal
$*N$	total population, billions
$*Y_D$	disposable personal income using personal tax liabilities, current dollars
$*$time	1 in 1948 QI, increments by one every quarter
$\hat{u}_{-1}$	previous period residual

State and local governments

(All flow variables measured in current dollars, seasonally adjusted annual rates)

Y_S — net income of citizens of States and localities

E_{ST} — total net expenditures of States and localities

*Y — GNP

*T_{FP} — Federal personal taxes, liability basis

*T_{FC} — Federal corporate profits tax accruals

*T_{FI} — Federal indirect taxes

*T_{FS} — Federal social insurance contributions

*T_{FE} — Federal estate and gift taxes

*e_T — Federal personal taxes on national income accounts basis less taxes on a liability basis

*G_{FP} — Federal transfer payments to persons less unemployment insurance benefits

*G_{FU} — unemployment insurance benefits

*G_{FS} — Federal subsidies less current surplus of government enterprises

*INT_F — Federal net interest payments

*G_{FG} — Federal grants-in-aid to State and local governments

E_{SW} — State and local compensation of employees

E_{SC} — State and local construction expenditures

E_{SO} — State and local other purchases

G_{SP} — State and local transfer payments

*INT_S — State and local net interest payments

G_{SS} — State and local surplus of government enterprises

T_{SP} — State and local personal taxes

T_{SC} — State and local corporate taxes

T_{SI} — State and local indirect taxes

T_{SS} — State and local social insurance contributions

*Y_H — personal income

*Y_C — corporate profits before tax (does not include IVA)

*R_C — Moody's Aaa corporate bond rate, per cent

*P_G — GNP deflator, decimal

*P_S — price deflator for State and local purchases, decimal

*N — population

*N_{20} — population under age 20, billions

*L_E — employed labor force, billions

*L_A — armed forces, billions

CONSUMPTION-INVENTORY BLOCK

Equations 1 and 2 of this block are identities adding up the components of GNP and consumer expenditures, respectively.

The next set of equations gets us from GNP to disposable income in four steps. Personal income less certain exogenous transfer payments depends on current and lagged GNP in such a way as to change less abruptly than GNP (Equation 3). After we add the price-wage block to the model, we plan to replace Equation 3 with one in which the relation of personal income and GNP depends on price, wage, and manhour changes. Taxable income depends on personal income and exemptions (Equation 4), income tax accruals are equal to taxable income multiplied by an exogenous tax rate (Equation 5), and disposable income depends, through an identity, on personal income, income tax accruals, and two categories of tax payments exogenous to this block.

Equations 7 through 10 get us from disposable income to total consumption (in our sense of including the services of durable goods) and its allocation. Equation 7 is the basic equation in the consumption sector. It relates our version of consumption to current and lagged disposable income with a long distributed lag. To guard against simultaneous equations bias, the relationship was actually estimated in ratio form with everything divided by current income [2, pp. 69–70]. We have experimented with wealth effects on consumption but were unable to get usable results due to collinearity between wealth and income. To some extent, the lag in income can serve as a proxy for wealth effects.

Equations 8 to 10 explain the distribution of total consumption among its three components —consumption of nondurables and services and the imputed services of autos and of other durables. These equations have been estimated with the sum of the coefficients for total consumption constrained to equal one, and the sum of all other sets of coefficients constrained to equal zero. This means that variables such as relative prices, interest rates, population, and the stocks of durables influence the distribution of consumption among its components, but not the over-all total. Equation 11 is the definition of the real income variable appearing in Equations 8 to 10.

The remaining consumption equations are identities. Equations 12 and 13 show the relation between consumption and consumer spending for autos and for other durables. Since stocks (K_{AR} and K_{DR}) are not measured at annual rates, whereas the other variables are, these equations imply that on a quarterly basis consumption in our sense equals between 6 and 7 per cent of the initial stock plus a fraction of current purchases. For durables other than autos, the fraction of current purchases is also between 6 and 7 per cent, but for autos it is nearly 12 per cent. All of these coefficients represent estimated depreciation rates plus an interest imputation. For other durables, depreciation rates come from a standard declining-balance formula based on data on lengths of life of durables in Goldsmith [7]. For autos depreciation rates come from a declining-balance formula with roughly double depreciation in the first quarter, based on a regression analysis of data compiled by Charles Friedman [5]. Autos are thus assumed to depreciate in value (and hence to yield services) at a much faster rate in the first quarter of their existence than in subsequent quarters.

Equations 14 and 15 define total consumer expenditures in real terms and total consumption in real terms. Equation 15 is listed simply to make clear the relation between the two consumption concepts; it is redundant in the complete consumption-inventory block since it is the sum of Equations 8–10.

Equations 16 and 17 explain stocks of autos and other durables by using declining-balance formulas. The depreciation rates are the ones already discussed in connection with Equations 12 and 13.

Equation 18 explains inventory investment. As described in the text, the equation estimates different inventory-sales ratios and different lags on the various components of final demand. Thus goods-in-process inventories connected with defense spending show up before ex-

penditures, whereas consumer expenditures have a small negative unanticipated effect in the current quarter.[2]

Equation 19 explains imports. This equation allows the average propensity to import to rise as GNP rises (as if imports were a luxury good). Relative price effects were tried in this equation, but they proved to be unimportant, perhaps because of errors of measurement in the import price index.

Equations

A. GNP and Consumption Identities

1. $Y = C_P + E_I - E_M + Z$ (identity)

2. $C_P = C_N + (E_{CAR} + E_{CDR}) P_{CAD}$ (identity)

B. Income Shares and Taxes

3. $\dfrac{Y_H - G_{FP}}{Y} = .789 - .0005 \text{ time} - .271 \left(\dfrac{\Delta Y}{Y_{-1}}\right)$

$$- .218 \left(\dfrac{\Delta Y_{-1}}{Y_{-2}}\right) - .105 \left(\dfrac{\Delta Y_{-2}}{Y_{-3}}\right)$$

4. $\ln\left(1 - \dfrac{Y_T}{Y_H}\right) = .123 - .3274 \ln\left(\dfrac{Y_H}{N}\right)$

$$+ .2808 \ln EX$$

5. $T_{FP} = t_h(Y_T)$

6. $Y_D = Y_H - T_{FP} - T_{FE} - T_{SP}$ (identity)

C. Total Consumption and its Components

Total consumption

7. $C_{TR}(.774 P_{CN} + .226 P_{CAD})$

$$= .3734 Y_D + \sum_{i=1}^{12} w_i Y_{D_{-i}} + .90 \, \hat{u}_{-1}$$

$w_1 = .0849$	$w_5 = .0584$	$w_9 = .0300$
$w_2 = .0785$	$w_6 = .0514$	$w_{10} = .0227$
$w_3 = .0718$	$w_7 = .0442$	$w_{11} = .0153$
$w_4 = .0651$	$w_8 = .0373$	$w_{12} = .0077$
	$\Sigma w_i = .5673$	

[2] In estimating this effect we made use of an instrumental variable, or two-stage technique, with new orders, lagged potential bank deposits, defense spending, and a number of other predetermined variables entering the first stage.

Components

8. $C_N/P_{CN} = .9518\,C_{TR} - .0191\,Y_{DR}$

$$+ \left(\frac{1}{10}\sum_{i=2}^{7} w_i\,R_{C_{-i}} - .0919\frac{P_{CN}}{P_{CAD}}\right)K_{AR_{-1}}$$

$$- .1625\,K_{AR_{-1}} - .1497\,K_{DR_{-1}} + 32.640\,N$$

9. $C_{AR} = .0369\,C_{TR} + .0205\,Y_{DR}$

$$+ \left(\frac{1}{10}\sum_{i=2}^{7} w_i'\,R_{C_{-i}} + .0781\frac{P_{CN}}{P_{CAD}}\right)K_{AR_{-1}}$$

$$+ .1778\,K_{AR_{-1}} - .1324\,K_{DR_{-1}} - 21.666\,N$$

10. $C_{DR} = .0112\,C_{TR} - .0014\,Y_{DR}$

$$+ \left(\frac{1}{10}\sum_{i=2}^{7} w_i''R_{C_{-i}} + .0138\frac{P_{CN}}{P_{CAD}}\right)K_{AR_{-1}}$$

$$- .0154K_{AR_{-1}} + .2821\,K_{DR_{-1}} - 10.965\,N$$

$w_2 = -.0154$		$w_2' = .0165$	
$w_3 = .0038$		$w_3' = .0004$	
$w_4 = .0163$		$w_4' = -.0103$	
$w_5 = .0222$		$w_5' = -.0157$	
$w_6 = .0214$		$w_6' = -.0158$	
$w_7 = .0140$		$w_7' = -.0106$	
$\Sigma w_i = .0623$		$\Sigma w_i' = -.0355$	
$w_2'' = -.0011$		$w_2 + w_2' + w_2'' = 0$	
$w_3'' = -.0041$		etc.	
$w_4'' = -.0060$			
$w_5'' = -.0065$			
$w_6'' = -.0056$			
$w_7'' = -.0035$			
$\Sigma w_i'' = -.0268$			

11. $Y_{DR} = Y_D/(.774\,P_{CN} + .226\,P_{CAD})$ (identity)

D. Relation of Real Consumer Expenditures to Real Consumption

12. $C_{AR} = .2551\,K_{AR_{-1}} + .11625\,E_{CAR}$ (identity)

13. $C_{DR} = .2675\,K_{DR_{-1}} + .06251\,E_{CDR}$ (identity)

14. $C_{PR} = C_N/P_{CN} + E_{CAR} + E_{CDR}$ (identity)

15. $C_{TR} = C_N/P_{CN} + C_{AR} + C_{DR}$ (identity)

E. Stocks of Consumer Durables

16. $K_{AR} = .9457\,K_{AR_{-1}} + .8884\,(E_{CAR}/4)$

(identity)

17. $K_{DR} = .9426\,(K_{DR_{-1}} + [E_{CDR}/4])$ (identity)

F. Inventory Investment

18. $E_{IR} = .424\,E_{IR_{-1}} - .138\,\Delta C_{PR}$

$$+ .573\,(\Delta C_{PR})_{-1} + .387\,\Delta\left(\frac{E_{FD}}{P_F}\right)_{+1}$$

$$+ \sum_{i=0}^{4} w_i\,\Delta\left(\frac{O_{PD}}{P_{PD}}\right)_{-i} - .276\,\Delta S_{TR}$$

$w_0 = -.020$		$w_3 = .335$
$w_1 = .214$		$w_4 = .224$
$w_2 = .331$		$\Sigma w_i = 1.084$

19. $E_I = E_{IR}(1.202\,P_{NB} - .095\,W_{NB}) + .009$

G. Imports

20. $E_M/Y = .665\,(E_M/Y)_{-1}$

$$+ \frac{1}{100}\left[.0009\frac{Y}{P_G}\right.$$

$$+ .0140\left(\frac{1}{1.05-U_M}\right) + 1.0095\right]$$

$$+ .0032\,D_{UDS} + .0027\,D_{USS}$$

H. Capacity Utilization, Materials Industries

21. $\Delta U_M = \dfrac{1}{(C_N/P_{CN})}\left(1.832\,\Delta E_{IR}\right.$

$$+ 1.905\,\Delta\,(E_{CAR}+E_{CDR})$$

$$+ .821\,\Delta\frac{C_N}{P_{CN}}\right) - .0156$$

Glossary

(Dollar amounts, in billions, seasonally adjusted at annual rates except where noted. * indicates exogenous to consumption-inventory block.)

C_{AR} consumption of the services of autos and parts, 1958 dollars

C_{DR} consumption of the services of durables except autos and parts, 1958 dollars

C_N expenditures on nondurables and services, current dollars

C_P total consumer expenditures, current dollars

C_{PR} total consumer expenditures, 1958 dollars

C_{TR} total "consumption" (see text), 1958 dollars

*D_{UDS} dummy variable for 1965 dock strike

$*D_{USS}$ dummy variable for 1959 steel strike

E_{CAR} consumer expenditures on autos and parts, 1958 dollars

E_{CDR} consumer expenditures on durables except autos and parts, 1958 dollars

$*E_{FD}$ Federal expenditures on defense goods, current dollars

E_I nonfarm inventory investment, current dollars

E_{IR} nonfarm inventory investment, constant dollars

E_M imports, current dollars

$*EX$ per capita exemptions under Federal personal income tax, in dollars

$*G_{FP}$ Federal transfer payments to persons, except unemployment benefits

K_{AR} stock of consumer autos and parts end of quarter, not at annual rates, 1958 dollars

K_{DR} stock of consumer durables except autos and parts, end of quarter, not at annual rates, 1958 dollars

$*N$ total U.S. population, billions

$*O_{PD}$ new orders for producers' durable equipment, current dollars

$*P_{CAD}$ implicit deflator for consumer durables (including autos), 1958 = 1.00

$*P_{CN}$ implicit deflator for consumer nondurables and services, 1958 = 1.00

$*P_F$ implicit deflator for Federal purchases, 1958 = 1.00

$*P_{NB}$ implicit deflator for nonfarm business GNP, 1958 = 1.00

$*P_{PD}$ implicit deflator for producers' durable equipment, 1958 = 1.00

$*P_G$ implicit deflator for GNP, 1958 = 1.00

$*R_C$ yield on seasoned Aaa corporate bonds, in per cent

$*S_{TR}$ man-days idle in excess of 10,000, in thousands

$*time$ time; 1948 I = 1, 1948 II = 2, etc.

$*T_{FE}$ Federal estate and gift tax payments, current dollars

T_{FP} Federal personal income tax liabilities, current dollars

$*t_h$ average tax rate under Federal personal income tax; 20 per cent = .2, etc.

$*T_{SP}$ State and local personal taxes, current dollars

U_M utilization rate for materials industries; 90 per cent = .9, etc.

$*W_{NB}$ average wage rate for nonfarm business, dollars per hour

Y GNP, current dollars

Y_D disposable personal income with taxes measured on a liability basis, current dollars

Y_{DR} disposable personal income divided by a weighted average of deflators for consumer expenditures

Y_H personal income, current dollars

Y_T taxable personal income, current dollars

$*Z$ autonomous spending; the sum of exports, government expenditures, fixed investment, and farm inventory investment

THE THREE BLOCKS COMBINED

The important equation of this block is number 5, which explains corporate dividend payments. Dividends have an effect on stock prices and will also be included in personal income when we finish the labor market side of the model. They depend on corporate cash flows with a distributed lag.

Corporate cash flows are described by the identity in Equation 3 and Federal corporate taxes by Equation 4. The equation for State and local corporate taxes is part of the investment block.

Equation 1 explains corporate profits. Except for statistical discrepancy and inventory valuation adjustment, this equation would be an identity, and Equation 2 is an informal way of dealing with the obscure residual items. Equations 6 through 10 then fill in the missing links in Equation 1. This treatment gives a very minor importance to indirect taxes, but our conclusions on this matter will change when we add the price and labor market blocks to the model. Both taxes would then have a direct effect on personal income, and indirect taxes will also influence output prices.

Equations

Corporate profits, cash flows, and dividends

1. $Y_C = Y - DEP - T_{FI} - T_{SI} + G_{FS} - G_{SS}$
$- T_{FS} - T_{SS} + Y_{CD} + INT + G_{FP}$
$+ G_{SP} - Y_H + ERR$

2. $\dfrac{ERR}{Y_{-1}} = -.0238 + .0386\, U_M$

$$- .0776 \left(\dfrac{Y}{Y_{-2}} - 1 \right) + .6585\, \hat{u}_{-1}$$

3. $Y_{CF} = Y_C + DEP_C - T_{FC} - T_{SC}$

4. $\ln\,(T_{FC} + \alpha_1\, z_k\, E_{PD}) = -.4161 + .7262 \ln t_c$
$+ 1.0177 \ln (Y_C - T_{SC}) + .8591\, \hat{u}_{-1}$

5. $Y_{CD} = .9906 + \displaystyle\sum_{i=0}^{7} w_i\, Y_{CF-i} + .5000\, \hat{u}_{-1}$

$w_0 = .0600$	$w_3 = .0309$	$w_6 = .0119$
$w_1 = .0485$	$w_4 = .0239$	$w_7 = .0061$
$w_2 = .0390$	$w_5 = .0177$	$\Sigma w_i = .2380$

Federal indirect and social insurance taxes

6. $T_{FI} = T_{FX} + T_{FCD}$

7. $\ln T_{FX} = 1.0883 + .6315 \ln C_P + 1.1027 \ln t_x$

8. $T_{FS} = T_{FO} + T_{FU} + T_{FSO}$

9. $\ln T_{FO} = \ln t_0 + .9473 \ln Y_H - .4384$

10. $\ln T_{FU} = \ln t_u + .4480 \ln Y_H$
$+ 1.2887 \ln t_{uic} + 2.9812$

Glossary

(All flow variables from national income accounts, seasonally adjusted annual rates, billions of current dollars.)

*Y	GNP
*DEP	total depreciation allowances
*DEP_C	corporate depreciation allowances
Y_C	corporate profits before tax (does not include IVA)
*Y_H	personal income
Y_{CD}	corporate dividend payments
Y_{CF}	corporate cash flows
*E_{PD}	expenditures on producers' durables equipment
*C_P	personal consumption expenditures

*INT	net interest paid by government and by consumers
ERR	Federal unemployment benefits less statistical discrepancy less net wage accruals less inventory valuation adjustment
T_{FI}	Federal indirect taxes
T_{FS}	Federal social insurance contributions
*G_{FS}	Federal subsides less current surplus of government enterprises
*G_{FP}	Federal transfer payments to persons less unemployment insurance benefits
T_{FC}	Federal corporate profits tax accruals
T_{FX}	Federal excise taxes
*T_{FCD}	Federal customs duties
T_{FO}	Federal social insurance contributions for old-age, survivors, disability insurance
T_{FU}	Federal social insurance contributions, unemployment insurance
*T_{FSO}	Federal social insurance contributions, other
*T_{SI}	State and local indirect taxes
*G_{SS}	State and local current surplus of government enterprises
*T_{SS}	State and local social insurance contributions
*G_{SP}	State and local transfer payments
*T_{SC}	State and local corporate taxes
*U_M	FRB capacity utilization rate for materials, decimal
*z_k	rate of tax credit for producers' durable equipment, decimal
*t_c	Federal corporate tax rate, decimal
*t_x	Federal excise tax rate, decimal
*t_0	Federal OASDI tax rate, decimal
*t_u	Federal unemployment insurance tax rate, decimal
*t_{uic}	labor force covered by unemployment insurance over total labor force, decimal
*α_1	proportion of producers' durable equipment eligible for tax credit, $= .4139$ from 1962–66
$\hat{u}_{-1}$	previous error term in appropriate equation

REFERENCES

1. A. Ando, and E. C. Brown, 1968. Personal income taxes and consumption following the 1964 tax reduction. *Studies in economic stabilization* (A. Ando, E. C. Brown, and A. F. Friedlaender, eds.); Washington: Brookings, 117–137.
2. A. Ando, and F. Modigliani, 1963. The "life cycle" hypothesis of saving: aggregate implications and tests. *American Economic Review, 53*(1): 55–84.
3. M. K. Evans, and L. R. Klein, 1967. *The Wharton econometric forecasting model.* Philadelphia: University of Pennsylvania. 1D.
4. C. S. Friedman, 1965. The stock of automobiles in the United States. *Survey of Current Business, 45*(10): 21–27.
5. M. Friedman, 1957. *A theory of the consumption function.* Princeton: Princeton University Press.
6. G. Fromm, and P. Taubman, 1968. *Policy simulations with an econometric model.* Washington: Brookings Institution. 2D.
7. R. W. Goldsmith, 1962. *The national wealth of the United States in the postwar period.* Princeton: Princeton University Press.
8. A. J. Tella, and P. A. Tinsley, 1968. The labor market and potential output of the FRB-MIT model: a preliminary report. *American Statistical Association, 1967 Proceedings of the Business and Economic Statistics Section*: 51–76. 2D.
9. M. Weidenbaum, 1961, The economic impact of the goverment spending process. *The Business Review, 8* (Spring): 3–47.

PART VI

METHODOLOGICAL ISSUES

Like all research methodologies, computer simulation has Jekyll-and-Hyde characteristics. It allows the model-builder to make substantively meaningful assumptions which are too complex to analyze by other methods; it offers great flexibility for creating intelligible output formats; it guarantees that the model's outputs follow logically from the model's assumptions; and it encourages the model-builder to analyze the causal structure of the modeled process. On the other hand, simulation provides few safeguards against the model-builder's human propensity for self-deception, and both the freedoms and constraints of simulation facilitate self-deception. Sufficient assumptions and temporal sequences must be specified even when the model-builder lacks adequate information to justify them; output flexibility lures model-builders into inventing a superficial realism; the mechanization of logic permits a model-builder to disclaim his personal responsibility for logical analysis; and the particularity of solutions adds ambiguity to the interpretation of model properties.

The particularity of solutions is also a source of technical difficulties in the exploration, analysis, and interpretation of model behavior. In one sense, the analysis of a simulation model is as difficult and complex as the analysis of empirical data from the real world: both are problems in inductive logic that contain irresolvable uncertainties and that can be treated with the same statistical techniques. The overwhelming majority of simulation studies have proceeded as if the simulation outputs were real-world data. However, simulation outputs are not real-world data, and the differences are sources of powerful (if unexploited) analytic leverage. A simulation model is completely deterministic and totally within the analyst's control; pseudorandom numbers are nonrandom and are exogenously controlled; the model can be subjected to conditions that would change or destroy the real process; independent variables can really be varied independently; the forms of probability distributions are known exactly; there are no measurement errors or unobservable causal links.

One result of these differences has been the creation of a body of literature devoted to analytic techniques for simulation models and to efficiency-increasing modifications of conventional statistics. Ten of the most relevant and suggestive articles are included in this section. The chapters by Fishman and Kiviat and by Frijda discuss model construction and general methodological strategy. The next six chapters discuss aspects of the conduct of simulation experiments: Bonini, and Jacoby and Harrison illustrate applications of experimental design; Clark and Brenner describe criteria for selecting stochastic variates; Fishman presents a technique for choosing a sample size; and Hoggatt searches for optimum parameter values. Finally, Starbuck and Hanna present alternative approaches for evaluating model accuracy and validity.

Unfortunately, the methodological literature is so extensive that no selection of ten articles can adequately represent it, and no existing textbook combines broad coverage with the kind of detailed exposition one needs in order to use specific techniques. Therefore the reader should supplement our selections by reading appropriate items from the bibliography appended to this introduction. Of particular interest are the articles on system identification and model synthesis, on decision-theoretic approaches to sample sizes, and on gradient search techniques.

The ideas presented in the articles on system identification are potentially applicable both to the study of the real-world system simulated and to the study of the simulation model. The rest of the cited articles assume that a simulation model already exists and that the objective is to investigate its behavior and to demonstrate that the input-output relations imbedded in the model resemble those of the real world. These postmodel problems are important, of course, but they do not have the relative importance implied by the literature cited. Equally important are the problems of analyzing and measuring the real-world system to obtain information on which to base the model, and the problems of intelligibly describing the model's structure and assumptions.

Premodel data collection forces the model-builder to decide what data to collect and how to collect them. Both are familiar issues in empirical research, and the familiar discussions of them are relevant, but both are affected by the fact that simulation is intended. That is, the fact that one contemplates building a simulation model instead of, say, a mathematical model indicates either that the real-world process differs from processes which are mathematically amenable or that one intends to represent aspects of the real-world which are mathematically awkward. Differences in the modeled situation or the modeled dimensions of the situation naturally imply differences in the kinds of data collected and differences in techniques for data acquisition. One such difference lies in simulation's relative emphasis on causal structure—simulation models frequently try to explicate structural details that mathematical models would leave inside a black box. The simulation model-builder must try to obtain data about causal structure, and such data are both expensive and readily distorted by measure-

ment interventions. Few real-world systems record and store structural data in the way they record and store input-output data, and some real-world systems, such as human brains, have inherently unobservable structures. The model-builder is likely to have to depend on inference from input-output time series, even though his resort to simulation suggests that the input-output relations are nonlinear and intricate. Obviously, data acquisition is affected by other distinguishing characteristics of simulation models, ranging from the acceptability of nonnumerical codes to the need for comparatively large numbers of observations.

Descriptions of simulation models are complicated by multiple objectives which are individually difficult to achieve. First, the computation procedure should be stated in sufficient detail to support an exact replication. This can be achieved in principle by a programming-language listing of the program, but it can only be achieved in practice if the programming language is available on many machines and if identical instructions produce identical results on different machines. Unfortunately, the desire to exploit fully the special advantages of different machines combines with local variations in hardware and software to make exact replication virtually impossible, and it is not uncommon for an attempted replication to yield surprising results. Consider, for example, the replication implications of Fetter and Thompson's experience with random number seeds (Chapter 19).

Since the computation procedure ordinarily incorporates details that the model-builder himself would not accept as representing the real-world process, the computation procedure is not the model. The second descriptive objective should be delineation of the limit of representation, the level of detail at which the simulation ceases to represent reality and starts to be only a computation scheme. This is nearly always achievable and practically never achieved because the model-builder becomes so immersed in programming technique that he loses his objectivity toward the representational characteristics of the simulation. Model construction involves progressive elaboration in which details are stated as the need for them is discovered; some details are specified after programming begins and others are specified after debugging uncovers deficiencies. Of course, the programming language formulation of one part of the simulation may drastically alter the formulation of another part, and the characteristics of the language itself facilitate or inhibit alternative formulations. The result is that substantive issues may not be considered until most substantively meaningful solutions have been excluded, and the model-builder is unlikely to perceive the perceptual focusing he imposed on himself.

The final descriptive objective should be to make the model intelligible to other social scientists. With the possible exception of economics, in which mathematics is nearly a lingua franca, descriptions in computer-oriented language are esoteric and the model must be translated into discipline-oriented language. Such translations are not one-to-one. Just as Eskimos have many words that translate as

"snow," computer-oriented languages incorporate logical distinctions that disciplinary languages cannot convey, and discipline-oriented languages differentiate among computationally equivalent processes. Moreover, a straightforward translation of a simulation can be as meaningful as a word-for-word translation of a haiku. One needs to convey the model's substantive gestalt as well as its operational structure, and one needs to display the operational structure at multiple levels of detail. If simulation modeling was undertaken rationally because the model-builder recognized deficiencies in potential verbal and mathematical modeling, it is by no means obvious how he should reconcile these deficiencies when restating his model in verbal or mathematical forms.

The reader should supplement his methodological reading by selections from the following bibliography.

INTRODUCTORY TEXTBOOKS

D. N. Chorafas, 1965. *Systems and simulation.*
G. W. Evans, II, G. F. Wallace, and G. L. Sutherland, 1967. *Simulation using digital computers.*
J. M. Hammersley, and D. C. Handscomb, 1964. *Monte Carlo methods.*
J. Klír, and M. Valach, 1967. *Cybernetic modelling.*
C. McMillan, and R. F. Gonzalez, 1965. *Systems analysis.*
F. F. Martin, 1968. *Computer modeling and simulation.*
R. C. Meier, W. T. Newell, and H. L. Pazer, 1969. *Simulation in business and economics.*
J. H. Mize, and J. G. Cox, 1968. *Essentials of simulation.*
T. H. Naylor, J. L. Balintfy, D. S. Burdick, and K. Chu, 1966. *Computer simulation techniques.*
J. Smith, 1968. *Computer simulation models.*
K. D. Tocher, 1963. *The art of simulation.*

GENERAL METHODOLOGICAL STRATEGY AND MODEL CONSTRUCTION

R. W. Conway, 1963. Some tactical problems in digital simulation.
M. H. David, 1965. *Design of simulation models of the household sector.*
J. J. Donovan, 1967. *Investigations in simulation and simulation languages.*
R. E. Gagné, and D. C. Baxter, 1968. Techniques for the design of linear digital simulations.
J. M. Hammersley, and D. C. Handscomb, 1964. *Monte Carlo methods.*
B. E. Howard, 1966. Nonlinear system simulation.
H. Kaufman, 1967. An experimental investigation of process identification by competitive evolution.
J. Klír, 1965. The general system as a methodological tool.
J. Klír, 1967. Processing of general system activity.
R. H. Kohr, 1967. On the identification of linear and nonlinear systems.
T. J. Manetsch, 1966. Transfer function representation of the aggregate behavior of a class of economic processes.
R. C. Meier, W. T. Newell, and H. L. Pazer, 1969. *Simulation in business and economics.*
I. I. Mitroff, 1969. Fundamental issues in the simulation of human behavior: a case in the strategy of behavioral science.
E. F. Moore, 1956. Gedanken-experiments on sequential machines.
G. A. Pask, 1962. The simulation of learning and decision-making behavior.
A. Svoboda, 1963. Synthesis of logical systems of given activity.
K. D. Tocher, 1963. *The art of simulation.*
L. E. Travis, 1962. *Observing how humans make mistakes to discover how to get computers to do likewise.*

MODEL SOLUTION

C. C. Holt, 1965. Validation and application of macroeconomic models using computer simulation.
M. R. Norman, 1967. *Solving a non-linear econometric model.*

EXPERIMENTAL DESIGN

H. Chernoff, 1969. Sequential designs.
A. L. Frank, 1968. The use of experimental design techniques in simulation.
T. H. Naylor, D. S. Burdick, and W. E. Sasser, 1967. Computer simulation experiments with economic systems: the problem of experimental design.
J. L. Overholt, 1969. Factorial designs.

SAMPLE SELECTION

C. E. Clark, 1960. *Importance sampling in Monte Carlo analyses.*
S. Ehrenfield, and S. Ben-Tuvia, 1962. The efficiency of statistical simulation procedures.
D. H. Evans, 1963. Applied multiplex sampling.
M. Francki, 1968. The problem of confidence and three methods of variance reduction in the simulation of queueing.
D. P. Gaver, Jr., 1969. *Statistical methods for improving simulation efficiency.*
J. H. Halton, and D. C. Handscomb, 1957. A method for increasing the efficiency of Monte Carlo integration.
J. H. Halton, 1960. On the efficiency of certain quasi-random sequences of points in evaluating multi-dimensional integrals.
J. M. Hammersley, 1956. Conditional Monte Carlo.
J. M. Hammersley, 1960. Monte Carlo methods for solving multivariable problems.
J. M. Hammersley, and J. G. Mauldon, 1956. General principles of antithetic variates.
J. M. Hammersley, and K. W. Morton, 1954. Poor man's Monte Carlo.
J. M. Hammersley, and K. W. Morton, 1956. A new Monte Carlo technique: antithetic variates.
D. C. Handscomb, 1958. Proof of the antithetic variates theorem for $n > 2$.
D. C. Handscomb, 1969. Variance reduction techniques: theoretical.
C. B. Haselgrove, 1961. A method for numerical integration.
H. Kahn, 1951. Modification of the Monte Carlo method.
H. Kahn, and A. W. Marshall, 1953. Methods of reducing sample size in Monte Carlo computations.
H. Kahn, 1956. Use of different Monte Carlo sampling techniques.
H. Kahn and I. Mann, 1957. *Monte Carlo.*
J. P. Kleijnen, 1968. *Increasing the reliability of estimates in the simulation of systems: negative and positive correlation between runs.*
K. W. Morton, 1957. A generalisation of the antithetic variate technique for evaluating integrals.
W. A. Moy, 1969. Variance reduction techniques: practical.
E. L. Pugh, 1964. *Some examples of stochastic distortion, a Monte Carlo technique.*
R. D. Richtmyer, 1958. *A non-random sampling method, based on congruences, for "Monte Carlo" problems.*
L. Rosenberg, 1967. Bernstein polynomials and Monte Carlo integration.
D. Teichroew, 1965. A history of distribution sampling prior to the era of the computer and its relevance to simulation.
H. F. Trotter, and J. W. Tukey, 1956. Conditional Monte Carlo for normal samples.
J. W. Tukey, 1957. Antithesis or regression?
J. G. Wendel, 1957. Groups and conditional Monte Carlo.

SAMPLE SIZE

M. E. Brenner, 1965. A relation between decision making penalty and simulation sample size for inventory systems.
M. E. Brenner, 1966. A cost model for determining the sample size in the simulation of inventory systems.
G. S. Fishman, 1968. The allocation of computer time in comparing simulation experiments.
S. E. Forbush, 1957. The use of sequential sampling procedures for acceptance tests of computers and applications to Monte Carlo battle games.
M. A. Geisler, 1964. The sizes of simulation samples required to compute certain inventory characteristics with stated precision and confidence.
M. J. Gilman, 1968. A brief survey of stopping rules in Monte Carlo simulations.

J. W. Horn, D. B. Stafford, D. R. Hinson, and G. L. Reed, 1964. *An investigation to correlate synthetic land use origin and destination techniques to field conducted origin and destination surveys, final report.*

R. H. Hurtubise, 1969. Sample sizes and confidence intervals associated with a Monte Carlo simulation model possessing a multinomial output.

I. W. Kabak, 1968. Stopping rules for queuing simulations.

A. W. Marshall, 1956. The use of multi-stage sampling schemes in Monte Carlo computations.

PARAMETER ESTIMATION AND OPTIMIZATION

D. S. Burdick, and T. H. Naylor, 1969. Response surface methods in economics.

B. C. Duer, 1966. The use of multidimensional search techniques in large scale simulation.

G. F. Healea, 1966. *Evolutionary methods as applied to simulation models.*

L. R. Klein, 1969. Estimation of interdependent systems in macroeconomics.

R. C. Meier, 1967. The application of optimum-seeking techniques to simulation studies: a preliminary evaluation.

J. Moshman, 1958. The application of sequential estimation to computer simulation and Monte Carlo procedures.

E. L. Pugh, 1965. *A gradient technique of adaptive Monte Carlo.*

P. A. Reese, 1968. *Steady state parameter estimation in computer simulated systems.*

J. E. Walsh, 1963. Use of linearized nonlinear regression for simulations involving Monte Carlo.

DATA ANALYSIS

R. F. Barton, 1967. A generalized responsiveness (elasticity) function for simulations.

R. E. Dear, 1961. *Multivariate analyses of variance and covariance for simulation studies involving normal time series.*

G. S. Fishman, 1968. *Digital computer simulation: input-output analysis.*

G. S. Fishman, and P. J. Kiviat, 1967. The analysis of simulation-generated time series.

A. C. Hoggatt, 1966. Statistical techniques for the computer analysis of simulation models.

E. P. Howrey, 1969. *Dynamic properties of a condensed version of the Wharton model.*

E. P. Howrey, and H. H. Kelejian, 1969. Computer simulation versus analytical solutions.

J. P. Kleijnen, 1968. *The use of multiple ranking and multiple comparison procedures in the simulation of business and economic systems.*

H. Mechanic, and W. McKay, 1966. *Confidence intervals for averages of dependent data in simulations II.*

H. F. Meissinger, 1960. The use of parameter influence coefficients in computer analysis of dynamic systems.

K. S. Miller, and F. J. Murray, 1953. A mathematical basis for an error analysis of differential analyzers.

T. H. Naylor, K. Wertz, and T. H. Wonnacott, 1967. Methods for analyzing data from computer simulation experiments.

T. H. Naylor, K. Wertz, and T. H. Wonnacott, 1969. Spectral analysis of data generated by simulation experiments with econometric models.

D. J. Nelson, 1963. A fundamental error theory for analog computers.

M. Pfaff, and A. B. Pfaff, 1969. *Statistical analysis of simulations of human systems.*

R. Vichnevetsky, 1967. Error analysis in the computer simulation of dynamic systems: variational aspects of the problem.

J. E. Walsh, 1956. Questionable usefulness of variance for measuring estimate accuracy in Monte Carlo importance sampling problems.

D. G. Watts, 1969. Spectral analysis.

SIMULATION ACCURACY

N. W. Bazley, and P. J. Davis, 1960. Accuracy of Monte Carlo methods in computing finite Markoff chains.

G. S. Fishman, 1968. Estimating reliability in simulation experiments.

A. V. Gafarian, and C. J. Ancker, Jr., 1966. Mean value estimation from digital computer simulation.

R. F. Gebhard, 1963. A limiting distribution of an estimate of mean queue length.

M. A. Geisler, 1964. A test of a statistical method for computing selected inventory model characteristics by simulation.

C. Levert, and J. van Galen, 1968. Mathematical and statistical details on the simulation of MARKOFF-type stochastic processes on an electronic computer.

J. I. Marcum, 1962. *Inference of Monte Carlo properties from the solution of a known problem.*

H. O. A. Wold, 1965. A graphic introduction to stochastic processes.

MODEL EVALUATION

J. F. Hanna, 1966. A new approach to the formulation and testing of learning models.

E. B. Hunt, 1965. The evaluation of somewhat parallel models.

J. L. McKenney, 1967. Critique of: "Verification of computer simulation models."

G. A. Miller, and J. G. Beebe-Center, 1956. Some psychological methods for evaluating the quality of translations.

T. H. Naylor, and J. M. Finger, 1967. Verification of computer simulation models.

G. R. Schink, 1968. *Estimation of forecast error in a dynamic and/or non-linear econometric model.*

W. E. Schrank, and C. C. Holt, 1967. Critique of: "Verification of computer simulation models."

R. L. Van Horn, 1969. The problem of validation.

29

THE STATISTICS OF DISCRETE-EVENT SIMULATION

GEORGE S. FISHMAN
PHILIP J. KIVIAT

I. INTRODUCTION

Many system simulation experiments are driven by input processes containing elements of random behavior. In such simulations, statistical reliability must be considered if experimental results are to be interpreted properly. Statistical considerations also enter into the evaluation of simulation model designs. This paper describes these considerations, identifying how and where they become important during the planning, performance, and analysis of simulation experiments. The description can be viewed as tracing the elements of a typical experiment from inception through analysis, defining statistical problems encountered and relating them to the formal body of statistical theory.

The problems described are inherent in all stochastic system simulation models. An experimental design's ability to reveal useful insights into a system depends to a great extent on how well these problems are solved. Failure to deal with them may cause errors in interpreting observed associations between system input and output. One common error is the underestimation of the statistical reliability of system response measurements; this error is caused by failure to account for autocorrelation in system

SOURCE: Reprinted from *SCi Simulation*, *10* (4): 185–195 (1968).

response time-series generated by a simulation model. Another frequent source of error is the assumption that random numbers generated within a simulation model are independent, when in fact the method of random number generation employed induces unwanted correlation.

Our aim is to promote awareness of problems, not to solve them. The study offers no general solutions, but provides references germane to the statistical problems described. Some references describe particular solutions; others offer methods of analysis.

To understand the role of statistics in system simulation experiments, a knowledge of how such experiments developed is helpful. System simulation may be regarded as an extension of Monte Carlo methods. These methods, which concern experiments with random numbers, began their systematic development during World War II when they were applied to problems related to the atomic bomb. The work involved direct simulation of probabilistic problems concerned with random neutron diffusion in fissionable material [11]. Shortly thereafter, it was proposed that Monte Carlo methods be applied to solve certain integral equations occurring in physics that were not amenable to analytical solution. Stochastic processes often existed whose parameters satisfied these equations. One could estimate these parameters (and hence the solution to the equations) by performing Monte Carlo experiments on the stochastic processes.

The reliability of parameter estimates was the dominant statistical problem in these Monte Carlo experiments. Since the estimates were generally the sum of independent, identically distributed random variables, their reliability was proportional to $n^{\frac{1}{2}}$—a 10-fold improvement in reliability required a 100-fold increase in sample size. For many problems, random sampling was prohibitively expensive even with digital computers. The crucial statistical problem was finding ways of reducing the variance of an estimator for a given sample size. A number of these variance reduction methods are described in [19]. A particularly useful variance reduction technique known as the method of antithetic variates is described in Hammersley and Handscomb [11].

The concept of system simulation became a reality in the early 1950's, when there was a shift in emphasis from looking at parts of a problem to examining the simultaneous interactions of all parts. This shift was at least partially due to the fact that system simulation experiments had become feasible on digital computers, which were undergoing order-of-magnitude advances in speed. Simulation made it possible to carry out fully integated system analyses which were generally far too complex to be carried out analytically. This was especially true for studies of the interactions among parts of a system.

In the past decade, the ability to model complex systems has greatly improved. Specialized computer simulation languages (such as GPSS, SIMSCRIPT, and SIMULA) offer convenient formats for describing system problems. Along with the improvements, however, have come a number of statistical problems, few of which have been satisfactorily solved. In fact, some of them have not even been recognized yet as serious problems.

Verification, validation, and *problem analysis* are tasks demanding careful statistical consideration. *Verification* determines whether a model with a particular mathematical structure and data base actually behaves as an experimenter

assumes it does. *Validation* tests whether a simulation model reasonably approximates a real system. *Problem analysis* seeks to insure the proper execution of the simulation and proper handling of its results; consequently it deals with a host of matters: the concise display of solutions, efficient allocation of computer time, proper design of tests of comparison, and correct estimates of sample sizes needed for specified levels of accuracy.

In other words, verification and validation insure that a simulation model is properly designed; only after a model has been verified and validated can an experimenter justifiably use a model to probe system behavior. Problem analysis mainly deals with the results of experimental probing.

Of the remaining sections of this paper, Section II provides some necessary definitions and motivation; Sections III and IV discuss problems associated with the design and proof-testing of a simulation model, and Section V considers problems associated with the use of simulation models.

The format of the last three sections is: presentation of problems, brief discussion of advised solutions, references to relevant literature.

II. SIMULATION MODELS

The concepts discussed from here on can best be understood in the context of a typical simulation model. This section defines a number of terms used in succeeding sections, examines a typical model to show these terms in their proper context, and indicates some problem areas connected with model structure and data systems that should concern every model-builder.

Every simulation model comprises two systems—a data system and a logical system. Both present the model-builder with problems; both contribute equally to the validity of a final simulation model.

When we first look at a simulation model, we see its logical structure—the way in which a system's operations have been analyzed and factored into discrete units, and how these units are combined so that the model can be made to reproduce the system's behavior. When we look at a model more deeply, we see that it contains sequences of data comparisons and logical tests. These tests cause a model to take different actions depending on numerical values that are either input from the world outside its boundaries or computed within the model. The model's behavior is conditioned by these data values, and its results are sensitive to data representations and methods of data generation.

Consider the simple one-machine shop with a waiting line, shown in Figure 1. Items arrive at the machine for processing; the arrow coming from the left shows the jobs arriving with average *arrival rate* λ. If the machine is free when a job arrives, it immediately begins service, which is performed at an average *service rate* μ. A job that arrives when the machine is engaged waits in line until it can be processed. The waiting line is pictured as a box; in a real system it might be a tote box or a pile of partially completed parts. When a job is completed, it leaves the service facility (arrow going to the right) freeing the machine for another job. If jobs are waiting in the line (queue), one is selected for service according to a *queue discipline* and the machine is engaged again. If no jobs are waiting, the machine remains idle until the next job arrives.

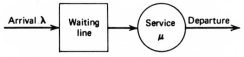

Figure 1   Simple machine-shop model.

Systems such as this, in which jobs arrive, possibly wait in queues, and are serviced, are called *queueing systems*. Almost all simulation models have queueing systems imbedded in them.

Simulating a system like the one described requires the definition of *events* that take place during its operation. Events occur at points in

time when system *activities* begin and end; if an activity has no duration, *e.g.*, a decision made at an instant in time, it only has one related event.

A gross representation of the logical structure of a queueing system is shown in Figure 2. The activities pictured are jobs arriving and jobs being serviced. Jobs arrive at the shop at random times. Let the first N jobs that arrive be denoted $j_1, j_2, ..., j_N$, and their arrival times be denoted $t_1, t_2, ..., t_N$. Then the times between job arrivals are: $d_1 = (t_1 - t_0), d_2 = (t_2 - t_1), ..., d_N = (t_N - t_{N-1})$. Inputs to the queueing system are simulated by *generating job arrivals* at the service facility; interarrival times rather than arrival times are usually used. When a job arrives, the time when the next job will arrive is computed *by random sampling from an interarrival time distribution.* Two data problems associated with this simulation are (1) determining the correct statistical sampling distribution and (2) generating random samples from it. Section IV discusses some problems concerned with selecting a sampling distribution. Methods for generating random samples from various statistical distributions can be found in references [4] and [24].

A sequence of job arrival times constitutes a sample from a *simulation input process.* Each arrival generates an interarrival time for the next job and a service time for itself. Figure 3 illustrates the arrival event in some detail, showing the sequence of simulation activities: the generation of an interarrival time and a service time and placement of a new arrival in process or in queue.[1]

When a job arrives, it is placed in service if the server is free; otherwise, it is placed in queue. Call the service times for the N jobs that

[1] The notation used in Figure 3 is taken from P. J. Kiviat, 1967, *Digital computer simulation: modeling concepts,* The Rand Corporation, RM-5378-PR.

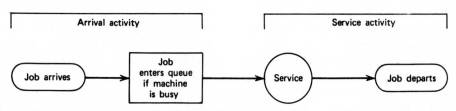

Figure 2   Basic queueing model.

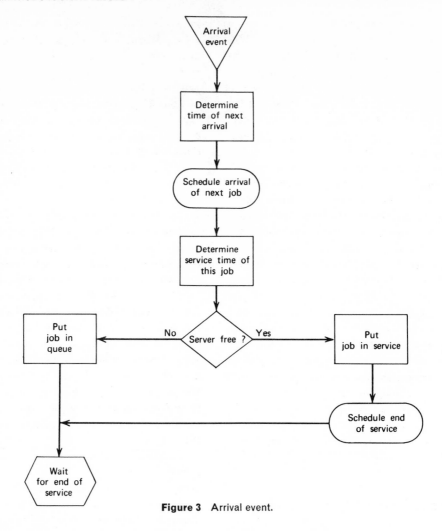

Figure 3 Arrival event.

enter the shop $s_1, s_2, ..., s_N$. The sequence of service times also constitutes a simulation input process, as random samples are drawn from some *service time distribution* whenever a job is processed. For each job that passes through the shop, two (random) quantities must be determined—d_i and s_i. The quantity d_i determines the time when a job enters the shop, and s_i determines the time it spends in process. In this model, both of the quantities d_i and s_i are generated when a job enters the shop; in a slightly modified version of the model the service time might not be generated until the job is actually put into service.

All simulation models are driven by some basic force, generally the arrival of a task, job, or request of some sort in the simulated system. Each job's progress through the system is

determined by two sets of factors: (1) its characteristics and (2) pressures exerted by the system. Job characteristics can be few or many; in our simple model there are two, an arrival time and a service time. These characteristics can be generated at one time or at different stages in a job's life as it passes through a simulated system. Regardless of where they are generated, they belong to a job and contribute to its simulated behavior.

A job with n characteristics can be described by a list of these characteristics, which we call an n-tuple. A job in our queueing model is characterized by a 2-tuple (d_i, s_i). A typical problem encountered when constructing a simulation model is the generation of job characteristics; an important problem encountered while checking out a simulation model is the examination of a sequence of generated *job characterizations*, as we call these *n*-tuples.

As figure 3 shows, a job does not necessarily have to pass directly through the shop; it can wait in line while other jobs are being processed. If T_i denotes the time that job i leaves the shop, then $w_i = T_i - t_i - s_i$ is the time it spends waiting for service. The sequences $T_1, T_2, ..., T_N$ and $w_1, w_2, ..., w_N$ are *simulation output processes*, sequences of variables whose values are determined by the activities that take place within the simulation model. If the model is designed so that certain jobs have priority over others, then low-priority jobs will have long waiting times; if it is designed with a service facility that shuts down periodically for repairs and rest periods, then the sequence of jobs that exit from the shop will reflect this.

A simulation model is designed to generate output processes that can be studied to observe a system's behavior as its data and/or logical structure are changed. Data influence a model through the selection of statistical sampling distributions, random sampling procedures, and *activity levels*. The rate at which jobs arrive and are serviced (λ and μ, respectively, in Figure 1) are activity levels that specify the intensity of system operations. Figures 3 and 4 illustrate some influences that model structure exerts on a simulation study.

The *operating rules* used to select a job from a waiting line clearly are part of the model structure and influence system behavior. A complex model generally contains many different kinds of operating rules; decision mechanisms, search-and-choice procedures, and scheduling heuristics are some that are found most frequently. We have chosen a queue discipline to illustrate the effect of an operating rule in a model. A rule under which jobs that have short processing times are selected first will produce a sequence of T_i's close to one another followed by sequences with greater values. The character of the output process will be different under this rule from the output under a rule that selects jobs in another way.

A simulation model must therefore be examined in two ways. Its data must be examined, both with respect to the particular representations chosen and the way the model selects samples in its simulation process; its structure

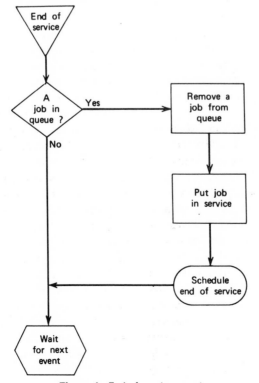

Figure 4   End of service event.

must be examined to see that mechanisms have been chosen that produce correct system response. Both data and structure are important; both pose statistical problems in analysis and evaluation. Section III treats in detail the problems outlined in the above example.

III. VERIFICATION

Data Verification

Inputs in most simulation experiments consist of jobs of some sort, each characterized by a sequence of random variables. In the simple queueing model each job is characterized by an interarrival time and a service time. Each job affects the system to an extent determined in part by the values of its corresponding 2-tuple. In general, simulation experiments measure the response of a system to different sequences of input n-tuples.

In most system simulation models the elements of job n-tuples are independent random variables, and sequences of n-tuples are independent multivariate random variables. The n-tuple elements are transformations of pseudo-random numbers drawn from a uniform distribution on the unit interval. To each n-tuple characterizing a job, there corresponds an n-tuple of uniformly distributed random variables. If the model design is proper, the elements of this latter n-tuple should be independent and uniformly distributed, and so should be the sequences of these n-tuples.

Absence of independence in generated samples implies that the assumptions of the model do not hold. Verifying assumptions of independence is the first statistical problem arising in system simulation experiments. Since the tests of independence in no way relate to proposed system structure, one may check the pseudorandom number generator separately from other considerations.

The most important hypothesis to test is that the pseudorandom number generator creates sequences of independent random variables. Suppose we collect m pseudorandom numbers. If we divide the unit interval into k class intervals and let x_i be the number of observations in interval i, then for sufficiently large m we may regard the statistic

$$X^2 = \frac{k}{m} \sum_{i=1}^{k} x_i^2 - m$$

as being χ^2 distributed with $(k-1)$ degrees of freedom.

Mann and Wald [17] who have studied the problem of choosing k according to some "best criterion," suggest

$$k = 4[2(m-1)^2/c^2]^{1/5}$$

where

$$(2\pi)^{-1/2} \int_{c}^{\infty} e^{-x^2/2} \, dx = \alpha$$

Cochran [1, 2] describes the sense in which this choice of k is best. For our purposes, the Mann and Wald criterion seems reasonable [17]. If X^2 exceeds $X^2_{k-1,\alpha}$, α being the confidence level we reject the hypothesis. This test or an equivalent one has been performed on most pseudorandom number generators and, therefore, our mentioning it is principally for completeness.

The χ^2 test also applies in testing the independence of n-tuples, but instead of working with the unit interval we divide the n-dimensional unit surface into k n-cubes of equal volume and define x_i as the number of n-tuples in the ith n-cube. MacLaren and Marsaglia [16] apply this test to the output of several pseudorandom number generators for pairs and triples. Their results show a number of standard generators to be suspect.

The χ^2 test concerns questions of randomness and makes no use of the way in which a particular method generates random numbers. Coveyou and MacPherson [5] who offer a unified theory of the statistical behavior of n-tuples of pseudorandom generators, conclude that currently there is no better method of generating n-tuples than the simple multiplicative congruence method, $r_{i+1} = r_i U(\bmod 2^p)$, with a carefully chosen multiplier, U. They describe how to choose the multiplier, and discuss the effects of computer word length on generated sequences.

A departure from the independence assumption can significantly affect experimental results. The following example illustrates this point. Let x and y be pseudorandom numbers that are suitably transformed; $g(x)$ is used as an interarrival time and $h(y)$ as a service time. Figure 5 shows the square over which the pair x, y are uniformly distributed.

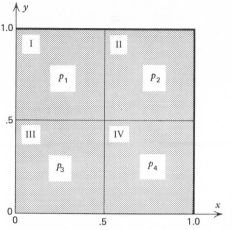

Figure 5 Space in which X and Y are jointly
distributed.

Let p_i be the probability of x, y being in the ith square. If pairs are independent, then

$$p_i = 1/4 \qquad i = 1, 2, .., 4.$$

Suppose, however, that p_1 is greater than $p_2, p_3,$ and p_4. If interarrival and service times are increasing functions of x and y, respectively, then we would expect short interarrival times and long service times to occur together more often than theory suggests. This would cause an upward bias in the waiting times and queue lengths observed in the simulation model.

In more complex models, the absence of independence among n-tuples is more difficult to assess. However, verifying that a data source satisfies the independence assumption will always be of value, if an incorrect interpretation of results is to be avoided. References [4], [5], and [16] offer helpful information to an experimenter in choosing a pseudorandom generator.

In some simulation experiments, correlated sampling is necessary. Suppose we are simulating the demand for aircraft tires; then tire wearout is clearly related to the number of aircraft landings. Simulations of economic behavior often contain autocorrelated input processes, e.g., autonomous investment. References [7] and [22] describe methods for generating correlated samples and [20] describes procedures for sampling from two kinds of autocorrelated processes.

Tocher [24] has pointed out that correlated sampling is often difficult to perform because of the onerous and often impossible task of collecting sufficient information to describe desired distributions. Verification and validation should clearly be applied to correlated sampling. The peculiar circumstances surrounding different kinds of correlated sampling make it difficult to suggest a generally applicable method. Since all sampling ultimately depends on sequences of independent uniformly distributed random numbers, the least that can be done is to test the hypothesis that successive numbers and sequences of numbers are independent.

Structure Verification

Verifying the structure of simulation models means examining substructure outputs and determining whether they behave acceptably. One value of this exercise is that it identifies unwanted system behavior. Very minor simplifying assumptions can generate output processes whose behavior differs considerably from what is desired. Structure verification is also valuable for determining whether one may substitute an analytical or simple simulation substructure for a complex one. This may be done if a behavioral equivalence can be established between the simple and complex structures. The advantages of substitution accrue from a better understanding of the analytic or simple simulation structure and from savings in computation time during simulation.

To make behavioral comparisons, we require a probability model. The model must be sufficiently general to include the variety of phenomena encountered in simulation models; yet it must be restrictive enough to permit reasonably straightforward hypothesis tesing. System simulations usually are concerned with series of interrelated events and an appropriate probability model must explicitly recognize interrelationships between past, present, and future events. Since these associations are time-dependent, we refer to them as intertemporal dependence.

In reference [10], the writers suggest the class of covariance stationary stochastic processes as a convenient model for studying simulation-generated time series. The reasons for this choice are the valuable conceptual insights that these processes afford as well as the ease with which certain of their sample statistics (principally the spectrum) can be used in hypothesis testing. We first formally define a covariance stationary process and then discuss the meaning of some of its population parameters.

Let X_t be a random variable generated by a simulation model and recorded at time t. If $\{X_t; t = 0, \pm 1, \pm 2, ., \pm \infty\}$ is a stochastic process such that $E(X_t X_{t+\tau})$ is finite and independent of t for all τ, then $\{X_t\}$ is *covariance stationary*. If the random variables X_t and $X_{t+\tau}$ are not independent for some $\tau \neq 0$, then $\{X_t\}$ is autocorrelated or linearly dependent. Output processes generally satisfy the covariance stationary assumptions and exhibit intertemporal dependence. The theory of covariance stationary processes provides a convenient framework within which to study the nature and extent of autocorrelation, the principal form of intertemporal dependence.

The *autocovariance function*

$$R_\tau = E(X_t X_{t+\tau}) - [E(X_t)]^2$$

summarizes all information concerning the autocorrelation present in $\{X_t\}$. The *spectrum*

$$g(\lambda) = (\pi)^{-1} \sum_{\tau = -\infty}^{\infty} R_\tau e^{-i\lambda\tau} \qquad 0 \leqslant \lambda \leqslant \pi$$

provides the same information and in the writers' opinion is the preferred function to examine both for conceptual and statistical reasons [10].

The autocovariance function R measures the covariance between the random variables X_t and $X_{t+\tau}$. For the class of processes with which we are concerned, this function diminishes, though not necessarily monotonically, as $|\tau|$ increases. This property accords with reality, where the influence of the past wears off as time elapses. The spectrum g permits us to study mean-square variation in a series of interrelated events in terms of a continuum of frequency components. Since

$$R_0 = \int_0^\pi g(\lambda)\, d\lambda,$$

we may regard the variance R_0 as being made up of infinitesimal contributions $g(\lambda)\, d\lambda$ in small bands $d\lambda$ around each frequency. The spectrum g may be considered a variance decomposition with each component being associated with a specific frequency. Low frequencies correspond to long fluctuations in $\{X_t\}$; high frequencies correspond to rapid fluctuations. If a peak occurs in a spectrum, the corresponding frequency influences the appearance of $\{X_t\}$ to a greater extent than the remaining frequencies. A process with a peak at a nonzero frequency in fact displays something of a periodic appearance with its period corresponding approximately to the frequency at which the peak appears.

When the subscript t denotes time and X_t is an observation at time t, observations are collected at equal intervals on the time axis. Since t is only an index, it need not necessarily refer to time; any series of events can generate a time series. For example, in the simple queueing problem t may denote the tth job to receive service, and X_t may be the waiting time of this job. Here $\{X_t\}$ is a series of waiting times arranged in the order in which their corresponding jobs receive service.

Interactions between input and structure may often create unwanted periodicities in the output. This possibility is not as remote as one would like to think, for Slutzky [23] long ago showed that the linear summation of purely random events can appear regularly periodic. Since peaks in a spectrum correspond to periodic components in $\{X_t\}$ and, since the sharper a peak is, the more regular its periodicity is, examining the sample spectrum permits an experimenter to determine whether any periodicities exist and to estimate the extent of their regularity.

Figure 6 shows the sample spectrum of queue length for a single-server queueing model with exponentially distributed interarrival times and constant service time. The peak at 0.05 cycles per hour and its harmonics suggest the presence of periodicity. This behavior can be explained as follows. Whenever jobs are queueing, a periodic reduction in queue length occurs every 20 hours. With a constant service time, jobs emerge from the service facility at a fixed periodic rate, creating a periodic appearance. If this efflux is the input to another service facility, then this input is periodic whenever jobs are queueing in the first facility.

Two points motivate our concern about periodicities. First, their presence may be contrary to our intentions. Second, since the output of one substructure is usually the input

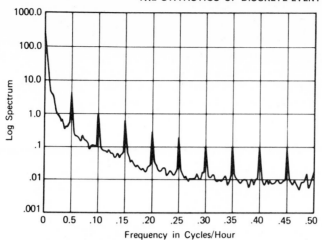

Figure 6 Estimated queue-length spectrum with constant service time.

to another, the effects of periodicity may propogate themselves throughout the remaining substructures. It is a property of substructures that they exhibit the characteristics of electromechanical systems and can have a natural or a resonant frequency. If a substructure is excited by a frequency close to its natural one, its response at that frequency is considerably exaggerated compared to that of others. The strength of a periodic component may therefore increase as it propogates through a system, obscuring the behavior of remaining components.

Conclusions drawn from the output of such a system may then be misleading. For example, one might suppose that the inputs to certain model subsystems are random phenomena, whereas they actually appear in a model as regular or strongly periodic impulses. If this is so, rules appropriate for controlling randomly varying inputs may be judged inappropriate. The performance of the rules will be judged in an environment different from that for which they were designed.

As mentioned earlier, economy of detail aids understanding and saves computation time. The ease with which computer simulation languages permit one to describe complex behavior carries with it the danger of too much detail. Since a detailed model has more built-in assumptions than a simple model, it generally requires a longer learning period for a prospective user. In addition, simulating these details can consume vast amounts of computer time. If several models offer the same response to a given input,

the simplest model is advantageous. It is desirable to test several models to determine the adequacy of each and then choose the simplest among the acceptable ones.

Suppose that a complex model behaves as required and that we wish to test the equivalence of a simpler model. If at all possible, the simpler model should be compared with the true environment. When this cannot be done, the responses of the simple and complex models should be compared for a given input. The comparison tests the hypothesis that certain population characteristics (for example, means, variances or spectra) are identical for both models.

Since intertemporal dependence is often an important characteristic of models, and since its mean-square variation is described by the spectrum, one may compare mean-square intertemporal dependence by testing the equivalence of spectra of two models. Jenkins [15] and Fishman and Kiviat [10] describe an appropriate testing procedure.

While it is true that higher-order effects may be dissimilar in the two models, a comparison of spectra can do much toward determining whether further comparisons are useful. The test is simple. In addition, when the null hypothesis of no difference is rejected, the comparison of spectra permits one to identify where in the structures of the two models the departures occur. With this knowledge, one may perhaps modify the simple structure to more closely match the complex one.

Verifying a model's structure protects an

experimenter against creating anomalous responses, allows for a justifiably simple design, and saves computer time. It is a natural imperative to verify both data and structure before a model is used in order to minimize complications that can arise in the course of an experiment. Failure to verify has created more than one embarrassing situation in interpreting output.

IV. VALIDATION

Data Validation

Validating a model means establishing that it resembles its actual system reasonably well. If a model describes some hypothetical system, then no validation can occur. Also, if no numerical data exist for an actual system, it is not possible to establish the quantitative congruence of a model with reality. The ideas of this section therefore only apply when numerical data exist for some or all of an actual system.

Sampling from a theoretical rather than an empirical distribution is generally considered preferable, since it exposes a simulated system to the universe of possible stimuli rather than merely to those that have occurred in the past. Often, graphical methods suffice to judge the validity of theoretical distributions. If, for example, we assume that data have the exponential distribution, then we would expect the cumulative empirical distribution to appear linear on semilogarithmic paper. If the normal distribution is assumed, we would expect the cumulative empirical distribution to appear linear on normal probability paper. Graphic examination is easy and revealing. Whenever applicable, it should be used.

The χ^2 test is often proposed for testing the appropriateness of a chosen sampling distribution, but Cochran [2], among other writers, has shown the inadequacy of this test when the sample size of the empirical data is limited and the theoretical distribution is skewed. As an alternative, Cochran suggests the variance test, which generally has greater power than the χ^2 goodness-of-fit test and does away with the need for class intervals.

As an example, we describe the variance test when the null hypothesis is that a set of independent observations $\{x_i, i = 1, 2, ..., N\}$ came

from an exponential distribution with parameter λ. Under this hypothesis we have

$$E(x_i) = 1/\lambda, \qquad \text{var}(x_i) = 1/\lambda^2$$

As our estimate of λ we use the maximum likelihood estimator

$$\hat{\lambda} = N / (\sum_{i=1}^{N} x_i)$$

The test statistic is

$$\sum_{i=1}^{N} \frac{(x_i - 1/\hat{\lambda})^2}{(1/\hat{\lambda}^2)}$$

which is approximately distributed as χ^2 with $(N-1)$ degrees of freedom. No class intervals are required in this test.

The χ^2 and variance tests both assume independent observations, an assumption that also simplifies Monte Carlo sampling. While its convenience for testing is apparent, the credibility of this assumption is seldom tested. If a sample record is "sufficiently long," one may estimate its spectrum and compare it with the uniform spectrum for an uncorrelated process.

For short records, spectrum comparisons are not possible. Here we suggest using nonparametic tests of randomness which do not require an investigator to make any assumptions about the underlying distribution of sample data. In addition, the appropriateness of the tests do not depend on the sample being large. Walsh [25] lists a number of nonparametric tests that can be applied to small samples.

The term "sufficiently long" has an irritating quality about it for simulation experimenters. Seldom is enough prior information available to estimate how long to run an experiment. Nevertheless, most writers on the statistical analysis of simulation experiments take the length of the sample record as adequate for the analyses they propose. In reference [9] a two-stage technique is described wherein one may estimate how long an experiment is to be run. The procedure is integrated into a test comparing means, but this should pose no problem in determining run lengths alone.

Structure Validation

Having tested assumptions about the data, there remains the task of validating the structure. If a model resembles reality fairly well, we expect that its simulated response to a simulated, but valid, input should exhibit behavior similar to that observed for the real system. A spectrum analysis is again instructive. Testing the homogeneity of spectra, one test for the actual system's output and the other for the simulated system's output, is easily accomplished as described in references [10] and [15].

The spectrum comparison applies to testing the homogeneity of the autocorrelation structure. Comparing means is also desirable since we would expect no difference if the simulation model adequately resembles the true system. Since the output processes are generally autocorrelated, a comparison of means requires more work and care than in the case of independent observations.

The procedures in reference [8] can easily be modified to compare the means of the simulated and real systems. The variance of the sample mean is shown to be proportional to the spectrum at zero frequency and, hence, testing means and testing spectra show a number of common features.

Validation, while desirable, is not always possible. Each investigator has the soul-searching responsibility of deciding how much importance to attach to his results. When no experience is available for comparison, an investigator is well advised to proceed in steps, first implementing results based on simple well-understood models and then using the results of this implementation to design more sophisticated models that yield stronger results. It is only through gradual development that a simulation can make any claim to approximate reality. Large-scale models that are not amenable to validation often lead to perplexing, if not misleading, results. This occurs partly because the complexity of a system confuses a model-builder and partly because of the tenuous nature of results based on cascaded approximations. Despite its difficulty, effort must be expended on model validation—first, to give credence to results within the validated range of model operations, and, second, to instill confidence in extrapolations beyond the range of model experience.

Verifying and validating a model comprise but a small share of the statistical problems in a simulation experiment. Once an experimenter accomplishes them, he can begin to exercise his model to get answers. His purpose is to collect data, reduce them, and make inferences about them, as efficiently as possible. We classify the statistical problems he encounters under problem analysis. The way he solves these problems strongly influences the quality of his results.

V. PROBLEM ANALYSIS

One purpose of system simulation experiments is to compare system responses to different operating rules. In the simple queueing problem, for example, we may wish to compare the mean queue lengths caused by given arrival and service rates when different rules are used to assign priorities to jobs. Another purpose is to determine functional relationships between input factors and system response. We may simply wish to get a "feel" for the way in which input and output relate, or we may wish to use a determined functional relationship in a further analysis. For example, we may determine a functional relationship when all inputs are unrestricted and then use this relationship to find the maximum response when constraints are placed on the inputs. In some studies, both purposes enter. For simplicity, we treat them separately.

Regardless of purpose, there are several statistical questions common to all problem analyses and to structural verification and validation as well. One question relates to the choice of sampling interval: What is the proper interval of simulated time between successive observations of a process of interest? Another question is: How can results be obtained efficiently with a given reliability? This topic is often discussed under the heading of "variance reduction techniques." Reliability estimation itself poses another statistical problem in system simulation experiments that must be solved before one can determine how long to run an experiment.

Other statistical questions are peculiar to particular kinds of experiments. When comparing experiments, one requires statistical testing procedures. When relating response to input, one asks where in the input ranges it is best to measure response so that its functional form can be most easily identified and its parameters most reliably estimated.

Measurements made in a simulation experiment can be of two kinds. One kind measures a system's response to all possible situations. Here the relevant statistic is a time-integrated average. The other measures a system's response to a specific set of initial conditions. Time-integrated averages appear to be the most common measurement. The simulation literature is principally concerned with them, and the discussion here retains this emphasis. The reader should not conclude from this that measurement of response to initial conditions is unimportant. In particular the lack of literature on the subject should be taken as a comment on its specialized nature, not its worth. As the use of simulation increases, there will be more concern for measurements of this kind and more will be written about them. As indicated, the discussion from here on will be of experiments performed with the first kind of measurements in mind. The remainder of this section uses the terms "time-integrated average" and "sample mean" interchangeably.

Sampling Interval

When t denotes time, the meaning of a time-integrated average is clear. When t is a more general ordering index, a time-integrated average refers to the mean value of a quantitative characteristic of a series of events indexed on t. The term time-integrated average remains appropriate since the ordering of events is related to time.

If the index denotes time, then the choice of sampling interval is crucial if we hope to extract useful information about the auto-correlation structure of a process in an efficient way. For our purposes a sampling interval should be small enough so that within it a process changes little, if at all. Process activity, not chronological time, dictates the choice of sampling interval. For each experiment, other than replications, it is wise to check the adequacy of the sampling interval, since too small an interval causes redundancy in the data and too large an interval loses information. Biasing an interval downward is more desirable than biasing it upward, since redundant data are far less harmful than lost information.

When t denotes an event in an ordered series, the role of the sampling interval is changed. Since we simply collect an observation every time an event occurs, it would seem that we could avoid choosing a sampling interval. It may occur, however, that successive events are so highly correlated that collecting information on each event is highly redundant. When this is the case a judicious choice of sampling interval reduces the number of observations without sacrificing any significant information.

Variance Reduction Techniques

It is naturally of interest to obtain experimental results with specified reliability at minimum cost. Development of variance reduction techniques was in fact the principal statistical activity in the early days of computer simulation (Monte Carlo) experiments. The importance of this activity continues to grow with the increasing complexity of experiments and their concomitant consumption of computer time.

Hammersley and Handscomb [11] discuss several variance-reduction techniques, among which the method of antithetic variates appears easiest to apply, and in [11, p. 20] show its use in a simulated queueing problem. Briefly, by generating ξ, a uniformly distributed random number, in one replication of an experiment and generating $1 - \xi$ in a second replication, the method induces negative correlation between the responses obtained in both replications. The variance of the average response of the two replications is consequently smaller than it would be if the replications were independent. Antithetic variates may also be used with more than two replications.

When the comparison of experiments is the purpose of a simulation exercise, one may improve the efficiency of the data-gathering procedure in another way. When testing the difference of two means, for example, one may reduce the variance of the difference by choosing the sample sizes as functions of the variances of the individual sample means, the computer times required to collect one observation in each experiment, and the degree of correlation between the sample means. Inducing a positive correlation between the sample means reduces the variance of their difference. This can be done, in some cases, by using the same set of random numbers for both experiments.

As mentioned in section IV, the choice of the number of observations to collect in each experiment is a major influence in minimizing the computer time needed to meet a specified level of accuracy. The two-stage procedure given in reference [9] offers a reasonably straightforward way of coming close to the most efficient sample sizes. When the sample sizes are chosen close to the efficient solution, a major saving in computer time accrues.

Estimating Reliability

Since experimental results are random variables, it is important that their reliability as estimates of population parameters be stated explicitly. Failure to do so obscures the fact that some results may be better than others. In addition, omitting reliability measures makes it impossible to determine how much longer to run an experiment in order to improve its reliability by some fixed amount.

Variance reduction techniques permit us to reduce the computer time necessary to obtain a result with a given reliability. We must also have a way of estimating the reliability of a result. This has long been a major problem area in simulation experiments.

If a sampling interval is chosen so that observations are independent, then the variance of a time-integrated average or sample mean is simply the population variance divided by T, the number of observations. In general, since simulation data are autocorrelated, the above approach requires finding a sampling interval such that successive observations are reasonably independent. Mechanic and McKay [18] have investigated this approach.

If, however, one treats a simulated process as a covariance stationary stochastic process (which it generally is), then the variance of the mean is $\pi g(0)/T$ where the function g is defined in section III, and T is the length of the simulation run. A procedure for estimating $g(0)$ is given in reference [8], but unfortunately it cannot easily be incorporated into the experimental run itself.

Another approach is to sum sample means from independent replications of the same experiment. The variance of this sum is, of course, inversely proportional to the number of replications. Using antithetic variates can reduce the variance even more by inducing negative correlation between sample means.

Comparison of Experiments

In an experiment, response is generally a large-sample, time-integrated average that satisfies the conditions for asymptotic normality. This fact greatly simplifies testing the difference of two means obtained under different operating rules, since the difference of the sample means is also asymptotically normal. Let the subscripts 1 and 2 denote experiments 1 and 2, respectively. Then for a given significance level α and tolerance δ, we have, under the null hypothesis of no difference in the means

$$\text{prob}(|\bar{X}_1 - \bar{X}_2| \leq \delta) = 1 - \alpha.$$

To test the null hypothesis, we require reasonably accurate estimates of the variances of the sample means. These can be obtained by procedures described in reference [9].

The comparison just described is the one most commonly applied in the analysis of experimental results. Multiple comparisons and ordering procedures are desirable when more than two sets of operating rules are being considered. Their appropriate statistical procedures are found in texts on the analysis of variance. To our knowledge, no study has yet appeared that makes a substantive contribution toward adapting these procedures to the peculiar environment of computer simulation experiments.

Response Measurement

In comparing experiments, one is concerned with the response of a system to different qualitative factors, such as operating rules. Alternatively, one may examine the system's response under given operating rules to changes in quantitative factors, such as different input activity levels. We refer to this analysis as response measurement. Its purpose is to find a functional form relating the variable parameters of an input process to an observed output, and to estimate the coefficients of the functional form.

Consider a simulation with one input x and one output y. For each experiment, x assumes a fixed value that is known exactly, whereas y assumes a value from a probability distribution whose parameters are functions of x; y is a random variable. In a queueing problem x might be the mean arrival rate and y the sample mean number of jobs in queue. If, for estimation purposes, we use the linear least-squares method, our functional relationship for the ith observation is

$$Y_i = \alpha + \beta X_i + \varepsilon_i$$

$$X_i = f(x_i)$$

$$Y_i = f(y_i)$$

To derive the best linear unbiased estimates of α and β with the linear least-squares method, we require

$$E(\varepsilon_i) = 0$$

$$E(\varepsilon_i \varepsilon_j) = 0, \qquad i \neq j$$

$$\mathrm{var}(Y_i) = c \qquad \text{for all } i$$

Some commonly used function forms are listed below.

	$f(x)$	$f(y)$
1	x	y
2	$\log x$	y
3	x	$\log y$
4	$\log x$	$\log y$

For a correctly chosen graph-paper form, the relationship between $f(x)$ and $f(y)$ will appear linear. Linear, semilog, and log-log graph paper may be used to find which relationship is most appropriate. Other forms may be examined, but for the moment we assume that one of the above forms will hold. Hoerl [14] describes several techniques for identifying the functional form that linearizes the relationship between x and y.

It is convenient to distinguish between two kinds of observations: those collected to determine the appropriate functional form, and those collected to estimate α and β with a given level of accuracy. The first set is a subset of the second.

To satisfy the above regression model, we require all y_i's to be independent and have a common variance. Independence can be gained by using different random number sequences in successive simulation runs with each set of input activity levels. For a given variance, the proper

length of a simulated run may be estimated by the two-stage procedure to which we have already alluded.

To find a functional form it is necessary to take observations for a number of input activity levels within the range of activity levels being considered. As one would expect, the number of such observations is inversely related to the variance of the observations. The more reliable the observations, the more confidence one can place in having identified an appropriate functional form for a given number of observations.

Once an appropriate functional form is found, one uses the observations already collected to estimate the coefficients. Additional observations may be collected and used to improve the reliability of the estimates. The objective at this step is efficiency—the conservation of computer time. If the computer times required to collect all y_i's with equal variance are the same, taking additional observations at the ends of the x range minimizes the computer time necessary to improve the reliability of the estimated coefficients by a given amount. In general, the computer times required to collect observations with common variance do differ, and, hence, the choice of where to collect observations is not simple. Little, if anything, has been published about this problem. Its solution will undoubtedly improve the efficient performance of simulation experiments.

It may occur that *a priori* theory suggests a model of the form,

$$Y_i = \alpha + \sum_{j=1}^{N} \beta_j X_i^j + \varepsilon_i$$

This model, unlike the one above, does not exclusively take observations at the end points of the independent variable range to minimize the sample size needed for a given accuracy. The points at which observations should be taken are given by the zeros of a polynomial which is the integral of one of the Legendre polynomials [13].

Response surface exploration, optimum seeking methods, and sequential experimentation are all topics germane to the analysis of computer simulation experiments. Cochran and Cox [3] describe the principles of response surface methodology, and Hill and Hunter [12] list a number of papers covering different aspects of the topic. Draper and Smith [6] describe procedures for applying a variety of linear regression analyses. Wilde [26] describes simple methods for finding maxima and minima. Cochran and Cox also discuss sequential experimentation. Although these methods contribute significantly to the statistical analysis of experiments, they remain to be integrated into a general procedure that takes due cognizance of the peculiarities of computer simulation experiments.

REFERENCES

1. W. G. Cochran, 1952. The χ^2 test of goodness of fit. *Annals of Mathematical Statistics, 23*(3): 315–345.
2. W. G. Cochran, 1954. Some methods for strengthening the common χ^2 tests. *Biometrics, 10*(4): 417–451.
3. W. G. Cochran, and G. M. Cox, 1950. *Experimental designs.* New York: Wiley, second edition, 1957.
4. A. Colker, F. A. Sorenson, M. L. Wolfson, and S. Zionts, 1962. *The generation of random samples from common statistical distributions.* Working paper, United States Steel Corporation Applied Research Laboratory, Report 25.17-016(1).
5. R. R. Coveyou, and R. D. MacPherson, 1967. Fourier analysis of uniform random number generators. *Journal of the Association for Computing Machinery, 14*(1): 100–119.
6. N. R. Draper, and H. Smith, 1966. *Applied regression analysis.* New York: Wiley.
7. E. C. Fieller, T. Lewis, and E. S. Pearson, 1955. *Correlated random normal deviates.* London: Cambridge University Press.
8. G. S. Fishman, 1967. Problems in the statistical analysis of simulation experiments: the comparison of means and the length of sample records. *Communications of the ACM, 10*(2): 94–99. MS.
9. G. S. Fishman, 1968. The allocation of computer time in comparing simulation experiments. *Operations Research, 16*(2): 280-295. See the erratum in *Operations Research, 16*(5): 1087. MS.
10. G. S. Fishman, and P. J. Kiviat, 1967. The analysis of simulation-generated time series. *Management Science, 13*(7): 525–557. MS.
11. J. M. Hammersley and D. C. Handscomb, 1964. *Monte Carlo methods.* New York: Wiley. MS.
12. W. J. Hill, and W. G. Hunter, 1966. A review of response surface methodology: a literature survey. *Technometrics, 8*(4): 571–590.
13. P. G. Hoel, 1958. Efficiency problems in polynomial estimation. *Annals of Mathematical Statistics, 29*(4): 1134–1145.
14. A. E. Hoerl, Jr., 1954. Fitting curves to data. *Chemical business handbook* (J. H. Perry, ed.); New York: McGraw-Hill, 20.55–20.77.
15. G. M. Jenkins, 1961. General considerations in the analysis of spectra. *Technometrics, 3*(2): 133–166.
16. M. D. MacLaren, and G. Marsaglia, 1965. Uniform random number generators. *Journal of the Association for Computing Machinery, 12*(1): 83–89.
17. H. B. Mann, and A. Wald, 1942. On the choice of the number of class intervals in the application of the chi square test. *Annals of Mathematical Statistics, 13*(3): 306–317.
18. H. Mechanic and W. McKay, 1966. *Confidence intervals for averages of dependent data in simulations II.* Working paper, IBM Advanced Systems Development Division, TR-17-202. MS.
19. H. A. Meyer, ed., 1956. *Symposium on Monte Carlo methods.* New York: Wiley.
20. T. H. Naylor, J. L. Balintfy, D. S. Burdick, and K. Chu, 1966. *Computer simulation techniques.* New York: Wiley. MG.
21. E. S. Page, 1965. On Monte Carlo methods in congestion problems. *Operations Research, 13*(2): 291–305. MS.
22. G. K. Pakov, 1960. *Generation of a random correlated quantity on a high-speed electronic computer.* Washington: U.S. Joint Publications Research Service, JPRS-5784.
23. E. Slutzky, 1937. The summation of random causes as the source of cyclic processes. *Econometrics, 5*(2): 105–146.
24. K. D. Tocher, 1963. *The art of simulation.* Princeton: Van Nostrand. MS.
25. J. E. Walsh, 1962. *Handbook of nonparametric statistics.* Princeton: Van Nostrand.
26. D. J. Wilde, 1964. *Optimum seeking methods.* Englewood Cliffs, N.J.: Prentice-Hall.

30

PROBLEMS OF COMPUTER SIMULATION[1]

NICO H. FRIJDA

Computer simulation of psychological processes has proved itself an important tool in the development of psychological theory. A number of successful programs parallel human problem-solving, pattern-recognition, or other behavior. Yet several methodological issues make it difficult to appreciate the contribution of these programs to psychology. In this paper some of these issues are discussed.

It may be useful to repeat the different functions in which computer simulation can be of value. First, computer programs can serve as unambiguous formulations of a theory. The program language is precise: the meaning of a given process is fully defined by what it does. Moreover, programming principles such as looping, nesting, and recursion enable one to express clearly complicated processes. Such programming already operates at the level of flow charting.

Second, computer simulation is a means to demonstrate and test the consistency and sufficiency of a theory. If the behavioral data which the theory wants to explain are in fact reproduced by running the program, the theory

SOURCE: Reprinted from *Behavioral Science, 12* (1): 59–67 (1967).
[1] This paper is based on a contribution to the Round Table Discussion on Computers in Psychology at the 15th International Conference of Applied Psychology.

has been proved capable of explaining these facts. Moreover, running the program under a variety of conditions may generate consequences of the theory which can be tested against new evidence. These consequences may be unforeseen and they may be quite important—such as the discovery of performance fluctuations without the introduction of stochastic elements [4]. Extensive experimentation is possible by running different versions of the program; decreasing or increasing fit with behavioral data can indicate the role of various components and parameters. An example is Gelernter's geometry program which was run with and without the diagram-based inference heuristic, with resulting difference in capability [7].

Third, computer simulation may serve as a heuristic in the search for models. The effort of getting a computer to perform a given task may lead to illuminating psychological hypotheses, even if no behavioral evidence has been taken into account. Moreover, a program which solves problems is by that sole virtue a candidate for a model and deserves the psychologists' attention. After all, proving theorems or recognizing patterns was until recently uniquely human or animal.

Computer programming principles of non-psychological origins may as such suggest psychological models. The TOTE is a clear example [12]; Yntema's model of immediate memory is another [20]. To regard problem solving as the functioning of sets of programs owes its existence, or at least a renewed impetus, to the way computers have been made to work.

Another source of psychological hypotheses resides in the necessity, evident during programming, to introduce specific conditions or auxiliary mechanisms. It may appear, for instance, that a given process can be realized only if the program is able to retain its prior efforts or to perform a given generalization. A theory may sound fine and plausible, but usually it is difficult to see what is needed to make it work. In the neuro-psychological field the simulation of Hebb's cell assemblies has demonstrated this quite clearly [17]. As a matter of fact, one of the most important functions of computer simulation resides in uncovering the implications of a theory. By implications we mean here: necessary assumptions or conditions without which the process could not be realized in the way desired.

In order to appreciate the contribution of a given simulation effort to psychological knowledge, there should be clarity in two respects. On the one hand, the relation of program to theory should be clear; otherwise it is not possible to make conclusions about theory adequacy on the basis of program success or failure. On the other hand, the criteria for correspondence between program output and observable behavior should be explicit; otherwise no evaluation of simulation success, and thereby of the program, can be made. I shall discuss the methodological issues in both problems.

THE RELATION BETWEEN PROGRAM AND THEORY

According to some formulations in the literature, a program *is* a theory. This seems an incorrect way of putting things. Rather, a program *represents* a theory. It does this with the help of a number of mechanisms which are irrelevant to the theory or which the theory might explicitly disclaim. The lower order subroutines and a number of technical necessities are determined by the particularities of the programming language, the mode of operation of the particular computer, and the special limitations

inherent in serially operating digital machines. Many operations, too, are just shortcuts for convenience or results of ignorance about the psychological mechanisms involved. Random selection by means of random number generators, scanning of serial lists to find a certain alternative, use of counters to check on capacities such as permissible depth or effort, or setting of a fixed number of working storage cells are examples.

Much in the program, then, is not theory. This has methodological consequences. Although parts of the program do not belong to the psychological theory, nothing in the program indicates when this is the case, and when it is not. Nothing in the program indicates from what level onward it is meant to be theory, and up to what level disagreement with psychological data or psychological plausibility is of no concern.

If the program does not show what is theory, the program's author has to. We are dependent upon the author's explicit statement of which routines embody his theory and how and under what conditions they function. Serious problems of communication arise in this connection. Descriptions of programs are usually presented in a discursive manner. Processes are described in more or less informal language and in a rather global way. Presentation is apt to be about as vague as in purely verbal theories. There is full loss of the program clarity, and it seems that one of the main advantages of computer simulation —unambiguous theory formulation—disappears at the moment it should manifest itself. One must take the author's word that the loosely indicated processes do what they are supposed to do and that what they do is what the theory prescribed. One must, moreover, take his word that the processes do what they are supposed to do *in the way and under the conditions stated.* By this proviso I mean without additional mechanisms not mentioned in the description. I will return to this point. Examples may be found in the most unsuspected quarters. One, for instance, is present in Simon and Kotovsky's otherwise beautiful paper on their letter series completion program [18]. "The pattern generator seeks periodicity in the sequence by looking for a relation that repeats at regular intervals" (p. 540), and "If this kind of periodicity is not found, the pattern generator looks for a relation that is interrupted at regular intervals" (p. 540) are the only descriptive statements concerning the main process of the program. It is true that the program is available for closer and convincing inspection. Few, however, understand the language and the programs are not easily obtained.

Finding a solution to this communication problem is not a simple matter. Global, informal description usually negates the benefits of computer simulation. Publishing the program itself, of course, is neither feasible nor useful. The best road seems to lie midway between the two. It will in general be possible to describe the relevant processes unambiguously by naming the subroutines concerned, by stating their precise input and output conditions, the conditions of their activation, and the transformations they achieve. It will in general also be possible to do this completely—in the sense of mentioning all tests, parameters, and so forth upon which these outputs depend—without leaving the level of theoretically relevant subroutines and without descending into technical detail. The original report on EPAM [4] and the latest report on the General Problem Solver [13] contain presentations of this kind.

This recommendation hides two requirements. The first is that the program structure reflects the structure of the theory. A description as meant here will be possible only if the program has been written in terms of independent, theory-relevant routines; only under this condition, that is, can one make sure that the description is faithful. The theory-relevant routines must, so to speak, be isolated from theoretically irrelevant auxiliary operations and must be as independent of technical realizations as possible. The goal is to specify fully the functions of each routine even without relating anything of the mode of operation of the lower order subroutines. Simulation programs are usually organized in this way—or reorganized if the original plan was jumbled [1]—but published work tends to follow this organization only incompletely.

The second requirement is quite important, though few published reports meet it. It is that the statement of the theoretically important program segments should contain all details about auxiliary operations and other conditions (such as memory storage registers or counters) which influence or codetermine the operation of the main routines.

Let us take an example. The success of GPS with logic tasks is highly dependent upon the ordering of the difference between present and desired state; or, Simon and Kotovsky's program [18] needs, for really successful operation, some fairly sophisticated routines to check on the correctness of its hypotheses. Since these features collaborate in determining the program's success or the success of the simulation effort, and since they do this at the same level as the main subroutines, they belong to the theory. Therefore, they should not only be mentioned; they should be stated explicitly as parts of the theory, if not in the specific form they have in the program, then at least in general functional terms.

Not to do so is not only misleading, it is also unwise. As indicated before, programming points to the implications of a given model. This can be one of the principal gains of computer simulation, which should not be lost or devaluated. For instance, natural language understanding by means of predicative analysis necessitates a series of specific memory cells for holding unfinished propositional phrases such as adverbs in search of a verb [10]. Here are implications as to memory load, then. As another example, recursive problem-solving routines, such as in the older version of GPS, presuppose elaborate retention of intermediate results in order to enable retracing of steps in case of failure [13], a presupposition whose psychological realism is doubtful. Or again, learning in a communication network proves possible only when behavior changes are based upon general strategies called "impatience" and "persistence," and not when based upon simple reinforcement of useful behaviors [11]. This major result of simulation effort is mentioned by its author only in passing; but such implications should serve as starting points for further research and tests of the validity of the model.

Details of this sort—the influence of auxiliary operations or even the specific mode of operation of the major routines—are in general hardly discussed. Simon and Kotovsky [18], for instance, do not describe the nature of the differences which distinguish the several versions of their program. These differences could have been one of the most interesting points of their study. Lack of necessary detail in program presentations is, I think, a shortcoming of very wide and general occurrence. In the case of simulation programs, it seriously detracts from the value of the work; performance as such is not so important here as convincing the reader that the reasons for this performance are plausible. Lack of information impairs the effect which computer simulation could have on psychology as a whole.

THE RELATION BETWEEN OUTPUT AND BEHAVIOR

Evaluation of program performance, the second major problem area, involves two activities: evaluation of the program's contribution to psychology; and evaluation of the fit between program output and behavior. These two, value of the theory and predictive accuracy, are separate in this case.

First, the value of a program as the embodiment of a theory depends largely upon the generality of the processes involved, upon the number of ad hoc assumptions and preprogrammed niceties. The theory of problem solving incorporated in GPS gains in appeal to the extent that the program was successful in several different problem areas. The program remains unconvincing qua theory to the extent that its success may depend upon similarities in task structure among a still quite limited set of mathematical tasks.

As for the fit between output and behavior, value, or fruitfulness for that matter, is of course highly dependent upon it. It is a function not only of degree of fit but also of number of correspondencies between output and behavior. There can be correspondence with respect to problem solution only, or to quantitative performance measures also—time, errors, orders of difficulty—or even to details of the process by which solution is sought or reached—introspections or intermediate results, such as used in Feldman's binary choice program [6] and in GPS [14].

The kind of correspondence one tries to achieve depends upon the nature of the tasks simulated and upon the intent of the investigator. With the more automatic processes such as recognition [19], immediate memory [2], or serial reproduction [5], performance measures and solution achievement are the only human output data available. For some purposes solution achievement is a sufficient criterion even with more complex tasks and even when some data process would conflict with some features of the machine process. Several question-answering programs, for example, are only simulations in so far as they prove that correct answers to questions in natural language can be produced by means of specific mechanisms. These mechanisms include the use of implication-rich data models in the case of SAD SAM [10], of search schemata in baseball [8], or of single relational representations and transitivity rules in SIR [16]. They are helpful for giving this proof, and for demonstrating the limitations and implications of the respective models.

DETAILED PROCESS SIMULATION

Sometimes one would want to reproduce not only the workings of one or two mechanisms but also the full stream of behavior during a given type of mental activity. One tries to achieve reproduction of the details of the process. Computer simulation seems ideally suited to so complex a task.

Efforts for mirroring this stream of behavior exist, with Newell, Shaw, and Simon's General Problem Solver [15], as the major example. The machine protocol was placed side by side with human protocols, and two or three comparisons were published. Laughery and Gregg's [9] paper is one of the few clear instances of program construction on the basis of protocol analysis. So is Feldman's work on binary choice. Besides these studies, very little attempt has been made to relate protocol data and programs systematically. Programs are usually constructed by drawing ideas from gross behavioral evidence. Analyzing introspective reports in systematic fashion has seldom been practised, at least to judge from published reports. This is a pity. Introspection gathered in a systematic way, this standby of the psychology of old, might play its role anew, precisely because programs can be fitted step by step from the protocol and reproduced.

To illustrate this approach, let me refer to the work which is in progress at the psychology laboratory of Amsterdam University. It concerns simulation of human information storage and retrieval.

We plunge, somewhere, into the mass of phenomena. We give our subjects some task and ask for introspection, in the traditional way of the Würzburgers. We ask, for instance, informal definition of concepts such as "What does 'lucidity' mean?" or "What is a cigarette?" We obtain protocols such as: "Eh, what is a cigarette . . . that is a long . . . thin object with white paper around it, and with tobacco in it, used to . . . be smoked for pleasure. Boy, what a complicated statement. I just see it, a vague kind of image. After saying that about white paper, I thought about cigarettes with yellow maize paper in France after the war, and then I thought of marihuana cigarettes. I had to search for the expression 'for pleasure'; I tried to classify things which you have just for fun. Also after describing the shape, I thought, now I should classify the function."

We try to transform this output into a program-oriented process description first by converting it into a series of short, simple statements containing the solution efforts, and second, by constructing a program-like description. In constructing the description, we try as much as possible to account for process comments such as "I just see it," "What a complicated statement," "I had to search for the expression." Comments such as these point, however vaguely, to the processes going on: verbal control processes, immediate nonverbal actualization of knowledge, and the like. Table 1 presents the resulting hypothesized sequence of subroutines. Defining a known concept is conceived as evocation of a mass of denotations, serial scanning of prominent elements in that mass, and testing the relevance of each in turn; naming relevant ones; checking the adequacy of the result by confronting the denotation of the definition words with the original denotation.

As a following step, other protocols are scanned to test the adequacy of the hypothesis. This can be done systematically by scoring the simple statements referred to above in terms of the subroutines whose output they are supposed to be. Deficiencies in terms of unclassifiable items, nonfitting items, or sequence violations rapidly manifest themselves. In the example given, several things became clear at once: test phase 4 did not always take the form given to it (an aspect may be rejected because it is unessential), and it did not always occur at the predicted place; the relevance test frequently followed naming. Program changes were made, which in this case had to be quite extensive. Modification of the content of the test phase necessitated flexible access to several relevance criteria dependent upon the type of solution proposal just made by the subject. The mobility of the test phase necessitated a much more hierarchical process structure than that given in Table 1, involving separation into executive and working routines as in GPS. The cycle of program correction is repeated until a sufficient fit seems to obtain, after which the routine denoted by "scanning prominent elements," "confronting denotations," and so forth, are to be spelled out and actual programming can begin.

It is clear that a very large part of the work is performed prior to writing the actual computer program. This is particularly true since process description at a fairly high level is what is really psychologically relevant. The yield of the work seems rather high, provided that all program changes which were dictated by the data are retained and reported. That a problem-solving executive had to be introduced, not because of programming convenience but because of the demands of the behavior data, is an interesting finding. Equally important is the emergence of arguments for flexible control procedures. It should be stressed that, although work up to this stage is entirely informal, results are nevertheless fruits of computer simulation. Only the flow chart structure of the hypotheses permits scanning of the protocol data in search of insufficiencies, and only the program model permits phrasing in terms of recurrent cycles and successive operations. The program functions clearly as a tool for analysis and search.

Although most of the psychological work occurs at this informal level, formal programming (in this case, ALGOL 60) is still necessary. There are two reasons for this. The first is that actual programming is the only way to make sure that everything really works; it is also the only

TABLE 1   Defining word meanings

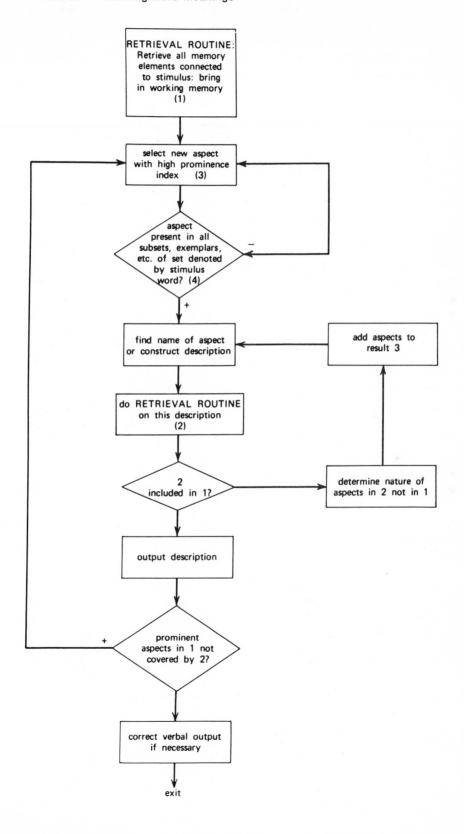

way to clear up mysterious notions such as "confronting denotations." The second reason is that only by formal programming can the necessary substructure be worked out—which must be done to discover the implications of the model. By "substructure" we mean the basic structure of data representation and of lower order search and retrieval processes. The substructure in the present case has to conform to a theory of human memory which is not very directly suggested by behavior data but which is in many ways constrained by them. A number of different memory problem-solving tasks (such as similarities, requests for supraordinate concepts, and so on) will be analyzed and programmed; considerations of parsimony will here be of primary concern. We hope the constraints mentioned will become more and more specific. The system is to absorb information from simple sentences and to produce, when questioned, protocols of retrieval activities similar to the one given as an example.

MATCHING HUMAN PROTOCOLS AND MACHINE PROTOCOLS

How is one to estimate the degree of fit between machine output and human output? There is hardly any methodology existing here. As much ingenuity as has been invested in the making of programs, as little has been spent on the assessment of their value. Next to high precision there always seem to be spots of rough approximations which undercut this very precision. We are left largely to our subjective impressions of what we consider good or bad correspondence.

When judging correspondence between machine output and human output we have to distinguish between those programs resulting only in quantitative performance data and those giving qualitative process details. With those giving only numerical results, one could be tempted to employ the usual significance tests. Their appropriateness, however, seems doubtful. The degrees of freedom of a computer program are extremely great. The construction of alternative models seems the only control, and a necessary one at that. Clarkson [3] is the only author I know of who actually tested his model (of portfolio selection) in this manner.

Detailed process simulation does not usually lend itself to significance tests. Common sense impression of similarity seems the only basis for judgement. There is nothing wrong with this use of common sense. The parallels between what subjects do and what the program does are often so striking (as with GPS or the Simon and Kotovsky program) as to render coincidence unlikely and to confer plausibility upon the machinery. This rough form of what has come to be called "Turing's test" [14] is a useful basis for evaluation.

In evaluating the degree of fit between machine protocol and human protocol, the investigator is confronted with problems of selection. On the one hand, he wants as faithfully as possible to simulate (and thus to understand) the human behavior. On the other hand, it is mostly trivial and unenlightening to aim at reproduction of all irrelevant human limitations or idiosyncrasies. Distractions, certain limitations of working memory, viscissitudes of information gathering, peculiarities of verbal expression, often contribute very little to understanding the processes in which we are interested. It is certainly admissible, and even wise, to select which data to simulate and which to discard even though this involves theoretical preconceptions and may entail the risk of discarding features which later may turn out to be consequences of the major process itself.

Problems of selection are most serious and essential in connection with generalizing simulation results. One has to make decisions where similarity is required and where data-specific differences can be neglected.

When a program is constructed on the basis of a given set of data, how can we make sure that it applies to other sets? With abstract tasks there is not too much difficulty. One varies the inputs for both subjects and program. With tasks yielding more qualitative data (such as memory tasks) checking gets complicated. How can a program constructed on the basis of definitions of a cigarette be checked on protocols of definitions of a cigar? The scoring system suggested above may offer a solution. Scoring the simple statements in terms of the subroutines whose outputs they are supposed to be permits construction of a quantitative index of fit. This is the case even when the content of the human protocols is different from what the machine would produce. Subroutine sequences should correspond to the requirements of the program, and deviations can be counted and weighed. Such an index permits the application of reliability tests of the scoring system used.

Of course, evaluation of programs and theories is not finished when output and human protocol are compared and are essentially alike. Any theory is useful only insofar as it gives rise to new investigation or leads to new integration of data. The same holds in connection with simulation. From the program written on the basis of protocols, we hope and expect cues for direct experiment. Our memory model, for instance, demands that the number of ways of access to the memory store be limited to sensory cues and names. This at once leads to experiments in which cue complexes are varied in concreteness and, for instance, reaction times are to be measured. A more consequential example of integration of computer simulation with other methods of research is given by another project, undertaken by Jan Elshout at the Amsterdam University psychology laboratory. Here, protocol analysis of problem-solving tasks will be related to factor analytic investigation of tests containing similar tasks (a Guildford type battery), as well as to performance on a concept formation criterion task. Parallels between the results of factor analysis and program components similar over different tasks will be looked for. The computer simulation here seems to be essential to carry process analysis beyond a purely verbal stage: it may show another of its aspects as a helpful technique in psychological research.

REFERENCES

1. F. B. Baker, 1964. An IPL-V program for concept attainment. *Educational and Psychological Measurement, 24*(1): 119–127.
2. G. H. Bower, with E. H. Galanter, E. J. Gibson, K. H. Pribram, E. A. Feigenbaum, H. B. Barlow, T. J. Voneida, A. W. Melton, F. Fremont-Smith, D. E. Broadbent, L. Weiskrantz, E. R. John, J. L. McGaugh, J. V. McConnell, P. Buser, B. Milner, D. R. Meyer, S. Kramer, D. P. Kimble, D. M. Rioch, R. A. Hinde, and J. J. Gibson, 1967. A descriptive theory of memory. *Conference on learning, remembering, and forgetting, Volume 2: the organization of recall* (D. P. Kimble, ed.); New York: New York Academy of Sciences, 112–185.
3. G. P. E. Clarkson, 1962. *Portfolio selection: a simulation of trust investment.* Englewood Cliffs, N.J.: Prentice-Hall. 8A.
4. E. A. Feigenbaum, 1959. *An information processing theory of verbal learning.* Working paper, Rand Corporation, P-1817; also doctoral dissertation, Carnegie-Mellon University. 3A.
5. E. A. Feigenbaum, and H. A. Simon, 1962. A theory of the serial position effect. *British Journal of Psychology, 53*(3): 307–320.
6. J. Feldman, 1962. Computer simulation of cognitive processes. *Computer applications in the behavioral sciences* (H. Borko, ed.); Englewood Cliffs, N. J.: Prentice-Hall, 336–359. MA.
7. H. L. Gelernter, J. R. Hansen, and D. W. Loveland, 1960. Empirical explorations of the geometry theorem machine. *Joint Computer Conference, Western Proceedings, 17*: 143–149.
8. B. F. Green, Jr., 1963. *Digital computers in research.* New York: McGraw-Hill. MG.
9. K. R. Laughery, and L. W. Gregg, 1962. Simulation of human problem-solving behavior. *Psychometrika, 27*(3): 265–282. 1A.
10. R. K. Lindsay, 1960. *The reading machine problem.* Doctoral dissertation, Carnegie-Mellon University. 7A.
11. W. H. McWhinney, 1964. Simulating the communication network experiments. *Behavioral Science, 9*(1): 80–84. 4B.
12. G. A. Miller, E. H. Galanter, and K. H. Pribram, 1960. *Plans and the structure of behavior.* New York: Holt, Rinehart and Winston. MA.
13. A. Newell, 1963. *A guide to the General Problem-Solver program GPS-2-2.* Working paper, Rand Corporation, RM-3337-PR. 7A.
14. A. Newell, and H. A. Simon, 1961. GPS, a program that simulates human thought. *Lernende Automaten* (H. Billing, ed.); Munich: R. Oldenbourg KG, 109–124. 1A.
15. A. Newell, and H. A. Simon, 1961. The simulation of human thought. *Current trends in psychological theory;* Pittsburgh: University of Pittsburgh Press, 152–179. 1A.
16. B. Raphael, 1964. *SIR: a computer program for semantic information retrieval.* Doctoral dissertation, Massachusetts Institute of Technology. 7A.

17. N. Rochester, J. H. Holland, L. H. Haibt, and W. L. Duda, 1956. Tests on a cell assembly theory of the action of the brain, using a large digital computer. *IEEE Transactions on Information Theory*, *IT-2*(3): S-80-93. 5A.

18. H. A. Simon, and K. Kotovsky, 1963. Human acquisition of concepts for sequential patterns. *Psychological Review*, *70*(6): 534–546. 3C.

19. L. Uhr, C. Vossler, and J. Uleman, 1962. Pattern recognition over distortions, by human subjects and by a computer simulation of a model for human form perception. *Journal of Experimental Psychology*, *63*(3): 227–234. 3C.

20. D. B. Yntema, and F. P. Trask, 1963. Recall as a search process. *Journal of Verbal Learning and Verbal Behavior*, *2*(1): 65–74.

31

EXPERIMENTAL DESIGN FOR A SIMULATION MODEL OF THE FIRM

CHARLES P. BONINI

Editors' Note: This paper is an excerpt from Charles Bonini's 1963 book *Simulation of information and decision systems in the firm*. Bonini's study does not fit our concept of a descriptive simulation because it devotes very little attention to the empirical bases for its assumptions, and the model's performance is not compared to the behaviors of actual firms. However, Bonini treats his model as an experimental subject whose characteristics he wants to understand, and he takes great advantage of the simulation's adaptability to experimental designs. The chapter is worth reading as an exercise in study design—and we are confident that its methodological significance can be understood—even though the variables may be no more than arbitrary terms to readers unfamiliar with the model. Some comprehension of Bonini's model can be gotten by reading Kaczka and Kirk's "Managerial climate, work groups, and organizational performance," Chapter 14.

INTRODUCTION

Our method of experimentation with the model is to make changes in the model and then to analyze the effects of these changes upon the behavior of the firm. In order to study the results in some systematic fashion, we must decide upon the proper method for analysis—i.e., the proper experimental design. Such considerations are the subject of this chapter.

It would be a relatively simple matter to make a series of independent alterations in the standard model, one at a time, and to note the effect of each of these alterations in turn. Such a procedure, however, has two serious drawbacks. These are:

1. Interaction effects would be ignored. It is possible that a change may have an effect upon the firm only if some other change is also effected. Thus, for example, much contagion of pressure may have an effect upon the firm only if the firm is operating in a highly variable environment. Such interaction effects are common and important, and should not be ignored.

2. There would be little generality in the results. If we were to make single changes in the model, the effects of these changes could be said to apply only to firms quite similar to our hypothetical one. While such observations would supply valuable insights into business organizations, they would have a very limited degree of generality. Ideally, we should like to test the effect of a particular change over a wide variety of firms (with different organization, different decision rules, different information systems, and so on). We can approximate this by testing the effect of one change in relation to all the other changes we make. Thus, for example, we can test the effect of contagion of

pressure on firms in a stable external environment and on firms in a variable environment; on firms with a "loose" industrial engineering department and on firms with a "tight" industrial engineering department; on firms using LIFO and on firms using average costing; and so on. In this way, our results will achieve a modest degree of generality.

The preceding discussion points to the need for a rather complex experimental design. But before we discuss the design we have chosen, let us delineate more explicitly the hypotheses to be tested.

HYPOTHESES

Since experimentation with our model involves introducing changes, the hypotheses to be tested are simply statements about the effects of the proposed changes. First, we shall hypothesize that the behavior of our firm is not affected by any of our changes. (Such hypotheses are known as *null hypotheses* in the statistical literature [8].) And we shall make the same statement about the effects of interactions of changes (the effect of changes taken two at a time). We would hope, of course, to reject the null hypotheses, at least in some of the cases. Rejection of the null hypothesis amounts to asserting that there is some significant effect for a given alteration or interaction (with a given chance of being wrong—called the *Type I error*).

Below are listed, in summary form, the eight changes we propose to make in the model. We wish to study the effects of:

1. Low vs. high variability in the external environment of the firm. More specifically, we are interested in the effect of small vs. large standard deviations in the probability distributions for sales and production cost.

2. Two different market trends for the firm; one a slow (2 per cent per year) growth upon which is superimposed a three-year cycle; the other a fast (10 per cent per year) but irregular growth.

3. A "loose" vs. "tight" industrial engineering department in the matter of changing standards.

4. An organization that is contagious to pressure as opposed to one that is not.

5. An organization in which the individuals are sensitive to pressure as opposed to one in which they are not.

6. An average cost method of inventory valuation versus a LIFO method.

7. Knowledge on the part of the sales force about the inventory position of the company vs. the absence of such knowledge.

8. The reliance primarily upon present vs. past information for control within the firm.

For ease in further reference and manipulation, we now tabulate this set of eight variations and associate them with letters and abbreviated names (Table 1). As noted in the table, we have denoted the case in the standard model by a zero, and the alternative by a one in each case.

TABLE 1   Variations in the Model

| Symbol | Changes to be Made in | Categories | |
		Standard Model 0	Alternatives 1
A	Inventory valuation	Average cost	LIFO
B	Contagious pressure	Little	Much
C	Sensitivity to pressure	Sensitive	Insensitive
D	Sales force knowledge of inventory	Knowledge	No knowledge
E	External-world variability	Stable	Variable
F	Market growth trend	Steady-cyclical growth	Fast-irregular growth
G	Industrial engineering department	Tight	Loose
H	Present vs. past in control	Present	Past

MAIN EFFECTS AND INTERACTIONS

We have referred, in the pages immediately preceding, to the main or major effects of a given change and to the interaction effects of a combination of changes. Some discussion will help to clarify these points.

In studying the variations in our model and in designating a suitable experimental design, it is necessary to clarify the major objectives which we wish to achieve. Recall that we wish to formulate and test theories or propositions about organizational behavior, and in particular about business firms. Such propositions may take any of the three following forms:

1. *Generalizations that are applicable to a wide variety of organizations (possibly all).* These are universal propositions. In our analysis we wish to be able to determine if the effect of any change has such generality. Thus, we estimate the effect of the change over all organizational arrangements (combinations of other changes). This estimated effect is called a *main effect* in the statistical terminology [2].

2. *Delimiting propositions that restrict a particular effect to a selected range of kinds of organizations and situations.* These are the kinds of propositions that assert that change G has some effect only if change B is also made (i.e., a loose industrial engineering department may result in higher cost only if there is also much contagion of pressure). Such a proposition is valid in some circumstances and not in others— it is dependent upon other organizational factors. In the statistical terminology, the effect of two (or more) factors acting together is called an *interaction effect* [3].

3. *Propositions isolating particular variations or patterns of simultaneous variation which produce no significant result on organizational behavior.* If certain main effects and interactions do not differ significantly from zero, then we may construe this as evidence that these changes or combinations of changes do not affect organizational behavior (at least over the range of organizational arrangements in the experiment). Such propositions are important also, for they distinguish between important factors meriting further attention by students of business and those which may be ignored as unimportant.

Using these general categories for guidance, we can determine some of the desiderata for an appropriate experimental design. Evidently, we want a design which enables us to study main effects and also higher-order interactions. In addition, we wish to determine when such effects are significantly different from zero. The factorial experimental design and the related analysis of variance seem suitably designed for our purposes; we shall turn presently to a discussion of these techniques.

BLOCK EFFECTS

In addition to testing each of our eight hypotheses (changes) over all the combinations of variations in the model, it would seem prudent to examine one other possible cause of variation— the effect upon the firm of initial condition for the firm. In order to simulate the behavior of the firm over time, it is necessary to give it some past history—that is, some initial or starting conditions. Might not, then, our results be influenced by our choice of starting conditions?

Thus, our experimental design should include a method to study the effect of initial conditions upon the behavior of the firm and upon the results of our main and interaction effects (above). In other words, we would like to achieve two results, in addition to those mentioned in the preceding section:

1. We would like to measure the effect, if any, of different initial conditions upon the behavior of the firm.

2. We would like to test our major hypotheses (abour effects of alterations in the model) over different input conditions, and eliminate results that may have come about because of specific starting conditions.

To achieve this, we have set up four cases (called *blocks* in the statistical terminology) of different starting conditions. The blocks have been chosen as follows:

Block 1 represents approximately "normal" starting conditions. Mean costs and sales are neither extremely high nor low. The firm should be moderately profitable.

Block 2 represents the same conditions as Block 1, modified slightly. The modification was achieved by adding or subtracting 0, 1, 2, or 3 per cent (determined randomly) from each of the conditions in Block 1.

Block 3 represents an extreme case. Mean costs are high and mean sales are low. Thus, all factors are set in such a fashion as to make the firm initially unprofitable.

Block 4 represents the opposite extreme. In this case, the data are set in such a way that the firm is immediately profitable. Mean costs are low and mean sales high.

These four conditions, representing normal and extreme situations, are a reasonable set of initial conditions over which to test the various hypotheses about the firm.

In addition, the number of salesmen of each type, the allocation of ability to salesmen, and the distribution of types of salesmen among sales districts were randomly changed in each of the four blocks to give an added dimension over which to test the various hypotheses.

THE FACTORIAL EXPERIMENTAL DESIGN

We have indicated in the two sections above that we desire an experimental technique that would enable us to estimate main effects and interactions of the various alterations in the model. In addition, we would like to include block effects which would represent the influence of initial conditions on the behavior of the firm. The factorial experimental design seems well suited for such an analysis.[1] We proceed to describe this technique.

Recall that there are eight changes to be made and that there are two cases for each change (the standard model and an alternative). We thus have a 2^8 factorial design. To include all the possible combinations would involve

[1] An experimental design of this sort is not the only procedure that could be used in such an analysis. Jay W. Forrester [7], utilizes merely comparative graphics in describing the results of his simulations. With an experiment of the above size, this would be impossible.

Cohen, Cyert, March, and Soelberg [3], on the other hand, discuss the utilization of a multiple regression technique for analyzing simulation studies. However, it seems more difficult to incorporate interaction effects into regression analysis than into our technique.

See also R. M. Cyert and J. G. March [4], Chapter 8.

$2^8 = 256$ experimental runs of the model to have even one complete *replicate* (i.e., one run for each combination).

The Model of the Experimental Design

We are considering the effects upon the behavior of the firm of changes in each of eight factors:

A: Inventory valuation;
B: Contagious pressure;
C: Sensitivity to pressure;
D: Sales force knowledge of inventory;
E: External-world variability;
F: Market growth trend;
G: Industrial engineering department;
H: Past vs. present in control.

As noted above, there are 256 cases:

1: all factors as in the standard model;
a: all factors as in the standard model except factor *A*;
b: all factors as in the standard model except factor *B*;
ab: all factors as in the standard model except factors *A* and *B*;

and so on, through

abcdefgh: all factors in the alternative case.

In the above notation, when a small letter is absent, the standard model case was used. When a small letter is present, the alternative case was used [5, p. 257]. (This applies for each of the small letters, *a* through *h*. Each represents a hypothesis.)

The equation of estimation is [9]; and [5]:

$$
\begin{aligned}
X_{abcdefghl} = M &+ A_a + B_b + C_c + D_d + E_e \\
&+ F_f + G_g + H_h \\
&+ (AB)_{ab} + (AC)_{ac} + (AD)_{ad} \\
&+ (AE)_{ae} + (AF)_{af} + (AG)_{ag} \\
&+ (AH)_{ah} \\
&+ (BC)_{bc} + (BD)_{bd} + (BE)_{be} \\
&+ (BF)_{bf} + (BG)_{bg} + (BH)_{bh} \\
&+ (CD)_{cd} + (CE)_{ce} + (CF)_{cf} \\
&+ (CG)_{cg} + (CH)_{ch} \\
&+ (DE)_{de} + (DF)_{df} + (DG)_{dg} \\
&+ (DH)_{dh} \\
&+ (EF)_{ef} + (EG)_{eg} + (EH)_{eh} \\
&+ (FG)_{fg} + (FH)_{fh} + (GH)_{gh} \\
&+ L_l + \varepsilon_{abcdefghl},
\end{aligned}
$$

where

$X_{abcdefghl}$ = the observed *response* in each case. It represents the resulting behavior of the firm.

M = the over-all *mean*.

A_a = the *main* effect of factor A.

$(AB)_{ab}$ = the *interaction* between factors A and B. It is a measure of the statistical dependency of factors A and B. When the interaction is different from zero, it means that the combination of A and B has some effect over and above the individual effects of A and B separately.

L_l = the block effects—that is, the effects of the different starting conditions.

$\varepsilon_{abcdefghl}$ = the experimental error term. It represents the difference between the observed response in each case and that predicted using the remainder of the above equation.

$a, b, c, \ldots, h$ = 0 for the standard model case, 1 for the alternative case. Thus, A_0 represents the main effect of factor A in the standard model case.

$l = 1, 2, 3, 4.$ l is the subscript, and takes on the value 1 for the first block, 2 for the second block, and so on.

Discussion. Note the absence of higher-order interactions in the above formulation. In general, in a factorial experiment, interactions such as (ABC) and even $(ABCDEFGH)$ could be estimated. In actual practice, this is rarely done. Interactions higher than first order are generally assumed to be zero.[2] In addition, their meaning would be difficult to decipher at the present state of knowledge.

Note also that there are 41 estimates to be made; one for the mean, M; eight for the main effects; 28 for the interactions; and four for the blocks (there are only 40 independent estimates, however, since the four block effects represent only three block contrasts).

[2] A detailed examination of the references cited in this chapter failed to reveal any illustrations in which the higher-order interactions were not ignored or assumed to be zero (except for very small problems such as the 2^3 design).

Assumptions. In order to use the experimental model as a basis for statistical inferences, we shall make the usual statistical assumptions (see [9]; and [1, pp. 220–223 and 268]):

1. The error terms, $\varepsilon_{abcdefghl}$ are normally and independently distributed with mean 0 and variance σ^2, uniform throughout.

2. The interaction terms are symmetrical, i.e., (AB) is equivalent to (BA). In addition, by the definitions of the main effects and interactions, we have:

3. $\displaystyle\sum_a A_a = \sum_b B_b = \sum_c C_c$
$$= \cdots = \sum_h H_h = \sum_l L_l = 0$$

and

$$\sum_a (AB)_{ab} = \sum_b (AB)_{ab} = \sum_a (AC)_{ac}$$
$$= \cdots = \sum_h (GH)_{gh} = 0.$$

This merely states that we measure the effect of each factor in terms of deviations from the over-all mean, M. Thus, the effect of factor A for the standard model (i.e., A_0), and the effect of factor A for the alternative case (i.e., A_1) average to zero.

And, finally, we are assuming:

4. The second-order and higher-order interactions are zero.

5. There are no interactions between the blocks and the other effects. This means that different starting conditions have an effect in themselves but should not interact with other changes.

Fractional Factorial Design

As noted earlier, to have one complete replicate of our experiment we would need 256 experimental observations (i.e., simulation runs of our model under different conditions). In order to keep our study within manageable proportions, it is necessary to economize on the number of observations. Fortunately, it is not necessary to obtain all 256 observations, if we take advantage of a technique called a *fractional factorial* design [6]. Such a technique enables us to estimate the main effects and low-order interaction effects in a factorial design, if we can assume that the higher-order interactions are zero.

Confounding. In order to explain how such fractional replications are possible, it is first necessary to introduce the concept of *confounding*. Essentially, we confound one effect with another if we use the same estimating equation (and the same data) to estimate both effects. (For example, if all the runs of A_0 were in Block 1, and all the runs of A_1 in Block 2, we could not distinguish between A_1 and A_0 from the difference between Block 1 and Block 2—that is, the A effect would be confounded with block effect.)

In utilizing a fractional factorial, we confound the higher-order interactions, such as $ABCDEFGH$, with main effects and low-order interactions. And since we assume that these higher-order interactions are negligible, we can unambiguously estimate the main effects and low-order interactions. The *aliases* of a given effect (or interaction) are those interactions which are confounded with the given effect [6]. (Thus, in the above illustration the block effect is the alias of the A effect.)

The National Bureau of Standards has published a listing of fractional factorial designs which has main effects and as many as possible first-order interactions measurable (in the sense that they are confounded with second-order and higher-order interactions) [10]. We have selected one of these designs.

The Actual Design. The actual design employed was a one-fourth replicate of eight factors in four blocks of 16 units each [10, p. 21]. Instead of the 256 observations needed for a complete replicate, we actually utilized one-fourth of the total, or 64 observations. The four blocks were used to estimate the effects of different starting conditions, as described earlier.

With this design, it is possible to estimate the main effects, the block effects, and all the first-order interactions. All main effects have third- or higher-order interactions as aliases. The first-order interactions are confounded with second- and higher-order interactions. The aliases of the block effects are the interactions $ABCDEF$, ACD, and BEF. This design represents a partitioning according to the interactions $ABCEG$, $ABDFH$, and $CDEFGH$. Since we are utilizing a one-fourth replicate, each of the main effects and first-order interactions will have

three aliases, which can be determined from the above partitioning factors.[3]

As mentioned above, there are 64 observations (experimental runs of our model) necessary to make the required estimates of main effects, block effects and interactions. These 64 observations are (from the National Bureau of Standards plan):

Block 1	Block 2	Block 3	Block 4
(l)	bdefh	acdefgh	abcg
abcfgh	acdeg	bde	fh
bcdeg	cfgh	abfh	ade
adefh	ab	cg	bcdefgh
efgh	bdg	acd	abcefh
abce	acdfh	bdfgh	eg
bcdfh	ce	abeg	adfgh
adg	abefgh	cefh	bcd
cdgh	bcefg	aef	abdh
abdf	aeh	bcegh	cdfg
beh	df	abcdfg	acegh
acefg	abcdgh	dh	bef
cdef	bch	agh	abdefg
abdegh	afg	bcf	cdeh
bfg	degh	abcdeh	acf
ach	abcdef	defg	bgh

where, as before, the presence of a small letter indicates the factor is in the alternate case (1 category), and the absence of the letter indicates the standard model case (0 category). The symbol (l) represents the observation when all factors are in the standard model case.

Tests of Statistical Significance

Once we have estimated the main effects, the block effects, and the interactions, it will be necessary to determine if these effects differ significantly from zero. That is, we must determine if there is a real effect or if the apparent effect could be attributable to chance.

We shall utilize the standard techniques of analysis of variance for these tests [1, pp. 268–

[3] The aliases of any effect may be obtained by multiplying the effect by the partitioning factors, treating a squared term as 1 (e.g., $A^2 = 1$). Thus, the aliases of AB are:
$$AB \times ABCEG = A^2 B^2 CEG = CEG$$
$$\text{(since } A^2 = B^2 = 1\text{);}$$
$$AB \times ABDFH = A^2 B^2 DFH = DFH;$$
$$AB \times CDEFGH = ABCDEFGH.$$

278; and 2, pp. 39–85]. Essentially, we break up the total sum of squares (of observations about the mean) into the parts attributable to each of the main effects, each of the interaction effects, and the block effects. The remaining sum of squares is the residual. We then utilize an F-ratio to test the significance of each effect.

We are making 40 independent estimates: 1 for the over-all mean; 8 for the main effects; 28 for the interaction effects; and 3 for the block contrasts. Since there are 64 observations, there remain 24 degrees of freedom with which to estimate σ^2—the variance of the experimental error.

SUMMARY

Experimentation with the model involves making alterations (one at a time and in combinations) in the model and noting the effects of these alterations. Since such an analysis would be quite complex, it is necessary to have a systematic procedure for formulating the experiment and examining the results. This chapter was a description of the technique—the experimental design—selected.

The eight changes to be made in the model were reformulated into eight hypotheses (null hypotheses) stating that the changes had no effects upon the behavior of the firm. The object of the experiment will be to determine if we can reject some or all of these hypotheses.

We are interested in estimating the main effects of a given alteration in the model. That is, we wish to know if the result of the change is general over a wide variety of situations (i.e., over all combinations of other alterations). In addition, we would like to estimate first-order interaction effects—results that occur only when two changes are effected simultaneously.

Also, we should like to measure the dependence of our results upon the initial starting conditions for the firm. To do this, four sets of initial starting conditions were designed. These are blocks, in the statistical sense.

The factorial experimental design was selected for making the above estimates and analyzing the block effects. To keep the experiment within manageable size, a fractional factorial was utilized. This involved 64 observations, one-fourth of the 256 required for a complete replicate. Interactions of second and higher order are assumed negligible, so that the main effects, first-order interactions, and block effects are measurable. Sufficient degrees of freedom remain to perform tests of statistical significance.

REFERENCES

1. R. L. Anderson, and T. A. Bancroft, 1952. *Statistical theory in research.* New York: McGraw-Hill.
2. W. G. Cochran, and G. M. Cox, 1950. *Experimental designs.* New York: Wiley, second edition, 1957.
3. K. J. Cohen, R. M. Cyert, J. G. March, and P. O. Soelberg, 1963. A general model of price and output determination. *Symposium on simulation models* (A. C. Hoggatt and F. E. Balderston, eds.); Cincinnati: South-Western, 250–289. 5D.
4. R. M. Cyert, and J. G. March, 1963. *A behavioral theory of the firm.* Englewood Cliffs, N.J.: Prentice-Hall. 2B.
5. O. L. Davies, 1956. Factorial experiments: elementary principles. *The design and analysis of industrial experiments* (O. L. Davies, ed.); London: Oliver and Boyd, 247–289.
6. O. L. Davies, 1956. Fractional factorial experiments. *The design and analysis of industrial experiments* (O. L. Davies, ed.); London: Oliver and Boyd, 440–494.
7. J. W. Forrester, 1961. *Industrial dynamics.* Cambridge, Mass.: MIT Press. MD.
8. P. G. Hoel, 1960. *Elementary statistics.* New York: Wiley.
9. E. Mansfield, 1958. *Notes on experimental design.* Lecture notes, Carnegie-Mellon University.
10. National Bureau of Standards, 1957. *Fractional factorial experiment designs for factors at two levels.* Washington: U.S. National Bureau of Standards, AMS-48.

32

MULTI-VARIABLE EXPERIMENTATION AND SIMULATION MODELS

JOAN E. JACOBY
STEPHEN HARRISON

INTRODUCTION

When a research worker is confronted by a simulation model of a segment of the universe, he rapidly discovers that his statistical techniques must be both modified and extended if he is to make an effective analysis of the model. All his tools are still essential, but simulation models possess characteristics that, on one hand, render insufficient some of the classical principles of experimental design and, on the other hand, present special opportunities in design economy. This paper discusses some of these modifications and extensions.

The frame of reference as well as the impetus to investigating these principles is the Air Battle Model (ABM), a large, two-sided, global air war game which is operated on a high-speed digital computer, and the Attrition Damage Assessment Model (ADAM), which is a one-sided air war game with emphasis on the attrition and damage routines of the ABM. Both of these simulations are literal, non-real time, stochastic, and, of course, extremely large.

These two simulation models, because they are large, literal, and stochastic, require large experimental programs. For example, the number of input variables in the ABM is of the order of 100. If these, represented at 2 levels, are to be tested by a factorial design, then the number of runs required is of the order of 2^{100}, and if each run takes a day or more, the implications in terms of available time and money are overwhelming. As models increase in size, so does the experimenter's problem, for the following two reasons: first, the number of variables tends to increase, hence the size of the experiment required to examine the system increases; second, despite the microsecond speeds of modern computers, overall game time is still appreciable. For, although it may take only a few microseconds to perform a computation, these microseconds accumulate until they result in a game run which may consume a day or more, as in the ABM. Hence the running time to complete an experiment (which is the ultimate measure of the size of the task) increases exponentially with the size of the model. Methods of shortcutting this time element are essential if any large scale simulation experimentation is to take place.

SOURCE: Reprinted from *Naval Research Logistics Quarterly*, 9 (2): 121–136 (1962).

Special Properties of Simulation Model

Even though some of the properties of simulation models require new directions in problem solving, others become extremely useful as aids to the ultimate task of describing and analyzing the model.

One such advantage is that a simulation model can be considered a closed system. A closed system should yield 100 percent information obtainable a priori, and should contain no ultimate surprises or unknowns as might be expected in an open, real-world system. In a theoretical sense, no experiments are ever required when dealing with a simulation model since all information is contained within it. Unfortunately, in practice, the comprehension of all aspects of a model is impossible, and as a result, the most one can hope to achieve is the recognition of functional relationships between certain subsets of variables which will eliminate a need for their independent variation in the experiment. A start can be made by delineating a topological tree, that is, by showing what connects to what. For even though the experimenter does not know all of the complexities of the model, he is still able to recognize connections between factors, convergent lines on a flow chart, and functional relationships. Hence, although one may not know how these lines are connected, for experimental purposes, it suffices that one knows where these lines are connected.

Following from this is the fact that often a cluster of variables seems to converge to a single node in a way described by a simple function. If many such clusters are recognizable, then by a progressive absorption of variables the size of the experiment can be reduced, and the sensitivity of those factors that converge to a node can be inferred.

Another useful property of the simulation model is that the random number sequences are strictly determined. This makes some control of the error variance possible. In the ABM, some 15 stochastic generators make on the order of 50,000 decisions in the course of one game. These generate an appreciable error variance. Whether the variance be high or low depends upon the way the stochastic generators link with the system. However, it is reasonable to assume that any error variance will be potentially low because the error being introduced in precisely known ways can also be manipulated so that its effects are scaled down, a useful technique for sensitivity studies.

One type of manipulation that is commonly used to decrease any error variance is the Monte Carlo swindle. An example of this may be seen in the use of the original random number input. If a design is constructed and each game run is started with the same set of random numbers, then a Monte Carlo swindle has been effected; for by this method an artificial correlation is generated between runs which suppresses much of the error variance. Another type of manipulation that could be used is the technique of sampling without replacement from the universe. In this case, the expectation distribution of events is predetermined and placed in the model before the game is run; drawings without replacement are then made randomly as the game proceeds. Hence, any variance which occurs is concerned largely with the order in which an event happens. A final extension of this idea leads to the construction of an expectation version of the model which results in zero variance or zero noise. In other words, if two replications were made, the outcomes would be identical.

If there is any disadvantage to a closed system, it appears not in a statistical sense, but rather in a realistic sense; for a closed system automatically places an upper bound on the usefulness of the results even though experimental difficulties have been overcome.

Experimental Designs

This paper discusses a few modifications of the old classical designs as well as new concepts to aid in the solution of the multivariable experimentation problem which characterizes so many large simulation models.

It will be shown that, depending on the purpose of the investigation and the a priori knowledge of the system, an experimenter can use the following types of design and statistical techniques:

Designs that sacrifice some interactions—fractional replications, $x_i(n-1)$ designs, nested hypercubes, compacted hypercubes, and modified orthogonal designs.

Designs that eliminate interactions—complete orthogonal designs, one-factor-at-a-time concept, and multi-level orthogonal designs.

Designs that sacrifice orthogonality—random balance, multiple balance, minimum correlation, skewed non-random balance, and technique of sequential bifurcation.

Split-plot techniques.

DESIGNS SACRIFICING SOME INTERACTIONS

It must be remembered that in all cases where some or all of the interactions are sacrificed, the decision for these omissions is based on a careful study of the model and the willingness of the experimenter to take a reasonable chance.

Most designs in the literature which confound or sacrifice interactions tend to start out from the complete factorial and then move downward eliminating first the higher order interactions which are supposedly of lesser interest. Moving in the opposite direction (i.e. starting from orthogonal designs and moving upward) seeks designs which preserve only a very few but explicitly desired, interactions. When a situation is encountered which includes a very high number of variables, as in the ABM, fractional replication designs do not begin to effect the kinds of economies which are required. They are, however, useful if the number of inputs is small, and are extremely valuable for more detailed sensitivity studies undertaken after an overall experiment has been run.

The second group, designs preserving special interaction subsets, ushers in the realm of real utility.

Interest is centered on such designs because, although a reduction in the number of game runs is necessary, it is obvious that the model contains some interactions that appear to be very important and, by necessity, should be estimated in a sensitivity-type experiment. Hence, an attempt is made by these designs to preserve compartments wherein these interactions may appear.

The first of these, designated $X_i(n-1)$ consists of $(n-1)$ variables arranged in a two-level orthogonal design, and the other consists of the design being duplicated with one set being associated with the remaining variable X_i at the low level, and the other set with variable X_i at the high level. Figure 1 shows the first order interaction matrix with the shaded portion indicating the interactions of X_i with each of the other variables. The use of this type of design enables the investigator to test the interaction and significance of one variable held either at a high or a low level against all other variables.

The *compacted hypercube* is a completely orthogonal hypercube. Table 1 gives an example of this design requiring 16 runs corresponding to the 16 cells shown, and examines 10 factors A-J at two levels each. The first order interaction matrix in Figure 2 shows the subset of interactions which the design yields. It gives, in effect, a chain of interactions:

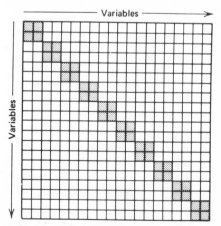

Figure 1 First-order interaction matrix of an $X_i(n-1)$ design.

Figure 2 First-order interaction matrix of a compacted hypercube design.

TABLE 1 Compacted Hypercube

		B_1						B_2					
		A_1			A_2			A_1			A_2		
D_1	C_1	E_1 F_1 G_1			E_2 F_1 G_1			E_1 F_2 G_2			E_2 F_2 G_2		
		H_1 I_1 J_1			H_2 I_2 J_1			H_2 I_1 J_2			H_1 I_2 J_2		
	C_2	E_2 F_1 G_2			E_1 F_1 G_2			E_2 F_2 G_1			E_1 F_2 G_1		
		H_1 I_1 J_2			H_2 I_2 J_2			H_2 I_1 J_1			H_1 I_2 J_1		
D_2	C_1	E_1 F_2 G_2			E_2 F_2 G_1			E_1 F_1 G_2			E_2 F_1 G_1		
		H_2 I_2 J_2			H_1 I_1 J_2			H_1 I_2 J_1			H_2 I_1 J_1		
	C_2	E_2 F_2 G_2			E_1 F_2 G_2			E_2 F_1 G_1			E_1 F_1 G_1		
		H_2 I_2 J_1			H_1 I_1 J_1			H_1 I_2 J_2			H_2 I_1 J_2		

MAIN EFFECTS: A B C D E F

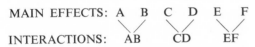

INTERACTIONS: AB   CD   EF

The *nested hypercube* designs are best illustrated by means of Table 2. The overall design at the left in Table 2 is the compacted hypercube already given. Each of the 16 cells has the structure shown on the right; that is, each cell contains a similar compacted design with a second set of variables. This second set is repeated identically in every cell. This looks like a split-plot, but it is not. It is simply a way of showing how the factor combinations are scheduled. The total number of factors in this example is 20, the total number of runs is 16^2 or 256. The most obvious property of this design is its vertigo-inducing powers in the experimenter. It is interesting because of the pattern of interactions to which it gives rise (all first order), as shown in Figure 3.[1]

The *modified orthogonal design* has the useful property of pin-pointing specific interactions, information concerning which is desired on a priori grounds. These are typically, but not necessarily, first order interactions. This is accomplished under the following assumptions:

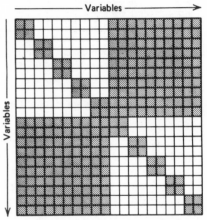

Figure 3 First-order interaction matrix of a nested hypercube design.

that first order interactions, if present will be on the whole, more influential than higher order interactions; and that there are no more than a few specific first order interactions which should stand out from the rest. If these assumptions are valid, then it is possible to construct an orthogonal design where the interaction desired will be contained within the original design. This is accomplished in the modified orthogonal by picking a larger design than necessary for orthogonal treatment, with the excess rows carefully selected so that a few desired interactions will appear and any residual rows used

---

[1] These interaction matrices are not necessarily constructed with the correct number of runs and columns, but merely convey the general idea.

as error. Table 3 demonstrates such a design wherein the interaction of AB may be located in row M. This, therefore, is the row to leave blank in order that the computed effect will give the interaction of AB. Figure 4 illustrates the pinpointing of specific interactions under investigation.

As noted, all these designs yielding interaction subsets make use of various kinds of a priori information. Generally, it is assumed that

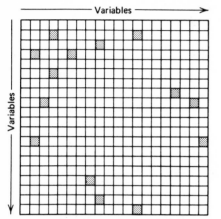

← Variables →

Variables

Figure 4 First-order interaction matrix of a modified orthogonal design.

higher order interactions tend to be less active; and that they are, in any case, less interesting and more difficult to interpret. More specifically, the knowledge of the system suggests which interactions are likely to be active.

DESIGNS ELIMINATING ALL INTERACTIONS

The most obvious example of these types of designs is the *completely orthogonal* $n(n-1)$ rectangle which examines a system of $(n-1)$ variables with n runs. A question of some interest is whether one should use a large organized experiment of the orthogonal type or a stepwise sequential type of design in which one factor is varied at a time. To answer this question, it is necessary to consider the advantages and disadvantages of a one-step sequential design as compared to a completely orthogonal design.

A great advantage of the sequential design is that an experiment need not be completed before analysis. This is worthy of consideration if, for any reason, the experiment cannot be completed; for, in the case of the organized or-

TABLE 2 Nested Hypercube Design

		B_1		B_2					L_1		L_2	
		A_1	A_2	A_1	A_2				K_1	K_2	K_1	K_2
D_1	C_1						N_1	M_1	$O_1 P_1 Q_1$ $R_1 S_1 T_1$	etc.		
	C_2			$E_2 F_2 G_1$ $H_2 I_1 J_1$				M_2				
D_2	C_1						N_2	M_1				
	C_2							M_2				

ONE CELL EXPANDED

$E_2 F_2 G_1 H_2 I_1 J_1$

TABLE 3　Modified Orthogonal Design

							Run No.									
	1	2	3	4	5	6	7	8	9	10	11	12	13	14	15	16
A	+	+	+	+	−	+	−	+	+	−	−	+	−	−	−	−
B	+	+	+	−	+	−	+	+	−	−	+	−	−	−	+	−
C	+	+	−	+	−	+	+	−	−	+	−	−	−	+	+	−
D	+	−	+	−	+	+	−	−	+	−	−	−	+	+	+	−
E	−	+	−	+	+	−	−	+	−	−	−	+	+	+	+	−
F	+	−	+	+	−	−	+	−	−	−	+	+	+	+	−	−
G	−	+	+	−	−	+	−	−	−	+	+	+	+	−	+	−
H	+	+	−	−	+	−	−	−	+	+	+	+	−	+	−	−
I	+	−	−	+	−	−	−	+	+	+	+	−	+	−	+	−
J	−	−	+	−	−	−	+	+	+	+	−	+	−	+	+	−
K	−	+	−	−	−	+	+	+	+	−	+	−	+	+	−	−
L	+	−	−	−	+	+	+	+	−	+	−	+	+	−	−	−
M	−	−	−	+	+	+	+	−	+	−	+	+	−	−	+	−
N	−	−	+	+	+	+	−	+	−	+	+	−	−	+	−	−
O	−	+	+	+	+	−	+	−	+	+	−	−	+	−	−	−
	−	−	−	−	−	−	−	−	−	−	−	−	−	−	−	−

thogonal design, no preliminary analysis is possible. In the *step-by-step design*, analysis is performed after each step. A design may be truncated because either machine time may run out or some combinations of conditions may prove unrunnable or over-flow some limit which falsifies the outcome.

A second advantage lies in the fact that an orthogonal design does not just ignore interaction estimates; rather, it confounds them with main effects. This, however, does not usually lead to any dangerous consequences since any inflation of Type I errors which might otherwise occur is prevented by the nature of the error variance, which also increases if there are any hidden interactions.

A third advantage is that, with a sequential type design, it is possible to learn as the experiment proceeds. In this respect, interactions may be added where main effects look interesting. This procedure, in one of its more sophisticated derivatives, has an extra attraction, should one be seeking a response surface maximum, rather than making a general sensitivity mapping.

A final advantage pertains to the consequences of blunders. For example, in the organized orthogonal design of the Plackett-Burman type, if a wrong number is written, the effect is disastrous [13]. A wave of falsification spreads throughout the entire analysis after the fashion of a stone cast into a pool. But in the one-factor-at-a-time approach, the effects of any blunder are localized.

There are, of course, disadvantages to a sequential type design. Potentially, the most serious is that concerning the error variance. In the orthogonal design, the basic error variance is inversely proportional to the square root of the size of the design; whereas, the error variance of the one-step-at-a-time approach does not diminish as the number of factors being tested increases. This is perhaps the major justification of the orthogonal design, and also an incentive to make the design as inclusive as possible. The effectiveness of using a large design, then, in reducing total error variance depends upon how much interaction contamination exists.

The second disadvantage of a sequential type design lies in the fact that the response of each factor is idiosyncratic. That is, the value produced for the sensitivity of a given factor is relative to the particular combination of settings of all the factors which existed when this factor was changed. Of course, if interactions are zero, this does not matter. The orthogonal design, in contrast, evaluates each factor effect against, as it were, a pooled background of all combinations of the other factors. It is as though each factor effect were obtained separately with all different combinations of the other factors, and the effects averaged. Without doubt, therefore, the estimates of factor effects obtained by the orthogonal design are more representative, less idiosyncratic, more stable, and more transferable; however, they are also less pure in that they are, to some extent, contaminated by whatever interactions show up.

A final decision as to which of the two designs is more attractive to large scale simulation experiments depends upon such questions as the following: Can we be guaranteed enough machine time? What is the likelihood of unrunnable combinations? Are contaminating interactions a serious menace? What is the basic error variance?

DESIGNS SACRIFICING ORTHOGONALITY

If experimental designs are to be considered in which the number of variables exceeds the number of runs made, then at least partial confounding between main effects is unavoidable. It does not follow that all interactions are completely confounded with main effects, though they may be. (What seems to happen is

that main effects and first order interactions are more uniformly partially confounded than higher order interactions.)

The utility of a design of this type depends upon the kind of response surface assumed. Consider a response surface where: the total number of factors is n, with $r \ll n$ of them being relatively active, the remainder relatively inactive; where interactions on the whole are less active than main effects, with increasing attenuation of higher order interactions; and where the error variance is not very large. Where this type of response surface can be assumed, a main-effect confounding design is not an unreasonable one to use to establish a rough approximation of the relative activity of the input variables. Figure 5 demonstrates what happens to estimates of effects as a result of the partial confounding inherent in the design with the kind of response surface postulated above. The white area indicates the true effects of the factors ranked in order of diminishing magnitude. The shaded area indicates the estimates obtained and ranked by running a hypothetical main-effects confounding experiment. It must be noted that discrimination has been lost; some of the variance of the more active variables has spilled over onto the less active variables, thereby causing the data to undergo a type of "Procrustean" distortion toward mediocrity. Nevertheless, the primary information has been preserved, namely, which variables are the more

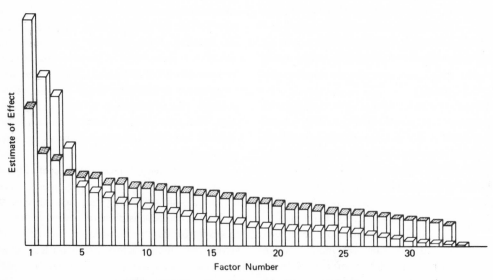

Figure 5   Effect of partial confounding on estimates.

active. Notice that not all the bars in the diagram are required to represent main-effects, some interactions could have been included if desired. The likelihood of preserving order is maximized by using a design such as the uniformly confounded minimum correlation variant of random balance.

Of course, the above example is idealistic in that noise is hardly in evidence and mutual confounding is rather uniform, with the result that the order of activity of the variables, as revealed by the experiment, corresponds to the true order. Under the less ideal conditions in the real world, there would undoubtedly be some distortion in the order of the variables, but the general sense of the experiment should be valid.

One may question the extent to which systems of interest meet the required constraints. It appears to the writers that this situation is typical and is encountered quite frequently. In exceptional cases, it might even be possible to apply a correction factor to the data to restore the disparity between the active and non-active factors. In order to do this, one would require not only low noise, but also advance a priori knowledge about the degree of difference of activity among the variables. In this case, the purpose of the experiment would be limited, in effect, to identifying the correct order of the variables with respect to activity. This is not currently the situation with simulation models of the ABM and ADAM type.

The following five varieties of main-effect confounding designs will be considered here: random balance, multiple balance designs, minimum correlation, skewed non-random balance, and bifurcation techniques. These five designs differ mainly in the way they distribute the confounding.

The admissibility of designs like random balance is purely a function of context. The designs are valid; it is simply a question of how frequently there exists in the real world the kind of conditions which these designs need. This is why experimenters should look to real world situations to decide the matter of utility of random balance type designs.

F. E. Satterthwaite's random balance may be regarded as the original master design of which the others are special cases [14, 15, 16, 17, 18].

In many cases of multivariate analysis a complete design, or even a fractional replication of a complete design, may be too large to handle. The principle of random balance states that the testing of a random sample of a design matrix should offer reasonable estimates of the results that would appear if it were possible to run the complete design.

Classical random balance designs have the following characteristics: (1) n variables, with r runs, and r not necessarily $\geqslant n$; (2) the value assigned to any variable in a given run is determined randomly; (3) the universe of reference need not be normal, but can be rectangular, logarithmic, or anything else one desires; (4) sampling may be with replacement, without replacement, of a single variable, or the joint selection of two or more variables, or from a discrete or continuous distribution; and (5) values are assigned to the different variables independently.

Random balance in the above pristine form can hardly survive the same kind of "what if" arguments that have been used to destroy many thorough-going randomization processes in statistics and experimental design. For example, what if one's selection of variable values happens to give a design with 100 percent mutual confounding; i.e., with all runs identical? Or, suppose that random numbers happened to give one or two absurdly high or low values? Arguments of this kind at once suggest that the randomization process be subject to certain constraints such as: (1) intercorrelations between factors should not be allowed to exceed a certain value; (2) each level of each factor should appear an equal number of times; and (3) variables may be grouped into independent factorial or fractional factorial designs. Hence even though random balance, in its simplest form, is a useful tool for exploratory investigation, the previous arguments cause the experimenter to seek other modifications leading to positions which are the reverse of random.

One such modification of random balance is that of multiple balance. These designs are useful when there exists the possibility of extreme unbalance among variables, which is considered undesirable. Under these circumstances, the variables may be grouped, and a

TABLE 4   A Minimum Correlation Design

Experimental Unit Number	Input Factors									
	A	B	C	D	E	F	G	H	I	J
1	+	+	+	+	+	+	+	+	+	+
2	+	+	+	+	−	−	−	−	−	−
3	+	−	−	−	+	+	+	−	−	−
4	−	+	−	−	+	−	−	+	+	−
5	−	−	+	−	−	+	−	+	−	+
6	−	−	−	+	−	−	+	−	+	+

factorial or fractional factorial design set up for each group. The subset of the combinations obtained in each group are then selected randomly and tested. For a detailed description of this design see the three articles by Budne [5, 6, 7].

Another extension of this theory lies in the minimum correlation design, which spreads confounding among and between all main effects so that any given main effect confounds all the other as equally as possible. The great merit of a design of this type is that one avoids freak effects which might arise all too easily in classical random balance; for example, one factor can confound one other factor highly and the rest not at all. Table 4 gives an example of a minimum correlation design.

It is possible to have uniform confounding in a design of this type, i.e., to have the main effects confounded equally. In Table 4 it can be shown that 1/3 of the m main effects are coincident for 2 out of the 6 runs, the remaining 2/3 are coincident for 4 out of 6 runs, whereas for orthogonality, 3 out of 6 coincident are required.[2]

It is convenient at this point to examine just exactly how interactions confound main effects and also each other. In this example, each first order interaction is confounded with 4 of the 10 variables and orthogonal to the rest. Con-

founding among the first order interactions themselves results in the situation shown in Table 5. Here each first order interaction is identical with two others. A further examination reveals that not only are these identities unique for each interaction, but that, even more, no main effect variable is repeated in these triple identities. For example, AB is identical with FH and GI, and BC is identical with EF and IJ; in neither case is an interaction identical to any other group but the one it is in, nor is any main effect repeated within the group. This, of course, implies that even though three first order interactions are totally confounded, one can still analyze the first order interactions, and with a priori knowledge, as well as test results, be able to choose that interaction alone which is important. Even if the investigator, through a priori knowledge of the system, could not decide among the three (all three being equally likely of significance), he could still console himself with the fact that of the 45 first order interactions possible, he has now narrowed his field down to 3.

Anyone attempting to experiment with more variables than runs is subject to this type of problem, and, therefore, must accept this confounding as part of the penalty to be paid. At the same time, it must also be remembered that these designs are exploratory and cannot be used for detailed investigation for which classical designs are required.

Although it is possible to obtain some estimate of interactions, even though confounded, one feels that probably one is stretching things quite far enough in trying to estimate main effects using less runs than variables.

[2] The fact that there are differences in the number of coincident runs does not destroy our statement concerning uniform confounding, since the degree of confounding is given by

$$\frac{|0.5 - p|}{0.5}$$

where $|0.5 - p|$ is the absolute difference between 0.5 and the proportion of pairs identical.

TABLE 5   Confounding of First Order Interactions in a Minimum Correlation Design

Interaction	Identical With							
AB					FH	GI		
AC				EH		GJ		
AD				EI	FJ			
AE		CH	DI					
AF	BH		DJ					
AG	BI	CJ						
AH	BF	CE						
AI	BG		DE					
AJ		CG	DF					
BC				EF				IJ
BD				EG			HJ	
BE		CF	DG					
BJ		CI	DH					
CD					FG		HI	
EJ					FI	GH		

However, the fact remains that many interactions are crudely estimatable; and in causal systems where one or two interactions are strongly positive, with the rest largely inactive, these should stand out sufficiently in the analysis to be observable.

An opposite derivation to that of minimum correlation is shown in Table 6, in which the confounding is deliberately skewed, such that it is high in some places and low in others. This is an example of a skewed non-random balance design: Inspection shows that columns A-G are confounded and columns H-R are mutually orthogonal. Designs of this type might be useful when, in a system of n variables, there exists a subset among which the most active will be found; there exists a second subset which a priori are assumed to be less active than the first subset; and there exists little or no interaction between the first subset of variables and the second subset of variables.

In a design of this type, an experimenter

TABLE 6   Skewed Non-Random Balance Design

Experimental Unit Number	Factors																	
	A	B	C	D	E	F	G	H	I	J	K	L	M	N	O	P	Q	R
1	+	+	+	+	+	+	+	+	−	+	−	−	−	+	+	+	−	+
2	+	−	+	+	+	+	+	+	+	−	+	−	−	−	+	+	+	−
3	+	+	−	+	+	+	+	−	+	+	−	+	−	−	+	+	+	+
4	+	+	+	−	+	+	+	+	−	+	+	−	+	−	−	−	+	+
5	+	+	+	+	−	−	−	+	+	−	+	+	−	+	−	−	−	+
6	+	−	−	−	−	−	−	+	+	+	−	+	+	−	−	−	−	−
7	−	+	−	−	−	−	+	−	+	+	+	−	+	+	−	+	−	−
8	−	−	+	−	−	+	−	−	−	+	+	+	−	+	+	−	+	−
9	−	−	−	+	+	−	−	−	−	−	+	+	+	−	+	+	−	+
10	−	−	−	+	+	−	−	+	−	−	−	+	+	+	−	+	+	−
11	−	−	+	−	−	+	−	−	+	−	−	−	+	+	+	−	+	+
12	−	+	−	−	−	−	+	−	−	−	−	−	−	−	−	−	−	−

would be able to investigate two groups of variables simultaneously. By assuming that there is little or no leak of interactions from one group to the other, each group can be analyzed separately, and a reasonable estimate of the order of importance of each variable within its own subset can be made. It must be emphasized, however, that the separation between groups must be large enough to eliminate or minimize any confounding of variables between the two groups. Clearly, one must be reasonably sure of his a priori information before attempting a design of this sort.

A final example of carrying the sacrifice of orthogonality to the limit appears in the technique in which some variables are totally confounded. One such technique to be presented here is that of sequential bifurcation. This technique is useful when a situation exists where there are a very large number of inputs of which only a few are active and the rest are silent. Then the experiment becomes a special search problem, and the procedure would be as follows (for purposes of exposition we are assuming a negligible error variance):

1. Orient all variables so that they all have the same sense where this is known, i.e., all point in the same direction so that variables which are significant and confounded will cumulate and reinforce each other rather than cancel each other.

2. Run everything at the lower level in one single run. This gives a basis for comparison in all later runs.

3. Make two further runs, the first run with the first half of the factors at the high level, and the second run with the second half of the factors at the high level.

4. Test that one of the two runs of step 3 which gives a significant difference from the original test run, depending upon which contains the two or three active variables. If 2 or 3 or more active variables are not in the same group, both groups will give significant differences and are then made into two further runs, each with half of the variables at a high level (i.e., a quarter of the original variables). In this way one tracks down the few significant inputs.

An example of this with 128 variables is presented in Figure 6. Figure 6 shows that, in a few steps, three significant variables have been isolated. A round number (in the binary sense) has been chosen to illustrate this division of variables into two groups of equal size at each branch of the tree. But these numbers do not need to be balanced in this way. It is simply that bifurcation each time is the most efficient way of proceeding. However, if a priori knowledge about the activity of the variables exists, then it would be more economical to make the split unevenly, putting the few hopefuls plus the

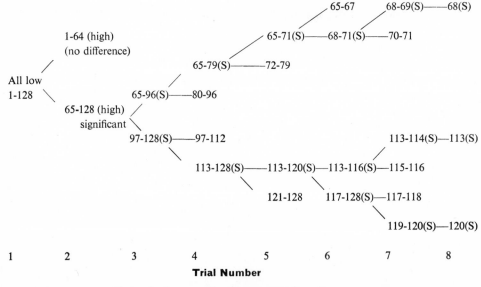

Figure 6 An example of sequential bifurcation.

number of half-way hopefuls in one group and all the rest in the other. One other point worthy of mention is that this technique is useful only in a closed system where the variables are known in advance and the splits can be made easily.

In conclusion, we might remind the reader that, hitherto, keeping main effects orthogonal has been a sacrosanct principle in purist statistical circles. The announcement of random balance designs, for example, generated a storm of controversy. But the locus of this storm was, we believe, misplaced. The question is not "are these designs correct" but rather "how often do real world systems meet the constraints?"

THE SPLIT-PLOT TECHNIQUES

The last statistical design technique to be considered here is the concept of split-plots. The question of plot-splitting is an entirely separate issue from that of deciding what main effects and interactions should be under investigation. The experimental designs used in conjunction with split-plots are not special designs; any design in the statistician's bag of tricks can be utilized in the split-plot situation, if conditions permit.

The decision to use the split-plot principle in large simulation models acknowledges that the utilization of a whole run as a plot is a prodigal waste of time and effort.

To extend the concept, it is not necessary to consider a run as a self-contained unit. By modifying the design, plots can overlap to game play 2, or even game play 3, thereby obtaining the same type of information as before, but increasing the number of combinations available for testing.

This is illustrated in Figure 7 below where 3 latin square designs are incorporated into 2 game plays.

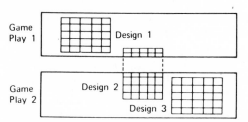

Figure 7 The concept of a split-plot within and between game plays.

If we consider the split-plot technique in terms of degrees of freedom it is seen that instead of thinking of each game play as 1 degree of freedom, we can now consider the degrees of freedom as being split up between and within game plays since each combination of the design does not necessarily utilize one game play.

A problem that may arise from this technique of plot-splitting is that of a sequence or time bias where feedback could distort the results. This problem, of course, could be remedied in a number of ways either by randomizing the ordering sequence, or by testing only those factors that are known a priori to be unrelated. The application of this concept to simulation models gives the experimenter the added advantage of being able to disperse variables within and among game runs while still being able to control the amount of variance.

CONCLUSION

In the development of the basic experimental techniques useful in the exploration of a response surface relative to a system of input variables, four basic lines of attack can be followed.

1. A prior consideration of the overall total number of input variables can be made in an attempt to reduce their number based upon the knowledge of the logic and inner workings of the model. This results in the following alternative outcomes:

(a) The number of initial variables which form the grand total of inputs to the model remains undiminished.

(b) One or more subsets of the grand total of variables are replaced in each case by a single input which we call a secondary variable.

(c) The total system of inputs is found to be decomposable into two or more subsystems with the property that no variable in any one subsystem interacts with that of any other subsystem.

These three alternatives are listed in the order of undesirability, (b) is preferable over (a) because it permits a small experiment, but (c) outranks them both because it permits a fragmentation of the experimental program into smaller pieces.

2. Possible tinkering with the stochastic processes inside the model can be considered to ensure that the error variance is small enough to make unnecessary more than one replication. In general, the error variance does not give much trouble. The large numbers of objects simulated by the model make its initial value of the order of only a few percent. The inputting of identical random numbers between runs reduces this still further, and the use of the split-plot principle allows the potential of a still further reduction through such possibilities as the filtering out a time-oriented component of the error variance. Suffice it to say, that it behooves the experimenter to fix the error variance so that it does not blunt the sensitivity of his experiment.

3. In constructing the actual experimental designs and design strategy, a basic two-step sequential strategy seems to be the most efficacious:

(a) First step: Use of gross wholistic-type design taking cognizance of all variables under consideration with the purpose of establishing the relative activity of the variables.

(b) Second step: Follow-up designs giving more detail in special areas established as interesting in the first step. Though too costly in the number of runs required for the first step in the experimental program, complete and fractional factorial designs are useful in the second step for detailed examination of subsets of variables which were proven interesting by the first step, and worthy of further study.

4. Wherever possible, in both of the above steps, the use of the split-plot principle forces as many variables as possible within game runs, thus minimizing the number of variables between game runs, and hence, the total number of runs required.

REFERENCES

1. F. J. Anscombe, 1959. Quick analysis methods for random balance screening experiments. *Technometrics*, *1*(2): 195–209.
2. K. A. Brownlee, 1949. *Industrial experimentation*. Brooklyn: Chemical Publishing, third American edition.
3. V. Chew, ed., 1958. *Experimental designs in industry*. New York: Wiley.
4. T. A. Budne, 1959. The application of random balance designs. *Technometrics*, *1*(2): 139–155.
5. T. A. Budne, 1959. Random balance, Part I—the missing statistical link in fact finding techniques. *Industrial Quality Control*, *15*(10): 5–10.
6. T. A. Budne, 1959. Random balance, Part II—techniques of analysis. *Industrial Quality Control*, *15*(11): 11–16.
7. T. A. Budne, 1959. Random balance, Part III—case histories. *Industrial Quality Control*, *15*(12): 16–19.
8. O. L. Davies, ed., 1956. *The design and analysis of industrial experiments*. London: Oliver and Boyd.
9. R. A. Fisher, 1946. *Statistical methods for research workers*. London: Oliver and Boyd, tenth edition.
10. R. A. Fisher, 1947. *The design of experiments*. London: Oliver and Boyd, fourth edition.
11. P. Hewett, B. Keigher, S. Meaker, and H. Montague, 1959. *A final report of the AG-1 sensitivity studies*. Working paper, Technical Operations, Incorporated, Operations Model Evaluation Group Staff Memorandum 59-4. 5C.
12. O. Kempthorne, 1952. *The design and analysis of experiments*. New York: Wiley.
13. R. L. Plackett, and J. P. Burman, 1946. The design of optimum multifactorial experiments. *Biometrika*, *33*(4): 305–325.
14. F. E. Satterthwaite, 1958. *Mathematical outline of polyvariable analysis*. Working paper, Statistical Engineering Institute.
15. F. E. Satterthwaite, 1958. *The research game*. Working paper, Statistical Engineering Institute.
16. F. E. Satterthwaite, 1959. *REVOP, or random evolutionary operation*. Working paper, Statistical Engineering Institute.
17. F. E. Satterthwaite, 1959. Random balance experimentation. *Technometrics*, *1*(2): 111–137.
18. F. E. Satterthwaite, and D. Shainin, 1959. *Polyvariable experimentation, a powerful tool for experimentation and control*. Working paper, Statistical Engineering Institute, second edition.
19. J. W. Tukey, 1960. Where do we go from here? *Journal of the American Statistical Association*, *55*(289): 80–93.
20. W. J. Youden, O. Kempthorne, J. W. Tukey, G. E. P. Box, J. S. Hunter, F. E. Satterthwaite, and T. A. Budne, 1959. Discussion of the papers of Messrs. Satterthwaite and Budne. *Technometrics* *1*(2): 157–193.

33

IMPORTANCE SAMPLING IN MONTE CARLO ANALYSES

CHARLES E. CLARK

The author has consulted with operations analysts concerning the statistical problems of Monte Carlo sampling. Inevitably importance sampling is suggested, and this procedure disturbs the analyst. The difficulty is not simply that importance sampling is not understood, but that superficially it appears absurd. For example, if a Monte Carlo analysis is to evaluate the effectiveness of a weapon, one of whose parameters is a reliability coefficient known to be between 0.50 and 0.75, the analyst might be told to carry out the simulation using 0.25 for the reliability coefficient. Such a proposal can be puzzling, and can generate resistance that is not easily overcome.

The limited understanding of importance sampling is unfortunate. The technique is easy to employ, at least in its simplest form. It can be highly efficient. When understood, it is a simple, natural procedure that does not require professional ability in statistics.

The following exposition was written for the author's clients. The discussion is intended to be an elementary presentation of fundamental statistical ideas that should be familiar to an operations analyst interested in Monte Carlo. The paper is an expository, largely nontechnical

SOURCE: Reprinted from *Operations Research*, 9 (5): 603–620 (1961).

discussion of statistical sampling problems that arise in Monte Carlo analyses. No statistical knowledge is presumed beyond recognition of the nature of a probability distribution. Techniques are not elaborated. In relatively simple Monte Carlo analyses the procedures discussed can be employed adequately by the non-mathematician. In the case of an elaborate Monte Carlo, the ideas of this paper should form the basis for coordination between the operations analysts and the mathematical statistician.

The paper starts with an informal statement of what is meant by a Monte Carlo analysis. There follows a digression on stratified sampling; this digression brings to light some important elements in the Monte Carlo analysis. Finally the discussion of importance sampling in Monte Carlo statistical analysis is presented through simple numerical illustrations.

MONTE CARLO ANALYSIS

This section indicates what is meant by a Monte Carlo analysis. The discussion introduces a simple example that will be used later as a numerical illustration.

Suppose that a machine starts at time zero and runs until the time of failure x. The time x is random with probability density $\lambda \exp(-\lambda x)$, $0 \leqq x < \infty$. At the time of failure the machine must be scrapped with probability p, $0 < p < 1$, but with probability $q = 1 - p$, the machine is repaired. If repaired, the machine runs from time x to $x + x'$ with x' distributed as x. Again the machine survives with probability q, and in case of survival the third failure occurs at time $x + x' + x''$ with x'' distributed as x. The process terminates when the machine is scrapped.

Suppose that we wish to know the probability that the machine will survive until time X (there may be failures before time X, but each of these failures is repaired). This probability can be computed analytically.[1] Alternatively one could use the following analysis. One would draw a random number from the exponential distribution with probability density $\lambda \exp(-\lambda x)$, and this number would simulate the time to the first failure. Another random number (uniformly distributed) would determine whether the machine could be repaired. If a repair is effected, a second generation from the exponential distribution would determine the time between the first and second failures. It is obvious how the simulation would continue until the machine would be scrapped. If such a process were carried out several times, the fraction of times that the machine survived to time X would be used as an estimate of the desired probability.

If one's interest were in this problem per se, the analytic solution is much to be preferred to the statistical sampling procedure. However, later in the paper we shall consider a Monte Carlo analysis of this problem. The fact that the problem can be handled analytically will permit evaluations of the Monte Carlo analysis that would be impossible in case of a problem appropriate for Monte Carlo analysis; typically a Monte Carlo analysis is used only when an analytic solution is not obtainable. In this paper, somewhat incorrectly, an "analytic" procedure is one that does not involve statistical sampling.

The statistical sampling procedure as described above is based upon a model whose random elements are given analytically. This distinguishes the problem from a typical survey statistics problem. If one were to estimate the tobacco consumption per capita from a sample, one might consider the consumption of an individual to be a random variable. But in that

case, the distribution of the random variable is unknown. One could not replace a survey of people by some desk procedure of simulating people and designating their consumptions by numbers read from a table. However, regardless of whether the sample data are obtained from a desk simulation or a field survey, the subsequent mathematical analysis of the sample data could be the same.

Some writers would distinguish between the machine-failure and tobacco-consumption problems by saying that that first can be solved by a Monte Carlo analysis, the term Monte Carlo indicating that one knows explicitly the distributions of all the random elements in the problem. In this sense the term Monte Carlo signifies that one could simulate the random process by a desk calculation that uses tables of random numbers or by a computer program that generates random numbers. With this definition Monte Carlo does not require any distinctive mathematical analysis. The techniques of analysis were in use before the term Monte Carlo was employed. The problems to be considered in this paper are Monte Carlo problems in the sense of the above definition. The objective of the paper could be stated as that of efficiency in Monte Carlo analyses. We shall retain this definition at present, but an alternative definition will appear below.

Monte Carlo analysis, as so defined, is *almost* a general, effective procedure that enables one to solve many problems too complex for mathematical analysis. But there is one unfortunate fact. Such Monte Carlo analysis is costly. In one problem it required a high-speed computer to run $1\frac{1}{2}$ hours to obtain a single sample value. At least 20 runs were required for even a small sample, and results were desired for hundreds of sets of model parameters.

There are ways to reduce the cost of such Monte Carlo analyses. Computer capabilities can be increased, and judicious adaptation of models can reduce costs. But a much easier way to reduce costs is through the employment of efficient sampling techniques. The nature and efficacy of importance sampling, one of these techniques, is the subject of this paper.

In importance sampling one considers a statistical sampling problem of the type designated above as a Monte Carlo problem. How-

[1] See [2, Appendix B]

ever, one does not carry out the sampling in the manner suggested by the problem. Rather a new random process is introduced in place of the original. The nature of this substitution will come to light in later sections of the paper. At present we merely remark that some writers reserve the term Monte Carlo for a method of analysis in which one creates a random variable whose expected value is the solution of a given problem. This random variable is artificial with respect to the given problem. In the machine-failure problem one is concerned with the random variable which is 1 if a machine is scrapped prior to time X, and which is 0 if the machine survives until time X (the expected value of this random variable is the probability that a machine is scrapped prior to time X). This random variable is given in the statement of the problem, and it is not created by the mathematician during the course of the analysis. However, in the solution constructed below by a Monte Carlo analysis, this random variable is not used. Rather the mathematician creates another random variable, whose expected value is the same as that of the given random variable, but whose expected value can be obtained at lower sampling cost.

STRATIFIED SAMPLING

The problem in the preceding section could be analyzed by simulating the histories of many machines, and computing statistics of the outcomes. The statistician would say that data were obtained by simple random sampling. But in costly statistical analyses it is usually possible to replace simple random sampling by some more efficient procedure. Before describing such a procedure for use in Monte Carlo analyses, we shall examine some features of stratified sampling. This digression will illustrate in simple form the basic idea to be employed in importance sampling.

As a hypothetical illustrative example we suppose that a hotel wishes to estimate the mean annual expenditure by its guests in barber shops and beauty parlors. It is known that the expenditures by women differ more widely than expenditures by men. Many men get a $2 haircut every 2 weeks at an annual cost of roughly $50; expenditures of as much as $100 or as little as $25 are found occasionally. Expenditures by

women can vary from nothing to over $500. The mean expenditure for women is harder to estimate than the mean for men.

We assume that 80 per cent of the hotel guests are men. Suppose that a sample of size 15 is to be taken (we use an absurdly small sample size to simplify the exposition). If simple random sampling were employed we would expect the sample to consist of 12 men (80 per cent of 15) and 3 women. However, suppose that one decided to obtain a stratified sample including 5 men and 10 women. Suppose the expenditures of the members of such a sample turned out to be in dollars:

Men: 50,   50,   50,   50,   100
Women: 0,   50,   100,   100,   200,   200,   200,   300,   500,   800

It is intuitively clear that such data will lead to a more accurate estimate of the overall average than would the expenditures of 12 men and 3 women.

To analyze these data we calculate $\bar{M}$ and $\bar{W}$, the means of the 5 male expenditures and the 10 female expenditures, respectively. The results are

$$\bar{M} = 60 \qquad \bar{W} = 245$$

These means emphasize the fact that stratified sampling is more advantageous than simple random sampling in the present situation. In the sample 30 per cent of the women have expenditures greater than the mean $\bar{W}$. This reflects the fact that a minority of the women have an important influence on the mean $\bar{W}$ and on the mean when both sexes are pooled into a single distribution. It is likely that the estimates to be made would be more accurate if an even greater fraction of the sample consisted of women. However the optimum fraction is not relevant to the following discussion.[2]

---

[2] The data suggest that the sample of women should be roughly 2.7 times as large as the sample of men. This ratio is obtained from $(0.2)(48.20)/(0.8)(17.89)$ in which 0.2 and 0.8 are the fractions of women and men respectively in the population, and 48.20 and 17.89 are empirical estimates of the standard deviations of the expenditures for women and men, respectively. A justification of this result is beyond the scope of this paper. Discussions of this analysis appear in [3], [4], and [5] and other discussions of stratified sampling.

We return to the problem of estimating the mean expenditure for all persons, male and female. If a simple random sample of size 15 had been drawn, one would divide the sum of the 15 data by 15. But this can not be done in the present instance because we have distorted the natural, simple random sampling procedure. However the analysis in the face of this distortion is obvious. Since 80 per cent of the guests are men, we compute the following weighted mean of $\bar{M}$ and $\bar{W}$, and we obtain an estimated mean expenditure of all hotel guests to be

$$\bar{x} = 0.8\bar{M} + 0.2\bar{W}$$
$$= (0.8)(60) + (0.2)(245) = 97$$

We could estimate the sampling error in this estimate. We shall not do so because the error analysis is not needed for our purposes.

We turn next to a cruder and more cumbersome analysis of the data given above. This alternative analysis is less appealing in the barber-beauty shop problem. However, interesting analogies with Monte Carlo analysis will appear.

Let us suppose that the sample was taken among the hotel guests registered at a specific time (we ignore the fact that the statistical properties of these guests may not accurately reflect the properties of all guests over a period of time). Let us suppose that when the sample was drawn, there were 80 men and 20 women registered at the hotel. If simple random sampling had been employed, 15 of the 100 guests, without consideration of sex, would have been selected in such a manner that each guest had the probability 0.15 of being included in the sample. Thus a random process is visualized that would select 15 guests. Before the process would be implemented, the particular 15 selected would be uncertain, but each of the 100 guests would have the probability 0.15 of being selected in the sample.

This simple random sampling process was not employed. Rather the natural process was distorted. Whereas any man M_i would have the probability

$$p(M_i) = 0.15$$

of being included in a simple random sample, the probability was distorted to

$$p^*(M_i) = 5/80 = 0.0625$$

under the distorted sampling procedure that selected 5 of the 80 male guests. For any individual woman W_i the probability of being included in a simple random sample is

$$p(W_i) = 0.15$$

and the probability of being included in a sample drawn by the distorted process is

$$p^*(W_i) = 10/20 = 0.5$$

Consider a particular man who was selected in the sample that was drawn. To be specific suppose that this man is the one with expenditure 100. We shall designate him by M_{100}. For analytic purposes to be revealed below, we compute for this man the weight

$$w(M_{100}) = p(M_{100})/p^*(M_{100})$$
$$= 0.15/0.0625 = 2.4$$

The interpretation of this weight is that M_{100} would expect to appear in simple random samples (if a large number of samples would be drawn) 2.4 times as often as in samples drawn under the distorted process. The distorted process underestimates the importance of M_{100} by the factor of 2.4. Suppose that the hotel guests numbered thousands, instead of 100, and that there were many duplicates of M_{100}. The distorted sampling process would include several duplicates of M_{100}, but in simple random sampling one would expect 2.4 times as many of such duplicates. Hence in the analysis, which will be carried out with use of formulas designed for simple random sampling, we will count M_{100} as 2.4 individuals.

Similarly, consider one of the women drawn into the sample, say W_{800}. For her we have the weight

$$w(W_{800}) = p(W_{800})/p^*(W_{800})$$
$$= 0.15/0.5 = 0.3$$

If many simple random samples would be drawn, this woman would be drawn into the sample approximately 30 per cent as often as she could expect to be chosen under the distorted process. One might say that the distorted process overestimates the importance of the lady by a factor of $1/0.3 = 3.33$. In the analysis we should downgrade the lady's importance by counting her as 0.3 of a person.

We return to the numerical sample. For each

person actually drawn into the sample we compute the weight. For each man the weight is 2.4 and for each woman the weight is 0.3. We compute the arithmetic mean of the 15 numbers in the sample, but we count each man as 2.4 men and each woman as 0.3 women. The result is a new estimate of $\bar{x}$, called $\bar{x}'$, computed as

$$\bar{x}' = \frac{\begin{array}{c}(2.4)(50) + \cdots + 2.4(100) \\ + (0.3)(0) + \cdots + (0.3)(800)\end{array}}{15} = 97$$

Fortunately $\bar{x}' = \bar{x}$. It is possible to prove that this equality is to be anticipated. Such a proof is not presented in this paper, but can be found in references [1] and [10] or [6].

The statistic $\bar{x}$ is simpler to comprehend than $\bar{x}'$. However the second statistic, or rather the basic ideas involved in the definition of $\bar{x}'$, can be employed in a wide variety of situations. In fact we can state the following general rule. As an estimator of a population expected value we could use a sample mean calculated from the elements of a simple random sample. Suppose, however, that instead of simple random sampling we use a sampling procedure in which the population elements have probabilities (or likelihoods) of inclusion within the sample, which are different from the probabilities under simple random sampling. For each element x of the population from which the sample is drawn, let $p(x)$ and $p^*(x)$ be the probabilities that the element x would be drawn into the sample under simple random sampling and the alternative sampling process, respectively. Consider the weight $w(x) = p(x)/p^*(x)$. We can still use the sample mean as an estimator of the population expected value if we weight each sample value by $w(x)$. This rule will be illustrated and clarified below.

IMPORTANCE SAMPLING IN MONTE CARLO ANALYSIS

We are ready to discuss importance sampling. The discussion continues through the medium of trivial numerical illustrations.

Consider the exponential distribution with probability density

$$p(x) = 0.01 \exp(-0.01x) \qquad (0 \leqq x < \infty) \quad (1)$$

We shall estimate the probability that a sample value from this distribution is less than 1. This probability is easy to obtain analytically, being $1 - \exp(-0.01) = 0.00995$ to five decimal places. However we shall estimate this probability by a Monte Carlo analysis in order to obtain a simple illustration involving sampling with distorted probability distributions.

Suppose we were to generate a simple random sample from the distribution (1). It would require a large sample to give an accurate estimate of the probability that a sample value from (1) is less than 1. This is due to the fact that approximately 1 per cent of the sample values would be less than 1. Hence hundreds of sample values would be required before we would know that the fraction is near 0.01.

In order to obtain a greater proportion of sample values within the interval of importance, namely $(0, 1)$, we shall distort the sampling procedure. We introduce the distribution with probability density

$$p^*(x) = \exp(-x) \qquad (2)$$

If we sample from this distribution, which superficially has no relevance to the problem, we shall achieve the result that a large fraction of the sample values will fall within the importance interval $(0, 1)$; the expected fraction is $1 - e^{-1} = 0.63$. Setting aside momentarily any question of the sanity of our operation, let us consider a sample from the distribution $p^*(x)$. Suppose that the first number generated from $p^*(x)$ were 2. Let us consider the likelihoods of generating this value 2 in both undistorted and distorted sampling. The likelihood in case of undistorted sampling is obtained from (1) as $p(2) = 0.01 \exp(-0.02) = 0.0098020$, and the likelihood of drawing this same value 2 in distorted sampling is obtained from (2) as $p^*(2) = 0.13534$. The ratio of these likelihoods is

$$p(2)/p^*(2) = 0.0098020/0.13534 = 0.07$$

approximately. This implies that in undistorted sampling one can expect approximately 7 per cent as many sample values in the interval $(2, 2 + dx)$ as would be obtained under distorted sampling. But this means that one can sample from $p^*(x)$, count the number of sample values between 2 and $2 + dx$ and multiply by 0.07; in this way one has an unbiased estimate of the

TABLE 1   Weights Related to the Use of $p^*(x)$ as a Distortion of $p(x)$

x	$p(x)$	$p^*(x)$	$w(x) = p(x)/p^*(x)$
0.1	0.0099900	0.90484	0.0110
0.2	0.0099800	0.81873	0.0122
0.3	0.0099700	0.74082	0.0135
0.4	0.0099600	0.67032	0.0149
0.5	0.0099501	0.60653	0.0164
0.6	0.0099402	0.54881	0.0181
0.8	0.0099302	0.49659	0.0200
0.8	0.0099203	0.44933	0.0221
0.9	0.0099104	0.40657	0.0244
1.0	0.0099005	0.36788	0.0269
2.0	0.0098020	0.13534	0.0724
3.0	0.0097045	0.049787	0.1949
4.0	0.0096080	0.018316	0.5246
5.0	0.0095123	0.0067379	1.412
6.0	0.0094176	0.0024788	3.799
7.0	0.0093239	0.00091188	10.22
8.0	0.0092311	0.00033546	27.52
9.0	0.0091393	0.00012341	74.56
10.0	0.0090484	0.000045400	199.3

number of sample values expected between 2 and $2 + dx$ under undistorted sampling (and with the same sample size). In practice, if 2 were generated under distorted sampling, one would accept 2 not as one value but as 0.07 of a value.

The numbers computed above for $x = 2$ appear in Table 1. This table also contains similar results for other values of x. For example, Table 1 gives the weight 1.412 for the sample value $x = 5$. This implies that a sample value within the interval $(5, 5 + dx)$ can be expected 41.2 per cent more often with undistorted sampling than with distorted sampling. Several such weights are listed in Table 1. The weights reflect the obvious fact that small sample values are more likely to be generated from $p^*(x)$ but large values are more likely from $p(x)$.

To illustrate the use of weighted sampling we have drawn a random sample of size 10 from $p^*(x)$. The sample values of x are listed in Table 2. In addition Table 2 gives each of the weights. Since we are estimating the probability that x is less than 1, we consider the six values of x in Table 2 that are less than 1. The value 0.31

is counted as 0.014 of an observation, 0.17 as 0.012 of an observation, etc. The sum of the weights for the six x's less than 1 is 0.096. Hence we count slightly less than one-tenth of an x less than 1. Since the sample size is 10, we estimate the probability that x in undistorted sampling will be less than 1 to be $0.096/10 = 0.0096$. This estimate is close to the true value 0.00995.

The procedure has been the following. If one were to sample from $p(x)$, approximately one out of a hundred sample values would be less than 1, and it would require a large sample to produce adequate data for an estimate of the probability that x is less than 1. We replaced $p(x)$ by $p^*(x)$ which generates a large fraction of its sample values less than 1. We observed that any sample value from $p^*(x)$ can be weighted in such a way as to represent a number of sample values from the distribution of $p(x)$. This number (weight) is in some cases a small fraction and in other cases much greater than 1. In the numerical illustration the distorted sampling produced 6 of 10 sample values less than 1. But the weighting procedure led to counting each of the 6 as a small fraction of a single value when the values are to be interpreted as from the distribution of $p(x)$. The mathematical justification of the weighting procedure and the estimate of the variance will not be made in this paper.[3]

COMMON DISTORTIONS OF TWO OR MORE RANDOM PROCESSES

In the preceding section we estimated a parameter of the distribution $p(x)$ given by (1). We did not generate a sample from this distribution; instead, our sample was from the distribution $p^*(x)$ given by (2). Let us observe that $p^*(x)$ can be regarded as a distortion of many distributions. Hence the sample of Table 2, drawn from $p^*(x)$, can be used for statistical analyses of many distributions.

To clarify this matter by a numerical illustration, we consider the distribution with probability density

$$p'(x) = 0.02 \exp(-0.02x) \qquad (0 \leqq x < \infty)$$

We shall estimate the probability that x, randomly drawn from $p'(x)$, is less than or equal to 1. Our new problem is identical with the problem in the preceding section, except that $p(x)$ is replaced by $p'(x)$.

[3] See [6], [7], or [8].

We shall use the same $p^*(x)$ as a distortion of $p'(x)$. We proceed as before and obtain Table 3 in place of Table 2. The sum of the weights in Table 3 for sample values in the interval $(0, 1)$ is 0.190. Dividing this sum by the sample size 10, we obtain 0.0190 as the estimate of the probability that x from $p'(x)$ is less than or equal to 1. This estimate can be compared with the true value 0.0198.

The salient feature is that two problems have been solved by use of the same sample (the first columns of Tables 2 and 3 are identical). In a serious Monte Carlo most of the computing time is used in obtaining the sample values from the distorted distribution; typically the time for statistical analysis is relatively insignificant. In our trivial example this does not happen to be true. But if we should assume that the major part of the computation consisted in the generation of the first column in Tables 2 and 3, we would conclude that we have solved two problems at the cost essentially of a single analysis.

In general, consider the probability distributions obtained by assigning a set of values to λ in $\lambda \exp(-\lambda x)$. Suppose that for each of these distributions we wish to know the probability that x is less than or equal to 1. All these problems can be solved from a single sample drawn from $p^*(x)$. If the number of values assigned to λ is large, the savings obtained from distorted

TABLE 2   Sample from $p^*(x)$ as a Distortion of $p(x)$

Sample x from $p^*(x)$	$p(x)$	$p^*(x)$	$w(x) = p(x)/p^*(x)$
2.71	0.009733	0.06654	0.146
0.31	0.009969	0.7334	0.014
0.17	0.009983	0.8437	0.012
0.02	0.009998	0.9802	0.010
0.59	0.009941	0.5543	0.018
0.54	0.009946	0.5828	0.017
4.15	0.009594	0.01576	0.609
0.91	0.009909	0.4025	0.025
2.72	0.009732	0.06588	0.148
1.15	0.009886	0.3166	0.031

$$\sum_{x<1} w(x) = 0.014 + 0.012 + 0.010 + 0.018 + 0.017 + 0.025 = 0.096$$

$$(10)^{-1} \sum w(x) = 0.0096.$$

TABLE 3   Sample from $p^*(x)$ as a Distortion of $p'(x)$

Sample x from $p^*(x)$	$p'(x)$	$p^*(x)$	$w(x) = p'(x)/p^*(x)$
2.71	0.01894	0.06654	0.285
0.31	0.01988	0.7334	0.027
0.17	0.01993	0.8437	0.024
0.02	0.01999	0.9802	0.020
0.59	0.01976	0.5543	0.036
0.54	0.01978	0.5828	0.034
4.15	0.01841	0.01576	1.17
0.91	0.01964	0.4025	0.049
2.72	0.01894	0.06588	0.288
1.15	0.01954	0.3166	0.062

$$\sum_{x<1} w(x) = 0.027 + 0.024 + 0.020 + 0.036 + 0.034 + 0.049 = 0.190$$

$$(10)^{-1} \sum w(x) = 0.0190$$

sampling can be tremendous. (However, if the values of λ differ greatly among themselves, it is possible that a common distortion of all the distributions may not be efficient for every λ. It might be necessary to group the values of λ into sets, and to handle the sets separately. Such technicalities are beyond the scope of this paper.)

COMPLEX STOCHASTIC PROCESSES

In the example given before, the efficiency of the Monte Carlo analysis can be greatly increased by distorted sampling. (We say that a first sampling procedure is k times as efficient as a second procedure if the sample sizes N_1 and N_2, respectively, required for a given sampling error satisfy $N_2 = kN_1$.) Unfortunately most Monte Carlo analyses are applied to more complex stochastic processes, and the dramatic savings are much harder to obtain. (But the procedure in the preceding section is no less efficient.) We shall illustrate this fact by an example of a stochastic process with two random elements.

Consider the random variable y, which is distributed uniformly between 0 and 200. The probability density of y is

$$P(y) = \begin{cases} \frac{1}{200}, & 0 \leq y \leq 200 \\ 0, & \text{otherwise} \end{cases}$$

We also use the random variable x with probability density $p(x)$ given by (1). We assume

x and y independently distributed. We shall study $z = x + y$, and we consider the estimation by Monte Carlo analysis of the probability that z is less than 1. To obtain values of z in the important interval $(0, 1)$ we shall distort the distributions of both x and y. The distortion of $p(x)$ will be the same used above. The distortion of $P(y)$ will be the probability density

$$P^*(y) = \begin{cases} 1, & 0 \leq y \leq \frac{1}{2} \\ \frac{1}{399}, & \frac{1}{2} < y \leq 200 \\ 0, & \text{otherwise} \end{cases}$$

Under distorted sampling for y, i.e., with y generated from the distribution with density P^*, the weight will be $P(y)/P^*(y) = 0.005$ if $0 \leq y \leq \frac{1}{2}$, and $P(y)/P^*(y) = 1.995$ if $\frac{1}{2} < y \leq 200$.

Suppose that one should generate under distorted sampling $x = 0.4$ and $y = 0.4$, and hence $z = 0.8$. Since x and y are independently distributed, the likelihood of this pair of drawings under undistorted sampling is $p(x)P(y)$, and the likelihood under distorted sampling is $p^*(x)P^*(y)$. Hence the weight associated with the pair of values is

$$p(x)P(y)/p^*(x)P^*(y)$$

This is the product of the weights associated with x and y individually. For $x = 0.4$, the weight is seen in Table 1 to be 0.0149, and for $y = 0.4$, the weight is given above as 0.005. Hence the weight associated with z determined as $0.4 + 0.4$ is $(0.0149)(0.005) = 0.0000745$.

Suppose that another pair of drawings gave $x = 0.2$ and $y = 0.6$, and hence again $z = 0.8$. One easily checks that the weight associated with the pair of generations is $(0.0122)(1.995) = 0.024339$. The important aspect of these results is that both pairs of generations produced the same z, namely $z = 0.8$, but the weights are different, indeed greatly different. Thus we do not have the monotonicity of the weight as a function of distance, which is apparent in Table 1. Such instability of the weights can greatly reduce the efficiency of sampling distortions.[4]

Let us reflect on this example. The generation of a value of z requires the generation of an x and a y. Under distorted sampling the weight associated with z is the product of the weights associated with x and y. Suppose that a small value of x is drawn. Since such a small x is more likely under distorted sampling, $w(x)$ is small. This tends to make the weight of z small. This is fortunate because our objective under distorted sampling is to get a large number of small values of z; furthermore, the large number of z's must have small weights associated with them to prevent bias in the statistical estimates.

However, this advantageous relation between x and $w(x)$ does not necessarily produce the same relation between z and $w(z)$. If a small x is added to a moderately large y, the sum is a z that is not small. However, the weight $w(z)$ might be small, being the product of a very small $w(x)$ and a value of $w(y)$ near 1. In other words, although there may be advantageous correlations between x and $w(x)$ as well as between y and $w(y)$, it is an unfortunate fact that the resulting correlation between $x + y$ and $w(x)w(y)$ may be weak. Thus we do not have the situation in which all small values of z have small weights and all large values of z have large weights. The serious implications of this non-monotonic relation between z and $w(z)$ may not be apparent. However, it can be proved that such instability of the weights can greatly reduce the efficiency of the distorted sampling.[5]

Consider a complex Monte Carlo. There will be many random variables $x_1, ..., x_n$, with n in some cases greater than 1000. Instead of the simple relation $z = x + y$, the outcome of the

process z is some complex function of $x_1, ..., x_n$. In general, the greater n, the more difficult it is to achieve an effective correlation between this function z and the product of the n weight factors.

In complex Monte Carlo analyses one tries to introduce distorted sampling of one or more of the random variables in the process. The objective is to obtain a relatively large amount of data within intervals of importance. Furthermore these data should have small weights to compensate for their large quantity. The data that fall outside the intervals of importance should be few in number but for that reason have large weights. For complex stochastic processes, it is often difficult to determine appropriate distortions.

A LESS UNREALISTIC ILLUSTRATION

We have described some aspects of the statistical sampling problem in Monte Carlo analysis. These discussions will be summarized through the medium of a numerical example that is intended to bridge the gap between formalism and realistic application.

We shall study the process described above in which the running time between failures of a machine is generated from the distribution with probability density $\lambda \exp(-\lambda x)$, $0 \leqq x < \infty$; at each time of failure the machine dies (is scrapped) with probability p but is repaired with probability $q = 1 - p$; in case of repair an additional running time is generated from the same exponential distribution; the process continues until death is generated at a time of failure. Let us suppose that the basic problem is to determine the 1 per cent quantile of the distribution of times to death. In other words we wish a lower tolerance limit for this time to death so that with 99 per cent confidence one can assume that a machine's life will exceed this tolerance limit. This 1 per cent quantile, which we shall denote by X, can be computed analytically.[6] For this reason our example is simpler than most Monte Carlo simulations. But the simplicity will permit analytic evaluations that are impossible if a simulation is complex.

---

[4] See [2, Appendix A].

[5] See [2, Appendix A].
[6] See [2, Appendix B].

The running times and death or survival at each failure could be simulated. The histories of several machines could be generated, and the time of death recorded for each history. From the record of these empirical times of death, one could estimate the 1 per cent quantile X. Such an estimate would have a large relative error unless the sample size were very large. This is due to the fact that very few of the empirical data would be within the interval of importance $(0, X)$.

To obtain a greater fraction of the empirical results within the importance interval $(0, X)$, we can distort the Monte Carlo process. We can replace the distribution of running times with one having a smaller expected time between failures. Furthermore we can increase the probability of death at each failure. We note that the expected value of the random variable with probability density $\lambda \exp(-\lambda x)$ is $1/\lambda$ [indeed, the integral from 0 to ∞ of $\lambda x \exp(-\lambda x)$ is $1/\lambda$.] Hence if the exponential distribution with parameter λ is replaced by the exponential distribution with parameter λ^* with $\lambda < \lambda^*$, the expected time between failures is reduced from $1/\lambda$ to $1/\lambda^*$. In addition we can replace the probability of death p by $p^* > p$.

Thus one would hope to employ importance sampling advantageously by increasing λ and p

to λ^* and p^*. But appropriate values for λ^* and p^* are not immediately obvious. Should both or only one of the parameters be distorted? How great should the distortions be? Before discussing how one might resolve these questions, we shall indicate the optimum distortions in a special case.

To particularize the discussion we shall use $\lambda = 1$ and $p = \frac{1}{2}$. For several pairs of values of λ^* and $q^* = 1 - p^*$, we have computed the efficiency of the distorted sampling relative to undistorted sampling. The reciprocals of these relative efficiencies appear in Table 4. For example Table 4 gives 0.00538 in case $\lambda^* = 80$ and $q^* = 0.005$. This means that if the sampling error is preassigned, and if a sample of size N is required under undistorted sampling to keep the error of estimate within the given limit of error, a sample size of $0.00538N$ would be adequate to attain the same accuracy if the parameters are distorted to $\lambda^* = 80$ and $q^* = 0.005$. The mathematical formulas from which Table 4 was derived are not presented in this paper.[7]

In a real problem, appropriate for Monte Carlo analysis, one cannot construct Table 4; if one could construct such a table, it is likely that

[7] See [2, Appendices].

TABLE 4   Variance of Sample Estimate in Distorted Sampling Divided by the Variance in Undistorted Sampling

λ^*	q^*							
	0.5	0.3	0.1	0.05	0.01	0.005	0.001	0.0005
1	1.00000	0.70904	0.55679	0.54068	0.64145	0.84770	14.58096	1087.46222
5	0.19739	0.13826	0.10571	0.10018	0.10013	0.10518	1.78017	3.33124
10	0.09908	0.06796	0.05075	0.04552	0.04653	0.04762	0.06128	0.08494
20	0.05055	0.03327	0.02370	0.02197	0.02100	0.02126	0.02470	0.02989
40	0.02770	0.01694	0.01097	0.00988	0.00919	0.00923	0.01027	0.01143
60	0.02167	0.01264	0.00763	0.00671	0.00610	0.00610	0.00668	0.00754
80	0.02032	0.01167	0.00687	0.00598	0.00540	0.00538	0.00580	0.00643
100	0.02132	0.01239	0.00743	0.00652	0.00590	0.00587	0.00622	0.00695
120	0.02409	0.01436	0.00896	0.00798	0.00729	0.00725	0.00758	0.00807
140	0.02854	0.01754	0.01145	0.01032	0.00949	0.00949	0.00981	0.01030
160	0.03492	0.02210	0.01499	0.01368	0.01278	0.01270	0.01303	0.01353
180	0.04361	0.02833	0.01982	0.01825	0.01718	0.01709	0.01743	0.01800

one could solve the problem analytically. Hence one must obtain good distortions of the model parameters partly by guesswork. Such guessing is not a simple matter. Table 4 reveals that some distortions would be disastrous.

In the face of our illustrative problem one might reason as follows. One cannot get a large fraction of small times to death x merely by increasing p. This is due to the fact that the first time to failure is generated before the probability p comes into play, and the first time to failure already exceeds X in a large fraction of the histories. Hence it is likely that large sampling savings will require a distortion of λ. It would be unwise to rely solely on a distortion of p.

Without further insight into the times that would be generated under undistorted sampling, one could not do much better than the following. We note that it could be disastrous to use too large values of λ^* and p^*; indeed, Table 4 indicates that $\lambda^* = 1$ and $q^* = 0.0005$ would be bad, and we remark, without proof, that similar unfortunate results are obtained if λ^* is increased beyond the range in Table 4. Hence one might generate two small samples of histories with small distortions to say $\lambda^* = 2$ and $q^* = 0.4$ in one sample and $\lambda^* = 3$ and $q^* = 0.3$ in the other. Estimates of the sampling errors in the two samples could suggest trial values of the parameters in a third sample. This timid, tentative, probing procedure has serious disadvantages. In the first place, the sampling errors in the estimates of the sampling errors would be great with small samples, and the empirical results might mislead one to believe, until further data were available, that a distortion of λ to 2 is better than a distortion to 3. More seriously, the analysis would be completed (with small savings) before one used parameters anywhere near the optimum. In some cases these difficulties cannot be circumvented.

In one can anticipate the results that would be obtained under simple random sampling, one can act more effectively. Suppose one had reason to believe that in undistorted sampling the expected value of the time to death is near 2 (it is 2) and that the 1 per cent quantile is near 0.020 (it is 0.020). Then one would know that in undistorted sampling much of the time-to-death data would be near 2, whereas we would like data near 0.020. This suggests a distortion of the times to death that decreases the expected value of the times to death by a factor of roughly 100. Use of $\lambda^* = 100$ would effect such a distortion. Hence for the sake of simplicity one could leave p undistorted and use $\lambda^* = 50$ or $\lambda^* = 25$ depending upon how timid one is in the face of the fact that it is worse, usually, to overestimate than to underestimate the optimum distortion.

The suggestion of the preceding paragraph can be implemented by two stage sampling. An initial sample can produce rough estimates of the expected value and 1 per cent quantile. A second sample can produce the desired accuracy with the economies of importance sampling.[8]

It is possible to devise less elementary procedures for arriving at a good estimate of an optimum distortion (but to the author's knowledge, current literature does not indicate any simple, generally applicable procedure for estimating accurately an optimum distortion). In general, elementary considerations often cannot be sharper than the above thoughts.

These thoughts lead to the suggestion that in the hands of a mathematical amateur, importance sampling can produce significant but moderate savings in computing time. If a Monte Carlo is so large that high computing costs are involved, it is likely that profit would result from professional mathematical assistance in the design of the statistical sampling procedures.[9]

ESTIMATES OF EXPECTED VALUES

The entire paper has been limited to the discussion of one problem, the estimation of the probability that the output of a Monte Carlo is less than X, where X is the 1 per cent quantile or some other quantile with a small percentage. This probability is an expected value (of the random variable, which is 1 if the time to death is less than X, and is 0 otherwise). In general, Monte Carlo analysis involves the estimation of expected values. However the different information requirements arise in the estimations of different expected values. Hence technical procedures vary from problem to problem.

[8] See [9, pp. 123–140].
[9] See [6], [7], and [8].

Consider, for example, the numerical example discussed in the preceding section. One might wish to know the expected value of the distribution of times to death. For an estimate of this expected value, the distortions used above would be bad. The large times of death are more important than the small ones in the sense that an efficient sample should contain more large times than would be generated in simple random sampling. One would in this case decrease λ and p. We shall not discuss this problem. Our purpose at this point is to warn the reader not to assume that all Monte Carlo statistical analyses are completely similar in details to the illustrations used in this paper.

REFERENCES

1. H. J. Arnold, B. D. Bucher, H. F. Trotter, and J. W. Tukey, 1956. Monte Carlo techniques in a complex problem about normal samples. *Symposium on Monte Carlo methods* (H. A. Meyer, ed.); New York: Wiley, 80–88. MS.
2. C. E. Clark, 1960. *Importance sampling in Monte Carlo analyses.* Working paper, System Development Corporation, TM-505. MS.
3. W. G. Cochran, 1953. *Sampling techniques.* New York: Wiley.
4. W. E. Deming, 1950. *Some theory of sampling.* New York: Wiley.
5. M. H. Hansen, W. N. Hurwitz, and W. G. Madow, 1953. *Sample survey methods and theory.* New York: Wiley, two volumes.
6. H. Kahn, 1954. *Applications of Monte Carlo.* Working paper, Rand Corporation, RM-1237-AEC, revised 1956. MS.
7. H. Kahn, 1956. Use of different Monte Carlo sampling techniques. *Symposium on Monte Carlo methods* (H. A. Meyer, ed.); New York: Wiley, 146–190. MS.
8. H. Kahn, and A. W. Marshall, 1953. Methods of reducing sample size in Monte Carlo computations. *Operations Research*, *1*(5): 263–278. MS.
9. A. W. Marshall, 1956. The use of multi-stage sampling schemes in Monte Carlo computations. *Symposium on Monte Carlo methods* (H. A. Meyer, ed.); New York: Wiley, 123–140. MS.
10. H. F. Trotter, and J. W. Tukey, 1956. Conditional Monte Carlo for normal samples. *Symposium on Monte Carlo methods* (H. A. Meyer, ed.); New York: Wiley, 64–79. MS.

34

SELECTIVE SAMPLING—A TECHNIQUE FOR REDUCING SAMPLE SIZE IN SIMULATION OF DECISION-MAKING PROBLEMS[1]

MICHAEL E. BRENNER[2]

There are many situations today in which industrial engineers and operations research analysts are faced with the need of simulating a system in order to make a decision (see, for example, [3]). The amount of simulation effort and the accuracy of the decision are interrelated. If the amount of simulation effort required to make a decision can be reduced for some fixed level of accuracy, the cost of obtaining a solution can be reduced and therefore more problems can be handled by means of simulation. If the accuracy of a decision can be improved for a given amount of simulation effort, better decisions can be made and therefore increase the confidence in the decision. This presentation describes a sampling method, *selective sampling*, which can be used either to reduce the simulation effort for a given level of accuracy or to increase the accuracy of a decision for a given amount of simulation effort.

SOURCE: Reprinted from *The Journal of Industrial Engineering*, *14* (6): 291–296 (1963).
[1] This article is an extract from the author's Doctor of Engineering dissertation [1].
[2] The author expresses his appreciation to Eliezer Naddor of The Johns Hopkins University and Ram Gnanadesikan of Bell Telephone Laboratories for helping to organize some of this presentation.

THE PROBLEM

Let us consider the situation in which simulation is needed and a decision must be made. A *decision* is defined here as the process of selecting some values of variables which management can control. The variables which management can control are denoted $u_1, u_2, ..., u_k$ or in general U. It is desired that the value of the controllable variables, U, be chosen such that the system is optimized according to some criterion. The values thus selected are called the *solution* and denoted U_o. In general when simulation is used, it is possible to obtain a *measure of the system*, such as the cost of operating the system, for a given set of values of the controllable variables. The measure of the system is a function of U and will be denoted $C(U)$. Then, the measure of the system at the optimum choice of U is $C(U_o)$. In order to make a decision the engineer must specify some set of values of U for which the system will be measured. It is necessary to adopt a procedure to determine the sequence and manner in which the designated set of U will be examined and to adopt a criterion for selecting that value of U which will be considered optimum.

It is important to distinguish between the

correct solution, U_o, and the solution obtained by simulation, U_0'. If we had perfect and complete information as well as the ability to reduce the information to a measure of the system, we would always select U_o as our solution. In simulation, however, we do not have perfect and complete information and it is possible to select as our solution some value of U, U_0', which is not the real optimum solution. If the procedure for examining the feasible set of values of U is a good procedure, then the cost incurred as a result of our simulation decision, $C(U_0')$, should be at most only slightly above the cost at the real optimum, $C(U_o)$. Specifying a procedure for selecting U_0' is beyond the scope of this presentation. The focus of this article is the procedure for obtaining the values of $C(U)$.

EVENTS

Simulation is used, among other reasons, when the real world system involves some stochastic occurrence, such as random demand for goods in inventory. Other types of stochastic occurrences could be the number of absent employees on a given day, the number of arrivals into a system, or the time required to complete processing a unit through a system. An *event* is defined here as the single occurrence of a specific value of the stochastic occurrence. The simulation model includes establishing a series of events and maintaining some records as to the repercussions of these events so that the value of system performance, $C(U)$, can be obtained. Selective sampling is a method for establishing the series of events within the simulation model for each level of U considered.

Let us say that there are m possible values of an event. The value of the individual event is denoted $b(x)$, where $x = 1,2,...,m$, with each level of x representing a different possible value of the event. For example, when $x = 1$, the value of the event, $b(1)$, might be no absentees. It is assumed that from records, historical or otherwise, we have knowledge as to the probability of the xth value of the event occurring and we will denote these probabilities by $p(x)$. For practical reasons only events for which $p(x) \geqslant .0001$ will be considered.

Any continuous probability density function would have to be converted into discrete form

for the simulation process. This conversion must be made cautiously, and it would be desirable to compare the discrete distribution against the original density function.

In simulation as it is discussed here there is a sampling process in which we establish a series of $b(x)$. The number of events simulated for a particular problem is the sample size and is denoted by n. Of the n events which are simulated, the number of times that the xth event occurs, in a particular sample, is denoted $v(x)$. The quantity, $v(x)$, is an integer.

The core of the Monte Carlo method [6, pp. 58–67] is the transformation of random numbers[3] into events. In order to transform random numbers into events the appropriate spectrum of random numbers is partitioned so that the portion of the random number spectrum which represents a particular event is proportionate to the probability that the event occurs. A random number is then selected, the spectrum examined to see which event the random number represents and the event is recorded. With this method, events can be artificially generated such that, in the long run, the events will occur in proportion to their probability. From these generated events an abstract but reasonable history of the system can be constructed.

As the size of the sample increases the relative frequency of the xth event, $v(x)/n$ will tend to more closely approximate $p(x)$. In a specific sample, especially for small or moderate values of n, $v(x)/n$ could vary considerably from $p(x)$ as a result of the random element in the usual Monte Carlo process itself. In terms of the above discussion, the focus of selective sampling is the process of establishing the $v(x)$.

CONCEPTS AND CRITERIA

In the Monte Carlo process as described above, the value of $v(x)/n$ will approximate $p(x)$ only to the extent that the particular sample allows. Also, the Monte Carlo method has no particular orientation toward decision making. Selective sampling derives its name from its two basic concepts. First, it helps in "selecting" the optimum solution, U_0'. Secondly, the values of

---

[3] Random numbers are taken to be numbers with a uniform distribution that pass reasonable statistical tests for randomness [5].

$v(x)$ are "selected" such that the relative frequency of each event is as close as possible to $p(x)$.

The first concept upon which selective sampling is based is the use of the same set of events for all levels of the decision variable which are considered in order to obtain a solution. Associated with the first level of U considered, there are n events from which a value of $C(U)$ is obtained. The exact same n events in the same sequence are then used for all remaining levels of U. This idea was discussed by Kahn and Marshall [2] and referred to as "correlated sampling." By using the same events for all levels of the decision variables, one source of variability is removed from the simulation in that all levels of the controllable variable are measured under the same conditions.

The other concept upon which selective sampling is based is that the relative frequency of the events simulated, $v(x)/n$, should conform as much as possible to the actual probability of the event occurring, $p(x)$. This idea was discussed by Naddor (4). The criterion adopted for adhering to this concept is that the $v(x)$ be chosen which minimize

$$z = \sum_{x=1}^{m} [v(x)/n - p(x)]^2 \qquad (1)$$

subject to the constraint $\Sigma\, v(x) = n$. The interpretation of this criterion is that the sum of squares of the deviations of the relative frequency of the xth event, $v(x)/n$, from its probability, $p(x)$, is minimized. The criterion is not unique but has been chosen as reasonable and objective.

An algorithm has been developed which produces values of $v(x)$ and satisfies the criterion in Equation 1. This algorithm can be found in Appendix A, which also contains a proof that the algorithm does indeed satisfy the criterion. The algorithm sets $v(x)$ equal to the integer closest to $np(x)$. If the $\Sigma\, v(x) > n$, then the $v(x)$ whose fractional parts in excess of 0.5 are smallest are reduced by one until $\Sigma\, v(x) = n$. Similarly, if $\Sigma\, v(x) < n$, then the $v(x)$ whose fractional parts less than 0.5 are greatest are increased by one until $\Sigma\, v(x) = n$.

Since selective sampling requires that values of $v(x)$ be established before the simulation is undertaken, it becomes necessary to determine the sequence in which the simulated events are considered to occur. The criterion chosen here for ordering the events is that all possible sequences of the set of values of the events should be equally likely. The procedure is to carry out the Monte Carlo process of random sampling in terms of sampling without replacement.[4]

Since the values of $v(x)$ are already determined, we could say that the probability of the xth event occurring in the simulation is $v(x)/n = p^*(x)$. Using the Monte Carlo method, the value of the first event could be determined. Now there are $n' = n-1$ events still to be sequenced. For the event that occurred, the number of times it would still occur is $v'(x) = v(x) - 1$. For every other event, the number of times it has yet to occur is $v'(x) = v(x)$. Now new values of $p^*(x)$ can be established as $p^*(x) = v'(x)/n'$. With the new set of probabilities the second event can be established by the Monte Carlo process. This approach means that the probability of an event occurring in the simulation is adjusted after the sequence of each event is established. The process of readjusting the probabilities is repeated after each event is sequenced until all n events have been sequenced, and this procedure is the means of sampling without replacement. Appendix B contains a subroutine in Fortran coding which selects values of $v(x)$ and orders the events.

EXAMPLE

In order to help clarify some of the ideas discussed in connection with selective sampling, let us look at a simple example. Suppose, for instance, that we have a situation in which $m = 2$, $p(1) = .20$ and $p(2) = .80$. Then, for a sample of size of $n = 4$, we have $np(1) = .8$ and $np(2) = 3.2$. We would therefore make $v(1) = 1$ and $v(2) = 3$, since they are respectively the

---

[4] The process of using the Monte Carlo method in conjunction with sampling without replacement is useful with a computer. For a hand simulation, $b(x)$, the values of an event, can be written on pieces of paper in accordance with the $v(x)$, mixed in a bowl, and drawn without replacement.

nearest integers. Going back to our criterion of Equation 1, we find that in this case,

$$z = [1 - 4(.2)]^2 + [3 - 4(.8)]^2$$
$$= .08.$$

Any other combination of integer values for $v(1)$ and $v(2)$ would increase the value of z to a value greater than .08.

With $v(1) = 1$ and $v(2) = 3$, we would determine whether the first event is $x = 1$ or $x = 2$ by means of the usual Monte Carlo process with $p^*(1) = \frac{1}{4}$ and $p^*(2) = \frac{3}{4}$. If the first event is a 1, then the next three events must be 2's because of the values of $v'(1) = 0$ and $v'(2) = 3$. If the initial event is a 2, then the second event can still be a 1 or 2. In using sampling without replacement, we would readjust the probabilities since only three events remain to be sequenced, namely $v'(1) = 1$ and $v'(2) = 2$, and with $n' = 3$ the adjusted probabilities become $p^*(1) = \frac{1}{3}$ and $p^*(2) = \frac{2}{3}$. Then, we would determine what the second event would be by using the Monte Carlo technique with the readjusted probabilities. The readjusting of the probabilities does, in fact, give us a procedure for sampling without replacement.

This example is completed in Table 1, which illustrates that using sampling without replacement in conjunction with the Monte Carlo method indeed makes each sequence equally likely. The generality of this result has not been included since it would be cumbersome to show while the end result is so obvious.

TABLE 1 An Example Showing the Equal Probability of Each Sequence for Selective Sampling

Sequence	Event No. 1	Event No. 2	Event No. 3	Event No. 4
A	$p(1) = \frac{1}{4}$	$p(2) = 1$	$p(2) = 1$	$p(2) = 1$
B	$p(2) = \frac{3}{4}$	$p(1) = \frac{1}{3}$	$p(2) = 1$	$p(2) = 1$
C	$p(2) = \frac{3}{4}$	$p(2) = \frac{2}{3}$	$p(1) = \frac{1}{2}$	$p(2) = 1$
D	$p(2) = \frac{3}{4}$	$p(2) = \frac{2}{3}$	$p(2) = \frac{1}{2}$	$p(1) = 1$

	Sequence	Probability
A	1, 2, 2, 2	$\frac{1}{4} \times 1 \times 1 \times 1 = \frac{1}{4}$
B	2, 1, 2, 2	$\frac{3}{4} \times \frac{1}{3} \times 1 \times 1 = \frac{1}{4}$
C	2, 2, 1, 2	$\frac{3}{4} \times \frac{2}{3} \times \frac{1}{2} \times 1 = \frac{1}{4}$
D	2, 2, 2, 1	$\frac{3}{4} \times \frac{2}{3} \times \frac{1}{2} \times 1 = \frac{1}{4}$

COMPARISON OF DIFFERENT SAMPLING METHODS

A series of experiments were conducted using as test subjects three inventory models for which analytical results as to the solution of the inventory system are available. Since solutions to these inventory models can be obtained analytically, simulation is not required. The experiments were conducted for the sake of learning more about different sampling methods. The known analytical solution to the inventory system has been used as a standard for comparing the sampling methods. In these experiments selective sampling was compared to two other methods, simple sampling and correlated sampling. Simple sampling, a direct, simple application of the Monte Carlo method, uses a different set of events for each level of the decision variable. Correlated sampling, as described earlier, uses the same events for each level of the decision variable but does not force the relative frequency of events, $v(x)/n$, to conform to the probabilities of the events, $p(x)$.

The experiments involved fifty trials for each of several sample sizes for each inventory model. Only one probability distribution, namely the Poisson, has been used for the events which in this case are the demands for goods in inventory. Two measures were taken in these experiments. First, the *average percent penalty* for a wrong decision was determined. The penalty for any decision is the cost of operation for the system in excess of the minimum cost which was determined from the analytical form of the model. The penalties were averaged over the fifty trials and taken as a percent of the cost of operation under the correct decision. Second, the worst decision, that is, the *maximum penalty*, in the fifty trials was also recorded.

The results reported here are for a few sets of conditions which are representative of all the results. Reference 1 contains a full description of the models, the details of the experiments and the complete results.

Model I is an inventory system in which orders are placed at fixed intervals of time, scheduling periods, so as to bring the level of stock up to some level, S, which is the controllable variable. The demand is probabilistic and is considered to occur at a uniform rate during the scheduling period. There is no delay between the placing of an order to replenish stocks and its arrival. The cost of carrying stock is being balanced against the cost of a shortage. A total of 120 conditions were tested for model I, including every combination of five cost ratios, four average daily rates of demand, and six sample sizes.

Table 2 shows some results of average percent penalty for model I with an average daily demand of five units and a ratio of unit shortage cost per day to unit carrying cost per day of 100. Of the 120 conditions tested selective sampling was preferred in 115.

TABLE 2   Some Results of Average Percent Penalty with Model I

	Sampling Method		
Sample Size	Simple	Correlated	Selective
10	34.8	19.0	7.0
100	5.2	1.5	0.0

Model II is similar to model I with one difference. In this model there is a delay, called the lead time, from the time of placing an order to replenish stocks until the time it arrives. A total of 180 conditions were tested for model II, including every combination of five cost ratios, two average daily demands, three lead times and six sample sizes.

For the results of model II reported, the average daily demand is again five units, the cost ratio is again 100, but there is now a two-day delay from the placing of an order until it arrives. Table 3 shows these results. Of the 180 conditions tested, selective sampling was preferred in 158.

TABLE 3   Some Results of Average Percent Penalty for Model II

	Sampling Method		
Sample Size	Simple	Correlated	Selective
10	199.5	108.5	68.6
100	10.7	6.1	4.7

Model III involves two controllable variables, a reorder point, s, and a recorder level, S, up to which the stock level is raised when an order is placed. There is no delay from placing an order until it arrives. In this model the costs of carrying stock, shortages and ordering are balanced. For model III there were 81 conditions tested, including every combination of 9 cost ratios, 3 average daily demands and 3 sample sizes.

The results for model III reported involve an average daily demand of 2 units, a ratio of shortage cost to carrying cost of 50, and a ratio of ordering cost to carrying cost of 40. Table 4 contains these results. Of the 81 conditions tested, selective sampling was preferred in 54.

TABLE 4   Some Results of Average Percent Penalty for Model III

	Sampling Method		
Sample Size	Simple	Correlated	Selective
10	28.1	22.6	24.9
200	2.7	2.2	1.4

In examining these results of average percent penalty, we can see that for models I and II selective sampling is consistently the best of the three methods. We can also notice that for the larger sample size the difference in performance between correlated and selective sampling decreases relative to simple sampling. With model III selective sampling becomes favored only for the larger sample size.

The results of the extreme performance, that is, the maximum penalty in fifty trials, are summarized in Table 5. In this table the total number of test conditions for each model are noted and the number of cases in which the penalty of the worst decision in fifty trials for selective sampling is smaller than for the other two sampling methods. Also the table shows the number of cases for which the penalty of the worst decision of selective sampling was at least as small as that of the other two methods. Considering the results of the experiments in terms of the maximum penalty, we can see that selective sampling displays more stability in that the maximum penalty for selective sampling in the fifty trials is usually smaller than that for the other two methods.

TABLE 5 Summary of Results Measuring Worst Decision

Model	Total Number of Test Conditions	Number of Cases in Which Selective Sampling had Smallest Value for Maximum Penalty	Number of Cases in Which Maximum Penalty for Selective Sampling at Least as Small as for Other Methods
I	120	119	120
II	180	127	162
III	81	48	64

One other experimental result is of interest. In general the computer running time for the tests with correlated and selective sampling was approximately one half of that with simple sampling. This reduction resulted from the process which establishes one set of events for all levels of the decision variables considered.

CONCLUSIONS

Overall the results of the experiments reported above indicate that under the conditions tested selective sampling is the best of the three methods tested. As seen from Tables 2, 3 and 4 the use of the same events (correlated sampling) for all levels of the controllable variable results in a smaller average percent penalty than simple sampling. Also using the same events and constraining the relative frequency of each event to correspond to its probability (selective sampling) results in an even smaller average percent penalty. Therefore, it is possible to achieve a given level of accuracy with a smaller sample size using selective sampling than by using the other methods, or, equivalently, it is possible to improve the accuracy for a given sample size. Also since selective sampling is more

stable in that it produces less extreme incorrect decisions, a smaller sample will also be less risky in the sense of extreme performance.

It is not appropriate to generalize the results of these experiments to all conditions. It does seem, however, that selective sampling offers a procedure for reducing sample size when obtaining decisions in problems of the type discussed.

The intent of this article is to provide those faced with real simulation problems involving decision making with a tool which makes the use of simulation more attractive. This article is also intended to stimulate industrial engineers and operations research analysts to look for methods which help to reduce the amount of simulation effort required to obtain a solution.

APPENDIX A:

A PROCEDURE FOR SELECTIVE SAMPLING

The Problem

Given a discrete probability distribution, $p(x)$, $x = 1, 2, ..., m$, and a sample size of n, find an integer function, $v(x)$, $x = 1, 2, ..., m$ which minimizes

$$z = \sum_x [v(x) - np(x)]^2 \qquad (A1)$$

subject to

$$\sum_x v(x) = n \qquad (A2)$$

The Solution

Let

$$h(x) = np(x) - [np(x)] \qquad (A3)$$

where $[np(x)]$ denotes the integer portion of $np(x)$. Obviously then, $0 \leqslant h(x) < 1$.

Let

$$J = \sum h(x) = n - \sum [np(x)] \qquad (A4)$$

Hence J is an integer and $0 \leqslant J \leqslant n$.

Let the m values that the random variable can take be referred to as x_i, $i = 1, 2, ..., m$. We will order the x_i such that

$$x_i \text{ precedes } x_j \text{ if } h(x_i) > h(x_j) \qquad (A5)$$

For the purposes of ordering, also let

$$x_i \text{ precede } x_j \text{ if } h(x_i) = h(x_j) \text{ and } \\ \text{if } b(x_i) > b(x_j) \qquad (A6)$$

The solution is then given by

$$
v(x_i) = \begin{cases} [np(x_i)]+1 & i = 1, 2, ..., J \\ [np(x_i)] & i = J+1, J+2, ..., m \end{cases}
$$

(A7)

The Proof

We first show that the constant Equation A2 is satisfied. From Equation A7 and Equation A4 we get immediately

$$
\sum_{i=1}^{m} v(x_i) = \sum_{i=1}^{J} \{[np(x_i)]+1\} + \sum_{i=J+1}^{m} [np(x_i)]
$$

$$
= J + \sum_{i=1}^{m} [np(x_i)]
$$

$$
= J + (n-J) = n
$$

To show that Equation A7 minimizes Equation A1, consider the situation for several values of J. If $J = 0$, then Equation A4 indicates $h(x_i) = 0$ for all i. Hence by Equation A3 $[np(x_i)] = np(x_i)$. Therefore for $J = 0$ by Equation A7 $v(x_i) = np(x_i)$ and by Equation A1 $z = 0$ and is indeed the minimum.

If $J = 1$, then by Equation A7 $v(x_1) = [np(x_1)]+1$ and $v(x_i) = [np(x_i)]$ for all other $i \neq 1$. Let the corresponding z in Equation A1 be designated by z_1. We will now show that if we allow some other $i \neq 1$ to have the value $v(x_i) = [np(x_i)]+1$, that this will result in a value of z_2 equal to or larger than z_1.

To show that $z_1 \leq z_2$ it suffices to show that for $i \neq 1$

$$
\{[np(x_1)]+1-np(x_1)\}^2 + \{[np(x_i)]-np(x_i)\}^2
$$
$$
\leq \{[np(x_1)]-np(x_1)\}^2
$$
$$
+ \{[np(x_i)]+1-np(x_i)\}^2 \quad (A8)
$$

Or by Equation A3 we must show

$$
[1-h(x_1)]^2 + [h(x_i)]^2
$$
$$
\leq [h(x_i)]^2 + [1-h(x_i)]^2 \quad (A9)
$$

By the ordering procedure Equations A5 and A6 we know that

$$
h(x_1) \geq h(x_i). \quad (A10)
$$

Equation A9 implies Equation A10 and hence the solution has been shown to be correct for $J = 1$.

This proof can be readily extended to other values of J.

APPENDIX B :

A SUBROUTINE FOR SELECTIVE SAMPLING

```
SUBROUTINE EVENTS (K1A, K2A,
   P, NNS, ND, RGDEM)
DIMENSION RGDEM (500), P(100, 10),
   IU(100), DF(100), CP(100), PP(100)
VNNS = NNS
SDF = 0.0
DO 400 KA = K1A, K2A
U = VNNS*P(KA, ND)
IU(KA) = U
FIU = IU(KA)
DF(KA) = U - FIU
400   SDF = SDF + DF(KA)
ISDF = SDF
FSDF = ISDF
IF(SDF - FSDF - 0.5) 410, 410, 405
405   ISDF = ISDF + 1
410   CONTINUE
DO 425 I = 1, ISDF
GDF = DF(K1A)
K3A = K1A
DO 420 KA = K1A, K2A
IF(DF(KA) - GDF) 420, 415, 415
415   GDF = DF(KA)
K3A = KA
420   CONTINUE
IU(K3A) = IU(K3A) + 1
425   DF(K3A) = 0.0
DO 445 I = 1, NNS
FNNS = NNS - I + 1
DO 426 KA = K1A, K2A
FIU = IU(KA)
426   PP(KA) = FIU/FNNS
CP(K1A) = PP(K1A)
K4A = K1A + 1
DO 430 KA = K4A, K2A
430   CP(KA) = CP(KA - 1) + PP(KA)
RN = RRN(0)
DO 435 KA = K1A, K2A
K = KA
IF(CP(KA) - RN) 435, 435, 440
435   CONTINUE
440   RGDEM(I) = K - 1
IU(K) = IU(K) - 1
445   CONTINUE
RETURN
END
```

Glossary of Terms

CP(KA)	cumulative value of PP(KA)
DF(KA)	decimal fraction of $np(x) - [np(x)]$
FIU	floating point form of IU
FNNS	balance of events to be sequenced
FSDF	floating point form of ISDF
GDF	greatest decimal fraction
ISDF	fixed point form of SDF, number of values of $v(x)$ to be increased by 1 unit
IU(KA)	fixed point form of U, $v(x)$
K	current value of KA
KA	index for value of event
K1A	lower bound of x of $p(x)$
K2A	upper bound of x of $p(x)$
K3A	index of KA associated with GDF
K4A	control to start DO loop
ND	index for number of probability distributions
NNS	sample size
P(KA, ND)	probability function of event
PP(KA)	probability of events remaining to be sequenced
RGDEM(I)	event
RN	current random number
RRN(O)	subsequent value of generated random number
SDF	sum of the decimal fractions
U	$np(x)$
VNNS	floating point form of NNS

REFERENCES

1. M. E. Brenner, 1963. *Correlated and selective sampling applied to the simulation of some inventory systems.* Doctoral dissertation, Johns Hopkins University. MS.
2. H. Kahn, and A. W. Marshall, 1953. Methods of reducing sample size in Monte Carlo computations. *Operations Research, 1*(5): 263–278. MS.
3. G. W. Morgenthaler, 1961. The theory and application of simulation in operations research. *Progress in operations research, Volume I* (R. L. Ackoff, ed.); New York: Wiley, 363–419. MG.
4. E. Naddor, 1963. Markov chains and simulations in an inventory system. *Journal of Industrial Engineering, 14*(2): 91–98. 7C.
5. Rand Corporation, 1955. *A million random digits with 100,000 normal deviates.* Glencoe, Ill.: Free Press.
6. M. Sasieni, A. Yaspan, and L. Friedman, 1959. *Operations research.* New York: Wiley.

35

PROBLEMS IN THE STATISTICAL ANALYSIS OF SIMULATION EXPERIMENTS: THE COMPARISON OF MEANS AND THE LENGTH OF SAMPLE RECORDS

GEORGE S. FISHMAN

1. INTRODUCTION

Statistical analysis of simulation experiments and, in particular, comparing means and determining the appropriate lengths of sample records is the subject of this paper. The stochastic processes in simulation experiments are usually autocorrelated and consequently the time series or sample records they generate cannot be analyzed by traditional statistical methods that apply to independent observations. The most common suggestion to reduce or eliminate autocorrelation is to perform linear transformations on the original time series. Traditional analysis is then applied assuming the transformed observations are uncorrelated [2]. Fishman and Kiviat [4] have pointed out, however, that this procedure throws away a considerable amount of valuable information about the behavior of a process, and that the transformed time series may be inappropriate for comparison purposes. In this

SOURCE: Reprinted from *Communications of the ACM*, *10* (2): 94–99 (1967).

paper, an alternative method is suggested for studying these time series by exploiting the autocorrelations rather than eliminating them. The approach centers on estimating the variances of the sample means for the original series from "sufficiently long" sample records and comparing these means for two independent experiments.

It is inevitable that stability considerations emerge early in the development of this method.

In performing two experiments for the same length of simulated time, there is no a priori reason to expect that the statistical quality of the two resulting time series or sample records will be the same. Suppose that the process being observed has the same variance, but is more auto-correlated in one experiment than in the other. The more autocorrelated process will generally show fewer changes in value during a given time than the other will. With fewer changes, there is less fluctuation around the mean of the process and consequently we cannot expect to obtain as good an estimate of the mean for the process with higher auto-correlation as we do for the other. This brings up two problems: how to determine the stability of the sample mean of an autocorrelated process, and more important, how to compare such information for two corresponding processes observed in two different simulation experiments.

The variance of the sample mean computed from a set of independent observations is inversely proportional to the number of observations. This is not true for autocorrelated data. For sufficiently long sample records, however, one may show that the variance of the sample mean for autocorrelated data is inversely proportional to a fraction of the number of observations. This fractional factor depends on the autocorrelation properties of the process. By analogy with the independent case, it seems natural to regard this fraction of the number of observations as the number of *equivalent independent observations*.

To develop this analogy, we introduce the concept of the *correlation time* of a process. If a process is observed for a time interval equal to *n* correlation times, then one may show that, from the point of view of the variance of the sample mean, this time series is equivalent to collecting *n*/2 independent observations. Using the correlation time together with the observation interval, we can define the number of *equivalent independent observations* contained in an auto-correlated time series. Comparing these measures for two autocorrelated samples allows us to draw inferences about the relative stability of their sample means just as we would with independent observations. The correlation time approach is analogous to a suggestion Yule made in which he defined the correlation time as the "coefficient of linkage" [6].

The most common comparison made between two simulation experiments is testing the difference of their means. For independent observations, the central limit allows us to treat the sample mean as a normal variate for large sample sizes. For autocorrelated observations an additional restriction must be met in order for the central limit theorem to apply. The meaning of this restriction in the current context is within the definition of a covariance stationary sequence as given in this paper and it

is suggested that the difference of the sample means be treated as a normal variate for a sufficiently long sample record.

So far we have implicitly assumed that the lengths of the time series are "sufficiently long" so that the effects of initial conditions are eliminated. In simulation work, it is often difficult to determine what minimum length of time suffices for meaningful analysis. As will be shown, the method suggested here has the advantage of providing this information about the adequacy of sample record lengths. The information gives us a basis for determining how long an experiment should be in order to estimate and compare means with given numbers of equivalent independent observations.

As stated earlier, we are interested in comparing means. In [4] it is pointed out that it is possible to compare the autocorrelation structure of two processes vis-à-vis their spectra. Such a comparison offers considerably more insight into the true nature of the process than does a comparison of means. There are circumstances, however, in which the latter comparison suffices as an initial step, and so we offer a method to facilitate this type of testing. Our emphasis should not be construed to mean that this comparison does away with the problem of comparing two experiments; a full recognition of the autocorrelation structure gives a much greater awareness of the characteristics of a process.

The theoretical tools of our analysis are presented in Section 2 and the relevant estimation and testing procedures are contained in Section 3. To show how the method works, two simulation experiments are compared in Section 4. While the example is simple, it illustrates the benefits of our suggested method quite well. The very same analysis can be performed on time series generated by considerably more complex simulation experiments.

2. DERIVATION OF PARAMETERS

In a wide variety of simulation experiments we are interested in observing a covariance stationary stochastic process $\{X(t), -\infty \leqq t \leqq \infty\}$. Assume that during an interval Δt the process shows little, if any, change so that observing $\{X(t)\}$ at periodic intervals Δt results in virtually no loss of information. For convenience, let Δt be unity and

$$X_t \equiv X(t) \tag{2.1}$$

so that the covariance stationary sequence $\{X_t, t = 0, \pm 1, \pm 2, ..., \pm \infty\}$ corresponds to the process $\{X(t)\}$ at all integer values of the parameter t. We have by definition: the mean

$$\mu = E(X_t) \tag{2.2}$$

the autocovariance function

$$R_\tau = E[(X_t - \mu)(X_{t-\tau} - \mu)],$$
$$\tau = 0, 1, 2, ..., \infty \tag{2.3}$$

the spectral density function

$$f(\lambda) = \frac{1}{\pi}\left[1 + 2\sum_{\tau=1}^{\infty}(R_\tau/R_0)\cos\lambda\tau\right],$$
$$0 \leq \lambda \leq \pi \tag{2.4}$$

and the spectrum

$$g(\lambda) = R_0 f(\lambda) \tag{2.5}$$

We also have the inverse relationship

$$R_\tau = \int_0^\pi g(\lambda)\cos\lambda\tau \, d\lambda \tag{2.6}$$

Let $\{X_t, t \in T\}$ be a time series of length T observed during the simulation experiment. The sample mean is

$$\bar{X} = \frac{1}{T}\sum_{t=1}^{T} X_t \tag{2.7}$$

and its variance is

$$\text{Var}(\bar{X}) = \frac{1}{T}\left[R_0 + 2\sum_{\tau=1}^{T-1}(1-\tau/T)R_\tau\right] \tag{2.8}$$

Substituting expression (2.6) into (2.8) gives

$$\text{Var}(\bar{X}) =$$

$$\frac{1}{T}\int_0^\pi g(\lambda)\left[1 + 2\sum_{\tau=1}^{T-1}(1-\tau/T)\cos\lambda\tau\right]d\lambda$$

$$= \frac{\pi}{T}\int_0^\pi g(\lambda)\left[\frac{\sin^2(\lambda T/2)}{\pi T\sin^2(\lambda/2)}\right]d\lambda$$

$$= \frac{\pi}{T}\int_0^\pi g(\lambda)K_T(\lambda, 0)\, d\lambda \tag{2.9}$$

where the averaging kernel K is

$$K_T(\lambda, \omega) = \frac{1}{2\pi T}\left\{\frac{\sin^2[(\lambda+\omega)T/2]}{\sin^2[(\lambda+\omega)/2]} + \frac{\sin^2[(\lambda-\omega)T/2]}{\sin^2[(\lambda-\omega)/2]}\right\} \tag{2.10}$$

One also has the limiting expression

$$\lim_{T\to\infty} T\text{Var}(\bar{X}) = \pi g(0) = \pi R_0 f(0) \tag{2.11}$$

The large sample variance of $\bar{X}$ is then

$$V \sim 2R_0\tau^*/T \tag{2.12}$$

where the *correlation time* τ^* is given by

$$\tau^* = \pi f(0)/2 \tag{2.13}$$

Observe that the variance V is inversely proportional to the sample record length just as in the case of independent observations. These results imply that if we are able to run the simulation experiment long enough, we may use the large sample variance given by expression (2.12) to measure the stability of the sample mean $\bar{X}$. How long is "long enough" depends on the shape of the spectral density function f which, in turn, depends on the extent of correlation in the sequence. Since this information is seldom available, we shall estimate empirically how long is "long enough." The method of estimation is described in Section 3.

The correlation time τ^* is the measure of autocorrelation alluded to earlier. The significance of τ^* can best be understood by reference to a particular nonrealizable sequence. If the sequence $\{X_t\}$ were perfectly autocorrelated over some integer τ^* time units, and uncorrelated with itself for intervals longer than τ^*, then

$$R_\tau = \begin{cases} R_0, & 0 \leq \tau < \tau^* \\ R_0/2, & \tau = \tau^* \\ 0, & \tau > \tau^* \end{cases} \tag{2.14}$$

$$f(\lambda) = \frac{1}{\pi}\left(1 + \cos\lambda\tau^* + 2\sum_{\tau=1}^{\tau^*-1}\cos\lambda\tau\right)$$

$$= \frac{\sin(\lambda\tau^*)\cos(\lambda/2)}{\pi\sin(\lambda/2)} \tag{2.15}$$

$$\tau^* = \pi f(0)/2 \tag{2.16}$$

the same formula as given by (2.13).

While this particular stochastic sequence is not physically realizable, it illustrates quite well the conceptual meaning of correlation time. The larger τ^*, the more autocorrelated the sequence. Now (2.13) allows us to conveniently determine the correlation time for any realizable covariance stationary sequence. While τ^* in such cases will not have the precise meaning as in our illustration, it does in effect measure the extent of autocorrelation.

As an example, consider the first-order Markov process

$$X_t = \alpha X_{t-1} + \varepsilon_t, \qquad 0 < \alpha < 1 \quad (2.17)$$

where $\{\varepsilon_t\}$ is a sequence of mutually independent identically distributed random variables. The autocorrelation and spectral density functions of $\{X_t\}$ are then

$$\rho_\tau = \alpha^\tau, \qquad \tau \geq 0, 1, ..., \infty \qquad (2.18a)$$

$$f(\lambda) = \frac{1-\alpha^2}{\pi(1-2\alpha\cos\lambda+\alpha^2)},$$

$$0 \leq \lambda \leq \pi \qquad (2.18b)$$

respectively. The correlation time is easily seen to be

$$\tau^* = \frac{1+\alpha}{2(1-\alpha)} \qquad (2.19)$$

Notice that the more influential is the past, the larger is α and, therefore, the greater is τ^*.

The quantity τ^* is also of interest in another way. Assume that $\{X_t\}$ is an uncorrelated sequence with variance R_0. Given a sample record of length N, the variance of the sample mean is R_0/N, which measures the precision of the estimator $\bar{X}$. If we equate this variance with the asymptotic variance for the autocorrelated case, we have

$$R_0/N = g(0)/T = 2R_0\tau^*/T \qquad (2.20)$$

and, consequently,

$$N = T/(2\tau^*) \qquad (2.21)$$

Expression (2.21) gives the number of *equivalent independent observations* in an autocorrelated sample record of length T with a correlation time of τ^*. That is, observing the sequence over the time interval $2\tau^*$ is equivalent to collecting one independent observation. The significance of these results is immediately apparent. If we can run the experiment long enough to use the large sample variance, then we can determine an equivalence between our results and those that

would have derived if we were analyzing independent observations.

Unfortunately we do not know the value of the spectrum at zero frequency, nor the variance of the sequence, and so cannot directly determine the number of equivalent independent observations. It is possible, however, to estimate $g(0)$ using statistical spectral analysis. This procedure has found wide applicability in the physical sciences and more recently in economics. The application of spectral analysis to simulation has been described in detail previously [4]. It is also possible to estimate the variance R_0 by a well-known formula. From these two sample values we may estimate the correlation time τ^* and consequently N, the number of equivalent independent observations.

3. ESTIMATION OF PARAMETERS

To estimate the asymptotic variance of the sample mean V, the correlation time τ^*, and the number of equivalent independent observations N, we use:

$$\hat{R}_\tau = \frac{1}{T-\tau}\sum_{t=1}^{T-\tau}(X_t - \bar{X})(X_{t+\tau} - \bar{X}) \qquad (3.1)$$

$$\hat{V} = \frac{1}{T}\left[\hat{R}_0 + 2\sum_{\tau=1}^{M}(1-\tau/M)\hat{R}_\tau\right]$$

$$M < T-1 \quad (3.2)$$

$$\hat{\tau}^* = T\hat{V}/(2\hat{R}_0) \qquad (3.3)$$

$$\hat{N} = T/(2\hat{\tau}^*) = \hat{R}_0/\hat{V} \qquad (3.4)$$

Note that our estimate of the large sample variance V contains M instead of $T-1$ lags. There are several reasons for this substitution. If the sample record length T is sufficiently large, then there is a quantity M such that the variance V will not change appreciably if more than M lags are used in the summation. This may be seen by looking at $\text{Var}(\bar{X})$ as given by (2.9) and the focusing power of the averaging kernel K.

Figure 1 shows the averaging kernel for two values of T. Observe that the kernel concentrates its mass closer to the origin for the larger T. One way to measure this concentration is to compute the bandwidth of the averaging kernel. Let the bandwidth $\beta_T(0)$ be defined as the width of a rectangle whose height is $K_T(0,0)$ and

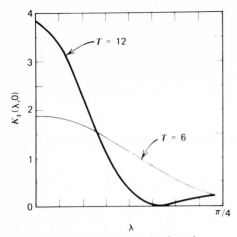

Figure 1 The averaging kernel:

$$K_T(\lambda, 0) = \frac{1}{\pi T}\left[\frac{\sin(\lambda T/2)}{\sin(\lambda/2)}\right]^2.$$

whose area is the area under the function K over the interval $\{0, \pi\}$. The bandwidth is therefore

$$\beta_T(0) = \int_0^\pi K_T(\lambda, 0)\, d\lambda \Big/ K_T(0, 0)$$

$$= \pi/T \qquad (3.5)$$

It is essentially a radian measure of the length of interval in which the averaging kernel concentrates virtually all its mass. In this case the interval is $\{0, \pi/T\}$.

It may be shown that the spectral density function f is relatively constant near the origin, and that the extent of this flatness is inversely related to the degree of autocorrelation in the sequence $\{X_t\}$. If this constancy extends over a greater interval than $\{0, \pi/M\}$, then the spectral average in (2.9) remains fairly constant as the length of the time series increases from M to T. Consequently, there is no need to include more than M autocovariances in the estimator $\hat{V}$. It should be observed, however, that the more autocorrelated the sequence $\{X_t\}$ is, the shorter is the interval which over the spectral density function f is flat and, therefore, the larger the M needed to accomplish the appropriate resolution must be.

The conservation of lags also stems from a peculiarity of spectral estimation. For a Gaussian sequence, the large sample variance of the statistic $T\hat{V}/\pi$ is

$$\mathrm{Var}\left(\frac{T\hat{V}}{\pi}\right) \sim \frac{4\pi}{T} g^2(0) \int_0^\pi K_M^2(\lambda, 0)\, d\lambda$$

$$= \frac{4M}{3T} g^2(0) \qquad (3.6)$$

The estimate is also assumed to be well resolved. Observe that if M were equal to $T-1$, then this variance would be independent of sample size as T increases and therefore would lack the desirable statistical property of consistency. This property requires that the ratio M/T approach zero as T increases.

If the sequence $\{X_t\}$ is Gaussian, the statistic $\hat{V}/V$ may be shown to be essentially the sum of χ^2-variates. The distribution of $\hat{V}/V$ may be approximated by that of a multiple of χ^2 with equivalent degrees of freedom [5]:

$$\mathrm{EDF}(0) = \frac{1.5T}{M} \qquad (3.7)$$

Note that the stability of $\hat{V}$, as measured by the equivalent degrees of freedom, is inversely related to M.

When the number of lags is inadequate for good resolution, we observe in practice that estimates of V increase in magnitude as M increases and stabilize in value when resolution is accomplished. This convergence will, however, be from above if the sequence contains a periodic component that causes a substantial peak in the spectrum in the low frequency range. To determine whether or not such periodicities are present, the entire spectrum should be estimated in a pilot analysis.

If we continue to estimate V for larger M, we observe that the estimates eventually decline. This curious phenomenon results from the neglect of the bias introduced by replacing the mean μ by the sample mean $\bar{X}$ in (3.1). The large sample bias in the autocovariance function [1] is

$$E(\hat{R}_\tau - R_\tau) \sim -2\tau^* R_0/T \qquad (3.8)$$

which in turn leads to

$$E(\hat{V}) \sim \frac{\pi}{T} \int_0^\pi \left(\frac{K_M(\lambda, 0) - 2M\tau^*}{\pi T}\right) g(\lambda)\, d\lambda \qquad (3.9)$$

As M increases, the bias term clearly increases and causes a reduction in the estimate of V. To avoid this, it is necessary to keep the number of lags M significantly smaller than the sample record length T. However, note that good resolution requires that M be sufficiently large so that the function g changes slowly at frequency π/M.

Testing the difference of the means is the most commonly applied test in the comparison of the results of two simulation experiments. It will often be the case in these experiments and, in particular, in queueing problems that the stochastic processes of interest are non-Gaussian. Under this circumstance the sample mean is not necessarily a Gaussian variate. Diananda [3] however, has established certain conditions about the nature of the autocorrelation in the sequence $\{X_t\}$ such that the central limit theorem holds for its sample mean. These conditions are general enough to include the covariance stationary sequence in Section 2 and consequently we may regard the sample mean to be asymptotically Gaussian distributed. This result simplifies the testing procedure considerably for we may now regard the difference of the sample mean as a Gaussian variate.

There remains one more problem to be dealt with before the testing procedure is feasible. The variances of the sample means are unknown. The most obvious solution is to replace them by their corresponding estimates. If the subscripts "1" and "2" denote the first and second experiments, respectively, the statistic for the null hypothesis is $(\bar{X}_1 - \bar{X}_2)(\hat{V}_1 + \hat{V}_2)^{-1/2}$ which we consider to be approximately Gaussian distributed with zero mean and unit variance. Here we neglect the effects of replacing V_1 and V_2 by their estimates assuming that the sample record length will suffice to make this neglect inconsequential. The reader is cautioned to bear in mind the approximate nature of the test and its crucial dependence on T being of sufficient magnitude.

4. APPLICATION OF TECHNIQUES

To illustrate the application of the techniques just described, we simulated a single-server queueing facility with Poisson mean arrival rate u_1 and exponentially distributed service times with mean $1/u_2$. The stochastic process of interest was "the sum of the service times on jobs waiting for service plus the remaining service time on the job being serviced." This measure of queue content reflects the backup of work time in the shop.

In the simulation experiment, we set

$$u_1 = 4 \text{ arrivals/hour}$$

and

$$u_2 = 5 \text{ jobs serviced/hour}$$

The experiment was performed twice, first using the shortest operation rule (SHOPN) and second using the first-come first-served principle (FCFS). In the first experiment, priority was given to the job that had the shortest processing time when a selection was made. In the second, jobs were assigned priority according to their order of arrival. Each sample record was 16,000 hours long with observations at hourly intervals. In order to focus on the estimation techniques, we initially consider only the first experiment. Later we shall compare both experiments.

The choice of a 16,000-hour sample record was quite arbitrary since no prior knowledge about the process's stochastic properties was available. Consequently, estimates of the asymptotic variance of the sample mean V, the correlation time τ^*, and the number of equivalent independent observations N were made for the first 1000, 2000, 4000, 8000 and 16,000 hours, and for seven different values of M.

Table 1 shows the estimates of the parameters μ, R_0 and TV for the first experiment. Estimates for TV rather than V are given because the former are theoretically comparable for different values of sample record length T, whereas the latter are scaled by the quantity $1/T$ and are therefore not similarly comparable.

Looking at the estimates of TV for the first 1000 hours, we observe that as the number of lags M increases, the corresponding estimates initially increase, remain fairly constant, then decrease sharply. Improved resolution accounts for the initial increase and stabilization, whereas the increasing influence of bias is responsible for the eventual decline. While the estimates of TV do appear to stabilize for M equal 200 and 300, the decline for greater M introduces some skepticism. We therefore

TABLE 1   Estimates of μ, R_0 and TV for Experiment 1

T	$\bar{X}$	$\hat{R}_0$	$T\hat{V}$ when M equals						
			50	100	150	200	300	400	500
1,000	2.02	4.72	172	289	377	424	415	317	193
2,000	1.84	4.37	150	229	281	310	300	249	196
4,000	1.93	4.62	155	229	273	297	306	294	277
8,000	2.03	5.31	185	268	307	333	355	349	336
16,000	1.83	4.40	144	202	227	244	264	266	258
Range	.20	.94	41	87	150	180	151	100	143

double the value of T and observe the resulting estimates.

Looking at the estimates of TV for the first 2000 hours, we observe the same phenomenon as the number of lags is increased. The increase and decrease here, however, are much less abrupt than for the 1000-hour estimates. It is interesting to note that the estimates of 4000, 8000 and 16,000 hours show no applicable decline as the number of lags is increased. This means that the influence of downward bias is considerably less for these three sample record lengths. One concludes from Table 1 that M should be at least 200, and that to a reasonable degree of accuracy T should be at least equal to 4000 in order to obtain well-resolved estimates that are relatively free of sample mean bias. These values of M and T are sufficient for us to use the large sample variance in our analysis. Using these values of M and T as minima, one may begin to build up the stability of the sample mean by increasing T to the desired level.

Considering the ranges of these estimates for the several different sample record lengths, we observe that the range of $\bar{X}$ is about 10% of the

value of its point estimates. The range of $\hat{R}_0$ is about 20% of its point estimates, and the ranges for TV vary from about 30–50% of their corresponding point estimates. Even more interesting, however, is the fact that there is considerable variation between estimates for T equal to 8000 and 16,000 hours. One would naturally expect convergence of these estimates for increasing record lengths. Using (3.6), one notes that the standard deviations of $T\hat{V}$ for 4000, 8000 and 16,000 hours are roughly 26, 18 and 13%, respectively, of the mean TV. While these results are not encouraging, our concern is with $\hat{V}$ itself which, as will be seen, becomes rather small compared to the sample mean.

Table 2 lists estimates of V, τ^* and N for 200 and 300 lags. The estimates were computed using (3.2), (3.3) and (3.4). Note that the estimates for 200 lags are substantially the same as those for 300 lags. Also observe that the estimates of N approximately double for successive values of T. This is to be expected since the quantity T is successively doubling in value and N is directly proportional to it.

In reference to our earlier point concerning

TABLE 2   Estimates of V, τ^* and N for Experiment 1

T	$\hat{V}$ where $M =$		$\hat{V}^{\frac{1}{2}}/\bar{X}$ where $M =$		$\hat{\tau}^*$ where $M =$		$\hat{N}$ where $M =$	
	200	300	200	300	200	300	200	300
1,000	.424	.415	.32	.32	44.9	44.0	11.1	11.4
2,000	.155	.150	.21	.21	35.5	34.3	28.2	29.2
4,000	.074	.077	.14	.15	32.1	33.1	62.3	60.4
8,000	.042	.044	.10	.10	31.4	33.4	127.4	119.8
16,000	.015	.107	.07	.07	27.7	30.0	288.8	266.7

stability, note that the ratio of the sample standard deviation $(\hat{V})^{1/2}$ and the sample mean $\bar{X}$ is 0.07 for 16,000 hours. If the actual variance were one hundred percent greater than the sample variance $\hat{V}$, this ratio would only be increased to about 0.10. We may safely conclude, therefore, that our results are reasonably stable.

In Section 3 it was pointed out that if $\{X_t\}$ is a Gaussian sequence, then the estimate $\hat{V}$ has a distribution that is reasonably approximated by that of a multiple of χ^2 with 1.5 T/M equivalent degrees of freedom. It is therefore possible to construct approximate confidence intervals for the variance of the sample mean V.

Unfortunately, we do not know the true value of R_0. This creates difficulties in deriving confidence intervals for the parameters τ^* and N. We approximate these intervals by replacing the variance R_0 by its estimate $\hat{R}_0$ for the several values of sample record length. Table 3 shows our approximate confidence intervals for the 90-percent probability level. As is to be expected, these intervals become smaller as length T increases and, furthermore, the respective confidence intervals for 200 and 300 lags become quite similar.

It is to be remarked if $\{X_t\}$ is non-Gaussian, these confidence intervals are to be considered as underestimates of the actual ones. In this regard the Gaussian confidence intervals serve only as a benchmark for measuring stability but are not very precise.

In order to illustrate the test for comparing two means, we repeated the experiment using the FCFS instead of the SHOPN rule. A sample rule was again collected at hourly intervals for 16,000 simulated hours. Table 4 shows the corresponding sample statistics for the two experiments. Note that the sample means are virtually identical, whereas the sample variances and consequently the estimates $T\hat{V}$ and $\hat{V}$ vary by about 15%. Perhaps the most interesting observation is the small variation in the estimated correlation times.

Treating the statistic $(\bar{X}_1 - \bar{X}_2)(\hat{V}_1 + \hat{V}_2)^{-1/2}$ as an approximately standardized Gaussian variate, we have for the .10 significance level

$$P(-.284 \leq \bar{X}_1 - \bar{X}_2 \leq .284) \approx .90 \qquad (4.1)$$

under the null hypothesis. The quantity $(\bar{X}_1 - \bar{X}_2)$ is equal to .011, which is well within the acceptance interval. Therefore, we accept

TABLE 3 Approximate 90 Percent Confidence Intervals for V, τ^* and N

		$\hat{V}$		$\hat{\tau}^*$		$\hat{N}$	
T	$EDF(0)$	a	b	a	b	b	a
			$M = 200$				
1,000	7.5	.215	1.297	22.8	137.5	3.6	21.9
2,000	15.0	.093	.320	21.3	73.3	13.6	47.0
4,000	30.0	.051	.108	12.2	46.8	42.7	90.8
8,000	60.0	.032	.058	23.8	43.6	91.8	168.1
16,000	120.0	.012	.019	22.7	34.8	227.4	352.4
			$M = 300$				
1,000	5.0	.187	1.811	19.9	191.9	2.6	25.2
2,000	10.0	.082	.381	25.8	87.1	11.5	53.3
4,000	20.0	.049	.141	21.1	61.0	32.8	94.8
8,000	40.0	.032	.067	24.0	50.4	79.3	166.8
16,000	80.0	.013	.022	23.6	39.7	201.3	339.6

Note: a refers to the lower confidence limit: b, to the upper confidence limit.

TABLE 4   Sample Statistics for the SHOPN and FCFS Experiments

$(T = 16,000; \ M = 300)$

Experiment	EDF (0)	$\bar{X}$	$\hat{R}_0$	$T\hat{V}$	$\hat{V}$	$\hat{\tau}^*$	$\hat{N}$
SHOPN	80	1.834	4.40	264	.017	30.0	267
FCFS	80	1.823	3.72	213	.013	28.6	280

the null hypothesis that the means of the two processes, generated by different job assignment rules, are not significantly different.

Suppose for a moment that $\hat{V}_1 + \hat{V}_2$ was an order of magnitude greater than the true variance $V_1 + V_2$. Then the correct probability interval in (4.1) would be $\pm .284 \ \sqrt{.1} = \pm .090$ which still contains the difference. We therefore conclude that the sample variances may be subject to rather large errors without upsetting the test results.

In view of the closeness of the sample means, the result of hypothesis testing is not surprising. Although we have no test at present for comparing correlation times, their small variation permits the reasonable conjecture that the correlation times of the two processes are the same, and consequently so are the numbers of equivalent independent observations. We may reasonably conclude, therefore, that the statistical quality of our results as far as means are concerned is essentially the same for both experiments.

5. CONCLUSIONS

A method has been given for estimating the minimum sample record length necessary to use the large sample variance of the sample mean. Also described is a meaningful way to compare the results concerning stability with those that would have been obtained with independent observations. In addition, it has been shown how to test the difference of the means of two autocorrelated processes.

The significance of the method should be apparent to investigators in simulation research who have, at one time or another, been faced with one or all of the problems discussed herein. While the authors have used a rather elementary simulation experiment to illustrate their ideas, there is no reason why the same logic may not be applied to considerably more complex experiments as long as the processes of interest may be observed periodically.

REFERENCES

1. M. S. Bartlett, 1955. Sampling fluctuations of means and correlation coefficients. *An introduction to stochastic processes;* Cambridge: Cambridge University Press, 254–259.
2. R. W. Conway, 1964. *An experimental investigation of priority assignment in a job shop.* Working paper, Rand Corporation, RM-3789-PR.
3. P. H. Diananda, 1953. Some probability limit theorems with statistical applications. *Proceedings of the Cambridge Philosophical Society, 49*(2): 239–246.
4. G. S. Fishman, and P. J. Kiviat, 1965. *Spectral analysis of time series generated by simulation models.* Working paper, Rand Corporation, RM-4393-PR. MS.
5. G. M. Jenkins, 1961. General considerations in the analysis of spectra. *Technometrics, 3*(2): 133–166.
6. G. U. Yule, 1945. On a method of studying time-series based on their internal correlations. *Journal of the Royal Statistical Society, Series A, 108*(I-II): 208–225.

36

ON STABILIZING A LARGE MICROECONOMIC SIMULATION MODEL[1]

AUSTIN CURWOOD HOGGATT

INTRODUCTION

In this paper we are concerned with the problem of using a computer and statistical methodology for the purpose of stating and measuring, in part, the nature of the transformation from the parameter space of a simulation into its behavior space. We are treating the problem of deriving implications concerning the behavior of a computer program. The model represents the activities of approximately 100 firms; there are suppliers who sell to wholesalers who sell to retailers who face a final market demand function. Wholesalers provide information and finance transactions, they underwrite the costs of linking the market by paying for costs of information under uncertainty. The model is a much revised version of the Hoggatt-Balderston market process simulator [1], and has been published by Professors L. Preston and N. Collins [6] who did most of the work of revision. It is

SOURCE: Reprinted from *Logistics Review and Military Logistics Journal*, *1* (3): 21–28 (1965).

[1] This is a reduced and revised version of a paper presented by the author with the assistance of Bernd J. Holtbrugge, "Statistical Techniques for the Computer Analysis of Simulation Models" at the Tenth Annual Meeting of O.R.S.A. in Hawaii, September 15, 1964. Another version of this paper appears in [4].

impossible to describe this model in detail here, but some feeling for its scope may be obtained from these gross statistics: there are 81 control parameters, 55 response variables are currently reported by the program, and the state space of the system requires 16,000 points for its definition. So far, the only way to describe such systems is to point to the program and leave the reader to plow through it. Thus we shall have to treat the model as a largely unknown system of pseudostochastic difference equations, a few properties of which we wish to understand.

In his now classical paper, "On the Experimental Attainment of Optimum Conditions" [2] G. E. P. Box provides us with methodology which is tailor-made for our application. He is concerned with the response of a system (dependent variables) to changes in control parameters (independent variables). He provides methods for calculating efficient sets of points for selecting the control parameters and methods for calculating non-linear regression functions which are maximum likelihood estimates for the expected response surface of the model for each individual dependent variable taken separately. The assumptions of his model are:

Let $X_1, ..., X_n$ be independent variables and Y be a dependent variable, then,

(1) $Y = f(X_1, ..., X_n) + u$

f can be expressed as the Taylor expansion of the functional relation of Y on X,

(2) Y and all X are continuous variables,

(3) $u:n(0, \sigma^2)$ is a normally distributed, homoscedastic, error function.

In the analysis which follows we shall adopt a statistical design which was developed by Dr. Louis B. Kahn for Shell Development Corporation and a program which is a revised version of a program written by the author to implement this design. The program estimates coefficients for zero, first and second order terms in f.

Statistical tests for the assumptions of the model are performed by the program. (1) is checked by analysis of variance which explicitly estimates the "lack of fit," (2) is true by definition for the variables under consideration, but (3) is assumed true without test for want of the resources required to pay for sufficient observations to provide a test.

Much has been said about the problem of the correspondence between a simulator and a real system. Kalman Cohen, for example, insists that the measure of the value of a model is the extent to which it duplicates the time path of the real system of which it is a counterpart [3]. The present writer would be happy to find models which duplicated the trends and frequency response of a real system leaving the search for exact duplication of time path to other researchers. For purposes of measuring frequency response of the present model we shall use the auto-correlation function. In empirical work,

stationarity is forced by detrending the data. We have measured the trends in the data but have been able to obtain our results without detrending the series prior to calculation of auto-correlations.

In the initial runs of this system a pervasive two period oscillation in market throughput was observed. This had some of the qualitative features actually observed by Ruth Mack in a multi-level market of a more complex sort [5]. As a means of demonstrating the control over the model which can be obtained via analysis of its structure, we shall concern ourselves with the problem of searching for the source of the observed oscillation and for parameter settings which can eliminate it. The correlogram for one of the early runs is shown in Figure 1. We have data on 13 such runs and in each of them the strong 2 period oscillation is evident. We conjecture that decision functions of the market participants are the source of the observed instabilities. Our problem then is to find ways in which we can vary these *functions* under the constraint that we still are able to employ analysis routines to study the results. One might consider the possibility of stepping inside each decision function and regarding its parameters as control variables. However, for the model in hand, each rule is complex in itself and we would be led into a research design involving some tens of parameters for which the results might be no less complex than the output of the model. Instead we shall take an approach to the problem which is less fine—but has the virtue of feasibility.

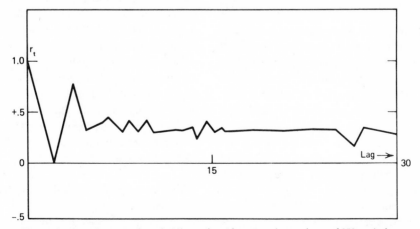

Figure 1   Correlogram of market throughput for an undamped run of 250 periods on the model which shows a strong oscillation in the throughput of the market.

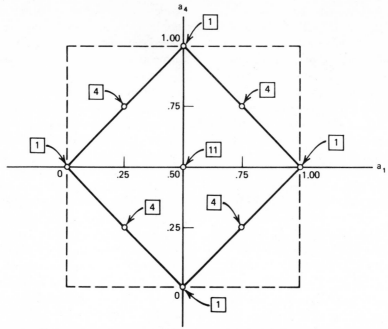

Figure 2 Spatial arrangement and frequency of observation on control points in the a_1–a_4 plane for the Box 4-variable design employed in the analysis of damping coefficients on decision rules. The design is seen to be cubic in form with the projection in the a_1–a_4 plane forming a square layout with the corners lying at the extremes of the design space. The numbers in □ stand for the frequency of observations for which the level remains fixed at the specified point in (a_1, a_4). It is a feature of this design that points at the corners of the 4-dimensional unit cube are not sampled. The design is symmetric in 4 space about the point (.50, .50, .50, .50).

Consider an arbitrary decision function, R, which specifies a calculation based on past history of the model and which results in a number, D_t, which represents a decision for period t. We embed this function in another such that a new decision, D_t^*, is produced by the process,

$$D_t^* = aD_t + (1-a) D_{t-1}^*   \qquad 0 \leqslant a \leqslant 1   \quad (1)$$

and then we replace D_t in all its instances with D_t^*. In the case where $a = 1$ we have the rule R operating as before and for $a = 0$ we have a constant decision function which repeats the decision of the initial period. For intermediate values between these two extremes we have a "damped" version of the original rule which preserves the qualitative aspects of the rule but which mutes its effect. One might choose to think of this as the imposition of a conservative, higher management review of the decision-making function which leads to a correction for an excessive desire for change on the part of subordinates.

Our scheme then is as follows. We treat the bid and offer rules for price and quantity in the manner of rule R above, assigning to each of them a parameter of the type exemplified by "a" in Equation 1. These four damping parameters will be the control parameters in a Box four variable design. The response variable of interest will be the intensity of the fall and recovery of the correlation of the initial lags in the correlogram of market throughput.

Our design requires 31 points. Fortunately, the control point where all damping coefficients are set to zero does not appear, so that there will always be some adaptability in the market, although most of it may be on the part of one class of participants. As we are concerned here with only the initial lags in the correlogram we reduce the run length to 80 periods.

Four new parameters are introduced into the model, viz.

a_1: damping coefficient for retail price quotation,

a_2: damping coefficient for retail *ex-anti* quantity quotation,

a_3: damping coefficient for supplier price quotation,

a_4: damping coefficient for supplier *ex-anti* quantity quotation.

The 31 points prescribed by the design are distributed about the surface and interior of the unit cube in four dimensions. A feeling for the "coverage" of the possible combinations of damping coefficients may be obtained from Figure 2 which portrays the arrangements of points as projected into the a_1, a_4 plane. For the purpose of standardization of the program, normalized values for control parameters are used. The transformations are:

$$X_i = 4a_i - 2 \qquad i = 1, ..., 4 \qquad (2)$$

and our regressions will be reported in terms of these normalized parameters.

Note that the strict application of the damping coefficient to the supplier quantity quotation rule could lead to quotations in excess of inventory in the event that the undamped decision was a cut in order to meet an inventory constraint. In this one case, the proposal for

upward adjustment resulting from application of the damping rule is overridden and the decision is set back to the level of the inventory constraint.

In Figure 3 we have listed the response of the system for each of the 31 runs of the design. Recall that we measure the intensity of oscillation by the difference, Δ, which is defined as autocorrelation of lag 2 minus autocorrelation of lag 1. The regression coefficients and their standard errors of estimate are shown in Figure 4 and the analysis of variance for a goodness of fit test is shown in Figure 5. Only β_4 and β_{14} are significant at the 99% level and we may expect that X_1 and X_4 are the dominant variables in the regression. Therefore, we pursue a partial analysis and fix the other two coefficients at the center of their range ($X_2 = X_3 = 0$). Then we have the reduced regression:

$$\Delta = .097 + .062X_4 - .060X_4 X_1 \qquad (3)$$

in which we have set the nonsignificant coefficients to zero also. Strictly speaking we should reestimate the relationship under the constraint that these coefficients are zero but for purposes of illustrating the technique this is not

Run Designation	R_2	R_1	$\Delta = R_2 - R_1$	Run Designation	R_2	R_1	$\Delta = R_2 - R_1$
18	.6030	.6452	$-.0422$	31	.6282	.5023	$+.1259$
3	.6675	.6921	$-.0246$	22	.5876	.4552	$+.1324$
5	.8250	.8481	$-.0231$	8	.7519	.6168	$+.1351$
1	.7706	.7829	$-.0123$	26	.5976	.4604	$+.1372$
12	.2386	.2445	$-.0058$	14	.6642	.5215	$+.1427$
23	.9763	.9774	$-.0010$	24	.6262	.4820	$+.1442$
28	.7322	.7133	$+.0189$	10	.4762	.3250	$+.1513$
29	.7297	.7106	$+.0192$	27	.6440	.4298	$+.2142$
2	.6623	.6380	$+.0243$	9	.6961	.4756	$+.2205$
30	.6365	.5963	$+.0402$	4	.5508	.3023	$+.2485$
20	.7082	.6673	$+.0409$	19	.1728	$-.0896$	$+.2624$
6	.8168	.7758	$+.0410$	21	.1861	$-.0887$	$+.2748$
17	.4000	.3514	$+.0487$	16	.3153	.0316	$+.2838$
13	.7789	.6875	$+.0914$	11	.6563	.3636	$+.2927$
7	.7709	.6588	$+.1120$	15	.4492	$-.0808$	$+.5300$
25	.6861	.5640	$+.1221$ ← median				

Figure 3 Table of first difference, Δ, for $R_2 =$ two period lagged correlation of sales to retailers, $R_1 =$ one period lagged correlation of sales to retailers, and $\Delta = R_2 - R_1$ for 31 design points involving damping coefficients on the price and quantity bidding rules for the retailers and suppliers. (Ordered low to high on Δ.) Source: Statistical program for serial correlation on data from runs 1 to 31 of Nov. 3, 1964.

$$\Delta = \beta_0 + \sum_{i=1}^{4} \beta_i X_i + \sum_{i=1}^{4} \sum_{j=i}^{4} \beta_{ij} X_i X_j$$

$\beta_0 = +.097$

$\beta_1 = -.014$

$\beta_2 = +.021$

$\beta_3 = +.006$

$\beta_4 = +.062$

$\beta_{11} = -.018$

$\beta_{12} = -.021$	$\beta_{22} = +.019$		
$\beta_{13} = -.003$	$\beta_{23} = +.043$	$\beta_{33} = +.032$	
$\beta_{14} = -.060$	$\beta_{24} = +.003$	$\beta_{34} = +.023$	$\beta_{44} = -.001$

Standard Errors of Estimate

$\sigma_i = .015$

$\sigma_{ii} = .014$

$\sigma_{ij} = .018$

Figure 4 Regression estimates for the dependence of $\Delta = R_2 - R_1$ of sales to retailers on the 4 damping coefficients associated with retailer and supplier quotation rules. Source: Box Analysis Run of Nov. 6, 1964.

necessary. Since we are interested in stabilizing the model, and since we are measuring stability by the nearness of Δ to zero we may obtain from Equation 3 an implicit function in the variables X_1, X_4 by setting Δ to zero. Explicitly we have:

$$X_4 = -.097/(.062 - .060 X_1) \qquad (4)$$

This function has been plotted for the design space in Figure 6 and it portrays an estimate of the locus of points for which the model does not exhibit the 2 period oscillation in market throughput. From this graph it is clear that for some values of X_1 in the design space the value of X_4 must lie outside the design space. In these cases, in order for smoothing to occur it would

be necessary for higher level management either to amplify or to change the direction of lower level decisions. We shall not pursue these radical policies further in this paper.

At this point we have shown that statistical analysis can contribute a great deal to the understanding and control of large complex simulation models. The efficiency of our technique is high. The search for stable control settings ended quickly given the guides to search provided by the Box design. Haphazard search of the parameter space of the model would have been prohibitive and most likely unrewarding. In this way a first step toward the analysis and control of simulators via the analysis of sampled data has been taken.

Source	Sum of Squares	Number of Degrees of Freedom	Mean Square
First order	.1091	4	.0273
Second order	.1538	10	.0154
Lack of fit	.1822	10	.0182
Experimental error	.0322	6	.0057
TOTAL	.4773	30	

Figure 5 Analysis of variance for the regression of $\Delta = R_2 - R_1$ (sales to retailers) for the 4-variable design involving damping coefficients a_1, a_2, a_3, a_4, on retailer and supplier quotation rules. Source: Box Analysis Run of Nov. 6, 1964.

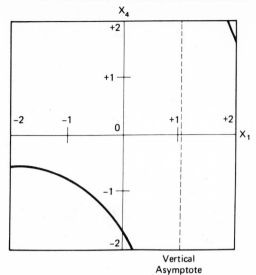

Figure 6   Estimated locus of points in (X_1, X_4) space for which expected value of $\Delta = R_2 - R_1 = 0$, given that $X_2 = X_3 = 0$.

REFERENCES

1. F. E. Balderston, and A. C. Hoggatt, 1962. *Simulation of market processes.* Berkeley: University of California. 7D.
2. G. E. P. Box, and K. B. Wilson, 1951. On the experimental attainment of optimum conditions. *Journal of the Royal Statistical Society, Series B*, *13*(1): 1–45.
3. K. J. Cohen, 1960. *Computer models of the shoe, leather, hide sequence.* Englewood Cliffs, N.J.: Prentice-Hall. 1D.
4. A. C. Hoggatt, 1966. Statistical techniques for the computer analysis of simulation models. *Studies in a simulated market* (L. E. Preston and N. R. Collins); Berkeley: University of California, 91–122. MS.
5. R. P. Mack, 1956. *Consumption and business fluctuations.* New York: National Bureau of Economic Research.
6. L. E. Preston, and N. R. Collins, 1966. *Studies in a simulated market.* Berkeley: University of California. 5D.

37

TESTING CASE-DESCRIPTIVE MODELS

WILLIAM H. STARBUCK

INTRODUCTION

The availability of large computers has fostered a new kind of model-building. A small but growing number of researchers are constructing models which attempt to describe causal processes in much greater detail than has been feasible heretofore. The ethic of these model-builders, to the extent that a common ethic exists, seems to be description for description's sake. Potential normative applications of their models are a secondary consideration. Similarly, the generality of their models is a secondary goal because they believe that the most effective way to achieve efficient and accurate generalizations is through detailed and elaborate analyses of individual cases.

This paper outlines a frame of reference for the builder of case-descriptive models and suggests a procedure for testing the models that are built.[1] Herbert Simon has proposed that a case-descriptive model be tested by giving a group of knowledgeable judges both the output of the model and the raw data that this output is supposed to represent, and asking the judges to decide which is output and which is data. If the judges cannot distinguish between the output and

the data, the model would be sufficient. The test procedure outlined below is similar to Simon's proposal except that: the model itself defines the characteristics of a judge—which aspects of the data should be emphasized—and the model is sufficient if even one judge mistakes output for data.

CASE-DESCRIPTIVE MODELS

A model is an attempt to represent a set of causal processes observed in the "real world." The set of causal processes represented constitutes a *referent situation*. And formally, a *model* is an operator that generates a set of variables X, given a set of variables Y, such that (a) the sets X and Y represent characteristics of a referent situation, and (b) the operator itself represents the causal processes of the referent situation.

A test is a critical examination of the model within the context of the model-builder's purpose. There seem to be three crude categories of models with respect to purpose. One can distinguish between *normative* and *descriptive* (or positive) models. Normative models are constructed with application in mind. In the purest case, the normative model is designed to answer a few predetermined questions. The ethical bases of the posed questions determine (a) which characteristics of the referent situation

SOURCE: Revised from *Behavioral Science*, 6 (3): 191–199 (1961).
[1] For another discussion of a related but slightly different problem, see [3].

should be included in the model and (b) how accurately these characteristics should be represented. Descriptive models are constructed for the purpose of describing and analyzing their referent situation. The model-builder frequently does not pose specific questions before constructing his model; or if he does pose questions beforehand, these questions have little ethical content. As a result, the builder of descriptive models is relatively unconstrained when selecting characteristics of the referent situation to represent, and he has no clear criterion for the accuracy with which these characteristics should be represented.[2]

Within the class of descriptive models, one can distinguish between *norm-descriptive* models and *case-descriptive* models. Norm-descriptive models are intended to be generalizations. They focus on an aggregate or an average, rather than an individual case. Frequently, norm-descriptive models are intended to be abstractions as well as generalizations: they are designed to assess the value of hypothetical, ideal relations between aggregate characteristics of the referent situations. In general, the builder of norm-descriptive models is as concerned with the simplicity and generality of his models as he is with their accuracy, and this is often an advantageous trade, the statistics of aggregation being what they are.

The case-descriptive models are the relatively new class of models described in the introduction. They are intended to be detailed analyses of one, or a few, specific cases. The model-builder seeks to represent the referent situation as accurately as possible. Case-descriptive models do not normally attempt to be abstractions, except in so far as every model is an abstraction; adherence to a specific piece of unaggregated data is not sympathetic with discovering ideal relationships. This does not mean that the builder of case-descriptive models is uninterested in generalization. Rather he believes that the most effective key to generalization—whether generalizations about individual cases or generalizations about an aggregate— is the detailed analysis of a specific case.

These three categories of models are neither

exhaustive nor clearly defined. They do, however, serve as a useful factoring against which the model-builder can measure his own objectives, and thereby decide what kinds of tests are most appropriate to his model.

Examples may make the three categories clearer. Consider the following problem: Human subjects are asked to predict which of two possible events will occur next in a series. The series of events is independent of the subjects' predictions.

A *normative* problem would be specification of the predictive strategy which the subjects should use. An appropriate model would represent the series of events and have just one output variable, the next prediction. If the model predicts correctly a large proportion of the time, it can be considered a good representation of the event series. Often, a specific degree of accuracy is stated as part of the objective, or can be derived from cost data.

One of the simplest models of the event series is a biased coin. If the bias were known, the optimum strategy would be "predict on every trial the event that occurs most frequently in the event series as a whole." Since the bias is not known, the strategy must be changed to "predict on trial N the event that has occurred most frequently in the previous $N-1$ trials." If N is odd and both events have occurred equally often, the dilemma can be resolved by flipping an unbiased coin. A standard for good performance can be inferred from the model itself, since the model implies a probability density function for the number of correct predictions.[3]

---

[2] A more elaborate discussion of the distinction between normative and descriptive models can be found in [8].

[3] Assume that the two events occur with known probabilities p and $1-p$. The a priori probability, $Q(N; p)$, of predicting the Nth event correctly is
$$Q(2k; p) = Q(2k+1; p)$$
$$= (1-p) \cdot \sum_{y=0}^{k-1} b(y; 2k-1, p)$$
$$+ p \cdot \sum_{y=k}^{2k-1} b(y; 2k-1, p)$$
and the a priori probability of predicting R out of N events correctly is
$$Pr[R; N, p] = Q(N; p) \cdot Pr[R-1; N-1, p]$$
$$+ [1 - Q(N; p)] \cdot Pr[R; N-1, p].$$
Since $Pr[0; 0, p] = 1$
and $Pr[0; N, p] = [1 - Q(N; P)] \cdot Pr[0; N-1, p],$
$$\sum_{\lambda=0}^{\infty} Pr[\lambda; N, p] \cdot S^\lambda =$$
$$\prod_{\lambda=1}^{N} [1 - Q(\lambda; p) + S \cdot Q(\lambda; p)]$$

A *descriptive* problem arising from the same basic situation would be analysis of the behavior of the human subjects. The model could be restricted to one output variable, the subjects' next prediction. However, there is no conclusive reason to bound the model at this point. The model could generate variables representing the subjects' emotional involvement or their verbal explanations for their predictions. The model-builder must try to explain any aspects of the situation that contribute to his understanding. The criterion for accuracy is even more unclear. Models must be judged on structure as well as output. Models that generate different numbers and kinds of outputs are not directly comparable. Frequently accuracy in generating one output must be sacrificed for accuracy in generating another output.

Two distinct approaches to this descriptive task have been made. A number of *norm-descriptive* models have been proposed [1, 4]. These models attempt to describe the aggregate behavior of several subjects who are presented with identical event series. They have three common characteristics: (1) They focus on one output variable, the Nth prediction. This variable is the most easily aggregated characteristic of the situation. (2) They are stochastic models. Stochastic treatment again reflects the aggregated nature of the output variable.[4] (3) The models are consistent with the empirical

---

at least for $|S| < 1$. Therefore $Pr[R; N, p]$ is the sum, over all combinations of R integers out of N, of terms of the form

$$\prod_i Q(i; p) \cdot \prod_j (1 - Q(j; p)),$$

where i is an index over the particular R integers in a combination, and j is an index over the N-R integers not in the combination ($j \neq i$).

Because p is not known, its value must be inferred from the event series. If the event corresponding to p has occurred x times in the preceding N trials, and if p and x have a priori uniform distributions, the a posteriori conditional distribution for p is

$$Pr[p; N, x] = (N+1) \cdot b(x; N, p).$$

Therefore the a posteriori distribution for R correct predictions in N trials is

$$Pr[R; N, x] =$$
$$(N+1) \cdot \int_0^1 Pr[R; N, p] \cdot b(x; N, p) \cdot dp$$

[4] Some model-builders take a position like that of Bush and Mosteller: "We tend to believe that behavior is intrinsically probabilistic" [1, p. 3]. However even a theorist who believes that behavior is basically deterministic, can accept a probabilistic model which is macroscopic.

---

observation that the proportion of subjects who predict a specific event is asymptotic to the frequency with which that event occurs.

At least one model-builder has attempted a *case-descriptive* model of the subjects' behavior. Julian Feldman analyzed in detail the behavior of three specific subjects and proposed different models for the behavior of each [5].[5] The outputs of the models include the subjects' stated reasons for their predictions as well as their predictions. Feldman's models are very complex since discrete changes were observed in the decision processes. Subjects used distinctly different decision processes after correct predictions than after incorrect predictions, and discrete changes in the subjects' hypotheses about the structure of the event series were frequent. It would be difficult to aggregate these models by calculation, and it would be practically impossible to aggregate the models analytically. Nevertheless, Feldman was able to take some steps toward a general model [7].

The need to test a model within the context of the model-builder's purpose is obvious. Descriptive models should not be expected to be as appropriate for answering specific questions as normative models that were constructed with these questions in mind. Norm-descriptive models should not be expected to represent specific cases as accurately as the appropriate case-descriptive models. Case-descriptive models should not be expected to generalize to new referent situations as effectively as norm-descriptive models.

There is a substantial body of literature relevant to the testing of normative and norm-descriptive models [10, 9]. But there is reason to question the relevance of this literature for case-descriptive models. The usual approach to testing focuses on the probable event. It asks, given the model, how likely is the set of observations. A "good" model is one with a high probability of generating the observations.

The builder of case-descriptive models can reasonably point out that he does not care how likely his observations are. He does not pretend to have constructed a generalization, and the

[5] Feldman reviews the norm-descriptive models in detail, and gives an especially relevant discussion of the testing of case-descriptive models (pp. 130–136). Also see [6].

rare event does happen. Because the represented processes are both discrete and complex, case-descriptive data more nearly represent one point in an N-dimensional space than N points in a one-dimensional space. Moreover, from a strictly pragmatic point of view, the functional forms that appear in case-descriptive models are much more complicated than those that have yielded to the likelihood treatment. The test procedure suggested below is both more consonant with the objectives of the builder of case-descriptive models and more amenable to computation than is the usual approach.

TESTING SIMULATIVE POWER

The purpose of a case-descriptive model is to represent causal processes, and the ideal test would be based on the accuracy with which the model represents these referent processes. However, causal processes are nearly always the subject of inference, not of observation. There is no standard for the structure of the referent situation per se that can serve as a criterion for the model's accuracy. Therefore it is necessary to adopt a surrogate criterion.

The obvious choice for a surrogate criterion is the simulative power of the model. A *simulation* is an operator that generates a set of variables X, such that (a) the set X represents characteristics of a referent situation and (b) the set X is indistinguishable from the corresponding characteristics of the referent situation. The word indistinguishable is used loosely. The variables in the model represent only measured characteristics of the referent situation, not the physical entities that comprise the referent situation, and distinguishableness is a binary property only with respect to an explicit criterion.

Characteristics of the referent situation may be either *observable* or *unobservable*—this being a function largely of the existing technology of measurement. Characteristic A is observable if its value can be measured without assuming specific causal relationships between characteristic A and other characteristics of the referent situation. Characteristic A is unobservable if (a) its value can only be measured in conjunction with the values of other characteristics or (b) no measurement technique is available for measuring its value. Here, the value of a characteristic

is the state of the characteristic with reference to any arbitrary class of states, and measurement is any empirical restriction on the value of the characteristic.

A simulation is a testable operator because it does not claim to represent unobservable characteristics of the referent situation. A simulation claims only to generate variables that are indistinguishable from specific corresponding characteristics of the referent situation. The subset of characteristics may be very small indeed, relative to the set of all characteristics of the referent situation.

In practice, no model takes full advantage of the available measurement techniques. The variables in the model represent *observed* and *unobserved* (latent) characteristics of the referent situation. Characteristic A is observed if it is observable and if measurements of its value are available for tests of the model. Characteristic A is unobserved if it is unobservable or if it is observable but no measurements are available.

At this point, it might be well to say something about the use of the word representation. A case-descriptive model is not an end in and of itself. Each model should be a foundation for other models which include additional observations and which accommodate more precise measurements. Some unobserved variables, although not observed in the strictest sense, may be partially observed. By incorporating these partially observed characteristics, the model becomes a more effective foundation for other models and, at the same time, a more credible statement about the referent situation. Any frequent participant in academic seminars will note that the degree of acceptance of the model being presented, and by implication its effectiveness as a representation, depends on the extent to which the model is consistent with partially observed variables.

This is one point at which Friedman's position breaks down.[6] As long as models are constructed without regard for their consistency with related models or with later refinements, one simulation is as good as another. Most model-builders like to feel that

[6] The essence of Professor Friedman's position is "... The only relevant test of the validity of a hypothesis is comparison of its predictions with experience" [8, pp. 8–9].

their models *represent* something, and recognize that theirs is not likely to be the last word said on the subject.

The archetype for the case-descriptive model is, then, a *simulative model* which is testable as a simulation and, at the same time, represents the referent situation. Formally, a simulative model is an operator that generates a set of variables X, given a set of variables Y, such that (a) the sets X and Y represent characteristics of the referent situation, (b) the set X is indistinguishable with respect to an explicit criterion from the corresponding characteristics of the referent situation, and (c) the operator itself represents the causal processes of the referent situation.

Being process models, case-descriptive models are necessarily dynamic. The generated variables X and the measurements of the referent situation are time series. On the assumption that the time series are discrete, the vector of measurements during time period T will be called an observation and denoted by an asterisk. $X(T)$ is the vector of generated variables at time T, and $X^*(T)$ is the vector of measurements at time T.

It is frequently argued that no examination of a model is a critical examination, a true test, unless the test is based on observations different from the observations used in developing the model. This may be a valuable comment on the testing of normative or norm-descriptive models; it is a much less valuable comment on the testing of case-descriptive models. First, rarely does a model-builder pretend to have explained all aspects of the referent situation. Nearly all models purport to be just what they are: defective contributions to the overall progress of human learning. Second, the effort invested in gathering detailed data to support a case-descriptive model is high relative to the work invested in developing the model itself. If the model is not consistent with the second set of observations, as in all probability it is not, it is better to spend time revising the model than to spend time criticizing the original model. Third, the value of the predictive criterion is that it exposes aspects of the referent situation that were not previously observed. But since the model-builder's perceptions are faulty, it does this at the risk of introducing more unobserved characteristics. As a result, the predictive criterion is more appropriate for models that aim at generality than it is for case-descriptive models. The basic objective of exposing unobserved characteristics can be achieved by including in the model as many observable characteristics as possible.

TESTING MICROPROCESSES

The causal processes in the referent situation generate a set of observed variables X_0^* and a set of unobserved variables U_0, given a set of observed variables Y_0^* and a set of unobserved variables V_0. In a practical sense, the set of observed variables X_0^* defines the referent situation.

The complete model of the referent situation will be called the *macroprocess*. The macroprocess is a set of causal functions that generates observed variables X_0 and unobserved variables U_0, given observed variables Y_0. For the time being, the sets X_0 and U_0 will be called endogenous variables and the set Y_0 will be called exogenous, although this terminology will be modified.

There are no unobserved exogenous variables V_0 in the specification of the model. Logically, this is a statement about the kinds of data that must be collected. Practically, it means that any characteristic of the referent situation that is not represented in the macroprocess or in the set Y_0 must either (a) have negligible effect on the set X_0 or (b) be constant over the time span being simulated [11, Appendix]. The same restriction is not true of the set, U_0, of unobserved variables represented in the model.

In general, the macroprocess can be factored into several mutually independent *microprocesses*. Formally, a microprocess is similar to the macroprocess. The Kth microprocess is a set of causal functions which generates observed variables X_K and unobserved variables U_K, given observed variables Y_K. X_K is the set of observed variables endogenous to the Kth microprocess; it is a subset of X_0. U_K is the set of unobserved variables endogenous to the Kth microprocess; it is a subset of U_0. Y_K is the set of observed variables exogenous to the Kth microprocess; it is composed of both (a) elements of Y_0 and (b) elements of X_0.

One important characteristic distinguishes a microprocess from an arbitrary subset of the macroprocess. A microprocess involves no unobserved variables except those that are endogenous to it; the only variables linking microprocesses are observed variables. The value of this characteristic is that a microprocess can be tested separately from other elements of the macroprocess. Tests of case-descriptive models should not only evaluate the goodness of the model; they should also identify sources of error. By testing the microprocesses independently, sources of error are associated with specific subsets of the macroprocess. However, it is not sufficient to test the individual microprocesses. A small error which appears insignificant when one microprocess is tested may be cumulative when two or more microprocesses are combined [2]. A thorough test procedure would sequentially examine all combinations of n microprocesses for $n = 1, 2, 3, \ldots$ until finally the macroprocess is tested as a unit.

The exogenous-endogenous terminology has been used rather loosely up to this point. Endogenous variables are variables generated by the model; they may be causally dependent on any characteristic of the referent situation. Exogenous variables are variables that are not generated by the model; they appear in the model because they influence the endogenous variables. There is a causal arrow that points from Y_0 to X_0. For the sufficiency test outlined below, this is the only constraint placed on the selection of exogenous variables. However, if the descriptive model is to be used normatively, exogenous variables must be selected more carefully. The character of the causal arrow from X_0 to Y_0 becomes important. A particular exogenous variable $Y_i(T)$ may be causally independent of the sets $X_0(T)$, $X_0(T-1)$, $X_0(T-2), \ldots X_0(T-L_i+1)$ but causally dependent on $X_0(T-L_i)$, $X_0(T-L_i-1)$, $X_0(T-L_i-2), \ldots X_0(-\infty)$. Such feedback from the referent process to its environment can radically affect a long-run normative projection. Therefore, it is meaningful to speak of the *order* of the model: the largest number of time periods for which the model can be validly projected. In the notation above, the order of the model is the smallest element in the set of causal lags, L_i. If X_0 is projected for n time periods into the future,

the order must be n or greater, and the causal functions defining Y_0 must not involve the variables $X_0(T)$, $X_0(T-1)$, $X_0(T-2), \ldots X_0(T-n+1)$.

TESTS OF SUFFICIENCY

X_0 is a probabilistic representation of X_0^*. It is probabilistic for four reasons. First, the characteristics of the referent situation are measured inaccurately. Rarely are the feasible states of a referent characteristic known exactly, and rarely can a referent characteristic be placed unambiguously in a defined state. Frequently measurements are crude; the feasible states of a referent characteristic are poorly defined and the actual state of the characteristic is ambiguous. An example of an accurately measurable characteristic is the state of a flipped coin: heads or tails. An example of a characteristic that is not accurately measurable is the amount of cooperative interaction during a period of group activity. Second, most models contain *stochastic generators*, elements whose state is randomly determined. For example, the model may generate variable X_1 with either causal function R_{11} or causal function R_{12}, the choice between R_{11} and R_{12} being random. Third, the model-builder may make outright errors in specifying the causal functions. And fourth, nearly all causal functions specified in the model are abstractions of the referent processes.

The first two sources of uncertainty will be called *loci of ignorance*. Loci of ignorance are aspects of the referent situation that the model-builder accepts as unknown, and that have ex ante measurable effects on the simulated variables. In principle, measurement inaccuracies and stochastic generators have measurable effects on X_0. The measurement dispersions of X_0^* and Y_0^* may not be known exactly, but they can usually be estimated by making multiple observations or by using a favorably designed measurement technique. The dispersions of stochastic generators are a similar case.

The second two sources of uncertainty are not loci of ignorance. The effects of an abstraction or an error are not ex ante measurable. A major reason for building models is to evaluate the uncertainty attached to the errors and abstractions. The builder of case-descriptive models does not accept abstraction as a desirable end in and of itself, only as a necessary truncation of his analysis. Outright errors are undesirable in any model.

The ideal objective of descriptive model-building is a set of functions that are both necessary and sufficient to explain the referent situation. There is, of course, no general test for this. A test of necessity implies that there are meaningful characterizations of all possible models, and measurements on enough observable variables to enable a unique choice among the possible models. A test of sufficiency, in the most general sense, implies that there are meaningful characterizations of all possible observations on all observable variables.

However, it is possible to test the sufficiency of a model (a) with respect to a specific set of observed endogenous variables, (b) over a specific sequence of observations, and (c) given the loci of ignorance specified in the model. X_0 defines the purpose of the model as a simulative device. The observations $X_0^*(T)$, $X_0^*(T+1), \ldots X_0^*(T+m)$ define the referent situation. The loci of ignorance define the maximum accuracy with which X_0 should be generated. The test focuses on the uncertainty introduced by abstraction and error.

The greater the uncertainty attached to the predictions of the model, the less can be said about the accuracy of the model. The statement that a model is sufficient is a statement that the model is an accurate description of the referent situation. If large loci of ignorance are present in the model, the model is more likely to be accepted as sufficient, but is less likely to be an accurate description of the referent situation.

Progress in description is made by reducing the sizes of loci of ignorance: through more measurements, more accurate measurements, and more detailed analyses of processes represented by stochastic generators. Through this process, models are subjected to increasingly rigorous tests of their accuracy. Gradually, the sufficiency tests become more rigorous. More variables are observed; more observations are accumulated; the sizes of loci of ignorance are reduced. The set of sufficient models becomes

smaller and smaller. In the long run, sufficiency converges toward necessity.

A case-descriptive model is, however, more than sufficient as defined by the sufficiency test. Incorporating in the model partially observed characteristics of the referent situation gives a weak assurance that the model will be consistent with later models.

THE SUFFICIENCY TEST

The set of unobserved endogenous variables U_0 can be factored into two subsets: the set of variables that change over time U_0', and the set of variables that do not change over time U_0''. The set U_0' is defined in terms of other variables by the causal functions of the model, as is the set X_0. Thus, the total number of causal functions in a microprocess is the sum of the number of variables in U_K' and the number of variables in X_K. The variables in the set U_0'' are free parameters; they are not determined by measurement and may exist only in the context of the specific model. However, logical limits may be imposed on these free parameters a priori.

The sufficiency criterion proposed here is: "Does a set U_K'' exist such that the model has a probability greater than zero of generating the sequence of observations?" For each time period a subset, $P_K(T)$, of the possible free parameter values will have probability greater than zero of generating $X_K^*(T)$, given all lagged values of X_K^*, and all current and lagged values of Y_K^*.[7] The intersection, P_K^*, of $P_K(T)$ over all T defines sufficiency. If P_K^* contains one or more points, the microprocess is sufficient. If P_K^* is null, the microprocess is not sufficient.

The test considers only the ranges of X_0^*, Y_0^*, and the stochastic generators. In order for the test to be meaningful, the density functions of the loci of ignorance must be bounded. The model-builder cannot use density functions with probability greater than zero for any value of the random variable (e.g., the Normal distribution).

The sufficiency test can be criticized as being both too tight and too loose. It is tight in the sense that the model must be able to generate every X_0^* for the entire sequence of observations. In comparison to tests usually given theoretical

---

[7] The regions $P_K(T)$ must be bounded by the logical limits imposed a priori on U_K''.

models, this is restrictive, but the builder of descriptive models should exchange something for the freedom to make specific rather than general models. The test is loose in the sense that only the ranges of the loci of ignorance are considered, not specific values. However, bounded density functions must be used, and improbable events sometimes occur.[8] Realistically, it seems probable that nearly all existing case-descriptive models would be rejected as insufficient if the tests were based on bounded, ex ante measured, loci of ignorance: fits now appear to be good only because the models include random error terms that cannot be characterized ex ante, and because large errors in some microprocesses are compensated by large errors in others.

This approach to testing suggests that the model-builder should focus his data gathering on measures of the ranges of random variables rather than on their precise values. The usual observational practice ignores measurements of loci of ignorance, leaving them to be inferred from the fit of the model. In fact, in the construction of case-descriptive models, it is as important to measure the loci of ignorance as it is to measure the variables X_0^* and Y_0^*.

Example. As an example of the mapping of the subset $P_K(T)$, consider the causal function:

$$X \leftarrow AY + B$$

[8] Of course, the test could be made tighter by changing the criterion to: "Does a set U_K'' exist such that the model has a probability greater than α of generating the sequence of observations?"

where A and B are parameters with logical limits:

$$0 \leqslant A$$
$$0 \leqslant B$$

At time period T, the measurements of X and Y indicate that:

$$0 \leqslant X_0 \leqslant X \leqslant X_1$$
$$0 \leqslant Y_0 \leqslant Y \leqslant Y_1$$

Therefore the region $P_K(T)$ is the region in $A - B$ space defined by the inequalities.

$$A \geqslant 0$$
$$B \geqslant 0$$
$$B \geqslant X_0 - AY_1$$
$$B \leqslant X_1 - AY_0$$

SUMMARY

This paper has attempted to outline a methodological ethic appropriate to the construction of case-descriptive models. The essence of the argument is that since the referent situations for case-descriptive models are essentially samples of size one, tests should focus on the sufficiency of the models using probability-not-zero as a criterion. This approach has computational as well as ethical advantages over the usual maximum likelihood criterion. The sufficiency test, however, does mean that the data-gathering process must focus more explicitly on loci of ignorance than would ordinarily be the case.

Since small errors tend to accumulate in large, complex models, it was suggested that the macroprocess be factored into microprocesses that can be tested sequentially.

REFERENCES

1. R. R. Bush, and F. Mosteller, 1955. *Stochastic models for learning.* New York: Wiley. 3C.
2. K. J. Cohen, 1960. *Computer models of the shoe, leather, hide sequence.* Englewood Cliffs, N.J.: Prentice-Hall. 1D.
3. K. J. Cohen, and R. M. Cyert, 1961. Computer models in dynamic economics. *Quarterly Journal of Economics,* 75(1): 112–127. MD.
4. W. K. Estes, and J. H. Straughan, 1954. Analysis of a verbal conditioning situation in terms of statistical learning theory. *Journal of Experimental Psychology,* 47(4): 225–234.
5. J. Feldman, 1959. *An analysis of predictive behavior in a two-choice situation.* Doctoral dissertation, Carnegie-Mellon University. 1A.
6. J. Feldman, 1961. Simulation of behavior in the binary choice experiment. *Joint Computer Conference, Western Proceedings,* 19: 133–144. 1A.
7. J. Feldman, F. Tonge, and H. Kanter, 1963. Empirical explorations of a hypothesis-testing model of binary choice behavior. *Symposium on simulation models* (A. C. Hoggatt and F. E. Balderston, eds.); Cincinnati: South-Western, 55–100. 1C.
8. M. Friedman, 1953. *Essays in positive economics.* Chicago: University of Chicago Press.
9. W. C. Hood, and T. C. Koopmans (eds.), 1953. *Studies in econometric method.* New York: Wiley.
10. T. C. Koopmans (ed.), 1950. *Statistical inference in dynamic economic models.* New York: Wiley.
11. H. A. Simon, and H. Guetzkow, 1955. A model of short- and long-run mechanisms involved in pressures toward uniformity in groups. *Psychological Review,* 62(1): 56–68.

38

INFORMATION-THEORETIC TECHNIQUES FOR EVALUATING SIMULATION MODELS

JOSEPH. F. HANNA

INTRODUCTION

It is widely recognized by those who do computer simulations that computer models, generally formulated as complex and rather opaque information processing programs, are exceedingly difficult to evaluate and that too little attention has been paid to this problem. Thus, in replying to the question, "How is one to estimate the degree of fit between machine output and human output?" Nico Frijda [2] notes that

There is hardly any methodology existing here. As much ingenuity as has been invested in the making of programs, as little has been spent on the assessment of their value. Next to high precision there always seem to be spots of rough approximations which undercut this very precision. We are left largely to our subjective impressions of what we consider good or bad correspondence.

This pessimistic view of existing procedures for evaluating simulation models is shared by the authors [6] of a recent book on computer simulation techniques, who write

The problem of validating computer simulation models is indeed a difficult one because it involves a host of practical, theoretical, statistical, and even philosophical complexities. Validation of simulation experiments is merely part of a more general problem, namely the validation of any kind of model or hypothesis. The basic questions are, "What does it mean to validate a hypothesis?" and "What criteria should be used to establish the validity of a hypothesis?" Since the scientific philosophers do not agree about the answers to these two questions, the reader will not be surprised to find that they remain unanswered in this book.

The present paper presents one approach to answering this second question: What criteria should be used to establish the *validity* (or more appropriately, the scientific *value*) of a hypothesis (specifically, a hypothesis formulated as a simulation model)? Roughly speaking, the proposal is to evaluate simulation models in terms of the amount of information they provide about the behavioral processes being simulated; the model with the maximum information content should be accepted over those containing less information. Stated so baldly, the proposal may strike the reader as trivial or tautological, but this would be a mistaken impression. In terms of a precisely stated concept of information content one can draw inferences regarding the most appropriate form of computer simulation output, as well as inferences regarding the relative merits of competing simulation models. Further, the precisely stated information measures clarify the distinction between a simulation model that is merely descriptive of phenomena and a simulation model that also has predictive or explanatory force.

In an early discussion of model testing, William Starbuck [7] distinguished three sorts of computer simulation models: normative models, norm-descriptive models, and case-descriptive models are intended to be generalizations. They focus upon an aggregate or an average, rather than an individual case. . . . The word of explanation. Quoting Starbuck, "Norm-descriptive models are intended to be generalizations. They focus upon an aggregate or an average, rather than an individual case . . . . The case-descriptive models are . . . intended to be detailed analyses of one, or a few, specific cases." In short, norm-descriptive models deal with behavioral processes that are common (at least hypothetically) to a general population, while case-descriptive models involve more detailed aspects of the behavioral processes: aspects which may be unique to a specific individual.

Following Starbuck, I will focus on problems of testing case-descriptive models because they appear, on the surface at least, to be especially intractable; the usual sorts of statistical tests, which depend on relatively large data samples from a homogeneous population, are simply not applicable to tests of models formulated for individual subjects. However, one advantage of the information measures presented in the present paper is that they apply both to case-descriptive and to norm-descriptive models, the principal difference in the two sorts of applications being the nature of the data. Indeed, from the present point of view there is no essential difference in the functions of case-descriptive and norm-descriptive models: both are intended to provide *information* about behavioral processes and the question is how to measure the amount of information that a specific model yields relative to a given body of data—independently of whether it is individual or group data.

My viewpoint contrasts sharply in this respect with that presented by Starbuck. He observes [7, p. 194] that, "the usual approach to model testing focuses on the probable event. It asks, given the model, how likely is the set of observations. A 'good' model is one with a high probability of generating the observations." Starbuck then goes on to argue that "The builder of case-descriptive models can reasonably point out that he really does not care how likely his observations are since (a) he does not pretend to have constructed a generalization, and (b) the rare event does happen." However, it seems to me that while points (a) and (b) are undoubtedly correct, it does not follow from them that the builder of case-descriptive models should not be concerned with assigning the "highest possible" probabilities to the behavior of individual subjects. Intuitively, the purpose of a model is, among other things, to decrease our surprise at what happens in the world. A "good" model—and this includes case-descriptive models—is one that explains (or describes) observed behavior, and this in turn means a model that makes our observations more plausible (or better understood) than they would have been without the model. This is not to deny that much behavior will be "unexpected" even when considered from the perspective of a "good" model, but the better model will on the average result in fewer surprising or unexplained phenomena.

Since the natural measure of information is a monotone increasing function of the likelihood, it follows that the most informative models are those that (on the average) assign the highest probability to observed phenomena. Thus, I would argue that even if one is solely interested in the isolated actions of a "unique" individual, one ought to search for models that assign high probabilities to those actions, and the adequacy of competing models ought to be judged in large part on the basis of one's success in achieving such high probabilities. This point will become clearer once the information measures are presented in detail. But before turning to that technical matter I would like to discuss in general terms some of the problems facing attempts to evaluate simulation models, and to indicate how the present approach to formulating and testing models can aid in resolving those problems.

SOME PROBLEMS IN TESTING CASE-DESCRIPTIVE MODELS

There is always a process of abstraction involved in formulating a model—even a case-descriptive model designed to simulate individual behavior. Roughly speaking, the model builder abstracts from the unlimited variability and detail of the perceptible world a class of stimulus variables and a class of response variables, and then hypothesizes some function that associates values of the response variables with observed or experimentally manipulatable values of the stimulus variables. Or in Starbuck's terminology [7]

Formally, a simulative model is an operator which generates a set of variables X, given a set of variables Y, such that (a) the sets of variables X and Y represent characteristics of the referent situation, (b) the set of variables X is indistinguishable with respect to an explicit criterion from the corresponding characteristics of the referent situation, and (c) the operator itself represents the causal processes relating the characteristics of the referent situation.

Thus, given a value Y^* of the stimulus (independent or exogenous) variables, the causal processes in the referent situation generate a value X^* of the response (dependent or endogenous) variables. Now the test of a simulation model is whether the value of the response variable that it generates when "fed" the observed value Y^* of the stimulus variable agrees with the observed response X^*. It should be noted, however, that we cannot reasonably expect perfect agreement between the model and the referent situation, even if the model is "perfect." This is because in specifying the referent situation for the model (specifically, the stimulus variables) one neglects (or abstracts from) factors that are actually involved in the referent causal processes. Starbuck distinguishes between sources of uncertainty that are ex ante measurable and those that are not, calling the former *loci of ignorance*. However, the term loci of ignorance will here be applied to all sources of uncertainty—measurement errors and neglected aspects of the referent situation alike. For specific loci of ignorance there is an upper limit on the accuracy attainable by any model. Once this limit has been reached greater accuracy can only be achieved by improvements in measurement techniques or by making finer discriminations of the characteristics of the referent situation—that is, by refining the data base.

Now there is a more general formulation of the above definition which sheds light on some of the problems of testing simulation models. Rather than view a model as an operator that generates values of the response variable X, given values of the stimulus variable Y, we may take explicit account of the stochastic elements that are introduced by the loci of ignorance, and view a model as an operator that determines a probability distribution over the range of X, given a value of Y. In this formulation, the random elements occasioned by both loci of ignorance—neglected factors and measurement errors—are explicitly included in the model. In general, the less precise one's measurements, and the more significant the neglected causal factors, the greater variance the resulting probability distribution will have. In the limit, if nothing is known about the causal factors influencing behavior, the model should attribute equal likelihood to all possible responses.

Historically, simulation models seem rarely to have been given this more general formulation. Rather than generating probabilities such models typically output a "response string" which may be viewed, depending on the nature of the simulation, as the protocol of a specific individual or as an ideal or average protocol. Feldman's [1] binary choice model is a good example; this model produced a string of responses that was intended to simulate the behavior of a concrete individual. The various chess- and checker-playing programs provide other examples of this type of model. Of course, these examples could be interpreted as degenerate stochastic models, where at each decision point the probability density is concentrated on a single response—namely, the response that the model outputs. However, such models are clearly not stochastic in spirit.

Now it seems to me that "deterministic" simulation models whose output consists of a protocol have several disadvantages when compared with "stochastic" simulation models whose output at each decision point is a probability distribution over the class of possible responses. These disadvantages are especially salient when viewed from the perspective of information theory. By way of illustration, let us consider some of the problems that Feldman encountered in his early attempt to simulate binary choice behavior.

i. Assessing Goodness-of-fit

One is always faced with the problem of assessing how adequately a model "simulates" observed behavior, but the problem is especially difficult for models whose output is simply a protocol. In such cases one is largely reduced to counting errors; either the simulated response agrees with the observation or it doesn't agree and there is usually little else one can say about it. The basic test of the model's adequacy is just the relative number of correct versus incorrect responses in the simulated output. For example, in discussing the deficiencies of his model Feldman [1] notes that "The segment of the model that has the highest number of errors relative to the number of times it is used is the guess opposite segment." Further examples are provided by the chess and checker programs designed to play book games; these are typically evaluated on the basis of the frequency with which the program makes the book move.

Now it is clear that simulation programs are intrinsically more informative than this means of evaluating them would indicate; it is usually possible at the very least for a simulation model to rank order the possible responses (moves, etc.) in terms of the same criterion that is used to generate a response (move, etc.). Thus, a chess program whose move at each play of the game is determined by maximizing some function can easily be revised so as to assign an ordering to the possible (legal) moves in terms of the values of this function. In general, the maximum value of the "strategy function" is associated with the simulated move, and the remaining possible moves can be ranked in decreasing order of their associated functional values. In effect, generating the rank order of possible moves would increase the information content of the simulation program. In addition to the information that a simulated move differed from the book move, one would have the information that the book move ranked second, or last, or whatever among the possible moves. Moreover, the information content of the program could be further increased by assigning probabilities to the possible moves rather than simply rank-ordering them. Given such probability assignments it is possible to speak in a precise way of the information content of a chess program relative to a particular book game or set of book games, and to evaluate alternative chess programs in terms of their relative information content.

A somewhat different argument for stochastic simulation models emerges from a consideration of the effect of *loci of ignorance*. Because of neglected causal factors and errors in measurement one would not expect, even if the world were fundamentally deterministic, that experimental results could be exactly replicated. Indeed, if we permit ourselves to formulate a thought experiment in which a given individual successively performs the *same experimental task*, and suppose that between performances all trace of earlier experimental runs is erased from the subject, we would not expect identical performances on every run—even in a deterministic universe. The key phrase here is "the same experimental task"; for in specifying the experimental task one performs an abstraction the net effect of which is to lump together as "the same" referent situations that are actually causally distinct. Now the causal factors incorporated in a simulation model consist at most of those variables that are explicitly considered to be relevant aspects of the referent situation (i.e., those variables that determine the "sameness" of referent situations). Thus, in general, any model that produces an actual protocol is generating predictions with a higher degree of precision than can be achieved given the loci of ignorance associated with the referent situation. Moreover, the effect of such overspecification is to lose information. In fact, it can be demonstrated (compare the following section) that the most informative model is one whose predictions have exactly the degree of precision permitted by the loci of ignorance associated with the referent situation. Thus, one can lose information due to overspecific as well as to underspecific predictions.

As a final note on this problem of assessing goodness-of-fit consider Starbuck's [7] proposed test of sufficiency. Roughly speaking, his test of sufficiency for a simulation model may be stated as follows: Do there exist parameter values (within the parameter space of the model) such that for those values the model has a nonzero probability of generating the sequence of observations? In other words, a model is judged adequate according to this criterion if it is not absolutely incompatible with the data. This criterion seems to me to be so weak as to have almost no force. In the first place, one can always formulate a model that meets the test by incorporating sufficiently powerful parameters in the model, that is, parameters that can "absorb" a great amount of information from the data (compare Def. 5 of the following section). In fact, the sufficiency test does not guard at all against unfalsifiable models—models that for appropriate parameter values could generate any preselected protocol. In the second place, the sufficiency test simply fails to take account of the bulk of the available evidence for discriminating among models: namely, it fails to take account of the actual likelihood that a model assigns to the observations. Starbuck's observation that "the improbable event occurs" does not seem to me to justify adopting such a weak criterion of adequacy. The improbable event clearly does not occur frequently (otherwise it would not be improbable) so that on the average one could expect that a "good" model (relative to the loci of ignorance) would assign high probabilities to observations. At the very least, the sufficiency test ought to be strengthened to the extent that a model is rejected if (on the average) it assigns a lower likelihood to observations than a random model (i.e., a model that assigns equal likelihood to all possible observations). In a sense, any model that is outperformed by a random model is *misinformative* (has a negative information content).

ii. Evaluating Subhypotheses

A second difficulty that Feldman encountered in evaluating his binary choice model was that of distributing responsibility for incorrect predictions among the various parts of the program. Often it is possible to correct false predictions by adjustments in different subprocesses of the overall program: for example, there may be different program parameters whose values can be adjusted in order to obtain the correct prediction and which, therefore, share the responsibility for having

generated an incorrect response. Thus, there is often no effective way to sort out the good from the bad subhypotheses of the simulation program. The early attempts to construct chess programs that would simulate book games illustrate this problem. The parameters of these models typically included weights attached to various board characteristics, for example, material balance, center control, and king safety. Because of the complex information processing and decision-making mechanisms associated with these parameters it was difficult to attribute responsibility for a bad move or a bad game to an improper weighting of any one board characteristic. Modification of a specific weight may result in a different game, but often it is difficult to say whether it is closer than the original to the book game being simulated.

Stochastic models have a definite advantage in meeting this problem because it is possible to measure the information content of the various subhypotheses and thereby to determine which of them are informative and should be retained and which of them are misinformative and should be abandoned or modified. Roughly speaking, the average information content of a hypothesis can be determined by fixing the remaining subhypotheses of the model and allowing the given subhypothesis to vary (this variation may involve a range of possible parameter values or it may simply be a question of including or excluding the hypothesis); if the average information content of the model with the given subhypothesis exceeds its information content without the subhypothesis, then the subhypothesis has positive information content, otherwise it has zero or negative information content (a more precise formulation of this measure will be presented in the following section). In this way the "effect" of any individual subhypothesis can be evaluated as well as the joint "effect" of any combination of two or more subhypotheses. Again, the result of assigning probabilities to possible protocols rather than generating simulated protocols is to increase the theoretical content and usefulness of the model.

iii. Setting Back on the Track

Feldman referred to a related problem of evaluating simulation models as that of "setting the program back on the track." Referring to chess and checker playing programs, Feldman [1] describes the problem as follows:

Because the decision of the chess or checker program at move m depends on the decisions at the preceding moves, $m-1$, $m-2$, ..., such a program, when it is playing a book game, must be "set back on the track" if its move deviates from the book move. The program and the book must have the same history if the program is to have a fair chance to make the same decision as that made in the book game. This "setting back on the track" may involve resetting a large number of parameters as well as changing the move itself.

As mentioned above, this problem is compounded by the fact that there are typically alternative ways of setting the program back on the track, and the selection of a particular route back onto the track may well influence the subsequent performance of the simulation program. There is also the problem of evaluating the significance of the program's performance when it is frequently set back on the track. Clearly, one-level prediction is not so difficult a feat as many-level prediction. Thus, it is more to the credit of a program that it was correct half the time but with long stretches of correct moves where no resetting was required, than it is if the program required resetting every other move (in which case it also would have been correct half the time).

From the present point of view "setting the program back on the track" poses no problem, since in assigning probabilities to possible moves the program never makes an incorrect move (except in the special case where the book move is assigned zero probability). Thus, the book move (or the subject's response) never has to be imposed on the model. Rather, at each decision point the program calculates the probability of the book move (observed response) conditional on the sequence of preceding book moves (responses). In principle, this technique requires the calculation of only one probability at each decision point and so is essentially as efficient in running time as a program that actually generates moves (or responses). Moreover, since the probabilities calculated at each decision point are conditional on the preceding sequence of moves (responses), their product is just the joint probability of the entire book game

(sequence of responses). Thus, by summing the logarithms of the trial-by-trial probabilities one can easily obtain a measure of the information content of a model relative to the total data.

iv. Estimating Parameters

When dealing with the type of case-descriptive model constructed by Feldman one is faced with formidable problems of parameter estimation. These difficulties are largely because of the fact that the output of the model (the simulated responses of the subject) is a discontinuous function of the parameter values; small changes in parameter values typically result in either no change in output or else in a significantly different output. As a result of this discontinuity, which Minski [5] has referred to as the "mesa phenomenon," familiar hill-climbing techniques of parameter estimation are largely ineffective. Moreover, because of the complexity of information flow in most computer simulation models it is difficult to acquire any feeling for what is happening in the model— to determine, for example, the "effect" or importance of various parameters.

This problem of parameter estimation and evaluation is closely related to the above-mentioned problem of evaluating subhypotheses of a model. In fact, the information measures described in the following section apply in like manner to these problems. For, measuring the "effect" of a specific parameter is simply a special case of measuring the "information content" of a subhypothesis.

Finally, since the probabilities assigned to observations by stochastic simulation models typically vary continuously with changes in parameter values, it is possible to employ hill-climbing procedures and thereby obtain reliable parameter estimates.

The following section contains a brief but precise formulation of the information measures mentioned in the preceding discussion.

INFORMATION MEASURES

Let $\Omega = \{\omega_1, ..., \omega_r\}$ be a set of mutually exclusive and exhaustive outcomes of some experiment. For instance, if the experiment consists of running a subject for N trials in a binary choice task (in which response latencies, etc. are not measured), then Ω contains 2^N outcomes, corresponding to the possible sequences of N binary responses. (Or Ω might be the set of possible chess games.)

In general, the elements of the outcome space will depend on a particular analysis or reduction of the data as well as on the physical design of the experiment. For instance, a binary choice model might be tested against the pooled trial-by-trial data from several subjects, the mean learning curve, asymptotic characteristics of the data, and so on. Thus, in the following, Ω might be the set of possible values of some statistic (or combination of statistics) of the data.

Let M be a stochastic simulation model, with parameter space $\mathscr{P}$, defined for the experimental situation represented by Ω. For each $\alpha \varepsilon \mathscr{P}$, M_α is the *instance of model* M determined by the parameter value α, and for each $\omega \varepsilon \Omega$, $M_\alpha(\omega)$ is the probability assigned by model instance M_α to outcome ω. If $\omega^* \varepsilon \Omega$ is an observed outcome of the experiment—for instance, the protocol of a particular subject or a particular book game—then $M_\alpha(\omega^*), \alpha \varepsilon \mathscr{P}$, is the likelihood function. In general, α may be a vector of parameters $\alpha = \langle \alpha_1, ..., \alpha_k \rangle$.

It should be noted that the following definitions are limited to those applications in which the outcome space Ω is finite and the likelihood function is everywhere nonzero.

Definition 1. The *coefficient of predictive power of model instance* M_α *relative to outcome* ω^* is
$$\rho_\alpha = 1 - \log_r(1/M_\alpha(\omega^*))$$

where r is the number of elements in the outcome space.

The motivation for adopting the coefficient of predictive power as a basis for evaluating simulation models is implicit in the following characteristics of the measure:

i.   The coefficient ρ_α is a monotone, increasing function of the likelihood.

ii.   Following Kullback [4], ρ_α is a measure of the information (in units r) in the observation ω^* for discriminating in favor of model instance M_α against a random model instance, where a random model instance assigns equal likelihood to all possible outcomes. Thus, the strengthened sufficiency test suggested above would amount to rejecting any model instance (relative to the

given observation ω^*) which resulted in a negative value of ρ_α.

iii.   From a slightly different point of view (compare [3]) ρ_α is a measure of the information content of model instance M_α relative to the observation ω^*.

iv.   For $\omega \varepsilon \Omega$, let $f(\omega)$ be the "true" relative frequency of outcome ω. More precisely, we may think of $f(\omega)$ as the expected frequency of ω in an infinite number of replications of the experiment, where the notion of a "replication" is determined relative to the loci of ignorance of the referent situation. (Of course, we can at best only obtain estimates of $f(\omega)$, and in case-descriptive situations we usually cannot even do that, but that is beside the point for the present purposes.) Then

(a)   the expected value of ρ_α is a maximum when $M_\alpha(\omega) = f(\omega)$, for all ω. Thus, the *true* model instance (i.e., the model instance that assigns to each outcome its limiting relative frequency) has the greatest expected predictive power; also, this means that the true model instance has the greatest information content and thereby supports my earlier argument against simulation models which generate overprecise predictions. And

(b)   the only monotone functions of the likelihood that satisfy condition (a) have the form $K + k \cdot \log M_\alpha(\omega^*)$. Thus, the coefficient of predictive power is unique up to a log-linear transformation of the likelihood (see [3, p. 370]).

v.   The predictive power coefficient is normalized: its range is $-\infty \leqslant \rho_\alpha \leqslant 1$, with $\rho_\alpha = 1$ if and only if the likelihood is 1, and $\rho_\alpha = 0$ if and only if the likelihood equals that of a random model instance. As a result of normalization, coefficients of predictive power associated with different referent situations or different statistics of the data can be meaningfully compared.

Definition 1 provides a means of comparing *model instances*, but it does not contain sufficient machinery for handling the complications introduced by free parameters whose values must be estimated from the data. The following definitions provide the required machinery for evaluating parameterized models.

Definition 2. *The coefficient of descriptive power of model M relative to outcome ω* is*

$$\delta_M = \operatorname*{Max}_{\alpha \varepsilon \mathscr{P}} \rho_\alpha$$

Notice that δ_M equals the predictive power of the instance(s) of model M whose parameter values are maximum likelihood estimates. By analogy with condition ii above, δ_M is a measure of the information in the observation ω^* (*after estimation of parameters*) for discriminating in favor of model M against a random model instance. Or by analogy with condition iii, an equally plausible interpretation of δ_M is as a measure of the a posteriori information content of model M relative to outcome $\omega.^*$ The dependence of δ_M on "information taken from (or transmitted by) the data" motivates the term *descriptive power*; its value clearly does not reflect predictive or explanatory power.

Let $g(\alpha), \alpha \varepsilon \mathscr{P}$, be a probability distribution reflecting a priori information about the true (or best) value of parameter α (in the absence of any information concerning the value of α, let g be the uniform distribution.) We may think of g as the output of a higher level (meta) model. In actual practice, the a priori distribution may be inferred from independent observations (previous data) or derived from an identification of parameters with aspects of the referent situation that can be independently measured (i.e., measured prior to the actual experiment). In any case, the *expected likelihood* determined by model M (in conjunction with distribution g) is

$$M(\omega^*) = \int_{\alpha \varepsilon \mathscr{P}} g(\alpha) \cdot M_\alpha(\omega^*)\, d\alpha \qquad (1)$$

provided that this integral exists. Now, treating M as a *model instance* (since it no longer has free parameters), we have by analogy with Def. 1 the following.

Definition 3. *The coefficient of predictive power of model M relative to outcome ω* and a priori distribution g is*

$$\rho_M = 1 - \log_r(1/M(\omega^*))$$

Again by analogy with condition ii above, the coefficient of predictive power is a measure of the information in observation ω^* (*before estimation of parameters*) for discriminating in favor of model M against a random model instance. Or by analogy with iii, it is a measure

of the a priori information content of M relative to ω^*. The independence of ρ_M from the data, the fact that it measures the degree to which the model yields accurate predictions, motivates the term *predictive* power. Of course, depending on the context, it would be equally appropriate to refer to ρ_M as a measure of explanatory power.

Although Def. 3 is a natural extension of the concept of predictive power as applied to model instances, there is an alternative measure of the predictive power of models: namely,

Definition 4. *The coefficient of mean predictive power of model M relative to outcome ω* and a priori distribution g is*

$$\bar{\rho}_M = \int_{\alpha \varepsilon \mathscr{P}} g(\alpha) \cdot \rho_\alpha \cdot d\alpha$$

where ρ_α is the coefficient of predictive power of model instance M_α relative to outcome ω^*.

Intuitively, $\bar{\rho}_M$ is a measure of the expected information content of the model instances $M_\alpha, \alpha \varepsilon \mathscr{P}$, while ρ_M is a measure of the information content of a model instance that is defined as the expectation of the model instances M_α. In some respects, $\bar{\rho}_M$ is a more sensitive measure than ρ_M, since for a given value of the likelihood $M(\omega^*), \rho_M \geqslant \bar{\rho}_M$, with equality holding if and only if the likelihood function $M_\alpha(\omega^*), \alpha \varepsilon \mathscr{P}$, is a constant. Moreover, for computer simulation models, which typically require nonanalytic parameter estimation procedures (e.g., hill climbing), the measure $\bar{\rho}_M$ is more stable than ρ_M: its value can be more reliably estimated from small samples of points in the parameter space. In the following definitions, I will use the symbol ρ_M indifferently to denote either predictive power or mean predictive power. In effect, each definition introduces two measures with essentially the same intuitive interpretations.

Since the coefficients ρ_M and δ_M are, respectively, measures of information content before and after estimation of parameters, their difference reflects the contribution of the parameters themselves. To be precise, $\delta_M - \rho_M$ is a measure of the information in the observation ω^* (*resulting from the parameter estimation process*) for discriminating in favor of model M against a random model instance, that is, a measure of the information "absorbed from (or transmitted by) the data in estimating parameters." If our goal is to maximize the information transmitted by the environment, by relevant characteristics of the referent situation, it is important to have such a measure in order to isolate the source of information. It seems to me that failure to make such a distinction between the *descriptive role* of a simulation model on the one hand, and its *predictive* or *explanatory* role on the other hand, represents a serious weakness of Starbuck's [7] satisfaction criterion; for, at best, the satisfaction criterion provides a measure of the model's capacity (after the fact) to simulate behavior, and depending upon the flexibility permitted by estimation of parameters this may or may not be a significant feat. Frijda [2] also blurs this distinction in his discussion of problems of computer simulation, for he remarks that,

. . . computer simulation is a means to demonstrate and test the consistency and sufficiency of a theory. If the behavioral data which the theory wants to explain are in fact reproduced by running the program, the theory has been proved capable of explaining those facts.

The definition of the term "explanation" does not seem to be at issue here; I would expect, for example, that Feldman's statement [1], "An acceptable explanation is an hypothesis that could have predicted the event," would be generally agreed to. But one is surely not permitted to make essential use of the event being explained in giving the explanation, and this is exactly what is involved when parameters are estimated from the same data against which the model is tested.

It might be supposed that the "number of free parameters" would be an adequate index of information transmitted by the data: the more free parameters one estimates, the greater the transmitted information. However, one can easily construct examples to show that this is not the case; the quantity of transmitted information is generally a nonmonotonic function of the number of free model parameters. For this reason, the measure $\delta_M - \rho_M$ is more adequate than the familiar notion of "degrees-of-freedom" as an index of the effect or power of parameters. Thus we have

Definition 5. *The coefficient of parameter effect of model M relative to outcome ω^* and a priori distribution g* is

$$\varepsilon_M = \delta_M - \rho_M$$

Notice that $0 \leqslant \varepsilon_M \leqslant \infty$, with $\varepsilon_M = 0$ when the likelihood function is a constant. Like the coefficients of predictive and descriptive power, the coefficient of parameter effect is normalized. Thus it makes sense to compare relative parameter effects for different statistics of the data.[1]

It is often convenient to have a measure of the information content of specific subhypotheses of a simulation model. Such a measure is presented in Def. 6, following the introduction of some preliminary concepts and notation.

We may view a subhypothesis as a generalized parameter of a model. When it is present in the model, the subhypothesis (which will often have the form of a program subroutine) will affect the likelihood function in different ways depending on the values taken on by its internal parameters. Thus, let α_1 represent the parameters internal to the given subhypothesis and let α_2 represent the remaining parameters of the simulation model. Let $g(\alpha_1, \alpha_2)$ be the a priori probability distribution over the "two-dimensional" parameter space, and let

$$g(\alpha_2) = \int g(\alpha_1, \alpha_2) \, d\alpha_1$$

be the marginal probability of the point α_2. Further, let ω^* be an observed outcome and α_2^* be a fixed value of parameter α_2. Then $M(\alpha_2^*)$ is a model all of whose parameters (namely, α_1) are internal to the given subhypothesis. In short, we are representing a two parameter model M as a one parameter model $M^* = M(\alpha_2^*)$ by fixing the value of one parameter. Thus, Def. 3 can be applied to yield the coefficient of predictive power ρ_{M*} of model M^* relative to outcome ω^* and a priori distribution g. In effect, ρ_{M*} is a measure of the predictive power (or normalized information content) of model M at the point α_2^*.

Now, let M_1 be the simulation model minus the given subhypothesis and let $M_1^* = M_1(\alpha_2^*)$

---

[1] In an earlier publication [3], the coefficient of parameter effect was further relativized by dividing by $1 - \rho_M$, thus resulting in a measure with limits $0 \leqslant \varepsilon_M \leqslant 1$.

be that instance of model M_1 determined by parameter value α_2^* (note that α_1 is *not* a parameter of model M_1). Then, $\rho_{M_1^*}$ is the coefficient of predictive power of model instance M_1^* and $\rho_{\alpha_1}(\alpha_2^*) = \rho_{M^*} - \rho_{M_1^*}$ (which may be negative) is a normalized measure of the *information content of the subhypothesis represented by* α_1 *at the point* α_2^*. Finally, we can compute the mean information content of the given subhypothesis by weighting its information content at individual points in the external parameter space according to the a priori distribution g. The precise statement is given by

Definition 6. *The coefficient of mean predictive power of subhypothesis* α_1 *relative to outcome* ω^* *and a priori distribution g is*

$$\mathbf{p}_{\alpha_1} = \int g(\alpha_2) \cdot \rho_{\alpha_1}(\alpha_2) \cdot d\alpha_2$$

Similar definitions can be formulated for the joint (mean) information content of any combination of subhypotheses of a model.

As an example of the application of Def. 6, consider two chess-playing programs that differ only in that the likelihood function of one program reflects the value of a particular board characteristic, say king safety, which the other program altogether ignores. Then, Def. 6 would provide a measure of the information content of this board characteristic (or more precisely, a measure of its information content when used in a certain way).

The coefficients of descriptive and predictive power together provide an objective means of comparing stochastic simulation models—a means that is independent of the number of free parameters. In fact, the two basic measures give rise to a number of distinct preference (dominance) relations, reflecting the different emphases that might be placed on descriptive power, predictive power, and parameter effect. For example, one model may be preferred to (dominate) another because it has greater predictive power, or because it has greater descriptive power, or because it has greater descriptive power but less parameter effect and so on. The three dominance relations presented in the following definition illustrate the spectrum of possibilities.

Definition 7. Let M_1 and M_2 be models defined for outcome space Ω, then (relative to outcome ω^* and a priori distributions g_1 and g_2)

(a) M_1 *weakly dominates* M_2 if $\delta_{M_1} \geqslant \delta_{M_2}$ and $\rho_{M_1} \geqslant \rho_{M_2}$;

(b) M_1 *dominates* M_2 if $\delta_{M_1} \geqslant \delta_{M_2}$ and $\varepsilon_{M_1} \leqslant \varepsilon_{M_2}$; and

(c) M_1 *strongly dominates* M_2 if $\rho_{M_1} \geqslant \delta_{M_2}$.

As suggested by the terminology, the above relations form a sequence of increasingly difficult hurdles for a given model to surmount in competition with alternative models. This is clear as regards dominance and weak dominance, since b logically implies a but not *vice versa*. Similarly, c is logically stronger than a, so that strong dominance entails weak dominance. Conditions b and c on the other hand, are logically independent: neither entails the other. It is easily seen, however, that strong dominance is a more stringent comparative test than dominance. For instance, if M_1 strongly dominates M_2, then M_1 strongly dominates a model (instance) which dominates M_2: namely, that model (instance) defined by the expected likelihood of M_1 (see Eq. 1). On the other hand, M_1 may dominate M_2 without dominating any model which strongly dominates M_2.

The distinction between conditions a and b reflects a basic opposition in the goals of model building. The primary goal is to accurately describe and predict (or explain) behavior. Thus, if a given model has both greater descriptive power and greater predictive power than a competing model, it comes closer to achieving this goal, regardless of the relative number of free parameters in the models. This is the intuitive import of the weak dominance relation. On the other hand, accurate description of observed behavior is not a significant feat if the model could have given an equally accurate description of any other behavior that might have occurred; in short, descriptive power is only significant to the extent that a model is descriptively falsifiable. (It seems to me that one of the major weaknesses of Starbuck's sufficiency test is its failure to take account of descriptive falsifiability.) This concern with falsifiability is reflected in the frequent emphasis placed on the *number of free parameters*: it is commonly felt that, because it can fit any arbitrary data, a model with many free parameters is unfalsifiable and, consequently, uninformative. However, in actual practice, the relative number of free parameters is not an adequate index of the relative falsifiability of competing models. Perhaps the most adequate measure of falsifiability in the present context is the mean descriptive power, given by

$$\bar{\delta}_M = 1/r \cdot \sum_{i=1}^{r} \delta_M(\omega_i) \tag{2}$$

To be precise, $\bar{\delta}_M$ measures nonfalsifiability, since the difficulty in falsifying a model increases with its mean descriptive power; in the limit, when $\bar{\delta}_M = 1$, every possible outcome can be described perfectly.

It would be difficult to calculate $\bar{\delta}_M$ in practice, since Eq. 2 involves an expectation over the outcome space as well as a search of the parameter space. In this respect, the dominance relation (condition b) represents a compromise: it is sensitive to the relative falsifiability of competing models (by virtue of its dependence on the coefficient of parameter effect), but it does not require computing an expectation over the outcome space. In effect, the dominance relation places a premium on predictive power, for condition b is equivalent to the following condition:

b') $\delta_{M_1} \geqslant \delta_{M_2}$ and $\delta_{M_1} - \delta_{M_2} \leqslant \rho_{M_1} - \rho_{M_2}$

which requires that M_1 surpass M_2 by a larger margin in predictive power than in descriptive power.

Notice, finally, that the dominance relations are only partial orders (i.e., reflexive and transitive, but not connected). Hence, it may happen that neither of two competing models weakly dominates the other. The choice between models which are "incomparable" relative to the dominance relations must be based on additional considerations, e.g. the relative priorities of predictive (explanatory) and descriptive power or the degree of falsifiability (which is inversely related to parameter effect).

SUMMARY

The above information measures provide a useful supplement to existing techniques for evaluating stochastic simulation models, but their most significant contribution, it seems to me, concerns the nature and purpose of simulation models. Specifically, the measures presented in Defs. 1–7

(a) Support the view that "stochastic" models are (in a precise sense) theoretically more informative than "deterministic" models, and, moreover, that a given body of data provides more evidence for discriminating among "stochastic" models than it provides for discriminating among "deterministic" models;

(b) Clarify the distinction between the use of a model to describe data and its use to explain or predict data;

(c) Provide a measure of the information content of specific subhypotheses or groups of subhypotheses of a model; and

(d) Provide a measure of "parameter effect" which is more reliable than "the number of free parameters" as an index of the descriptive falsifiability of a model.

Thus, if our goal in building simulation models is to gain information about the causally relevant characteristics of the referent situation, then we should avoid models whose predictions are overprecise. And if our goal is to explain or predict rather than simply to describe data, then we should take explicit account of the information that comes from *that same data* (through parameter estimation) as against information that comes from *independent* characteristics of the referent situation.

REFERENCES

1. J. Feldman, 1961. Simulation of behavior in the binary choice experiment. *Joint Computer Conference, Western Proceedings, 19*: 133–144. 1A.
2. N. H. Frijda, 1967. Problems of computer simulation. *Behavioral Science, 12*(1): 59–67. MA.
3. J. F. Hanna, 1966. A new approach to the formulation and testing of learning models. *Synthese, 16*(3): 344–380. MS.
4. S. Kullback, 1959. *Information theory and statistics.* New York: Wiley.
5. M. L. Minsky, 1963. Steps toward artificial intelligence. *Computers and thought* (E. A. Feigenbaum, and J. Feldman, eds.); New York: McGraw-Hill, 406–450.
6. T. H. Naylor, J. L. Balintfy, D. S. Burdick, and K. Chu, 1966. *Computer simulation techniques.* New York: Wiley. MG.
7. W. H. Starbuck, 1961. Testing case-descriptive models. *Behavioral Science, 6*(3): 191–199. MS.

REFERENCES: Publications cited in text but not included in the Simulation Bibliography (Chapter 2).

R. P. Abelson, and M. J. Rosenberg, 1958. Symbolic psycho-logic: a model of attitudinal cognition. *Behavioral Science, 3*(1): 1–13.

L. E. Albright, J. R. Glennon, and W. J. Smith, 1963. *The use of psychological tests in industry.* Cleveland: Howard Allen.

R. M. Alt, 1949. The internal organization of the firm and price formation: an illustrative case. *Quarterly Journal of Economics, 63*(1): 92–110.

R. L. Anderson, and T. A. Bancroft, 1952. *Statistical theory in research.* New York: McGraw-Hill.

T. W. Anderson, 1958. Principal components. *An introduction to multivariate statistical analysis;* New York: Wiley, 272–287.

A. Ando, and E. C. Brown, 1968. Personal income taxes and consumption following the 1964 tax reduction. *Studies in economic stabilization* (A. Ando, E. C. Brown, and A. F. Friedlaender, eds.); Washington: Brookings, 117–137.

A. Ando, and F. Modigliani, 1963. The "life cycle" hypothesis of saving: aggregate implications and tests. *American Economic Review, 53*(1): 55–84.

F. J. Anscombe, 1959. Quick analysis methods for random balance screening experiments. *Technometrics, 1*(2): 195–209.

R. C. Atkinson, G. H. Bower, and E. J. Crothers, 1965. *An introduction to mathematical learning theory.* New York: Wiley.

F. B. Baker, 1964. An IPL-V program for concept attainment. *Educational and Psychological Measurement, 24*(1): 119–127.

R. F. Bales, 1959. Small-group theory and research. *Sociology today* (R. K. Merton, L. Broom, and L. S. Cottrell, eds.); New York: Basic Books, 293–305.

Baltimore Regional Planning Council, 1963. *A projection of planning factors for land use and transportation.* Baltimore: Maryland State Planning Department, Technical Report No. 9.

H. Barger, and L. R. Klein, 1954. A quarterly model for the United States economy. *Journal of the American Statistical Association, 49*(267): 413–437.

T. H. Barker, 1966. *A computer program for simulation of perceptrons and similar neural networks: users manual.* Ithaca, N.Y.: Cornell University Cognitive Systems Research Program.

C. I. Barnard, 1938. *The functions of the executive.* Cambridge, Mass.: Harvard University Press.

C. F. Barnes, Jr., 1961. Integrating land use and traffic forecasting. *Highway Research Board Bulletin, 297*: 1–13.

M. S. Bartlett, 1955. Sampling fluctuations of means and correlation coefficients. *An introduction to stochastic processes;* Cambridge: Cambridge University Press, 254–259.

M. S. Bartlett, 1957. Measles periodicity and community size. *Journal of the Royal Statistical Society, Series A, 120*(1): 48–60.

G. K. Bennett, and M. Gelink, 1956. *Short employment tests.* New York: Psychological Corporation.

L. Benson, 1957. Research problems in American political historiography. *Common frontiers of the social sciences* (M. Komarovsky, ed.); Glencoe, Ill.: Free Press, 113–183.

L. Benson, 1961. *The concept of Jacksonian democracy.* Princeton: Princeton University Press.

B. R. Berelson, P. F. Lazarsfeld, and W. N. McPhee, 1954. *Voting.* Chicago: University of Chicago Press.

M. S. Blumberg, 1961. "DPF concept" helps predict bed needs. *Modern Hospital, 97*(6): 75–81.

K. E. Boulding, 1955. *Economic analysis.* New York: Harper, third edition.

L. E. Bourne, Jr., and R. C. Haygood, 1959. The role of stimulus redundancy in concept identification. *Journal of Experimental Psychology, 58*(3): 232–238.

G. H. Bower, and T. R. Trabasso, 1964. Concept identification. *Studies in mathematical psychology* (R. C. Atkinson, ed.); Stanford: Stanford University Press, 32–94.

G. H. Bower, with E. H. Galanter, E. J. Gibson, K. H. Pribram, E. A. Feigenbaum, H. B. Barlow, T. J. Voneida, A. W. Melton, F. Fremont-Smith, D. E. Broadbent, L. Weiskrantz, E. R. John, J. L. McGaugh, J. V. McConnell, P. Buser, B. Milner, D. R. Meyer, S. Kramer, D. P. Kimble, D. M. Rioch, R. A. Hinde, and J. J. Gibson, 1967. A descriptive theory of memory. *Conference on learning, remembering, and forgetting, Volume 2: the organization of recall* (D. P. Kimble, ed.); New York: New York Academy of Sciences, 112–185.

G. E. P. Box, and K. B. Wilson, 1951. On the experimental attainment of optimum conditions. *Journal of the Royal Statistical Society, Series B, 13*(1): 1–45.

D. Braybrooke, and C. E. Lindblom, 1963. *A strategy of decision*. New York: Free Press.

A. A. Brown, F. T. Hulswit, and J. D. Kettelle, 1956. A study of sales operations. *Operations Research*, *4*(3): 296–308.

R. Brown, 1962. Models of attitude change. *New directions in psychology, Volume I* (R. Brown, E. H. Galanter, E. H. Hess, and G. Mandler); New York: Holt, Rinehart, and Winston, 1–85.

K. A. Brownlee, 1949. *Industrial experimentation*. Brooklyn: Chemical Publishing, third American edition.

C. Bücher, 1901. *Industrial evolution*. New York: Holt.

J. S. Bruner, J. J. Goodnow, and G. A. Austin, 1956. *A study of thinking*. New York: Wiley.

V. E. Buck, 1963. *Job pressures on managers: sources, subjects, and correlates*. Doctoral dissertation, Cornell University.

T. A. Budne, 1959. The application of random balance designs. *Technometrics*, *1*(2): 139–155.

T. A. Budne, 1959. Random balance, Part I—the missing statistical link in fact finding techniques. *Industrial Quality Control*, *15*(10): 5–10.

T. A. Budne, 1959. Random balance, Part II—techniques of analysis. *Industrial Quality Control*, *15*(11): 11–16.

T. A. Budne, 1959. Random balance, Part III—case histories. *Industrial Quality Control*, *15*(12): 16–19.

Bureau of Public Roads, 1954. *Manual of procedures for home interview traffic study*. Washington: Bureau of Public Roads, revised edition.

Bureau of the Census, 1960. *Current Industrial Reports, Series M22A (60)-9*. Washington: U.S. Department of Commerce.

R. R. Bush, and W. K. Estes, eds., 1959. *Studies in mathematical learning theory*. Stanford: Stanford University Press.

D. W. Bushaw, and R. W. Clower, 1957. Toward a generalized theory of price determination and a unified theory of price and quantity determination. *Introduction to mathematical economics;* Homewood, Ill.: Irwin, 176–190.

E. R. Caianiello, A. deLuca, and L. M. Ricciardi, 1967. Reverberations and control of neural nets. *Kybernetik*, *4*(1): 10–18.

A. Campbell, P. E. Converse, W. E. Miller, and D. E. Stokes, 1960. *The American voter*. New York: Wiley.

E. H. Chamberlin, 1946. Duopoly and oligopoly. *The theory of monopolistic competition;* Cambridge, Mass.: Harvard University Press, fifth edition, 30–55.

E. H. Chamberlin, 1946. Selling costs and the theory of value: group equilibrium. *The theory of monopolistic competition;* Cambridge, Mass.: Harvard University Press, fifth edition, 149–171.

E. H. Chamberlin, 1946. Selling costs vs. production costs. *The theory of monopolistic competition;* Cambridge, Mass.: Harvard University Press, fifth edition, 117–129.

V. Chew, ed., 1958. *Experimental designs in industry*. New York: Wiley.

Chicago Area Transportation Study, 1960. Estimated land use in 1980. *Final report, Volume II: data projections;* Chicago: Chicago Area Transportation Study, 16–33.

C. W. Churchman, and H. B. Eisenberg, 1964. Deliberation and judgment. *Human judgments and optimality* (M. W. Shelly, II, and G. L. Bryan, eds.); New York: Wiley, 45–53.

W. G. Cochran, 1952. The χ^2 test of goodness of fit. *Annals of Mathematical Statistics*, *23*(3): 315–345.

W. G. Cochran, 1953. *Sampling techniques*. New York: Wiley.

W. G. Cochran, 1954. Some methods for strengthening the common χ^2 tests. *Biometrics*, *10*(4): 417–451.

W. G. Cochran, and G. M. Cox, 1950. *Experimental designs*. New York: Wiley, second edition in 1957.

K. J. Cohen, and F. Tonge, 1961. *A work problem in computer simulation*. Course note, Carnegie-Mellon University.

J. S. Coleman, 1964. *Introduction to mathematical sociology*. New York: Free Press.

A. Colker, F. A. Sorenson, M. L. Wolfson, and S. Zionts, 1962. *The generation of random samples from common statistical distributions*. Working paper, United States Steel Corporation Applied Research Laboratory, Report 25.17-016(1).

Commission on Hospital Care, 1947. *Hospital care in the United States*. New York: The Commonwealth Fund.

P. E. Converse, A. Campbell, W. E. Miller, and D. E. Stokes, 1961. Stability and change in 1960: a reinstating election. *American Political Science Review*, *55*(2): 269–280.

R. W. Conway, 1964. *An experimental investigation of priority assignment in a job shop*. Working paper, Rand Corporation, RM-3789-PR.

W. W. Cooper, 1951. A proposal for extending the theory of the firm. *Quarterly Journal of Economics*, *65*(1): 87–109.

R. L. Cosgriff, and G. E. Briggs, 1960. *Accomplishments in human operator simulation*. New York: American Society of Mechanical Engineers, Paper No. 60-AV-40.

R. R. Coveyou, and R. D. MacPherson, 1967. Fourier analysis of uniform random number generators. *Journal of the Association for Computing Machinery*, *14*(1): 100–119.

R. M. Cyert, and J. G. March, 1955. Organizational structure and pricing behavior in an oligopolistic market. *American Economic Review*, *45*(1): 129–139.

R. M. Cyert, and J. G. March, 1956. Organizational factors in the theory of oligopoly. *Quarterly Journal of Economics*, *70*(1): 44–64.

R. M. Cyert, H. A. Simon, and D. B. Trow, 1956. Observation of a business decision. *Journal of Business*, *29*(4): 237–248.

F. N. David, and J. Neyman, 1938. Extension of the Markoff theorem on least squares. *Statistical Research Memoirs, 2*: 105–116.

O. L. Davies, ed., 1956. *The design and analysis of industrial experiments.* London: Oliver and Boyd.

O. L. Davies, 1956. Factorial experiments: elementary principles. *The design and analysis of industrial experiments* (O. L. Davies, ed.); London: Oliver and Boyd, 247–289.

O. L. Davies, 1956. Fractional factorial experiments. *The design and analysis of industrial experiments* (O. L. Davies, ed.); London: Oliver and Boyd, 440–494.

O. A. Davis, M. A. H. Dempster, and A. B. Wildavsky, 1966. On the process of budgeting: an empirical study of Congressional appropriations. *Papers on non-market decision making* (G. Tullock, ed.); Charlottesville: University of Virginia, 63–132.

T. J. Davis, 1958. *Cycles and trends in textiles.* Washington: U.S. Government Printing Office.

J. Dean, 1951. Findings of empirical studies on cost. *Managerial economics;* New York: Prentice-Hall, 292–296.

A. D. DeGroot, 1946. *Thought and choice in chess.* Amsterdam: North-Holland; English translation published in 1965 by Mouton.

W. E. Deming, 1950. *Some theory of sampling.* New York: Wiley.

D. A. D'Esopo, H. L. Dixon, and B. Lefkowitz, 1960. A model for simulating an air-transportation system. *Naval Research Logistics Quarterly, 7*(3): 213–220.

P. H. Diananda, 1953. Some probability limit theorems with statistical applications. *Proceedings of the Cambridge Philosophical Society, 49*(2): 239–246.

N. R. Draper and H. Smith, 1966. *Applied regression analysis.* New York: Wiley.

J. S. Duesenberry, G. Fromm, L. R. Klein, and E. Kuh, eds., 1965. *The Brookings quarterly econometric model of the United States.* Chicago: Rand McNally.

K. Duncker, 1945. On problem solving. *Psychological Monographs, 58*(5): 1–112.

W. K. Estes, and J. H. Straughan, 1954. Analysis of a verbal conditioning situation in terms of statistical learning theory. *Journal of Experimental Psychology, 47*(4): 225–234.

A. Etzioni, 1961. *A comparative analysis of complex organizations.* New York: Free Press.

E. A. Feigenbaum, and H. A. Simon, 1962. A theory of the serial position effect. *British Journal of Psychology, 53*(3): 307–320.

W. Feller, 1957. *An introduction to probability theory and its applications,* New York: Wiley, Volume 1, second edition.

L. Festinger, S. Schachter, and K. Back, 1950. *Social pressures in informal groups.* New York: Harper.

E. C. Fieller, T. Lewis, and E. S. Pearson, 1955. *Correlated random normal deviates.* London: Cambridge University Press.

R. A. Fisher, 1946. *Statistical methods for research workers.* London: Oliver and Boyd, tenth edition.

R. A. Fisher, 1947. *The design of experiments.* London: Oliver and Boyd, fourth edition.

A. G. Frank, 1959. Goal ambiguity and conflicting standards. *Human Organization, 17*(4): 8–13.

B. Friedman, 1949. A simple urn model. *Communications on Pure and Applied Mathematics, 2*(1): 59–70.

C. S. Friedman, 1965. The stock of automobiles in the United States. *Survey of Current Business, 45*(10): 21–27.

M. Friedman, 1953. *Essays in positive economics.* Chicago: University of Chicago Press.

M. Friedman, 1957. *A theory of the consumption function.* Princeton: Princeton University Press.

I. Friend, and P. Taubman, 1964. A short-term forecasting model. *Review of Economics and Statistics, 46*(3): 229–236.

D. B. Fry, and P. Denes, 1958. The solution of some fundamental problems in mechanical speech recognition. *Language and Speech, 1*(1): 35–58.

H. L. Gelernter, J. R. Hansen, and D. W. Loveland, 1960. Empirical explorations of the geometry theorem machine. *Joint Computer Conference, Western Proceedings, 17*: 143–149.

H. B. Gerard, 1954. The anchorage of opinions in face-to-face groups. *Human Relations, 7*(3): 313–325.

E. E. Ghiselli, and R. P. Barthol, 1953. The validity of personality inventories in the selection of employees. *Journal of Applied Psychology, 37*(1): 18–20.

R. W. Goldsmith, 1962. *The national wealth of the United States in the postwar period.* Princeton: Princeton University Press.

G. Gordon, 1961. *Preliminary manual for GPS—a general purpose systems simulator.* White Plains, N.Y.: IBM.

L. V. Gordon, 1963. *Gordon personal inventory.* New York: Harcourt, Brace and World.

L. V. Gordon, 1963. *Gordon personal profile.* New York: Harcourt, Brace and World.

R. A. Gordon, 1948. Short-period price determination in theory and practice. *American Economic Review, 38*(3): 265–288.

M. E. Goss, 1961. Influence and authority among physicians in an outpatient clinic. *American Sociological Review, 26*(1): 39–50.

D. A. Grant, 1962. Testing the null hypothesis and the strategy and tactics of investigating theoretical models. *Psychological Review, 69*(1): 54–61.

C. H. Graves, 1965. Two multiple regression models of small-area population change. *Highway Research Record, 102*: 42–53.

D. Gross, and J. Ray, 1965. A general purpose forecast simulator. *Management Science, 11*(6): B-119–135.

J. T. Gullahorn, 1956. Measuring role conflict. *American Journal of Sociology, 61*(4): 299–303.

J. T. Gullahorn, and J. E. Gullahorn, 1963. Role conflict and its resolution. *Sociological Quarterly, 4*(1): 32–48.

H. Gulliksen, 1950. *Theory of mental tests.* New York: Wiley.

E. R. Guthrie, and G. P. Horton, 1946. *Cats in a puzzle box.* New York: Rinehart.

L. Guttman, 1950. The basis for Scalogram analysis. *Meaasurement and prediction* (S. A. Stouffer, L. Guttman, E. A. Suchman, P. F. Lazarsfeld, S. A. Star, and J. A. Clausen); Princeton: Princeton University Press, 60–90.

S. M. Halpin, and M. Pilisuk, 1967. *Prediction and choice in the Prisoner's Dilemma.* Lafayette, Ind.: Purdue University, Institute paper No. 174.

J. R. Hamburg, 1959. Land use projection for predicting future traffic. *Highway Research Board Bulletin, 224*: 72–84.

J. R. Hamburg, and R. H. Sharkey, 1961. *Land use forecast.* Working paper, Chicago Area Transportation Study, Report 3.2.6.10.

M. H. Hansen, W. N. Hurwitz, and W. G. Madow, 1953. *Sample survey methods and theory.* New York: Wiley, two volumes.

W. G. Hansen, 1959. How accessibility shapes land use. *Journal of the American Institute of Planners, 25*(2): 73–76.

S. I. Hayakawa, 1949. *Language in thought and action.* New York: Harcourt, Brace.

K. E. Heanue, L. B. Hamner, and R. M. Hall, 1965. Adequacy of clustered home interview sampling for calibrating a gravity model trip distribution formula. *Highway Research Record, 88*: 116–136.

E. S. Hedges, ed., 1960. *Tin and its alloys.* London: Arnold.

E. Heidbreder, 1924. An experimental study of thinking. *Archives of Psychology, 11*(73): 1–175.

B. G. Hickman, Jr., 1951. *Cyclical fluctuations in the cotton textile industry.* Doctoral dissertation, University of California at Berkeley.

W. J. Hill, and W. G. Hunter, 1966. A review of response surface methodology: a literature survey. *Technometrics, 8*(4): 571–590.

L. A. Hiller, Jr., and L. M. Isaacson, 1959. *Experimental Music.* New York: McGraw-Hill.

J. Hilsenrath, G. G. Ziegler, C. G. Messina, P. J. Walsh, and R. J. Herbold, 1966. *OMNITAB: a computer program for statistical and numerical analysis.* Washington: U.S. Government Printing Office, National Bureau of Standards Handbook 101.

A. A. Hirsch, 1964. *Predicting housing starts: Professor Maisel's model modified.* Working paper, U.S. Department of Commerce, Staff Working Paper in Economics and Statistics No. 5.

P. G. Hoel, 1958. Efficiency problems in polynomial estimation. *Annals of Mathematical Statistics, 29*(4): 1134–1145.

P. G. Hoel, 1960. *Elementary statistics.* New York: Wiley.

A. E. Hoerl, Jr., 1954. Fitting curves to data. *Chemical business handbook* (J. H. Perry, ed.); New York: McGraw-Hill, 20.55.-20.77.

G. C. Homans, 1961. *Social behavior.* New York: Harcourt, Brace and World.

W. C. Hood, and T. C. Koopmans (eds.), 1953. *Studies in econometric method.* New York: Wiley.

C. L. Hull, 1943. *Principles of behavior.* New York: Appleton-Century-Crofts.

H. H. Hyman, 1959. *Political socialization.* Glencoe, Ill.: Free Press.

International Tin Council, 1956. *Statistical Yearbook, 1956.* London: International Tin Council.

International Tin Council, 1960. *Statistical Yearbook, 1960.* London: International Tin Council.

International Tin Council, 1961. *Statistical Yearbook, 1961.* London: International Tin Council.

G. M. Jenkins, 1961. General considerations in the analysis of spectra. *Technometrics, 3*(2): 133–166.

O. Kempthorne, 1952. *The design and analysis of experiments.* New York: Wiley.

M. D. Kilbridge, 1961. Non-productive work as a factor in the economic division of labor. *Journal of Industrial Engineering, 12*(3): 155–159.

M. D. Kilbridge, 1962. A model for industrial learning costs. *Management Science, 8*(4): 516–527.

M. D. Kilbridge, and L. Wester, 1961. The balance delay problem. *Management Science, 8*(1): 69–84.

L. R. Klein, 1953. *A textbook of econometrics.* Evanston, Ill.: Row, Peterson.

F. Klemm, 1959. *A history of Western technology.* New York: Scribner.

T. Kloek, and L. B. M. Mennes, 1960. Simultaneous equations estimation based on principal components of predetermined variables. *Econometrica, 28*(1): 45–61.

T. C. Koopmans (ed.), 1950. *Statistical inference in dynamic economic models.* New York: Wiley.

T. C. Koopmans, 1957. Implications of tool developments for future research. *Three essays on the state of economic science;* New York: McGraw-Hill, 208–217.

K. E. Knorr, 1945. *Tin under control.* Stanford: Stanford University.

S. Kullback, 1959. *Information theory and statistics.* New York: Wiley.

F. C. Lane, 1934. *Venetian ships and shipbuilders of the renaissance.* Baltimore: Johns Hopkins Press.

N. J. Langer, ed., 1961. *Metal statistics 1961.* New York: American Metal Market.

P. F. Lazarsfeld, 1950. The logical and mathematical foundation of latent structure analysis. *Measurement and prediction* (S. A. Stouffer, L. Guttman, E. A. Suchman, P. F. Lazarsfeld, S. A. Star, and J. A. Clausen); Princeton: Princeton University Press, 362–412.

H. J. Leavitt, and B. M. Bass, 1964. Organizational psychology. *Annual Review of Psychology, 15*: 371–398.

M. Levine, 1966. Hypothesis behavior by humans during discrimination learning. *Journal of Experimental Psychology, 71*(3): 331–338.

K. Lewin, 1935. The psychological situations of reward and punishment. *A dynamic theory of personality;* New York: McGraw-Hill, 114–170.

R. Likert, 1961. *New patterns of management.* New York: McGraw-Hill.

R. Likert, and S. E. Seashore, 1963. Making cost control work. *Harvard Business Review, 41*(6): 96–108.

C. E. Lindblom, 1959. The science of "muddling through." *Public Administration Review, 19*(2): 79–88.

D. Longley, 1964. An analogue computer application in operations research. *Electronic Engineering, 36*: 378–381.

A. J. Lott, and B. E. Lott, 1965. Group cohesiveness as interpersonal attraction: a review of relationships with antecedent and consequent variables. *Psychological Bulletin, 64*(4): 259–309.

R. D. Luce, 1959. *Individual choice behavior.* New York: Wiley.

R. D. Luce, and H. Raiffa, 1957. *Games and decisions.* New York: Wiley.

D. D. McCracken, 1962. *A guide to ALGOL programming.* New York: Wiley.

R. P. Mack, 1956. *Consumption and business fluctuations.* New York: National Bureau of Economic Research.

M. D. MacLaren, and G. Marsaglia, 1965. Uniform random number generators. *Journal of the Association for Computing Machinery, 12*(1): 83–89.

W. N. McPhee, 1963. *Formal theories of mass behavior.* New York: Free Press.

S. J. Maisel, 1963. A theory of fluctuations in residential construction starts. *American Economic Review, 53*(3): 359–383.

H. B. Mann, and A. Wald, 1942. On the choice of the number of class intervals in the application of the chi square test. *Annals of Mathematical Statistics, 13*(3): 306–317.

E. Mansfield, 1958. *Notes on experimental design.* Lecture notes, Carnegie-Mellon University.

E. Mansfield, 1961. Technical change and the rate of imitation. *Econometrica, 29*(4): 741–766.

J. G. March, and H. A. Simon, 1958. *Organizations.* New York: Wiley.

H. M. Markowitz, B. Hausner, and H. W. Karr, 1963. *SIMSCRIPT: a simulation programming language.* Englewood Cliffs, N.J.: Prentice-Hall.

H. A. Meyer, ed., 1956. *Symposium on Monte Carlo methods.* New York: Wiley.

W. H. Miernyk, and M. Zymelman, 1961. *Inventories in the textile cycle.* Washington: U.S. Government Printing Office.

N. E. Miller, 1944. Experimental studies of conflict. *Personality and the behavior disorders.* (J. McV. Hunt, ed.); New York: Ronald, Volume I, 431–465.

F. C. Mills, 1955. *Statistical methods.* New York: Holt, third edition.

M. L. Minsky, 1963. Steps toward artificial intelligence. *Computers and thought* (E. A. Feigenbaum, and J. Feldman, eds.); New York: McGraw-Hill, 406–450.

O. K. Moore, and S. B. Anderson, 1954. Modern logic and tasks for experiments on problem solving behavior. *Journal of Psychology, 38*(1): 151–160.

W. M. Morgenroth, 1964. A method for understanding price determinants. *Journal of Marketing Research, 1*(3): 17–26.

F. Mosteller, H. Hyman, P. J. McCarthy, E. S. Marks, and D. B. Truman, 1949. *The pre-election polls of 1948.* New York: Social Science Research Council.

A. Nataf, 1968. Aggregation. *International encyclopedia of the social sciences* (D. L. Sills, ed.); New York: Macmillan, Volume 1, 162–168.

National Bureau of Standards, 1957. *Fractional factorial experiment designs for factors at two levels.* Washington: U.S. National Bureau of Standards, AMS-48.

T. M. Newcomb, 1961. *The acquaintance process.* New York: Holt, Rinehart, and Winston.

A. Newell, ed., 1961. *Information processing language-V manual.* Englewood Cliffs, N.J.: Prentice-Hall; second edition in 1964.

N. J. Nilsson, 1965. *Learning machines.* New York: McGraw-Hill.

C. E. Osgood, 1953. *Method and theory in experimental psychology.* New York: Oxford University Press.

A. S. Otis, 1928. *Manual of directions for the Otis self-administering tests of mental ability.* New York: Harcourt, Brace and World.

G. K. Pakov, 1960. *Generation of a random correlated quantity on a high-speed electronic computer.* Washington: U.S. Joint Publications Research Service, JPRS-5784.

A. G. Papandreou, 1952. Some basic problems in the theory of the firm. *A survey of contemporary economics* (B. F. Haley, ed.); Homewood, Ill.: Irwin, Volume 2, 183–219.

M. Pilisuk, and P. Skolnick, 1968. Inducing trust: a test of the Osgood proposal. *Journal of Personality and Social Psychology, 8*(2): 121–133.

M. Pilisuk, P. Potter, A. Rapoport, and J. A. Winter, 1965. War hawks and peace doves: alternate resolutions of experimental conflicts. *Journal of Conflict Resolution, 9*(4): 491–508.

M. Pilisuk, J. A. Winter, R. Chapman, and N. Haas, 1967. Honesty, deceit, and timing in the display of intentions. *Behavioral Science*, *12*(3): 205–215.

R. L. Plackett, and J. P. Burman, 1946. The design of optimum multifactorial experiments. *Biometrika*, *33*(4): 305–325.

J. Popkin, 1965. The relationship between new orders and shipments: an analysis of the machinery and equipment industries. *Survey of Current Business*, *45*(3): 24–32.

K. R. Popper, 1959. *The logic of scientific discovery*. New York: Basic Books.

Rand Corporation, 1955. *A million random digits with 100,000 normal deviates*. Glencoe, Ill.: Free Press.

An. Rapoport and C. Orwant, 1962. Experimental games: a review. *Behavioral Science*, *7*(1): 1–37.

M. D. Richards, and P. S. Greenlaw, 1966. *Management decision making*. Homewood, Ill.: Irwin.

F. J. Roethlisberger, 1941. *Management and morale*. Cambridge: Harvard University Press.

A. Salz, 1934. Specialization. *Encyclopaedia of the social sciences* (E. R. A. Seligman, ed.); New York: Macmillan, Volume 14, 279–285.

A. L. Samuel, 1959. Some studies in machine learning using the game of checkers. *IBM Journal of Research and Development*, *3*(3): 210–229.

M. Sasieni, A. Yaspan, and L. Friedman, 1959. *Operations research*. New York: Wiley.

F. E. Satterthwaite, 1958. *Mathematical outline of polyvariable analysis*. Working paper, Statistical Engineering Institute.

F. E. Satterthwaite, 1958. *The research game*. Working paper, Statistical Engineering Institute.

F. E. Satterthwaite, 1959. Random balance experimentation. *Technometrics*, *1*(2): 111–137.

F. E. Satterthwaite, 1959. *REVOP, or random evolutionary operation*. Working paper, Statistical Engineering Institute.

F. E. Satterthwaite, and D. Shainin, 1959. *Polyvariable experimentation, a powerful tool for experimentation and control*. Working paper, Statistical Engineering Institute, second edition.

L. R. Sayles, 1958. *Behavior of industrial work groups*. New York: Wiley.

R. Schlaifer, 1959. *Probability and statistics for business decisions*. New York: McGraw-Hill.

E. Schwartz, 1962. Financing current operations, Part I. *Corporation finance;* New York: St. Martin's 232–250.

S. E. Seashore, 1954. *Group cohesiveness in the industrial work group*. Ann Arbor, Mich.: Institute for Social Research.

O. G. Selfridge, 1959. Pandemonium: a paradigm for learning. *Mechanisation of thought processes* (D. V. Blake and A. M. Uttley, eds.); London: H. M. Stationery Office, Volume 1, 513–531.

M. D. Seversky, 1966. Retail forecasting. *Datamation*, *12*(8): 28–34.

H. A. Simon, 1955. A behavioral model of rational choice. *Quarterly Journal of Economics*, *69*(1): 99–118.

H. A. Simon, 1957. *Administrative behavior*. New York: Macmillan, second edition.

H. A. Simon, 1957. Amounts of fixation and discovery in maze learning behavior. *Psychometrika*, *22*(3): 261–268.

H. A. Simon, 1957. *Models of man*. New York: Wiley.

H. A. Simon, 1960. *The new science of management decision*. New York: Harper.

H. A. Simon, 1962. A note on mathematical models for learning. *Psychometrika*, *27*(4): 417–418.

H. A. Simon, 1964. On the concept of organizational goal. *Administrative Science Quarterly*, *9*(1): 1–22.

H. A. Simon, and H. Guetzkow, 1955. A model of short- and long-run mechanisms involved in pressures toward uniformity in groups. *Psychological Review*, *62*(1): 56–68.

E. Slutzky, 1937. The summation of random causes as the source of cyclic processes. *Econometrica*, *5*(2): 105–146.

A. Smith, 1776. On the division of labor. *An inquiry into the nature and causes of the wealth of nations;* London: Strahan and Cadell, Book 1, Chapter 1.

B. L. Smith, 1965. Gravity model theory applied to a small city using a small sample of origin-destination data. *Highway Research Record*, *88*: 85–115.

T. C. Sorensen, 1965. *Kennedy*. Scranton: Harper and Row.

A. B. Sosslau and G. E. Brokke, 1960. Appraisal of sample size based on Phoenix O-D survey data. *Highway Research Board Bulletin*, *253*: 114–127.

South Dakota Department of Highways, 1956. *Sioux Falls origin and destination traffic study, 1956*. Pierre: South Dakota Department of Highways Research and Planning Division.

South Dakota Department of Highways, 1960. *Parking survey, Sioux Falls central business district*. Pierre: South Dakota Department of Highways Research and Planning Division.

T. M. Stanback, Jr., 1954. *Short run instability in the cotton broadwoven goods industry*. Doctoral dissertation, Duke University.

T. M. Stanback, Jr., 1958. The textile cycle: characteristics and contributing factors. *Southern Economic Journal*, *25*(2): 174–188.

E. S. Stanton, 1964. Psychological testing in industry: a critical evaluation. *Personnel Journal*, *43*(1): 27–32.

W. H. Starbuck, 1965. *The heteroscedastic normal*. Lafayette, Ind.: Purdue University, Institute paper no. 106.

S. A. Stouffer, 1940. Intervening opportunities: a theory relating mobility and distance. *American Sociological Review*, *5*(6): 845–867.

F. L. Strodtbeck, 1949. Equal opportunity intervals: a contribution to the method of intervening opportunity analysis. *American Sociological Review*, *14*(4): 490–497.

F. K. Tan, and J. M. Burling, 1967. Manufacturing planning using simulation. *Conference of the AIIE, Proceedings of the Eighteenth Annual:* 261–266.

H. Theil, and A. L. Nagar, 1961. Testing the independence of regression disturbances. *Journal of the American Statistical Association, 56*(296): 793–806.

J. D. Thompson, O. W. Avant, and E. D. Spiker, 1960. How queuing theory works for the hospital. *Modern Hospital, 94*(3): 75–78.

Ja. D. Thompson, and A. Tuden, 1959. Strategies, structures, and processes of organizational decision. *Comparative studies in administration* (J. D. Thompson et al., eds.); Pittsburgh: University of Pittsburgh Press, 195–216.

L. L. Thurstone, 1927. A law of comparative judgment. *Psychological Review, 34*(4): 273–286.

E. B. Titchener, 1896. *An outline of psychology.* New York: Macmillan.

E. C. Tolman, 1939. Prediction of vicarious trial and error by means of the schematic sowbug. *Psychological Review, 46*(4): 318–336.

T. R. Trabasso, 1963. Stimulus emphasis and all-or-none learning in concept identification. *Journal of Experimental Psychology, 65*(4): 398–406.

E. C. Tolman, 1948. Cognitive maps in rats and men. *Psychological Review, 55*(4): 189–208.

J. W. Tukey, 1960. Where do we go from here? *Journal of the American Statistical Association, 55*(289): 80–93.

D. S. Tull, 1965. The carry-over effects of advertising. *Journal of Marketing, 29*(2): 46–53.

W. O. Turner, 1963. Traffic simulation. *Bell Laboratories Record, 41*(9): 346–350.

A. M. Voorhees, 1959. Use of mathematical models in estimating travel. *Proceedings of the American Society of Civil Engineers, Journal of the Highway Division, 85*(HW4): 129–141.

J. E. Walsh, 1962. *Handbook of nonparametric statistics.* Princeton: Van Nostrand.

J. N. Washburne, 1940. *Manual for interpretation of the Washburne social adjustment inventory.* New York: Harcourt, Brace and World.

J. B. Watson, 1925. *Behaviorism.* New York: Norton.

M. Weidenbaum, 1961. The economic impact of the government spending process. *The Business Review, 8* (Spring): 3–47.

S. Weintraub, 1942. Monopoly equilibrium and anticipated demand. *Journal of Political Economy, 50*(3): 427–434.

R. H. Wiant, 1961. A simplified method for forecasting urban traffic. *Highway Research Board Bulletin, 297*: 128–145.

A. B. Wildavsky, 1964. *The politics of the budgetary process.* Boston: Little Brown.

D. J. Wilde, 1964. *Optimum seeking methods.* Englewwood Cliffs, N.J.: Prentice-Hall.

O. E. Williamson, 1963. Managerial discretion and business behavior. *American Economic Review, 53*(5): 1032–1057.

T. A. Wilson, and O. Eckstein, 1964. Short-run productivity behavior in U.S. manufacturing. *Review of Economics and Statistics, 46*(1): 41–54.

B. J. Winer, 1962. *Statistical principles in experimental design.* New York: McGraw-Hill.

R. Wyman, 1962. A nerve net simulation. *Behavioral Science, 7*(2): 250–252.

W. J. Youden, O. Kempthorne, J. W. Tukey, G. E. P. Box, J. S. Hunter, F. E. Satterthwaite, and T. A. Budne, 1959. Discussion of the papers of Messrs. Satterthwaite and Budne. *Technometrics, 1*(2): 157–193.

D. B. Yntema, and F. P. Trask, 1963. Recall as a search process. *Journal of Verbal Learning and Verbal Behavior, 2*(1): 65–74.

G. U. Yule, 1945. On a method of studying time-series based on their internal correlations. *Journal of the Royal Statistical Society, Series A, 108*(I-II): 208–225.

Index

Introduction

This is an unusual index. The entries are hierarchically arranged. The total number of entries is small compared with the book's size. Methodological entries predominate out of proportion to their true frequencies in the text. Distinctions are made between concepts that some authors do not see as distinct, and some distinctions made in the separate chapters are not preserved. More often than not, the editors have substituted their own terminology.

One reason for this distortion is the book's methodological purpose. Since the reader is assumed to be primarily interested in the design, implementation, and evaluation of computer simulations, the index makes comparatively fine distinctions among methodological concepts and cites even minor passages that discuss or illustrate methodological issues. The index's major headings separate the methodological entries from the behaviorally substantive entries and gather the entries into categories.

A second reason for distortion lies in the book's multidisciplinary coverage. An ordinary index that would take its entries from the chapters themselves would be confusing—because different disciplines use the same terms differently—and very long—because different disciplines use different terms similarly, and many cross-references would be needed to identify these similarities. The present index attempts to eliminate the terminological idiosyncracies of different disciplines and to apply a uniform conceptual treatment across all chapters.

The index's brevity and hierarchical structure are intended to satisfy the need for cross-references: associated concepts ought to be found near each other, and readers ought to be able to keep the index's overall structure in mind. However, this design does imply that one should not attempt to use the index until he has read through the whole index and grasps its general plan.

One cannot impose order on chaos without exposing one's own prejudices, and this index is very much a function of the editors' beliefs, values, and interpretations. In fact, the index is more a statement about how the editors interpret the text—what the editors think one should notice when he reads—than it is an exhaustive and impersonal listing of words and phrases from the various chapters. Naturally, the editors see no disadvantage in this, but readers should beware.